INCREASED SERVICES COVERAGE

A significant increase in the number of non-manufacturing examples and applications provides a better balance and treatment of services and manufacturing throughout. The service process examples are closer to the kind of processes students will encounter in their jobs after graduation, giving students a glimpse at future employment opportunities.

- Chapter 2 includes a new section on New Service and Product Development, and

- Chapter 3 introduces the Customer Contact model, which shows the relationship between customer contact and process complexity for front office and back office designs.

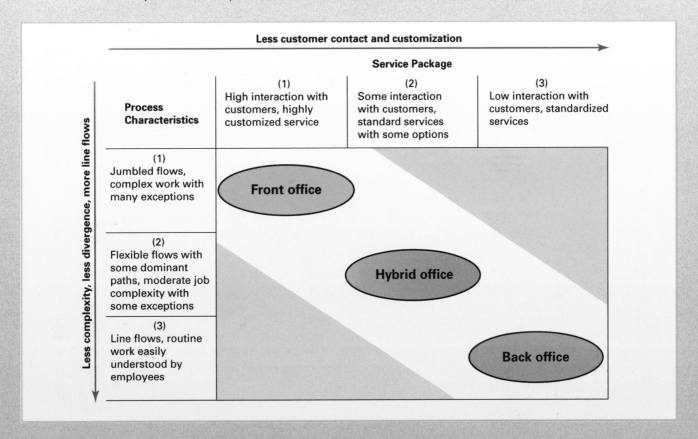

ENHANCED STUDENT CD-ROM RESOURCES

The Student CD-ROM contains extensive tools, activities, and resources to enhance student skills and understanding of each chapter.

Resources include: PowerPoint Slides, Video Clips, Special software packages that allow students to do "What if" scenarios (OM Explorer, Active Models, SimQuick), links to popular software downloads (Microsoft Project 2002, SmartDraw), Supplemental Topics, Written Tours, and a link to our Companion Website which includes chapter specific self-study quizzes, In the News Articles, Internet Exercises, and Virtual Company Tours.

HAVE YOU THOUGHT ABOUT *Customizing* THIS BOOK?

THE PRENTICE HALL JUST-IN-TIME PROGRAM IN DECISION SCIENCE

You can combine chapters from this book with chapters from any of the Prentice Hall titles listed on the following page to create a text tailored to your specific course needs. You can add your own material or cases from our extensive case collection. By taking a few minutes to look at what is sitting on your bookshelf and the content available on our Web site, you can create your ideal textbook.

The Just-In-Time program offers:

- ➠ **Quality of Material to Choose From**—In addition to the books listed, you also have the option to include any of the cases from Prentice Hall Custom Business Resources, which gives you access to cases (and teaching notes where available) from Darden, Harvard, Ivey, NACRA, and Thunderbird. Most cases can be viewed online at our Web site.

- ➠ **Flexibility**—Choose only that material you want, either from one title or several titles (plus cases) and sequence it in whatever way you wish.

- ➠ **Instructional Support**—You have access to the text-specific CD-ROM that accompanies the traditional textbook and desk copies of your JIT book.

- ➠ **Outside Materials**—There is also the option to include up to 20% of the text from materials outside of Prentice Hall Custom Business Resources.

- ➠ **Cost Savings**—Students pay only for material you choose. The base price is $6.00, plus $2.00 for case material, plus $.09 per page. The text can be shrink-wrapped with other Pearson textbooks for a 10% discount. Outside material is priced at $.10 per page plus permission fees.

- ➠ **Quality of Finished Product**—Custom cover and title page—including your name, school, department, course title, and section number. Paperback, perfect bound, black-and-white printed text. Customized table of contents. Sequential pagination throughout the text.

Visit our Web site at www.prenhall.com/custombusiness and create your custom text on our bookbuildsite or download order forms online.

THE PRENTICE HALL
Just-In-Time program

You can customize your textbook with chapters from any of the following Prentice Hall titles: *

BUSINESS STATISTICS
- Berenson/Levine/Krehbiel, BASIC BUSINESS STATISTICS, 9/e
- Groebner/Shannon/Fry/Smith, BUSINESS STATISTICS, 6/e
- Levine/Stephan/Krehbiel/Berenson, STATISTICS FOR MANAGERS USING MICROSOFT EXCEL, 4/e
- Levine/Krehbiel/Berenson, BUSINESS STATISTICS: A FIRST COURSE, 3/e
- Newbold/Carlson/Thorne, STATISTICS FOR BUSINESS AND ECONOMICS, 5/e
- Shannon/Groebner/Fry/Smith, A COURSE IN BUSINESS STATISTICS, 3/e

PRODUCTION/OPERATIONS MANAGEMENT
- Anupindi/Chopra/Deshmukh/Van Mieghem/Zemel, MANAGING BUSINESS PROCESS FLOWS
- Handfield/Nichols, Jr., SUPPLY CHAIN MANAGEMENT
- Haksever/Render/Russell/Murdick, SERVICE MANAGEMENT AND OPERATIONS, 2/e
- Hanna/Newman, INTEGRATED OPERATIONS MANAGEMENT
- Heineke/Meile, GAMES AND EXERCISES IN OPERATIONS MANAGEMENT
- Heizer/Render, OPERATIONS MANAGEMENT, 7/e
- Krajewski/Ritzman, OPERATIONS MANAGEMENT, 7/e
- Latona/Nathan, CASES AND READINGS IN POM
- Russell/Taylor, OPERATIONS MANAGEMENT, 4/e
- Schmenner, PLANT AND SERVICE TOURS IN OPERATIONS MANAGEMENT, 5/e
- Nicholas, PROJECT MANAGEMENT, 2/e

MANAGEMENT SCIENCE/SPREADSHEET MODELING
- Eppen/Gould, INTRODUCTORY MANAGEMENT SCIENCE, 5/e
- Moore/Weatherford, DECISION MODELING WITH MICROSOFT EXCEL, 6/e
- Render/Stair/Hanna, QUANTITATIVE ANALYSIS FOR MANAGEMENT, 8/e
- Render/Stair/Balakrishnan, MANAGERIAL DECISION MODELING WITH SPREADSHEETS
- Render/Stair, CASES AND READINGS IN MANAGEMENT SCIENCE
- Taylor, INTRODUCTION TO MANAGEMENT SCIENCE, 8/e

For more information, or to speak to a customer service representative, contact us at 1-800-777-6872.

www.prenhall.com/custombusiness

* Selection of titles on the JIT program is subject to change

OPERATIONS MANAGEMENT
PROCESSES AND VALUE CHAINS

SEVENTH EDITION

OPERATIONS MANAGEMENT
PROCESSES AND VALUE CHAINS

SEVENTH EDITION

LEE J. KRAJEWSKI
University of Notre Dame

LARRY P. RITZMAN
Boston College

PEARSON

Prentice Hall

Upper Saddle River, NJ 07458

Library of Congress Cataloging-in-Publication Data

Krajewski, Lee J.
    Operations management: strategy and analysis / Lee J. Krajewski, Larry P. Ritzman.—
    7th ed.
        p. cm.
    Includes bibliographical references and index.
    ISBN: 0-13-143664-3
    1. Production management   I. Ritzman, Larry P.   II. Title.

    TS155.K788 2004
    658.5—dc22   2003069025

Executive Editor: Tom Tucker
Editor-in-Chief: PJ Boardman
Project Manager: Erika Rusnak
Editorial Assistant: Dawn Stapleton
Senior Media Project Manager: Nancy Welcher
Executive Marketing Manager: Debbie Clare
Marketing Assistant: Amanda Fisher
Managing Editor (Production): Cynthia Regan
Production Editor: Kerri M. Tomasso
Manufacturing Buyer: Diane Peirano
Design Manager: Maria Lange
Designer: Steve Frim
Interior Design: Heather Peres
Cover Design: Carmen Dibartolomeo
Cover Illustration/Photo: (top to bottom): Bob Krist/Getty Images, Inc.; David Joel/Getty Images, Inc.;
    Michael Newman/Photoedit, Inc.
Photo Researcher: Elaine Soares
Image Permission Coordinator: Debbie Latronica
Manager, Print Production: Christy Mahon
Composition/Full-Service Project Management: Sue Katkus and Natalie Hansen, PreMediaONE,
    A Black Dot Group Company
Printer/Binder: Courier-Kendallville

Credits and acknowledgments borrowed from other sources and reproduced, with permission, in this text-book appear on appropriate page within text (or on page 831).

Microsoft® and Windows® are registered trademarks of the Microsoft Corporation in the U.S.A. and other countries. Screen shots and icons reprinted with permission from the Microsoft Corporation. This book is not sponsored or endorsed by or affiliated with the Microsoft Corporation.

Pearson Education LTD.
Pearson Education Singapore, Pte. Ltd
Pearson Education, Canada, Ltd
Pearson Education-Japan

Pearson Education Australia PTY, Limited
Pearson Education North Asia Ltd
Pearson Educación de Mexico, S.A. de C.V.
Pearson Education Malaysia, Pte. Ltd

10 9 8 7 6 5 4 3 2 1
ISBN 0-13-143664-3

ABOUT THE AUTHORS

LEE J. KRAJEWSKI is the William R. and F. Cassie Daley Professor of Manufacturing Strategy at the University of Notre Dame. Prior to joining Notre Dame, Lee was a faculty member at The Ohio State University, where he received the University Alumni Distinguished Teaching Award and the College of Business Outstanding Faculty Research Award. He initiated the Center for Excellence in Manufacturing Management and served as its director for four years. In addition, he received the National President's Award and the National Award of Merit of the American Production and Inventory Control Society. He served as President of the Decision Sciences Institute and was elected a Fellow of the Institute in 1988. He received the Distinguished Service Award in 2003.

Lee received his Ph.D. from the University of Wisconsin. Over the years, he has designed and taught courses at both graduate and undergraduate levels on topics such as manufacturing strategy, introduction to operations management, operations design, and manufacturing planning and control systems.

Lee served as the editor of *Decision Sciences,* was the founding editor of the *Journal of Operations Management,* and has served on several editorial boards. Widely published himself, Lee has contributed numerous articles to such journals as *Decision Sciences,* the *Journal of Operations Management, Management Science, Harvard Business Review,* and *Interfaces,* to name just a few. He has received five bestpaper awards. Lee's areas of specialization include operations strategy, manufacturing planning and control systems, supply-chain management, and master production scheduling.

LARRY P. RITZMAN is the Thomas J. Galligan, Jr. Professor in Operations and Strategic Management at Boston College, where he recently received the Distinguish Service Award from the School of Management. He is a Professor Emeritus at The Ohio State University where he served for twenty-three years. He received several awards for both teaching and research, including the Pace Setters' Club Award for Outstanding Research. He received his doctorate at Michigan State University, having had prior industrial experience at the Babcock and Wilcox Company. Over the years, he has been privileged to teach and learn more about operations management with numerous students at all levels—undergraduate, MBA, executive MBA, and doctorate.

Particularly active in the Decision Sciences Institute, Larry has served as Council Coordinator, Publications Committee Chair, Track Chair, Vice President, Board Member, Executive Committee Member, Doctoral Consortium Coordinator, and President. He was elected a Fellow of the Institute in 1987 and earned the Distinguished Service Award in 1996. He has received three best-paper awards. He is a frequent reviewer, discussant, and session chair for several other professional organizations.

Larry's areas of particular expertise are service processes, operations strategy, production and inventory systems, forecasting, multistage manufacturing, and layout. An active researcher, Larry's publications have appeared in such journals as *Decision Sciences, Journal of Operations Management, Production and Operations Management, Harvard Business Review,* and *Management Science.* He has served in various editorial capacities for several journals.

BRIEF CONTENTS

CONTENTS

PREFACE

This seventh edition is a complete redesign of the general outline and approach of the first six editions. It is a revision that is really a revision—providing readers with something really new and topical. While many improvements are made, the three most important new thrusts are:

1. *Processes and Value Chains.* While the seventh edition maintains its perspective on the big picture and the strategic importance of operations, it shifts its overall approach to a process orientation. This new paradigm starts at the level of a process and then transitions to the level of value chains, which involve the linkages of processes. The term "value chain" applies equally well to non-manufacturing processes. It is also finding widespread usage in practice.

2. *Services.* While the overall approach of the seventh edition focuses on processes, a second major emphasis is the coverage of service processes. We significantly increased the emphasis on service operations and the number of non-manufacturing examples and applications. These service process examples are closer to the sort of processes students will encounter in their jobs after graduation, instead of examples such as making hamburgers. Students can relate with our examples, and can envision future employment opportunities.

3. *All Majors.* Processes are the fundamental unit of work in all organizations. This unifying theme opens up operations management to all students, regardless of their majors or career paths. It creates an excellent "buy-in" for a course in operations management, because students understand that processes underlie activities throughout any organization, not just in one functional area or department.

We wrote this book for an introductory course at either the undergraduate or MBA level. The book is suitable for undergraduates because it provides the pedagogical structure (clear explanations, step-by-step examples of quantitative techniques, numerous solved problems and homework problems, and the like). The book is suitable for MBA students because of its managerial perspective, strong coverage of processes and value chains, cases and experiential exercises, and significant computer software and internet resources. Students at either level need to understand the interrelated processes of a firm, how each part of an organization must design and manage processes, and how the processes should be connected with customers and suppliers. The book conveys the essential ideas and techniques but is supplemented by a rich set of pedagogical features that allow students to go much deeper into any given topic. This depth comes from accessing the various resources on the Student CD-ROM and online at our Companion Website. These additional resources create opportunities in and out of the classroom for various forms of active learning: experiential exercises, cases, virtual tours, discussion questions, Active Models, OM Explorer activities, SimQuick simulations, video discussions, and internet exercises. The focus on a process also provides an excellent vehicle for student teams to do field projects that relate course concepts to practice.

Our goal is to help students become effective managers in today's competitive, global environment. They discover the challenge of both managing activities throughout the organization. Second, we seek to help students discover the excitement of the dynamic field of operations management. We engage students by offering interesting examples at numerous firms that bring operations alive, presenting new technologies for enhancing decision-making and data gathering, and including realistic cases that encourage open debate of important issues. Third, we want students to understand what managers do about processes, to understand the many cross-functional links, and to learn more about the tools that managers can use to make better decisions.

● ORGANIZATION

We organized the text into four major parts: "Competing with Operations," "Designing and Improving Processes," "Designing Value Chains," and "Operating Value Chains." The flow of topics is summarized in the road map of Figure 1.6. These four parts build upon each other as described below.

Part 1: Competing With Operations   The first three chapters of the text are major revisions and set the stage for the body of the text. They show how a firm's operations can provide a sound basis for its competitiveness in the marketplace, and bring out the pivotal role of sound processes.

Chapter 1, "Operations as a Competitive Weapon," introduces the reader to the concept of a process and how processes are nested within each other at an organization. It also introduces the concept of a value chain and outlines the flow of the text. These concepts are brought to life with an ad agency example. Key points are that processes are found in services as well as manufacturing, that processes are customer focused (both internal and external), and that processes always have suppliers (both internal and external). Another point of this chapter is that operations management is about making decisions, which is reinforced by Supplement A, "Decision Making."

Chapter 2, "Operations Strategy," follows the theme of customer-focused processes by introducing the concept of competitive priorities at the <u>process</u> level, thereby adding a strategic dimension to effective processes. This chapter also has a new section on New Service or Product Development, which introduces the concepts of service packages and product strategy. Quality function deployment is a way to capture the voice of the customer.

Chapter 3, "Process Design Strategies," is a major revision and reorientation. It focuses just on the strategic issues involved in designing processes, and gives considerably more attention to service processes as distinct from manufacturing processes. A key aspect is the introduction of the customer-contact matrix, which shows the relationship between customer contact and process complexity for front-office and back-office designs. Examples from the financial services industry illustrate the different types of service process structures. The product-process matrix then addresses manufacturing processes, and shows how their design relates with volume and customization.

Part 2: Designing and Improving Processes   This section contains five chapters and two supplements. The focus is on the design of effective processes and improving existing ones. Figure 4.2, "A Systematic Approach to Process Analysis," provides the integrating theme. The sequence of the chapters in Part 2 generally follows the flow of this figure.

Chapter 4, "Process Analysis," is completely new, with a considerable amount of fresh material to bring home our process orientation, with considerable attention to service processes. It brings together in one place the analytic tools from the sixth edition on Process Management and Total Quality Management (TQM), including the homework problems and cases that go with them. Emphasis is placed on flowcharts, process charts, and TQM data analysis tools. This chapter (along with the other chapters in Part 1 and Part 2) equips student teams for field projects on process analysis, if that approach makes sense for the instructor. The chapter's distinctive orientation focuses on (1) "lifting the lid" of the organization and looking at its underlying processes, and (2) managing processes throughout the organization to achieve continual improvements and adaptations. This chapter is the first of a succession of chapters with significant computer-assisted means of analysis. Here we show examples of process analysis, using OM Explorer, SmartDraw, PowerPoint, and simulation.

Simulation is explored further in Supplement B, "Simulation." It now has a new section on how to create Excel simulations for simple situations, and how to use the SimQuick software page (accessed on the Student CD-ROM) for simulating more complex situations.

Chapter 5, "Process Performance and Quality," combines into one streamlined chapter the sixth edition's chapter on TQM with the chapter on Statistical Process Control (SPC). Building on the process analysis approach in Chapter 4, it makes clear that you do not know whether or not the process is performing poorly until data are recorded on key metrics and compared to prescribed performance targets. This chapter underwent a significant amount of revision, including the addition of service examples throughout. A major addition to this chapter is a section on Six Sigma as a program for process improvement based on statistical analysis and its unique problem solving approach.

Chapter 6, "Process Capacity," is the first of two chapters addressing step 5 (redesigning the process) of Figure 4.2. Capacity is one process dimension that can be changed to improve effectiveness. This chapter now views capacity issues at the process level, and considers both capital and human resources as part of the capacity decision. As with the other chapters, it gives considerable attention to service processes. For example, the decision on capacity customers and the calculations on capacity requirements are related directly to services and the customer-contact model. The chapter covers the Theory of Constraints, economies and diseconomies of scale, capacity strategies, and a systematic approach to capacity planning. We describe useful quantitative techniques, such as decision trees, simulation, and techniques in OM Explorer. Supplement C, "Waiting Lines," is linked to Chapter 6 as well as to the central issue of redesigning processes.

Chapter 7, "Process Layout," is the next process design issue that can improve effectiveness. This chapter views layout issues at the process level, and gives even more attention to service processes. For example, developing block plans is now illustrated with a division of a state government department. Customer satisfaction is seen as a key performance criterion, particularly when customer contact is high. The terminology is revised to be more intuitive for both service and manufacturing processes. Active Model 7.1, one of several such Excel spreadsheets that are added to the Student CD-ROM to enhance the book's Examples, gives new insight on devising good process layouts.

Chapter 8, "Planning and Managing Projects," was revised to link with step 6 (implement changes) of Figure 4.2, without losing sight of the usefulness of the project management approach in general. Understanding project management is needed by students regardless of their major or future career path. The chapter benefits from more nonmanufacturing examples, as with many of the other chapters. Active Models and OM Explorer Solvers add considerable computer support. Access to the MS Project (60-day evaluation) package is also provided.

Part 3: Designing Value Chains   We define value chains in Chapter 1, but the chapters up through Part 2 focus on internal (to a company) processes. Part 3, which consists of three chapters, examines value chains as linkages between processes at both the internal and external levels. We start off with supply-chain (or value-chain) strategies from a big picture perspective and follow that with issues associated with location of facilities. We close with a discussion of lean systems because this design strategy nicely draws together the issues and concepts already discussed in conjunction with individual processes.

Chapter 9, "Supply-Chain Design," was significantly enhanced. Figure 9.2, "External Value-Chain Linkages", brings forward the concept of linking processes. Both internal as well as external customers must be satisfied. Designing the customer relationship, order fulfillment, and supplier relationship processes are each examined. This chapter provides a good balance between non-manufacturing and manufacturing examples. For example, supply chains for service firms are discussed from the perspective of a real floral shop. In addition, we introduce new material on vendor-managed inventories and the bullwhip effect. The *Brunswick Distribution* case is another important addition, because it brings out the connections between supply-chain decisions and a firm's financial statements.

Chapter 10, "Location," is revised to view location decisions as part of the design of value chains. Managers must help determine where to locate new facilities (including global operations). As with the other chapters, it gives considerable attention to service processes. For example, the new opener is about how Starbucks locates new stores. In addition, all three Managerial Practices are about service providers. Location decisions for both a single facility, as well as one within a larger network, are examined. Active Model 10.1, which brings out important insights on the center-of-gravity model, is indicative of this new kind of learning support. Updated Web sites give some interesting links on location software and location factors, and the new *R. U. Reddie for Location* case adds to our library of short cases.

Chapter 11, "Lean Systems" now has more of a service orientation and fits into our new paradigm. The chapter shows how the principles of lean systems can be used for non-manufacturing processes and how the Toyota Production System can improve manufacturing processes. The chapter serves as a capstone for Part 3 because it demonstrates how the concepts already discussed for individual processes in Part 2 can be drawn together for an effective value-chain design.

Part 4: Operating Value Chains   The last section of the text addresses how to operate value chains. There are five chapters and three supplements. We begin with a chapter on information technology because it is a key enabler for operating effective value chains. We follow that with a chapter on forecasting, which is needed to do any planning, and aggregate planning, which utilizes forecasts to plan for the resources needed to satisfy the external customer demands. Inventory management, resource planning, and scheduling complete the progression from the intermediate range of planning to the short-term execution of plans. All this planning and execution results in the Outcomes depicted at the end of the road map in Figure 1.6.

Chapter 12, "Information Technology and Value Chains," is a major change from the past editions in that it focuses on the information technology, Enterprise Resource Planning (ERP), and e-commerce as it relates to operating value chains. It adds some substance to the external value-chain linkages in Figure 9.1.

Chapter 13, "Forecasting," spans the full range of forecasting approaches. It begins with qualitative techniques and concludes with time series models. Three solvers and four tutors in OM Explorer, plus the new Active Model 13.1, provide computer power to understanding and implementing these models. The chapter has the latest information on CPFR, combination forecasts and focus forecasting. The chapter presents forecasting as an essential part of managing value chains effectively. As with the other chapters, it gives considerable attention to service providers.

Chapter 14, "Aggregate Planning," presents aggregate planning as an essential part of managing value chains effectively. As with the other chapters, it gives more attention to service providers than in previous editions. The revised definition of product families and the focus on package delivery services in Managerial Practice 14.1 are good examples. The chapter is supported by Supplement D, "Linear Programming." Supplement D is enhanced by Active Model D.1, which provides a deeper understanding of graphic analysis and sensitivity analysis.

Chapter 15, "Inventory Management," has two major revisions. First, we added material addressing the situation where both demand and lead times are uncertain. This important new feature adds a number of sections, four new screenshots, and new OM Explorer capabilities. Second, we added a new experiential exercise, *Swift Electronic Supply*, which provides an opportunity for students to apply inventory models through an in-class simulation. Supplement E, "Special Inventory Models," covers other more specialized inventory models. This supplement is enhanced by the addition of three new Active Models.

Chapter 16, "Resource Planning," has more emphasis on service operations by devoting a complete section on Service Resource Planning and adding new material on Distribution Requirements Planning. The new chapter now has parallel sections on manufacturing resource planning and service resource planning. Supplement F,

"Master Production Scheduling," now on the Student CD-ROM, provides in-depth information on an important interface between manufacturing and marketing.

Chapter 17, "Scheduling," also has more of a service focus. For instance, the use of Gantt charts is demonstrated with a hospital operating room. We start off discussing demand scheduling, then progresses to employee scheduling, and finally conclude with operations scheduling.

SPECIAL FEATURES OF THE BOOK

The following are highlights of our coverage of the ever-changing field of operations management. These changes are based on extensive feedback from professors and students. All of these changes support the overall text philosophy.

- **Central Role of Processes and Value Chains.** We focus on processes—the fundamental unit of work in all organizations. It is all about processes, and the value chains created with them! This unifying theme builds bridges between chapters and opens up the topics in operations management to all students, regardless of their majors or career paths.

- **Pedagogical Structure.** Provides colorful and instructive formatting—not only in the textbook itself but also in the Student CD-ROM and the Companion Website. The book includes full color, clear explanations, step-by-step examples of quantitative techniques, solved problems, and numerous homework exercises. Students learn a framework for solving problems and experience the use of powerful decision-making tools.

- **Active Learning.** Motivating students to learn and apply OM concepts to processes and value chains is an important ingredient to a successful course. We have retained several popular and time-tested features that give students a deeper understanding of realistic business issues and enable them to become active participants in and out of the classroom. For example, Active Models, OM Explorer tutors, end-of-chapter cases, and experiential exercises involve the students in actually applying the concepts and theories explained in the text. The multiple activities available at the textbook's Companion Website expand learning beyond the textbook and the classroom.

- **A Balanced Perspective.** We believe that OM texts should address both the "big picture" strategic issues and also the analytic tools that facilitate decision making. It is not just about "concepts" or just about "numbers", but recognizes both dimensions. We provide a balanced treatment of services and manufacturing throughout the text.

- **Flexibility.** For those who want the flexibility to expand or enrich their courses, the Student CD-ROM and Companion Website offer many possibilities. The book's flexibility allows instructors to design courses that match sequencing preferences and the unique needs of the student body.

- **Chapter Opening Vignettes.** Each chapter opens with an example of how a company actually dealt with the specific process issues addressed in the chapter. See Chapter 5, "Process Performance and Quality," which also illustrates how the video series is linked to the text.

- **Managerial Practices.** Boxed inserts show operations management in action at various firms. Balanced between service providers and manufacturers, these updated inserts present current examples of how companies–successfully or unsuccessfully–deal with the process and the value-chain issues facing them.

- **Examples.** Numerous examples throughout each chapter are a popular feature and are designed to help students understand the quantitative material presented. Each example concludes with the "Decision Point," which focuses on the decision implications for managers. Whenever a new technique is presented, an example is immediately provided to walk the student through the solution. Often, an OM Explorer Tutor or an Active Model reinforces the example.

- **Solved Problems.** At the end of each chapter, detailed solutions demonstrate how to solve problems with the techniques presented in each chapter. These solved problems reinforce basic concepts and serve as models for students to refer to when doing the problems that follow.

- **The Big Picture.** Four, full-color two-page spreads help visualize the facilities of King Soopers Bakery (Chapter 3), Coors Field baseball stadium (Chapter 8), and the Lower Florida Keys Hospital and Chaparral Steel (see *Written Tours* on the Student CD-ROM).

- **Cases.** All chapters have at least one case that can serve as a basis for classroom instruction or provide an important capstone problem to the chapter, challenging students to grapple with the issues of the chapter in a less structured and more comprehensive way. Many of the cases can be used as in-class exercises without prior student preparation.

- **Cross-Functional Cases.** Two cross-functional cases have been newly developed. These unique learning experiences demonstrate how all function areas must be coordinated for a winning formula. The *Brunswick Distributing Co.* shows how various operating decisions relate to popular business performance measures through an Excel spreadsheet. It could be used in Chapter 1 to introduce the impact of operations decisions on business performance, or in Chapter 9 to support the importance of distribution and supply-chain issues. The second case, *R. U. Reddie for Location*, links the value-chain considerations of facility location covered in Chapter 10 with the financial considerations of cash flows and internal rate of return. A third cross-functional case, *Fitness Plus (B)*, is provided on the Student CD-ROM.

- **Experiential Learning Exercises.** There are six experiential learning modules: *Min-Yo Garment Company* (Chapter 2), *Statistical Process Control with a Coin Catapult* (Chapter 5), *The Pizza Connection* case (Chapter 7), *Sonic Distributors* (Chapter 9), *Yankee Fork and Hoe Company* case (Chapter 13), and *Swift Electronic Supply* (Chapter 15). Each of these experiences is an in-class exercise that actively involves the students. Each has been thoroughly tested in class and proven to be a valuable learning tool. The *Swift Electronic Supply* exercise has been newly created.

- **Across the Organization.** Each chapter begins and ends with a discussion of how the topic of the chapter is important to professionals throughout the organization. In every chapter, cross-functional connections link operations management to accounting, finance, human resources, marketing, and management information systems.

- **Screen Captures.** The streamlined book still includes many screen captures demonstrating the use of OM Explorer, Microsoft Project, PowerPoint, and SmartDraw. The text integrates these packages into the analysis of meaningful problems. See Chapter 4 for SmartDraw and PowerPoint, Chapter 8 for Microsoft Project, and Chapter 14 for OM Explorer.

- **Company URLs.** The URLs are provided for all companies featured in the Opening Vignettes and the Managerial Practices allowing students to explore them more fully beyond what is said in the text.

- **Margin Items.** A number of margin items exist:

  Questions from Managers. These voices from the real world highlight key concepts being presented.

  Definitions. Short definitions of boldfaced terms are provided for easy reference.

  Icons. These icons accompanied by brief content descriptions, indicate where the OM Explorer Tutors, Active Models, or Video Clips apply. Just click on to the Student CD-ROM for access.

● **Student CD-ROM Resources.** The Student CD-ROM, packaged free with each new copy of the text, contains many tools, activities, and resources designed for each chapter and supplement. They are recommended to enhance skills and understanding on a chapter-by-chapter basis. Resources include the following:

Textbook Supplements. Six self-contained, fully supported supplements on specialized topics: Master Production Scheduling, Learning Curve Analysis, Measuring Output Rates, Acceptance Sampling Plans, Financial Analysis, and Computer-Integrated Manufacturing.

PowerPoint Slides. View the comprehensive set of slides customized for the concepts and techniques of each chapter and supplement.

Video Clips. Video clips that bring to life the text material by viewing actual organizations in action. They are identified with icons on where they should be viewed relative to the text content. These video clips are abstracts of the full-length videos in our video library. View them directly from the Student CD-ROM, even if the instructor does not have time to show the full-length video in class.

OM Explorer. This is a complete decision support software package designed *specifically for this text*. It has the look and feel of an Excel worksheet environment. The package includes both tutors and solvers.

> *Tutors.* There are over 60 tutors that provide coaching for all of the difficult analytical methods presented in the text. They accompany problem scenarios, called "Examples," that demonstrate a particular technique. Each tutor is identified by an icon and a brief description. A tutor supplies a new example for learning and practicing the technique.

> *Tutor Exercises.* There are many tutor exercises provided that pose different questions that can be answered using one or more tutors. They are provided on a chapter-by-chapter basis on the Student CD-ROM.

> *Solvers.* There are over 40 solvers, which are powerful routines to solve problems that are often encountered in practice. They are particularly useful for experiential exercises and homework problems.

Active Models. A new package of 29 Active Model spreadsheets has been added to bring new insights for a selected number of Examples. Their purpose is to bring out new insights on the same problem scenario given in an Example, whereas the tutors give you the opportunity to practice the technique on an entirely new problem. Several of the Active Models are illustrated as exercises at the end of chapters.

SimQuick Simulation Package. The SimQuick simulation package is now loaded on the Student CD-ROM, along with its users' manual. This easy-to-use, PC-based simulation package is essentially an Excel spreadsheet with several macros. Models can be created for a variety of issues dealing with processes and value chains.

SimQuick Exercises. Exercises are provided at the end of many chapters, illustrating how to apply simulation to the problems addressed in the chapter. The full problem scenarios for the SimQuick exercises are available on the Student CD-ROM. The Extend exercises are accessible through an optional package with the book.

Microsoft Project. The 60-day evaluation version of MS Project, software that is quite popular in practice for managing projects, can be ordered from Microsoft at **www.microsoft.com/project**. This link is included on the CD-ROM. Your instructor may have ordered a 120-day evaluation version as a supplement to the textbook. Microsoft Project can be used to solve the problems and the case at the end of Chapter 8, in addition to any problems, cases, or projects that the instructor may assign.

SmartDraw. Use the link to download a 30-day trial of SmartDraw, a software package often used in practice to prepare flowcharts.

Fitness Plus (B). Download this sequel to the *Fitness Plus (A)* case in the text, to get further into cross-functional issues related with capacity.

Written Tours. See how the management of the Lower Florida Keys Health System and Chaparral Steel design their processes and value chains.

Key Equations. Find the key equations given at the end of each chapter here in one convenient place as a Word document.

- **Internet Resources.** The Companion Website at **www.prenhall.com/ krajewski** contains many other resources to enhance your understanding of the text material. The Internet has become a critical tool for success in business. Students can go online to build research skills and reinforce their understanding of operations management concepts. This element appears at the end of each chapter and describes the many tools and activities at the Companion Website that are designed specifically for each chapter. Resources include:

Self-Study Quizzes. See the compendium of true/false, multiple-choice, and essay questions that give feedback on how well you have mastered the concepts and techniques in each chapter and supplement.

In the News. See current articles that apply to each chapter and supplement.

Internet Exercises. Try out the different links on how actual businesses handle the topics covered in each chapter.

Virtual Tours. Take virtual tours of actual sites at different companies, as applied to content and managerial issues of specific chapters. Also see the "Web Links to Company Facility Tours" for additional tours of company facilities.

● ENHANCED INSTRUCTIONAL SUPPORT SYSTEM

- **Instructor's Solutions Manual.** The Instructor's Solutions Manual was created by the authors and checked by Don Knox Jr. of Wayland Baptist University, so as to keep it current and to eliminate any errors. It provides complete solutions to all discussion questions, problems, and notes for each case, experiential exercise, and cross-functional case. Selected computer screenshots are included to illustrate the different software capabilities that are available. Each case note includes a brief synopsis of the case, a description of the purposes for using the case, recommendations for analysis and goals for student learning from the case, and detailed teaching suggestions for assigning and discussing the case with students. The Solutions Manual is intended for instructors who may in turn choose to share parts of it with students, possibly through an online course. An electronic version of the whole manual is available on the **Instructor's Resource CD-ROM** and is also available for download at **www.prenhall.com**.

- **Instructor's Resource Manual.** The Instructor's Resource Manual, by Tom Wood of James Madison University, includes sample course outlines, a summary of the various ancillaries that go with the text, Annotated Chapter Outlines for each chapter and supplement, and in-class exercises called "Applications." Solutions to the in-class Applications are supplied as transparency masters. Due to the numerical aspects of the Applications, many instructors prefer to use overhead transparencies to show the solutions to Applications after students have had time to develop their own answers. An electronic version of the Instructor's Resource Manual is available on the

Instructor's Resource CD-ROM and is also available for download at www.prenhall.com.

- **Test Item File.** The Test Item File, by Ross Fink of Bradley University, contains true/false, multiple choice, fill-in-the-blank, short answer, and problem questions for each chapter and supplement. An electronic version of the Test Item File in Microsoft Word, Web CT and Blackboard formats is available on the **Instructor's Resource CD-ROM** and for download at **www.prenhall.com.**

- **TestGEN.** The print test item file is designed for use with the TestGen test-generating software. Updated by Ross Fink at Bradley University, this computerized package allows instructors to custom design, save, and generate classroom tests. The test program permits instructors to edit, add, or delete questions from the test banks; edit existing graphics and create new graphics; analyze test results; and organize a database of tests and student results. This new software allows for greater flexibility and ease of use. It provides many options for organizing and displaying tests, along with a search and sort feature. This software is available on the **Instructor's Resource CD-ROM** and for download at **www.prenhall.com.**

- **PowerPoint Presentations.** An extensive set of PowerPoint slides have been created by Jeff Heyl of Lincoln University in New Zealand. This impressive set of slides illuminates and builds upon key concepts in the text. The PowerPoints are available to adopters in electronic form on the **Instructor's Resource CD-ROM** and **Student CD-ROM,** and can also be downloaded at www.prenhall.com.

- **Video Package.** The video package contains the following videos: TQM at Parkroyal Christchurch, Process Choice at the King Soopers Bakery, Queuing at 1st Bank Villa Italia, Inventory and Textbooks, Service Scheduling at Air New Zealand, Project Management at Nantucket Nectars, and Managing Information Technology at Prentice Hall. The videos provide pedagogical value in that they incorporate summary "bullet point" screens and interviews with managers regarding significant issues Abstracts of these videos have been created as video clips by Jeff Heyl of Lincoln University in New Zealand.

- **Instructor's Resource CD-ROM.** The Instructor's Resource CD-ROM includes electronic files for the complete Instructor's Solutions Manual, the Test Item File, the computerized Test Item File, Web CT-, Blackboard- and Course Compass-formatted Test Item File, PowerPoint presentations, and the Instructor's Resource Manual. Providing these materials as Microsoft Word and PowerPoint files, rather than just as .pdf files, allows the instructor to customize portions of the material and to provide them to students as appropriate.

- **WebCT, Blackboard, CourseCompass.** Prentice Hall now makes its WebCT, Blackboard, and CourseCompass course content available on the Instructor's Resource CD and at **www.prenhall.com.** Instructors can use the student and instructor's resources as building blocks for their online courses. To learn more, contact your local Prentice Hall representative.

ACKNOWLEDGMENTS

We wish to thank various people at Prentice Hall who made up the publishing team. Those most closely involved with the project and for whom we hold the greatest admiration include Tom Tucker, Executive Editor of Decision Sciences, who supervised the overall project; Dawn Stapleton, the Editorial Assistant who kept us moving forward on our manuscript revisions; Nancy Welcher, the Senior Media Project Manager, who artfully created the Companion Website and produced all Internet and CD-ROM materials; Erika Rusnak, the Editorial Project Manager, who coordinated the ancillaries; Kerri

Tomasso, Production Editor, who managed to assemble an excellent product on time from a seemingly endless array of components; Debbie Clare, Executive Marketing Manager, whose marketing insights and promotional efforts make all the work of the publishing team worthwhile. Special thanks go to the terrific work of the folks at PreMediaONE, including Cathy Townsend, Natalie Hansen, and Sue Katkus. Don Knox of Wayland Baptist University contributed his expertise to checking the text and Solutions Manual for accuracy. We are especially appreciative for the creations of Howard Weiss, who added the Active Models and revised parts of the OM Explorer software.

We also thank our colleagues who provided extremely useful guidance for this significantly revised edition. They include the following:

Peter Ward,
Ohio State University

Madeleine E. Pullman,
Cornell University

Joy Field,
Boston College

Henry Aigbedo,
Oakland University

Danny Johnson,
Iowa State University

Karen C. Eboch,
Bowling Green State University

Dennis Krumweide,
Idaho State University

Kudos go to Larry Meile, of Boston College, for his contributions to the Internet Exercises. Brooke Saladin's cases continue to make it easy for instructors to add interest and excitement to their classes. Three graduate students at Boston College also provided valued inputs. Melissa Grills, Sadik Culcuoglu, and Leo Festino were not only exemplary students from whom a professor can learn much, but made special inputs on spreadsheets, screenshots, and managerial practices. Special thanks go to Boston College colleagues, whose research collaboration gave us many insights about service processes. We also gratefully acknowledge six graduate students at the University of Notre Dame. Carl Liu, David Ngata and Akash Trivedi were instrumental in developing the *Swift Electronics Supply* and the *Brunswick Distributors* cases. Celina Celada helped refine our Internet Exercises and Tiffany Tipps helped with research on the practical examples and managerial practices used in the text. Victor Unda Vila programmed some spreadsheets for the inventory mangement chapter. In addition, Deborah Robinson made sure everything was in order before shipping materials to the publisher at the last moment.

Finally, we thank our families for not abandoning us during our days of seclusion even when the weather for fishing was perfect. Our wives, Judie and Barb, have provided love, stability, encouragement, and a sense of humor that were needed when we were transforming the sixth edition into the seventh.

Lee J. Krajewski
University of Notre Dame

Larry P. Ritzman
Boston College

CHAPTER

1

Operations As a Competitive Weapon

CHAPTER OUTLINE

LEARNING GOALS   *After reading this chapter, you should be able to . . .*

IDENTIFY OR DEFINE
1. the set of decisions that operations managers make.
2. the trends and challenges facing operations management.
3. the customer–supplier relationships between processes.

DESCRIBE OR EXPLAIN
4. operations in terms of inputs, processes, outputs, information flows, suppliers, and customers.
5. the importance of taking a process view to operations in a firm.
6. operations as a function alongside finance, accounting, marketing, management information systems, and human resources.
7. how operations can be used as a competitive weapon.

FEDEX

FedEx (www.fedex.com) is a $17 billion-a-year delivery service company that thrives on speed and reliability. FedEx delivers 4.5 million packages a day—25 percent of the world's package delivery business. Because 70 percent of the packages that FedEx delivers go by plane, it can charge premium prices for the service. For the past 25 years, companies have used FedEx delivery services when they suddenly realized that they were short of critical parts or that they were low on goods demanded by customers. Companies have traditionally chosen FedEx because of its technological superiority in tracking packages.

The Internet, however, has changed the way business is conducted. Many businesses are now using complex Web-based processes designed to eliminate much of the unpredictability in their operations by communicating directly with customers and suppliers. E-mail reliably delivers documents instantaneously, and low-cost truck lines, discount air carriers, and even ocean vessels can now track shipments via the Internet.

While these technological advances have been an advantage to some firms, they have cut into the demand for FedEx's traditional services. The growth potential now is in ground transportation services, presently dominated by United Parcel Service. This demand is fueled by Internet companies such as Amazon.com that rely heavily on ground transportation services to deliver packages directly to the customer's door and by the vast business-to-business supply networks energized by Web-based purchasing systems. To remain competitive in this changing environment, FedEx created two new services: FedEx Ground and FedEx Home Delivery. FedEx Ground focuses on business-to-business deliveries via a recently procured trucking company; FedEx Home Delivery specializes in deliveries to residences. The processes that produce those services strive for low-cost operations and dependable deliveries—a change from the goals of past operations, which stress speed. In addition, FedEx will rely on its core competency in technology. It invested $100 million in processes that will coordinate the flow of goods from a company such as Cisco with shipments from suppliers of major components, all to be delivered to a customer within a short window of time for assembly of the final product. FedEx is relying on its operations to compete successfully in a dynamic environment being reshaped by the Internet.

Source: O'Reilly, Brian. "They've Got Mail!" *Fortune* (February 7, 2000), pp. 101–112.

An employee of FedEx Home Delivery division drops off a package at a residence. Emphasizing low-cost operations and dependable deliveries, FedEx changed its operations strategy to reflect technology changes.

Operations management deals with processes that produce goods and services that people use every day. *Processes* are the fundamental activities that organizations use to do work and achieve their goals. FedEx must receive packages from customers, sort them by destination, move them to their destination by air or ground transportation, keep track of progress, and bill the customer for the service. The changes at FedEx provide one example of designing processes for competitive operations. Major processes were created for the new ground delivery services that satisfy the needs of customers. The new delivery system involves the coordination of processes from all areas of the firm.

Every organization, whether public or private, service or manufacturing, must manage processes to add value for customers. That is the focus of this book. We explain what managers of processes do, the decisions they make, and some of the tools and concepts that they can use. By selecting appropriate techniques and strategies, managers can design and operate processes to give companies a competitive edge. Helping you understand how to make operations a competitive weapon begins with this chapter and continues throughout the book.

What processes have you been involved with?

As you read this introductory chapter about operations management, think about how the effective management of processes is important to various departments across the organization, such as . . .

➤ **accounting,** which prepares financial and cost accounting information that aids managers in designing and operating processes.

➤ **finance,** which manages the cash flows and capital investment requirements that are created by the firm's processes.

➤ **human resources,** which hires and trains employees to match process needs, location decisions, and planned output levels.

➤ **management information systems,** which develops information systems and decision support systems for the firm's processes.

➤ **marketing,** which helps create the demand that operations must satisfy, link customer demand with staffing and production plans, and keep the operations function focused on satisfying customers' needs.

➤ **operations,** which designs and operates processes that transform inputs into services or products to give the firm a sustainable competitive advantage.

WHAT IS A PROCESS?

A **process** is any activity or group of activities that takes one or more inputs, transforms and adds value to them, and provides one or more outputs for its customers. Every business is composed of a set of processes. You might be wondering why we have chosen to look at "processes" as the unit of analysis, as opposed to departments or even the firm. The answer is that a process view of the firm is much more relevant to the way firms actually do work. Departments typically have their own set of objectives, set of resources with capabilities to achieve those objectives, and managers and employees responsible for their performance. Some processes, such as billing, may be contained wholly within a department, such as accounting in this example. The concept of a process, however, can be much more expansive. A process can have its own set of objectives, involve a work flow that cuts across departmental boundaries, and require resources from several departments. Such is the case with product development, which may involve coordination between engineering, marketing, and operations. You will see examples throughout the text of companies that have discovered that they can use the performance of their processes to competitive advantage. As you proceed through the text, you will notice that the key to success in many organizations is a keen understanding of how their processes do work.

process Any activity or group of activities that takes one or more inputs, transforms and adds value to them, and provides one or more outputs for its customers.

A PROCESS VIEW

It is important to take a process view of organizations because an organization is only as effective as its processes. To get a better understanding of processes, let us take a look at what happens at an ad agency. Suppose that a client contacts her account executive (AE) at an ad agency about her need for a memorable ad for the next Super Bowl football game. The AE gathers all of the pertinent information and passes it along to a creative design team and a media planning team, which prepare an ad layout and a media exposure plan acceptable to the client. The AE also gives the information to the accounting department, which prepares an account for billing purposes. The creative design team passes the layout design to a production team, which prepares the final layout for publication and delivers it to the selected media outlets according to the schedule developed by the media team and approved by the client. The design team, media team, and production team send their billable hours and expense items to the accounting department, which prepares an invoice that is approved by the AE and then sent to the client for payment.

Figure 1.1 shows a process view of the ad agency at two levels. The red-outlined box represents the ad agency as an aggregate process. Viewed at this level, the ad agency requires inputs from external sources and produces advertisements for external clients. The inputs from external sources are resources used by the ad agency's processes and include employees, managers, money, equipment, facilities, materials, services, land, and

A design team discusses an ad campaign for a new Ortho product at an ad agency. The design team must coordinate with the media planning team and the production team to produce an ad that satisfies the client.

energy. The output is the Super Bowl ad for its client. However, inside the red box we see a more detailed process view: the firm has four processes (many others are not shown). The client interface process includes the AE and his interactions with the client. The advertisement design and planning process creates the ad and plans its exposure during the Super Bowl and subsequent showings. The production process acquires the actors and actresses, prepares the production set and props, coordinates the schedules of all involved in the production of the ad, films the content, prepares a video, and delivers the ad to the media outlets on time. The arrows in the diagram indicate information and work flows between the processes. They also indicate feedback on performance.

As we look at the four processes, we see that each has inputs and each has outputs. At the process level, we see that the inputs could be the resources from external sources mentioned earlier, or they may be very specific to the tasks of the process received from other processes. For example, the advertisement design and planning process receives detailed information about the ad requirements from the client interface process, and the production process receives the ad layout and media plan from the advertisement design and planning process. Billable hours for the ad are an output of the production process, and a complete invoice for the client is an output of the accounting process. It is clear that among primary and supporting processes, the output of one process is the

---

FIGURE 1.1   **Process View of an Ad Agency**

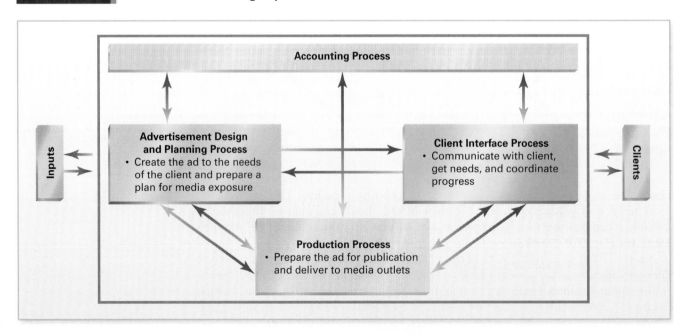

input of another. It follows that performance failures in one process can have major influences on other processes.

NESTED PROCESSES

Our process view of the ad agency is helpful; however, even at that level of detail, we may not have a clear enough picture of what is going on. Let us peel away a little more of the layers. Consider the advertisement design and planning process. Figure 1.2 shows that there are really two separate processes involved. The creative design process receives a work order from the AE, after which the creative design director assembles the team. The work order includes details of the ad's objective, the overall message of the ad, the evidence supporting the claims, and the intended audience. The design team comes up with several designs, gets feedback from the AE, prepares a final design, gets feedback from the client through the client interface process, and revises the design as needed. This process has its own set of inputs and outputs, separate from the media planning process. The work order for the media planning process, which includes the information in the creative design director's work order plus information about the size of the ad and the intended duration of the campaign, goes to the media director, who selects a media planner. The media planner prepares several plans, gets feedback from the AE, prepares a final plan, gets feedback from the client, and revises the plan as needed.

Processes, such as the advertisement design and planning process, can be broken down into subprocesses, which in turn can be broken down further. For example, "preparing an ad design" is itself a process within the creative design process. We refer to this concept of a process within a process as a **nested process**. It may be helpful to separate one part of a process from another for several reasons. One person or one department may be unable to do all parts of the process, or different parts of the process may require different skills. That was the case in the advertisement design and planning process. The skills needed for creative ad designs are quite different from the skills needed for effective media planning. Another reason could be that one part of the process provides services requiring considerable customer contact, which requires special employee skills and attitudes, whereas another part is unobservable by the customer. Finally, some parts of the process may be designed for routine work while other parts of the process may be geared for customized work. The nested process concept reinforces the need to understand the interconnectivity of activities within a business and the nature of each processes inputs and outputs.

nested process   The concept of a process within a process.

CUSTOMER–SUPPLIER RELATIONSHIPS

Processes should be designed with a customer focus. Processes provide outputs—often services (which can take the form of information)—to their customers. Every process and every person in an organization has customers. Some are **external customers,** who may be either end users or intermediaries (such as manufacturers, financial institutions, or retailers) buying the firm's finished services or products. The client of the ad agency

external customers   A customer who is either an end user or an intermediary (such as manufacturers, financial institutions, or retailers) buying the firm's finished services or products.

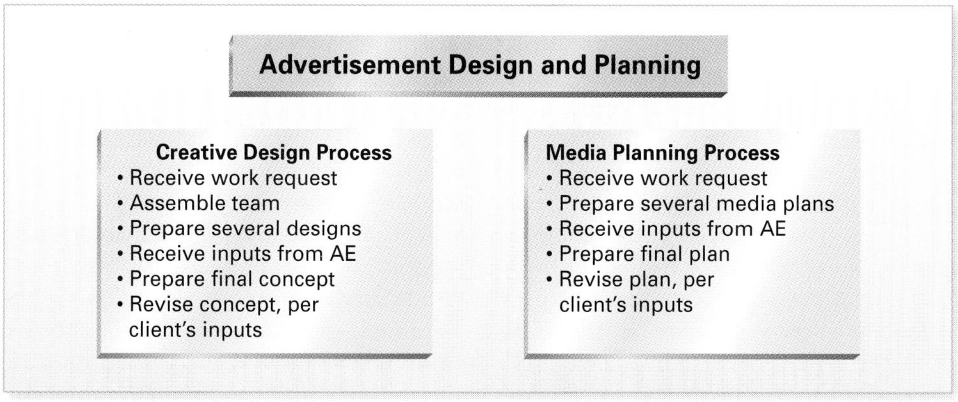

FIGURE 1.2

Nested Processes

Advertisement Design and Planning

Creative Design Process
- Receive work request
- Assemble team
- Prepare several designs
- Receive inputs from AE
- Prepare final concept
- Revise concept, per client's inputs

Media Planning Process
- Receive work request
- Prepare several media plans
- Receive inputs from AE
- Prepare final plan
- Revise plan, per client's inputs

internal customers   One or more employees or processes that rely on inputs from other employees or processes in order to perform their work.

external suppliers   The businesses or individuals who provide the resources, services, products, and materials for the firm's short term and long term needs.

internal suppliers   The employees or processes that supply important information or materials to a firm's processes.

is an example of an external customer. Others are **internal customers,** who may be employees or processes that rely on inputs from other employees or processes in order to perform their work. The production process is an internal customer of the advertisement design and planning process. Either way, internal or external, processes must be designed and managed with the customer in mind. A continuing question for all managers: Is this process meeting or exceeding the customer's expectations?

In similar fashion, every process and every person in an organization relies on suppliers. **External suppliers** may be other businesses or individuals who provide the resources, services, products, and materials for the firm's short term and long term needs. For example, the ad agency needs bank loans, office supplies, computer equipment, software, and new personnel to support the needs of its processes over time. Processes also have **internal suppliers,** who may be employees or processes that supply them with important information or materials. In the ad agency, the advertisement design and planning process supplies an ad design and media plan to the production process. Understanding the customer–supplier relationships between processes is important to becoming an effective manager.

SERVICE AND MANUFACTURING PROCESSES

There are two major types of processes: service and manufacturing. Service processes pervade the business world. Judging on statistics from the major industrialized countries in the world, 80 percent of the jobs in business are in services. Consequently, service processes have a prominent place in our discussion of operations management in this text. Manufacturing processes, however, are also important because, without them, the products we enjoy as part of our daily lives would not exist. In addition, manufacturing gives rise to a host of service opportunities. Services related to products now represent 10 to 30 times the annual dollar volume of the underlying product sales. See Managerial Practice 1.1 for some examples. Consequently, both types of processes are important to anyone interested in a career in business.

Why do we distinguish between service and manufacturing processes? The answer lies at the heart of the design of competitive processes. While Chapter 3, "Process Design Strategy" shares all the secrets of process design, there are two key differences between service and manufacturing processes: (1) the nature of their output and (2) the degree of customer contact. Service processes tend to produce intangible, perishable outputs that we refer to as services. For example, the output from the auto finance department of a bank would be a car loan, and the output from the U.S. Postal Service is the delivery of your letter. The outputs from service processes typically cannot be held in a finished goods inventory to insulate the process from erratic customer demands. Manufacturing processes, on the other hand, produce physical, durable outputs that we call products. For example, an assembly line produces a 350 Z sports car, and a tailor produces an outfit for the rack at an upscale clothing store. The outputs from manufacturing processes can be produced, stored, and transported in anticipation of future demands if the situation dictates it. The nature of a process's outputs bears heavily on its effective design.

A second key difference between service processes and manufacturing processes is the degree of customer contact. Service processes tend to have a higher degree of customer contact. Customers may take an active role in the process itself, as in the case of shopping in a supermarket, or they may be in close contact with the service provider to communicate specific service needs, as in the case of a medical clinic. Manufacturing processes tend to have less customer contact, leaving the primary contacts with customers to retailers or distributors. For example, washing machines are produced to forecasts of retail needs and the process requires little information from the ultimate consumers (you and me), except indirectly through market surveys and market focus groups. Nonetheless, the distinction between service and manufacturing processes on the basis of customer contact is not perfect. Some service processes have nested subprocesses where there may be low customer contact, as in the central offices of an insurance provider where insurance products and policies are designed and produced, while others may have high customer contact, as in the branch offices where insurance

Employees in the billing department at the Huntington Hospital in Pasadena, California, are part of a low customer contact process.

agents deal with customers daily. Likewise, some manufacturing processes require high customer contact. Such is the case in the production of unique engine parts for a specific model of automobile, such as the Ford Explorer. Before large scale production can begin, the quality of the part must be verified by Ford. The supplier can accomplish this by successfully executing some pilot runs of the process. There must be close coordination between Ford and the supplier until the quality has been verified and even beyond that, as weekly shipments must be coordinated with Ford's assembly schedules. The important point is that managers must recognize the degree of customer contact required when designing processes.

While there tends to be differences between service and manufacturing processes, there are also many similarities. Taken at the level of the firm, service providers do not just offer services and manufacturers do not just offer products. Patrons of a restaurant expect good service and good food. A customer purchasing new computers for his business expects a good product as well as good warranty, maintenance, replacement, and financial services. Managerial Practice 1.1 gives examples of major manufacturing companies that offer services along with their products. At the process level, the managers of service processes as well as manufacturing processes must be concerned with issues of process design, quality, productivity, capacity, staffing levels, forecasting, location, and layout, just to name a few of the decision areas we will explore in this text. Further, while service processes do not use finished goods inventories, they do inventory their inputs. For example, hospitals need to keep inventories of their medical supplies and day-to-day materials needed for the operation of the hospital's processes. Some manufacturing processes, on the other hand, do not inventory their outputs because they are very costly. Such would be the case with low-volume customized products (e.g., tailored suits) or products with short shelf lives (e.g., daily newspapers). With all of these differences and similarities between the two major types of processes, the importance of taking a process view of a firm is very clear.

VALUE CHAINS

Most services or products are produced through a series of interrelated business activities. Our process view of a firm is helpful for understanding how services or products are produced and why it is important for cross-functional coordination, but it does not shed any light on the strategic benefits of the processes. The missing strategic insight is that processes must add value for their customers. The cumulative work of the processes of a firm is a **value chain**, which is the interrelated series of processes that produces a service or product. The concept of the value chain can also be seen at the activity level: Each activity in a process should add value to the preceding activities. Adding the concept of value chains to the concept of taking a

value chain An interrelated series of processes that produces a service or product.

MANAGERIAL PRACTICE 1.1

MANUFACTURERS DO NOT JUST OFFER PRODUCTS

Despite the high marks that U.S. manufacturers achieved in productivity increases during the 1990s and despite thriving economic expansion, the growth in sales for many manufacturing sectors has stagnated. For example, the annual growth in sales of industrial machinery dropped from 5.2 percent in the 1960s to 2 percent in the 1990s. Thanks to past purchases and longer product life spans, the installed base of products has been expanding over the years. Today, the number of U.S. autos in service is 200 million, while new sales have been flat at 15 million vehicles a year. This pattern is repeated across many manufacturing sectors. Revenues from related service-based activities now represent 10 to 30 times the annual dollar volume of underlying product sales. In corporate computing, the average company puts 20 percent of its annual personal-computer budget into purchasing the equipment itself; the rest goes to technical support, administration, and other maintenance activities. New distribution channels, such as the Internet, have also emerged to threaten manufacturers. Dozens of companies like Amazon.com, Autobytel.com, and eBay are becoming electronic intermediaries with powerful advantages, putting new pressure on manufacturers and traditional channels.

The upshot is that smart manufacturers are getting increasingly involved with related services. Product sales are seen as a way to open the door to providing future services. Four basic models for providing related services are proving successful for some companies. Honeywell (www.honeywell.com), using the *embedded services* model, builds traditional services into its product with new digital technologies. Its Airplane Information Management System (AIMS) ties airplane systems together with a microprocessor and software. AIMS performs a variety of tasks that used to be performed manually by Honeywell's customers, reducing the need for expensive flight engineers and allowing Honeywell to charge a premium for its products. GE (www.ge.com) uses the *comprehensive services* model. In the locomotive market, for example, it provides financing, supplies parts, provides boxcar-scheduling and routing services and helps manage maintenance facilities. The Finnish company Nokia (www.nokia.com/main.html) uses the *integrated services* model, which combines products and services into a seamless customer offering. It seeks to address all of the equipment and service needs of its customers—cellular carriers. Its products include handsets, transmission equipment, and switches for the carriers. Its services include managing customer networks, meeting zoning requirements for new transmission towers, and providing technical support. The fourth approach is the *distribution control* model. Coca-Cola (www.coke.com/gateway.html) is a good example. It has gained control over lucrative distribution activities. Today, it controls 70 percent of its U.S. bottling and distribution, and it is expanding its control overseas.

Such models blur the line between manufacturers and service providers, because these manufacturers do not just offer products.

Honeywell's AIMS architecture, which acts as the "brains" of the 777 aircraft, is the centerpiece of an advanced avionics system designed to meet stringent requirements for functionality, maintainability, and reliability. Here, two lab technicians inspect newly assembled, liquid crystal cockpit displays that are an integral part of the AIMS system.

Source: Wise, Richard and Peter Baumgartner. "Go Downstream: The New Profit Imperative in Manufacturing." *Harvard Business Review* (September–October 1999), pp. 133–141.

process view to businesses is important because processes are consumers of resources and need to be assessed not only in terms of the value they add but also the amount of employees, managers, equipment, facilities, materials, services, land, and energy that they consume in the creation of that value.

The concept of value chains reinforces the interconnectedness of processes to business performance. A weak link in the chain imperils the value provided by the chain. The concept of value chains also focuses attention on the type of processes in the value chain. For example, a **core process** is a chain of activities that delivers value to external customers. These processes interact with external customers and build relationships with them, develop new services and products, interact with external suppliers, and produce the service or product for the external customer. Examples include reservation handling, new car designing, Web-based purchasing, and loan processing. Another type of process is a **support process,** which provides vital resources and inputs to the core processes and therefore is essential to the management of the business. Examples include budgeting, recruiting, and scheduling. It is sometimes debatable as to what is core and what is supporting. Generally, if the process is directly involved in the service or product for the external customer, it is a core process. We discuss the concept of core processes further in Chapter 2, "Operations Strategy."

Figure 1.3 shows the linkages between the core and support processes in a firm. In this text we focus on four core processes:

- *Customer Relationship Process.* Sometimes referred to as *customer relationship management,* the **customer relationship process** identifies, attracts, builds relationships with external customers, and facilitates the placement of orders by customers. Traditional functions, such as marketing and sales, may be a part of this process. The client interface process for the ad agency is an example of the customer relationship process.
- *New Service/Product Development Process.* The **new service/product development process** designs and develops new services or products. These services or products may be developed to external customer specifications or conceived from inputs received from the market in general through the customer relationship process. The advertisement design and planning process for the ad agency is an example of the new service/product development process.
- *Order Fulfillment Process.* The **order fulfillment process** includes the activities required to produce and deliver the service or product to the external customer. The production process in the ad agency is an example of the order fulfillment process.

core process A chain of activities that delivers value to external customers.

support process A process that provides vital resources and inputs to the core processes and therefore is essential to the management of the business.

customer relationship process A process that identifies, attracts, builds relationships with external customers, and facilitates the placement of orders by customers, sometimes referred to as customer relationship management.

new service/product development process A process that designs and develops new services or products from inputs received from external customer specifications or from the market in general through the customer relationship process.

order fulfillment process A process that includes the activities required to produce and deliver the service or product to the external customer.

FIGURE 1.3   Internal Value-Chain Linkages Showing Work and Information Flows

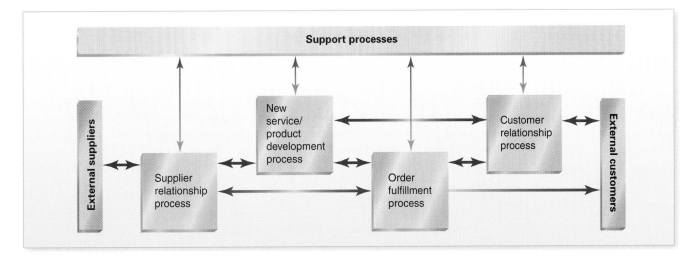

TABLE 1.1   EXAMPLES OF SUPPORT PROCESSES

Capital Acquisition	The provision of financial resources for the organization to do its work and to execute its strategy.
Budgeting	The process of deciding how funds will be allocated over a period of time.
Recruitment and Hiring	The acquisition of people to do the work of the organization.
Evaluation and Compensation	The assessment and payment of people for the work and value they provide to the company.
Human Resource Support and Development	The preparation of people for their current jobs and future skill and knowledge needs.
Regulatory Compliance	The processes that ensure that the company is meeting all laws and legal obligations.
Information Systems	The movement and processing of data and information to expedite business operations and decisions.
Enterprise and Functional Management	The systems and activities that provide strategic direction and ensure effective execution of the work of the business.

Source: Pande, Peter S., Robert P. Neuman, and Roland R. Cavanagh, *The Six Sigma Way,* New York: McGraw-Hill, 2000, page 161.

supplier relationship process
A process that selects the suppliers of services, materials, and information and facilitates the timely and efficient flow of these items into the firm.

• *Supplier Relationship Process.* The **supplier relationship process** selects the suppliers of services, materials, and information and facilitates the timely and efficient flow of these items into the firm. Working effectively with suppliers can add significant value to the services or products of the firm. Fair prices must be negotiated, deliveries must be scheduled on time, and ideas and insights from critical suppliers to the new service/product development process are just a few of the ways value can be created.

Of course, each of these core processes has nested processes within it. We will explore some of these processes in later chapters of this text.

Firms also have many support processes. Accounting (actually, invoice preparation) was used as an example in the ad agency. Support processes provide key resources, capabilities, or other inputs that allow the core processes to function. Table 1.1 provides some examples of support processes.

It is important to realize that a need registered by an internal or external customer jump-starts a process into action. These needs may be actual work orders (as in the work request from the AE at the ad agency to the director of the creative design process) or they may be forecasts of future needs. Regardless, in reality, many of these needs may be present at any process at any time, making for a very complicated management challenge.

WHAT IS OPERATIONS MANAGEMENT?

operations management   The systematic design, direction, and control of processes that transform inputs into services and products for internal, as well as external, customers.

The term **operations management** refers to the systematic design, direction, and control of processes that transform inputs into services and products for internal, as well as external, customers. Broadly speaking, operations management underlies all departments in a business because departments are composed of many processes. If you aspire to manage a department or a particular process in your discipline, or if you just want to understand how the process you are a part of fits into the overall fabric of the business, you need to understand the principles of operations management. In this regard, there is at least a little bit of operations management in all of us. Narrowly interpreted, *operations* refers to a particular department (or more likely several departments) associated with the order fulfillment process. Operations managers oversee the processes that are required to produce and deliver the service or product to the external customer. Given our discussion of value chains, it is clear that operations managers are closely involved with the other areas of a firm.

OPERATIONS MANAGEMENT AS A FUNCTION

As a firm grows in size, different departments must be created that assume responsibility for certain clusters of processes. Often, these departments are organized around *functions* (sometimes called *functional areas*). Figure 1.4 shows that operations is one of several functions within an organization. Each function is specialized, having its own knowledge and skill areas, primary responsibilities, processes, and decision domains. Regardless of how lines are drawn, departments and functions remain interrelated. As we have said, many processes are enterprise wide and cut across departmental boundaries. Thus, coordination and effective communication are essential to achieving organizational goals.

In large organizations, the *operations* (or *production*) *department* is usually responsible for the actual transformation of inputs into finished services or products. *Accounting* collects, summarizes, and interprets financial information. *Distribution* deals with the movement, storage, and handling of inputs and outputs. *Engineering* develops service and product designs and production methods. *Finance* secures and invests the company's capital assets. *Human resources* (or *personnel*) hires and trains employees. *Marketing* generates demand for the company's output.

Some organizations never need to perform certain functions. Other organizations may save money by contracting for a function, such as legal services or engineering, when they need it, rather than maintain an in-house department. In small businesses, the owners might manage one or more functions, such as marketing or operations.

Operations serves as an excellent career path to upper-management positions in many organizations. One survey of manufacturing firms showed over 45 percent of the chief executives appointed had operations background. In manufacturing firms, the head of operations usually holds the title chief operations officer (COO) or vice-president of manufacturing (or production or operations). The corresponding title in a service organization might be COO or vice president (or director) of operations. Reporting to the head of operations are the managers of departments, such as customer service, production and inventory control, quality assurance, and check processing.

How does operations differ from other functions?

OPERATIONS MANAGEMENT AS A SET OF DECISIONS

Decision making is an essential aspect of all management activity, including operations management. Although the specifics of each situation vary, decision making generally involves the same basic steps: (1) recognize and clearly define the problem, (2) collect the information needed to analyze possible alternatives, (3) choose the most attractive alternative, and (4) implement the chosen alternative. Some decisions are strategic in nature, while others are tactical. Strategic plans are developed further in the future than tactical plans. Thus, strategic decisions are less structured and have long-term consequences; whereas tactical decisions are more structured, routine, and repetitive and have short-term consequences. What sets operations managers apart,

What types of decisions are involved in managing operations?

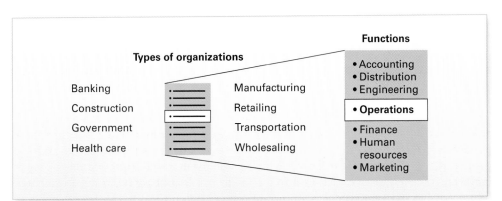

FIGURE 1.4

Operations Management As a Function

however, are the types of decisions that they make or participate in making. In this text we cover the major decisions operations managers make in practice. At the strategic level, operations managers are involved in the development of new capabilities and the maintenance of existing capabilities to best serve the firm's external customers now and in the future. Operations managers design new processes that have strategic implications and they are deeply involved in the development and organization of value chains linking external suppliers and external customers to the firm's internal processes. Operations managers are often responsible for key performance measures such as cost, quality, and others we discuss throughout the text. These decisions have strategic impact because they affect the very processes the firm uses to gain a competitive edge.

While strategic decisions have a lot of glamour, we must not lose sight of the fact that great strategic decisions lead nowhere if the tactical decisions that support them fail. Operations managers are also involved in many important tactical decisions, including process improvement and performance measurement, managing and planning projects, generating production and staffing plans, managing inventories, and scheduling resources. You will find numerous examples of these decisions, and the implications of making them, throughout the text. You will also experience the decision-making tools practicing managers use to recognize and define the problem and then choose the best alternative from the various alternatives available. In addition to the chapters in the text, there are three other sources for learning and experiencing decision-making tools that have application in practice.

- *Supplements in the Text.* We have singled out several of the most often used decision-making methods for inclusion in the text as supplements to various chapters. We begin with "Decision Making" which discusses traditional decision-making tools that have application for many operating decisions that we discuss in the text. The other supplements are "Simulation," "Waiting Lines," "Linear Programming"and "Special Inventory Models." Explore these supplements—you may find just the tool you need to analyze a tough problem.
- *Supplements on the Student CD-ROM.* Several other decision-making tools can be found on the Student CD-ROM. These supplements include "Master Production Scheduling," "Learning Curve Analysis," "Measuring Output Rates," "Acceptance Sampling Plans," "Financial Analysis," and "Computer-Integrated Manufacturing." Whenever we think any of these tools are useful for a particular decision problem, we will remind you to look for them on the Student CD-ROM.
- *OM Explorer and Other Computer Applications.* The Student CD-ROM contains a unique set of decision tools we call OM Explorer. This package contains 41 powerful computer routines to solve problems often encountered in practice. It also has 63 tutors that provide coaching for all of the difficult analytical techniques in the text. See Figure 1.5 for an example of a Tutor. The Student CD-ROM also contains many Active Models, which are spreadsheets designed to help you learn more about important decision-making techniques, and a spreadsheet-based simulation package called SimQuick. In addition, it contains a web link to a 60-day evaluation version of MS Project, which is a popular, project planning software package, and a Web link to a 30-day trial version of SmartDraw, which is a useful package for drawing charts and diagrams. Whenever we think you could benefit from these packages, we will let you know as you read the text.

The operations manager's decisions should reflect corporate strategy. Plans, policies, and actions should be linked to those in other functional areas so as to be supportive of the firm's goals and objectives. These linkages are facilitated by taking a process view of a firm. Regardless of whether you aspire to be an operations manager in the narrow view, or you just want to use the principles of operations management to be a more effective manager, it is important to realize that the effective management of people, capital, information, and materials is critical to the success of any process. As you study operations management, keep two principles in mind.

1. Each part of an organization, not just the operations function, must design and operate processes and deal with quality, technology, and staffing issues.
2. Each part of an organization has its own identity and yet is connected with operations.

Introduction

OM Explorer

Tutor 1.1 - Productivity Measures

The state ferry service charges $18 per ticket, plus a $3 surcharge to fund planned equipment upgrades. It expects to sell 4,700 tickets during the eight-week summer season. During that period, the ferry service will experience $110,000 in labor costs. Materials required for each passage sold (tickets, a tourist-information sheet, and the like) cost $1.30. Overhead during the period comes to $79,000.

a. What is the *multifactor* productivity ratio?
b. If ferry-support staff work an average of 310 person-hours per week for the 8 weeks of the summer season, what is the *labor* productivity ratio? Calculate labor productivity here on an hourly basis.

Click here to continue.

Inputs

FIGURE 1.5b

Tutor 1.1 - Productivity Measures

Enter data in yellow-shaded areas.

a. Multifactor productivity is the ratio of the value of output to the value of input.

Step 1. Enter the number of tickets sold during a season, the price per ticket, and the surcharge per ticket. To compute value of output, multiply tickets sold by the sum of price and surcharge.

Tickets sold: Value of output:
Price:
Surcharge:

Step 2. Enter labor costs, materials costs per passenger, and overhead cost. For value of input, add labor costs, materials costs times number of passengers, and overhead costs.

Labor costs: Materials costs: Overhead:

                                    Value of input:

Step 3. To calculate multifactor productivity, divide value of output by value of input.

                    Multifactor productivity:

b. Labor productivity is the ratio of the value of output to labor hours. The value of output is computed in part a, step 1.

Step 1. Enter person-hours per week and the number of weeks in the season; multiply the two together to calculate labor hours of input.

Hours per week: Weeks:

                            Labor hours of input:

Step 2. To calculate labor productivity, divide value of output by labor hours of input.

                            Labor productivity:

Click here to view the Results sheet.

FIGURE 1.5a

Using Tutors in OM Explorer
The icon next to Example 1.1 means that there is a *tutor* spreadsheet in OM Explorer, software that was packaged on the Student CD-ROM that came with your text. Open up the Tutor menu for Chapter 1 and select *Tutor 1.1: Productivity*. You will be presented with three worksheets for this Tutor. The Introduction describes an entirely new example. The Inputs requires you to enter your inputs and answers in the areas shaded in yellow, and the Results gives the correct answers in the areas shaded in green. There are 63 such tutors throughout the book. Most of them are for more complex techniques than demonstrated here. Use them when you are not sure about an example, when you want to test your understanding, or when you want to do some "what-if" analysis on a different problem.

TRENDS AND CHALLENGES IN OPERATIONS MANAGEMENT

Several business trends are currently having a great impact on operations management: productivity improvement; global competitiveness; technological change; and environmental, ethical, and diversity issues. In this section, we look at these trends and their challenges for operations managers.

FIGURE 1.5c

Using Tutors in OM Explorer

Results

Tutor 1.1 - Productivity Measures

a. Multifactor productivity is the ratio of the value of output to the value of input.

Step 1. Enter the number of tickets sold during a season, the price per ticket, and the surcharge per ticket. To compute value of output, multiply tickets sold by the sum of price and surcharge.

Tickets sold:	4,700	Value of output:	$98,700
Price:	$18		
Surcharge:	$3		

Step 2. Enter labor costs, materials costs per passenger, and overhead cost. For value of input, add labor costs, materials costs times number of passengers, and overhead costs.

| Labor costs: | $110,000 | Materials costs: | $1.30 | Overhead: | $79,000 |

Value of input: $195,110

Step 3. To calculate multifactor productivity, divide value of output by value of input.

Multifactor productivity: 0.51

b. Labor productivity is the ratio of the value of output to labor hours. The value of output is computed in part a, step 1.

Step 1. Enter person-hours per week and the number of weeks in the season; multiply the two together to calculate labor hours of input.

| Hours per week: | 310 | Weeks: | 8 |

Labor hours of input: 2,480

Step 2. To calculate labor productivity, divide value of output by labor hours of input.

Labor productivity: $39.80

PRODUCTIVITY IMPROVEMENT

Productivity is a basic measure of performance for economies, industries, firms, and processes. **Productivity** is the value of outputs (services and products) produced divided by the values of input resources (wages, cost of equipment, and the like) used:

productivity The value of outputs (services and products) produced divided by the values of input resources (wages, costs of equipment, and the like).

$$\text{Productivity} = \frac{\text{Output}}{\text{Input}}$$

Is productivity increasing faster in manufacturing or in services?

It is interesting, and even surprising, to break out productivity improvements between the service and manufacturing sectors. For example, in the United States, employment in the service sector has grown rapidly, outstripping the manufacturing sector. However, productivity gains have been much lower. The sector's lagging productivity slows economic growth. Other major industrial countries, such as Japan and Germany, have experienced the same problem. There are signs of improvement. The surge of investment across national boundaries can stimulate productivity gains by exposing firms to greater competition. The increased investment in information technology by service providers will also increase productivity. Nonetheless, productivity improvement is a particular concern for service providers. If productivity growth stagnates, so does the overall standard of living regardless of which part of the world you live in.

As a manager, how can you measure the productivity of your processes? Many measures of productivity are possible, and all are rough approximations. For example, value of output can be measured by what the customer pays or simply by the number of units produced or customers served. The value of inputs can be judged by their cost or simply by the number of hours worked.

Managers usually pick several reasonable measures and monitor trends to spot areas needing improvement. For example, a manager at an insurance firm might measure office productivity as the number of insurance policies processed per employee per week. A manager at a carpet company might measure the productivity of installers as the number of square yards of carpet installed per hour. Both of these measures reflect *labor productivity*, which is an index of the output per person or hour worked. Similar measures may be used for *machine productivity*, where the denominator is the number of machines. Accounting for several inputs simultaneously is also possible. *Multifactor producitivity* is an index of the output provided by more than one of the resources used in production. For example, it may be the value of the output divided by the sum of labor, materials, and overhead costs. When developing such a measure, you must convert the quantities to a common unit of measure, typically dollars.

Productivity Calculations

EXAMPLE 1.1

Calculate the productivity for the following operations:

a. Three employees process 600 insurance policies in a week. They work 8 hours per day, 5 days per week.

b. A team of workers make 400 units of a product, which is valued by its standard cost of $10 each (before markups for other expenses and profit). The accounting department reports that for this job the actual costs are $400 for labor, $1,000 for materials, and $300 for overhead.

ACTIVE MODEL 1.1

Active Model 1.1 on the Student CD-ROM provides additional insight on labor productivity for the insurance company.

SOLUTION

a. $\text{Labor productivity} = \dfrac{\text{Policies processed}}{\text{Employee hours}}$

$$= \frac{600 \text{ policies}}{(3 \text{ employees})(40 \text{ hours/employee})} = 5 \text{ policies/hour}$$

TUTOR 1.1

Tutor 1.1 on the Student CD-ROM provides a new example to practice productivity measurement.

b. $\text{Multifactor productivity} = \dfrac{\text{Quantity at standard cost}}{\text{Labor cost} + \text{Materials cost} + \text{Overhead cost}}$

$$= \frac{(400 \text{ units})(\$10/\text{unit})}{\$400 + \$1,000 + \$300} = \frac{\$4,000}{\$1,700} = 2.35$$

DECISION POINT   These measures must be compared with both performance levels in prior periods and with future goals. If they are not living up to expectations, the process should be investigated for improvement opportunities. (See Figure 1.5 for an example of Tutor 1.1).

The way processes are managed plays a key role in productivity improvement. Managers must examine productivity from the level of the value chain because it is the collective performance of individual processes that makes the difference. The challenge is to increase the value of output relative to the cost of input. If processes can generate more output or output of better quality using the same amount of input, their productivity increases. If they can maintain the same level of output while reducing the use of resources, their productivity also increases. Nonetheless, the performance of the value chain depends on the effective management and coordination of all processes in the chain.

GLOBAL COMPETITION

Businesses accept the fact that, to prosper, they must view customers, suppliers, facility locations, and competitors in global terms. Most products today are global composites of materials and services from throughout the world. Your Gap polo shirt is sewn in Honduras from cloth cut in the United States. Sitting in a Cineplex theater (Canadian), you munch a Nestle's Crunch bar (Swiss) while watching a Columbia Pictures movie (Japanese).

Strong global competition affects industries everywhere. For example, U.S. manufacturers have experienced declining shares of the domestic and international markets in steel, appliances and household durable goods, machinery, and chemicals. With the value of world trade in services now at more than $1.5 trillion per year, banking, law, data processing, airlines, and consulting services operations are beginning to face many of the same international pressures as manufacturers. And regional trading blocs, such as the European Union (EU) and North American Free Trade Agreement (NAFTA), further change the competitive landscape in both services and manufacturing. Regardless of which area of the world you live in, if you face international competition, the challenge is to produce services or products that can compete on a global market, and to design the processes to back them up.

RAPID TECHNOLOGICAL CHANGE

What can be done to compete better in terms of technology?

An important trend in operations management is accelerating *technological change*. It affects the design of new services and products and a firm's processes. Many new opportunities are coming from advances in computer technology. Robots and various forms of information technology are but two examples. E-commerce is dramatically changing many sales and purchasing processes. U.S. firms alone spend hundreds of billions of dollars each year on information technology. The *Internet*—part of the telecommunications "information highway"—has emerged as a vital tool linking firms internally and linking firms externally with customers, strategic partners, and critical suppliers. This computer network has global e-mail and data exchange capabilities, with almost 200 countries already linked to it. The exploding rate of technological opportunities poses an enormous potential, but also many challenges. How can new technology be used to its greatest advantage? How must processes be redesigned? Further, introducing any new technology involves risk, and employee attitudes toward it depend on how the change is managed. The right choices and effective management of technology can give a firm a competitive advantage.

ETHICAL, WORKFORCE DIVERSITY, AND ENVIRONMENTAL ISSUES

How do ethics and the environment affect operations?

Businesses face more ethical quandaries than ever before, intensified by an increasing global presence and rapid technological change. Companies are locating new operations, and have more suppliers and customers, in other countries. Potential ethical dilemmas arise when business can be conducted by different rules. Some countries are more sensitive than others about lavish entertainment, conflicts of interest, bribery, discrimination against minorities and women, poverty, minimum-wage levels, unsafe workplaces, and workers' rights. Managers must decide in such cases whether or not to design and operate processes that do more than just meet local standards that are lower than those back home. In addition, technological change brings debates about data protection and customer privacy, such as on the Internet. In an electronic world, businesses are geographically far from their customers, and a reputation of trust may become even more important.

One expert suggests a more ethical approach to business in which firms

- have responsibilities that go beyond producing goods and services at a profit,
- help solve important social problems,
- respond to a broader constituency than shareholders alone,
- have impacts beyond simple marketplace transactions, and
- serve a range of human values that go beyond the merely economic.

Environmental issues, such as toxic wastes, poisoned drinking water, poverty, air quality, and global warming are getting more emphasis. In the past, many people viewed environmental problems as quality-of-life issues; in the 2000s, many people see them as survival issues. Interest in a clean, healthy environment is increasing. Industrial nations have a particular burden because their combined populations, representing only 25 percent of the total global population, consume 70 percent of all resources. Just seven nations, including the United States and Japan, produce almost half of all

greenhouse gases. The United States and some European nations now spend 2 percent of their gross domestic products on environmental protection, a level that environmentalists believe should be increased.

The challenge is clear: Consideration of ethics, workforce diversity, and the environment are becoming part of every manager's job. When designing and operating processes, they should consider integrity, respect for the individual, and respecting the customer along with more conventional performance measures such as productivity, quality, cost, and profit.

ROAD MAP FOR COMPETITIVE OPERATIONS

This text is about managing processes for competitive advantage. Even though processes often cut across departmental boundaries, they have certain general properties that, once understood, can be exploited for advantage regardless of the functions involved. Figure 1.6 shows a road map for competitive operations that spans both service operations and manufacturing operations.

Our text has four major parts: "Competing with Operations," "Designing and Improving Processes," "Designing Value Chains," and "Operating Value Chains." The flow of topics reflects our philosophy of first understanding how a firm's operations can provide a sound basis for its competitiveness in the marketplace before tackling the essential process design decisions that will support its strategies. Once it is clear how firms design and improve internal processes, and how these designs get implemented, we extend the discussion to examine the design of value chains that link processes between firms. In the last part, we focus on the effective operation of value chains, which involves information technology and a host of planning and control tools that assist managers in achieving the desired performance from their value chains. The performance of the value chains determine the outcomes, which include the services or products the firm produces, the financial results, and the feedback from its customers. These outcomes are considered in the firm's strategic plan, which closes the loop and demonstrates the strategic importance of operations.

Figure 1.6 shows how each chapter relates to others in its part. It is typically not possible to cover all of the chapters in one course. Next, we briefly discuss the chapters in each part to get a better overview of the topics covered in this text.

PART 1: COMPETING WITH OPERATIONS

We have already discussed the importance of taking a process view of businesses, and we have incorporated the concept of value chains. We continue the discussion of processes and value chains in "Operations Strategy" (Chapter 2) by presenting the big picture of how corporate strategy affects a firm's operations. This chapter provides a

FIGURE 1.6 **Operations Road Map**

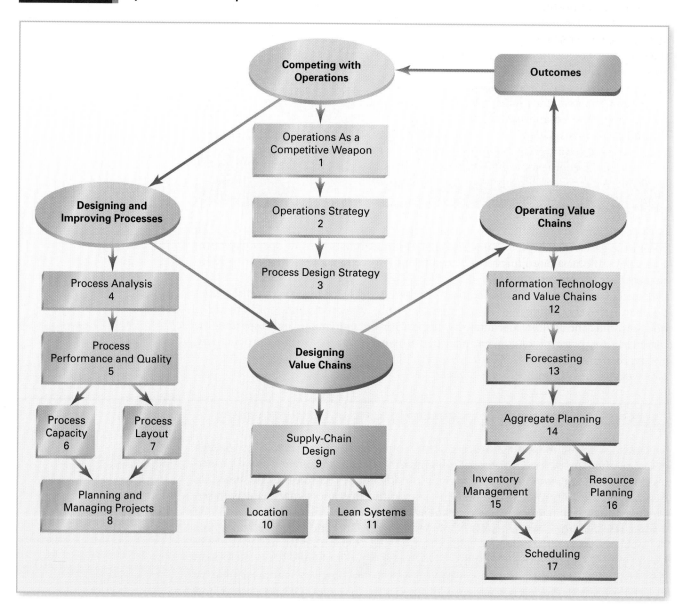

framework that links the operating characteristics of processes at all levels to the strategies and objectives of the firm, thereby defining the way the processes add value to the service or product. We use this framework throughout the text to reinforce the idea that effective process designs and operations require top-notch customer service, whether the customers are internal or external. "Process Design Strategy" (Chapter 3) is a key chapter in this part because it focuses on the strategic aspects of process design. In addition to addressing manufacturing processes, this chapter also explores a customer contact model, which shows the relationship between customer contact and process complexity for nonmanufacturing processes. The three chapters in Part 1 show how operations can provide a sound basis for the competitiveness of a firm, whether it is a service provider or a manufacturer.

PART 2: DESIGNING AND IMPROVING PROCESSES
After the framework is in place for understanding how the operational characteristics of processes add value, our road map takes us to the point where we discover how new processes are designed and existing processes are improved. This part of the text con-

tains five chapters and follows our six-step *systematic approach to process analysis:* (1) identify the opportunity, (2) define the scope, (3) document the process, (4) evaluate performance, (5) redesign the process, and (6) implement the changes. "Process Analysis" (Chapter 4) introduces this six-step approach and reveals the tools useful for understanding how a process works and where it might be improved (step 3) and how process performance can be measured (step 4). "Process Performance and Quality" (Chapter 5) builds on the metrics identified in step 4 of the systematic approach to process analysis and leads into step 5. It discusses total quality management (TQM) and the time-honored approach of statistical process control (SPC), and it shows how SPC and programs such as Six Sigma can be used to determine when process performance has gone astray, perhaps signaling a need to redesign the process. Once a process has been redesigned, the tools of this chapter can be used to determine if the process has actually been improved. "Process Capacity" (Chapter 6) is the first of two chapters that address step 5 of the systematic approach to process analysis. Capacity is one possible dimension of processes that can be changed to improve effectiveness. The other chapter is "Process Layout" (Chapter 7), which can have profound implications for the processes of service providers as well as manufacturers. We conclude this part with "Planning and Managing Projects" (Chapter 8), which addresses step 6 of the systematic approach to process analysis. The way new processes are introduced or existing processes are changed is through projects. The chapter discusses the three major phases of projects: defining and organizing the project, planning the project, and monitoring and controlling the project. The tools of project management we discuss in this text can be used for any project and are not restricted to process design or redesign projects. In the five chapters of Part 2, we focus on key aspects of internal processes and present a framework for analyzing them, redesigning them, and implementing the changes. This same framework can be applied to any of the processes we discuss later in the text.

PART 3: DESIGNING VALUE CHAINS

In Chapter 1, we define the concept of a value chain and in Part 2 we focus on processes internal to a firm. Think of these ideas and concepts as building blocks. Our road map now brings us to a point where we get a better understanding of how these building blocks come together in the business world. This part of the text, which consists of three chapters, expands the presentation of value chains to include processes that are external to the firm. "Supply-Chain Design" (Chapter 9) shows how value chains that include the processes of external customers and suppliers can be designed for competitive advantage. Next, the issues associated with the design of value chains that are related to spatial considerations, such as global operations or competitive factors, are discussed in "Location" (Chapter 10). We close this part with "Lean Systems" (Chapter 11), which explores the just-in-time design strategy for value chains in services and manufacturing. This chapter serves to draw together many of the issues and concepts we discussed in conjunction with individual processes. The three chapters of Part 3 focus on the key decisions that managers make in designing world-class value chains.

PART 4: OPERATING VALUE CHAINS

The last point in our road map is just as important as the first because it addresses the mechanisms available to operate value chains at their most efficient levels. There are six chapters in this final part of the text. We begin with "Information Technology and Value Chains" (Chapter 12) because information technology, which includes enterprise resource planning (ERP) systems and Web applications, is the enabler for operating effective value chains. We follow this chapter with "Forecasting" (Chapter 13), which provides many useful forecasting tools for developing the forecasts that are so important for planning and scheduling processes. "Aggregate Planning" (Chapter 14) discusses how firms utilize the forecasts to generate production plans and staffing plans, which are required to provide the level of resources required for the firm's processes. "Inventory Management" (Chapter 15) focuses on the tools needed to manage retail and distribution inventories in value chains. "Resource Planning" (Chapter 16) examines material requirements planning (MRP), which is a widely used system for managing manufacturing inventories and estimating resource requirements for processes, and demonstrates how those principles can also be used in service firms. We conclude this part of the text with "Scheduling" (Chapter 17), which reveals the approaches firms use to schedule processes and employees to perform the work they are intended to do. The six chapters in Part 4 show how firms can effectively manage their value chains to their full potential.

OUTCOMES

The road map in Figure 1.6 ultimately takes us to *outcomes*, which consist of the services or products the firm produces, the rewards the firm receives from the marketplace, and the feedback from external customers. In addition to the services or products for external customers, outcomes include performance measures, such as financial measures, service or product performance measures, and customer perceptions of their experiences. Financial measures include profits, return on assets (ROA), and earnings per share of stock (EPS), just to name a few. The financial measures are important because stockholders are significant constituents of the firm and must be recognized in all major process design or redesign decisions.

The performance measures are important to the firm's external customers because they compete on the basis of cost, quality, time, and flexibility (see Chapter 2, "Operations Strategy"). The actual measures a firm tracks may be different depending on whether the firm is a service provider or a manufacturer, and there may be many of them; however, they give the firm a handle on how things are going relative to the needs of external customers. "Process Analysis" (Chapter 4) and "Process Performance and Quality" (Chapter 5) get into the tools for tracking these measures.

Finally, customer perceptions are a very important outcome because the firm does not want to lose customers. Often, these measures are collected in varied ways, including market surveys (mail, phone, or e-mail); market focus groups; and simple customer feedback cards the customer can fill out just after the business transaction is completed. Questions such as, "Were you satisfied with your overall experience with our company?" or "Was the salesperson courteous and knowledgeable?" or "Did we meet your expectations regarding the time to receive your order?" provide some clues to the level of performance the firm is achieving in the eyes of the customer. Information on the financial measures, service/product performance measures, and customer perception measures flows to the strategy level of the firm, thereby closing the loop as Figure 1.6 shows.

The outcomes are actually the collective outcomes of many processes that culminate in the performance of the firm. We will address the nature of process-level outcomes throughout the text; however, the next stop in our road map, "Operations Strategy" (Chapter 2), will show how these process-level outcomes add value to the firm as a whole.

OPERATIONS MANAGEMENT ACROSS THE ORGANIZATION

We have described operations management as designing and operating processes in both services and manufacturing, as one of several functional areas within an organization, and as a set of decisions. In this final section, we describe operations management as an interfunctional imperative and a competitive weapon for organizations.

OPERATIONS MANAGEMENT AS AN INTERFUNCTIONAL IMPERATIVE

Operations managers need to build and maintain solid relationships both interorganizationally and intraorganizationally. We discuss interorganizational relationships, such as those with suppliers, later in the text (see Part 3, "Designing Value Chains"). Here, our focus is on intraorganizational relationships, which call for cross-functional coordination.

Too often, managers allow artificial barriers to be erected between functional areas and departments. In these situations, jobs or tasks move sequentially from marketing to engineering to operations. The result is often slow or poor decision making because each department bases its decisions solely on its own limited perspective, not the organization's overall perspective. A new approach being tried by many organizations, which we have referred to as a process view, is to replace sequential decision making with more cross-functional coordination and flatter organizational structures. For example, Hallmark Cards formed cross-functional teams and cut its product development time by 50 percent.

CROSS-FUNCTIONAL COORDINATION. Cross-functional coordination between processes is essential to effective management. For example, consider how other functional areas interact with operations. Perhaps the strongest connection is with the marketing function, which determines the need for new services and products and the demand for existing ones. Operations managers must bring together human and capital resources to handle demand effectively. The operations manager must consider facility locations and relocations to serve new markets, and the design of layouts for service organizations must match the image that marketing seeks to convey to the customer. Marketing and sales make delivery promises to customers, which must be related to current operations capabilities. Marketing demand forecasts guide the operations manager in planning output rates and capacities.

The operations manager also needs feedback from the accounting function to understand current performance. Financial measures help the operations manager assess labor costs, the long-term benefits of new technologies, and quality improvements. Accounting can help the operations manager monitor the production system's vital signs by developing multiple tracking methods. The operations manager can then identify problems and prescribe remedies. Accounting also has an impact on the operations function because of the order fulfillment process, which begins when the customer places an order and is completed when operations delivers the order to the external customer and then provides information to accounting for billing.

In securing and investing the company's capital assets, finance influences operations' decisions about investments in new technology, layout redesign, capacity expansion, and even inventory levels. Similarly, human resources interacts with operations to hire and train workers and aids in changeovers related to new process and job designs. Human resources can help make promotions and transfers into and out of operations easier, thereby encouraging cross-functional understanding. Engineering can also have a big impact on operations. In designing new services or products engineering needs to consider technical trade-offs. It must ensure that the designs do not create costly specifications or exceed operations capabilities.

ACHIEVING CROSS-FUNCTIONAL COORDINATION. Several approaches may be used to achieve cross-functional coordination. Each organization should select some blend of them to get everyone pulling in the same direction.

How can coordination be achieved with other functional areas?

- A unified strategy should be developed by management as a starting point, giving each department a vision of what it must do to help fulfill the overall organizational strategy.
- The organizational structure and management hierarchy can be redesigned to promote cross-functional coordination, guided by a process view of the organization. Drawing departmental lines around areas of specialization tends to work against integration by creating insular views and "turf battles." A better option may be to organize around major product lines or processes.
- The goal-setting process and reward systems can encourage cross-functional coordination. So can bringing people together from different functional areas—through task forces or committees—to make decisions and solve problems.
- Improvements to information systems also can boost coordination.
Information must in part be tailored to the needs of each functional manager.

However, sharing information helps harmonize the efforts of managers from different parts of the organization and enables them to make decisions consistent with organizational goals.

- Informal social systems are another device that can be used to encourage better understanding across functional lines. Joint cafeteria facilities, exercise rooms, and social events can help build a sense of camaraderie, as can corporate training and development programs.
- Employee selection and promotion also can help foster more cross-functional coordination by encouraging broad perspectives and common goals. Of course, employees must first be competent in their own skill areas.

The best mix of approaches depends on the organization. Some organizations need more coordination than others. The need is greatest when functions are dispersed (owing to organizational structure or geographical distance), organizations are large, and many services or products are customized. The need is also crucial in service organizations that have high customer contact and provide services directly to the customer.

OPERATIONS MANAGEMENT AS A COMPETITIVE WEAPON

In the global era, business and government leaders are increasingly recognizing the importance of involving the whole organization in making strategic decisions. Because the organization usually commits the bulk of its human and financial assets to operations, operations is an important function in meeting global competition. More than 35 years ago, Wickham Skinner suggested that operations could be either a competitive weapon or a millstone (see Skinner, 1969). He concluded that, all too often, operations policies covering inventory levels, schedules, and capacity reflect incorrect assumptions about corporate strategy and may work against a firm's strategic goals. This lack of understanding can waste a firm's resources for years.

Largely because of foreign competition and the explosion of new technologies, recognition is growing that a firm competes not only by offering new services and products, creative marketing, and skillful finance, but also with unique competencies in operations and sound management of core processes. The organization that can offer superior services and products at lower prices is a formidable competitor.

What are companies doing to make operations a competitive weapon?

To conclude this chapter, Managerial Practice 1.2 demonstrates what four companies are doing to improve quality and productivity and how management can use operations as a competitive weapon. These examples offer insight into the role that operations managers play in an organization.

The steps taken by these companies cover almost every type of decision (shown in parentheses) in operations management. Note that each decision category in operations management plays a vital role in gaining competitive advantage. These descriptions indicate that there are many ways to succeed with operations, not one single magic formula.

MANAGERIAL PRACTICE 1.2

MEETING THE COMPETITIVE CHALLENGE

Continental Airlines

In 1994, Continental Airlines (www.continental.com) was in poor financial condition, quickly running out of customers and cash. Over 40,000 jobs were at stake. Today, Continental is flying high, thanks to what it has done to better design and operate its processes. The key in the turnaround was to get many processes redesigned fast in a coordinated fashion, so that everyone pulled together (*planning and managing projects*). After years of a low-cost approach (*operations strategy*), quality and customer-response policies were improved dramatically. Continental revised its processes to focus on adding customer value rather than on cutting costs. The hard part was figuring out how to improve the customer's experience so that revenues increased faster than costs (*operations as a competitive weapon*). The airline set up a toll-free hotline to handle employee suggestions on how to improve operations, such as speeding up the reservation process (*process analysis*). Management sought to change the customer's experience by selecting places where people want to go, at the times they wanted to go, and in clean, attractive airplanes.

It also chose 15 or so key measures to track and compare against competitors (*process performance and quality*), including on-time arrivals, baggage handling, and customer complaints. Maintenance was improved, providing better capacity utilization (*process capacity*). Planes were fixed so that they were not breaking down when they needed to be flying. In one year, the maintenance budget dropped from $777 million to $395 million, and the airline jumped from worst to first in the industry in dispatch reliability. It decided to build up its Houston, Newark, and Cleveland hubs (*location*). Finally to improve reliability, it fostered better cross-functional communication between the people who made the flight schedule (*scheduling*) and the operating departments who controlled the mechanics, crews, and parts inventory (*inventory management*).

A traveler prints her e-ticket at an automated Continental Airlines machine in an airport. Improvements such as this have speeded up the check-in process and have added customer value.

GTE Corporation

GTE's operation (www.gte.com) in Florida's Tampa–Sarasota region is typical of companies that are doing more with less. Over the past five years, although the area's population and telephone system have grown by about 7 percent annually, GTE still employs the same number of service people, about 250. Laptop computers (*process analysis*) let repair crews plan their daily schedules (*scheduling*) and give customers more accurate times of arrival. The support staff (*process analysis*) has dropped from 45 to 11, as software-driven "expert" systems (*information technology and value chains*) take customer requests and arrange them in the most efficient order.

Merlin Metalworks, Inc.

Merlin Metalworks (www.merlinbike.com) began as a three-person company in 1986, and it keeps growing. Its manufacturing facility now covers more than 12,000 square feet (*process capacity*) in a new plant in Cambridge, Massachusetts (*location*). The heart of its business is bike frames, which are made from titanium to make them tough, durable, and rust-proof (*process analysis*). The Merlin process, praised by reviews in *Bicycle Guide* and *Bicycling* stresses precision and attention to detail during manufacturing. Welding is critical to the process and is carefully monitored (*process measurement and quality*). The company invested $100,000 in one machine just to cut the bottom bracket threads exactly straight and uses a proprietary butting technology. Merlin uses almost 50 different tube sizes in its frame and makes all its frames (*process analysis*). Merlin makes about 100 style and size combinations; 20 percent will be custom-built (*operations strategy*). Merlin's growing size as a titanium customer allows it to dictate precisely the types of titanium tubing that it will buy for use in its frames (*supply-chain design*).

Sharp Corporation

Sharp Corporation (www.sharp-world.com), a $14 billion consumer-electronic giant, was once regarded

(continued)

MANAGERIAL PRACTICE 1.2 *continued*

as a second-tier competitor by its Japanese rivals. Today, however, its consistent pursuit of technological creativity, particularly in the area of specialized optoelectronics, is giving it a competitive advantage. Each year, nearly one-third of Sharp's research and design budget is spent on 10 to 15 Gold Badge projects *(planning and managing projects)*. Such projects cut across product groups. All project members are vested with the authority of the company president and wear gold-colored badges so that they can call on people throughout Sharp for assistance. Sharp is organized around functional lines so that applied research and manufacturing occur in a single unit where economies of scale *(process capacity)* can be

exploited. To assure cross-functional coordination product managers are given the responsibility—but not the authority—for coordinating the entire set of value-chain processes *(supply-chain design)*.

Sources: "The Mechanic Who Fired Continental." *Fortune* (December 20, 1999), "Right Away and All at Once: How We Saved Continental." *Harvard Business Review* (September–October 1998), pp. 162–175; "Riding High." *Business Week* (October 9,1995); "Boston Becoming a Hub to High-End Bike Industry." *The Boston Globe* (July 28, 1999); and "Creating Corporate Advantage." *Harvard Business Review* (May–June 1998), pp. 71–84.

CHAPTER HIGHLIGHTS

- Every organization must manage processes and the operations by which these processes are performed. Processes are the fundamental activity that organizations use to do work and achieve their goals. Value is added for the customer by transforming inputs into outputs for customers. Inputs include human resources (workers and managers), capital resources (equipment and facilities), purchased materials and services, land, and energy. Outputs are goods and services.

- The concept of processes applies not just to an entire organization but also to the work of each department and individual. Each has work processes, customers, and suppliers (whether internal or external).

- A process can be broken down into subprocesses, which in turn can be broken down further. A process within a process is known as a *nested process*.

- The nature of the output and the degree of customer contact are two key differences between service and manufacturing processes. Understanding these differences is important in the design of effective processes. Nonetheless, there

are many similarities in the way service and manufacturing processes are managed.

- The concept of value chains reinforces the interconnectedness of processes to business performance. The firm's core processes provide a direct link from external suppliers to external customers. Support processes provide vital resources to the core processes.

- Operations managers are involved with decisions at the strategic and tactical levels. All decisions should reflect corporate strategy. Linking decisions to other functional areas is facilitated by taking a process view of the firm.

- Productivity improvement (particularly in services); intense global competition; rapid technological change; and emerging ethical, workforce diversity, and environmental issues and major challenges for operations managers.

- Operations managers must deal with both intraorganizational and interorganizational relationships. For operations to be used successfully as a competitive weapon, it must address interfunctional concerns. Tomorrow's managers in every functional area must understand operations.

STUDENT CD-ROM AND INTERNET RESOURCES

The Student CD-ROM and the Companion Website at **www.prenhall.com/krajewski** contain many tools, activities, and resources designed for this chapter. The following items are recommended to enhance your skills and improve your understanding of the material in this chapter.

STUDENT CD-ROM RESOURCES

➤ **PowerPoint Slides.** View the comprehensive set of slides customized for this chapter's concepts and techniques.

➤ **OM Explorer Tutor.** OM Explorer contains a tutor spreadsheet (see Figure 1.5) that will help you learn more about productivity measures. See Chapter 1 in the OM Explorer menu. See also the Tutor exercise on productivity measures.

➤ **Active Model.** There is an active model spreadsheet that provides additional insight on productivity measurement. See Operations As a Competitive Weapon in the Active Models menu for this routine. Also see the Active Model exercise at the end of this chapter.

INTERNET RESOURCES

➤ **Self-Study Quizzes.** See the compendium of true or false, multiple choice, and essay questions that allows online tests or gives feedback on how well you have mastered the concepts in this chapter.

➤ **In the News.** See articles that apply to this chapter.

➤ **Internet Exercises.** Try out five different links to explore global competition, using services as a competitive weapon in manufacturing, and environmental leadership.

➤ **Virtual Tours.** Compare the manufacturing processes at Thompson-Shore Bindery to those of the ski producer, K2 Corporation. Also see the "Web Links to Company Facility Tours" for additional tours of company facilities.

KEY EQUATION

Productivity is the ratio of output to input, or

$$\text{Productivity} = \frac{\text{Output}}{\text{Input}}$$

KEY TERMS

core process 9
customer relationship process 9
external customers 5
external suppliers 6
internal customers 6
internal suppliers 6

nested process 5
new service/product development
    process 9
operations management 10
order fulfillment process 9
process 3

productivity 14
supplier relationship process 10
support process 9
value chain 7

SOLVED PROBLEM I

Student tuition at Boehring University is $100 per semester credit hour. The state supplements school revenue by matching student tuition dollar for dollar. Average class size for a typical three-credit course is 50 students. Labor costs are $4,000 per class, materials costs are $20 per student per class, and overhead costs are $25,000 per class.

a. What is the *multifactor* productivity ratio for this course process?

b. If instructors work an average of 14 hours per week for 16 weeks for each three-credit class of 50 students, what is the *labor* productivity ratio?

SOLUTION

a. Multifactor productivity is the ratio of the value of output to the value of input resources.

$$\text{Value of output} = \left(\frac{50 \text{ students}}{\text{class}}\right)\left(\frac{3 \text{ credit hours}}{\text{student}}\right)\left(\frac{\$100 \text{ tuition} + \$100 \text{ state support}}{\text{credit hour}}\right)$$

$$= \$30,000/\text{class}$$

$$\text{Value of input} = \text{Labor} + \text{Materials} + \text{Overhead}$$

$$= \frac{\$4,000 + (\$20/\text{student} \times 50 \text{ students}) + \$25,000}{\text{class}}$$

$$= \$30,000/\text{class}$$

$$\frac{\text{Multifactor}}{\text{productivity}} = \frac{\text{Output}}{\text{Input}} = \frac{\$30,000/\text{class}}{\$30,000/\text{class}} = 1.00$$

b. Labor productivity is the ratio of the value of output to labor hours. The value of output is the same as in part (a), or $30,000/class, so

$$\text{Labor hours of input} = \left(\frac{14 \text{ hours}}{\text{week}}\right)\left(\frac{16 \text{ weeks}}{\text{class}}\right) = 224 \text{ hours/class}$$

$$\text{Labor productivity} = \frac{\text{Output}}{\text{Input}} = \frac{\$30,000/\text{class}}{224 \text{ hours/class}}$$

$$= \$133.93/\text{hour}$$

SOLVED PROBLEM 2

Natalie Attired makes fashionable garments. During a particular week employees worked 360 hours to produce a batch of 132 garments, of which 52 were "seconds" (meaning that they were flawed). Seconds are sold for $90 each at Attired's Factory Outlet Store. The remaining 80 garments are sold to retail distribution, at $200 each. What is the *labor* productivity ratio of this manufacturing process?

SOLUTION

$$\text{Value of Output} = (52 \text{ defective} \times \$90/\text{defective}) + (80 \text{ garments} \times \$200/\text{garment})$$

$$= \$20,680$$

$$\text{Labor hours of input} = 360 \text{ hours}$$

$$\text{Labor productivity} = \frac{\text{Output}}{\text{Input}} = \frac{\$20,680}{360 \text{ hours}}$$

$$= \$57.44 \text{ in sales per hour}$$

DISCUSSION QUESTIONS

1. Consider your last (or current) job.
   a. What activities did you perform?
   b. Who were your customers (internal and external), and how did you interact with them?
   c. How could you measure the customer value you were adding by performing your processes?
   d. Was your position in accounting, finance, human resources, management information systems, marketing, operations, or other? Explain.

2. Make a list of possible endings to this sentence: "The responsibility of a business is to _____" (for example, "...*make money*" or "...*provide health care for its employees*"). Make a list of the responsibilities that you would support and a list of those that you would not support. Form a small group, and compare your lists with those of the others in the group. Discuss the issues and try to arrive at a consensus. An alternative discussion question: "The responsibility of a student is to _____."

3. Multinational corporations are formed to meet global competition. Although they operate in several countries, workers do not have international unions. Some union leaders complain that multinationals are in a position to play off their own plants against each other to gain concessions from labor. What responsibilities do multinational corporations have to host countries? To employees? To customers? To shareholders? Would you support provisions of international trade treaties to address this problem? Form a small group, and compare your views with those of the others in the group. Discuss the issues and try to obtain a consensus.

PROBLEMS

An icon in the margin next to a problem identifies the software that can be helpful but is not mandatory. The software is available on the Student CD-ROM that is packaged with every new copy of the textbook.

1. 🔖 **OM Explorer** (Refer to Solved Problem 1.) Under Coach Bjourn Toulouse, several football seasons for the Big Red Herrings have been disappointing. Only better recruiting will return the Big Red Herrings to winning form. Because of the current state of the program, Boehring University fans are unlikely to support increases in the $192 season ticket price. Improved recruitment will increase overhead costs to $30,000 per class section from the current $25,000 per class section. The university's budget plan is to cover recruitment costs by increasing the average class size to 75 students. Labor costs will increase to $6,500 per three-credit course. Material costs are about $25 per student for each three-credit course. Tuition will be $200 per semester credit, which is matched by state support of $100 per semester credit.

   a. What is the productivity ratio? Compared to the result obtained in Solved Problem 1, did productivity increase or decrease for the course process?

   b. If instructors work an average of 20 hours per week for 16 weeks for each three-credit class of 75 students, what is the *labor* productivity ratio?

2. Suds and Duds Laundry washed and pressed the following numbers of dress shirts per week.

Week	Work crew	Total Hours	Shirts
1	Sud and Dud	24	68
2	Sud and Jud	46	130
3	Sud, Dud, and Jud	62	152
4	Sud, Dud, and Jud	51	125
5	Dud and Jud	45	131

Calculate the *labor* productivity ratio for each week.

Explain the labor productivity pattern exhibited by the data.

3. Compact disc players are produced on an automated assembly line process. The standard cost of compact disc players is $150 per unit (labor, $30; materials, $70; and overhead, $50). The sales price is $300 per unit.

   a. To achieve a 10 percent multifactor productivity improvement by reducing materials costs only, by what percentage must those costs be reduced?

   b. To achieve a 10 percent multifactor productivity improvement by reducing labor costs only, by what percentage must those costs be reduced?

   c. To achieve a 10 percent multifactor productivity improvement by reducing overhead costs only, by what percentage must those costs be reduced?

Advanced Problem

4. The Big Black Bird Company (BBBC) has a large order for special plastic-lined military uniforms to be used in an urgent Mideast operation. Working the normal two shifts of 40 hours, the BBBC production process usually produces 2,500 uniforms per week at a standard cost of $120 each. Seventy employees work the first shift and 30 the second. The contract price is $200 per uniform. Because of the urgent need, BBBC is authorized to use around-the-clock production, six days per week. When each of the two shifts works 72 hours per week, production increases to 4,000 uniforms per week but at a cost of $144 each.

   a. Did the productivity ratio increase, decrease, or remain the same? If it changed, by what percentage did it change?

   b. Did the labor productivity ratio increase, decrease or remain the same? If it changed, by what percentage did it change?

   c. Did weekly profits increase, decrease, or remain the same?

ACTIVE MODEL EXERCISE

This Active Model appears on the Student CD-ROM. It allows you to evaluate the important elements of productivity.

QUESTIONS

1. If the insurance company can process 60 (10 percent) more policies per week, by what percentage will the productivity rise?
2. Suppose the 8-hour day includes a 45-minute lunch. What is the revised productivity measure, excluding lunch?
3. If an employee is hired, what will be the weekly number of polices processed if the productivity of five is maintained?
4. Suppose that, during the summer, the company works for only four days per week. What will be the weekly number of policies processed if the productivity of five is maintained?

ACTIVE MODEL 1.1

Productivity Using Data from Example 1.1

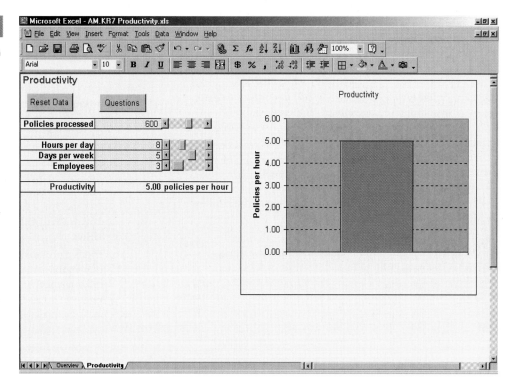

CASE CHAD'S CREATIVE CONCEPTS

Chad's Creative Concepts designs and manufactures wood furniture. Founded by Chad Thomas on the banks of Lake Erie in Sandusky, Ohio, the company began by producing custom-made wooden furniture for vacation cabins located along the coast of Lake Erie and on nearby Kelly's Island and Bass Island. Being an "outdoors" type himself, Chad Thomas originally wanted to bring "a bit of the outdoors" inside. Chad's Creative Concepts developed a solid reputation for creative designs and high-quality workmanship. Sales eventually encompassed the entire Great Lakes region. Along with growth came additional opportunities.

Traditionally, the company had focused entirely on custom-made furniture, with the customer specifying the kind of wood from which the piece would be made. As the company's reputation grew and sales increased, the sales force began selling some of the more popular pieces to retail furniture outlets. This move into retail outlets led Chad's Creative Concepts into the production of a more standard line of furniture. Buyers of this line were much more price sensitive and imposed more stringent delivery requirements than did clients for the custom line. Custom-designed furniture, however, continued to dominate sales, accounting for 60 percent of volume and 75 percent of dollar sales. Currently, the company operates a single manufacturing process in Sandusky, where both custom and standard furniture is manufactured. The equipment is mainly general purpose in nature in order to provide the flexibility needed for producing custom pieces of furniture. The layout puts together saws in one section of the facility, lathes in another, and so on. The quality of the finished product reflects the quality of the wood chosen and the craftsmanship of individual workers. Both custom and standard furniture compete for processing time on the same equipment by the same craftspeople.

During the past few months, sales of the standard line have steadily increased, leading to more regular scheduling of this product line. However, when scheduling trade-offs had to be made, custom furniture was always given priority because of its higher sales and profit margins. Thus, scheduled lots of standard furniture pieces were left sitting around the plant in various stages of completion.

As he reviews the progress of Chad's Creative Concepts, Chad Thomas is pleased to note that the company has grown. Sales of custom furniture remain strong, and sales of standard pieces are steadily increasing. However, finance and accounting have indicated that profits are not what they should be. Costs associated with the standard line are rising. Dollars are being tied up in inventory, both of raw materials and work in process. Expensive public warehouse space has to be rented to accommodate the inventory volume. Thomas also is concerned with increased lead times for both custom and standard orders, which are causing longer promised delivery times. Capacity is being pushed, and no space is left in the plant for expansion. Thomas decides that the time has come to take a careful look at the overall impact that the new standard line is having on his manufacturing process.

QUESTIONS

1. What types of decisions must Chad Thomas make daily for his company's operations to run effectively? Over the long run?
2. How did sales and marketing affect operations when they began to sell standard pieces to retail outlets?
3. How has the move to producing standard furniture affected the company's financial structure?
4. What might Thomas have done differently to avoid some of the problems he now faces?

Source: This case was prepared by Dr. Brooke Saladin, Wake Forest University, as a basis for classroom discussion.

SELECTED REFERENCES

Bowen, David E., Richard B. Chase, Thomas G. Cummings and Associates. *Service Management Effectiveness*. San Francisco: Jossey-Bass, 1990.

Buchholz, Rogene A, "Corporate Responsibility and the Good Society: From Economics to Ecology." *Business Horizons* (July–August 1991), pp. 19–31.

Collier, David A. *The Service Quality Solution*. Milwaukee: ASQC Quality Press, and Burr Ridge, IL: Irwin Professional Publishing, 1994.

Hayes, Robert H., and Gary P. Pisano. "Beyond World-Class: The New Manufacturing Strategy." *Harvard Business Review* (January–February 1994), pp. 77–86.

Heskett, James L., W. Earl Sasser, Jr., and Christopher Hart. *Service Breakthroughs: Changing the Rules of the Game*. New York: Free Press, 1990.

"The Horizontal Corporation." *Business Week* (December 20, 1993), pp. 76–81.

Kaplan, Robert S., and David P. Norton. *Balanced Scoreboard*. Boston, MA: Harvard Business School Press, 1997.

Pande, Peter S., Robert P. Neuman, and Roland R. Cavanagh. *The Six Sigma Way*. New York: McGraw-Hill, 2000.

Porter, Michael. *Competitive Advantage*. New York: The Free Press, 1987.

Post, James E. "Managing As If the Earth Mattered." *Business Horizons* (July–August 1991), pp. 32–38.

Roach, Stephen S. "Services Under Siege—The Restructuring Imperative." *Harvard Business Review* (September–October 1991), pp. 82–91.

Rummler, Geary A., and Alan P. Brache. *Improving Performance*. San Francisco: Jossey-Bass Publishers, 1995.

Schmenner, Roger W. *Service Operations Management*. Englewood Cliffs, NJ: Prentice Hall, 1995.

Skinner, Wickham. "Manufacturing—Missing Link in Corporate Strategy." *Harvard Business Review* (May–June 1969), pp. 136–145.

"Time for a Reality Check in Asia." *Business Week* (December 2, 1996), pp. 58–66.

van Biema, Michael, and Bruce Greenwald. "Managing Our Way to Higher Service-Sector Productivity." *Harvard Business Review* (July–August 1997), pp. 87–95.

Womack, James P., Daniel T. Jones, and Daniel Roos. *The Machine That Changed the World*. New York: HarperPerennial, 1991.

Decision Making

LEARNING GOALS   *After reading this supplement, you should be able to . . .*

IDENTIFY OR DEFINE

1. break-even analysis, using both the graphic and algebraic approaches.
2. a preference matrix.
3. the maximin, maximax, Laplace, minimax regret, and expected value decision rules.
4. the value of perfect information.

DESCRIBE OR EXPLAIN

5. using break-even analysis to evaluate new services and products and different processes.
6. how to construct a payoff table.
7. how to draw and analyze a decision tree.

Operations managers make many choices as they deal with various decision areas (see Chapter 1, "Operations As a Competitive Weapon"). Although the specifics of each situation vary, decision making generally involves the same basic steps: (1) recognize and clearly define the problem, (2) collect the information needed to analyze possible alternatives, and (3) choose and implement the most feasible alternative.

Sometimes, hard thinking in a quiet room is sufficient. At other times, reliance on more formal procedures is needed. Here, we present four such formal procedures: break-even analysis, the preference matrix, decision theory, and the decision tree.

➤ Break-even analysis helps the manager identify how much change in volume or demand is necessary before a second alternative becomes better than the first alternative.
➤ The preference matrix helps a manager deal with multiple criteria that cannot be evaluated with a single measure of merit, such as total profit or cost.
➤ Decision theory helps the manager choose the best alternative when outcomes are uncertain.
➤ A decision tree helps the manager when decisions are made sequentially—when today's best decision depends on tomorrow's decisions and events.

BREAK-EVEN ANALYSIS

break-even point The volume at which total revenues equal total costs.

break-even analysis The use of the break-even point; can be used to compare processes by finding the volume at which two different processes have equal total costs.

To evaluate an idea for a new service or product, or to assess the performance of an existing one, determining the volume of sales at which the service or product breaks even is useful. The **break-even point** is the volume at which total revenues equal total costs. Use of this technique is known as **break-even analysis.** Break-even analysis can also be used to compare processes by finding the volume at which two different processes have equal total costs.

EVALUATING SERVICES OR PRODUCTS

We begin with the first purpose: to evaluate the profit potential of a new or existing service or product. This technique helps the manager answer questions, such as the following:

- Is the predicted sales volume of the service or product sufficient to break even (neither earning a profit nor sustaining a loss)?
- How low must the variable cost per unit be to break even, based on current prices and sales forecasts?
- How low must the fixed cost be to break even?
- How do price levels affect the break-even volume?

Break-even analysis is based on the assumption that all costs related to the production of a specific service or product can be divided into two categories: variable costs and fixed costs.

variable cost The portion of the total cost that varies directly with volume of output.

fixed cost The portion of the total cost that remains constant regardless of changes in levels of output.

The **variable cost,** c, is the portion of the total cost that varies directly with volume of output: costs per unit for materials, labor, and usually some fraction of overhead. If we let Q equal the number of customers served or units produced per year, total variable cost $= cQ$. The **fixed cost,** F, is the portion of the total cost that remains constant regardless of changes in levels of output: the annual cost of renting or buying new equipment and facilities (including depreciation, interest, taxes, and insurance); salaries; utilities; and portions of the sales or advertising budget. Thus, the total cost of producing a service or good equals fixed costs plus variable costs times volume, or

$$\text{Total cost} = F + cQ$$

The variable cost per unit is assumed to be the same no matter how small or large Q is, and thus, total cost is linear. If we assume that all units produced are sold, total annual revenues equal revenue per unit sold, p, times the quantity sold, or

$$\text{Total revenue} = pQ$$

If we set total revenue equal to total cost, we get the break-even point as

$$pQ = F + cQ$$
$$(p - c)Q = F$$
$$Q = \frac{F}{p - c}$$

We can also find this break-even quantity graphically. Because both costs and revenues are linear relationships, the break-even quantity is where the total revenue line crosses the total cost line.

Finding the Break-Even Quantity

A hospital is considering a new procedure to be offered at $200 per patient. The fixed cost per year would be $100,000, with total variable costs of $100 per patient. What is the break-even quantity for this service? Use both algebraic and graphic approaches to get the answer.

SOLUTION

The formula for the break-even quantity yields

$$Q = \frac{F}{p - c} = \frac{100,000}{200 - 100} = 1,000 \text{ patients}$$

ACTIVE MODEL A.1
Active Model A.1 on the Student CD-ROM provides additional insight on this break-even example and its extensions.

To solve graphically we plot two lines—one for costs and one for revenues. Two points determine a line, so we begin by calculating costs and revenues for two different output levels. The following table shows the results for $Q = 0$ and $Q = 2,000$. We selected zero as the first point because of the ease of plotting total revenue (0) and total cost (F). However, we could have used any two reasonably spaced output levels.

TUTOR A.1
Tutor A.1 on the Student CD-ROM provides a new example to practice break-even analysis.

QUANTITY (PATIENTS) (Q)	TOTAL ANNUAL COST ($) (100,000 + 100Q)	TOTAL ANNUAL REVENUE ($) (200Q)
0	100,000	0
2,000	300,000	400,000

We can now draw the cost line through points (0, 100,000) and (2,000, 300,000). The revenue line goes between (0, 0) and (2,000, 400,000). As Figure A.1 indicates, these two lines intersect at 1,000 patients, the break-even quantity.

Graphic Approach to Break-Even Analysis

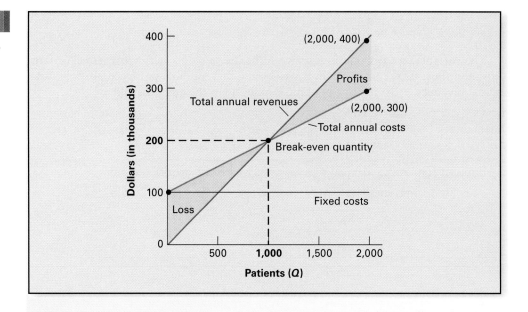

DECISION POINT Management expects the number of patients needing the new procedure will exceed the 1,000-patient break-even point but first wants to learn how sensitive the decision is to demand levels before making a final choice.

sensitivity analysis A technique for systematically changing parameters in a model to determine the effects of such changes.

Break-even analysis cannot tell a manager whether to pursue a new service or product idea or drop an existing line. The technique can only show what is likely to happen for various forecasts of costs and sales volumes. To evaluate a variety of "what-if" questions, we use an approach called **sensitivity analysis**, a technique for systematically changing parameters in a model to determine the effects of such changes. The concept can be applied later to other techniques, such as linear programming (see Supplement D, "Linear Programming"). Here we assess the sensitivity of total profit to different pricing strategies, sales volume forecasts, or cost estimates.

EXAMPLE A.2   Sensitivity Analysis of Sales Forecasts

If the most pessimistic sales forecast for the proposed service in Figure A.1 were 1,500 patients, what would be the procedure's total contribution to profit and overhead per year?

SOLUTION

The graph shows that even the pessimistic forecast lies above the break-even volume, which is encouraging. The product's total contribution, found by subtracting total costs from total revenues, is

$$pQ - (F + cQ) = 200(1,500) - [100,000 + 100(1,500)]$$
$$= \$50,000$$

DECISION POINT Even with the pessimistic forecast, the new procedure contributes $50,000 per year. After having the proposal evaluated by the present value method (see OM Explorer's *Financial Analysis* Solver and Supplement J, "Financial Analysis" on the Student CD-ROM), management added the new procedure to the hospital's services.

EVALUATING PROCESSES

Often, choices must be made between two processes or between an internal process and buying services or materials on the outside (see Chapter 3, "Process Design Strategy"). In such cases, we assume that the decision does not affect revenues. The manager must study all the costs and advantages of each approach. Rather than find the quantity at which total costs equal total revenues, the analyst finds the quantity for which the total costs for two alternatives are equal. For the make-or-buy decision, it is the quantity for which the total "buy" cost equals the total "make" cost. Let F_b equal the fixed cost (per year) of the buy option, F_m equal the fixed cost of the make option, c_b equal the variable cost (per unit) of the buy option, and c_m equal the variable cost of the make option. Thus, the total cost to buy is $F_b + c_b Q$ and the total cost to make is $F_m + c_m Q$. To find the break-even quantity, we set the two cost functions equal and solve for Q:

$$F_b + c_b Q = F_m + c_m Q$$
$$Q = \frac{F_m - F_b}{c_b - c_m}$$

The make option should be considered, ignoring qualitative factors, only if its variable costs are lower than those of the buy option. The reason is that the fixed costs for making the service or product are typically higher than the fixed costs for buying. Under these circumstances, the buy option is best if production volumes are less than the break-even quantity. Beyond that quantity, the make option becomes best.

Break-Even Analysis for Make-or-Buy Decisions

EXAMPLE A.3

The manager of a fast-food restaurant featuring hamburgers is adding salads to the menu. There are two options, and the price to the customer will be the same for each. The make option is to install a salad bar stocked with vegetables, fruits, and toppings and let the customer assemble the salad. The salad bar would have to be leased and a part-time employee hired. The manager estimates the fixed costs at $12,000 and variable costs totaling $1.50 per salad. The buy option is to have preassembled salads available for sale. They would be purchased from a local supplier at $2.00 per salad. Offering preassembled salads would require installation and operation of additional refrigeration, with an annual fixed cost of $2,400. The manager expects to sell 25,000 salads per year.

What is the break-even quantity?

SOLUTION

The formula for the break-even quantity yields

$$Q = \frac{F_m - F_b}{c_b - c_m}$$
$$= \frac{12,000 - 2,400}{2.0 - 1.5} = 19,200 \text{ salads}$$

Figure A.2 shows the solution from OM Explorer's *Break-Even Analysis* Solver. The break-even quantity is 19,200 salads. As the 25,000-salad sales forecast exceeds this amount, the make option is preferred. Only if the restaurant expected to sell fewer than 19,200 salads would the buy option be better.

DECISION POINT   Management chose the make option, after considering other qualitative factors, such as customer preferences and demand uncertainty. A deciding factor was that the 25,000-salad sales forecast is well above the 19,200-salad break-even quantity.

ACTIVE MODEL A.2

Active Model A.2 on the Student CD-ROM provides additional insight on this make-or-buy example and its extensions.

TUTOR A.2

Tutor A.2 on the Student CD-ROM provides a new example to practice break-even analysis on make-or-buy decisions.

FIGURE A.2   **Break-Even Analysis Solver for Example A.3**

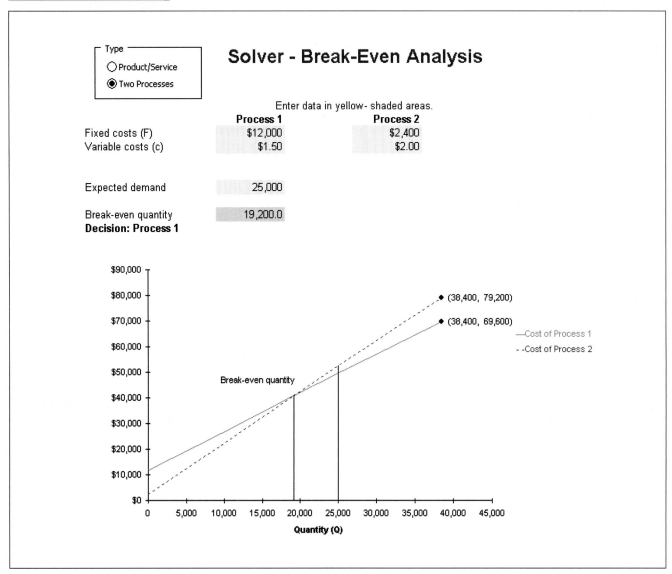

PREFERENCE MATRIX

preference matrix   A table that allows the manager to rate an alternative according to several performance criteria.

Decisions often must be made in situations where multiple criteria cannot be naturally merged into a single measure (such as dollars). For example, a manager deciding in which of two cities to locate a new plant would have to consider such unquantifiable factors as quality of life, worker attitudes toward work, and community reception in the two cities. These important factors cannot be ignored. A **preference matrix** is a table that allows the manager to rate an alternative according to several performance criteria. The criteria can be scored on any scale, such as from 1 (worst possible) to 10 (best possible) or from 0 to 1, as long as the same scale is applied to all the alternatives being compared. Each score is weighted according to its perceived importance, with the total of these weights typically equaling 100. The total score is the sum of the weighted scores (weight × score) for all the criteria. The manager can compare the scores for alternatives against one another or against a predetermined threshold.

Evaluating an Alternative with a Preference Matrix

The following table shows the performance criteria, weights, and scores (1 = worst, 10 = best) for a new product: a thermal storage air conditioner. If management wants to introduce just one new product and the highest total score of any of the other product ideas is 800, should the firm pursue making the air conditioner?

TUTOR A.3

Tutor A.3 on the Student CD-ROM provides a new example to practice with preference matrixes.

PERFORMANCE CRITERION	WEIGHT (A)	SCORE (B)	WEIGHTED SCORE (A × B)
Market potential	30	8	240
Unit profit margin	20	10	200
Operations compatibility	20	6	120
Competitive advantage	15	10	150
Investment requirement	10	2	20
Project risk	5	4	20
		Weighted score =	750

SOLUTION

Because the sum of the weighted scores is 750, it falls short of the score of 800 for another product. This result is confirmed by the output from OM Explorer's *Preference Matrix* Solver in Figure A.3.

Solver - Preference Matrix

Replace the labels Criterion 1, Criterion 2, etc. with descriptions of your own criteria. Use the buttons above the list if you want to insert a criterion (between existing ones), add a criterion (at the end of the list), or remove a criterion. (You will not be able to reduce the number of criteria below two).

Enter the relative weights for the criteria. Remember that the weights must add up to 100. Enter the score for each criterion. Formulas in the weighted score column do the rest. The Final Weighted Score is the overall score for the product, procedure, or strategy you're considering.

Insert a Criterion	Add a Criterion	Remove a Criterion

	Weight (A)	Score (B)	Weighted Score (A x B)
Market potential	30	8	240
Unit profit margin	20	10	200
Operations compatability	20	6	120
Competitive advantage	15	10	150
Investment requirement	10	2	20
Project risk	5	4	20

	Final Weighted Score	750

FIGURE A.3

Preference Matrix Solver for Example A.4

DECISION POINT Management should drop the thermal storage air-conditioner idea. Another new product idea is better, considering the multiple criteria, and management only wanted to introduce just one new product at the time.

Not all managers are comfortable with the preference matrix technique. It requires the manager to state criteria weights before examining the alternatives, although the proper weights may not be readily apparent. Perhaps only after seeing the scores for several alternatives can the manager decide what is important and what is not. Because a low score on one criterion can be compensated for or overridden by high scores on others, the preference matrix method also may cause managers to ignore important signals. In Example A.4, the investment required for the thermal storage air conditioner might exceed the firm's financial capability. In that case, the manager should not even be considering the alternative, no matter how high its score.

DECISION THEORY

decision theory   A general approach to decision making when the outcomes associated with alternatives are often in doubt.

Decision theory is a general approach to decision making when the outcomes associated with alternatives are often in doubt. It helps operations managers with decisions on process, capacity, location, and inventory because such decisions are about an uncertain future. Decision theory can also be used by managers in other functional areas. With decision theory, a manager makes choices using the following process.

1. List the feasible *alternatives*. One alternative that should always be considered as a basis for reference is to do nothing. A basic assumption is that the number of alternatives is finite. For example, in deciding where to locate a new retail store in a certain part of the city, a manager could theoretically consider every grid coordinate on the city's map. Realistically, however, the manager must narrow the number of choices to a reasonable number.

2. List the *events* (sometimes called *chance events* or *states of nature*) that have an impact on the outcome of the choice but are not under the manager's control. For example, the demand experienced by the new facility could be low or high, depending not only on whether the location is convenient to many customers but also on what the competition does and general retail trends. Then group events into reasonable categories. For example, suppose that the average number of sales per day could be anywhere from 1 to 500. Rather than have 500 events, the manager could represent demand with just 3 events: 100 sales/day, 300 sales/day, or 500 sales/day. The events must be mutually exclusive and exhaustive, meaning that they do not overlap and that they cover all eventualities.

payoff table   A table that shows the amount for each alternative if each possible event occurs.

3. Calculate the *payoff* for each alternative in each event. Typically, the payoff is total profit or total cost. These payoffs can be entered into a **payoff table,** which shows the amount for each alternative if each possible event occurs. For 3 alternatives and 4 events, the table would have 12 payoffs (3 × 4). If significant distortions will occur if the time value of money is not recognized, the payoffs should be expressed as present values or internal rates of return (see OM Explorer's *Financial Analysis* solver and Supplement J, "Financial Analysis" on the Student CD-ROM). For multiple criteria with important qualitative factors, use the weighted scores of a preference matrix approach as the payoffs.

4. Estimate the likelihood of each events, using past data, executive opinion, or other forecasting methods. Express it as a *probability*, making sure that the probabilities sum to 1.0. Develop probability estimates from past data if the past is considered a good indicator of the future.

5. Select a *decision rule* to evaluate the alternatives, such as choosing the alternative with the lowest expected cost. The rule chosen depends on the amount of information the manager has on the event probabilities and the manager's attitudes toward risk.

Using this process, we examine decisions under three different situations: certainty, uncertainty, and risk.

DECISION MAKING UNDER CERTAINTY

The simplest situation is when the manager knows which event will occur. Here the decision rule is to pick the alternative with the best payoff for the known event. The best alternative is the highest payoff if the payoffs are expressed as profits. If the payoffs are expressed as costs, the best alternative is the lowest payoff.

Decisions Under Certainty

A manager is deciding whether to build a small or a large facility. Much depends on the future demand that the facility must serve, and demand may be small or large. The manager knows with certainty the payoffs that will result under each alternative, shown in the following payoff table. The payoffs (in $000) are the present values (see Supplement J, "Financial Analysis" on the Student CD-ROM) of future revenues minus costs for each alternative in each event.

	POSSIBLE FUTURE DEMAND	
ALTERNATIVE	**LOW**	**HIGH**
Small facility	200	270
Large facility	160	800
Do nothing	0	0

What is the best choice if future demand will be low?

SOLUTION

In this example, the best choice is the one with the highest payoff. If the manager knows that future demand will be low, the company should build a small facility and enjoy a payoff of $200,000. The larger facility has a payoff of only $160,000. The "do nothing" alternative is dominated by the other alternatives; that is, the outcome of one alternative is no better than the outcome of another alternative for each event. Because the "do nothing" alternative is dominated, the manager does not consider it further.

DECISION POINT   If management really knows future demand, it would build the small facility if demand will be low and the large facility if demand will be high. If demand is uncertain, it should consider other decision rules.

DECISION MAKING UNDER UNCERTAINTY

Here, we assume that the manager can list the possible events but cannot estimate their probabilities. Perhaps a lack of prior experience makes it difficult for the firm to estimate probabilities. In such a situation, the manager can use one of four decision rules.

1. *Maximin.* Choose the alternative that is the "best of the worst." This rule is for the *pessimist*, who anticipates the "worst case" for each alternative.

2. *Maximax.* Choose the alternative that is the "best of the best." This rule is for the *optimist* who has high expectations and prefers to "go for broke."

3. *Laplace.* Choose the alternative with the best *weighted payoff*. To find the weighted payoff, give equal importance (or, alternatively, equal probability) to each event. If there are n events, the importance (or probability) of each is $1/n$, so they add up to 1.0. This rule is for the *realist*.

4. *Minimax Regret.* Choose the alternative with the best "worst regret." Calculate a table of regrets (or opportunity losses), in which the rows represent the alternatives and the columns represent the events. A regret is the difference between a given payoff and the best payoff in the same column. For an event, it shows how much is lost by picking an alternative to the one that is best for this event. The regret can be lost profit or increased cost, depending on the situation.

EXAMPLE A.6   Decisions Under Uncertainty

TUTOR A.4

Tutor A.4 on the Student CD-ROM provides a new example to make decisions under uncertainty.

Reconsider the payoff matrix in Example A.5. What is the best alternative for each decision rule?

SOLUTION

a. *Maximin*. An alternative's worst payoff is the *lowest* number in its row of the payoff matrix, because the payoffs are profits. The worst payoffs ($000) are

ALTERNATIVE	WORST PAYOFF
Small facility	200
Large facility	160

The best of these worst numbers is $200,000, so the pessimist would build a small facility.

b. *Maximax*. An alternative's best payoff ($000) is the *highest* number in its row of the payoff matrix, or

ALTERNATIVE	BEST PAYOFF
Small facility	270
Large facility	800

The best of these best numbers is $800,000, so the optimist would build a large facility.

c. *Laplace*. With two events, we assign each a probability of 0.5. Thus, the weighted payoffs ($000) are

ALTERNATIVE	WEIGHTED PAYOFF
Small facility	0.5(200) + 0.5(270) = **235**
Large facility	0.5(160) + 0.5(800) = **480**

The best of these weighted payoffs is $480,000, so the realist would build a large facility.

d. *Minimax Regret*. If demand turns out to be low, the best alternative is a small facility and its regret is 0 (or 200 − 200). If a large facility is built when demand turns out to be low, the regret is 40 (or 200 − 160).

	REGRET		
ALTERNATIVE	LOW DEMAND	HIGH DEMAND	MAXIMUM REGRET
Small facility	200 − 200 = **0**	800 − 270 = **530**	530
Large facility	200 − 160 = **40**	800 − 800 = **0**	40

The column on the right shows the worst regret for each alternative. To minimize the maximum regret, pick a large facility. The biggest regret is associated with having only a small facility and high demand.

DECISION POINT   The pessimist would choose the small facility. The realist, optimist, and manager choosing to minimize the maximum regret would build the large facility.

DECISION MAKING UNDER RISK

Here we assume that the manager can list the events and estimate their probabilities. The manager has less information than with decision making under certainty, but more information than with decision making under uncertainty. For this intermediate situation, the *expected value* decision rule is widely used. The expected value for an alternative is found by weighting each payoff with its associated probability and then adding the weighted payoff scores. The alternative with the best expected value (highest for profits and lowest for costs) is chosen.

This rule is much like the Laplace decision rule, except that the events are no longer assumed to be equally likely (or equally important). The expected value is what the *average* payoff would be if the decision could be repeated time after time. Of course, the expected value decision rule can result in a bad outcome if the wrong event occurs. However, it gives the best results if applied consistently over a long period of time. The rule should not be used if the manager is inclined to avoid risk.

Decisions Under Risk	EXAMPLE A.7

Reconsider the payoff matrix in Example A.5. For the expected value decision rule, which is the best alternative if the probability of small demand is estimated to be 0.4 and the probability of large demand is estimated to be 0.6?

SOLUTION

The expected value for each alternative is

ALTERNATIVE	EXPECTED VALUE
Small facility	$0.4(200) + 0.6(270) = \mathbf{242}$
Large facility	$0.4(160) + 0.6(800) = \mathbf{544}$

Figure A.4 confirms this $544 expected value for the large facility, using OM Explorer's *Decision Theory* Solver. With the drop-down menu, it can also show the choices for the other four decision rules that we covered.

Solver - Decision Theory

Enter data in yellow-shaded areas.

This solver can accommodate between two and five events and between two and six alternatives. Replace the event and alternative names with your own (delete any unused labels). Then enter the payoff estimates directly in the first table. Also, enter probabilities for the events if you plan to use the Expected Value decision rule. Using the dropdown menu, you can then view the alternative chosen for each decision rule, and the payoff that goes with its choice.

Payoff Scenarios

	1:	2:	3:	4:	5:
	Low Demand	High Demand			
Probabilities---->	0.4	0.6			
Small Facility	200	270			
Large Facility	160	800			

Use the dropdown list to select the decision rule >>>   `Expected Value ▼`

Selected decision rule indicates you should select: `Large Facility`

Expected Payoff   `$544`

FIGURE A.4

Decision Theory Solver for Example A.7

DECISION POINT   Management would choose a large facility if it used this expected value decision rule, because it provides the best long-term results if consistently applied over time.

VALUE OF PERFECT INFORMATION

Suppose that a manager has a way of improving the forecasts—say, through more expensive market research or studying past trends. Assume that the manager, although unable to affect the probabilities of the events, can predict the future without error. The **value of perfect information** is the amount by which the expected payoff will improve if the manager knows which event will occur. It can be found with the following procedure:

value of perfect information
The amount by which the expected payoff will improve if the manager knows which event will occur.

1. Identify the best payoff for each event.
2. Calculate the expected value of these best payoffs by multiplying the best payoff for each event by the probability that the event will occur.
3. Subtract the expected value of the payoff without perfect information from the expected value of the payoff with perfect information. This difference is the value of perfect information.

EXAMPLE A.8   Value of Perfect Information

TUTOR A.5
Tutor A.5 on the Student CD-ROM provides a new example to determine the value of perfect information.

What is the value of perfect information to the manager in Example A.7?

SOLUTION

The best payoff for each event is the highest number in its column of the payoff matrix, or

EVENT	BEST PAYOFF
Low demand	200
High demand	800

The expected values, with and without perfect information, are

$$EV_{perfect} = 200(0.4) + 800(0.6) = 560$$
$$EV_{imperfect} = 160(0.4) + 800(0.6) = 544$$

Therefore, the value of perfect information is $560,000 − $544,000 = $16,000.

DECISION POINT   Management will not pay more than $16,000 for any effort to improve forecast accuracy, even if it ensures a perfect forecast.

DECISION TREES

The decision tree method is a general approach to a wide range of OM decisions, such as product planning, process analysis, process capacity, and location. It is particularly valuable for evaluating different capacity expansion alternatives when demand is uncertain and sequential decisions are involved. For example, a company may expand a facility in 2005 only to discover in 2009 that demand is much higher than forecasted. In that case, a second decision may be necessary to determine whether to expand again or build a second facility.

decision tree   A schematic model of alternatives available to the decision maker, along with their possible consequences.

A **decision tree** is a schematic model of alternatives available to the decision maker, along with their possible consequences. The name derives from the tree-like appearance of the model. It consists of a number of square *nodes*, representing decision points, that are left by *branches* (which should be read from left to right), representing the alternatives. Branches leaving circular, or chance, nodes represent the events. The probability of each chance event, *P(E)*, is shown above each branch. The probabilities for all branches leaving a chance node must sum to 1.0. The conditional payoff, which is the payoff for each possible alternative-event combination, is shown at the end of each combination. Payoffs are given only at the outset, before the analysis begins, for the end points of each alternative-event combination. In Figure A.5, for example, payoff 1 is the financial outcome the manager expects if alternative 1 is chosen and then chance event 1 occurs. No payoff can be associated yet with any branches farther to the left, such as alternative 1 as a whole, because it is followed by a chance event and is not an end point. Payoffs often are expressed as the present value (see Supplement J,

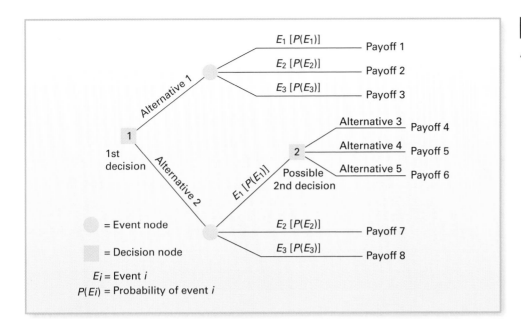

"Financial Analysis" in the Student CD-ROM) of net profits. If revenues are not affected by the decision, the payoff is expressed as net costs.

After drawing a decision tree, we solve it by working from right to left, calculating the *expected payoff* for each node as follows:

1. For an event node, we multiply the payoff of each event branch by the event's probability. We add these products to get the event node's expected payoff.
2. For a decision node, we pick the alternative that has the best expected payoff. If an alternative leads to an event node, its payoff is equal to that node's expected payoff (already calculated). We "saw off," or "prune," the other branches not chosen by marking two short lines through them. The decision node's expected payoff is the one associated with the single remaining unpruned branch.

We continue this process until the leftmost decision node is reached. The unpruned branch extending from it is the best alternative to pursue. If multistage decisions are involved, we must await subsequent events before deciding what to do next. If new probability or payoff estimates are obtained, we repeat the process.

Various software is available for drawing decision trees. PowerPoint can be used to draw decision trees, although it does not have the capability to analyze the decision tree. More extensive capabilities, in addition to OM Explorer, are found with SmartDraw (**www.smartdraw.com**), Applied Decision Analysis DPL Software (**www.adainc.com/software**), PrecisionTree decision analysis from Palisade Corporation (**www.palisade.com/html/ptree.html**), and TreePlan (**www.ourworld.compuserve.com/homepages/decision**).

Analyzing a Decision Tree

EXAMPLE A.9

ACTIVE MODEL A.3

Active Model A.3 on the Student CD-ROM provides additional insight on this decision tree example and its extensions.

A retailer must decide whether to build a small or a large facility at a new location. Demand at the location can be either small or large, with probabilities estimated to be 0.4 and 0.6, respectively. If a small facility is built and demand proves to be high, the manager may choose not to expand (payoff = $223,000) or to expand (payoff = $270,000). If a small facility is built and demand is low, there is no reason to expand and the payoff is $200,000. If a large facility is built and demand proves to be low, the choice is to do nothing ($40,000) or to stimulate demand through local advertising. The response to advertising may be either modest or sizable, with their probabilities estimated to be 0.3 and 0.7, respectively. If it is modest, the payoff is estimated to be only $20,000; the payoff grows to $220,000 if the response is sizable. Finally, if a large facility is built and demand turns out to be high, the payoff is $800,000.

Draw a decision tree. Then analyze it to determine the expected payoff for each decision and event node. Which alternative—building a small facility or building a large facility—has the higher expected payoff?

SOLUTION

The decision tree in Figure A.6 shows the event probability and the payoff for each of the seven alternative-event combinations. The first decision is whether to build a small or a large facility. Its node is shown first, to the left, because it is the decision the retailer must make now. The second decision node—whether to expand at a later date—is reached only if a small facility is built and demand turns out to be high. Finally, the third decision point—whether to advertise—is reached only if the retailer builds a large facility and demand turns out to be low.

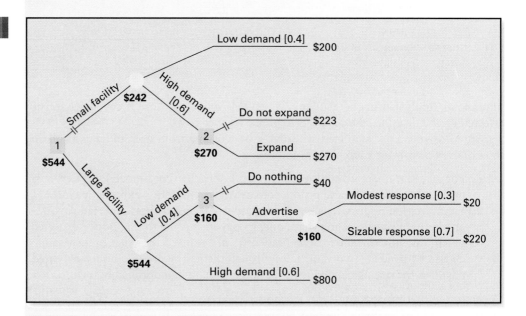

FIGURE A.6

Decision Tree for Retailer

Analysis of the decision tree begins with calculation of the expected payoffs from right to left, shown on Figure A.6 beneath the appropriate event and decision nodes.

1. For the event node dealing with advertising, the expected payoff is 160, or the sum of each event's payoff weighted by its probability [0.3(20) + 0.7(220)].
2. The expected payoff for decision node 3 is 160 because *Advertise* (160) is better than *Do nothing* (40). Prune the *Do nothing* alternative.
3. The payoff for decision node 2 is 270 because *Expand* (270) is better than *Do not expand* (223). Prune *Do not expand*.
4. The expected payoff for the event node dealing with demand, assuming that a small facility is built, is 242 [or 0.4(200) + 0.6(270)].
5. The expected payoff for the event node dealing with demand, assuming that a large facility is built, is 544 [or 0.4(160) + 0.6(800)].
6. The expected payoff for decision node 1 is 544 because the large facility's expected payoff is largest. Prune *Small facility*.

DECISION POINT   The retailer should build the large facility. This initial decision is the only one made now. Subsequent decisions are made after learning whether demand actually is low or high.

SUPPLEMENT HIGHLIGHTS

- Break-even analysis can be used to evaluate the profit potential of services and products. It can also be used to compare alternative processes. Sensitivity analysis can be used to predict the effect of changing forecasts, costs, or prices.

- At times, decision alternatives cannot be evaluated in light of a single performance measure such as profit or cost. The preference matrix is a method of rating alternatives according to several objectives. The technique calls for important objectives to receive more weight in the decision, but determining in advance which objectives are important may be difficult.

- Applications of decision theory in operations management include decisions on process, capacity, location, and inventory. Decision theory is a general approach to decision making under conditions of certainty, uncertainty, or risk.

STUDENT CD-ROM AND INTERNET RESOURCES

The Student CD-ROM and the Companion Website at **www.prenhall.com/krajewski** contain many tools, activities, and resources designed for this supplement. The following items are recommended to enhance your skills and improve your understanding of the material in this supplement.

STUDENT CD-ROM RESOURCES

- ➤ **PowerPoint Slides.** View this comprehensive set of slides customized for this supplement's concepts and techniques.
- ➤ **OM Explorer Tutors.** OM Explorer contains six tutor spreadsheets that will help you learn about break-even analysis (for evaluating processes, products, or services); the preference matrix; decisions under uncertainty; decisions under risk; and location decisions under risk. See Supplement A in the OM Explorer.
- ➤ **OM Explorer Solvers.** OM Explorer contains three spreadsheets designed to solve general problems involving break-even analysis, decision theory, and the preference matrix. See Decision Making in the OM Explorer menu for these routines.
- ➤ **Active Models.** There are three active model spreadsheets that provide additional insight on break-even analysis,

make-or-buy analysis, and decision trees. See Decision Making in the Active Models menu for these routines.
- ➤ **SmartDraw.** Use the link to download a 30-day trial of SmartDraw, a software package that can help prepare decision trees.
- ➤ **Supplement J.** "Financial Analysis." Learn about several tools for evaluating decisions that involve large capital investments.

INTERNET RESOURCES

- ➤ **Self-Study Quizzes.** See the compendium of true or false, multiple choice, and essay questions that give feedback on how well you have mastered the concepts in this supplement.
- ➤ **In the News.** See articles that apply to this supplement.
- ➤ **Internet Exercises.** Try out this link to see how decision-making tools help to plan for starting a new business. Another exercise explores payoff tables and decision trees.
- ➤ **Virtual Tours:** See the "Web Links to Company Facility Tours" for various tours of company facilities.

KEY EQUATIONS

1. Break-even volume: $Q = \dfrac{F}{p - c}$

2. Evaluating processes, make-or-buy indifference quantity: $Q = \dfrac{F_m - F_b}{c_b - c_m}$

KEY TERMS

break-even analysis 32
break-even point 32
decision theory 38
decision tree 42

fixed cost 32
payoff table 38
preference matrix 36
sensitivity analysis 34

value of perfect information 41
variable cost 32

SOLVED PROBLEM I

The owner of a small manufacturing business has patented a new device for washing dishes and cleaning dirty kitchen sinks. Before trying to commercialize the device and add it to her existing product line, she wants reasonable assurance of success. Variable costs are estimated at $7 per unit produced and sold. Fixed costs are about $56,000 per year.

a. If the selling price is set at $25, how many units must be produced and sold to break even? Use both algebraic and graphic approaches.

b. Forecasted sales for the first year are 10,000 units if the price is reduced to $15. With this pricing strategy, what would be the product's total contribution to profits in the first year?

SOLUTION

a. Beginning with the algebraic approach, we get

$$Q = \frac{F}{p - c} = \frac{56,000}{25 - 7}$$
$$= 3,111 \text{ units}$$

Using the graphic approach, shown in Figure A.7, we first draw two lines:

$$\text{Total revenue} = 25Q$$
$$\text{Total cost} = 56,000 + 7Q$$

The two lines intersect at $Q = 3,111$ units, the break-even quantity.

b.

$$\text{Total profit contribution} = \text{Total revenue} - \text{Total cost}$$
$$= pQ - (F + cQ)$$
$$= 15(10,000) - [56,000 + 7(10,000)]$$
$$= \$124,000$$

FIGURE A.7

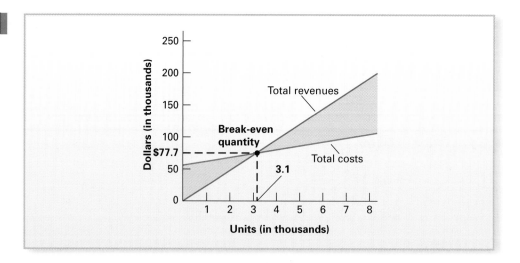

SOLVED PROBLEM 2

Binford Tool Company is screening three new product ideas, A, B, and C. Resource constraints allow only one of them to be commercialized. The performance criteria and ratings, on a scale of 1 (worst) to 10 (best), are shown in the following table. The Binford managers give equal weights to the performance criteria. Which is the best alternative, as indicated by the preference matrix method?

PERFORMANCE CRITERION	RATING		
	PRODUCT A	PRODUCT B	PRODUCT C
1. Demand uncertainty and project risk	3	9	2
2. Similarity to present products	7	8	6
3. Expected return on investment (ROI)	10	4	8
4. Compatibility with current manufacturing process	4	7	6
5. Competitive advantage	4	6	5

SOLUTION

Each of the five criteria receives a weight of 1/5 or 0.20.

PRODUCT	CALCULATION	TOTAL SCORE
A	$(0.20 \times 3) + (0.20 \times 7) + (0.20 \times 10) + (0.20 \times 4) + (0.20 \times 4)$	= 5.6
B	$(0.20 \times 9) + (0.20 \times 8) + (0.20 \times 4) + (0.20 \times 7) + (0.20 \times 6)$	= 6.8
C	$(0.20 \times 2) + (0.20 \times 6) + (0.20 \times 8) + (0.20 \times 6) + (0.20 \times 5)$	= 5.4

The best choice is product B. Products A and C are well behind in terms of total weighted score.

SOLVED PROBLEM 3

Adele Weiss manages the campus flower shop. Flowers must be ordered three days in advance from her supplier in Mexico. Although Valentine's Day is fast approaching, sales are almost entirely last-minute, impulse purchases. Advance sales are so small that Weiss has no way to estimate the probability of low (25 dozen), medium (60 dozen), or high (130 dozen) demand for red roses on the big day. She buys roses for $15 per dozen and sells them for $40 per dozen. Construct a payoff table. Which decision is indicated by each of the following decision criteria?

TUTOR A.6

Tutor A.6 on the Student CD-ROM examines decisions under uncertainty for a location example.

    a. Maximin
    b. Maximax
    c. Laplace
    d. Minimax regret

SOLUTION

The payoff table for this problem is

ALTERNATIVE	DEMAND FOR RED ROSES		
	LOW (25 DOZEN)	MEDIUM (60 DOZEN)	HIGH (130 DOZEN)
Order 25 dozen	$625	$625	$625
Order 60 dozen	$100	$1,500	$1,500
Order 130 dozen	($950)	$450	$3,250
Do nothing	$0	$0	$0

    a. Under the maximin criteria, Weiss should order 25 dozen, because if demand is low, Weiss's profits are $625.

    b. Under the maximax criteria, Weiss should order 130 dozen. The greatest possible payoff, $3,250, is associated with the largest order.

    c. Under the Laplace criteria, Weiss should order 60 dozen. Equally weighted payoffs for ordering 25, 60, and 130 dozen are about $625, $1,033, and $917, respectively.

    d. Under the minimax regret criteria, Weiss should order 130 dozen. The maximum regret of ordering 25 dozen occurs if demand is high: $3,250 − $625 = $2,625. The maximum regret of ordering 60 dozen occurs if demand is high: $3,250 − $1,500 = $1,750. The maximum regret of ordering 130 dozen occurs if demand is low: $625 − (−$950) = $1,575.

SOLVED PROBLEM 4

White Valley Ski Resort is planning the ski lift operation for its new ski resort. Management is trying to determine whether one or two lifts will be necessary; each lift can accommodate 250 people per day. Skiing normally occurs in the 14-week period from December to April, during which the lift will operate seven days per week. The first lift will operate at 90 percent capacity if economic conditions are bad, the probability of which is believed to be about a 0.3. During normal times the first lift will be utilized at 100 percent capacity, and the excess crowd will provide 50 percent utilization of the second lift. The probability of normal times is 0.5. Finally, if times are really good, the probability of which is 0.2, the utilization of the second lift will increase to 90 percent. The equivalent annual cost of installing a new lift, recognizing the time value of money and the lift's economic life, is $50,000. The annual cost of installing two lifts is only $90,000 if both are purchased at the same time. If used at all, each lift costs $200,000 to operate, no matter how low or high its utilization rate. Lift tickets cost $20 per customer per day.

a. Should the resort purchase one lift or two?
b. What is the value of perfect information?

SOLUTION

a. The decision tree is shown in Figure A.8. The payoff ($000) for each alternative-event branch is shown in the following table. The total revenues from one lift operating at 100 percent capacity are $490,000 (or 250 customers × 98 days × $20/customer-day).

ALTERNATIVE	ECONOMIC CONDITION	PAYOFF CALCULATION (REVENUE − COST)
One lift	Bad times	0.9(490) − (50 + 200) = 191
	Normal times	1.0(490) − (50 + 200) = 240
	Good times	1.0(490) − (50 + 200) = 240
Two lifts	Bad times	0.9(490) − (90 + 200) = 151
	Normal times	1.5(490) − (90 + 400) = 245
	Good times	1.9(490) − (90 + 400) = 441

b. The value of perfect information is

ECONOMIC CONDITION	BEST PAYOFF	PROBABILITY	WEIGHTED PAYOFF
Bad times	$191,000	0.3	$ 57,300
Normal times	$245,000	0.5	$122,500
Good times	$441,000	0.2	$ 88,200

Expected value with perfect information	$268,000
Without perfect information, part (a)	$256,000
The value of perfect information is	$ 12,000

FIGURE A.8

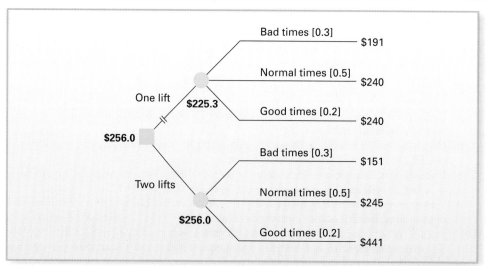

PROBLEMS

An icon in the margin next to a problem identifies the software that can be helpful, but is not mandatory. The software is available on the Student CD-ROM that is packaged with every new copy of the textbook.

Problems 1 through 11 show a variety of applications for break-even analysis. Problems 1 through 4 apply break-even analysis to product or service planning decisions (discussed in Chapter 2, "Operations Strategy"). Problems 12 and 13 demonstrate use of the preference matrix for service or product planning, and Problem 14 applies the preference matrix to location decisions. Decision theory Problems 15, 16, and 19 through 22 apply to capacity decisions (discussed in Chapter 6, "Process Capacity"). Problems 17 and 18 involve the use of decision trees to evaluate fairly complex service or product planning decisions.

Break-Even Analysis

1. ◗ **OM Explorer** Mary Williams, owner of Williams Products, is evaluating whether to introduce a new product line. After thinking through the production process and the costs of raw materials and new equipment, Williams estimates the variable costs of each unit produced and sold at $6 and the fixed costs per year at $60,000.

   a. If the selling price is set at $18 each, how many units must be produced and sold for Williams to break even? Use both graphic and algebraic approaches to get your answer.

   b. Williams forecasts sales of 10,000 units for the first year if the selling price is set at $14.00 each. What would be the total contribution to profits from this new product during the first year?

   c. If the selling price is set at $12.50, Williams forecasts that first-year sales would increase to 15,000 units. Which pricing strategy ($14.00 or $12.50) would result in the greater total contribution to profits?

   d. What other considerations would be crucial to the final decision about making and marketing the new product?

2. ◗ **OM Explorer** A product at the Jennings Company has enjoyed reasonable sales volumes, but its contributions to profits have been disappointing. Last year, 17,500 units were produced and sold. The selling price is $22 per unit, c is $18, and F is $80,000.

   a. What is the break-even quantity for this product? Use both graphic and algebraic approaches to get your answer.

   b. Jennings is considering ways to either stimulate sales volumes or decrease variable costs. Management believes that sales can be increased by 30 percent or that c can be reduced to 85 percent of its current level. Which alternative leads to higher contributions to profits, assuming that each is equally costly to implement? (*Hint:* Calculate profits for both

alternatives and identify the one having the greatest profits.)

   c. What is the percent change in the per-unit profit contribution generated by each alternative in part (b).

3. An interactive television service that costs $10 per month to provide can be sold on the information highway for $15 per client per month. If a service area includes a potential of 15,000 customers, what is the most a company could spend on annual fixed costs to acquire and maintain the equipment?

4. A restaurant is considering adding fresh brook trout to its menu. Customers would have the choice of catching their own trout from a simulated mountain stream or simply asking the waiter to net the trout for them. Operating the stream would require $10,600 in fixed costs per year. Variable costs are estimated to be $6.70 per trout. The firm wants to break even if 800 trout dinners are sold per year. What should be the price of the new item?

5. ◗ **OM Explorer** Gabriel Manufa. . . . . must implement a manufacturing process that . . . . . the amount of toxic by-products. Two process . . . . . n identified that provide the same level of to. . . . . . . ct reduction. The first process would inc. . . . . . of fixed costs and $600 per unit of varia. . . . . second process has fixed costs of $120, ... ble costs of $900 per unit.

   a. What is the break-even quan . . . . . which the first process is more attractiv .

   b. What is the difference in total . . . . . the quantity produced is 800 units?

6. ◗ **OM Explorer** A news clipping service is considering modernization. Rather than manually clipping and photocopying articles of interest and mailing them to its clients, employees electronically input stories from most widely circulated publications into a database. Each new issue is searched for key words, such as a client's company name, competitors' names, type of business, and the company's products, services, and officers. When matches occur, affected clients are instantly notified via an on-line network. If the story is of interest, it is electronically transmitted, so the client often has the story and can prepare comments for follow-up interviews before the publication hits the street. The manual process has fixed costs of $400,000 per year and variable costs of $6.20 per clipping mailed. The price charged the client is $8.00 per clipping. The computerized process has fixed costs of $1,300,000 per year and variable costs of $2.25 per story electronically transmitted to the client.

   a. If the same price is charged for either process, what is the annual volume beyond which the automated process is more attractive?

   b. The present volume of business is 225,000 clippings per year. Many of the clippings sent with the current process are not of interest to the client or are multiple copies of the same story appearing in several publications. The news clipping service believes that by improving service and by lowering the price to $4.00 per story, modernization will increase volume to 900,000 stories transmitted per year. Should the clipping service modernize?

  c. If the forecasted increase in business is too optimistic, at what volume will the new process break even?

7. 🌑 **OM Explorer** Hahn Manufacturing has been purchasing a key component of one of its products from a local supplier. The current purchase price is $1,500 per unit. Efforts to standardize parts have succeeded to the point that this same component can now be used in five different products. Annual component usage should increase from 150 to 750 units. Management wonders whether it is time to make the component in-house, rather than to continue buying it from the supplier. Fixed costs would increase by about $40,000 per year for the new equipment and tooling needed. The cost of raw materials and variable overhead would be about $1,100 per unit, and labor costs would be $300 per unit produced.

  a. Should Hahn make rather than buy?

  b. What is the break-even quantity?

  c. What other considerations might be important?

8. Techno Corporation is currently manufacturing an item at variable costs of $5.00 per unit. Annual fixed costs of manufacturing this item are $140,000. The current selling price of the item is $10.00 per unit, and the annual sales volume is 30,000 units.

  a. Techno can substantially improve the item's quality by installing new equipment at additional annual fixed costs of $60,000. Variable costs per unit would increase by $1.00, but, as more of the better-quality product could be sold, the annual volume would increase to 50,000 units. Should Techno buy the new equipment and maintain the current price of the item? Why or why not?

  b. Alternatively, Techno could increase the selling price to $11.00 per unit. However, the annual sales volume would be limited to 45,000 units. Should Techno buy the new equipment and raise the price of the item? Why or why not?

9. The Tri-County Generation and Transmission Association is a nonprofit cooperative organization that provides electrical service to rural customers. Based on a faulty long-range demand forecast, Tri-County overbuilt its generation and distribution system. Tri-County now has much more capacity than it needs to serve its customers. Fixed costs, mostly debt service on investment in plant and equipment, are $82.5 million per year. Variable costs, mostly fossil fuel costs, are $25 per megawatt-hour (MWh, or million watts of power used

for one hour). The new person in charge of demand forecasting prepared a short-range forecast for use in next year's budgeting process. That forecast calls for Tri-County customers to consume 1 million MWh of energy next year.

  a. How much will Tri-county need to charge its customers per MWh to break even next year?

  b. The Tri-County customers balk at that price and conserve electrical energy. Only 95 percent of forecasted demand materializes. What is the resulting surplus or loss for this nonprofit organization?

10. 🌑 **OM Explorer** Earthquake, drought, fire, economic famine, flood, and a pestilence of TV court reporters have caused an exodus from the City of Angels to Boulder, Colorado. The sudden increase in demand is straining the capacity of Boulder's electrical system. Boulder's alternatives have been reduced to buying 150,000 MWh of electric power from Tri-County G&T at a price of $75 per MWh, or refurbishing and recommissioning the abandoned Pearl Street Power Station in downtown Boulder. Fixed costs of that project are $10 million per year, and variable costs would be $35 per MWh. Should Boulder build or buy?

11. Tri-County G&T sells 150,000 MWh per year of electrical power to Boulder at $75 per MWh, has fixed costs of $82.5 million per year, and has variable costs of $25 per MWh. If Tri-County has 1,000,000 MWh of demand from its customers (other than Boulder) what will Tri-County have to charge to break even?

Preference Matrix

12. 🌑 **OM Explorer** The Forsite Company is screening three ideas for new services. Resource constraints allow only one idea to be commercialized at the present time. The following estimates have been made for the five performance criteria that management believes to be most important.

	Rating		
Performance Criterion	Service A	Service B	Service C
Capital equipment investment required	0.6	0.8	0.3
Expected return on investment (ROI)	0.7	0.3	0.9
Compatibility with current workforce skills	0.4	0.7	0.5
Competitive advantage	1.0	0.4	0.6
Compatibility with EPA requirements	0.2	1.0	0.5

  a. Calculate a total weighted score for each alternative. Use a preference matrix and assume equal weights for each performance criterion. Which alternative is best? Worst?

  b. Suppose that the expected ROI is given twice the weight assigned to each of the remaining criteria. (Sum of weights should remain the same as in part (a).) Does this modification affect the ranking of the three potential services?

TABLE A.1

ANALYSIS OF NEW PRODUCT IDEAS

Performance Criterion	Rating				
	Product A	Product B	Product C	Product D	Product E
Compatibility with current manufacturing	8	7	3	6	9
Expected return on investment (ROI)	3	8	4	7	7
Compatibility with current workforce skills	9	5	7	6	5
Unit profit margin	7	6	9	2	7

13. ◥ **OM Explorer** You are in charge of analyzing five new product ideas and have been given the information shown in Table A.1 (1 = worst, 10 = best). Management has decided that criteria 2 and 3 are equally important and that criteria 1 and 4 are each four times as important as criterion 2. Only two new products can be introduced, and a product can be introduced only if its score exceeds 70 percent of the maximum possble total points. Which product ideas do you recommend?

14. ◥ **OM Explorer** Soft-Brew, Inc., collected the following information on where to locate a brewery (1 = poor, 10 = excellent).

Location Factor	Factor Weight	Location Score	
		A	B
Construction costs	10	8	5
Utilities available	10	7	7
Business services	10	4	7
Real estate cost	20	7	4
Quality of life	20	4	8
Transportation	30	7	6

    a. Which location, A or B, should be chosen on the basis of the total weighted score?

    b. If the factors were weighted equally, would the choice change?

Decision Theory

15. ◥ **OM Explorer** Build-Rite Construction has received favorable publicity from guest appearances on a public TV home improvement program. Public TV programming decisions seem to be unpredictable, so Build-Rite cannot estimate the probability of continued benefits from its relationship with the show. Demand for home improvements next year may be either low or high. But Build-Rite must decide now whether to hire more employees, do nothing, or develop subcontracts with other home improvement contractors. Build-Rite has developed the following payoff table.

Alternative	Demand for Home Improvements		
	Low	Moderate	High
Hire	($250,000)	$100,000	$625,000
Subcontract	$100,000	$150,000	$415,000
Do nothing	$ 50,000	$ 80,000	$300,000

Which alternative is best, according to each of the following decision criteria?

    a. Maximin

    b. Maximax

    c. Laplace

    d. Minimax regret

16. ◥ **OM Explorer** Once upon a time in the Old West, Fletcher, Cooper, and Wainwright (the Firm) was deciding whether to make arrows, barrels, or Conestoga wagons. The Firm understood that demand for products would vary, depending on U.S. government policies concerning the development of travel routes to California. If land routes were chosen and treaties with Native Americans could not be negotiated, the demand for arrows would be great. Success in those negotiations would favor demand for Conestoga wagons. If the water route was chosen, the success of negotiations would be irrelevant. Instead, many barrels would be needed to contain goods during the long sea voyage around Cape Horn. Although the Firm was expert at forecasting the effect of policy on its business, it could not estimate the probability of the U.S. government favoring one policy over another. Based on the Firm's forecasted demand, which alternative is best, according to each of the following decision criteria?

    a. Maximin

    b. Maximax

    c. Laplace

	Forecasted Demand		
Policy	**Arrows**	**Barrels**	**Conestoga Wagons**
Land, no treaty	9,000,000	300,000	5,000
Land, with treaty	5,000,000	200,000	50,000
Sea	2,500,000	500,000	3,000

	Product		
Price and Costs	**Arrows**	**Barrels**	**Conestoga Wagons**
Fixed costs	$60,000	$80,000	$100,000
Variable costs per unit	$0.05	$1.50	$50
Price per unit	$0.15	$3.00	$75

17. Returning to Problem 16, assume that Fletcher, Cooper, and Wainwright has contributed to the reelection campaign and legal defense fund for the Chairman of the House Ways and Means Committee. In return, the Firm learns that the probability of choosing the sea route is 0.2, the probability of developing the land route and successful treaty negotiations is 0.3, and the probability of developing the land route and unsuccessful negotiations is 0.5.

   a. Draw a decision tree to analyze the problem. Calculate the expected value of each product alternative.

   b. The Chariman informs Fletcher, Cooper and Wainwright that a more accurate forecast of events is available "for a price." What is the value of perfect information?

Decision Tree

18. Analyze the decision tree in Figure A.9. What is the expected payoff for the best alternative? First, be sure to infer the missing probabilities.

19. A manager is trying to decide whether to buy one machine or two. If only one is purchased and demand proves to be excessive, the second machine can be purchased later. Some sales will be lost, however, because the lead time for producing this type of machine is six months. In addition, the cost per machine will be lower if both are purchased at the same time. The probability of low demand is estimated to be 0.20. The after-tax net present value of the benefits from purchasing the two machines together is $90,000 if demand is low and $180,000 if demand is high.

   If one machine is purchased and demand is low, the net present value is $120,000. If demand is high, the manager has three options. Doing nothing has a net present value of $120,000; subcontracting, $160,000; and buying the second machine, $140,000.

   a. Draw a decision tree for this problem.

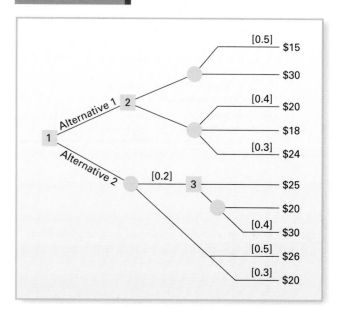

   b. How many machines should the company buy initially? What is the expected payoff for this alternative?

20. A manager is trying to decide whether to build a small, medium, or large facility. Demand can be low, average, or high, with the estimated probabilities being 0.25, 0.40, and 0.35, respectively.

   A small facility is expected to earn an after-tax net present value of just $18,000 if demand is low. If demand is average, the small facility is expected to earn $75,000; it can be increased to average size to earn a net present value of $60,000. If demand is high, the small facility is expected to earn $75,000 and can be expanded to average size to earn $60,000 or to large size to earn $125,000.

   A medium-sized facility is expected to lose an estimated $25,000 if demand is low and earn $140,000 if demand is average. If demand is high, the medium-sized facility is expected to earn a net present value of $150,000; it can be expanded to a large size for a net payoff of $145,000.

   If a large facility is built and demand is high, earnings are expected to be $220,000. If demand is average for the large facility, the present value is expected to be $125,000; if demand is low, the facility is expected to lose $60,000.

   a. Draw a decision tree for this problem.

   b. What should management do to achieve the highest expected payoff?

21. A manufacturing plant has reached full capacity. The company must build a second plant—either small or large—at a nearby location. The demand is likely to be high or low. The probability of low demand is 0.3. If demand is low, the large plant has a present value of $5

million and the small plant, $8 million. If demand is high, the large plant pays off with a present value of $18 million and the small plant with a present value of only $10 million. However, the small plant can be expanded later if demand proves to be high, for a present value of $14 million.

a. Draw a decision tree for this problem.

b. What should management do to achieve the highest expected payoff?

22. Benjamin Moses, chief engineer of Offshore Chemicals, Inc., must decide whether to build a new processing facility based on an experimental technology. If the new facility works, the company will realize a net profit of $20 million. If the new facility fails, the company will lose $10 million. Benjamin's best guess is that there is a 40 percent chance that the new facility will work.

a. What decision should Benjamin Moses make?

b. How much should he be willing to pay for perfect information?

SELECTED REFERENCES

Bonini, Charles P., Warren H. Hausman, and Harold Bierman, Jr. *Quantitative Analysis for Management.* Burr Ridge Parkway, IL: Irwin/McGraw-Hill, 1996.

Clemen, Robert T. *Making Hard Decisions: An Introduction to Decision Analysis.* Boston: PWS-Kent, 1991.

Operations Strategy

LEARNING GOALS   *After reading this chapter, you should be able to . . .*

IDENTIFY OR DEFINE
  1. an operations strategy.
  2. the nine different competitive priorities used in operations strategies.
  3. the steps in the new service/product development process.

DESCRIBE OR EXPLAIN
  4. the role of operations strategy as a source of competitive strength in a global marketplace.
  5. how to link marketing strategy to operations strategy through the use of competitive priorities.
  6. how operations strategy is a pattern of decisions directed at processes, systems, and procedures in order to develop the capabilities to achieve certain competitive priorities.

STARBUCKS

Want to go for a coffee? You say that you want something special, such as espresso or cappuccino? Perhaps, then, we should go to Starbucks (www.starbucks.com) as millions of others do. Who would have thought that someone could turn a pedestrian product like coffee into an upscale consumer accessory? Entrepreneur Howard Schultz did, 15 years ago, when he purchased the 17-store Seattle chain and turned it into a global success. Now the chain has 5,689 outlets in 28 countries generating a total of $2.6 billion a year in sales in 2001 and more than $180 million in profits. Average growth in profits has been a phenomenal 30 percent a year. Apparently there is something very special going on here.

What is the secret to this outstanding performance? Much of it has to do with the Starbucks service strategy. Consider what you get when you shop at a Starbucks. Certainly you get your choice of exotic coffees, lattes, cappuccino, or espresso. You can also have a sandwich, dessert, a CD of your favorite pop artist, or even packaged coffee for a special occasion. There are some new innovations to look for. You may choose to use an automated espresso machine or a prepaid Starbucks card to speed service. Transaction times are cut in half with the card. You may even wish to use Starbucks Express at some stores, which uses Web technology to provide faster service. Customers can preorder and prepay for beverages and pastries via phone or the Web site, and the order will be available for pickup with their name on the package. In about 1,200 locations in North America and Europe, you can access the Internet while enjoying your java. You also get upscale surroundings (some customers say they are "hip") that are conducive for conversation and socializing and friendly service from a cadre of *baristas*.

The strategy goes beyond the actual services and goods that are offered to customers. Starbucks likes to cluster stores in a good market to increase total revenue and market share. For example, there is a Starbucks store for every 9,400 people in Seattle. In Manhattan's 24 square miles, there are 124 Starbucks stores or about 1 store for every 12,000 people. It is cheaper to deliver to and manage stores located close together. Starbucks is capable of designing and opening a new store in 16 weeks or less and recouping the initial investment in three years.

While the Starbucks business model has been very successful, there are challenges that must be dealt with. For example, to maintain its growth in a saturated home market, Starbucks must look to international markets. Starbucks expects to double its number of stores worldwide to 10,000, most of the new ones overseas. Global expansion poses risks, not the least of which is lower profitability per store. Most of the international stores are operated by partners, thereby reducing the share Starbucks gets. Also, the profile of customers is changing. The chain's successes were largely built upon the baby boomer set. However, a new generation of younger potential customers is more adverse to the power and image of the Starbucks brand and is turned off by the image of latte-sipping sophisticates and piped-in soft rock music. Three-dollar cups of coffee are not an attraction, and they feel unwanted in Starbucks stores, where the only other people in the store like them are behind the counter. The business model also relies on employing lots of low-wage workers. Keeping them happy is a key to the successful delivery of the services provided at the Starbucks stores; an exceptional challenge in an environment that traditionally has low pay and long, hard hours.

Many of the new innovations that Starbucks is adding to the services at selected stores are an attempt to attract the new generation of customers. This is an example of how successful companies must constantly evaluate their strategies and update the goods and services they offer to reflect changes in demographics and customer desires. Nonetheless, it remains to be seen whether Starbucks will continue its phenomenal growth. Let's go get that coffee.

Source: Holmes, Stanley. "Planet Starbucks." *Business Week* (September 9, 2002), pp. 100–110.

A smiling Starbuck's employee fills a coffee grinder for the opening of a new store in Beijing. Starbucks is increasingly looking to international markets for expansion.

Starbucks' amazing growth story is an example of a customer-driven operations strategy in action. Core processes focus on critical activities, ranging from the acquisition of select coffee beans to the delivery of a variety of goods and services to the delight of customers. Managerial challenges abound as customer desires change, requiring managers to revisit the very strategy that historically brought them success and to redesign processes to support the new directions. This chapter explores operations strategy and its importance for business success.

Figure 2.1 shows how corporate strategy is linked to the functional strategies of the firm and serves as an outline of this chapter. Developing a customer-driven operations strategy begins with *corporate strategy*, which coordinates the firm's overall goals with its core processes. It determines the markets the firm will serve and the responses the firm will take to changes in the business and socioeconomic environment. It provides the resources to develop the firm's core competencies and core processes, and it identifies the strategy the firm will employ in international markets. Based on the corporate strategy, a *market analysis* categorizes the firm's customers, identifies their needs, and assesses competitors' strengths. This information is used to develop *competitive priorities* for processes that deal with external as well as internal customers. These competitive priorities help managers develop the services or products and the processes needed to be competitive in the marketplace. We will discuss the concept of competitive priorities in more detail later. Nonetheless, competitive priorities are important to the design of new services or products, the processes that will deliver them, and the functional strategies that provide the means by which the capabilities of the firm's processes are developed.

Within the umbrella of Figure 2.1 we focus on **operations strategy**, which specifies the means by which operations implements the firm's corporate strategy. Basically, operations strategy links long- and short-term operations decisions to corporate strategy. As

operations strategy The means by which operations implements the firm's corporate strategy.

FIGURE 2.1   **Competitive Priorities: Link Between Corporate Strategy and Functional Area Strategies**

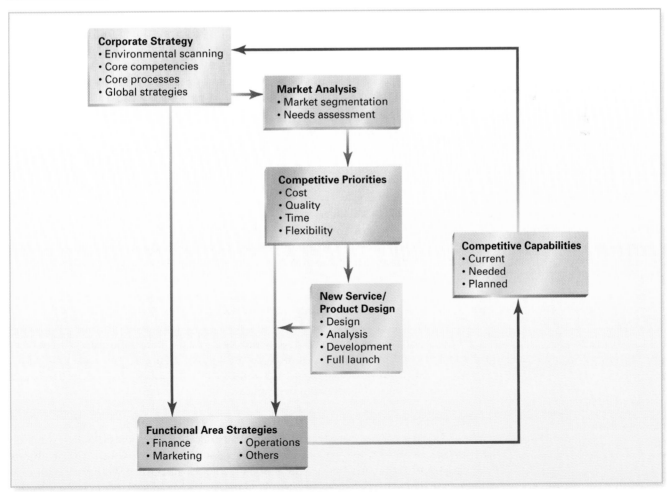

we will see throughout the text, these operations decisions include the design and operation of the firm's processes. Continuous cross-functional interaction must occur in implementing operations strategy. For example, Starbucks' operations manager needs feedback from marketing to determine how much capacity should be planned for a new store, and the operations manager must work with finance regarding the timing and funding of the new store. Thus, in identifying the operational capabilities needed for the future, operations managers must work closely with the managers of other functional areas.

As you read this chapter on operations strategy, think about how operation strategy is important to various departments across the organization, such as . . .

> **engineering,** which must design the services and products and the processes needed to produce them.
> **finance,** which performs the financial analyses of alternative service or product designs.
> **management information systems,** which designs the systems that provide market data and competitor information in a global format.
> **marketing,** which determines the services and products the firm needs to produce to be competitive in the marketplace.
> **operations,** which must determine the best operations strategies and manage the processes that produce the services or products to achieve the firm's market strategy.

CORPORATE STRATEGY

Corporate strategy specifies the business or businesses that the company will pursue, isolates new opportunities and threats in the environment, and identifies the growth objectives that it should achieve. Also addressed is business strategy, or how a firm can differentiate itself from the competition. Choices could include producing standardized versus customized services or products or competing on the basis of cost advantage versus responsive delivery. Corporate strategy provides an overall direction that serves as the framework for carrying out all the organization's functions.

STRATEGIC CONSIDERATIONS

Developing a corporate strategy involves three considerations: (1) monitoring and adjusting to changes in the business environment, (2) identifying and developing the firm's core competencies, and (3) developing the firm's core processes.

How can management identify and deal with environmental change when formulating corporate strategy?

ENVIRONMENTAL SCANNING.   The external business environment in which a firm competes changes continually, and an organization needs to adapt to those changes. Adaptation begins with *environmental scanning*, the process by which managers monitor trends in the socioeconomic environment (including the industry, the marketplace, and society) for potential opportunities or threats. A crucial reason for environmental scanning is to stay ahead of the competition. Competitors may be gaining an edge by broadening service or product lines, improving quality, or lowering costs. New entrants into the market or competitors that offer substitutes for a firm's service or product may threaten continued profitability. Other important environmental concerns include economic trends, technological changes, political conditions, social changes (such as attitudes toward work), the availability of vital resources, and the collective power of customers or suppliers.

core competencies   The unique resources and strengths that an organization's management considers when formulating strategy.

CORE COMPETENCIES.   Good managerial skill alone cannot overcome environmental changes. Rather, corporate strategy must address them. Firms succeed by taking advantage of what they do particularly well—that is, the organization's unique strengths. **Core competencies** are the unique resources and strengths that an organization's management considers when formulating strategy. They reflect the collective

Newspaper printing presses represent a large capital investment. For this reason, many newspapers have divested themselves of their printing processes to focus on their core competencies.

learning of the organization, especially in how to coordinate diverse processes and integrate multiple technologies. These competencies include the following:

1. *Workforce.* A well-trained and flexible workforce allows organizations to respond to market needs in a timely fashion. This competency is particularly important in service organizations, where the customer comes in direct contact with the employees.

2. *Facilities.* Having well-located facilities—offices, stores, and plants—is a primary advantage because of the long lead time needed to build new ones. Expansion into new services or products may be accomplished quickly. In addition, flexible facilities that can handle a variety of services or products at different levels of volume provide a competitive advantage.

3. *Market and Financial Know-How.* An organization that can easily attract capital from stock sales, market and distribute its services or products, or differentiate them from similar services or products on the market has a competitive edge.

4. *Systems and Technology.* Organizations with expertise in information systems will have an edge in industries that are data—and information—intensive, such as banking. Particularly advantageous is expertise in Internet technologies and applications, such as business-to-consumer and business-to-business systems. Having the patents on a new technology is also a big advantage.

CORE PROCESSES.   A firm's core competencies should determine its core processes. In Chapter 1, "Operations As a Competitive Weapon," we discussed four core processes: *customer relationship, new service/product development, order fulfillment,* and *supplier relationship.* Many companies have all four of these core processes. However, many other companies have selected to focus on a subset of them as their core processes, so as to better match their core competencies. For example, in the newspaper industry, all four processes were tightly integrated. A newspaper typically attracted its own customers—both readers and advertisers (customer relationship). It developed most of its product—the news stories printed on its pages (new service/product development). It also managed its own production, delivery, and supply processes (order fulfillment and supplier relationship). However, many newspaper companies found that it was very difficult to be good at all four processes and still be competitive on price, quality, and delivery. Today, much of the typical newspaper's product is outsourced to wire services, syndicated columnists, and publishers of specialty magazine inserts. In addition, many newspapers have divested themselves of the order fulfillment process, leaving the capital intensive printing and delivery processes to specialty printers. All of this allows the newspapers to focus on the customer relationship process, helping to connect readers to advertisers, and a portion of the new service/product development process, editing of the daily newspaper and developing stories of local interest. A similar situation exists in the banking industry, particularly in the credit card business. Companies are specializing in finding customers and maintaining relationships with them. For example, American Airlines' credit card program reaches out and achieves a special affinity to customers through its marketing database. Specialized credit card companies, such as CapitalOne, focus on service innovation by creating new features and pricing programs. Finally, many companies are taking over the order fulfillment process by managing the processing of credit card transactions and call centers. In the remainder of the text, we will continue to make reference to the four core processes; however, the important point is that every firm must evaluate their core competencies and choose to focus on those processes that provide the greatest competitive strength.

GLOBAL STRATEGIES

What role does operations play in entering international markets?

Identifying opportunities and threats today requires a global perspective. A global strategy may include buying foreign services or parts, combating threats from foreign competitors, or planning ways to enter markets beyond traditional national boundaries. Although warding off threats from global competitors is necessary, firms should also actively seek to penetrate foreign markets. Two effective global strategies are strategic alliances and locating abroad.

STRATEGIC ALLIANCES.   One way for a firm to open foreign markets is to create a *strategic alliance*. A strategic alliance is an agreement with another firm that may take one of three forms. One form of strategic alliance is the *collaborative effort*, which often arises when one firm has core competencies that another needs but is unwilling (or unable) to duplicate. Such arrangements are common in buyer–supplier relationships, as when a U.S. firm supplies parts to a foreign manufacturer, but also may be used in nontraditional ways.

Another form of strategic alliance is the *joint venture*, in which two firms agree to produce a service or product jointly. This approach often is used by firms to gain access to foreign markets. Finally, *technology licensing* is a form of strategic alliance in which one company licenses its service or production methods to another. Licenses may be used to gain access to foreign markets.

LOCATING ABROAD.   Another way to enter global markets is to locate operations in a foreign country. However, managers must recognize that what works well in their home country might not work well elsewhere. The economic and political environment or customers' needs may be very different. For example, McDonald's is known for the consistency of its products—a Big Mac tastes the same anywhere in the world. However, a family-owned chain, Jollibee Foods Corporation, has become the dominant fast-food chain in the Philippines. Jollibee caters to a local preference for sweet-and-spicy flavors, which it incorporates into its fried chicken, spaghetti, and burgers. Jollibee's strength is its understanding of local tastes and claims that its burger is similar to the one a Filipino would cook at home. McDonald's responded by introducing its own Filipino-style spicy burger, but competition is stiff. McDonald's experience demonstrates that, to be successful, corporate strategies must recognize customs, preferences, and economic conditions in other countries.

● MARKET ANALYSIS

One key to success in formulating a customer-driven operations strategy for both service and manufacturing firms is understanding what the customer wants and how to provide it better than the competition does. *Market analysis* first divides the firm's customers into market segments and then identifies the needs of each segment. In this section, we define and discuss the concepts of market segmentation and needs assessment.

MARKET SEGMENTATION

Market segmentation is the process of identifying groups of customers with enough in common to warrant the design and provision of services or products that the larger group wants and needs. For instance, The Gap, Inc., a major provider of casual clothes, has targeted teenagers and young adults and, for its GapKids stores, the parents or guardians of infants through 12-year-olds. In general, to identify market segments, the analyst must determine the characteristics that clearly differentiate each segment. A sound marketing program can then be devised and an effective operating strategy developed to support it.

Once the firm has identified a market segment, it can incorporate the needs of customers into the design of the service or product and the processes for its production. The following characteristics are among those that can be used to determine market segments.

1. *Demographic Factors.* Age, income, educational level, occupation, and location can differentiate markets.

2. *Psychological Factors.* Factors such as pleasure, fear, innovativeness, and boredom can serve to segment markets.

3. *Industry Factors.* Customers may utilize specific technologies (e.g., electronics, robotics, or microwave telecommunications); use certain materials (e.g., rubber, oil, or wood); or participate in a particular industry (e.g., banking, health care, or automotive). These factors are used for market segmentation when the firm's customers use its goods or services to produce other goods or services.

At one time, managers thought of customers as a homogeneous mass market. Managers now realize that two customers may use the same product for very different reasons. Identifying the key factors in each market segment is the starting point in devising a customer-driven operations strategy.

NEEDS ASSESSMENT

The second step in market analysis is to make a *needs assessment*, which identifies the needs of each segment and assesses how well competitors are addressing those needs. Once it has made this assessment, the firm can differentiate itself from its competitors. The needs assessment should include both the tangible and the intangible service or product attributes and features that a customer desires. Each market segment has market needs that can be related to the service or product process, or demand attributes. Market needs may be grouped as follows:

- *Service or Product Needs.* Attributes of the service or product, such as price, quality, and degree of customization desired.
- *Delivery System Needs.* Attributes of the processes and the supporting systems and resources needed to deliver the service or product, such as availability, convenience, courtesy, safety, accuracy, reliability, delivery speed, and delivery dependability.
- *Volume Needs.* Attributes of the demand for the service or product, such as high or low volume, degree of variability in volume, and degree of predictability in volume.
- *Other Needs.* Other attributes, such as reputation and number of years in business, after-sale technical support, ability to invest in international financial markets, competent legal services, and service or product design capability.

We will discuss these market needs further when we explore new service or product development.

COMPETITIVE PRIORITIES AND CAPABILITIES

What are the key priorities managers assign to processes so as to be competitive in the marketplace?

A customer-driven operations strategy reflects a clear understanding of the firm's long-term goals as embodied in its corporate strategy. It requires a cross-functional effort by all areas of the firm to understand the needs of the firm's external customers and to specify the operating capabilities the firm needs to outperform its competitors. A customer-driven operations strategy also addresses the needs of the internal customers of the firm's processes because the overall performance of the firm is dependent upon the performance of its core and supporting processes. **Competitive priorities** are the critical dimensions a process must possess to satisfy its internal or external customers, both now and in the future. We focus on nine broad competitive dimensions, which fall into four groups:

competitive priorities The critical dimensions that a process must possess to satisfy its internal or external customers, both now and in the future.

Cost	1. Low-cost operations
Quality	2. Top quality
	3. Consistent quality
Time	4. Delivery speed
	5. On-time delivery
	6. Development speed
Flexibility	7. Customization
	8. Variety
	9. Volume flexibility

Competitive priorities are planned, but not necessarily yet obtained, for a process or group of processes. They are abilities that must be present so as to maintain or build market share or to allow other internal processes to be successful. Not all nine dimensions are critical for a given process; management selects the ones that are most important. **Competitive capabilities** are the cost, quality, time, and flexibility dimensions that a process actually possesses and is able to deliver. When the capability falls short of the priority attached to it, management must find ways to close the gap or else revise the priority. We will have more to say about closing the gap later in this chapter.

competitive capabilities The cost, quality, time, and flexibility dimensions that a process actually possesses and is able to deliver.

A firm is composed of many processes that must be coordinated to provide the overall desirable outcome for the external customer (see Chapter 1, "Operations As a Competitive Weapon"). To link to corporate strategy, management assigns selected competitive priorities to each process (or group of processes) that are consistent with the current and future needs of external customers, as well as the process's internal customers. By doing so, management communicates the level of importance that it has attached to the development of certain capabilities for each process. Operations strategy is about developing the capabilities the firm's processes need to achieve customer satisfaction, whether the customer is internal or external.

COST

low-cost operations Delivering a service or producing a product at the lowest possible cost to the satisfaction of the process's external or internal customers.

Lowering prices can increase demand for services or products, but it also reduces profit margins if the service or product cannot be produced at lower cost. **Low-cost operations** is delivering a service or producing a product at the lowest possible cost to the satisfaction of the process's external or internal customers. To reduce costs, processes must be designed and operated to make them very efficient, often addressing workforce, methods, scrap or rework, overhead, and other factors to lower the cost per unit of the service or product (see Chapter 4, "Process Analysis"). Often, lowering costs requires a completely new process, which may require investment in new automated facilities or technology (see Chapter 6, "Process Capacity" and Chapter 12, "Information Technology and Value Chains"). Managerial Practice 2.1 shows how Costco uses the low-cost operations priority (along with other competitive priorities) to strategic advantage.

MANAGERIAL PRACTICE 2.1

USING OPERATIONS FOR PROFIT AT COSTCO

Looking for bargains on items ranging from watermelons to symphonic baby grand pianos? One company addressing those needs is Costco (www.costco.com), a wholesale club with 347 stores that generate $31 billion in annual revenue and $542 million in annual profits. Its closest competitor is Wal-Mart's Sam's Club, whose 200 more stores generate $1 billion less in annual revenue. Individual and business customers pay Costco from $45 to $100 a year for a membership and the privilege of buying staple items in bulk quantities and other select items at big discounts.

What makes Costco so successful? It has linked the needs of its customers to its operations by developing a customer-driven operations strategy that supports its retailing concept. Costco's competitive priorities are low-cost operations, quality, and flexibility. A visit to one of Costco's stores will show how these competitive priorities manifest themselves.

Low-Cost Operations

Customers come to Costco because of low prices, which are possible because processes are designed for efficiency. The store is actually a warehouse where products are stacked on pallets with little signage. New products can replace old products efficiently. In addition, Costco managers are tough price negotiators with suppliers because they buy in high volumes. Suppliers are expected to change factory runs to produce specially built packages that are bigger but cheaper per unit. Costco's profit margins are low, but annual profits are high because of the volume.

Quality

Customers are not looking for high levels of customer service, but they are looking for high value. In addition to low prices, Costco backs everything it sells with a return-anything-at-any-time guarantee. Customers trust Costco, which has generated an 86 percent membership renewal rate—the highest in the industry. To support the need for high value, operations must ensure that products are of high quality and undamaged when placed in the store.

Flexibility

One of the key aspects of Costco's operations is the fact that it carries only 4,000 carefully selected items in a typical store, while a Wal-Mart Superstore carries 125,000 items. However, items change frequently to provide return customers with a "surprise" aspect to the shopping experience. Processes must be flexible to accommodate a dynamic store layout. In addition, the supply chain must be carefully managed because the products are constantly changing.

Japanese shoppers push carts full of their purchases at Costco's outlet in Makuhari, east of Tokyo. By expanding operations in Japan, Costco is eager to attract shoppers to the American style of buying in bulk.

Source: "Inside the Cult of Costco." *Fortune* (September 6, 1999), pp. 184–190.

QUALITY

Quality is a dimension of a service or product that is defined by the external and internal customers. Today, more than ever, quality has important market implications. Two important competitive priorities deal with quality: top quality and consistent quality.

TOP QUALITY.   The first, **top quality**, is delivering an outstanding service or product. This priority may require a high level of customer contact, and high levels of helpfulness, courteousness, and availability of servers from a service process. Alternatively,

top quality   Delivering an outstanding service or product.

it may require superior product features, close tolerances, and greater durability from a manufacturing process. Processes delivering top quality need to be designed to more demanding requirements than other processes. For example, Club Med and a no-frills motel both provide a room, bed, and bath for their guests. However, the processes at Club Med (the all-inclusive resorts with entertaining, dining, recreation, and hotel processes) have much more demanding requirements for customer service than does the no-frills motel. Likewise, Ferrari and Isuzu both provide vehicles that will get you from one location to another; however, the difference in the ride is eye-popping. Will anyone debate the claim that Ferrari's processes have to deal with superior product features and more demanding requirements?

consistent quality   Producing services or products that meet design specifications on a consistent basis.

CONSISTENT QUALITY.   The second quality priority, **consistent quality**, is producing services or products that meet design specifications on a consistent basis. External customers want services or products that consistently meet the specifications they contracted for, have come to expect, or saw advertised. For example, bank customers expect that the bank's accounting process will not make errors when recording transactions. Similarly, customers of a foundry expect castings to meet tolerances for length, diameter, and surface finish. Internal customers also want consistency in the outputs of their internal or external suppliers. The payroll department needs the correct hours each employee worked from each of the other departments, and the purchasing department needs consistent quality materials from suppliers. To compete on the basis of consistent quality, managers need to design and monitor processes to reduce errors. Although consistent quality is as important now as it has ever been, it is increasingly expected by customers, both internal and external.

TIME

As the saying goes, "time is money." Some companies do business at "Internet speed," while others thrive on consistently meeting delivery promises. Three competitive priorities deal with time: delivery speed, on-time delivery, and development speed.

delivery speed   Quickly filling a customer's order.

lead time   A measure often used for delivery speed.

DELIVERY SPEED.   The first, **delivery speed**, is quickly filling a customer's order. Delivery speed is often measured by the elapsed time between the receipt of a customer order and filling it, often referred to as **lead time**. You increase delivery speed by reducing lead times. An acceptable lead time can be minutes for an ambulance, hours for a report from the legal department, several weeks for scheduling elective surgery, and a year for a complex, customized machine. A cushion of backup capacity is one way to reduce lead times (see Chapter 6, "Process Capacity"). Manufacturing processes sometimes have another way: storing inventory (see Chapter 15, "Inventory Management" and Chapter 16, "Resource Planning").

on-time delivery   Meeting delivery-time promises.

ON-TIME DELIVERY.   The second time priority, **on-time delivery**, is meeting delivery-time promises. An airline, for example, might measure on-time delivery as the percent of flights that arrive at the gate within 15 minutes of the scheduled arrival. Manufacturers may measure on-time delivery as the percent of customer orders shipped when promised, with 95 percent often considered as the goal. On-time delivery is important for many processes, especially just-in-time processes where inputs are required at very specific times (see Chapter 11, "Lean Systems").

development speed   Quickly introducing a new service or product.

DEVELOPMENT SPEED.   The third time priority, **development speed**, is quickly introducing a new service or product. Development speed is measured by the elapsed time from idea generation through the final design and introduction of the service or product. Achieving a high level of development speed requires a high level of cross-functional coordination because marketing, sales, service or product designers, and operations typically are involved. Sometimes critical external suppliers are asked to participate in the process. Getting the new service or product to market first gives the firm an edge on the competition that is difficult to overcome in a rapidly changing business environment, and it may involve international connections. For example, The

Limited can get a new product idea for a sweater, design the sweater, transmit the design to Hong Kong where it is produced, ship the sweater back to the United States, and put the sweater on the store shelves in less than 25 weeks.

TIME-BASED COMPETITION. Many companies focus on the competitive priorities of delivery speed and development speed for their processes, which is a strategy called **time-based competition.** To implement the strategy, managers carefully define the steps and time needed to deliver a service or produce a product and then critically analyze each step to determine whether they can save time without hurting quality. In Part 2, "Designing and Improving Processes," we provide the framework and tools to analyze processes to improve performance regarding any of the competitive priorities, including those relating to time.

time-based competition A strategy that focuses on the competitive priorities of delivery speed and development speed.

FLEXIBILITY

Flexibility is a characteristic of a firm's processes that enables them to react to their customers' needs quickly and efficiently. Some processes require one or more of the following types of flexibility: customization, variety, and volume flexibility.

CUSTOMIZATION. **Customization** is satisfying the unique needs of each customer by changing service or product designs. For example, the advertisement design and planning process in an ad agency (see Chapter 1, "Operations As a Competitive Weapon") must be able to satisfy customers needing ads, where requests can range from selling cat litter using a herd of live cats to informing the public of the dangers of secondhand smoke. Customization typically implies that the service or product has low volume. There are some exceptions to that generalization. For example, a customized plastic bottle design for a shampoo manufacturer may be produced in large volumes until the design of the bottle is changed. Nonetheless, processes with a customization priority must be able to work closely with their customers (external or internal) and then devote their resources to their unique needs. Managerial Practice 2.2 shows how one company's need for high degrees of customization in its processes involves process modifications caused by product design changes and very long lead times.

customization Satisfying the unique needs of each customer by changing service or product designs.

VARIETY. The second flexibility priority is **variety,** which is handling a wide assortment of services or products efficiently. Variety differs from customization in that the services or products are not necessarily unique to specific customers and may have repetitive demands. For example, Amazon.com has a customer relationship process (see Chapter 1, "Operations As a Competitive Weapon") that has the ability to allow customers access to thousands of services and products through the Internet. Likewise, a manufacturing process that produces an assortment of parts for tables, chairs, and cabinets has a variety priority. Processes with a variety priority must have the capability to focus on the needs of their internal or external customers and to efficiently shift their focus across a variety of predefined services or products.

variety Handling a wide assortment of services or products efficiently.

VOLUME FLEXIBILITY. The third flexibility priority is **volume flexibility** which is accelerating or decelerating the rate of production of services or products quickly to handle large fluctuations in demand. Volume flexibility is an important priority that often supports other competitive priorities, such as delivery speed or development speed. The need for this priority is driven by the severity and frequency of demand fluctuations. For example, the time between demand peaks might be hours, as with the swings in demand at a large postal facility where processes are required for receiving, sorting, and dispatching mail to a multitude of branch locations. It may be months, as with the processes at ski resorts or the processes that manufacture lawn fertilizers. It may even be years, as with political campaigns or with home construction as the home-building industry goes through its cycles.

volume flexibility Accelerating or decelerating the rate of production of services or products quickly to handle large fluctuations in demand.

Understanding how competitive priorities and competitive capabilities can be used to improve competitiveness is an important message of this text. We will use the concept of competitive priorities and capabilities throughout the discussion of the topics to

MANAGERIAL PRACTICE 2.2

BUILDING AIRCRAFT CARRIERS TO CUSTOMER ORDER

Arguably the most technically challenging and toughest to manufacture product is a nuclear-powered aircraft carrier. Consider the newest addition to the U.S. Navy's Nimitz-class carriers, the USS *Ronald Reagan*, which measures a fifth of a mile from bow to stern, has 4½ acres of flight deck, can plow through the ocean at more than 35 mph, and can carry 50 fighter planes and 20 support aircraft. Each ship in the Nimitz class (there are nine at present) costs more than $4 billion, and involves 47,000 tons of precision-welded steel up to 4 inches thick, more than a million different parts, 900 miles of wire and cable, about 40 million skilled-worker hours, thousands of engineers, and more than seven years to build. Such a product requires an enormous amount of technological skill and coordination and processes that can be efficient with low volumes.

The world's only producer of full-sized aircraft carriers, nuclear or otherwise, is Northrup Grumman Newport News, situated along the James River in Virginia. The shipyard has 550 acres of sheds, cranes, dry docks, and piers and employs 17,800 employees, many of whom are from families that have worked in the yard for generations. Over the years, Newport News had to design their processes with high degrees of flexibility so as to handle the changes in aircraft carrier designs. Building aircraft carriers is not the same as building fleets of standard supertankers or cargo ships because each aircraft carrier differs significantly in design from its predecessors, has tons of specialized equipment, houses munitions lockers and nuclear reactors, must provide quarters for 6,000 people, and provide more than 18,000 meals a day. The design changes can be dramatic. For example, two years of planning before construction began on the *Reagan* resulted in 1,362 major changes from its predecessor, including a new bow and an expanded flight control tower, which weighs 717 tons. The need to have flexibility required Newport News to redesign their processes. The first carriers in the Nimitz class were largely hand-built by skilled craftsmen, piece by piece in dry dock. Pipes, ducts, and cables were run only after large sections of the superstructure were constructed. However, major sections of the *Reagan* were designed using 3-D computer drafting software, constructed from huge prebuilt modules built indoors, and then taken to the building site and hoisted in place. The software avoided the need for mock-ups because the designer could actually dynamically simulate the use of various compartments or the operation of equipment with computer-generated manikins. Modular construction with 3-D computer design capability is very efficient and allows for design changes to be more easily incorporated.

The long lead time associated with the construction of an aircraft carrier also poses process considerations for Newport News. For example, one of the first jobs in the construction schedule is to order the long lead time equipment, such as major nuclear reactor components. However, after seven years have passed, the equipment could be outdated and modifications must be made to the superstructure of the aircraft carrier to accommodate the new specifications. Processes must be capable of handling changes such as this. Also, a key resource for a manufacturing operation focusing on customization is the workforce, which must be highly skilled. While at any one time 2,700 employees may have been working on the *Reagan*, the individuals and the jobs changed over time. There was lots of work for welders early on, but toward the end it was the painters who were in demand. Welders can wield a paintbrush, but painters typically cannot operate a blowtorch. Newport News has managed to get a flexible United Steelworkers labor contract and it is the sole contractor for the refurbishing of the entire nuclear aircraft carrier fleet, both of which help to mitigate the problem.

The aircraft carrier USS *Ronald Reagan* under construction beneath the large crane in the north yard of Northrup Grumman Newport News Shipbuilding Company in Newport News, Virginia. The manufacturing processes must be flexible to incorporate technological advances and design changes over the long construction lead time.

Source: Siekman, Philip. "Build to Order: One Aircraft Carrier." *Fortune* (July 22, 2002), pp. 180(B)–180(J).

follow so that you will see how strategy, designing of processes and value chains, and operating value chains all fit together. However, there are two things to keep in mind. First, our nine competitive dimensions are aggregate terms that may represent a multitude of required detailed, process-specific capabilities in any given situation. For example, low-cost operations may be broken down to requirements for high worker productivity, low overhead cost, and adherence to budgets for a service process. For a manufacturing process, that same competitive priority may be broken down to requirements for high equipment utilization, worker productivity, low inventory levels, and high levels of defect-free output. Whatever the competitive priority or competitive capability might be for a particular process, it can be categorized under one of our nine aggregate competitive priorities. Second, there is some overlap between our groups of competitive dimensions. *Quality* and *time* are good examples. Many managers will consider "quality" to include our "top quality" and "consistent quality" dimensions plus other operating capabilities the external customer considers important, such as delivery speed and on-time delivery. Indeed, many of the competitive priorities are correlated. For example, low-cost operations and consistent quality (less rework or scrap) are often interrelated. While grouping competitive dimensions together might be convenient for general conversation, from a managerial perspective it is necessary to be specific regarding the abilities the processes require because it allows us to focus the analysis of performance problems where it is needed. Consequently, as you read the text, you will sometimes see references to competitive priorities or competitive capabilities at a more detailed level than the nine competitive dimensions we have just discussed.

USING COMPETITIVE PRIORITIES: AN AIRLINE EXAMPLE

Competitive priorities are a useful tool for translating the goals of corporate strategy to the level of the processes that actually do the work. Competitive priorities are attached to the firm's services or products to reflect what the external customer considers important in the business transaction. The key word here is *priorities* because these are target capabilities the firm must demonstrate to the external customer to not only win the current business but also future business. Appropriate competitive priorities must also be assigned to the firm's core and supporting processes that not only reflect the needs of the external customers but also the needs of internal customers.

To get a better understanding of how competitive priorities are used, let us look at a major airline as an example. We will consider two market segments: first-class passengers and coach passengers. Core services for both market segments are ticketing and seat selection, baggage handling, and transportation to the customer's destination. However, the peripheral services are quite different. A needs assessment of both market segments would reveal that, relative to coach passengers, first-class passengers require separate airport lounges; preferred treatment during check-in, boarding, and deplaning; more comfortable seats; better meals and beverages; more personal attention (cabin attendants who refer to customers by name); more frequent service from attendants; high levels of courtesy; and low volumes (adding to the feeling of being special). Coach passengers, however, are satisfied with standardized services (no surprises), courteous flight attendants, and low prices. Both market segments expect the airline to hold to its schedule. Consequently, we can say that the competitive priorities for the first-class segment are *top quality* and *on-time delivery*, whereas the competitive priorities for the coach market segment are *low-cost operations*, *consistent quality*, and *on-time delivery*.

The airline knows what its collective capabilities must be as a firm, but how does that get communicated to each of its core processes? Let us focus on four core processes: customer relationship, new service/product development, order fulfillment, and supplier relationship (see Chapter 1, "Operations As a Competitive Weapon"). Recognizing that each core process could have many nested processes within, competitive priorities are assigned to each core process to achieve the service required to provide complete customer satisfaction. Here are some possible assignments, just to give you an idea of how this works.

A Continental Airlines flight attendant hands out meals to coach passengers on a flight from New York to Atlanta. Coach cabin customers look for standardized services, courteous flight attendants, and low prices.

CUSTOMER RELATIONSHIP.   This process is involved in high levels of customer contact through ticketing (both electronic and telephone), elite lounge service, and boarding. It also has marketing and sales functions. Possible competitive priorities would include

- *Top Quality*. High levels of customer contact and lounge service for the first-class passengers.
- *Consistent Quality*. The information and service must be error free.
- *Delivery Speed*. Customers want immediate information regarding flight schedules and other ticketing information.
- *Variety*. The process must be capable of handling the service needs of all market segments and promotional programs, such as frequent-flier services.

NEW SERVICE DEVELOPMENT.   New service packages must continually be developed to remain ahead of the competition. Such packages would include tours to the world's vacation paradises, new routes, or new dinner service. Competitive priorities might include

- *Development Speed*. It is important to get to market fast to preempt the competition.
- *Customization*. The process must be able to create unique services.
- *Top Quality*. New services must be carefully designed because the future of the airline depends on them. This requires a lot of energy and ingenuity.

ORDER FULFILLMENT.   This process is responsible for delivering the service to the customer's satisfaction. It is a huge process in an airline, involving scheduling, gate operations, maintenance, cabin service, pilot operations, and baggage handling. It has many nested processes, and many competitive priorities, which might include

- *Low-Cost Operations*. Airlines compete on price and must keep costs in check.
- *Top Quality*. The service provided to first-class passengers must be top notch. To a large extent, this involves well-trained and experienced cabin attendants and high-quality meal and beverage service.
- *Consistent Quality*. Once the quality level is set, it is important to achieve it every time.
- *On-Time Delivery*. The airline strives to arrive at its destination on schedule, otherwise the passenger's connections to other flights might not be possible.
- *Variety*. Maintenance operations are required for a variety of aircraft models.

SUPPLIER RELATIONSHIP.   This process is responsible for acquiring all of the inputs the airline requires to do business, which range from human resources to capital goods. Competitive priorities might include

- *Low-Cost Operations.* The cost of acquiring inputs must be kept to a minimum to allow for the competitive pricing in the airline industry.
- *Consistent Quality.* The quality of the inputs must adhere to the required specifications. In addition, the information provided to the suppliers must be accurate.
- *On-Time Delivery.* Inputs must be delivered to tight schedules, particularly meal services.
- *Variety.* Many different inputs must be acquired, including maintenance items, meals and beverages, and even aircraft.
- *Volume Flexibility.* The process must be able to handle variations in supply quantities efficiently.

As you can see, competitive priorities can be used at the process level to provide the managers of those processes a clear picture of what capabilities their processes require so that the firm can be competitive.

NEW SERVICE OR PRODUCT DEVELOPMENT

New services or products are essential to the long-term survival of firms. Times change, people change, technologies change, and services or products must change. In this regard, *new* refers to both brand new services or products or major changes to existing services or products. The new service/product development process is often a core process in a firm, which must serve internal as well as external customers (see Chapter 1, "Operations As a Competitive Weapon"). In this section, we will discuss the nature and importance of the new service/product development process. For this discussion, we will occasionally refer to a firm's services or products as its "offerings." We begin our discussion with the various strategies firms use to compete with new offerings.

How do firms use new services and products to compete?

DEVELOPMENT STRATEGIES

There are a number of ways firms can bring value to customers beyond low prices and good quality for a given service or product. Here are several development strategies that have proven successful:

- *Product Variety.* Amazon.com and Wal-Mart in retail, Dell in computers, Honda in motorcycles, and Campbell in soups are just a few companies that have established their niches in part through product variety. This strategy requires processes that have the flexibility to offer a wide band of offerings without compromising cost, quality, or speed.
- *Design.* eBay in Web auctions, Saks Fifth Avenue in retailing, Ralph Lauren in clothes, Stickley in furniture, and Kenwood in stereo equipment are examples of companies that have used design as a competitive edge. Aesthetic appeal, safety, ease of use, ease of maintenance, and service or product features are characteristics that distinguish a firm's services or products from their competitors. Competing on the basis of design often requires an emphasis on top quality and development speed to ensure that the firm stays ahead of the competition.
- *Innovation.* Firms that compete with innovative offerings must have the capability to develop new technologies and then to translate them into new products. LASIK surgery, virtual CAT scans, handheld computers, cell phones, global positioning systems, and digital cameras are examples of innovative offerings that have opened new markets. Innovation requires significant research and development activities by technology engineers and the ability to get the new offerings to market fast. With innovative services or products, the firm that is a "first mover" often obtains a strong competitive advantage for a long time to come.
- *Service.* Manufacturers can win customer orders by providing value-added services to complement their products, such as financial services, repair contracts, consulting, and delivery services. Dell, for example, helps customers design their information infrastructure. Automobile manufacturers consider car dealerships as

part of the total process that begins with the construction of an automobile and ends by delivering it to the ultimate consumer. Through the dealership, the manufacturers offer assistance in product selection and delivery, financing, warranty repairs, and maintenance services. The customer's total experience includes the comfort feeling that lingers after the transaction is completed, which is affected by the helpfulness and courteousness of the salesperson, the design of the showroom, and the personal attention received before, during, and after the purchase.

Development strategies go beyond specifying the variety, design, innovation, or service thrust. Firms must also define the market position of the firm relative to its competitors and the type of relationship the firm wishes to pursue with its customers. Market positioning decisions entail choosing to be a *leader* (be the first to introduce a service or product, consistent with an innovation thrust); *middle-of-the-road* (wait until the leaders have introduced a service or product); or *laggard* (wait and see if the service or product idea catches on in the market). The market position decision determines when the firm will initiate the new service/product development process relative to competitors in the market. Customer relationship decisions, at the extremes, entail choosing to build long-term partnerships with customers or to have an encounter-by-encounter transactional basis. Long-term relationships involve services or products specific to a particular customer while an encounter-by-encounter basis involves services or products with appeal to a broader range of customers. The customer relationship decision determines the nature of the firm's offerings to its customers. We now turn to a discussion of how firms define their service or product offerings.

SERVICE AND PRODUCT DEFINITION

New services and products are important to any developed economy. This is especially true for services, given that more than half of the gross domestic product of developed economies is in the service sector. Globalization, technological advancement, and changing customer requirements increase the need for firms to compete on a widening array of new service and product offerings. The benefits from providing new services and products include

- enhancing the profitability of existing offerings,
- attracting new customers to the firm,
- improving the loyalty of existing customers, and
- opening markets of opportunity.

New services and products provide the foundation for future growth in the dynamic business environment that firms face today.

SERVICE PACKAGE.   One of the more difficult aspects of managing a service process is defining what it is the process provides to its internal or external customers. Recall the last time you had a pleasurable experience at a hotel. What did the hotel building, lobby area, and your room look like? Was the meal you ordered from room service tasty and in ample proportions? Did the hotel have a swimming pool, restaurant, and concierge? Was it easy to park at the hotel and was the bellhop friendly and informative? Your experience at the hotel was a collection of goods and services delivered by the hotel's many processes. We call this collection a **service package**, which consists of the following four features.

1. *Supporting Facility.* The physical resources that must be in place before a service can be offered are known as the supporting facility. For example, the hotel building, the lobby, and your room would be considered supporting facilities. Other examples include a bus, a golf course, and a movie theater. Supporting facilities would include bricks and mortar (e.g., buildings and rooms), machines and equipment, and human resources.

2. *Facilitating Goods.* The material purchased or consumed by the customer or the items provided by the customer to receive a service are known as facilitating goods. The food you ordered from room service is a facilitating good. Other examples include

What goes into making a pleasurable service experience?

service package A collection of goods and services provided by a service process to its external or internal customers.

your own golf clubs for a round of golf, popcorn and condiments at the movie theater, and your tax records for a tax accountant. These items are not the service; however, they are needed to provide the service.

3. *Explicit Services.* The benefits that are readily observable by the senses and consist of essential features of the service are known as explicit services. The explicit services you received from room service included the preparation of the food by the chef and the delivery of the meal to your room by the bellhop. Taking a swim in the swimming pool, experiencing a prepared meal and the table service at the restaurant, and getting advice on tours from the concierge are additional examples of explicit services at the hotel. Other examples of explicit services include the delivery of a package to your home, a washed car, and the preparation of a tax-deferred annuity portfolio.

4. *Implicit Services.* Psychological benefits that the customer may sense only vaguely or nonessential features of the service are known as implicit services. A jovial bellhop may provide a sense of friendliness and comfort, and just sitting in the hotel lobby absorbing the glamour of the lavish surroundings may provide a vague sense of awe and well-being. Other examples include the use of an appointment system in a doctor's office (fairness and control); a well-lighted parking area (safety); and entertainment while waiting in a line, as at Disney World (make the time delays seem shorter).

Designing the service package requires a careful analysis of customer requirements and a good understanding of the competitive priorities for success. Compare the service package of the hotel you visited to that of a bargain motel, which has a stucco facade and a small lobby, no room service, no swimming pool, and no bellhop. The motel is attractive to guests who want consistent quality and low prices, while the upscale hotel is attractive to guests who want top quality and a variety of services. The motel's service package is much less complex than the upscale hotel's service package; the processes in each case must be designed with the service package and competitive priorities in mind (see Chapter 3, "Process Design Strategy").

QUALITY FUNCTION DEPLOYMENT.   A key input into the definition of services and products is that of the customer's needs and wants. This input can be used to define new services and products or refine existing ones. A technique used by manufacturing companies and by some service companies to refine existing offerings is **quality function deployment (QFD)**, which is a means of translating customer requirements into the appropriate technical requirements for each stage of service or product development and production. Bridgestone Tire and Mitsubishi Heavy Industries originated QFD in the late 1960s and early 1970s when they used charts that took customer requirements into account in the product design process. In 1978, Yoji Akao and Shigeru Mizuno published the first work on this subject, showing how design considerations could be "deployed" to every element of competition. Since then, more than 200 U.S. companies have used the approach, including Digital Equipment, Texas Instruments, Hewlett-Packard, AT&T, ITT, Ford, Chrysler, General Motors, Procter & Gamble, Polaroid, and Deere & Company.

This approach seeks answers to the following six questions.

1. *Voice of the Customer.* What do our customers need and want?
2. *Competitive Analysis.* In terms of our customers, how well are we doing relative to our competitors?
3. *Voice of the Engineer.* What technical measures relate to our customers' needs?
4. *Correlations.* What are the relationships between the voice of the customer and the voice of the engineer?
5. *Technical Comparison.* How does our service or product performance compare to that of our competition?
6. *Trade-Offs.* What are the potential technical trade-offs?

How can the voice of the customer be brought into the service/product development process?

quality function deployment (QFD)   A means of translating customer requirements into the appropriate technical requirements for each stage of service or product development and production.

The competitive analysis provides a place to start looking for ways to gain a competitive advantage. Then the relationships between customer needs and engineering attributes need to be specified. Finally, the fact that improving one performance measure may detract from another must be recognized.

The QFD approach provides a way to set targets and debate their effects on quality. Engineering uses the data to focus on significant service or product design features. Marketing uses this input to determine marketing strategies. Operations uses the information to identify the processes that are crucial to improving quality as perceived by the customer. As a result, QFD encourages interfunctional communication for the purpose of improving the quality of services and products.

DEVELOPMENT PROCESS

How do firms develop new services or products?

The new service/product development process begins with consideration of the development strategy and ends with the launch of the new offering. Figure 2.2 shows the four stages of the new service/product development process.

DESIGN. The first stage, *design*, is critical because it links the creation of new services or products to the corporate strategy of the firm. As we have already discussed, the corporate strategy specifies the long-term objectives and the markets the firm wishes to compete in. Within that framework, the development strategy specifies the thrust the firm wants to take with its offerings. Given the development strategy, ideas for new offerings are generated and screened for feasibility and market worthiness. For services, these ideas specify how the customer interfaces with the service provider, the service benefits and outcomes for the customer, the value of the service, and how the service will be delivered. The specific service package is then formulated for the best idea, the competitive priorities are assigned to the processes, and the manner in which the service package will be delivered is proposed and checked for feasibility. We will have more to say about how the service is delivered when we address the topic of service process design (see Chapter 3, "Process Design Strategy").

For manufactured products, the new ideas include a specification of the product's architecture. There are two basic types: modular and integrated. Using a modular architecture, the product is an assembly of components; several varieties of products can be made quickly using the same standardized components. This approach supports competitive priorities of product variety and delivery speed; however, such architecture may cause lower product performance because of the pressure to use existing components in new products. In addition, such designs may be easier for competitors to copy. Alternatively, with the integrated product architecture, the product's functions are performed by only a few components that are specifically designed for it. Integrated product structures often lead to higher product performance and are not easily imitated; however, the design lead time is high and the ability to produce a variety of products is limited. The most promising new product idea is selected for more detailed attention, which includes diagramming the product's assembly, providing specifications for the product's performance dimensions, and investigating the manufacturability and the cost of the new product. It is in this stage that firms engage the inputs of their manufacturing engineers in an activity referred to as *design for manufacturing*. Even though the detailed specifics of the product and process have not yet been developed, this interaction of designers and manufacturing engineers can avoid design mistakes that would be costly if not discovered until production begins.

ANALYSIS. The second stage, *analysis*, involves a critical review of the new offering and how it will be produced to make sure that it fits the corporate strategy, is compatible with regulatory standards, presents an acceptable market risk, and satisfies the needs of the intended customers. The resource requirements for the new offering must be examined from the perspective of the core capabilities of the firm and the need to acquire additional resources or secure strategic partnerships with other firms. If the analysis reveals that the new offering has good market potential and that the firm has

FIGURE 2.2 New Service or Product Development Process

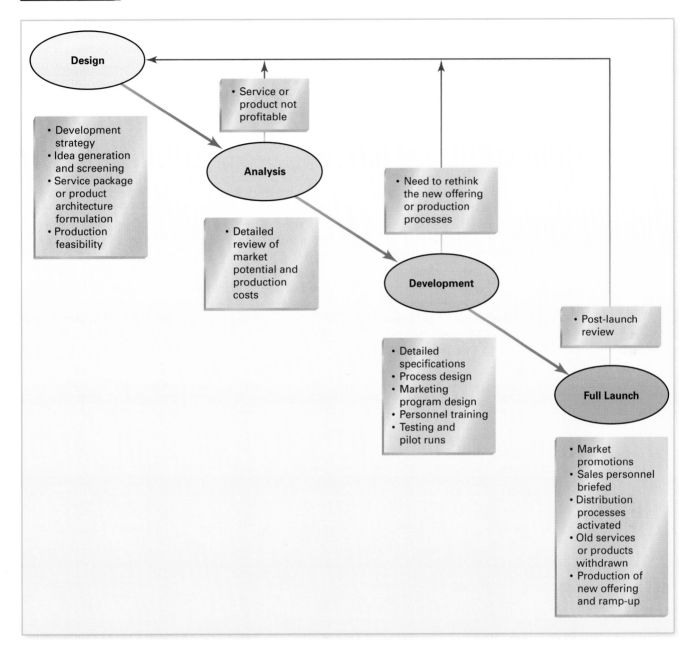

the capability (or can acquire it), the authorization is given to proceed to the next stage in the new service/product development process.

DEVELOPMENT. The third stage, *development*, brings more specificity to the new offering. Here the new offering and the required competitive priorities are used as inputs to the design (or redesign) of the processes that will be involved in delivering the new offering. The processes are diagrammed; each activity is designed to meet its required competitive priorities and to add value to the service or product (see Chapter 4, "Process Analysis"). Once the new offering is specified and the processes have been designed, the market program can be designed. Finally, personnel are trained and some pilot runs can be conducted to iron out the kinks in the production of the new offering. As this stage in the development process is executed, it is possible that some unforeseen problems may arise, thereby forcing a reconsideration of the service or product or the processes required to produce it. For example, a new service package for an airline may include adding a new route from South Bend, Indiana to Columbus, Ohio at 5 P.M. on weekdays. It would be delivered with a Boeing 737 airplane because of the space and comfort such a plane offers relative to smaller commuter aircraft. Suppose, during development, it was discovered that the airline's fleet of 737s was already being used to capacity and shifting the schedules of any of them would result in scheduling conflicts with the flight attendants and pilots. An entire network of flights and schedules would be affected. Nonetheless, the new flight could be offered if the airline contracted with a regional provider that uses smaller commuter aircraft. Passenger comfort and service delivery costs would be affected. Such a change to the service package and the processes required to deliver it would require further thought and analysis.

concurrent engineering
A concept that brings product engineers, process engineers, marketers, buyers, information specialists, quality specialists, and suppliers together to work jointly to design a service or product and the required processes that will meet customer expectations.

To avoid costly mismatches between the design of a new offering and the capability of the processes required to produce it, many firms engage in a concept called **concurrent engineering**, which brings product engineers, process engineers, marketers, buyers, information specialists, quality specialists, and suppliers together to work jointly to design a product and the required processes that will meet customer expectations. For example, Ford Motor Company gives full responsibility for each new product to a program manager who forms a product team representing every relevant part of the organization. Each department can raise concerns or anticipate problems while there is still time to alter the product or the manufacturing processes. Changes are much simpler and less costly at this stage than after the product is introduced to the external customers. However, it may be discovered during this stage that problems exist with the product design or the process capability to deliver the product as desired. The new product proposal may have to be scrapped or completely rethought.

FULL LAUNCH.   The final stage, *full launch*, involves the coordination of many of the firm's processes. Promotions for the new offering must be initiated, sales personnel briefed, distribution processes activated, and old services or products that the new offering is to replace must be withdrawn. A particular strain is placed on the processes needed to produce the offering during a period referred to as *ramp-up*, when the production processes must increase volume to meet demands while coping with quality problems and last-minute design changes. Competitive priorities may change over time for the production processes. For example, consider a high-volume standardized product, such as color ink-jet desktop printers. In the early stages of the ramp-up period, when the printers just entered the mass market, the manufacturing processes required consistent quality, delivery speed, and volume flexibility. In the later stages of the ramp-up period, when demands were high, the competitive priorities became low-cost operations, consistent quality, and on-time delivery. A postlaunch review will compare the competitive priorities of the processes with their competitive capabilities and may signal a need to rethink the original product idea. The review also gets inputs from customers, who will divulge their experiences and may share ideas for new offerings.

The new service/product development process is an ongoing activity for many firms. Anytime a change is suggested to the firm's offerings or the processes for producing them, the development process is initiated.

MASS CUSTOMIZATION

What are the operations implications of being a mass customizer?

A firm's service or product strategy addresses certain competitive priorities that will win orders from customers. One such competitive priority is *variety*. We all want a wide variety of options when choosing a particular service or product. For example, suppose you want to paint your living room a new color. You need to complement all of the existing furnishings, wall decorations, and carpet. You go to your local paint retail store and select a color from a book of hundreds of options that span every color of the rainbow. The store can give you all the paint you need in your selected color while you wait. How can the store provide that service economically? Certainly the store cannot stock all of the hundreds of colors in sufficient quantities for any job. The store stocks the base colors and pigments separately and mixes them as needed, thereby supplying an unlimited variety of colors without maintaining the inventory required to match each customer's particular color needs. The paint retailer is practicing a strategy known as **mass customization**, whereby a firm's flexible processes generate a wide variety of services or products at reasonably low costs. Essentially, the firm allows customers to select from a variety of standard options to create the service or product of their choice. A key for the paint retailer is the separation of the paint mixing process from the paint production process. See Chapter 3, "Process Design Strategy," for the implications of the mass-customization strategy on a firm's processes.

mass customization A strategy whereby a firm's flexible processes generate a wide variety of services or products at reasonably low costs.

POSTPONEMENT

A key to being a successful mass customizer is postponing the task of differentiating a service or product for a specific customer until the last possible moment. **Postponement** is an organizational concept whereby some of the final activities in the provision of a service or product are delayed until the orders are received. Doing so allows the greatest application of standard modules of the service package or product before specific customization. Mass customization with postponement is applied to services, as well as to manufactured products.

postponement An organizational concept whereby some of the final activities in the provision of a service or product are delayed until the orders are received.

SERVICES. With mass customization, a service package should be designed so that it consists of independent modules that can be assembled into different forms easily and inexpensively. For example, the Ritz-Carlton, an upscale chain of hotels, records the preferences expressed by customers during their stay and uses them to tailor the services the customers receive on their next visit. Requests for items such as hypoallergenic pillows, additional towels, or even chocolate chip cookies are recorded for future use. When the customer checks in, special services and facilitating goods such as these are added to the customized service package.

Online retailers also use mass customization and postponement. Travelocity, an online travel agency, was built around the Sabre travel reservation system and uses massive standardized database systems and secure channels for searching and booking travel itineraries for individual customers. Using its slick customer interface systems, Travelocity postpones the actual assembly of itineraries until the very last moment when the customer actively participates in the choice of a final package from a wide variety of standardized elements. Travelocity uses its databases proactively to e-mail travel information to customers and to maintain personal travel pages for customers.

MANUFACTURING. The costs of inventory and transportation often determine the extent that a manufacturer uses mass customization and postponement. With postponement, manufacturing processes can avoid building up inventories of finished goods in anticipation of future orders because they will wait for a specific customer order, and they can deliver the product directly to the customer rather than first shipping to a warehouse and then to the customer. The Hewlett-Packard Company provides a good example of mass customization. Hewlett-Packard postpones assembly of its printers with the country-specific power supply and packaging of the appropriate manuals until the last step in the process, which is performed by the distributor in the region where the printer is being delivered.

Being a successful mass customizer such as Hewlett-Packard may require the redesign of products or processes. Benneton, a major producer of sweaters, realized that a process redesign would save millions of dollars in inventory write-offs because they stocked sweaters in colors that nobody wanted. Rather than dyeing the yarn before manufacturing the sweater, Benneton reversed the dyeing and knitting processes so that sweaters were dyed after the customer (usually large retail buyers) placed their orders or the color preferences of consumers for the upcoming season had been determined. By redesigning their processes Benneton was able to postpone the final production of the sweaters until the last moment, thereby reducing costs and becoming a mass customizer.

A couple checks in at the Ritz-Carlton where services are customized to individual preferences.

INTERNET IMPLICATIONS

The Internet has been a valuable technology for mass-customization strategies. Web pages can be designed to attract customers and allow them to configure their own services or products easily and quickly. Customers to Amazon.com fill baskets of goods from a vast array of possibilities, each one different from the next customer's. Dell sells computers through a Web page that allows consumers to configure their own computers from a large variety of options. Fleet Corporation, a large bank, offers investment services along with its banking services for its Internet customers. Ford and GM are building systems to permit customers to configure their own automobiles over the Internet. Each of these ventures provides customers an enormous amount of choice in the services or products they buy, but they also put a lot of pressure on the processes that must produce them. Flexibility and short response times are prized qualities for mass-customization processes.

OPERATIONS STRATEGY AS A PATTERN OF DECISIONS

Operations strategy translates service or product plans and competitive priorities for each market segment into decisions affecting the processes that support those market segments. Figure 2.3 shows how corporate strategy provides the umbrella for key operations management decisions. The operations manager must select a service or manufacturing strategy for each process. This strategy determines how the firm's processes are organized to handle the volume and variety of services or products for each specific market segment. This initial choice sets in motion a series of other decisions that govern the design of the processes, systems, and procedures that support the operations strategy. These decisions are not static; they must be constantly reevaluated according to the dynamics of the marketplace. We cover these decisions in detail throughout this text. Nonetheless, from a strategic perspective, operations managers are responsible for making the decisions that ensure the firm has the capability to address the competitive priorities of new and existing market segments as they evolve. Furthermore, the pattern of decisions for one organization may be different from that of another, even if they are both in the same industry, because of differences in core competencies, market segments served, and degree of Web integration. Each process must be analyzed from the perspective of the customers it serves, be they external or internal.

The operations management decisions shown in Figure 2.3 contribute to the development of the firm's capability to successfully compete in the marketplace. Once competitive priorities for a process are determined, it is necessary to assess the competitive capabilities the process actually possesses. If there is a gap between a competitive priority and the process's capability to achieve that competitive priority, the gap must be

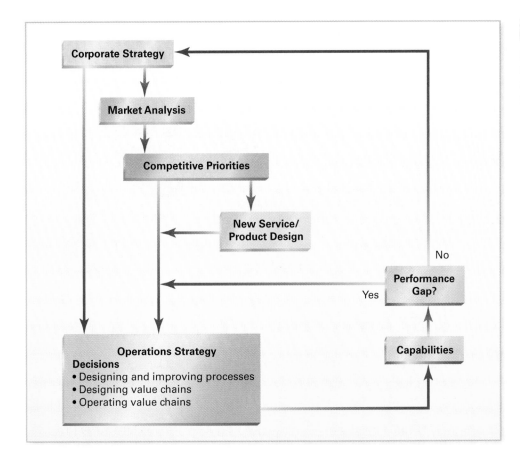

closed by an effective operations strategy. For example, suppose the management of a bank's credit card division decided to embark on a marketing campaign to significantly increase its business, while keeping costs low. A key process in this division is the billing and payments process. The competitive priorities for that process became (1) low operating expenses *(low cost operations)*, (2) a rapid increase in volume *(volume flexibility)*, (3) fast merchant statement cycle times *(delivery speed)*, and (4) error-free processing *(top quality and consistent quality)*. An assessment of the capability of the billing and payments process to meet those priorities revealed that the process was doing fine with respect to the accuracy of processing transactions and the merchant statement cycle time, which was already down to a respectable 48 hours. Nonetheless, the cost of operations was too high and the process needed to be redesigned to handle larger volumes. To close the gap between the competitive priorities and competitive capabilities, management eliminated some activities, such as the microfilming and storage of billing statements and cut back on the amount of mailing by going online for many transactions. Additional capacity was acquired to handle larger volumes of transactions, while maintaining the flexibility to adjust to seasonal variations. As this example demonstrates, developing capabilities and closing gaps is the thrust of operations strategy.

OPERATIONS STRATEGY ACROSS THE ORGANIZATION

Corporate strategy affects every functional area of a firm. It views the organization as a system of interconnected parts, or functional areas, each working in concert with the others to achieve desired goals. Operations strategy, which supports corporate strategy, also requires a close connection among the functional areas. A key area is *management information systems*, which designs the systems that provide market data and competitor information in a global environment. However, this connectivity transcends information flows and extends to full collaboration on decisions. As we have indicated, operations

Low-cost operations, volume flexibility, delivery speed, top quality, and consistent quality are key competitive priorities for a billing and payments process.

strategy specifies the overall service or manufacturing strategy and involves a pattern of decisions that affect the processes, systems, and procedures of the firm. Consequently, when *marketing* wants to add a new service or product, it should coordinate with *operations* to ensure that the firm has the ability to support the new endeavor. Adding new services or products without the ability to produce them can lead to poor performance.

Often, new investments are required to support new endeavors or to improve existing operations. An operations strategy may require investments in new equipment and other financial support for improvements, both of which must be coordinated with *finance*. In addition, finance is interested in the operations strategy because it affects the ability of the firm to generate revenues, which contribute to its financial performance.

Invariably, operations strategies involve the design of new processes or the redesign of existing ones. *Engineering* works with operations to arrive at the designs that achieve the appropriate competitive priorities. Engineering also is heavily involved in the design of new services and products and must do so in light of the ability of the firm to produce them.

CHAPTER HIGHLIGHTS

- Corporate strategy involves monitoring and adjusting to changes in the external environment and exploiting core competencies through the development of core processes. Firms taking a global view may form strategic alliances through collaborative efforts, joint ventures, or licensing of technology.

- Market analysis is key to formulating a customer-driven operations strategy. Market segmentation and needs assessment are methods of pinpointing elements of a service or product that satisfy customers.

- Customer-driven operations strategy requires translating market needs, as embodied in competitive priorities for a firm's processes, into desirable capabilities for the operations function, called competitive capabilities. There are nine priorities: low-cost operations, top quality, consistent quality, delivery speed, on-time delivery, development speed, customization, variety, and volume flexibility. Trade-offs among them are sometimes necessary. Management must decide on which dimensions the firm's processes should excel.

- With time-based competition, managers seek to save time on the various steps taken to deliver a service or product.

- A new service or product development strategy involves selecting whether the firm will compete on the basis of product variety, design, innovation, or service. It also specifies the desired market position and the nature of the relationship the firm wants to maintain with its customers.

- The new service/product development process has four stages: design, analysis, development, and full launch.

- Concurrent engineering during product planning involves operations and other functions early in the development and testing of a new product.

- Mass customization, a strategy whereby a firm's flexible processes generate a wide variety of services or products at reasonably low costs, often involves a concept called postponement. The Internet has facilitated the application of mass customization.

- Operations strategy is a pattern of decisions, starting with a choice of service or manufacturing strategy and addressing the many processes that support it so as to close any gaps between competitive priorities and competitive capabilities.

STUDENT CD-ROM AND INTERNET RESOURCES

The Student CD-ROM and the Companion Website at **www.prenhall.com/krajewski** contain many tools, activities, and resources designed for this chapter. The following items are recommended to enhance your skills and improve your understanding of the material in this chapter.

STUDENT CD-ROM RESOURCES

➤ **Power Point Slides.** View the comprehensive set of slides customized for this chapter's concepts and techniques.
➤ **Written Tours.** See how the Lower Florida Keys Health System Community Hospital offers a customized service package and why Chaparral Steel's processes are designed as they are for competitive operations.

INTERNET RESOURCES

➤ **Study-Guide Quizzes.** See the compendium of true or false, multiple choice, and essay questions that allows online tests or gives you feedback on how well you have mastered the concepts of this chapter.
➤ **In the News.** See the articles that apply to this chapter.
➤ **Internet Exercises.** Try out seven different links to explore operations strategy topics including competitive priorities, service and manufacturing strategies, top quality, product variety, and joint ventures.
➤ **Virtual Tours.** Compare the operations strategy of Baja Spas to that of Hershey Foods. Also see the "Web Links to Company Facility Tours" for additional tours of company facilities.

KEY TERMS

competitive capabilities 62
competitive priorities 62
concurrent engineering 74
consistent quality 64
core competencies 58
customization 65
delivery speed 64

development speed 64
lead time 64
low-cost operations 62
mass customization 75
on-time delivery 64
operations strategy 57
postponement 75

quality function deployment (QFD) 71
service package 70
time-based competition 65
top quality 63
variety 65
volume flexibility 65

DISCUSSION QUESTIONS

1. The onset of exponential growth in the development of information technologies has encouraged the birth of many "dot-com" companies. The Internet has enabled these companies to reach customers in very effective ways. Consider Amazon.com, whose Web site enjoys millions of "hits" each day and puts customers in touch with more than 18 million services and products. What are Amazon.com's competitive priorities and what should its operations strategy focus on?

2. A local hospital declares that it is committed to provide *care* to patients arriving at the emergency unit in less than 15 minutes and that it will never turn away patients who need to be hospitalized for further medical care. What implications does this commitment have for strategic operations management decisions (e.g., decisions relating to capacity and workforce)?

3. FedEx has built its business on quick, dependable delivery of items being shipped by air from one business to another. Its early advantages included global tracking of shipments using Web technology. The advancement of Internet technology has enabled competitors to become much more sophisticated in order tracking. In addition, the advent of dot-com business has put pressure on increased ground transportation deliveries. Explain how this change in the environment could affect FedEx's oper-

ations strategy, especially relative to UPS, which has a strong hold on the business-to-consumer ground delivery business.

4. Understanding the service package enables management to identify ways to gain competitive advantage in the marketplace. What do you consider to be the components of the service package in the provision of

    a. an automobile insurance policy.
    b. dental work to install a crown.
    c. an airline flight.

5. Suppose that you were conducting a market analysis for a new textbook about technology management. What would you need to know to identify a market segment? How would you make a needs assessment? What should be the collection of services and products?

6. Although all nine of the competitive priorities discussed in the chapter are relevant to a company's success in the marketplace, explain why a company should not necessarily try to excel in all of them. What determines the choice of the competitive priorities that a company should emphasize?

7. Choosing which processes are core to a firm's competitive position is a key strategic decision. For example, Nike, a popular sporting shoe company, focuses on the customer

relationship, new product development, and supplier relationship processes and leaves the order fulfillment process to others. Edmonds, a top-quality shoe company, considers all four processes to be core processes. What considerations would you make in determining which processes should be core to your manufacturing company?

8. A local fast-food restaurant processes several customer orders at once. Service clerks cross paths, sometimes nearly colliding, while they trace different paths to fill customer orders. If customers order a special combination of toppings on their hamburgers, they must wait quite some time while the special order is cooked. How would you modify the restaurant's operations to achieve competitive advantage? Because demand surges at lunchtime, volume flexibility is a competitive priority in the fast-food business. How would you achieve volume flexibility?

9. Kathryn Shoemaker established Grandmother's Chicken Restaurant in Middlesburg five years ago. It features a unique recipe for chicken, "just like grandmother used to make." The facility is homey, with relaxed and friendly service. Business has been good during the past two years, for both lunch and dinner. Customers normally wait about 15 minutes to be served, although complaints about service delays have increased. Shoemaker is currently considering whether to expand the current facility or open a similar restaurant in neighboring Uniontown, which has been growing rapidly.

   a. What types of strategic plans must Shoemaker make?
   b. What environmental forces could be at work in Middleburg and Uniontown that Shoemaker should consider?
   c. What are the possible distinctive competencies of Grandmother's?

10. For 20 years, Russell's Pharmacy has been located on the town square of River City, the only town for 20 miles in any direction. River City's economy is dominated by agriculture and generally rises and falls with the price of corn. But Russell's Pharmacy enjoys a steady business. Jim Russell is on a first-name basis with the entire town. He provides friendly, accurate service; listens patiently to health complaints; and knows the family health history of everyone. He keeps an inventory of the medicines required by regular customers, but sometimes has a one-day delay to fill new prescriptions. However, he cannot obtain drugs at the same low price as the large pharmacy

chains can. There's trouble right here in River City. Several buildings around the town square are now abandoned or used as storerooms for old cars. The town is showing signs of dying off right along with the family farm. Twenty miles upstream, situated on a large island in the river, is the growing town of Large Island. Russell is considering a move to the Conestoga Mall in Large Island.

   a. What types of strategic plans must Russell make?
   b. What environmental forces could be at work that Russell should consider?
   c. What are the possible core competencies of Russell's Pharmacy?

11. Wild West, Inc., is a regional telephone company that inherited nearly 100,000 employees and 50,000 retirees from AT&T. Wild West has a new mission: to diversify. It calls for a 10-year effort to enter the financial services, real estate, cable TV, home shopping, entertainment, and cellular communication services markets—and to compete with other telephone companies. Wild West plans to provide cellular and fiber-optic communication services in markets with established competitors, such as the United Kingdom, and in markets with essentially no competition, such as Russia and former Eastern Bloc countries.

   a. What types of strategic plans must Wild West make? Is the "do-nothing" option viable? If Wild West's mission appears too broad, which businesses would you trim first?
   b. What environmental forces could be at work that Wild West should consider?
   c. What are the possible core competencies of Wild West? What weaknesses should it avoid or mitigate?

12. You are in the process of choosing a bank to open a checking with interest account. Several banks in your community offer competitive checking services with the same interest payment. Identify the nature of the service package that would guide your choice.

13. You are designing a grocery delivery business. Via the Internet, your company will offer staple and frozen foods in a large metropolitan area and then deliver them within a customer-defined window of time. You plan to partner with two major food stores in the area. What should be your competitive priorities and what capabilities do you want to develop in your operations?

EXPERIENTIAL LEARNING MIN-YO GARMENT COMPANY

The Min-Yo Garment Company is a small firm in Taiwan that produces sportswear for sale in the wholesale and retail markets. Min-Yo's garments are unique because they offer fine embroidery and fabrics with a variety of striped and solid patterns. Over the 20 years of its existence, the Min-Yo Garment Company has become known as a quality producer of sports shirts with dependable deliveries. However, during that same period, the nature of the apparel industry was undergoing change. In the past, firms could be successful producing stan-

dardized shirts in high volumes with few pattern or color choices and long production lead times. Currently, with the advent of regionalized merchandising and intense competition at the retail level, buyers of the shirts are looking for shorter lead times and much more variety in patterns and colors. Consequently, many more business opportunities are available today than ever before to a respected company such as Min-Yo.

Even though the opportunity for business success seemed bright, the management meeting last week was gloomy. Mr.

Min-Yo Lee, president and owner of Min-Yo Garment, expressed concerns over the performance of the company: "We are facing strong competition for our products. Large apparel firms are driving prices down on high-volume licensed brands. Each day more firms enter the customized shirt business. Our profits are lower than expected, and delivery performance is deteriorating. We must reexamine our capabilities and decide what we can do best."

PRODUCTS

Min-Yo has divided its product line into three categories: licensed brands, subcontracted brands, and special garments.

Licensed Brands. Licensed brands are brands that are owned by one company but, through a licensing agreement, are produced by another firm that also markets the brand in a specific geographic region. The licenser may have licensees all over the world. The licensee pays the licenser a fee for the privilege of marketing the brand in its region, and the licenser agrees to provide some advertising for the product, typically through media outlets that have international exposure. A key aspect of the licensing agreement is that the licensee must agree to provide sufficient quantities of product at the retail level. Running out of stock hurts the image of the brand name.

Presently, only one licensed brand is manufactured by Min-Yo. The brand, called the Muscle Shirt, is owned by a large "virtual corporation" in Italy that has no manufacturing facilities of its own. Min-Yo has been licensed to manufacture Muscle Shirts and sell them to large retail chains in Taiwan. The retail chains require prompt shipments at the end of each week. Because of competitive pressures from other licensed brands, low prices are important. Min-Yo sells each Muscle Shirt to retail chains for $6.

The demand for Muscle Shirts averages 900 shirts per week. The following demand for Muscle Shirts has been forecasted for the next 12 weeks.

WEEK	DEMAND	WEEK	DEMAND
1*	700	7	1,100
2	800	8	1,100
3	900	9	900
4	900	10	900
5	1,000	11	800
6	1,100	12	700

*In other words, the company expects to sell 700 Muscle Shirts at the end of week 1.

Min-Yo has found that its forecasts of Muscle Shirts are accurate to within ±200 shirts per week. If demand exceeds supply in any week, the excess demand is lost. No backorders are taken, and there is no cost penalty to Min-Yo for lost sales.

Subcontracted Brands. Manufacturers in the apparel industry often face uncertain demand. To maintain level production at their plants, many manufacturers seek subcontractors to produce their brands. Min-Yo is often considered as a subcontractor because of its reputation in the industry. Although price is a consideration, the owners of subcontracted brands emphasize dependable delivery and the ability of the subcontractor to adjust order quantities on short notice.

Currently, Min-Yo manufactures only one subcontracted brand, called the Thunder Shirt because of its bright colors.

Thunder Shirts are manufactured to order for a company in Singapore. Min-Yo's price to this company is $7 per shirt. When orders are placed, usually twice a month, the customer specifies the delivery of certain quantities in each of the next two weeks. The last order the customer placed is overdue, forcing Min-Yo to pay a penalty charge. To avoid another penalty, 200 shirts must be shipped in week 1. The company is expected to specify the quantities it requires for weeks 2 and 3 at the beginning of week 1. The delivery schedule containing the orders for weeks 4 and 5 is expected to arrive at the beginning of week 3, and so on. The customer has estimated its average weekly needs for the year to be 200 shirts per week, although its estimates are frequently inaccurate.

Because of the importance of this large customer to Min-Yo and the lengthy negotiations of the sales department to get the business, management always tries to satisfy its needs. Management believes that, if Min-Yo Garment ever refuses to accept an order from this company, Min-Yo will lose its business. Under the terms of the sales contract, Min-Yo agreed to pay this customer $1 for every shirt not shipped on time for each week the shipment of the shirt is delinquent. *Delinquent shipments must be made up.*

Special Garments. Special garments are made only to customer order because of their low volume and specialized nature. Customers come to Min-Yo Garment to manufacture shirts for special promotions or special company occasions. Min-Yo's special garments are known as Dragon Shirts because of the elaborate embroidery and oriental flair of the designs. Because each shirt is made to a particular customer's specifications and requires a separate setup, special garments cannot be produced in advance of a firm customer order.

Although price is not a major concern for the customers of special garments, Min-Yo sells Dragon Shirts for $8 a shirt to ward off other companies seeking to enter the custom shirt market. Its customers come to Min-Yo because the company can produce almost any design with high quality and deliver an entire order on time. When placing an order for a Dragon Shirt, a customer specifies the design of the shirt (or chooses from Min-Yo's catalog), supplies specific designs for logos, and specifies the quantity of the order and the delivery date. In the past, management checked to see if such an order could be fitted into the schedule and either accepted or rejected it on that basis. If Min-Yo accepts an order for delivery at the *end* of a certain week and fails to meet this commitment, it pays a penalty of $2 per shirt for each week delivery is delayed. This penalty is incurred weekly until the delinquent order is delivered. The company tried to forecast demand for specific designs of Dragon Shirts but has given up.

Table 2.1, Min-Yo's current open-order file, shows a past-due order of Thunder Shirts that has already been promised for delivery. Orders for Dragon Shirts (none shown here) are specified by order number to emphasize that each order quantity is unique.

TABLE 2.1		
MIN-YO OPEN-ORDER FILE* (AS OF THE END OF WEEK 0)		
Week of Delivery	**Product Type**	**Quantity**
1	Thunder	200 (past due)

*All orders are to be delivered at the *end* of the week indicated, after production for the week has been completed and before the next week's production is started.

MANUFACTURING

Process.   Min-Yo Garment has the latest process technology in the industry—a machine, called a garment maker, which is run by one operator on each of three shifts. This single machine process can make every garment Min-Yo produces; however, the changeover times consume a substantial amount of capacity. Company policy is to run the machine three shifts a day, five days a week. If there is insufficient business to keep the machine busy, the workers are idle because Min-Yo has made a definite commitment to never fire or lay off a worker. By the same token, the firm has a policy of never working on weekends. Thus, the capacity of the process is 5 days × 24 hours = 120 hours per week. The hourly wage is $10 per hour, so the firm is committed to a fixed labor cost of $10 × 120 = $1,200 per week. Once the machine has been set up to make a particular type of garment, it can produce them at the rate of 10 garments per hour, regardless of type. The cost of the material in each garment, regardless of type, is $4. Raw materials are never a problem and can be obtained overnight.

Scheduling the Garment Maker.   Scheduling at Min-Yo Garment is done once each week, after production for the week has been completed and shipped, after new orders from customers have arrived, and before production for the next week has started. Scheduling results in two documents. The first is a profit and loss (P&L) statement for the week that factors in sales and production costs, including penalty charges and inventory carrying costs, as shown in Table 2.2. The inventory carrying cost for *any type of product* is $0.10 per shirt per week left in inventory after shipments for the week have been made.

The second document, a production schedule, is shown in Table 2.3. The schedule shows what management wants the garment maker process to produce for each week in the future. Because the schedule loses validity (owing to uncertainty) the farther into the future that it is projected, it is reformulated each week. Note that the schedule specifies two things that are important in the "action" bucket (the next period for which definite, *irrevocable* commitments must be made). The first is the number of hours (setup + run) that are allocated to each product to be produced. The garment maker can produce 10 shirts per hour, so the hours required to produce a particular product is calculated by adding the setup time to the production quantity divided by 10. For example, in Table 2.3, the setup times for Muscle Shirts and Thunder Shirts are 8 and 10 hours, respectively. The time spent on Muscle Shirts is 8 + 800/10 = 88 hours. For Thunder Shirts, it is 10 + 200/10 = 30 hours. The total time spent by the garment maker process on all products in a week *cannot exceed 120 hours.*

The second important piece of information is a circled number indicating the sequence in which products are to be produced. This information is important because, at the end of a week, the garment maker process will be set up for the last product produced. If the same product is to be produced first the following week, no new setup will be required (as indicated by this number sequence). The only exception to this rule is Dragon Shirts. As each order is unique, a new setup is required for each Dragon Shirt order. Table 2.3 shows that in week 0 the sequence was Muscle Shirts followed by Thunder Shirts.

TABLE 2.2								
P&L STATEMENT (WEEK 0)								
(1)	(2)	(3)	(4)	(5)	(6)	(7)	(8)	(9)
Product	Price	Beginning Inventory	Production	Available[2]	Demand	Sales[3]	Ending Inventory[1] (past due)	Inventory/ Past-Due Cost[4]
Muscle	$6	550	800	1,350	750	$4,500	600	$ 60
Thunder	7	—	200	200	400	1,400	(200)	200
Dragon	8	—	—	—	—	—	—	—
Totals			1,000			$5,900		$260

Sales (total of column 7) $5,900
Costs:
  Labor $1,200
  Materials (total of column 4 × $4)   4,000
  Inventory/past due (total of column 9)   260
    Total cost $5,460
  Contribution to profit $ 440 ($5,900 − $5,460)
  Cumulative contribution $ 440 (add to next period's contribution)

[1]Past due refers to the quantity of shirts not shipped as promised.

[2]Available = column 3 + column 4.

[3]Sales = column 6 × column 2 when demand < available; column 5 × column 2, otherwise.

[4]Inventory cost = 0.10 times number of shirts in ending inventory. Past-due cost equals number of shirts not shipped when promised times the penalty ($1 for Thunder Shirts, $2 for the Dragon Shirts).

Week—Product	0	1	2	3	4	5	6	7	8	9	10
TABLE 2.3 PRODUCTION SCHEDULE (WEEK 0)											
Muscle	800 ①										
Hours	88										
Thunder	200 ②										
Hours	30										
Dragon											
Hours											
Total hours scheduled	118										

THE SIMULATION

At Min-Yo Garment Company, the executive committee meets weekly to discuss the new order possibilities and the load on the garment maker process. The executive committee consists of top management representatives from finance, marketing, and operations. You will be asked to participate on a team and play the role of a member of the executive committee in class. During this exercise, you must decide how far into the future to plan. Some decisions, such as the markets you want to exploit, are long term in nature. Before class, you may want to think about the markets and their implications for manufacturing. Other decisions are short term and have an impact on the firm's ability to meet its commitments. The instructor will give each team the latest company data, including the setup times for each product, before the simulation begins. In class, the simulation will proceed as follows.

1. You will start by specifying the production schedule for week 1, based on the forecasts for week 1 in the case narrative for Muscle Shirts and additional information on new and existing orders for the customized shirts. This decision is to be made in collaboration with your executive committee colleagues in class.

2. When all the teams have finalized their production plans for week 1, the instructor will supply the *actual* demands for Muscle Shirts in week 1. At this point, one of the members of the executive committee is to complete the P&L statement for week 1, assuming that the production schedule for week 1 has been completed. Blank copies of Table 2.2 will be provided.

3. While the P&L statement for week 1 is being completed, the instructor will announce the new order requests for Thunder Shirts and Dragon Shirts to be shipped in week 2 and the weeks beyond.

4. You should look at your order requests, accept those that you want, and reject the rest. Add those that you accept for delivery in future periods to your open-order file (blank copies will be provided). You are then irrevocably committed to them and their consequences.

5. You should then make out a new production schedule, specifying at least what you want your garment maker process to do in the next week (it will be for week 2 at that time).

6. The instructor will impose a time limit for each period of the simulation. When the time limit for one period has been reached, the simulation will proceed to the next week.

CASE   BSB, INC., THE PIZZA WARS COME TO CAMPUS

Renee Kershaw, manager of food services at a medium-sized private university in the Southeast, has just had the wind taken out of her sails. She had decided that, owing to the success of her year-old pizza service, the time had come to expand pizza-making operations on campus. However, yesterday the university president announced plans to begin construction of a student center on campus that would house, among other facilities, a new food court. In a departure from past university policy, this new facility would permit and accommodate food-service operations from three private organizations: Dunkin' Donuts, Taco Bell, and Pizza Hut. Until now, all food service on campus had been contracted out to BSB, Inc.

CAMPUS FOOD SERVICE

BSB, Inc. is a large, nationally operated food-services company serving client organizations. The level of service provided varies, depending on the type of market being served and the particular contract specifications. The company is organized into three market-oriented divisions: corporate, airline, and university or college. Kershaw, of course, is employed in the university or college division.

At this particular university, BSB, Inc. is under contract to provide food services for the entire campus of 6,000 students and 3,000 faculty, staff, and support personnel. Located in a city of approximately 200,000 people, the campus was built on land donated by a wealthy industrialist. Because the campus is somewhat isolated from the rest of the town, students wanting to shop or dine off campus have to drive into town.

The campus itself is a "walking" campus, with dormitories, classrooms, and supporting amenities such as a bookstore, sundry shop, barber shop, branch bank, and food-service facilities—all within close proximity. Access to the campus by car is limited, with peripheral parking lots provided. The university also provides space, at a nominal rent, for three food-service facilities. The primary facility, a large cafeteria housed on the ground floor of the main administration building, is located in the center of campus. This cafeteria is open for breakfast, lunch, and dinner daily. A second location, called the Dogwood Room, on the second floor of the administration building, serves an upscale luncheon buffet on weekdays only. The third facility is a small grill located in the corner of a recreational building near the dormitories. The grill is open from 11 A.M. to 10 P.M. daily and until midnight on Friday and Saturday nights. Kershaw is responsible for all three operations.

THE PIZZA DECISION

BSB, Inc. has been operating the campus food services for the past 10 years—ever since the university decided that its mission and core competencies should focus on education, not on food service. Kershaw has been at this university for 18 months. Previously, she had been assistant manager of

food services at a small university in the Northeast. After 3 to 4 months of getting oriented to the new position, she had begun to conduct surveys to determine customer needs and market trends.

An analysis of the survey data indicated that students were not as satisfied with the food service as Kershaw had hoped. A large amount of the food being consumed by students, broken down as follows, was not being purchased at the BSB facilities:

Percent of food prepared in dorm rooms	20
Percent of food delivered from off campus	36
Percent of food consumed off campus	44

The reasons most commonly given by students were (1) lack of variety in food offerings and (2) tight, erratic schedules that did not always fit with cafeteria serving hours. Three other findings from the survey were of concern to Kershaw: (1) the large percentage of students with cars, (2) the large percentage of students with refrigerators and microwave ovens in their rooms, and (3) the number of times students ordered food delivered from off campus.

Percent of students with cars on campus	84
Percent of students with refrigerators or microwaves in their rooms	62
Percent of food that students consume outside BSB, Inc. facilities	43

In response to the market survey, Kershaw decided to expand the menu at the grill to include pizza. Along with expanding the menu, she also started a delivery service that covered the entire campus. Now students would have not only greater variety, but also the convenience of having food delivered quickly to their rooms. To accommodate these changes, a pizza oven was installed in the grill and space was allocated to store pizza ingredients, to make cut-and-box pizzas, and to stage premade pizzas that were ready to cook. Existing personnel were trained to make pizzas, and additional personnel were hired to deliver them by bicycle. In an attempt to keep costs down and provide fast delivery, Kershaw limited the combinations of toppings available. That way a limited number of "standard pizzas" could be preassembled and ready to cook as soon as an order was received.

THE SUCCESS

Kershaw believed that her decision to offer pizza service in the grill was the right one. Sales over the past 10 months had steadily increased, along with profits. Follow-up customer surveys indicated a high level of satisfaction with the reasonably priced and speedily delivered pizzas. However, Kershaw realized that success brought with it other challenges.

The demand for pizzas had put a strain on the grill's facilities. Initially, space was taken from other grill activities to accommodate the pizza oven, preparation, and staging areas. As the demand for pizzas grew, so did the need for space and equipment. The capacities of existing equipment and space allocated for making and cooking pizzas now were insufficient to meet demand, and deliveries were being delayed. To add to the problem, groups were beginning to order pizzas in volume for various on-campus functions.

Finally, a closer look at the sales data showed that pizza sales were beginning to level off. Kershaw wondered whether the capacity problem and resulting increase in delivery times were the reasons. However, something else had been bothering her. In a recent conversation, Mack Kenzie, the grill's supervisor, had told Kershaw that over the past couple of months requests for pizza toppings and combinations not on the menu had steadily increased. She wondered whether her on-campus market was being affected by the "pizza wars" off campus and the proliferation of specialty pizzas.

THE NEW CHALLENGE

As she sat in her office, Kershaw thought about yesterday's announcement concerning the new food court. It would increase competition from other types of snack foods (Dunkin' Donuts) and fast foods (Taco Bell). Of more concern, Pizza Hut was going to put in a facility offering a limited menu and providing a limited selection of pizzas on a "walk-up-and-order" basis. Phone orders would not be accepted nor would delivery service be available.

Kershaw pondered several crucial questions: Why had demand for pizzas leveled off? What impact would the new food court have on her operations? Should she expand her pizza operations? If so, how?

QUESTIONS

1. Does BSB, Inc. enjoy any competitive advantages or core competencies?
2. Initially, how did Renee Kershaw choose to use her pizza operations to compete with off-campus eateries? What were her competitive priorities?
3. What impact will the new food court have on Kershaw's pizza operations? What competitive priorities might she choose to focus on now?
4. If she were to change the competitive priorities for the pizza operation, what are the gaps between the priorities and capabilities of her processes? How might that affect her operating processes and capacity decisions?
5. What would be a good service strategy for Kershaw's operations on campus to meet the food court competition?

Source: This case was prepared by Dr. Brooke Saladin, Wake Forest University, as a basis for classroom discussion.

SELECTED REFERENCES

Berry, W. L., C. Bozarth, T. Hill, and J. E. Klompmaker. "Factory Focus: Segmenting Markets from an Operations Perspective." *Journal of Operations Management*, vol. 10, no. 3 (1991), pp. 363–387.

Blackburn, Joseph. *Time-Based Competition: The Next Battle-Ground in American Manufacturing.* Homewood, IL: Business One-Irwin, 1991.

Collier, David A. *The Service Quality Solution.* Milwaukee: ASQC Quality Press, and Burr Ridge, IL: Irwin Professional Publishing, 1994.

Feitzinger, Edward, and Hau L. Lee. "Mass Customization at Hewlett-Packard: The Power of Postponement." *Harvard Business Review*, vol. 75, no. 1 (1997), pp. 116–121.

Fitzsimmons, James A., and Mona Fitzsimmons. *Service Management for Competitive Advantage.* New York: McGraw-Hill, 2001.

Goldstein, Susan Meyer, Robert Johnson, JoAnn Duffy, and Jay Rao. "The Service Concept: The Missing Link in Service Design Research?" *Journal of Operations Management*, vol. 20 (2002), pp. 121–134.

Gilmore, James H., and B. Joseph Pine II. "The Four Faces of Mass Customization." *Harvard Business Review*, vol. 75, no. 1 (1997), pp. 91–101.

Hammer, Michael, and Steven Stanton. "How Process Enterprises Really Work." *Harvard Business Review* (November–December 1999), pp. 108–120.

Hayes, Robert H., and G. P. Pisano. "Manufacturing Strategy: At the Intersection of Two Paradigm Shifts." *Production and Operations Management*, vol. 5, no. 1 (1996), pp. 25–41.

Heim, Gregory R., and Kingshuk K. Sinha. "Service Process Configurations in Electronic Retailing: A Taxonomic Analysis of Electronic Food Retailers." *Production and Operations Management*, vol. 11, no. 1 (Spring 2002), pp. 54–74.

Heskett, James L., and Leonard A. Schlesenger. "The Service-Driven Service Company." *Harvard Business Review* (September–October 1991), pp. 71–81.

Hill, Terry. *Manufacturing Strategy: Text and Cases,* 3d ed. Homewood, IL: Irwin/McGraw-Hill, 2000.

Kellogg, Deborah L., and Winter Nie. "A Framework for Strategic Service Management." *Journal of Operations Management*, vol. 13 (1995), pp. 323–337.

Menor, Larry J., Mohan V. Tatikonda, and Scott E. Sampson. "New Service Development: Areas for Exploitation and Exploration." *Journal of Operations Management*, vol. 20 (2002), pp. 135–157.

O'Reilly, Brian. "They've Got Mail!" *Fortune* (February 7, 2000), pp. 101–112.

Pine, B. Joseph II, Bart Victor, and Andrew C. Boynton. "Making Mass Customization Work." *Harvard Business Review* (September–October 1993), pp. 108–119.

Prahalad, C. K., and Venkatram Ramaswamy. "Co-opting Customer Competence." *Harvard Business Review* (January–February 2000), pp. 79–87.

Roth, Aleda V., and Marjolijn van der Velde. "Operations As Marketing: A Competitive Service Strategy." *Journal of Operations Management*, vol. 10, no. 3 (1993), pp. 303–328.

Safizadeh, H. M., L. P. Ritzman, D. Sharma, and C. Wood. "An Empirical Analysis of the Product–Process Matrix." *Management Science*, vol. 42, no. 11 (1996), pp. 1576–1591.

Skinner, Wickham. "Manufacturing Strategy on the 'S' Curve." *Production and Operations Management*, vol. 5, no. 1 (1996), pp. 3–14.

Stalk, George, Jr., P. Evans, and P. E. Schulman. "Competing on Capabilities: The New Rules of Corporate Strategy," *Harvard Business Review* (March–April 1992), pp. 57–69.

Vickery, S. K., C. Droge, and R. E. Markland. "Production Competence and Business Strategy: Do They Affect Business Performance?" *Decision Sciences*, vol. 24, no. 2 (1993), pp. 435–456.

Ward, Peter T., Deborah J. Bickford, and G. Keong Leong. "Configurations of Manufacturing Strategy, Business Strategy, Environment and Structure." *Journal of Management*, vol. 22, no. 4 (1996), pp. 597–626.

Wheelwright, Steven C., and H. Kent Bowen. "The Challenge of Manufacturing Advantage." *Production and Operations Management*, vol. 5, no. 1 (1996), pp. 59–77.

Womack, J. P., D. T. Jones, and D. Roos. *The Machine That Changed the World.* New York: Rawson Associates, 1990.

Process Design Strategy

LEARNING GOALS
After reading this chapter, you should be able to . . .

IDENTIFY OR DEFINE
1. five main process design decisions.
2. dimensions of customer contact.
3. customer-contact matrix and product-process matrix.
4. basic transformation processes in manufacturing.
5. five process choices.
6. automation, capital intensity, economies of scope, and focus.
7. process reengineering and process improvement.

DESCRIBE OR EXPLAIN
8. fitting process design decisions together.
9. positioning a service process on the customer-contact matrix.
10. relating process choice with inventory strategy.
11. the pros and cons of customer involvement.
12. when less vertical integration is appropriate.

DUKE POWER

Duke Power (www.duke-energy. com) is a true pioneer of the enterprise process. The electric utility arm of Duke Energy, Duke Power serves nearly 2 million customers in North and South Carolina. In 1995, with deregulation looming, the company realized that its processes had to do a much better job of customer service. But the existing organizational structure of Customer Operations, the business unit responsible for delivering electricity to customers, was getting in the way of process improvements. The unit was divided into four regional profit centers, and regional vice presidents had little time for wrestling with process improvements for customer service. And even if they had, there was no way to coordinate their efforts across regions.

To resolve the problem, Duke Power identified the five core processes that together encompassed the essential work of Customer Operations: developing market strategies, maintaining customers, providing reliability and integrity, delivering products and services, and calculating and collecting revenues. Each process was assigned an owner, and the five process owners, like the four existing regional vice presidents, now report directly to the head of Customer Operations. Process owners are senior managers with end-to-end responsibility for enterprise processes, and they embody the company's commitment to better process management.

With the new structure, regional vice presidents continue to manage their own workforces—the process owners have only small staffs—but process owners have been given vast authority over the design and operation of the processes. They decide how work will proceed at every step. Then they establish performance targets and set budgets among regions. In other words, while regions have authority over people, they are evaluated on how well they meet goals set by process owners. This structure requires a new collaborative style of management, in which the process managers and regional vice presidents act as partners rather than rivals. Teams are composed of individuals with broad process knowledge, and they are measured on performance. They take over most of the managerial responsibilities usually held by supervisors. Supervisors, in turn, become more like coaches. Because the same employees are often involved in several processes, sometimes simultaneously, processes overlap. Process owners promote process improvements and continually seek to add value to the customer.

The new structure at Duke Power requires collaboration between process managers and the regional VPs. Teamwork is essential in the design and operation of processess.

Source: Stanton, Steven. "How Process Enterprises Really Work." *Harvard Business Review* (November–December 1999), pp. 108–117.

One essential issue in the design of processes is deciding how to provide services or make products. Deciding on processes involves many different choices in selecting human resources, equipment, outsourced services, and materials. Processes are involved in how marketing prepares a market analysis, how accounting bills customers, how a retail store provides services on the sales floor, and how a manufacturing plant performs its assembly operations. Process decisions can affect an organization's ability to compete over the long run.

Process decisions are also strategic in nature: As we saw in Chapter 2, they should further a company's long-term competitive goals. In making process decisions, managers focus on controlling such competitive priorities as quality, flexibility, time, and cost. For example, firms can improve their ability to compete on the basis of time by examining each step of their processes and finding ways to respond more quickly to their customers. Productivity and, therefore, cost can be improved. Service to customers (whether internal or external) is affected by choices made when processes are designed. Process management is an ongoing activity, with the same principles applying to both first-time and redesign choices. Thus, the processes at Duke Power are in constant change.

We begin by defining five basic process decisions: process structure, customer involvement, vertical integration, resource flexibility, and capital intensity. We discuss these decisions for both service and manufacturing processes, methods of focusing operations, and the impact of job design. We pay particular attention both to ways in which services strategy, capital intensity, and customer contact affect service operations and to methods for focusing operations. We conclude with two basic change strategies of analyzing and modifying processes—reengineering and process improvement.

As you read about process design strategies, think about why they are important to the various departments and functions across the organization, such as . . .

- ➤ **accounting,** which seeks better ways to perform its work processes and provides cost information to evaluate process improvement proposals.
- ➤ **finance,** which seeks better processes to perform its work, does financial analyses of new process proposals, and looks for ways to raise funds for major process changes.
- ➤ **human resources,** which melds process and job design decisions into an effective whole and seeks employees with the skills needed by the firm's processes.
- ➤ **management information systems,** which identifies how information technologies can support the exchange of information.
- ➤ **marketing,** which makes significant input into the service and product design that must be connected to process design, maintains many front-office processes of its own, and explores opportunities to expand market share by encouraging ongoing customer dialogue.
- ➤ **operations,** which designs and manages its processes in order to maximize customer value and enhance a firm's core competencies.

◉ WHAT IS PROCESS DESIGN?

A process involves the use of an organization's resources to provide something of value. No service can be provided and no product can be made without a process, and no process can exist without at least one service or product.

Process design is the selection of the inputs, resources, work flows, and methods that transform inputs into outputs. Input selection begins by deciding which processes are to be done in-house and which processes are to be done outside and purchased as materials and services. Process design decisions also deal with the proper mix of human skills and equipment and which parts of the processes are to be performed by each. Decisions about processes must be consistent with competitive priorities (see Chapter 2, "Operations Strategy") and the organization's ability to obtain the resources necessary to support them.

process design The selection of the inputs, resources, work flows, and methods that transform inputs into outputs.

Process design decisions must be made when

- a gap exists between competitive priorities and competitive capabilities.
- a new or substantially modified service or product is being offered.
- quality must be improved.
- competitive priorities have changed.
- demand for a service or product is changing.
- current performance is inadequate.
- the cost or availability of inputs has changed.
- competitors are gaining by using a new process.
- new technologies are available.

Not all such situations lead to changes in current processes. Process design decisions must also take into account other choices, such as quality, capacity, layout, and inventory. Moreover, as Managerial Practice 3.1 shows, it also applies to how new services and products are developed.

The impact on the environment is another increasingly important consideration. It is a very important concern in Europe and growing in the United States. A good example

MANAGERIAL PRACTICE 3.1

THE SERVICE/PRODUCT DEVELOPMENT PROCESS AT NETSCAPE

The advent of the World Wide Web opens up a whole new approach to the product development process. Traditionally, design implementation begins once a product's concept has been determined in its entirety. This approach still works well when technology, customer preferences, and competitive conditions are predictable and stable. However, when new technologies or competitors appear overnight, and when a company's customers can easily switch to new suppliers, a different development process is needed. The Internet makes possible a more flexible, more dynamic development process. Designers, for example, can continue shaping products even after implementation has begun. Companies can incorporate rapidly evolving customer requirements and changing technologies into their designs until the last possible moment before a product is introduced to the market.

A good example is in the Internet industry itself, where there is considerable turbulence in technology and competing products. Founded in 1994, Netscape (www.netscape.com) pioneered the easy-to-use Web browser—that is, a software interface that provides access to the World Wide Web. Navigator was designed and updated in a rapidly evolving industry in which fast-changing technology makes product development a project manager's nightmare. Even the most basic design decisions about a product must be continually revised as new information arises. Netscape thus introduced Navigator 2.0 in January of 1996 and immediately began to develop Navigator 3.0. The Netscape

development group produced the first 3.0 prototype in just six weeks. This Beta 0 version was put on the company's internal project Web site for testing by the development staff. Although many of the product's functions were not yet available, the Beta 0 version captured enough of the essence of the new product to get meaningful feedback for change. Two weeks later, the development team issued an updated version, Beta 1, again for internal development staff only. By early March, with major bugs worked out, the first public release, Beta 2, appeared on Netscape's Internet Web site. Additional public refinements followed every few weeks until the official release date in August, with gradual refinements appearing in each beta iteration.

This iterative testing process was extremely useful to Netscape because the development team could react to user feedback and changes in customer preferences throughout the design process. It also allowed the development team to monitor competing products; such as Microsoft's Explorer. Microsoft has since adopted a similar process. For example, more than 650,000 customers tested a beta version of Microsoft's Windows 2000 and shared their ideas for changing product features. The beta tests also helped clear the glitches from early versions of the software.

Two designers at Netscape, where the use of the World Wide Web opened up a new way to develop Navigator.

Source: Iansiti, Marco, and Alan MacCormack. "Developing Products on Internet Time." *Harvard Business Review* (September–October 1997), pp. 108–117.

is McDonald's. It made subtle changes in the processes used to package food, reducing waste by more than 30 percent since 1990 and becoming one of the country's leading buyers of recycled materials. The greening of McDonald's entailed replacing "clamshell" boxes with special lightweight paper; introducing shorter napkins; and relying less on plastics in straws, dining trays, and playground equipment. McDonald's is now looking at a plan to turn waste into fertilizer, so that eating out could generate less waste than eating at many homes.

Concerns for ecology in process design are also increasing in the manufacturing sector. General Motors found in 1991 that it was generating 88 pounds of waste and trash for each car assembled. By examining its processes with a particular focus on waste, the amount of solid waste dropped to only 15 pounds in 1994. In their plant in Fairfax, Kansas, where the Grand Prix is assembled, the processes were generating only 1 pound of waste per car. A focus on pollution and waste gained momentum internationally when the International Organization of Standards adopted ISO 14001 in 1996. **ISO 14001** is a set of standards on how a company goes about eliminating pollution, such as setting up a formal system and database for monitoring environmental performance. Since 1996, over 250,000 firms have been certified in more than 50 countries, with the rate of certification growing at least 50,000 each year. Recent research shows that certified manufacturers who scrutinize their processes for pollution abatement report higher performance on their various competitive capabilities, suggesting a "win–win" situation (Melnyk, Sroufe, and Calantone 2003).

> **ISO 14001** A set of standards on how a company goes about eliminating pollution.

There are three principles concerning process design that are particularly important.

1. The key to successful process design is to make choices that fit the situation and that make sense together. They should not work for cross-purposes, with one process optimized at the expense of other processes. A more effective process is one that matches key process characteristics and has a close *strategic fit*.
2. Although this section of the text focuses on individual processes, they are the building blocks that eventually create the firm's whole value chain. The cumulative effect on customer satisfaction and competitive advantage is huge.
3. Whether processes in the value chain are performed internally or by outside suppliers, a decision we examine in this chapter, management must pay particular attention to the interfaces between processes. Having to deal with these interfaces underscores the need for cross-functional coordination (see Chapter 1, "Operations As a Competitive Weapon") and coordination with suppliers and customers (see Chapter 9, "Supply-Chain Design").

MAJOR PROCESS DESIGN DECISIONS

Process decisions directly affect the process itself and indirectly the services and the products that it provides. Whether dealing with processes for offices, service providers, or manufacturers, operations managers must consider five common process decisions.

Figure 3.1 shows that they are all important steps towards an effective process design.

- **Process structure** determines how processes are designed relative to the kinds of resources needed, how resources are partitioned between them, and their key characteristics. Beginning points for making these decisions for services are the desired amount and type of customer contact and the competitive priorities that the process design must achieve. Beginning points for manufacturing are the volume level and amount of customization and once again the competitive priorities. Understanding these connections helps the manager detect possible misalignments in processes, paving the way for reengineering and process improvements.
- **Customer involvement** reflects the ways in which customers become part of the process and the extent of their participation.
- **Vertical integration** is the degree to which a firm's own production system or service facility handles the entire value chain. The more that the processes are performed in-house rather than by suppliers or customers, the greater is the degree of vertical integration.
- **Resource flexibility** is the ease with which employees and equipment can handle a wide variety of products, output levels, duties, and functions.
- **Capital intensity** is the mix of equipment and human skills in a process. The greater the relative cost of equipment, the greater is the capital intensity.

> **process structure** A process decision that determines how processes are designed relative to the kinds of resources needed, how resources are partitioned between them, and their key characteristics.
>
> **customer involvement** The ways in which customers become part of the process and the extent of their participation.
>
> **vertical integration** The degree to which a firm's own production system or service facility handles the entire value chain.
>
> **resource flexibility** The ease with which employees and equipment can handle a wide variety of products, output levels, duties, and functions.
>
> **capital intensity** The mix of equipment and human skills in a process.

FIGURE 3.1   Major Decisions for Effective Process Design

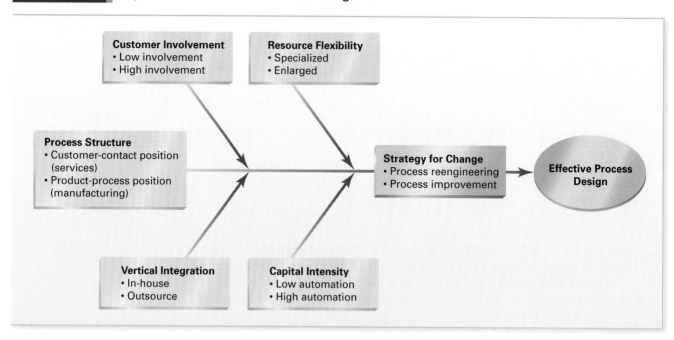

These five decisions are best understood at the process or subprocess level, rather than at the firm level. Process decisions act as building blocks that are used in different ways to achieve effective process designs.

PROCESS STRUCTURE IN SERVICES

How can operations strategy best be implemented?

One of the first decisions a manager makes in designing a well-functioning process is to choose a process type that best achieves the relative importance to be placed on it for quality, time, flexibility, and cost (see Chapter 2, "Operations Strategy"). Strategies for designing processes can be quite different, depending on whether a service is being provided or a product is being manufactured. We begin with service processes, given their huge share of the workforce in industrialized countries.

NATURE OF SERVICE PROCESSES: CUSTOMER CONTACT

An effective service process design in one situation can be a poor choice in another. A process design that gets customers in and out of a fast-food restaurant quickly would not be the right process design strategy for a five-star restaurant, where customers seek a leisurely dining experience. Further, a good design strategy for the servers at a restaurant might be totally inappropriate for a process back in the restaurant's business office. Economists sometimes put service organizations into different industry classifications, such as financial services, health services, education, and the like. Such distinctions help in the understanding of aggregate economic data and perhaps even some general tendencies on process design choices within a firm. However, the classifications are not very helpful when it gets down to designing an individual process. For example, there is no standard blueprint for how work should be done in the banking industry. To get insights, we must start at the process level and recognize key contextual variables associated with the process. Only by starting at the process level can we recognize patterns of appropriate designs and see how decisions should be grouped together.

A good process design for a service process depends first and foremost on the type and amount of customer contact. **Customer contact** is the extent to which the customer is present, is actively involved, and receives personal attention during the service

customer contact   The extent to which the customer is present, is actively involved, and receives personal attention during the service process.

A bank's branch manager talks with a customer at his desk. The customer at this high-contact process is not only present but also is actively involved and receiving personal attention.

process. In contrast with a manufacturing process, the customer can be very much a part of the process itself. Figure 3.2 shows several dimensions of customer contact. The nested-process concept applies to customer contact, because some parts of a process can have low contact and other parts of a process can have high contact. Further, even a subprocess can be high on some dimensions and low on others.

Figure 3.2 shows only the two extremes of customer contact, but they really represent a continuum. Thus, many levels are possible on each of the five dimensions. Only when they are taken together can you truly measure the kind and extent of customer contact. For example, the customer may not be physically present, but may still have high contact by being actively involved in the process, such as with eBay and other forms of Internet interactions that are managed without any face-to-face contact.

The first dimension is whether or not the customer is physically present at the process. Customer contact at a process is important, regardless of whether the customer is internal or external, and regardless of whether the service process is at a manufacturing or service organization. The amount of contact can be approximated as the percentage of the total time the customer is at the process, relative to the total time to complete the service. The higher the percentage of time that the customer is present, the

FIGURE 3.2   **Different Dimensions of Customer Contact in Service Processes**

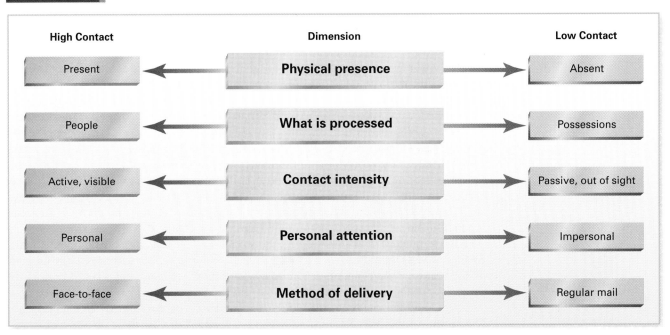

High Contact	Dimension	Low Contact
Present	**Physical presence**	Absent
People	**What is processed**	Possessions
Active, visible	**Contact intensity**	Passive, out of sight
Personal	**Personal attention**	Impersonal
Face-to-face	**Method of delivery**	Regular mail

higher the customer contact. Face-to-face interaction, sometimes called a *moment of truth* or *service encounter,* brings the customer and service providers together. At that time, customer attitudes about the quality of the service provided are shaped. Many processes requiring *physical presence* are found in health care, hospitality services, and passenger transportation. Physical presence also exists at a manufacturer's service processes, such as when a marketing representative (internal customer) receives information for putting together a bid on a customized product. During a face-to-face meeting with an industrial engineer and accountant, they collectively make some key decisions on how the product will be manufactured and priced. When physical presence is required, either the customer comes to the service facility, or the service providers and equipment go to the customer. In the first case the service operation is fixed in place, and in the second case the service provider and equipment are mobile. Either way allows the customer to be present while the service is being created.

A second dimension is *what is being processed* at the service encounter. *People-processing services* involve tangible actions to customers in person. The service is provided *to* the person, rather than *for* the person, and so it requires physical presence. Customers become part of the process, making the service's production simultaneous with its consumption. *Possession-processing services* (many such processes are found in e-commerce, freight transportation, equipment installation, maintenance and repair, and warehousing) involve tangible actions to physical objects that provide value to the customer. The object must be present during the processing, but not the customer. The service is consumed after the process is finished, rather than simultaneously with the service's creation. Customer contact is also established with *information-based services,* which collect, manipulate, analyze, and transmit data that has value to the customer. Such processes are common in insurance, news, banking, education, and legal services. Internet processes also fit within this category, where there is no face-to-face contact during the execution of the service. Figure 3.2 does not list information processing in either the low- or high-contact category. Although often a low-contact process, examples of information-processing services exist where the customer is quite active and contact is high without face-to-face contact, as we discover in the next dimension.

The *intensity of customer contact* goes one step beyond physical presence and what is processed. It deals with the extent to which the process accommodates the customer, and it involves considerable interaction and service customization. **Active contact** means that the customer is very much part of the creation of the service and affects the service process itself. The customer can personalize the service to suit her particular needs and even might decide in part how the process is performed. Active contact usually means the process is visible to the customer. Many processes for dental services or psychiatric services involve active contact. **Passive contact** means that the customer is not involved in tailoring the process to meet special needs or in how the process is performed. Even if the customer is present, he may simply be sitting in a waiting room, standing in line, or perhaps lying in a hospital bed. Many processes where the customer is present but the contact is passive can be found in public transportation or theaters. Interaction with service personnel is limited.

A fourth dimension is the extent of *personal attention* provided. High-contact processes are more intimate, and they exhibit mutual confiding and trust between the service provider and the customer. They also can mean a richer interchange of information between the customer and the service provider. When contact is more personal, the customer often *experiences* the service rather than just receiving it. The customer is changed in some way. Impersonal contact lies at the other end of the customer-contact continuum. At a less intimate process, for example, the customer might move through a standardized work flow or stand in line at a ticket counter.

A final dimension of customer contact is the *method used* to be in contact. A high-contact process would use face-to-face or the telephone, assuring more clarity in identifying customer needs and in delivering the service. A low-contact process would likely use a less personable means to deliver the service. Regular mail or standardized e-mail messages would be the preferred way to exchange information for low-contact process. The advent of the Internet and the widening channels of electronic distribution chan-

active contact The customer is very much part of the creation of the service and affects the service process itself.

passive contact The customer is not involved in tailoring the process to meet special needs or in how the process is performed.

nels allows processes that traditionally had high customer contact to be converted into low-contact processes. Retail banking is a good example, where customers can go to the traditional branch bank or they now can do their banking online.

CUSTOMER-CONTACT MATRIX

The customer-contact matrix, shown in Figure 3.3, brings together three elements: the degree of customer contact, the service design package (see Chapter 2, "Operations Strategy"), and the process. It synchronizes the service to be provided with the delivery process. The matrix is the starting point for evaluating and improving a process.

How should a service process fit with customer contact?

CUSTOMER CONTACT AND SERVICE DESIGN. The horizontal dimension of the matrix represents the service provided to the customer in terms of customer contact, the service design, and the competitive priorities. A key competitive priority is how much customization is needed. Positions on the left side of the matrix represent high customer contact and highly customized services. The customer is more likely to be present and active, with competitive priorities calling for more customization. The process is visible to the customer, who receives more personal attention. The right side of the matrix represents low customer contact, passive involvement, less personalized attention, and a process out of the customer's sight.

PROCESS COMPLEXITY, DIVERGENCE, AND FLOW. The vertical dimension of the customer-contact matrix deals with three characteristics of the process itself: (1) complexity, (2) divergence, and (3) flow. Each process can be analyzed on these three dimensions.

Process complexity is the number and intricacy of the steps required to perform the process. Complexity depends in part on how broadly the process is defined. At a bank, for example, the *auto finance* process is complex because it involves many steps. One

process complexity The number and intricacy of the steps required to perform the process.

FIGURE 3.3   **Customer-Contact Matrix for Processes**

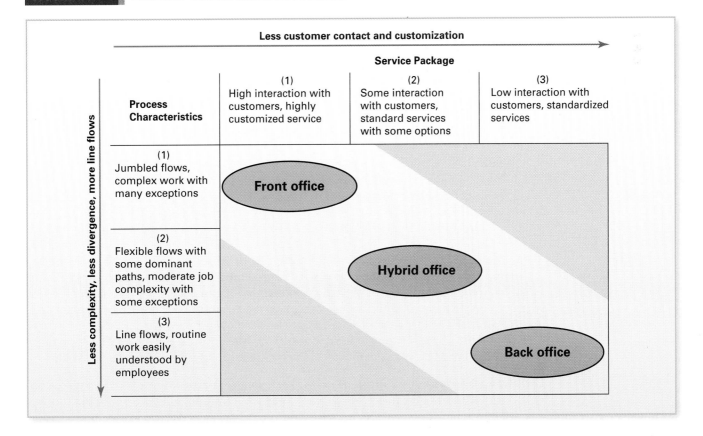

of the subprocesses nested within auto finance is *credit application*. It is not as complex because it is just one part of the auto finance process, and thus involves fewer steps. Nested within credit application, in turn, is the *loan documentation* process. It is even less complex because it represents just one small part of the overall auto finance process. Focusing on a more narrowly defined nested process reduces the number of steps to be performed if they are all to be completed by the same service provider (or team). However, even just a few steps can still be complex if they are intricate.

process divergence   The extent to which the process is highly customized with considerable latitude as to how it is performed.

Process divergence is the extent to which the process is highly customized with considerable latitude as to how it is performed. If the process changes with each customer, virtually every performance of the service is unique. Examples of highly divergent service processes where many steps in them change with each customer are found in consulting, law, and architecture. For an architect's nested processes, completing the home design can take on a different character for each customer, even if there are many common activities. They involve much judgment and discretion, depending on what the situation and customer dictate. Services that involve interpretative skills, as with creating art works, also are highly divergent because the execution of the process is individualized. A service with low divergence, on the other hand, is repetitive and standardized. The work is performed exactly the same with all customers. Certain hotel services and telephone services are highly standardized to assure uniformity. At many hotels, every step from room cleaning to checkout is standardized with documentation and rules governing how the process is performed.

process flow   The manner in which work progresses through the sequence of steps in a process, which could range from highly diverse to linear.

line flow   The customers, materials, or information move linearly from one operation to the next, according to a fixed sequence.

Closely related to divergence is how the customer, object, or information being processed flows through the service facility. **Process flow** is the manner in which work progresses through the sequence of steps in a process, which could range from highly diverse to linear. A **line flow** means that the customers, materials, or information move linearly from one operation to the next, according to a fixed sequence. When there is considerable diversity, the work flow appears jumbled, with the path of one customer often crisscrossing the path that the next one will take. When diversity is low and the process standardized, line flows are a natural consequence. With line flows, the work invariably goes from one workstation to the next in the same sequence for every customer or job.

A process can be analyzed as to its complexity, divergence, and work flow. A physician's service, for example, can be complex. It can also be divergent, as the doctor defines the steps performed based on the information collected during the diagnosis and then takes one or more actions. The patient may be routed to testing areas that vary with the patient, creating jumbled flows rather than line flows. Some services are low in complexity, but high in divergence. For example, a teacher simply transmits knowledge, but the actual ways used can be highly individualized and can vary with each topic covered.

SERVICE PROCESS STRUCTURING

Figure 3.3 shows that there are several desirable positions in the matrix that effectively connect the service product with the process. The manager has three process structures, which form a continuum, to choose from: (1) *front office,* (2) *hybrid office,* and (3) *back office.* Figure 3.4 illustrates each type of service process position with an example from the financial services industry. It is unlikely that a process can be a top performer if a process lies too far from one of these diagonal positions, occupying instead one of the extreme positions represented by the light blue triangles in the matrix (refer to Figure 3.3). Such positions represent too much of a disconnect between the service design and process design. A much more likely position is somewhere within the yellow area, or band, that stretches down from the front-office position to the back-office position. Some deviation from the diagonal is expected and even desirable, allowing for special niches. However, the extreme positions are to be avoided.

front office   A process with high customer contact where the service provider interacts directly with the internal or external customer.

FRONT OFFICE. A **front-office** process has high customer contact where the service provider interacts directly with the internal or external customer. Because the customization of the service and variety of service options, the process is more complex

FIGURE 3.4   **Service Process Structures in the Financial Services Industry**

Front Office *Sale of financial services*	Hybrid Office *Creation of quarterly performance reports*	Back Office *Production of monthly client fund balance reports*
• Research customer finances • Work with customer to understand customer needs • Make customized presentation to customer addressing specific customer needs • Involve specialized staff offering variety of services • Continuing relationship with customer, reaction to changing customer needs	• Data obtained electronically • Report calculated using standardized process • Report reviewed using standardized diagnostic systems • Manager provides written analysis and recommendations in response to individual employee performance • Manager meets with employee to discuss performance	• Data obtained electronically • Report run using standardized process • Results checked for "reasonableness" using well-established policies • Hard copies and electronic files forwarded to analysts • Process repeated monthly with little variation

and many of the steps in it have considerable divergence. Work flows are jumbled, and they vary from one customer to the next. More freedom is allowed or inherent in the steps and sequence of the process. There are many exceptions to the usual work pattern. Not only are there more steps in the process, but employees find them more difficult to understand. There is more service variety and services are more customized, at least to the extent of having many standard service modules (as with mass customization). The high-contact service process tends to be adapted or tailored to each customer, and the customer has more choice in how each step of the service process is carried out and sometimes even where the service encounter occurs. An example of a front office, as illustrated by the first column in Figure 3.4, is the process of the sale of financial services to municipalities. This process is highly customized to meet specific customer needs, with customer contact, complexity, and divergence all quite high. The process flow is jumbled, depending on customer requirements.

HYBRID OFFICE. A hybrid office tends to be in the middle on the five dimensions in Figure 3.3, or perhaps high on some contact measures and low on others. A **hybrid-office** process has moderate levels of customer contact and standard services, with some options available from which the customer chooses. The work flow progresses from one workstation to the next, with some dominant paths apparent. The work is reasonably complex, and some customization exists in how the process is performed. An example of a hybrid office, as illustrated by the second column in Figure 3.4, is the process of evaluating employee performance on a quarterly basis. This portion of the process is not particularly complex, in that the reports are fairly standardized and the process is repeated periodically according to a well-established process. Some parts of the performance analysis are even computerized. On the other hand, this portion of the process aggregates information from a variety of sources, both quantitative and qualitative, and is therefore more complex than the back-office process discussed next. Furthermore, the manager's written analyses and meetings with employees are highly customized and tailored to the individual.

hybrid office   A process with moderate levels of customer contact and standard services with some options available.

BACK OFFICE. A **back-office** process has low customer contact and little service customization. The work is standardized and routine, with line flows from one service provider to the next until the service is completed. An example of a back-office process,

back office   A process with low customer contact and little service customization.

An employee uses a FedEx computer in a back-office process. The work being performed is standardized and repeated frequently, with no direct customer contact.

as illustrated by the third column of Figure 3.4, is the monthly production of client fund balance reports. The process is very standardized, repeated frequently, and requires very little variation. When completed, and checked for reasonableness, the reports are sent to the analysts. Customer contact is quite low, as are process complexity and divergence. The process has a line flow.

CHANGING POSITION

After analyzing a process and determining its position on the matrix, it may be apparent that it is improperly positioned, either too far to the left or right, or too far to the top or bottom. A process's position on the customer-contact matrix is not fixed and immutable. Opportunities for improvement can become apparent after identifying the current process's position. Maybe the service design calls for more customization and customer contact. Increased customization and customer contact usually allows for a niche strategy, with profits sustained less on the basis of volume and more on margins. Perhaps, instead, the process is too complex and divergent, with unnecessarily jumbled flows. Maybe the competitive capabilities of customization, variety, or cost are not measuring up to the importance assigned to them by the competitive capabilities. Reducing divergence and complexity might allow a more volume-oriented position that reduces costs and improves productivity.

Figure 3.5 shows how service design, customer contact, and process characteristics (complexity, divergence, and flow) can be realigned for the dining process at a mid-priced family restaurant. The changes on the left move the process in the direction of a front office, whereas the changes on the right are more in the direction of a back office.

PROCESS STRUCTURE IN MANUFACTURING

Many processes at a manufacturing firm are actually services to internal or external customers, and so the previous discussion on services applies to them. Here we focus instead on the manufacturing processes themselves. Because of the differences between service and manufacturing processes, we need a different view on process structure.

FIGURE 3.5   Process Repositioning at a Restaurant

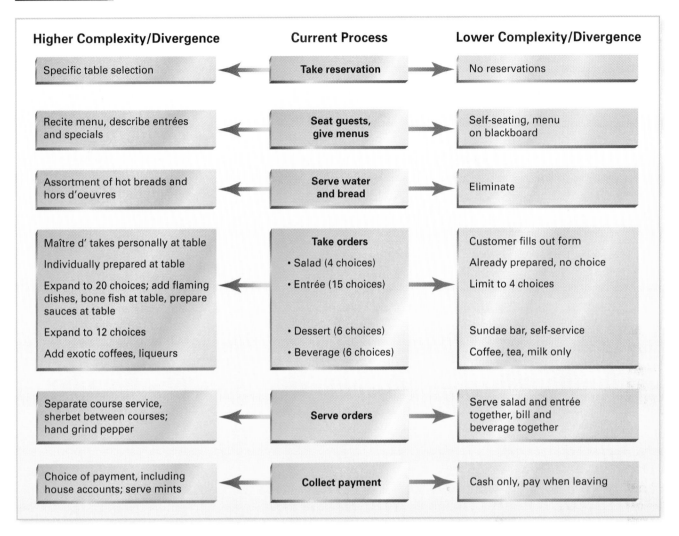

Source: Adapted from Shostack, G. Lynn. "Service Positioning Through Structural Change." *Journal of Marketing,* vol. 51, no. 1 (1987), pp. 34–43. Printed with permission.

NATURE OF MANUFACTURING PROCESSES

Manufacturing processes convert materials into goods that have a physical form. The transformation processes change the properties of materials on one or more of the following dimensions:

1. change the material's physical properties,
2. change the material's shape,
3. machine parts to a fixed dimension,
4. obtain a surface finish,
5. assemble or join parts and materials.

More specific processes exist within each category. For example, changing the material's physical properties could be a chemical reaction, cold working, hot working, heat treatment, or refining/extraction. Because materials are being moved, stored, and packed, the material-handling supporting processes take on critical importance. So do inspection processes that make sure the products measure up to specifications.

When you look at what is being done at the process level, it is much easier to discern whether it is providing a service or manufacturing a product. This clarity is lost when the whole company is classified as either a manufacturer or a service provider,

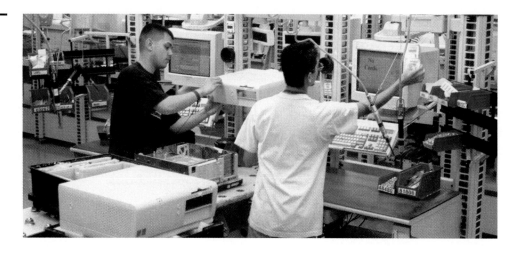

Employees at Dell's Metric 12 facility in Austin, Texas, work in groups of two to assemble computers. Assembly and the joining of parts or materials is one of the basic processes in manufacturing.

because it often performs both types of processes. For example, the process of cooking the meat at a McDonald's store is a manufacturing process, because it changes the material's physical properties (dimension 1). So is the process of assembling the hamburger with the bun, which is assembling or joining parts and materials (dimension 5). However, most of the other processes visible or invisible to McDonald's customers are service processes. Whether to call the whole McDonald's organization a manufacturer or a service provider can be debated, whereas classifications at the process level are much less ambiguous.

PRODUCT-PROCESS MATRIX

The product-process matrix, shown in Figure 3.6, brings together three elements: (1) volume, (2) product design, and (3) process. It synchronizes the product to be manufactured with the manufacturing process itself.

How should a manufacturing process fit with volume?

A good design for a manufacturing process depends first and foremost on volume. Customer contact, a primary feature of the customer-contact matrix for services, normally is not a consideration for manufacturing processes. Some exceptions are possible, such as a manufacturing process that produces a highly customized product and is coupled with an active external-customer interface process. For many manufacturing processes, high product customization means lower volumes for many of the steps in the process. If customization, top quality, and product variety are strongly emphasized, the likely result is lower volume for any particular step in the manufacturing process.

The vertical dimension of the product-process matrix deals with the same three characteristics in the customer-contact matrix: complexity, divergence, and flow. Each manufacturing process should be analyzed on these three dimensions, just as was done for a service process.

MANUFACTURING PROCESS STRUCTURING

Figure 3.6 shows that there are several desirable positions (often called *process choices*) in the product-process matrix that effectively connect the manufactured product with the process. **Process choice** is the way of structuring the process by organizing resources around the process or organizing them around the products. Organizing around the process means, for example, that all milling machines are grouped together and process all products or parts needing that kind of transformation. Organizing around the product means bringing together all the different human resources and equipment needed for a specific product and dedicating them to producing just that product. The manager has five process choices, which form a continuum, to choose from: (1) *project process*, (2) *job process*, (3) *batch process*, (4) *line process*, and (5) *continuous process*. As with the customer-contact matrix, it is unlikely that a manufacturing process can be a top performer if its position is too far from the diagonal. The fundamental message in Figure 3.6 is that the best choice for a manufacturing

process choice A way of structuring the process by organizing resources around the process or organizing them around the products.

FIGURE 3.6   Product-Process Matrix for Processes

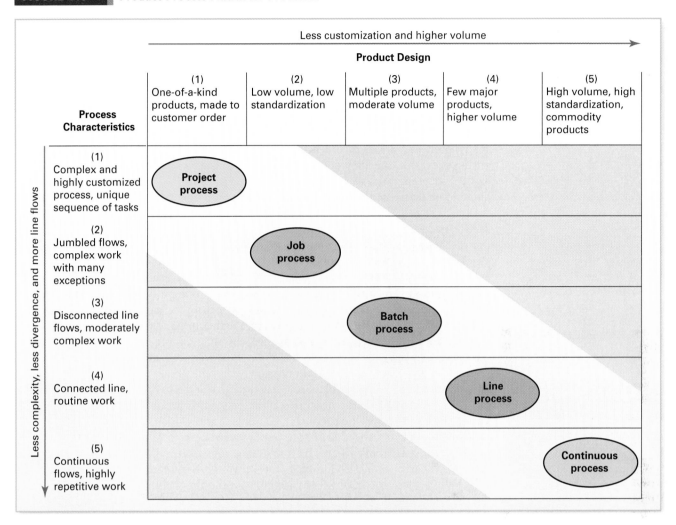

process depends on the volume and degree of customization required of the process. The process choice might apply to an entire manufacturing process or just one sub-process nested within it. For example, one step of the process might be a job process where a specific part is machined (along with parts for many different products), whereas another step might be a line process where the part is assembled with other parts and materials to create the final product. We now concentrate on the differences among the five choices for manufacturing processes.

PROJECT PROCESS. An example of a project process is producing power-generation equipment for an electric utility company (such as Duke Power in the chapter opener) that is designed to meet specific customer requirements for output rates; types of fuel (oil, coal, gas, or nuclear) to consume; and environmental protection devices. A **project process** is characterized by a high degree of product customization, the large scope of each product, and the release of substantial resources once it is completed. It is associated with a highly customized, one-of-a-kind product, typically engineered to customer specifications. A project process lies at the high-customization, low-volume end of the product-process matrix. It is both complex and divergent, with the sequence of steps performed specifically to create the customized product or one of the parts going into the product. Process flows are defined with each new project. Although some projects may look similar, each is unique. Project processes are valued on the basis of their capabilities to do certain kinds of work, rather than their ability to produce specific products at low cost. Project processes tend to take a long time and to be large. Many

VIDEO CLIP 3.1

Video Clip 3.1 on the Student CD-ROM introduces three different process choices suited to different product volumes and variety.

project process   A process characterized by a high degree of product customization, the large scope of each product, and the release of substantial resources once it is completed.

interrelated tasks must be completed, requiring close coordination (see Chapter 8, "Planning and Managing Projects"). Resources needed for a project are assembled and then released for further use after the project is finished. Project processes typically make heavy use of certain skills and resources at particular stages and then have little use for them the rest of the time.

Project processes are not limited to manufacturing, but also are found in most service organizations. Examples include building a shopping center, planning a major event, running a political campaign, putting together a comprehensive training program, constructing a new hospital, doing a management consulting job, leasing and constructing facilities for a large insurance company, or forming a project team to do an assignment (such as a student team doing a course project). They are not manufacturing processes, but they definitely have the characteristics of a project process. The key to designing these service processes, however, must begin with the amount of customer contact needed in the project, as suggested by the customer-contact matrix.

JOB PROCESS. Next in the continuum of process choices is the job process. Examples are machining a metal casting for a customized order or producing customized cabinets. A **job process** creates the flexibility needed to produce a wide variety of products in significant quantities, with considerable complexity and divergence in the steps performed. Customization is relatively high and volume for any one product is low. However, volumes are not as low as for a project process, which by definition does not produce in quantity. The workforce and equipment are flexible to handle considerable task divergence. As with a project process, companies choosing job processes often bid for work. Typically, they make products to order and do not produce them ahead of time. The specific needs of the next customer are unknown, and the timing of repeat orders from the same customer is unpredictable. Each new order is handled as a single unit—as a job.

A job process primarily organizes all like resources around itself (rather than allocating them out to specific products); equipment and workers capable of certain types of work are located together. These resources process all jobs requiring that type of work. Because customization is high and most jobs have a different sequence of steps, this process choice creates jumbled flows through the operations rather than a line flow. While there is considerable variability in the flows through a job process, there can be some line flows within it. Some subprocesses nested within the process can be identical for all jobs or customers. Also, some customers handled by a job process place repeat orders from time to time. These conditions create some line flows and higher volumes than are found with project processes. Some front-office processes that create services can be interpreted to be job processes, such as providing emergency room care.

BATCH PROCESS. Examples of a batch process are making standard components that feed an assembly line or some processes that manufacture capital equipment. A **batch process** differs from the job process with respect to volume, variety, and quantity. The primary difference is that volumes are higher because the same or similar products or parts going into them are produced repeatedly. Some of the components going into the final product may be processed in advance. Another difference is that a narrower range of products is provided. A third difference is that production lots are handled in larger quantities (or *batches*) than are with job processes. A batch of one product (or component part going into it or perhaps other products) is processed, and then production is switched to the next one. Eventually the first product is produced again. A batch process has average or moderate volumes, but process divergence is still too great to warrant dedicating a separate process for each product. The process flow is jumbled, with no standard sequence of steps throughout the facility. However, more dominant paths emerge than at a job process, and some segments of the process have a line flow.

Some hybrid-office processes can be seen as batch processes, such as scheduling air travel for a group, some subprocesses for mortgage loans, the order fulfillment process of an importer/distributor, or placing purchase orders at a public relations agency. However, not all batch processes are hybrid offices—the type and extent of customer contact must be brought into the equation.

job process A process with the flexibility needed to produce a wide variety of products in significant quantities, with considerable complexity and divergence in the steps performed.

batch process A process that differs from the job process with respect to volume, variety, and quantity.

LINE PROCESS. Products created by a line process include the assembly of computers, automobiles, appliances, and toys. A **line process** lies between the batch and continuous processes on the continuum; volumes are high and products are standardized, which allows resources to be organized around particular products. There is not much divergence in the process or line flows, and little inventory is held between the processing steps. Each step performs the same process over and over, with little variability in the products manufactured.

Production orders are not directly linked to customer orders, as is the case with project and job processes. Standard products are produced in advance of their need and held in inventory so that they are ready when a customer places an order. Product variety is possible by careful control of the addition of standard options to the main product. Examples of a line process in services are found in many back offices, where customer contact is low.

> **line process** A process that lies between the batch and continuous processes on the continuum; volumes are high and products are standardized, which allows resources to be organized around particular products.

CONTINUOUS PROCESS. Examples of a continuous process are petroleum refining; chemical processes; and processes making steel, soft drinks, and food (such as Borden's huge pasta-making plant). A **continuous process** is the extreme end of high-volume standardized production, with rigid line flows. Process divergence is negligible. Its name derives from the way materials move through the process. Usually, one primary material (such as a liquid, a gas, or a powder) moves without stopping through the process. The process seems more like a separate entity than a series of connected steps. The process is often capital-intensive and operates around the clock to maximize utilization and to avoid expensive shutdowns and start-ups.

> **continuous process** The extreme end of high-volume standardized production, with rigid line flows.

PRODUCTION AND INVENTORY STRATEGIES

Strategies for manufacturing processes differ from those in services, not only because of low customer contact and involvement, but also because of the ability to use inventories. Make-to-stock, assemble-to-order, and make-to-order strategies are three approaches to inventory that should be coordinated with process choice.

MAKE-TO-STOCK STRATEGY. Manufacturing firms that hold items in stock for immediate delivery, thereby minimizing customer delivery times, use a **make-to-stock strategy.** This strategy is feasible for standardized products with high volumes and reasonably accurate forecasts. It is the inventory strategy of choice for continuous or line processes. For example, in Figure 3.7, which depicts a final automobile assembly process, both the midsized 6-cylinder and the compact 4-cylinder models are assembled on the same line. Their volumes are sufficient to warrant a make-to-stock strategy. The process flow for the two products is straightforward, with four nested processes devoted to the two products.

This strategy is also applicable to situations in which the process produced a unique product for a specific customer if the volumes are high enough. For example, a company producing a sensor for the transmission of the Ford Explorer would have enough

> **make-to-stock strategy** A strategy that involves holding items in stock for immediate delivery, thereby minimizing customer delivery times.

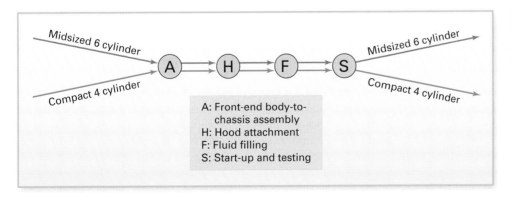

FIGURE 3.7

Automobile Assembly Process

volume to operate a production line specifically for that sensor and would carry a stock of the finished product for the scheduled shipments to the factory. Other examples of products produced with a make-to-stock strategy include garden tools, electronic components, soft drinks, and chemicals.

Combining a line process with the make-to-stock strategy is sometimes called **mass production.** It is what the popular press commonly envisions as the classical manufacturing process, because the environment is stable and predictable, with workers repeating narrowly defined task with low divergence. However, a line process is only one of five process choices. Further, mass customization (see Chapter 2, "Operations Strategy") is another possibility as is the assemble-to-order strategy, which we consider next.

mass production   A term sometimes used in the popular press for a line process that uses the make-to-stock strategy.

ASSEMBLE-TO-ORDER STRATEGY.   The **assemble-to-order strategy** is an approach to producing a wide variety of products from relatively few assemblies and components after the customer orders are received. Typical competitive priorities are variety and fast delivery times. The assemble-to-order strategy often involves a line process for assembly and a batch process for fabrication. Because they are devoted to manufacturing standardized components and assemblies in high volumes, the fabrication processes focus on creating appropriate amounts of inventories for the assembly processes. Once the specific order from the customer is received, the assembly processes create the product from standardized components and assemblies produced by the fabrication processes.

Stocking finished products would be economically prohibitive because the numerous possible options make forecasting relatively inaccurate. Thus, the principle of *postponement* (see Chapter 2, "Operations Strategy") is applied. For example, a manufacturer of upscale upholstered furniture can produce hundreds of a particular style of sofa, with no two alike, to meet customers' selections of fabric and wood. Other examples include paint (any color can be produced at the paint store by mixing standard pigments) and prefabricated homes for which the customer chooses among color and trim options.

assemble-to-order strategy   A strategy for producing a wide variety of products from relatively few assemblies and components after the customer orders are received.

MAKE-TO-ORDER STRATEGY.   Manufacturers that make products to customer specifications in low volumes tend to use the **make-to-order strategy,** coupling it with project or job processes. It is a more complex process than assembling a final product from standard components, such as assembling a Dell computer to customer order. Many different types of manufacturing processes might be used, other than primarily "assembly or joining parts and materials." The process is viewed with a make-to-order strategy as a set of subprocesses that can be used in many different ways to satisfy the unique needs of customers. This strategy provides a high degree of customization and typically uses project or job processes. The processes are complex, with high divergence. Because most products, components, and assemblies are custom-made, the manufacturing process must be flexible to accommodate the variety. Specialized medical equipment, castings, and expensive homes are suited to the make-to-order strategy.

make-to-order strategy   A strategy used by manufacturers that make products to customer specifications in low volumes.

CHANGING POSITION

Just as a service process can be repositioned in the customer-contact matrix, so can a manufacturing process be moved in the product-process matrix. Changes can be made either in the horizontal direction by changing the degree of customization and volume or they can be moved in the vertical direction by changing the process complexity or divergence. The production and inventory strategy can also be changed. Process flows can be made more linear by dedicating human and capital resources to a specific product or perhaps a group of very similar products. In that way, the sequence of tasks becomes the same. There is little divergence because, essentially, the same product is made repetitively with no deviations.

THE BIG PICTURE: PROCESS CHOICE AT KING SOOPERS BAKERY

In the Big Picture illustration on pages 106–107, we literally lifted the roof of the multiproduct bakery King Soopers, a division of Kroger Company, in Denver, Colorado, to show process choice at work. King Soopers makes three types of baked goods—custom-decorated cakes, pastries, and bread—with widely varying volumes and degrees of customization. It uses three different manufacturing processes to meet varying demand.

As you can see from the bar graph of relative volumes to the right (Figure 3.8), the custom cake process is a low-volume process. It starts with basic cakes of the appropriate sizes, which are made from a batch process (not shown). From that point on, the product is highly customized and cakes are produced to order. The process choice is best described as a *job process*. Customers may choose some standard selections from a catalog but often request one-of-a-kind designs. Frosting colors and cake designs are limited only by the worker's imagination.

The pastry process has higher volumes but not high enough for each product to have dedicated resources. The process choice is best described as a *batch process*. Dough is mixed in relatively small batches and sent to the proofing room (not shown), where general-purpose equipment feeds the batch of dough through rollers. Special fixtures, each unique to the product being made, cut the dough into the desired shapes. A great deal of product variety is handled, with each batch comprising about 1,000 units before a change is made to the next type of pastry.

The bread line is a high-volume process, making 7,000 loaves per hour. The bread is a standardized product made to stock, and production is not keyed to specific customer orders. The process choice is a *line process*. Because of the rigid line flows, it is not a batch process, even though a batch of dough is made each day. Once the line starts, it must run until empty so that no dough is left in the mixers overnight and no bread is left in the oven. The line usually does not operate around the clock and, in this sense, is less like a continuous process.

VIDEO CLIP 3.2
Video Clip 3.2 on the Student CD-ROM summarizes the three different process choices at the King Soopers Bakery.

CUSTOMER INVOLVEMENT

The second key decision in process design strategy is customer involvement. It reflects the ways in which customers become part of the process and the extent of their participation. It is important for many service processes, particularly if customer contact is (or should be) high.

A good place to begin increasing customer involvement is making more of the process visible to the customer. Letting customers see what normally is hidden from them is part of the service design at Harvey's, a Canadian fast-food chain. There you can see workers in a sanitary and neat workplace broiling your meat, and you can pick the kinds of additional ingredients desired. An even bolder step is to let your customers participate in selected back-office processes, in effect converting them into front offices.

How much should customers be involved in the process?

POSSIBLE DISADVANTAGES

Customer involvement is not always a good idea. In some cases giving the customer more active contact in a service process will just be disruptive, making the process less efficient. Dealing with the unique needs of each customer can make the process more complex and divergent. Managing the timing and volume of customer demands becomes more challenging if the customer is physically present and expects prompt delivery. Quality measurement also becomes more difficult. Exposing the facilities and employees to the customer can have important implications (favorable or unfavorable)

PASTRY PROCESS

Moderate capital intensity and moderate resource flexibility

- Batch process
- Moderate volume
- Moderate automation
- Moderately difficult and moderately expensive to change or reset equipment

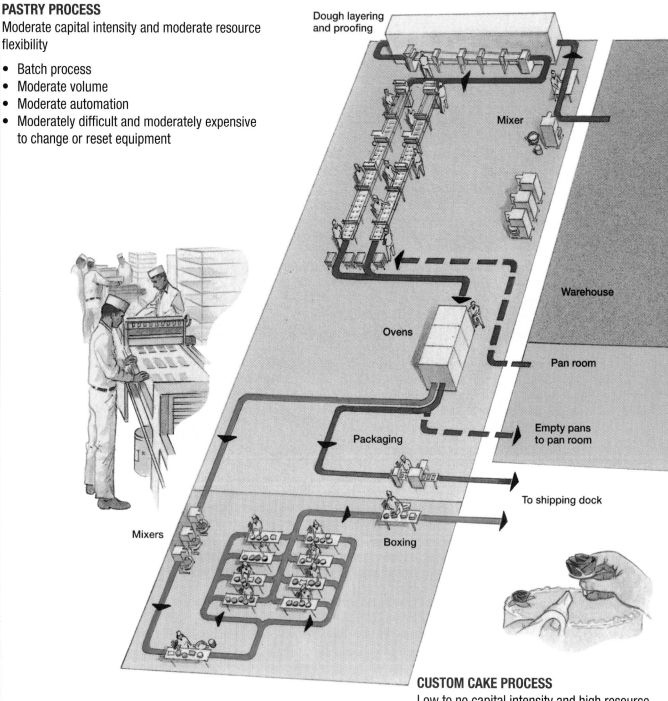

Dough layering and proofing

Mixer

Warehouse

Pan room

Ovens

Packaging

Empty pans to pan room

To shipping dock

Mixers

Boxing

CUSTOM CAKE PROCESS

Low to no capital intensity and high resource flexibility

- Job process
- Low volume
- Low to no automation
- Easy and inexpensive to change capacity

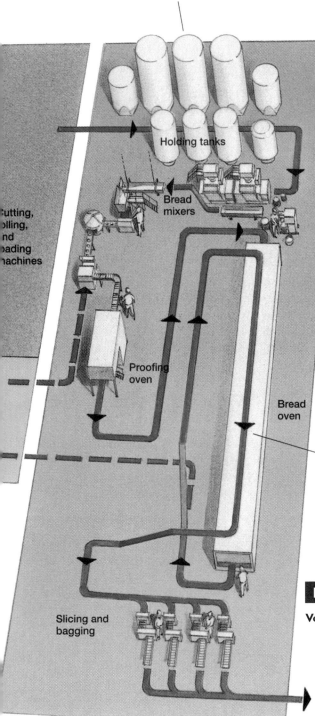

Bulk storage tanks

Holding tanks

Bread mixers

Cutting, oiling, and loading machines

Proofing oven

Bread oven

Cooling conveyor

Slicing and bagging

BREAD PROCESS
High capital intensity and low resource flexibility

- Line process
- High volume
- Difficult and expensive to change capacity

FIGURE 3.8

Volumes at King Soopers

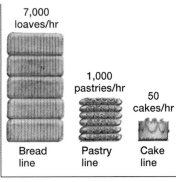

7,000 loaves/hr

1,000 pastries/hr

50 cakes/hr

Bread line	Pastry line	Cake line

High   Low

A college student is waiting for his meal at a restaurant in the UCLA food court in Los Angeles, California. A good place to begin increasing customer involvement is making the process more visible to the customer.

for perceived quality. No longer buffered from external influences, service provider productivity can drop, and costs can increase. Such changes make interpersonal skills a prerequisite to the service provider's job, but higher skill levels come at a cost. Revising the facility layout might be a necessary investment, now that managing customer perceptions becomes an important part of the process.

If customer involvement requires physical presence, customers may determine the time and location that the service is to be provided. If the service is delivered to the customer, decisions involving the location become part of the process design. Will the customer be served only on the service provider's premises, will the service providers go to the customer's premises, or will the service be provided at a third location? Having many smaller decentralized facilities closer to the various customer concentration areas may be required if the customer comes to the service providers. Otherwise, the service capability must be mobile. Either approach increases costs. Although certified public accountants frequently work on their clients' premises, both the time and the place are likely to be known well in advance, and travel becomes a cost consideration.

POSSIBLE ADVANTAGES

Despite these possible disadvantages, the advantages of a more customer-focused process might increase the net value to the customer. Some customers seek active participation in and control over the service process, particularly if they will enjoy savings in both price and time. The manager must assess whether advantages outweigh disadvantages, judging them in terms of the competitive priorities and customer satisfaction. The manager must also be aware of the possible use of emerging technologies in facilitating more customer involvement.

IMPROVED COMPETITIVE CAPABILITIES. Depending on the situation, more customer involvement can mean better quality, faster delivery, greater flexibility, and even lower cost. Quality can be improved for some services if the customer seeks to be more active and to receive more personal attention. Customers can come face-to-face with the service providers, where they can ask questions, make special requests on the spot, provide additional information, and even offer advice. Such a change creates a more personal relationship with the service provider and makes the customer part of assuring the competitive priority of consistent quality. Customer involvement can speed up the delivery or at least reduce the perceived waiting time.

If customization and variety are highly valued, customer involvement might help. Some processes can be designed to allow the customers to come up with their own service or product specifications or even become involved in the design of the product. A good example is in the custom-designed and custom-built home industry: The customer is heavily involved in the design process and inspects the work in process at various times. If a wide variety of services or products are available, the customers can make their own selections to fit their own preferences. In effect, they "pick their own groceries."

Just as active customer contact and personalized attention can increase costs, there are some ways that it can reduce costs. Self-service is the choice of many retailers, such as gasoline stations, supermarkets, and bank services. Sometimes referred to as the "salad-bar approach" to productivity, it substitutes customer efforts for those of the service provider. Manufacturers of products (such as toys, bicycles, and furniture) may also prefer to let the customer perform the final assembly because product, shipping, and inventory costs frequently are lower, as are losses from damage. The savings are passed on to the customers as lower prices. Of course, some customers prefer a more passive role, such as full-service at a gasoline station during a wintry day, despite the higher cost.

EMERGING TECHNOLOGIES. In a market where customers are technology enabled, companies can now engage in an active dialogue with customers and make them partners in creating value. Customers are a new source of competence for such processes. To harness customer competencies, companies must involve customers in an ongoing dialogue. They must also revise some of their traditional processes, such as pricing and billing systems, to account for their customer's new role. For example, in business-to-business relationships, the Internet changes the roles that companies play with other businesses. Ford's suppliers now are close collaborators in the process of developing new vehicles and no longer are passive providers of materials and services. The same is true for distributors. Wal-Mart does more than just distribute Procter & Gamble's products: It shares daily sales information and works with Proctor & Gamble in managing inventories and warehousing operations.

● VERTICAL INTEGRATION

All businesses buy at least some inputs to their processes (such as professional services, raw materials, or manufactured parts) from other producers. King Soopers is no exception and buys such materials as flour, sugar, butter, and water. Management decides the level of vertical integration by looking at all the processes performed between the acquisition of raw materials or outside services and the delivery of finished products or services. The more processes in the value chain that the organization performs itself, the more vertically integrated it is. If it does not perform some processes itself, it must rely on **outsourcing,** or paying suppliers and distributors to perform those processes and provide needed services and materials. When managers opt for more vertical integration, there is by definition less outsourcing. These decisions are sometimes called **make-or-buy decisions,** with a *make* decision meaning more integration and a *buy* decision meaning more outsourcing. After deciding what to outsource and what to do in-house, management must find ways to coordinate and, integrate the various processes and suppliers involved (see Chapter 9, "Supply-Chain Design").

BACKWARD AND FORWARD INTEGRATION

Vertical integration can be in two directions, as Figure 3.9 illustrates for King Soopers. **Backward integration** represents a firm's movement upstream toward the sources of raw materials and parts, such as a major grocery chain having its own plants to produce house brands of ice cream, frozen pizza dough, and peanut butter. **Forward integration** means that the firm acquires more channels of distribution, such as its own distribution centers (warehouses) and retail stores. It can also mean that the firm goes even further by acquiring its business customers. For example, King Soopers could acquire some of its own grocery stores that sell its products.

Which services and products should be created in-house?

outsourcing Allotting work to suppliers and distributors to provide needed services and materials and to perform those processes that the organization does not perform itself.

make-or-buy decisions Decisions that either involve more integration (a *make* decision) or more outsourcing (a *buy* decision).

backward integration A firm's movement upstream toward the sources of raw materials and parts.

forward integration A firm's movement downstream by acquiring more channels of distribution, such as its own distribution centers (warehouses) and retail stores.

FIGURE 3.9

Vertical Integration at King Soopers

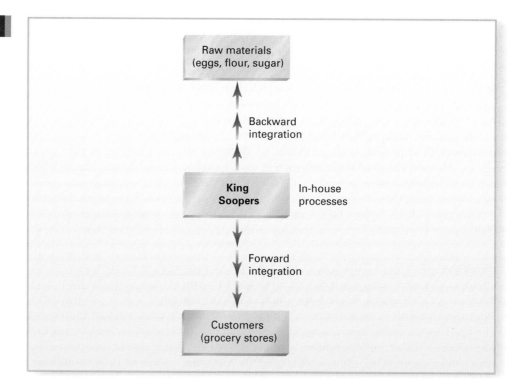

ADVANTAGES OF VERTICAL INTEGRATION AND OUTSOURCING

The advantages of vertical integration are the disadvantages of more outsourcing. Similarly, the advantages of more outsourcing are disadvantages of more vertical integration. Managers must study the options carefully before making choices. Break-even analysis (see Supplement A, "Decision Making"; also see Active Model A.2 and Tutor A.2 on the Student CD-ROM) and financial analysis (see Supplement J, "Financial Analysis," on the Student CD-ROM) are good starting points. However, the need for strategic fit is fundamental to all choices and must reflect qualitative as well as quantitative factors if analyses are to be complete.

ADVANTAGES OF VERTICAL INTEGRATION. More vertical integration can sometimes improve market share in another way, by allowing a firm to enter foreign markets more easily than it could otherwise. A firm can also achieve savings if it has the skills, volume, and resources to perform processes at lower cost and produce higher-quality goods and services than outsiders can. Doing the work in-house may mean better quality and more timely delivery—and taking better advantage of the firm's human resources, equipment, and space. Extensive vertical integration is generally attractive when input volumes are high because high volumes allow task specialization and greater efficiency. It is also attractive if the firm has the relevant skills and views the processes that it is integrating as particularly important to its future success, as seen in Managerial Practice 3.2.

Management must identify, cultivate, and exploit its core competencies to prevail in global competition. Recall that core competencies are the collective learning of the firm, especially its ability for coordinating diverse processes and integrating multiple technologies (see Chapter 2, "Operations Strategy"). They define the firm and provide its reason for existence. Management must look upstream toward its suppliers and downstream toward its customers and bring in-house those processes that give it the right core competencies—those that allow the firm to organize work and deliver value better than its competitors. Management should also realize that if the firm outsources a critical process, it may lose control over that area of its business—and perhaps the ability to bring the work in-house later.

Such a risk is particularly high for front-office processes that engage the external (rather than the internal) customer. The customer relationship process, one of the five core processes (see Chapter 1, "Operations As a Competitive Weapon"), should nor-

MANAGERIAL PRACTICE 3.2

CHOOSING THE RIGHT AMOUNT OF VERTICAL INTEGRATION

More Integration (Less Outsourcing)

The Citgo Petroleum Corporation's (www.citgo.com) triangular emblem is more visible at U.S. gas stations thanks to its addition of 14,000 new U.S. outlets, surpassing the number bearing the rival Texaco star. The red, white, and blue emblem is a symbol of a massive push into the United States by parent Petroleos de Venezuela (PDVSA), the $22 billion Venezuelan state oil company. It also signals a drive by key producers in OPEC to lock up shares in global markets by investing heavily in "downstream" refining and retailing as the cartel loses its hold on crude supplies and prices. "We believe that the fundamentals of the oil business indicate that you should be as integrated as possible," says the PDVSA president.

Tulsa-based Citgo, PDVSA's $10 billion U.S. refining and marketing subsidiary, has been growing at double-digit rates. To add to its six refineries in the United States, it is discussing ventures with Phillips Petroleum Company, Mobil Corporation, and others that could add retailing strength. In Europe, it has a joint refining venture with Germany's Veba. PDVSA's strategy of increased vertical integration is being embraced by other big OPEC members. Saudi Arabia and Kuwait, for example, are buying into refineries in markets such as the Philippines and India.

Less Integration (More Outsourcing)

Li & Fung (www.lifung.com), Hong Kong's largest export trading company, has a predominantly American and European customer base. This multinational firm outsources most of its manufacturing, using what is called "dispersed manufacturing" or "borderless manufacturing." It still performs the higher-value-added processes in Hong Kong, but outsources lower-value-added processes to the best possible locations around the world. Thus, it retains processes for designing products, buying and inspecting raw materials, managing factories and developing production schedules, and controlling quality. But it does not manage the workers, and it does not own the factories.

Li & Fung's approach goes beyond outsourcing to suppliers and letting them worry about contracting for raw materials. Any single factory is small and does not have the buying power to demand fast deliveries and good prices. Li & Fung may know, for instance, that the Limited is going to order 100,000 garments but does not yet know the style or colors. The firm reserves undyed yarn from its yarn supplier and locks up capacity at supplier mills for weaving. Because this approach is more complicated, Li & Fung was forced to get smart about logistics and dissecting the value chain. It is an innovator in supply-chain management techniques, using a host of information-intensive service processes for product development, sourcing, shipping, handling, and logistics. For its enterprise process of executing and tracking orders, it has its own standardized, fully computerized operating system, and everybody in the company uses it. Essentially, therefore, Li & Fung manages information and the relationships among 350 customers and 7,500 suppliers and does so with a lot of phone calls, faxes, and on-site vists. In time, the firm will need a sophisticated information system with an open architecture that can handle work in Hong Kong and New York, as well as in places like Bangladesh, where you cannot always count on a good phone line.

The competitive priorities of customization and fast delivery usually do not match up well together, but Li & Fung achieves both by organizing around small, customer-focused units. One unit might be a theme-store division that serves a handful of customers, such as Warner Brothers stores and Rainforest Café. Its retailing customers are in consumer-driven, fast-moving markets and face the problem of obsolete inventory with a vengeance. If a retailer shortens its buying cycle from three months to five weeks, it gains eight weeks to develop a better sense of where the market is heading. Forecasting accuracy improves, and there is less need for markdowns of obsolete inventory at the end of the selling season. Such payoffs to Li & Fung's customers make it a valued supplier. During the last decade, the focus was on supplier partnerships to improve cost and quality. In today's faster-paced markets, the focus has shifted to innovation, flexibility, and speed.

Sources: "Stepping on the Gas with Citgo." *Business Week* (March 11, 1996); "Fast, Global, and Entrepreneurial: Supply Chain Management, Hong Kong Style: An Interview with Victor Fung." *Harvard Business Review* (September–October 1998), pp. 103–115.

---

mally be kept in-house, even if volumes are low and the processes are divergent. Clearly hearing "the voice of the customer" assures effective dialogue with the customer. It is part of the need to keep processes customer focused, which begins with satisfying the external customer.

ADVANTAGES OF OUTSOURCING. Outsourcing offers several advantages to firms. It is particularly attractive to those that have low volumes. For example, **LoanCity.com,** an online mortgage company, set up shop in August, 1999. It started life with zero revenue but planned to serve more than a million customers in a few years. Any online operation of that size would require a sprawling computing center, which in turn would require a few million dollars of hardware, software licenses, and a staff of as many as 20 specialists. Instead, the company hired an application service provider, or ASP, to set up and run the various business-software packages needed to handle its sales, accounting, and human resource processes. It uses the Internet to connect to the applications needed on machines located at its ASP. Outsourcing can also provide better quality and cost savings. For example, foreign locations sometimes offer lower wages and yield higher productivity.

Firms are doing more outsourcing than ever before. The NCNB bank in Charlotte, North Carolina, outsourced the processing of card transactions and saved $5 million per year. Merrill Lynch, Sears Roebuck, and Texaco outsource their mailroom and photocopying operations to Pitney Bowes Management Services. Many firms do the same with payroll, security, cleaning, and other types of services, rather than employ personnel to provide these services. One recent survey showed that 35 percent of more than 1,000 large corporations have increased the amount of outsourcing they do.

Two factors are contributing to this trend: global competition and information technology. Globalization creates more supplier options, and advances in information technology make coordination with suppliers easier. IKEA, the largest retailer of home furnishings, has 30 buying offices around the world to seek out suppliers. Its Vienna-based business service department runs a computer database that helps suppliers locate raw materials and new business partners. Cash registers at its stores around the world relay sales data to the nearest warehouse and its operational headquarters in Älmhult, Sweden, where its information systems provide the data needed to control its shipping patterns worldwide.

virtual corporation A situation in which competitors enter into short-term partnerships to respond to market opportunities.

THE VIRTUAL CORPORATION. Information technology allows suppliers to come together as a virtual corporation. In a **virtual corporation**, competitors actually enter into short-term partnerships to respond to market opportunities. Teams in different organizations and at different locations collaborate on design, production, and marketing, with information going electronically from place to place. They disband when the project is completed. Virtual corporations allow firms to change their positions flexibly in response to quickly changing market demands.

network companies Companies that contract with other firms for most of their production and for many of their other functions.

An extreme case of outsourcing is **network companies,** which contract with other firms for most of their production and for many of their other functions. Li & Fung, which we discussed in Managerial Practice 3.2, is a good example. The name comes from their employees spending most of their time on the telephone or at the computer, coordinating suppliers. If demand for the network company's services or products changes, its employees simply pass this message along to suppliers, who change their output levels. Network companies can move in and out of markets, riding the waves of fashion and technology. However, network companies are vulnerable to new competition because the investment barriers to enter their businesses are low and because they lose business if their suppliers integrate forward or their customers integrate backward.

● RESOURCE FLEXIBILITY

How flexible should a process's human resources and equipment be?

Just as managers must account for customer contact when making customer involvement decisions, so must they account for process divergence and diverse process flows when making resource flexibility decisions. High task divergence and jumbled process flows require more flexibility of the process's resources—its employees, facilities, and equipment. Employees need to perform a broad range of duties, and equipment must be general purpose. Otherwise, resource utilization will be too low for economical operations.

WORKFORCE

flexible workforce A workforce whose members are capable of doing many tasks, either at their own workstations or as they move from one workstation to another.

Operations managers must decide whether to have a **flexible workforce.** Members of a flexible workforce are capable of doing many tasks, either at their own workstations or as they move from one workstation to another. However, such flexibility often comes at a cost, requiring greater skills and thus more training and education. Nevertheless, benefits can be large: Worker flexibility can be one of the best ways to achieve reliable customer service and alleviate capacity bottlenecks. Resource flexibility helps to absorb the feast-or-famine workloads in individual operations that are caused by low-volume production, divergent tasks, jumbled routings, and fluid scheduling.

The type of workforce required also depends on the need for volume flexibility. When conditions allow for a smooth, steady rate of output, the likely choice is a permanent workforce that expects regular full-time employment. If the process is subject to hourly, daily, or seasonal peaks and valleys in demand, the use of part-time or temporary employees to supplement a smaller core of full-time employees may be the best solution. However, this approach may not be practical if knowledge and skill requirements are too high for a temporary worker to grasp quickly. Controversy is growing over the practice of replacing full-time workers with temporary or part-time workers.

EQUIPMENT

Low volumes mean that process designers should select flexible, general-purpose equipment. Figure 3.10 illustrates this relationship by showing the total cost lines for two different types of equipment that can be chosen for a process. Each line represents the total annual cost of the process at different volume levels. It is the sum of fixed costs and variable costs (see Supplement A, "Decision Making"). When volumes are low (because customization is high), process 1 is the best choice. It calls for inexpensive general-purpose equipment, which keeps investment in equipment low and makes fixed costs (F_1) small. Its variable unit cost is high, which gives its total cost line a relatively steep slope. Process 1 does the job, but not at peak efficiency. However, volumes are not high enough for total variable costs to overcome the benefit of low fixed costs.

Conversely, process 2 is the best choice when volumes are high and customization is low. Its advantage is low variable unit cost, as reflected in the flatter total cost line. This efficiency is possible when customization is low because the equipment can be designed for a narrow range of products or tasks. Its disadvantage is high equipment investment and, thus, high fixed costs (F_2). When annual volume produced is high enough, spreading these fixed costs over more units produced, the advantage of low variable costs more than compensates for the high fixed costs.

The break-even quantity in Figure 3.10 is the quantity at which the total costs for the two alternatives are equal. At quantities beyond this point, the cost of process 1 exceeds that of process 2. Unless the firm expects to sell more than the break-even amount, which is unlikely with high customization and low volume, the capital investment of process 2 is not warranted.

TUTOR 3.1

Tutor 3.1 on the Student CD-ROM demonstrates how to do break-even analysis for equipment selection.

FIGURE 3.10

Relationship Between Process Costs and Product Volume

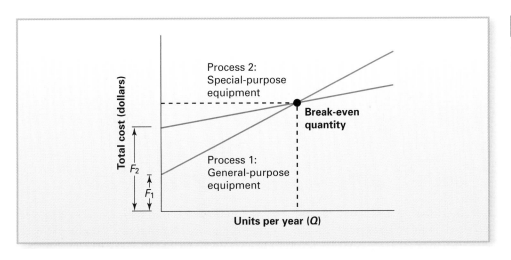

CAPITAL INTENSITY

How much should a firm depend on machinery and automated processes?

automation A system, process, or piece of equipment that is self-acting and self-regulating.

For either the design of a new process or the redesign of an existing one, managers must determine the amount of capital intensity required. Capital intensity is the mix of equipment and human skills in the process; the greater the relative cost of equipment, the greater is the capital intensity. As the capabilities of technology increase and its costs decrease, managers face an ever-widening range of choices, from operations utilizing very little automation to those requiring task-specific equipment and very little human intervention. **Automation** is a system, process, or piece of equipment that is self-acting and self-regulating. Although automation is often thought to be necessary to gain competitive advantage, it has both advantages and disadvantages. Thus, the automation decision requires careful examination.

AUTOMATING MANUFACTURING PROCESSES

Substituting labor-saving capital equipment and technology for labor has been a classic way of improving productivity and quality consistency in manufacturing processes. If investment costs are large, automation works best when volume is high, because more customization typically means reduced volume. Gillette, for example, spent $750 million on the production lines and robotics that gave it a capacity to make 1.2 billion Mach3 razor cartridges a year. The equipment is complicated and expensive. Fortunately, sales of core blade and razor products has climbed 10 percent on a worldwide basis, thanks largely to high demand for the flagship Mach3 product. Only with such high volumes could this continuous process produce the product at a price low enough that consumers could afford to buy it.

One big disadvantage of capital intensity can be the prohibitive investment cost for low-volume operations. Look again at Figure 3.10. Process 1, which uses general-purpose equipment, is not capital-intensive and therefore has small fixed costs, F_1. Although its variable cost per unit produced is high, as indicated by the slope of the total cost line, process 1 is well below the break-even quantity if volumes are low. Generally, capital-intensive operations must have high utilization to be justifiable. Also, automation does not always align with a company's competitive priorities. If a firm offers a unique product or high-quality service, competitive priorities may indicate the need for skilled servers, hand labor, and individual attention rather than new technology. A case in point is Gillette's downstream processes that package and store the razor cartridges. It customizes the packaging for different regions of the world, so that volumes for any one type of package is much lower. As a result of the low volumes, Gillette does not use expensive automation for these processes. In fact, it outsources them.

fixed automation A manufacturing process that produces one type of part or product in a fixed sequence of simple operations.

FIXED AUTOMATION. Manufacturers use two types of automation: fixed and flexible (or programmable). Particularly appropriate for line and continuous process choices, **fixed automation** produces one type of part or product in a fixed sequence of simple operations. Until the mid-1980s, most U.S. automobile plants were dominated by fixed automation—and some still are. Chemical processing plants and oil refineries also utilize this type of automation.

Operations managers favor fixed automation when demand volumes are high, product designs are stable, and product life cycles are long. These conditions compensate for the process's two primary drawbacks: large initial investment cost and relative inflexibility. The investment cost is particularly high when a single, complex machine (called a *transfer machine*) must be capable of handling many operations. Because fixed automation is designed around a particular product, changing equipment to accommodate new products is difficult and costly. However, fixed automation maximizes efficiency and yields the lowest variable cost per unit if volumes are high.

flexible (or programmable) automation A manufacturing process that can be changed easily to handle various products.

FLEXIBLE AUTOMATION. Flexible (or **programmable**) **automation** can be changed easily to handle various products. The ability to reprogram machines is useful for both low-customization and high-customization processes. In the case of high customization, a machine that makes a variety of products in small batches can be programmed to alternate between products. When a machine has been dedicated to a particular product or family of products, as in the case of low customization and a line flow, and the product is at the end of its life cycle, the machine can simply be reprogrammed with a new sequence of operations for a new product.

Cummins Engine Company, a manufacturer of diesel engines based in Columbus, Indiana, utilizes such flexibility to handle frequent design modifications. For example, in the first 18 months after introducing new compression brakes for its engines, Cummins' engineers made 14 design changes to the brakes. If the brakes had been made on less-flexible machines, these improvements probably would have taken several years and millions of dollars to implement—and, in fact, might not have been made.

AUTOMATING SERVICE PROCESSES

Using capital inputs as a labor-saving device is also possible for service processes. In educational services, for example, long-distance learning technology now can supplement or even replace the traditional classroom experience by using books, computers, Web sites, and videos as facilitating goods that go with the service. Justifying technology need not be limited to cost reduction. Sometimes it can actually increase complexity and task divergence by making available a wide menu of choices to the customer. Automated teller machines (ATMs) for banks initially just did cash dispensing and deposit services. Now they also offer funds transfer and investment services. Technology in the future surely will make possible even a greater degree of customization and variety in services than currently only human providers can now deliver. Beyond cost and variety considerations, the process designer must understand the customer and how much close contact is valued. If the customers seek a visible presence and personal attention, technologies reduced to sorting through a variety of options on the Internet or over the telephone might be a poor choice.

The need for volume to justify expensive automation is just as valid for service processes as for manufacturing processes. Increasing the volume lowers the cost per dollar of sales. Volume is essential for many capital-intensive processes in the transportation, communications, and utilities industries. A jetliner idled because of low demand is very expensive, a reality reflected in the 2002 income statements of airline companies. Managers must carefully assess both volume and investment dollars in deciding how much automation makes sense. While buying larger, more standardized equipment might be tempting, it may not provide a good strategic fit.

It is often correctly assumed that volumes are higher in back-office processes, where customer contact is low. Physical contact, personalized treatment, and face-to-face communication often create divergent tasks and low volume. However, this is not always the case. A recent study of financial services shows that high volumes are just as likely in front offices as in back offices. As a result, automation is not concentrated in the back office, but is just as likely found in front-office processes. Automation of financial services comes primarily from information technology, which can flexibly handle a wide array of processes at multiple locations. This flexibility acts much like flexible (programmable) automation does for certain manufacturing processes—variety and customization of the services does not rule it out. With financial services, the technology handles a variety of service processes, rather than different manufactured parts, but it achieves enough cumulative volume. Another factor allowing technology in both the front offices and back offices of financial services is the low investment cost. For example, the typical capital cost might be $300,000 per employee in a manufacturing process. In financial service processes, it might be only in the range of $50,000 per employee. In terms of Figure 3.10, the break-even volume for introducing the technology is much lower.

ECONOMIES OF SCOPE

If capital intensity is high, resource flexibility is low. King Soopers produces a high-volume product (loaves of bread) efficiently on an automated (high-capital-intensity) bread line, with few people monitoring its operation; but the process has low resource

Should more economies of scope be sought?

flexibility. In contrast, the custom cake line produces a low volume of product because it requires high customization. To complete the unique customer orders, resources must be flexible, and because the process requires hand work, capital intensity is low.

In certain types of manufacturing operations, such as machining and assembly, programmable automation breaks this inverse relationship between resource flexibility and capital intensity (see Supplement K, "Computer-Integrated Manufacturing"). It makes possible both high capital intensity and high resource flexibility, creating economies of scope. **Economies of scope** reflect the ability to produce multiple products more cheaply in combination than separately. In such situations, two conflicting competitive priorities—customization and low price—become more compatible. However, taking advantage of economies of scope requires that a family of parts or products have enough collective volume to utilize equipment fully. Adding a product to the family results in one-time programming (and sometimes fixture) costs. (*Fixtures* are reusable devices that maintain exact tolerances by holding the product firmly in position while it is processed.)

Economies of scope also apply to service processes. Consider, for example, Disney's approach to the Internet. When the company's managers entered the volatile Internet world, their businesses were only weakly tied together. They wanted plenty of freedom to evolve in and even shape emerging markets. They wanted flexibility and agility, not control, in these fast-moving markets. Disney's Infoseek business, in fact, was not even fully owned. However, once its Internet markets became more crystallized, managers at Disney moved to reap the benefits of economies of scope. They aggressively linked their Internet processes with one another and with other parts of Disney. They bought the rest of the Infoseek business and then combined it with Internet businesses, such as Disney Travel Online, into a single business (**Go.com**). They made their content Web sites accessible from a single portal (Go Network) and created new links to established businesses like ESPN. A flexible technology that handles many services together can be less expensive than handling each one separately, particularly when the markets are not too volatile.

economies of scope
Economies that reflect the ability to produce multiple products more cheaply in combination than separately.

STRATEGIC FIT

The process designer should understand how the five major process decisions tie together, so as to spot ways of improving poorly designed processes. The choices should fit the situation and each other. When there is more of a *strategic fit,* the process will be more effective. We examine services and manufacturing processes, looking for ways to test for strategic fit.

DECISION PATTERNS FOR SERVICE PROCESSES

How can the key process design decisions be coordinated for service processes?

The common denominator for decisions on service processes is primarily customer contact. Figure 3.11 shows how the process structure and the other key process decisions are tied to customer contact. High customer contact at a front-office service process means

1. *Process Structure.* The customer (internal or external) is present, actively involved, and receives personal attention. These conditions create processes with high complexity, high divergence, and jumbled process flows.

2. *Customer Involvement.* When customer contact is high, customers are more likely to become part of the process. The service created for each customer is unique.

3. *Vertical Integration.* When a process has high contact with external customers, it is a core process and more likely to be done in-house (increasing vertical integration). With internal customers, vertical integration opportunities are better if volumes are high, which is a situation often more likely found in back offices. However, exceptions are possible, such as in financial services where high volumes are also found in front offices.

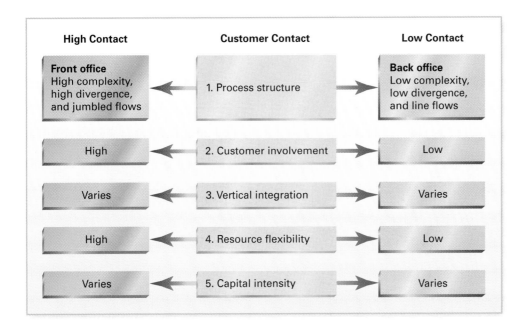

FIGURE 3.11

Decision Patterns for Service Processes

4. *Resource Flexibility.* High process divergence and jumbled process flows fit with more flexibility from the process's resources—its workforce, facilities, and equipment.

5. *Capital Intensity.* When volume is higher, automation and capital intensity are more likely. While higher volume is usually assumed to be found in the back office, it is just as likely to be in the front office for financial services. Information technology is a major type of automation at many service processes, which brings together both resource flexibility and automation.

Of course, these are general tendencies rather than rigid prescriptions. Exceptions can be found, but these relationships provide a way of understanding how process decisions can be linked coherently.

DECISION PATTERNS FOR MANUFACTURING PROCESSES

The common denominator for decisions on manufacturing processes is volume. Figure 3.12 summarizes the relationships between volume and the five key process decisions. High volumes at a manufacturing process typically mean

How can the key process design decisions be coordinated for manufacturing processes?

1. *Process Choice.* The high volumes at King Soopers' bread line, combined with a standard product, make a line flow possible. It is just the opposite with the King Soopers' custom cakes, where a job process produces cakes to specific customer orders.

2. *Customer Involvement.* Customer involvement is not a factor in most manufacturing processes, except for choices made on product variety and customization. Less discretion is allowed with line or continuous processes, so as to avoid the unpredictable demands required by customized orders.

3. *Vertical Integration.* High volumes create more opportunities for vertical integration.

4. *Resource Flexibility.* When volumes are high and process divergence is low, there is no need for flexibility to utilize resources effectively, and specialization can lead to more efficient processes. King Soopers' bread line can make just one product—bread.

5. *Capital Intensity.* High volumes justify the large fixed costs of an efficient operation. The King Soopers bread line is capital-intensive. It is automated from dough mixing to placement of the product on shipping racks. Expanding this process would be very expensive. By way of contrast, the King Soopers' custom cake process is labor-intensive and requires little investment to equip the workers.

FIGURE 3.12   Decision Patterns for Manufacturing Processes

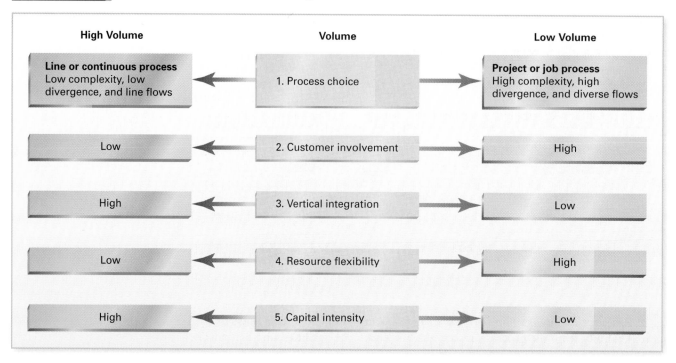

JOB DESIGN

Should jobs be specialized or enlarged?

Process structure, resource flexibility, and capital intensity influence how a manager designs jobs that go into a process. In particular, the manager must decide how much the jobs should be specialized or enlarged. A job with a high degree of **specialization** involves a narrow range of tasks, low complexity, low divergence, and, presumably, great efficiency and high quality. For example, an appliance repairperson specializing in refrigerators can quickly diagnose problems and make the correct repairs based on previous experience. Specialization results in such benefits as

specialization   The degree to which a job involves a narrow range of tasks, low complexity, low divergence, and, presumably, great efficiency and high quality.

- less training time per employee because methods and procedures are limited,
- faster work pace, leading to more output in less time, and
- lower wages because education and skill requirements are lower.

However, the arguments against job specialization suggest that narrowly defined jobs lead to

- poor employee morale, high turnover, and lower quality because of the monotony and boredom of repetitive work;
- the need for more management attention because the total activity is broken into a large number of jobs for a large number of employees, all of whom have to be coordinated to produce the entire service or product; and
- less flexibility to handle changes or employee absences.

ALTERNATIVES TO SPECIALIZATION. Considerable process specialization is usually associated with competitive priorities of low cost and consistent quality, with little product variety; with back offices; with line or continuous processes; with low resource flexibility; and with high capital intensity. A low degree of process specialization is typically associated with competitive priorities of customization, top quality, and volume flexibility; with front offices; with project or job processes; with high resource flexibility; and with low capital intensity. However, there are notable exceptions. Some firms (e.g., Motorola and AT&T) are having success with less specialization, even with process characteristics that seem to call for more specialization, by using three alternative strategies: (1) job enlargement, (2) job rotation, and (3) job enrichment.

Job Enlargement. The *horizontal* expansion of a job—that is, increasing the range of tasks at the same level—is called **job enlargement**. The employee completes a larger proportion of the total work required for the service or product. Typically, this approach requires that workers have various skills, and it is often accompanied by training programs and wage increases. Besides reducing boredom, job enlargement has the potential to increase employee satisfaction because the worker feels a greater sense of responsibility, pride, and accomplishment.

For example, the Capita Credit unit of AT&T Capital Credit Corporation, which leases telecommunications, computer, and other equipment, is organized so that teams of workers perform three major leasing functions for a customer: receiving applications and checking credit ratings, drawing up contracts, and collecting payments. Other financial institutions often devote three separate departments to these functions and design the jobs with a high degree of specialization. Employees at Capita Credit feel responsible for the quality of the service they provide and understand how their activities contribute to the success of the business as a whole. With this job design, Capita Credit processes up to 250 applications a day, more than double the number of a bank using the traditional job design processes.

Job Rotation. A system whereby workers exchange jobs periodically, thus getting more diverse experience in task assignment, is called **job rotation**. This approach is most effective when the jobs require an equal level of skill. For example, workers at a family restaurant may rotate duties from busing tables to cooking meals to taking orders. Because workers learn many aspects of the job, job rotation increases the skills of the workforce, giving management the flexibility to replace absent workers or to move workers to different workstations as necessary. In addition, rotating jobs can give each worker a better appreciation of the production problems of others and the value of passing only good quality to the next person.

Job Enrichment. The most comprehensive approach to job design is **job enrichment**, which entails a *vertical* expansion of job duties. That is, workers have greater control and responsibility for an entire process, not just a specific skill or operation. This approach supports the development of *employee empowerment* and *self-managed teams*, whereby employees make basic decisions about their jobs. For example, a chef at an elegant restaurant may be given the responsibility of purchasing ingredients at the market and arranging her own work schedule. Job enrichment generally increases job satisfaction because it gives workers a sense of achievement in mastering many tasks, recognition and direct feedback from users of the output, and responsibility for the quality of the output.

GAINING FOCUS

In the past, many firms were willing to endure the additional complexity that went with size. New services or products were added to a facility in the name of better utilizing fixed costs and keeping everything under the same roof. The result was a jumble of competitive priorities, process structures, and technologies. In the effort to do everything, nothing was done well.

FOCUS BY PROCESS SEGMENTS. A facility's process often can neither be characterized nor actually designed for one set of competitive priorities and one process choice. King Soopers had three processes under one roof, but management segmented them into three separate operations that were relatively autonomous. At a services facility, some parts of the process might seem like a front office and other parts like a back office. Such arrangements can be effective, provided that sufficient focus is given to each process. **Plants within plants (PWPs)** are different operations within a facility with individualized competitive priorities, processes, and workforces under the same roof. Boundaries for PWPs may be established by physically separating subunits or simply by revising organizational relationships. At each PWP, customization, capital intensity volume, and other relationships are crucial and must be complementary. The

---

job enlargement The horizontal expansion of a job, increasing the range of tasks at the same level.

job rotation A system whereby workers exchange jobs periodically, thus getting more diverse experience in task assignment.

job enrichment A vertical expansion of job duties; workers have greater control and responsibility for an entire process, not just a specific skill or operation.

How can operations be focused?

plants within plants (PWPs) Different operations within a facility with individualized competitive priorities, processes, and workforces under the same roof.

advantages of PWPs are fewer layers of management, greater ability to rely on team problem solving, and shorter lines of communication between departments.

cell A group of two or more dissimilar workstations located close to each other that process a limited number of parts or models with similar process requirements.

Another way of gaining focus is with the use of cells. A **cell** is a group of two or more dissimilar workstations located close to each other that process a limited number of parts or models with similar process requirements. A cell has line flows, even though the operations around it may have flexible flows (see Chapter 7, "Process Layout"). The small size of focused factories, PWPs, and cells offers a flexible, agile system that competes better on the basis of short lead times.

FOCUSED SERVICE OPERATIONS. Service industries also have implemented the concepts of focus, PWPs, and cells. Specialty retailers, such as Gap and The Limited, opened stores that have smaller, more accessible spaces. These focused facilities have generally chipped away at the business of large department stores. Using the same philosophy, some department stores are focusing on specific customers or products. Remodeled stores create the effect of many small boutiques under one roof.

focused factories The result of a firm's splitting large plants that produced all the company's products into several specialized smaller plants.

FOCUSED FACTORIES. Hewlett-Packard, S. C. Johnson and Sons, Japan's Ricoh and Mitsubishi, and Britain's Imperial Chemical Industries PLC are some of the firms that have created **focused factories,** splitting large plants that produced all the company's products into several specialized smaller plants. The theory is that narrowing the range of demands on a facility will lead to better performance because management can concentrate on fewer tasks and lead a workforce toward a single goal. In some situations, a plant that used to produce all the components of a product and assemble them may split into one that produces the components and one that assembles them, so that each can focus on its own individual process technology.

● STRATEGIES FOR CHANGE

The five major process design decisions represent broad, strategic issues. Decisions that are made must be translated into actual process designs or redesigns. We conclude with two different but complementary philosophies for process design: (1) process reengineering and (2) continuous process improvement. Let us first examine process reengineering, which has been getting considerable attention in management circles during the last decade.

PROCESS REENGINEERING

Do some of the organization's key processes need reengineering?

reengineering The fundamental rethinking and radical redesign of processes to improve performance dramatically in terms of cost, quality, service, and speed.

Reengineering is the fundamental rethinking and radical redesign of processes to improve performance dramatically in terms of cost, quality, service, and speed. Process reengineering is about reinvention, rather than incremental improvement. It is strong medicine and not always needed or successful. Pain, in the form of layoffs and large cash outflows for investments in information technology, almost always accompanies massive change. However, reengineering processes can have big payoffs. For example, Bell Atlantic reengineered its telephone business. After five years of effort, it cut the time to connect new customers from 16 days to just hours. The changes caused Verizon to lay off 20,000 employees, but the company is decidedly more competitive.

A process selected for reengineering should be a core process, such as a firm's order-fulfillment activities. Reengineering then requires focusing on that process, often using cross-functional teams, information technology, leadership, and process analysis. Let us examine each element of the overall approach.

CRITICAL PROCESSES. The emphasis of reengineering should be on core business processes (see Chapter 1, "Operations As a Competitive Weapon"), rather than on functional departments, such as purchasing or marketing. By focusing on processes, managers may spot opportunities to eliminate unnecessary work and supervisory activities, rather than worry about defending turf. Because of the time and energy involved, reengineering should be reserved for essential processes, such as new-product development or customer service. Normal process-improvement activities can be continued with the other processes.

STRONG LEADERSHIP. Senior executives must provide strong leadership for reengineering to be successful. Otherwise, cynicism, resistance ("we tried that before"), and boundaries between departments can block radical changes. Managers can help overcome resistance by providing the clout necessary to ensure that the project proceeds within a strategic context. Executives should set and monitor key performance objectives for the process. Top management should also create a sense of urgency, making a case for change that is compelling and constantly refreshed.

CROSS-FUNCTIONAL TEAMS. A team, consisting of members from each functional area affected by the process change, is charged with carrying out a reengineering project. For instance, in reengineering the process of handling an insurance claim, three departments should be represented: customer service, adjusting, and accounting. Reengineering works best at high-involvement workplaces, where self-managing teams and employee empowerment are the rule rather than the exception. Top-down and bottom-up initiatives can be combined—top-down for performance targets and bottom-up for deciding how to achieve them.

INFORMATION TECHNOLOGY. Information technology is a primary enabler of process engineering (see Chapter 12, "Information Technology and Value Chains"). Most reengineering projects design processes around information flows, such as customer order fulfillment. The process owners who will actually be responding to events in the marketplace need information networks and computer technology to do their jobs better. The reengineering team must determine who needs the information, when they need it, and where.

CLEAN-SLATE PHILOSOPHY. Reengineering requires a "clean-slate" philosophy—that is, starting with the way the customer wants to deal with the company. To ensure a customer orientation, teams begin with internal and external customer objectives for the process. Often, teams first establish a price target for the service or product, deduct profits desired, and then find a process that provides what the customer wants at the price the customer will pay. Reengineers start from the future and work backward, unconstrained by current approaches.

PROCESS ANALYSIS. Despite the clean-slate philosophy, a reengineering team must understand things about the current process: what it does, how well it performs, and what factors affect it. Such understanding can reveal areas in which new thinking will provide the biggest payoff. The team must look at every procedure involved in the process throughout the organization, recording each step, questioning why it is done, and then eliminating everything that is not necessary. Information on standing relative to the competition, process by process, is also valuable.

Like many new techniques and concepts in operations management, reengineering was highly touted in the early 1990s, almost as a recipe for instant competitive advantage. It has led to many successes and will continue to do so. However, actual experience gives a better picture of the method. It is not simple or easily done, nor is it appropriate for all processes or all organizations. Many firms cannot invest the time and resources to implement a radical, clean-slate approach. Moderate gains that better fit corporate strategy and culture might give greater cumulative results than the pursuit of breakthrough. Significant process improvements that have nothing to do with information technology can be realized. A firm must not only improve cross-functional processes but also the processes within each functional area. Finally, the best understanding of a process, and how to improve it, often lies with the people who perform the work each day, not cross-functional teams or top management.

PROCESS IMPROVEMENT

process improvement The systematic study of the activities and flows of each process to improve it.

Process improvement is the systematic study of the activities and flows of each process to improve it. Its purpose is to "learn the numbers," understand the process, and dig out the details. Once a process is really understood, it can be improved. The relentless pressure to provide better quality at a lower price means that companies must continually review all aspects of their operations. As the chief executive of Dana Corporation, a $4.9 billion producer of automotive parts, put it, "You have to get productivity improvements forever." Process improvement goes on, whether or not a process is reengineered.

Each aspect of the process is examined. An individual or a whole team examines the process, using the tools described in Chapter 4, "Process Analysis." Once the process is understood, they brainstorm different aspects of it, listing as many solutions as possible. They are guided by the principle that the process *can* be improved—that there is *always* a better way. One must look for ways to streamline tasks, eliminate whole processes entirely, cut expensive materials or services, improve the environment, or make jobs safer. One must find the ways to trim costs and delays and to improve customer satisfaction.

PROCESS DESIGN STRATEGY ACROSS THE ORGANIZATION

Processes are everywhere and are the basic unit of work. They are found in accounting, finance, human resources, management information systems, marketing, and operations. Managers in all departments must make sure that their processes are adding as much customer value as possible. They must be open to change in their processes, whether coming from a major reengineering effort or simply from an ongoing effort at process improvement. Managers must also understand that enterprise processes cut across organizational lines, regardless of whether the firm is organized along functional, product, regional, or process lines.

Managerial Practice 3.1 showed processes at work within Netscape's engineering and management information systems functions, using the Internet in the process to design and update its products. Duke Power, our chapter opener, is another example. Its customer operations unit had five core processes that cut across boundaries between its four regions. The calculate and collect revenues process is most closely aligned with accounting, the deliver products and services process with operations, the develop market strategies process and maintain customers process with marketing, and the provide reliability and integrity process with quality assurance (see Chapter 5, "Process Performance and Quality"). Cross-functional coordination paid off in better performance. This payoff came in part by reorganizing to create process owners but also by creating a new collaborative style of management. The process owners and regional vice presidents acted as partners rather than rivals.

CHAPTER HIGHLIGHTS

- Process design deals with *how* to make a service or product. Many choices must be made concerning the best mix of human resources, equipment, outside services, and materials.

- Process design is of strategic importance and is closely linked to a firm's long-term success. It involves the selection of inputs, resources, work flows, and methods used to produce services and goods.

- Process decisions are made in the following circumstances: gaps exist between competitive priorities and competitive capabilities, a new service or product is to be offered or an existing one modified, quality improvements are necessary, competitive priorities are changed, demand levels change, current performance is inadequate, competitor capabilities change, new technology is available, or cost or availability of inputs changes.

- The five major process design decisions are process structure, customer involvement, vertical integration, resource flexibility, and degree of capital intensity. *Process structure* is how processes are designed relative to the kinds of resources needed, how resources are partitioned between processes, and key process characteristics. *Customer involvement* is the extent to which customers are allowed to interact with the process. *Vertical integration* involves decisions about whether to outsource certain processes. *Resource flexibility* is the degree to which equipment is general purpose and individuals can handle a wide variety of work. *Capital intensity* is the mix of capital equipment and human skills in a process.

- Customer contact varies along five dimensions: physical contact, what is processed, contact intensity, personal attention, and method of delivery.

- For service processes, the customer-contact matrix brings together the degree of customer contact, the service design package, and process characteristics. Three key process characteristics are process complexity, divergence, and flow. Service processes can be revised so that they are improperly positioned in the matrix.

- Three basic process structures in services are the front office, the hybrid office, and the back office. A front office has high customer contact; it matches up with a process with high complexity, high divergence, and jumbled flows. A back office has low customer contact; it matches up with a process with low complexity, low divergence, and line flows.

- For manufacturing processes, the product-process matrix brings together volume, the product design, and process characteristics. Basic process choices are project, job, batch, line, and continuous. Manufacturing processes can be revised if they are poorly positioned in the matrix.

- Customer involvement has potential disadvantages, such as less efficiency with a more complex and divergent process.

Time and location must also be considered. Potential advantages are improved competitive capabilities, particularly in light of emerging technologies.

- Fixed automation maximizes efficiency for high-volume products with long life cycles, but flexible (programmable) automation provides economies of scope. Flexibility is gained and setups are minimized because the machines can be reprogrammed to follow new instructions.

- The process design should achieve strategic fit. For service processes, the starting point is with customer contact. If it is high, the normal choice is a front office, high customer involvement, and more resource flexibility. Vertical integration and capital intensity depend on volume, and in the case of vertical integration, whether the front office is for external customers. For manufacturing processes, the starting point is volume. High volume means a line or continuous process, less customer involvement, more vertical integration, less resource flexibility, and more capital intensity.

- Job design and process decisions are related, particularly in determining the extent of specialization versus enlargement.

- Focusing operations avoids confusion among competitive priorities, process choices, and technologies. Focused facilities, plants within plants, and cells are ways to achieve focus in both service and manufacturing operations.

- Process reengineering uses cross-functional teams to rethink the design of critical processes. Process improvement is a systematic analysis of activities and flows that occurs continuously.

STUDENT CD-ROM AND INTERNET RESOURCES

The Student CD-ROM and the Companion Website at **www.prenhall.com/krajewski** contain many tools, activities, and resources designed for this chapter. The following items are recommended to enhance your skills and improve your understanding of the material in this chapter.

STUDENT CD-ROM RESOURCES

➤ **PowerPoint Slides.** View this comprehensive set of slides customized for this chapter's concepts and techniques.
➤ **Video Clips.** See the two video clips customized for this chapter to learn more about process choice.
➤ **OM Explorer Tutors.** OM Explorer contains one tutor spreadsheet that will help you learn about break-even analysis applied to equipment selection. See Chapter 3 in the OM Explorer menu. See also the Tutor exercise on break-even analysis for equipment selection.
➤ **Written Tours.** See how the management of Lower Florida Keys Health System builds resource flexibility into its highly divergent emergency room processes, whereas the management at Chaparral Steel opts for considerable automation of its high-volume Bar Mill process.

➤ **Supplement K.** "Computer-Integrated Manufacturing." Read about how complex computer systems can give manufacturers more resource flexibility in some of their processes.

INTERNET RESOURCES

➤ **Self-Study Quizzes.** See the compendium of true or false, multiple choice, and essay questions that give feedback on how well you have mastered the concepts in this chapter.
➤ **In the News.** See the articles that apply to this chapter.
➤ **Internet Exercises.** Try out the links covering outsourcing at Ryder and continuous process improvement at Freightliner. Other exercises are available on additional aspects of process design.
➤ **Virtual Tours.** Check out three different process choices at the Kokomo Opalescent Glass Factory, Buck Knives, and a sugar-processing facility. Also see the "Web Links to Company Facility Tours" for additional tours of company facilities.

KEY TERMS

active contact 94	focused factories 120	outsourcing 109
assemble-to-order strategy 104	forward integration 109	passive contact 94
automation 114	front office 96	plants within plants (PWPs) 119
back office 97	hybrid office 97	process choice 100
backward integration 109	ISO 14001 91	process complexity 95
batch process 102	job enlargement 119	process design 89
capital intensity 91	job enrichment 119	process divergence 96
cell 120	job process 102	process flow 96
continuous process 103	job rotation 119	process improvement 122
customer contact 92	line flow 96	process structure 91
customer involvement 91	line process 103	project process 101
economies of scope 116	make-or-buy decisions 109	reengineering 120
fixed automation 114	make-to-order strategy 104	resource flexibility 91
flexible (or programmable)	make-to-stock strategy 103	specialization 118
automation 114	mass production 104	vertical integration 91
flexible workforce 112	network companies 112	virtual corporation 112

DISCUSSION QUESTIONS

1. To give utilities an incentive to spend money on new pollution-control technology, the EPA proposes that flue gas emission limits be changed to require slightly cleaner stacks than the older technology is capable of producing. To comply, some utilities will install the new technology. Some will not. Utilities that reduce emissions below the new requirements will receive "credits," which they can sell to utilities that choose not to install the pollution-control technology. These utilities can then continue business as usual, so long as they have purchased enough credits to account for the extra pollution they create. The price of the credits will be determined by the free market.

   Form sides and discuss the ethical, environmental, and political issues and trade-offs associated with this proposition.

2. The Dewpoint Chemical Company is deciding where to locate a fertilizer plant near the Rio Grande. What are the ethical, environmental, and political issues and trade-offs associated with locating a fertilizer plant on the north bank versus the south bank of the Rio Grande?

PROBLEMS

An icon in the margin next to a problem identifies the software that can be helpful, but is not mandatory. The software is available on the Student CD-ROM that is packaged with every new copy of the textbook. Problems 3 and 4 apply break-even analysis (discussed in Supplement A, "Decision Making") to process design.

1. Rate a service process with which you are familiar on each of the five dimensions of customer contact. Use a seven-point scale, where 1 = very low and 7 = very high. Explain your ratings, and then calculate a combined score for the overall customer contact. Did you use equal weights in calculating the combined score? Why or why not? Where is your process positioned on the customer-contact matrix? Is it properly aligned? Why or why not?

2. Select one of the three processes shown in the Big Picture and video for King Soopers (bread, pastry, or customer cake). What kind of transformation process, process choice, and inventory strategy are involved? Is the process properly aligned? Explain.

3. OM Explorer Dr. Gulakowicz is an orthodontist. She estimates that adding two new chairs will increase fixed costs by $150,000, including the annual equivalent cost of the capital investment and the salary of one more technician. Each new patient is expected to bring in $3,000 per year in additional revenue, with variable costs estimated at $1,000 per patient. The two new chairs will allow her to expand her practice by as many as 200 patients annually. How many patients would have to be added for the new process to break even?

4. OM Explorer Two different manufacturing processes are being considered for making a new product. The first process is less capital-intensive, with fixed costs of only $50,000 per year and variable costs of $700 per unit. The second process has fixed costs of $400,000 but varible costs of only $200 per unit.

   a. What is the break-even quantity, beyond which the second process becomes more attractive than the first?

   b. If the expected annual sales for the product is 800 units, which process would you choose?

CASE   CUSTOM MOLDS, INC.

Custom Molds, Inc. manufactures custom-designed molds for plastic parts and produces custom-made plastic connectors for the electronics industry. Located in Tucson, Arizona, Custom Molds was founded by the father and son team of Tom and Mason Miller in 1987. Tom Miller, a mechanical engineer, had more than 20 years of experience in the connector industry with AMP, Inc., a large multinational producer of electronic connectors. Mason Miller had graduated from the University of Arizona in 1986 with joint degrees in chemistry and chemical engineering.

The company was originally formed to provide manufacturers of electronic connectors with a source of high-quality, custom-designed molds for producing plastic parts. The market consisted mainly of the product design and development divisions of those manufacturers. Custom Molds worked closely with each customer to design and develop molds to be used in the customer's product development processes. Thus, virtually every mold had to meet exacting standards and was somewhat unique. Orders for multiple molds would arrive when customers moved from the design and pilot-run stage of development to large-scale production of newly designed parts.

As the years went by, Custom Molds' reputation grew as a designer and fabricator of precision molds. Building on this reputation, the Millers decided to expand into the limited manufacture of plastic parts. Ingredient-mixing facilities and injection-molding equipment were added, and by the mid-1990s Custom Molds developed its reputation to include being a supplier of high-quality plastic parts. Because of limited capacity, the company concentrated its sales efforts on supplying parts that were used in limited quantities for research and development efforts and in preproduction pilot runs.

PRODUCTION PROCESSES

By 1997, operations at Custom Molds involved two distinct processes: one for fabricating molds and one for producing plastic parts. Although different, in many instances these two processes were linked, as when a customer would have Custom Molds both fabricate a mold and produce the necessary parts to support the customer's research and design efforts. All fabrication and production operations were housed in a single facility. The layout was characteristic of a typical job shop, with like processes and similar equipment grouped in various places in the plant. Figure 3.13 shows a schematic of the plant floor. Multiple pieces of various types of high-precision machinery, including milling, turning, cutting, and drilling equipment, were located in the mold-fabrication area.

Fabricating molds is a skill-oriented, craftsman-driven process. When an order is received, a design team, comprising a design engineer and one of 13 master machinists, reviews the design specifications. Working closely with the customer, the team establishes the final specifications for the mold and gives them to the master machinist for fabrication. It is always the same machinist who was assigned to the design team. At

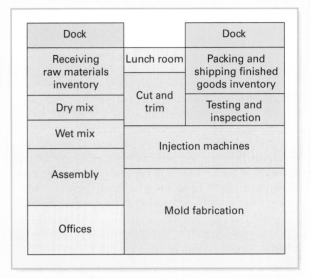

FIGURE 3.13   **Plant Layout**

the same time, the purchasing department is given a copy of the design specifications, from which it orders the appropriate raw materials and special tooling. The time needed to receive the ordered materials is usually three to four weeks. When the materials are received for a particular mold, the plant master scheduler reviews the workload of the assigned master machinist and schedules the mold for fabrication.

Fabricating a mold takes from two to four weeks, depending on the amount of work the machinist already has scheduled. The fabrication process itself takes only three to five days. Upon completion, the mold is sent to the testing and inspection area, where it is used to produce a small number of parts on one of the injection molding machines. If the parts meet the design specifications established by the design team, the mold is passed on to be cleaned and polished. It is then packed and shipped to the customer. One day is spent inspecting and testing the mold and a second day cleaning, polishing, packing, and shipping it to the customer. If the parts made by the mold do not meet design specifications, the mold is returned to the master machinist for retooling and the process starts over. Currently, Custom Molds has a published lead time of nine weeks for delivery of custom-fabricated molds.

The manufacturing process for plastic parts is somewhat different from that for mold fabrication. An order for parts may be received in conjunction with an order for a mold to be fabricated. In instances where Custom Molds has previously fabricated the mold and maintains it in inventory, an order may be just for parts. If the mold is already available, the order is reviewed by a design engineer, who verifies the part and raw material specifications. If the design engineer has any questions concerning the specifications, the customer is contacted and any revisions to specifications are mutually worked out and agreed upon.

Upon acceptance of the part and raw material specifications, raw material orders are placed and production is scheduled for the order. Chemicals and compounds that support plastic-parts manufacturing are typically ordered and received within one week. Upon receipt, the compounds are first dry-mixed and blended to achieve the correct composition. Then the mixture is wet-mixed to the desired consistency (called *slurry*) for injection into molding machines. When ready, the slurry is transferred to the injection molding area by an overhead pipeline and deposited in holding tanks adjacent to the injection machines. The entire mixing process takes only one day.

When the slurry is staged and ready, the proper molds are secured—from inventory or from the clean and polish operation if new molds were fabricated for the order—and the parts are manufactured. Although different parts require different temperature and pressure settings, the time to produce a part is relatively constant. Custom Molds has the capacity to produce 5,000 parts per day in the injection-molding department; historically, however, the lead time for handling orders in this department has averaged one week. Upon completion of molding, the parts are taken to the cut and trim operation, where they are disconnected and leftover flashing is removed. After being inspected, the parts may be taken to assembly or transferred to the packing and shipping area for shipment to the customer. If assembly of the final parts is not required, the parts can be on their way to the customer two days after being molded.

Sometimes the final product requires some assembly. Typically, this entails attaching metal leads to plastic connectors. If assembly is necessary, an additional three days is needed before the order can be shipped. Custom Molds is currently quoting a three-week lead time for parts not requiring fabricated molds.

THE CHANGING ENVIRONMENT

In early 2003, Tom and Mason Miller began to realize that the electronics industry they supplied, along with their own business, was changing. Electronics manufacturers had traditionally used vertical integration into component-parts manufacturing to reduce costs and ensure a timely supply of parts. By the 1990s, this trend had changed. Manufacturers were developing strategic partnerships with parts suppliers to ensure the timely delivery of high-quality, cost-effective parts. This approach allowed funds to be diverted to other uses that could provide a larger return on investment.

The impact on Custom Molds could be seen in sales figures over the past three years. The sales mix was changing. Although the number of orders per year for mold fabrication remained virtually constant, orders for multiple molds were declining, as shown in the following table:

| | NUMBER OF ORDERS | | |
Order Size	Molds 2000	Molds 2001	Molds 2002
1	80	74	72
2	60	70	75
3	40	51	55
4	5	6	5
5	3	5	4
6	4	8	5
7	2	0	1
8	10	6	4
9	11	8	5
10	15	10	5
Total orders	230	238	231

The reverse was true for plastic parts, for which the number of orders per year had declined but for which the order sizes were becoming larger, as illustrated in the following table:

| | NUMBER OF ORDERS | | |
Order Size	Parts 2000	Parts 2001	Parts 2002
50	100	93	70
100	70	72	65
150	40	30	35
200	36	34	38
250	25	27	25
500	10	12	14
750	1	3	5
1,000	2	2	8
3,000	1	4	9
5,000	1	3	8
Total orders	286	280	277

During this same period, Custom Molds began having delivery problems. Customers were complaining that parts orders were taking four to five weeks instead of the stated three weeks and that the delays were disrupting production schedules. When asked about the situation, the master scheduler said that determining when a particular order could be promised for delivery was very difficult. Bottlenecks were occurring during the production process, but where or when they would occur could not be predicted. They always seemed to be moving from one operation to another.

Tom Miller thought that he had excess labor capacity in the mold-fabrication area. So, to help push through those orders that were behind schedule, he assigned one of the master machinists the job of identifying and expediting those late orders. However, that tactic did not seem to help much. Complaints about late deliveries were still being received. To add to the problems, two orders had been returned recently because of the number of defective parts. The Millers knew that something had to be done. The question was "What?"

QUESTIONS

1. What are the major issues facing Tom and Mason Miller?
2. What are the competitive priorities for Custom Molds' processes and the changing nature of the industry?
3. What alternatives might the Millers pursue? What key factors should they consider as they evaluate these alternatives?

Source: This case was prepared by Dr. Brooke Saladin, Wake Forest University, as a basis for classroom discussion.

SELECTED REFERENCES

Alster, Norm. "What Flexible Workers Can Do." *Fortune* (February 13, 1989), pp. 62–66.

Bowen, John, and Robert C. Ford. "Managing Service Organizations: Does Having a 'Thing' Make a Difference?" *Journal of Management*, vol. 28, no. 3 (2002), pp. 447–469.

Brown, Donna. "Outsourcing: How Corporations Take Their Business Elsewhere." *Management Review* (February 1992), pp. 16–19.

Byrne, John A. "The Virtual Corporation." *Business Week* (February 8, 1993), pp. 98–102.

Collier, David A. *Service Management: The Automation of Services*. Reston, VA: Reston, 1985.

Collier, D. A., and Meyer, S. "An Empirical Comparison of Service Matrices." *International Journal of Operations and Production Management*, vol. 20, no. 5–6 (2000), pp. 705–729.

Collier, D. A., and Meyer, S. "A Positioning Matrix for Services." *International Journal of Operations and Production Management*, vol. 18, no. 12 (1998), pp. 1223–1244.

Collins, Jim. *Good to Great: Why Some Companies Make the Leap . . . and Others Don't*. New York: HarperCollins, 2001.

Cook, David P., Chon-Huat Goh, and Chen H. Chung. "Service Typologies: A State of the Art Survey." *Production and Operations Management*, vol. 8, no. 3 (1999), pp. 318–338.

Dixon, J. Robb, Peter Arnold, Janelle Heineke, Jay S. Kim, and Paul Mulligan. "Business Process Reengineering: Improving in New Strategic Directions." *California Management Review* (Summer 1994), pp. 1–17.

Ellis, Christian M., and Lea A. P. Tonkin. "Mature Teams Rewards and the High-Performance Workplace: Change and Opportunity." *Target*, vol. 11, no. 6 (1995).

Fitzsimmons, James A, and Mona J. Fitzsimmons. *Service Management: Operations, Strategy, and Information Technology*. New York: McGraw-Hill, 1998.

Gephart, Martha A. "The Road to High Performance." *Training and Development*, vol. 49 (June 1995), pp. 29–44.

Goldhar, J. D., and Mariann Jelinek. "Plan for Economies of Scope." *Harvard Business Review* (November–December 1983), pp. 141–148.

Grover, Varun, and Manoj K. Malhotra, P. S. "Business Process Reengineering: A Tutorial on the Concept, Evolution, Method, Technology and Application." *Journal of Operations Management*, vol. 15, no. 3 (1997), pp. 194–213.

Hall, Gene, Jim Rosenthal, and Judy Wade. "How to Make Reengineering Really Work." *Harvard Business Review* (November–December 1993), pp. 119–131.

Hammer, M. "Reengineering Work: Don't Automate, Obliterate." *Harvard Business Review*, vol. 68, no. 4 (1990), pp. 104–112.

Hammer, M. *Beyond Reengineering*. New York: Harper Business, 1996.

Hammer, Michael, and James Champy. *Reengineering the Corporation: A Manifesto for Business Revolution*. New York: HarperBusiness, 1993.

Harrigan, K. R. *Strategies for Vertical Integration*. Lexington, MA: D. C. Heath, 1983.

Katzenbach, Jon R., and Douglas K. Smith. "The Discipline of Teams." *Harvard Business Review* (March–April 1993), pp. 111–120.

Kellogg, Deborah L., and Winter Nie. "A Framework for Strategic Service Management." *Journal of Operations Management*, vol. 13, no. 4 (1995), pp. 323–337.

Klassen, R. D., and C. P. McLauglin. "The Impact of Environmental Management on Firm Performance." *Management Science*, vol. 42, no. 8 (1990), pp. 1100–1214.

Leibs, Scott. "A Little Help from Their Friends." *Industry Week*, February 2, 1998.

Lovelock, Christopher H., and George S. Yip. "Developing Global Strategies for Service Businesses." *California Management Review*, vol. 38, no. 2 (1996), pp. 64–86.

"Making It by the Billions." *The Boston Globe*, August 9, 1998.

Makowe, J. *Beyond the Bottom Line*. New York: Simon & Schuster, 1994.

Malhotra, Manoj K., and Larry P. Ritzman. "Resource Flexibility Issues in Multistage Manufacturing." *Decision Sciences*, vol. 21, no. 4 (1990), pp. 673–690.

Melnyk, S. A., Robert P. Sroufe, and Roger Calantone. "Assessing the Impact of Environmental Management Systems on Corporate and Environmental Performance." *Journal of Operations Management*, vol. 21, no. 3 (2003), pp. 329–351.

Mersha, Tigineh. "Enhancing the Customer Contact Model." *Journal of Operations Management*, vol. 9, no. 3 (1990), pp. 391–405.

Metters, Richard, Kathryn King-Metters, and Madeleine Pullman. *Successful Service Operations Management*. Mason, OH: South-Western, 2003.

Narasimhan, Ram, and Jayanth Jayaram. "Reengineering Service Operations: A Longitudinal Case Study." *Journal of Operations Management*, vol. 17, no. 1 (1998), pp. 7–22.

Normann, Richard, and Rafael Ramirez. "From Value Chain to Value Constellation: Designing Interactive Strategy." *Harvard Business Review* (July–August 1993), pp. 65–77.

Port, Otis. "The Responsive Factory." *Business Week*, Enterprise 1993, pp. 48–51.

Porter, Michael E. "The Competitive Advantage of Nations." *Harvard Business Review* (March–April 1990), pp. 73–93.

Prahalad, C. K., and Gary Hamel. "The Core Competence of the Corporation." *Harvard Business Review*, vol. 90, no. 3 (1990), pp. 79–91.

"Process, Process, Process." *Planning Review* (special issue), vol. 22, no. 3 (1993), pp. 1–56.

Quinn, J. B. "The Productivity Paradox Is False: Information Technology Improves Services Performance." *Advances in Services Marketing and Management*, vol. 5 (1996), pp. 71–84.

"Reengineering: The Hot New Managing Tool." *Fortune* (August 23, 1994), pp. 41–48.

Roth, Aleda V., and Marjolijn van der Velde. *The Future of Retail Banking Delivery Systems*. Rolling Meadows, Ill.: Bank Administration Institute, 1988.

Safizadeh, M. Hossen, Larry P. Ritzman, and Debasish Mallick. "Revisiting Alternative Theoretical Paradigms in Manufacturing." *Production and Operations Management*, vol. 9, no. 2 (2000), pp. 111–127.

Schmenner, Roger W. *Service Operations Management*. Englewood Cliffs, NJ: Prentice Hall, 1998.

Shostack, G. Lynn. "Service Positioning Through Structural Change." *Journal of Marketing*, vol. 51, no. 1 (1987), pp. 34–43.

Silvestro, R. L. Fitzgerald, R. Johnston, and Chris Voss. "Toward a Classification of Service Processes." *International Journal of Service Industry Management*, vol. 3 (1992), pp. 62–75.

Skinner, Wickham. "Operations Technology: Blind Spot in Strategic Management." *Interfaces*, vol. 14 (January–February 1984), pp. 116–125.

"Somebody Else's Problem." *The Wall Street Journal*, November 15, 1999.

Tonkin, Lea A. P. "Outsourcing: A Tool, Not a Solution." *Target*, vol. 15, no. 2 (1999), pp. 44–45.

Wemmerlöv, U. "A Taxonomy for Service Processes and Its Implications for System Design." *International Journal of Service Industry Management*, vol. 1, no. 1 (1990), pp. 20–40.

Wheelwright, Steven C., and Robert H. Hayes. "Competing Through Manufacturing." *Harvard Business Review* (January–February 1985), pp. 99–109.

"When the Going Gets Rough, Boeing Gets Touchy-Feely." *Business Week* (January 17, 1994), pp. 65–67.

Process Analysis

LEARNING GOALS *After reading this chapter, you should be able to . . .*

IDENTIFY OR DEFINE

1. flowcharts, service blueprints, and process charts.
2. metrics for process evaluation.
3. Pareto charts, cause-and-effect diagrams, and process simulation.

DESCRIBE OR EXPLAIN

4. a systematic way to analyze processes.
5. benchmarking to create better processes.
6. keys for effective process management.

OMGEO

When a Hong Kong investment manager buys stock from a broker in Tokyo, chances are the deal passes through Omgeo (www. omgeo.com). Omgeo's name (pronounced OM-gee-oh) combines the Latin word *omni*, meaning "in all ways or places" with the Greek word *geo*, meaning "earth." Omgeo is the leading provider of complete global trade management services. In 2002, it processed over one million trades per day and serviced 6,000 broker–dealers, custodian banks, and investment managers in 40 countries. The Depository Trust & Clearing Corporation (DTCC) and Thomson Financial created Omgeo in 2000 as a new joint venture. DTCC (www.dtcc.com) is an institution set up and owned by financial services firms to settle their trades. A unit of Thomson Financial (www.thomson.com) originally marketed this posttrade, presettlement service in the late 1980s as a money saver for institutional investors. The dozens of scribbled faxes, telexes, and phone calls made for the typical trade cost from $10 to $12, but Thomson's process allowed it to charge only 20 cents to $1 per trade—and investment managers essentially got the

service free. Its behind-the-scenes service was an improvement over previous processes for making trades, but Figure 4.1 shows that it was still a tangle of communications between brokers (such as Goldman Sachs), big investors (such as Royal London Asset Management), and banks (such as the Deutsche Bank) every time a trade was placed. It took three to five days to settle a trade in the United States, when money and securities officially changed hands.

But every process can be improved, in part by critically analyzing the current process for improvement possibilities. Omgeo made a major improvement over the old process, with the goal being able to complete the whole process in potentially just one day. A key factor to the new process was the Internet and new information technology solutions. With the revised process, steps 1 through 3 were done the same way. However, steps 4 through 9 were replaced by entering all of the information into a central database that the broker, investment manager, and custodian banks all have access to in real time (e.g., central matching). The revised process ended the need to tack message after message onto a cumbersome file. It cut

some of the grinding monotony of processing trades and saved employees time. It also saved vast amounts of money by reducing human errors. Royal London Asset Management, currently live on Omgeo Central Trade Manager (CTM), is able to move a trade through to step 8 (settlement notification) in 3 hours. Before, when using Omgeo's old process, it took 20 hours to move one trade that far along the trade cycle. Now, they have 17 extra hours to identify and fix trade errors and get them done on the same day.

Central trade matching information technology replaces many of the steps that were performed sequentially. With central matching, the allocations from the institutional investment manager and trade details from the broker are submitted into a central engine, and the details of the trades are automatically compared to assure that there are no errors. The CTM engine provides straight-through processing of the work flow in back-office operations.

Sources: Healy, Beth. "One Day, Not Three: A Push to Trade Faster." *The Boston Globe* (July 19, 2000); Pressroom at **www.omgeo.com**, September, 2002.

The five main process design decisions covered in Chapter 3 represent broad, strategic issues. The changes leading to the creation of Omgeo involved processes with considerable customer contact, and they reflect strategies favoring more vertical integration and automation. The strategy for change was definitely in the "process reengineering" rather than "process improvement" category. The process was so totally revamped that a new company was formed to implement it, and information technology was a primary enabler of the new process.

Here our attention turns to analyzing a process in detail and determining exactly how each step in a process will be performed. Process analysis is needed for both process reengineering and process improvement. It also closely connects with monitoring process performance over time (see Chapter 5, "Process Performance and Quality"). We begin with a systematic approach for analyzing a process that identifies opportunities for improvement, documents the current process, evaluates the process to spot performance gaps, redesigns the process to eliminate the gaps, and implements the desired changes. The goal is continual improvement and never being satisfied with current performance levels. Three supporting techniques—flowcharts, service blueprints, and process charts—can give good insights into the current process and proposed changes.

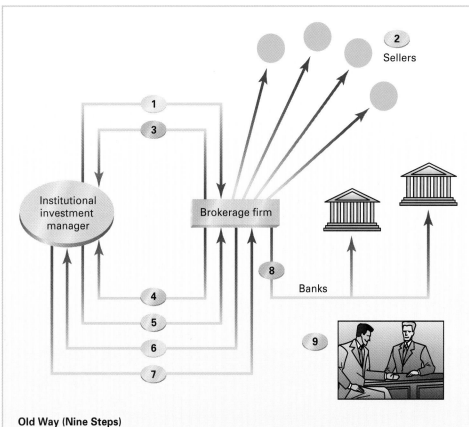

FIGURE 4.1

Old Way and New Way with Omgeo

Old Way (Nine Steps)
1. Institutional investment manager calls brokerage firm to buy 1 million shares of IBM.
2. Broker calls or e-mails five or six clients to find sellers of IBM shares.
3. Broker calls back the investment manager, says he has sellers offering 1 million shares at $104. The two agree to buy the shares at that price, locking in the sale.
4. Broker sends electronic notice of execution to the investment manager's trading desk.
5. Investment manager e-mails back allocation details, saying which portfolios the stock should be sent to.
6. Broker takes the allocation notice, adds commissions, fees, and taxes to the trade price; sends confirmation back to investment manager.
7. Investment manager affirms that message.
8. Broker sends message to custodian banks of all parties involved in the trade.
9. DTCC actually "settles" trade, overseeing the transfer of money and shares.

New Way (Four Steps)
Steps 1, 2, and 3 are the same.
4. After all parties agree to the terms of the trade, the information is entered into a central database that broker, investment manager, and custodian banks all have access to in real time.

Data analysis tools, such as checklists, bar charts, Pareto charts, and cause-and-effect diagrams allow the analyst to go from problem symptoms to root causes. Simulation is a more advanced technique that can evaluate dynamically the process's performance. We conclude with some of the keys to managing processes effectively, assuring that changes are implemented and an infrastructure is set for making continual process improvements. Processes must be managed to gain a competitive advantage.

As you read about process analysis, think about why it is important to the various departments and functions across the organization, such as . . .

➤ **accounting,** which manages key support processes and provides information to evaluate process performance.
➤ **finance,** which assures that sizeable deployments of existing capital to process redesigns will yield good returns that are aligned with the firm's value strategy.

Omgeo employees have instigated a number of customer surveys on a worldwide level and throughout the financial community. One result of Omgeo's surveys is that they have devised a better way to communicate Omgeo's product release schedule. Here, employees discuss this aspect of their overall straight-through processing operation.

➤ **human resources,** which connects the firm's processes with the people who perform them by hiring and training people with the necessary skills and knowledge and by setting job goals.

➤ **management information systems,** which offers information technology solutions that often can improve processes and monitor their performance.

➤ **marketing,** which helps manage core processes, such as new service/product development and the external customer interface, and connects with the order fulfillment process.

➤ **operations,** which designs and manages the order fulfillment process for both service providers and manufacturers and seeks seamless connections with other core and supporting processes in the firm.

A SYSTEMATIC APPROACH

How can processes be analyzed, understood, and redesigned?

Processes are perhaps the least understood and managed aspect of a business. No matter how talented and motivated people are, a firm cannot gain competitive advantage with faulty processes. Work gets done somehow. Just as Samuel Clemens (Mark Twain) said of the Mississippi River, a process just keeps rolling on. However, there is one big difference. Most processes can be improved if someone thinks of the way and it is effectively implemented. Long-term success comes from managers and employees who understand their businesses in detail. All too often, highly publicized efforts that seem to offer quick-fix solutions fail to live up to expectations over the long haul, be they programs for conceptualizing a business vision, conducting culture-transformation campaigns, or providing leadership training. Within the field of operations management, there have been many important innovations over the last several decades, such as work-simplification or better-methods programs, statistical process control, optimization techniques, statistical forecasting techniques, material requirements planning, flexible automation, lean manufacturing, total quality management, reengineering, Six-Sigma programs, enterprise resource planning, and e-commerce. We cover all of these important approaches in the following chapters because they can add significant customer value to a process. However, they are best viewed as just part of a total system for the effective design and management of work processes, rather than cure-alls that work in all situations. Here we cover a basic, yet very important ingredient in this total approach—a systematic approach to continually improving processes. Processes will either adapt to the changing needs of its customers or cease to exist. Processes must be adaptive, both reactively and proactively, if the firm is to be a *learning organization* that nimbly adapts to changing conditions and improves itself.

Figure 4.2 shows a six-step blueprint for process analysis. **Process analysis** is the documentation and detailed understanding of how work is performed and how it can

process analysis The documentation and detailed understanding of how work is performed and how it can be redesigned.

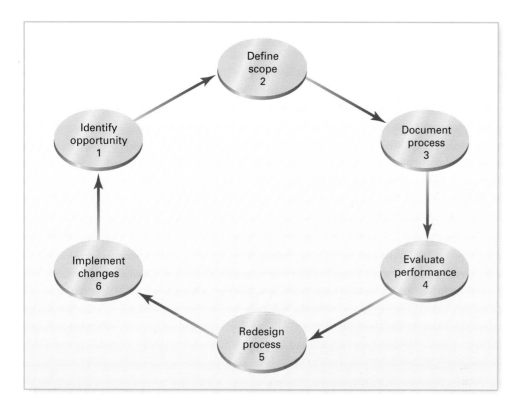

FIGURE 4.2

A Systematic Approach to Process Analysis

be redesigned. The intent is to continually improve processes, judging their performance on multiple measures. Process analysis begins with identifying a new opportunity for improvement and ends with implementing a revised process. The last step goes back to the first step, thus creating a cycle of continual improvement.

IDENTIFY OPPORTUNITIES

In order to identify opportunities, particular attention must be given to the four core processes: supplier relationship, new service/product development, order fulfillment, and customer relationship. Each of these processes, and the subprocesses nested within them, are involved in delivering value to the external customers. Are the customers currently satisfied with the services or products that they receive, or is there room for improvement? How about internal customers? Customer satisfaction must be monitored periodically, either with a formal measurement system or with informal checks or studies. Managers sometimes develop an inventory of their core and support processes, providing a guide for what processes need scrutiny.

Another way to identify opportunities is by looking at the strategic issues. Are there gaps between a process's competitive priorities and its current competitive capabilities? Do multiple measures of cost, top quality, quality consistency, delivery speed, and on-time delivery meet or exceed expectations? Is there a good *strategic fit* in the process? If the process provides a service, does its position on the customer-contact matrix (see Figure 3.3) seem appropriate? How does the degree of customer contact match up with process structure, customer involvement, vertical integration, resource flexibility, and capital intensity (see Figure 3.11)? Similar questions should be asked for manufacturing processes regarding the strategic fit between process choice, volume, and customization. A "no" answer points to a possible improvement opportunity.

Another way to identify opportunities is from the employees who actually perform the process or from its internal suppliers or internal customers. They should be encouraged to bring forward their ideas to managers, staff specialists (such as industrial engineers), or perhaps pass on their ideas through a formal suggestions system. A **suggestion system** is a voluntary system by which employees submit their ideas on process improvements. Usually, a specialist follows through to evaluate the proposals, makes sure worthy suggestions are implemented, and provides feedback to the persons

suggestion system A voluntary system by which employees submit their ideas on process improvements.

originating the suggestions. Sometimes the person or team making a good suggestion are rewarded, either monetarily or by special recognition.

DEFINE SCOPE

The second step in process analysis establishes the boundaries of the process to be analyzed. Is it a broadly defined process that stretches across the whole organization, involving many steps and many employees? Is it instead a more narrowly bracketed nested subprocess that is just part of one person's job? The process's scope can be too narrow or too broad. Limiting it to just a small subprocess can overlook important breakthroughs in the process design. A broadly defined process that outstrips the resources available, sometimes called trying to "boil the ocean," is doomed because it will increase frustration without producing any results.

The resources that management assigns to improving or reengineering the process should match the process's scope. For a small nested process involving only one employee, perhaps the employee is asked to redesign the process herself. Staff specialists can sometimes provide her with time standards, current performance measures, information technology options, purchasing costs, wage and overhead rates, and the like. For a large reengineering project that deals with a major core process, managers typically establish one or more teams (see Chapter 8, "Planning and Managing Projects"). A **design team** consists of knowledgeable, team-oriented individuals who work at one or more steps in the process, do the process analysis, and are motivated to make the necessary changes. Other resources may be internal or external *facilitators* who do not work on the process, but are full-time specialists. Facilitators know process analysis methodology, and they can guide and train the design team. If the process is extensive and cuts across several departmental lines, perhaps a *steering team* is also formed. It consists of several managers from the various departments, headed by a project manager, who oversees the process analysis.

design team A group of knowledgeable, team-oriented individuals who work at one or more steps in the process, do the process analysis, and are motivated to make the necessary changes.

DOCUMENT PROCESS

Once the process scope is established, the analyst should document it. This documentation begins by developing a list of the process's inputs, suppliers (internal or external), outputs, and customers (internal or external). This information then can be shown as a diagram, with a more detailed breakdown given in a table.

Documentation next moves to understanding the different steps performed in the process, using one or more of the diagrams, tables, and charts described later in this chapter. When breaking down the process into the steps performed, the analyst notes the degrees and types of customer contact, process complexity, and process divergence along the various steps in the process. Attention is also given to what steps are visible to the customer and to where in the process work is handed off from one department to the next.

EVALUATE PERFORMANCE

It is important to have performance measures that can evaluate a process, getting clues on how it can be improved. **Metrics** are performance measures that are established for the process and the steps within it. A good place to start is with the competitive priorities, but they need to be made specific. The analyst creates multiple measures of quality, customer satisfaction, throughput time, cost, errors, safety, environmental measures, on-time delivery, flexibility, and the like.

For example, Omgeo (see the chapter opener) gave particular emphasis to the competitive priorities of low-cost operations, consistent quality, and delivery speed. Specific metrics dealing only with delivery speed for the posttrade process include

metrics Performance measures that are established for a process and the steps within it.

1. average response times to messages, such as trade entry, allocations, confirmations, and affirmations/rejections;
2. average time from receipt of trades to market close;
3. regional confirmation generation time compared against market and security type averages.

After identifying metrics, information is collected on how the process is currently performing on each one. Measurement can be as simple as making a reasoned guess, asking a knowledgeable person, or simply taking notes while observing the process. More extensive studies could involve collecting data for several weeks, consulting cost accounting data, or checking data recorded in information systems. In addition, techniques for analyzing wait times and delays (see Supplement B, "Simulation" and Supplement C, "Waiting Lines") can provide important information. Other valuable techniques include work sampling, time studies, and learning curve analysis (see Supplement G, "Learning Curve Analysis" and Supplement H, "Measuring Output Rates" on the Student CD-ROM). Chapter 5, "Process Performance and Quality," goes one step further, presenting ways to measure and track process performance over time.

REDESIGN PROCESS

Documenting a process is not a value-added activity, unless the process is better understood and then improved. A careful analysis of the process and its performance on the selected metrics should uncover *disconnects*, or gaps, between actual and desired performance. Performance gaps can be caused by illogical, missing, or extraneous steps. They can be caused by a poor selection of metrics that reinforce the silo mentality of individual departments when the process spans across several departments. A *silo mentality* means that a department focuses on its own tasks without understanding the role and processes of departments outside its own organizational boundaries. The analyst or design team should dig deep to find the root causes of such performance gaps.

Having identified the performance gaps, it is necessary to shift from analytical thinking to creative thinking, generating a long list of ideas for possible improvements. A questioning and critical attitude is needed to spot breakthroughs. These ideas are then sifted through and analyzed. Ideas that are justifiable, where benefits outweigh costs, are reflected in a new process design. The new design should be documented "as proposed." Combining the new process design with the documentation of the current process gives the analysts intelligible before and after pictures. The new documentation should make clear how the revised process will work and the performance that is expected for the various metrics.

When do you shift from analytical to creative thinking?

IMPLEMENT CHANGES

Once the new process is approved, it must be implemented. Implementation is more than developing a plan and carrying it out. Many processes have been redesigned effectively, but never get implemented. People often resist change, arguing that "we have always done it that way" or "we tried that before." Widespread participation in process analysis is essential, not only because of the work involved but also because it builds commitment. It is much easier to implement something that is partly your own idea. In addition, special expertise may be needed, such as for developing software. New jobs and skills may be needed, involving training and investments in new technology. Implementation brings to life the steps needed to bring the redesigned process online. Implementation of any new process or redesigned process is a project, often with complex relationships between activities and significant allocations of resources. Management or the steering committee must make sure that the implementation project goes according to schedule (see Chapter 8, "Planning and Managing Projects"). Management support and encouragement are essential, particularly if the extent of change is large.

Managerial Practice 4.1 shows how design teams aggressively improved manufacturing processes at the Freudenberg–NOK plant. The approach applies equally well to service processes.

DOCUMENTING THE PROCESS

Three techniques are effective for documenting and evaluating processes: (1) flowcharts, (2) service blueprints, and (3) process charts. They allow you to lift the lid and peer inside at how an organization does its work. You can see how a process operates,

How can processes be documented?

MANAGERIAL PRACTICE 4.1

PROCESS ANALYSIS AT WORK

Process analysis helps the Freudenberg–NOK (www. freudenberg-nok.com) autoparts factory in Ligonier, Indiana, become more competitive. This plant makes 123,000 parts a month for Ford Motor Company's Aerostar vans and Ranger pickup trucks. A key element of the approach is quick-hit teams of plant workers, managers, and people from other functional areas who come up with ways to improve operations in different sections of the plant. These teams make *kaizen*, a Japanese term for continuous improvement, pay off through productivity improvements. Other elements are worker cooperation (bolstered by a no-layoff pledge), strong management backing, measurable goals and results, continuity between teams so that unfinished "to-do" lists are passed on to the next team, and a bias for immediate action on many fronts, rather than costly, technological big fixes. The multiple, small changes add up. For example, a typical 12-member team worked between Monday and Thursday to propose and test ways to improve the engine-mount line of the factory. After a training session, the team members grabbed their stopwatches

and white lab coats and headed for the shop floor. They analyzed the current process, talked with the operators, and brainstormed ideas for improvement. Subteams were formed to attack different problems simultaneously. On Thursday, the team presented its results to plant management. It had cut work-in-process inventory by 50 percent and improved productivity by some 20 percent. It had also increased capacity somewhat, although it fell short of its 20 percent goal. In one year, 40 such teams move through this factory. "What we are doing today is what any company will have to do to survive a decade from now," says the chief executive of Freudenberg–NOK, a $420 million German–Japanese joint venture with 14 U.S. plants that make rubber seals, vibration dampers, and engine mounts. He expects kaizen teams to help the company more than double sales by 2000 without adding people or factory space.

Source: "Improving the Soul of an Old Machine," *Business Week* (October 25, 1993).

at any level of detail, and how well it is performing. Trying to create one of these charts might even reveal that there is no established process at all, with work getting done in a haphazard way. These techniques show the current mosaic of the process. It may not be a pretty picture, but it is how work actually gets done. They lend themselves to finding performance gaps, to brainstorming for process improvements, and to documenting the *after* look of a redesigned process.

FLOWCHARTS

flowchart A diagram that traces the flow of information, customers, equipment, or materials through the various steps of a process.

A **flowchart** traces the flow of information, customers, equipment, or materials through the various steps of a process. Flowcharts are also known as flow diagrams, process maps, relationship maps, or blueprints. Flowcharts have no precise format and typically are drawn with boxes (with a brief description of the step inside), and with lines and arrows to show sequencing. The rectangle ($\square$) shape is the usual choice for a box, although other shapes ($\bigcirc$, $\bigcirc$, $\bigcirc$, ∇, or $\diagup\!\square$) can differentiate between different types of steps (operation, delay, storage, inspection, and the like). Alternately, colors and shading can call attention to different types of steps, such as those particularly

A consultant discusses the proposal for a new organizational development program with clients during a follow-up meeting. The use of flowcharts can help in understanding this step as just one part of the overall process of the sales process for a consulting company.

high on process complexity or on process divergence. Divergence is also communicated when an outgoing arrow from a step splits into two or more arrows that lead to different boxes. While many representations are acceptable, there must be an understanding on the conventions used, whether established by past practice, given as a key somewhere in the flowchart, or described in the text that accompanies the flowchart. It is also important to communicate *what* (information, customer order, customer, materials, or the like) is tracked through the process.

Microsoft PowerPoint offers many different formatting choices if it is used to flowchart (see the Flowchart submenu under AutoShapes). Other powerful software packages for flowcharting and drawing many other diagrams (such as organization charts and decision trees) are SmartDraw (**www.smartdraw.com**), Microsoft Visio (**www.microsoft.com/office/visio**), and Micrografx (**www.adainc.com/software**). Often, free downloads are available at such sites on a trail basis. For example, a link is provided on your CD-ROM to SmartDraw.

Flowcharts can be created for several levels in the organization. For example, at the strategic level, they could show the core processes and their linkages, such as in Figure 1.3. At this level, the flowcharts would not have much detail; however, they would give a bird's eye view of the overall business. Just identifying what is a core process is often helpful. Let us now turn to the process level, where we get into the details of the process being analyzed, as bracketed by the process's scope. Figure 4.3, drawn with SmartDraw, shows such a process. This process is complex, because it consists of many steps that have subprocesses nested within them. Rather than representing everything in one flowchart, Figure 4.3 presents a more aggregate view of the whole process. It describes the sales process for a consulting firm that specializes in organizational development and corporate education programs. Four different departments (accounting, consulting, marketing, and sales) interact with the external customer (client). The process goes through three main phases: generating business leads, client agreement and service delivery, and billing and collection.

Nested processes can then be created for steps that were more aggregated. For example, Figure 4.4 flowcharts a nested process within the client agreement and service delivery step in Figure 4.3. Figure 4.4 brings out more details, such as invoicing the customer for 50 percent of the total estimated cost of the service before the service is delivered, and then putting together a final invoice for the remainder after the service is finished.

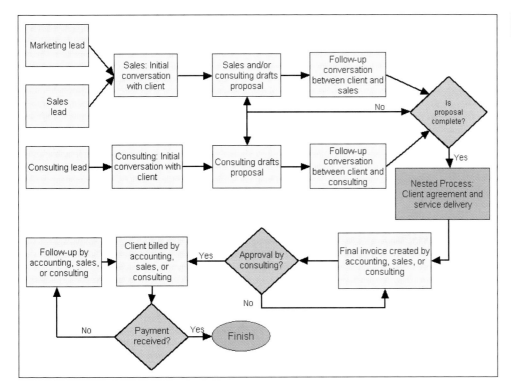

FIGURE 4.3

Flowchart of the Sales Process for a Consulting Company (Created with SmartDraw)

FIGURE 4.4

Flowchart of the Nested Subprocess of Client Agreement and Service Delivery (Created with SmartDraw)

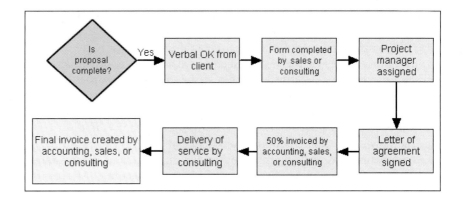

Figure 4.3 illustrates one other feature. The diamond shape (◇) represents a yes/no decision or outcome, such as the results of an inspection or a recognition of different kinds of customer requirements. In Figure 4.3, it represents three yes/no decision points: (1) whether the proposal is complete, (2) whether consulting approves the invoice, and (3) whether payment is received. These yes/no decision points are more likely to appear when a process is high in divergence.

Figure 4.5, which was created with PowerPoint, shows still another format that is most appropriate when the process spans across several department boundaries. The flowchart illustrates the order-filling process of a manufacturing company. The process starts when an order is generated by a customer and ends when the payment is received by the company. All functions contributing to this process are included in the flow-

FIGURE 4.5   **Flowchart of the Process Showing Handoffs Between Departments (Created with PowerPoint)**

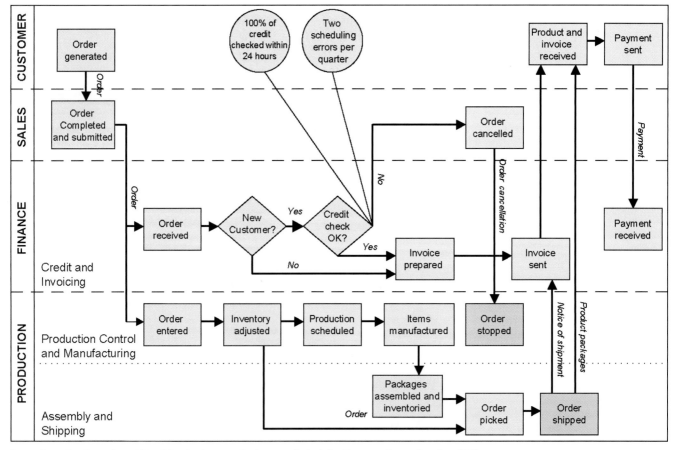

Source: Rummler, Geary A., and Alan P. Brache. *Improving Performance,* 2nd ed. San Francisco: Jossey-Bass, Inc., 1995.

chart. The rows represent different departments or functional areas, and the steps are placed in the department row where they are performed. This approach points out the *handoffs* from one department to another department, because the outgoing arrow from a step goes to another row. Other ways to show handoffs, such as using special arrows, are possible. Handoffs are where cross-functional coordination is at particular risk due to the silo mentality of focusing just on one's own department. It is here where misunderstandings, backlogs, and errors are more likely. In this way, flowcharts allow the process analyst and managers to look at the horizontal organization, rather than the vertical organization and departmental boundaries implied by an organizational chart. Flowcharts show how organizations produce their outputs though a myriad of cross-functional work processes, allowing the design team to see all the critical interfaces between functions and departments.

Most work flows across traditional departmental boundaries. Consider a nested manufacturing process that produces a handhold fitting. This fitting goes into a pressure vessel that, in turn, is part of a utility boiler that power plants use to generate the electricity that we use everyday. The handhold fitting must withstand pressure when the boiler is operating. However, it must be removable to allow workers to reach inside the pressure vessel for maintenance or initial installation. The handhold fitting might begin in the forge shop of the manufacturing plant, where it is heated and then extruded into the correct approximate shape, much like a barbell with a handhold fitting at each end, with a bar connected to them. These then are moved to another department, the machine shop, where they are sawed in half to create two fittings. The fittings are then moved to another section of the machine shop, where threads are put on the bar. After cleaning and inspection, the part moves to still another department where it is assembled into the final product. Thus, for one small component, such as a handhold fitting, the component moves from one department to the next (from the forge shop to the machine shop to the assembly area) in the manufacturing plant.

SERVICE BLUEPRINTS

A good design for service processes depends first and foremost on the type and amount of customer contact. Recognizing this principle, a **service blueprint** is a special flowchart of a service process that shows which of its steps have high customer contact. Figure 4.6 illustrates one type of service blueprint for an automobile repair process. Its

> **service blueprint** A special flowchart of a service process that shows which of its steps have high customer contact.

FIGURE 4.6   Service Blueprint for Automobile Repair (Created with SmartDraw)

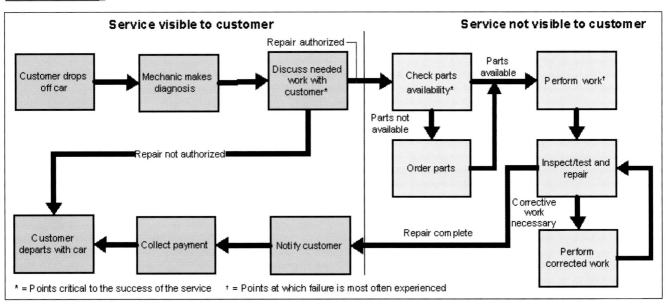

Source: J. L. Heskett and R. Anthony, "Note on Service Mapping," Harvard Business School Publishing, No. 693–065, Winter 1993/1994, p. 5.

special feature is the line of visibility that identifies which steps are visible to the customer (and thus more of a front-office process) and those that are not visible (the back office). This particular service blueprint also identifies points critical to the success of the service and points where failure most often occurs.

Figure 4.7 is a more complex service blueprint. It shows the steps taken by a consulting company that specializes in inventory appraisals and inventory liquidations. Its external customers are large banks that make asset-based loans. The banks' customers, in turn, are companies seeking a loan based on the value of their assets (including inventories). Figure 4.7 describes the consulting company's current inventory evaluation and appraisal process. This process is part of two core processes: the customer relationship process and the order fulfillment process (see Chapter 1, "Operations As a Competitive Weapon"). Drawn with SmartDraw, it not only shows the steps in its current inventory evaluation and appraisal process, but also which steps are visible to its external customers (the banks) and its customers' customers (the company seeking a loan). The steps visible to the banks are in *blue* and partitioned with the vertical dashed lines. The steps visible to the company seeking a loan are in *yellow,* partitioned off by the top vertical dashed line and the horizontal dashed lines. The steps in gray are not visible to external customers.

The process begins with a call from a bank seeking this service by the consulting company. There are three main steps in the overall process.

1. The bank contacts to the consulting company and they agree on the contract.
2. The consulting company performs the inventory evaluation on the site of the company seeking a loan from the bank.
3. The consulting company prepares the final report and presents it to the bank.

Of course, visibility is just one aspect of customer contact, and it may not adequately capture how actively the customer is involved or how much personal attention is required. A service blueprint can use colors, shading, or box shapes, instead of the line of visibility, to show the extent and type of customer contact. Another approach to service blueprinting is to tag each step with a number, and then have an accompanying table that describes in detail the customer contact for the numbered steps.

FIGURE 4.7   **Service Blueprint of Consulting Company's Inventory Appraisal Process (Created with SmartDraw)**

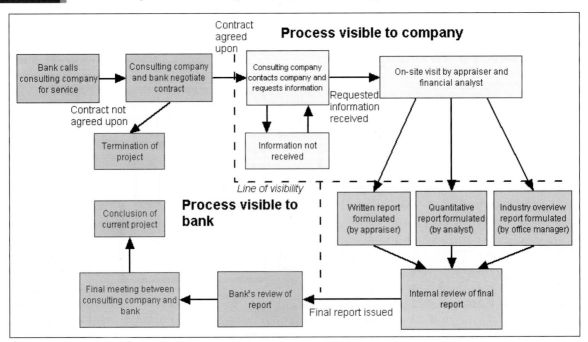

PROCESS CHARTS

A process chart drills down to the job level for an individual person, a team, or a focused nested process. It concentrates in more detail on a smaller number of steps than does a flowchart. A **process chart** is an organized way of documenting all of the activities performed by person, by a machine, at a workstation, with a customer, or on materials. For our purposes, we group these activities into five categories.

> **process chart** An organized way of documenting all of the activities performed by a person, by a machine, at a workstation, with a customer, or on materials.

- *Operation.* Changes, creates, or adds something. Drilling a hole and serving a customer are examples of operations.
- *Transportation.* Moves the study's subject from one place to another (sometimes called *materials handling*). The subject can be a person, a material, a tool, or a piece of equipment. A customer walking from one end of a counter to the other, a crane hoisting a steel beam to a location, and a conveyor carrying a partially completed product from one workstation to the next are examples of transportation.
- *Inspection.* Checks or verifies something but does not change it. Getting customer feedback, checking for blemishes on a surface, weighing a product, and taking a temperature reading are examples of inspections.
- *Delay.* Occurs when the subject is held up awaiting further action. Time spent waiting for a server, time spent waiting for materials or equipment; cleanup time; and time that workers, machines, or workstations are idle because there is nothing for them to do are examples of delays.
- *Storage.* Occurs when something is put away until a later time. Supplies unloaded and placed in a storeroom as inventory, equipment put away after use, and papers put in a file cabinet are examples of storage.

Depending on the situation, other categories can be used. For example, subcontracting for outside services might be a category, or temporary storage and permanent storage might be two separate categories. Choosing the right category for each activity requires taking the perspective of the subject charted. A delay for the equipment could be inspection or transportation for the operator.

To complete a chart for a new process, the analyst must identify each step performed. If the process is an existing one, the analyst can actually observe the steps, categorizing each step according to the subject being studied. The analyst then records the distance traveled and the time taken to perform each step. After recording all the activities and steps, the analyst summarizes the number of steps, times, and distances data. Figure 4.8 shows a process chart prepared using OM Explorer's *Process Chart* solver. It is for a patient with a twisted ankle being treated at a hospital. The process begins at the entrance and ends with the patient exiting after picking up the prescription.

After a process is charted, the analyst sometimes estimates the annual cost of the entire process. It becomes a benchmark against which other methods for performing the process can be evaluated. Annual labor cost can be estimated by finding the product of (1) time in hours to perform the process each time, (2) variable costs per hour, and (3) number of times the process is performed each year, or

$$\begin{pmatrix} \text{Annual} \\ \text{labor cost} \end{pmatrix} = \begin{pmatrix} \text{Time to perform} \\ \text{the process in hours} \end{pmatrix} \begin{pmatrix} \text{Variable costs} \\ \text{per hour} \end{pmatrix} \begin{pmatrix} \text{Number of times process} \\ \text{performed per year} \end{pmatrix}$$

In the case of the patient in Figure 4.8, this conversion would not be necessary, with total patient time being sufficient. What is being tracked is the patient's time, not the time and costs of the service providers.

You can design your own process chart spreadsheets to bring out issues that are particularly important for the process being analyzed, such as categories for customer contact, process divergence, and the like. Performance measures other than time and distance traveled, such as error rates, also might be tracked as appropriate.

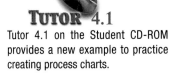

TUTOR 4.1

Tutor 4.1 on the Student CD-ROM provides a new example to practice creating process charts.

FIGURE 4.8

Process Chart for Emergency Room Admission (Created with OM Explorer)

Process:	Emergency room admission
Subject:	Ankle injury patient
Beginning:	Enter emergency room
Ending:	Leave hospital

	Insert Step
	Append Step
	Remove Step

Summary

Activity	Number of Steps	Time (min)	Distance (ft)
Operation ●	5	23.00	
Transport ➡	9	11.00	815
Inspect ■	2	8.00	
Delay ▶	3	8.00	
Store ▼	--	--	

Step No.	Time (min)	Distance (ft)	●	➡	■	▶	▼	Step Description
1	0.50	15.0			X			Enter emergency room, approach patient window
2	10.00		X					Sit down and fill out patient history
3	0.75	40.0			X			Nurse escorts patient to ER triage room
4	3.00					X		Nurse inspects injury
5	0.75	40.0			X			Return to waiting room
6	1.00						X	Wait for available bed
7	1.00	60.0			X			Go to ER bed
8	4.00						X	Wait for doctor
9	5.00				X			Doctor inspects injury and questions patient
10	2.00	200.0			X			Nurse takes patient to radiology
11	3.00		X					Technician x-rays patient
12	2.00	200.0			X			Return to bed in ER
13	3.00					X		Wait for doctor to return
14	2.00		X					Doctor provides diagnosis and advice
15	1.00	60.0			X			Return to emergency entrance area
16	4.00		X					Check out
17	2.00	180.0			X			Walk to pharmacy
18	4.00		X					Pick up prescription
19	1.00	20.0			X			Leave the building

⦿ EVALUATING PERFORMANCE

Metrics and performance information must be gathered to finish the documentation of a process (see step 4 in Figure 4.2). Metrics can be displayed in various ways. Sometimes they can be added directly on the flowchart or process chart. Figure 4.5 is an example of adding metrics with circled entries. They establish the goals for the credit check: (1) all credit checks completed within 24 hours and (2) no more than two scheduling errors per quarter. When the number of metrics gets unwieldy, another approach is to create a supporting table that goes with the chart. Its rows are the steps in the flowchart, service blueprint, or process charts. The columns are the current performance, goals, and performance gaps for various metrics.

DATA ANALYSIS TOOLS

There are various ways to get a fuller understanding on a particular metric. Here we present six such methods: (1) checklists, (2) histograms and bar charts, (3) Pareto charts, (4) scatter diagrams, (5) cause-and-effect diagrams, and (6) graphs. These tools help the analyst identify the root causes behind a particular performance gap. Many of them were developed initially with a focus on quality issues, but they apply equally well to the full range of performance measures.

CHECKLISTS Data collection through the use of a checklist is often the first step in the analysis of a metric. A **checklist** is a form used to record the frequency of occurrence of certain service or product characteristics related to performance. The characteristics may be measurable on a continuous scale (e.g., weight, customer satisfaction on a 1-to-7 scale, unit cost, scrap loss percentage, time, or length) or on a yes-or-no basis (e.g., customer complaint, posting error, paint discoloration, or inattentive servers).

checklist A form used to record the frequency of occurrence of certain service or product characteristics related to performance.

HISTOGRAMS AND BAR CHARTS. The data from a checklist often can be presented succinctly and clearly with histograms or bar charts. A **histogram** summarizes data measured on a continuous scale, showing the frequency distribution of some quality characteristic (in statistical terms, the central tendency and dispersion of the data). Often the mean of the data is indicated on the histogram. A **bar chart** is a series of bars representing the frequency of occurrence of data characteristics measured on a yes-or-no basis. The bar height indicates the number of times a particular quality characteristic was observed.

histogram A summarization of data measured on a continuous scale, showing the frequency distribution of some quality characteristic (in statistical terms, the central tendency and dispersion of the data).

bar chart A series of bars representing the frequency of occurrence of data characteristics measured on a yes-or-no basis.

PARETO CHARTS. When managers discover several process problems that need to be addressed, they have to decide which should be attacked first. Vilfredo Pareto, a nineteenth-century Italian scientist whose statistical work focused on inequalities in data, proposed that most of an "activity" is caused by relatively few of its factors. In a restaurant quality problem, the activity could be customer complaints and the factor could be "discourteous waiter." For a manufacturer, the activity could be product defects and a factor could be "missing part." Pareto's concept, called the 80–20 rule, is that 80 percent of the activity is caused by 20 percent of the factors. By concentrating on the 20 percent of the factors (the "vital few"), managers can attack 80 percent of the quality problems. Of course, the exact percentages vary with each situation, but inevitably there are relatively few factors causing most of the performance shortfalls.

The few vital factors can be identified with a **Pareto chart**, a bar chart on which the factors are plotted in decreasing order of frequency along the horizontal axis. The chart has two vertical axes, the one on the left showing frequency (as in a histogram) and the one on the right showing the cumulative percentage of frequency. The cumulative frequency curve identifies the few vital factors that warrant immediate managerial attention.

Pareto chart A bar chart on which the factors are plotted in decreasing order of frequency along the horizontal axis.

Pareto Chart for a Restaurant

EXAMPLE 4.1

The manager of a neighborhood restaurant is concerned about the smaller numbers of customers patronizing his eatery. The number of complaints have been rising, and he would like some means of finding out what issues to address and of presenting the findings in a way his employees can understand.

SOLUTION

The manager surveyed his customers over several weeks and collected the following data:

COMPLAINT	FREQUENCY
Discourteous server	12
Slow service	42
Cold dinner	5
Cramped tables	20
Smoky air	10

Figure 4.9 is a bar chart and Figure 4.10 is a Pareto chart, both created with OM Explorer's *Bar, Pareto, and Line Charts* solver. They present the data in a way that shows which complaints

ACTIVE MODEL 4.1
Active Model 4.1 on the Student CD-ROM provides additional insights on this Pareto chart example and its extensions.

TUTOR 4.2
Tutor 4.2 on the Student CD-ROM provides a new example on creating Pareto charts.

are the more prevalent (the vital few). These charts are set up for a quality metric, but you can reformat them for other "yes-or-no" metrics. Just click on "unprotect sheet" under the spreadsheet's Tools menu, and then make your revisions. Another approach is to create your own spreadsheets from scratch. More advanced software with point-and-click interfaces include Minitab (**www.minitab.com/index.htm**), SAS (**www.sas.com/rnd/app/qc.html**), and Microsoft Visio (**www.microsoft.com/office/visio**).

FIGURE 4.9

Bar Chart

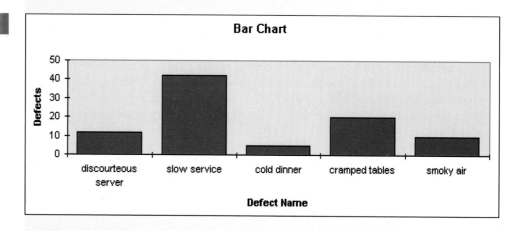

FIGURE 4.10

Pareto Chart

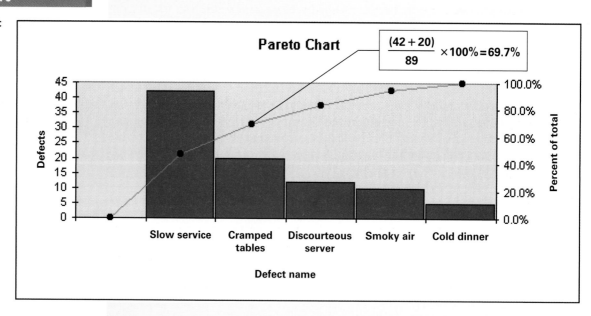

DECISION POINT It was clear to the manager and all employees which complaints, if rectified, would cover most of the quality problems in the restaurant. First, slow service will be addressed by training the existing staff, adding another server, and improving the food preparation process. Removing some decorative, but otherwise unnecessary, furniture from the dining area and spacing the tables better will solve the problem with cramped tables. The Pareto chart shows that these two problems, if rectified, will account for almost 70 percent of the complaints.

SCATTER DIAGRAMS. Sometimes managers suspect but are not sure that a certain factor is causing a particular quality problem. A **scatter diagram**, which is a plot of two variables showing whether they are related, can be used to verify or negate the suspicion. Each point on the scatter diagram represents one data observation. For example, the manager of a castings shop may suspect that casting defects are a function of the

scatter diagram A plot of two variables showing whether they are related.

diameter of the casting. A scatter diagram could be constructed by plotting the number of defective castings found for each diameter of casting produced. After the diagram is completed, any relationship between diameter and number of defects could be observed.

CAUSE-AND-EFFECT DIAGRAMS. An important aspect of process analysis is linking each metric to the inputs, methods, and process steps that build a particular attribute into the service or product. One way to identify a design problem that needs to be corrected is to develop a **cause-and-effect diagram** that relates a key performance problem to its potential causes. First developed by Kaoru Ishikawa, the diagram helps management trace disconnects directly to the operations involved. Operations that have no bearing on a particular problem are not shown on the diagram.

cause-and-effect diagram
A diagram that relates a key performance problem to its potential causes.

The cause-and-effect diagram sometimes is called a *fishbone diagram*. The main performance gap is labeled as the fish's "head," the major categories of potential causes as structural "bones," and the likely specific causes as "ribs." When constructing and using a cause-and-effect diagram, an analyst identifies all the major categories of potential causes for the problem. For example, these might be personnel, machines, materials, and processes. For each major category, the analyst lists all the likely causes of the performance gap. For example, under personnel might be listed "lack of training," "poor communication," and "absenteeism." Brainstorming helps the analyst identify and properly classify all suspected causes. The analyst then systematically investigates the causes listed on the diagram for each major category, updating the chart as new causes become apparent. The process of constructing a cause-and-effect diagram calls management and worker attention to the primary factors affecting product or service quality. Example 4.2 demonstrates the use of a cause-and-effect diagram by an airline.

Analysis of Flight Departure Delays   **EXAMPLE 4.2**

The operations manager for Checker Board Airlines at Port Columbus International Airport noticed an increase in the number of delayed flight departures.

SOLUTION

To analyze all the possible causes of that problem, he constructed a cause-and-effect diagram, shown in Figure 4.11. The main problem, delayed flight departures, is the "head" of the diagram. He brainstormed all possible causes with his staff, and together they identified several major categories: equipment, personnel, materials, procedures, and "other factors," which are beyond managerial control. Several suspected causes were identified for each major category.

DECISION POINT The operations manager, having a good understanding of the process, suspected that most of the flight delays were caused by problems with materials. Consequently, he had food service, fueling, and baggage-handling operations examined. He learned that there were not enough tow trucks for the baggage-transfer operations and that planes were delayed waiting for baggage from connecting flights.

GRAPHS. Graphs represent data in a variety of pictorial formats, such as line charts and pie charts. *Line charts* represent data sequentially with data points connected by line segments to highlight trends in the data. Line charts are used in control charts (see Chapter 5, "Process Performance and Quality") and forecasting (see Chapter 13, "Forecasting"). Pie charts represent process factors as slices of a pie; the size of each slice is in proportion to the number of occurrences of the factor. Pie charts are useful for showing data from a group of factors that can be represented as percentages totaling 100 percent.

graphs Representations of data in a variety of pictorial forms, such as line charts and pie charts.

FIGURE 4.11   **Cause-and-Effect Diagram for Flight Departure Delays**

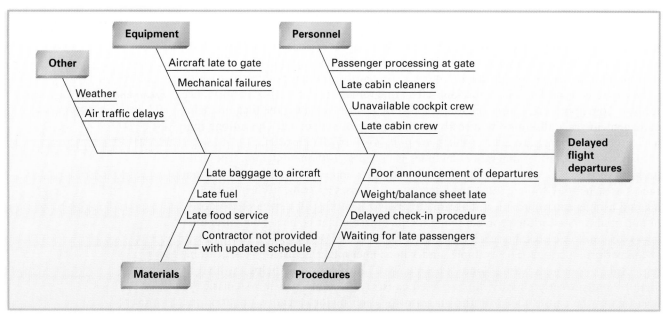

DATA SNOOPING

Each of the tools for improving quality may be used independently, but their power is greatest when they are used together. In solving a quality problem, managers often must act as detectives, sifting data to clarify the issues involved and deducing the causes. We call this process *data snooping*. Example 4.3 demonstrates how the tools for improving quality can be used for data snooping.

EXAMPLE 4.3   Identifying Causes of Poor Headliner Quality

The Wellington Fiber Board Company produces headliners, the fiberglass components that form the inner roof of passenger cars. Management wanted to identify which defects were most prevalent and to find the cause.

SOLUTION

Figure 4.12 shows the sequential application of several tools for improving quality.

Step 1. A checklist of different types of defects was constructed from last month's production records.

Step 2. A Pareto chart prepared from the checklist data indicated that broken fiber board accounted for 72 percent of the quality defects. The manager decided to dig further into the problem of broken fiber board.

Step 3. A cause-and-effect diagram for broken fiber board identified several potential causes for the problem. The one strongly suspected by the manager was employee training.

Step 4. The manager reorganized the production reports into a bar chart according to shift because the personnel on the three shifts had varied amounts of experience.

DECISION POINT   The bar chart indicated that the second shift, with the least experienced workforce, had most of the defects. Further investigation revealed that workers were not using proper procedures for stacking the fiber boards after the press operation, causing

FIGURE 4.12   **Application of the Tools for Improving Quality**

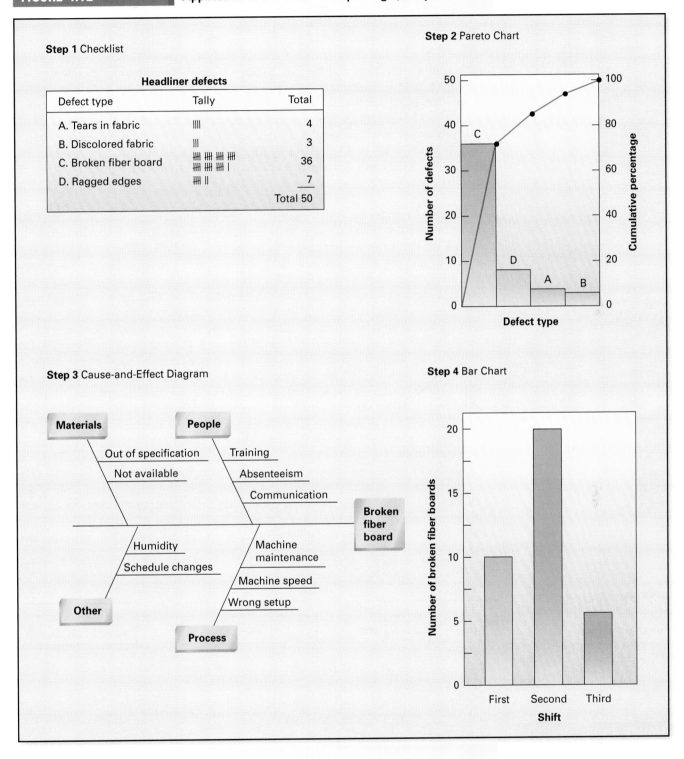

Step 1 Checklist

Headliner defects

Defect type	Tally	Total
A. Tears in fabric	IIII	4
B. Discolored fabric	III	3
C. Broken fiber board	IIII IIII IIII IIII IIII IIII IIII I	36
D. Ragged edges	IIII II	7
		Total 50

Step 2 Pareto Chart

Step 3 Cause-and-Effect Diagram

Step 4 Bar Chart

cracking and chipping. The manager initiated additional training sessions focused on board handling after the press operation. Although the second shift was not responsible for all the defects, finding the source of many defects enabled the manager to improve the quality of her operations.

process simulation   The act of reproducing the behavior of a process, using a model that describes each step of the process.

SIMULATION

A simulation model goes one step further than possible with the data analysis tools, because it can show how the process performs dynamically over time. **Process simulation** is the act of reproducing the behavior of a process, using a model that describes each step of the process. Once the process is modeled, the analyst can make changes in the model to measure the impact on certain metrics, such as response time, waiting lines, resource utilization, and the like. To learn more about how simulation works, see Supplement B, "Simulation," which follows this chapter. More advanced capabilities are possible using software packages such as SimQuick (**www.nd.edu/~dhartvig/ simquick/top.htm**), Extend (**www.imaginethatinc.com**), SIMPROCESS (**www.caciasl. com**), ProModel (**www.promodel.com**), and Witness (**www.lanner.com/corporate**). Here we illustrate process simulation with the SimQuick software (provided on the Student CD-ROM) and Extend (which might be packaged with your book on an option basis).

SIMQUICK. Consider the following process within a small bank: Customers enter the bank, get into a single line, are served by a teller, and finally leave the bank. Currently, this bank has one teller working from 9 A.M. to 11 A.M. Management is concerned that the wait in line seems to be too long. Therefore, they are considering two process improvement ideas: adding an additional teller during these hours or installing a new automated check-reading machine that can help the single teller serve customers more quickly.

A first step in simulating this process with SimQuick is to draw a flowchart of the process using SimQuick's building blocks. Figure 4.13(a) shows that the one-teller bank (both the original and the variation with a check-reading machine) can be modeled with four building blocks: an entrance (modeling the arrival of customers at the bank), a buffer (modeling the waiting line), a work station (modeling the teller), and a final buffer (modeling served customers). The two-teller variation can be modeled with five building blocks, as shown in Figure 4.13(b).

Information describing each building block is entered into SimQuick tables. In these models there are three key pieces of information to enter: when people arrive at the door, how long the teller takes to serve a customer, and the maximum length of the line. The first two pieces of information are described by statistical distributions. Each of the three models is run 30 times, simulating the hours from 9 A.M. to 11 A.M. Statistics are collected by SimQuick and summarized. Figure 4.14 shows the key results for the model of the original one-teller process as output by SimQuick (many other statistics are collected, but they are not displayed here).

FIGURE 4.13a

Flowchart of Bank (Modeled with SimQuick)
(a) Flowchart for one-teller bank

FIGURE 4.13b

(b) Flowchart for two-teller bank

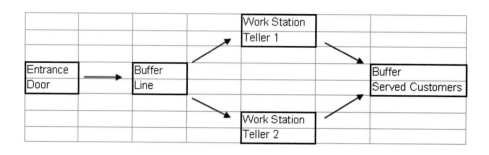

Element Types	Element Names	Statistics	Overall Means
Entrance(s)	Door	Service level	0.90
Buffer(s)	Line	Mean inventory	4.47
		Mean cycle time	11.04

FIGURE 4.14

Simulation Results of Bank (Modeled with SimQuick)

The numbers shown are averages across the 30 simulations. The service level for Door tells us that 90 percent of the simulated customers who arrived at the bank were able to get into Line (hence 10 percent found line full and immediately left). The mean inventory for Line tells us that there were, on average, 4.47 simulated customers standing in line. The mean cycle time tells us that our simulated customers waited an average of 11.04 minutes in line.

When we run the model with two tellers, we find that the service level increases to 100 percent, the mean inventory in Line decreases to 0.37 customers, and the mean cycle time drops to 0.71 minutes. All dramatic improvements. When we run the one-teller model with the faster check-reading machine we find that the service level is 97 percent, the mean inventory in Line is 2.89 customers, and the mean cycle time is 6.21 minutes. These statistics, together with cost information, should help management select the best process. All the details for this model (as well as many others) appear in the book *SimQuick: Process Simulation with Excel*, which is included, along with the SimQuick software, on the Student CD-ROM that comes with this text.

EXTEND. Figure 4.15(a) shows a simulation model created with the Extend simulation package. The analyst creates the steps in the process model much like with a flowchart. This particular model is for a process that manufactures stained-glass panels. The products are collections of cut pieces of colored and textured glass

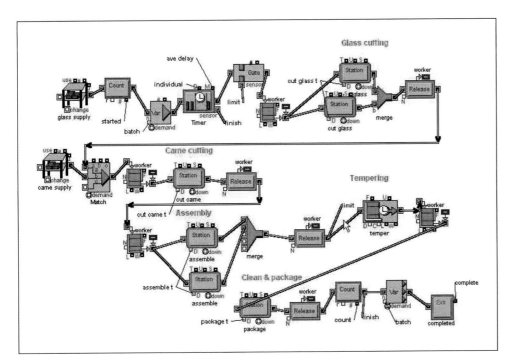

FIGURE 4.15a

Artistic Glass Works (Modeled with Extend)
(a) Simulation model

arranged in attractive patterns and held in place by strips of lead or brass "came." The five basic steps in the batch process are glass cutting, came cutting, assembly, tempering, and clean and package. Other modules (such as count, merge, and release) are shown in Figure 4.15(a) to correctly model the process using the Extend modeling conventions. Input data on process times, workforce size, batch size, and the capacities must also be entered for each step. Having formulated the model, the process can be simulated with the click of a mouse on your personal computer to gather information on the different metrics of interest. Figure 4.15(b) shows some of the simulated output over the history of a year (or 2,000 work hours) for total output (green line) and work-in-process (WIP) inventory (blue line). The simulation shows that the current process will produce 492 panels for the whole year, and the average WIP will be about 16.5 units. Figure 4.15(c) reports on the *throughput time*, the time elapsing between the start of a unit's production and its completion. It shows metrics for both the individual throughput times (red dots) and the cumulative average. The average throughput time will average just less than 62 hours per batch of panels produced. If management seeks better performance on these metrics, it should explore ways of improving the process by simulating revised models that reflect different improvement ideas.

FIGURE 4.15b

Artistic Glass Works (Modeled with Extend)
(b) Production and WIP inventory

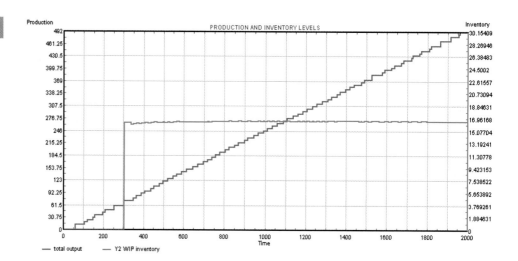

FIGURE 4.15c

(c) Throughput time

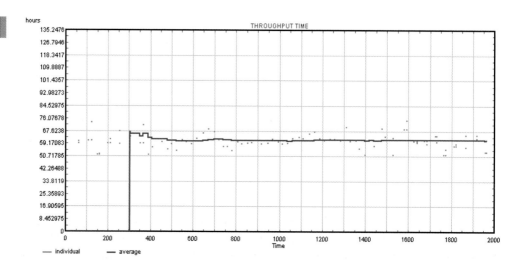

REDESIGNING THE PROCESS

A doctor pinpoints an illness after a thorough diagnosis of the patient, and then the doctor recommends treatments based on the diagnosis; so it is with processes. After a process is documented, metrics data collected, and disconnects identified, the process analyst or design team puts together a set of changes that will make the process better. This is the step where the people directly involved in the process are brought in, which is particularly important in order to get their good ideas and inputs.

A QUESTIONING ATTITUDE

Sometimes ideas for reengineering or improving a process become apparent after documenting the process and carefully examining the areas of substandard performance, handoffs between departments, and steps where customer contact is high. Example 4.3 illustrates how such documentation pointed to a better way of handling the fiber boards through better training. In other cases, the better solution is less evident from such analysis. Ideas can be uncovered (because there is always a better way) by asking six questions about each step in the process, and the process as a whole.

1. *What* is being done?
2. *When* is it being done?
3. *Who* is doing it?
4. *Where* is it being done?
5. *How* is it being done?
6. *How well* does it do on the various metrics of importance?

Answers to these questions are challenged by asking still another series of questions that bring value to this step. *Why* is the process even being done? *Why* is it being done where it is being done? *Why* is it being done when it is being done? Such questioning often leads to creative answers and breakthroughs in process design.

Creativity can also be stimulated by having a **brainstorming session,** a time when a group of people, knowledgeable on the process and its disconnects, propose ideas for change in a rapid-fire manner. It is sometimes called the "get crazy" phase of process analysis when ideas are sought that invert existing rules and examine totally new approaches. A facilitator records the group's ideas on a flipchart, so that all can see. Participants are discouraged from evaluating any of the ideas generated during the brainstorming session. The purpose is to encourage creativity and to get as large a list of ideas as possible, no matter how far-fetched the ideas may seem at the time. The creative part of the mind is emphasized, rather than the judicial part. The participating group need not be limited to the design team. Others can be included, as long as they have seen or heard the process documentation. Often, a presentation of the process documentation is given as a prelude to the brainstorming session.

After the brainstorming session is over, the design team moves into the "get real" phase where they evaluate analytically the different ideas. It identifies the changes that give the best payoffs into the process redesign. The redesign could involve issues of capacity, layout, technology, or even location, all of which are discussed in more detail in the following chapters. The redesigned process is documented once again, this time as the "after" view of the process. This helps to visualize the future design and to provide proof on concept. Expected payoffs are carefully estimated, along with risks. For changes involving investments, the time value of money must be considered (see Supplement J, "Financial Analysis," on the Student CD-ROM). The impact on people (skills, degree of change, training requirements, and resistance to change) must also be factored in the evaluation of the new design.

BENCHMARKING

Benchmarking can be another valuable source for process redesign efforts. **Benchmarking** is a systematic procedure that measures a firm's processes, services, and products against those of industry leaders. Companies use benchmarking to understand

How should the process be redesigned?

brainstorming session
A time when a group of people, knowledgeable on the process and its disconnects, propose ideas for change in a rapid-fire manner.

How good are the company's processes relative to that of its competitors?

benchmarking A systematic procedure that measures a firm's processes, services, and products against those of industry leaders.

better how outstanding companies do things so that they can improve their own processes. Typical measures used in benchmarking include cost per unit, service upsets (breakdowns) per customer, processing time per unit, customer retention rates, revenue per unit, return on investment, and customer satisfaction levels. Those involved in improvement efforts rely on benchmarking to formulate goals and targets for performance. Benchmarking consists of four basic steps.

1. *Planning.* Identify the process, service, or product to be benchmarked and the firm(s) to be used for comparison; determine the performance metrics for analysis; and collect the data.
2. *Analysis.* Determine the gap between the firm's current performance and that of the benchmark firm(s) and identify the causes of significant performance gaps.
3. *Integration.* Establish goals and obtain the support of managers who must provide the resources for accomplishing the goals.
4. *Action.* Develop cross-functional teams of those most affected by the changes, develop action plans and team assignments, implement the plans, monitor progress, and recalibrate benchmarks as improvements are made.

Benchmarking focuses on setting quantitative goals for improvement. *Competitive* benchmarking is based on comparisons with a direct industry competitor. *Functional* benchmarking compares areas such as administration, customer service, and sales operations with those of outstanding firms in any industry. For instance, Xerox benchmarked its distribution function against L.L.Bean's because Bean is renowned as a leading retailer in distribution efficiency and customer service.

Internal benchmarking involves using an organizational unit with superior performance as the benchmark for other units. This form of benchmarking can be advantageous for firms that have several business units or divisions, as is the case of Xerox in Managerial Practice 4.2. All forms of benchmarking are best applied in situations where a long-term program of continuous improvement is pursued.

Collecting benchmarking data can sometimes be a challenge. Internal benchmarking data is surely the most accessible, assuming that the firm is sufficiently large to have multiple business units or similar processes in several parts of the organization. Functional benchmarking data are often collected by professional associations or consulting firms. Confidentiality makes competitive benchmarking data at the process level the most difficult to obtain because of the desire to protect proprietary interest. One way of benchmarking is always available—tracking the performance of a process over time.

● MANAGING PROCESSES

Processes must be managed. Failure to do so is failure to effectively manage the business. Implementing a beautifully rewired process is not the end, but the beginning to continually monitoring and improving processes. Poorly managed processes will quickly fall in disrepair. Metrics goals must be continually evaluated and reset to fit changing requirements. The following seven mistakes should be avoided when managing processes.[1]

1. *Not Connecting with Strategic Issues.* Is particular attention being paid to core processes, competitive priorities, impact of customer contact and volume, and strategic fit during process analysis?
2. *Not Involving the Right People in the Right Way.* Is process analysis turned over to the experts either inside or outside the organization, rather than closely involving the people performing the process, or those closely connected to it as internal customers and suppliers?

---

[1]Rummler, Geary A. and Alan P. Brache. *Improving Performance.* San Francisco: Jossey-Bass, Inc., Second Edition, 1995, pp. 126–133.

MANAGERIAL PRACTICE 4.2

BENCHMARKING TO IMPROVE A SALES PROCESS

Xerox (www.xerox.com) has an almost religious belief in benchmarking processes and sharing best practices. Benchmarking means identifying who is best at something (in your company, in your industry, or in the world), not by guesswork or reputation but by the numbers. Sharing best practices means identifying who is doing the process best and then adapting their ideas to your own operations. Xerox applies benchmarking not only to the cost side of the ledger but also to the revenue side. Headquartered in Dublin, Ireland, Xerox Europe, a 100 percent-owned subsidiary of Xerox Corporation, sells more than $5.3 billion worth of products and services annually, mostly in Europe. A team was formed, charged with learning where sales performance was best for different products and how these results were achieved. The team consisted of a couple of dozen people from the sales, service, and administrative staffs, of whom a third worked for Marlow and two-thirds for operating divisions across Europe, the Middle East, and Africa. Team members gathered all kinds of sales data, making country-by-country (division) comparisons. They needed just a couple of weeks to find eight cases in which one division dramatically outperformed the others. Somehow, France sold five times more color copiers than its sister divisions, Switzerland's sales of Xerox's top-of-the-line Docu-Print machines were ten times those of any other country, Austria suffered only a 4-percent attrition rate when service contracts came up for renewal, and so on. The team then found out how these benchmark results were achieved and what specific processes were used. Country managers were then told to pick three or four best practices to implement. They were given the ambitious goal of achieving 70 percent of the benchmark standard during the first year. In most cases, country managers visited benchmark divisions and installed their methods in a matter of weeks. The results were breathtaking. By copying France's practices in selling color copiers, chiefly by improving sales training and pushing color copiers through dealer channels as well as direct sales, Switzerland increased its unit sales by 328 percent, Holland by 300 percent, and Norway by 152 percent.

Clearly, a lot more knowledge is lying around organizations than many managers are aware of, regardless of the functional area and type of process involved. Putting this knowledge to work improves both the process and the bottom line.

In 2000, the American Productivity and Quality Center named Xerox one of five global organizations that serve as models for implementing knowledge management successful. It said that Xerox changed the way the business world looks at benchmarking and knowledge sharing.

Xerox has invested in excess of £400 million ($692 million) to create 4,100 jobs in two new facilities in Ireland. Benchmarking has helped Xerox create state-of-the-art facilities. Here, teams of technicians explore ways to improve products at the Electronics facility at the Xerox Technology Park in Dundalk.

Source: "Beat the Budget and Astound Your CFO." *Fortune* (October 28, 1996), p. 187.

3. *Not Giving the Design Teams and Process Analysts a Clear Charter, and Then Holding Them Accountable.* Does management set expectations for change and maintain pressure for results? Does it allow paralysis in process improvement efforts by requiring excessive analysis?

4. *Not Satisfied Unless Fundamental "Reengineering" Changes Are Made.* Is radical change the expectation at the expense of incremental change? If so, the cumulative effect of many small improvements is lost. Process management efforts should not be limited to downsizing or to reorganization, even though jobs may be eliminated or the structure changed. It should not be limited to big

technological innovation projects, particularly if automation just calcifies an illogical process, even though technological change occurs often.

5. *Not Considering the Impact on People.* Are the changes aligned with the attitudes and skills of the people who must implement the redesigned process? It is crucial to understand and deal with the *people side* of process changes.

6. *Not Giving Attention to Implementation.* Are processes redesigned, but never implemented? A great job of flowcharting and benchmarking a process is only of academic interest if the proposed changes are not implemented. Sound project management practices (see Chapter 8, "Planning and Managing Projects") are required.

7. *Not Creating an Infrastructure for Continuous Process Improvement.* Is there a measurement system to monitor key metrics over time? Managers must check to see if the anticipated benefits of a redesigned process are actually being realized.

Managers must make sure that their organization spots new performance gaps in the continual search for process improvements. Process redesign efforts need to be part of periodic reviews and even annual plans. Measurement is the particular focus of Chapter 5, "Process Performance and Quality." It covers how a performance tracking system is the basis for feedback and improvement efforts. The essence of a learning organization is the intelligent use of such feedback.

PROCESS ANALYSIS ACROSS THE ORGANIZATION

All parts of an organization need to be concerned about process analysis simply because they are doing work, and process analysis focuses on how work is actually done. Are they providing the most value to their customers (internal or external), or can they be improved? Operations and sales are often the first areas that come to mind because they are so closely connected with the core processes. However, support processes in accounting, finance, and human resources are crucial to success. They get involved with process analysis not just within their own domains, but also outside their departments. Accounting is a key source of information on actual performance on various metrics in the order fulfillment process and processes nested within it. Finance gets involved when process redesigns require funds for substantial investments in new technology or equipment. Human resources gets involved when process redesigns mean that new skills and knowledge must be acquired, either through hiring, transfers, or training. Reward systems might need to be restructured. Top management also gets involved when processes are only partially within their domain, and also require the baton to be handed off to other departments. It is here where disconnects are often the worst and opportunities for improvement the greatest. These areas are what some call the *white spaces* in the organization chart that lie between departmental silos.

CHAPTER HIGHLIGHTS

- Process analysis creates a detailed understanding of how work is performed and redesigned. It is the foundation of continual improvement efforts.

- The six steps in a systematic approach to process analysis are: identify opportunities, define the scope, document the process, evaluate performance, redesign the process, and implement the changes.

- Identifying opportunities involves reviewing the four core processes and strategic issues. The four core processes are supplier relationships, new service/product development, order fulfillment, and customer relationships. Strategic

issues include gaps between competitive priorities and competitive capabilities, or lack of strategic fit.

- Managers must put into place a plan for redesigning processes, making sure that the resources assigned match up with the project scope.

- Three techniques that are particularly effective in documenting processes are flowcharts, service blueprints, and process charts.

- Performance data on the selected metrics must be collected, so as to spot disconnects and areas on substandard performance, paving the way to process redesign ideas.

- Six methods for analyzing data for a particular metric are checklists, histograms and bar charts, Pareto charts, scatter diagrams, cause-and-effect diagrams, and graphs. Their power is greatest when used together to identify the root causes of problem symptoms.

- Finding ways to redesign a process begins with a questioning attitude about each step in the process and about the process as a whole. Brainstorming sessions and benchmarking often are the source of breakthrough ideas for process change. Benchmarking can be competitive, functional, or internal, depending on the information source.

- Managers must understand and manage the processes over which they responsible, and they must also participate in improving processes that connects with other departments or functional areas. Important elements of good management practice are connecting process analysis with strategic issues, involving the right people, giving design teams clear charters, accounting for behavioral aspects of process changes, and creating an infrastructure that assures continual improvement efforts.

STUDENT CD-ROM AND INTERNET RESOURCES

The Student CD-ROM and the Companion Website at **www.prenhall.com/krajewski** contain many tools, activities, and resources designed for this chapter. The following items are recommended to enhance your skills and improve your understanding of the material in this chapter.

STUDENT CD-ROM RESOURCES

- **PowerPoint Slides.** View this comprehensive set of slides customized for this chapter's concepts and techniques.
- **OM Explorer Tutors.** OM Explorer contains two tutor spreadsheets that will help you learn about process charts and Pareto charts. See Chapter 4 in the OM Explorer menu. See also the two Tutor Exercises on process charts and Pareto charts.
- **OM Explorer Solvers.** OM Explorer contains one spreadsheet designed to solve general problems involving process charts and one spreadsheet for bar, Pareto, and line charts. See Process Analysis in the OM Explorer menu for these routines.
- **Active Models.** There is an active model spreadsheet that provides additional insights on Pareto charts. See Process Analysis in the Active Models menu for this routine.
- **SimQuick.** Learn the basics of building simulation models for processes by working through Example 1 in *SimQuick: Process Simulation with Excel.* This simple bank process example is followed by other examples including waiting lines, inventory in supply chains, manufacturing, and project management.

- **SmartDraw.** Use the link to download a 30-day trial of SmartDraw, a software package often used in practice to prepare flowcharts.
- **Supplement G.** "Learning Curve Analysis." Learn about how to account for learning effects when estimating requirements for new or revised processes.
- **Supplement H.** "Measuring Output Rates." Learn about several tools for estimating the time it takes for each step in a process.
- **Supplement J.** "Financial Analysis." Learn about several tools for evaluating revised processes that involve large capital investments.

INTERNET RESOURCES

- **Self-Study Quizzes.** See the compendium of true or false, multiple choice, and essay questions that give you feedback on how well you have mastered the concepts in this chapter.
- **In the News.** See the articles that apply to this chapter.
- **Internet Exercises.** Try out the exercises available on various aspects of process analysis.
- **Virtual Tours.** See the "Web Links to Company Facility Tours" for various tours of company facilities.

KEY TERMS

bar chart 143
benchmarking 151
brainstorming session 151
cause-and-effect diagram 145
checklist 143
design team 134

flowchart 136
graphs 145
histogram 143
metrics 134
Pareto chart 143
process analysis 132

process chart 141
process simulation 148
scatter diagram 144
service blueprint 139
suggestion system 133

SOLVED PROBLEM 1

Create a flowchart for the following telephone-ordering process at a retail chain that specializes in selling books and music CDs. It provides an ordering system via the telephone to its time-sensitive customers besides its regular store sales.

First, the automated system greets customers and identifies if they have a tone or pulse phone. Customers choose 1 if they have a tone phone; otherwise, they wait for the first available service representative to process their request. If customers have a tone phone, they complete their request by choosing options on the phone. First, the system checks if customers have an existing account or not. Customers choose 1 if they have an existing account or choose 2 if they want to open a new account. Customers wait for the service representative to open a new account if they choose 2.

Next, customers choose between the options of making an order, canceling an order, or talking to a customer representative for questions and/or complaints. If customers choose to make an order, then they specify the order type as a book or a music CD, and a specialized customer representative for books or music CDs picks up the phone to get the order details. If customers choose to cancel an order, then they wait for the automated response. By entering the order code via phone, customers can cancel the order. The automated system says the name of the ordered item and asks for the confirmation of the customer. If the customer validates the cancellation of the order, then the system cancels the order; otherwise, the system asks the customer to input the order code again. After responding to the request, the system asks whether the customer has additional requests; if not, the process terminates.

SOLUTION

Figure 4.16 shows the flowchart created with the SmartDraw software.

SOLVED PROBLEM 2

An automobile service is having difficulty providing oil changes in the 29 minutes or less mentioned in its advertising. You are to analyze the process of changing automobile engine oil. The subject of the study is the service mechanic. The process begins when the mechanic directs the customer's arrival and ends when the customer pays for the services.

SOLUTION

Figure 4.17 shows the completed process chart. The process is broken into 21 steps. A summary of the times and distances traveled is shown in the upper right-hand corner of the process chart.

The times add up to 28 minutes, which does not allow much room for error if the 29-minute guarantee is to be met and the mechanic travels a total of 420 feet.

SOLVED PROBLEM 3

What improvement can you make in the process shown in Figure 4.17?

SOLUTION

Your analysis should verify the following three ideas for improvement. You may also be able to come up with others.

- **a. Move Step 17 to Step 21.** Customers should not have to wait while the mechanic cleans the work area.
- **b. Store Small Inventories of Frequently Used Filters in the Pit.** Steps 7 and 10 involve travel to the storeroom. If the filters are moved to the pit, a copy of the reference material must also be placed in the pit. The pit will have to be organized and well lighted.
- **c. Use Two Mechanics.** Steps 10, 12, 15, and 17 involve running up and down the steps to the pit. Much of this travel could be eliminated. The service time could be shortened by having one mechanic in the pit working simultaneously with another working under the hood.

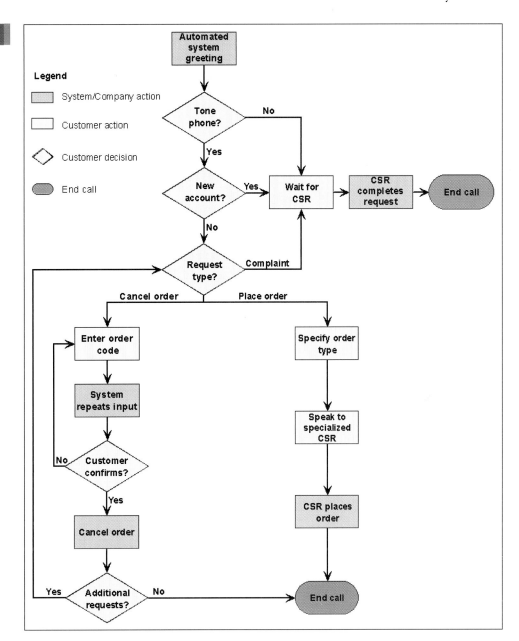

FIGURE 4.16

Flowchart of Telephone Ordering Process

SOLVED PROBLEM 4

Vera Johnson and Merris Williams manufacture vanishing cream. Their packaging process has four steps: mix, fill, cap, and label. They have had the reported defects analyzed, which shows the following.

Defect	Frequency
Lumps of unmixed product	7
Over- or underfilled jars	18
Jar lids did not seal	6
Labels rumpled or missing	29
Total	60

Draw a Pareto chart to identify the vital defects.

FIGURE 4.17

Process Chart for Changing Engine Oil

Process:	Changing engine oil
Subject:	Mechanic
Beginning:	Direct customer arrival
Ending:	Total charges, receive payment

Insert Step

Append Step

Remove Step

Summary

Activity		Number of Steps	Time (min)	Distance (ft)
Operation	●	7	16.50	
Transport	➡	8	5.50	420
Inspect	■	4	5.00	
Delay	▶	1	0.70	
Store	▼	1	0.30	

Step No.	Time (min)	Distance (ft)	●	➡	■	▶	▼	Step Description
1	0.80	50.0		X				Direct customer into service bay
2	1.80		X					Record name and desired service
3	2.30				X			Open hood, verify engine type, inspect hoses, check fluids
4	0.80	30.0		X				Walk to customer in waiting area
5	0.60		X					Recommend additional services
6	0.70					X		Wait for customer decision
7	0.90	70.0		X				Walk to storeroom
8	1.90		X					Look up filter number(s), find filter(s)
9	0.40				X			Check filter number(s)
10	0.60	50.0		X				Carry filter(s) to service pit
11	4.20		X					Perform under-car services
12	0.70	40.0		X				Climb from pit, walk to automobile
13	2.70		X					Fill engine with oil, start engine
14	1.30				X			Inspect for leaks
15	0.50	40.0		X				Walk to pit
16	1.00				X			Inspect for leaks
17	3.00		X					Clean and organize work area
18	0.70	80.0		X				Return to auto, drive from bay
19	0.30						X	Park the car
20	0.50	60.0		X				Walk to customer waiting area
21	2.30		X					Total charges, receive payment

SOLUTION

Defective labels account for 48.33 percent of the total number of defects:

$$\frac{29}{60} \times 100\% = 48.33\%$$

Improperly filled jars account for 30 percent of the total number of defects:

$$\frac{18}{60} \times 100\% = 30.00\%$$

The cumulative percent for the two most frequent defects is

$$48.33\% + 30.00\% = 78.33\%$$

Lumps represent $\frac{7}{60} \times 100\% = 11.67\%$ of defects; the cumulative percentage is

$$78.33\% + 11.67\% = 90.00\%$$

Defective seals represent $\frac{6}{60} \times 100\% = 10\%$ of defects; the cumulative percentage is

$$10\% + 90\% = 100.00\%$$

The Pareto chart is shown in Figure 4.18.

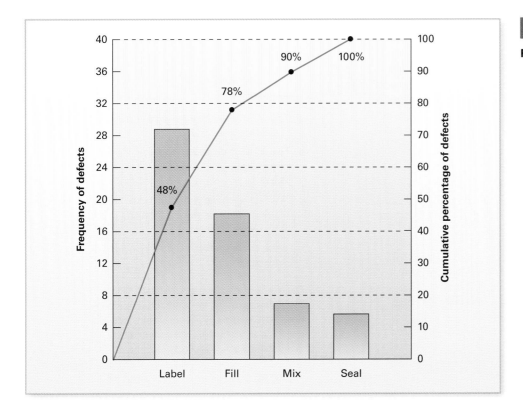

FIGURE 4.18

Pareto Chart

DISCUSSION QUESTIONS

1. Continuous improvement recognizes that many small improvements add up to sizable benefits. Will continuous improvement take a company at the bottom of an industry to the top? Explain.

2. The Hydro-Electric Company (HEC) has three sources of power. A small amount of hydroelectric power is generated by damming wild and scenic rivers; a second source of power comes from burning coal, with emissions that create acid rain and contribute to global warming; the third source of power comes from nuclear fission. HEC's coal-fired plants use obsolete pollution-control technology, and an investment of several hundred million dollars would be required to update it. Environmentalists urge HEC to promote conservation and purchase power from suppliers that use the cleanest fuels and technology.

However, HEC is already suffering from declining sales, which have resulted in billions of dollars invested in idle equipment. Its large customers are taking advantage of laws that permit them to buy power from low-cost suppliers. HEC must cover the fixed costs of idle capacity by raising rates charged to its remaining customers or face defaulting on bonds (bankruptcy). The increased rates motivate even more customers to seek low-cost suppliers, the start of a death spiral for HEC. To prevent additional rate increases, HEC implements a cost-cutting program and puts its plans to update pollution controls on hold.

Form sides, and discuss the ethical, environmental, and political issues and trade-offs associated with HEC's strategy.

PROBLEMS

An icon next to a problem identifies the software that can be helpful, but is not mandatory. The software is available on the Student CD-ROM that is packaged with every new copy of the textbook.

1. **OM Explorer** Your class has volunteered to work for Referendum 13 on the November ballot, which calls for free tuition and books for all college courses except operations management. Support for the referendum includes assembling 10,000 yard signs (preprinted water-resistant paper signs to be glued and stapled to a wooden stake) on a fall Saturday. Construct a flowchart and a process chart for yard sign assembly. What inputs in terms of materials, human effort, and equipment are involved? Estimate the amount of volunteers, staples, glue, equipment, lawn and garage space, and pizza required.

2. **SmartDraw** Prepare a flowchart for the three processes at King Soopers. (See The Big Picture section in Chapter 3, the Video Clip 3.2 and the *Process Choice at the King Soopers Bakery* video.)

3. **OM Explorer** Suppose that you are in charge of a large mailing to the alumni of your college, inviting them to contribute to a scholarship fund. The letters and envelopes have been individually addressed (mailing labels were not used). The letters are to be folded and stuffed into the correct envelopes, the envelopes are to be sealed, and a large commemorative stamp is to be placed in the upper right-hand corner of each envelope. Make a process chart for this activity, assuming that it is a one-person operation. Estimate how long it will take to stuff, seal, and stamp 2,000 envelopes. Assume that the person doing this work is paid $8.00 per hour. How much will it cost to process 2,000 letters, based on your

time estimate? Consider how each of the following changes individually would affect the process:

- Each letter has the greeting "Dear Alumnus or Alumna," instead of the person's name.
- Mailing labels are used and have to be put on the envelopes.
- Prestamped envelopes are used.
- Envelopes are stamped by a postage meter.
- Window envelopes are used.
- A preaddressed envelope is included with each letter for contributions.

a. Which of these changes would reduce the time and cost of the process?

b. Would any of these changes be likely to reduce the effectiveness of the mailing? If so, which ones? Why?

c. Would the changes that increase time and cost be likely to increase the effectiveness of the mailing? Why or why not?

d. What other factors need to be considered for this project?

4. Diagrams of two self-service gasoline stations, both located on corners, are shown in Figure 4.19 (a) and (b). Both have two rows of four pumps and a booth at which an attendant receives payment for the gasoline. At neither station is it necessary for the customer to pay in advance. The exits and entrances are marked on the diagrams. Analyze the flows of cars and people through each station.

a. Which station has the more efficient flows from the standpoint of the customer?

FIGURE 4.19

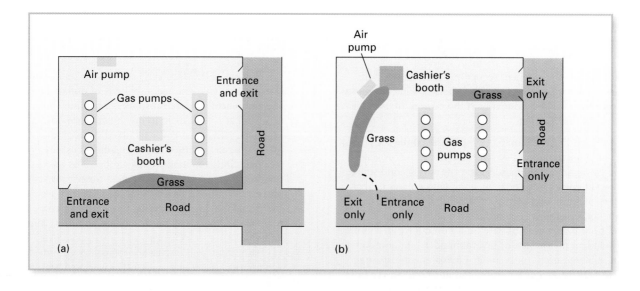

(a)

(b)

b. Which station is likely to lose more potential customers who cannot gain access to the pumps because another car is headed in the other direction?

c. At which station can a customer pay without getting out of the car?

5. ✎ **OM Explorer** The management of the Just Like Home restaurant has asked you to analyze some of its processes. One of these processes is making a single-scoop ice cream cone. Cones can be ordered by a server (for table service) or by a customer (for takeout).

Figure 4.20 illustrates the process chart for this operation.

- The ice cream counter server earns $10 per hour (including variable fringe benefits).
- The process is performed 10 times per hour (on average).
- The restaurant is open 363 days a year, 10 hours a day.

a. Complete the summary (top-right) portion of the chart.

b. What is the total labor cost associated with the process?

c. How can this operation be made more efficient? Draw a process chart of the improved process. What are the annual labor savings if this new process is implemented?

6. As a graduate assistant, your duties include grading and keeping records for operations management course homework assignments. Five sections for 40 students each are offered each semester. A few graduate students attend sections 3 and 4. Graduate students must complete some extra work to higher standards for each assignment. Every student delivers (or is supposed to deliver) directly to (under) the door of your office one homework assignment every Tuesday. Your job is to correct the homework, record grades, sort the papers by class section, sort by student last name in alphabetical order, and return the homework papers to the appropriate instructors (not necessarily in that order). There are some complications. A fair majority of the students sign their names legibly, others identify their work with the

FIGURE 4.20

Process:	Making one ice cream cone
Subject:	Server at counter
Beginning:	Walk to cone storage area
Ending:	Give it to server or customer

Summary

Activity	Number of Steps	Time (min)	Distance (ft)
Operation ●			
Transport ➡			
Inspect ■			
Delay ▶			
Store ▼			

Insert Step
Append Step
Remove Step

Step No.	Time (min)	Distance (ft)	●	➡	■	▶	▼	Step Description
1	0.20	5.0		X				Walk to cone storage area
2	0.05		X					Remove empty cone
3	0.10	5.0		X				Walk to counter
4	0.05		X					Place cone in holder
5	0.20	8.0		X				Walk to sink area
6	0.50					X		Ask dishwasher to wash scoop
7	0.15	8.0		X				Walk to counter with clean scoop
8	0.05		X					Pick up empty cone
9	0.10	2.5		X				Walk to flavor ordered
10	0.75		X					Scoop ice cream from container
11	0.75		X					Place ice cream in cone
12	0.25				X			Check for stability
13	0.05	2.5		X				Walk to order placement area
14	0.05		X					Give server or customer the cone

correct I.D. number, and a few do neither. Rarely do students identify their section number or graduate status. Prepare a list of process chart steps and place them in an efficient sequence.

7. 🖱 **OM Explorer** At the Department of Motor Vehicles, the process of getting license plates for your car begins when you enter the facility and take a number. You walk 50 feet to the waiting area. During your wait, you count about 30 customers waiting for service. You notice that many customers become discouraged and leave. When a number is called, if a customer stands, the ticket is checked by a uniformed person, and the customer is directed to the available clerk. If no one stands, several minutes are lost while the same number is called repeatedly. Eventually, the next number is called, and more often than not, that customer has left too. The DMV clerk has now been idle for several minutes but does not seem to mind.

An unkempt man walks over to the ticket dispenser, picks up several tickets from the floor, and returns to his seat. A new arrival, carrying a stack of paper and looking like a car dealer, walks directly to the unkempt man. Some sort of transaction takes place. A few more numbers are called and it is the car dealer's number! After 4 hours, your number is called and checked by the uniformed person. You walk 60 feet to the clerk, and the process of paying city sales taxes is completed in 4 minutes. The clerk then directs you to the waiting area for paying state personal property tax, 80 feet away. With a sinking heart, you take a different number and sit down with some different customers who are just renewing licenses. You notice the same unkempt man. A 1-hour, 40-minute wait this time, and after a walk of 25 feet you pay property taxes in a process that takes 2 minutes. Now that you have paid taxes you're eligible to pay registration and license fees. That department is 50 feet away, beyond the employees' cafeteria. As you walk by the cafeteria, you notice the unkempt man having coffee with a uniformed person.

The registration and license customers are called in the same order in which personal property taxes were paid. There is only a 10-minute wait and a 3-minute process. You receive your license plates, take a minute to abuse the license clerk, and leave exactly 6 hours after arriving.

Make a process chart to depict this process, and suggest improvements.

8. Refer to the process chart for the automobile oil change in Solved Problem 2. Calculate the annual labor cost if:

• The mechanic earns $40 per hour (including variable fringe benefits).

• The process is performed twice per hour (on average)

• The shop is open 300 days a year, 10 hours a day.

a. What is the total labor cost associated with the process?

b. If steps 7, 10, 12, and 15 were eliminated, estimate the annual labor savings associated with implementing this new process.

9. 🖱 **OM Explorer** The manager of Perrotti's Pizza collects data concerning customer complaints about delivery. Pizza is arriving late, or the wrong pizza is being delivered.

Problem	Frequency
Topping stuck to box lid	17
Pizza is late	35
Wrong topping or combination	9
Wrong style of crust	6
Wrong size	4
Pizza is partially eaten	3
Pizza never showed up	6

a. Use a Pareto chart to identify the "few vital" delivery problems.

b. Use a cause-and-effect diagram to identify potential causes of late pizza delivery.

10. 🖱 **OM Explorer** Smith, Schroeder, and Torn (SST) is a short-haul household furniture moving company. SST's labor force, selected from the local community college football team, is temporary and part-time. SST is concerned with recent complaints, as tabulated on the following tally sheet.

Complaint	Tally
Broken glass	///// ///// ///
Delivered to wrong address	///// ////
Furniture rubbed together while on truck	///// ///// ///// /////
Late delivery	/////
Late arrival for pickup	///// ///// ///// ///
Missing items	///// ///// ///// ///// ///// /
Nicks and scratches from rough handling	///// /////
Soiled upholstery	///// ///

a. Draw a bar chart and a Pareto chart to identify the most serious moving problems.

b. Use a cause-and-effect diagram to identify potential causes of complaints.

11. 🖱 **OM Explorer** Rick DeNeefe, manager of the Golden Valley Bank credit authorization department, recently noticed that a major competitor was advertising that applications for equity loans could be approved within two working days. As fast credit approval was a competitive priority, DeNeefe wanted to see how well his department was doing relative to the competitor's. Golden Valley stamps each application with the date and time it is received and again when a decision is made. A total of 104 applications were received in March. The time required for each decision, rounded to the nearest hour, is shown in the following table. Golden Valley's employees work 8 hours per day.

Decision Process Time	Frequency
7–9 hours	8
10–12 hours	19
13–15 hours	28
16–18 hours	10
19–21 hours	25
22–24 hours	4
25–27 hours	10
Total	104

a. Draw a bar chart for these data.

b. Analyze the data. How is Golden Valley Bank doing with regard to this competitive priority?

12. **OM Explorer** Last year, the manager of the service department at East Woods Lincoln–Mercury instituted a customer opinion program to find out how to improve service.

One week after service on a vehicle was performed, his assistant would call the customer to find out whether the work had been done satisfactorily and how service could be improved. After a year of gathering data, the assistant discovered that the complaints could be grouped into the following five categories.

Complaint	Frequency
Unfriendly atmosphere	5
Long wait for service	17
Price too high	20
Incorrect bill	8
Need to return to correct problem	50
Total	100

a. Draw a bar chart and a Pareto chart to identify the significant service problems.

b. Use a cause-and-effect diagram to identify potential causes of complaints.

13. Oregon Fiber Board makes roof liners for the automotive industry. The manufacturing manager is concerned about product quality. She suspects that one particular defect, tears in the fabric, is related to production-run size. An assistant gathers the following data from production records.

Run	Size	Defects (%)	Run	Size	Defects (%)
1	1,000	3.5	11	6,500	1.5
2	4,100	3.8	12	1,000	5.5
3	2,000	5.5	13	7,000	1.0
4	6,000	1.9	14	3,000	4.5
5	6,800	2.0	15	2,200	4.2
6	3,000	3.2	16	1,800	6.0
7	2,000	3.8	17	5,400	2.0
8	1,200	4.2	18	5,800	2.0
9	5,000	3.8	19	1,000	6.2
10	3,800	3.0	20	1,500	7.0

a. Draw a scatter diagram for these data.

b. Does there appear to be a relationship between run size and percent defects? What implications does this have for Wellington's business?

14. Grindwell, Inc., a manufacturer of grinding tools, is concerned about the durability of its products, which depends on the permeability of the sinter mixtures used in production. Suspecting that the carbon content might be the source of the problem, the plant manager collected the following data.

Carbon Content (%)	Permeability Index
5.5	16
3.0	31
4.5	21
4.8	19
4.2	16
4.7	23
5.1	20
4.4	11
3.6	20

a. Draw a scatter plot for these data.

b. Is there a relationship between permeability and carbon content?

c. If low permeability is desirable, what does the scatter plot suggest with regard to the carbon content?

15. The operations manager for Superfast Airlines at Port Columbus International Airport noticed an increase in the number of delayed flight departures. She brainstormed possible causes with her staff:

• Aircraft late to gate
• Acceptance of late passengers
• Passengers arrive late at gate
• Passengers processing delays at gate
• Late baggage to aircraft
• Other late personnel or unavailable items
• Mechanical failures

Draw a cause-and-effect diagram to organize the possible causes of delayed flight departures into the following major categories: equipment, personnel, material, procedures, and "other factors" beyond managerial control. Provide a detailed set of causes for each major cause identified by the operations manager, and incorporate them in your cause-and-effect diagram.

16. **OM Explorer** Plastomer, Inc., specializes in the manufacture of high-grade plastic film used to wrap food products. Film is rejected and scrapped for a variety of reasons (e.g., opacity, high carbon content, incorrect thickness or gauge, scratches, etc.). During the past month, management collected data on the types of rejects and the amount of scrap generated by each type. The following table presents the results.

Type of Defect	Amount of Scrap (lb)
Air bubbles	500
Bubble breaks	19,650
Carbon content	150
Unevenness	3,810
Thickness or gauge	27,600
Opacity	450
Scratches	3,840
Trim	500
Wrinkles	10,650

Draw a Pareto chart to identify which type of defect management should attempt to eliminate first.

17. Management of a shampoo bottling company introduced a new 13.5-ounce pack and used an existing machine, with some modifications, to fill it. To measure filling consistency by the modified machine (set to fill 13.85 ounces), an analyst collected the following data (volume in ounces) for a random sample of 100 bottles.

13.0	13.3	13.6	13.2	14.0	12.9	14.2	12.9	14.5	13.5
14.1	14.0	13.7	13.4	14.4	14.3	14.8	13.9	13.5	14.3
14.2	14.1	14.0	13.9	13.9	14.0	14.5	13.6	13.3	12.9
12.8	13.1	13.6	14.5	14.6	12.9	13.1	14.4	14.0	14.4
13.1	14.1	14.2	12.9	13.3	14.0	14.1	13.1	13.6	13.7
14.0	13.6	13.2	13.4	13.9	14.5	14.0	14.4	13.9	14.6
12.9	14.3	14.0	12.9	14.2	14.8	14.5	13.1	12.7	13.9
13.6	14.4	13.1	14.5	13.5	13.3	14.0	13.6	13.5	14.3
13.2	13.8	13.7	12.8	13.4	13.8	13.3	13.7	14.1	13.7
13.7	13.8	13.4	13.7	14.1	12.8	13.7	13.8	14.1	14.3

a. Draw a histogram for these data.

b. Bottles with less than 12.85 ounces or more than 14.85 ounces are considered to be out of specification. Based on the sample data, what percent of the bottles filled by the machine will be out of specification?

Advanced Problem

18. This problem should be solved as a team exercise.
   Shaving is a process that most men perform each morning. Assume that the process begins at the bathroom sink with the shaver walking (say, 5 feet) to the cabinet) where his shaving supplies are stored) to pick up bowl, soap, brush, and razor. He walks back to the sink, runs the water until it gets warm, lathers his face, shaves, and inspects the results. Then, he rinses the razor, dries his face, walks over to the cabinet to return the bowl, soap, brush, and razor, and comes back to the sink to clean it up and complete the process.

   a. ✎ OM Explorer Develop a process chart for shaving. (Assume suitable values for the time required for the various activities involved in the process.)

   b. Brainstorm to generate ideas for improving the shaving process. (Do not try to evaluate the ideas until the group has compiled as complete a list as possible. Otherwise, judgment will block creativity.)

19. ✎ OM Explorer At Conner Company, a custom manufacturer of printed circuit boards, the finished boards are subjected to a final inspection prior to shipment to its customers. As Conner's quality assurance manager, you are responsible for making a presentation to management on quality problems at the beginning of each month. Your assistant has analyzed the reject memos for all the circuit boards that were rejected during the past month. He has given you a summary statement listing the reference number of the circuit board and the reason for rejection from one of the following categories:

   A = Poor electrolyte coverage

   B = Improper lamination

   C = Low copper plating

   D = Plating separation

   E = Improper etching

For 50 circuit boards that had been rejected last month, the summary statement showed the following:

C B C C D E C C B A D A C C C B C A C D C A C C B

A C A C B C C A C A A C C D A C C C E C C A B A C

   a. Prepare a tally sheet (or checklist) of the different reasons for rejection.

   b. Develop a Pareto chart to identify the more significant types of rejection.

   c. Examine the causes of the most significant type of defect, using a cause-and-effect diagram.

ACTIVE MODEL EXERCISE

This Active Model appears on your CD-ROM. It allows you to evaluate the structure of a Pareto chart.

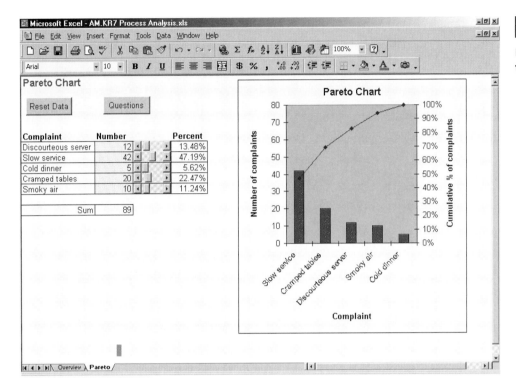

ACTIVE MODEL 4.1

Pareto Chart Using Data from Example 4.1

QUESTIONS

1. What percentage of overall defects does discourteous service account for?
2. What percentage of overall defects do the three most common complaints account for?
3. How does it affect the chart if we could eliminate discourteous service?

SIMULATION EXERCISES

These simulation exercises require the use of the SimQuick and Extend LT simulation packages. SimQuick is on the Student CD-ROM that is packaged with every new copy of the textbook. Extend LT is an optional simulation package that your instructor may or may not have ordered.

1. A manufacturing cell consists of 6 workstations. Raw materials are taken from inventory and proceed through the cell in a fixed route, starting with workstation 1 and ending with workstation 6. The finished product is then stored in an inventory. Management has the option of assigning 2, 3, or 6 workers to the cell. For example, if 2 workers are in the cell, one would be assigned to workstations 1, 2, and 3 while the other would be assigned to the other machines. The workers would be highly flexible in that they can do several different tasks. Use SimQuick to find the mean throughput for each option. See Example 19 in *SimQuick: Process Simulation with Excel* for details of this problem and additional exercises.

2. Consider the process at the Artistic Glass Works, which is introduced as Figure 4.13. Use the Extend LT simulator to evaluate the current process and other designs. See the full Artistic Glass Works case on the optional CD-ROM, along with the basic model and information on how to use it. Answer the various questions asked about the current and proposed process.

CASE   JOSÉ'S AUTHENTIC MEXICAN RESTAURANT

"Two bean tacos, a chicken burrito grande, and a side order of Spanish rice, please," Ivan Karetski called his table's order into the kitchen as he prepared the beverage orders. Business was brisk. Karetski liked it that way. Lots of customers meant lots of tips and, as a struggling graduate student, the extra income was greatly appreciated. Lately, however, his tips had been declining.

José's is a small, 58-seat restaurant that offers a reasonably broad range of Mexican food prepared and presented in a traditional Mexican style. It is located in New England in a mature business district on the edge of a large metropolitan area. The site is adjacent to a central artery and offers limited free off-street parking. The restaurant's interior decoration promotes the Mexican theme: The walls appear to be made of adobe and are draped with serapes, the furniture is Spanish-Mexican style, and flamenco guitar and mariachi alternate as background music.

Patrons enter the restaurant through a small vestibule that opens directly into the dining area; there is no separate waiting area. Upon arrival, patrons are greeted by a hostess and either seated directly or apprised of the expected wait. Seating at José's is usually immediate except for Friday and Saturday nights when waits of as long as 45 minutes can be encountered. Because space inside for waiting is very limited patrons must remain outside until their party is called. José's does not take reservations.

After seating patrons, the hostess distributes menus and fills glasses with water. If standards are being met, the waiter assigned to the table greets the patrons within one minute of their being seated. (Being a traditional Mexican restaurant, all its waitstaff are male.) The waiter introduces himself, announces the daily specials, and takes the beverage orders. After delivering the beverages, the waiter takes the meal orders.

The menu consists of 23 main entrees which are assembled from eight basic stocks (chicken, beef, beans, rice, corn tortillas, flour tortillas, tomatoes, and lettuce) and a variety of other ingredients (fruits, vegetables, sauces, herbs, and spices). Before the dining hours begin, the cook prepares the basic stocks so that they can be quickly combined and finished off to complete the requested meals. The typical amount of time needed to complete a meal once it has been ordered is 12 minutes. A good portion of this time is for final cooking, so several meals may be in preparation at the same time. As can be imagined, one of the skills a good cook needs is to be able to schedule production of the various meals ordered at a table so that they are ready at approximately the same time. Once all the meals and any side dishes have been completed by the cook, the waiter checks to see that all meals are correct and pleasing to the eye, corrects any mistakes, and adds any finishing touches. When everything is in order, he assembles them on a tray and delivers them to the table. From this point on, the waiter keeps an eye on the table to detect when any additional service or assistance is needed.

When the diners at the table appear to be substantially finished with their main meal, the waiter approaches, asks if he can clear away any dishes, and takes any requests for dessert or coffee. When the entire meal has been completed, the waiter presents the bill and shortly thereafter collects payment. José's accepts cash or major credit card but no checks.

Karetski feels that his relationship with the cook is important. As the cook largely controls the quality of the food, Karetski wants to stay on good terms with him. He treats the cook with respect, tries to place the items on his order slip in the sequence of longest preparation time, and makes sure to write clearly so that the orders are easy to read. Although it is not his job, he helps out by fetching food stocks from the refrigerator or the storage area when the cook is busy and by doing some of the food preparation himself. The cook has been irritable lately, complaining of the poor quality of some of the ingredients that have been delivered. Last week, for example, he received lettuce that appeared wilted and chicken that was tough and more bone than meat. During peak times, it can take more than 20 minutes to get good meals delivered to the table.

Karetski had been shown the results of a customer survey that management conducted last Friday and Saturday during the evening mealtime. The following table shows a summary of the responses.

CUSTOMER SURVEY RESULTS

Were you seated promptly?	Yes 70	No 13
Was your waiter satisfactory?	Yes 73	No 10
Were you served in a reasonable time?	Yes 58	No 25
Was your food enjoyable?	Yes 72	No 11
Was your dining experience worth the cost?	Yes 67	No 16

As Karetski carried the tray of drinks to the table, he wondered whether the recent falloff in tips was due to anything that he could control.

QUESTIONS

1. How should quality be defined at this restaurant?
2. What are the restaurant's costs of poor quality?
3. Use some of the tools for process analysis to assess the situation at José's.

Source: This case was prepared by Larry Meile, Boston College, as a basis for classroom discussion.

SELECTED REFERENCES

Anupindi, Ravi, Sunil Chopra, Sudhakar D. Deshmukj, Jan A. Van Mieghem, and Eitan Zemel. *Managing Business Process Flows*. Upper Saddle River, NJ: Prentice Hall, 1999.

Banker, R. D., J. M. Field, R. G. Schroeder, and K. K. Sinha. "Impact of Work Teams on Manufacturing Performance: A Longitudinal Field Study." *Academy of Management Journal*, vol. 39, no. 4 (1996), pp. 867–890.

Collier, D. A. *The Service/Quality Solution*. Burr Ridge, IL: Irwin Professional Pulishing, 1993.

Deming, W. Edwards. "Improvement of Quality and Productivity Through Action by Management." *National Productivity Review*, vol. 1, no. 1 (Winter 1981–1982), pp. 12–22.

Ellis, Christian M., and Lea A. P. Tonkin. "Mature Teams Rewards and the High-Performance Workplace: Change and Opportunity." *Target*, vol. 11, no. 6 (1995).

Fitzsimmons, James A., and Mona J. Fitzsimmons. *Service Management: Operations, Strategy, and Information Technology*. New York: McGraw-Hill, 1998.

Gephart, Martha A. "The Road to High Performance." *Training and Development*, vol. 49 (June 1995) pp. 29-44.

Hartvigsen, David. *SimQuick: Process Simulation with Excel*. 2d ed. Upper Saddle River, NJ: Prentice Hall, 2004.

Katzenbach, Jon R., and Douglas K. Smith. "The Discipline of Teams." *Harvard Business Review* (March–April 1993), pp. 111–120.

Kingman-Brundage, Jane. "Technology, Design, and Service Quality." *International Journal of Service Industry Management*, vol. 2, no. 3 (1991), pp. 47–59.

Liebs, Scott. "A Little Help from Their Friends." *Industry Week* (February 2, 1998).

Lovelock, Christopher H., and George S. Yip. "Developing Global Strategies for Service Businesses." *California Management Review*, vol. 38, no. 2 (1996), pp. 64–86.

Metters, Richard, Kathryn King-Metters, and Madeleine Pullman. *Successful Service Operations Management*. Mason, OH: South-Western, 2003.

Pande, Peter S., Robert P. Neuman, and Roland R. Cavanagh. *The Six Sigma Way*. New York: McGraw-Hill, 2000.

Port, Otis. "The Responsive Factory," *Business Week*, Enterprise 1993, pp. 48–51.

"Process, Process, Process." *Planning Review* (special issue), vol. 22, no. 3 (1993), pp. 1–56.

Pullman, Madeleine E., and William L. Moore. "Optimal Service Design: Integrating Marketing and Operations Perspectives." *International Journal of Service Industry Management*, vol. 10, no. 2 (1999), pp. 239–260.

Rampersad, Hubert K. *Total Performance Scorecard*. Butterworth Heinemann. New York: Butterworth-Heinemann, 2003.

Rummler, Geary A., and Alan P. Brache. *Improving Performance*. San Francisco: Jossey-Bass Inc., Second Edition, 1995.

Schmenner, Roger W. *Service Operations Management*. Englewood Cliffs, NJ: Prentice Hall, 1998.

Senge, P. *The Fifth Discipline: The Art and Practice of the Learning Organization*. New York: Doubleday, 1990.

Shostack, G. Lynn. "Service Positioning Through Structural Change." *Journal of Marketing*, vol. 51, no. 1 (1987), pp. 34–43.

"When the Going Gets Rough, Boeing Gets Touchy-Feely." *Business Week* (January 17, 1994), pp. 65–67.

Simulation

LEARNING GOALS   *After reading this supplement, you should be able to . . .*

IDENTIFY OR DEFINE

1. problems best suited for simulation models.
2. the Monte Carlo simulation process.

DESCRIBE OR EXPLAIN

3. how to create a simulation model and use it to help make a decision.
4. how to create a simple simulation model with an Excel spreadsheet.
5. the advanced capabilities of SimQuick and Extend.

simulation The act of reproducing the behavior of a system using a model that describes the processes of the system.

The act of reproducing the behavior of a system using a model that describes the processes of the system is called **simulation**. Once the model has been developed, the analyst can manipulate certain variables to measure the effects of changes on the operating characteristics of interest. A simulation model cannot prescribe what should be done about a problem. Instead, it can be used to study alternative solutions to the problem. The alternatives are systematically used in the model, and the relevant operating characteristics are recorded. After all the alternatives have been tried, the best one is selected.

Waiting-line models (see Supplement C, "Waiting Lines") are not simulation models because they describe the operating characteristics with known equations. With simulation the equations describing the operation characteristics are unknown. Using a simulation model, the analyst actually generates customer arrivals, puts customers into waiting lines, selects the next customer to be served by using some priority discipline, serves that customer, and so on. The model keeps track of the number in line, waiting time, and the like during the simulation and calculates the averages and variances at the end.

Simulation also may be used in other ways. For example, pilots are tested periodically on flight simulators. The cockpit of the simulator is identical to that of a real plane, but it is inside a large building. Through the use of computer graphics and other visual and mechanical effects, a pilot seems to be actually flying a plane. The pilot's reactions to various unexpected situations are measured and evaluated.

REASONS FOR USING SIMULATION

Simulation is useful when waiting-line models become too complex. There are other reasons for using simulation for analyzing processes. First, when the relationship between the variables is nonlinear or when there are too many variables or constraints to handle with optimizing approaches, simulation models can be used to estimate operating characteristics or objective function values and analyze a problem.

Second, simulation models can be used to conduct experiments without disrupting real systems. Experimenting with a real system can be very costly. For example, a simulation model can be used to estimate the benefits of purchasing and installing a new flexible manufacturing system without first installing such a system. Also, the model could be used to evaluate different configurations or processing decision rules without disrupting production schedules.

time compression The feature of simulation models that allows them to obtain operating characteristic estimates in much less time than is required to gather the same operating data from a real system.

Third, simulation models can be used to obtain operating characteristic estimates in much less time than is required to gather the same operating data from a real system. This feature of simulation is called **time compression**. For example, a simulation model of airport operations can generate statistics on airplane arrivals, landing delays, and terminal delays for a year in a matter of minutes on a computer. Alternative airport designs can be analyzed and decisions made quickly.

Finally, simulation is useful in sharpening managerial decision-making skills through gaming. A descriptive model that relates managerial decisions to important operating characteristics (e.g., profits, market share, and the like) can be developed. From a set of starting conditions, the participants make periodic decisions with the intention of improving one or more operating characteristics. (For example, see the Min-Yo Garment Company exercise at the end of Chapter 2, "Operations Strategy.") In such an exercise, a few hours' "play" can simulate a year's time. Gaming also enables managers to experiment with new ideas without disrupting normal operations.

Although simulation is used extensively, some analysts still think of it as the method of last resort. Mathematical analysis is preferred because it yields the optimal solution to a problem, whereas simulation requires the analyst to try various alternatives and possibly obtain a suboptimal solution. In addition, simulation modeling usually is very expensive because of the detail required in the computer model. Spending thousands of hours on programming and debugging complex models is not uncommon. Optimizing approaches, if they apply, usually are less expensive.

THE SIMULATION PROCESS

The simulation process includes data collection, random-number assignment, model formulation, and analysis. This process is known as **Monte Carlo simulation,** after the European gambling capital, because of the random numbers used to generate the simulation events.

Monte Carlo simulation A simulation process that uses random numbers to generate simulation events.

DATA COLLECTION

Simulation requires extensive data gathering on costs, productivities, capacities, and probability distributions. Typically, one of two approaches to data collection is used. Statistical sampling procedures are used when the data are not readily available from published sources or when the cost of searching for and collecting the data is high. Historical search is used when the data are available in company records, governmental and industry reports, professional and scientific journals, or newspapers.

Data Collection for a Simulation

EXAMPLE B.1

The Specialty Steel Products Company produces items, such as machine tools, gears, automobile parts, and other specialty items in small quantities to customer order. Because the products are so diverse, demand is measured in machine-hours. Orders for products are translated into required machine-hours, based on time standards for each operation. Management is concerned about capacity in the lathe department. Assemble the data necessary to analyze the addition of one more lathe machine and operator.

SOLUTION

Historical records indicate that lathe department demand varies from week to week as follows:

WEEKLY PRODUCTION REQUIREMENTS (HR)	RELATIVE FREQUENCY
200	0.05
250	0.06
300	0.17
350	0.05
400	0.30
450	0.15
500	0.06
550	0.14
600	0.02
Total	1.00

To gather these data, all weeks with requirements of 175.00–224.99 hours were grouped in the 200-hour category, all weeks with 225.00–274.99 hours in the 250-hour category, and so on. The average weekly production requirements for the lathe department are

$$200(0.05) + 250(0.06) + 300(0.17) + \cdots + 600(0.02) = 400 \text{ hours}$$

Employees in the lathe department work 40 hours per week on 10 machines. However, the number of machines actually operating during any week may be less than 10. Machines may need repair, or a worker may not show up for work. Historical records indicate that actual machine-hours were distributed as follows:

REGULAR CAPACITY (HR)	RELATIVE FREQUENCY
320 (8 machines)	0.30
360 (9 machines)	0.40
400 (10 machines)	0.30

The average number of operating machine-hours in a week is

$$320(0.30) + 360(0.40) + 400(0.30) = 360 \text{ hours}$$

The company has a policy of completing each week's workload on schedule, using overtime and subcontracting if necessary. The maximum amount of overtime authorized in any week is 100 hours, and requirements in excess of 100 hours are subcontracted to a small machine shop in town. Lathe operators receive $10 per hour for regular time. However, management estimates that the cost for overtime work is $25 per hour per employee, which includes premium-wage, variable-overhead, and supervision costs. Subcontracting costs $35 per hour, exclusive of materials costs.

To justify adding another machine and worker to the lathe department, weekly savings in overtime and subcontracting costs should be at least $650. These savings would cover the cost of the additional worker and provide for a reasonable return on machine investment. Management estimates from prior experience that with 11 machines the distribution of weekly capacity machine-hours would be

REGULAR CAPACITY (HR)	RELATIVE FREQUENCY
360 (9 machines)	0.30
400 (10 machines)	0.40
440 (11 machines)	0.30

RANDOM-NUMBER ASSIGNMENT

Before we can begin to analyze this problem with simulation, we must specify a way to generate demand and capacity each week. Suppose that we want to simulate 100 weeks of lathe operations with 10 machines. We would expect that 5 percent of the time (5 weeks of the 100) we would have a demand for 200 hours. Similarly, we would expect that 30 percent of the time (30 weeks of the 100) we would have 320 hours of capacity. However, we cannot use these averages of demand in our simulation because a real system does not operate that way. Demand may be 200 hours one week but 550 hours the next.

We can obtain the effect we want by using a random-number table to determine the amount of demand and capacity each week. A **random number** is a number that has the same probability of being selected as any other number (see the Table of Random Numbers in Appendix 2 for five-digit random numbers).

The events in a simulation can be generated in an unbiased way if random numbers are assigned to the events in the same proportion as their probability of occurrence. We expect a demand of 200 hours 5 percent of the time. If we have 100 random numbers (00–99), we can assign 5 numbers (or 5 percent of them) to the event "200 hours demanded." Thus, we can assign the numbers 00–04 to that event. If we randomly choose numbers in the range of 00–99 enough times, 5 percent of the time they will fall in the range of 00–04. Similarly, we can assign the numbers 05–10, or 6 percent of the numbers, to the event "250 hours demanded." In Table B.1 we show the allocation of the 100 random numbers to the demand events in the same proportion as their probability of occurrence. We similarly assigned random numbers to the *capacity* events for 10 machines. The capacity events for the 11-machine simulation would have the same random-number assignments, except that the events would be 360, 400, and 440 hours, respectively.

MODEL FORMULATION

Formulating a simulation model entails specifying the relationships among the variables. Simulation models consist of decision variables, uncontrollable variables, and dependent variables. **Decision variables** are controlled by the decision maker and will change from one run to the next as different events are simulated. For example, the number of lathe machines is the decision variable in the Specialty Steel Products problem in Example B.1. **Uncontrollable variables,** however, are random events that the

TABLE B.1 RANDOM-NUMBER ASSIGNMENTS TO SIMULATION EVENTS

Event					
Weekly Demand (hr)	Probability	Random Number	Existing Weekly Capacity (hr)	Probability	Random Numbers
200	0.05	00–04	320	0.30	00–29
250	0.06	05–10	360	0.40	30–69
300	0.17	11–27	400	0.30	70–99
350	0.05	28–32			
400	0.30	33–62			
450	0.15	63–77			
500	0.06	78–83			
550	0.14	84–97			
600	0.02	98–99			

decision maker cannot control. At Specialty Steel Products, the weekly production requirements and the *actual* number of machine-hours available are uncontrollable variables for the simulation analysis. Dependent variables reflect the values of the decision variables and the uncontrollable variables. At Specialty Steel Products, operating characteristics such as idle time, overtime, and subcontracting hours are dependent variables.

The relationships among the variables are expressed in mathematical terms so that the dependent variables can be computed for any values of the decision variables and uncontrollable variables. For example, in the simulation model for Specialty Steel Products, the methods of determining weekly production requirements and actual capacity availability must be specified first. Then the methods of computing idle-time hours, overtime hours, and subcontracting hours for the values of production requirements and capacity hours can be specified.

Formulating a Simulation Model

EXAMPLE B.2

Formulate a simulation model for Specialty Steel Products that will estimate idle-time hours, overtime hours, and subcontracting hours for a specified number of lathes. Design the simulation model to terminate after 20 weeks of simulated lathe department operations.

SOLUTION

Let us use the first two rows of random numbers in the random number table for the demand events and the third and fourth rows for the capacity events (see the Table of Random Numbers in Appendix 2). Because they are five-digit numbers, we use only the first two digits of each number for our random numbers. The choice of the rows in the random-number table was arbitrary. The important point is that we must be consistent in drawing random numbers and should not repeat the use of numbers in any one simulation.

To simulate a particular capacity level, we proceed as follows:

Step 1. Draw a random number from the first two rows of the table. Start with the first number in the first row, then go to the second number in the first row, and so on.

Step 2. Find the random-number interval for production requirements associated with the random number.

Step 3. Record the production hours (PROD) required for the current week.

Step 4. Draw another random number from row 3 or 4 of the table. Start with the first number in row 3, then go to the second number in row 3, and so on.

Step 5. Find the random-number interval for capacity (CAP) associated with the random number.

Step 6. Record the capacity hours available for the current week.

Step 7. If CAP ≥ PROD, then IDLE HR = CAP − PROD.

Step 8. If CAP < PROD, then SHORT= PROD − CAP.
If SHORT ≤ 100, then OVERTIME HR = SHORT
and SUBCONTRACT HR = 0.
If SHORT > 100, then OVERTIME HR = 100
and SUBCONTRACT HR = SHORT − 100.

Step 9. Repeat steps 1–8 until you have simulated 20 weeks.

ANALYSIS

Table B.2 contains the simulations for the two capacity alternatives at Specialty Steel Products. We used a unique random-number sequence for weekly production requirements for each capacity alternative and another sequence for the existing weekly capacity to make a direct comparison between the capacity alternatives.

Based on the 20-week simulations, we would expect average weekly overtime hours (highlighted in red) to be reduced by 41.5 − 29.5 =12 hours and subcontracting hours (highlighted in gray) to be reduced by 18 − 10 = 8 hours per week. The average weekly savings would be

$$
\begin{aligned}
\text{Overtime:} &\quad (12 \text{ hours}) (\$25/ \text{hour}) = \$300 \\
\text{Subcontracting:} &\quad (8 \text{ hours}) (\$35/ \text{hour}) = \underline{280} \\
&\quad \text{Total savings per week} = \$580
\end{aligned}
$$

TABLE B.2 20-WEEK SIMULATIONS OF ALTERNATIVES

				10 Machines				11 Machines			
Week	Demand Random Number	Weekly Production (hr)	Capacity Random Number	Existing Weekly Capacity (hr)	Idle Hours	Overtime Hours	Sub-contract Hours	Existing Weekly Capacity (hr)	Idle Hours	Overtime Hours	Sub-contract Hours
1	71	450	50	360		90		400		50	
2	68	450	54	360		90		400		50	
3	48	400	11	320		80		360		40	
4	99	600	36	360		100	140	400		100	100
5	64	450	82	400		50		440		10	
6	13	300	87	400	100			440	140		
7	36	400	41	360		40		400			
8	58	400	71	400				440	40		
9	13	300	00	320	20			360	60		
10	93	550	60	360		100	90	400		100	50
11	21	300	47	360	60			400	100		
12	30	350	76	400	50			440	90		
13	23	300	09	320	20			360	60		
14	89	550	54	360		100	90	400		100	50
15	58	400	87	400				440	40		
16	46	400	82	400				440	40		
17	00	200	17	320	120			360	160		
18	82	500	52	360		100	40	400		100	
19	02	200	17	320	120			360	160		
20	37	400	19	320	___	80	___	360	___	40	___
				Total	490	830	360		890	590	200
				Weekly average 24.5		41.5	18.0		44.5	29.5	10.0

TABLE B.3
COMPARISON OF 1,000-WEEK SIMULATIONS

	10 Machines	11 Machines
Idle hours	26.0	42.2
Overtime hours	48.3	34.2
Subcontract hours	18.4	8.7
Cost	$1,851.50	$1,159.50

This amount falls short of the minimum required savings of $650 per week. Does that mean that we should not add the machine and worker? Before answering, let us look at Table B.3 which shows the results of a *1,000-week* simulation for each alternative. The costs (highlighted in blue) are quite different from those of the 20-week simulations. Now the savings are estimated to be $1,851.50 − $1,159.50 = $692 and exceed the minimum required savings for the additional investment. This result emphasizes the importance of selecting the proper run length for a simulation analysis. We can use statistical tests to check for the proper run length.

Simulation analysis can be viewed as a form of hypothesis testing, whereby the results of a simulation run provide sample data that can be analyzed statistically. Data can be recorded and compared with the results from other simulation runs. Statistical tests also can be made to determine whether differences in the alternative operating characteristics are statistically significant. Commonly used statistical methods include *analysis of variance, t-tests,* and *regression analysis.* These techniques require replication of each simulation experiment. For example, if we wanted to test the null hypothesis that the difference between total weekly costs is zero, we would have to run the simulation model several times for each capacity alternative. Each time, we would use a different set of random numbers to generate weekly production requirements and weekly existing capacity. The number of replications is analogous to the sample size in statistical terminology. If we can show that the weekly cost for 11 machines is significantly different (in a statistical sense) from the weekly cost for 10 machines, we can be more confident of the estimate of the difference between the two.

Even though a difference between simulation experiments may be statistically significant, it may not be *managerially* significant. For example, suppose that we developed a simulation model of a car-wash operation. We may find, by changing the speed of the car wash from 3 to 2.75 minutes per car, that we can reduce the average waiting time per customer by 0.20 minute. Even though this may be a statistically significant difference in the average waiting time, the difference is so small that customers may not even notice it. What is managerially significant often is a judgment decision.

COMPUTER SIMULATION

The manual simulation of the lathe process in Examples B.1 and B.2 demonstrates the basics of simulation. However, there is only one step in the process, two uncontrollable variables (weekly production requirements and the actual number of machine-hours available), and 20 time periods in the simulation. It is important to simulate a process long enough to achieve **steady state,** so that the simulation is repeated over enough time that the average results for performance measures remain constant. In Figure 4.15c achieving steady state explains why the simulation was continued over 2,000 hours and the averages were not plotted in the graph until after the first 300 hours. Visually plotting the averages shows that steady state was achieved. Manual simulations can be excessively time-consuming, particularly if there are many subprocesses, many services or products with unique flow patterns, many uncontrollable variables, complex logic for releasing new jobs and assigning work, and the like.

steady state The state that occurs when the simulation is repeated over enough time that the average results for performance measures remain constant.

Simulating these real-world situations manually can become too time-consuming and therefore requires a computer instead. Simple simulation models, say with one or two uncontrollable variables, can be developed using Excel. Its ability to generate random numbers—coupled with adding formulas elsewhere in the worksheet to specify relations between demand, customer served, inventory, and output—allow the Monte Carlo simulation approach to be implemented. Even more computer power comes from commercial, prewritten simulation software.

SIMULATION WITH EXCEL SPREADSHEETS

The starting point in creating an Excel simulation is generating random numbers, the computer equivalent of using Appendix 2 for manual simulations. Equally important is random-number assignment, which translates a random number into a value for an uncontrollable variable.

GENERATING RANDOM NUMBERS. Random numbers can be created from 0 to 1 by entering the formula =RAND() into a cell of the Excel spreadsheet. This formula then can be copied to other cells in the spreadsheet as needed. Figure B.1 shows a table of 100 random numbers generated with the RAND() function in the range A3:J12. They were formatted to show four-digit numbers, although the format can be changed as desired. These random numbers are fractions from 0 to 1, rather than the two-digit integer numbers from 0 through 99 in Table B.1. If you attempt to replicate Figure B.1, or reopen an Excel file that was created earlier and saved, you will see a different set of random numbers. To use the same exact set or *stream* of random numbers, such as for experiments that compare the effectiveness of different policies, you should *freeze* the random numbers. First, select with your mouse the cells holding the random numbers that you wish frozen. For example, cover A3:J12 in Figure B.1. Next, click on Edit/Copy in the menu at the top of your spreadsheet. Click next on Edit/Paste Special and choose the Values option. When you click on OK, a copy of the numbers in these cells is pasted over the same cells with the =RAND() formulas in them. The result is that they are fixed in place and will not change from one use of the spreadsheet to the next. Each simulation is conducted with the same stream of random numbers. In fact, the numbers in Figure B.1 were frozen using this procedure.

RANDOM-NUMBER ASSIGNMENT. A second capability that is needed for Excel simulations is to translate random numbers into values for the uncontrollable variables. It is equivalent to identifying the random-number interval in which a random number falls and then selecting the value of the uncontrollable variable assigned to that interval (see Table B.1 for the demand or capacity variables). In an Excel spreadsheet, the Lookup feature of Excel serves this purpose. Read about the VLOOKUP() function under Excel's Help Topics and check out the function by selecting Insert/Function/

FIGURE B.1

A Spreadsheet with 100 Random Numbers Generated with RAND()

	A	B	C	D	E	F	G	H	I	J	K	L
1	Random Number Table Using RAND()											
2												
3	0.2858	0.0287	0.7906	0.5752	0.6719	0.3756	0.7136	0.3506	0.2184	0.8734		
4	0.9377	0.2569	0.7606	0.3411	0.2013	0.5270	0.1037	0.1589	0.6092	0.2768		
5	0.9230	0.8938	0.8995	0.7370	0.2308	0.8001	0.2189	0.7370	0.5849	0.2935		
6	0.3684	0.8174	0.9635	0.0082	0.3211	0.8143	0.5237	0.4769	0.2235	0.6465		
7	0.8164	0.9626	0.9041	0.8596	0.5203	0.2763	0.0405	0.6229	0.7908	0.2328		
8	0.0699	0.9116	0.3194	0.6435	0.7507	0.7179	0.8473	0.6650	0.2683	0.2505		
9	0.7434	0.9540	0.9654	0.7457	0.5739	0.2974	0.0448	0.5035	0.8662	0.6522		
10	0.1528	0.8228	0.2987	0.1987	0.2209	0.3466	0.4633	0.2702	0.0172	0.2614		
11	0.5384	0.3741	0.9467	0.1050	0.6346	0.6695	0.0598	0.8396	0.8366	0.1351		
12	0.7628	0.8358	0.4549	0.0945	0.3317	0.6182	0.0260	0.1718	0.9218	0.1020		
13												

Lookup & Reference/VLOOKUP. Example B.3 demonstrates the use of both the VLOOKUP() and RAND() functions.

Excel Simulation Model for BestCar Auto Dealer

EXAMPLE B.3

The BestCar automobile dealership sells new automobiles. The BestCar store manager believes that the number of cars sold weekly has the following probability distribution:

WEEKLY SALES (CARS)	RELATIVE FREQUENCY (PROBABILITY)
0	0.05
1	0.15
2	0.20
3	0.30
4	0.20
5	0.10
Total	1.00

The selling price per car is $20,000. Design a simulation model that determines the probability distribution and mean of the weekly sales.

SOLUTION

Figure B.2 simulates 50 weeks of sales at BestCar. A longer run length, say 500 or 1,000 weeks, would be prudent, but here we keep it small for demonstration purposes. The bottom right of the spreadsheet shows that the average weekly sales is 2.88 cars, for $57,600 per week. The distribution of the simulated weekly demand is shown in cells B17:E22. For example, 13 of the 50 weeks experienced a demand for 3 cars, which translates into 26 percent of the weeks (see cell D20). The chance that sales are not more than 3 cars is 60 percent (see cell E20).

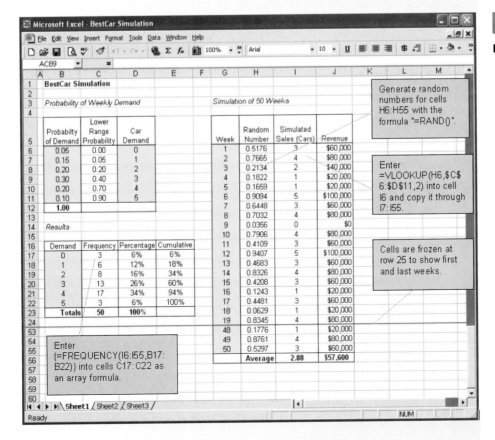

FIGURE B.2

BestCar Simulation Model

The first step in creating this spreadsheet is to input the probability distribution, including the cumulative probabilities associated with it. These inputs values are highlighted in yellow in cells B6:B11 of the spreadsheet, with corresponding demands in D6:D11. The lower range of cumulative probabilities is calculated in cells C6:C11 by entering 0 in C6 and then entering the formula "=C6+B6" into cell C7 and copying it to cells C8:C11. The cumulative values provide a basis to associate random numbers to the corresponding demand, using the VLOOKUP() function. For example, the first random number for week 1 has the value 0.5176 and will result in a demand of 3 cars, because 0.5176 is greater than the lower range for a demand of 3 cars, but smaller than the lower range for demand of 4 cars. In a similar way, any random number with a value greater than 0.70 but smaller than 0.90 will correspond to a demand of 4 cars.

The next step is to create a table with four columns. Column G identifies each of the 50 weeks to be simulated in cells G6:G55. Column H generates the random numbers, one for each of the 50 weeks. To create the random numbers, we enter the formula "=RAND()" into cell H6 of our spreadsheet and then copy it to the cells H7:H55. After generating the random numbers, we need to match these numbers with the corresponding demand values. We can do this by using the VLOOKUP function. We enter the formula "=VLOOKUP(H6,$C$6:$D$11,2)" into cell I6 and copy it through I7:I55. With this use of the VLOOKUP function, Excel's logic identifies (or "looks up") for each week's random number (in column H) which demand it corresponds to in the lookup array defined by $C6:$D$11. Once it finds the probability range (defined by column C) in which the random number fits, it posts the car demand (in column D) for this range back into the week's sales (in column I). When searching the lookup array, it moves down through column C until it finds a cell that has a value greater than the random number. It goes back to the previous cell, gets the corresponding demand value from column D, and returns it to the cell in column I. The weekly revenue column is the fourth column in the simulation table, created in cells J6:J55 by multiplying the weekly demand values (column I) by average selling price ($20,000). The average car sales is calculated in cell I56 using the =AVERAGE(I6:I55) function, and the average revenue in cell J56 using the =AVERAGE(J6:J55) function. Note that Figure B.2 only shows the first 19 weeks and the last 3 weeks. This compression is possible using the Window/Freeze Panes option. Here, the window is frozen up through week 19 (start of row 25). You can scroll down or up to show just a few of the last weeks or most of them, depending on how much you want to display.

Finally, the results table is created at the lower left portion of the spreadsheet to summarize the simulation output. By entering the FREQUENCY function into cells C17:C22, we calculate the number of observations in each demand category out of a total of 50 observations. The function looks through the simulated demand values in cells I6:I55 and compares them to the demand categories in cells B17:B22, which are defined as the bin array of the FREQUENCY function. Percentage and cumulative columns next to the frequency column show the frequencies in percentage and cumulative percentage terms.

SIMULATION WITH TWO UNCONTROLLABLE VARIABLES. Going beyond one variable is usually necessary to be able to evaluate different decision alternatives. For example, Figure B.3 shows a simulation model of the inventory replenishment rule for futons. The weekly demand and lead time are both uncontrollable variables, and their probability distributions are input to the top of the spreadsheet, along with the inventory holding, ordering, and stockout cost parameters. There are two decision variables, the order size and the reorder point. The order size is the quantity ordered each time a new order is placed with the supplier. The reorder point is the level to which the inventory is allowed to drop before a replenishment order is placed. The order size is set at 50 units in Figure B.3 and the reorder point is 35 units. The results of the simulation are summarized at the bottom of the spreadsheet. Of particular interest are the values of the dependent variables. The average holding cost is $44.91 per week, the average ordering cost is $3.20 per week, and the average stockout cost is $186.00 per week. The manager can try out different values of the order size and reorder point to seek a less costly result just by changing the input values of the two decision variables. The manager should notice the high stockout cost and might want to try a higher reorder point. The annotations in

FIGURE B.3 Inventory Simulation Model

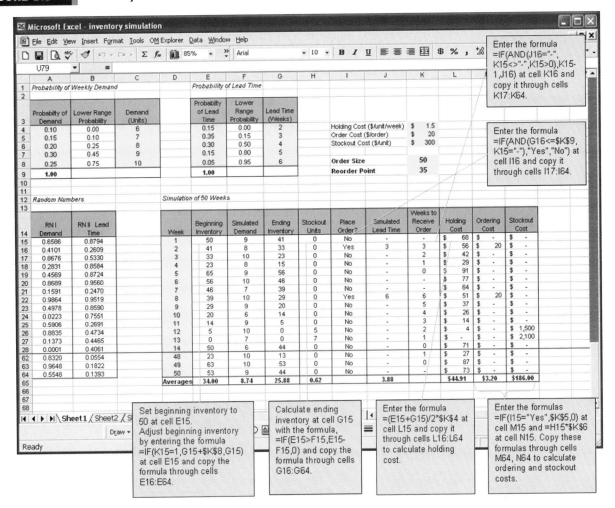

Figure B.3 show that the formulas become much more complex when the simulation model must reflect multiple decision and uncontrollable variables. For more information on the logic of inventory replenishment systems, see Chapter 15, "Inventory Management."

SIMULATION WITH MORE ADVANCED SOFTWARE

Simulation programming can be done in a variety of computer languages, including general-purpose programming languages such as VISUAL BASIC, FORTRAN, or C^{++}. The advantage of general-purpose programming languages is that they are available on most computer systems. Special simulation languages, such as GPSS, SIMSCRIPT, and SLAM, are also available. These languages simplify programming because they have macroinstructions for the commonly used elements of simulation models. These macroinstructions automatically contain the computer instructions needed to generate arrivals, keep track of waiting lines, and calculate the statistics on the operating characteristics of a system.

Simulation is also possible with powerful PC-based packages, such as SimQuick (**www.nd.edu/~dhartvig/simquick/top.htm**), Extend (**www.imaginethatinc.com**), SIMPROCESS (**www.caciasl.com**), ProModel (**www.promodel.com**), and Witness (**www.lanner.com/corporate**). Here we illustrate process simulation with the SimQuick software (provided on the Student CD-ROM) and Extend (which might be packaged with your textbook on an optional basis).

SIMQUICK. SimQuick, for example, is an easy-to-use package that is simply an Excel spreadsheet with some macros. Models can be created for a variety of simple processes, such as waiting lines, inventory control, and projects. Here we consider the passenger security process at one terminal of a medium-sized airport between the hours of 8 A.M. and 10 A.M. The process works as follows. Passengers arriving at the security area immediately enter a single line. After waiting in line, each passenger goes through one of two inspection stations, which involves walking through a metal detector and running any carry-on baggage through a scanner. After completing this inspection, 10 percent of the passengers are randomly selected for an additional inspection, which typically involves a more thorough search of the person's carry-on baggage. There are two stations for this additional inspection, and selected passengers go through only one of them. Management is interested in examining the effect of increasing the percentage of passengers that undergo the second inspection. In particular, they want to compare the waiting times for the second inspection when 10 percent, then 15 percent, and then 20 percent of the passengers are randomly selected for this inspection. Management also wants to know how opening a third station for the second inspection would affect these waiting times.

A first step in simulating this process with SimQuick is to draw a flowchart of the process using SimQuick's building blocks. SimQuick has five building blocks that can be combined in a wide variety of ways. Four of these types are used to model this process. An *entrance* is used to model the arrival of passengers at the security process. A *buffer* is used to model each of the two waiting lines, one before each type of inspection, as well as the passengers that have finished the process. Each of the four inspection stations is modeled with a *work station*. Finally, the random selection of passengers for the second inspection is modeled with a *decision point*. Figure B.4 shows the flowchart.

Information describing each building block is entered into SimQuick tables. In this model there are three key types of information to enter: when people arrive at the

Flowchart of Passenger Security Process (Modeled with SimQuick)

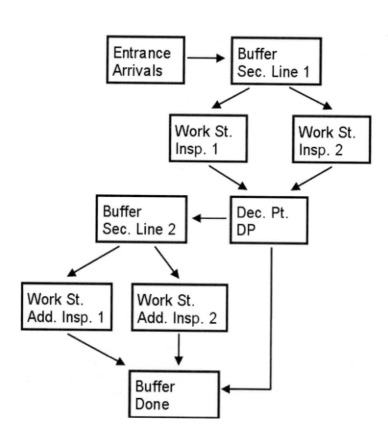

Element Types	Element Names	Statistics	Overall Means
Entrance(s)	Arrivals	Objects entering process	237.23
Buffer(s)	Line 1	Mean inventory	5.97
		Mean cycle time	3.12
	Line 2	Mean inventory	0.10
		Mean cycle time	0.53
	Done	Final inventory	224.57

Simulation Results of Passenger Security Process (Modeled with SimQuick)

entrance, how long inspections take at the four stations, and what percentage of passengers are randomly selected for the additional inspection. All of this information must be entered into SimQuick in the form of statistical distributions. The first two types of information are determined by observing the real process from 8 A.M. and 10 A.M. The third type of information is a policy decision (10 percent, 15 percent, or 20 percent).

The original model is run 30 times, simulating the hours from 8 A.M. to 10 A.M. Statistics are collected by SimQuick and summarized. Figure B.5 provides some key results for the model of the present process as output by SimQuick (many other statistics are collected, but not displayed here).

The numbers shown are averages across the 30 simulations. The number 237.23 is the average number of passengers that enter line 1 during the simulated two hours. The two mean inventory statistics tell us there were, on average, 5.97 simulated passengers standing in line 1 and 0.10 standing in line 2. The two mean cycle time statistics tell us that the simulated passengers in line 1 waited an average of 3.12 minutes, while those in line 2 waited 0.53 minutes. The final inventory statistic tells us that, on average, 224.57 simulated passengers passed through the security process in the simulated two hours. The next step is to change the percentage of simulated passengers selected for the second inspection to 15 percent, and then to 20 percent, and rerun the model. Of course, these process changes will increase the average waiting time for the second inspection, but by how much? The final step is to rerun these simulations with one more work station and see the effect of this on the waiting time for the second inspection. All the details for this model (as well as many others) appear in the book *SimQuick: Process Simulation with Excel,* which is included, along with the SimQuick software, on the CD-ROM that comes with this textbook.

EXTEND. Going one step further than SimQuick, the Extend package helps users create models and then use them to answer a variety of "what-if" questions. The output graphs on performance measures actually show what is occurring as the simulation takes place. An animation option can be clicked on to show customers or jobs working their way from one subprocess to the next subprocess over the whole simulation horizon. The user must invest time to fully understand the Extend modeling features because of its large range of capabilities. Its versatility also means that it can be applied to most issues about processes. Example B.4 demonstrates some of its capabilities for a layout problem.

EXAMPLE B.4   Security Inspection at the Sharpville Plant

The chief of security at the Sharpville plant of a large defense contractor is concerned. The security inspection at the plant entrance is creating delays. Currently, there is one main security gate and all employees are required to show identification and allow a visual search of their vehicle when entering the plant. Each day, approximately 800 salaried and hourly workers enter the plant prior to the 8:00 A.M. shift. As Figure B.6 shows, arriving vehicles enter one of two lanes to be inspected on a first-come, first-served basis. The plant allocates space for approximately 40 cars in each lane on the plant's property ahead of the gate.

Employees commute to work by personal vehicle (cars), vanpools, or bus. Approximately 300 vehicles are inspected each morning between 7:00 A.M. and 8:00 A.M., with the peak occurring just after 7:30 A.M. Figure B.7 gives the arrival rates based on data collected over several days. Approximately 10 percent of the entering vehicles are vans, each carrying about 10 people. The Sharpville plant sponsors seven buses from areas with very high concentrations of workers. Unlike the cars and vans, buses are formally scheduled to arrive at 7:30, although in reality they arrive up to five minutes early or late. Given the relatively large number of people in each bus, management decided to give the buses priority. One inspection lane was designated as an "express" lane for buses (Lane 1). Visitors to the plant also used this lane. All other employee vehicles (cars and vanpools) use the second lane (Lane 0). This lane has up to three checkpoint positions; the number in use depends on the availability of guards. Usually, two guards were available for morning inspections, and one guard performed inspections at Checkpoint 1, while another inspected at Checkpoint 2. When the buses begin to arrive, the second guard shifts to the express lane (Lane 1), leaving only one guard in Lane 0. Inspection times are as follows:

VEHICLE	INSPECTION TIME (SEC)	
	AVERAGE	STANDARD DEVIATION
Cars	10	3
Vanpools	30	9
Buses	50	10

FIGURE B.6   Security Inspection Layout

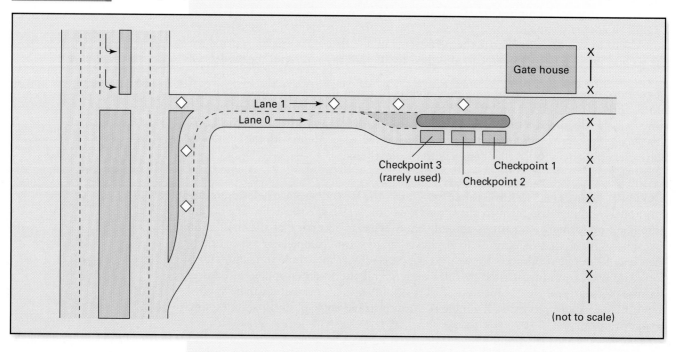

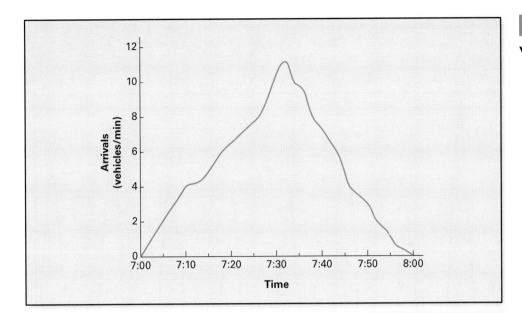

a. During the 7:00 A.M. to 8:00 A.M. interval, what is the average time to service each type of vehicle?
b. What is the average line length in each lane? What is the maximum line length in each lane?
c. What is the guard utilization?

SOLUTION

Here we use the Extend software to model and simulate this process during the 7:00 A.M. to 8:00 A.M. arrival hour over the course of 10 days. Figure B.8(a) shows the simulation model for this inspection process, with the three types of vehicles arriving and going into one of two lanes for inspection. Figure B.8(b) shows how the length of the lines behaves. Every day the number of

FIGURE B.8a   **Extend Model for Security Inspection Process**

(a) Simulation model

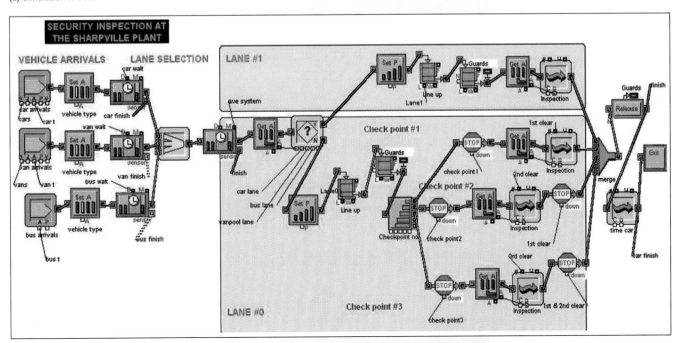

(b) Waiting lines for 10 simulated arrival periods

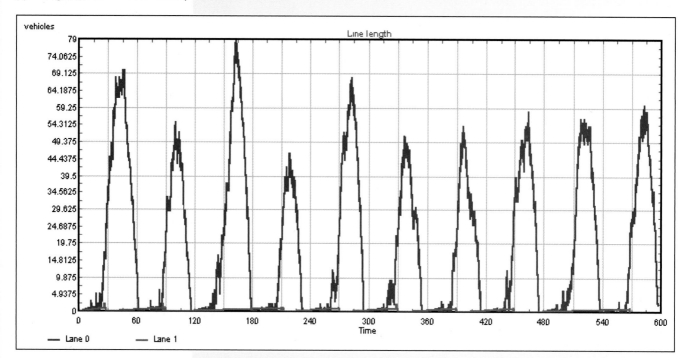

vehicles in the waiting lines exceeds 40, which means that some vehicles must wait in line on the highway. Figure B.8(c) reports additional performance measures. The average service time (waiting and inspection) is 4.018 minutes, but it is particularly high for vans. Lane 0, where cars and vans are inspected, is the critical bottleneck, with the maximum wait time reaching 11.2 minutes and the maximum waiting line reaching 79 vehicles.

FIGURE B.8c

(c) Performance measures

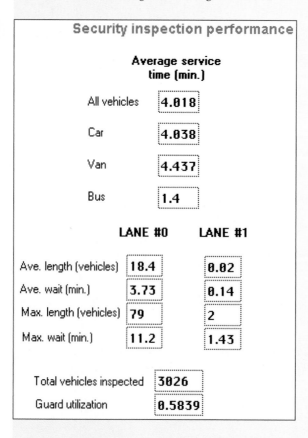

DECISION POINT Management must make some changes, such as adding capacity, redesigning the process, changing the priority rules, or spreading out the arrival-time pattern. The current process is causing significant employee frustration and is creating a potentially dangerous traffic problem.

Source: This case and simulation experience was provided by Professor Robert Klassen, University of Western Ontario.

SUPPLEMENT HIGHLIGHTS

- Simulation is used to model the important operating characteristics of complex waiting-line situations. Information that is not attainable through the use of waiting-line formulas, such as the maximum number in line and the effect of disruptions to steady-state operations, also can be collected.

- Simulation models consist of decision variables (e.g., number of servers), uncontrollable variables (e.g., incidence of machine breakdowns), and dependent variables (e.g., utilization or the maximum number in line). Dependent variables reflect the behavior of the system defined by the decision variables as it is affected by uncontrollable variables. For example, simulation of three machines (decision variable) may show that when one machine breaks down for two hours (uncontrollable

variable), the maximum number in line grows to seven customers (dependent variable).

- Computer support is required for most real simulation problems, so as to handle more complex situations and ensure steady state. Excel simulations can be created for relatively simple situations.

- For more complex situations, general-purpose and special-purpose programming languages are available. Of particular interest are two PC-based packages—SimQuick and Extend. *SimQuick: Process Simulation with Excel* is a user-friendly package with considerable power that is available on the Student CD-ROM, which is packaged with every new copy of the textbook. Extend is a prewritten simulator with a graphic interface.

STUDENT CD-ROM AND INTERNET RESOURCES

The Student CD-ROM and the Companion Website at **www.prenhall.com/krajewski** contain many tools, activities, and resources designed for this supplement. The following items are recommended to enhance your skills and improve your understanding of the material in this supplement.

 STUDENT CD-ROM RESOURCES

➤ **PowerPoint Slides.** View this comprehensive set of slides customized for this supplement's concepts and techniques.

 INTERNET RESOURCES

➤ **Self-Study Quizzes.** See the compendium of true or false, multiple choice, and essay questions that give feedback on how well you have mastered the concepts in this supplement.
➤ **In the News.** See articles that apply to this supplement.
➤ **Internet Exercises.** Try out the exercises available on various simulation applications.
➤ **Virtual Tours.** See the "Web Links to Company Facility Tours" for various tours of company facilities.

KEY TERMS

decision variables 172
Monte Carlo simulation 171
random number 172

simulation 170
steady state 175
time compression 170

uncontrollable variables 172

SOLVED PROBLEM

A manager is considering production of several products in an automated facility. The manager would purchase a combination of two robots. The two robots (named Mel and Danny) in series are capable of doing all the required operations. Every batch of work will contain 10 units. A waiting line of several batches will be maintained in front of Mel. When Mel completes his portion of the work, the batch will then be transferred directly to Danny.

Each robot incurs a setup before it can begin processing a batch. Each unit in the batch has equal run time. The distributions of the setup times and run times for Mel and Danny are identical. But, as Mel and Danny will be performing different operations, simulation of each batch requires four random numbers from the table. The first random number determines Mel's setup time, the second determines Mel's run time per unit, and the third and fourth random numbers determine Danny's setup and run times, respectively.

Setup Time (min)	Probability	Run Time per Unit (sec)	Probability
1	0.10	5	0.10
2	0.20	6	0.20
3	0.40	7	0.30
4	0.20	8	0.25
5	0.10	9	0.15

Estimate how many units will be produced in an hour. Then use the first column of random numbers to simulate 60 minutes of operation for Mel and Danny.

SOLUTION

Except for the time required for Mel to set up and run the first batch, we assume that the two robots run simultaneously. The expected average setup time per batch is

$$[(0.1 \times 1 \ \text{min}) + (0.2 \times 2 \ \text{min}) + (0.4 \times 3 \ \text{min}) + (0.2 \times 4 \ \text{min}) + (0.1 \times 5 \ \text{min})]$$
$$= 3 \ \text{minutes} \quad \text{or} \quad 180 \ \text{seconds per batch}$$

The expected average run time per batch (of 10 units) is

$$[(0.1 \times 5 \ \text{sec}) + (0.2 \times 6 \ \text{sec}) + (0.3 \times 7 \ \text{sec}) + (0.25 \times 8 \ \text{sec}) + (0.15 \times 9 \ \text{sec})]$$
$$= 7.15 \ \text{seconds}/\text{unit} \times 10 \ \text{units}/\text{batch} = 71.5 \ \text{seconds per batch}$$

Thus, the total of average setup and run times per batch is 251.5 seconds. In an hour's time we might expect to complete about 14 batches $(3,600/251.5 \ \text{seconds} = 14.3)$. However, this estimate is probably too high.

Keep in mind that Mel and Danny operate in sequence and that Danny cannot begin to do work until it has been completed by Mel (see batch 2 of Table B.4). Nor can Mel start a new batch until Danny is ready to accept the previous one. Refer to batch 6, where Mel completes

TABLE B.4   SIMULATION RESULTS FOR MEL AND DANNY

		Mel						Danny				
Batch No.	Start Time	Random No.	Setup	Random No.	Process	Completion Time	Start Time	Random No.	Setup	Random No.	Process	Completion Time
1	0:00	71	4 min	50	7 sec	5 min 10 sec	5:10	21	2 min	94	9 sec	8 min 40 sec
2	5:10	50	3 min	63	8 sec	9 min 30 sec	9:30	47	3 min	83	8 sec	13 min 50 sec
3	9:30	31	3 min	73	8 sec	13 min 50 sec	13:50	04	1 min	17	6 sec	15 min 50 sec
4	13:50	96	5 min	98	9 sec	20 min 20 sec	20:20	21	2 min	82	8 sec	23 min 40 sec
5	20:20	25	2 min	92	9 sec	23 min 50 sec	23:50	32	3 min	53	7 sec	28 min 0 sec
6	23:50	00	1 min	15	6 sec	25 min 50 sec	28:00	66	3 min	57	7 sec	32 min 10 sec
7	28:00	00	1 min	99	9 sec	30 min 30 sec	32:10	55	3 min	11	6 sec	36 min 10 sec
8	32:10	10	2 min	61	8 sec	35 min 30 sec	36:10	31	3 min	35	7 sec	40 min 20 sec
9	36:10	09	1 min	73	8 sec	38 min 30 sec	40:20	24	2 min	70	8 sec	43 min 40 sec
10	40:20	79	4 min	95	9 sec	45 min 50 sec	45:50	66	3 min	61	8 sec	50 min 10 sec
11	45:50	01	1 min	41	7 sec	48 min 00 sec	50:10	88	4 min	23	6 sec	55 min 10 sec
12	50:10	57	3 min	45	7 sec	54 min 20 sec	55:10	21	2 min	61	8 sec	58 min 30 sec
13	54:20	26	2 min	46	7 sec	57 min 30 sec	58:30	97	5 min	31	7 sec	64 min 40 sec

this batch at time 25:50 but cannot begin the seventh batch until Danny is ready to accept the sixth batch at time 28:00.

Mel and Danny completed only 12 batches in one hour. Even though the robots used the same probability distributions and therefore have perfectly balanced production capacities, Mel and Danny did not produce the expected capacity of 14 batches because Danny was sometimes idle while waiting for Mel (see batch 2) and Mel was sometimes idle while waiting for Danny (see batch 6). This loss-of-throughput phenomenon occurs whenever variable processes are closely linked, whether those processes are mechanical, such as Mel's and Danny's, or functional, such as production and marketing. The simulation shows the need to place between the two robots sufficient space to store several batches to absorb the variations in process times. Subsequent simulations could be run to show how many batches are needed.

PROBLEMS

1. Comet Dry Cleaners specializes in same-day dry cleaning. Customers drop off their garments early in the morning and expect them to be ready for pickup on their way home from work. There is a risk, however, that the work needed on a garment cannot be done that day, depending on the type of cleaning required. Historically, an average of 20 garments have had to be held over to the next day. The outlet's manager is contemplating expanding to reduce or eliminate that backlog. A simulation model was developed with the following distribution for garments per day:

Number	Probability	Random Numbers
50	0.10	00–09
60	0.25	10–34
70	0.30	35–64
80	0.25	65–89
90	0.10	90–99

With expansion, the maximum number of garments that could be dry-cleaned per day is

Number	Probability	Random Numbers
60	0.30	00–29
70	0.40	30–69
80	0.30	70–99

In the simulation for a specific day, the number of garments needing cleaning (NGNC) is determined first. Next, the maximum number of garments that could be dry-cleaned (MNGD) is determined. If MNGD ≥ NGNC, all garments are dry-cleaned for that day. If MNGD < NGNC, then (NGNC − MNGD) garments must be added to the number of garments arriving the next day to obtain the NGNC for the next day. The simulation continues in this manner.

   a. Assuming that the store is empty at the start, simulate 15 days of operation. Use the following random numbers, the first determining the number of arrivals and the second setting the capacity:

   (49, 77), (27, 53), (65, 08), (83, 12), (04, 82), (58, 44), (53, 83), (57, 72), (32, 53), (60, 79), (79, 30), (41, 48), (97, 86), (30, 25), (80, 73)

Determine the average daily number of garments held overnight, based on your simulation.

   b. If the cost associated with garments being held over is $25 per garment per day and the added cost of expansion is $200 per day, is expansion a good idea?

2. The Precision Manufacturing Company is considering the purchase of an NC machine and has narrowed the possible choices to two models. The company produces several products, and batches of work arrive at the NC machine every six minutes. The number of units in the batch has the following discrete distribution:

Number of Units in Batch	Probability
3	0.1
6	0.2
8	0.3
14	0.2
18	0.2

The distributions of the setup times and processing times for the two NC models follow. Assume that the work in a batch shares a single setup and that each unit in the batch has equal processing time. Simulate two hours (or 10 batch arrivals) of operation for the two NC machines. Use the following random numbers, the first one for the number of units in a batch, the second one for setup times, and the third one for run times:

   (71, 21, 50), (50, 94, 63), (96, 93, 95), (83, 09, 49), (10, 20, 68), (48, 23, 11), (21, 28, 40), (39, 78, 93), (99, 95, 61), (28, 14, 48)

Which one would you recommend if both machines cost the same to purchase, operate, and maintain?

NC MACHINE 1			
Setup Time (min)	Probability	Run Time Per Unit (sec)	Probability
1	0.10	5	0.10
2	0.20	6	0.20
3	0.40	7	0.30
4	0.20	8	0.25
5	0.10	9	0.15

NC MACHINE 2			
Setup Time (min)	Probability	Run Time Per Unit (sec)	Probability
1	0.05	3	0.20
2	0.15	4	0.25
3	0.25	5	0.30
4	0.45	6	0.15
5	0.10	7	0.10

3. In Problem 2, what factors would you consider if the initial cost of NC Machine 1 was $4,000 less than that of NC Machine 2?

4. The 30 management professors at Omega University (ΩU) find out that telephone calls made to their offices are not being picked up. A call-forwarding system redirects calls to the management office after the fourth ring. A department office assistant answers the telephone and takes messages. An average of 90 telephone calls per hour are placed to the management faculty, and each telephone call consumes about one minute of the assistant's time. The calls arrive according to a Poisson distribution, with an average of 1.5 calls per minute, as shown in Figure B.9 (a). Because the professors spend much of their time in class and in conferences, there is only a 40 percent chance that they will pick up a call themselves, as shown in Figure B.9 (b). If two or more telephone calls are forwarded to the office during the same minute, only the first call will be answered.

a. Without using simulation, make a preliminary guess of what proportion of the time the assistant will be on the telephone and what proportion of the telephone calls will not be answered.

b. Now use random numbers to simulate the situation for one hour starting at 10:00 A.M. Table B.5 will get you started.

c. What proportion of the time is the office assistant on the telephone? What proportion of the telephone calls are not answered? Are these proportions close to what you expected?

5. The management chair at ΩU is considering installing a voice-mail system. Monthly operating costs are $25 per voice-mailbox, but the system will reduce the amount of time the office assistant spends answering the telephone by 60 percent. The department has 32 telephones. Use the results of your simulation in Problem 4 to estimate the proportion of the assistant's time presently spent answering the telephone. The office assistant's salary (and overhead) is $3,000 per month. Should the management chair order the voice-mail system?

6. Weekly demand at a local E-Z Mart convenience store for 1-gallon jugs of low-fat milk for the last 50 weeks has varied between 60 and 65 jugs, as shown in the following table. Demand in excess of stock cannot be back-ordered.

Demand (jugs)	Number of Weeks
60	5
61	7
62	17
63	11
64	6
65	4
Total	50

FIGURE B.9

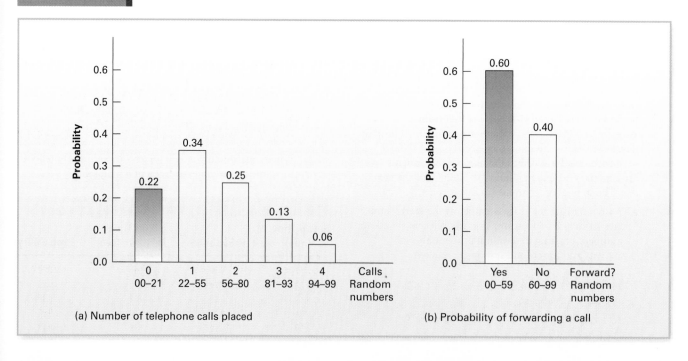

(a) Number of telephone calls placed

(b) Probability of forwarding a call

TABLE B.5 OFFICE ASSISTANT SIMULATION

Time	RN	Number of Calls Made	RN	1st Call Forwarded? (Yes/No)	RN	2d Call Forwarded? (Yes/No)	RN	3d Call Forwarded? (Yes/No)	RN	4th Call Forwarded? (Yes/No)	Number of Calls Not Answered	Assistant Idle (✔)
10:00	68	2	30	Yes	54	Yes					1	
10:01	76	2	36	Yes	32	Yes					1	
10:02	68	2	04	Yes	07	Yes					1	
10:03	98	4	08	Yes	21	Yes	28	Yes	79	No	2	
10:04	25	1	77	No							0	✔
10:05	51	1	23	Yes							0	
10:06	67	2	22	Yes	27	Yes					1	
10:07	80	2	87	No	06	Yes					0	
10:08	03	0									0	✔
10:09	03	0									0	✔
10:10	33	1	78	No							0	✔

a. Assign random numbers between 00 and 99 to simulate the demand probability distribution.

b. E-Z Mart orders 62 jugs every week. Simulate the demand for this item for 10 weeks, using the random numbers 97, 2, 80, 66, 99, 56, 54, 28, 64, and 47. Determine the shortage or excess stock for each week.

c. What is the average shortage and the average excess stock for the 10 weeks?

7. The Brakes-Only Service Shop promises its customers same-day service by working overtime if necessary. The shop's two mechanics can handle a total of 12 brake jobs a day during regular hours. Over the past 100 days, the number of brake jobs at the shop varied between 10 and 14, as shown in the following table:

Demand (jobs)	Number of Days
10	10
11	30
12	30
13	20
14	10
Total	100

a. Assign random numbers between 00 and 99 to simulate the demand probability distribution for brake jobs.

b. Simulate the demand for the next 10 days, using the random numbers 28, 83, 73, 7, 4, 63, 37, 38, 50, and 92.

c. On how many days will overtime work be necessary? On how many days will the mechanics be underutilized?

d. What percent of days, on average, will overtime work be necessary?

8. A machine center handles four types of clients: A, B, C, and D. The manager wants to assess the number of machines required to produce goods for these clients.

Setup times for changeover from one client to another are negligible. Annual demand and processing times are uncertain; demand may be low, normal, or high. The probabilities for these three events are shown in the following tables:

CLIENT A			
Demand (units/yr)	Probability	Processing Time (hr/unit)	Probability
3,000	0.10	10	0.35
3,500	0.60	20	0.45
4,200	0.30	30	0.20

CLIENT B			
Demand (units/yr)	Probability	Processing Time (hr/unit)	Probability
500	0.30	60	0.25
800	0.50	90	0.50
900	0.20	100	0.25

CLIENT C			
Demand (units/yr)	Probability	Processing Time (hr/unit)	Probability
1,500	0.10	12	0.25
3,000	0.50	15	0.60
4,500	0.40	20	0.15

CLIENT D			
Demand (units/yr)	Probability	Processing Time (hr/unit)	Probability
600	0.40	60	0.30
650	0.50	70	0.65
700	0.10	80	0.05

a. Explain how simulation could be used to generate a probability distribution for the total number of machine hours required per year to serve the clients.

b. Simulate one year, using the following random numbers. For example, use random number 88 for client A's demand and 24 for client A's processing time.

$$88, 24, 33, 29, 52, 84, 37, 92$$

9. The sales activity at BestCar (see Example B.3) has changed. Weekly sales are now estimated to be distributed as follows:

Weekly Sales Cars	Relative Frequency Probability
0	0.02
1	0.03
2	0.05
3	0.10
4	0.15
5	0.30
6	0.20
7	0.10
8	0.05
Total	1.00

Create an Excel model that simulates 500 weeks at BestCar. It should calculate from the simulated experience the average number of cars and revenue per week and also a frequency table on car sales.

10. Keep the same weekly sales distribution for BestCar as in Example B.3, but assume that the price of cars is distributed as follows:

Sales Price (Price/Car)	Relative Frequency (Probability)
$18,000	0.15
$20,000	0.35
$22,000	0.35
$24,000	0.10
$26,000	0.05
Total	1.00

Create an Excel model that simulates 500 weeks at BestCar. It should calculate from the simulated experience the average number of cars and revenue per week and also a frequency table on car sales.

SIMULATION EXERCISES

These simulation exercises require the use of the SimQuick and Extend simulation packages. SimQuick is on the Student CD-ROM that is packaged with every new copy of the textbook. Extend LT is an optional simulation package that your instructor may or may not have ordered.

1. The management of a grocery store is concerned about the waiting time of customers between the hours of 5 P.M. and 8 P.M. on week nights. Three checkout lanes are typically open; each register clerk can handle customers with any number of items, and there is a bagger always available. The checkout times are normally distributed, with a mean of 3 minutes per customer and a standard deviation of 0.5 minutes. The time between customer arrivals is exponentially distributed, with a mean of 1 minute and a standard deviation of 1 minute. The owner of the store is considering the purchase of a new barcode scanner that would reduce the mean checkout time to 2.6 minutes with a standard deviation of 0.5 minutes. Use SimQuick on the Student CD-ROM to assess the effect the new scanner would have on the mean number of customers in the system and the mean waiting time per customer. See Example 2 in *SimQuick: Process Simulation with Excel* for more details about this problem and additional exercises.

2. Consider the inspection process at the Sharpville plant, which is introduced as Example B.4. Use the Extend simulator to evaluate the basic process, and then analyze the impact of various changes in the process such as increased staffing, changing the flow pattern, reconfiguring the inspection checkpoints, and changing the mix of vehicles requiring inspection. For the full case and its requirements, see the *Security Inspection at the Sharpville Plant* case on the optional CD-ROM, which includes the basic model and how to use it.

SELECTED REFERENCES

Abdou, G., and S. P. Dutta. "A Systematic Simulation Approach for the Design of JIT Manufacturing Systems." *Journal of Operations Management,* vol. 11, no. 3 (1993), pp. 25–38.

Brennan, J. E., B. L. Golden, and H. K. Rappoport. "Go with the Flow: Improving Red Cross Bloodmobiles Using Simulation Analysis." *Interfaces,* vol. 22, no. 5 (1992), p. 1.

Christy, D. P., and H. J. Watson. "The Application of Simulation: A Survey of Industry Practice." *Interfaces,* vol. 13, no. 5 (October 1983), pp. 47–52.

Conway, R., W. L. Maxwell, J. D. McClain, and S. L. Worona. *XCELL & Factory Modeling System Release 4.0.* San Francisco: Scientific Press, 1990.

Ernshoff, J. R., and R. L. Serson. *Design and Use of Computer Simulation Models.* New York: Macmillan, 1970.

Hartvigsen, David. *SimQuick: Process Simulation with Excel.* 2d ed. Upper Saddle River, NJ: Prentice Hall, 2004.

Imagine That! (**www.imaginethatinc.com**). *Extend Simulation Package.* San Jose, CA.

Law, A. M., and W. D. Kelton. *Simulation Modeling and Analysis,* 2d ed. New York: McGraw-Hill, 1991.

Meier, R. C., W. T. Newell, and H. L. Pazer. *Simulation in Business and Economics.* Englewood Cliffs, NJ: Prentice Hall, 1969.

MicroAnalysis and Design Software Inc. "Hospital Overcrowding Solutions Are Found with Simulation." *Industrial Engineering* (December 1993), p. 557.

Naylor, T. H., et al. *Computer Simulation Techniques.* New York: John Wiley & Sons, 1966.

Pritsker, A. A. B., C. E. Sigal, and R. D. Hammesfahr. *SLAM II: Network Models for Decision Support.* Upper Saddle River, NJ: Prentice Hall, 1989.

Solomon, S. L. *Simulation of Waiting Lines.* Englewood Cliffs, NJ: Prentice Hall, 1983.

Swedish, Julian. "Simulation Brings Productivity Enhancements to the Social Security Administration." *Industrial Engineering* (May 1993), pp. 28–30.

Winston, Wayne L. "Simulation Modeling Using @RISK." Belmont, CA: Wadsworth Publishing Company, 1996.

Process Performance and Quality

LEARNING GOALS   *After reading this chapter, you should be able to . . .*

IDENTIFY OR DEFINE

1. the four major costs of poor process performance and quality.
2. *quality* from the customer's perspective.
3. the basic principles of TQM or Six-Sigma programs.

DESCRIBE OR EXPLAIN

4. the differences between common causes and assignable causes of variation in process performance and why that distinction is important.
5. how to construct control charts and use them to determine if a process is out of statistical control.
6. how to determine if a process is capable of producing a service or product to specifications.

PARKROYAL CHRISTCHURCH

The Parkroyal Christchurch, a luxury hotel in Christchurch, New Zealand, has 297 guest rooms, three restaurants, three lounges, and 338 employees to serve 2,250 guests each week who purchase an average of 2,450 meals. Even though the operation is complex, service performance and quality get top priority at the Parkroyal because customers demand it. Customers have many opportunities to evaluate the quality of service they are receiving. For example, prior to the guest's arrival, the reservation staff has gathered a considerable amount of information about the guest's particular likes and dislikes. This information (e.g., preference for firm pillows or extra towels) is distributed to housekeeping and other hotel processes and is used to customize the service that each guest receives. Upon arrival, a guest is greeted by a porter who opens the car door and unloads the luggage. Then the guest is escorted to the receptionist who registers the guest and assigns the room. Finally, when the guest goes to dinner, servers and cooks must also live up to the high standard of quality that distinguishes the Parkroyal from its competitors.

How can such a level of quality be sustained? The Parkroyal has empowered employees to take preventive and, if necessary, corrective action without management approval. Also, management and employees use line charts, histograms, and other graphs to track performance and identify areas needing improvement. In the restaurants, photos of finished dishes remind employees of presentation and content. Finally, in this service business with high customer contact, employee recruiting, training, and motivation are essential for achieving and sustaining high levels of service quality.

Exceptional hospitality is a key characteristic of any top-quality hotel. Here, a guest is helped with her luggage by a white-gloved bellhop.

Source: Operations Management in Action video.

The challenge for business today is to satisfy its customers through the exceptional performance of its processes. The Parkroyal Christchurch is but one example of a company that has met the challenge by designing and operating processes that provide a service package to the total satisfaction of customers. Failure to delight customers, be they internal or external, is a process failure regardless of whether it produces a service or a product. Evaluating process performance is an important element of process analysis, the fourth step in Figure 5.1. This chapter first addresses the costs of poor process performance and quality and then focuses on the philosophies and tools that many companies have embraced to evaluate process performance and reduce those costs.

As you read this chapter, think about how process quality and performance is important to various departments across the organization, such as . . .

➤ **accounting,** which must measure and estimate the costs of poor quality and provide error-free data to its internal customers.

➤ **finance,** which must assess the cash flow implications of process performance programs such as TQM and Six Sigma and provide defect-free financial reports to its internal customers.

➤ **human resources,** which recruits employees who value quality work and manages the processes that motivates and trains them.

➤ **management information systems,** which designs the systems for tracking process performance data.

➤ **marketing,** which uses quality and performance data for promotional purposes and manages processes that have direct contact with external customers.

➤ **operations,** which designs and implements programs such as TQM and Six Sigma and manages processes that produce services or products.

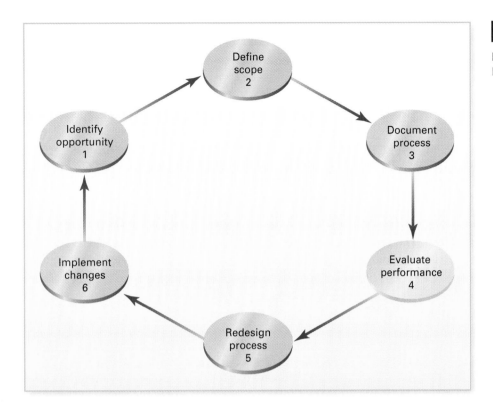

FIGURE 5.1

Evaluating Process Performance

COSTS OF POOR PROCESS PERFORMANCE AND QUALITY

Any instance when a process fails to satisfy its customer is considered a **defect**. According to the California Academy of Family Physicians, defects for the processes in a doctor's practice are defined as "anything that happened in my office that should not have happened, and that I absolutely do not want to happen again." Obviously, this definition covers process failures that the patient sees, such as poor communication and errors in dosage for prescriptions, and failures the patient does not see, such as incorrect charting. Many companies have spent significant time, effort, and expense on systems, training, and organizational changes to improve the performance and quality of their processes. They believe that it is important to have the ability to determine the current levels of performance of their processes so that any gaps between a process's competitive priorities and its competitive capabilities can be determined. Gaps reflect the potential for dissatisfied customers and additional costs for the firm. Most experts estimate losses in the range of 20 to 30 percent of gross sales for unsatisfactory services or products. These costs, attributable to poor process performance and quality, can be broken down into four major categories: prevention, appraisal, internal failure, and external failure.

defect Any instance when a process fails to satisfy its customer.

What are the costs of poor process performance and quality?

PREVENTION COSTS

Prevention costs are associated with preventing defects before they happen. They include the costs of redesigning the process to remove the causes of poor performance, redesigning the service or product to make it simpler to produce, training employees in the methods of continuous improvement, and working with suppliers to increase the quality of purchased items or contracted services. In order to improve performance, firms have to invest additional time, effort, and money.

prevention costs Costs associated with preventing defects before they happen.

APPRAISAL COSTS

Appraisal costs are incurred in assessing the level of performance attained by the firm's processes. Appraisal helps management identify performance problems. As preventive measures improve performance, appraisal costs decrease, because fewer resources are

appraisal costs Costs incurred in assessing the level of performance attained by the firm's processes.

needed for quality inspections and the subsequent search for causes of any problems that are detected.

INTERNAL FAILURE COSTS

internal failure costs Costs resulting from defects that are discovered during the production of a service or product.

Internal failure costs result from defects that are discovered during the production of a service or product. They fall into two main categories: *rework costs*, which are incurred if some aspect of a service must be performed again or if a defective item must be rerouted to some previous operation(s) to correct the defect and *yield losses*, which are incurred if a defective item must be scrapped. For example, an analysis of the viability of acquiring a company might be sent back to the mergers and acquisitions department if an assessment of the company's history of environmental compliance is missing. Likewise, if the final inspector at an automobile paint shop discovers that the paint on a car has a poor finish, the car may have to be completely resanded and repainted. The additional time spent correcting such a mistake results in lower productivity for the sanding and painting departments. In addition, the car may not be finished by the date on which the customer is expecting it.

EXTERNAL FAILURE COSTS

external failure costs Costs that arise when a defect is discovered after the customer has received the service or product.

External failure costs arise when a defect is discovered after the customer has received the service or product. For instance, suppose that you have the oil changed in your car and that the oil filter is improperly installed, causing the oil to drain onto your garage floor. You might insist that the company pay for the car to be towed and restore the oil and filter immediately. External failure costs to the company include the towing and additional oil and filter costs, as well as the loss of future revenue because you decide never to take your car back there for service. Dissatisfied customers talk about bad service or products to their friends, who in turn tell others. If the problem is bad enough, consumer protection groups alert the media. The potential impact on future profits is difficult to assess, but without doubt external failure costs erode market share and profits. Encountering defects and correcting them after the product is in the customer's hands is costly.

warranty A written guarantee that the producer will replace or repair defective parts or perform the service to the customer's satisfaction.

External failure costs also include warranty service and litigation costs. A **warranty** is a written guarantee that the producer will replace or repair defective parts or perform the service to the customer's satisfaction. Usually, a warranty is given for some specified period. For example, television repairs are usually guaranteed for 90 days and new automobiles for five years or 50,000 miles, whichever comes first. Warranty costs must be considered in the design of new services or products.

TOTAL QUALITY MANAGEMENT

How do customers perceive the quality of services or products?

total quality management (TQM) A philosophy that stresses three principles for achieving high levels of process performance and quality: customer satisfaction, employee involvement, and continuous improvement in performance.

quality A term used by customers to describe their general satisfaction with a service or product.

Total quality management (TQM) is a philosophy that stresses three principles for achieving high levels of process performance and quality: customer satisfaction, employee involvement, and continuous improvement in performance. As Figure 5.2 indicates, TQM also involves a number of important elements that are covered in other chapters and supplements in this text: service/product design (see Chapter 2, "Operations Strategy"); process design (see Chapter 3, "Process Design Strategy"); purchasing (see Chapter 9, "Supply-Chain Design"); and benchmarking and problem-solving tools (see Chapter 4, "Process Analysis," and Supplement A, "Decision Making"). Here we focus on the three main principles of TQM.

CUSTOMER SATISFACTION

Customers, internal or external, are satisfied when their expectations regarding a service or product have been met or exceeded. Often, customers use the general term **quality** to describe their level of satisfaction with a service or product. Quality has multiple dimensions in the mind of the customer, which cut across the nine competitive

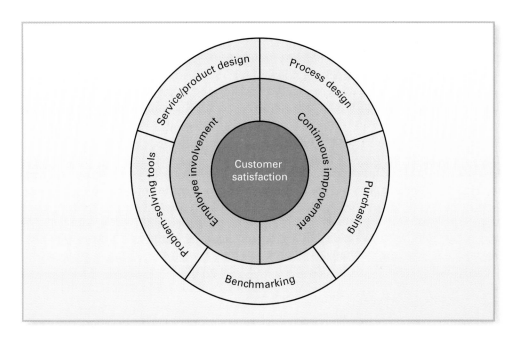

FIGURE 5.2

TQM Wheel

priorities we introduced in Chapter 2, "Operations Strategy." One or more of the following definitions apply at any one time.

CONFORMANCE TO SPECIFICATIONS. While customers evaluate the service or product they receive, it is the processes that produced the service or product that are really being judged. In this case, a process failure would be the process's inability to meet certain advertised or implied performance standards. Conformance to specifications may relate to consistent quality, on-time delivery, or delivery speed. Bell Canada measures the performance of its call center process by the length of time it takes to process a call (called "handle time"). If the average time exceeds the standard of 23 seconds, managers work with the employees to reduce the time. Customers become agitated if they cannot get access to an operator quickly. Seagate, however, advertises that its high-performance Cheetah disk drives have a mean time between failures of 1.2 million hours. All of the components of the disk drive must conform to Seagate's individual specifications to achieve the desired performance of the complete product. Consistent quality is very important. Customers measure quality by the performance of the product; however, each of the manufacturing processes at Seagate and its suppliers are being evaluated.

VALUE. Another way customers define quality is through value, or how well the service or product serves its intended purpose at a price customers are willing to pay. The service/product design process plays a role here, as do the competitive priorities of top

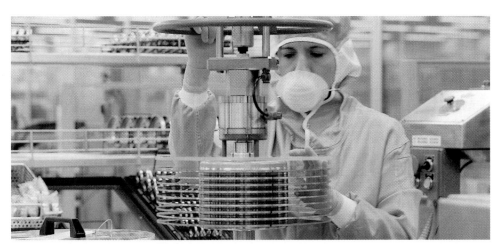

An employee at a hard disk factory wears a special suit and a mask to avoid contaminating the product. Maintaining a dust-free environment is critical to the quality of disk drives.

quality and low-cost operations, which must be balanced to produce value for the customer. How much value a service or product has in the mind of the customer depends on the customer's expectations before purchasing it. A complicated trust set up by a reputable law firm may cost $3,000; however, if the trust is flexible enough so that it will not have to be changed over time, the price may be worth it. Likewise, purchasing a Honda Civic for $13,000 may have more value for a customer than purchasing a Jaguar for $45,000 because the intended purpose for the car is to provide a child with transportation while attending school.

VIDEO CLIP 5.1
Video Clip 5.1 on the Student CD-ROM shows how a hotel learns about what it takes to satisfy its customers.

FITNESS FOR USE. In assessing fitness for use, or how well the service or product performs its intended purpose, the customer may consider the convenience of a service or the mechanical features of a product. Other aspects of fitness for use include appearance, style, durability, reliability, craftsmanship, and serviceability. For example, you may judge your dentist's quality of service on the basis of the age of her equipment because new dental technology greatly reduces the discomfort associated with visits to the dentist. Or you may define the quality of the entertainment center you purchased on the basis of how easy it was to assemble and how well it housed your equipment.

SUPPORT. Often the service or product support provided by the company is as important to customers as the quality of the service or product itself. Customers get upset with a company if financial statements are incorrect, responses to warranty claims are delayed, or advertising is misleading. Good product support can reduce the consequences of quality failures in other areas. For example, if you just had a brake job done, you would be upset if the brakes began squealing again a week later. If the manager of the brake shop offers to redo the work at no additional charge, the company's intent to satisfy the customer is clear.

PSYCHOLOGICAL IMPRESSIONS. People often evaluate the quality of a service or product on the basis of psychological impressions: atmosphere, image, or aesthetics. In the provision of services, where the customer is in close contact with the provider, the appearance and actions of the provider are very important. Nicely dressed, courteous, friendly, and sympathetic employees can affect the customer's perception of service quality. For example, rumpled, discourteous, or grumpy waiters can undermine a restaurant's best efforts to provide high-quality service. In manufacturing, product quality often is judged on the basis of the knowledge and personality of salespeople, as well as the product image presented in advertisements.

These five consumer-driven definitions of quality are applicable to all processes, including those that rely on the Internet to sell merchandise ranging from textbooks to mortgages directly to consumers (see Chapter 12, "Information Technology and Value Chains"). How does the customer in such situations define service quality? The following factors influence a customer's perception of service on the Internet:

- *Web Page.* A good Web site is easy to navigate and convenient to use and place orders *(fitness for use, psychological impressions)*. It also provides ample information about the service or product that the customer wants to purchase and information about other similar or related items the customer may be interested in *(value)*. Billing is accurate *(support)*.
- *Product Availability.* Having a wide variety of selections and having the specific documents or product the customer wants to purchase ready to ship are keys to good service marks *(value)*.
- *Delivery Performance.* Often delivery of purchases is promised within a certain time frame *(conformance to specifications)* and the faster the better *(value)*. Deliveries are made at a time and location convenient to the customer, such as a home residence between the hours of 4 and 6 P.M. *(fitness for use, value, conformance to specifications)*. Delivery of digitized documents may be instantaneous.
- *Personal Contact.* The opportunity to talk to a live person is often comforting to a customer who is doubtful of the right choice *(psychological impressions)*.

With nearly an estimated $4 billion in online revenues lost annually because of poor service quality, it is clear that factors such as these are very important for the success of processes relying on the Internet.

Attaining quality in all areas of a business is a difficult task. To make things even more difficult, consumers change their perceptions of quality. In general, a business's success depends on the accuracy of its perceptions of consumer expectations and its ability to bridge the gap between those expectations and operating capabilities. Good quality pays off in higher profits. High-quality services and products can be priced higher than comparable lower-quality ones and yield a greater return for the same sales dollar. Poor quality erodes the firm's ability to compete in the marketplace and increases the costs of producing its service or product. For example, by improving conformance to specifications, a firm can increase its market share *and* reduce the cost of its services or products, which in turn increase profits. Management is better able to compete on both price and quality.

EMPLOYEE INVOLVEMENT

One of the important elements of TQM is employee involvement, as shown in Figure 5.2. A program in employee involvement includes changing organizational culture and encouraging teamwork.

CULTURAL CHANGE. The challenge of quality management is to instill an awareness of the importance of quality in all employees and to motivate them to improve service or product quality. With TQM, everyone is expected to contribute to the overall improvement of quality—from the administrator who finds cost-saving measures to the salesperson who learns of a new customer need to the engineer who designs a product with fewer parts to the manager who communicates clearly with other department heads. In other words, TQM involves all the functions that relate to a service or product.

One of the main challenges in developing the proper culture for TQM is to define *customer* for each employee. In general, customers are internal or external (see Chapter 1, "Operations As a Competive Weapon"). External customers are the people or firms who buy the service or product. In this sense, the entire firm is a single unit that must do its best to satisfy external customers. However, communicating external customers' concerns to everyone in the organization is difficult. Some employees, especially those having little contact with external customers, may have difficulty seeing how their jobs contribute to the whole effort. It is helpful to point out to employees that each employee also has one or more internal customers—employees in the firm who rely on the output of other employees. For example, a machinist who drills holes in a component and passes it on to a welder has the welder as her customer. Even though the welder is not an external customer, he will have many of the same definitions of quality as an external customer, except that they will relate to the component instead of a complete product. All employees must do a good job of serving their internal customers if external customers ultimately are to be satisfied. The concept of internal customers works if each internal customer demands only value-added activities of their internal suppliers: that is, activities that the external customer will recognize and pay for. The notion of internal customers applies to all parts of a firm and enhances cross-functional coordination. For example, accounting must prepare accurate and timely reports for management, and purchasing must provide high-quality materials on time for operations.

In TQM, everyone in the organization must share the view that quality control is an end in itself. Errors or defects should be caught and corrected at the source, not passed along to an internal customer. For example, a consulting team should make sure their billable hours are correct before submitting them to the accounting department. This philosophy is called *quality at the source*. In addition, firms should avoid trying to "inspect quality into the product" by using inspectors to weed out unsatisfactory services or defective products after all operations have been performed. In some manufacturing firms, workers have the authority to stop a production line if they spot quality problems.

How can employees be included in the quality improvement process?

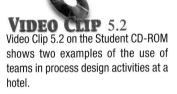

VIDEO CLIP 5.2
Video Clip 5.2 on the Student CD-ROM shows two examples of the use of teams in process design activities at a hotel.

How can a company develop teams?

teams Small groups of people who have a common purpose, set their own performance goals and approaches, and hold themselves accountable for success.

employee empowerment An approach to teamwork that moves responsibility for decisions farther down the organizational chart—to the level of the employee actually doing the job.

quality circles Another name for problem-solving teams; small groups of supervisors and employees who meet to identify, analyze, and solve process and quality problems.

special-purpose teams Groups that address issues of paramount concern to management, labor, or both.

self-managing team A small group of employees who work together to produce a major portion, or sometimes all, of a service or product.

continuous improvement The philosophy of continually seeking ways to improve processes based on a Japanese concept called *kaizen.*

TEAMS. Employee involvement is a key tactic for improving processes and quality. One way to achieve employee involvement is by the use of **teams**, which are small groups of people who have a common purpose, set their own performance goals and approaches, and hold themselves accountable for success. Teams differ from the more typical "working group" because

- the members have a common commitment to an overarching purpose that all believe in and that transcends individual priorities;
- the leadership roles are shared rather than held by a single, strong leader;
- performance is judged not only by individual contributions but also by collective "work products" that reflect the joint efforts of all the members;
- open-ended discussion, rather than a managerially defined agenda, is prized at meetings; and
- the members of the team do real work together, rather than delegating to subordinates.

The three approaches to teamwork most often used are problem-solving teams, special-purpose teams, and self-managing teams. All three use some amount of **employee empowerment**, which moves responsibility for decisions farther down the organizational chart—to the level of the employee actually doing the job.

First introduced in the 1920s, problem-solving teams, also called **quality circles**, became more popular in the late 1970s after the Japanese had used them successfully. Problem-solving teams are small groups of supervisors and employees who meet to identify, analyze, and solve process and quality problems. The philosophy behind this approach is that the people who are directly responsible for providing the service or making the product will be best able to consider ways to solve a problem. Also, employees take more pride and interest in their work if they are allowed to help shape it. The teams typically consist of 5 to 12 volunteers drawn from different areas of a department or from a group of employees assigned to a particular task, such as credit application processing or automobile assembly. The teams meet several hours a week to work on quality and process problems and make suggestions to management. Such teams are used extensively by Japanese-managed firms in the United States. The Japanese philosophy is to encourage employee input while maintaining close control over their job activities. Although problem-solving teams can successfully reduce costs and improve quality, they die if management fails to implement many of the suggestions generated.

An outgrowth of the problem-solving teams, **special-purpose teams** address issues of paramount concern to management, labor, or both. For example, management may form a special-purpose team to design and introduce new work policies or new technologies or to address customer service problems. Essentially, this approach gives workers a voice in high-level decisions. Special-purpose teams first appeared in the United States in the early 1980s.

The **self-managing team** approach takes worker participation to its highest level: A small group of employees work together to produce a major portion, or sometimes all, of a service or product. Members learn all the tasks involved in the operation, rotate from job to job, and take over managerial duties such as work and vacation scheduling, ordering supplies, and hiring. In some cases, team members design the process and have a high degree of latitude as to how it takes shape. Self-managing teams essentially change the way work is organized because employees have control over their jobs. Some self-managing teams have increased productivity by 30 percent or more in their firms.

CONTINUOUS IMPROVEMENT

Continuous improvement, based on a Japanese concept called *kaizen,* is the philosophy of continually seeking ways to improve processes. Continuous improvement involves identifying benchmarks of excellent practice and instilling a sense of employee ownership in the process. The focus can be on reducing the length of time required to process requests for loans at a bank, the amount of scrap generated at a milling machine, or the number of employee injuries at a construction site. Continuous improvement also can focus on problems with customers or suppliers, such as external customers who request frequent changes in shipping quantities or internal suppliers who fail to maintain high quality. The bases of the continuous improvement philosophy are the beliefs that virtually any aspect of a process can be improved and that the people most closely associated with a process are in the best position to identify the changes that should be made. The idea is not to wait until a massive problem occurs before acting.

GETTING STARTED. Instilling a philosophy of continuous improvement in an organization may be a lengthy process, and several steps are essential to its eventual success.

1. Train employees in the methods of statistical process control (SPC) and other tools for improving quality and performance. We discuss SPC later in this chapter.
2. Make SPC methods a normal aspect of daily operations.
3. Build work teams and employee involvement.
4. Utilize problem-solving tools within the work teams.
5. Develop a sense of operator ownership in the process.

Note that employee involvement is central to the philosophy of continuous improvement. However, the last two steps are crucial if the philosophy is to become part of everyday operations. Problem solving addresses the aspects of processes that need improvement and evaluates alternatives for achieving improvements. A sense of operator ownership emerges when employees feel as though they own the processes and methods they use and take pride in the quality of the service or product they produce. It comes from participation on work teams and in problem-solving activities, which instill in employees a feeling that they have some control over their workplace and tasks.

PROBLEM-SOLVING PROCESS. Most firms actively engaged in continuous improvement train their work teams to use the **plan–do–check–act cycle** for problem solving. Another name for this approach is the Deming Wheel. Figure 5.3 shows this cycle, which lies at the heart of the continuous improvement philosophy. The cycle comprises the following steps.

plan–do–check–act cycle
A cycle, also called the Deming Wheel, used by firms actively engaged in continuous improvement to train their work teams in problem solving.

1. *Plan.* The team selects a process (e.g., activity, method, machine, or policy) that needs improvement. The team then documents the selected process, usually by analyzing data (see Chapter 4, "Process Analysis"), sets qualitative goals for improvement, and discusses various ways to achieve the goals. After assessing the benefits and costs of the alternatives, the team develops a plan with quantifiable measures for improvement.

2. *Do.* The team implements the plan and monitors progress. Data are collected continuously to measure the improvements in the process. Any changes in the process are documented, and further revisions are made as needed.

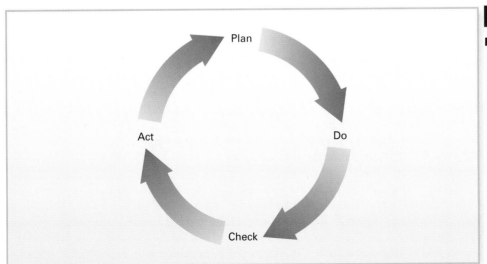

FIGURE 5.3

Plan–Do–Check–Act Cycle

3. *Check.* The team analyzes the data collected during the *do* step to find out how closely the results correspond to the goals set in the *plan* step. If major shortcomings exist, the team may have to reevaluate the plan or stop the project.

4. *Act.* If the results are successful, the team documents the revised process so that it becomes the standard procedure for all who may use it. The team may then instruct other employees in the use of the revised process.

Problem-solving projects often focus on those aspects of processes that do not add value to the service or product. Value is added in processes such as machining a part or serving a customer on a Web page. No value is added in activities such as inspecting parts for quality defects or routing requests for loan approvals to several different departments. The idea of continuous improvement is to reduce or eliminate activities that do not add value and, thus, are wasteful. For example, suppose that a firm has identified three non-value-added activities in the manufacture of its products: inspection of each part, repair of defects, and handling of materials between operations. The time that parts spend in each activity is not adding value to the product and, hence, is not generating revenue for the firm. Continuous improvement projects might focus on reducing materials handling time by rearranging machine locations to minimize the distances traveled by materials or improving the methods for producing the parts to reduce the need for inspection and rework.

STATISTICAL PROCESS CONTROL

Evaluating the performance of processes requires a variety of data gathering approaches. We have already discussed checklists, histograms and bar charts, Pareto charts, scatter diagrams, cause-and-effect diagrams, and graphs (see Chapter 4, "Process Analysis").

statistical process control (SPC) The application of statistical techniques to determine whether a process is delivering what the customer wants.

Statistical process control (SPC) is the application of statistical techniques to determine whether a process is delivering what the customer wants. In SPC, tools called control charts are used primarily to detect production of defective services or products or to indicate that the process has changed and that services or products will deviate from their design specifications unless something is done to correct the situation. SPC can also be used to inform management of process changes that have changed output of the process for the better. Some examples of process changes that can be detected by SPC are

- a decrease in the average number of complaints per day at a hotel,
- a sudden increase in the proportion of defective gear boxes,
- an increase in the time to process a mortgage application,
- a decline in the number of scrapped units at a milling machine, and
- an increase in the number of claimants receiving late payment from an insurance company.

Let us consider the last situation. Suppose that the manager of the accounts payable department of an insurance company notices that the proportion of claimants receiving late payment has risen from an average of 0.01 to 0.03. The first question is whether the rise is a cause for alarm or just a random occurrence. Statistical process control can help the manager decide whether further action should be taken. If the rise in the proportion is large, the manager should not conclude that it was just a random occurrence and should seek other explanations of the poor performance. Perhaps the number of claims significantly increased, causing an overload on the employees in the department. The decision might be to hire more personnel. Or perhaps the procedures being used are ineffective or the training of employees is inadequate. SPC is an integral part of TQM. Managerial Practice 5.1 shows how TQM and SPC are used to produce chocolate products.

acceptance sampling The application of statistical techniques to determine whether a quantity of material should be accepted or rejected based on the inspection or test of a sample.

Another approach to quality management, **acceptance sampling** is the application of statistical techniques to determine whether a quantity of material should be accepted

MANAGERIAL PRACTICE 5.1

TQM AND SPC HELP ADM COCOA MAINTAIN A SWEET BUSINESS

ADM Cocoa produces chocolate drops and other chocolate products for a wide variety of customers in the confectionery, dairy, and baking industries. The production process for chocolate drops is a highly automated line process. Some 500,000 pounds of cocoa beans are unloaded, cleaned, and roasted each day. The roasted beans are ground into a liquid, called *liquor,* which is then blended with other ingredients according to a particular recipe for a given product to form a paste. The paste is heated to a specified temperature and then is pumped to a depositing machine that forms the paste into drops and controls their cooling. The drops then are packaged for delivery.

ADM utilizes TQM techniques with SPC to make sure the process produces what the customer wants. The characteristics of agricultural commodities used for raw materials in the production of chocolate differ. For example, the fat content of cocoa beans varies according to the conditions under which the beans were grown. Fat content is crucial to determining the proper amount of each additive for blending into a specific product. ADM samples each batch of liquor just before the blending operation to measure fat content. If the sample is unacceptable, the

liquor is reprocessed until it has the proper fat content. Because the fat content is standardized, the blending operation also can be standardized from batch to batch.

ADM's customers depend on receiving consistent quantities of chocolate drops. Customers have specifications such as 4,000 ± 200 drops per pound and gear their production processes accordingly. An essential step in production of the drops is the operation of the depositing machine. Every hour, a random sample of 100 drops is taken from the production line, the total weight is recorded, and the average number of drops per pound is estimated. If the result is unacceptable, the operator of the machine explores the possible reasons for the problem (e.g., the temperature of the paste entering the depositing machine or the setting of the aperture that forms the drops). Adjustments require 15 minutes to take effect because of the amount of time needed to clear the defective products. Operators must be well trained in both statistical process control techniques and machine operations because a mistake in the adjustment means that at least 30 minutes of production will be lost.

Heated chocolate is poured from a holding tank into the depositing machine that forms the chocolate drops.

Source: Krajewski, David. Archer Daniels Midland Company, 2003. www.admworld.com.

or rejected based on the inspection or test of a sample (see Supplement I, "Acceptance Sampling Plans" on the Student CD-ROM). In this section, we explore the techniques of statistical process control to understand better the role they play in decision making.

VARIATION OF OUTPUTS

No two services or products are exactly alike because the processes used to produce them contain many sources of variation, even if the processes are working as intended. Nonetheless, it is important to minimize the variation in outputs because variation is what the customer sees and feels. For example, suppose a physician submits claims on the behalf of his patients to a particular insurance company. In some cases he gets payment in 4 weeks, and in other cases 20 weeks, even though the request is for the same treatment. Since the physician must cover his expenses while he waits for payment, the variation in the time for reimbursement is intolerable. The time to process a request for payment varies because of the load on the insurance company's processes, the medical history of the patient, and the skills and attitudes of the employees. Similarly, in manufacturing, the diameter of two crankshafts may vary because of differences in tool wear, material hardness, operator skill, or temperature during the period in which they were produced. Whether the process is producing services or products, nothing can be done to eliminate variation in output completely; however, management can investigate the *causes* of variation to minimize it.

COMMON CAUSES. There are two basic categories of variation in output: common causes and assignable causes. **Common causes of variation** are the purely random, unidentifiable sources of variation that are unavoidable with the current process. For example, the time required to process specimens at an intensive care unit lab in a hospital will vary. If you measured the time to complete an analysis of a large number of patients and plotted the results, the data would tend to form a pattern that can be described as a *distribution*. Such a distribution may be characterized by its mean, spread, and shape.

common causes of variation
The purely random, unidentifiable sources of variation that are unavoidable with the current process.

1. The *mean* is the sum of the observations divided by the total number of observations:

$$\bar{x} = \frac{\sum_{i=1}^{n} x_i}{n}$$

where

x_i = observation of a quality characteristic (such as time)

n = total number of observations

$\bar{x}$ = mean

2. The *spread* is a measure of the dispersion of observations about the mean. Two measures commonly used in practice are the range and the standard deviation. The *range* is the difference between the largest observation in a sample and the smallest. The *standard deviation* is the square root of the variance of a distribution. An estimate of the population standard deviation based on a sample is given by

$$\sigma = \sqrt{\frac{\Sigma(x_i - \bar{x})^2}{n-1}} \quad \text{or} \quad \sigma = \sqrt{\frac{\Sigma x_i^2 - \frac{(\Sigma x_i)^2}{n}}{n-1}}$$

where

σ = standard deviation of a sample

n = total number of observations in the sample

$\bar{x}$ = mean

x_i = observation of a quality characteristic

Relatively small values for the range or the standard deviation imply that the observations are clustered near the mean.

3. Two common *shapes* of process distributions are symmetric and skewed. A *symmetric* distribution has the same number of observations above and below the mean. A *skewed* distribution has a preponderance of observations either above or below the mean.

If process variability comes solely from common causes of variation, a typical assumption is that the distribution is symmetric, with most observations near the center.

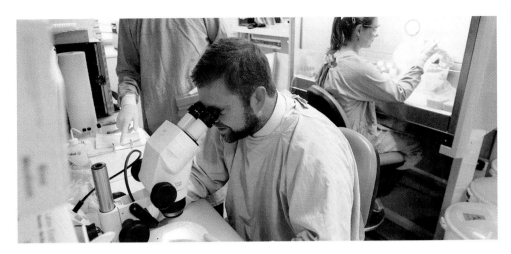

A doctor and his assistants measure immune responses in a medical lab. The time required to do lab work on patient samples can vary.

ASSIGNABLE CAUSES. The second category of variation, **assignable causes of variation,** also known as *special causes,* includes any variation-causing factors that can be identified and eliminated. Assignable causes of variation include an employee needing training or a machine needing repair. Let us return to the example of the lab analysis process. Figure 5.4 shows how assignable causes can change the distribution of output for the analysis process. The green curve is the process distribution when only common causes of variation are present. The purple lines depict a change in the distribution because of assignable causes. In Figure 5.4 (a), the purple line indicates that the process took more time than planned in many of the cases, thereby increasing the average time of each analysis. In Figure 5.4 (b), an increase in the variability of the time for each case affected the spread of the distribution. Finally, in Figure 5.4 (c), the purple line indicates that the process produced a preponderance of the tests in less than average time. Such a distribution is skewed—that is, it is no longer symmetric to the average value. A process is said to be in statistical control when the location, spread, or shape of its distribution does not change over time. After the process is in statistical control, managers use SPC procedures to detect the onset of assignable causes so that they can be eliminated.

assignable causes of variation Any variation-causing factors that can be identified and eliminated.

PERFORMANCE MEASUREMENTS. To detect abnormal variations in process output, employees must be able to measure performance variables. Performance can be evaluated in two ways. One way is to measure **variables**—that is, service or product characteristics, such as weight, length, volume, or time, that can be *measured.* For example, United Parcel Service managers monitor the length of time drivers spend delivering packages. Similarly, inspectors at Harley-Davidson measure the diameter of a piston to determine whether the product adheres to the specifications (within the allowable tolerance) and identify differences in diameter over time. The advantage of measuring a performance

What trade-offs are involved in using attribute measurements instead of variable measurements of performance?

variables Service or product characteristics, such as weight, length, volume, or time, that can be *measured.*

FIGURE 5.4   **Effects of Assignable Causes on the Process Distribution for the Lab Analysis Process**

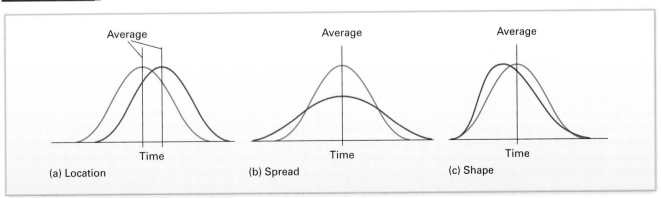

characteristic is that if a service or product misses its performance specifications, the inspector knows by how much. The disadvantage is that such measurements typically involve special equipment, employee skills, exacting procedures, and time and effort.

Another way to evaluate performance is to measure **attributes**—that is service or product characterstics that can be quickly *counted* for acceptable performance. The method allows inspectors to make a simple yes–no decision about whether a service or product meets the specifications. Attributes often are used when performance specifications are complex and measuring by variables is difficult or costly. Some examples of attributes that can be counted are the number of insurance forms containing errors that cause underpayments or overpayments, the proportion of radios inoperative at the final test, the proportion of airline flights arriving within 15 minutes of scheduled times, and the number of stove-top assemblies with spotted paint. The advantage of attribute counts is that less effort and fewer resources are needed than for measuring variables. The disadvantage is that, even though attribute counts can reveal that process performance has changed, they may not be of much use in indicating by how much. For example, a count may determine that the proportion of airline flights arriving within 15 minutes of their scheduled times has declined, but the result may not show how much beyond the 15-minute allowance the flights are arriving. For that, the actual deviation from the scheduled arrival, a variable, would have to be measured. Managerial Practice 5.2 provides examples of attribute quality measures used in the insurance industry.

SAMPLING. The most thorough approach to inspection is to inspect each service or product at each stage of the process for quality. This method, called *complete inspection*, is used when the costs of passing defects to an internal or external customer outweigh the inspection costs. Firms often use automated inspection equipment that can record, summarize, and display data. Many companies have found that automated inspection equipment can pay for itself in a reasonably short time.

A well-conceived **sampling plan** can approach the same degree of protection as complete inspection. A sampling plan specifies a **sample size,** which is a quantity of randomly selected observations of process outputs; the time between successive samples; and decision rules that determine when action should be taken. Sampling is appropriate when inspection costs are high because of the special knowledge, skills, procedures, or expensive equipment required to perform the inspections.

SAMPLING DISTRIBUTIONS. The purpose of sampling is to calculate a variable or attribute measure for some performance variable of the sample. That measure is then used to assess the performance of the process itself. For example, in the lab analysis process example, an important performance variable is the time it takes to get results to the critical care unit. Suppose that management wants the process to produce analyses so that the average time is 25 minutes. That is, it wants the process distribution to have a mean of 25 minutes. An inspector periodically taking a sample of five analyses and calculating the sample mean (a variable measure) could use it to determine how well the process is doing.

Plotting a large number of these means would show that they have their own distribution, with a mean centered on 25 minutes, as did the process distribution, but with much less variability. The reason is that means offset the highs and lows of the individual times. Figure 5.5 shows the relationship between the sampling distribution and the process distribution for the analysis times.

Some sampling distributions (e.g., for means with sample sizes of 4 or more and proportions with sample sizes of 20 or more) can be approximated by the *normal* distribution, allowing the use of the normal tables (see the "Normal Distribution" appendix). For example, suppose you wanted to determine the probability that a sample mean will be more than 2.0 standard deviations *greater* than the mean. Go to the "Normal Distribution" appendix and note that the entry in the table for 2.0 standard deviations is 0.9772. Consequently, the probability is $1.0000 - 0.9772 = 0.0228$, or 2.28 percent. The probability that the sample mean will be more than 2.0 standard deviations lower than the mean is also 2.28 percent because the normal distribution is

attributes   Service or product characteristics that can be quickly *counted* for acceptable performance.

sampling plan   A plan that specifies a sample size, the time between successive samples, and decision rules that determine when action should be taken.

sample size   A quantity of randomly selected observations of process outputs.

MANAGERIAL PRACTICE 5.2

QUALITY MEASURES IN THE INSURANCE INDUSTRY

Unisys, a major provider of computers and computer services, is expanding into the fast-growing computerized insurance outsourcing business. In addition to health insurance claims processing for government agencies, which it has been doing for a long time, Unisys secured a contract to run Florida's state employee health insurance business, which required organizing a network of doctors and hospitals. To secure the contract, Unisys had to beat out Blue Cross/Blue Shield of Florida, Inc., which appealed the decision and lost. Nonetheless the delay reduced the amount of time Unisys had to get the system up and running. Things did not run smoothly, and the Florida Department of Management Services fined Unisys for not meeting performance standards.

What quality measures did the state of Florida use to make its case? The number of incidences of conflicting information given to customers by Unisys and its subcontractors and several deficiencies in the process that compromised the security of confidential customer information both played a role. However, failure to meet two measures of performance and quality significantly influenced the state's decision to levy the fines.

- *Percentage of Claims Processed in Error.* This is an attribute measure because a claim is either processed correctly or it is not. A simple count of the number of incorrectly processed claims in a sample divided by the total number of claims in the sample, multiplied by 100, will produce this quality measure. A Coopers & Lybrand audit found that Unisys made errors in 8.5 percent of the claims it processed, as opposed to an industry standard of 3.5 percent.

- *Percent of Claims Processed Within a Given Time Limit.* This is also an attribute measure. A claim is "defective" if processing time is longer than the contractual time limit. In the contract with Unisys, at most, 5 percent of the claims could take longer than 30 days to process. In one month's sample, 13 percent of the claims exceeded the 30-day limit.

Both of these quality measures can be tracked by using the SPC techniques presented in this chapter. Since that incident, Unisys has corrected the problems and has expanded its insurance outsourcing business. Unisys is one of the leading providers of outsourcing services with over 400 of the world's leading insurance companies as clients.

Source: "Unisys: Nobody Said Diversifying Was Easy." *Business Week* (July 15, 1996), p. 32. www.unisys.com, 2003.

Office workers are processing claims for an insurance company. Processing claims without errors, and doing so in a timely fashion, are important quality measures.

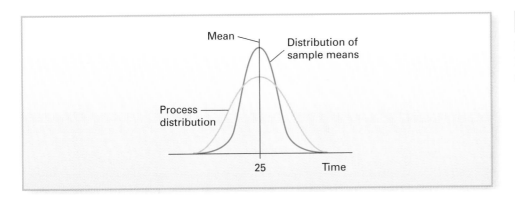

FIGURE 5.5

Relationship Between the Distribution of Sample Means and the Process Distribution

symmetric to the mean. The ability to assign probabilities to sample results is important for the construction and use of control charts.

CONTROL CHARTS

control chart A time-ordered diagram that is used to determine whether observed variations are abnormal.

To determine whether observed variations are abnormal, we can measure and plot the performance measure taken from the sample on a time-ordered diagram called a **control chart**. A control chart has a nominal value, or central line, which can be the process's historic average or a target that managers would like the process to achieve, and two control limits based on the sampling distribution of the quality measure. The control limits are used to judge whether action is required. The larger value represents the *upper control limit* (UCL) and the smaller value represents the *lower control limit* (LCL). Figure 5.6 shows how the control limits relate to the sampling distribution. A sample statistic that falls between the UCL and the LCL indicates that the process is exhibiting common causes of variation; a statistic that falls outside the control limits indicates that the process is exhibiting assignable causes of variation.

Observations falling outside the control limits do not always mean poor quality. For example, in Figure 5.6 the assignable cause may be a new billing process introduced to reduce the number of incorrect bills sent to customers. If the proportion of incorrect bills, the performance measure from a sample of bills, falls *below* the LCL of the control chart, the new procedure has likely changed the billing process for the better and a new control chart should be constructed.

Managers or employees responsible for evaluating a process can use control charts in the following ways:

1. Take a random sample from the process and calculate a variable or attribute performance measure.
2. If the statistic falls outside the chart's control limits, look for an assignable cause.
3. Eliminate the cause if it degrades performance; incorporate the cause if it improves performance. Reconstruct the control chart with new data.
4. Repeat the procedure periodically.

Sometimes problems with a process can be detected even though the control limits have not been exceeded. Figure 5.7 contains five examples of control charts. Chart (a) shows a process that is in statistical control. No action is needed. However, chart (b) shows a pattern called a *run*, or a sequence of observations with a certain characteristic. A typical rule is to take remedial action when there is a trend of five or more observations, even if the points have not yet exceeded the control limits.

FIGURE 5.6

Relationship of Control Limits to Sampling Distribution and Observations from Three Samples

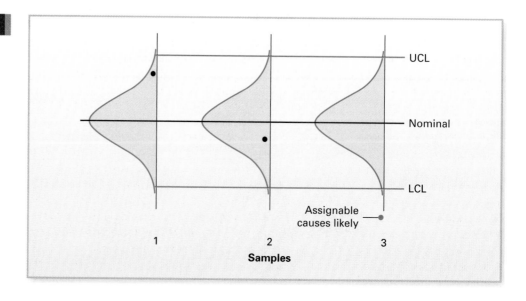

FIGURE 5.7   **Control Chart Examples**

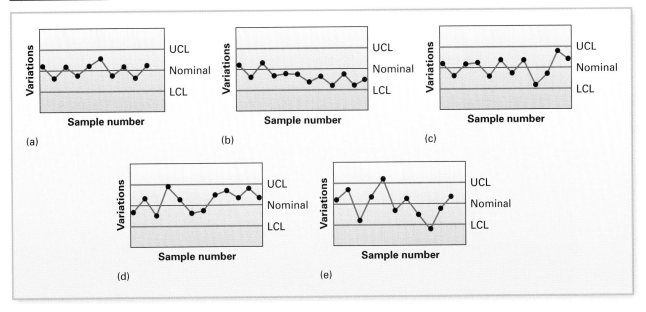

Chart (c) shows that the process has taken a sudden change from its normal pattern. The last four observations are unusual: three rising toward the UCL and the fourth remaining above the nominal value. A manager should be concerned with such sudden changes even though the control limits have not been exceeded. Chart (d) demonstrates another situation in which action is needed even though the limits have not been exceeded. Whenever a run of five or more observations above or below the nominal value occurs, the operator should look for a cause. The probability is very low that such a result could take place by chance. Finally, chart (e) indicates that the process went out of control twice because two sample results fell outside the control limits. The probability that the process distribution has changed is high. We discuss more implications of being out of statistical control when we discuss process capability later in this chapter.

Control charts are not perfect tools for detecting shifts in the process distribution because they are based on sampling distributions. Two types of error are possible with the use of control charts. A **type I error** occurs when the employee concludes that the process is out of control based on a sample result that falls outside the control limits, when in fact it was due to pure randomness. A **type II error** occurs when the employee concludes that the process is in control and only randomness is present, when actually the process is out of statistical control.

Management can control these errors by the choice of control limits. The choice would depend on the costs of looking for assignable causes when none exist versus the cost of not detecting a shift in the process. For example, setting control limits at three standard deviations from the mean reduces the type I error because there is a very small chance that a sample result will fall outside of the control limits unless the process is out of statistical control. However, the type II error may be significant because more subtle shifts in the nature of the process distribution will go undetected because of the wide spread in the control limits. Alternatively, the spread in the control limits can be reduced to two standard deviations, thereby increasing the likelihood of sample results falling outside of the control limits. Now the type II error is smaller, but the type I error is larger because there is a good chance that employees will search for assignable causes when the sample result occurred solely by chance. As a general rule, managers will use wider limits when the cost for searching for assignable causes is large relative to the cost of not detecting a shift in the process distribution.

type I error An error that occurs when the employee concludes that the process is out of control based on a sample result that falls outside the control limits, when in fact it was due to pure randomness.

type II error An error that occurs when the employee concludes that the process is in control and only randomness is present, when actually the process is out of statistical control.

STATISTICAL PROCESS CONTROL METHODS

Statistical process control (SPC) methods are useful for both measuring the current process performance and detecting whether the process has changed in a way that will affect performance. In this section, we first discuss mean and range charts for variable measures of performance and then consider control charts for attributes measures.

CONTROL CHARTS FOR VARIABLES

Control charts for variables are used to monitor the mean and the variability of the process distribution.

R-chart A chart used to monitor process variability.

R-CHARTS. A range chart, or **R-chart,** is used to monitor process variability. To calculate the range of a set of sample data, the analyst subtracts the smallest from the largest measurement in each sample. If any of the data fall outside the control limits, the process variability is not in control.

The control limits for the R-chart are

$$\text{UCL}_R = D_4\overline{R} \quad \text{and} \quad \text{LCL}_R = D_3\overline{R}$$

where

$\overline{R}$ = average of several past R values and the central line of the control chart

D_3, D_4 = constants that provide three standard deviation (three-sigma) limits for a given sample size

Values for D_3 and D_4 are contained in Table 5.1 and change as a function of the sample size. Note that the spread between the control limits narrows as the sample size increases. This change is a consequence of having more information on which to base an estimate for the process range.

x̄-chart A chart used to see if the process is generating output on average consistent with a target value management has set for the process or whether its current performance, with respect to the average of the performance measure, is consistent with past performance.

x̄-CHARTS. An $\overline{x}$-chart (read "x-bar chart") is used to see if the process is generating output on average consistent with a target value management has set for the process or whether its current performance, with respect to the average of the performance measure, is consistent with past performance. A target value is useful when a process is completely redesigned and past performance is no longer relevant. When the assignable causes of process variability have been identified and the process variability is in

| TABLE 5.1 | FACTORS FOR CALCULATING THREE-SIGMA LIMITS FOR THE x̄-CHART AND R-CHART |

Size of Sample (n)	Factor for UCL and LCL for x̄-Charts (A_2)	Factor for LCL for R-Charts (D_3)	Factor for UCL for R-Charts (D_4)
2	1.880	0	3.267
3	1.023	0	2.575
4	0.729	0	2.282
5	0.577	0	2.115
6	0.483	0	2.004
7	0.419	0.076	1.924
8	0.373	0.136	1.864
9	0.337	0.184	1.816
10	0.308	0.223	1.777

Source: 1950 ASTM Manual on Quality Control of Materials, copyright © American Society for Testing Materials. Reprinted with permission.

statistical control, the analyst can then construct an $\bar{x}$-chart. The control limits for the $\bar{x}$-chart are

$$\text{UCL}_{\bar{x}} = \bar{\bar{x}} + A_2 \bar{R} \quad \text{and} \quad \text{LCL}_{\bar{x}} = \bar{\bar{x}} - A_2 \bar{R}$$

where

$\bar{\bar{x}}$ = central line of the chart, which can be either the average of past sample means or a target value set for the process

A_2 = constant to provide three-sigma limits for the sample mean

The values for A_2 are contained in Table 5.1. Note that the control limits use the value of $\bar{R}$; therefore, the $\bar{x}$-chart must be constructed *after* the process variability is in control. Analysts can develop and use $\bar{x}$- and R-charts in the following way:

Step 1. Collect data on the variable quality measurement (such as time, weight, or diameter) and organize the data by sample number. Preferably, at least 20 samples should be taken for use in constructing a control chart.

Step 2. Compute the range for each sample and the average range, $\bar{R}$, for the set of samples.

Step 3. Use Table 5.1 to determine the upper and lower control limits of the R-chart.

Step 4. Plot the sample ranges. If all are in control, proceed to step 5. Otherwise, find the assignable causes, correct them, and return to step 1.

Step 5. Calculate $\bar{x}$ for each sample and determine the central line of the chart, $\bar{\bar{x}}$.

Step 6. Use Table 5.1 to determine the parameters for $\text{UCL}_{\bar{x}}$ and $\text{LCL}_{\bar{x}}$ and construct the $\bar{x}$-chart.

Step 7. Plot the sample means. If all are in control, the process is in statistical control in terms of the process average and process variability. Continue to take samples and monitor the process. If any are out of control, find the assignable causes, correct them, and return to step 1. If no assignable causes are found after a diligent search, assume that the out-of-control points represent common causes of variation and continue to monitor the process.

Using $\bar{x}$- and R-Charts to Monitor a Process

EXAMPLE 5.1

The management of West Allis Industries is concerned about the production of a special metal screw used by several of the company's largest customers. The diameter of the screw is critical to the customer. Data from five samples are shown in the accompanying table. The sample size is 4. Is the process in statistical control?

ACTIVE MODEL 5.1

Active Model 5.1 on the Student CD-ROM provides additional insight on the x-bar and R-charts and their uses for the metal screw problem.

SOLUTION

Step 1. For simplicity, we have taken only 5 samples. In practice, more than 20 samples would be desirable. The data are shown in the following table.

TUTOR 5.1

Tutor 5.1 on the Student CD-ROM provides a new example to practice the use of x-bar and R-charts.

	DATA FOR THE $\bar{x}$- AND R-CHARTS: OBSERVATIONS OF SCREW DIAMETER (IN.)					
	OBSERVATION					
SAMPLE NUMBER	1	2	3	4	R	$\bar{x}$
1	0.5014	0.5022	0.5009	0.5027	0.0018	0.5018
2	0.5021	0.5041	0.5024	0.5020	0.0021	0.5027
3	0.5018	0.5026	0.5035	0.5023	0.0017	0.5026
4	0.5008	0.5034	0.5024	0.5015	0.0026	0.5020
5	0.5041	0.5056	0.5034	0.5047	0.0022	0.5045
				Average	0.0021	0.5027

Range Chart from the OM Explorer $\bar{x}$- and R-Chart Solver for the Metal Screw, Showing that the Process Variability is in Control

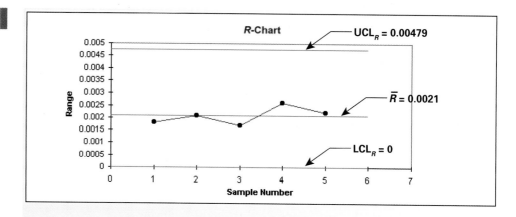

Step 2. Compute the range for each sample by subtracting the lowest value from the highest value. For example, in sample 1 the range is $0.5027 - 0.5009 = 0.0018$ in. Similarly, the ranges for samples 2, 3, 4, and 5 are 0.0021, 0.0017, 0.0026, and 0.0022 in., respectively. As shown in the table, $\bar{R} = 0.0021$.

Step 3. To construct the R-chart, select the appropriate constants from Table 5.1 for a sample size of 4. The control limits are

$$UCL_R = D_4\bar{R} = 2.282(0.0021) = 0.00479 \text{ in.}$$

$$LCL_R = D_3\bar{R} = 0(0.0021) = 0 \text{ in.}$$

Step 4. Plot the ranges on the R-chart, as shown in Figure 5.8. None of the sample ranges falls outside the control limits. Consequently, the process variability is in statistical control. If any of the sample ranges had fallen outside of the limits, or an unusual pattern had appeared (see Figure 5.7) we would have had to search for the causes of the excessive variability, correct them, and repeat step 1.

Step 5. Compute the mean for each sample. For example, the mean for sample 1 is

$$\frac{0.5014 + 0.5022 + 0.5009 + 0.5027}{4} = 0.5018 \text{ in.}$$

Similarly, the means of samples 2, 3, 4, and 5 are 0.5027, 0.5026, 0.5020, and 0.5045 in., respectively. As shown in the table, $\bar{\bar{x}} = 0.5027$.

Step 6. Now construct the $\bar{x}$-chart for the process average. The average screw diameter is 0.5027 in. and the average range is 0.0021 in., so use $\bar{\bar{x}} = 0.5027$, $\bar{R} = 0.0021$, and A_2 from Table 5.1 for a sample size of 4 to construct the control limits:

$$UCL_{\bar{x}} = \bar{\bar{x}} + A_2\bar{R} = 0.5027 + 0.729(0.0021) = 0.5042 \text{ in.}$$

$$LCL_{\bar{x}} = \bar{\bar{x}} - A_2\bar{R} = 0.5027 - 0.729(0.0021) = 0.5012 \text{ in.}$$

Step 7. Plot the sample means on the control chart, as shown in Figure 5.9.

The $\bar{x}$-Chart from the OM Explorer $\bar{x}$- and R-Chart Solver for the Metal Screw, Showing That Sample 5 Is Out of Control

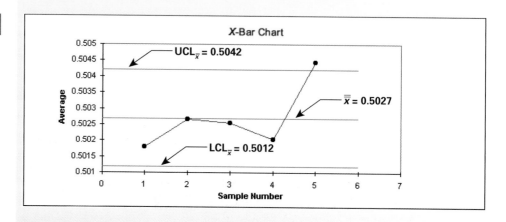

The mean of sample 5 falls above the UCL, indicating that the process average is out of control and that assignable causes must be explored, perhaps using a cause-and-effect diagram (see Chapter 4, "Process Analysis").

DECISION POINT   A new employee operated the lathe machine that makes the screw on the day the sample was taken. Management initiated a training session for the employee. Subsequent samples showed that the process was back in statistical control.

If the standard deviation of the process distribution is known, another form of the $\bar{x}$-chart may be used:

$$\text{UCL}_{\bar{x}} = \bar{\bar{x}} + z\sigma_{\bar{x}} \quad \text{and} \quad \text{LCL}_{\bar{x}} = \bar{\bar{x}} - z\sigma_{\bar{x}}$$

where

$\sigma_{\bar{x}} = \sigma/\sqrt{n}$ = standard deviation of sample means

σ = standard deviation of the process distribution

n = sample size

$\bar{\bar{x}}$ = central line of the chart, which can be either the average
     of past sample means or a target value set for the process

z = normal deviate (number of standard deviations from the average)

The analyst can use an R-chart to be sure that the process variability is in control before constructing the $\bar{x}$-chart. The advantage of using this form of the $\bar{x}$-chart is that the analyst can adjust the spread of the control limits by changing the value of z. This approach can be useful for balancing the effects of type I and type II errors.

Designing an $\bar{x}$-Chart Using the Process Standard Deviation   EXAMPLE 5.2

The Sunny Dale Bank monitors the time required to serve customers at the drive-by window because it is an important quality factor in competing with other banks in the city. After analyzing the data gathered in an extensive study of the window operation, bank management determined that the mean time to process a customer at the peak demand period has been 5 minutes, with a standard deviation of 1.5 minutes. Management wants to monitor the mean time to process a customer by periodically using a sample size of six customers. Assume that the process variability is in statistical control. Design an $\bar{x}$-chart that has a type I error of 5 percent. That is, set the control limits so that there is a 2.5 percent chance a sample result will fall below the LCL and a 2.5 percent chance that a sample result will fall above the UCL. After several weeks of sampling, two successive samples came in at 3.70 and 3.68 minutes, respectively. Is the customer service process in statistical control?

SOLUTION

$$\bar{\bar{x}} = 5.0 \text{ minutes}$$
$$\sigma = 1.5 \text{ minutes}$$
$$n = 6 \text{ customers}$$
$$z = 1.96$$

The process variability is in statistical control, so we proceed directly to the $\bar{x}$-chart. The control limits are

$$\text{UCL}_{\bar{x}} = \bar{\bar{x}} + z\sigma/\sqrt{n} = 5.0 + 1.96(1.5)/\sqrt{6} = 6.20 \text{ minutes}$$
$$\text{LCL}_{\bar{x}} = \bar{\bar{x}} - z\sigma/\sqrt{n} = 5.0 - 1.96(1.5)/\sqrt{6} = 3.80 \text{ minutes}$$

The value for z can be obtained in the following way. The normal distribution table (see the "Normal Distribution" appendix) gives the proportion of the total area under the normal curve from $-\infty$ to z. We want a type I error of 5 percent, or 2.5 percent of the curve above the UCL and 2.5 percent below the LCL. Consequently, we need to find the z value in the table that leaves only 2.5 percent in the upper portion of the nomal curve (or 0.9750 in the table). The value is 1.96. The two new samples are below the LCL of the chart, implying that the average time to serve a customer has dropped. Assignable causes should be explored to see what caused the improvement.

DECISION POINT   Management studied the time period over which the samples were taken and found that the supervisor of the process was experimenting with some new procedures. Management decided to make the new procedures a permanent part of the customer service process. After all employees were trained in the new procedures, new samples were taken and the control chart reconstructed.

CONTROL CHARTS FOR ATTRIBUTES

Of the alternative attribute process charts available, which one can best be used in a given situation?

Two charts commonly used for performance measures based on attributes measures are the p- and c-chart. The p-chart is used for controlling the proportion of defects generated by the process. The c-chart is used for controlling the number of defects when more than one defect can be present in a service or product.

p-chart   A chart used for controlling the proportion of defective services or products generated by the process.

p-CHARTS.   The p-chart is a commonly used control chart for attributes. The performance characteristic is counted rather than measured, and the entire service or item can be declared good or defective. For example, in the banking industry, the attributes counted might be the number of nonendorsed deposits or the number of incorrect financial statements sent to customers. The method involves selecting a random sample, inspecting each item in it, and calculating the sample proportion defective, p, which is the number of defective units divided by the sample size.

Sampling for a p-chart involves a yes–no decision: The process output either is or is not defective. The underlying statistical distribution is based on the binomial distribution. However, for large sample sizes, the normal distribution provides a good approximation to it. The standard deviation of the distribution of proportion defective, σ_p, is

$$\sigma_p = \sqrt{\overline{p}(1 - \overline{p})/n}$$

where

n = sample size

$\overline{p}$ = central line on the chart, which can be either the historical average population proportion defective or a target value

We can use σ_p to arrive at the upper and lower control limits for a p-chart:

$$\text{UCL}_p = \overline{p} + z\sigma_p \quad \text{and} \quad \text{LCL}_p = \overline{p} - z\sigma_p$$

where

z = normal deviate (number of standard deviations from the average)

The chart is used in the following way. Periodically, a random sample of size n is taken, and the number of defective services or products is counted. The number of defectives is divided by the sample size to get a sample proportion defective, p, which is plotted on the chart. When a sample proportion defective falls outside the control limits, the analyst assumes that the proportion defective generated by the process has changed and searches for the assignable cause. Observations falling below the LCL_p indicate that the process may actually have improved. The analyst may find no assignable cause because there is always a small chance that an out-of-control proportion will have occurred randomly. However, if the analyst discovers assignable causes, those sample data should not be used to calculate the control limits for the chart.

Using a *p*-Chart to Monitor a Process

The operations manager of the booking services department of Hometown Bank is concerned about the number of wrong customer account numbers recorded by Hometown personnel. Each week a random sample of 2,500 deposits is taken, and the number of incorrect account numbers is recorded. The results for the past 12 weeks are shown in the following table. Is the booking process out of statistical control? Use three-sigma control limits.

ACTIVE MODEL 5.2
Active Model 5.2 on the Student CD-ROM provides additional insight on the *p*-chart and its uses for the booking services department.

SAMPLE NUMBER	WRONG ACCOUNT NUMBERS	SAMPLE NUMBER	WRONG ACCOUNT NUMBERS
1	15	7	24
2	12	8	7
3	19	9	10
4	2	10	17
5	19	11	15
6	4	12	3
		Total	147

TUTOR 5.2
Tutor 5.2 on the Student CD-ROM provides a new example to practice the use of the *p*-chart.

SOLUTION

Step 1. Construct the *p*-chart, using past data to calculate $\bar{p}$.

$$\bar{p} = \frac{\text{Total defectives}}{\text{Total number of observations}} = \frac{147}{12(2,500)} = 0.0049$$

$$\sigma_p = \sqrt{\bar{p}(1 - \bar{p})/n} = \sqrt{0.0049(1 - 0.0049)/2,500} = 0.0014$$

$$\text{UCL}_p = \bar{p} + z\sigma_p = 0.0049 + 3(0.0014) = 0.0091$$

$$\text{LCL}_p = \bar{p} - z\sigma_p = 0.0049 - 3(0.0014) = 0.0007$$

Step 2. Calculate the sample proportion defective. For sample 1, the proportion of defectives is 15/2,500 = 0.0060.

Step 3. Plot each sample proportion defective on the chart, as shown in Figure 5.10.

Sample 7 exceeds the UCL; thus, the process is out of control and the reasons for the poor performance that week should be determined.

DECISION POINT Management explored the circumstances when sample 7 was taken. The encoding machine used to print the account numbers on the checks was defective that week. The following week the machine was repaired; however, the recommended preventive maintenance was not performed for months prior to the failure. Management reviewed the performance of the maintenance department and instituted changes to the maintenance procedures for the encoding machine. After the problem was corrected, an analyst recalculated the control limits using the data without sample 7. Subsequent weeks were sampled and the booking process was determined to be in statistical control. Consequently, the *p*-chart provides a tool to indicate when a process needs adjustment.

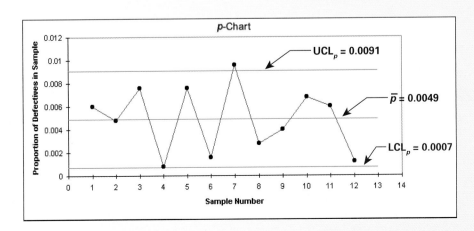

FIGURE 5.10

The *p*-Chart from the OM Explorer *p*-Chart Solver for Wrong Account Numbers, Showing That Sample 7 Is Out of Control

c-CHARTS. Sometimes services or products have more than one defect. For example, a roll of carpeting may have several defects, such as tufted or discolored fibers or stains from the production process. Other situations in which more than one defect may occur include accidents at a particular intersection, bubbles in a television picture tube face panel, and complaints from one patron at a hotel. When management is interested in reducing the number of defects per unit or service encounter, another type of control chart, the *c*-chart, is useful.

c-chart A chart used for controlling the number of defects when more than one defect can be present in a service or product.

The underlying sampling distribution for a *c*-chart is the Poisson distribution. It is based on the assumption that defects occur over a continuous region on the surface of a product or a continuous time interval for the provision of a service and that the probability of two or more defects at any one location on the surface or at any instant of time is negligible. The mean of the distribution is $\bar{c}$ and the standard deviation is $\sqrt{\bar{c}}$. A useful tactic is to use the normal approximation to the Poisson so that the central line of the chart is $\bar{c}$ and the control limits are

$$\text{UCL}_c = \bar{c} + z\sqrt{\bar{c}} \quad \text{and} \quad \text{LCL}_c = \bar{c} - z\sqrt{\bar{c}}$$

EXAMPLE 5.4   Using a c-Chart to Monitor Defects per Unit

TUTOR 5.3

Tutor 5.3 on the Student CD-ROM provides a new example to practice the use of the *c*-chart.

The Woodland Paper Company produces paper for the newspaper industry. As a final step in the process, the paper passes through a machine that measures various product quality characteristics. When the paper production process is in control, it averages 20 defects per roll.

a. Set up a control chart for the number of defects per roll. For this example, use two-sigma control limits.
b. Five rolls had the following number of defects: 16, 21, 17, 22, and 24, respectively. The sixth roll, using pulp from a different supplier, had 5 defects. Is the paper production process in control?

SOLUTION

a. The average number of defects per roll is 20. Therefore

$$\text{UCL}_c = \bar{c} + z\sqrt{\bar{c}} = 20 + 2(\sqrt{20}) = 28.94$$
$$\text{LCL}_c = \bar{c} - z\sqrt{\bar{c}} = 20 - 2(\sqrt{20}) = 11.06$$

The control chart is shown in Figure 5.11.
b. Because the first roll had only 16 defects, or less than the UCL, the process is still in control. Five defects, however, is less than the LCL, and therefore, the process is technically "out of control." The control chart indicates that something good has happened.

FIGURE 5.11

The c-Chart from the OM Explorer c-Chart Solver for Defects per Roll of Paper

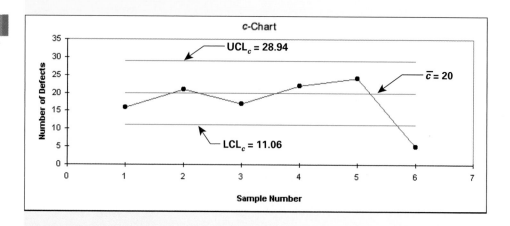

DECISION POINT The supplier for the first 5 samples has been used by Woodland Paper for many years. The supplier for the sixth sample is new to the company. Management decided to continue using the new supplier for a while, monitoring the number of defects to see if it stays low. If the number remains below the LCL for 20 consecutive samples, management will make the switch permanent and recalculate the control chart parameters.

PROCESS CAPABILITY

Statistical process control techniques help managers achieve and maintain a process distribution that does not change in terms of its mean and variance. The control limits on the control charts signal when the mean or variability of the process changes. However, a process that is in statistical control may not be producing services or products according to their design specifications because the control limits are based on the mean and variability of the *sampling distribution*, not the design specifications. **Process capability** refers to the ability of the process to meet the design specifications for a service or product. Design specifications often are expressed as a **nominal value**, or target, and a **tolerance**, or allowance above or below the nominal value. For example, the administrator of an intensive care unit lab might have a nominal value for the turnaround time of results to the attending physicians of 25 minutes and a tolerance of ± 5 minutes because of the need for speed under life-threatening conditions. The tolerance gives an *upper specification* of 30 minutes and a *lower specification* of 20 minutes. The lab process must be capable of providing the results of analyses within these specifications, otherwise it will produce a certain proportion of "defects." The administrator is also interested in detecting occurrences of turnaround times of less than 20 minutes because something might be learned that can be built into the lab process in the future. For the present, the physicians are pleased with results that arrive within 20 to 30 minutes.

What determines whether a process is capable of producing the services or products that customers demand?

process capability The ability of the process to meet the design specifications for a service or product.

nominal value A target for design specifications.

tolerance An allowance above or below the nominal value.

DEFINING PROCESS CAPABILITY

Figure 5.12 shows the relationship between a process distribution and the upper and lower specifications for the lab process turnaround time under two conditions. In Figure 5.12 (a), the process is capable because the extremes of the process distribution fall

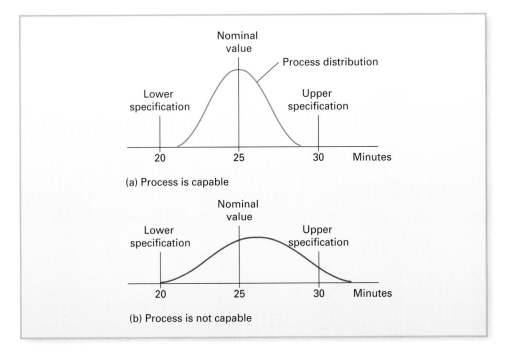

(a) Process is capable

(b) Process is not capable

FIGURE 5.12

Relationship Between Process Distribution and Specifications

within the upper and lower specifications. In Figure 5.12 (b) the process is not capable because the lab process produces too many reports with long turnaround times.

Figure 5.12 shows clearly why managers are so concerned with reducing process variability. The less variability—represented by lower standard deviations—the less frequently bad output is produced. Figure 5.13 shows what reducing variability means for a process distribution that is a normal probability distribution. The firm with two-sigma quality (the tolerance limits equal the process distribution mean ±2 standard deviations) produces 4.56 percent defects, or 45,600 defects per million. The firm with four-sigma quality produces only 0.0063 percent defectives, or 63 defects per million. Finally, the firm with six-sigma quality produces only 0.0000002 percent defects, or 0.002 defects per million.

How can a manager determine quantitatively whether a process is capable? Two measures commonly are used in practice to assess the capability of a process: process capability ratio and process capability index.

PROCESS CAPABILITY RATIO. A process is *capable* if it has a process distribution whose extreme values fall within the upper and lower specifications for a service or product. As a general rule, most values of any process distribution fall within ±3 standard deviations of the mean. For example, if the process distribution is normal, 99.74 precent of the values fall within ±3 standard deviations. In other words, the range of values of the quality measure generated by a process is approximately 6 standard deviations of the process distribution. Hence, if a process is capable, the difference between the upper and lower specification, called the *tolerance width*, must be greater than 6 standard deviations. The **process capability ratio** C_p, is defined as

$$C_p = \frac{\text{Upper specification} - \text{Lower specification}}{6\sigma}$$

where

σ = standard deviation of the process distribution

A C_p value of 1.0 implies that the firm is producing three-sigma quality (0.26 percent defects) and that the process is consistently producing outputs within specifications even though some defects are generated. C_p values greater than 1.0 imply higher levels of quality achievement. Firms striving to achieve greater than three-sigma

process capability ratio, C_p
The tolerance width divided by 6 standard deviations (process variability).

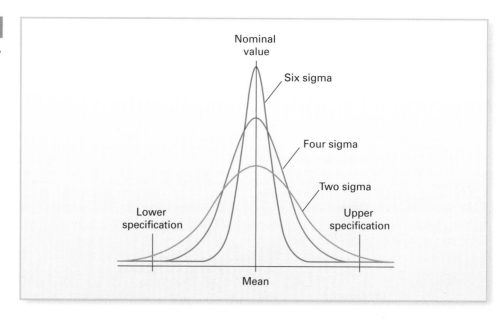

quality use a critical value for the ratio that is greater than 1.0. For example, a firm targeting six-sigma quality will use 2.0, a firm targeting five-sigma quality will use 1.67, and a firm striving for four-sigma quality will use 1.33. Processes producing services or products with less than three-sigma quality will have C_p values less than 1.0.

PROCESS CAPABILITY INDEX. The process is capable only when the capability ratio is greater than the critical value and the process distribution is centered on the nominal value of the design specifications. For example, the lab process may have a process capability ratio greater than 1.33 for turnaround time. However, if the mean of the distribution of process output, $\bar{\bar{x}}$, is closer to the upper specification, lengthy turnaround times may still be generated. Likewise, if $\bar{\bar{x}}$ is closer to the lower specification, very quick results may be generated. Thus, we need to compute a capability index that measures the potential for the output of the process to fall outside of either the upper or lower specifications.

The **process capability index, C_{pk}** is defined as

$$C_{pk} = \text{Minimum of} \left[\frac{\bar{\bar{x}} - \text{Lower specification}}{3\sigma}, \frac{\text{Upper specification} - \bar{\bar{x}}}{3\sigma} \right]$$

> **process capability index, C_{pk}**
> An index that measures the potential for a process to generate defective outputs relative to either upper or lower specifications.

We take the minimum of the two ratios because it gives the *worst-case* situation. If C_{pk} is greater than the critical value (say, 1.33 for four-sigma quality) and the process capability ratio is also greater than the critical value, we can finally say the process is capable. If C_{pk} is less than the critical value, either the process average is close to one of the tolerance limits and is generating defective output, or the process variability is too large.

The capability index will always be less than or equal to the capability ratio. Because of this, the capability index can be used as a first check for capability; if the capability index passes the test, the process can be declared capable. If it does not pass, the process capability ratio must be calculated to see if the process variability is a source of the problem. When C_{pk} equals C_p, the process is centered between the upper and lower specifications and, hence, the mean of the process distribution is centered on the nominal value of the design specifications.

USING CONTINUOUS IMPROVEMENT TO DETERMINE THE CAPABILITY OF A PROCESS

To determine the capability of a process to produce outputs within the tolerances, use the following steps.

Step 1. Collect data on the process output, and calculate the mean and the standard deviation of the process output distribution.

Step 2. Use the data from the process distribution to compute process control charts, such as an $\bar{x}$- or an R-chart.

Step 3. Take a series of random samples from the process and plot the results on the control charts. If at least 20 consecutive samples are within the control limits of the charts, the process is in statistical control. If the process is not in statistical control, look for assignable causes and eliminate them. Recalculate the mean and standard deviation of the process distribution and the control limits for the charts. Continue until the process is in statistical control.

Step 4. Calculate the process capability index and the process capability ratio, if necessary. If the results are acceptable, document any changes made to the process and continue to monitor the output by using the control charts. If the results are unacceptable, further explore assignable causes for reducing the variance in the output or centering the process distribution on the nominal value. As changes are made, recalculate the mean and standard deviation of the process distribution and the control limits for the charts and repeat step 3.

EXAMPLE 5.5   Assessing the Process Capability of the Intensive Care Unit Lab

ACTIVE MODEL 5.3

Active Model 5.3 on the Student CD-ROM provides additional insight on the process capability problem at the intensive care unit lab.

TUTOR 5.4

Tutor 5.4 on the Student CD-ROM provides a new example to practice the process capability measures.

The intensive care unit lab process has an average turnaround time of 26.2 minutes and a standard deviation of 1.35 minutes. The nominal value for this service is 25 minutes with an upper specification limit of 30 minutes and a lower specification limit of 20 minutes. The administrator of the lab wants to have four-sigma performance for her lab. Is the lab process capable of this level of performance?

SOLUTION

The administrator began by taking a quick check to see if the process is capable by applying the process capability index:

$$\text{Lower specification calculation} = \frac{26.2 - 20.0}{3(1.35)} = 1.53$$

$$\text{Upper specification calculation} = \frac{30.0 - 26.2}{3(1.35)} = 0.94$$

$$C_{pk} = \text{Minimum of } [1.53, \ 0.94] = 0.94$$

Since the target value for four-sigma performance is 1.33, the process capability index told her that the process was not capable. However, she did not know if the problem was the variability of the process, the centering of the process, or both. The options available to improve the process depended on what is wrong.

She next checked the process variability with the process capability ratio:

$$C_p = \frac{30 - 20}{6(1.35)} = 1.23$$

The process variability did not meet the four-sigma target of 1.33. Consequently, she initiated a study to see where variability was introduced to the process. Two activities, report preparation and specimen slide preparation, were identified as having inconsistent procedures. These procedures were modified to provide consistent performance. New data were collected and the average turnaround was now 26.1 minutes with a standard deviation of 1.20 minutes. She now had the process variability at the four-sigma level of performance, as indicated by the process capability ratio:

$$C_p = \frac{30.0 - 20.0}{6(1.20)} = 1.39$$

However, the process capability index indicated there were still some problems to resolve:

$$C_{pk} = \text{Minimum of } \left[\frac{(26.1 - 20)}{3(1.20)}, \ \frac{(30 - 26.1)}{3(1.20)} \right] = 1.08$$

DECISION POINT   The lab process was still not at the level of four-sigma performance on turnaround time. The lab administrator searched for the causes of the off center turnaround time distribution. She discovered that there were periodic backlogs at a key piece of testing equipment. Acquiring a second machine provided the capacity to reduce the turnaround times to four-sigma capability.

How can quality engineering help improve the quality of services and products?

quality engineering   An approach originated by Genichi Taguchi that involves combining engineering and statistical methods to reduce costs and improve quality by optimizing product design and manufacturing processes.

QUALITY ENGINEERING

Originated by Genichi Taguchi, **quality engineering** is an approach that involves combining engineering and statistical methods to reduce costs and improve quality by optimizing product design and manufacturing processes. Taguchi believes that unwelcome costs are associated with *any* deviation from a quality characteristic's target value.

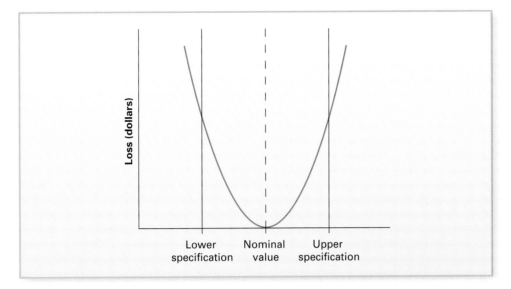

FIGURE 5.14

Taguchi's Quality Loss Function

Taguchi's view is that there is a **quality loss function** of zero when the quality characteristic of the service or product is exactly on the target value and that the value rises exponentially as the quality characteristic gets closer to the tolerance limits. The rationale is that a service or product that barely conforms to the specifications is more like a defective service or product than a perfect one. Figure 5.14 shows Taguchi's quality loss function schematically. Taguchi concluded that managers should continually search for ways to reduce *all* variability from the target value in the production process and not be content with merely adhering to specification limits.

quality loss function   The rationale that a service or product that barely conforms to the specifications is more like a defective service or product than a perfect one.

SIX SIGMA

We have seen how TQM and SPC can improve process performance and quality. Nonetheless, another approach, relying heavily on the principles and tools of TQM, has been gaining in popularity. **Six Sigma** is a comprehensive and flexible system for achieving, sustaining, and maximizing business success. Six Sigma is driven by close understanding of customer needs; disciplined use of facts, data, and statistical analysis; and diligent attention to managing, improving, and reinventing business processes. While many of the principles and tools of Six Sigma are similar to those of TQM, the approach has more formality than TQM. General Electric views Six Sigma as a strategy, a discipline, and a set of tools. It is a strategy because it focuses on what the customer wants, whether the customer is internal or external. It aims at total customer satisfaction. Consequently, it helps to achieve better business results as measured by market share, revenue, and profits. It is a discipline because it has a formal sequence of steps, called the Six Sigma Improvement Model, to accomplish the desired improvement in process performance. The goal is to simplify processes and close the gaps between a process's competitive priorities and its competitive capabilities. Finally, it is a set of tools because it makes use of powerful tools such as those we have discussed in this chapter and in Chapter 4, "Process Analysis." The tools help detect if process performance has gone astray and they provide a means to monitor performance on an ongoing basis.

Motorola is credited with developing Six Sigma more than 20 years ago to improve its manufacturing capability in a world marketplace that was becoming increasingly competitive. Management noticed that some customers were complaining about the quality of Motorola's products and that competitor products were outperforming its products. Motorola initially responded by setting higher goals for each of its processes so as to reduce the number of defects to one-tenth the previous level of performance. To achieve such a goal required that they work smarter, not just harder. Motorola began by

Six Sigma   A comprehensive and flexible system for achieving, sustaining, and maximizing business success.

soliciting new ideas and benchmarking their competitors and followed that with extensive changes to employee compensation and reward programs, training programs, and critical processes. The results were impressive. At one plant, after 10 months the defect rate improved 70 percent and the yield improved 55 percent. The procedures for achieving those impressive results were documented and refined and became known as Six Sigma. Its name relates to the goal of achieving such a low degree of variation in a process's output relative to its specifications that even if the process's average shifts 1.5 standard deviations there would be only 3.4 defects (items falling outside of the specifications) per million opportunities. Without a shift in the process average, a process generating Six-Sigma quality would have only 0.002 defects per million opportunities.

Although Six Sigma was rooted in an effort to improve manufacturing processes, credit General Electric with popularizing the application of the approach to nonmanufacturing processes such as sales, human resources, customer service, and financial services. The concept of eliminating defects is the same, although the definition of "defect" depends on the process involved. For example, a human resource department's failure to meet a hiring target counts as a defect. Applying Six Sigma to service processes is more challenging than for manufacturing processes for the following reasons:

1. The "work product" is much more difficult to see because it often consists of information, requests, orders, proposals, presentations, meetings, invoices, designs, and ideas. Service processes are often involved with computers and networks, sometimes international, that make the process "virtual" and difficult to document. This makes it difficult for people working in diverse functional areas such as sales, marketing, and software development to understand that they are actually part of a process that needs analysis.

2. Service processes can be changed quickly. Responsibilities can be shifted, forms revised, and new steps added without capital investment. Service processes in many companies evolve, adapt, and grow almost continuously.

3. Hard facts on service process performance are often hard to come by. The data that do exist are often anecdotal or subjective. Big stacks of unprocessed documents are often easy to see; however, measuring backlogs, rework, delays, and the costs of working on them is difficult. For example, streamlining a loan closure process is complicated because the process may involve many different people, each only devoting a small slice of their workday.

Despite the challenges, Six Sigma has been successfully applied to a host of service processes, including financial services, human resource processes, marketing processes, and health care administrative processes. Managerial Practice 5.3 shows how Six Sigma was applied at a health care facility.

SIX SIGMA IMPROVEMENT MODEL

The Six Sigma Improvement Model is a five-step procedure that leads to improvements in process performance. The model can be applied to projects involving incremental improvements to processes or to projects requiring major changes, including a redesign of an existing process or the development of a new process. The elements of the Six Sigma Improvement Model have been discussed in Chapter 2, "Operations Strategy;" Chapter 3, "Process Design Strategy;" and Chapter 4, "Process Analysis."

- *Define.* Determine the characteristics of the process's output that are critical to customer satisfaction and identify any gaps between these characteristics and the process's capabilities. These gaps provide opportunities for improvement. There may be a mismatch in the process's positioning in the customer-contact matrix (see Figure 3.3) or the product-process matrix (see Figure 3.6). Get a picture of the current process by documenting it.
- *Measure.* Quantify the work the process does that affects the gap. Select what to measure, identify data sources, and prepare a data collection plan.
- *Analyze.* Use the data on measures to perform process analysis, which may be focused on incremental process improvement or major process redesign. Use data analysis tools, such as Pareto charts, scatter diagrams, and cause-and-effect

MANAGERIAL PRACTICE 5.3

APPLYING THE SIX-SIGMA PROCESS AT SCOTTSDALE HEALTHCARE'S OSBORN HOSPITAL

Dozens of leading companies, including General Electric, Seagate Technology, Bombardier, and AlliedSignal have adopted the Six-Sigma process pioneered by Motorola in the 1980s. While the initial applications have focused on manufacturing processes, many recent applications have been in service processes. The health care industry is a case in point.

The dynamics of supply versus demand in emergency services may be more evident in Scottsdale, Arizona, than most other markets. Thousands of snow birds, retirement-aged visitors from the north, flock to the sunny climate of Scottsdale during the onset of the traditional flu season. Combined with permanent residents, this population creates a huge demand for emergency services at the emergency department (ED) of hospitals such as Scottsdale Healthcare's Osborn Hospital. In one 6-month period, hospitals in the area reported more than 12,000 hours during which they closed their doors to new patients and diverted ambulance services to other hospitals. Osborn's ED, one of the busiest of trauma centers, experienced an increase of 74 percent in its diversion rate and an alarming 272 percent increase in the number of patients who voluntarily left the ED before receiving any attention. Patients that leave before being seen by a doctor demonstrate a low customer satisfaction with the ED process; those that did remain long enough to be served also gave the ED low satisfaction marks in exit surveys. The hospital estimated that it could lose $500,000 each quarter that this condition existed.

Six Sigma consultants first mapped the ED process to identify potential problem areas. Three processes nested within the ED process presented potential bottlenecks so significant that they could increase the probability of diverting patients to other hospitals. The process variables of concern were registration time, lab/radiology turnaround, and the time to transfer patients to inpatient beds when they require admission. Data were collected on these process variables for analysis. Improvements to the processes were identified and studied for feasibility. Some of the proposed improvements were implemented. For example, the analysis revealed that the average time to transfer a patient out of the ED was 80 minutes; however, for 40 of those minutes the inpatient bed was actually ready and waiting. This result prompted the hospital to change its procedures for inpatient bed transfers. Having identified the key process variables with Six Sigma tools enabled hospital administrators to redesign their processes.

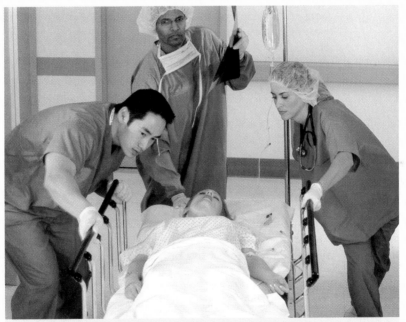

Hospital personnel at a trauma center rush a patient to the emergency room. Six Sigma can be used to improve service processes such as those in a trauma center.

Source: Lazarus, Ian R., and Keith Butler. "The Promise of Six Sigma." *Managed Healthcare Executive* (October 2001), pp. 22–26.

diagrams and the statistical process control tools in this chapter to determine where improvements are necessary. Whether or not major redesign is necessary, establish procedures to make the desired outcome routine.

● *Improve.* Modify or redesign existing methods to meet the new performance objectives. Implement the changes (see Chapter 8, "Planning and Managing Projects").

● *Control.* Monitor the process to make sure that high performance levels are maintained. Use data analysis tools such as Pareto charts, bar charts, scatter diagrams, as well as the statistical process control tools in this chapter.

Successful users of Six Sigma have found that it is essential to rigorously follow the steps in the Six Sigma Improvement Model, which is sometimes referred to as the *DMAIC process* using the first letter of each step in the model.

IMPLEMENTATION

Implementing a successful Six Sigma program begins with an understanding that Six Sigma is not a product you can buy—it requires a lot of time and commitment. Here are some lessons that Motorola, General Electric, and other leaders in Six Sigma have learned about implementing the program.

- *Top-Down Commitment.* Corporate leaders must show their commitment to the program and take a visible role in auditing processes and searching for ways to improve the business. They must set an example for everyone in the organization.
- *Measurement Systems to Track Progress.* Management must be committed to providing the means to track results and to use those means along with their employees to measure process performance.
- *Tough Goal Setting.* Establish the highest standards for the organization by regularly benchmarking "best-in-class" companies so as to assess the critical dimensions of customer satisfaction for the services or products the organization produces against those of the competition.
- *Education.* Employees must be trained in the "whys" and the "how-tos" of quality and what it means to customers, both internal and external. This is accomplished by a unique application of "train-the-trainer" programs. Successful firms using Six Sigma develop a cadre of internal teachers who then are responsible for teaching and assisting teams involved in a process improvement project. These teachers have different titles depending on their experience and level of achievement. Green Belts devote part of their time to teaching and helping teams with their projects and the rest of their time to their normally assigned duties. Black Belts are full time teachers and leaders of teams involved in Six Sigma projects. Finally, Master Black Belts are full time teachers who review and mentor Black Belts. Selection criteria for Master Black Belts are quantitative skills and the ability to teach and mentor. According to the Six-Sigma Academy, a typical Black Belt can undertake five to six projects a year, with average savings in the range of $175,000 per project.
- *Communication.* Successes are as important to understand as failures. Communicating organizational successes is a critical step in ensuring that the firm can build upon them in the future.
- *Customer Priorities.* Never lose sight of the customer's priorities, which are translated into competitive priorities for the firm's processes. These priorities are targets for the capabilities of the firm's processes and identify where gaps exist.

Successful firms using Six Sigma are mindful of these lessons; however, they are never satisfied. Continuous improvement or redesign of existing processes must be on the minds of all employees.

INTERNATIONAL QUALITY DOCUMENTATION STANDARDS

From a quality perspective, how can an organization prepare to do business in foreign markets?

Once a company has gone through the effort of making its processes capable, it must document its level of quality so as to better market its services or products. This is especially important in international trade. However, if each country had its own set of standards, companies selling in international markets would have difficulty complying with quality documentation standards in the countries where they did business. To overcome this problem, the International Organization for Standardization devised a set of standards called ISO 9000 for companies doing business in the European Union. Subsequently, a new set of documentation standards, ISO 14000, was devised for environmental management systems.

THE ISO 9000 DOCUMENTATION STANDARDS

ISO 9000 is a set of standards governing documentation of a quality program. Companies become certified by proving to a qualified external examiner that they have complied with all the requirements. Once certified, companies are listed in a directory so that potential customers can see which companies have been certified and to what level. Compliance with ISO 9000 standards says *nothing* about the actual quality of a product. Rather, it indicates to customers that companies can provide documentation to support whatever claims they make about quality.

ISO 9000 actually consists of five documents: ISO 9000–9004. ISO 9000 is an overview document, which provides guidelines for selection and use of the other standards. ISO 9001 is a standard that focuses on 20 aspects of a quality program for companies that design, produce, install, and service products. These aspects include management responsibility, quality system documentation, purchasing, product design, inspection, training, and corrective action. It is the most comprehensive and difficult standard to attain. ISO 9002 covers the same areas as ISO 9001 for companies that produce to the customer's designs or have their design and service activities at another location. ISO 9003 is the most limited in scope and addresses only the production process. ISO 9004 contains guidelines for interpreting the other standards.

> **ISO 9000** A set of standards governing documentation of a quality program.

ISO 14000: AN ENVIRONMENTAL MANAGEMENT SYSTEM

The **ISO 14000** documentation standards require participating companies to keep track of their raw materials use and their generation, treatment, and disposal of hazardous wastes. Although not specifying what each company is allowed to emit, the standards require companies to prepare a plan for ongoing improvement in their environmental performance. ISO 14000 is a series of five standards that cover a number of areas, including the following:

> **ISO 14000** Documentation standards that require participating companies to keep track of their raw materials use and their generation, treatment, and disposal of hazardous wastes.

- *Environmental Management System*. Requires a plan to improve performance in resource use and pollutant output.
- *Environmental Performance Evaluation*. Specifies guidelines for the certification of companies.
- *Environmental Labeling*. Defines terms such as *recyclable, energy efficient*, and *safe for the ozone layer*.
- *Life-Cycle Assessment*. Evaluates the lifetime environmental impact from the manufacture, use, and disposal of a product.

To maintain their certification, companies must be inspected by outside, private auditors on a regular basis.

BENEFITS OF ISO CERTIFICATION

Completing the certification process can take as long as 18 months and involve many hours of management and employee time. The cost of certification can exceed $1 million for large companies. Despite the expense and commitment involved in ISO certification, it bestows significant external and internal benefits. The external benefits come from the potential sales advantage that companies in compliance have. Companies looking for a supplier will more likely select a company that has demonstrated compliance with ISO documentation standards, all other factors being equal. Registered companies report an average of 48 percent increased profitability and 76 percent improvement in marketing. Consequently, more and more firms are seeking certification to gain a competitive advantage. Hundreds of thousands of manufacturing sites worldwide are ISO 9000 certified.

Internal benefits relate directly to the firm's TQM program. The British Standards Institute, a leading third-party auditor, estimates that most ISO 9000-registered companies experience a 10 percent reduction in the cost of producing a product because of the quality improvements they make while striving to meet the documentation requirements. Certification in ISO 9000 requires a company to analyze and document its procedures, which is necessary in any event for implementing continuous improvement, employee involvement, and similar programs. The internal benefits can be significant. The guidelines and requirements of the ISO documentation standards provide companies with a jump start in pursuing TQM programs.

MALCOLM BALDRIGE NATIONAL QUALITY AWARD

Malcolm Baldrige National Quality Award An award named for the late secretary of commerce, who was a strong proponent of enhancing quality as a means of reducing the trade deficit; the award promotes, recognizes, and publicizes quality strategies and achievements.

Regardless of where a company does business, it is clear that all organizations have to produce high-quality products and services if they are to be competitive. To emphasize that point, in August 1987, Congress signed into law the Malcolm Baldrige National Quality Improvement Act, creating the **Malcolm Baldrige National Quality Award** (**www.quality.nist.gov**). Named for the late secretary of commerce, who was a strong proponent of enhancing quality as a means of reducing the trade deficit; the award promotes, recognizes, and publicizes quality strategies and achievements.

The application and four-stage review process for the Baldrige award is rigorous, but often the process helps companies define what quality means for them. The seven major criteria for the award are

1. *Leadership*. Leadership system, values, expectations, and public responsibilities.
2. *Strategic Planning*. The effectiveness of strategic and business planning and deployment of plans, focusing on performance requirements.
3. *Customer and Market Focus*. How the company determines customer and market requirements and achieves customer satisfaction.
4. *Information Analysis*. The effectiveness of information systems to support customer-driven performance excellence and marketplace success.
5. *Human Resource Focus*. The success of efforts to realize the full potential of the workforce to create a high-performance organization.
6. *Process Management*. The effectiveness of systems and processes for assuring the quality of products and services.
7. *Business Results*. Performance results and competitive benchmarking in customer satisfaction, financials, human resources, suppliers, and operations.

Customer satisfaction underpins these seven criteria. Criterion 7, business results, is given the most weight in selecting winners.

PROCESS PERFORMANCE AND QUALITY ACROSS THE ORGANIZATION

Total quality management and Six Sigma are powerful approaches for improving performance and quality in service and manufacturing companies. The payoffs can be great; however, everyone must be involved. For example, Merrill Lynch Credit Corporation (MLCC), a winner of the Malcolm Baldrige National Quality Award, found out that focusing on quality management and performance excellence using TQM throughout the organization has significant rewards. MLCC, which originates over $4 billion in loans a year and manages a portfolio of nearly $10 billion, has 8 core and 10 support processes, involving 830 employees, that need to be coordinated. Communication from top to bottom in the organization is critical. Each year senior managers translate the company's strategic imperatives into a few critical objectives, which are accompanied by specific targets and measures. These objectives become the basis for determining employee performance plans, which in turn facilitate the communication loop between top management and the employees. Employees are empowered to take initiative and responsibility, especially in being flexible in responding rapidly to customer needs and in individual development. Employees receive an average of 74 hours of training a year, emphasizing the need to keep abreast of changes in technology to better serve customers.

A key element of MLCC's quality initiative is the "voice of the client" process, which identifies customer satisfaction drivers for each market segment and credit category. These priority customer requirements provide the basis for key performance measures for the eight core processes. In addition, data snooping is used to analyze customer satisfaction data to detect trends (see Chapter 4, "Process Analysis"). Negative trends and recurring problems trigger process improvement teams to develop countermeasures and to prevent recurrences. Clients receive feedback on the resolution of the problem within five working days. MLCC's complete organizational commitment is exemplary of the pervasiveness of TQM, and it has paid off. In the two years after the initiation of the TQM philosophy, net income rose 100 percent, return on equity increased 74 percent, and return on assets improved 36 percent.

CHAPTER HIGHLIGHTS

- A defect is any instance when a process fails to satisfy a customer. The four main cost categories associated with poor process performance and quality are prevention, appraisal, internal failure, and external failure. If performance and quality is to be improved, prevention costs must increase. Appraisal, internal failure, and external failure costs all decline if performance is improved through preventive measures.

- Total quality management stresses three principles: customer satisfaction, employee involvement, and continuous improvements in performance.

- The consumer's view of quality may be defined in a variety of ways. The customer may make a quantitative judgment about whether a service or product meets specified design characteristics. In other situations, qualitative judgments about value, fitness for the customer's intended use, product or service support, and aesthetics may take on greater importance. One responsibility of marketing is to listen to customers and report their changing perceptions of quality.

- Quality can be used as a competitive weapon. High-performance design and consistent quality are competitive priorities associated with quality. World-class competition requires businesses to produce quality services or products efficiently.

- Responsibility for process performance and quality is shared by all employees in the organization. Employee involvement programs include leadership in changing organizational culture, individual development, awards and incentives, and teamwork.

- Continuous improvement involves identifying benchmarks of excellent practice and instilling a sense of ownership in employees so that they will continually identify product, services, and process improvements that should be made.

- A key to achieving customer satisfaction in a service or product is to reduce output variability. When a process is in a state of statistical control, outputs subject to common causes of variation follow a stable probability distribution. When assignable causes of variation are present, the process is out of statistical control. Statistical process control (SPC) methods are used to detect the presence of assignable causes of variation.

- Statistical process control charts are useful for measuring the current performance of a process and for detecting whether the process has changed to the detriment of quality. Thus, R-charts are used to monitor process variability, $\bar{x}$- and p-charts identify abnormal variations in the process average, and c-charts are used for controlling the number of defects when a service or product process could result in multiple defects per unit of output. The presence of abnormal variation triggers a search for assignable causes.

- Process variability should be in control before process average control charts are constructed. The reason is that the average range is used in the calculation of control limits for process average control charts. Crucial decisions in the design of control charts are sample size and control limits.

- The central line of a control chart can be the average of past averages of the performance measurement or a management target related to service or product specifications. The spread in control limits affects the chances of detecting a shift in the process average or range, as well as the chances of searching for assignable causes when none exist.

- A process can be in statistical control but still not be capable of producing all of its output defect free. The process capability ratio and the process capability index are quantitative measures used to assess the capability of a process.

- Six Sigma is a comprehensive and flexible system for achieving, sustaining, and maximizing business success through intensive data analysis and process management, improvement and reengineering. While Six Sigma uses most of the principles and tools of TQM, it is a more formal approach that incorporates an improvement decision model and a structured approach to teaching and mentoring employees engaged in process improvement projects. Motorola is credited with developing the initial procedures for Six Sigma, which has been successfully applied to many service and manufacturing processes.

- The Malcolm Baldrige National Quality Award promotes, recognizes, and publicizes the quality strategies and achievements of outstanding American manufacturers, service providers, and small businesses.

- ISO 9000 is a set of standards governing the documentation of quality programs. ISO 14000 standards require participating companies to keep track of their raw materials use and their generation, treatment, and disposal of hazardous wastes.

STUDENT CD-ROM AND INTERNET RESOURCES

The Student CD-ROM and the Companion Website at **www.prenhall.com/krajewski** contain many tools, activities, and resources designed for this chapter. The following items are recommended to enhance your skills and improve your understanding of the material in this chapter.

STUDENT CD-ROM RESOURCES

➤ **PowerPoint Slides.** View the comprehensive set of slides customized for this chapter's concepts and techniques.
➤ **Video Clips.** See the two video clips customized for this chapter to learn more about defining customer satisfaction and using teams at a hotel.
➤ **OM Explorer Tutors.** OM Explorer contains six tutor spreadsheets to enhance your understanding of $\bar{x}$- and R-charts, p-charts, c-charts, process capability, constructing operating characteristic (OC) curves, and calculating the average outgoing quality level (AOQL). See Chapter 5 and Supplement I in the OM Explorer menu. See also the Tutor exercises on quality.
➤ **OM Explorer Solvers.** OM Explorer contains five spreadsheets designed to solve general problems involving $\bar{x}$- and R-charts, p-charts, c-charts, process capability, and single-sampling plans. See Process Performance and Quality and Acceptance Sampling Plans in the OM Explorer menu.
➤ **Active Models.** There are three active model spreadsheets that provide additional insights on x-bar and R-charts, p-charts, and process capability. See Process Performance and Quality in the Active Models menu for these routines. See also the Active Model Exercise at the end of this chapter for a demonstration of the p-chart model.

➤ **SimQuick Exercise.** Learn how to build simulation models of a quality inspection station and a machine that periodically breaks down. See Examples 23 and 24 in *SimQuick: Process Simulation with Excel*.
➤ **Written Tours.** See how the management of Lower Florida Keys Health System designs its processes to achieve high levels of process performance and quality and how Chaparral Steel builds quality into its products at each step of the manufacturing process.
➤ **Supplement I.** "Acceptance Sampling Plans." Use this supplement to learn how to design single-sampling plans and estimate the average outgoing quality of your plan.

INTERNET RESOURCES

➤ **Self-Study Quizzes.** See the compendium of true or false, multiple choice, and essay questions that allows online tests or gives you feedback on how well you have mastered the concepts of this chapter.
➤ **In the News.** See the articles that apply to this chapter.
➤ **Internet Exercises.** Try out 12 different links to explore quality topics including global and industry quality awards, international quality documentation standards, definitions of quality in services and manufacturing, product safety, the role of the Internet in quality, using quality as a competitive weapon, and using SPC in practice.
➤ **Virtual Tours.** Compare the processes used to achieve top quality at Steinway Pianos and Verne Q. Powell Flutes, and discover the quality measures used at Stickley Furniture. Also see the "Web Links to Company Facility Tours" for additional tours of company facilities.

KEY EQUATIONS

1. Mean: $\bar{x} = \dfrac{\sum_{i=1}^{n} x_i}{n}$

2. Standard deviation of a sample:

$$\sigma = \sqrt{\frac{\sum(x_i - \bar{x})^2}{n-1}} \quad \text{or} \quad \sigma = \sqrt{\frac{\sum x^2 - \dfrac{(\sum x_i)^2}{n}}{n-1}}$$

3. Control limits for variable process control charts

   a. R-chart, range of sample:

   $$\text{Upper control limit} = \text{UCL}_R = D_4\bar{R}$$
   $$\text{Lower control limit} = \text{LCL}_R = D_3\bar{R}$$

   b. $\bar{x}$-chart, sample mean:

   $$\text{Upper control limit} = \text{UCL}_{\bar{x}} = \bar{\bar{x}} + A_2\bar{R}$$
   $$\text{Lower control limit} = \text{LCL}_{\bar{x}} = \bar{\bar{x}} - A_2\bar{R}$$

   c. When the standard deviation of the process distribution, σ, is known:

   $$\text{Upper control limit} = \text{UCL}_{\bar{x}} = \bar{\bar{x}} + z\sigma_{\bar{x}}$$
   $$\text{Lower control limit} = \text{LCL}_{\bar{x}} = \bar{\bar{x}} - z\sigma_{\bar{x}}$$

   where

   $$\sigma_{\bar{x}} = \frac{\sigma}{\sqrt{n}}$$

4. Control limits for attribute process control charts

   a. p-chart, proportion defective:

   $$\text{Upper control limit} = \text{UCL}_p = \bar{p} + z\sigma_p$$
   $$\text{Lower control limit} = \text{LCL}_p = \bar{p} - z\sigma_p$$

   where

   $$\sigma_p = \sqrt{\bar{p}(1-\bar{p})/n}$$

b. *c*-chart, number of defects:

$$\text{Upper control limit} = \text{UCL}_c = \bar{c} + z\sqrt{\bar{c}}$$
$$\text{Lower control limit} = \text{LCL}_c = \bar{c} - z\sqrt{\bar{c}}$$

5. Process capability ratio:

$$C_p = \frac{\text{Upper specification} - \text{Lower specification}}{6\sigma}$$

6. Process capability index:

$$C_{pk} = \text{Minimum of}$$

$$\left[\frac{\bar{\bar{x}} - \text{Lower specification}}{3\sigma}, \frac{\text{Upper specification} - \bar{\bar{x}}}{3\sigma} \right]$$

KEY TERMS

acceptance sampling 202
appraisal costs 195
assignable causes of variation 205
attributes 206
c-chart 216
common causes of variation 204
continuous improvement 200
control chart 208
defect 195
employee empowerment 200
external failure costs 196
internal failure costs 196
ISO 9000 225
ISO 14000 225

Malcolm Baldrige National Quality
 Award 226
nominal value 217
p-chart 214
plan–do–check–act cycle 201
prevention costs 195
process capability 217
process capability index C_{pk} 219
process capability ratio C_p 218
quality 196
quality circles 200
quality engineering 220
quality loss function 221
R-chart 210

sample size 206
sampling plan 206
self-managing team 200
Six Sigma 221
special-purpose teams 200
statistical process control (SPC) 202
teams 200
tolerance 217
total quality management (TQM) 196
type I error 209
type II error 209
variables 205
warranty 196
$\bar{x}$-chart 210

SOLVED PROBLEM I

The Watson Electric Company produces incandescent light bulbs. The following data on the number of lumens for 40-watt light bulbs were collected when the process was in control.

	OBSERVATION			
SAMPLE	**1**	**2**	**3**	**4**
1	604	612	588	600
2	597	601	607	603
3	581	570	585	592
4	620	605	595	588
5	590	614	608	604

a. Calculate control limits for an *R*-chart and an $\bar{x}$-chart.
b. Since these data were collected, some new employees were hired. A new sample obtained the following readings: 570, 603, 623, and 583. Is the process still in control?

SOLUTION

a. To calculate $\bar{x}$, compute the mean for each sample. To calculate *R*, subtract the lowest value in the sample from the highest value in the sample. For example, for sample 1,

$$\bar{x} = \frac{604 + 612 + 588 + 600}{4} = 601$$
$$R = 612 - 588 = 24$$

SAMPLE	$\bar{x}$	R
1	601	24
2	602	10
3	582	22
4	602	32
5	604	24
Total	2,991	112
Average	$\bar{\bar{x}} = 598.2$	$\bar{R} = 22.4$

The R-chart control limits are

$$\mathrm{UCL}_R = D_4 \bar{R} = 2.282(22.4) = 51.12$$
$$\mathrm{LCL}_R = D_3 \bar{R} = 0(22.4) = 0$$

The $\bar{x}$-chart control limits are

$$\mathrm{UCL}_{\bar{x}} = \bar{\bar{x}} + A_2 \bar{R} = 598.2 + 0.729(22.4) = 614.53$$
$$\mathrm{LCL}_{\bar{x}} = \bar{\bar{x}} - A_2 \bar{R} = 598.2 - 0.729(22.4) = 581.87$$

b. First check to see whether the variability is still in control based on the new data. The range is 53 (or 623–570), which is outside the UCL for the R-chart. Even though the sample mean, 594.75, is within the control limits for the process average, process variability is not in control. A search for assignable causes must be conducted.

SOLVED PROBLEM 2

The data processing department of the Arizona Bank has five data entry clerks. Each day their supervisor verifies the accuracy of a random sample of 250 records. A record containing one or more errors is considered defective and must be redone. The results of the last 30 samples are shown in the table. All were checked to make sure that none were out of control.

SAMPLE	NUMBER OF DEFECTIVE RECORDS	SAMPLE	NUMBER OF DEFECTIVE RECORDS	SAMPLE	NUMBER OF DEFECTIVE RECORDS
1	7	11	18	21	17
2	5	12	5	22	12
3	19	13	16	23	6
4	10	14	4	24	7
5	11	15	11	25	13
6	8	16	8	26	10
7	12	17	12	27	14
8	9	18	4	28	6
9	6	19	6	29	11
10	13	20	11	30	9
				Total	300

a. Based on these historical data, set up a p-chart using $z = 3$.

b. Samples for the next four days showed the following:

SAMPLE	NUMBER OF DEFECTIVE RECORDS
31	17
32	15
33	22
34	21

What is the supervisor's assessment of the data-entry process likely to be?

SOLUTION

a. From the table, the supervisor knows that the total number of defective records is 300 out of a total sample of 7,500 [or 30(250)]. Therefore, the central line of the chart is

$$\bar{p} = \frac{300}{7,500} = 0.04$$

The control limits are

$$\text{UCL}_p = \bar{p} + z\sqrt{\frac{\bar{p}(1-\bar{p})}{n}} = 0.04 + 3\sqrt{\frac{0.04(0.96)}{250}} = 0.077$$

$$\text{LCL}_p = \bar{p} - z\sqrt{\frac{\bar{p}(1-\bar{p})}{n}} = 0.04 - 3\sqrt{\frac{0.04(0.96)}{250}} = 0.003$$

b. Samples for the next four days showed the following:

SAMPLE	NUMBER OF DEFECTIVE RECORDS	PROPORTION
31	17	0.068
32	15	0.060
33	22	0.088
34	21	0.084

Samples 33 and 34 are out of control. The supervisor should look for the problem and, upon identifying it, take corrective action.

SOLVED PROBLEM 3

The Minnow County Highway Safety Department monitors accidents at the intersection of Routes 123 and 14. Accidents at the intersection have averaged three per month.

a. Which type of control chart should be used? Construct a control chart with three-sigma control limits.

b. Last month, seven accidents occurred at the intersection. Is this sufficient evidence to justify a claim that something has changed at the intersection?

SOLUTION

a. The safety department cannot determine the number of accidents that did *not* occur, so it has no way to compute a proportion defective at the intersection. Therefore, the administrators must use a *c*-chart for which

$$\text{UCL}_c = \bar{c} + z\sqrt{\bar{c}} = 3 + 3\sqrt{3} = 8.20$$

$$\text{LCL}_c = \bar{c} - z\sqrt{\bar{c}} = 3 - 3\sqrt{3} = -2.196$$

There cannot be a negative number of accidents, so the LCL in this case is adjusted to zero.

b. The number of accidents last month falls within the UCL and LCL of the chart. We conclude that no assignable causes are present and that the increase in accidents was due to chance.

SOLVED PROBLEM 4

Pioneer Chicken advertises "lite" chicken with 30 percent fewer calories. (The pieces are 33 percent smaller.) The process average distribution for "lite" chicken breasts is 420 calories, with a standard deviation of the population of 25 calories. Pioneer randomly takes samples of six chicken breasts to measure calorie content.

a. Design an $\bar{x}$-chart, using the process standard deviation.

b. The product design calls for the average chicken breast to contain 400 ± 100 calories. Calculate the process capability index (target = 1.33) and the process capability ratio. Interpret the results.

SOLUTION

a. For the process standard deviation of 25 calories, the standard deviation of the sample mean is

$$\sigma_{\bar{x}} = \frac{\sigma}{\sqrt{n}} = \frac{25}{\sqrt{6}} = 10.2 \text{ calories}$$

$$\text{UCL}_{\bar{x}} = \bar{\bar{x}} + z\sigma_{\bar{x}} = 420 + 3(10.2) = 450.6 \text{ calories}$$

$$\text{LCL}_{\bar{x}} = \bar{\bar{x}} - z\sigma_{\bar{x}} = 420 - 3(10.2) = 389.4 \text{ calories}$$

b. The process capability index is

$$C_{pk} = \text{Minimum of} \left[\frac{\bar{\bar{x}} - \text{Lower specification}}{3\sigma}, \frac{\text{Upper specification} - \bar{\bar{x}}}{3\sigma} \right]$$

$$= \text{Minimum of} \left[\frac{420 - 300}{3(25)} = 1.60, \frac{500 - 420}{3(25)} = 1.07 \right] = 1.07$$

The process capability ratio is

$$C_p = \frac{\text{Upper specification} - \text{Lower specification}}{6\sigma} = \frac{500 \text{ calories} - 300 \text{ calories}}{6(25)} = 1.333$$

Because the process capability ratio is greater than 1.33, the process should be able to produce the product reliably within specifications. However, the process capability index is 1.07, so the current process is not centered properly for four-sigma performance. The mean of the process distribution is too close to the upper specification.

DISCUSSION QUESTIONS

1. Considerable success has been achieved by companies practicing TQM. What are the major hurdles to continuing quality improvements that manufacturers and service providers face?

2. Recently, the Polish General Corporation, well-known for manufacturing appliances and automobile parts, initiated a $13 billion project to produce automobiles. A great deal of learning on the part of management and employees was required. While pressure was mounting to get a new product to market in early 2005, the production manager of the newly formed automobile division insisted on almost a year of trial runs before sales started because workers have to do their jobs 60 to 100 times before they can memorize the right sequence. The launch date was set for early 2006. What are the consequences of using this approach to entering the market with a new product?

3. Form a group and choose a service provider or manufacturer and a functional area, such as accounting, finance, or marketing. Define a process important to that functional area (see Chapter 3, "Process Design Strategy") and then identify a key performance measure for that process. How can SPC be used to manage that process?

PROBLEMS

An icon next to a problem identifies the software that can be helpful, but not mandatory. The software is available on the Student CD-ROM that is packaged with every new copy of the textbook.

1. ◆ **OM Explorer** At Quickie Car Wash, the wash process is advertised to take less than 7 minutes. Consequently, management has set a target average of 390 seconds for the wash process. Suppose the average range for a sample of nine cars is 10 seconds. Use Table 5.1 to establish control limits for sample means and ranges for the car wash process.

2. ◆ **OM Explorer** At Isogen Pharmaceuticals, the filling process for its asthma inhaler is set to dispense 150 milliliters (ml) of steroid solution per container. The average range for a sample of 4 containers is 3 ml. Use Table 5.1 to establish control limits for sample means and ranges for the filling process.

3. ◆ **OM Explorer** Garcia's Garage desires to create some colorful charts and graphs to illustrate how reliably its mechanics "get under the hood and fix the problem." The historic average for the proportion of customers that return for the same repair within the 30-day warranty period is 0.10. Each month, Garcia tracks 100 customers to see whether they return for warranty repairs. The results are plotted as a proportion to report progress toward the goal. If the control limits are to be set at two standard deviations on either side of the goal, determine the control limits for this chart. In March, 8 of the 100 customers in the sample group returned for warranty repairs. Is the repair process in control?

4. ◆ **OM Explorer** The Canine Gourmet Company produces delicious dog treats for canines with discriminating tastes. Management wants the box-filling line to be set so that the process average weight per packet is 45 grams. To make sure that the process is in control, an inspector at the end of the filling line periodically selects a random box of 10 packets and weighs each packet. When the process is in control, the range in the weight of each sample has averaged 6 grams.

   a. Design an R- and an $\bar{x}$-chart for this process.

   b. The results from the last five samples of 10 packets are

Sample	$\bar{x}$	R
1	44	9
2	40	2
3	46	5
4	39	8
5	48	3

   Is the process in control? Explain.

5. ◆ **OM Explorer** The Marlin Company produces plastic bottles to customer order. The quality inspector randomly selects four bottles from the bottle machine and measures the outside diameter of the bottle neck, a critical quality dimension that determines whether the bottle cap will fit properly. The dimensions (in.) from the last six samples are

	Bottle			
Sample	**1**	**2**	**3**	**4**
1	0.604	0.612	0.588	0.600
2	0.597	0.601	0.607	0.603
3	0.581	0.570	0.585	0.592
4	0.620	0.605	0.595	0.588
5	0.590	0.614	0.608	0.604
6	0.585	0.583	0.617	0.579

   a. Assume that only these six samples are sufficient, and use the data to determine control limits for an R- and an $\bar{x}$-chart.

   b. Suppose that the specification for the bottle neck diameter is 0.600 ± 0.050 in. If the population standard deviation is 0.012 in., and the firm is seeking four-sigma quality, is the process capable of producing the bottle?

6. In an attempt to judge and monitor the quality of instruction, the administration of Mega-Byte Academy devised an examination to test students on the basic concepts that all should have learned. Each year, a random sample of 10 graduating students is selected for the test. The average score is used to track the quality of the educational process. Test results for the past 10 years are shown in Table 5.2.

   Use these data to estimate the center and standard deviation for this distribution. Then calculate the two-sigma control limits for the process average. What comments would you make to the administration of the Mega-Byte Academy?

7. ◆ **OM Explorer** As a hospital administrator of a large hospital, you are concerned with the absenteeism among nurse's aides. The issue has been raised by registered nurses, who feel they often have to perform work normally done by their aides. To get the facts, absenteeism data were gathered for the last two weeks, which is considered a representative period for future conditions. After taking random samples of 64 personnel files each day, the following data were produced:

Day	Aides Absent	Day	Aides Absent
1	4	9	7
2	3	10	2
3	2	11	3
4	4	12	2
5	2	13	1
6	5	14	3
7	3	15	4
8	4		

TABLE 5.2
TEST SCORES ON EXIT EXAM

Year	Student 1	2	3	4	5	6	7	8	9	10	Average
1	63	57	92	87	70	61	75	58	63	71	69.7
2	90	77	59	88	48	83	63	94	72	70	74.4
3	67	81	93	55	71	71	86	98	60	90	77.2
4	62	67	78	61	89	93	71	59	93	84	75.7
5	85	88	77	69	58	90	97	72	64	60	76.0
6	60	57	79	83	64	94	86	64	92	74	75.3
7	94	85	56	77	89	72	71	61	92	97	79.4
8	97	86	83	88	65	87	76	84	81	71	81.8
9	94	90	76	88	65	93	86	87	94	63	83.6
10	88	91	71	89	97	79	93	87	69	85	84.9

Since your assessment of absenteeism is likely to come under careful scrutiny, you would like a type I error of only 1 percent. You want to be sure to identify any instances of unusual absences. If some are present, you will have to explore them on behalf of the registered nurses.

a. Design a p-chart.

b. Based on your p-chart and the data from the last two weeks, what can you conclude about the absenteeism of nurses' aides?

8. OM Explorer A textile manufacturer wants to set up a control chart for irregularities (e.g., oil stains, shop soil, loose threads, and tears) per 100 square yards of carpet. The following data were collected from a sample of twenty 100-square-yard pieces of carpet.

Sample	1	2	3	4	5	6	7	8	9	10
Irregularities	11	8	9	12	4	16	5	8	17	10

Sample	11	12	13	14	15	16	17	18	19	20
Irregularities	11	5	7	12	13	8	19	11	9	10

a. Using these data, set up a c-chart with $z = 3$.

b. Suppose that the next five samples had 15, 18, 12, 22, and 21 irregularities. What do you conclude?

9. OM Explorer The IRS is concerned with improving the accuracy of tax information given by its representatives over the telephone. Previous studies involved asking a set of 25 questions of a large number of IRS telephone representatives to determine the proportion of correct responses. Historically, the average proportion of correct responses has been 70 percent. Recently, IRS representatives have been receiving more training. On April 1, the set of 25 tax questions were again asked of 20 randomly selected IRS telephone representatives. The proportions of correct answers were 0.88, 0.76, 0.64, 1.00, 0.76, 0.76, 0.72, 0.88, 0.50, 0.50, 0.40, 1.00,

0.88, 1.00, 0.64, 0.76, 0.76, 0.88, 0.40, and 0.76. Interpret the results of that study.

10. OM Explorer A travel agency is concerned with the accuracy and appearance of itineraries prepared for its clients. Defects can include errors in times, airlines, flight numbers, prices, car rental information, lodging, charge card numbers, and reservation numbers, as well as typographical errors. As the possible number of errors is nearly infinite, the agency measures the number of errors that do occur. The current process results in an average of three errors per itinerary.

a. What are the two-sigma control limits for these defects?

b. A client scheduled a trip to Dallas. Her itinerary contained six errors. Interpret this information.

11. OM Explorer Jim's Outfitters, Inc., makes custom fancy shirts for cowboys. The shirts could be flawed in various ways, including flaws in the weave or color of the fabric, loose buttons or decorations, wrong dimensions, and uneven stitches. Jim randomly examined 10 shirts, with the following results:

Shirt	Defects
1	8
2	0
3	7
4	12
5	5
6	10
7	2
8	4
9	6
10	6

a. Assuming that 10 observations are adequate for these purposes, determine the three-sigma control limits for defects per shirt.

b. Suppose that the next shirt has 13 flaws. What can you say about the process now?

12. ◗ **OM Explorer** The Big Black Bird Company produces fiberglass camper tops. The process for producing the tops must be controlled so as to keep the number of dimples low. When the process was in control, the following defects were found in randomly selected sheets over an extended period of time.

Top	Dimples
1	7
2	9
3	14
4	11
5	3
6	12
7	8
8	4
9	7
10	6

   a. Assuming 10 observations are adequate for these purposes, determine the three-sigma control limits for dimples per camper top.

   b. Suppose that the next camper top has 15 dimples. What can you say about the process now?

13. ◗ **OM Explorer** The production manager at Sunny Soda, Inc., is interested in tracking the quality of the company's 12-ounce bottle filling line. The bottles must be filled within the tolerances set for this product because the dietary information on the label shows 12 ounces as the serving size. The design standard for the product calls for a fill level of 12.00 ± 0.10 ounces. The manager collected the following sample data (in fluid ounces per bottle) on the production process:

	Observation			
Sample	1	2	3	4
1	12.00	11.97	12.10	12.08
2	11.91	11.94	12.10	11.96
3	11.89	12.02	11.97	11.99
4	12.10	12.09	12.05	11.95
5	12.08	11.92	12.12	12.05
6	11.94	11.98	12.06	12.08
7	12.09	12.00	12.00	12.03
8	12.01	12.04	11.99	11.95
9	12.00	11.96	11.97	12.03
10	11.92	11.94	12.09	12.00
11	11.91	11.99	12.05	12.10
12	12.01	12.00	12.06	11.97
13	11.98	11.99	12.06	12.03
14	12.02	12.00	12.05	11.95
15	12.00	12.05	12.01	11.97

   a. Are the process average and range in statistical control?

   b. Is the process capable of meeting the design standard at four-sigma quality? Explain.

14. ◗ **OM Explorer** The Money Pit Mortgage Company is interested in monitoring the performance of the mortgage process. Fifteen samples of five completed mortgage transactions each were taken during a period when the process was believed to be in control. The times to complete the transactions were measured. The means and ranges of the mortgage process transaction times, measured in days, are as follows.

Sample	1	2	3	4	5	6	7	8	9	10	11	12	13	14	15
Mean	17	14	8	17	12	13	15	16	13	14	16	9	11	9	12
Range	6	11	4	8	9	14	12	15	10	10	11	6	9	11	13

Subsequently, samples of size 5 were taken from the process every week for the next 10 weeks. The times were measured and the following results obtained.

Sample	16	17	18	19	20	21	22	23	24	25
Mean	11	14	9	15	17	19	13	22	20	18
Range	7	11	6	4	12	14	11	10	8	6

   a. Construct the control charts for the mean and the range, using the original 15 samples. Were these samples sufficient for developing the control chart? Explain your answer.

   b. On the control charts, plot the sample values subsequently obtained and comment on whether the process is in control.

   c. In part (b), if you concluded that the process was out of control, would you attribute it to a drift in the mean, or an increase in the variability, or both? Explain your answer.

15. ◗ **OM Explorer** The Money Pit Mortgage Company of Problem 14 made some changes to the process and undertook a process capability study. The following data were obtained for 15 samples of size 5. Based on the individual observations, management estimated the process standard deviation to be 4.21 (days) for use in the process capability analysis. The lower and upper specification limits (in days) for the mortgage process times were 5 and 25.

Sample	1	2	3	4	5	6	7	8	9	10	11	12	13	14	15
Mean	11	12	8	16	13	12	17	16	13	14	17	9	15	14	9
Range	9	13	4	11	10	9	8	15	14	11	6	6	12	10	11

   a. Calculate the process capability ratio and the process capability index values.

   b. Suppose management would be happy with three-sigma performance. What conclusions is management likely to draw from the capability analysis? Can valid conclusions about the process be drawn from the analysis?

c. What remedial actions, if any, do you suggest that management take?

16. 🖱 **OM Explorer** Webster Chemical Company produces mastics and caulking for the construction industry. The product is blended in large mixers and then pumped into tubes and capped. Management is concerned about whether the filling process for tubes of caulking is in statistical control. The process should be centered on eight ounces per tube. Several samples of eight tubes were taken, each tube was weighed, and the weights in Table 5.3 were obtained.

   a. Assume that only six samples are sufficient and develop the control charts for the mean and the range.

   b. Plot the observations on the control chart and comment on your findings.

17. 🖱 **OM Explorer** Management at Webster, in Problem 16, is now concerned as to whether caulking tubes are being properly capped. If a significant proportion of the tubes are not being sealed, Webster is placing its customers in a messy situation. Tubes are packaged in large boxes of 144. Several boxes are inspected, and the following numbers of leaking tubes are found:

Sample	Tubes	Sample	Tubes	Sample	Tubes
1	3	8	6	15	5
2	5	9	4	16	0
3	3	10	9	17	2
4	4	11	2	18	6
5	2	12	6	19	2
6	4	13	5	20	1
7	2	14	1	Total	72

   Calculate p-chart three-sigma control limits to assess whether the capping process is in statistical control.

18. 🖱 **OM Explorer** At Webster Chemical Company, lumps in the caulking compound could cause difficulties in dispensing a smooth bead from the tube. Even when the process is in control, an average of four lumps per tube of caulk will remain. Testing for the presence of lumps destroys the product, so an analyst takes random samples. The following results are obtained.

Tube No.	Lumps	Tube No.	Lumps	Tube No.	Lumps
1	6	5	6	9	5
2	5	6	4	10	0
3	0	7	1	11	9
4	4	8	6	12	2

Determine the c-chart two-sigma upper and lower control limits for this process.

19. 🖱 **OM Explorer** A critical dimension of a certain service is its time. Periodically, random samples of three service instances are measured for time. The results of the last four samples are in the following table.

Sample	Time (Secs)		
1	495	501	498
2	512	508	504
3	505	497	501
4	496	503	492

   a. Assuming that management is willing to use three-sigma limits, and using only the historical information contained in the four samples, show that the process producing the service is in statistical control.

   b. Suppose that the standard deviation of the process distribution is 5.77. If the specifications for the time of the service are 500 ± 18 sec, is the process capable? Why or why not? Assume three-sigma quality.

20. 🖱 **OM Explorer** An automatic lathe produces rollers for roller bearings, and the process is monitored by statistical process control charts. The central line of the chart for the sample means is set at 8.50 and for the mean range at 0.31 mm. The process is in control, as established by samples of size 5. The upper and lower specifications for the diameter of the rollers are $(8.50 + 0.25)$ and $(8.50 - 0.25)$ mm, respectively.

   a. Calculate the control limits for the mean and range charts.

   b. If the standard deviation of the process distribution is estimated to be 0.13 mm, is the process capable of meeting specifications? Assume four-sigma quality.

				TABLE 5.3				
				OUNCES OF CAULKING PER TUBE				
				Tube Number				
Sample	1	2	3	4	5	6	7	8
1	7.98	8.34	8.02	7.94	8.44	7.68	7.81	8.11
2	8.33	8.22	8.08	8.51	8.41	8.28	8.09	8.16
3	7.89	7.77	7.91	8.04	8.00	7.89	7.93	8.09
4	8.24	8.18	7.83	8.05	7.90	8.16	7.97	8.07
5	7.87	8.13	7.92	7.99	8.10	7.81	8.14	7.88
6	8.13	8.14	8.11	8.13	8.14	8.12	8.13	8.14

c. If the process is not capable, what percent of the output will fall outside the specification limits? (*Hint:* Use the normal distribution.)

Advanced Problems

21. **OM Explorer** Canine Gourmet Super Breath dog treats are sold in boxes labeled with a net weight of 12 ounces (340 grams) per box. Each box contains eight individual 1.5-ounce packets. To reduce the chances of shorting the customer, product design specifications call for the packet-filling process average to be set at 43.5 grams so that the average net weight per box will be 348 grams. Tolerances are set for the box to weigh 348 ± 12 grams. The standard deviation for the *packet-filling* process is 1.01 grams. The target process capability ratio is 1.33. One day, the packet-filling process average weight drifts down to 43.0 grams. Is the packaging process capable? Is an adjustment needed?

22. **OM Explorer** The Precision Machining Company makes hand-held tools on an assembly line that produces one product every minute. On one of the products, the critical quality dimension is the diameter (measured in thousandths of an inch) of a hole bored in one of the assemblies. Management wants to detect any shift in the process average diameter from 0.015 in. Management considers the variance in the process to be in control. Historically, the average range has been 0.002 in., regardless of the process average. Design an x-chart to control this process, with a center line at 0.015 in. and the control limits set at three sigmas from the center line.

   Management has provided the results of 80 minutes of output from the production line, as shown in Table 5.4. During this 80 minutes, the process average changed once. All measurements are in thousandths of an inch.

   a. Set up an $\bar{x}$-chart with $n = 4$. The frequency should be sample four, then skip four. Thus, your first sample would be for minutes 1–4, the second would be for minutes 9–12, and so on. When would you stop the process to check for a change in the process average?

   b. Set up an $\bar{x}$-chart with $n = 8$. The frequency should be sample eight, then skip four. When would you stop the process now? What can you say about the desirability of large samples on a frequent sampling interval?

23. **OM Explorer** Using the data from Problem 22, continue your analysis of sample size and frequency by trying the following plans.

   a. Using the $\bar{x}$-chart for $n = 4$, try the frequency sample four, then skip eight. When would you stop the process in this case?

   b. Using the $\bar{x}$-chart for $n = 8$, try the frequency sample eight, then skip eight. When would you consider the process to be out of control?

   c. Using your results from parts a and b, determine what trade-offs you would consider in choosing between them.

24. **OM Explorer** The manager of the customer service department of Omega Credit Card Service Company is concerned about the number of defects produced by the billing process. Every day a random sample of 250 statements was inspected for errors regarding incorrect entries involving account numbers, transactions on the customer's account, interest charges, and penalty charges. Any statement with one or more of these errors was considered a defect. The study lasted 30 days and yielded the data in Table 5.5. Based on the data, what can you tell the manager about the performance of the billing process? Do you see any nonrandom behavior in the billing process? If so, what might cause this behavior?

TABLE 5.4
SAMPLE DATA FOR PRECISION MACHINING COMPANY

Minutes	Diameter											
1–12	15	16	18	14	16	17	15	14	14	13	16	17
13–24	15	16	17	16	14	14	13	14	15	16	15	17
25–36	14	13	15	17	18	15	16	15	14	15	16	17
37–48	18	16	15	16	16	14	17	18	19	15	16	15
49–60	12	17	16	14	15	17	14	16	15	17	18	14
61–72	15	16	17	18	13	15	14	14	16	15	17	18
73–80	16	16	17	18	16	15	14	17				

TABLE 5.5
SAMPLE DATA FOR OMEGA CREDIT CARD SERVICE

Samples	Number of Errors in Sample of 250									
1–10	4	9	6	12	8	2	13	10	1	9
11–20	4	6	8	10	12	4	3	10	14	5
21–30	13	11	7	3	2	8	11	6	9	5

TABLE 5.6									
SAMPLE DATA FOR RED BARON AIRLINES									
Samples	Number of Late Planes in Sample of 300 Arrivals and Departures								
1–10	3	8	5	11	7	2	12	9	1	8
11–20	3	5	7	9	12	5	4	9	13	4
21–30	12	10	6	2	1	8	4	5	8	2

25. **OM Explorer** Red Baron Airlines serves hundreds of cities each day, but competition is increasing from smaller companies affiliated with major carriers. One of the key competitive priorities is on-time arrivals and departures. Red baron defines *on time* as any arrival or departure that takes place within 15 minutes of the scheduled time. To stay on top of the market, management has set the high standard of 98 percent on-time performance. The operations department was put in charge of monitoring the performance of the airline. Each week, a random sample of 300 flight arrivals and departures was checked for schedule performance. Table 5.6 contains the numbers of arrivals and departures over the last 30 weeks that did not meet Red Baron's definition of on-time service. What can you tell management about the quality of service? Can you identify any nonrandom behavior in the process? If so, what might cause the behavior?

26. **OM Explorer** Beaver Brothers, Inc., is conducting a study to assess the capability of its 150-gram bar soap production line. A critical quality measure is the weight of the soap bars after stamping. The upper and lower specification limits are 162 and 170 grams, respectively. As a part of an initial capability study, 25 samples of size 5 were collected by the quality assurance group and the observations in Table 5.7 were recorded.

After analyzing the data by using statistical control charts, the quality assurance group calculated the process capability ratio, C_p, and the process capability index, C_{pk}. It then decided to improve the stamping

process, especially the feeder mechanism. After making all the changes that were deemed necessary, 18 additional samples were collected. The summary data for these samples are

$$\bar{\bar{x}} = 163 \text{ grams}$$
$$\bar{R} = 2.326 \text{ grams}$$
$$\sigma = 1 \text{ gram}$$

All sample observations were within the control chart limits. With the new data, the quality assurance group recalculated the process capability measures. It was pleased with the improved C_p but felt that the process should be centered at 166 grams to ensure that everything was in order. Its decision concluded the study.

a. Draw the control charts for the data obtained in the initial study and verify that the process was in statistical control.

b. What were the values obtained by the group for C_p and C_{pk} for the initial capability study? Comment on your findings and explain why further improvements were necessary.

c. What are the C_p and C_{pk} after the improvements? Comment on your findings, indicating why the group decided to change the centering of the process.

d. What are the C_p and C_{pk} at the conclusion of the study? Comment on your findings.

 ACTIVE MODEL EXERCISE

This Active Model appears on the Student CD-ROM. It allows you to see the effects of sample size and z-values on control charts.

QUESTIONS

1. Has the booking process been in statistical control?
2. Suppose we use a 95 percent p-chart. How do the upper- and lower-control limits change? What are your conclusions about the booking process?
3. Suppose that the sample size is reduced to 2,000 instead of 2,500. How does this affect the chart?
4. What happens to the chart as we reduce the z-value?
5. What happens to the chart as we reduce the confidence?

TABLE 5.7					
SAMPLE DATA FOR BEAVER BROTHERS, INC.					
Sample	OBS.1	OBS.2	OBS.3	OBS.4	OBS.5
1	167.0	159.6	161.6	164.0	165.3
2	156.2	159.5	161.7	164.0	165.3
3	167.0	162.9	162.9	164.0	165.4
4	167.0	159.6	163.7	164.1	165.4
5	156.3	160.0	162.9	164.1	165.5
6	164.0	164.2	163.0	164.2	163.9
7	161.3	163.0	164.2	157.0	160.6
8	163.1	164.2	156.9	160.1	163.1
9	164.3	157.0	161.2	163.2	164.4
10	156.9	161.0	163.2	164.3	157.3
11	161.0	163.3	164.4	157.6	160.6
12	163.3	164.5	158.4	160.1	163.3
13	158.2	161.3	163.5	164.6	158.7
14	161.5	163.5	164.7	158.6	162.5
15	163.6	164.8	158.0	162.4	163.6
16	164.5	158.5	160.3	163.4	164.6
17	164.9	157.9	162.3	163.7	165.1
18	155.0	162.2	163.7	164.8	159.6
19	162.1	163.9	165.1	159.3	162.0
20	165.2	159.1	161.6	163.9	165.2
21	164.9	165.1	159.9	162.0	163.7
22	167.6	165.6	165.6	156.7	165.7
23	167.7	165.8	165.9	156.9	165.9
24	166.0	166.0	165.6	165.6	165.5
25	163.7	163.7	165.6	165.6	166.2

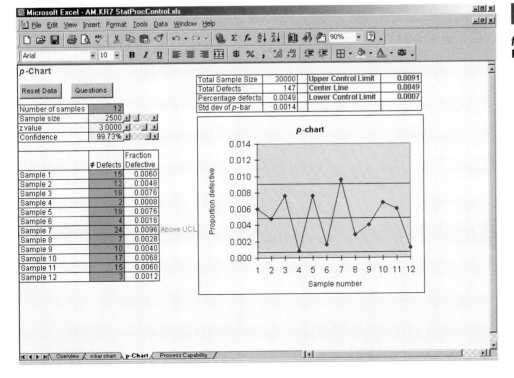

ACTIVE MODEL 5.2

p-Chart Using Data from Example 5.3

SIMULATION EXERCISES

These simulation exercises require the use of the SimQuick and Extend simulation packages. SimQuick is on the Student CD-ROM that is packaged with every new copy of the textbook. Extend is an optional simulation package that your instructor may or may not have ordered.

1. **SimQuick** Management is evaluating the advantages of replacing a machine in a printed circuit board process. The boards are passed, one at a time, to a workstation where a worker installs a few components. Each board is then passed to a quality control station where the installation is tested. Ninety percent of the boards pass this test and are then put into finished goods inventory. Those that fail are returned to the worker to be immediately reworked and retested. Management would like to know the advantages of investing in a new machine that would have 95 percent of its output pass the test. Use SimQuick to determine the additional throughput of the process with a new machine. See Example 23 in *SimQuick: Process Simulation with Excel* for details of this problem and additional exercises.

2. **Extend** Best Burger is a small regional fast-food chain in an industry that has become increasingly competitive. An increasing number of complaints are being made about its slow service, particularly in the drive-through operations. A management team has been formed to improve this process and is using statistical process control methods to monitor service times and track the effects of changes. Use the Extend simulator and control chart techniques to analyze their process. See the *Service Quality at Best Burger* case on the Extend CD-ROM, which includes the basic model and how to use it. Answer the various questions asked about the process and improvements made to it.

EXPERIENTIAL LEARNING STATISTICAL PROCESS CONTROL WITH A COIN CATAPULT

EXERCISE A: CONTROL CHARTS FOR VARIABLES

Materials

1 ruler
1 pen or pencil
1 coin (a quarter will do nicely)
1 yardstick
An exercise worksheet
Access to a calculator

Tasks

Divide into teams of two to four. If four people are on a team,
one person holds the yardstick and observes the action,
one person adjusts the catapult and launches the coin,
one person observes the maximum height for each trial, and
one person records the results.

If teams of less than four are formed, provide a support for the yardstick and combine the other tasks as appropriate.

Practice

To catapult the coin, put a pen or pencil under the 6-in. mark of the ruler. Put the coin over the 11-in. mark. Press both ends of the ruler down as far as they will go. Let the end that holds the coin snap up, catapulting the coin into the air. The person holding the yardstick should place the stick so that it is adjacent to, but does not interfere with, the trajectory of the coin. To observe the maximum height reached by the coin, the observer should

stand back with his or her eye at about the same level as the top of the coin's trajectory. Practice until each person is comfortable with his or her role. The person operating the catapult should be sure that the pen or pencil fulcrum has not moved between shots and that the launch is done as consistently as possible.

Step 1

Gather data. Take four samples of five observations (launches) each. Record the maximum height reached by the coin in the first data table on the worksheet. When you have finished, determine the mean and range for each sample, and compute the mean of the means $\bar{\bar{x}}$ and the mean of the ranges $\bar{R}$.

Step 2

Develop an R-chart. Using the data gathered and the appropriate D_3 and D_4 values, compute the upper and lower three-sigma control limits for the range. Enter these values and plot the range for each of the four samples on the range chart on the worksheet. Be sure to indicate an appropriate scale for range on the y axis.

Step 3

Develop an $\bar{x}$ chart. Now, using the data gathered and the appropriate value for A_2, compute the upper and lower three-sigma control limits for the sample means. Enter these values and plot the mean for each of the four samples on the $\bar{x}$ chart on the worksheet. Again, indicate an appropriate scale for the y axis.

Step 4

Observe the process.   Once a control chart has been established for a process, it is used to monitor the process and to identify when it isn't running "normally." Collect two more samples of five trials each, as you did to collect the first set of data. Plot the range and the sample mean on the charts you constructed on the worksheet each time you collect a sample. What have you observed that affects the process? Does the chart indicate that the process is operating the way it did when you first collected data?

Step 5

Observe a changed process.   Now change something (for instance, move the pencil out to the 8-in. mark). Collect data for samples 7 and 8. Plot the range and the sample mean on the charts you constructed on the worksheet as you complete each sample. Can you detect a change in the process from your control chart? If the process has changed, how sure are you that this change is real and not just due to the particular sample you chose?

EXERCISE B: CONTROL CHARTS FOR ATTRIBUTES

Materials

1 ruler
1 pen or pencil
1 coin (a quarter will do nicely)
1 paper or plastic cup (with a 4-in. mouth)
An exercise worksheet
Access to a calculator

Tasks

Divide into teams of two or three. If three people are on a team,
one person adjusts the catapult and launches the coin,
one person observes the results and fetches the coin, and
one person records the results.

If teams of two are formed, combine the tasks as appropriate.

Practice

The object is to flip a coin into a cup using a ruler. To catapult the coin, put a pen or pencil under the 6-in. mark of the ruler.

Put a coin over the 11-in. mark and let its weight hold that end of the ruler on the tabletop. Strike the raised end of the ruler with your hand to flip the coin into the air. Position a cup at the place where the coin lands so that on the next flip, the coin will land inside. You will have to practice several times until you find out how hard to hit the ruler and the best position for the cup. Be sure that the pen or pencil fulcrum has not moved between shots and that the launch is done as consistently as possible.

Step 1

Gather data.   Try to catapult the coin into the cup 10 times for each sample. Record each trial in the data table on the worksheet as a hit (H) when the coin lands inside or a miss (M) when it does not. The proportion of misses will be the number of misses divided by the sample size, *n*—in this case 10. A miss is a "defect," so the proportion of misses is the proportion defective, *p*.

Step 2

Develop a p-chart.   Compute the upper and lower three-sigma control limits for the average fraction defective. Plot these values and the mean for each of the four samples on the *p*-chart on the worksheet.

Step 3

Observe the process.   Once a chart has been established for a process, it is used to monitor the process and to identify abnormal behavior. Exchange tasks so that someone else is catapulting the coin. After several practice launches, take four more samples of 10. Plot the proportion defective for this person's output. Is the process still in control? If it is not, how sure are you that it is out of control? Can you determine the control limits for a 95 percent confidence level? With these limits, was your revised process still in control?

Source: The basis for Exercise A was written by J. Christopher Sandvig, Western Washington University, as a variation of the "Catapulting Coins" exercise from *Games and Exercises for Operations Management* by Janelle Heinke and Larry Meile (Prentice Hall, 1995). Given these foundations, Larry Meile of Boston College wrote Exercise A. He also wrote Exercise B as a new extension.

SELECTED REFERENCES

Besterfield, Dale. *Quality Control*, 6th ed. Upper Saddle River, NJ: Prentice Hall, 2001.

Brown Ed. "The Best Business Hotels." *Fortune* (March 17, 1997), pp. 204–205.

Collier, David A., *The Service Quality Solution*. New York: Irwin Professional Publishing; Milwaukee: ASQC Quality Press, 1994.

Crosby, Philip B. *Quality Is Free: The Art of Making Quality Certain*. New York: McGraw-Hill, 1979.

Deming, W. Edwards. *Out of the Crisis*. Cambridge, MA: Massachusetts Institute of Technology Center for Advanced Engineering Study, 1986.

Denton, D. Keith. "Lessons on Competitiveness: Motorola's Approach." *Production and Inventory Management Journal* (Third Quarter 1991), pp. 22–25.

Duncan, Acheson J. *Quality Control and Industrial Statistics*, 5th ed. Homewood, IL: Irwin, 1986.

Feigenbaum, A.V. *Total Quality Control: Engineering and Management*, 3d ed. New York: McGraw-Hill, 1983.

Hartvigsen, David. *SimQuick: Process Simulation with Excel*. 2d ed. Upper Saddle River, NJ: Prentice Hall, 2004.

Juran, J.M., and Frank Gryna, Jr. *Quality Planning and Analysis*, 2d ed. New York: McGraw-Hill, 1980.

Kalinosky, Ian S., "The Total Quality System—Going Beyond ISO 9000." *Quality Progress* (June 1990), pp. 50–53.

Katzenbach, Jon R., and Douglas K. Smith. "The Discipline of Teams." *Harvard Business Review* (March–April 1993), pp. 111–120.

Lazarus, Ian R., and Keith Butler. "The Promise of Six Sigma." *Managed Healthcare Executive* (October 2001), pp. 22–26.

Lucier, Gregory T., and Sridhar Seshadri. "GE Takes Six Sigma Beyond the Bottom Line." *Strategic Finance* (May 2001), pp. 41–46.

Miller, Bill. "ISO 9000 and the Small Company: Can I Afford It?" *APICS—The Performance Advantage* (September 1994), pp. 45–46.

Mitra, Amitava. *Fundamentals of Quality Control and Improvement*, 2d ed. Upper Saddle River, NJ: Prentice Hall, 1998.

Nakhai, Benham, and Joao S. Neves. "The Deming, Baldrige, and European Quality Awards." *Quality Progress* (April 1994), pp. 33–37.

Neves, Joao S., and Benham Nakhai. "The Evolution of the Baldrige Award." *Quality Progress* (June 1994), pp. 65–70.

Pande, Peter S., Robert P. Neuman, and Roland R. Cavanagh. *The Six Sigma Way*. New York: McGraw-Hill, 2000.

Rabbitt, John T., and Peter A. Bergh. *The ISO 9000 Book*. White Plains, NY: Quality Resources, 1993.

Roth, Daniel. "Motorola Lives!" *Fortune* (September 27, 1999). pp. 305–306.

Rust, Roland T., Timothy Keiningham, Stephen Clemens, and Anthony Zahorik. "Return on Quality at Chase Manhattan Bank," *Interfaces*, vol. 29, no. 2 (March-April 1999), pp. 62–72.

Sanders, Lisa. "Going Green with Less Red Tape." *Business Week* (September 23, 1996), pp. 75-76.

Sester, Dennis. "Motorola: A Tradition of Quality." *Quality* (October 2001), pp. 30–34.

Sullivan, Lawrence P. "The Power of Taguchi Methods." *Quality Progress*, vol. 20, no. 6 (1987), pp. 76–79.

"Why Online Browsers Don't Become Buyers." *Computerworld* (November 29, 1999), p. 14.

Process Capacity

LEARNING GOALS   *After reading this chapter, you should be able to...*

IDENTIFY OR DEFINE
1. capacity measures.
2. capacity.
3. capacity utilization.
4. bottlenecks and theory of constraints.
5. capacity gaps.

DESCRIBE OR EXPLAIN
6. economies and diseconomies of scale.
7. capacity cushions, timing and sizing options, and decision linkages.
8. a systematic approach to capacity planning.
9. how waiting-line models, simulation, and decision trees assist capacity decisions.

JPMORGAN CHASE

In 1995, the Chemical Banking Corporation and the venerable Chase Manhattan Corporation, the bank of the Rockefellers, merged. With combined assets of $297 billion, the new Chase (www.chase.com) dwarfed even Citicorp, the largest U.S. bank until this merger. Combining two operations that competed directly in two markets, the new Chase Bank had more than $163 billion in overall deposits and some 4 million consumer accounts. One primary motivation for increasing its capacity was cost savings. Chase expected to cut 12,000 employees and $1.5 billion in annual expenses by the first quarter of 1999. Back in 1991, Chemical itself had merged with Manufacturers Hanover Corporation, which cut 6,200 jobs and $750 million in annual costs. By late 1999, Chase expanded its capacity again when Chase Global Investor Services acquired Morgan Stanley's Trust Company. By January 2001, it had acquired JPMorgan and considerable expertise in investment banking, becoming JPMorgan Chase & Co. (www.jpmorganchase.com). The Morgan Stanley acquisition, for example, gave $400 billion of assets in trust to Chase to manage. Overall, the merger-related cost savings are expected to reach $3.8 billion. By the end of 2001, more than three quarters of these savings had been captured. In addition to economies-of-scale benefits, the acquisition added almost 330 highly trained professional staff to its firm. In the investment banking industry where it is often said that "the assets go home at night," management estimates that it costs about $250,000 per person to recruit, train, and retain such professionals.

A doubling of capacity is by no means unique, as the banking industry is in the biggest wave of consolidation in its history. In part, consolidation is a sensible response to excess capacity. Banking is also becoming a technology-driven business. More than ever, financial products and services, from loans to credit cards, are marketed through computers and telephones instead of through bank branches. Banks able to make large investments in technology gain an unparalleled ability to reach customers nationwide. Unprecedented capital investments create the need to spread costs over a broader customer base. The electronic revolution also undermines a bank's traditional role of intermediary between borrowers and savers, making it easier for both kinds of customers to get together directly. Lower profit margins in retail banking encourage moves into wholesale business, such as investment banking, where size and large capacity can, to some extent, be equated with strength. The trend toward megabanks has been obvious in North America but now has gripped France, Germany, and even Japan—though banks there are moving toward union at a typically sedate pace. Dealing with a product—money—that moves across borders electronically, banks are quick to feel the forces of globalization and technological change.

Although these reasons for large size can be impressive, there can also be qualms about capacity getting too big. When that happens, customers may withdraw their accounts and turn to smaller banks that meet a variety of personal and business banking needs. To protect revenue, large banks must offer the same exceptional service that small banks offer. Small banks almost have it easier than big banks because they are accustomed to giving a high degree of personalized service. A large bank must try to provide the same level and type of service that customers want.

Sources: "The Bank-Merger Splurge," *The Economist* (August 28, 1999); Letter to Shareholders, JPMorgan Chase 2001 Annual Report.

Analysts on the trading floor at JPMorgan Chase. Acquiring such highly trained professional staff was another benefit of acquiring Morgan Stanley, beyond the expected economy-of-scale benefits. The use of information technology is a visible component of these trading processes.

A process may be well designed in terms of customer involvement, work flows, resource flexibility, and use of technology. Perhaps it was recently reengineered, and yet, recent measurements of process performance may be disappointing. Cost might be high or customer satisfaction low. What could be wrong? The answer might be that the capacity at one or more steps in the process is too low, too high, or poorly utilized. Adjusting capacity is an important aspect of redesigning a process, the fifth step in Figure 6.1. The new JPMorgan Chase's experience demonstrates how important

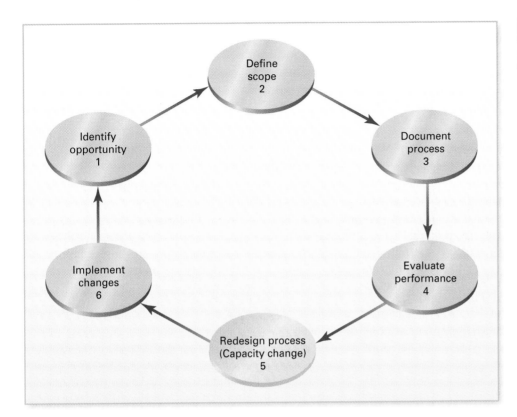

FIGURE 6.1

Redesigning a Process Through Capacity Change

capacity plans are to an organization's future. **Capacity** is the maximum rate of output for a process. Managers must provide the capacity to meet current and future demand; otherwise, the organization will miss opportunities for growth and profits.

Capacity plans are made at two levels. Long-term capacity plans deal with investments in new facilities and equipment. These plans cover at least two years into the future, but construction lead times alone can force much longer time horizons. U.S. firms invest more than $600 billion annually in *new* plant and equipment. Service industries account for more than 68 percent of the total. Such sizable investments require top-management participation and approval because they are not easily reversed. Short-term capacity plans focus on workforce size, overtime budgets, inventories, and other types of decisions. Concepts in this chapter apply to both long-term and short-term capacity plans. However, we explore short-term capacity issues more fully in later chapters on operating value chains (see Chapter 14, "Aggregate Planning;" Chapter 16, "Resource Planning;" and Chapter 17, "Scheduling").

As you read about process capacity, think about why it is important to the various departments and functions across the organization, such as . . .

capacity   The maximum rate of output for a process.

> **accounting,** which prepares the cost accounting information needed to evaluate capacity expansion decisions.
> **finance,** which performs the financial analysis of proposed capacity expansion investments and raises funds to support them.
> **human resources,** which must hire and train employees to support capacity plans.
> **management information systems,** which designs the databases used in determining work standards that help in calculating capacity gaps.
> **marketing,** which provides demand forecasts needed to identify capacity gaps.
> **operations,** which must select capacity strategies that provide the capacity levels to meet future demand most effectively.
> **purchasing,** which obtains outside capacity that is outsourced to suppliers upstream in the value chain.

CAPACITY PLANNING

Capacity planning is central to the long-term success of an organization. Too much capacity can be as agonizing as too little, as Managerial Practice 6.1 demonstrates. When choosing a capacity strategy, managers have to consider questions such as the following: How much of a cushion is needed to handle variable, uncertain demand? Should we expand capacity before the demand is there or wait until demand is more certain? A systematic approach is needed to answer these and similar questions and to develop a capacity strategy appropriate for each situation.

MEASURES OF CAPACITY

How should the maximum rate of output be measured?

No single capacity measure is applicable to all types of situations. A retailer measures capacity as annual sales dollars generated per square foot; an airline measures capacity as available seat-miles (ASMs) per month; a theater measures capacity as number of seats; and a job shop measures capacity as number of machine hours. In general, capacity can be expressed in one of two ways: output measures or input measures.

Output measures are the usual choice for high-volume processes that produce only one type of product. However, many processes produce more than one service or product. For example, a restaurant may be able to handle 100 take-out customers *or* 50 sit-down customers per hour. It might also handle 50 take-out *and* 25 sit-down customers or many other combinations of the two types of customers. As the amount of customization and variety in the product mix becomes excessive, output-based capacity measures become less useful. Output measures are best utilized when the firm provides a relatively small number of standardized services and products or when applied to individual processes within the overall firm. For example, a bank would have one capacity measure for processes that serve customers with B2C e-commerce and another measure for customers served with traditional brick-and-mortar facilities (see Chapter 12, "Information Technology and Value Chains").

Input measures are the usual choice for low-volume, flexible processes. For example, in a photocopy shop, capacity can be measured in machine hours or number of machines. Just as product mix can complicate output capacity measures, so too can demand complicate input measures. Demand, which invariably is expressed as an output rate, must be converted to an input measure. Only after making the conversion can a manager compare demand requirements and capacity on an equivalent basis. For example, the manager of a copy center must convert its annual demand for copies from different clients to the number of machines required.

UTILIZATION. Capacity planning requires a knowledge of the current capacity of a process and its utilization. **Utilization,** or the degree to which equipment, space, or labor is currently being used, is expressed as a percent:

utilization The degree to which equipment, space, or labor is currently being used.

$$\text{Utilization} = \frac{\text{Average output rate}}{\text{Maximum capacity}} \times 100\%$$

The average output rate and the capacity must be measured in the same terms—that is, time, customers, units, or dollars. The utilization rate indicates the need for adding extra capacity or eliminating unneeded capacity. The greatest difficulty in calculating utilization lies in defining *maximum capacity,* the denominator in the ratio. A number, such as servicing 40 customers per day, does not indicate how long that rate can be sustained. Being able to handle 40 customers for a one-week peak is quite different than sustaining it for six months. Here we refer to capacity as the greatest level of output that a process can *reasonably sustain* for a longer period, using realistic employee work schedules and the equipment currently in place. In some processes, this capacity level implies a one-shift operation; in others, it implies a three-shift operation. A process can be operated above its capacity level using marginal methods of production, such as excessive overtime, extra shifts, temporarily reduced maintenance activities, over-

MANAGERIAL PRACTICE 6.1

THE AGONY OF TOO MUCH—AND TOO LITTLE—CAPACITY

Carnival Cruise Line (www.carnivalcorp.com) has a fleet of cruise ships that ply the waters off Florida. The capacity of these ships is huge. The *Destiny* is its largest, which displaces 100,000 tons and can carry over 3,100 passengers. But Carnival has been sailing in choppy seas during the last year, plagued by three onboard fires and technical problems. The most pressing problem, however, is the glut of new ships being added throughout the industry. Carnival alone is bringing in a cadre of 15 new amenity-filled ships, boosting its fleet to 61. With other cruise lines also adding to their fleets, the number of available beds jumped by 12 percent in 2000. But historically, passenger volume has grown at only about 8 percent annually. Carnival argues that with the baby boomers now approaching their peak cruise-vacation years, the industry has lots of room to grow beyond the 6.5 million people who will book a cruise this year. "What is important to us is that we're building over the next five years $6.5 billion worth of new ships," says COO Frank.

"We're going to continue to grow our business, and we're going to grow it profitably." Not everyone is convinced. Some experts worry about the overcapacity issue and Carnival's decreasing return on investment. During 2000, the company's share prices plunged by more than 50 percent. For now, Carnival is filling its berths by slashing prices. After years of rising prices in this industry, the capacity glut is causing the steep discounts. For a seven-day cruise, the cheapest fare has dropped from $599 to

$549, and discounted tickets have gone as low as $359. Carnival is also adding a variety of shorter and cheaper voyages as a way to expand the market, because high utilization is a key to success when its resources are so capital-intensive.

The aircraft industry experienced the opposite problem in the late 1980s—not enough capacity. The world's airlines reequipped their fleets to carry more passengers on existing planes and vied to buy a record number of new commercial passenger jets. Orders received by Boeing (www.boeing.com), Airbus (www.airbus.com), and McDonnell Douglas surged to more than 2,600 planes. McDonnell Douglas alone had a backlog of some $18 billion in firm orders for its MD-80 and new MD-11 widebody—enough to keep its plant fully utilized for more than three years. Despite the number of orders, Douglas's commercial aircraft division announced a startling loss, Airbus struggled to make money, and even mighty Boeing fought to improve subpar margins. Capacity shortage caused many problems for McDonnell Douglas: Its suppliers were unable to keep pace, its doubled workforce was inexperienced and less productive, and considerable work had to be subcontracted to other plants. The result was that costs skyrocketed and profits plummeted. In 1997, Boeing acquired McDonnell Douglas.

The Carnival *Destiny* cruise ship, built for Miami-based Carnival Cruise Lines, returns to its Italian shipyard following four days of trial testing at sea. This $400-million-plus ship is nearly three football fields in length. Its huge capacity and steep investment cost make high utilization a key factor for success.

Sources: "Carnival Isn't Shipshape These Days," *Business Week* (April 24, 2000); "Floating Fantasy," *The Economist* (January 10, 1998).

staffing, and subcontracting. Although they help with temporary peaks, these options cannot be sustained for long. Employees do not want to work excessive overtime for extended periods, overtime and night-shift premiums drive up costs, and quality drops.

Operating processes close to (or even temporarily above) their capacity can result in low customer satisfaction, minimal profits, and even losing money despite high sales levels. Such was the case with the aircraft manufacturers mentioned in Managerial Practice 6.1. Similarly, Cummins Engine Company reacted a few years ago to an unexpected demand surge caused by the weakened dollar by working at peak capacity: The plant operated three shifts, often seven days a week. Overtime soared and exhausted workers dragged down productivity. Productivity also suffered when Cummins called back less-skilled workers, laid off during an earlier slump. These factors together caused Cummins to report a quarterly loss of $6.2 million, even as sales jumped.

INCREASING MAXIMUM CAPACITY. Most processes involve multiple operations, and often their capacities are not identical. A **bottleneck** is an operation that has the lowest capacity of any operation in the process and thus limits the system's output. Figure 6.2(a) shows a process where operation 2 is a bottleneck that limits the output to 50 units per hour. In effect, the process can produce only as fast as the slowest operation. Figure 6.2(b) shows the process when the capacities are perfectly balanced, making every operation a bottleneck. True expansion of a process's capacity occurs only when bottleneck capacity is increased. In Figure 6.2(a), initially adding capacity at operation 2 (and not operation 1 or 3) will increase system capacity. However, when operation 2's capacity reaches 200 units per hour, as in Figure 6.2(b), all three operations must be expanded simultaneously to increase capacity further.

A front-office process with high customer contact and divergence does not enjoy the simple line flows shown in Figure 6.2. Its operations may service many different customer types, and the demands on any one operation could vary considerably from one day to the next. Bottlenecks can still be identified by computing the average utilization of each operation. However, the variability in workload also creates *floating bottlenecks*. One week the mix of work may make operation 1 a bottleneck, and the next week it may make operation 3 the constraint. This type of variability increases the complexity of day-to-day scheduling. In this situation, management prefers lower utilization rates, which allow greater slack to absorb unexpected surges in demand.

The long-term capacity of bottleneck operations can be expanded in various ways. Investments can be made in new equipment and in brick-and-mortar facility expansions. The bottleneck's capacity also can be expanded by operating it more hours per week, such as going from a one-shift operation to multiple shifts, or going from five workdays per week to six or seven workdays per week. Managers also might relieve the bottleneck by redesigning the process, either through process reengineering or process improvement (see Chapter 3, "Process Design Strategy").

THEORY OF CONSTRAINTS

Long-term capacity expansions are not the only way to ease bottlenecks. Overtime, temporary or part-time employees, and temporarily outsourcing during peak periods are short-term options. Managers should also explore ways to increase the effective capacity utilization at bottlenecks, without experiencing the higher costs and poor customer service usually associated with maintaining output rates at full capacity. The key is to carefully monitor short-term schedules (see Chapter 17, "Scheduling"), keeping bottleneck resources as busy as practical. They should minimize the idle time lost at bottlenecks because jobs or customers are delayed at upstream operations in the process, or because the necessary materials or tools are temporarily unavailable. They

bottleneck An operation that has the lowest capacity of any operation in the process and thus limits the system's output.

FIGURE 6.2 Capacity Bottlenecks at a Three-Operation Facility

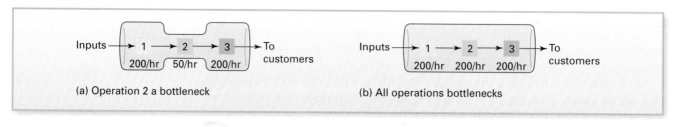

(a) Operation 2 a bottleneck

(b) All operations bottlenecks

should also minimize the time spent unproductively for setups, which is changing over from one service or product to another. When a changeover is made at a bottleneck operation, the number of units or customers processed before the next changeover should be large compared to the number processed at less critical operations. Maximizing the number processed per setup means that there will be fewer setups per year and, thus, less total time lost to setups.

Developing schedules that focus on bottlenecks has great potential for improving a firm's financial performance. The **theory of constraints** (TOC), sometimes referred to as the **drum–buffer–rope method,** is an approach to management that focuses on whatever impedes progress toward the goal of maximizing the flow of total value-added funds or sales less discounts and variable costs. The impediments, or bottlenecks, might be overloaded processes for new service development, order fulfillment, or the external customer interface. The fundamental idea is to focus on the bottlenecks to increase their throughput, thereby increasing the flow of total value-added funds. In terms of TOC, the key to the performance of the overall system lies in how the bottlenecks are scheduled.

With TOC, the bottlenecks are scheduled to maximize their throughput of services or products while adhering to promised completion dates. For example, manufacturing garden rakes involves the attachment of a bow to the head. Rake heads must be processed on the blanking press, welded to the bow, cleaned, and attached to the handle to make the rake, which is packaged and finally shipped to Sears, Kmart or Wal-Mart according to a specific delivery schedule. Suppose that the delivery commitments for all styles of rakes for the next month indicate that the welder is loaded at 105 percent of its capacity but that the other processes will be used at only 75 percent of their capacities. According to TOC, the welder is a bottleneck resource, whereas the blanking, cleaning, handle attaching, packaging, and shipping processes are nonbottleneck resources. Any idle time on the welder is a lost opportunity to generate total value-added funds. To maximize throughput of the rake manufacturing system, managers should focus on the welder schedule.

Application of TOC involves the following steps.

1. *Identify the System Bottleneck(s).* For the rake example, the bottleneck is the welder because it is restricting the firm's ability to meet the shipping schedule and, hence, total value-added funds.

2. *Exploit the Bottleneck(s).* Create schedules that maximize the throughput of the bottleneck(s). For the rake example, schedule the welder to maximize its utilization while meeting the shipping commitments to the extent possible.

3. *Subordinate All Other Decisions to Step 2.* Nonbottleneck resources should be scheduled to support the schedule of the bottleneck and not produce more than it can handle. That is, the blanking press should not produce more than the welder can handle, and the activities of the cleaning and subsequent operations should be based on the output rate of the welder.

4. *Elevate the Bottleneck(s).* After the scheduling improvements in steps 1–3 have been exhausted and the bottleneck is still a constraint to throughput, management should consider increasing the capacity of the bottleneck. For example, if welding is still a constraint after exhausting schedule improvements, consider increasing its capacity by adding another shift or another welding machine.

5. *Do Not Let Inertia Set In.* Actions taken in steps 3 and 4 will improve the welder throughput and may alter the loads on other processes. Consequently, the system constraint(s) may have shifted.

Details on the scheduling method used in TOC can be found in Simons and Simpson III (1997).

Many manufacturers have applied the principles of the theory of constraints, including National Semiconductor, Dresser Industries, Allied-Signal, Bethlehem Steel, Johnson Controls, Rockwell Automotive, and Bal Seals (see Managerial Practice 6.2).

theory of constraints (TOC)
An approach to management that focuses on whatever impedes progress toward the goal of maximizing the flow of total value-added funds or sales less discounts and variable costs. **Also referred to as drum–buffer–rope method.**

drum–buffer–rope method
See theory of constraints.

MANAGERIAL PRACTICE 6.2

USE OF THEORY OF CONSTRAINTS AT BAL SEAL

Bal Seal (www.balseal.com) designs, prototypes, and produces seals and springs for different industries, such as aerospace, automotive, medical and dental equipment, transportation, and electronics. Bal Seal has locations in both the United States and Europe (www.balseal.nl). Its engineers specialize in unique sealing solutions and provide considerable product variety. Its manufacturing processes were best characterized as batch processes. Before discovering TOC, process measurements focused on departmental efficiency. Bal Seals was experiencing troublesome difficulties with excessive inventory, long lead times, and an entire production crew that was routinely working 55 to 58 hours per week. Despite operating well above capacity, the on-time shipment rate hovered just in the 80 to 85 percent range.

What was wrong? Bal Seal put together a team and learned about TOC and the critical thinking processes associated with it. The results were dramatic and highly visible. Almost immediately, bloated inventories began to dry up. Some production workers were concerned, because having inventory all over the place provided a sense of security. They also were worried about efficiency ratings and reduced pay. One member of the design team met with each direct production worker and explained that it was okay to have nothing to do. Under this new way of utilizing capacity and managing production rates, only the constraint must be kept productive all the time. The other work centers were tied to that constraint, and it was their job to be available and ready when work came their way. Under TOC, extra capacity surfaced everywhere except at the constraint. Where the company had been able to produce a maximum of 65,000 parts per week, after TOC total production was up to 100,000 per week. Even at this higher throughput rate, nonconstraint work centers were operating well below capacity most of the time. Other almost immediate effects were reduced customer response times (from six weeks to eight days) and improved on-time shipments up to 97 percent. Customer satisfaction increased, although initially customers questioned whether Bal Seal's performance was just a temporary condition. Time has proven the permanence of the improvements. Now that the order fulfillment process is shipshape, the next challenge is to address the customer relationship process, because its salespeople were simply order-takers. The goal is for them to become more proactive, increase active customer contact, and seek out additional business to take advantage of the plant's higher production rate. The lessons of TOC can be applied there as well.

Source: "Theory of Constraints Case Study: Bal Seal Engineering." www.goldratt.com/balsealerp.htm (December 2002).

Service organizations, such as Delta Airlines, United Airlines, and the U.S. Air Force, have also used TOC to advantage. The U.S. Air Force health care system, for example, has 120 medical facilities and a patient base of around 3 million people, and it is continually seeking performance improvements. When it comes to health care, there is an overriding need to provide services at the highest quality. But productivity and cost are other key metrics. A major problem has been mismatches between changing demand and the capacity of certain resources. A team was put together to redesign their health care delivery process. Team members represented all levels, including U.S. Air Force headquarters, the command level, and individual hospitals. The team members understood the details and challenges of their processes. The team concluded that the critical constraint was the surgeons and the operating rooms, the highest-cost and highest-value portions of their processes. They developed plans that subordinated all other considerations to these key resources. These examples show that TOC thinking is quite scalable, from individual processes at a single Bal Seals plant to a 120-facility medical care system.

What is the maximum reasonable size for a facility?

ECONOMIES OF SCALE

economies of scale A concept that states that the average unit cost of a service or good can be reduced by increasing its output rate.

A concept known as **economies of scale** states that the average unit cost of a service or good can be reduced by increasing its output rate. Managerial Practice 6.3 illustrates the importance of economies of scale for the airlines industry in China and South America. There are four principal reasons why economies of scale can drive costs down when output increases: Fixed costs are spread over more units, construction costs are reduced, costs of purchased materials are cut, and process advantages are found.

MANAGERIAL PRACTICE 6.3

ECONOMIES OF SCALE AT WORK

China Southern Airlines

In light of the fierce battle for market share in China's aviation market, China Southern Airlines (www.cs-air.com/en) has a powerful objective: to be the strongest airline in China. The key to attaining this objective, according to company president Wang Changshun, is to embrace economies of scale. With the reform and opening of China in the early 1980s, its civil aviation industry grew with a number of smaller airlines that were saddled with high operational costs. Profitability of all airlines dropped, and services deteriorated. Against this backdrop, China Southern Airlines (CSA) has taken advantage of economies of scale. In 1998, CSA purchased Guizhou Airlines, converting it into an aviation base in Southwest China. In 2000, a merger with Zhong Yuan Airlines resulted in CSA seeing its market share in Zhengzhou jump to more than 64 percent. In that same year, CSA began churning a profit. Furthermore, its total assets doubled and the number of passengers carried increased by 26 percent. As of late 2002, CSA controlled approximately 25 percent of the domestic market share and was in the process of merging with China Northern Airlines and Xinjiang Airlines to form the New China Southern Airlines Group. It is estimated that, after restructuring, CSA will have a fleet of 180 airplanes serving more than 600 routes. This restructuring will help reduce operational costs and concentrate marketing efforts on major routes. It will also lay a solid foundation for CSA to extend its regional and international routes and strengthen multilateral code-share agreements with other airlines. The new CSA would not only be the largest airline in China, with more than 40 percent of the domestic market share, but also one of the largest in Asia.

South American Airlines

In the mid-1990s, many of the airlines in the Latin America region expanded their capacity, expecting demand to rise. But it shrank in the wake of Brazil's devaluation crisis in early 1999 at the same time as the airlines were facing ever more competition from airlines in the United States, which enjoy bigger economies of scale. Brazil's domestic flights in the first quarter of 2000 showed only 58 percent of seats were taken, much below the 65 percent occupation that is the industry's typical break-even quantity. Without enough volume over which to spread fixed costs, the results were inevitable. A rescue plan for Aerolineas Argentinas (www.aerolineas.com.ar) announced big cuts in domestic and international services. After restructuring its operations, the carrier decided in mid-2002 to fly again some of its international routes. TAM (www.tam.com.br) and Transbrasil (www.transbrasil.com.br), two of Brazil's four big airlines, were discussing an "operational partnership" to cut the overlap between their flights, a step widely seen as leading to an eventual merger and significant cuts. Unfortunately for Transbrasil, an agreement was not reached and the carrier went bankrupt. Vasp (www.vasp.com.br), another of Brazil's big four, announced the suspension of its flights to North America and Europe after Boeing had demanded some of its airplanes back because Vasp was not keeping up its lease payments. The president of the Brazilian Development Bank suggested that there might be room for only one large local airline in Brazil, pointing to Canada and Mexico, where in each case two big local airlines have merged. With the weakening of the South American region's economy, a consolidation of the industry would benefit the remaining airlines due to the higher volumes associated with strong economies of scale.

A China Southern Airlines (CSA) jetliner taking off at the Guangzhou Baiyun International Airport, China, previously known as Canton. This Boeing 777-2000 plane, along with the others waiting to take off, are part of an expanding fleet. The capacity expansion allows CSA to gain economies of scale that reduce operational costs while garnering over 40 percent of the domestic market share.

Sources: "China Southern Airlines President Addresses IATA Confab," *Business Wire* (June 7, 2002); "Rival Operations," *Wall Street Journal* (June 6, 1990); "South American Airlines," *The Economist* (May 6, 2000); "Transbrasil Will Probably Lose Operating Certificate," *Aviation Daily* (October 12, 2002).

An operating room scrub technician, orthopedic surgeon, and general surgeon prepare for surgery on a patient at a forward-deployed location in support of Operation Enduring Freedom. The U.S. Air Force understands that surgeons are a key to planning the capacity of its processes.

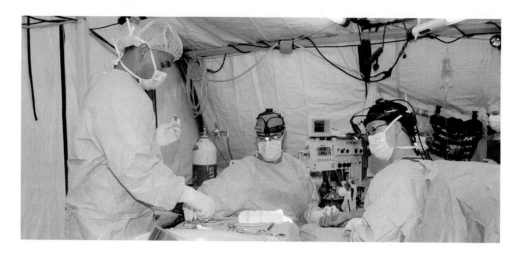

SPREADING FIXED COSTS. In the short term, certain costs do not vary with changes in the output rate. These fixed costs include heating costs, debt service, and management salaries. Depreciation of plant and equipment already owned is also a fixed cost in the accounting sense. When the output rate—and, therefore, the facility's utilization rate—increase, the average unit cost drops because fixed costs are spread over more units.

REDUCING CONSTRUCTION COSTS. Certain activities and expenses are required in building small and large facilities alike: building permits, architects' fees, rental of building equipment, and the like. Doubling the size of the facility usually does not double construction costs. The construction cost of equipment or a facility often increases relative to its surface area, whereas its capacity increases in proportion to its cubic volume.

CUTTING COSTS OF PURCHASED MATERIALS. Higher volumes can reduce the costs of purchased materials and services. They give the purchaser a better bargaining position and the opportunity to take advantage of quantity discounts. Retailers such as Wal-Mart and Toys "Я" Us reap significant economies of scale because their national and international stores sell huge volumes of each item. Producers that rely on a vast network of suppliers (e.g., Toyota) and food processors (e.g., Kraft General Foods) also can buy inputs for less because of the quantity they order.

FINDING PROCESS ADVANTAGES. High-volume production provides many opportunities for cost reduction. At a higher output rate, the process shifts toward a line process, with resources dedicated to individual products. Firms may be able to justify the expense of more efficient technology or more specialized equipment. The benefits from dedicating resources to individual services or products may include speeding up the learning effect, lowering inventory, improving process and job designs, and reducing the number of changeovers.

DISECONOMIES OF SCALE

diseconomies of scale   When the average cost per unit increases as the facility's size increases.

At some point, a facility can become so large that **diseconomies of scale** set in; that is, the average cost per unit increases as the facility's size increases. The reason is that excessive size can bring complexity, loss of focus, and inefficiencies that raise the average unit cost of a service or product. There may be too many layers of employees and bureaucracy, and management loses touch with employees and customers. The organization is less agile and loses the flexibility needed to respond to changing demand. Many large companies become so involved in analysis and planning that they innovate less and avoid risks. The result is that small companies outperform corporate giants in numerous industries.

Figure 6.3 illustrates the transition from economies of scale to diseconomies of scale. The 500-bed hospital shows economies of scale because the average unit cost at its *best operating level,* represented by the blue dot, is less than that of the 250-bed hospital. However, further expansion to a 750-bed hospital leads to higher average unit costs and diseconomies of scale. One reason the 500-bed hospital enjoys greater economies of scale than the 250-bed hospital is that the cost of building and equipping it is less than twice the cost for the smaller hospital. The 750-bed facility would enjoy similar savings. Its higher average unit costs can be explained only by diseconomies of scale, which outweigh the savings realized in construction costs.

Figure 6.3 does not mean that the optimal size for all hospitals is 500 beds. Optimal size depends on the number of patients per week to be served. On the one hand, a hospital serving a small community would have lower costs by choosing a 250-bed capacity rather than the 500-bed capacity. On the other hand, assuming the same cost structure, a large community will be served more efficiently by two 500-bed hospitals than by one 1,000-bed facility.

An example of going too far with huge facilities was the Incredible Universe superstores of Tandy Corporation. This Fort Worth-based electronics retailer opened its first superstore in 1992. The average store packed some 85,000 products into 185,000 square feet, or more than four times the average at rival Circuit City stores. The superstores never were profitable. Tandy opted to sell all 17 Incredible Universe stores at bargain-basement prices and focus on Radio Shack. The lack of focus and huge size of the superstores made it impossible to generate enough sales per square foot to make the stores profitable.

CAPACITY STRATEGIES

Operations managers must examine three dimensions of capacity strategy before making capacity decisions: (1) sizing capacity cushions, (2) timing and sizing expansion, and (3) linking process capacity and other operating decisions.

How much capacity cushion is best for various processes?

SIZING CAPACITY CUSHIONS. Average utilization rates should not get too close to 100 percent. When they do, that usually is a signal to increase capacity or decrease order acceptance so as to avoid declining productivity. The **capacity cushion** is the amount of reserve capacity that a process has to handle sudden increases in demand or temporary losses of production capacity; it measures the amount by which the average utilization (in terms of total capacity) falls below 100 percent. Specifically,

capacity cushion The amount of reserve capacity that a process has to handle sudden increases in demand or temporary losses of production capacity; it measures the amount by which the average utilization (in terms of total capacity) falls below 100 percent.

$$\text{Capacity cushion} = 100\% - \text{Utilization rate (\%)}$$

Historically, U.S. manufacturers have maintained an average cushion of 18 percent. The appropriate size of the cushion varies by industry. In the capital-intensive paper industry, where machines can cost hundreds of millions of dollars each, cushions well under 10 percent are preferred. The less capital-intensive hotel industry breaks even with a 60 to 70 percent utilization (40 to 30 percent cushion), and begins to suffer

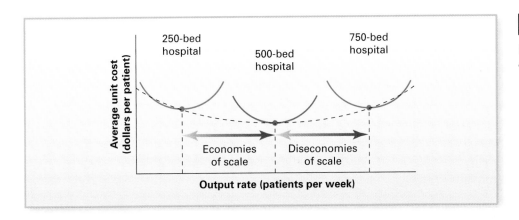

FIGURE 6.3

Economies and Diseconomies of Scale

customer-service problems when the cushion drops to 20 percent. The more capital-intensive cruise ship industry, such as Carnival Cruise Line, prefers cushions as small as 5 percent. Large cushions are particularly vital for front-office processes where customers expect fast delivery times.

Businesses find large cushions appropriate when demand varies. In certain service industries (e.g., groceries), demand on some days of the week is predictably higher than on other days, and there are even hour-to-hour patterns. Long customer waiting times are not acceptable because customers grow impatient if they have to wait in a supermarket checkout line for more than a few minutes. Prompt customer service requires supermarkets to maintain a capacity cushion large enough to handle peak demand.

Large cushions also are necessary when future demand is uncertain, particularly if resource flexibility is low. One large bank operated its computer for six months at an average 77 percent load on the central processing unit (CPU) during peak demand. Top management believed that the capacity cushion was more than ample and rejected a proposal to expand capacity. During the next six months, however, the average CPU utilization during peaks unexpectedly surged to 83 percent, causing a dramatic decline in customer service. The 17 percent capacity cushion proved to be too small to meet the bank's customer-service objectives. Simulation and waiting-line analysis (see Supplement B, "Simulation" and Supplement C, "Waiting Lines") can help managers anticipate better the relationship between capacity cushion and customer service.

Another type of demand uncertainty occurs with a changing product mix. Though total demand might remain stable, the load can shift unpredictably from one work center to another as the mix changes.

Supply uncertainty also favors large capacity cushions. Capacity often comes in large increments, so expanding even by the minimum amount possible may create a large cushion. Firms also need to build in excess capacity to allow for employee absenteeism, vacations, holidays, and any other delays. Penalty costs for overtime and subcontracting can create the need for further increases in capacity cushions.

The argument in favor of small cushions is simple: Unused capacity costs money. For capital-intensive firms, minimizing the capacity cushion is vital. Studies indicate that businesses with high capital intensity achieve a low return on investment when the capacity cushion is high. This strong correlation does not exist for labor-intensive firms, however. Their return on investment is about the same because the lower investment in equipment makes high utilization less critical. Small cushions have other advantages; they reveal inefficiencies that may be masked by capacity excesses—problems with absenteeism, for example, or unreliable suppliers. Once managers and workers have identified such problems, they often can find ways to correct them.

Should an expanionist or a wait-and-see strategy be followed?

TIMING AND SIZING EXPANSION. The second issue of capacity strategy is when to expand and by how much. Figure 6.4 illustrates two extreme strategies: the *expansionist strategy*, which involves large, infrequent jumps in capacity, and the *wait-and-see strategy*, which involves smaller, more frequent jumps.

FIGURE 6.4   Two Capacity Strategies

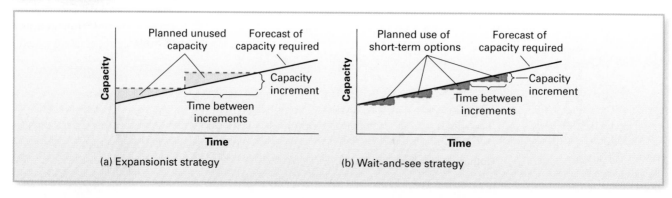

(a) Expansionist strategy

(b) Wait-and-see strategy

The timing and sizing of expansion are related; that is, if demand is increasing and the time between increments increases, the size of the increments must also increase. The expansionist strategy, which stays ahead of demand, minimizes the chance of sales lost to insufficient capacity. The wait-and-see strategy lags behind demand, relying on short-term options, such as use of overtime, temporary workers, subcontractors, stockouts, and postponement of preventive maintenance to meet any shortfalls.

Several factors favor the expansionist strategy. Expansion may result in economies of scale and a faster rate of learning, thus helping a firm reduce its costs and compete on price. This strategy might increase the firm's market share or act as a form of preemptive marketing. By making a large capacity expansion or announcing that one is imminent, the firm uses capacity to preempt expansion by other firms. These other firms must sacrifice some of their market share or risk burdening the industry with overcapacity. To be successful, however, the preempting firm must have the credibility to convince the competition that it will carry out its plans—and must signal its plans before the competition can act.

The conservative wait-and-see strategy is to expand in smaller increments, such as by renovating existing facilities rather than building new ones. Because the wait-and-see strategy follows demand, it reduces the risks of overexpansion based on overly optimistic demand forecasts, obsolete technology, or inaccurate assumptions regarding the competition.

However, this strategy has its own risks, such as being preempted by a competitor or being unable to respond if demand is unexpectedly high. The wait-and-see strategy has been criticized as a short-term strategy typical of some U.S. management styles. Managers on the fast track to corporate advancement tend to take fewer risks. They earn promotions by avoiding the big mistake and maximizing short-term profits and return on investment. The wait-and-see strategy fits this short-term outlook but can erode market share over the long run.

Management may choose one of these two strategies or one of the many between these extremes. With strategies in the more moderate middle, firms may expand more frequently (on a smaller scale) than with the expansionist strategy but do not always lag behind demand as with the wait-and-see strategy. An intermediate strategy could be to *follow the leader*, expanding when others do. If others are right, so are you, and nobody gains a competitive advantage. If they make a mistake and overexpand, so have you, but everyone shares in the agony of overcapacity.

LINKING PROCESS CAPACITY AND OTHER DECISIONS. Capacity decisions should be closely linked to strategies and processes throughout the organization. When managers make decisions about location, resource flexibility, and inventory, they must consider the impact on capacity cushions. Capacity cushions buffer the organization against uncertainty, as do resource flexibility, inventory, and longer customer lead times. If a system is well balanced and a change is made in some other decision area, then the capacity cushion may need change to compensate. For example, capacity cushions at a process can be lowered if less emphasis is placed on fast deliveries (*competitive priorities*), yield losses (*quality*) drop, investment in capital-intensive equipment increases or worker flexibility increases (*process design*), and if inventory is used more to smooth the output rate (*aggregate planning*).

> How should capacity and competitive priorities be linked? How should capacity and other types of decisions be linked?

A SYSTEMATIC APPROACH TO CAPACITY DECISIONS

Although each situation is somewhat different, a four-step procedure generally can help managers make sound capacity decisions. In describing this procedure, we assume that management has already performed the preliminary steps of determining the process's existing capacity and assessing whether its current capacity cushion is appropriate.

> How can capacity plans be systematically developed?

1. Estimate future capacity requirements.
2. Identify gaps by comparing requirements with available capacity.

3. Develop alternative plans for filling the gaps.

4. Evaluate each alternative, both qualitatively and quantitatively, and make a final choice.

STEP 1: ESTIMATE CAPACITY REQUIREMENTS

capacity requirement   What the process capacity should be for some future time period to meet the demand of its customers (external or internal), allowing for the desired capacity cushion.

planning horizon   The set of consecutive time periods considered for planning purposes.

A process's **capacity requirement** is what its capacity should be for some future time period to meet the demand of its customers (external or internal), allowing for the desired capacity cushion. It can be expressed in one of two ways: with an output measure or with an input measure. Either way, the foundation for the estimate is forecasts of demand, productivity, competition, and technological change. These forecasts normally need to be made for several time periods in a **planning horizon,** which is the set of consecutive time periods considered for planning purposes. Long-term capacity plans need to consider more of the future (perhaps a whole decade) than do short-term plans. Depending on the situation, each time period within the time horizon could be a year, month of the year, day of the week, or even hour of the day. A time period is likely to be a year when planning equipment purchases or a new facility, or it can be an hour of the day for scheduling the workforce at a call center that experiences predictable hour-to-hour demand fluctuations. Unfortunately, the farther ahead you look, the more chance you have of making an inaccurate forecast (see Chapter 13, "Forecasting").

USING OUTPUT MEASURES.   The simplest way to express capacity requirements is as an output rate. As discussed earlier, output measures are appropriate for high-volume processes with little product variety or process divergence. Here, demand forecasts for future years are used as a basis for extrapolating capacity requirements into the future. If demand is expected to double in the next five years (and the current capacity cushion is appropriate), then the capacity requirements also double. For example, if a process's current capacity requirement is 50 customers per day, then the requirement in five years would be 100 customers per day. Example 6.1 shows how to calculate capacity requirements when the current capacity cushion is not what is desired.

EXAMPLE 6.1   Estimating Capacity Requirements when Using Output Measures

A process currently services an average of 50 customers per day. Observations in recent weeks show that its utilization is about 90 percent, allowing for just a 10 percent capacity cushion. If demand is expected to double in five years, what capacity requirement should be planned? Management wants to increase the capacity cushion to 20 percent because customer service has been inadequate and there is a good deal of customer contact in the process.

SOLUTION

This year's capacity requirement, allowing instead for a 20-percent capacity cushion, is 62.5 (or $50/[1.0 - 0.20]$) customers per day. Essentially, you should divide by the desired utilization rate. (It is incorrect to multiply 50 by 1.20 because we are expressing C, which is the desired capacity cushion, as a proportion of the *total* capacity and not just the productive portion of it.) Five years from now, if demand doubles, the customer requirement will be 125 (or 62.5×2) customers per day.

DECISION POINT   Increasing the capacity cushion from 10 to 20 percent means better customer service, but the capacity requirement that must be provided for five years from now is well above 100 customers per day. Management must find ways to provide the added capacity.

USING INPUT MEASURES. Output measures may be insufficient when

- product variety and process divergence is high,
- the product or service mix is changing,
- productivity rates are expected to change, or
- significant learning effects are expected (see Supplement G, "Learning Curve Analysis," on the Student CD-ROM).

In such cases, it is more appropriate to calculate capacity requirements using an input measure, such as the number of employees, machines, computers, trucks, or the like. Using an input measure for the capacity requirement brings together demand forecasts, process time estimates, and the desired capacity cushion. When just one service or product is processed at an operation and the time period is a particular year, the capacity requirement, M, is

$$\text{Capacity requirement} = \frac{\text{Processing hours required for year's demand}}{\text{Hours available from a single capacity unit (such as an employee or machine) per year, after deducting desired cushion}}$$

$$M = \frac{Dp}{N[1 - (C/100)]}$$

where

D = demand forecast for the year (number of customers serviced or units of product)

p = processing time (in hours per customer served or unit produced)

N = total number of hours per year during which the process operates

C = desired capacity cushion (expressed as a percent)

M is the number of input units required and should be calculated for each year in the time horizon. The processing time, p, depends on the process and methods selected to do the work (see Chapter 4, "Process Analysis"). Various techniques are available to estimate p (see Supplement H, "Measuring Output Rates," on the Student CD-ROM). The denominator is the total number of hours, N, available for the year from one unit of capacity (an employee or machine), multiplied by a proportion that accounts for the desired capacity cushion, C. The proportion is simply $1.0 - C$, where C is converted from a percent to a proportion by dividing by 100. For example, a 20-percent capacity cushion means that $1.0 - C$ equals 0.80.

If multiple services or products are involved, extra time usually is needed to change over from one service or product to the next. **Setup time** is the time required to change a machine from making one service or product to making another. Setup time is derived from process decisions, as is processing time (see Chapter 4, "Process Analysis"). The total setup time is found by dividing the number of units forecast per year, D, by the number of units made in each lot (number of units processed between setups), which gives the number of setups per year, and then multiplying by the time per setup. For example, if the annual demand is 1,200 units and the average lot size is 100, there are $1{,}200/100 = 12$ setups per year. Accounting for both processing and setup time when there are multiple services (products), we get

setup time The time required to change a machine from making one service or product to making another.

$$\text{Capacity requirement} = \frac{\text{Processing } and \text{ setup hours required for year's demand, summed over all services or products}}{\text{Hours available from a single capacity unit per year, after deducting desired cushion}}$$

$$M = \frac{[Dp + (D/Q)s]_{\text{product 1}} + [Dp + (D/Q)s]_{\text{product 2}} + \cdots + [Dp + (D/Q)s]_{\text{product } n}}{N[1 - (C/100)]}$$

where

Q = number of units in each lot

s = setup time (in hours) per lot

What to do when M is not an integer depends on the situation. For example, it is impossible to buy a fractional machine. In this case, round up the fractional part, unless it is cost efficient to use short-term options, such as overtime or stockouts to cover any shortfalls. If, instead, the capacity unit is the number of employees at a process, a value of 23.6 may be achieved using just 26 employees and a modest use of overtime (equivalent to having 60 percent of another full-time person). Here, the fractional value should be retained as useful information.

EXAMPLE 6.2   Estimating Capacity Requirements when Using Input Measures

TUTOR 6.1

Tutor 6.1 on the Student CD-ROM provides a new example to practice calculating capacity requirements when using input measures.

A copy center in an office building prepares bound reports for two clients. The center makes multiple copies (the lot size) of each report. The processing time to run, collate, and bind each copy depends on, among other factors, the number of pages. The center operates 250 days per year, with one eight-hour shift. Management believes that a capacity cushion of 15 percent (beyond the allowance built into time standards) is best. It currently has three copy machines. Based on the following table of information, determine how many machines are needed at the copy center.

ITEM	CLIENT X	CLIENT Y
Annual demand forecast (copies)	2,000	6,000
Standard processing time (hour/copy)	0.5	0.7
Average lot size (copies per report)	20	30
Standard setup time (hours)	0.25	0.40

SOLUTION

$$M = \frac{[Dp + (D/Q)s]_{\text{product 1}} + [Dp + (D/Q)s]_{\text{product 2}} + \cdots + [Dp + (D/Q)s]_{\text{product } n}}{N[1 - (C/100)]}$$

$$= \frac{[2,000(0.5) + (2,000/20)(0.25)]_{\text{client X}} + [6,000(0.7) + (6,000/30)(0.40)]_{\text{client Y}}}{[(250 \text{ days/year})(1 \text{ shift/day})(8 \text{ hours/shift})](1.0 - 15/100)}$$

$$= \frac{5,305}{1,700} = 3.12$$

Rounding up to the next integer gives a requirement of four machines.

DECISION POINT   The copy center's capacity is being stretched and no longer has the desired 15 percent capacity cushion. Not wanting customer service to suffer, management decided to use overtime as a short-term solution to handle past-due orders. If demand continues at the current level or grows, it will acquire a fourth machine.

STEP 2: IDENTIFY GAPS

capacity gap   Any difference (positive or negative) between projected demand and current capacity.

A **capacity gap** is any difference (positive or negative) between projected demand and current capacity. Identifying gaps requires use of the correct capacity measure. Complications arise when multiple operations and several resource inputs are involved. Expanding the capacity of some operations may increase overall capacity. However, if one operation is a bottleneck, capacity can be expanded only if the capacity of the bottleneck operation is expanded.

STEP 3: DEVELOP ALTERNATIVES

base case   The act of doing nothing and losing orders from any demand that exceeds current capacity.

The next step is to develop alternative plans to cope with projected gaps. One alternative, called the **base case**, is to do nothing and simply lose orders from any demand that exceeds current capacity. Other alternatives are various timing and sizing options for adding new capacity, including the expansionist and wait-and-see strategies illustrated in Figure 6.4. Additional possibilities include expanding at a different location and using short-term options, such as overtime, temporary workers, and subcontracting.

STEP 4: EVALUATE THE ALTERNATIVES

In this final step, the manager evaluates each alternative, both qualitatively and quantitatively.

QUALITATIVE CONCERNS. Qualitatively, the manager has to look at how each alternative fits the overall capacity strategy and other aspects of the business not covered by the financial analysis. Of particular concern might be uncertainties about demand, competitive reaction, technological change, and cost estimates. Some of these factors cannot be quantified and have to be assessed on the basis of judgment and experience. Others can be quantified, and the manager can analyze each alternative by using different assumptions about the future. One set of assumptions could represent a worst case, in which demand is less, competition is greater, and construction costs are higher than expected. Another set of assumptions could represent the most optimistic view of the future. This type of "what-if" analysis allows the manager to get an idea of each alternative's implications before making a final choice.

QUANTITATIVE CONCERNS. Quantitatively, the manager estimates the change in cash flows for each alternative over the forecast time horizon compared to the base case. **Cash flow** is the difference between the flows of funds into and out of an organization over a period of time, including revenues, costs, and changes in assets and liabilities. The manager is concerned here only with calculating the cash flows attributable to the project.

cash flow The difference between the flows of funds into and out of an organization over a period of time, including revenues, costs, and changes in assets and liabilities.

Evaluating the Alternatives

EXAMPLE 6.3

TUTOR 6.2

Tutor 6.2 on the Student CD-ROM provides a new example to practice projecting cash flows for capacity decisions.

Grandmother's Chicken Restaurant is experiencing a boom in business. The owner expects to serve a total of 80,000 meals this year. Although the kitchen is operating at 100 percent capacity, the dining room can handle a total of 105,000 diners per year. Forecasted demand for the next five years is 90,000 meals for next year, followed by a 10,000-meal increase in each of the succeeding years. One alternative is to expand both the kitchen and the dining room now, bringing their capacities up to 130,000 meals per year. The initial investment would be $200,000, made at the end of this year (year 0). The average meal is priced at $10, and the before-tax profit margin is 20 percent. The 20 percent figure was arrived at by determining that, for each $10 meal, $6 covers variable costs and $2 goes toward fixed costs (other than depreciation). The remaining $2 goes to pretax profit.

What are the pretax cash flows from this project for the next five years compared to those of the base case of doing nothing?

SOLUTION

Recall that the base case of doing nothing results in losing all potential sales beyond 80,000 meals. With the new capacity, the cash flow would equal the extra meals served by having a 130,000-meal capacity, multiplied by a profit of $2 per meal. In year 0, the only cash flow is $-\$200,000$ for the initial investment. In year 1, the 90,000-meal demand will be completely satisfied by the expanded capacity, so the incremental cash flow is $(90,000 - 80,000)(2) = \$20,000$. For subsequent years, the figures are as follows:

Year 2:	Demand $= 100,000$; Cash flow $= (100,000 - 80,000)2 = \$40,000$
Year 3:	Demand $= 110,000$; Cash flow $= (110,000 - 80,000)2 = \$60,000$
Year 4:	Demand $= 120,000$; Cash flow $= (120,000 - 80,000)2 = \$80,000$
Year 5:	Demand $= 130,000$; Cash flow $= (130,000 - 80,000)2 = \$100,000$

If the new capacity were smaller than the expected demand in any year, we would subtract the base case capacity from the new capacity (rather than the demand).

DECISION POINT   Before deciding on this capacity alternative, the owner should account for the time value of money, applying such techniques as the present value or internal rate of return methods (see Supplement J, "Financial Analysis," on the Student CD-ROM). The owner should also examine the qualitative concerns. For example, the homey atmosphere that the restaurant has projected may be lost with expansion. Furthermore, other alternatives should be considered (see Solved Problem 2).

TOOLS FOR CAPACITY PLANNING

What tools can help in planning capacities?

Capacity planning requires demand forecasts for an extended period of time. Unfortunately, forecast accuracy declines as the forecasting horizon lengthens. In addition, anticipating what competitors will do increases the uncertainty of demand forecasts. Finally, demand during any period of time is not evenly distributed; peaks and valleys of demand may (and often do) occur within the time period. These realities necessitate the use of capacity cushions. In this section, we introduce three tools that deal more formally with demand uncertainty and variability: (1) waiting-line models, (2) simulation, and (3) decision trees. Waiting-line models and simulation account for the random, independent behavior of many customers, in terms of both their time of arrival and their processing needs. Decision trees allow anticipation of events, such as competitors' actions.

WAITING-LINE MODELS

Waiting-line models often are useful in capacity planning, such as selecting an appropriate capacity cushion for a high customer-contact process. Waiting lines tend to develop in front of a work center, such as an airport ticket counter, a machine center, or a central computer. The reason is that the arrival time between jobs or customers varies, and the processing time may vary from one customer to the next. Waiting-line models use probability distributions to provide estimates of average customer delay time, average length of waiting lines, and utilization of the work center. Managers can use this information to choose the most cost-effective capacity, balancing customer service and the cost of adding capacity.

Supplement C, "Waiting Lines", follows this chapter and provides a fuller treatment of these models. It introduces formulas for estimating important characteristics of a waiting line, such as average customer waiting time and average facility utilization for different facility designs. For example, a facility might be designed to have one or multiple lines at each operation and to route customers through one or multiple operations. Given the estimating capability of these formulas and cost estimates for waiting and idle time, managers can select cost-effective designs and capacity levels that also provide the desired level of customer service.

Figure 6.5 shows output from OM Explorer's Solver for waiting lines. The process modeled, a professor meeting students during office hours, has an arrival rate of three students per hour and a service rate of six students per hour. The output shows that the capacity cushion is 50 percent (1 − average server utilization of 0.50). This result is expected because the processing rate is double the arrival rate. What might not be expected is that a typical student spends 0.33 hours either in line or talking with the professor, and the probability of having two or more students at the office is 0.125. These numbers might be surprisingly high, given such a large capacity cushion.

SIMULATION

More complex waiting-line problems must be analyzed with simulation (see Supplement B, "Simulation"). It can identify the process's bottlenecks and appropriate

FIGURE 6.5

Solver Output for Waiting Line During Office Hours

Solver - Waiting Lines

Enter data in yellow shaded areas.

◉ Single-server model   ○ Multiple-server model   ○ Finite-source model

Servers	1	(Number of servers is assumed to be 1 in single-server model.)
Arrival Rate (λ)	3	
Service Rate (μ)	6	

Probability of zero customers in the system (P_0)	0.5000
Probability of [at most ▼] 2 customers in the system (P_n)	0.8750
Average utilization of the server (ρ)	0.5000
Average number of customers in the system (L)	1.0000
Average number of customers in line (L_q)	0.5000
Average waiting/service time in the system (W)	0.3333
Average waiting time in line (W_q)	0.1667

capacity cushions, even for complex processes with random demand patterns and predictable surges in demand during a typical day. The SimQuick simulation package (**www.nd.edu/~dhartvig/simquick/top.htm**), provided on the Student CD-ROM, allows you to build dynamic models and systems. Figure 6.6 demonstrates an optional package, the Extend simulation package (**www.imaginethatinc.com**), which is another powerful simulation tool. Figure 6.6 (a) graphs the waiting lines at three operations (review, violations, and payment) that exist in a driver's license renewal process. Figure 6.6 (b) focuses on the violations operation, giving the kind of statistics provided by waiting-line models. The operation's utilization is 0.91 (a nine percent cushion) and the lines are very long, with an average of over 17 customers waiting in line during the day. Most would agree that this level of service is unacceptable and that capacity is insufficient. Other simulation packages can be found with Simprocess (**www.caciasl.com**), ProModel (**www.promodel.com**), and Witness (**www.lanner.com/corporate**).

FIGURE 6.6a   **Extend Model for Automobile License Renewals**

Waiting lines for three simulated days

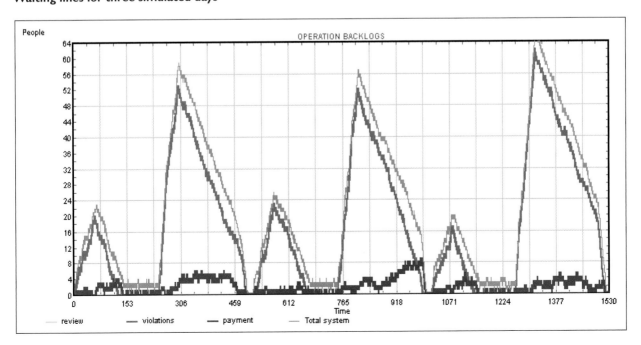

FIGURE 6.6b

Extend Model for Automobile License Renewals Utilization at violations subprocess

Source: This simulation example was provided by Professor Robert Klassen, University of Western Ontario.

Resource Pool	Cost	**Results**	Comments

Stores the resource pool available for use in the model.

[OK]

[Cancel]

__Resource pool__

Current: 1

Available: 1

Utilization: 0.986926

__Items waiting__

Current: 0

Average number: 17.37551

Average wait: 19.13933

DECISION TREES

A decision tree can be particularly valuable for evaluating different capacity expansion alternatives when demand is uncertain and sequential decisions are involved (see Supplement A, "Decision Making"). For example, the owner of Grandmother's Chicken Restaurant (see Example 6.3) may expand the restaurant now, only to discover in year 4 that demand growth is much higher than forecasted. In that case, she needs to decide whether to expand further. In terms of construction costs and down time, expanding twice is likely to be much more expensive than building a large facility from the outset. However, making a large expansion now, when demand growth is low, means poor facility utilization. Much depends on the demand.

Figure 6.7 shows a decision tree for this view of the problem, with new information provided. Demand growth can be either low or high, with probabilities of 0.40 and 0.60, respectively. The initial expansion in year 1 (square node 1) can either be small or large. The second decision node (square node 2), whether to expand at a later date, is reached only if the initial expansion is small and demand turns out to be high. If demand is high and if the initial expansion was small, a decision must be made about a second expansion in year 4. Payoffs for each branch of the tree are estimated. For example, if the initial expansion is large, the financial benefit is either $40,000 or $220,000, depending on whether demand is low or high. Weighting these payoffs by the probabilities yields an expected value of $148,000. This expected payoff is higher than the $109,000 payoff for the small initial expansion, so the better choice is to make a large expansion in year 1.

For software support for decision tree analysis, see SmartDraw (**www.smartdraw. com**), Precision Tree decision analysis (**www.palisade.com/html/ptree.html**), and Decision Programming Language (**www.adainc.com/software**).

FIGURE 6.7

A Decision Tree for Capacity Expansion

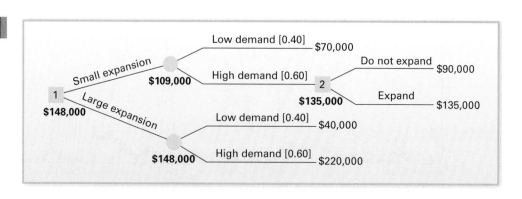

PROCESS CAPACITY ACROSS THE ORGANIZATION

Managers make capacity choices at the organization level, as illustrated by JPMorgan Chase in our chapter opener. They also must make capacity decisions at the individual-process level in accounting, finance, human resources, management information systems, marketing, operations, and purchasing. Capacity issues can cut across departmental lines, because relieving a bottleneck in one part of an organization does not have the desirable effect unless a bottleneck in another part of the organization is also addressed. Managers everywhere must understand capacity measures, economies and diseconomies of scale, capacity cushions, timing-and-sizing strategies, and trade-offs between customer service and capacity utilization. They also must understand how such capacity decisions link with other decisions that have to be made about their processes.

CHAPTER HIGHLIGHTS

- Capacity planning is an important aspect of redesigning processes.

- Long-term capacity planning is crucial to an organization's success because it often involves large investments in facilities and equipment and because such decisions are not easily reversed.

- Capacity can be stated in terms of either output or input measures. Output measures giving the number of services or products completed in a time period are useful when a process provides *standardized* services or products. However, a statement of the number of *customized* services or products completed in a time period is meaningless, because the work content per unit varies. Demand for customized services and products must be translated into input measures, such as number of employees, machines, or trucks.

- Operating a process at full capacity calls for extraordinary effort, using marginal production methods that usually is not sustainable. The operation having the lowest capacity is called a bottleneck and limits the capacity of the entire system. Variable workloads and changing product mix complicate measuring capacity and can cause different operations to become bottlenecks under varying circumstances. Such floating bottlenecks make determining a process's capacity difficult.

- Focusing capacity and scheduling decisions on bottleneck resources with an approach called the theory of constraints (TOC) can help maximize the flow of total value-added funds.

- Economies of scale derive from spreading fixed costs, reducing construction costs, reducing purchased materials

costs, and obtaining process advantages. Diseconomies of scale cause some firms to focus their operations and move to smaller, rather than larger, facilities.

- The desirable amount of capacity cushion varies, depending on competitive priorities, cost of unused capacity, resource flexibility, supply uncertainties, shelf life, variability and uncertainty of demand, and other factors.

- Three capacity strategies for timing and sizing expansion are expansionist, wait and see, and follow the leader. The expansionist strategy is attractive when there are economies of scale, learning effects, and a chance for preemptive marketing. The wait-and-see strategy minimizes risk by relying more on short-term options. The follow-the-leader strategy maintains the current balance between competitors.

- Capacity choices must be linked to other management decisions about processes and value chains.

- The four steps in capacity planning are (1) estimate capacity requirements, (2) identify gaps, (3) develop alternatives, and (4) evaluate the alternatives.

- Waiting-line models help the manager choose the capacity level (including the capacity cushion) that best balances customer service and the cost of adding more capacity. As waiting-line problems involve more servers, mathematical models quickly become very complex. Simulation is used to analyze most multiple-server waiting-fine situations. Decision trees are schematic models that can be helpful in evaluating different capacity-expansion alternatives when demand is uncertain and sequential decisions are involved.

STUDENT CD-ROM AND INTERNET RESOURCES

The Student CD-ROM and the Companion Website at **www.prenhall.com/krajewski** contain many tools, activities, and resources designed for this chapter. The following items are recommended to enhance your skills and improve your understanding of the material in this chapter.

 STUDENT CD-ROM RESOURCES

➤ **PowerPoint Slides.** View this comprehensive set of slides customized for this chapter's concepts and techniques.

➤ **OM Explorer Tutors.** OM Explorer contains two tutor spreadsheets that will help you learn about capacity (capacity requirements and projecting cash flows) and three spreadsheets about waiting lines (single-servers, multiple-server, and finite-source models). See Chapter 6 and Supplement C in the OM Explorer menu. See also the Tutor Exercise on capacity requirements.

➤ **OM Explorer Solvers.** OM Explorer contains one spreadsheet to help with general capacity planning problems on capacity requirements and one on analyzing waiting lines. See Process Capacity and Waiting Lines in the OM Explorer menu for these routines.

➤ **SimQuick.** Learn the basics of waiting lines and manufacturing processes (including how to estimate their capacities) by building simulation models. Examples in *SimQuick: Process Simulation with Excel* include a bank, a fast-food restaurant, a call center, and jewelry box manufacturing.

➤ **SmartDraw.** Use the link to download a 30-day trial of SmartDraw, a software package often used in practice to prepare decision trees.

➤ **Written Tours.** See how the Lower Florida Keys Health System designs its process capacity for a 10 percent cushion during the peak season and how Chaparral Steel defines the capacity for its capital-intensive processes in terms of a three-shift operation, seven days per week.

➤ **Supplement G.** "Learning Curve Analysis." Learn about how to account for learning effects when estimating future capacity requirements.

➤ **Supplement H.** "Measuring Output Rates." See how processing times can be estimated as inputs to capacity planning.

➤ **Supplement J.** "Financial Analysis." Learn about several tools for evaluating capacity expansions that involve large capital investments.

INTERNET RESOURCES

➤ **Self-Study Quizzes.** See the compendium of true or false, multiple choice, and essay questions that give feedback on how well you have mastered the concepts in this chapter.

➤ **In the News.** See the articles that apply to this chapter.

➤ **Internet Exercises.** Try out two different links on capacity issues at AOL and Texaco. Other exercises are available on additional aspects of capacity and waiting lines.

➤ **Virtual Tours.** Check out capacity issues at Camarillo, California, Sanitary District and waiting lines at Paris Companies Cleaners. Also see the "Web Links to Company Facility Tours" for additional tours of company facilities.

KEY EQUATIONS

1. Utilization, expressed as a percent:

$$\text{Utilization} = \frac{\text{Average output rate}}{\text{Maximum capacity}} \times 100\%$$

2. Capacity cushion, C, expressed as a percent:

$$C = 100\% - \text{Utilization rate}(\%)$$

3. **a.** Capacity requirement for one service or product:

$$M = \frac{Dp}{N[1 - (C/100)]}$$

b. Capacity requirement for multiple services or products:

$$M = \frac{\{[Dp + (D/Q)s]_{\text{product1}} + [Dp + (D/Q)s]_{\text{product2}} + \cdots + [Dp + (D/Q)s]_{\text{product}n}\}}{N[1 - (C/100)]}$$

KEY TERMS

base case 258
bottleneck 248
capacity 245
capacity cushion 253
capacity gap 258

capacity requirement 256
cash flow 259
diseconomies of scale 252
drum-buffer-rope method 249
economies of scale 250

planning horizon 256
setup time 257
theory of constraints (TOC) 249
utilization 246

SOLVED PROBLEM I

You have been asked to put together a capacity plan for a critical bottleneck operation at the Surefoot Sandal Company. Your capacity measure is number of machines. Three products (men's, women's, and children's sandals) are manufactured. The time standards (processing and setup), lot sizes, and demand forecasts are given in the following table. The firm operates two

8-hour shifts, 5 days per week, 50 weeks per year. Experience shows that a capacity cushion of 5 percent is sufficient.

Time Standards

Product	Processing (hr/pair)	Setup (hr/pair)	Lot Size (pairs/lot)	Demand Forecast (pairs/yr)
Men's sandals	0.05	0.5	240	80,000
Women's sandals	0.10	2.2	180	60,000
Children's sandals	0.02	3.8	360	120,000

a. How many machines are needed?

b. If the operation currently has two machines, what is the capacity gap?

SOLUTION

a. The number of hours of operation per year, N, is

$$N = (2 \text{ shifts/day}) (8 \text{ hours/shift}) (250 \text{ days/machine-year})$$
$$= 4,000 \text{ hours/machine-year}$$

The number of machines required, M, is the sum of machine-hour requirements for all three products divided by the number of productive hours available for one machine:

$$M = \frac{[Dp + (D/Q)s]_{\text{men}} + [Dp + (D/Q)s]_{\text{women}} + [Dp + (D/Q)s]_{\text{children}}}{N[1 - (C/100)]}$$

$$= \frac{\begin{array}{c}[80,000(0.05) + (80,000/240)0.5] + [60,000 \ (0.10) + (60,000/180)2.2] \\ + [120,000(0.02) + (120,000/360)3.8]\end{array}}{4,000[1 - (5/100)]}$$

$$= \frac{14,567 \ \text{hours/year}}{3,800 \ \text{hours/machine-year}} = 3.83 \quad \text{or} \quad 4 \text{ machines}$$

b. The capacity gap is 1.83 machines (3.83 − 2). Two more machines should be purchased, unless management decides to use short-term options to fill the gap.

The *Capacity Requirements Solver* in OM Explorer confirms these calculations, as Figure 6.8 shows, using only the "Expected" scenario for the demand forecasts.

SOLVED PROBLEM 2

The base case for Grandmother's Chicken Restaurant (see Example 6.3) is to do nothing. The capacity of the kitchen in the base case is 80,000 meals per year. A capacity alternative for Grandmother's Chicken Restaurant is a two-stage expansion. This alternative expands the kitchen at the end of year 0, raising its capacity from 80,000 meals per year to that of the dining area (105,000 meals per year). If sales in year 1 and 2 live up to expectations, the capacities of both the kitchen and the dining room will be expanded at the *end* of year 3 to 130,000 meals per year. This upgraded capacity level should suffice up through year 5. The initial investment would be $80,000 at the end of year 0 and an additional investment of $170,000 at the end of year 3. The pretax profit is $2 per meal. What are the pretax cash flows for this alternative through year 5, compared with the base case?

SOLUTION

Table 6.1 shows the cash inflows and outflows. The year 3 cash flow is unusual in two respects. First, the cash inflow from sales is $50,000 rather than $60,000. The increase in sales over the base is 25,000 meals (105,000 − 80,000) instead of 30,000 meals (110,000 − 80,000) because the restaurant's capacity falls somewhat short of demand. Second, a cash outflow of $170,000 occurs at the end of year 3, when the second-stage expansion occurs. The net cash flow for year 3 is $50,000 − $170,000 = −$120,000.

FIGURE 6.8

Using the *Capacity Requirements Solver* **for Solved Problem I**

Solver - Capacity Requirements

Enter data in yellow-shaded areas.

Shifts/Day	2
Hours/Shift	8
Days/Week	5
Weeks/Year	50
Cushion (as %)	5%
Current capacity	2

Components [3]

↑ More Components
↓ Fewer Components

Components	Processing (hr/unit)	Setup (hr/lot)	Lot Size (units/lot)	Demand Forecasts Pessimistic	Expected	Optimistic
Men's sandals	0.05	0.5	240		80,000	
Women's sandals	0.10	2.2	180		60,000	
Children's sandals	0.02	3.8	360		120,000	

Productive hours from
one capacity unit for a year   3,800

	Pessimistic		Expected		Optimistic	
	Process	Setup	Process	Setup	Process	Setup
Men's sandals	0	0.0	4,000	166.7	0	0.0
Women's sandals	0	0.0	6,000	733.3	0	0.0
Children's sandals	0	0.0	2,400	1,266.7	0	0.0
	0	0.0	12,400	2,166.7	0	0.0
Total hours required		0.0		14,566.7		0.0

| Total capacity requirements (M) | 0.00 | 3.83 | 0.00 |
| Rounded | 0 | 4 | 0 |

Scenarios that can be met with current systems/capacity: **Pessimistic, Optimistic**

| If capacity increased by | 0% |
| Expanded current capacity | 3,800 |

| Total capacity requirements (M) | 0.00 | 3.83 | 0.00 |
| Rounded | 0 | 4 | 0 |

Scenarios that can be met with expanded current capacity: **Pessimistic, Optimistic**

TABLE 6.1
CASH FLOWS FOR TWO-STAGE EXPANSION AT GRANDMOTHER'S CHICKEN RESTAURANT

Year	Projected Demand (meals/yr)	Projected Capacity (meals/yr)	Calculation of Incremental Cash Flow Compared to Base Case (80,000 meals/yr)	Cash Inflow (outflow)
0	80,000	80,000	Increase kitchen capacity to 105,000 meals =	($80,000)
1	90,000	105,000	90,000 − 80,000 = (10,000 meals)($2/meal) =	$20,000
2	100,000	105,000	100,000 − 80,000 = (20,000 meals)($2/meal) =	$40,000
3	110,000	105,000	105,000 − 80,000 = (25,000 meals)($2/meal) =	$50,000
			Increase total capacity to 130,000 meals =	($170,000)
				($120,000)
4	120,000	130,000	120,000 − 80,000 = (40,000 meals)($2/meal) =	$80,000
5	130,000	130,000	130,000 − 80,000 = (50,000 meals)($2/meal) =	$100,000

DISCUSSION QUESTIONS

1. What are the economies of scale in class size? As class size increases, what symptoms of diseconomies of scale appear? How are these symptoms related to customer contact?

2. A young boy has set up a lemonade stand on the corner of College Street and Air Park Boulevard. Temperatures in the area climb to 100° during the summer. The intersection is near a major university and a large construction site. Explain to this young entrepreneur how his business might benefit from economies of scale. Explain also some conditions that might lead to diseconomies of scale.

3. Consider the Lower Florida Keys Health System and the Chaparral Steel tours on the Student CD-ROM. The organizations are quite different in terms of customization as a competitive priority, size of markets served, capital intensity, ability to use inventory to smooth output rates, and degree of certainty in future demands. What are the likely differences between these two organizations on whether output or input capacity measures are used, on desired capacity cushions, and on the need to exploit economies of scale? Explain.

PROBLEMS

An icon next to a problem identifies the software that can be helpful, but is not mandatory. The software is available on the Student CD-ROM that is packaged with every new copy of the textbook.

1. **OM Explorer** The Dahlia Medical Center has 30 labor rooms, 15 combination labor and delivery rooms, 3 delivery rooms, and 1 special delivery room reserved for complicated births. All of these facilities operate around the clock. Time spent in labor rooms varies from hours to days, with an average of about a day. The average uncomplicated delivery requires about one hour in a delivery room.

   During an exceptionally busy three-day period, 115 healthy babies were born at or received by Dahlia Medical Center. Sixty babies were born in separate labor and delivery rooms, 45 were born in combined labor and delivery rooms, 6 were born en route to the hospital, and only 4 babies required a labor room and the complicated-delivery room. Which of the facilities (labor rooms, labor and delivery rooms, or delivery rooms) had the greatest utilization rate?

2. **OM Explorer** The Clip Joint operates four barber's chairs in the student center. During the week before semester break and the week before graduation, The Clip Joint experiences peak demands. Military-style haircuts take 5 minutes each, and other styles require 20 minutes each. Operating from 9 A.M. to 6 P.M. on the six days before semester break, The Clip Joint completes 500 military-style haircuts and 400 other haircuts. During a comparable six-day week before graduation, The Clip Joint completes 700 military-style haircuts and 300 other haircuts. In which week is utilization higher?

3. A process currently services an average of 50 customers per day. Observations in recent weeks show that its utilization is about 90 percent, allowing for just a 10 percent capacity cushion. If demand is expected to be 75 percent of the current level in five years and management wants to have a capacity cushion of just 5 percent, what capacity requirement should be planned?

4. An airline company must plan its fleet capacity and its long-term schedule of aircraft usage. For one flight segment, the average number of customers per day is 70, which represents a 65 percent utilization rate of the equipment assigned to the flight segment. If demand is expected to increase to 84 customers for this flight segment in three years, what capacity requirement should be planned? Assume that management deems a capacity cushion of 25 percent appropriate.

5. **OM Explorer** An automobile brake supplier operates on two 8-hour shifts, five days per week, 52 weeks per year. Table 6.2 shows the time standards, lot sizes, and demand forecasts for three components. Because of demand uncertainties, the operations manager obtained three demand forecasts (pessimistic, expected, and optimistic). The manager believes that a 20 percent capacity cushion is best.

   a. What is the minimum number of machines needed? The expected number? The maximum number?

   b. If the operation currently has three machines and the manager is willing to expand capacity by 20 percent through short-term options in the event that the optimistic demand occurs, what is the capacity gap?

6. **OM Explorer** Up, Up, and Away is a producer of kites and wind socks. Relevant data on a bottleneck operation in the shop for the upcoming fiscal year are given in the following table:

Item	Kites	Wind Socks
Demand forecast	30,000 units/year	12,000 units/year
Lot size	20 units	70 units
Standard processing time	0.3 hour/unit	1.0 hour/unit
Standard setup time	3.0 hours/lot	4.0 hours/lot

The shop works two shifts per day, eight hours per shift, 200 days per year. There currently are four machines, and a 25 percent capacity cushion is desired. How many machines should be purchased to meet the upcoming year's demand without resorting to any short-term capacity solutions?

TABLE 6.2
CAPACITY INFORMATION FOR AUTOMOTIVE BRAKE SUPPLIER

	Time Standard			Demand Forecast		
Component	Processing (hr/wait)	Setup (hr/lot)	Lot Size (units/lot)	Pessimistic	Expected	Optimistic
A	0.05	1.0	60	15,000	18,000	25,000
B	0.20	4.5	80	10,000	13,000	17,000
C	0.05	8.2	120	17,000	25,000	40,000

7. **◆ OM Explorer** Tuff-Rider, Inc., manufactures touring bikes and mountain bikes in a variety of frame sizes, colors, and component combinations. Identical bicycles are produced in lots of 100. The projected demand, lot size, and time standards are shown in the following table:

Item	Touring	Mountain
Demand forecast	5,000 units/year	10,000 units/year
Lot size	100 units	100 units
Standard processing time	¼ hour/unit	½ hour/unit
Standard setup time	2 hours/lot	3 hours/lot

The shop currently works eight hours a day, five days a week, 50 weeks a year. It has five workstations, each producing one bicycle in the time shown in the table. The shop maintains a 15 percent capacity cushion. How many workstations will be required next year to meet expected demand without using overtime and without decreasing the firm's current capacity cushion?

8. **◆ OM Explorer** Worcester Athletic Club is considering expanding its facility to include two adjacent suites. The owner will remodel the suites in consideration of a seven-year lease. Expenditures for rent, insurance, utilities, and exercise equipment leasing would increase by $45,000 per year. This expansion would increase Worcester's lunchtime rush hour capacity from the present 150 members to 225 members. A maximum of 30 percent of the total membership attends the Athletic Club during any one lunch hour. Therefore, Worcester's facility can presently serve a total membership of 500. Membership fees are $40 per month. Based on the following membership forecasts, determine what before-tax cash flows the expansion will produce for the next several years:

Year	1	2	3	4	5	6	7
Membership	450	480	510	515	530	550	600

9. Arabelle is considering expanding the floor area of her high-fashion import clothing store, The French Prints of Arabelle, by increasing her leased space in the upscale Cherry Creek Mall from 2,000 square feet to 3,000 square feet. The Cherry Creek Mall boasts one of the country's highest ratios of sales value per square foot. Rents (including utilities, security, and similar costs) are $110 per square foot per year. Salary increases related to French Prints' expansion are shown in the following table, along with projections of sales per square foot. The purchase cost of goods sold averages 70 percent of the sales price. Sales are seasonal, with an important peak during the year-end holiday season.

Year	Quarter	Sales (per sq ft)	Incremental Salaries
1	1	$ 90	$12,000
	2	60	8,000
	3	110	12,000
	4	240	24,000
2	1	99	12,000
	2	66	8,000
	3	121	12,000
	4	264	24,000

a. If Arabelle expands French Prints at the end of year 0, what will her quarterly pretax cash flows be through year 2?

b. Project the quarterly pretax cash flows assuming that the sales pattern (10 percent annually compounded increase) continues through year 3.

10. The Astro World amusement park has the opportunity to expand its size now (the end of year 0) by purchasing adjacent property for $250,000 and adding attractions at a cost of $550,000. This expansion is expected to increase attendance by 30 percent over projected attendance without expansion. The price of admission is $30, with a $5 increase planned for the beginning of year 3. Additional operating costs are expected to be $100,000 per year. Estimated attendance for the next five years, *without expansion*, follows:

Year	1	2	3	4	5
Attendance	30,000	34,000	36,250	38,500	41,000

a. What are the pretax combined cash flows for years 0 through 5 that are attributable to the park's expansion?

b. Ignoring tax, depreciation, and the time value of money, determine how long it will take to recover (pay back) the investment.

11. Kim Epson operates a full-service car wash, which operates from 8 A.M. to 8 P.M. seven days a week. The car wash has two stations: an automatic washing and drying station and a manual interior cleaning station. The automatic washing and drying station can handle 30 cars per hour. The interior cleaning station can handle 200 cars per day. Based on a recent year-end review of operations, Kim estimates that future demand for the interior cleaning station for the seven days of the week, expressed in average number of cars per day, would be as follows:

Day	Mon.	Tues.	Wed.	Thurs.	Fri.	Sat.	Sun.
Cars	160	180	150	140	280	300	250

By installing additional equipment (at a cost of $50,000) Kim can increase the capacity of the interior cleaning station to 300 cars per day. Each car wash generates a pretax contribution of $4.00. Should Kim install the additional equipment if she expects a pretax payback period of three years of less?

12. Roche Brothers is considering a capacity expansion of its supermarket. The landowner will build the addition to suit in return for $200,000 upon completion and a five-year lease. The increase in rent for the addition is $10,000 per month. The annual sales projected through year 5 follow. The current effective capacity is equivalent to 500,000 customers per year. Assume a 2 percent pretax profit on sales.

Year	1	2	3	4	5
Customers	560,000	600,000	685,000	700,000	715,000
Average Sales per Customer	$50.00	$53.00	$56.00	$60.00	$64.00

a. If Roche expands its capacity to serve 700,000 customers per year now (end of year 0), what are the projected annual incremental pretax cash flows attributable to this expansion?

b. If Roche expands its capacity to serve 700,000 customers per year at the end of year 2, the landowner will build the same addition for $240,000 and a three-year lease at $12,000 per month. What are the projected annual incremental pretax cash flows attributable to this expansion alternative?

Advanced Problems

Problems 13, 16, and 17 require reading of Supplement A, "Decision Making". Problems 14 and 17 require reading of Supplement J, "Financial Analysis," on the Student CD-ROM.

13. A manager is trying to decide whether to buy one machine or two. If only one machine is purchased and demand proves to be excessive, the second machine can be purchased later. Some sales would be lost, however, because the lead time for delivery of this type of machine is six months. In addition, the cost per machine will be lower if both machines are purchased at the same time. The probability of low demand is estimated to be 0.30 and that of high demand to be 0.70. The after-tax net present value of the benefits (NPV) from purchasing two machines together is $90,000 if demand is low and $170,000 if demand is high.

If one machine is purchased and demand is low, the NPV is $120,000. If demand is high, the manager has three options. Doing nothing, which has an NPV of $120,000; subcontracting, with an NPV of $140,000; and buying the second machine, with an NPV of $130,000.

a. Draw a decision tree for this problem.

b. What is the best decision and what is its expected payoff?

14. **OM Explorer** Several years ago, River City built a water purification plant to remove toxins and filter the city's drinking water. Because of population growth, the demand for water next year will be more than the plant's capacity of 120 million gallons per year. Therefore, the city must expand the facility. The estimated demand over the next 20 years is given in Table 6.3.

The city planning commission is considering three alternatives.

• *Alternative 1.* Expand enough at the end of year 0 to last 20 years. This means an 80 million gallon increase (200 − 120).

• *Alternative 2.* Expand at the end of year 0 and at the end of year 10.

• *Alternative 3.* Expand at the end of years 0, 5, 10, and 15.

Each alternative would provide the needed 200 million gallons per year at the end of 20 years, when the value of the plant would be the same regardless of the alternative chosen. There are significant economies of scale in construction costs: A 20 million gallon expansion would cost $18 million; a 40 million gallon expansion, $30 million; and an 80 million gallon expansion, only $50 million. The level of future interest rates is uncertain,

	TABLE 6.3				
	WATER DEMAND				
Year	Capacity	Year	Capacity	Year	Capacity
0	120	7	148	14	176
1	124	8	152	15	180
2	128	9	156	16	184
3	132	10	160	17	188
4	136	11	164	18	192
5	140	12	168	19	196
6	144	13	172	20	200

leading to uncertainty about the hurdle rate. The city believes that it could be as low as 12 percent and as high as 16 percent (see Supplement A, "Decision Making").

a. Compute the cash flows for each alternative, compared to a base case of doing nothing. (*Note:* As a municipal utility, the operation pays no taxes.)

b. Which alternative minimizes the present value of construction costs over the next 20 years if the discount rate is 12 percent? 16 percent?

c. Because the decision involves public policy and compromise, what political considerations does the planning commission face?

15. Two new alternatives have come up for expanding Grandmother's Chicken Restaurant (see Solved Problem 2). They involve more automation in the kitchen and feature a special cooking process that retains the original-recipe taste of the chicken. Although the process is more capital-intensive, it would drive down labor costs, so the pretax profit for *all* sales (not just the sales from the capacity added) would go up from 20 to 22 percent. This gain would increase the pretax profit by 2 percent of each sales dollar through $800,000 (80,000 meals × $10) and by 22 percent of each sales dollar between $800,000 and the new capacity limit. Otherwise, the new alternatives are much the same as those in Example 6.3 and Solved Problem 2.

• *Alternative 1.* Expand both the kitchen and the dining area now (at the end of year 0), raising the capacity to 130,000 meals per year. The cost of construction, including the new automation, would be $336,000 (rather than the earlier $200,000).

• *Alternative 2.* Expand only the kitchen now, raising its capacity to 105,000 meals per year. At the end of year 3, expand both the kitchen and the dining area to the 130,000 meals-per-year volume. Construction and equipment costs would be $424,000, with $220,000 at the end of year 0 and the remainder at the end of year 3. As with alternative 1, the contribution margin would go up to 22 percent.

   With both new alternatives, the salvage value would be negligible. Compare the cash flows of all alternatives. Should Grandmother's Chicken Restaurant expand with the new or the old technology? Should it expand now or later?

16. Acme Steel Fabricators has experienced booming business for the past five years. The company fabricates a wide range of steel products, such as railings, ladders, and light structural steel framing. The current manual method of materials handling is causing excessive inventories and congestion. Acme is considering the purchase of an overhead rail-mounted hoist system or a forklift truck to increase capacity and improve manufacturing efficiency.

   The annual pretax payoff from the system depends on future demand. If demand stays at the current level, the probability of which is 0.50, annual savings from the overhead hoist will be $10,000. If demand rises, the hoist will save $25,000 annually because of operating efficiencies in addition to new sales. Finally, if demand falls, the hoist will result in an estimated annual loss of $65,000. The probability is estimated to be 0.30 for higher demand and 0.20 for lower demand.

   If the forklift is purchased, annual payoffs will be $5,000 if demand is unchanged, $10,000 if demand rises, and −$25,000 if demand falls.

a. Draw a decision tree for this problem and compute the expected value of the payoff for each alternative.

b. Which is the best alternative, based on the expected values?

17. The vice president of operations at Dintell Corporation, a major supplier of passenger-side automotive air bags, is considering a $50 million expansion at the firm's Fort Worth production complex. The most recent economic projections indicate a 0.60 probability that the overall market will be $400 million per year over the next five years and a 0.40 probability that the market will be only $200 million per year during the same period. The marketing department estimates that Dintell has a 0.50 probability of capturing 40 percent of the market and an equal probability of obtaining only 30 percent of the market. The cost of goods sold is estimated to be 70 percent of sales. For planning purposes, the company currently uses a 12 percent discount rate, a 40 percent tax rate, and the MACRS depreciation schedule (see Supplement J, "Financial Analysis," on the CD-ROM.). The criteria for investment decisions at Dintell are (1) the net expected present value must be greater than zero; (2) there must be at least a 70 percent chance that the net present value will be positive; and (3) there must be no more than a 10 percent chance that the firm will lose more than 20 percent of the initial value.

a. Based on the stated criteria, determine whether Dintell should fund the project.

b. What effect will a probability of 0.70 of capturing 40 percent of the market have on the decision?

c. What effect will an increase in the discount rate of 15 percent have on the decision? A decrease of 10 percent?

d. What effect will the need for another $10 million in the third year have on the decision?

SIMULATION EXERCISES

These simulation exercises require the use of the SimQuick and Extend LT simulation packages. SimQuick is on the Student CD-ROM that is packaged with every new copy of the textbook. Extend LT is an optional simulation package that your instructor may or may not have ordered.

1. A jewelry box is made from the following parts: two identical square pieces (the top and bottom), four identical rectangular pieces (the sides), and a hinge. At the beginning of the process is a pile of sheets of wood. One sheet at a time is taken to the cutter, which cuts four square pieces and eight rectangular pieces. The four square pieces are sent to a buffer inventory, which feeds the TB finishing machine that makes them into tops and bottoms. The parts are then taken to a buffer inventory. The eight rectangular pieces are also sent to a buffer inventory, which feeds the S finishing machine that makes them into sides. After this operation, the sides are taken to another buffer inventory. The final workstation is the box assembly, which assembles the top, bottom, and sides to make a finished jewelry box. Management knows that the S finishing machine is a bottleneck. Use SimQuick to determine the increase in throughput if the S finishing machine is replaced with a faster one. See Example 20 in *SimQuick: Process Simulation with Excel* for details about this problem and additional exercises.

2. Consider the process at the Canadian provincial department of motor vehicles, which is introduced in Figure 6.6. Use the Extend simulator to identify bottlenecks, capacity cushions, and ways of improving the effectiveness of the process. See the full *Provincial Automobile License Renewals* case on the optional CD-ROM, along with the basic model and information on how to use it. Answer the various questions asked about the capacity of the process.

CASE   FITNESS PLUS, PART A

Fitness Plus, Part B, explores alternatives to expanding a new downtown facility and is included in the Instructor's Manual. If you are interested in this topic, ask your instructor for a preview.

Fitness Plus is a full-service health and sports club in Greensboro, North Carolina. The club provides a range of facilities and services to support three primary activities: fitness, recreation, and relaxation. Fitness activities generally take place in four areas of the club: the aerobics room, which can accommodate 35 people per class; a room equipped with free weights; a workout room with 24 pieces of Nautilus equipment; and a large workout room containing 29 pieces of cardiovascular equipment. This equipment includes nine staircase steppers, six treadmills, six life-cycle bikes, three airdyne bikes, two cross-aerobics machines, two rowing machines, and one climber. Recreational facilities comprise eight racquetball courts, six tennis courts, and a large outdoor pool. Fitness Plus also sponsors softball, volleyball, and swim teams in city recreation leagues. Relaxation is accomplished through yoga classes held twice a week in the aerobics room, whirlpool tubs located in each locker room, and a trained massage therapist.

Situated in a large suburban office park, Fitness Plus opened its doors in 1991. During the first two years, membership was small and use of the facilities was light. By 1992, membership had grown as fitness began to play a large role in more and more people's lives. Along with this growth came increased use of club facilities. Records indicate that, in 1995, an average of 15 members per hour checked into the club during a typical day. Of course, the actual number of members per hour varied by both day and time. On some days during a slow period, only 6 to 8 members would check in per hour. At a peak time, such as Mondays from 4:00 P.M. to 7:00 P.M., the number would be as high as 40 per hour.

The club was open from 6:30 A.M. to 11:00 P.M. Monday through Thursday. On Friday and Saturday, the club closed at 8:00 P.M., and on Sunday the hours were 12:00 P.M. to 8:00 P.M.

As the popularity of health and fitness continued to grow, so did Fitness Plus. By May 2000, the average number of members arriving per hour during a typical day had increased to 25. The lowest period had a rate of 10 members per hour; during peak periods, 80 members per hour checked in to use the facilities. This growth brought complaints from members about overcrowding and unavailability of equipment. Most of these complaints centered on the Nautilus, cardiovascular, and aerobics fitness areas. The owners began to wonder whether the club was indeed too

small for its membership. Past research had indicated that individuals work out an average of 60 minutes per visit. Data collected from member surveys showed the following facilities usage pattern: 30 percent of the members do aerobics, 40 percent use the cardiovascular equipment, 25 percent use the Nautilus machines, 20 percent use the free weights, 15 percent use the racquetball courts, and 10 percent use the tennis courts. The owners wondered whether they could use this information to estimate how well existing capacity was being utilized.

If capacity levels were being stretched, now was the time to decide what to do. It was already May, and any expansion of the existing facility would take at least four months. The owners knew that January was always a peak membership enrollment month and that any new capacity needed to be ready by then. However, other factors had to be considered. The area was growing both in terms of population and geographically. The downtown area had just received a major facelift, and many new offices and businesses were moving back to it, causing a resurgence in activity.

With this growth came increased competition. A new YMCA was offering a full range of services at a low cost. Two new health and fitness facilities had opened within the past year in locations 10 to 15 minutes from Fitness Plus. The first, called the Oasis, catered to the young adult crowd and restricted the access of children under 16 years old. The other facility, Gold's Gym, provided excellent weight and cardiovascular training only.

As the owners thought about the situation, they had many questions: Were the capacities of the existing facilities constrained, and if so, where? If capacity expansion was necessary, should the existing facility be expanded? Because of the limited amount of land at the present site, expansion of some services might require reducing the capacity of others. Finally, owing to increased competition and growth downtown, was now the time to open a facility to serve that market? A new facility would take six months to renovate, and the financial resources were not available to do both.

QUESTIONS

1. What method would you use to measure the capacity of Fitness Plus? Has Fitness Plus reached its capacity?
2. Which capacity strategy would be appropriate for Fitness Plus? Justify your answer.
3. How would you link the capacity decision being made by Fitness Plus to other types of operating decisions?

SELECTED REFERENCES

Bakke, Nils Arne, and Ronald Hellberg. "The Challenges of Capacity Planning." *International Journal of Production Economics*, 31–30 (1993), pp. 243–264.

Bowman, Edward H. "Scale of Operations—An Empirical Study." *Operations Research* (June 1958), pp. 320–328.

Goldratt, E. Y., and J. Cox. *The Goal.* New York: North River, 1984.

Hammesfahr, R. D. Jack, James A. Pope, and Alireza Ardalan. "Strategic Planning for Production Capacity." *International Journal of Operations and Production Management,* vol. 13, no. 5(1993), pp. 41–53.

Hartvigsen, David. *SimQuick: Process Simulation with Excel.* 2d ed. Upper Saddle River, NJ: Prentice Hall, 2004.

"How Goliaths Can Act Like Davids." *Business Week/Enterprise* (1993), pp. 192–200.

"Intel's $10 Billion Gamble." *Fortune* (November 11, 2002), pp. 90–102.

Klassen, Kenneth J., and Thomas R. Rohleder. "Combining Operations and Marketing to Manage Capacity and Demand in Services." *The Service Industries Journal,* vol. 21, no. 2 (2001), pp. 1–30.

"Logan's Roadhouse." *Business Week* (May 27, 1996), p. 113.

Ritzman, Larry P., and M. Hossein Safizadeh. "Linking Process Choice with Plant-Level Decisions About Capital and Human Resources." *Production and Operations Management,* vol. 8, no. 4(1999), pp. 374–392.

Simons, Jacob, Jr., and Wendell P. Simpson III. "An Exposition of Multiple Constraint Scheduling As Implemented in the Goal System (Formerly Disaster™)." *Production and Operations Management,* vol. 8, no. 1 (Spring 1997), pp. 3–22.

"Wow! That's Some Bank." *Business Week* (September 11, 1995), pp. 36–39.

Waiting Lines

LEARNING GOALS *After reading this supplement, you should be able to . . .*

IDENTIFY OR DEFINE
1. the elements of a waiting-line problem in a real situation.
2. the single-server, multiple-server, and finite-source models.

DESCRIBE OR EXPLAIN
3. how to use waiting-line models to estimate the operating characteristics of a process.
4. how waiting lines can be used to make managerial decisions.

Anyone who has had to wait at a stoplight, at McDonald's, or at the registrar's office has experienced the dynamics of waiting lines. Perhaps one of the best examples of effective management of waiting lines is that of Walt Disney World. One day there may be only 25,000 customers, but on another day there may be 90,000. Careful analysis of process flows, technology for people-mover (materials handling) equipment, capacity, and layout keeps the waiting times for attractions to acceptable levels.

The analysis of waiting lines is of concern to managers because it affects process design, capacity planning, and process performance. In this supplement we discuss why waiting lines form, the uses of waiting-line models in operations management, and the structure of waiting-line models. We also discuss the decisions managers address with the models. Waiting lines can also be analyzed using computer simulation. Software such as SimQuick, a simulation package included in the Student CD-ROM, or Excel spreadsheets can be used to analyze the problems in this supplement (see Supplement B, "Simulation", for more details).

WHY WAITING LINES FORM

waiting line One or more "customers" waiting for service.

VIDEO CLIP C.1
Video Clip C.1 on the Student CD-ROM shows how variable arrival and service rates cause a bank teller line to grow and shrink.

A **waiting line** is one or more "customers" waiting for service. The customers can be people or inanimate objects, such as machines requiring maintenance, sales orders waiting for shipping, or inventory items waiting to be used. A waiting line forms because of a temporary imbalance between the demand for service and the capacity of the system to provide the service. In most real-life waiting-line problems, the demand rate varies; that is, customers arrive at unpredictable intervals. Most often, the rate of producing the service also varies, depending on customer needs. Suppose that bank customers arrive at an average rate of 15 per hour throughout the day and that the bank can process an average of 20 customers per hour. Why would a waiting line ever develop? The answers are that the customer arrival rate varies throughout the day and the time required to process a customer can vary. During the noon hour, 30 customers may arrive at the bank. Some of them may have complicated transactions, requiring above-average process times. The waiting line may grow to 15 customers for a period of time before it eventually disappears. Even though the bank manager provided for more than enough capacity on average, waiting lines can still develop.

Waiting lines can develop even if the time to process a customer is constant. For example, a subway train is computer controlled to arrive at stations along its route. Each train is programmed to arrive at a station, say, every 15 minutes. Even with the constant service time, waiting lines develop while riders wait for the next train or cannot get on a train because of the size of the crowd at a busy time of the day. Consequently, variability in the rate of demand determines the sizes of the waiting lines in this case. In general, if there is no variability in the demand or service rates and enough capacity has been provided, no waiting lines form.

USES OF WAITING-LINE THEORY

Waiting-line theory applies to service as well as manufacturing firms, relating customer arrival and service-system processing characteristics to service-system output characteristics. In our discussion, we use the term *service* broadly—the act of doing work for a customer. The service system might be hair cutting at a hair salon, satisfying customer complaints, or processing a production order of parts on a certain machine. Other examples of customers and services include lines of theatergoers waiting to purchase tickets, trucks waiting to be unloaded at a warehouse, machines waiting to be repaired by a maintenance crew, and patients waiting to be examined by a physician. Regardless of the situation, waiting-line problems have several common elements.

STRUCTURE OF WAITING-LINE PROBLEMS

Analyzing waiting-line problems begins with a description of the situation's basic elements. Each specific situation will have different characteristics, but four elements are common to all situations:

1. an input, or **customer population,** that generates potential customers;
2. a waiting line of customers;
3. the **service facility,** consisting of a person (or crew), a machine (or group of machines), or both necessary to perform the service for the customer; and
4. a **priority rule,** which selects the next customer to be served by the service facility.

Figure C.1 shows these basic elements. The **service system** describes the number of lines and the arrangement of the facilities. After the service has been performed, the served customers leave the system.

CUSTOMER POPULATION

A customer population is the source of input to the service system. If the potential number of new customers for the service system is appreciably affected by the number of customers already in the system, the input source is said to be *finite*. For example, suppose that a maintenance crew is assigned responsibility for the repair of 10 machines. The customer population for the maintenance crew is 10 machines in working order. The population generates customers for the maintenance crew as a function of the failure rates for the machines. As more machines fail and enter the service system, either waiting for service or being repaired, the customer population becomes smaller and the rate at which it can generate another customer falls. Consequently, the customer population is said to be finite.

Alternatively, an *infinite* customer population is one in which the number of customers in the system does not affect the rate at which the population generates new customers. For example, consider a mail-order operation for which the customer population consists of shoppers who have received a catalog of products sold by the company. Because the customer population is so large and only a small fraction of the shoppers place orders at any one time, the number of new orders it generates is not appreciably affected by the number of orders waiting for service or being processed by the service system. In this case, the customer population is said to be infinite.

Customers in waiting lines may be *patient* or *impatient*, which has nothing to do with the colorful language a customer may use while waiting in line for a long time on a hot day. In the context of waiting-line problems, a patient customer is one who enters

customer population   An input that generates potential customers.

service facility   A person (or crew), a machine (or group of machines), or both necessary to perform the service for the customer.

priority rule   A rule that selects the next customer to be served by the service facility.

service system   The number of lines and the arrangement of the facilities.

FIGURE C.1	**Basic Elements of Waiting-Line Models**

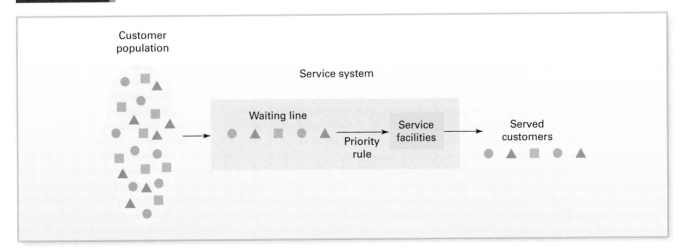

the system and remains there until being served; an impatient customer is one who either decides not to enter the system (balks) or leaves the system before being served (reneges). For the methods used in this supplement, we make the simplifying assumption that all customers are patient.

THE SERVICE SYSTEM

The service system may be described by the number of lines and the arrangement of facilities.

VIDEO CLIP C.2

Video Clip C.2 on the Student CD-ROM demonstrates the basic elements of waiting lines at a bank.

NUMBER OF LINES. Waiting lines may be designed to be a *single line or multiple lines*. Figure C.2 shows an example of each arrangement. Generally, single lines are utilized at airline counters, inside banks, and at some fast-food restaurants; whereas multiple lines are utilized in grocery stores, at drive-in bank operations, and in discount stores. When multiple servers are available and each one can handle general transactions, the single-line arrangement keeps servers uniformly busy and gives customers a sense of fairness. Customers believe that they are being served on the basis of when they arrived, and not on how well they guessed their waiting time when selecting a particular line. The multiple-line design is best when some of the servers provide a limited set of services. In this arrangement, customers select the services they need and wait in the line where that service is provided, such as at a grocery store where there are special lines for customers paying with cash or having fewer than 10 items.

Sometimes, queues are not organized neatly into "lines." Machines that need repair on the production floor of a factory may be left in place, and the maintenance crew comes to them. Nonetheless, we can think of such machines as forming a single line or multiple lines, depending on the number of repair crews and their specialties. Likewise, passengers who telephone for a taxi also form a line even though they may wait at different locations.

ARRANGEMENT OF SERVICE FACILITIES. Service facilities consist of the personnel and equipment necessary to perform the service for the customer. Figure C.3 shows examples of the five basic types of service facility arrangements. Managers should

---

FIGURE C.2

Waiting-Line Arrangements

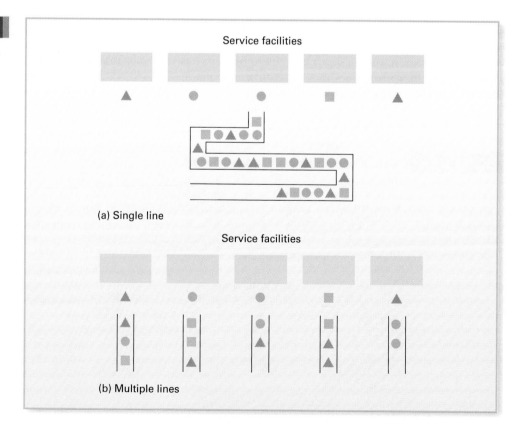

FIGURE C.3   Examples of Service Facility Arrangements

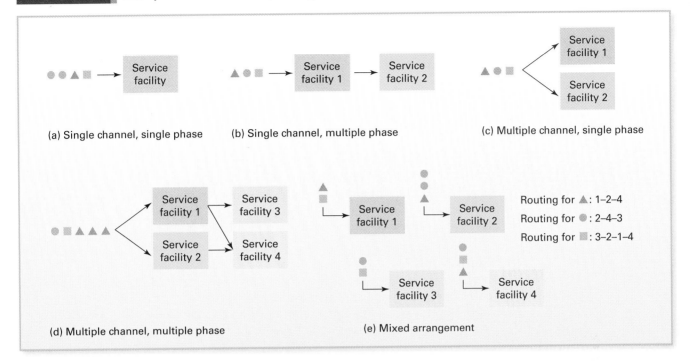

(a) Single channel, single phase   (b) Single channel, multiple phase   (c) Multiple channel, single phase

(d) Multiple channel, multiple phase   (e) Mixed arrangement

choose an arrangement based on customer volume and the nature of services performed. Some services require a single step, also called a **phase,** whereas others require a sequence of steps.

In the *single-channel, single-phase* system, all services demanded by a customer can be performed by a single-server facility. Customers form a single line and go through the service facility one at a time. Examples are a drive-through car wash and a machine that must process several batches of parts.

The *single-channel, multiple-phase* arrangement is used when the services are best performed in sequence by more than one facility, yet customer volume or other constraints limit the design to one channel. Customers form a single line and proceed sequentially from one service facility to the next. An example of this arrangement is a McDonald's drive-through, where the first facility takes the order, the second takes the money, and the third provides the food.

The *multiple-channel, single-phase* arrangement is used when demand is large enough to warrant providing the same service at more than one facility or when the services offered by the facilities are different. Customers form one or more lines,

phase   A single step in providing a service.

Customers wait in line to buy tickets at the central ticket office on the campus of UCLA. The ticket office uses the "single-line" waiting-line arrangement.

depending on the design. In the single-line design, customers are served by the first available server, as in the lobby of a bank. If each channel has its own waiting line, customers wait until the server for their line can serve them, as at a bank's drive-through facilities.

The *multiple-channel, multiple-phase* arrangement occurs when customers can be served by one of the first-phase facilities but then require service from a second-phase facility, and so on. In some cases, customers cannot switch channels after service has begun; in others they can. An example of this arrangement is a laundromat. Washing machines are the first-phase facilities, and dryers are the second-phase facilities. Some of the washing machines and dryers may be designed for extra-large loads, thereby providing the customer a choice of channels.

The most complex waiting-line problem involves customers who have unique sequences of required services; consequently, service cannot be described neatly in phases. A *mixed* arrangement is used in such a case. In the mixed arrangement, waiting lines can develop in front of each facility, as in a job shop, where each customized job may require the use of various machines and different routings.

PRIORITY RULE

The priority rule determines which customer to serve next. Most service systems that you encounter use the first-come, first-served (FCFS) rule. The customer at the head of the waiting line has the highest priority, and the customer who arrived last has the lowest priority. Other priority disciplines might take the customer with the earliest promised due date (EDD) or the customer with the shortest expected processing time (SPT). We focus on FCFS in this supplement and discuss EDD and SPT elsewhere (see Chapter 17, "Scheduling").

preemptive discipline A rule that allows a customer of higher priority to interrupt the service of another customer.

A **preemptive discipline** is a rule that allows a customer of higher priority to interrupt the service of another customer. For example, in a hospital emergency room, patients with the most life-threatening injuries receive treatment first, regardless of their order of arrival. Modeling of systems having complex priority disciplines is usually done using computer simulation (see Supplement B, "Simulation").

PROBABILITY DISTRIBUTIONS

The sources of variation in waiting-line problems come from the random arrivals of customers and the variations in service times. Each of these sources can be described with a probability distribution.

ARRIVAL DISTRIBUTION

Customers arrive at service facilities randomly. The variability of customer arrivals often can be described by a Poisson distribution, which specifies the probability that n customers will arrive in T time periods:

$$P(n) = \frac{(\lambda T)^n}{n!} e^{-\lambda T} \quad \text{for } n = 0, 1, 2, \ldots$$

where

$P(n)$ = probability of n arrivals in T time periods

λ = average number of customer arrivals per period

e = 2.7183

The mean of the Poisson distribution is λT, and the variance also is λT. The Poisson distribution is a discrete distribution; that is, the probabilities are for a specific number of arrivals per unit of time.

Calculating the Probability of Customer Arrivals

EXAMPLE C.1

Management is redesigning the customer service process in a large department store. Accommodating four customers is important. Customers arrive at the desk at the rate of two customers per hour. What is the probability that four customers will arrive during any hour?

SOLUTION

In this case $\lambda = 2$ customers per hour, $T = 1$ hour, and $n = 4$ customers. The probability that four customers will arrive in any hour is

$$P(4) = \frac{[2(1)]^4}{4!} e^{-2(1)} = \frac{16}{24} e^{-2} = 0.090$$

DECISION POINT The manager of the customer service desk can use this information to determine the space requirements for the desk and waiting area. There is a relatively small probability that four customers will arrive in any hour. Consequently, seating capacity for two or three customers should be more than adequate unless the time to service each customer is lengthy. Further analysis on service times is warranted.

Another way to specify the arrival distribution is to do it in terms of customer **interarrival times**—that is, the time between customer arrivals. If the customer population generates customers according to a Poisson distribution, the *exponential distribution* describes the probability that the next customer will arrive in the next T time periods. As the exponential distribution also describes service times, we discuss the details of this distribution in the next section.

interarrival times The time between customer arrivals.

SERVICE TIME DISTRIBUTION

The exponential distribution describes the probability that the service time of the customer at a particular facility will be no more than T time periods. The probability can be calculated by using the formula

$$P(t \leq T) = 1 - e^{-\mu T}$$

where

μ = average number of customers completing service per period

t = service time of the customer

T = target service time

The mean of the service time distribution is $1/\mu$, and the variance is $(1/\mu)^2$. As T increases, the probability that the customer's service time will be less than T approaches 1.0.

For simplicity, let us look at a single-channel, single-phase arrangement.

Calculating the Service Time Probability

EXAMPLE C.2

The management of the large department store in Example C.1 must determine if more training is needed for the customer service clerk. The clerk at the customer service desk can serve an average of three customers per hour. What is the probability that a customer will require less than 10 minutes of service?

SOLUTION

We must have all the data in the same time units. Because $\mu = 3$ customers per *hour*, we convert minutes of time to hours, or $T = 10$ minutes $= 10/60$ hour $= 0.167$ hour. Then

$$P(t \leq T) = 1 - e^{-\mu T}$$
$$P(t \leq 0.167 \text{ hour}) = 1 - e^{-3(0.167)} = 1 - 0.61 = 0.39$$

DECISION POINT   The probability that the clerk will require only 10 minutes or less is not very high, which leaves the possibility that customers may experience lengthy delays. Management should consider additional training for the clerk so as to reduce the time it takes to process a customer request.

Some characteristics of the exponential distribution do not always conform to an actual situation. The exponential distribution model is based on the assumption that each service time is independent of those that preceded it. In real life, however, productivity may improve as human servers learn about the work. Another assumption underlying the model is that very small, as well as very large, service times are possible. However, real-life situations often require a fixed-length start-up time, some cutoff on total service time, or nearly constant service time.

USING WAITING-LINE MODELS TO ANALYZE OPERATIONS

Operations managers can use waiting-line models to balance the gains that might be made by increasing the efficiency of the service system against the costs of doing so. In addition, managers should consider the costs of *not* making improvements to the system: long waiting lines or long waiting times may cause customers to balk or renege. Managers should therefore be concerned about the following operating characteristics of the system.

1. *Line Length.* The number of customers in the waiting line reflects one of two conditions. Short lines could mean either good customer service or too much capacity. Similarly, long lines could indicate either low server efficiency or the need to increase capacity.

2. *Number of Customers in System.* The number of customers in line and being served also relates to service efficiency and capacity. A large number of customers in the system causes congestion and may result in customer dissatisfaction, unless more capacity is added.

3. *Waiting Time in Line.* Long lines do not always mean long waiting times. If the service rate is fast, a long line can be served efficiently. However, when waiting time seems long, customers perceive the quality of service to be poor. Managers may try to change the arrival rate of customers or design the system to make long wait times seem shorter than they really are. For example, at Walt Disney World, customers in line for an attraction are entertained by videos and also are informed about expected waiting times, which seems to help them endure the wait.

4. *Total Time in System.* The total elapsed time from entry into the system until exit from the system may indicate problems with customers, server efficiency, or capacity. If some customers are spending too much time in the service system, there may be a need to change the priority discipline, increase productivity, or adjust capacity in some way.

5. *Service Facility Utilization.* The collective utilization of service facilities reflects the percentage of time that they are busy. Management's goal is to maintain high utilization and profitability without adversely affecting the other operating characteristics.

The best method for analyzing a waiting-line problem is to relate the five operating characteristics and their alternatives to dollars. However, placing a dollar figure on certain characteristics (such as the waiting time of a shopper in a grocery store) is difficult. In such cases, an analyst must weigh the cost of implementing the alternative under consideration against a subjective assessment of the cost of *not* making the change.

We now present three models and some examples showing how waiting-line models can help operations managers make decisions. We analyze problems requiring the single-server, multiple-server, and finite-source models, all of which are single phase. References to more advanced models are cited at the end of this supplement.

SINGLE-SERVER MODEL

The simplest waiting-line model involves a single server and a single line of customers. To further specify the model, we make the following assumptions:

1. The customer population is infinite and all customers are patient.
2. The customers arrive according to a Poisson distribution, with a mean arrival rate of λ.
3. The service distribution is exponential, with a mean service rate of μ.
4. The mean service rate exceeds the mean arrival rate.
5. Customers are served on a first-come, first-served basis.
6. The length of the waiting line is unlimited.

With these assumptions, we can apply various formulas to describe the operating characteristics of the system:

$$\rho = \text{Average utilization of the system}$$
$$= \frac{\lambda}{\mu}$$
$$P_n = \text{Probability that } n \text{ customers are in the system}$$
$$= (1 - \rho)\rho^n$$
$$L = \text{Average number of customers in the service system}$$
$$= \frac{\lambda}{\mu - \lambda}$$
$$L_q = \text{Average number of customers in the waiting line}$$
$$= \rho L$$
$$W = \text{Average time spent in the system, including service}$$
$$= \frac{1}{\mu - \lambda}$$
$$W_q = \text{Average waiting time in line}$$
$$= \rho W$$

Calculating the Operating Characteristics of a Single-Channel, Single-Phase System

EXAMPLE C.3

The manager of a grocery store in the retirement community of Sunnyville is interested in providing good service to the senior citizens who shop in his store. Presently, the store has a separate checkout counter for senior citizens. On average, 30 senior citizens per hour arrive at the counter, according to a Poisson distribution, and are served at an average rate of 35 customers per hour, with exponential service times. Find the following operating characteristics:

a. Probability of zero customers in the system
b. Utilization of the checkout clerk
c. Number of customers in the system
d. Number of customers in line
e. Time spent in the system
f. Waiting time in line

ACTIVE MODEL C.1

Active Model C.1 on the Student CD-ROM provides additional insight on the single-server model and its uses for this problem.

SOLUTION

The checkout counter can be modeled as a single-channel, single-phase system. Figure C.4 shows the results from the *Waiting-Lines* Solver from OM Explorer. Manual calculations of the equations for the *single-server model* are demonstrated in Solved Problem 1 at the end of the supplement.

FIGURE C.4

Waiting-Lines Solver for Single-Channel, Single-Phase System

Solver - Waiting Lines

Enter data in yellow-shaded areas.

◉ Single-server model   ○ Multiple-server mode   ○ Finite-source model

Servers		(Number of servers s assumed to be 1 in single-server model)
Arrival Rate (λ)	30	
Service Rate (μ)	35	

Probability of zero customers in the system (P_0)	0.1429
Probability of [exactly ▼] 0 customers in the system	0.1429
Average utilization of the server (ρ)	0.8571
Average number of customers n the system (L)	6.0000
Average number of customers n line (L_q)	5.1429
Average waiting/service time in the system (W)	0.2000
Average waiting time in line (W_q)	0.1714

Both the average waiting time in the system (W) and the average time spent waiting in line (W_q) are expressed in hours. To convert the results to minutes, simply multiply by 60 minutes/hour. For example, $W = 0.20(60) = 12.00$ minutes, and $W_q = 0.1714(60) = 10.28$ minutes.

EXAMPLE C.4   Analyzing Service Rates with the Single-Server Model

The manager of the Sunnyville grocery in Example C.3 wants answers to the following questions:

    a. What service rate would be required to have customers average only eight minutes in the system?

    b. For that service rate, what is the probability of having more than four customers in the system?

    c. What service rate would be required to have only a 10 percent chance of exceeding four customers in the system?

SOLUTION

The *Waiting-Lines* Solver from OM Explorer could be used iteratively to answer the questions. Here we show how to solve the problem manually.

    a. We use the equation for the average time in the system and solve for μ.

$$W = \frac{1}{\mu - \lambda}$$

$$8 \text{ minutes} = 0.133 \text{ hour} = \frac{1}{\mu - 30}$$

$$0.133\mu - 0.133(30) = 1$$

$$\mu = 37.52 \text{ customers/hour}$$

    b. The probability that there will be more than four customers in the system equals 1 minus the probability that there are four or fewer customers in the system.

TUTOR C.1

Tutor C.1 on the Student CD-ROM provides a new example to practice the single-server model.

$$P = 1 - \sum_{n=0}^{4} P_n$$
$$= 1 - \sum_{n=0}^{4} (1 - \rho)\rho^n$$

and

$$\rho = \frac{30}{37.52} = 0.80$$

Then,

$$P = 1 - 0.2(1 + 0.8 + 0.8^2 + 0.8^3 + 0.8^4)$$
$$= 1 - 0.672 = 0.328$$

Therefore, there is a nearly 33 percent chance that more than four customers will be in the system.

c. We use the same logic as in part (b), except that μ is now a decision variable. The easiest way to proceed is to find the correct average utilization first, and then solve for the service rate.

$$P = 1 - (1 - \rho)(1 + \rho + \rho^2 + \rho^3 + \rho^4)$$
$$= 1 - (1 + \rho + \rho^2 + \rho^3 + \rho^4) + \rho(1 + \rho + \rho^2 + \rho^3 + \rho^4)$$
$$= 1 - 1 - \rho - \rho^2 - \rho^3 - \rho^4 + \rho + \rho^2 + \rho^3 + \rho^4 + \rho^5$$
$$= \rho^5$$

or

$$\rho = P^{1/5}$$

If $P = 0.10$,

$$\rho = (0.10)^{1/5} = 0.63$$

Therefore, for a utilization rate of 63 percent, the probability of more than four customers in the system is 10 percent. For $\lambda = 30$, the mean service rate must be

$$\frac{30}{\mu} = 0.63$$
$$\mu = 47.62 \text{ customers/hour}$$

DECISION POINT. The service rate would only have to increase modestly to achieve the eight-minute target. However, the probability of having more than four customers in the system is too high. The manager must now find a way to increase the service rate from 35 per hour to approximately 48 per hour. She can increase the service rate in several different ways, ranging from employing a high school student to help bag the groceries to installing electronic point-of-sale equipment that reads the prices from bar-coded information on each item.

MULTIPLE-SERVER MODEL

With the multiple-server model, customers form a single line and choose one of s servers when one is available. The service system has only one phase. We make the following assumption in addition to those for the single-server model: There are s identical servers, and the service distribution for each server is exponential, with a mean service time of $1/\mu$. It should always be the case that $s\mu$ exceeds λ.

With these assumptions, we can apply several formulas to describe the operating characteristics of the service system:

ρ = Average utilization of the system

$$= \frac{\lambda}{s\mu}$$

P_0 = Probability that zero customers are in the system

$$= \left[\sum_{n=0}^{s-1} \frac{(\lambda/\mu)^n}{n!} + \frac{(\lambda/\mu)^s}{s!} \left(\frac{1}{1-\rho} \right) \right]^{-1}$$

P_n = Probability that n customers are in the system

$$
= \begin{cases}
\dfrac{(\lambda/\mu)^n}{n!} P_0 & 0 < n < s \\[2mm]
\dfrac{(\lambda/\mu)^n}{s! s^{n-s}} P_0 & n \geq s
\end{cases}
$$

L_q = Average number of customers in the waiting line

$$
= \frac{P_0 (\lambda/\mu)^s \rho}{s!(1-\rho)^2}
$$

W_q = Average waiting time of customers in line

$$
= \frac{L_q}{\lambda}
$$

W = Average time spent in the system, including service

$$
= W_q + \frac{1}{\mu}
$$

L = Average number of customers in the service system

$$
= \lambda W
$$

EXAMPLE C.5   Estimating Idle Time and Hourly Operating Costs with the Multiple-Server Mo

ACTIVE MODEL C.2

Active Model C.2 on the Student CD-ROM provides additional insight on the multiple-server model and its uses for this problem.

TUTOR C.2

Tutor C.2 on the Student CD-ROM provides a new example to practice the multiple-server model.

The management of the American Parcel Service terminal in Verona, Wisconsin, is concerned about the amount of time the company's trucks are idle, waiting to be unloaded. The terminal operates with four unloading bays. Each bay requires a crew of two employees, and each crew costs $30 per hour. The estimated cost of an idle truck is $50 per hour. Trucks arrive at an average rate of three per hour, according to a Poisson distribution. On average, a crew can unload a semitrailer rig in one hour, with exponential service times. What is the total hourly cost of operating the system?

SOLUTION

The *multiple-server model* is appropriate. To find the total cost of labor and idle trucks, we must calculate the average number of trucks in the system.

Figure C.5 shows the results for the American Parcel Service problem using the *Waiting-Lines* Solver from OM Explorer. Manual calculations using the equations for the *multiple-server model* are demonstrated in Solved Problem 2 at the end of this supplement. The results show that the four-bay design will be utilized 75 percent of the time and that the average number of trucks either being serviced or waiting in line is 4.53 trucks. We can now calculate the hourly costs of labor and idle trucks:

Labor cost:	$30(s) = $30(4)	= $120.00
Idle truck cost:	$50(L) = $50(4.53)	= 226.50
	Total hourly cost	= $346.50

DECISION POINT   Management must now assess whether $346.50 per day for this operation is acceptable. Attempting to reduce costs by eliminating crews will only increase the waiting time of the trucks, which is more expensive per hour than the crews. However, the service rate can be increased through better work methods; for example, L can be reduced and daily operating costs will be less.

LITTLE'S LAW

Little's law   A fundamental law that relates the number of customers in a waiting-line system to the waiting time of customers.

One of the most practical and fundamental laws in waiting-line theory is **Little's law**, which relates the number of customers in a waiting-line system to the waiting time of customers. Using the same notation we used for the single-server and multiple-server models, Little's law can be expressed as $L = \lambda W$ or $L_q = \lambda W_q$. This relationship holds

FIGURE C.5

Waiting-Lines Solver for Multiple-Server Model

Solver - Waiting Lines

Enter data in yellow-shaded areas.

○ Single-server model   ● Multiple-server model   ○ Finite-source model

Servers	4
Arrival Rate (λ)	3
Service Rate (μ)	1

Probability of zero customers in the system (P_0)	0.0377
Probability of [exactly ▼] 0 customers in the system	0.0377
Average utilization of the server (ρ)	0.7500
Average number of customers in the system (L)	4.5283
Average number of customers in line (L_q)	1.5283
Average waiting/service time in the system (W)	1.5094
Average waiting time in line (W_q)	0.5094

---

for a wide variety of arrival processes, service-time distributions, and numbers of servers. The practical advantage of Little's law is that you only need to know two of the parameters to estimate the third. For example, consider the manager of a motor vehicle licensing facility who has received many complaints about the time people must spend either having their licenses renewed or getting new license plates. It would be difficult to get data on the times individual customers spend at the facility. However, the manager can have her assistant monitor the number of people who arrive at the facility each hour and compute the average (λ). The manager also could periodically count the number of people in the sitting area and at the stations being served and compute that average (L). Using Little's law, she can then estimate W, the average time each customer spent in the facility. If the time a customer spends at the facility is unreasonable, the manager can focus on either adding capacity or improving the work methods to reduce the time spent serving the customers.

Likewise, Little's law can be used for manufacturing processes. Suppose that a production manager knows the average lead time of a unit of product through a manufacturing process (W) and the average number of units per hour that arrive at the process (λ). The production manager can then estimate the average work in process (L) using Little's law. Knowing the relationship between the arrival rate, the lead time, and the work in process, he has a basis for measuring the effects of process improvements on the work in process at his facility. For example, adding some capacity to a bottleneck in the process can reduce the lead time of the product, thereby reducing the work in process inventory.

Customers of the motor vehicle administration in Beltsville, Maryland, wait for their number to be called. Little's law can be used to estimate the average time each customer spends in the facility.

While Little's law is applicable in many situations in both service and manufacturing environments, it is not applicable in situations where the customer population is finite, which we address next.

FINITE-SOURCE MODEL

We now consider a situation in which all but one of the assumptions of the single-server model are appropriate. In this case, the customer population is finite, having only N potential customers. If N is greater than 30 customers, the single-server model with the assumption of an infinite customer population is adequate. Otherwise, the finite-source model is the one to use. The formulas used to calculate the operating characteristics of this service system are

P_0 = Probability that zero customers are in the system

$$= \left[\sum_{n=0}^{N} \frac{N!}{(N-n)!} \left(\frac{\lambda}{\mu} \right)^n \right]^{-1}$$

ρ = Average utilization of the server

$$= 1 - P_0$$

L_q = Average number of customers in the waiting line

$$= N - \frac{\lambda + \mu}{\lambda} (1 - P_0)$$

L = Average number of customers in the service system

$$= N - \frac{\mu}{\lambda} (1 - P_0)$$

W_q = Average waiting time in line

$$= L_q \left[(N - L)\lambda \right]^{-1}$$

W = Average time spent in the system, including service

$$= L \left[(N - L)\lambda \right]^{-1}$$

EXAMPLE C.6   Analyzing Maintenance Costs with the Finite-Source Model

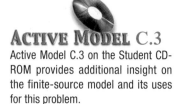

ACTIVE MODEL C.3
Active Model C.3 on the Student CD-ROM provides additional insight on the finite-source model and its uses for this problem.

TUTOR C.3
Tutor C.3 on the Student CD-ROM provides a new example to practice the finite-source model.

The Worthington Gear Company installed a bank of 10 robots about three years ago. The robots greatly increased the firm's labor productivity, but recently, attention has focused on maintenance. The firm does no preventive maintenance on the robots because of the variability in the breakdown distribution. Each machine has an exponential breakdown (or interarrival) distribution with an average time between failures of 200 hours. Each machine hour lost to downtime costs $30, which means that the firm has to react quickly to machine failure. The firm employs one maintenance person, who needs 10 hours on average to fix a robot. Actual maintenance times are exponentially distributed. The wage rate is $10 per hour for the maintenance person, who can be put to work productively elsewhere when not fixing robots. Determine the daily cost of labor and robot downtime.

SOLUTION

The *finite-source model* is appropriate for this analysis because there are only 10 machines in the customer population and the other assumptions are satisfied. Here, $\lambda = 1/200$, or 0.005 breakdown per hour, and $\mu = 1/10 = 0.10$ robot per hour. To calculate the cost of labor and robot downtime, we need to estimate the average utilization of the maintenance person and L, the average number of robots in the maintenance system. Figure C.6 shows the results for the Worthington Gear Problem using the *Waiting-Lines* Solver from OM Explorer. Manual computations using the equations for the *finite-source model* are demonstrated in Solved Problem 3 at the end of this supplement. The results show that the maintenance person is utilized only 46.2 percent of the time, and the average number of robots waiting in line or being repaired is 0.76 robot. However, a failed robot will spend an average of 16.43 hours in the repair system, of which 6.43 hours of that time is spent waiting for service.

FIGURE C.6

Waiting-Lines Solver for Finite-Source Model

Solver - Waiting Lines

Enter data in yellow-shaded areas.

○ Single-server model   ○ Multiple-server model   ● Finite-source model

Customers	10
Arrival Rate (λ)	0.005
Service Rate (μ)	0.1

Probability of zero customers in the system (P_0)	0.5380
Probability of [fewer than ▼] 0 customers in the system	#N/A
Average utilization of the server (ρ)	0.4620
Average number of customers in the system (L)	0.7593
Average number of customers in line (L_q)	0.2972
Average waiting/service time in the system (W)	16.4330
Average waiting time in line (W_q)	6.4330

The daily cost of labor and robot downtime is

Labor cost:	($10/hour)(8 hours/day)(0.462 utilization)	= $ 36.96
Idle robot cost:	(0.76 robot)($30/robot hour)(8 hours/day)	= 182.40
	Total daily cost	= $219.36

DECISION POINT. The labor cost for robot repair is only 20 percent of the idle cost of the robots. Management might consider having a second repair person on call in the event two or more robots are waiting for repair at the same time.

● DECISION AREAS FOR MANAGEMENT

After analyzing a waiting-line problem, management can improve the service system by making changes in one or more of the following areas.

1. *Arrival Rates.* Management often can affect the rate of customer arrivals, λ, through advertising, special promotions, or differential pricing. For example, a telephone company uses differential pricing to shift residential long-distance calls from daytime hours to evening hours.

2. *Number of Service Facilities.* By increasing the number of service facilities, such as tool cribs, toll booths, or bank tellers; or by dedicating some facilities in a phase to a unique set of services, management can increase system capacity.

3. *Number of Phases.* Managers can decide to allocate service tasks to sequential phases if they determine that two sequential service facilities may be more efficient than one. For instance, in assembly lines a decision concerns the number of phases or workers needed along the assembly line. Determining the number of workers needed on the line also involves assigning a certain set of work elements to each one (see Chapter 7, "Process Layout"). Changing the facility arrangement can increase the service rate, μ, of each facility and the capacity of the system.

4. *Number of Servers per Facility.* Managers can influence the service rate by assigning more than one person to a service facility.

5. *Server Efficiency.* By adjusting the capital-to-labor ratio, devising improved work methods, or instituting incentive programs, management can increase the efficiency of servers assigned to a service facility. Such changes are reflected in μ.

VIDEO CLIP C.3

Video Clip C.3 on the Student CD-ROM explains how waiting line analysis can be used in a service setting.

6. *Priority Rule.* Managers set the priority rule to be used, decide whether to have a different priority rule for each service facility, and decide whether to allow preemption (and, if so, under what conditions). Such decisions affect the waiting times of the customers and the utilization of the servers.

7. *Line Arrangement.* Managers can influence customer waiting times and server utilization by deciding whether to have a single line or a line for each facility in a given phase of service.

Obviously, these factors are interrelated. An adjustment in the customer arrival rate, λ, might have to be accompanied by an increase in the service rate, μ, in some way. Decisions about the number of facilities, the number of phases, and waiting-line arrangements also are related.

For each of the problems we analyzed with the waiting-line models, the arrivals had a Poisson distribution (or exponential interarrival times), the service times had an exponential distribution, the service facilities had a simple arrangement, and the priority discipline was first come, first served. Waiting-line theory has been used to develop other models in which these criteria are not met, but these models are very complex. Many times, the nature of the customer population, the constraints on the line, the priority rule, the service-time distribution, and the arrangement of the facilities are such that waiting-line theory is no longer useful. In these cases, simulation often is used (see Supplement B, "Simulation").

SUPPLEMENT HIGHLIGHTS

- Waiting lines form when customers arrive at a faster rate than they are being served. Because customer arrival rates vary, long waiting lines may occur even when the system's designed service rate is substantially higher than the average customer arrival rate.

- Four elements are common to all waiting-line problems; a customer population, a waiting line, a service system, and a priority rule for determining which customer is to be served next.

- Waiting-line models have been developed for use in analyzing service systems. If the assumptions made in creating a waiting-line model are consistent with an actual situation, the model's formulas can be solved to predict the performance of the system with respect to server utilization, average customer waiting time, and the average number of customers in the system.

- Little's law is a useful relationship between the number of customers in a waiting-line system and the waiting time of those customers.

STUDENT CD-ROM AND INTERNET RESOURCES

The Student CD-ROM and the Companion Website at **www.prenhall.com/krajewski** contain many tools, activities, and resources designed for this supplement. The following items are recommended to enhance your skills and improve your understanding of the material in this supplement.

STUDENT CD-ROM RESOURCES

➤ **PowerPoint Slides.** View the comprehensive set of slides customized for this supplement's concepts and techniques.
➤ **Video Clips.** See the three video clips customized for this supplement to learn more about the effects of variable arrival and service rates, the basics of multiple server systems, and the use of waiting line analysis in service settings.
➤ **OM Explorer Tutors.** OM Explorer contains three tutor programs that will help you learn how to use the single-server, multiple-server, and finite-source models. See the Supplement C folder in OM Explorer.

➤ **OM Explorer Solvers.** OM Explorer has a program designed to solve general problems involving waiting lines. See the Waiting Lines folder in OM Explorer.
➤ **Active Models.** There are three active model spreadsheets that provide additional insights on the single-server, multiple-server, and finite-source models. See Waiting Lines in the Active Models menu for these routines.
➤ **SimQuick.** Learn the basics of building waiting line models for practical problems by exploring the many examples contained in *SimQuick: Process Simulation with Excel.*

INTERNET RESOURCES

➤ **Self-Study Quizzes.** See the compendium of true or false, multiple choice, and essay questions that allows online tests or gives you feedback on how well you have mastered the concepts in this supplement.
➤ **In the News.** See the articles that apply to this supplement.

➤ **Internet Exercises.** Try out an Internet exercise that addresses the issue of long wait times for a Web page to load.

➤ **Virtual Tours.** Learn about the waiting lines that develop at West Park Health Care Center. Also see the "Web Links to Company Facility Tours" for additional tours of company facilities.

KEY EQUATIONS

1. Customer arrival Poisson distribution: $P_n = \dfrac{(\lambda T)^n}{n!} e^{-\lambda T}$

2. Service-time exponential distribution: $P[t \leq T] = 1 - e^{-\mu T}$

	Single-Server Model	Multiple-Server Model	Finite-Source Model
Average utilization of the system	$\rho = \dfrac{\lambda}{\mu}$	$\rho = \dfrac{\lambda}{s\mu}$	$\rho = 1 - P_0$
Probability that n customers are in the system	$P_n = (1 - \rho)\rho^n$	$P_n = \begin{cases} \dfrac{(\lambda/\mu)^n}{n!} P_0 & 0 < n < s \\ \dfrac{(\lambda/\mu)^n}{s!\, s^{n-s}} P_0 & n \geq s \end{cases}$	
Probability that zero customers are in the system	$P_0 = 1 - \rho$	$P_0 = \left[\displaystyle\sum_{n=0}^{s-1} \dfrac{(\lambda/\mu)^n}{n!} + \dfrac{(\lambda/\mu)^s}{s!}\left(\dfrac{1}{1-\rho}\right) \right]^{-1}$	$P_0 = \left[\displaystyle\sum_{n=0}^{N} \dfrac{N!}{(N-n)!}\left(\dfrac{\lambda}{\mu}\right)^n \right]^{-1}$
Average number of customers in the service system	$L = \dfrac{\lambda}{\mu - \lambda}$	$L = \lambda W$	$L = N - \dfrac{\mu}{\lambda}(1 - P_0)$
Average number of customers in the waiting line	$L_q = \rho L$	$L_q = \dfrac{P_0(\lambda/\mu)^s \rho}{s!(1-\rho)^2}$	$L_q = N - \dfrac{\lambda + \mu}{\lambda}(1 - P_0)$
Average time spent in the system, including service	$W = \dfrac{1}{\mu - \lambda}$	$W = W_q + \dfrac{1}{\mu}$	$W = L\left[(N - L)\lambda\right]^{-1}$
Average waiting time in line	$W_q = \rho W$	$W_q = \dfrac{L_q}{\lambda}$	$W_q = L_q\left[(N - L)\lambda\right]^{-1}$

KEY TERMS

customer population 277
interarrival times 281
Little's law 286

phase 279
preemptive discipline 280
priority rule 277

service facility 277
service system 277
waiting line 276

SOLVED PROBLEM I

A photographer at the post office takes passport pictures at an average rate of 20 pictures per hour. The photographer must wait until the customer blinks or scowls, so the time to take a picture is exponentially distributed. Customers arrive at a Poisson-distributed average rate of 19 customers per hour.

   a. What is the utilization of the photographer?

   b. How much time will the average customer spend at the photograph step of the passport issuing process?

SOLUTION

a. The assumptions in the problem statement are consistent with a single-server model. Utilization is

$$\rho = \frac{\lambda}{\mu} = \frac{19}{20} = 0.95$$

b. The average customer time spent at the photographer's station is

$$W = \frac{1}{\mu - \lambda} = \frac{1}{20 - 19} = 1 \text{ hour}$$

SOLVED PROBLEM 2

The Mega Multiplex Movie Theater has three concession clerks serving customers on a first-come, first-served basis. The service time per customer is exponentially distributed with an average of 2 minutes per customer. Concession customers wait in a single line in a large lobby, and arrivals are Poisson distributed with an average of 81 customers per hour. Previews run for 10 minutes before the start of each show. If the average time in the concession area exceeds 10 minutes, customers become dissatisfied.

a. What is the average utilization of the concession clerks?
b. What is the average time spent in the concession area?

SOLUTION

a. The problem statement is consistent with the multiple-server model, and the average utilization rate is

$$\rho = \frac{\lambda}{s\mu} = \frac{81 \text{ customers/hour}}{(3 \text{ servers})\left(\dfrac{60 \text{ minutes/server hour}}{2 \text{ minutes/customer}}\right)} = 0.90$$

The concession clerks are busy 90 percent of the time.

b. The average time spent in the system, W, is.

$$W = W_q + \frac{1}{\mu}$$

Here,

$$W_q = \frac{L_q}{\lambda} \quad L_q = \frac{P_0(\lambda/\mu)^s \rho}{s!(1-\rho)^2} \quad \text{and} \quad P_0 = \left[\sum_{n=0}^{s-1} \frac{(\lambda/\mu)^n}{n!} + \frac{(\lambda/\mu)^s}{s!}\left(\frac{1}{1-\rho}\right)\right]^{-1}$$

We must solve for P_0, L_q, and W_q, in that order, before we can solve for W:

$$P_0 = \left[\sum_{n=0}^{s-1} \frac{(\lambda/\mu)^n}{n!} + \frac{(\lambda/\mu)^s}{s!}\left(\frac{1}{1-\rho}\right)\right]^{-1}$$

$$= \frac{1}{1 + \dfrac{(81/30)}{1} + \dfrac{(2.7)^2}{2} + \left[\dfrac{(2.7)^3}{6}\left(\dfrac{1}{1-0.9}\right)\right]}$$

$$= \frac{1}{1 + 2.7 + 3.645 + 32.805} = \frac{1}{40.15} = 0.0249$$

$$L_q = \frac{P_0(\lambda/\mu)^s \rho}{s!(1-\rho)^2} = \frac{0.0249(81/30)^3(0.9)}{3!(1-0.9)^2} = \frac{0.4411}{6(0.01)} = 7.352 \text{ customers}$$

$$W_q = \frac{L_q}{\lambda} = \frac{7.352 \text{ customers}}{81 \text{ customers/hour}} = 0.0908 \text{ hour}$$

$$W = W_q + \frac{1}{\mu} = 0.0908 \text{ hour} + \frac{1}{30} \text{ hour} = (0.1241 \text{ hour})\left(\frac{60 \text{ minutes}}{\text{hour}}\right)$$

$$= 7.45 \text{ minutes}$$

With three concession clerks, customers will spend an average of 7.45 minutes in the concession area.

SOLVED PROBLEM 3

The Severance Coal Mine serves six trains having exponentially distributed interarrival times averaging 30 hours. The time required to fill a train with coal varies with the number of cars, weather-related delays, and equipment breakdowns. The time to fill a train can be approximated by a negative exponential distribution with a mean of 6 hours 40 minutes. The railroad requires the coal mine to pay very large demurrage charges in the event that a train spends more than 24 hours at the mine. What is the average time a train will spend at the mine?

SOLUTION

The problem statement describes a finite-source model, with $N = 6$. The average time spent at the mine is $W = L[(N-L)\lambda]^{-1}$, with $1/\lambda = 30$ hours/train, $\lambda = 0.8$ train/day, and $\mu = 3.6$ trains/day. In this case,

$$P_0 = \left[\sum_{n=0}^{N} \frac{N!}{(N-n)!}\left(\frac{\lambda}{\mu}\right)^n\right]^{-1} = \frac{1}{\displaystyle\sum_{n=0}^{6} \frac{6!}{(6-n)!}\left(\frac{0.8}{3.6}\right)^n}$$

$$= \frac{1}{\left[\frac{6!}{6!}\left(\frac{0.8}{3.6}\right)^0\right] + \left[\frac{6!}{5!}\left(\frac{0.8}{3.6}\right)^1\right] + \left[\frac{6!}{4!}\left(\frac{0.8}{3.6}\right)^2\right] + \left[\frac{6!}{3!}\left(\frac{0.8}{3.6}\right)^3\right] + \left[\frac{6!}{2!}\left(\frac{0.8}{3.6}\right)^4\right] + \left[\frac{6!}{1!}\left(\frac{0.8}{3.6}\right)^5\right] + \left[\frac{6!}{0!}\left(\frac{0.8}{3.6}\right)^6\right]}$$

$$= \frac{1}{1 + 1.33 + 1.48 + 1.32 + 0.88 + 0.39 + 0.09} = \frac{1}{6.49} = 0.1541$$

$$L = N - \frac{\mu}{\lambda}(1 - P_0) = 6 - \left[\frac{3.6}{0.8}(1 - 0.1541)\right] = 2.193 \text{ trains}$$

$$W = L[(N-L)\lambda]^{-1} = \frac{2.193}{(3.807)0.8} = 0.72 \text{ day}$$

Arriving trains will spend an average of 0.72 day at the coal mine.

PROBLEMS

An icon next to a problem identifies the software that can be helpful, but is not mandatory. The software is available on the Student CD-ROM that is packaged with every new copy of the textbook.

1. **OM Explorer** The Solomon, Smith, and Samson law firm produces many legal documents that must be typed for clients and the firm. Requests average 8 pages of documents per hour, and they arrive according to a Poisson distribution. The secretary can type 10 pages per hour on average according to an exponential distribution.

   a. What is the average utilization rate of the secretary?

   b. What is the probability that more than 4 pages are waiting or being typed?

   c. What is the average number of pages waiting to be typed?

2. **OM Explorer** Benny's Arcade has six video game machines. The average time between machine failures is 50 hours. Jimmy, the maintenance engineer, can repair a machine in 15 hours on the average. The machines have an exponential failure distribution, and Jimmy has an exponential service-time distribution.

   a. What is Jimmy's utilization?

   b. What is the average number of machines out of service, that is, waiting to be repaired or being repaired?

   c. What is the average time a machine is out of service?

3. **OM Explorer** Moore, Aiken, and Payne is a dental clinic serving the needs of the general public on a first-come, first-served basis. The clinic has three dental chairs, each staffed by a dentist. Patients arrive at the rate of five per hour, according to a Poisson distribution, and do not balk or renege. The average time required for a dental checkup is 30 minutes, according to an exponential distribution.

   a. What is the probability that no patients are in the clinic?

   b. What is the probability that six or more patients are in the clinic?

   c. What is the average number of patients waiting?

   d. What is the average total time that a patient spends in the clinic?

4. **OM Explorer** Fantastic Styling Salon is run by two stylists, Jenny Perez and Jill Sloan, each capable of serving five customers per hour, on average. Eight customers, on average, arrive at the salon each hour.

   a. If all arriving customers wait in a common line for the next available stylist, how long would a customer wait in line, on average, before being served?

   b. Suppose that 50 percent of the arriving customers want to be served only by Perez and that the other 50 percent want only Sloan. How long would a customer wait in line, on average, before being served by Perez? By Sloan? What is the average customer waiting time in the line?

   c. Do you observe a difference in the answers to parts (a) and (b)? If so, why? Explain.

5. **OM Explorer** You are the manager of a local bank where three tellers provide services to customers. On average, each teller takes three minutes to serve a customer. Customers arrive, on average, at a rate of 50 per hour. Having recently received complaints from some customers that they have had to wait for a long time before being served, your boss asks you to evaluate the service system. Specifically, you must provide answers to the following questions:

   a. What is the average utilization of the three-teller service system?

   b. What is the probability that no customers are being served by a teller or are waiting in line?

   c. What is the average number of customers waiting in line?

   d. On average, how long does a customer wait in line before being served?

   e. On average, how many customers would be at a teller's station and in line?

6. **OM Explorer** Jake Tweet hosts a psychology talk show on KRAN radio. Jake's advice averages 10 minutes per caller but varies according to an exponential distribution. The average time between calls is 25 minutes, exponentially distributed. Generating calls in this local market is difficult, so Jake does not want to lose any calls to busy signals. The radio station has only three telephone lines. What is the probability that a caller receives a busy signal?

7. **OM Explorer** The supervisor at the Precision Machine Shop wants to determine the staffing policy that minimizes total operating costs. The average arrival rate at the tool crib, where tools are dispensed to the workers, is 8 machinists per hour. Each machinist's pay is $20 per hour. The supervisor can staff the crib either with a junior attendant who is paid $5 per hour and can process 10 arrivals per hour or with a senior attendant who is paid $12 per hour and can process 16 arrivals per hour. Which attendant should be selected, and what would be the total estimated hourly cost?

8. **OM Explorer** The daughter of the owner of a local hamburger restaurant is preparing to open a new fast-food restaurant called Hasty Burgers. Based on the arrival rates at her father's outlets, she expects customers to arrive at the drive-in window according to a Poisson distribution, with a mean of 20 customers per hour. The service rate is flexible; however, the service times are expected to follow an exponential distribution. The drive-in window is a single-server operation.

   a. What service rate is needed to keep the average number of customers in the service system (waiting line and being served) to 4?

   b. For the service rate in part (a), what is the probability that more than 4 customers are in line and being served?

   c. For the service rate in part (a), what is the average waiting time in line for each customer? Does this average seem satisfactory for a fast-food business?

Advanced Problems

9. **OM Explorer** Three employees in the maintenance department are responsible for repairing the video games at Pinball Wizard, a video arcade. A maintenance worker can fix one video game machine every 8 hours on average, with an exponential distribution. An average of one video game machine fails every three hours, according to a Poisson distribution. Each down machine costs the Wizard $10 per hour in lost income. A new maintenance worker would cost $8 per hour.

Should the manager hire any new personnel? If so, how many? What would you recommend to the manager, based on your analysis?

10. **OM Explorer** The College of Business and Public Administration at Benton University has a copy machine on each floor for faculty use. Heavy use of the five copy machines causes frequent failures. Maintenance records show that a machine fails every 2.5 days (or $\lambda = 0.40$ failure/day). The college has a maintenance contract with the authorized dealer of the copy machines. Because the copy machines fail so frequently, the dealer has assigned one person to the college to repair them. This person can repair an average of 2.5 machines per day. Using the finite-source model, answer the following questions:

   a. What is the average utilization of the maintenance person?

   b. On average, how many copy machines are being repaired or waiting to be repaired?

   c. What is the average time spent by a copy machine in the repair system (waiting and being repaired)?

11. **OM Explorer** You are in charge of a quarry that supplies sand and stone aggregates to your company's construction sites. Empty trucks from construction sites arrive at the quarry's huge piles of sand and stone aggregates and wait in line to enter the station, which can load either sand or aggregate. At the station, they are filled with material, weighed, checked out, and proceed to a construction site. Currently, nine empty trucks arrive per hour, on average. Once a truck has entered a loading station, it takes six minutes for it to be filled, weighed, and checked out. Concerned that trucks are spending too much time waiting and being filled, you are evaluating two alternatives to reduce the average time the trucks spend in the system. The first alternative is to add side boards to the trucks (so that more material could be loaded) and to add a helper at the loading station (so that filling time could be reduced) at a total cost of $50,000. The arrival rate of trucks would change to six per hour, and the filling time would be reduced to four minutes. The second alternative is to add another loading station at a cost of $80,000. The trucks would wait in a common line and the truck at the front of the line would move to the next available station.

   Which alternative would you recommend if you want to reduce the current average waiting time in the system?

SELECTED REFERENCES

Cooper, Robert B. *Introduction to Queuing Theory*. 2d ed. New York: Elsevier-North Holland, 1980.

Hartvigsen, David. *SimQuick: Process Simulation with Excel*. 2d ed. Upper Saddle River, NJ: Prentice Hall, 2004.

Hillier, F.S., and G.S. Lieberman. *Introduction to Operations Research*. 2d ed. San Francisco: Holden-Day, 1975.

Little, J.D.C. "A Proof for the Queuing Formula: $L = \lambda W$." *Operations Research*, vol. 9, (1961), pp 383–387.

Moore, P.M. *Queues, Inventories and Maintenance*. New York: John Wiley & Sons, 1958.

Saaty, T.L. *Elements of Queuing Theory with Applications*. New York: McGraw-Hill, 1961.

Process Layout

CHAPTER OUTLINE

LEARNING GOALS   *After reading this chapter, you should be able to ...*

IDENTIFY OR DEFINE

1. layout planning and the questions it addresses.
2. performance criteria for evaluating layouts.
3. a step-by-step approach in designing flexible-flow layouts.

DESCRIBE OR EXPLAIN

4. four basic layout types and when each is best.
5. how cells help create hybrid layouts.
6. different strategies in warehouse and office layouts.
7. how to balance operations for line-flow processes.

RIVERTOWN CROSSINGS

A 35-year-old mother does not know it, but the Internet has made her trips to the mall a little easier. In 2000, RiverTown Crossings (www.rivertowncrossings.com) opened its doors in Grandville, Michigan. Since then, she rarely ventures beyond just one section of the mall—the one with Abercrombie Kids, Gap Kids, Gymboree, and other kids' clothing stores. She can shop in that wing and find almost everything she needs. In an effort to compete with the allure of online shopping, the mall owner, General Growth Properties, Inc. (www.generalgrowth.com), selected a layout that runs counter to decades of retailing wisdom: It clustered competing stores together. Shoppers were asking for such clusters long before Web retailing took off, and General Growth began experimenting with the idea three years ago. Now, all of its new malls will have clusters.

Worried about a future when shoppers point and click instead of park and walk and wait in line, developers are finally trying to make it more convenient to shop in malls. Some owners are revising their existing layouts by removing large fixtures, such as planters and fountains, to clear sight lines to storefronts. Others are adding directories that are easier to understand than current mall maps. A few malls in the design stages are opting to put anchor department stores closer together—a layout that cuts down on walking. A few malls are trying to offer shoppers elements of the Web using high-tech directories. At the Dayton Mall, in Ohio, sleek electronic kiosks give shoppers e-mail access and let them search for names of stores carrying types of merchandise, such as "sweaters." The kiosks also have printers that can spit out a map with a store's location highlighted.

Beneath the new layout designs is an old retailing secret: The traditional mall was designed to be difficult. This planned inconvenience made customers who wanted to comparison-shop walk from one end of the mall to the other, so that they had every chance to make impulse purchases in between. Many developers left little to chance in directing the traffic flow to their advantage, using plants, carpeting, and other fixtures to set winding routes past stores.

Revising the layout of existing malls to make them more convenient is costly. Most of them are jungles of escalators, fountains, and play areas—and those are the easy obstacles. The tougher problem is figuring out how to rearrange similar stores that are probably operating on long leases. After all, a mall developer cannot simply order four shoe store tenants to pick up and move. And many retailers still prefer to keep their distance from competitors. RiverTown's Hallmark Gold Crown store is located on the first level on the north end of the mall, while an American Greetings store is on the second level on the south end. Hallmark Cards' location strategy calls for space between its stores and competitors.

Source: "Making Malls (Gasp!) Convenient." *Wall Street Journal* (February 8, 2000).

The internet has revolutionized the way traditional businesses design their processes, even to the point of layout design. RiverTown Crossings Mall has clustered company stores to improve comparison shopping, a convenience that Web retailing already offers online customers.

F acility layout decisions translate the broader decisions about a firm's competitive priorities, process, design, quality, and capacity of processes into actual physical arrangements of people, equipment, and space. In this chapter, we examine layout of processes in a variety of settings, along with techniques of layout analysis.

Revising layouts can be an important aspect of designing and improving processes, the fifth step in Figure 7.1. They put other decisions on processes in tangible, physical form, converting flowcharts and capacity plans into brick and mortar. The new layout of RiverTown Crossings demonstrates the impact of layout on customer attitudes and satisfaction.

As you read about the layout of processes, think about why it is important to the various departments and functions across the organization, such as . . .

➤ **accounting,** which seeks effective layouts for its offices and provides cost information on layout changes elsewhere in the organization.

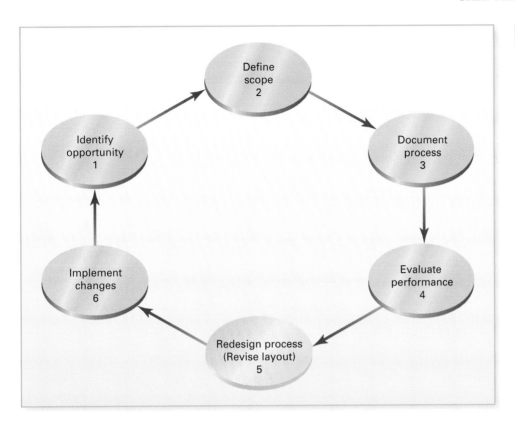

FIGURE 7.1

**Redesigning a Process
Through Layout Revision**

➤ **distribution,** which seeks warehouse layouts that make materials handling easier and make customer response times shorter.

➤ **finance,** which performs the financial analysis of proposed capacity expansion investments in new or revised layouts.

➤ **human resources,** which considers how layout designs affect employee attitudes and behavior.

➤ **management information systems,** which designs decision support systems for improving layout design.

➤ **marketing,** which uses layout as a tool to expand market share for high customer-contact processes.

➤ **operations,** which seeks layouts of operations that best balance multiple performance criteria.

⦿ WHAT IS LAYOUT PLANNING?

Layout planning involves decisions about the physical arrangement of economic activity centers needed by a facility's various processes. An **economic activity center** can be anything that consumes space: a person or group of people, a customer reception area, a teller window, a machine, a workbench or workstation, a department, a stairway or an aisle, a time card rack, a cafeteria or a storage room, and so on. The goal of layout planning is to allow customers, workers, and equipment to operate most effectively. Before a manager can make decisions regarding physical arrangement, four questions must be addressed.

  1. *What Centers Should the Layout Include?* Centers should reflect process decisions and maximize productivity. For example, a customer information desk near the entrance of a bank or hotel can better guide customers to the desired services.

  2. *How Much Space and Capacity Does Each Center Need?* Inadequate space can reduce productivity, deprive employees of privacy, and even create safety hazards. However, excessive space is wasteful, can reduce productivity, and can isolate employees unnecessarily.

What are some key layout questions that need to be addressed?

layout planning Planning that involves decisions about the physical arrangement of economic activity centers needed by a facility's various processes.

economic activity center Anything that consumes space; for example, a person or a group of people, a customer reception area, a teller window, a machine, a workbench or workstation, a department, a stairway or an aisle, a time card rack, a cafeteria or a storage room.

3. *How Should Each Center's Space Be Configured?* The amount of space, its shape, and the elements in a center are interrelated. For example, placement of a desk and chair relative to the other furniture is determined by the size and shape of the office, as well as the activities performed there. Providing a pleasing atmosphere also should be considered as part of the layout configuration decisions, especially in retail outlets and offices.

4. *Where Should Each Center Be Located?* Location can significantly affect productivity. For example, employees who must frequently interact with one another face to face should be placed in a central location rather than in separate, remote locations to reduce time lost traveling back and forth.

The location of a center has two dimensions: (1) *relative location,* or the placement of a center relative to other centers and (2) *absolute location,* or the particular space that the center occupies within the facility. Both affect a center's performance. Look at the grocery store layout in Figure 7.2 (a). It shows the location of five departments, with the dry groceries department allocated twice the space of each of the others. The location of frozen foods relative to bread is the same as the location of meats relative to vegetables, so the distance between the first pair of departments equals the distance between the second pair of departments. Relative location is normally the crucial issue when travel time, materials handling cost, and communication effectiveness are important.

Now look at the plan in Figure 7.2(b). Although the relative locations are the same, the absolute locations have changed. This modified layout might prove unworkable. For example, the cost of moving the meats to the upper-left corner could be excessive; or customers might react negatively to the placement of vegetables in the bottom-left corner, preferring them to be near the entrance.

● STRATEGIC ISSUES

How should layout reflect competitive priorities?

Layout choices can help immensely in communicating an organization's product plans and competitive priorities. As Managerial Practice 7.1 illustrates, if a retailer plans to upgrade the quality of its merchandise, the store layout should convey more exclusiveness and luxury.

Layout has many practical and strategic implications. Altering a layout can affect an organization and how well it meets its competitive priorities by

- increasing customer satisfaction and sales at a retail store,
- facilitating the flow of materials and information,
- increasing the efficient utilization of labor and equipment,
- reducing hazards to workers,
- improving employee morale, and
- improving communication.

The type of operation determines layout requirements. For example, in warehouses, materials flows and stockpicking costs are dominant considerations. In retail stores, customer convenience and sales may dominate, whereas communication effectiveness and team building may be crucial in an office.

FIGURE 7.2

Identical Relative Locations and Different Absolute Locations

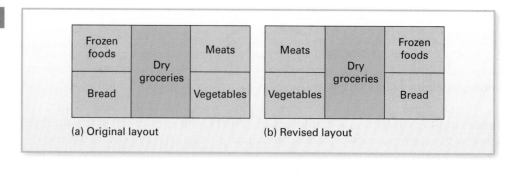

(a) Original layout   (b) Revised layout

MANAGERIAL PRACTICE 7.1

RETAILERS MATCH LAYOUTS TO STRATEGIES

The Limited

The Limited, Inc. (www.limited.com), the specialty clothing retailer with more than 4,500 stores across North America, uses the look of its stores to match its strategy. Once a small outlet geared to teenagers, the store has quadrupled in size and changed its look to that of a European boutique in order to attract older customers. From the grainy wood floors to the black lacquered display cases, the store serves as a stage for trendy sportswear for women. While rivals left their store layouts basically unchanged, The Limited tripled the size of its stores and spent millions on a fresh look. The look is intended to entice customers to spend more time in its stores and pay more for merchandise.

In 1999, The Limited spun off Limited Too, a rapidly growing retailer that sells apparel, swimwear, underwear, lifestyle, and personal care products for active fashion-wear girls between 7 and 14 years. The company markets and sells Limited Too brand-name merchandise exclusively in its 408 stores, through its catazine and on its Web site (www.limitedtoo.com). The layout of these stores is quite different. They are colorful and fun with a high-energy atmosphere. The lighting, which includes handmade globe lights with broken glass color mosaics, enhances the excitement. Limited Too added a new high-tech element in select stores: full spectrum digital lighting. It uses a light-emitting diode (LED)-based system. Unlike conventional techniques that use gels and moving parts to produce colors, this system generates colors and colored-lighting effects via microprocessor-controlled red, green, and blue LEDs. The system has no moving parts and generates almost no heat. Limited Too is using the digital lighting to highlight its signature and most eye-catching layout element: a 3-D banner soffit curved-wall projection that is 5 feet high and about 50 feet long. The color-changing digital lights bring the banner soffit to life and reflect the playful, youthful spirit of the store.

Wal-Mart

Wal-Mart, the discount giant that is the largest U.S. retailer, experimented with a prototype store in Rogers, Arkansas, to appeal to customers who are as concerned about service as about low prices. With wide aisles, less-cramped racks, sitting areas for customers, and attractive displays, the store looks more like an upscale department store than a discount store. As in department stores, the displays organize related products—such as shower curtains, towels, and ceramic bathroom accessories—into visual "vignettes" that encourage sales of "multiples" of related products. Unlike department stores, however, the store has the same bargain-basement prices and wide selection offered in all its outlets. Many retailing executives consider Wal-Mart the leader in attention to the layout details that help shape shoppers' attitudes. The chain is particularly adapt at striking the delicate balance needed to convince customers that its prices are low without making people feel that its stores are cheap.

Wal-Mart's Web site (www.walmart.com) provides a virtual storefront that is quite consistent with the shopping experience at its brick-and-mortar physical store. Behind the Amazon.com-like site architecture is the floor plan of your local superstore: products organized by department in aisles, with checkout registers and customer service at the door. While the Web site might be exactly right for its target customers, some critics believe the site reflects a legacy mind-set and that Wal-Mart's excellence in the brick-and-mortar physical world seems to have imposed a mental straitjacket on its efforts in the virtual world.

Color Kinetics lighting brings Limited Too's cool, colorful graphics to life through C-Series fixtures, which illuminate the store's soffit.

Sources: "Lighting Goes High-Tech," *Chain Store Age* (January 1, 2000); "The Business Logic of Site Architecture," *The Industry Standard* (April 17, 2000).

Among the several fundamental layout choices available to managers are whether to plan for current or future (and less predictable) needs, whether to select a single-story or multistory design, whether to open the planning process to employee suggestions, what type of layout to choose, and what performance criteria to emphasize. Because of their strategic importance, we focus on the last two choices.

LAYOUT TYPES

What layout type is best for our processes?

The choice of layout type depends largely on process structure—the position of the processes on the customer-contact matrix for service providers and on the product-process matrix for manufacturing processes (see Chapter 3, "Process Design Strategy"). There are four basic types of layout: (1) flexible flow, (2) line flow, (3) hybrid, and (4) fixed position.

flexible-flow layout A layout that organizes resources (employees and equipment) by function rather than by service or product.

FLEXIBLE-FLOW LAYOUTS. Front office and job processes with highly divergent work flows have low volume and high customization. For such processes, the manager should choose a **flexible-flow layout,** which organizes resources (employees and equipment) by function rather than by service or product. For example, in the metal-working job processes shown in Figure 7.3(a), all drills are located in one area of the machine shop and all milling machines are located in another area. The flexible-flow layout is most common when the operation must intermittently serve many different customer types or manufacture many different products or parts. Demand levels are too low or unpredictable for management to set aside human and capital resources exclusively for a particular type of customer or product line. Advantages of the flexible-flow layout over the line-flow layout, illustrated by Figure 7.3(b), where centers are arranged in a linear path, include: general-purpose and less capital-intensive resources, more flexibility to handle changes in product mix, more specialized employee supervision when job content requires a good deal of technical knowledge, and higher equipment utilization. When volumes are low, dedicating resources to each service or product (as done with a line-flow layout) would require more equipment than would pooling the requirements for all products.[1] A major challenge in designing a flexible-flow layout is to locate centers so that they bring some order to the apparent chaos of divergent processes with jumbled work flows.

FIGURE 7.3   **Two Layout Types**

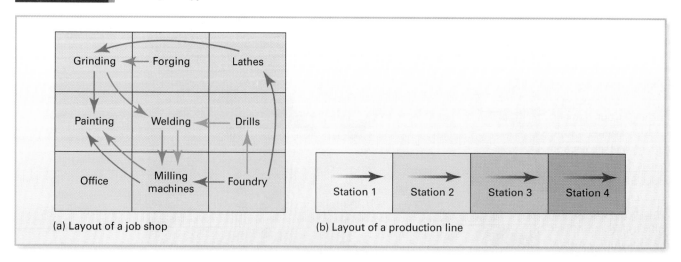

(a) Layout of a job shop

(b) Layout of a production line

---

[1]However, management would not allow utilization to get too high. A larger capacity cushion for divergent processes absorbs the more unpredictable demands of customized services and products.

LINE-FLOW LAYOUTS. Back offices and line processes typically have linear work flows and repetitive tasks. For such processes, the manager should dedicate resources to individual services, products, or tasks. This strategy is achieved by a **line-flow layout,** illustrated by Figure 7.3(b), in which workstations or departments are arranged in a linear path. As in an automated car wash, the customer or product moves along in a smooth, continuous flow. Resources are arranged around the customer's or product's route, rather than shared across many of them. (Later, we demonstrate that some such layouts, called *mixed-model lines*, can handle several products as long as their processing requirements are similar and not too divergent.) Although line-flow layouts often follow a straight line, a straight line is not always best, and layouts may take an L, O, S, or U shape. The layout often is called a *production line* or an *assembly line*. The difference between the two is that an assembly line is limited to assembly processes, whereas a production line can be used to perform other processes, such as machining.

Such layouts often rely heavily on specialized, capital-intensive resources. When volumes are high, the advantages of line-flow layouts over flexible-flow layouts include: faster processing rates, lower inventories, and less unproductive time lost to changeovers and materials handling. There is less need to decouple one operation from the next, allowing management to cut inventories. The Japanese refer to a line process as *overlapped operations,* whereby materials move directly from one operation to the next without waiting in queues.

For line-flow layouts, deciding where to locate centers is easy because operations must occur in a prescribed order. Centers can simply be placed to follow the work flow, which ensures that all interacting pairs of centers are as close together as possible or have a common boundary. The challenge of line-flow layout is to group activities into workstations and achieve the desired output rate with the least resources. The composition and number of workstations are crucial decisions, which we explore later in the chapter.

HYBRID LAYOUTS. More often than not, the layout combines elements of both divergent and line-flow processes. This intermediate strategy calls for a **hybrid layout,** in which some portions of the facility are arranged in a flexible-flow layout and others are arranged in a line-flow layout. Hybrid layouts are used in facilities that have both fabrication and assembly operations, as would be the case if both types of layout shown in Figure 7.3 were in the same building. Fabrication operations—in which components are made from raw materials—have a jumbled flow, whereas assembly operations—in which components are assembled into finished products—have a line flow. Operations managers also create hybrid layouts when introducing cells and flexible automation, such as a flexible manufacturing system (FMS). A *cell* is two or more dissimilar workstations located close together through which a limited number of parts or models are processed with line flows (see Chapter 3, "Process Design Strategy"). We cover two special types of cells—group technology (GT) cells and one-worker, multiple-machines (OWMM) cells—later in this chapter. An *FMS* is a group of computer-controlled workstations at which materials are automatically handled and machine loaded (see Supplement K, "Computer-Integrated Manufacturing" on the Student CD-ROM). These technologies help achieve repeatability, even when product volumes are too low to justify dedicating a single line to one product, by bringing together all resources needed to make a family of parts in one center.

FIXED-POSITION LAYOUT. The fourth basic type of layout is the **fixed-position layout.** In this arrangement, the service or manufacturing site is fixed in place; employees, along with their equipment, come to the site to do their work. Many project processes have this arrangement. This type of layout makes sense when the product is particularly massive or difficult to move, as in building a new office complex, shipbuilding, assembling locomotives, making huge pressure vessels, building dams, or repairing home furnaces. A fixed-position layout minimizes the number of times that the product must be moved and often is the only feasible solution.

line-flow layout A layout in which workstations or departments are arranged in a linear path.

hybrid layout An arrangement in which the service or manufacturing site is fixed in place; employees along with their equipment, come to the site to do their work.

fixed-position layout An arrangement in which service or manufacturing site is fixed in place; employees along with their equipment, come to the site to do their work.

A financial consultant discusses brochures with a young couple at their home. This process has a fixed-position layout because the consultant goes to customer sites to provide his services.

PERFORMANCE CRITERIA

What performance criteria should be emphasized?

Other fundamental choices facing the layout planner concern *performance criteria*, which may include one or more of the following factors:

- customer satisfaction,
- level of capital investment,
- requirements for materials handling,
- ease of stockpicking,
- work environment and "atmosphere,"
- ease of equipment maintenance,
- employee and internal customer attitudes,
- amount of flexibility needed, and
- customer convenience and level of sales.

Managers must decide early in the process which factors to emphasize in order to come up with a good layout solution. In most cases, multiple criteria are used. For example, a warehouse manager may emphasize case in stockpicking, flexibility, and amount of space needed (capital investment).

CUSTOMER SATISFACTION. When customer contact (either external or internal) is high and the customer is present and actively involved when a service is being provided, customer satisfaction is a key performance measure. The layout uses "spatial language" to communicate the competitive priorities associated with the service. Customer loyalty, emotional connect, customer convenience, and level of sales can all be influenced by the layout. For example, a retail store manager may emphasize atmosphere, customer satisfaction, flexibility, and sales as the top performance criteria. Sales are particularly important to the layout of retail facilities, where managers place items with high-profitability per cubic foot of shelf space in the most prominent display areas and impulse-buy items near the entrance of the checkout counter. A good layout, as designed for The Pizza Connection case that appears later in this chapter, depends on how the various measures of customer satisfaction are met and how well it communicates the competitive priorities that the owner wants the customers to experience. Of course, capital expenditure and flexibility considerations also enter the equation.

CAPITAL INVESTMENT. Floor space, equipment needs, and inventory levels are assets that the firm buys or leases. These expenditures are an important criterion in all settings. If an office layout is to have partitions to increase privacy, the cost rises. Even increasing space for filing cabinets can add up. A four-drawer lateral file occupies about nine square feet, including the space needed to open it. At $25 per square foot, that translates into a floor space "rental" of $225 a year.

MATERIALS HANDLING. Relative locations of centers should restrict large flows to short distances. Centers between which frequent trips or interactions are required should be placed close to one another. In a manufacturing plant, this approach minimizes materials handling costs. In a warehouse, stockpicking costs are reduced by storing items typically needed for the same order next to one another. In a retail store, customer convenience improves if items are grouped predictably to minimize customer search and travel time. In an office, communication and cooperation often improve when people or departments that must interact frequently are located near one another, because telephone calls and memos can be poor substitutes for face-to-face communication. Spatial separation is one big reason why cross-functional coordination between departments can be challenging.

FLEXIBILITY. A flexible layout allows a firm to adapt quickly to changing customer needs and preferences and is best for many situations. **Layout flexibility** means either that the facility remains desirable after significant changes occur or that it can be easily and inexpensively adapted in response to changes. The changes can be in the mix of customers served by a store, goods made at a plant, space requirements in a warehouse, or organizational structure in an office. Using modular furniture and partitions, rather than permanent load-bearing walls, is one way to minimize the cost of office layout changes. So can having wide bays (fewer columns), heavy-duty floors, and extra electrical connections in a plant.

> **layout flexibility** The property of a facility to remain desirable after significant changes occur or to be easily and inexpensively adapted in response to changes.

For retailers, the height of flexibility is the kiosks that display a variety of novelty and specialty items on sale in the center aisles of malls. They have an ever-changing array of merchandise that transform once-utilitarian passageways into retailing hot spots. The kiosks are right where the customers have to walk and create a stream of impulse purchases. Unlike large retailers who are often locked into a product up to a year in advance, kiosk operations are better able to follow trends, such as Pokemon. If the fad lasts only a few months, that is fine for a temporary retailer. Over the past 15 years, seasonal and temporary carts, kiosks, and stores have ballooned into a $10 billion business.

OTHER CRITERIA. Other criteria that may be important include labor productivity, machine maintenance, work environment, and organizational structure. Labor productivity can be affected if certain workstations can be operated by common personnel in some layouts but not in others. Downtime spent waiting for materials can be caused by materials handling difficulties resulting from poor layout.

CREATING HYBRID LAYOUTS

When volumes are not high enough to justify dedicating a single line of multiple workers to a single customer type or product, managers still may be able to derive the benefits of line-flow layout— simpler materials handling, low setups, and reduced labor costs—by creating line-flow layouts in some portions of the facility. Two techniques for creating hybrid layouts are one-worker, multiple-machines (OWMM) cells and group technology (GT) cells. They are special types of cells, which we described earlier as a way to focus operations (see Chapter 3, "Process Design Strategy").

> Can some miniature line-flow layouts be created in a facility?

ONE WORKER, MULTIPLE MACHINES

If volumes are not sufficient to keep several workers busy on one production line, the manager might set up a line small enough to keep one worker busy. A one-person cell is the theory behind the **one-worker, multiple-machines (OWMM) cell**, in which a worker operates several different machines simultaneously to achieve a line flow. Having one worker operate several identical machines is not unusual. However, with an OWMM cell, several different machines are in the line.

> **one-worker, multiple-machines (OWMM) cell** A one-person cell in which a worker operates several different machines simultaneously to achieve a line flow.

FIGURE 7.4

One-Worker, Multiple-Machines (OWMM) Cell

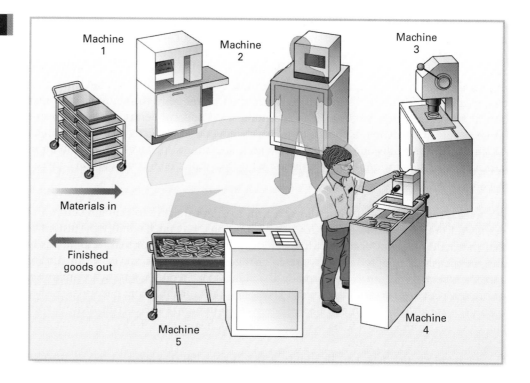

Figure 7.4 illustrates a five-machine OWMM cell that is being used to produce a flanged metal part, with the machines encircling one operator in the center. (A U shape also is common.) The operator moves around the circle, performing tasks (typically loading and unloading) that have not been automated. Different products or parts can be produced in an OWMM cell by changing the machine setups. If the setup on one machine is especially time-consuming for one part, management can add a duplicate machine to the cell for use whenever that part is being produced.

An OWMM arrangement reduces both inventory and labor requirements. Inventory is cut because, rather than piling up in queues, materials move directly into the next operation. Labor is cut because more work is automated. The addition of several low-cost automated devices can maximize the number of machines included in an OWMM arrangement: automatic tool changers, loaders and unloaders, start and stop devices, and fail-safe devices that detect defective parts or products. Japanese manufacturers are applying the OWMM concept widely because of their desire to achieve low inventories.

GROUP TECHNOLOGY

group technology (GT) An option for achieving line-flow layouts with low-volume processes; this technique creates cells not limited to just one worker and has a unique way of selecting work to be done by the cell.

A second option for achieving line-flow layouts with low-volume processes is **group technology (GT)**. This manufacturing technique creates cells not limited to just one worker and has a unique way of selecting work to be done by the cell. The GT method groups parts or products with similar characteristics into *families* and sets aside groups of machines for their production. Families may be based on size, shape, manufacturing or routing requirements, or demand. The goal is to identify a set of products with similar processing requirements and minimize machine changeover or setup. For example, all bolts might be assigned to the same family because they all require the same basic processing steps regardless of size or shape.

Once parts have been grouped into families, the next step is to organize the machine tools needed to perform the basic processes on these parts into separate cells. The machines in each cell require only minor adjustments to accommodate product changeovers from one part to the next in the same family. By simplifying product routings, GT cells reduce the time a job is in the shop. Queues of materials waiting to be worked on are shortened or eliminated. Frequently, materials handling is automated so that, after loading raw materials into the cell, a worker does not handle machined parts until the job has been completed.

Figure 7.5 compares process flows before and after creation of GT cells. Figure 7.5(a) shows a shop floor where machines are grouped according to function: lathing, milling, drilling, grinding, and assembly. After lathing, a part is moved to one of the milling machines, where it waits in line until it has a higher priority than any other job competing for the machine's capacity. When the milling operation on the part has been finished, the part is moved to a drilling machine, and so on. The queues can be long, creating significant time delays. Flows of materials are very jumbled because the parts being processed in any one area of the shop have so many different routings.

By contrast, the manager of the shop shown in Figure 7.5(b) has identified three product families that account for a majority of the firm's production. One family always requires two lathing operations followed by one operation at the milling machines. The second family always requires a milling operation followed by a grinding operation. The third family requires the use of a lathe, a milling machine, and a drill press. For simplicity, only the flows of parts assigned to these three families are shown. The remaining parts are produced at machines outside the cells and still have jumbled routings. Some equipment might have to be duplicated, as when a machine is required for one or more cells and for operations outside the cells. However, by creating three GT cells, the manager has definitely created more line flows and simplified routings.

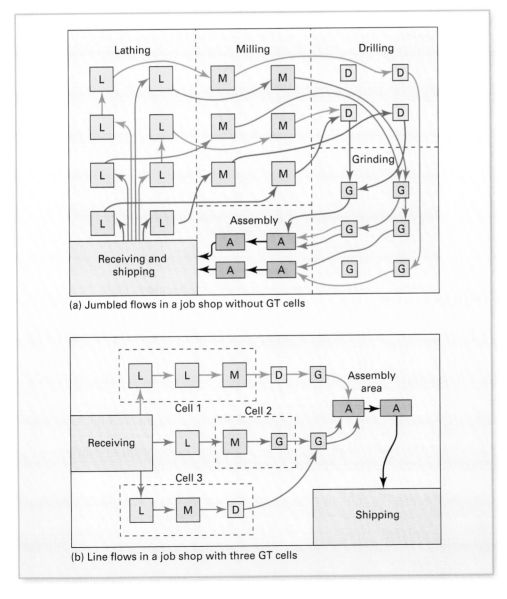

(a) Jumbled flows in a job shop without GT cells

(b) Line flows in a job shop with three GT cells

FIGURE 7.5

Process Flows Before and After the Use of GT Cells

Source: Groover, Mikell P. *Automation, Production Systems, and Computer-Aided Manufacturing.* Englewood Cliffs, NJ: Prentice Hall, 1980, pp. 540–541. Reprinted by permission.

DESIGNING FLEXIBLE-FLOW LAYOUTS

How can a better flexible-flow layout be found for a facility?

The approach to designing a layout depends on whether a flexible-flow layout or a line-flow layout has been chosen. A fixed-position format basically eliminates the layout problem, wheres the design of the hybrid layout partially uses flexible-flow layout principles and partially uses line-flow layout principles.

Flexible-flow layout involves three basic steps, whether the design is for a new layout or for revising an existing layout: (1) gather information, (2) develop a block plan, and (3) design a detailed layout.

STEP 1: GATHER INFORMATION

The Office of Budget Management (OBM), which is a major division in a large state government, consists of 120 employees assigned to six different departments. It is one of several divisions occupying a relatively new office tower. This building was constructed to bring together, under one roof, most of the divisions in the state government. It was justified also by the substantial cost reduction that resulted from vacating leased space elsewhere. The building was designed to accommodate growth expectations, so that more space was allocated to OBM than justified by its original size. Currently, however, workloads have expanded to the extent that 30 new employees must be hired and somehow housed in the space allocated to OBM. While changing the layout, it also makes sense to review the layout to make sure that it is arranged as effectively as possible. The goal is to improve communication among people who must interact and to create a good work environment. Three types of information are needed to begin designing the revised layout for OBM: (1) space requirements by center, (2) available space, and (3) closeness factors.

SPACE REQUIREMENTS BY CENTER. OBM has grouped its processes into six different departments: administration, social services, institutions, accounting, education, and internal audit. The exact space requirements of each department, in square feet, are as follows.

Department	Area Needed (ft^2)
1. Administration	3,500
2. Social services	2,600
3. Institutions	2,400
4. Accounting	1,600
5. Education	1,500
6. Internal audit	3,400
Total	15,000

The layout designer must tie space requirements to capacity and staffing plans; calculate the specific equipment and space needs for each center; and allow circulation space, such as aisles and the like. At OBM, a way must be found to include all 150 employees in its assigned area and minimize adverse reactions to space reductions or relocations. Consulting with the managers and employees involved can help avoid excessive resistance to change and make the transition smooth.

block plan *A plan that allocates space and indicates placement of each department.*

AVAILABLE SPACE. A **block plan** allocates space and indicates placement of each department. To describe a new facility layout, the plan need only provide the facility's dimensions and space allocations. When an existing facility layout is being modified, the current block plan also is needed. OBM's available space is 150 feet by 100 feet, or 15,000 square feet. The designer could begin the design by dividing the total amount of space into six equal blocks (2,500 square feet each), even though education needs only 1,500 square feet and administration needs 3,500 square feet. The equal-space approximation shown in Figure 7.6 is sufficient until the detailed layout stage, when larger departments (such as administration) are assigned more space than smaller departments.

CLOSENESS FACTORS. The layout designer must also know which centers need to be located close to one another. The following table shows OBM's **closeness matrix**, which gives a measure of the relative importance of each pair of centers being located close together. The metric used depends on the type of processes involved and the organizational setting. It can be a qualitative judgment on a scale from 0 to 10 that the manager uses to account for multiple performance criteria, as in the OBM's case. Only the right-hand portion of the matrix is used. The closeness factors are indicators of the need for proximity based on an analysis of information flows and the need for face-to-face meetings. They give clues as to which departments should be located close together. For example, the most important interaction is between the administration and internal audit departments for OBM, with a score of 10. This closeness factor is given in the first row and last column. Thus, the designer should locate departments 1 and 6 close together, which is not the arrangement in the current layout. Taking into account entries in both the columns and rows, there are five factor scores for each section. For the general case of the number of centers (n) in a layout, there are $n - 1$ closeness factors found either in the row or column assigned to the center.

closeness matrix A table that gives a measure of the relative importance of each pair of centers being located close together.

| | Closeness Factors | | | | | |
Department	1	2	3	4	5	6
1. Administration	–	3	6	5	6	10
2. Social services		–	8	1	1	
3. Institutions			–	3	9	
4. Accounting				–	2	
5. Education					–	1
6. Internal audit						–

At a manufacturing plant, the closeness factor could be the number of trips (or some other measure of materials movement) between each pair of centers per day. This information can be gleaned by conducting a statistical sampling, polling supervisors and materials handlers, or using the routings and ordering frequencies for typical items made at the plant.

OTHER CONSIDERATIONS. Finally, the information gathered for OBM includes performance criteria that depend on the *absolute* location of a department. OBM has two criteria based on absolute location.

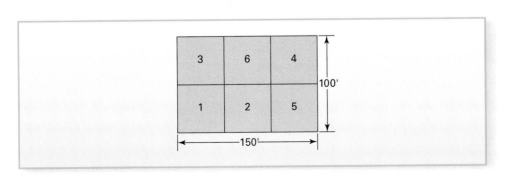

FIGURE 7.6

Current Block Plan for the Office of Budget Management

1. Education (department 5) should remain where it is because it is next to the office library.
2. Administration (department 1) should remain where it is because that location has the largest conference room, which administration uses very often. Relocating the conference room would be very costly.

Noise levels and management preference are other potential sources of performance criteria that depend on absolute location. The closeness matrix cannot reflect these criteria because it reflects only *relative* location considerations. The layout designer must list these criteria separately.

STEP 2: DEVELOP A BLOCK PLAN

The second step in layout design is to develop a block plan that best satisfies performance criteria and area requirements. The most elementary way to do so is by trial and error. Because success depends on the designer's ability to spot patterns in the data, this approach does not guarantee the selection of the best or even a nearly best solution. When supplemented by the use of a computer to evaluate solutions, however, research shows that such an approach compares quite favorably with more sophisticated computerized techniques.

EXAMPLE 7.1   Developing a Block Plan

Develop an acceptable block plan for the Office of Budget Management, using trial and error. The goal is to locate the departments that have the greatest interaction between them (largest closeness factor) as close to each other as possible.

SOLUTION

A good place to start is with the largest closeness ratings (say, 8 and above). Beginning with the largest factor scores and working down the list, you might plan to locate departments as follows:

   a. Departments 1 and 6 close together,
   b. Departments 3 and 5 close together,
   c. Departments 2 and 3 close together.

Departments 1 and 5 should remain at their current locations because of the "other considerations."

If after several attempts you cannot meet all three requirements, drop one or more and try again. If you can meet all three easily, add more (such as for interactions below 8).

The block plan in Figure 7.7 shows a trial-and-error solution that satisfies all three requirements. We started by keeping departments 1 and 5 in their original locations. As the first requirement is to locate departments 1 and 6 close to each other, we put 6 in the upper-left corner of the

---

FIGURE 7.7

Proposed Block Plan

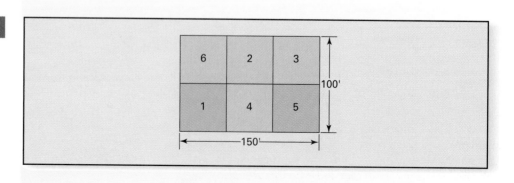

layout. The second requirement is to have departments 3 and 5 close to each other, so we placed 3 in the space just above the 5, and so on.

DECISION POINT. This solution fell into place easily for this particular problem, but it might not be the best layout. Management wants to consider several alternative layouts before making a final choice and needs some measure of effectiveness with which to compare the alternative layouts.

APPLYING THE WEIGHTED-DISTANCE METHOD

When *relative* locations are a primary concern, such as for effective information flow, communication, material handling, and stockpicking, the weighted-distance method can be used to compare alternative block plans. The **weighted-distance method** is a mathematical model used to evaluate flexible-flow layouts based on proximity factors. A similar approach, called the *load-distance method*, can be used to evaluate facility locations (see Chapter 10, "Location"). The objective is to select a layout (or facility location) that minimizes the total weighted distances. The distance between two points is expressed by assigning the points to grid coordinates on a block diagram or map. An alternative approach is to use time rather than distance.

weighted-distance method
A mathematical model used to evaluate flexible-flow layouts based on proximity factors.

DISTANCE MEASURES. For a rough calculation, which is all that is needed for the weighted-distance method, either a Euclidean or rectilinear distance measure may be used. **Euclidean distance** is the straight-line distance, or shortest possible path, between two points. To calculate this distance, we create a graph. The distance between two points, say, points A and B, is

$$d_{AB} = \sqrt{(x_A - x_B)^2 + (y_A - y_B)^2}$$

where

$$d_{AB} = \text{distance between points } A \text{ and } B$$
$$x_A = x\text{-coordinate of point } A$$
$$y_A = y\text{-coordinate of point } A$$
$$x_B = x\text{-coordinate of point } B$$
$$y_B = y\text{-coordinate of point } B$$

Euclidean distance The straight-line distance, or shortest possible path, between two points.

Rectilinear distance measures distance between two points with a series of 90-degree turns, as along city blocks. The distance traveled in the *x*-direction is the absolute value of the difference in *x*-coordinates. Adding this result to the absolute value of the difference in the *y*-coordinates gives

$$d_{AB} = |x_A - x_B| + |y_A - y_B|$$

rectilinear distance The distance between two points with a series of 90-degree turns, as along city blocks.

For assistance in calculating distances using either measure, see Tutor 7.1 in OM Explorer.

TUTOR 7.1

Tutor 7.1 on the Student CD-ROM provides an example to calculate both Euclidean and rectilinear distance measures.

CALCULATING A WEIGHTED-DISTANCE SCORE. The designer seeks to minimize the weighted-distance (*wd*) score by locating centers that have high-closeness ratings close together.

To calculate a layout's *wd* score, we use either of the distance measures and simply multiply the proximity scores by the distances between centers. The sum of those products becomes the layout's final *wd* score—the lower the better. The location of a center is defined by its *x*-coordinate and *y*-coordinate.

EXAMPLE 7.2   Calculating the Weighted-Distance Score

ACTIVE MODEL 7.1

Active Model 7.1 on the Student CD-ROM allows evaluation of the impact of swapping OBM departmental positions.

How much better, in terms of the *wd* score, is the proposed block plan that was shown in Figure 7.7 than the current plan that was shown in Figure 7.6? Use the rectilinear distance measure.

SOLUTION

The accompanying table lists each pair of departments that has a nonzero closeness factor in the closeness matrix. For the third column, calculate the rectilinear distances between the departments in the current layout. For example, departments 3 and 5 in Figure 7.6 are in the upper-left corner and bottom-right corner of the building, respectively. The distance between the centers of these blocks is three units (two horizontally and one vertically). For the fourth column, we multiply the weights (closeness factors) by the distances, and then add the results for a total *wd* score of 112 for the current plan. Similar calculations for the proposed plan in Figure 7.7 produce a *wd* score of only 82. For example, between departments 3 and 5 is just one unit of distance (one vertically and zero horizontally).

DEPARTMENT PAIR	CLOSENESS FACTOR (*w*)	CURRENT PLAN DISTANCE (*d*)	CURRENT PLAN WEIGHTED-DISTANCE SCORE (*wd*)	PROPOSED PLAN DISTANCE (*d*)	PROPOSED PLAN WEIGHTED-DISTANCE SCORE (*wd*)
1, 2	3	1	3	2	6
1, 3	6	1	6	3	18
1, 4	5	3	15	1	5
1, 5	6	2	12	2	12
1, 6	10	2	20	1	10
2, 3	8	2	16	1	8
2, 4	1	2	2	1	1
2, 5	1	1	1	2	2
3, 4	3	2	6	2	6
3, 5	9	3	27	1	9
4, 5	2	1	2	1	2
5, 6	1	2	2	3	3
			Total **112**		Total **82**

To be exact, we could multiply the two *wd* total scores by 50 because each unit of distance represents 50 feet. However, the relative difference between the two totals remains unchanged.

DECISION POINT   The *wd* score for the proposed layout makes a sizeable drop from 112 to 82, but management is not sure the improvement outweighs the cost of relocating four of the six departments (that is, all departments but 1 and 5).

Although the *wd* score for the proposed layout in Example 7.2 represents an almost 27 percent improvement, the designer may be able to do better. Furthermore, the designer must determine whether the revised layout is worth the cost of relocating four of the six departments. If relocation costs are too high, a less-expensive proposal must be found.

OM Explorer can help identify some more attractive proposals. The output in Figure 7.8 shows the *wd* score for the proposed plan and offers some clues about a better layout. Department pairs with the largest closeness factors are listed first, allowing you to check whether these strongest interactions are between departments closest together. The lowest possible distance is one for any department pair.

Figure 7.8 shows that much of the 82 score comes from relationship between departments 1 and 3 (18). This department pair is the first going down the list from the top that currently has a distance greater than one. The next department pair is departments 1 and 5, which currently has two units of distance between them. One option that puts department 1 closer to departments 3 and 5 is to switch the locations of departments 3 and 4. The output in Figure 7.9 indicates that the *wd* score for this second revision not only drops to 80, but requires that only three departments must be

FIGURE 7.8

First Proposed Block Plan of Figure 7.7 (Analyzed with Flexible-Flow Layout Solver)

Solver - Flexible-Flow Layout

● Rectilinear Distances   ○ Euclidean Distances

Department Pair	Closeness Factor	Distance	Score
1,6	10	1	10
3,5	9	1	9
2,3	8	1	8
1,3	6	3	18
1,5	6	2	12
1,4	5	1	5
1,2	3	2	6
3,4	3	2	6
4,5	2	1	2
2,4	1	1	1
2,5	1	2	2
5,6	1	3	3
Total			82

Block plan:

6	2	3
1	4	5

relocated compared with the original layout in Figure 7.6. Perhaps this second proposal is the best compromise.

STEP 3: DESIGN A DETAILED LAYOUT

After finding a satisfactory block plan, the layout designer translates it into a detailed representation, showing the exact size and shape of each center; the arrangement of elements (e.g., desks, machines, and storage areas); and the location of aisles, stairways, and other service space. These visual representations can be two-dimensional drawings, three-dimensional models, or computer-aided graphics. This step helps decision makers discuss the proposal and problems that might otherwise be overlooked. Such visual representations can be particularly important when evaluating high customer-contact processes, such as for The Pizza Connection case at the end of this chapter.

FIGURE 7.9

Second Proposed Block Plan of Figure 7.7 (Analyzed with Flexible-Flow Layout Solver)

Solver - Flexible-Flow Layout

● Rectilinear Distances   ○ Euclidean Distances

Department Pair	Closeness Factor	Distance	Score
1,6	10	1	10
3,5	9	1	9
2,3	8	1	8
1,3	6	1	6
1,5	6	2	12
1,4	5	3	15
1,2	3	2	6
3,4	3	2	6
4,5	2	1	2
2,4	1	1	1
2,5	1	2	2
5,6	1	3	3
Total			80

Block plan:

6	2	4
1	3	5

OTHER DECISION SUPPORT TOOLS

The spreadsheet approach of OM Explorer is a useful tool, and counts on the power of the human mind to recognize patterns in the data. However, larger problems can get quite complex. For example, a facility with 20 departments has 2.43×10^{18} possible solutions if each of the 20 departments can be assigned to any of the 20 locations. Several more advanced software packages are now available for designing more complex flexible-flow layouts.

The **automated layout design program (ALDEP)** is a computer software package that constructs a good layout from scratch, adding one department at a time. Being a heuristic method, it generally provides good—but not necessarily the best—solutions. The program picks the first department randomly. The second department must have a strong closeness factor with the first, the third must have a strong rating with the second, and so on. When no department has a strong rating with the department just added, the system again randomly selects the next department. The program computes a score (somewhat different from the wd score used earlier) for each solution generated and prints out the layouts having the best scores for the manager's consideration.

Another powerful computer software package, the **computerized relative allocation of facilities technique (CRAFT)**, is a heuristic method that begins with the closeness matrix and an initial block layout. Working from an initial block plan (or starting solution), CRAFT evaluates all possible paired exchanges of departments. The exchange that causes the greatest reduction in the total wd score is incorporated into a new starting solution. This process continues until no other exchanges can be found to reduce the wd score. The starting solution at this point is also the final solution and is printed out with the wd score.

WAREHOUSE LAYOUTS

Warehouses are one of the invisible nerve centers of e-commerce. Warehouses are similar to manufacturing plants in that materials are moved between activity centers. Much of the preceding discussion on flexible-flow layouts applies to warehouses. However, warehouses are a special case because a warehouse's central process is one of storage. Basically, a warehouse receives items at the dock and moves them to a storage area. Later, stockpickers withdraw inventory to fill individual customer orders.

Various options are available for warehouse layouts. First, various ways of utilizing space offer additional layout options. For example, an 82,000-square-foot, 32-foot-high racked warehouse can handle the same volume as a 107,000-square-foot, low-ceilinged warehouse, with the higher stockpicking productivity of the high-ceilinged warehouse offsetting the added rack and equipment costs. Another space-saving design assigns all incoming materials to the nearest available space, rather than to a predetermined area where all like items are clustered. A computer system tracks the location of each item. When it is time to retrieve an item, the system prints its location on the shipping bill and identifies the shortest route for the stockpicker. Canadiana Outdoor Products, in Brampton, Ontario, introduced a computer system with terminals mounted on lift trucks. This arrangement allows drivers to track the exact location and contents of each storage bin in the warehouse. With this new system, Canadiana can handle quadrupled sales with less storage space.

Second, different layout patterns offer still more layout options. The most basic layout pattern is the *out-and-back pattern,* as illustrated in Figure 7.10. Items are picked one at a time, with the stockpicker traveling back and forth from the dock to

automated layout design program (ALDEP) A computer software package that constructs a good layout from scratch, adding one department at a time.

computerized relative allocation of facilities technique (CRAFT) A heuristic method that begins with the closeness matrix and an initial block layout, and makes a series of paired exchanges of departments to find a better block plan.

What type of layout makes sense for a warehouse?

FIGURE 7.10

Out-and-Back Warehouse Layout

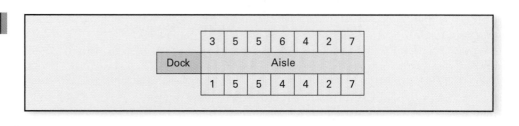

Three Views of the Layout at a Modern Warehouse that Holds About 16 Million Books in Inventory and Processes Between 2,000 and 5,000 Orders per Day

Cases of the fastest-selling titles are stacked outside the flow racks in the "golden zone," where the 80 fastest-selling titles are stored. These titles comprise about 50 percent of all shipments. Whole cases are picked here in response to specific orders.

A floor-level conveyor transports boxes of books to the packaging area. There, the boxes pass over a computerized weight-in-motion scale, which compares the total weight of the package to the sum of weights of individual titles.

Returned books are temporarily sorted in the 5,400 locations in the returns staging carousel. The number of returns is surprisingly large, comprising about 12.5 percent of the overall volume. Returns from schools and colleges occur when bookstores order more books than they actually sell to students.

the storage area. In Figure 7.10, storage area 1 could be where toasters are stored, storage area 2 could be for air conditioners, and so forth. Some items require more space than others, depending on their size and inventory requirements. In general, the high-volume items are stored closest to the dock with this layout pattern. In a *route collection system*, the stockpicker selects a variety of items to be shipped to a customer. In a *batch-picking system*, the stockpicker gathers the quantity of an item required to satisfy a group of customer orders to be shipped in the same truck or rail car. Finally, in the *zone system*, the stockpicker gathers all needed items in her assigned zone and places them on a powered conveyor line. Figure 7.11 illustrates the zone system for a warehouse. The conveyor line consists of five feeder lines and one trunk line. When the merchandise arrives at the control station, an operator directs it to the correct tractor trailer for outbound shipment. The advantage of the zone system is that pickers need not travel throughout the warehouse to fill orders. They are responsible only for their own zones.

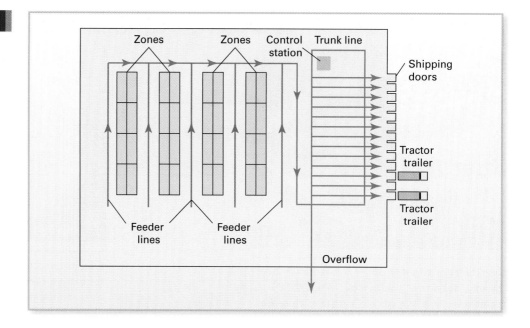

OFFICE LAYOUTS

What is the best trade-off between proximity and privacy for an office layout?

More than 40 percent of the U.S. workforce is employed in offices, and office layout can affect both productivity and the quality of work life. In a recent survey, three-fourths of 1,400 employees polled said that productivity could be raised by improvements in their work environments.

PROXIMITY. Accessibility to coworkers and supervisors can enhance communication and develop mutual interest. Conversations tend to become more formal as individuals are placed farther apart. The famous Hawthorne study in 1939 showed that the physical work setting influences group formation. In the study, management used spatial language to tell workers in the experimental group that they were important. Management changed both absolute and relative locations of the workers by moving them to a separate room and away from the watchful eyes of a supervisor. The revised layout facilitated contact between workers and the setting of group norms. More recent studies confirm that proximity to others can help clarify what is expected of an employee on the job and in other ways.

Most formal procedures for designing office layouts try to maximize the proximity of workers whose jobs require frequent interaction. This approach can be implemented with the weighted-distance method. Certain procedures can be used to identify natural clusters of workers to be treated as a center in a block plan. The goal of such approaches is to design layouts around work flows and communication patterns.

PRIVACY. Another key factor in office design—and one that is somewhat culturally dependent—is privacy. Outside disruptions and crowding can hurt a worker's performance. At Sperry Rand's and McDonald's world headquarters, employee reactions to open offices were favorable. However, when a newspaper company tried to increase worker proximity by going from private work spaces to an open-plan office, the results were disappointing. Employees felt as if they were in a fishbowl and that they had little control over their environment. Studies at several state government departments revealed a strong link between privacy and satisfaction with the supervisor and the job.

OPTIONS IN OFFICE LAYOUT. Providing both proximity and privacy for employees poses a dilemma for management. Proximity is gained by opening up the work area. Privacy is gained by more liberal space standards, baffled ceilings, doors, partitions, and thick carpeting that absorbs noise—expensive features that reduce layout flexibility. Thus, management must generally arrive at a compromise between proximity and

Office space at Microsoft's Redman, Washington, facility is designed to support the variety of needs of its employees. Software developers need private, quiet space while marketing personnel need open spaces conducive to face-to-face interactions.

privacy. No single type of space fits all workers. For example, Microsoft in Redmond, Washington, has found that software developers do their best work in a private, quiet space. But its sales and marketing people work in a mixture of private and open spaces; the emphasis is on facilitating interactions among sales and marketing personnel and providing good spaces for meetings with customers. Its product support offices are about 90 percent open space.

Four different approaches are available: traditional layouts, office landscaping, activity settings, and electronic cottages. The choice requires an understanding of work requirements, the workforce itself, and top management's philosophy of work.

Traditional layouts call for closed offices for management and those employees whose work requires privacy and open areas (or bullpens) for all others. The resulting layout may be characterized by long hallways lined with closed doors, producing considerable isolation, and by open areas filled uniformly with rows of desks. In traditional layouts, each person has a designated place. With these layouts, location, size, and furnishings signify the person's status in the organization.

An approach developed in Germany during the late 1950s puts everyone (including top management) in an open area. The headquarters of Johnson Wax is designed with open offices. So is Hewlett-Packard's Waltham, Massachusetts, plant. Shoulder-high dividers partition the space. The idea is to achieve closer cooperation among employees at *all* levels. However, the corporate nurse still keeps earplugs on hand for employees bothered by noise. An extension of this concept is called *office landscaping:* Attractive plants, screens, and portable partitions increase privacy and cluster or separate groups. Movable workstations and accessories help maintain flexibility. Because the workstations (or cubicles) are only semiprivate, employees might have trouble concentrating or might feel uncomfortable trying to hold sensitive discussions. Construction costs are as much as 40 percent less than for traditional layouts, and rearrangement costs are less still.

Activity settings represent a relatively new concept for achieving both proximity and privacy. The full range of work needs is covered by multiple workplaces, including a library, teleconferencing facility, reception area, conference room, special graphics area, and shared terminals. Employees move from one activity setting to the next as their work requires during the day. Each person also gets a small, personal office as a home base.

Some futurists expect more and more employees to work at home or in neighborhood offices connected to the main office by computer. Called *telecommuting* or *electronic cottages,* this approach represents a modern-day version of the cottage industries that existed prior to the Industrial Revolution. Besides saving on commuting time, it offers flexibility in work schedules. Many working men and women with children, for example, prefer such flexibility. More than nine million Americans already have a taste of this arrangement, working at least part of the week at home. However, telecommuting can have drawbacks, such as lack of equipment, too many family disruptions, and too few opportunities for socialization and politicking. Some managers at Hartford Insurance complained that they could not supervise—much less get to know—employees they could not see. Managerial Practice 7.2 discusses the telecommuting policy of two other companies, Pacific Bell and DKM, Inc.

MANAGERIAL PRACTICE 7.2

TELECOMMUTING AT PACIFIC BELL AND DKM, INC.

Pacific Bell

Pacific Bell (www.pacbell.com), a subsidiary of Pacific Telesis Group, in turn a subsidiary of SBC Communications, has a formal telecommuting policy. More than 1,000 of its managers work fairly regularly from sites other than their primary offices. The company opened two full-blown satellite offices four years ago, each able to accommodate 18 managers who communicate with coworkers and the outside world via personal computers, modems, facsimile machines, copying equipment, and laser printers.

One of the managers in sales support, for example, works at a neighborhood satellite just 15 minutes from his home. He used to make a 26-mile commute to the downtown Los Angeles office, which took an hour when everything went well and up to 2.5 hours when it rained. Free from the time-consuming commute and the distractions of Pacific Telesis's main office, he feels that he is functioning more efficiently. He prefers working at an office to working at home, where there are distractions, such as doing dishes, mowing the lawn, or seeing what's in the refrigerator. Like other sateliite workers, he visits the main office from time to time.

DKM, Inc.

DKM, Inc. (www. dkminc.com) is a manufacturing consulting firm in the Los Angeles basin. The first thing a new employee receives is a notebook computer—a symbol of the firm's commitment to virtual work arrangements. Especially considering the Los Angeles traffic snarls, it does not make sense to have employees come to the office if the client is 10 minutes from home. The firm pays for a second phone line in each employee's home office and, if necessary, springs for a printer or scanner. As a result, DKM's consultants can meet at a manufacturer's plant in the morning and finish up their day's work at home in the afternoon. There are additional Web-based services that help bring together far-flung employees, such as free Web-scheduling service SchedulePlus. Among other things, telecommuting employees use the site to reserve time in the office conference room and avoid scheduling conflicts. Others bounce their ideas around with others in real time using the free ICQ Internet chat service (www.placeware. com) or the Web conferencing service Place-Ware (www. icq. com). For a fee of $400 annually per seat at the "virtual conference," you can present PowerPoint slides on a common Web page that all meeting participants can access. It also lets you receive answers to yes or no questions in real time to gauge the thoughts of others.

Virtual work arrangements are becoming popular in consulting firms. Here an employee at DKM receives her new laptop computer and instructions on how to use the firm's Web services.

Source: "Tools of the Remote Trade." *Business Week* (March 27, 2000), p. F20.

DESIGNING LINE-FLOW LAYOUTS

Line-flow layouts raise management issues entirely different from those of flexible-flow layouts. Often called a production or assembly line, a line-flow layout arranges workstations in sequence. The product moves from one station to the next until its completion at the end of the line. Typically, one worker operates each station, performing repetitive tasks. Little inventory is built up between stations, so stations cannot operate independently. Thus, the line is only as fast as its slowest workstation. In other words, if the slowest station takes five minutes per customer or unit, the line's fastest possible output is one customer or unit every five minutes.

How can a better line-flow layout for a process be determined?

LINE BALANCING

Line balancing is the assignment of work to stations in a line so as to achieve the desired output rate with the smallest number of workstations. Normally, one worker is assigned to a station. Thus, the line that produces at the desired pace with the fewest workers is the most efficient one. Line balancing must be performed when a line is set up initially, when a line is rebalanced to change its hourly output rate, or when product or process changes. The goal is to obtain workstations with well-balanced workloads (e.g., every station takes roughly five minutes per customer or unit processed).

The analyst begins by separating the work into **work elements,** which are the smallest units of work that can be performed independently. The analyst then obtains the time standard (see Supplement H, *"Measuring Output Rate,"* on the Student CD-ROM) for each element and identifies the work elements, called **immediate predecessors,** that must be done before the next element can begin.

line balancing The assignment of work to stations in a line so as to achieve the desired output rate with the smallest number of workstations.

work elements The smallest units of work that can be performed independently.

immediate predecessors Work elements that must be done before the next element can begin.

PRECEDENCE DIAGRAM. Most lines must satisfy some technological precedence requirements; that is, certain work elements must be done before the next can begin. However, most lines also allow for some latitude and more than one sequence of operations. To help you visualize immediate predecessors better, let us run through the construction of a **precedence diagram.**[2] We denote the work elements by circles, with the time required to perform the work shown below each circle. Arrows lead

precedence diagram A diagram that allows one to visualize immediate predecessors better; work elements are denoted by circles, with the time required to perform the work shown below each circle.

Factory workers in Dong Guan, Guangdong Province, China, assemble electronic boards. Each worker performs the same set of tasks at her station on each electronic board that is assembled.

---

[2]Precedence relationships and precedence diagrams are important in the entirely different context of project scheduling (see Chapter 8, "Planning and Managing Projects").

from immediate predecessors to the next work element. Example 7.3 illustrates a manufacturing process, but a back office with a line-flow process can be approached in a similar way.

EXAMPLE 7.3   Constructing a Precedence Diagram

Green Grass, Inc., a manufacturer of lawn and garden equipment, is designing an assembly line to produce a new fertilizer spreader, the Big Broadcaster. Using the following information on the production process, construct a precedence diagram for the Big Broadcaster.

WORK ELEMENT	DESCRIPTION	TIME (sec)	IMMEDIATE PREDECESSOR(S)
A	Bolt leg frame to hopper	40	None
B	Insert impeller shaft	30	A
C	Attach axle	50	A
D	Attach agitator	40	B
E	Attach drive wheel	6	B
F	Attach free wheel	25	C
G	Mount lower post	15	C
H	Attach controls	20	D, E
I	Mount nameplate	18	F, G
		Total 244	

SOLUTION

Figure 7.12 shows the complete diagram. We begin with work element A, which has no immediate predecessors. Next, we add elements B and C, for which element A is the only immediate predecessor. After entering time standards and arrows showing precedence, we add elements D and E, and so on. The diagram simplifies interpretation. Work element F, for example, can be done anywhere on the line after element C is completed. However, element I must await completion of elements F and G.

DECISION POINT   Management now has enough information to develop a line-flow layout that clusters work elements to form workstations, with a goal being to balance the workloads and, in the process, minimize the number of workstations required.

What should be a line's output rate?

DESIRED OUTPUT RATE.   The goal of line balancing is to match the output rate to the staffing or production plan. For example, if the plan calls for 4,000 units (customers or products) per week and the line operates 80 hours per week, the desired output rate ideally would be 50 units (4,000/80) per hour. Matching output to demand ensures on-time delivery and prevents buildup of unwanted inventory or customer

FIGURE 7.12

Precedence Diagram for Assembling the Big Broadcaster

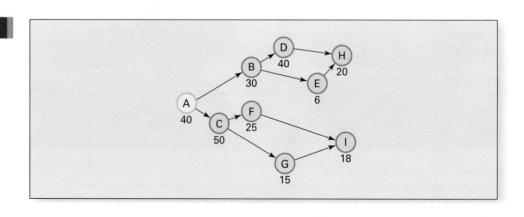

delays. However, managers should avoid rebalancing a line too frequently because each time a line is rebalanced many workers' jobs on the line must be redesigned, temporarily hurting productivity and sometimes even requiring a new detailed layout for some stations.

CYCLE TIME. After determining the desired output rate for a line, the analyst can calculate the line's cycle time. A line's **cycle time** is the maximum time allowed for work on a unit at each station.[3] If the time required for work elements at a station exceeds the line's cycle time, the station will be a bottleneck, preventing the line from reaching its desired output rate. The target cycle time is the reciprocal of the desired hourly output rate:

$$c = \frac{1}{r}$$

where

c = cycle time in hours per unit

r = desired output rate in units per hour

cycle time The maximum time allowed for work on a unit at each station.

For example, if the line's desired output rate is 60 units per hour, the cycle time is $c = 1/60$ hour per unit, or one minute.

THEORETICAL MINIMUM. To achieve the desired output rate, managers use line balancing to assign every work element to a station, making sure to satisfy all precedence requirements and to minimize the number of stations, n, formed. If each station is operated by a different worker, minimizing n also maximizes worker productivity. Perfect balance is achieved when the sum of the work-element times at each station equals the cycle time, c, and no station has any idle time. For example, if the sum of each station's work-element times is one minute, which is also the cycle time, there is perfect balance. Although perfect balance usually is unachievable in practice, owing to the unevenness of work-element times and the inflexibility of precedence requirements, it sets a benchmark, or goal, for the smallest number of stations possible. The **theoretical minimum (TM)** for the number of stations is

$$\text{TM} = \frac{\Sigma t}{c}$$

where

Σt = total time required to assemble each unit (the sum of all work-element standard times)

Σc = cycle time

theoretical minimum (TM) A benchmark or goal for the smallest number of stations possible, where the total time required to assemble each unit (the sum of all work-element standard times) is divided by the cycle time.

For example, if the sum of the work-element times is 15 minutes and the cycle time is 1 minute, TM = 15/1, or 15 stations. Any fractional values obtained for TM are rounded up because fractional stations are impossible.

IDLE TIME, EFFICIENCY, AND BALANCE DELAY. Minimizing n automatically ensures (1) minimal idle time, (2) maximal efficiency, and (3) minimal balance delay. Idle time is the total unproductive time for all stations in the assembly of each unit:

$$\text{Idle time} = nc - \Sigma t$$

---

[3]Except in the context of line balancing, *cycle time* has a different meaning. It is the elapsed time between starting and completing a job. Some researchers and practitioners prefer the term *lead time*.

where

$$n = \text{number of stations}$$

$$c = \text{cycle time}$$

$$\Sigma t = \text{total standard time required to assemble each unit}$$

Efficiency is the ratio of productive time to total time, expressed as a percent:

$$\text{Efficiency(\%)} = \frac{\Sigma t}{nc}(100)$$

balance delay The amount by which efficiency falls short of 100 percent.

Balance delay is the amount by which efficiency falls short of 100 percent:

$$\text{Balance delay(\%)} = 100 - \text{Efficiency}$$

As long as c is fixed, we can optimize all three goals by minimizing n.

EXAMPLE 7.4   Calculating the Cycle Time, Theoretical Minimum, and Efficiency

TUTOR 7.2

Tutor 7.2 on the Student CD-ROM provides another example to calculate these line-balancing measures.

Green Grass's plant manager has just received marketing's latest forecasts of Big Broadcaster sales for the next year. She wants its production line to be designed to make 2,400 spreaders per week for at least the next three months. The plant will operate 40 hours per week.

   a. What should be the line's cycle time?
   b. What is the smallest number of workstations that she could hope for in designing the line for this cycle time?
   c. Suppose that she finds a solution that requires only five stations. What would be the line's efficiency?

SOLUTION

   a. First convert the desired output rate (2,400 units per week) to an hourly rate by dividing the weekly output rate by 40 hours per week to get $r = 60$ units per hour. Then the cycle time is

$$c = \frac{1}{r} = \frac{1}{60} \text{ hour/unit} = 1 \text{ minute/unit}$$

   b. Now calculate the theoretical minimum for the number of stations by dividing the total time, Σt, by the *cycle* time, $c = 1$ minute $= 60$ seconds. Assuming perfect balance, we have

$$\text{TM} = \frac{\Sigma t}{c} = \frac{244 \text{ seconds}}{60 \text{ seconds}} = 4.067 \quad \text{or} \quad 5 \text{ stations}$$

   c. Now calculate the efficiency of a five-station solution, assuming for now that one can be found:

$$\text{Efficiency(\%)} = \frac{\Sigma t}{nc}(100) = \frac{244}{5(60)}(100) = 81.3\%$$

DECISION POINT Thus, if the manager finds a solution with five stations, that is the minimum number of stations possible. However, the efficiency (sometimes called the *theoretical maximum efficiency*) will be only 81.3 percent. Perhaps the line should be operated less than 40 hours per week and the employees transferred to other kinds of work when the line does not operate.

FINDING A SOLUTION. Often, many assembly-line solutions are possible, even for such simple problems as Green Grass's. As for flexible-flow layouts, computer assistance is available. For example, one software package considers every feasible combination of work elements that does not violate precedence or cycle-time requirements. The combination that minimizes the station's idle time is selected. If any work elements remain unassigned, a second station is formed, and so on.

The approach that we use here is even simpler. We select a work element from a list of candidates and assign it to a station. We repeat this process until all stations have been formed, using k as a counter for the station being formed.

Step 1. Start with station $k = 1$. Make a list of candidate work elements to assign to station k. Each candidate must satisfy three conditions.

1. It has not yet been assigned to this or any previous station.
2. All its predecessors have been assigned to this or a previous station.
3. Its time does not exceed the station's idle time, which accounts for all work elements already assigned. If no work elements have been assigned, the station's idle time equals the cycle time.

If no such candidates can be found, go to step 4.

Step 2. Pick a candidate. Two decision rules are commonly used for selecting from the candidate list.

1. Pick the candidate with the *longest work-element time*. This heuristic rule assigns as quickly as possible those work elements most difficult to fit into a station and saves work elements having shorter times for fine tuning the solution.
2. Pick the candidate having the *largest number of followers*. Figure 7.12 shows, for example, that work element C has three followers and E has one follower. This rule helps keep options open for forming subsequent stations. Otherwise, precedence requirements may leave only a few possible sequences of work elements, all causing an unnecessary amount of station idle time as a result.

Assign the candidate chosen to station k. If two or more candidates are tied, arbitrarily choose one of them.

Step 3. Calculate the cumulative time of all tasks assigned so far to station k. Subtract this total from the cycle time to find the station's idle time. Go to step 1, and generate a new list of candidates.

Step 4. If some work elements are still unassigned, but none are candidates for station k, create a new station, station $k + 1$, and go to step 1. Otherwise, you have a complete solution.

Finding a Solution   EXAMPLE 7.5

Find a line-balancing solution for the Green Grass, Inc., problem. Use the manual solution procedure, the longest work-element time rule to pick candidates, and a cycle time of one minute.

SOLUTION

The following worksheet shows how to proceed, and the first few iterations reveal the pattern. Beginning with the first station, S1 ($k = 1$), the precedence diagram shows that only element A can be a candidate. It is the only one with all immediate predecessors (none, in this case) already assigned. With element A assigned, station S1 has an idle time of 20 seconds ($60 - 40$). Elements B and C cannot now become candidates for station S1, because their times exceed 20 seconds, and so S1 is complete. For the second station ($k = 2$), elements B and C are candidates, and we choose C because it has the larger work-element time. With station S2 now consisting of element C, its idle time equals 10 seconds ($60 - 50$). No candidates remain because adding the time of

FIGURE 7.13

Big Broadcaster Precedence Diagram Solution Using Longest Work-Element Time Rule

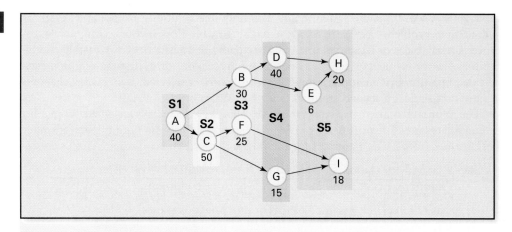

element B, F, or G brings the work content of S2 over the cycle time ($c = 60$). We continue through the procedure until we have assigned all work elements. The final solution calls for only five stations, as shown in Figure 7.13. As n = TM = 5, we can do no better than this with a 60-second cycle time.

	WORKSHEET			
STATION (STEP 1)	**CANDIDATE (STEP 2)**	**CHOICE (STEP 3)**	**CUMULATIVE TIME (SEC) (STEP 4)**	**IDLE TIME (c = 60 SEC) (STEP 4)**
S1	A	A	40	20
S2	B, C	C	50	10
S3	B, F, G	B	30	30
	E, F, G	F	55	5
S4	D, E, G	D	40	20
	E, G	G	55	5
S5	E, I	I	18	42
	E	E	24	36
	H	H	44	16

When implementing this solution, we must observe precedence requirements within each station. For example, the worker at station S5 can do element I at any time but cannot start element H until element E is finished.

OTHER CONSIDERATIONS

In addition to balancing a line for a given cycle time, managers must also consider four other options: (1) pacing, (2) behavioral factors, (3) number of models produced, and (4) cycle times.

PACING. The movement of product from one station to the next as soon as the cycle time has elapsed is called **pacing**. Pacing manufacturing processes allows materials handling to be automated and requires less inventory storage area. However, it is less flexible in handling unexpected delays that require either slowing down the entire line or pulling the unfinished work off the line to be completed later.

BEHAVIORAL FACTORS. The most controversial aspect of line-flow layouts is behavioral response. Studies have shown that installing production lines increases absenteeism, turnover, and grievances. Paced production and high specialization (say, cycle times of less than two minutes) lower job satisfaction. Workers generally favor inventory buffers as a means of avoiding mechanical pacing. One study even showed that productivity increased on unpaced lines.

pacing   The movement of product from one station to the next as soon as the cycle time has elapsed.

What can be done to humanize product layouts?

NUMBER OF MODELS PRODUCED. A **mixed-model line** produces several items belonging to the same family. In contrast, a single-model line produces one model with no variations. Mixed-model production enables a plant to achieve both high-volume production *and* product variety. However, it complicates scheduling and increases the need for good communication about the specific parts to be produced at each station.

CYCLE TIMES. A line's cycle time depends on the desired output rate (or sometimes on the maximum number of workstations allowed). In turn, the maximum line efficiency varies considerably with the cycle time selected. Thus, exploring a range of cycle times makes sense. A manager might go with a particularly efficient solution even if it does not match the output rate. The manager can compensate for the mismatch by varying the number of hours the line operates through overtime, extending shifts, or adding shifts. Multiple lines might even be the answer.

Should a mixed-model line be considered?

mixed-model line A production line that produces several items belonging to the same family.

MANAGING PROCESS LAYOUT ACROSS THE ORGANIZATION

Layouts are found in every area of a business because every facility has a layout. Good layouts can improve coordination across departmental lines and functional area boundaries. Each process in a facility has a layout that should be carefully designed. The layouts of retail operations, such as the mall at RiverTown Crossings or one of the stores at The Limited, can affect customer attitudes and therefore sales. How a manufacturing or warehousing process is laid out affects materials handling costs, throughput times, and worker productivity. Redesigning layouts can require significant capital investments, which need to be analyzed from an accounting and financial perspective. Layouts also affect employee attitudes, whether on a production line or in an office.

CHAPTER HIGHLIGHTS

- Layout decisions go beyond placement of economic activity centers. Equally important are which centers to include, how much space they need, and how to configure their space.

- There are four layout types: flexible flow, line flow, hybrid, and fixed position. Management's choice should reflect process structure. Hybrid layouts include OWMM, GT cells, and FMS.

- Customer satisfaction, capital investment, materials handling cost, and flexibility are important criteria in judging most layouts. Entirely different criteria, such as encouraging sales or communication, might be emphasized for stores or offices.

- If volumes are too low to justify dedicating a line to a single product, obtaining overlapped operations may still be possible. In such cases, the one-worker, multiple-machines (OWMM) concept or group technology (GT) cells, where machines are arranged to produce families of parts, may be feasible.

- Designing a flexible-flow layout involves gathering the necessary information, developing an acceptable block plan, and translating the block plan into a detailed layout. Information needed for flexible-flow layouts includes space requirements by center, available space, the block plan for existing layouts, closeness factors, and performance criteria relating to absolute location concerns. A manual approach

to finding a block plan begins with listing key requirements, which may be based on high closeness ratings or on other considerations. Trial and error is then used to find a block plan that satisfies most of the requirements. A weighted-distance (*wd*) score is helpful in evaluating the plan for relative location concerns. Several computer-based models, such as ALDEP and CRAFT, are now available to aid layout decision making.

- The simplest warehouse situation is the out-and-back pattern. Other patterns are the route collection, batch picking, and the zone systems.

- The effect of a layout on people is particularly apparent in offices. Layout affects productivity and the quality of work life. Four approaches to proximity–privacy trade-offs are traditional layouts, office landscaping, activity settings, and electronic cottages.

- In line-flow layouts, workstations are arranged in a somewhat naturally occurring, commonsense sequence as required for high-volume production of only one product or type of customer. Management concerns include line balance, pacing, behavior, number of models, and cycle times.

- In line balancing, tasks are assigned to stations so as to satisfy all precedence and cycle-time constraints while minimizing the number of stations required. Balancing minimizes idle time, maximizes efficiency, and minimizes delay.

The desired output rate from a line depends not only on demand forecasts but also on frequency of rebalancing, capacity utilization, and job specialization. One approach to line balancing is to create one station at a time. A work element selected from a list of candidates is added to a station at each iteration. Two commonly used decision rules for making this choice are the longest work-element time and largest number of followers rules.

STUDENT CD-ROM AND INTERNET RESOURCES

The Student CD-ROM and the Companion Website at **www.prenhall.com/krajewski** contain many tools, activities, and resources designed for this chapter. The following items are recommended to enhance your skills and improve your understanding of the material in this chapter.

STUDENT CD-ROM RESOURCES

➤ **PowerPoint Slides.** View this comprehensive set of slides customized for this chapter's concepts and techniques.
➤ **OM Explorer Tutors.** OM Explorer contains two tutor spreadsheets that will help you learn about distance measures and line balancing. See Chapter 7 in the OM Explorer menu. See also the Tutor Exercise on distance measures.
➤ **OM Explorer Solvers.** OM Explorer contains one spreadsheet to help with flexible-flow layout problems. See Process Layout in the OM Explorer menu for this routine.
➤ **Active Model.** There is an active model spreadsheet that evaluates paired exchanges (swaps) of departments using the weighted-distance method. See Process Layout in the Active Models menu for this routine.
➤ **SmartDraw.** Use the link to download a 30-day trial of SmartDraw, a software package that can help to prepare detailed layouts and floor plans.

➤ **Written Tours.** See how the flexible-flow layout at the Lower Florida Keys Health System differs from the line-flow layout at Chaparral Steel.
➤ **Supplement H:** "Measuring Output Rates." See how processing times for work elements can be estimated when planning line-flow layouts.

INTERNET RESOURCES

➤ **Self-Study Quizzes.** See the compendium of true or false, multiple choice, and essay questions that give feedback on how well you have mastered the concepts in this chapter.
➤ **In the News.** See the articles that apply to this chapter.
➤ **Internet Exercises.** Try out the links to Newport News's fixed-position layout and Royal Cake Company's layout for producing cakes and cookies. Other exercises are available on additional aspects of forecasting.
➤ **Virtual Tours.** Check out the plant layout at Casework Furniture Manufacturing for midvolume furniture construction. Also see the "Web Links to Company Facility Tours" for additional tours of company facilities.

KEY EQUATIONS

1. Euclidean distance: $d_{AB} = \sqrt{(x_A - x_B)^2 + (y_A - y_B)^2}$

2. Rectilinear distance: $d_{AB} = |x_A - x_B| + |y_A - y_B|$

3. Cycle time: $c = \dfrac{1}{r}$

4. Theoretical minimum number of workstations: $\text{TM} = \dfrac{\Sigma t}{c}$

5. Idle time (in seconds): $nc - \Sigma t$

6. Efficiency (%): $\dfrac{\Sigma t}{nc}(100)$

7. Balance delay (%): $100 - \text{Efficiency}$

KEY TERMS

automated layout design program (ALDEP) 314
balance delay 322
block plan 308
closeness matrix 309
computerized relative allocation of facilities technique (CRAFT) 314
cycle time 321
economic activity center 299
Euclidean distance 311

fixed-position layout 303
flexible-flow layout 302
group technology (GT) 306
hybrid layout 303
immediate predecessors 319
layout flexibility 305
layout planning 299
line balancing 319
line-flow layout 303
mixed-model line 325

one-worker, multiple-machines (OWMM) cell 305
pacing 324
precedence diagram 319
rectilinear distance 311
theoretical minimum (TM) 321
weighted-distance method 311
work elements 319

SOLVED PROBLEM 1

A defense contractor is evaluating its machine shop's current flexible-flow layout. Figure 7.14 shows the current layout, and the table shows the closeness matrix for the facility measured as the number of trips per day between department pairs. Safety and health regulations require departments E and F to remain at their current locations.

TRIPS BETWEEN DEPARTMENTS

DEPARTMENT	A	B	C	D	E	F
A	—	8	3		9	5
B		—		3		
C			—		8	9
D				—		3
E					—	3
F						—

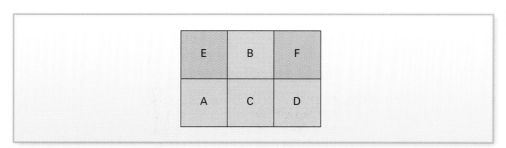

FIGURE 7.14

Current Layout

a. Use trial and error to find a better layout.
b. How much better is your layout than the current layout in terms of the *wd* score? Use rectilinear distance.

SOLUTION

a. In addition to keeping departments E and F at their current locations, a good plan would locate the following department pairs close to each other: A and E, C and F, A and B, and C and E. Figure 7.15 was worked out by trial and error and satisfies all these requirements. Start by placing E and F at their current locations. Then, because C must be as close as possible to both E and F, put C between them. Place A directly south of E, and B next to A. All of the heavy traffic concerns have now been accommodated. Department D is located in the remaining space.

DEPARTMENT PAIR	NUMBER OF TRIPS (1)	CURRENT PLAN DISTANCE (2)	CURRENT PLAN *wd* SCORE (1) × (2)	PROPOSED PLAN DISTANCE (3)	PROPOSED PLAN *wd* SCORE (1) × (3)
A, B	8	2	16	1	8
A, C	3	1	3	2	6
A, E	9	1	9	1	9
A, F	5	3	15	3	15
B, D	3	2	6	1	3
C, E	8	2	16	1	8
C, F	9	2	18	1	9
D, F	3	1	3	1	3
E, F	3	2	6	2	6
			wd = 92		*wd* = 67

b. The table reveals that the *wd* score drops from 92 for the current plan to 67 for the revised plan, a 27 percent reduction.

FIGURE 7.15

Proposed Layout

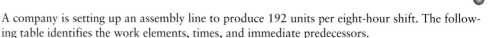

E	C	F
A	B	D

SOLVED PROBLEM 2

A company is setting up an assembly line to produce 192 units per eight-hour shift. The following table identifies the work elements, times, and immediate predecessors.

WORK ELEMENT	TIME (SEC)	IMMEDIATE PREDECESSOR(S)
A	40	None
B	80	A
C	30	D, E, F
D	25	B
E	20	B
F	15	B
G	120	A
H	145	G
I	130	H
J	115	C, I
	Total 720	

a. What is the desired cycle time?
b. What is the theoretical minimum number of stations?
c. Use the largest work-element time rule to work out a solution, and show your solution on a precedence diagram.
d. What are the efficiency and balance delay of the solution found?

SOLUTION

a. Substituting in the cycle-time formula, we get

$$c = \frac{1}{r} = \frac{8 \text{ hours}}{192 \text{ units}} (3,600 \text{ seconds/hours}) = 150 \text{ seconds/unit}$$

b. The sum of the work-element times is 720 seconds, so

$$\text{TM} = \frac{\Sigma t}{c} = \frac{720 \text{ seconds/unit}}{150 \text{ seconds/unit-station}} = 4.8 \text{ or } 5 \text{ stations}$$

which may not be achievable.

c. The precedence diagram is shown in Figure 7.16. Each row in the following table represents one iteration of application of the largest work-element time rule in assigning work elements to workstations.

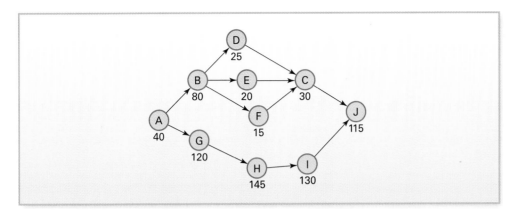

FIGURE 7.16

Precedence Diagram

STATION	CANDIDATE(S)	CHOICE	WORK-ELEMENT TIME (SEC)	CUMULATIVE TIME (SEC)	IDLE TIME (c = 150 SEC)
S1	A	A	40	40	110
	B	B	80	120	30
	D, E, F	D	25	145	5
S2	E, F, G	G	120	120	30
	E, F	E	20	140	10
S3	F, H	H	145	145	5
S4	F, I	I	130	130	20
	F	F	15	145	5
S5	C	C	30	30	120
	J	J	115	145	5

d. Calculating the efficiency, we get

$$\text{Efficiency} = \frac{\Sigma t}{nc}(100) = \frac{720 \text{ seconds/unit}}{5[150 \text{ seconds/unit}]}(100)$$
$$= 96\%$$

Thus, the balance delay is only 4 percent (100 − 96).

DISCUSSION QUESTIONS

1. Identify the types of layout performance criteria that might be most important in the following settings.

   a. Airport
   b. Bank
   c. Classroom
   d. Office of product designers
   e. Law firm
   f. Fabrication of sheet-metal components
   g. Parking lot
   h. Human resources department

2. Consider the Lower Florida Keys Health System and the Chaparral Steel written tours on the Student CD-ROM. The organizations are quite different in terms of facility layout. Which one has a flexible-flow layout? Which one has a line-flow layout? How do these layout designs relate to process choice? Explain.

PROBLEMS

An icon next to a problem identifies the software that can be helpful, but is not mandatory. The software is available on the Student CD-ROM that is packaged with every new copy of the textbook.

1. **OM Explorer** Baker Machine Company is a job shop that specializes in precision parts for firms in the aerospace industry. Figure 7.17 shows the current block plan for the key manufacturing centers of the 75,000-square-foot facility. Referring to the closeness matrix below the figure, use rectilinear distance (the current distance from inspection to shipping and receiving is three units) to calculate the change in the weighted distance, *wd*, score if Baker exchanges the locations of the tool crib and inspection.

FIGURE 7.17 | Current Layout

3	4	2
1	5	6

CLOSENESS MATRIX

Trips Between Departments

Department	1	2	3	4	5	6
1. Burr and grind	—	8	3		9	5
2. NC equipment		—		3		
3. Shipping and receiving			—		8	9
4. Lathes and drills				—		3
5. Tool crib					—	3
6. Inspection						—

2. ● **OM Explorer** Use trial and error to find a particularly good block plan for Baker Machine (see Problem 1). Because of excessive relocation costs, shipping and receiving (department 3) must remain at its current location. Compare *wd* scores to evaluate your new layout, again assuming rectilinear distance.

3. ● **OM Explorer** The head of the information systems group at Conway Consulting must assign six new analysts to offices. The following closeness matrix shows the expected frequency of contact between analysts. The block plan in Figure 7.18 shows the available office locations (1–6) for the six analysts (A–F). Assume equal-sized offices and rectilinear distance. Owing to their tasks, analyst A must be assigned to location 4 and analyst D to location 3. What are the best locations for the other four analysts? What is the *wd* score for your layout?

CLOSENESS MATRIX

Contacts Between Analysts

Analyst	A	B	C	D	E	F
Analyst A	—		6			
Analyst B		—		12		
Analyst C			—	2	7	
Analyst D				—		4
Analyst E					—	
Analyst F						—

4. ● **OM Explorer** Richard Garber is the head designer for Matthews and Novak Design Company. Garber has been called in to design the layout for a newly constructed office building. From statistical samplings over the past three months, Garber developed the closeness matrix shown for daily trips between the department's offices.

CLOSENESS MATRIX

Trips Between Departments

Department	A	B	C	D	E	F
A	—	25	90			185
B		—			105	
C			—		125	125
D				—	25	
E					—	105
F						—

a. If other factors are equal, which two offices should be located closest together?

b. Figure 7.19 shows an alternative layout for the department. What is the total weighted-distance score for this plan based on rectilinear distance and assuming that offices A and B are three units of distance apart?

c. Swapping which two departments will most improve the total weighted-distance score?

5. ● **OM Explorer** A firm with four departments has the following closeness matrix and the current block plan shown in Figure 7.20.

FIGURE 7.18 | Proposed Layout

1	2	3
4	5	6

FIGURE 7.19 | Alternative Layout

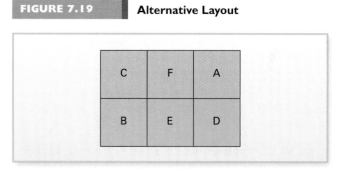

C	F	A
B	E	D

FIGURE 7.20 | Current Block Plan

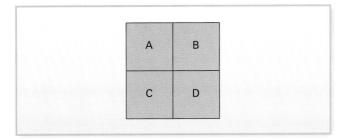

a. What is the weighted-distance score for the current layout (assuming rectilinear distance)?

CLOSENESS MATRIX

Trips Between Departments

Department	A	B	C	D
A	—	12	10	8
B		—	20	6
C			—	0
D				—

b. Develop a better layout. What is its total weighted-distance score?

6. OM Explorer The department of engineering at a university in New Jersey must assign six faculty members to their new offices. The closeness matrix shown indicates the expected number of contacts per day between professors. The available office spaces (1–6) for the six faculty members are shown in Figure 7.21. Assume equal-sized offices. The distance between offices 1 and 2 (and between offices 1 and 3) is 1 unit.

CLOSENESS MATRIX

Contacts Between Professors

Professor	A	B	C	D	E	F
A	—		4			
B		—		12		10
C			—	2	7	
D				—		4
E					—	
F						—

a. Because of their academic positions, professor A must be assigned to office 1, professor C must be assigned to office 2, and professor D must be assigned to office 6. Which faculty members should be assigned to offices 3, 4, and 5, respectively, to minimize the total weighted-distance score (assuming rectilinear distance)?

b. What is the weighted-distance score of your solution?

FIGURE 7.21 | Available Space

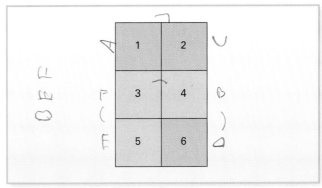

7. OM Explorer Use the longest work element time rule to balance the assembly line described in the following table and Figure 7.22 so that it will produce 40 units per hour. Break ties using the largest number of followers rule.

a. What is the cycle time?

b. What is the theoretical minimum number of workstations?

c. Which work elements are assigned to each workstation?

d. What are the resulting efficiency and balance delay percentages?

Work Element	Time (sec)	Immediate Predecessor(s)
A	40	None
B	80	A
C	30	A
D	25	B
E	20	C
F	15	B
G	60	B
H	45	D
I	10	E, G
J	75	F
K	15	H, I, J
	Total 415	

8. OM Explorer Johnson Cogs wants to set up a line to serve 60 customers per hour. The work elements and their precedence relationships are shown in the following table.

a. What is the theoretical minimum number of stations?

b. How many stations are required if the longest work-element time method is used?

c. How many stations are required if the largest number of followers method is used?

d. Suppose that a solution requiring five stations is obtained. What is its efficiency?

FIGURE 7.22   **Precedence Diagram**

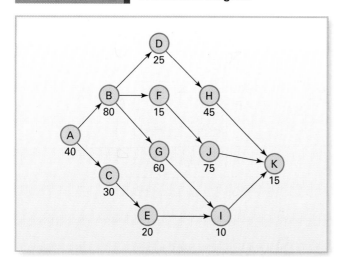

Work Element	Time (sec)	Immediate Predecessor(s)
A	40	None
B	30	A
C	50	A
D	40	B
E	6	B
F	25	C
G	15	C
H	20	D, E
I	18	F, G
J	30	H, I
	Total 274	

9. ● **OM Explorer** The Baxter Bicycle Company is installing a line to produce a new line of BMX bicycles, and you, as the operations manager, are responsible for designing the line. The line has to produce 576 units per day, and the company operates three 8-hour shifts each day. The work elements, time requirements, and immediate predecessor(s) are as follows:

Work Element	Time (sec)	Immediate Predecessor(s)
A	75	None
B	50	A
C	30	B
D	25	B
E	45	B
F	55	D
G	70	D
H	50	F, G
I	25	E
J	90	C, H, I

a. What is the theoretical number of stations?

b. If you balance the line using the longest work-element time rule, which elements are assigned to station 3?

10. ● **OM Explorer** The *trim line* at PW is a small subassembly line that, along with other such lines, feeds into the final chassis line. The entire assembly line, which consists of more than 900 workstations, is to make PW's new E cars. The trim line itself involves only 13 work elements and must handle 20 cars per hour. In addition to the usual precedence constraints, there are two *zoning constraints*. First, work elements K and L should be assigned to the same station; both use a common component, and assigning them to the same station conserves storage space. Second, work elements H and J cannot be performed at the same station. Work-element data are as follows:

Work Element	Time (min)	Immediate Predecessor(s)
A	1.8	None
B	0.4	None
C	1.6	None
D	1.5	A
E	0.7	A
F	0.5	E
G	0.8	B
H	1.4	C
I	1.4	D
J	1.4	F, G
K	0.5	H
L	1.0	J
M	0.8	I, K, L

a. Draw a precedence diagram.

b. What cycle time (in minutes) results in the desired output rate?

c. What is the theoretical minimum number of stations?

d. Using trial and error, balance the line as best you can.

e. What is the efficiency of your solution?

11. ● **OM Explorer** An assembly line must produce 40 microwave ovens per hour. The following data give the necessary information:

Work Element	Time (sec)	Immediate Predecessor(s)
A	20	None
B	55	A
C	25	B
D	40	B
E	5	B
F	35	A
G	14	D, E
H	40	C, F, G

a. Draw a precedence diagram.

b. What cycle time (in seconds) ensures the desired output rate?

c. What is the theoretical minimum number of stations? the theoretical maximum efficiency?

d. Use the longest work-element rule to design the line. What is its efficiency?

e. Can you find any way to improve the line's balance? If so, explain how.

Advanced Problems

12. ◆ **OM Explorer** CCI Electronics makes various products for the communications industry. One of its manufacturing plants makes a device for sensing when telephone calls are placed. A from–to matrix is shown in Table 7.1; the current layout appears in Figure 7.23. Management is reasonably satisfied with the current layout, although it has heard some complaints about the placement of departments D, G, K, and L. Use information in the from–to matrix to create a closeness matrix, and then find a revised block plan for moving only the four departments about which complaints have been made. Show that the weighted-distance score is improved. Assume rectilinear distance.

13. A paced assembly line has been devised to manufacture calculators, as the following data show:

Station	Work Element Assigned	Work Element Time (min)
S1	A	2.7
S2	D, E	0.6, 0.9
S3	C	3.0
S4	B, F, G	0.7, 0.7, 0.9
S5	H, I, J	0.7, 0.3, 1.2
S6	K	2.4

a. What is the maximum hourly output rate from this line? (*Hint:* The line can go only as fast as its slowest workstation.)

b. What cycle time corresponds to this maximum output rate?

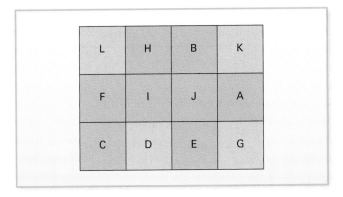

FIGURE 7.23 **Current Block Plan**

c. If a worker is at each station and the line operates at this maximum output rate, how much idle time is lost during each 10-hour shift?

d. What is the line's efficiency?

14. ◆ **OM Explorer** The manager of Sugar Hams wants to organize the tasks involved in the preparation and delivery of hams. The manager plans to produce 60 hams per 10-hour workday. The following table presents work-element times and precedence relationships.

Work Element	Time (min)	Immediate Predecessor(s)
A	3	None
B	5	A
C	2	B
D	7	B
E	7	C, D
F	6	E
G	2	D, E
H	3	F
I	8	G
J	6	H
K	3	I, J
L	8	K

TABLE 7.1
FROM–TO MATRIX

Trips Between Departments

Department	A	B	C	D	E	F	G	H	I	J	K	L
A. Network lead forming	—											80
B. Wire forming and subassembly		—							50	70		
C. Final assembly			—			120						
D. Inventory storage				—	40							
E. Presoldering			80		—						90	
F. Final testing						—	120					
G. Inventory storage		30					—	40	50			
H. Coil winding								—	80			
I. Coil assembly			70		40				—		60	
J. Network preparation	90									—		
K. Soldering			80								—	
L. Network insertion			60									—

TABLE 7.2
BIG BROADCASTER ASSEMBLY

Work Element	Description	Time (sec)	Immediate Predecessor(s)	Work Element	Description	Time (sec)	Immediate Predecessor(s)
	Attach leg frame				*Attach free wheel*		
A	Bolt leg frame to hopper	51	None	L	Slip on free wheel	30	G
B	Insert impeller shaft into hopper	7	A	M	Place washer over axle	6	L
C	Attach agitator to shaft	24	B	N	Secure with cotter pin	15	M
D	Secure with cotter pin	10	C	0	Push on hub cap	9	N
	Attach axle				*Mount lower post*		
E	Insert bearings into housings	25	A	P	Bolt lower handle post to hopper	27	G
F	Slip axle through first bearing and shaft	40	E	Q	Seat post in square hole	13	P
G	Slip axle through second bearing	20	D, F	R	Secure leg to support strap	60	Q
	Attach drive wheel				*Attach controls*		
H	Slip on drive wheel	35	G	S	Insert control wire	28	K, O, R
I	Place washer over axle	6	H	T	Guide wire through slot	12	S
J	Secure with cotter pin	15	I	U	Slip T handle over lower post	21	T
K	Push on hub cap	9	J	V	Attach on–off control	26	U
				W	Attach lever	58	V
				X	Mount nameplate	29	R
						Total 576	

a. Construct a precedence diagram for this process.

b. What cycle time corresponds to the desired output rate?

c. Try to identify the best possible line-balancing solution. What work elements are assigned to each station?

d. What is the impact on your solution if the time for work element D increases by three minutes? Decreases by three minutes?

15. ⬤ **OM Explorer** Green Grass, Inc., is expanding its product line to include a new fertilizer spreader called the Big Broadcaster. Operations plans to make the Big Broadcaster on a new assembly line, with most parts purchased from outside suppliers. The plant manager obtained the information shown in Table 7.2 concerning work elements, labor standards, and immediate predecessors for the Big Broadcaster.

a. Construct a precedence diagram for the Big Broadcaster.

b. Find a line-balancing solution using the longest work-element time rule so that the line will produce 2,400 Big Broadcasters per week with one shift of 40 hours.

c. Calculate the efficiency and balance delay of your solution.

16. The associate administrator at Getwell Hospital wants to evaluate the layout of the outpatient clinic. Table 7.3 shows the interdepartmental flows (patients/day) between departments; Figure 7.24 shows the current layout.

a. Determine the effectiveness of the current layout, as measured by the total *wd* score, using rectilinear distances.

b. Try to find the best possible layout based on the same effectiveness measure.

c. What is the impact on your new solution if it must be revised to keep department 1 at its present location?

d. How should the layout developed in part (c) be revised if the interdepartmental flow between the examining room and the X-ray department is increased by 50 percent? Decreased by 50 percent?

TABLE 7.3
CLOSENESS MATRIX

Trips Between Departments

Department	1	2	3	4	5	6	7	8
1. Reception	—	25	35	5	10	15		20
2. Business office		—	5	10	15			15
3. Examining room			—	20	30	20		10
4. X-ray				—	25	15		25
5. Laboratory					—	20		25
6. Surgery						—	40	
7. Postsurgery							—	15
8. Doctor's office								—

FIGURE 7.24   **Current Layout**

ACTIVE MODEL EXERCISE

This Active Model appears on the Student CD-ROM. It allows you to see the effects of performing paired swaps of departments.

QUESTIONS

1. What is the current total weighted-distance score?
2. Use the swap button one swap at a time. If the swap helps, move to the next pair. If the swap does not help, hit the swap button once again to put the departments back. What is the minimum weighted-distance score after all swaps have been tried?
3. Look at the two data tables, and use the yellow-shaded column to put departments in spaces. What space assignments lead to the minimum cost? What is this cost?

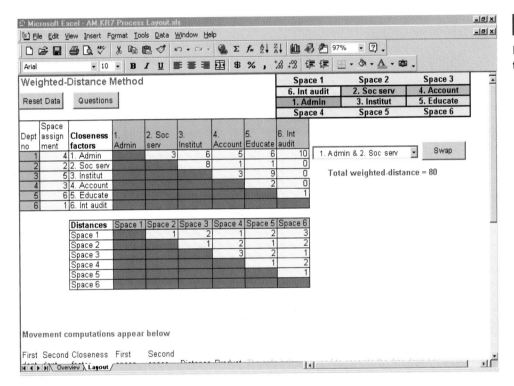

ACTIVE MODEL 7.1

Process Layout Using Data from Example 7.1

CASE   HIGHTEC, INC.

"It's hard to believe," thought Glenn Moore as he walked into the employee lunch area, "that it has been only six years since I founded Hightec." He was not interested in lunch because it was only 9:30 A.M. His purpose was to inspect the new microcomputer, which had just been purchased to improve management of the company's inventory and accounting functions. The computer had to be housed at the rear of the employee lunch area, right next to the coffee, hot soup, and hot chocolate vending machines. There was absolutely no room for the computer elsewhere.

Hightec is a manufacturer of transducers, which convert gas or liquid pressure into an electrical signal. Another form of the device converts weight or force into an electrical signal. A typical customer order is for only 3 to 10 units. The firm currently rents a 12,000-square-foot, L-shaped building, housing four basic sections: the office area, an engineering area, a machine shop, and an assembly area. The 80 employees comprise machinists, engineers, assemblers, secretaries, and salespeople.

Although Moore concentrated on finance and marketing during the first two years of Hightec's existence, his activities now are more concerned with production costs, inventory, and capacity. Sales have been increasing about 30 percent per year, and this growth is expected to continue. Specific symptoms of Hightec's problems include the following.

- Space limitations have delayed the purchase of a numerical control machine and a more efficient testing machine. Both promise greater capacity and higher productivity, and their costs are easily justified.
- The machine shop is so crowded that equipment not in constant use had to be moved into the inventory storage area.
- More machines are being operated on second and third shifts than would normally be justified. Productivity is falling, and quality is slipping.
- Approximately 10 percent of the workforce's time is spent moving materials to and from the inventory storage area, where inventory at all stages of production is kept. The chaotic supply room makes finding wanted parts difficult, and considerable time is lost searching.
- Approximately 1,000 square feet of storage space must be rented outside the plant.
- Lack of capacity has forced Moore to forgo bidding on several attractive jobs. One salesperson is particularly disgruntled because she lost a potentially large commission.
- Several office workers have complained about the cramped quarters and lack of privacy. The quality of employee space also leaves an unfavorable impression on prospective customers who visit the plant.
- Additional help was just hired for the office. To make room for their desks, Moore had to discard his favorite tropical plant, which started as a cutting when Hightec was formed and had sentimental value.

THE OPTIONS

Glenn Moore has identified three options for increasing capacity at Hightec. The first is to renew the rental contract on the current facility for another five years and rent portable units to ease the cramped conditions. He discarded this option as being inadequate for a growing problem. The second option is to purchase land and build a new 19,000-square-foot facility. The most attractive site would cost $100,000 for land, and the construction cost is estimated at $40 per square foot. His cost of capital is about 15 percent.

The third option is to renew the rental contract on the current building for another five years and rent an adjacent 7,000-square-foot building only 30 feet from the current one. The rental cost of both buildings would be $2,800 per month. Moore's choice of this third option would necessitate building a $15,000 corridor connecting the buildings. However, Moore estimates the relocation costs (such as for moving and installing the machines and the loss of regular-time capacity) to be $20,000 less than with the second alternative.

THE LAYOUT

Regardless of which option Moore chooses, he must improve on the existing layout. It suffers in terms of materials handling costs and departmental coordination. When Moore initially designed the existing layout, he located the office first and then fit the other departments around it as best he could. The main consideration for the other departments was not to have the machine shop next to the cleaning room. Moore put together the information needed for planning the new layout, as shown in Table 7.4 and Figure 7.25. The projected area requirements should be sufficient for the next five years. Both layouts provide for 19,000 square feet. The closeness matrix emphasizes materials handling and communication patterns.

Glenn Moore walked back to the office with a fresh cup of coffee in his hand. He hated hot chocolate, and it was too early for soup. He wondered what he should do next.

FIGURE 7.25   Available Space for Option 2 and Option 3

(a) Available space for new plan (Option 2)

(b) Available space for renting buildings (Option 3)

TABLE 7.4
CLOSENESS MATRIX

Department	Closeness Rating Between Departments															Area Needed (blocks*)
	1	2	3	4	5	6	7	8	9	10	11	12	13	14	15	
1. Administrative office	—	1	6	5		6	5	3	3	3	3	4	5	3		3
2. Conference room		—														1
3. Engineering and materials mgt.			—	4			3	6	5	5	4	5	5		3	2
4. Production manager				—		6	6	6	6	6	4	4	5	3	6	1
5. Lunch room					—											2
6. Computer						—	6					3	4			1
7. Inventory storage							—	6	3	3	3	3				2
8. Machine shop								—	6		4	3		4		6
9. Assembly area									—	6	6	4		4	6	7
10. Cleaning										—	3	3				1
11. Welding											—	3				1
12. Electronic												—	5			1
13. Sales and accounting													—	3		2
14. Shipping and receiving														—		1
15. Load test															—	1

*Each block represents approximately 585 square feet.

Whatever the choice, he wanted a more attractive work environment for the engineering and materials-management staffs, currently located in a cramped, open-office setting. Attracting creative people in these areas had been difficult. He made a mental note that the adjacent building also is quite drab.

QUESTIONS

1. Which expansion option would you recommend to Glenn Moore? Justify your position.
2. Design an effective block plan and evaluate it. Cite any qualitative considerations that you believe make your design attractive.

CASE   THE PIZZA CONNECTION

Dave Collier owns and operates The Pizza Connection in Worthington, Ohio. The restaurant is a franchise of a large, national chain of pizza restaurants; its product and operations are typical of the industry. As Figure 7.26 shows, the facility is divided into two areas: customer contact and pizza production. Customers enter the facility and wait to be seated by a hostess. In the case of a carry-out order, the customer goes directly to the cashier at the front of the facility to place an order or to pick up a previously phoned-in order. Dine-in customers are served by waiters and waitresses; upon completion of their meal and receipt of the check from the server, they proceed to the cashier to pay their bill and leave. During peak hours at lunch and dinner, the cashier's area becomes quite crowded with customers waiting for carry-out orders and dine-in customers trying to pay their bills.

The pizza production area is somewhat of a hybrid layout. Major operations that comprise the pizza production process, such as the preparation tasks, baking, and the cut

and box tasks, are grouped together. These individual work centers are arranged in a flexible-flow pattern around the production area.

Historically, Collier's operation has been very successful, benefiting from the rise in popularity of pizza that swept across the country during the past few years. To help take advantage of this trend, the franchiser's home office provided coordinated national and regional marketing and advertising support. It also provided strong product development support. This resulted in a new line of specialty pizzas designed to expand pizza's market appeal.

Recently, however, Collier has noticed a decline in sales. Over the past few months the number of customers has been declining steadily. After doing some research, he came to the following conclusions, which he felt explained the decline in sales.

To begin with, customer demand had changed. Providing high-quality pizza at a reasonable price no longer was enough. The customers now demanded speed, convenience,

FIGURE 7.26

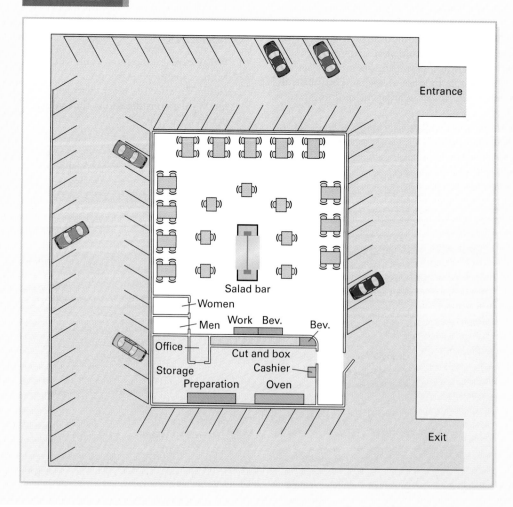

and alternative dining options. If they were dine-in patrons, they wanted to be able to get in, eat, and get out quickly. Phoned-in, carry-out customers wanted their orders ready when they arrived. Also, restaurant "parties" were a growing trend. Little league baseball teams, youth soccer teams, and birthdays all had been part of a growing demand for "party space" in restaurants. The busy, fast-paced lifestyle of today's families was contributing to moving celebrations out of the home and into restaurants and activity centers such as Putt-Putt or the Discovery Zone.

Besides these changing market demands, Collier had seen competition for the consumer's dining dollar increase significantly in the geographic area his restaurant served. The number of dining establishments in the area had more than tripled during the last two years. They ranged from drive-through to dine-in options and covered the entire spectrum from Mexican to Chinese and chicken to burgers.

Collier wondered how he should respond to what he had learned about his market. He thought that a reconfiguration of the restaurant's layout would enable him to address some of these changing customer demands. He hoped that a change in facilities would also help with labor turnover problems. Collier was having difficulty keeping trained servers, which he knew was driving up labor costs and causing a deterioration in service to his customers.

QUESTIONS

1. Reconfigure the layout shown in Figure 7.26 to respond to customers' demands for speed and convenience.
2. Explain how your new layout addresses the issues that Dave Collier identified.
3. How can the effectiveness of this new layout be measured?

Source: This case was prepared by Dr. Brooke Saladin, Wake Forest University, as a basis for classroom discussion.

SELECTED REFERENCES

Barry, Curt. "One Warehouse or Two?" *Catalog Age* (March 1, 2002).

Berry, L., L. Carbone, and S. Haeckel. "Managing the Total Customer Experience." *MIT Sloan Management Review,* vol. 43, no. 3 (Spring 2002), pp. 85–89.

Bitner, Mary Jo. "Evaluating Service Encounters: The Effects of Physical Surroundings and Employee Response." *Journal of Marketing,* vol. 54 (April 1990), pp. 69–82.

Bitner, Mary Jo. "Servicescapes: The Impact of Physical Surroundings on Customers and Employees." *Journal of Marketing,* vol. 56 (April 1992), pp. 57–71.

"Bloomie's Tries Losing the Attitude." *Business Week* (November 13, 1995), p. 52.

Bozer, Y. A., and R. D. Meller. "A Reexamination of the Distance-Based Layout Problem." *IIE Transactions.* vol. 29, no. 7 (1997), pp. 549–580.

Carbone, L., and S. Haeckel. "Engineering Customer Experience." *Marketing Management,* vol. 3, no. 3 (Winter 1994). pp. 8–19.

"Cool Offices." *Fortune* (December 9, 1996), pp. 204–210.

Cross, Kim. "The Wearable Warehouse." www.business2.com/articles/mag/0,1640,14548,FF.html (February 2001).

"Cummins Engine Flexes Its Factory." *Harvard Business Review* (March–April 1990), pp. 120–127.

"Deck the Malls with Kiosks." *Business Week* (December 13, 1999), p. 86.

Faaland, B. H., T. D. Klastorin, T. G. Schmitt, and A. Shtub. "Assembly Line Balancing with Resource Dependent Task Times." *Decision Sciences,* vol. 23, no. 2 (1992), pp. 343–363.

Francis, Richard L., Leon F. McGinnis, Jr., and John A. White. *Facility Layout and Location: An Analytical Approach,* 2d ed. Englewood Cliffs, NJ: Prentice Hall, 1992.

Frazier, G. V., and M. T. Spriggs, "Achieving Competitive Advantage Through Group Technology." *Business Horizons,* vol. 39, no. 3 (1996), pp. 83–90.

Gupta, S., and M. Vajic. "The Contextual and Dialectical Nature of Experiences," p.33–51 in Fitzsimmons and Fitzsimmons (eds.), *New Service Development.* Thousand Oaks, CA: Sage Publications Inc., 1999.

Heragu, Sunderesh. *Facilities Design.* Boston, MA: PWS Publishing Company, 1997.

"How Nokia Thrives By Breaking the Rules." *Wall Street Journal* (January 3, 2003).

Hyer, N. L., and K. H. Brown. "The Discipline of Real Cells." *Journal of Operations Management,* vol. 17, no. 5 (1999), pp. 557–574.

"Making Malls (Gaspl) Convenient." *Wall Street Journal* (February 8, 2000).

Oldham, G. R., and D. J. Brass. "Employee Reactions to an Open-Plan Office: A Naturally Occurring Quasi-Experiment." *Administrative Science Quarterly,* vol. 24 (1979), pp. 267–294.

Pesch, Michael J., Larry Jarvis, and Loren Troyer. "Turning Around the Rust Belt Factory: The $1.98 Solution." *Production and Inventory Management Journal* (Second Quarter 1993).

Pine, B., and J. Gilmore. *The Experience Economy.* Boston, MA: Harvard Business School Press, 1999.

Pinto, Peter D., David Dannenbring, and Basheer Khumawala. "Assembly Line Balancing with Processing Alternatives." *Management Science,* vol. 29, no. 7 (1983), pp. 817–830.

Pullman, Madeleine E., and Michael A. Gross. "Making the Connection: An Exploration of the Relationship Between Customer Loyalty and Experience Design Elements." Working Paper, Colorado State University, February 2003.

"Retailing: Confronting the Challenges that Face Bricks-and-Mortar Stores." *Harvard Business Review* (July–August 1999), p. 159.

Schuler, Randall S., Larry P. Ritzman, and Vicki L. Davis. "Merging Prescriptive and Behavioral Approaches for Office Layout." *Journal of Operations Management,* vol. 1, no. 3 (1981), pp. 131–142.

Stone, Phillip J., and Robert Luchetti, "Your Office Is Where You Are." *Harvard Business Review* (March–April 1985), pp. 102–117.

Sule, D. R. *Manufacturing Facilities: Location, Planning, and Design.* Boston, MA: PWS Publishing Company, 1994.

Suresh, N. C., and J. M. Kay, eds. *Group Technology and Cellular Manufacturing: A State-of-the-Art Synthesis of Research and Practice.* Boston, MA: Kluwer Academic Publishers, 1997.

"The Most Devastating Retailer in the World." *The New Yorker* (September 2000).

"Tools of the Remote Trade." *Business Week* (March 27, 2000), p. F20.

Wakefield, K., and G. Blodgett. "The Effect of the Servicescape on Customers' Behavioral Intentions in Leisure Service Settings." *Journal of Services Marketing,* vol. 10, no. 6 (1996), pp. 45–61.

Wasserman, V., Rafaeli, A., and A. Kluger. "Aesthetic Symbols As Emotional Cues," pp. 140–165 in Fineman, S. (ed.), *Emotion in Organizations.* London: Sage Publications, 2000.

Winarchick, C., and R. D. Caldwell. "Physical Interactive Simulation: A Hands-On Approach to Facilities Improvements." *IIE Solutions,* vol. 29, no. 5 (1997), pp. 34–42.

"Will This Open Space Work?" *Harvard Business Review* (May–June 1999), p. 28.

Wolf, M. J. *The Entertainment Economy: How Mega-Media Forces Are Transforming Our Lives.* New York: Times Books, Random House, 1999.

Planning and Managing Projects

LEARNING GOALS   *After reading this chapter, you should be able to . . .*

IDENTIFY OR DEFINE
1. the three major activities associated with the successful planning and managing of projects.
2. the sequence of critical activities that determine the duration of a project.
3. the options available to project managers to alleviate resource problems.

DESCRIBE OR EXPLAIN
4. how to diagram the network of interrelated activities in a project.
5. how to compute the probability of completing a project on time.
6. how to determine a minimum-cost project schedule.

BECHTEL GROUP, INC.

Bechtel Group, Inc. (www.bechtel.com) is a $11.6 billion-a-year construction contractor that specializes in large projects. In business for more than a century, the venerable company led the Six Companies consortium that built Hoover Dam early in the twentieth century and has built scores of rail systems, refineries, airports, and power plants since then.

Bechtel has the capability to manage projects throughout the world. Here, a crane assists the construction of two boilers for a steam power generating facility in Alexandria, Egypt.

Bechtel led the rebuilding of Kuwait's oil and gas infrastructure after Desert Storm and became the first U.S. company to be granted a construction license in China, which enabled it to work with Motorola on a number of projects including the construction of a $650 million state-of-the-art semiconductor manufacturing complex at Tianjin. Bechtel's customers choose the company because of its ability to deliver projects on time. They also choose the company because of its capability for delivery speed. For example, Wisconsin's Kewaunee nuclear power plant needed to replace its two steam generators, a common problem with aging nuclear power plants. Bechtel's crews cut the domes off the two generators, refurbished the domes, brought in new generator lower assemblies, and welded everything into place in just 71 days, thereby minimizing the time that Kewaunee would be out of service. Many of Bechtel's customers want to set up facilities nationwide or around the world with short lead times and do not have the time to deal with local contractors. Bechtel satisfies their needs.

Bechtel must set up a project process for each major project it undertakes with on-time delivery and short delivery lead times in mind. Because of the complexity of many ongoing projects with diverse needs, processes must also be flexible enough to respond to changes in schedules or requirements. Communication is a major issue; it takes an average of five days to get a piece of paper from Bechtel's Singapore office to a project in Thailand. Paperwork ranging from routine requests for information to detailed architectural drawings can suffer unnecessary delays when it must be copied and faxed or sent by mail, thereby delaying decisions and lengthening a project. Bechtel has thus initiated a Web-based communications system that provides access to project information electronically. Members of the project team can access schedules, progress reports, drawings, and messages at one Web site without having to rely on faxes. Decisions on various issues can be made quickly, thereby reinforcing Bechtel's competitive priorities.

Source: The Bechtel Report 2003; Bechtel Global Report 2002; **www.bechtel.com.**

---

project An interrelated set of activities that have a definite starting and ending point, which results in a unique outcome for a specific allocation of resources.

Companies such as Bechtel are experts at managing projects. They have mastered the ability to schedule activities and monitor progress within strict time, cost, and performance guidelines. A **project** is an interrelated set of activities that has a definite starting and ending point, which results in a unique outcome for a specific allocation of resources. A project process is the mechanism for completing a project (See Chapter 3, "Process Design Strategy"). Typical competitive priorities for such processes include on-time delivery and customization.

Projects can be complex and challenging to manage. Projects often cut across organizational lines because they need the skills of multiple professions and organizations. Furthermore, each project is unique, even if it is routine, requiring new combinations of skills and resources in the project process. For example, projects for adding a new branch office, installing new computers in a department, or developing a sales promotion may be initiated several times a year. Each project may have been done many times before; however, differences will arise with each replication. Uncertainties, such as the advent of new technologies or the activities of competitors, can change the character of projects and require responsive countermeasures. Finally, projects are temporary because personnel, materials, and facilities are organized to complete them within a specified time frame and then are disbanded.

Projects are common in everyday life as well as in business. Planning weddings, remodeling bathrooms, writing term papers, and organizing surprise parties are examples of small projects in everyday life. Conducting company audits, planning mergers, creating advertising campaigns, reengineering processes, developing new services or products, and establishing a strategic alliance are examples of large projects in business. The techniques for planning and managing projects that we address in this chapter are powerful tools for a wide variety of applications. One important use of these techniques is the implementation of process changes resulting from a process analysis, as Figure 8.1 shows. Whatever changes are needed, a project is the mechanism for actually making the changes.

Nonetheless, since planning and managing projects is such a pervasive activity, we will not restrict our discussion to process improvement projects. In this chapter, we discuss three major activities associated with managing any project: (1) defining and organizing projects, (2) planning projects, and (3) monitoring and controlling projects.

As you read this chapter, think about how the planning and managing of projects is important to various departments across the organization, such as . . .

➤ **accounting,** which supplies activity cost data for the financial analysis of projects.
➤ **finance,** which manages projects for financing new business acquisitions.
➤ **human resources,** which manages projects for initiating new training and development programs.
➤ **management information systems,** which manages projects for designing new information systems to support reengineered processes.
➤ **marketing,** which manages projects to design and execute new product advertising campaigns.
➤ **operations,** which manages projects to introduce new technologies for the production of services and products.

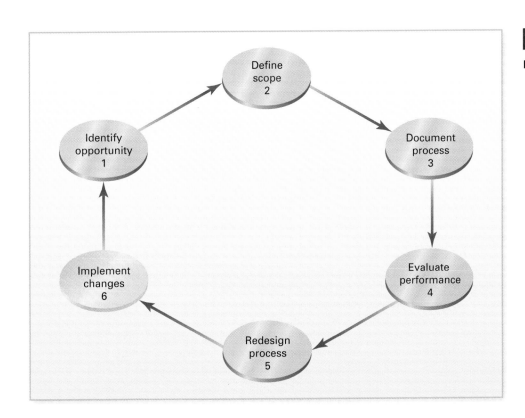

FIGURE 8.1

Implementing Changes

DEFINING AND ORGANIZING PROJECTS

Successful projects begin with a clear definition of scope, objectives, and tasks. However, a successful project begins with a clear understanding of its organization and how personnel are going to work together to complete the project. In this section, we will address three important activities in this initial phase of planning and managing projects: (1) defining the scope and objectives, (2) selecting the project manager and team, and (3) planning the project format for meetings and communication.

DEFINING THE SCOPE AND OBJECTIVES

A thorough statement of project scope, time frame, and allocated resources is essential to managing the project process. This statement is often referred to as the *project objective statement*. The scope provides a succinct statement of project objectives and captures the essence of the desired project outcomes in the form of major deliverables, which are concrete outcomes of the project. These deliverables become the focus of management attention during the life of the project. For example, suppose a firm wants to reengineer its billing process. Major deliverables for the project might include a list of all affected processes in both the firm and entities exterior to the firm; revision of the billing process and a new process flowchart; an implementation plan; a staffing plan; and a new, fully operational billing process. Each of the deliverables requires activities to achieve it; therefore, it is important to avoid many changes to the scope of the project once it is underway. Changes to the scope of a project inevitably increase costs and delay completion. For example, adding a requirement to recommend an e-commerce software solution to the reengineering project after it has started might require a reanalysis of the recommended changes to the existing internal processes and a consultant to recommend a software package. Such a change will not only delay the completion of a project but will add to the needed resources to complete it. Collectively, changes to scope are called *scope creep* and, in sufficient quantity, are primary causes of failed projects.

The time frame for a project should be as specific as possible. For example, "by the first quarter, 2007," is too vague for most purposes. Some people could interpret it as the beginning and others the end. Even though it should be considered only as a target at this early stage of the project plan, the time frame should be much more specific, as in "the billing process reengineering project should be completed by January 1, 2007."

Although specifying an allocation of resources to a project may be difficult at the early stages of planning, it is important for managing the project process. The allocation could be expressed as a dollar figure or as full-time equivalents of personnel time. For example, in the billing process reengineering project, the allocated resources might be $250,000. Avoid statements such as "with available resources" because they are too vague and imply that there are sufficient resources to complete the project when there may not be. A specific statement of allocated resources makes it possible to make adjustments to the scope of the project as it proceeds.

SELECTING THE PROJECT MANAGER AND TEAM

Project managers should be good motivators, teachers, and communicators. They should be able to organize a set of disparate activities and work with personnel from a variety of disciplines. These qualities are important because project managers have the responsibility to see that their projects are completed successfully. The project manager is responsible for establishing the project goals and providing the means to achieve them. The project manager must also specify how the work will be done and ensure that any necessary training is conducted. Finally, the project manager evaluates progress and takes appropriate action when schedules are in jeopardy.

The project team is a group of people led by the project manager. Members of the project team may represent entities internal to the firm (such as marketing, finance, accounting, or operations) or entities external to the firm (such as customers, suppliers, or consultants). A clear definition of who is on the team is essential as is a clear understanding of their specific roles and responsibilities, such as helping to create the project plan, performing specific tasks, and reporting progress and problems. Everyone performing work for the project should be a part of the project team. Consequently, the size and makeup of the team may fluctuate during the life of the project.

PLANNING THE PROJECT FORMAT

A key activity for any project process is making decisions. The managers of successful project processes specify the format for how the team will make decisions and who will make them. Such a format sets down guidelines for meetings, for resolving issues, and for communication among team members.

MEETINGS. One of the quickest ways to undermine morale in a project team is to hold too many meetings. The project manager should specify a standard meeting time and an attendance policy. An agenda should be provided in advance and, at the meeting, the issues should be discussed and meted out for further resolution if necessary.

RESOLVING ISSUES. The project manager should specify in advance how decisions will be made (by consensus, majority, or project manager). Invariably, team members will raise issues at each meeting. These issues should be logged and someone given the responsibility, with a deadline, to resolve them. Sometimes an issue will need to be resolved by a senior manager not on the team.

COMMUNICATION. It will typically save a lot of time on large projects if the method of communication is thought out in advance. For example, team members can communicate by e-mail for most issues that do not require immediate responses and by voice mail for issues with more immediacy. In addition, the question of who should get what information is an important operating issue, if not a political one. The project manager needs to determine the nature of the interim information that senior managers need and when they should get it.

Managerial Practice 8.1 shows that defining and organizing projects takes on critial importance when dealing with global teams.

PLANNING PROJECTS

Once the project has been defined and the project process organized, the team must formulate a plan that identifies the specific tasks to be accomplished and a schedule for their completion. Planning projects involves five steps: (1) *defining the work breakdown structure*, (2) *diagramming the network*, (3) *developing the schedule*, (4) *analyzing cost–time trade-offs*, and (5) *assessing risks*.

DEFINING THE WORK BREAKDOWN STRUCTURE

The **work breakdown structure (WBS)** is a statement of all work that has to be completed. Perhaps the single most important contributor to delay is the omission of work that is germane to the successful completion of the project. The project manager must work closely with the team to identify all work tasks. Typically, in the process of accumulating work tasks, the team generates a hierarchy to the work breakdown. Major work components are broken down to smaller tasks by the project team. Figure 8.2 shows a WBS for the start of a new business. The level 1 activities are major work components that can be broken down into smaller tasks. For example, "proceed with start-up plan" can be divided into three tasks at level 2, and "establish business structure" can be further divided into five tasks at level 3. It is easy to conclude that the total WBS for starting a new business may include more than 100 tasks. Regardless of the project, care must be taken to include all important tasks in the WBS to avoid project delays. Often overlooked are the tasks required to plan the project, get management approval at various stages, run pilot tests of new services or products, and prepare final reports.

work breakdown stucture (WBS) A statement of all work that has to be completed.

MANAGERIAL PRACTICE 8.1

VIRTUAL GLOBAL TEAMING AT BAXTER INTERNATIONAL

Baxter International (www.baxter.com) is an $8 billion company that produces services and products for the health care industry in facilities located in 22 countries worldwide. Baxter produces thousands of services and products, such as online continuing education courses for a wide variety of health care professionals, products and technologies for blood centers, transfusion services, intravenous therapy services, and vaccines for serious infectious diseases. One product, however, provided the vehicle for Baxter to learn some interesting lessons in the management of projects.

BaxHealth is a software package produced by Baxter that is used by companies to manage their environmental, health, and safety initiatives. When management decided to develop the next generation of the software package, the assignment to the software development team was to develop a top-quality product at the lowest cost possible and to get the product to the market in a compressed time frame. The software development team would have normally had the capability to deliver the project on time and within budget; however, a recent merger placed a heavy load on software development. Shortly after the BaxHealth project began, it became clear that the project team was not going to be able to deliver the project on time. In a bold move, the team decided to enlist the help of a software development firm in India. Now, part of the project team was in Deerfied, Illinois, and the other part was in Bangalore, India. Steps were taken to transform the two separate international teams into a single, high-performing team.

- Establishing planning at all levels of the project, not just at the aggregate level.
- Establishing the processes that would foster consistent and open communication among team members, so as to minimize biases and finger-pointing.
- Defining a rigorous development process, establishing discipline, and providing leadership throughout the project, so as to ensure that the same planning and management procedures were being employed everywhere.

- Setting clear and measurable team and individual goals.
- Developing an integrated project plan and schedule that reflected all time demands placed on team members, even those outside the BaxHealth project.

Communications became a critical element of the project success. Language, international regulations, culture, and different time zones had to be taken into consideration. Each week, the project management team communicated the status of the project with respect to goals, risks, and progress to all team members. Since the team was spread out internationally, walking down the hall to discuss problems was not an option. E-mail, fax, Web pages, and the phone had to fill the need to communicate. In many regards, the BaxHealth project team was a virtual team.

The BaxHealth software package was reengineered and launched in 18 months, which was on schedule. Baxter learned that the management of virtual, global project teams requires solid project management principles, excellent communication with the entire global team, and an agreement by all to follow the same process. The approach requires patience and personal accountability from all team members. Nonetheless, after the project was over, Baxter examined the product development process for improvements. For example, the team learned that it would have been better to have the Bangalore development team work with the Deerfield team in Illinois in the early stages of the project, so as to reduce the time it takes to achieve a "one team" spirit. Many other improvements were identified that will be incorporated in future development projects.

Source: Seguy, Robert J., Mary Ann Latko, Jay Baima, and Errol Jones. "Virtual Global Teaming: Baxter International Builds a Successful Model." *Target* (Second Quarter 2002), pp. 23–31.

What tools are available for scheduling and controlling projects?

activity   The smallest unit of work effort consuming both time and resources that the project manager can schedule and control.

An **activity** is the smallest unit of work effort consuming both time and resources that the project manager can schedule and control. Each activity in the WBS must have an "owner" who is responsible for doing the work. *Task ownership* avoids confusion in the execution of activities and assigns responsibility for timely completion. The team should have a defined procedure for assigning tasks to team members, which can be democratic (consensus of the team) or autocratic (project manager).

DIAGRAMMING THE NETWORK

Network planning methods can help managers monitor and control projects. These methods treat a project as a set of interrelated activities that can be visually displayed

FIGURE 8.2   **Work Breakdown Structure for a New Business**

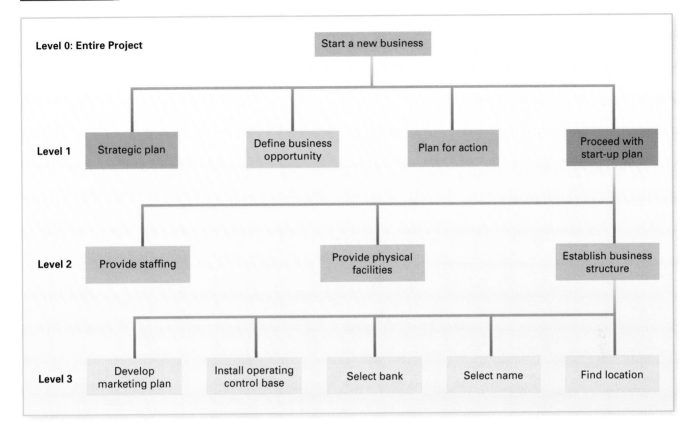

Source: Abstracted from MS Project 2000 template for a new business.

in a **network diagram,** which consists of nodes (circles) and arcs (arrows) that depict the relationships between activities. Two network planning methods were developed in the 1950s. The **program evaluation and review technique (PERT)** was created for the U.S. Navy's Polaris missile project, which involved 3,000 separate contractors and suppliers. The **critical path method (CPM)** was developed as a means of scheduling maintenance shutdowns at chemical-processing plants. Although early versions of PERT and CPM differed in their treatment of activity–time estimates, today the differences between PERT and CPM are minor. For purposes of our discussion, we refer to them collectively as PERT/CPM. These methods offer several benefits to project managers, including the following.

1. Considering projects as networks forces project teams to identify and organize the data required and to identify the interrelationships between activities. This process also provides a forum for managers of different functional areas to discuss the nature of the various activities and their resource requirements.

2. Networks enable project managers to estimate the completion time of projects, an advantage that can be useful in planning other events and in conducting contractual negotiations with customers and suppliers.

3. Reports highlight the activities that are crucial to completing projects on schedule. They also highlight the activities that may be delayed without affecting completion dates, thereby freeing up resources for other, more critical activities.

4. Network methods enable project managers to analyze the time and cost implications of resource trade-offs.

network diagram   A network planning method, designed to depict the relationships between activities, that consists of nodes (circles) and arcs (arrows).

program evaluation and review technique (PERT)   A network planning method created for the U.S. Navy's Polaris missile project in the 1950s, which involved 3,000 separate contractors and suppliers.

critical path method (CPM)   A network planning method developed in the 1950s as a means of scheduling maintenance shutdowns at chemical-processing plants.

precedence relationship A relationship that determines a sequence for undertaking activities; it specifies that one activity cannot start until a preceding activity has been completed.

activity-on-arc (AOA) network An approach used to create a network diagram that uses arcs to represent activities and nodes to represent events.

event The point at which one or more activities are to be completed and one or more other activities are to begin.

activity-on-node (AON) network An approach used to create a network diagram, in which nodes represent activities and arcs represent the precedence relationships between them.

ESTABLISHING PRECEDENCE RELATIONSHIPS. Diagramming the project as a network requires establishing the precedence relationships between activities. A **precedence relationship** determines a sequence for undertaking activities; it specifies that one activity cannot start until a preceding activity has been completed. For example, brochures announcing a conference for executives must first be designed by the program committee (activity A) before they can be printed (activity B). In other words, activity A must *precede* activity B. For large projects, this task is essential because incorrect or omitted precedence relationships will result in costly delays. The precedence relationships are represented by a network diagram.

SELECTING A NETWORK DIAGRAM APPROACH. Two different approaches may be used to create a network diagram. The first approach, the **activity-on-arc** (**AOA**) **network,** uses arcs to represent activities and nodes to represent events. An **event** is the point at which one or more activities are to be completed and one or more other activities are to begin. An event consumes neither time nor resources. Because the AOA approach emphasizes activity connection points, we say that it is *event oriented*. Here, the precedence relationships require that an event not occur until all preceding activities have been completed. Conventionally, AOA networks number events sequentially from left to right.

The second approach is the **activity-on-node (AON) network,** in which nodes represent activities and arcs represent the precedence relationships between them. This approach is *activity oriented*. Here, precedence relationships require that an activity not begin until all preceding activities have been completed. In AON networks, when there are multiple activities with no predecessors, it is usual to show them emanating from a common node called *start*. When there are multiple activities with no successors, it is usual to show them connected to a node called *finish*. We have used AON networks to describe assembly lines (see Chapter 7, "Process Layout").

Figure 8.3 shows the AOA and AON approaches for several commonly encountered activity relationships. In Figure 8.3(a), activity S must be completed before activity T, which in turn must be completed before activity U can be started. For example, in the AOA diagram, event 1 might be "the start of the project" and event 2 "the completion of activity S." The arrows in the AOA diagram denote both precedence and the activity itself. The arrow for activity 5 starts from event 1 and ends at event 2, indicating that the sequence of events is from 1 to 2. In the AON diagram, the arrows represent precedence relationships only. The direction of the arrows indicates the sequence of activities, from S to T to U.

Figure 8.3 (b) shows that activities S and T can be worked simultaneously, but both must be completed before activity U can begin. In Figure 8.3 (c), neither activity T nor U can begin until activity S has been completed. Multiple dependencies also can be identified. For example, Figure 8.3(d) shows that U and V cannot begin until both S and T have been completed.

Sometimes the AOA approach requires the addition of a *dummy activity* to clarify the precedence relationships between two activities. Figure 8.3 (e) shows an example of this situation. Activity U cannot begin until both S and T have been completed; however, V depends only on the completion of T. A dummy activity, which has an activity time of zero and requires no resources, must be used to clarify the precedence between T and V and between S and T and U. A dummy activity also is used when two activities have the same starting and ending nodes. For example, in Figure 8.3 (f), both activities T and U cannot begin until S has been completed, and activity V cannot begin until both T and U have been completed. The dummy activity enables activities T and U to have unique beginning nodes. This distinction is important for computer programs because activities often are identified by their beginning and ending nodes. Without dummy activities, the computer could not differentiate activities that have identical beginning and ending nodes from each other, which is essential when the activities have different time requirements.

FIGURE 8.3	AOA and AON Approaches to Activity Relationships

AOA	AON	Activity Relationships
(a)		S precedes T, which precedes U.
(b)		S and T must be completed before U can be started.
(c)		T and U cannot begin until S has been completed.
(d)		U and V cannot begin until both S and T have been completed.
(e)		U cannot begin until both S and T have been completed; V cannot begin until T has been completed.
(f)		T and U cannot begin until S has been completed and V cannot begin until both T and U have been completed.

Diagramming a Hospital Project

EXAMPLE 8.1

St. Adolf's Hospital is a private hospital that first started serving the community 30 years ago. Judy Kramer, executive director of the board of St. Adolf's, initiated a strategic assessment of the hospital's service package, so as to identify the gaps in its capability to provide top-quality service. The study revealed a gap in the hospital's capability to provide the level of service required by the community, particularly because of the lack of bed space and small, inefficient lab facilities. However, expansion at its present location was impossible.

In the interest of better serving the public in Benjamin County, the board of St. Adolf's Hospital decided to relocate from Christofer to Northville. The move to Northville will involve constructing a new hospital and making it operational. Judy Kramer must prepare for a hearing, scheduled for next week, before the Central Ohio Hospital Board (COHB) on the proposed project. The hearing will address the specifics of the total project, including time and cost estimates for its completion.

With the help of her team, Kramer has developed a WBS consisting of 11 major project activities. Each team member was assigned the responsibility for certain activities, with Kramer taking overall responsibility as project manager. The team also has specified the immediate predecessors (those activities that must be completed before a particular activity can begin) for each activity, as shown in the following table.

ACTIVITY	DESCRIPTION	IMMEDIATE PREDECESSOR(S)	RESPONSIBILITY
A	Select administrative and medical staff	—	Johnson
B	Select site and do site survey	—	Taylor
C	Select equipment	A	Adams
D	Prepare final construction plans and layout	B	Taylor
E	Bring utilities to the site	B	Burton
F	Interview applicants and fill positions in nursing, support staff, maintenance, and security	A	Johnson
G	Purchase and take delivery of equipment	C	Adams
H	Construct the hospital	D	Taylor
I	Develop an information system	A	Simmons
J	Install the equipment	E, G, H	Adams
K	Train nurses and support staff	F, I, J	Johnson

    a. Draw the AON network diagram.
    b. Draw the AOA network diagram.

SOLUTION

    a. The AON network diagram for the hospital project, based on Kramer's 11 activities and their precedence relationships, is shown in Figure 8.4. It depicts activities as circles, with arrows indicating the sequence in which they are to be performed. Activities A and B emanate from a *start* node because they have no immediate predecessors. The arrows connecting activity A to activities C, F, and I indicate that all three require completion of activity A before they can begin. Similarly, activity B must be completed before activities D and E can begin, and so on. Activity K connects to a *finish* node because no activities follow it. The start and finish nodes do not actually represent activities. They merely provide beginning and ending points for the network.
    b. The AOA network diagram is shown in Figure 8.5. Event 1 is the start of the project. Activities A and B have no immediate predecessors; therefore, the arrows representing

FIGURE 8.4

AON Network Diagram for the St. Adolf's Hospital Project

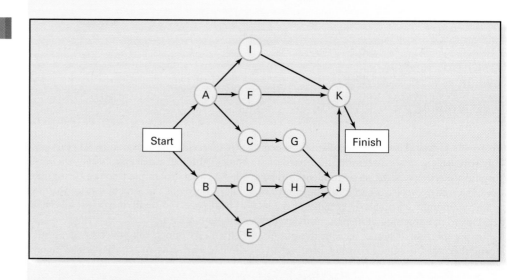

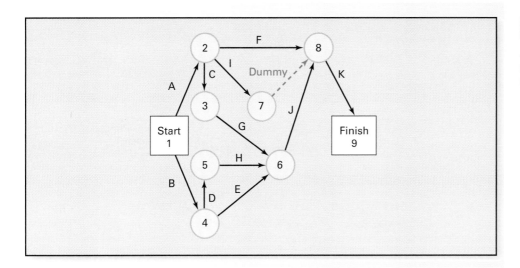

FIGURE 8.5

AOA Network Diagram for the St. Adolf's Hospital Project

those activities both have event 1 as their base. Event 2 signals the completion of activity A. Because activities C, F, and I all require the completion of A, the arrows representing these activities leave the node representing event 2. Similarly, the arrows for activities D and E leave the node for event 4, which signals the completion of activity B. The arrow for activity G leaves event 3, and event 6 is needed to tie activities G, H, and E together because they must be completed before activity J can begin.

Properly representing the relationship for activity K requires the use of a dummy activity. Activities I and F both emanate from event 2, and both must be completed before K can begin. Activities I and F will have the same beginning and ending nodes unless a dummy activity is used. Thus, event 7 signals the end of activity I and event 8 the end of activity F, with a dummy activity joining them. Now all activities are uniquely defined, and the network shows that activities F, I, and J must be completed before activity K can begin. Event 9 indicates the completion of the project.

Both the AON and the AOA methods can accurately represent all the activities and precedence relationships in a project. Regardless of the method used, modeling a large project as a network forces the project team to identify the necessary activities and recognize the precedence relationships. If this preplanning is skipped, unexpected delays often occur.

In the remainder of our discussion of PERT/CPM, we use the AON convention, although AOA diagrams also can be applied to all procedures.

DEVELOPING THE SCHEDULE

Next, the project team must make time estimates for activities. When the same type of activity has been done many times before, time estimates are apt to have a relatively high degree of certainty. There are several ways to get time estimates in such an environment. First, statistical methods can be used if the project team has access to data on actual activity times experienced in the past (see Supplement H, "Measuring Output Rates," in the Student CD-ROM). Second, if activity times improve with the number of replications, the times can be estimated using learning curve models (see Supplement G, "Learning Curves Analysis," on the Student CD-ROM). Finally, the times for first-time activities are often estimated using managerial opinions based on similar prior experiences (see Chapter 13, "Forecasting"). If there is a high degree of uncertainty in the estimates, probability distributions for activity times can be used. We discuss two approaches for incorporating uncertainty in project networks when we address risk assessment later. For now, we assume that the activity times are known with certainty. Figure 8.6 shows the estimated time for each activity of the St. Adolf's Hospital project.

Which activities determine the duration of an entire project?

FIGURE 8.6

Network Showing Activity Times for the St. Adolf's Hospital Project

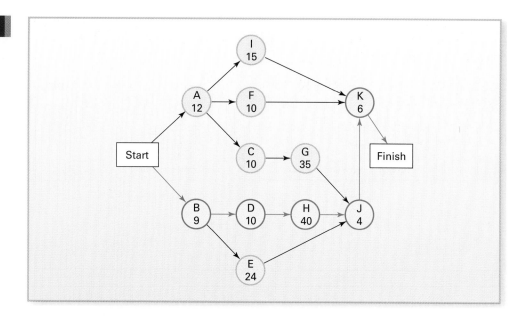

path The sequence of activities between a project's start and finish.

critical path The sequence of activities between a project's start and finish that takes the longest time to complete.

A crucial aspect of project management is estimating the time of completion. If each activity in relocating the hospital were done in sequence, with work proceeding on only one activity at a time, the time of completion would equal the sum of the times for all the activities, or 175 weeks. However, Figure 8.6 indicates that some activities can be carried on simultaneously given adequate resources. We call each sequence of activities between the project's start and finish a **path**. The network describing the hospital relocation project has five paths: A–F–K, A–I–K, A–C–G–J–K, B–D–H–J–K, and B–E–J–K. The **critical path** is the sequence of activities between a project's start and finish that takes the longest time to complete. Thus, the activities along the critical path determine the completion time of the project; that is, if one of the activities on the critical path is delayed, the entire project will be delayed. The estimated times for the paths in the hospital project network are

Path	Estimated Time (wk)
A–F–K	28
A–I–K	33
A–C–G–J–K	67
B–D–H–J–K	69
B–E–J–K	43

The activity string B–D–H–J–K is estimated to take 69 weeks to complete. As the longest, it constitutes the critical path and is shown in red in Figure 8.6.

Because the critical path defines the completion time of the project, Judy Kramer and the project team should focus on these activities. However, projects can have more than one critical path. If activity A, C, or G were to fall behind by two weeks, the string A–C–G–J–K would become a second critical path. Consequently, the team should be aware that delays in activities not on the critical path could cause delays in the entire project.

Manually finding the critical path in this way is easy for small projects; however, computers must be used for large projects. Computers calculate activity slack and prepare periodic reports, enabling managers to monitor progress. **Activity slack** is the maximum length of time that an activity can be delayed without delaying the entire project. Activities on the critical path have zero slack. Constantly monitoring the progress of activities with little or no slack enables managers to identify activities that

activity slack The maximum length of time that an activity can be delayed without delaying the entire project.

need to be expedited to keep the project on schedule. Activity slack is calculated from four times for each activity: (1) earliest start time, (2) earliest finish time, (3) latest start time, and (4) latest finish time.

EARLIEST START AND EARLIEST FINISH TIMES. The earliest start and earliest finish times are obtained as follows.

1. The **earliest finish time (EF)** of an activity equals its earliest start time plus its estimated duration, t, or $EF = ES + t$.
2. The **earliest start time (ES)** for an activity is the earliest finish time of the immediately preceding activity. For activities with more than one preceding activity, ES is the latest of the earliest finish times of the preceding activities.

To calculate the duration of the entire project, we determine the EF for the last activity on the critical path.

earliest finish time (EF) An activity's earliest start time plus its estimated duration, t, or $EF = ES + t$.

earliest start time (ES) The earliest finish time of the immediately preceding activity.

Calculating Earliest Start and Earliest Finish Times

EXAMPLE 8.2

Calculate the earliest start and finish times for the activities in the St. Adolf's Hospital project. Figure 8.7 contains the activity times.

FIGURE 8.7   **Network Diagram Showing Earliest Start and Earliest Finish Times for the St. Adolf's Hospital Project**

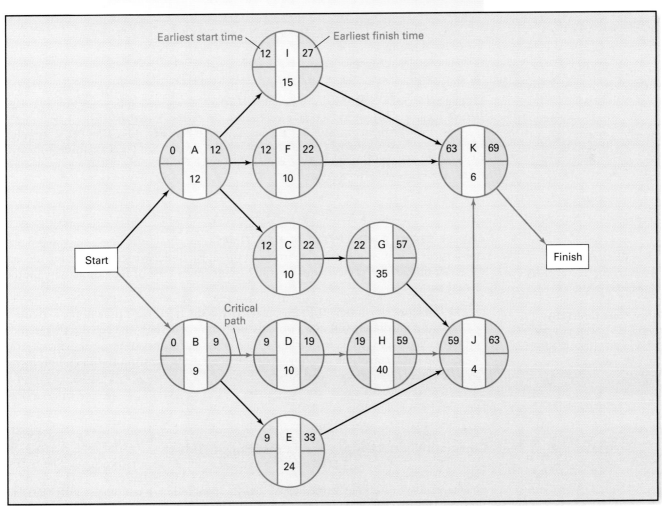

SOLUTION

We begin at the start node at time zero. Because activities A and B have no predecessors, the earliest start times for these activities are also zero. The earliest finish times for these activities are

$$EF_A = 0 + 12 = 12 \quad \text{and} \quad EF_B = 0 + 9 = 9$$

Because the earliest start time for activities I, F, and C is the earliest finish time of activity A,

$$ES_I = 12, \quad ES_F = 12, \quad \text{and} \quad ES_C = 12$$

Similarly,

$$ES_D = 9 \quad \text{and} \quad ES_E = 9$$

After placing these ES values on the network diagram, as shown in Figure 8.7, we determine the EF times for activities I, F, C, D, and E:

$$EF_I = 12 + 15 = 27, \quad EF_F = 12 + 10 = 22, \quad EF_C = 12 + 10 = 22$$
$$EF_D = 9 + 10 = 19, \quad \text{and} \quad EF_E = 9 + 24 = 33$$

The earliest start time for activity G is the latest EF time of all immediately preceding activities. Thus,

$$
\begin{array}{ll}
ES_G = EF_C & ES_H = EF_D \\
\quad = 22 & \quad = 19 \\
EF_G = ES_G + t & EF_H = ES_H + t \\
\quad = 22 + 35 & \quad = 19 + 40 \\
\quad = 57 & \quad = 59
\end{array}
$$

DECISION POINT   The project team can now determine the earliest time any activity can be started. Because activity J has several predecessors, the earliest time that activity J can begin is the latest of the EF times of any of its preceding activities: EF_G, EF_H, EF_E. Thus $EF_J = 59 + 4 = 63$. Similarly, $ES_K = 63$ and $EF_K = 63 + 6 = 69$. Because activity K is the last activity on the critical path, the earliest the project can be completed is week 69. The earliest start and finish times for all activities are shown in Figure 8.7.

LATEST START AND LATEST FINISH TIMES. To obtain the latest start and latest finish times, we must work backward from the finish node. We start by setting the latest finish time of the project equal to the earliest finish time of the last activity on the critical path.

latest finish time (LF)   The latest start time of the activity that immediately follows.

latest start time (LS)   The latest finish time of an activity minus its estimated duration, t, or $LS = LF - t$.

1. The **latest finish time (LF)** for an activity is the latest start time of the activity that immediately follows. For activities with more than one activity that immediately follow, LF is the earliest of the latest start times of those activities.
2. The **latest start time (LS)** for an activity equals its latest finish time minus its estimated duration, t, or $LS = LF - t$.

EXAMPLE 8.3   Calculating Latest Start and Latest Finish Times

For the St. Adolf's Hospital project, which activity should Kramer start immediately? In addition, calculate the latest start and latest finish times for each activity from Figure 8.7.

SOLUTION

We begin by setting the latest finish activity time of activity K at week 69, which is its earliest finish time as determined in Example 8.2. Thus, the latest start time for activity K is

$$LS_K = LF_K - t = 69 - 6 = 63$$

If activity K is to start no later than week 63, all its predecessors must finish no later than that time. Consequently,

$$LF_I = 63, \quad LF_F = 63, \quad \text{and} \quad LF_J = 63$$

The latest start times for these activities are shown in Figure 8.8 as

$$LS_I = 63 - 15 = 48, \quad LS_F = 63 - 10 = 53, \quad \text{and} \quad LS_J = 63 - 4 = 59$$

After obtaining LS_J, we can calculate the latest start times for the immediate predecessors of activity J:

$$LS_G = 59 - 35 = 24, \quad LS_H = 59 - 40 = 19, \quad \text{and} \quad LS_E = 59 - 24 = 35$$

FIGURE 8.8   **Network Diagram Showing Data Needed for Activity Slack Calculation for the St. Adolf's Hospital Project**

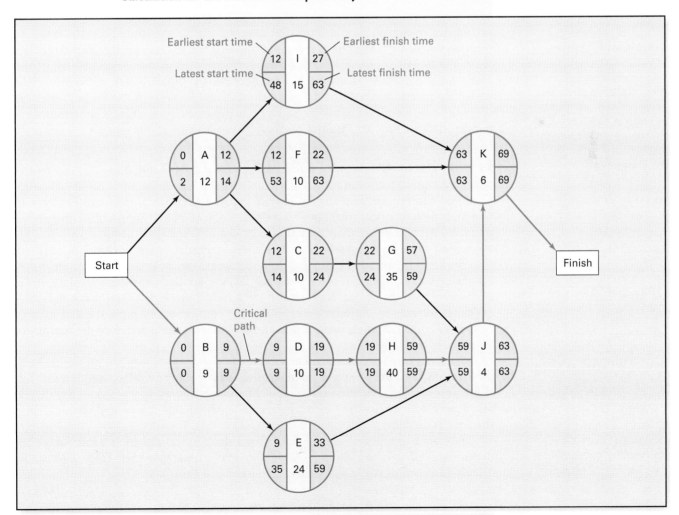

Similarly, we can now calculate the latest start times for activities C and D:

$$LS_C = 24 - 10 = 14 \quad \text{and} \quad LS_D = 19 - 10 = 9$$

Activity A has more than one immediately following activity: I, F, and C. The earliest of the latest start times is 14 for activity C. Thus,

$$LS_A = 14 - 12 = 2$$

Similarly, activity B has two immediate followers, D and E. Because the earliest of the latest start times of these activities is 9,

$$LS_B = 9 - 9 = 0$$

DECISION POINT   The earliest or latest start dates can be used for developing a project schedule. For example, Kramer should start activity B immediately because the latest start date is 0; otherwise, the project will not be completed by week 69. When the LS is greater than the ES for an activity, that activity could be scheduled for any date between ES and LS. Such is the case for activity E, which could be scheduled to start anytime between week 9 and week 35, depending on the availability of resources. The earliest start and earliest finish times and the latest start and latest finish times for all activities are shown in Figure 8.8.

Gantt chart   A project schedule, usually created by the project manager using computer software, that superimposes project activities, with their precedence relationships and estimated duration times, on a time line.

PROJECT SCHEDULE.   The project manager, often with the assistance of computer software, creates the project schedule by superimposing project activities, with their precedence relationships and estimated duration times, on a time line. The resulting diagram is called a **Gantt chart**. Figure 8.9 shows a Gantt chart for the hospital project created with Microsoft Project, a popular software package for project management. The critical path is shown in red. The chart clearly shows which activities can be undertaken simultaneously and when they should be started. In this example, the schedule calls for all activities to begin at their earliest start times. Gantt charts are popular because they are intuitive and easy to construct.

ACTIVITY SLACK.   Information on slack can be useful because it highlights activities that need close attention. In this regard, activity slack is the amount of schedule slippage that can be tolerated for an activity before the entire project will be delayed. Activities on the critical path have zero slack. Slack at an activity is reduced when the estimated time duration of an activity is exceeded or when the scheduled start time for the activity must be delayed because of resource considerations. For example, activity G in the hospital project is estimated to have 2 weeks of slack. Suppose that the orders for the new equipment are placed in week 22, the activity's earliest start date. If the supplier informs the project team that it will have a 2-week delay in the normal delivery time, the activity time becomes 37 weeks, consuming all the slack and making activity G critical. Management must carefully monitor the delivery of the equipment to avoid delaying the entire project.

Sometimes managers can manipulate slack to overcome scheduling problems. Slack information helps the project team make decisions about the reallocation of resources. When resources can be used on several different activities in a project, they can be taken from activities with slack and given to activities that are behind schedule until the slack is used up.

There are two types of activity slack. **Total slack** for an activity is a function of the performance of activities leading to it. It is shared by other activities. Total slack can be calculated in one of two ways for any activity:

total slack   Slack shared by other activities; calculated as $S = LS - ES$ or $S = LF - EF$.

$$S = LS - ES \quad \text{or} \quad S = LF - EF$$

FIGURE 8.9

MS Project Gantt Chart for the St. Adolf's Hospital Project Schedule

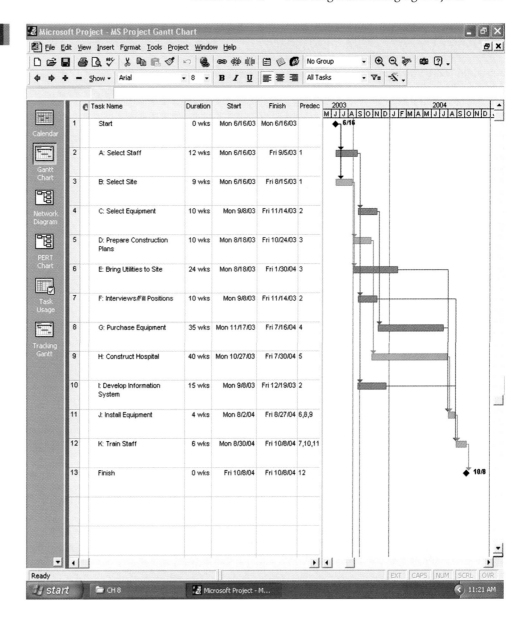

Free slack is the amount of time that an activity's earliest finish time can be delayed without delaying the earliest start time of any activity that immediately follows. The distinction between the two types of slack is important for making resource-allocation decisions. If an activity has total slack but no free slack, any slippage in its start date will affect the slack of other activities. However, the start date for an activity with free slack can be delayed without affecting the schedules of other activities.

free slack The amount of time that an activity's earliest finish time can be delayed without delaying the earliest start time of any activity that immediately follows.

Calculating Activity Slack

EXAMPLE 8.4

Calculate the slack for the activities in the St. Adolf's Hospital project. Use the date that was provided in Figure 8.8.

SOLUTION

The following table from Microsoft Project shows the total slack and the free slack for each activity. Figure 8.10 shows activities B, D, H, J, and K are on the critical path because they have zero slack.

FIGURE 8.10

Schedule Table Showing Activity Slacks for the St. Adolf's Hospital Project

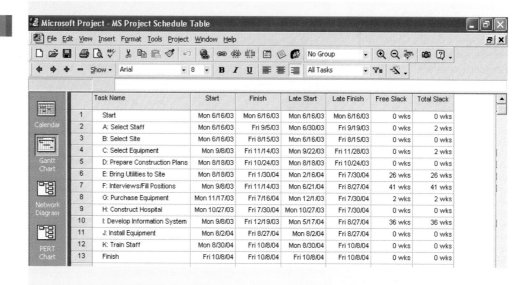

	Task Name	Start	Finish	Late Start	Late Finish	Free Slack	Total Slack
1	Start	Mon 6/16/03	Mon 6/16/03	Mon 6/16/03	Mon 6/16/03	0 wks	0 wks
2	A: Select Staff	Mon 6/16/03	Fri 9/5/03	Mon 6/30/03	Fri 9/19/03	0 wks	2 wks
3	B: Select Site	Mon 6/16/03	Fri 8/15/03	Mon 6/16/03	Fri 8/15/03	0 wks	0 wks
4	C: Select Equipment	Mon 9/8/03	Fri 11/14/03	Mon 9/22/03	Fri 11/28/03	0 wks	2 wks
5	D: Prepare Construction Plans	Mon 8/18/03	Fri 10/24/03	Mon 8/18/03	Fri 10/24/03	0 wks	0 wks
6	E: Bring Utilities to Site	Mon 8/18/03	Fri 1/30/04	Mon 2/16/04	Fri 7/30/04	26 wks	26 wks
7	F: Interviews/Fill Positions	Mon 9/8/03	Fri 11/14/03	Mon 6/21/04	Fri 8/27/04	41 wks	41 wks
8	G: Purchase Equipment	Mon 11/17/03	Fri 7/16/04	Mon 12/1/03	Fri 7/30/04	2 wks	2 wks
9	H: Construct Hospital	Mon 10/27/03	Fri 7/30/04	Mon 10/27/03	Fri 7/30/04	0 wks	0 wks
10	I: Develop Information System	Mon 9/8/03	Fri 12/19/03	Mon 5/17/04	Fri 8/27/04	36 wks	36 wks
11	J: Install Equipment	Mon 8/2/04	Fri 8/27/04	Mon 8/2/04	Fri 8/27/04	0 wks	0 wks
12	K: Train Staff	Mon 8/30/04	Fri 10/8/04	Mon 8/30/04	Fri 10/8/04	0 wks	0 wks
13	Finish	Fri 10/8/04	Fri 10/8/04	Fri 10/8/04	Fri 10/8/04	0 wks	0 wks

ACTIVE MODEL 8.1

Active Model 8.1 on the Student CD-ROM provides additional insight on Gantt charts and their uses for the St. Adolf's Hospital project.

DECISION POINT. The total slack at an activity depends on the performance of activities leading to it. If the project team decides to schedule activity A to begin in week 2 instead of immediately, the total slack for activities C and G would be zero. Thus, total slack is shared among all activities on a particular path. The table also shows that several activities have free slack. For example, activity G has two weeks of free slack. If the schedule goes as planned to week 22 when activity G is scheduled to start, and the supplier for the equipment asks for a 2-week extension on the delivery date, the project team knows that the delay will not affect the schedule for the other activities. Nonetheless, activity G would be on the critical path.

ANALYZING COST–TIME TRADE-OFFS

How do project planning methods increase the potential to control costs and provide better customer service?

Keeping costs at acceptable levels is almost always as important as meeting schedule dates. In this section, we discuss the use of PERT/CPM methods to obtain minimum-cost schedules.

The reality of project management is that there are always cost–time trade-offs. For example, a project can often be completed earlier than scheduled by hiring more workers or running extra shifts. Such actions could be advantageous if savings or additional revenues accrue from completing the project early. *Total project costs* are the sum of direct costs, indirect costs, and penalty costs. These costs are dependent either on activity times or on project completion time. *Direct costs* include labor, materials, and any other costs directly related to project activities. Managers can shorten individual activity times by using additional direct resources, such as overtime, personnel, or equipment. *Indirect costs* include administration, depreciation, financial, and other variable overhead costs that can be avoided by reducing total project time: The shorter the duration of the project, the lower the indirect costs will be. Finally, a project may incur penalty costs if it extends beyond some specific date, whereas a bonus may be provided for early completion. Thus, a project manager may consider *crashing*, or expediting, some activities to reduce overall project completion time and total project costs. Managerial Practice 8.2 shows how substantial project penalty costs can be.

normal time (NT) The time necessary to complete an activity under normal conditions.

COST TO CRASH. To assess the benefit of crashing certain activities—from either a cost or a schedule perspective—the project manager needs to know the following times and costs.

normal cost (NC) The activity cost associated with the normal time.

1. The **normal time (NT)** is the time necessary to complete an activity under normal conditions.

crash time (CT) The shortest possible time to complete an activity.

2. The **normal cost (NC)** is the activity cost associated with the normal time.
3. The **crash time (CT)** is the shortest possible time to complete an activity.
4. The **crash cost (CC)** is the activity cost associated with the crash time.

crash cost (CC) The activity cost associated with the crash time.

MANAGERIAL PRACTICE 8.2

PROJECT DELAYS ARE COSTLY FOR AMTRAK AND ITS SUPPLIERS

Amtrak (www.amtrak.com), also known as the National Railroad Passenger Corporation, is a $1.84 billion-a-year federally funded corporation whose mandate is to provide passenger rail service to major cities. Competition in the transportation industry is fierce; passengers can use airplanes, buses, cars, and trains to get to their destinations. To gain a larger share of transportation services in the Northeast, Amtrak initiated the Acela Regional project in 1996, with a goal of providing high-speed electric rail service between Boston and Washington, DC, by December 1999. The project included enhancements to existing rail infrastructure, particularly the 156-mile stretch between New Haven and Boston. Amtrak and its contractors erected 12,200 catenary poles, strung 1,550 miles of electrical wire across three states, and built 25 power stations. In addition, Amtrak installed 115 miles of continuous welded rail, laid 455,000 concrete ties, and poured 500,000 tons of ballast to allow for the faster acceleration and higher top speeds than could be achieved with existing diesel technology. However, unexpected problems caused the delay of service to December, 2000.

A key deliverable in the project was the Acela Express train, which is capable of 150 mile-per-hour speeds and includes such amenities as modem jacks at every seat and microbrews on tap. Each train has two locomotives, a business-class car, six coach-class cars, and a café car. In September 1999, Amtrak, though on schedule with the electrification part of the project, discovered that the delivery of 20 locomotives was going to be delayed. The development of the locomotives, which were designed and manufactured by a consortium of two companies, began in 1996 and was on schedule until it was discovered during testing that the wheels underwent excessive wear. Additional design and testing would add several months to the promised delivery date. Without the locomotives, Amtrak could not test the rails and electrification improvements on schedule. The inaugural of the new service would have to be delayed, causing Amtrak to lose some needed revenue.

The contract between Amtrak and the consortium specified penalties for late delivery of the locomotives. The fines started at $1,000 per day per train and went as high as $13,500 per day per train as delays continued. The fines were over and above compensation for certain other damages to Amtrak caused by nonperformance of the consortium. The Acela Regional service has been a success for Amtrak, outperforming the revenues generated by the old trains by 55 to 65 percent.

Amtrak's Acela Express train stands at Platform 9 at South Station in Boston. Regular passenger service between Washington, DC, and Boston began in December 2000.

Source: "Fast Train to Nowhere?" *Business Week* (September 27, 1999), p. 56, (Updated January 2003.)

Our cost analysis is based on the assumption that direct costs increase linearly as activity time is reduced from its normal time. This assumption implies that for every week the activity time is reduced, direct costs increase by a proportional amount. For example, suppose that the normal time for activity C in the hospital project is 10 weeks and is associated with a direct cost of $4,000. If, by crashing activity C, we can reduce its time to only 5 weeks at a crash cost of $7,000, the net time reduction is 5 weeks at a net cost increase of $3,000. We assume that crashing activity C costs $3,000/5 = $600 per week—an assumption of linear marginal costs that is illustrated in Figure 8.11. Thus, if activity C were expedited by 2 weeks (i.e., its time reduced from 10 weeks to 8 weeks), the estimated direct costs would be $4,000 + 2($600) = $5,200. For any activity, the cost to crash an activity by one week is

FIGURE 8.11

Cost–Time Relationships in Cost Analysis

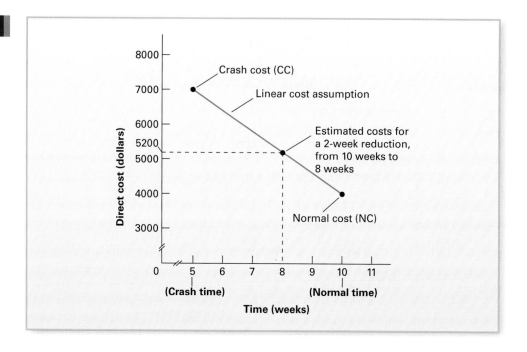

$$\text{Cost to crash per week} = \frac{CC - NC}{NT - CT}$$

Table 8.1 contains direct cost and time data, as well as the costs of crashing per week for the activities in the hospital project.

MINIMIZING COSTS. The objective of cost analysis is to determine the project schedule that minimizes total project costs. Suppose that project indirect costs are $8,000 per week. Suppose also that, after week 65, the Central Ohio Hospital Board imposes on St. Adolf's a penalty cost of $20,000 per week if the hospital is not fully operational. With a critical path completion time of 69 weeks, the hospital faces potentially large penalty costs unless the schedule is changed. For every week that the project is shortened—to week 65—the hospital saves one week of penalty *and* indirect costs, or $28,000. For reductions beyond week 65, the savings are only the weekly indirect costs of $8,000.

TABLE 8.1   DIRECT COST AND TIME DATA FOR THE ST. ADOLF'S HOSPITAL PROJECT

Activity	Normal Time (NT)	Normal Cost (NC)	Crash Time (CT)	Crash Cost (CC)	Maximum Time Reduction (wk)	Cost of Crashing per Week
A	12	$ 12,000	11	$ 13,000	1	$ 1,000
B	9	50,000	7	64,000	2	7,000
C	10	4,000	5	7,000	5	600
D	10	16,000	8	20,000	2	2,000
E	24	120,000	14	200,000	10	8,000
F	10	10,000	6	16,000	4	1,500
G	35	500,000	25	530,000	10	3,000
H	40	1,200,000	35	1,260,000	5	12,000
I	15	40,000	10	52,500	5	2,500
J	4	10,000	1	13,000	3	1,000
K	6	30,000	5	34,000	1	4,000
	Totals	$1,992,000		$2,209,500		

In determining the **minimum-cost schedule,** we start with the normal time schedule and crash activities along the critical path, whose length equals the length of the project. We want to determine how much we can add in crash costs without exceeding the savings in indirect and penalty costs. The procedure involves the following steps:

Step 1. Determine the project's critical path(s).

Step 2. Find the activity or activities on the critical path(s) with the lowest cost of crashing per week.

Step 3. Reduce the time for this activity until (a) it cannot be further reduced, (b) another path becomes critical, or (c) the increase in direct costs exceeds the savings that result from shortening the project. If more than one path is critical, the time for an activity on each path may have to be reduced simultaneously.

Step 4. Repeat this procedure until the increase in direct costs is larger than the savings generated by shortening the project.

> **minimum-cost schedule** A schedule determined by starting with the normal time schedule and crashing activities along the critical path, in such a way that the costs of crashing do not exceed the savings in indirect and penalty costs.

| **Finding a Minimum-Cost Schedule** | **EXAMPLE 8.5** |

Determine the minimum-cost schedule for the St. Adolf's Hospital project. Use the information that was provided in Table 8.1 and Figure 8.8.

SOLUTION

The projected completion time of the project is 69 weeks. The project costs for that schedule are $1,992,000 in direct costs, 69($8,000) = $552,000 in indirect costs, and (69 − 65)($20,000) = $80,000 in penalty costs, for total project costs of $2,624,000. The five paths in the network have the following normal times.

ACTIVE MODEL 8.2
Active Model 8.2 on the Student CD-ROM provides additional insight on cost analysis for the St. Adolf's Hospital project.

A – I – K:	33 weeks	B – D – H – J – K:	69 weeks
A – F – K:	28 weeks	B – E – J – K:	43 weeks
A – C – G – J – K:	67 weeks		

It will simplify our analysis if we can eliminate some paths from further consideration. If all activities on A–C–G–J–K were crashed, the path duration would be 47 weeks. Crashing all activities on B–D–H–J–K results in a duration of 56 weeks. Because the *normal* times of A–I–K, A–F–K, and B–E–J–K are less than the minimum times of the other two paths, we can disregard those three paths; they will never become critical regardless of the crashing we may do.

STAGE I

Step 1. The critical path is B–D–H–J–K.

Step 2. The cheapest activity to crash per week is J at $1,000, which is much less than the savings in indirect and penalty costs of $28,000 per week.

Step 3. Crash activity J by its limit of 3 weeks because the critical path remains unchanged. The new expected path times are

A–C–G–J–K: 64 weeks   and   B–D–H–J–K: 66 weeks

The net savings are 3($28,000) − 3($1,000) = $81,000. The total project costs are now $2,624,000 − $81,000 = $2,543,000.

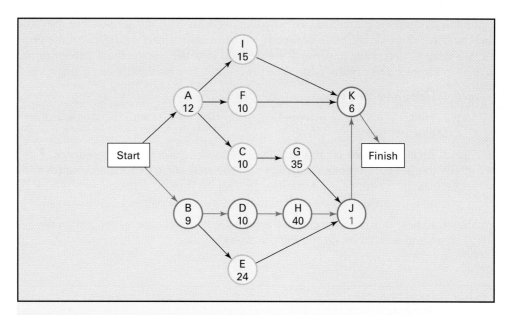

STAGE 2

Step 1. The critical path is still B–D–H–J–K.

Step 2. The cheapest activity to crash per week now is D at $2,000.

Step 3. Crash D by 2 weeks. The first week of reduction in activity D saves $28,000 because it eliminates a week of penalty costs, as well as indirect costs. Crashing D by a second week saves only $8,000 in indirect costs because, after week 65, there are no more penalty costs. These savings still exceed the cost of crashing D by 2 weeks. Updated path times are

$$\text{A–C–G–J–K: 64 weeks} \quad \text{and} \quad \text{B–D–H–J–K: 64 weeks}$$

The net savings are $28,000 + $8,000 − 2($2,000) = $32,000. Total project costs are now $2,543,000 − $32,000 = $2,511,000.

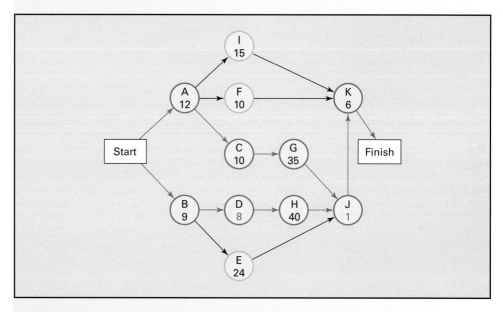

STAGE 3

Step 1. After crashing D, we now have two critical paths. *Both* critical paths must now be shortened to realize any savings in indirect project costs. If one is shortened and the other is not, the length of the project remains unchanged.

Step 2. Our alternatives are to crash one of the following combinations of activities—(A, B); (A, H); (C, B); (C, H); (G, B); (G, H)—or to crash activity K, which is on both critical paths

(J has already been crashed). We consider only those alternatives for which the cost of crashing is less than the potential savings of $8,000 per week. The only viable alternatives are (C, B) at a cost of $7,600 per week and K at $4,000 per week. We choose activity K to crash.

Step 3. We crash activity K to the greatest extent possible—a reduction of I week—because it is on both critical paths. Updated path times are

A–C–G–J–K: 63 weeks   and   B–D–H–J–K: 63 weeks

The net savings are $8,000 − $4,000 = $4,000. Total project costs are $2,511,000 − $4,000 = $2,507,000.

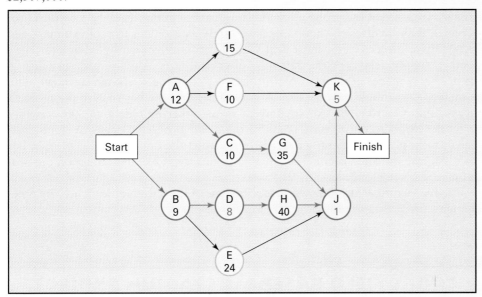

STAGE 4

Step 1. The critical paths are B–D–H–J–K and A–C–G–J–K.

Step 2. The only viable alternative at this stage is to crash activities B and C simultaneously at a cost of $7,600 per week. This amount is still less than the savings of $8,000 per week.

Step 3. Crash activities B and C by 2 weeks, the limit for activity B. Updated path times are

A–C–G–J–K: 61 weeks   and   B–D–H–J–K: 61 weeks

Net savings are 2($8,000) − 2($7,600) = $800. Total project costs are $2,507,000 − $800 = $2,506,200.

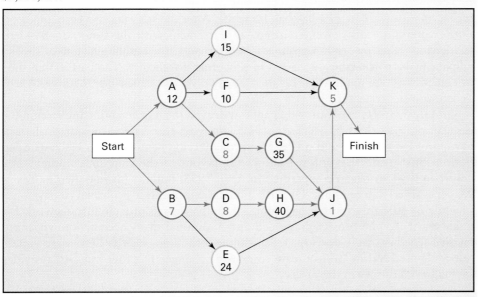

DECISION POINT   Because the crash costs exceed weekly indirect costs, any other combination of activities will result in a net increase in total project costs. The minimum-cost schedule is 61 weeks, with a total cost of $2,506,200. To obtain this schedule, the project team must crash activities B, D, J, and K to their limits and activity C to 8 weeks. The other activities remain at their normal times. This schedule costs $117,800 less than the normal-time schedule.

ASSESSING RISKS

risk-management plan   A plan that identifies the key risks to a project's success and prescribes ways to circumvent them.

Risk is a measure of the probability and consequence of not reaching a defined project goal. Risk involves the notion of uncertainty as it relates to project timing and costs. Often, project teams must deal with uncertainty caused by labor shortages, weather, supply delays, or the outcomes of critical tests. A major responsibility of the project manager at the start of a project is to develop a **risk-management plan.** Team members should have an opportunity to describe the key risks to the project's success and prescribe ways to circumvent them, either by redefining key activities or by developing contingency plans in the event problems occur. A good risk-management plan will quantify the risks and predict their impact on the project. For each risk, the outcome is either acceptable or unacceptable, depending on the project manager's tolerance level for risk.

The Big Picture, which follows, describes some of the uncertainties in activity times that may affect a major project.

● THE BIG PICTURE: COORS FIELD BASEBALL STADIUM PROJECT

Play ball! is a familiar call in the spring, and the people of Denver, Colorado, wanted to hear those words directed at their own National League baseball team. The Denver Metropolitan Major League Baseball Stadium District, a political subdivision of the state, was created by the Colorado Legislature in June 1989. It was given the authority and responsibility to promote the acquisition of a major league franchise and develop a baseball stadium. A key requirement of the National League for granting a franchise is that the community either have a state-of-the-art ballpark dedicated to baseball or commit to building one. One of the first challenges, then, was to secure from the community a financial commitment to build a new stadium.

The district prepared a financial plan and recommended using a sales tax levy contingent on the awarding of a baseball franchise. After the sales tax had been approved by the voters, the district entered into an agreement with the Colorado Baseball Partnership (team ownership group), which provided for building a state-of-the-art ballpark if the partnership succeeded in procuring a franchise. The partnership then proceeded with the application for the franchise. At the same time, the district proceeded with site selection.

On July 5, 1991, the National League approved the partnership's application for the Colorado Rockies baseball franchise, allowing the district to initiate the tax levy, purchase the land, and proceed with the development of Coors Field. The Big Picture illustration that follows shows the layout of the stadium complex. The Colorado Rockies began competition in April 1993, initially playing their games in Denver's Mile High Stadium. On such a complex project, it is normal to develop a schedule of milestones at the beginning of the project to provide a framework for managing it. As the project proceeded and additional tasks become known, more detailed schedules were developed. Scheduling techniques such as CPM were important tools used by the project team to manage change. The following list provides the major milestones in the project.

June 2, 1989	District legislation becomes effective
May 10, 1990	Architect selected
May 15, 1990	Request for proposals for site selection
July 11, 1990	Plan for finance prepared
August 14, 1990	Sales tax election—voters approve tax
September 1, 1990	National League deadline for franchise applications
September 18, 1990	Colorado delegation presentation to National League in New York
March 13, 1991	Lower downtown site selected
March 26, 1991	National League selection committee visit to Denver
July 5, 1991	National League awards franchise to Colorado Baseball Partnership, 1993, Ltd.
December 31, 1991	Largest portion of land purchased
February 13, 1992	Final lease negotiations start
April 1, 1992	Schematic design of ballpark starts
April 21, 1992	Contractor selected
October 8, 1992	Architect presents exterior elevations of ballpark to the public
October 16, 1992	Construction starts
November 11, 1992	Satellite site location of home plate
November 30, 1992	Mass excavation commences
February 2, 1993	Agreement on final terms of lease
February 15, 1993	Caissons and foundation start
June 8, 1993	Playing field turf planted at a farm in northeastern Colorado
July 14, 1993	Last parcel of land purchased
September 24, 1993	First steel raised
October 6, 1993	Final seating capacity set
March 11, 1994	First bricks placed
September 19, 1994	Scoreboard installed
October 25, 1994	Sod transplanted to playing field
February 27, 1995	Sports lighting turned on at night
March 31, 1995	Field ready for opening day

Construction of the stadium started on October 16, 1992. One of the techniques the contractor used to help manage the progress of the thousands of construction activities was the critical path method (CPM). However, planned start times and the durations of many construction activities had to be altered because of nonconstruction-related occurrences. For example, land acquisition took longer than anticipated because one property owner refused to sell a parcel of land on the site slated to become the home-plate entrance to the stadium. Consequently, construction had to begin out of sequence in order to maintain construction progress and avoid changing the scheduled completion date. In addition, owing to the enthusiastic response of baseball fans to the Colorado Rockies, the district altered its estimates of needed seating capacity three times before finally settling on 50,000. Each change required a design modification, which then caused a change in construction activities. Eventually, the stadium took 29 months to construct and cost more than $215.5 million.

To ensure community input on key components of project design, District Executive Director John Lehigh and his team held regular meetings with six different citizen advisory committees representing traffic and transportation, stadium design, handicapped person accessibility, ballpark operations, environmental concerns, art and decorations, media access, and neighborhood interests and concerns. These meetings generated numerous recommendations, to which the project design team responded during the project. For example, neighborhood residents' concerns about the stadium location prompted extensive parking and traffic studies, resulting in a traffic-management plan that helped mitigate concerns. The results were good. On April 26, 1995, the citizens of

THE BIG PICTURE COORS FIELD

Construction of the ballpark required 57,000 cubic yards of concrete, 700,000 masonry blocks, 1,400,000 bricks, and 9,000 tons of steel. Before construction could begin, quantities of these materials had to be estimated, suppliers selected, and delivery schedules determined. Quantities and schedules then had to be changed when the seating capacity was increased. Construction started in October 1992 and was completed in March 1995.

Seating (A). From the start in 1993, attendance figures at the Colorado Rockies games at Mile High Stadium consistently surpassed expectations, with average crowds of over 57,000 fans per game exceeding the seating capacity of 43,000 planned for Coors Field. The seating capacity was increased by 500, then by 1,500, and finally by another 5,000 one year after construction began on the stadium, resulting in a total of over 50,000 seats. The final design called for 18,300 seats in the main concourse, 3,200 in left field, 2,300 in center field, 2,600 in right field, 18,500 in the upper deck, 4,400 in the club mezzanine, and 700 in the suites. Included in these figures are 500 wheelchair seats with 500 companion seats and 500 seats without arms for disabled fans.

The Playing Field (B). Creating the playing field involved a number of sequential steps. Once the site had been excavated, 10,000 feet of drainage pipes were positioned throughout the site and 3,000 tons of pea gravel spread on top to improve drainage. The pipes can drain 5 inches of rain an hour. The 3-acre playing field was made from 6,000 tons of sand in an organic peat growing mixture. Forty-five miles of wire were installed beneath the surface to lengthen the growing season of the turf. The sod, a bluegrass/ryegrass blend, was planted at a turf farm in June 1993 and transplanted to Coors Field in October 1994.

Lighting (C). Coors Field is illuminated by 528 metal halide lamp fixtures, which can be individually controlled for optimal lighting. The 200-watt lights were attached to the structural steel support trusses prior to erection to reduce labor time.

Parking (D). A major component of the stadium project was planning efficient traffic flows and parking. A detailed analysis of vehicle access and parking was conducted before construction began. As the stadium seating capacity was increased after construction began, so was the parking capacity. The present parking capacity is 5,500 on-site spots.

Entrance (E). The ballpark was designed to make access and egress convenient for the fans. The ballpark has two gentle sloping ramps, numerous stair towers, 11 passenger elevators, 7 escalators, and 2 freight elevators. To accommodate the fans during the game, the ballpark has 35 separate concession stands, numerous portable stands, 35 women's restrooms, 31 men's restrooms, and 8 family restrooms.

Denver watched the Colorado Rockies beat the New York Mets in what has been billed as the finest ballpark in the major leagues.

PERT/CPM networks can be used to quantify risks associated with project timing. Often, the uncertainty associated with an activity can be reflected in the activity's time duration. For example, an activity in a new product development project might be developing the enabling technology to manufacture it, an activity that may take from eight months to a year. To incorporate uncertainty into the network model, probability distributions of activity times can be used. There are two approaches: computer simulation and statistical analysis. With simulation, the time for each activity is randomly chosen from its probability distribution (see Supplement B, "Simulation"). The critical path of the network is determined and the completion date of the project computed. The procedure is repeated many times, which results in a probability distribution for the completion date. See the Simulation Exercises section at the end of this chapter for examples of how simulation can be used to incorporate uncertainty in a project network.

The statistical analysis approach requires that activity times be stated in terms of three reasonable time estimates:

> **How can uncertainty in time estimates be incorporated into project planning?**

1. The **optimistic time** (*a*) is the shortest time in which an activity can be completed, if all goes exceptionally well.
2. The **most likely time** (*m*) is the probable time required to perform an activity.
3. The **pessimistic time** (*b*) is the longest estimated time required to perform an activity.

In the remainder of this section, we will discuss how to calculate activity statistics using these three time estimates and how to analyze project risk using probabilities.

optimistic time (*a*) The shortest time in which an activity can be completed, if all goes exceptionally well.

most likely time (*m*) The probable time required to perform an activity.

pessimistic time (*b*) The longest estimated time required to perform an activity.

CALCULATING TIME STATISTICS. With three time estimates—the optimistic, the most likely, and the pessimistic—the project manager has enough information to estimate the probability that an activity will be completed on schedule. To do so, the project manager must first calculate the mean and variance of a probability distribution for each activity. In PERT/CPM, each activity time is treated as though it were a random variable derived from a beta probability distribution. This distribution can have various shapes, allowing the most likely time estimate *(m)* to fall anywhere between the pessimistic *(b)* and optimistic *(a)* time estimates. The most likely time estimate is the *mode* of the beta distribution, or the time with the highest probability of occurrence. This condition is not possible with the normal distribution, which is symmetrical, because the normal distribution requires the mode to be equidistant from the end points of the distribution. Figure 8.12 shows the difference between the two distributions.

Two key assumptions are required. First, we assume that *a*, *m*, and *b* can be estimated accurately. The estimates might best be considered values that define a reasonable time range for the activity duration negotiated between the project manager and the team members responsible for the activities. Second, we assume that the standard deviation, σ, of the activity time is one-sixth the range $b - a$. Thus, the chance that actual activity times will fall between *a* and *b* is high. Why does this assumption make sense? If the activity time followed the normal distribution, six standard deviations would span approximately 99.74 percent of the distribution.

Even with these assumptions, derivation of the mean and variance of each activity's probability distribution is complex. These derivations show that the mean of the beta distribution can be estimated by using the following weighted average of the three time estimates:

$$t_e = \frac{a + 4m + b}{6}$$

Note that the most likely time has four times the weight of the pessimistic and optimistic estimates.

FIGURE 8.12   Differences Between Beta and Normal Distributions for Project Analysis

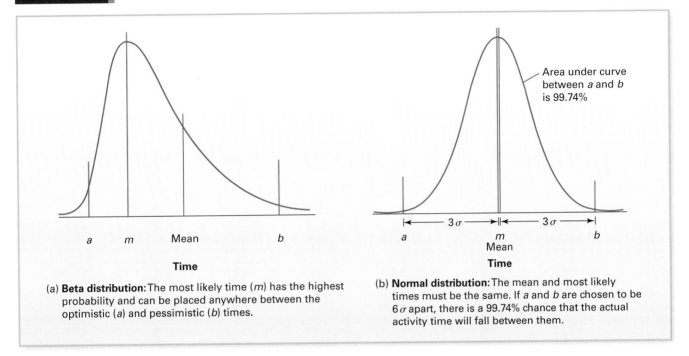

(a) **Beta distribution:** The most likely time (*m*) has the highest probability and can be placed anywhere between the optimistic (*a*) and pessimistic (*b*) times.

(b) **Normal distribution:** The mean and most likely times must be the same. If *a* and *b* are chosen to be 6σ apart, there is a 99.74% chance that the actual activity time will fall between them.

The variance of the beta distribution for each activity is

$$\sigma^2 = \left(\frac{b-a}{6}\right)^2$$

The variance, which is the standard deviation squared, increases as the difference between *b* and *a* increases. This result implies that the less certain a person is in estimating the actual time for an activity, the greater will be the variance.

Calculating Means and Variances   **EXAMPLE 8.6**

Suppose that the project team has arrived at the following time estimates for activity B (site selection and survey) of the St. Adolf's Hospital project:

$$a = 7 \text{ weeks}, \quad m = 8 \text{ weeks}, \quad \text{and} \quad b = 15 \text{ weeks}$$

a. Calculate the expected time for activity B and the variance.
b. Calculate the expected time and variance for the other activities in the project.

SOLUTION

a. The expected time for activity B is

$$t_e = \frac{7 + 4(8) + 15}{6} = \frac{54}{6} = 9 \text{ weeks}$$

Note that the expected time (9 weeks) does not equal the most likely time (8 weeks) for this activity. These times will be the same only when the most likely time is equidistant from the optimistic and pessimistic times. We calculate the variance for activity B as

$$\sigma^2 = \left(\frac{15-7}{6}\right)^2 = \left(\frac{8}{6}\right)^2 = 1.78$$

b. The following table shows expected activity times and variances for the activities listed in the project description.

	TIME ESTIMATES (wk)			ACTIVITY STATISTICS	
ACTIVITY	**OPTIMISTIC (a)**	**MOST LIKELY (m)**	**PESSIMISTIC (b)**	**EXPECTED TIME (t_e)**	**VARIANCE (σ^2)**
A	11	12	13	12	0.11
B	7	8	15	9	1.78
C	5	10	15	10	2.78
D	8	9	16	10	1.78
E	14	25	30	24	7.11
F	6	9	18	10	4.00
G	25	36	41	35	7.11
H	35	40	45	40	2.78
I	10	13	28	15	9.00
J	1	2	15	4	5.44
K	5	6	7	6	0.11

DECISION POINT   The project team should notice that the greatest uncertainty lies in the time estimate for activity I, followed by the estimates for activities E and G. These activities should be analyzed for the source of the uncertainties and actions should be taken to reduce the variance in the time estimates. For example, activity I, developing an information system, may entail the use of a consulting firm. The availability of the consulting firm for the time period scheduled for activity I may be in doubt because of the firm's other commitments. To reduce the risk of delay in the project, the project team could explore the availability of other reputable firms or scale down the requirements for the information system and undertake much of that activity themselves.

ANALYZING PROBABILITIES. Because time estimates for activities involve uncertainty, project managers are interested in determining the probability of meeting project completion deadlines. To develop the probability distribution for project completion time, we assume that the duration time of one activity does not depend on that of any other activity. This assumption enables us to estimate the mean and variance of the probability distribution of the time duration of the entire project by summing the duration times and variances of the activities along the critical path. However, if one work crew is assigned two activities that can be done at the same time, the activity times will be interdependent. In addition, if other paths in the network have small amounts of slack, one of them might become the critical path before the project is completed. In such a case, we should calculate a probability distribution for those paths.

Because of the assumption that the activity duration times are independent random variables, we can make use of the central limit theorem, which states that the sum of a group of independent, identically distributed random variables approaches a normal distribution as the number of random variables increases. The mean of the normal distribution is the sum of the expected activity times on the path. In the case of the critical path, it is the earliest expected finish time for the project:

$$T_E = \Sigma \text{ (Expected activity times on the critical path)} = \text{Mean of normal distribution}$$

Similarly, because of the assumption of activity time independence, we use the sum of the variances of the activities along the path as the variance of the time distribution for that path. That is, for the critical path,

$$\sigma^2 = \Sigma \text{ (Variances of activities on the critical path)}$$

To analyze probabilities of completing a project by a certain date using the normal distribution, we use the z-transformation formula:

$$z = \frac{T - T_E}{\sqrt{\sigma^2}}$$

where

$$T = \text{due date for the project}$$

Given the value of z, we use the Normal Distribution appendix to find the probability that the project will be completed by time T, or sooner. An implicit assumption in this approach is that no other path will become critical during the time span of the project.

The procedure for assessing the probability of completing any activity in a project by a specific date is similar to the one just discussed. However, instead of the critical path, we would use the longest time path of activities from the start node to the activity node in question.

Calculating the Probability of Completing a Project by a Given Date   **EXAMPLE 8.7**

Calculate the probability that St. Adolf's Hospital will become operational in 72 weeks, using (a) the critical path and (b) path A–C–G–J–K.

SOLUTION

a. The critical path B–D–H–J–K has a length of 69 weeks. From the table in Example 8.6, we obtain the variance of path B–D–H–J–K: $\sigma^2 = 1.78 + 1.78 + 2.78 + 5.44 + 0.11 = 11.89$. Next, we calculate the z-value:

$$z = \frac{72 - 69}{\sqrt{11.89}} = \frac{3}{3.45} = 0.87$$

ACTIVE MODEL 8.3
Active Model 8.3 on the Student CD-ROM provides additional insight on probability analysis for the St. Adolf's Hospital project.

Using the Normal Distribution appendix, we find that the probability is about 0.81 that the length of path B–D–H–J–K will be no greater than 72 weeks. Because this path is the critical path, there is a 19 percent probability that the project will take longer than 72 weeks. This probability is shown graphically in Figure 8.13.

b. From the table in Example 8.6, we determine that the sum of the expected activity times on path A–C–G–J–K is 67 weeks and that $\sigma^2 = 0.11 + 2.78 + 7.11 + 5.44 + 0.11 = 15.55$. The z-value is

$$z = \frac{72 - 67}{\sqrt{15.55}} = \frac{5}{3.94} = 1.27$$

The probability is about 0.90 that the length of path A–C–G–J–K will be no greater than 72 weeks.

DECISION POINT   The project team should be aware that there is a 10 percent chance that path A–C–G–J–K will cause a delay in the project. Although the probability is not high for that path, activities A, C, and G bear watching during the first 57 weeks of the project to make sure that there is no more than 2 weeks of slippage in their schedules. This is especially true for activity G, which has a high time variance.

FIGURE 8.13

Probability of Completing the St. Adolf's Hospital Project on Schedule

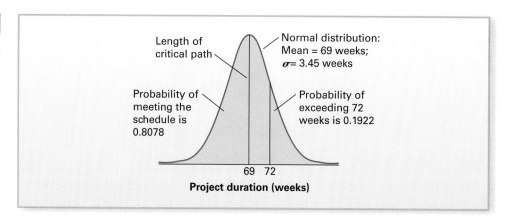

MONITORING AND CONTROLLING PROJECTS

Once project planning is over, the challenge becomes keeping the project on schedule within the budget of allocated resources. In this section, we discuss how to monitor project status and resource usage. In addition, we identify the features of project management software useful for monitoring and controlling projects.

MONITORING PROJECT STATUS

A good tracking system will help the project team accomplish its project goals. Often, the very task of monitoring project progress motivates the team as it sees the benefits of its planning efforts come to fruition. It also focuses attention on the decisions that must be made as the project unfolds. Effective tracking systems collect information on three topics: open issues, risks, and schedule status.

OPEN ISSUES AND RISKS. One of the duties of the project manager is to make sure that issues that have been raised during the project actually get resolved in a timely fashion. The tracking system should remind the project manager of due dates for open issues and who was responsible for seeing that they are resolved. Likewise, it should provide the status of each risk to project delays specified in the risk-management plan, so that the team can review them at each meeting. The project manager should also enter new issues or risks into the system as they arise. To be effective, the tracking system requires team members to update information periodically regarding their respective responsibilities. Although the tracking system can be computerized, it can also be as simple as using e-mail, voice mail, or meetings to convey the necessary information.

SCHEDULE STATUS. Even the best laid project plans can go awry. Monitoring slack time in the project schedule can help the project manager control activities along the critical path. Suppose in the hospital project that activity A is completed in 16 weeks rather than the anticipated 12 weeks and that activity B takes 10 weeks instead of the expected 9 weeks. Table 8.2 shows how these delays affect slack times as of the sixteenth week of the project. Activities A and B are not shown because they have already been completed.

Negative slack occurs when the assumptions used to compute planned slack are invalid. Activities C, G, J, and K, which depend on the timely completion of activities A and B, show negative slack because they have been pushed beyond their planned latest start dates. The activities at the top of Table 8.2 are more critical than those at the bottom because they are the furthest behind schedule and affect the completion time of the entire project. To meet the original completion target of week 69, the project manager must try to make up two weeks of time somewhere along path C–G–J–K. Moreover, one week will have to be made up along path D–H. If that time is made up, there will be two critical paths: C–G–J–K and D–H–J–K. Many project managers work with computer scheduling programs that generate slack reports like the one shown in Table 8.2.

TABLE 8.2   SLACK CALCULATIONS AFTER ACTIVITIES A AND B HAVE BEEN COMPLETED

Activity	Duration	Earliest Start	Latest Start	Slack
C	10	16	14	−2
G	35	26	24	−2
J	4	61	59	−2
K	6	65	63	−2
D	10	10	9	−1
H	40	20	19	−1
E	24	10	35	25
I	15	16	48	32
F	10	16	53	37

MONITORING PROJECT RESOURCES

The resources allocated to a project are consumed at an uneven rate that is a function of the timing of the schedules for the project's activities. Projects have a *life cycle* that consists of four major phases: (1) definition and organization, (2) planning, (3) execution, and (4) close out. Figure 8.14 shows that each of the four phases requires different resource commitments.

We have already discussed the activities associated with the project definition and organization and project planning phases. The phase that takes the most resources is the *execution phase*, during which managers focus on activities pertaining to deliverables. The project schedule becomes very important because it shows when each resource devoted to a given activity will be required. Monitoring the progress of activities throughout the project is important to avoid potential overloading of resources. Problems arise when a specific resource, such as a construction crew or staff specialist, is required on several activities with overlapping schedules. Project managers have several options to alleviate resource problems, including

- *Resource Leveling.* The attempt to reduce the peaks and valleys in resource needs by shifting the schedules of conflicting activities within their earliest and latest start dates. If an activity must be delayed beyond its latest start date, the

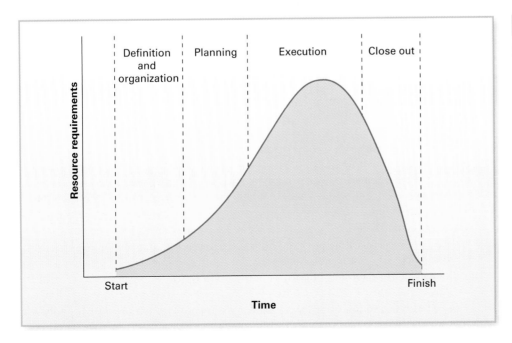

FIGURE 8.14

Project Life Cycle

completion date of the total project will be delayed unless activities on the critical path can be reduced to compensate. The crashing techniques we discussed in the cost–time trade-off section of this chapter might help to bring the schedule back on track, but there is the possibility of added costs to consider.

- *Resource Allocation.* The attempt to shift resources from activities with slack to those on the critical path where resources are overloaded. A slack report such as the one in Table 8.2 identifies potential candidates for resource shifting. However, efficiency can be compromised if shifted employees do not have all the skills required for their new assignments.
- *Resource Acquisition.* The addition of more of an overloaded resource to maintain the schedule of an activity.

close out An activity that includes writing final reports, completing remaining deliverables, and compiling the team's recommendations for improving the project process.

The project **close out** is an activity that many project managers forget to include in their consideration of resource usage. The purpose of this final phase in the project life cycle is to write final reports and complete remaining deliverables. A very important aspect of this phase, however, is compiling the team's recommendations for improving the project process of which they were a part. Many team members will be assigned to other projects where they can apply what they have learned.

PROJECT MANAGEMENT SOFTWARE

Project management software is accessible to most organizations and is being used extensively in government, services, and manufacturing. Ford Motor Company used computerized network planning for retooling assembly lines, and Chrysler Corporation used it for building a new assembly plant. Other users include the San Francisco Opera Association, the Walt Disney Company, and Procter & Gamble.

Bechtel Group, Inc. had to purchase a sophisticated software package because of the complexity of its scheduling problems. However, with the advent of personal computers, off-the-shelf project management software has become accessible to many companies. Large projects, as well as small projects, are routinely managed with the assistance of standard computerized scheduling packages. Software costs have come down, and user–computer interfaces are friendly. Standard software programs may differ in terms of their output reports and may include one or more of the following capabilities:

- *Gantt Charts and PERT/CPM Diagrams.* The graphics capabilities of software packages allow for visual displays of project progress on Gantt charts and PERT/CPM network diagrams. Most packages allow the user to display portions of the network on the video monitor to analyze specific problems.
- *Project Status and Summary Reports.* These reports include budget variance reports that compare planned to actual expenses at any stage in the project, resource histograms that graphically display the usage of a particular resource over time, status reports for each worker by task performed, and summary reports that indicate project progress to top management.
- *Tracking Reports.* These reports identify areas of concern, such as the percentage of activity completion with respect to time, budget, or labor resources. Most software packages allow multiple projects to be tracked at the same time. This feature is important when resources must be shared jointly by several projects.
- *Project Calendar.* This feature allows the project manager to lay out calendars based on actual workdays, weekends, and vacations and enables the software to present all schedules and reports in terms of the project calendar.
- *What-If Analysis.* Some packages allow the project manager to enter proposed changes to activity times, precedence relationships, or start dates to see what effect the changes might have on the project completion date.

Today there are more than 200 software packages, most of which are user friendly and available for the PC.

PLANNING AND MANAGING PROJECTS ACROSS THE ORGANIZATION

Projects are big and small. They are contained within a single department or they can cut across several departments. Many organizations have several projects ongoing at any one time, addressing issues of concern to finance, marketing, accounting, human resources, information systems, or operations. Regardless of the scope, projects are completed with the use of a project process. The size of the project team may be small and the need for project management software marginal, but successful projects will use the principles we discussed in this chapter regardless of the discipline the project addresses.

The applicability of project processes is pervasive across all types of organizations and disciplines. Managers often find themselves working with counterparts from other departments. For example, consider a project to develop a corporate database at a bank. Because no department knows exactly what services a customer is receiving from the other departments, the project will consolidate information about corporate customers from many areas of the bank into one corporate database. From this information, corporate banking services could be designed not only to better serve the corporate customers but also to provide a basis for evaluating the prices that the bank charges. Marketing is interested in knowing all the services a customer is receiving, so that it can package and sell other services that the customer may not be aware of. Finance is interested in how profitable a customer is to the bank and whether the provided services are appropriately priced. The project team should consist of representatives from marketing, the finance departments with a direct interest in corporate clients, and management information systems. Projects such as this are becoming more common as companies take advantage of the Internet to provide services and products directly to the customer.

CHAPTER HIGHLIGHTS

- A project is an interrelated set of activities that often transcends functional boundaries. A project process is the organization and management of the resources dedicated to completing a project. Managing projects involves defining and organizing, planning, and monitoring and controlling the project.

- Project planning involves defining the work breakdown structure, diagramming the network, developing a schedule, analyzing cost–time trade-offs, and assessing risks.

- Project planning and scheduling focuses on the critical path: the sequence of activities requiring the greatest cumulative amount of time for completion. Delay in critical activities will delay the entire project.

- Cost–time trade-offs can be analyzed with network planning methods such as PERT/CPM under the assumption of linear marginal costs.

- Risks associated with the completion of activities on schedule can be incorporated in project networks by recognizing three time estimates for each activity and then calculating expected activity times and variances. The probability of completing the schedule by a certain date can be computed with this information.

- Monitoring and controlling projects involves the use of activity-time slack reports and reports on actual resource usage. Overloads on certain resources can be rectified by resource leveling, allocation, or acquistion.

STUDENT CD-ROM AND INTERNET RESOURCES

The Student CD-ROM and the Companion Website at **www.prenhall.com/krajewski** contain many tools, activities, and resources designed for this chapter. The following items are recommended to enhance your skills and improve your understanding of the material in this chapter.

STUDENT CD-ROM RESOURCES

- **PowerPoint Slides:** View the comprehensive set of slides customized for this chapter's concepts and techniques.

- ▶ **OM Explorer Tutors:** OM Explorer contains five tutor spreadsheets to enhance your understanding of learning curves, time–study sample sizes, normal times for an activity, standard times for an activity, and the work sampling approach. See the Supplement G and Supplement H folders in OM Explorer.

- ▶ **OM Explorer Solvers:** OM Explorer contains four spreadsheets designed to solve project planning problems under four conditions: (1) activity times are known with certainty, (2) activity times are uncertain and must be estimated with a probability distribution, (3) project budgeting and cash flow estimates are required, or (4) crash costs are important. OM Explorer also has three spreadsheets designed to solve general problems involving time study, work sampling, and learning curves. See the Planning and Managing Projects, Measuring Output Rates, and Learning Curves folders in OM Explorer.

➤ **Active Models:** There are three active model spreadsheets that provide additional insights on Gantt charts, cost analysis, and probability analysis. See Planning and Managing Projects, in the Active Models menu for these routines. Also see the Active Model Exercise later in this chapter for an example of the Gantt chart active model.

➤ **SimQuick:** Learn the basics of building simulation models for planning and managing projects by working through Examples 25 and 26 in *SimQuick: Process Simulation with Excel*. These examples are among many other examples addressing waiting lines, inventory in supply chains, and manufacturing.

➤ **MS Project:** Your instructor may have ordered the 120-day evaluation version of MS Project software that is often used in practice for managing projects. It can be used to solve most of the problems, as well as the case at the end of the chapter, in addition to any problems or cases the instructor may add. Alternatively, you can use the link on the Student CD-ROM to order a 60-day evaluation version from Microsoft.

➤ **SmartDraw:** Use the link to download a trial version of SmartDraw, a software package often used in practice to prepare network diagrams.

➤ **Supplement G:** "Learning Curve Analysis." This supplement provides the background to estimate the time or resources to perform an activity consisting of the production of a given number of identical units.

➤ **Supplement H:** "Measuring Output Rates." This supplement presents several tools for estimating the time to perform a repetitive task after all learning effects have worn off.

 INTERNET RESOURCES

➤ **Self-Study Quizzes:** See the compendium of true or false, multiple choice, and essay questions that allows online tests or gives you feedback on how well you have mastered the concepts of this chapter.

➤ **In the News:** See the articles that apply to this chapter.

➤ **Internet Exercises:** Try out three different links to project management topics, including scheduling at the Olympics and managing construction projects.

➤ **Virtual Tours:** Explore the management of a project process at the Rieger Orgelbau Pipe Organ Factory. Also see the "Web Links to Company Facility Tours" for additional tours of company facilities.

➤ **Critical Tools:** Visit the Web site for Critical Tools at **www.criticaltools.com**. Explore the add-ons to Microsoft's MS Project, such as WBS Chart and PERT Chart Expert. Find links to user groups, training opportunities, and the MS Project Web site.

➤ **Project Management Institute:** Visit the Web site for a major organization promoting the use of the project management approach at **www.pmi.org**.

KEY EQUATIONS

1. Start and finish times:

$$ES = \max(EF \text{ times of all activities immediately preceding activity})$$

$$EF = ES + t$$

$$LS = LF - t$$

$$LF = \min(LS \text{ times of all activities immediately following activity})$$

2. Activity slack:

$$S = LS - ES \quad \text{or} \quad S = LF - EF$$

3. Project costs:

$$\text{Crash cost per unit of time} =$$

$$\frac{\text{Crash cost} - \text{Normal cost}}{\text{Normal time} - \text{Crash time}} = \frac{CC - NC}{NT - CT}$$

4. Activity time statistics:

$$t_e = \frac{a + 4m + b}{6} \quad \text{(Expected activity time)}$$

$$\sigma^2 = \left(\frac{b - a}{6}\right)^2 \quad \text{(Variance)}$$

5. z-transformation formula:

$$z = \frac{T - T_E}{\sqrt{\sigma^2}}$$

where

$$T = \text{due date for the project}$$

$$T_E = \text{(expected activity times on the critical path)}$$

$$= \text{mean of normal distribution}$$

$$\sigma^2 = \Sigma\text{(variances of activities on the critical path)}$$

KEY TERMS

activity 346
activity-on-arc (AOA) network 348
activity-on-node (AON) network 348
activity slack 352
close out 374
crash cost (CC) 358
crash time (CT) 358
critical path 352
critical path method (CPM) 347
earliest finish time (EF) 353
earliest start time (ES) 353

event 348
free slack 357
Gantt chart 356
latest finish time (LF) 354
latest start time (LS) 354
minimum-cost schedule 361
most likely time (m) 368
network diagram 347
normal cost (NC) 358
normal time (NT) 358
optimistic time (a) 368

path 352
pessimistic time (b) 368
precedence relationship 348
program evaluation and review technique (PERT) 347
project 342
risk-management plan 364
total slack 356
work breakdown structure (WBS) 345

SOLVED PROBLEM I

Your company has just received an order from a good customer for a specially designed electric motor. The contract states that, starting on the thirteenth day from now, your firm will experience a penalty of $100 per day until the job is completed. Indirect project costs amount to $200 per day. The data on direct costs and activity precedence relationships are given in Table 8.3.

TABLE 8.3 ELECTRIC MOTOR PROJECT DATA

Activity	Normal Time (days)	Normal Cost ($)	Crash Time (days)	Crash Cost ($)	Immediate Predecessor(s)
A	4	1,000	3	1,300	None
B	7	1,400	4	2,000	None
C	5	2,000	4	2,700	None
D	6	1,200	5	1,400	A
E	3	900	2	1,100	B
F	11	2,500	6	3,750	C
G	4	800	3	1,450	D, E
H	3	300	1	500	F, G

a. Draw the project network diagram.
b. What completion date would you recommend?

SOLUTION

a. The AON network diagram, including normal activity times, for this procedure is shown in Figure 8.15. Keep the following points in mind while constructing a network diagram.

1. Always have start and finish nodes.
2. Try to avoid crossing paths to keep the diagram simple.
3. Use only one arrow to directly connect any two nodes.
4. Put the activities with no preducessors at the left and point the arrows from left to right.
5. Use scratch paper and be prepared to revise the diagram several times before you come up with a correct and uncluttered diagram.

FIGURE 8.15

AON Network Diagram for the Electric Motor Project

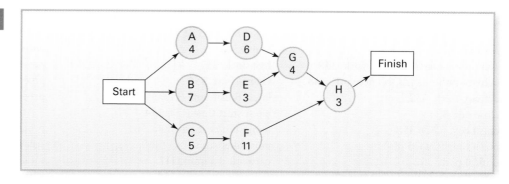

b. With these activity durations, the project will be completed in 19 days and incur a $700 penalty. Determining a good completion date requires the use of the minimum-cost schedule procedure. Using the data provided in Table 8.3, you can determine the maximum crash-time reduction and crash cost per day for each activity. For example, for activity A

$$\text{Maximum crash time} = \text{Normal time} - \text{Crash time} = 4 \text{ days} - 3 \text{ days} = 1 \text{ day}$$

$$\frac{\text{Crash cost}}{\text{per day}} = \frac{\text{Crash cost} - \text{Normal cost}}{\text{Normal time} - \text{Crash time}} = \frac{\text{CC} - \text{NC}}{\text{NT} - \text{CT}} = \frac{\$1,300 - \$1,000}{4 \text{ days} - 3 \text{ days}} = \$300$$

ACTIVITY	CRASH COST PER DAY ($)	MAXIMUM TIME REDUCTION (DAYS)
A	300	1
B	200	3
C	700	1
D	200	1
E	200	1
F	250	5
G	650	1
H	100	2

Table 8.4 summarizes the analysis and the resultant project duration and total cost. The critical path is C–F–H at 19 days which is the longest path in the network. The cheapest of these activities to crash is H, which costs only an extra $100 per day to crash. Doing so saves $200 + $100 = $300 per day in indirect and penalty costs. If you crash this activity two days (the maximum), the lengths of the paths are now

A–D–G–H: 15 days,   B–E–G–H: 15 days, and   C–F–H: 17 days

The critical path is still C–F–H. The next cheapest critical activity to crash is F at $250 per day. You can crash F only two days because at that point you will have three critical paths. Further reductions in project duration will require simultaneous crashing of more than one activity (D, E, and F). The cost to do so, $650, exceeds the savings, $300. Consequently, you should stop. Note that every activity is critical. The project costs are minimized when the completion date is day 15. However, there may be some goodwill costs associated with disappointing a customer who wants delivery in 12 days.

TABLE 8.4   PROJECT COST ANALYSIS

Stage	Crash Activity	Resulting Critical Path(s)	Time Reduction (days)	Project Duration (days)	Project Direct Costs, Last Trial	Crash Cost Added	Total Indirect Costs	Total Penalty Costs	Total Project Costs
0	—	C–F–H	—	19	$10,100	—	$3,800	$700	$14,600
1	H	C–F–H	2	17	$10,100	$200	$3,400	$500	$14,200
2	F	A–D–G–H B–E–G–H C–F–H	2	15	$10,300	$500	$3,000	$300	$14,100

SOLVED PROBLEM 2

An advertising project manager has developed the network diagrams shown in Figure 8.16 for a new advertising campaign. In addition, the manager has gathered the time information for each activity, as shown in the accompanying table.

Network Diagrams for an Advertising Program

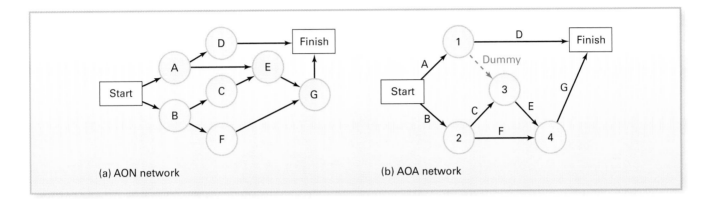

(a) AON network   (b) AOA network

ACTIVITY	TIME ESTIMATES (wk)			IMMEDIATE PREDECESSOR(S)
	OPTIMISTIC	MOST LIKELY	PESSIMISTIC	
A	1	4	7	—
B	2	6	7	—
C	3	3	6	B
D	6	13	14	A
E	3	6	12	A, C
F	6	8	16	B
G	1	5	6	E, F

a. Calculate the expected time and variance for each activity.
b. Calculate the activity slacks and determine the critical path, using the expected activity times.
c. What is the probability of completing the project within 23 weeks?

SOLUTION

a. The expected time for each activity is calculated as follows:

$$t_e = \frac{a + 4m + b}{6}$$

ACTIVITY	EXPECTED TIME (wk)	VARIANCE
A	4.0	1.00
B	5.5	0.69
C	3.5	0.25
D	12.0	1.78
E	6.5	2.25
F	9.0	2.78
G	4.5	0.69

b. We need to calculate the earliest start, latest start, earliest finish, and latest finish times for each activity. Starting with activities A and B, we proceed from the beginning of the network and move to the end, calculating the earliest start and finish times:

ACTIVITY	EARLIEST START (wk)	EARLIEST FINISH (wk)
A	0	0 + 4.0 = 4.0
B	0	0 + 5.5 = 5.5
C	5.5	5.5 + 3.5 = 9.0
D	4.0	4.0 + 12.0 = 16.0
E	9.0	9.0 + 6.5 = 15.5
F	5.5	5.5 + 9.0 = 14.5
G	15.5	15.5 + 4.5 = 20.0

Based on expected times, the earliest finish for the project is week 20, when activity G has been completed. Using that as a target date, we can work backward through the network, calculating the latest start and finish times (shown graphically in Figure 8.17):

ACTIVITY	LATEST START (wk)	LATEST FINISH (wk)
G	15.5	20.0
F	6.5	15.5
E	9.0	15.5
D	8.0	20.0
C	5.5	9.0
B	0.0	5.5
A	4.0	8.0

We now calculate the activity slacks and determine which activities are on the critical path:

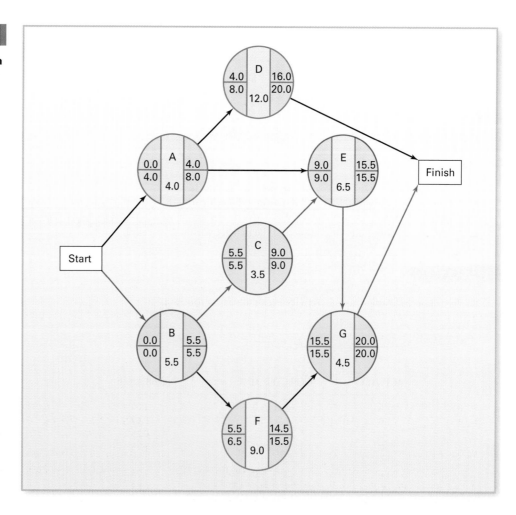

FIGURE 8.17

AON Network Diagram with All Time Estimates Needed to Calculate Slack

	START		FINISH		ACTIVITY SLACK	CRITICAL PATH
ACTIVITY	EARLIEST	LATEST	EARLIEST	LATEST		
A	0.0	4.0	4.0	8.0	4.0	No
B	0.0	0.0	5.5	5.5	0.0	Yes
C	5.5	5.5	9.0	9.0	0.0	Yes
D	4.0	8.0	16.0	20.0	4.0	No
E	9.0	9.0	15.5	15.5	0.0	Yes
F	5.5	6.5	14.5	15.5	1.0	No
G	15.5	15.5	20.0	20.0	0.0	Yes

The paths, and their total expected times and variances, are

PATH	TOTAL EXPECTED TIME (wk)	TOTAL VARIANCE
A–D	4 + 12 = 16	1.00 + 1.78 = 2.78
A–E–G	4 + 6.5 + 4.5 = 15	1.00 + 2.25 + 0.69 = 3.94
B–C–E–G	5.5 + 3.5 + 6.5 + 4.5 = 20	0.69 + 0.25 + 2.25 + 0.69 = 3.88
B–F–G	5.5 + 9 + 4.5 = 19	0.69 + 2.78 + 0.69 = 4.16

The critical path is B–C–E–G, with a total expected time of 20 weeks. However path B–F–G is 19 weeks and has a large variance. In this solution, we used the AON notation, showing the start and finish times within the node circles. The same results can be obtained with the AOA notation, except that times are typically shown in a box drawn near the arc (arrow). For example:

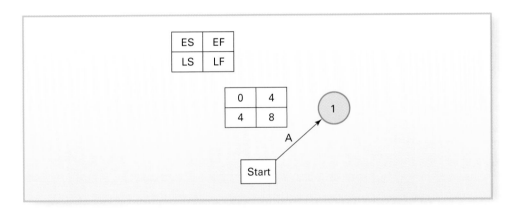

c. We first calculate the z-value:

$$z = \frac{T - T_E}{\sqrt{\sigma^2}} = \frac{23 - 20}{\sqrt{3.88}} = 1.52$$

Using the Normal Distribution appendix, we find that the probability of completing the project in 23 weeks or less is 0.9357. Because the length of path B–F–G is very close to that of the critical path and has a large variance, it might well become the critical path during the project.

DISCUSSION QUESTIONS

1. One of your colleagues comments that software is the ultimate key to project management success. How would you respond?

2. When a large project is mismanaged, it makes news. Form a discussion group and identify penalties associated with a mismanaged project in your experience or in recent headlines. Identify the cause of the problem, such as inaccurate time estimates, changed scope, unplanned or improperly sequenced activities, inadequate resources, or poor management—labor relations.

3. Describe a project in which you participated. What activities were involved and how were they interrelated? How would you rate the project manager? What is the basis of your evaluation?

PROBLEMS

In the following problems, network diagrams can be drawn in the AOA or AON format. Your instructor will indicate which is preferred. An icon next to a problem identifies the software that can be helpful, but is not mandatory. OM Explorer and a link to MS Project are available on the Student CD-ROM that is packaged with every new copy of the textbook. Your instructor will indicate which package, if any, is to be used.

1. ◗ **OM Explorer** Consider the following data for a project.

Activity	Activity Time (days)	Immediate Predecessor(s)
A	2	—
B	4	A
C	5	A
D	2	B
E	1	B
F	8	B, C
G	3	D, E
H	5	F
I	4	F
J	7	G, H, I

    a. Draw the network diagram.

    b. Calculate the critical path for this project.

    c. How much total slack is in activities G, H, and I?

2. ◗ **OM Explorer** The following information is known about a project.

Activity	Activity Time (days)	Immediate Predecessor(s)
A	7	—
B	2	A
C	4	A
D	4	B, C
E	4	D
F	3	E
G	5	E

    a. Draw the network diagram for this project.

    b. Determine the critical path and project duration.

3. ◗ **OM Explorer** A project has the following precedence relationships and activity times.

Activity	Activity Time (wks)	Immediate Predecessor(s)
A	4	—
B	10	—
C	5	A
D	15	B, C
E	12	B
F	4	D
G	8	E
H	7	F, G

    a. Draw the network diagram.

    b. Calculate the total slack for each activity. Which activities are on the critical path?

4. ◗ **OM Explorer** The following information is available about a project.

Activity	Activity Time (days)	Immediate Predecessor(s)
A	3	—
B	4	—
C	5	—
D	4	—
E	7	A
F	2	B, C, D
G	4	E, F
H	6	F
I	4	G
J	3	G
K	3	H

    a. Draw the network diagram.

    b. Find the critical path.

5. ◗ **OM Explorer** The following information has been gathered for a project.

Activity	Activity Time (wks)	Immediate Predecessor(s)
A	4	—
B	7	A
C	9	B
D	3	B
E	14	D
F	10	C, D
G	11	F, E

    a. Draw the network diagram.

    b. Calculate the total slack for each activity and determine the critical path. How long will the project take?

6. ◗ **OM Explorer** Consider the following project information.

Activity	Activity Time (wks)	Immediate Predecessor(s)
A	4	—
B	3	—
C	5	—
D	3	A, B
E	6	B
F	4	D, C
G	8	E, C
H	12	F, G

    a. Draw the network diagram for this project.

    b. Specify the critical path.

    c. Calculate the total slack for activities A and D.

    d. What happens to the slack for D if A takes five weeks?

7. ◗ **OM Explorer** Barbara Gordon, the project manager for Web Ventures, Inc., compiled a table showing time estimates for each of the company's manufacturing activities of a project, including optimistic, most likely, and pessimistic.

   a. Calculate the expected time, t_e, for each activity.

   b. Calculate the variance, σ^2, for each activity.

Activity	Optimistic	Most Likely	Pessimistic
A	3	8	19
B	12	15	18
C	2	6	16
D	4	9	20
E	1	4	7

8. ◗ **OM Explorer** Recently, you were assigned to manage a project for your company. You have constructed a network diagram depicting the various activities in the project (Figure 8.18). In addition, you have asked your team to estimate the amount of time that they would expect each of the activities to take. Their responses are shown in the following table.

Activity	Time Estimates (days)		
	Optimistic	Most Likely	Pessimistic
A	5	8	11
B	4	8	11
C	5	6	7
D	2	4	6
E	4	7	10

   a. What is the expected completion time of the project?

   b. What is the probability of completing the project in 21 days?

   c. What is the probability of completing the project in 17 days?

FIGURE 8.18

AON Network Diagram

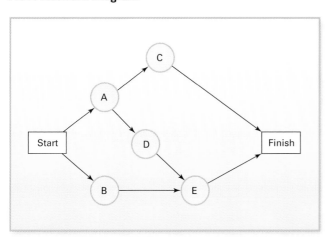

9. In Solved Problem 2, estimate the probability that the noncritical path B–F–G will take more than 20 weeks. *Hint:* Subtract from 1.0 the probability that B–F–G will take 20 weeks or less.

10. ◗ **OM Explorer** Consider the following data for a project never before attempted by your company.

Activity	Expected Time t_e(wk)	Immediate Predecessor(s)
A	5	—
B	3	—
C	2	A
D	5	B
E	4	C, D
F	7	D

   a. Draw the network diagram for this project.

   b. Identify the critical path and estimate the project's duration.

   c. Calculate the total slack for each activity.

11. ◗ **OM Explorer** The director of continuing education at Bluebird University has just approved the planning for a sales training seminar. Her administrative assistant has identified the various activities that must be done and their relationships to each other, as shown in Table 8.5.

   Because of the uncertainty in planning the new course, the assistant also has supplied the following time estimates for each activity.

Activity	Time Estimates (days)		
	Optimistic	Most Likely	Pessimistic
A	5	7	8
B	6	8	12
C	3	4	5
D	11	17	25
E	8	10	12
F	3	4	5
G	4	8	9
H	5	7	9
I	8	11	17
J	4	4	4

TABLE 8.5
ACTIVITIES FOR THE SALES TRAINING SEMINAR

Activity	Description	Immediate Predecessor(s)
A	Design brochure and course announcement	—
B	Identify prospective teachers	—
C	Prepare detailed outline of course	—
D	Send brochure and student applications	A
E	Send teacher applications	B
F	Select teacher for course	C, E
G	Accept students	D
H	Select text for course	F
I	Order and receive texts	G, H
J	Prepare room for class	G

The director wants to conduct the seminar 47 working days from now. What is the probability that everything will be ready in time?

12. Table 8.6 contains information about a project. Shorten the project three weeks by finding the minimum-cost schedule. Assume that project indirect costs and penalty costs are negligible. Identify activities to crash while minimizing the additional crash costs.

13. ◆ OM Explorer Information concerning a project is given in Table 8.7. Indirect project costs amount to $250 per day. The company will incur a $100 per day penalty for each day the project lasts beyond day 14.

   a. What is the project's duration if only normal times are used?

   b. What is the minimum-cost schedule?

   c. What is the critical path for the minimum-cost schedule?

14. ◆ OM Explorer Jason Ritz, district manager for Gumfull Foods, Inc., is in charge of opening a new fast-food outlet in the college town of Clarity. His major concern is the hiring of a manager and a cadre of hamburger cooks, assemblers, and dispensers. He also has to

coordinate the renovation of a building that was previously owned by a pet-supplies retailer. He has gathered the data shown in Table 8.8.

Top management has told Ritz that the new outlet is to be opened as soon as possible. Every week that the project can be shortened will save the firm $1,200 in lease costs. Ritz thought about how to save time during the project and came up with two possibilities. One was to employ Arctic, Inc., a local employment agency, to locate some good prospects for the manager's job. This approach would save three weeks in activity A and cost Gumfull Foods $2,500. The other was to add a few workers to shorten the time for activity B by two weeks at an additional cost of $2,700.

Help Jason Ritz by answering the following questions.

   a. How long is the project expected to take?

   b. Suppose that Ritz has a personal goal of completing the project in 14 weeks. What is the probability that this will happen?

   c. What additional expenditures should be made to reduce the project's duration? Use the expected time for each activity as though it were certain.

15. ◆ OM Explorer The diagram in Figure 8.19 was developed for a project that you are managing. Suppose that you are interested in finding ways to speed up the project at minimal additional cost. Determine the schedule for completing the project in 25 days at minimum cost. Penalty and project-overhead costs are negligible. Time and cost data for each activity are shown in Table 8.9

16. ◆ OM Explorer Paul Silver, owner of Sculptures International, just initiated a new art project. The following data are available for the project.

TABLE 8.6
PROJECT ACTIVITY AND COST DATA

Activity	Normal Time (wks)	Crash Time (wks)	Cost to Crash ($ per week)	Immediate Predecessor(s)
A	7	6	200	None
B	12	9	250	None
C'	7	6	250	A
D	6	5	300	A
E	1	1	—	B
F	1	1	—	C, D
G	3	1	200	D, E
H	3	2	350	F
I	2	2	—	G

TABLE 8.7
PROJECT ACTIVITY AND COST DATA

Activity	Normal Time (days)	Normal Cost ($)	Crash Time (days)	Crash Cost ($)	Immediate Predecessor(s)
A	5	1,000	4	1,200	—
B	5	800	3	2,000	—
C	2	600	1	900	A, B
D	3	1,500	2	2,000	B
E	5	900	3	1,200	C, D
F	2	1,300	1	1,400	E
G	3	900	3	900	E
H	5	500	3	900	G

FIGURE 8.19

AON Network Diagram

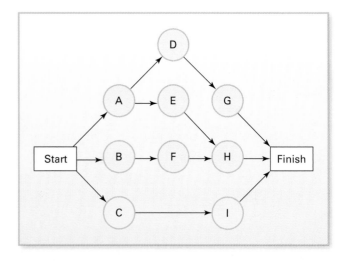

TABLE 8.8
DATA FOR THE FAST-FOOD OUTLET PROJECT

Activity	Description	Immediate Predecessor(s)	Time (wk)		
			a	m	b
A	Interview at college for new manager	—	2	4	6
B	Renovate building	—	5	8	11
C	Place ad for employees and interview applicants	—	7	9	17
D	Have new manager prospects visit	A	1	2	3
E	Purchase equipment for new outlet and install	B	2	4	12
F	Check employee applicant references and make final selection	C	4	4	4
G	Check references for new manager and make final selection	D	1	1	1
H	Hold orientation meetings and do payroll paperwork	E, F, G	2	2	2

Activity	Activity Time (days)	Immediate Predecessor(s)
A	4	—
B	1	—
C	3	A
D	2	B
E	3	C, D

a. Draw the network diagram for the project.

b. Determine the project's critical path and duration.

c. What is the total slack for each activity?

17. ◗ **OM Explorer** Reliable Garage is completing production of the J2000 kit car. The following data are available for the project.

Activity	Activity Time (days)	Immediate Predecessor(s)
A	2	—
B	6	A
C	4	B
D	5	C
E	7	C
F	5	C
G	5	F
H	3	D, E, G

TABLE 8.9
PROJECT ACTIVITY AND COST DATA

	Normal		Crash	
Activity	Time (days)	Cost ($)	Time (days)	Cost ($)
A	12	1,300	11	1,900
B	13	1,050	9	1,500
C	18	3,000	16	4,500
D	9	2,000	5	3,000
E	12	650	10	1,100
F	8	700	7	1,050
G	8	1,550	6	1,950
H	2	600	1	800
I	4	2,200	2	4,000

a. Draw the network diagram for the project.

b. Determine the project's critical path and duration.

c. What is the total slack for each activity?

18. ◗ **OM Explorer** The following information concerns a new project your company is undertaking.

Activity	Activity Time (days)	Immediate Predecessor(s)
A	10	—
B	11	—
C	9	A, B
D	5	A, B
E	8	A, B
F	13	C, E
G	5	C, D
H	10	G
I	6	F, G
J	9	E, H
K	11	I, J

a. Draw the network diagram for this project.

b. Determine the critical path and project completion time.

Advanced Problems

19. ◗ **OM Explorer** The project manager of Good Public Relations has gathered the data shown in Table 8.10 for a new advertising campaign.

a. How long is the project likely to take?

b. What is the probability that the project will take more than 38 weeks?

c. Consider the path A–E–G–H–J. What is the probability that this path will exceed the expected project duration?

20. ◗ **SmartDraw** Michaelson Construction builds houses. Create a network showing the precedence relationships for the activities listed in Table 8.11.

21. ◗ **SmartDraw** Fronc is a wedding coordinator. Beatrice Wright and William Bach have asked Fronc to help them organize their wedding. Create a network

TABLE 8.10
ACTIVITY DATA FOR ADVERTISING PROJECT

Time Estimates (days)

Activity	Optimistic	Most Likely	Pessimistic	Immediate Predecessor(s)
A	8	10	12	—
B	5	8	17	—
C	7	8	9	—
D	1	2	3	B
E	8	10	12	A, C
F	5	6	7	D, E
G	1	3	5	D, E
H	2	5	8	F, G
I	2	4	6	G
J	4	5	8	H
K	2	2	2	H

showing the precedence relationships for the activities listed in Table 8.12.

22. **OM Explorer** The information in Table 8.13 is available about a large project.

   a. Determine the critical path and the expected completion time of the project.

   b. Plot the total project cost, starting from day 1 to the expected completion date of the project, assuming the earliest start times for each activity. Compare that result to a similar plot for the latest start times. What implication does the time differential have for cash flows and project scheduling?

TABLE 8.11
MICHAELSON CONSTRUCTION BUILDING ACTIVITIES

Activity	Description	Activity	Description
Start			
A	Appliance installation	M	Roughing-in plumbing
B	Building permit	N	Outside painting
C	Carpets and flooring	O	Interior painting
D	Dry wall	P	Roof
E	Electrical wiring	Q	Siding
F	Foundation	R	Final wood trim
G	Framing	S	Pouring sidewalks, driveway, basement, and garage floors
H	Heating and air conditioning	T	Doors
I	Insulation	U	Windows
J	Kitchen and bath cabinets	V	Bath fixtures
K	Lighting fixtures	W	Lawn sprinkler system
L	Moving in	X	Landscaping

TABLE 8.12
WILL AND BEA WRIGHT-BACH WEDDING ACTIVITIES

Activity	Description	Activity	Description
Start	Accept proposal	O	Order cake, mints, cashews
A	Select and print announcements	P	Photographer
B	Blood tests	Q	Reserve reception hall
C	Color theme selection	R	Rings
D1	Wedding dress	S	Bachelor party
D2	Bridesmaids' dresses	T	Tuxedo rental
D3	Bride's mother's dress	U	Ushers
D4	Groom's mother's dress	V	Reserve church
E	Establish budget and net worth of parents	W	Wedding ceremony
F	Flowers	X	Select groomsmen, ring bearer
G	Gifts for wedding party	Y	Select bridesmaids, flower girls
H	Honeymoon planning	Z	Rehearsal and prenuptial dinner
I	Mailed invitations	AA	Prenuptial agreement
J	Guest list	BB	Groom's nervous breakdown
K	Caterer	CC	Register for china, flatware, gifts
L	Marriage license	DD	Dance band
M	Menu for reception	EE	Thank you notes
N	Newspaper photograph, society page announcement	FF	Finish

TABLE 8.13
ACTIVITY AND COST DATA

Activity	Activity Time (days)	Activity Cost ($)	Immediate Predecessor(s)
A	3	100	—
B	4	150	—
C	2	125	A
D	5	175	B
E	3	150	B
F	4	200	C, D
G	6	75	C
H	2	50	C, D, E
I	1	100	E
J	4	75	D, E
K	3	150	F, G
L	3	150	G, H, I
M	2	100	I, J
N	4	175	K, M
O	1	200	H, M
P	5	150	N, L, O

 ACTIVE MODEL EXERCISE

This Active Model appears on the Student CD-ROM. It allows you to evaluate the sensitivity of the project time to changes in activity times and activity predecessors.

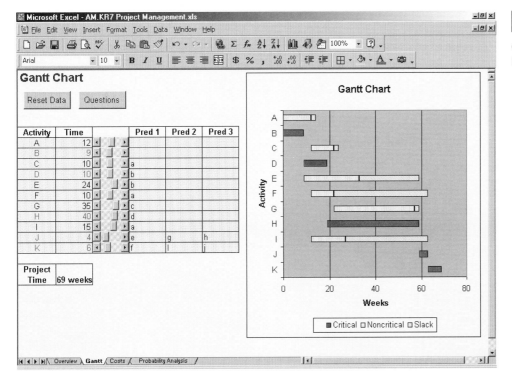

ACTIVITY MODEL 8.1

Gantt Chart Using Data from Example 8.2

QUESTIONS

1. Activity B and activity K are critical activities. Describe the difference that occurs on the graph when you increase activity B versus when you increase activity K.
2. Activity F is not critical. Use the scroll bar to determine how many weeks you can increase activity F until it becomes critical.
3. Activity A is not critical. How many weeks can you increase activity A until it becomes critical? What happens when activity A becomes critical?
4. What happens when you increase activity A by one week after it becomes critical?
5. Suppose that building codes may change and, as a result, activity C would have to be completed before activity D could be started. How would this affect the project?

SIMULATION EXERCISES

These simulation exercises require the use of the SimQuick and Extend simulation packages. SimQuick is on the Student CD-ROM that is packaged with every new copy of the textbook. Extend is an optional simulation package that your instructor may or may not have ordered.

1. **SimQuick** Management is concerned about the completion time of a software development project. There are eight major tasks with highly uncertain duration times. Use SimQuick to determine the minimum, average, and maximum time duration of this project. See Example 25 in *SimQuick: Process Simulation with Excel*, for details of this problem and additional exercises.

2. **Extend** Connect Telecom is a rapidly growing international supplier of consumer-oriented telecommunications products, including wireless telephones and digital answering machines. Senior management plans to introduce approximately 10 new products over the next two years. The director of marketing wants to establish more formal project plans for this new wave of product introductions. Many tasks are involved, such as selecting marketing personnel for training, preparing a separate media plan, reviewing TV commercials, and the like. The project team has a list of activities and time estimates (most likely, pessimistic, and optimistic). Use the Extend simulator and PERT/CPM methods to analyze their project. See the *New Product Introduction at Connect Telecom* case on the Extend CD-ROM, which includes the basic model and how to use it. Answer the various questions asked about the project, recognizing the uncertainty in activity times.

CASE   THE PERT STUDEBAKER

The new director of service operations for Roberts's Auto Sales and Service (RASAS) started work at the beginning of the year. It is now mid-February. RASAS consists of three car dealerships that sell and service several makes of American and Japanese cars, two auto parts stores, a large body shop and car painting business, and an auto salvage yard. Vikky Roberts, owner of RASAS, went into the car business when she inherited a Studebaker dealership from her father. The Studebaker Corporation was on the wane when she obtained the business, but she was able to capitalize on her knowledge and experience to build her business into the diversified and successful miniempire it is today. Her motto, "Sell 'em today, repair 'em tomorrow!" reflects a strategy that she refers to in private as "Get 'em coming and going."

Roberts has always retained a soft spot in her heart for Studebaker automobiles. They were manufactured in South Bend, Indiana, from 1919 to 1966, and many are still operable today because of a vast number of collectors and loyal fans. Roberts has just acquired a 1963 Studebaker Avanti that needs a lot of restoration. She has also noted the public's growing interest in the restoration of vintage automobiles.

Roberts is thinking of expanding into the vintage car restoration business and needs help in assessing the feasibility of such a move. She also wants to restore her 1963 Avanti to mint condition, or as close to mint condition as possible. If she decides to go into the car restoring business, she can use the Avanti as an exhibit in sales and advertising and take it to auto shows to attract business for the new shop.

Roberts believes that many people want the thrill of restoring an old car themselves but they do not have the time to run down all the old parts. Still, others just want to own a vintage auto because it is different and many of them have plenty of money to pay someone to restore an auto for them.

Roberts wants the new business to appeal to both types of people. For the first group, she envisions serving as a parts broker for NOS ("new old stock"), new parts that were manufactured many years ago and are still packaged in their original cartons. It can be a time-consuming process to find the right part. RASAS could also machine new parts to replicate those that are hard to find or that no longer exist.

In addition, RASAS could assemble a library of parts and body manuals for old cars to serve as an information resource for do-it-yourself restorers. The do-it-yourselfers could come to RASAS for help in compiling parts lists, and RASAS could acquire the parts for them. For others, RASAS would take charge of the entire restoration.

Roberts asks the new director of service operations to take a good look at her Avanti and determine what needs to be done to restore it to the condition it was in when it came from the factory more than 40 years ago. She wants to restore it in time to exhibit it at the National Studebaker Meet in Springfield, Missouri. If the car wins first prize in its category, it will be a real public relations coup for RASAS—especially if Roberts decides to enter this new venture. Even if she does not, the car will be a showpiece for the rest of the business.

Roberts asks the director of service operations to prepare a report about what is involved in restoring the car and whether it can be done in time for the Springfield meet in 45 working days using PERT/CPM. The parts manager, the body shop manager, and the chief mechanic have provided the following estimates of times and tasks that need to be done, as well as cost estimates.

- Order all needed material and parts (upholstery, windshield, carburetor, and oil pump). Time: 2 days. Cost (phone calls and labor): $100.
- Receive upholstery material for seat covers. Cannot be done until order is placed. Time: 30 days. Cost: $250.
- Receive windshield. Cannot be done until order is placed. Time: 10 days. Cost: $130.
- Receive carburetor and oil pump. Cannot be done until order is placed. Time: 7 days. Cost: $180.
- Remove chrome from body. Can be done immediately. Time: 1 day. Cost: $50.
- Remove body (doors, hood, trunk, and fenders) from frame. Cannot be done until chrome is removed. Time: 1 day. Cost: $150.
- Have fenders repaired by body shop. Cannot be done until body is removed from frame. Time: 4 days. Cost: $200.
- Repair doors, trunk, and hood. Cannot be done until body is removed from frame. Time: 6 days. Cost: $300.
- Pull engine from chassis. Do after body is removed from frame. Time: 1 day. Cost: $50.
- Remove rust from frame. Do after the engine has been pulled from the chassis. Time: 3 days. Cost: $300.
- Regrind engine valves. Have to pull engine from chassis first. Time: 5 days. Cost: $500.
- Replace carburetor and oil pump. Do after engine has been pulled from chassis and after carburetor and oil pump have been received. Time: 1 day. Cost: $50.
- Rechrome the chrome parts. Chrome must have been removed from the body first. Time: 3 days. Cost: $150.
- Reinstall engine. Do after valves are reground and carburetor and oil pump have been installed. Time: 1 day. Cost: $150.
- Put doors, hood, and trunk back on frame. The doors, hood, and trunk must have been repaired. The frame also has to have had its rust removed. Time: 1 day. Cost: $80.
- Rebuild transmission and replace brakes. Do so after the engine has been reinstalled and the doors, hood, and trunk are back on the frame. Time: 4 days. Cost: $700.
- Replace windshield. Windshield must have been received. Time: 1 day. Cost: $70.
- Put fenders back on. The fenders must already have been repaired and the transmission rebuilt and the brakes replaced. Time: 1 day. Cost: $60.
- Paint car. Cannot be done until the fenders are back on and windshield replaced. Time: 4 days. Cost: $1,700.

- Reupholster interior of car. Must have first received upholstery material. Car must also have been painted. Time: 7 days. Cost: $1,200.
- Put chrome parts back on. Car has to have been painted and chrome parts rechromed. Time: 1 day. Cost: $50.
- Pull car to Studebaker show in Springfield, Missouri. Must have completed reupholstery of interior and have put the chrome parts back on. Time: 2 days. Cost: $500.

Roberts wants to limit expenditures on this project to what could be recovered by selling the restored car. She has already spent $1,500 to acquire the car.

In addition, she wants a brief report on some of the aspects of the proposed business, such as how it fits in with RASAS's other businesses and what RASAS's operations task should be with regard to cost, quality, customer service, and flexibility.

According to *Turning Wheels,* a publication for owners and drivers of Studebakers, and other books on car restoration, there are various categories of restoration. A basic restoration gets the car looking great and running, but a mint condition restoration puts the car back in original condition— as it was "when it rolled off the line." When restored cars compete, a car in mint condition has an advantage over one that is just a basic restoration. As cars are restored, they can also be customized. That is, something is put on the car that could not have been on the original. Customized cars compete in a separate class. Roberts wants a mint condition restoration, without customization. (The proposed new business would accept any kind of restoration a customer wanted.)

The total budget cannot exceed $8,500 including the $1,500 Roberts has already spent. In addition, Roberts can-not spend more than $1,700 in any week given her present financial position. Even though much of the work will be done by Roberts's own employees, labor and materials costs must be considered. All relevant costs have been included in the cost estimates.

QUESTIONS

1. **OM Explorer** Using the information provided, prepare the report that Roberts requested, assuming that the project will begin immediately. Assume 45 working days are available to complete the project, including transporting the car to Springfield before the meet begins. Your report should briefly discuss the aspects of the proposed new business, such as the competitive priorities (see Chapter 2 "Operations Strategy"), that Roberts asked about.

2. **OM Explorer** Construct a table containing the project activities, with a letter assigned to each activity, the time estimates, and the precedence relationships from which you will assemble the network diagram.

3. **SmartDraw** Draw an AON network diagram of the project similar to Figure 8.8. Determine the activities on the critical path and the estimated slack for each activity.

4. **OM Explorer** Prepare a project budget showing the cost of each activity and the total for the project. Can the project be completed within the budget? Are there any cash-flow problems? If so, how might Roberts overcome them?

Source: This case was prepared by and is used by courtesy of Professor Sue Perrott Siferd, Arizona State University.

SELECTED REFERENCES

Bloom, R "Software for Project Management," *Transportation & Distribution,* vol. 34, 1993, pp. 33–34.

Branston, Lisa. "Construction Firms View the Web As a Way to Get Out From Under a Mountain of Paper." *The Wall Street Journal* (November 15, 1999).

Caland, D. I. *Project Management: Strategic Design and Implementation.* New York: McGraw-Hill, 1994.

Day, P. J. *Microsoft Project 4.0 for Windows and the Macintosh: Setting Project Management Standards.* New York: Van Nostrand Reinhold, 1995.

Hartvigsen, David. *SimQuick: Process Simulation with Excel.* 2nd ed. Upper Saddle River, NJ: Prentice Hall, 2004.

IPS Associates. *Project Management Manual.* Boston: Harvard Business School Publishing, 1996.

Kerzner, Harold. *Applied Project Management: Best Practices on Implementation.* New York: John Wiley & Sons, 2000.

Kerzner, Harold. *Project Management: A Systems Approach to Planning, Scheduling, and Controlling,* 6th ed. New York: John Wiley & Sons, 1998.

Lewis, J. P. *Mastering Project Management.* New York: McGraw-Hill, 1998.

Littlefield, T. K., and P.H. Randolph, "PEAT Duration Times: Mathematical or MBO." *Interfaces,* vol. 21, no. 6 (1991), pp. 92–95.

Meredith, Jack R., and Samuel J. Mantel. *Project Management: A Managerial Approach,* 4th ed. New York: John Wiley & Sons, 2000.

Nichols, John M. *Managing Business and Engineering Projects.* Englewood Cliffs, N.J: Prentice Hall, 1990.

"Project Management Body of Knowledge." Available for free download at the Project Management Institute at **www.pmi.org**.

"Project Management Software Buyer's Guide." *Industrial Engineering* (March 1995), pp. 36–37.

CHAPTER

9

Supply-Chain Design

LEARNING GOALS   *After reading this chapter, you should be able to . . .*

IDENTIFY OR DEFINE

1. the nature of supply-chains for service providers, as well as for manufacturers.
2. the key design issues associated with supply-chain processes.
3. the critical supply-chain measures.

DESCRIBE OR EXPLAIN

4. the strategic importance of supply-chain design and give real examples of its application in service situations, as well as in manufacturing situations.
5. how the Internet has enabled the development of virtual supply chains.
6. how efficient supply chains differ from responsive supply chains and the environments best suited for each type of supply chain.

DELL COMPUTER CORPORATION

The Dell Computer Corporation (www.dell.com), a mass customizer of personal computers, is experiencing phenomenal growth and profitability in an industry that traditionally has low profit margins. In 1996, Dell was selling laptops, desktops, and servers at the rate of $1 million a day. Today, Dell's Web site sells more than $30 million in products a day. This success has defined Dell as a leader among PC makers. What is Dell's secret? In a single word—speed. A customer's order for a customized computer can be on a delivery truck in 36 hours. This capability allows Dell to keep parts costs and inventories low—5 days of sales—thereby enabling it to sell at prices 10 to 15 percent below those of competitors. Compaq, Gateway, and IBM average from 50 to 90 days of inventory.

A primary factor in filling customers orders is Dell's manufacturing operations and the performance of its suppliers. Dell's manufacturing process is flexible enough to postpone the ordering of components and the assembly of computers until an order is booked. In addition, Dell's warehousing plan calls for the bulk of its components to be warehoused within 15 minutes of its Austin (Texas), Limerick (Ireland), and Penang (Malaysia) plants. Dell's top 33 suppliers, which supply 90 percent of its goods, use a Web site for data on how they measure up to Dell's standards, what orders they have shipped, and the best way to ship. Dell links the supplier Web site to its order placement Web site so that as customers place orders, the suppliers know when to ship components such as motherboards or liquid-crystal displays. Dell's focus is on how fast the inventory moves, not on how much is there. At Austin, Dell does not actually have to order the components because the suppliers restock the warehouse and manage their own inventories. Dell uses the components as needed and is not billed for them until they leave the warehouse. This system of suppliers and manufacturing operations has proven to be a great advantage over competitors. For example, a software package called Factory Planner manages the factory schedule so that machines are built while the parts needed for the next 2 hours of orders are being shipped from suppliers' hubs. The hub has 15 minutes to confirm that it has the needed parts, and 1 hour and 15 minutes to get them to the plant.

Dell's efficient operations carry over to service providers who also are used to lower costs and reduced lead time. For example, Dell might send an e-mail message to UPS requesting that a computer monitor from Sony be sent to a certain customer as part of a purchased computer system. UPS pulls a monitor from the monitor supplier's stocks and schedules it to arrive with the PC, saving Dell shipping and inventory costs.

Such careful management of the materials and services from the suppliers through production to the customer lets Dell operate more efficiently than any other computer company.

Sources: "The Power of Virtual Integration: An Interview with Dell Computer's Michael Dell." *Harvard Business Review* (March–April, 1998), pp. 72–85; Roth, Daniel. "Dell's Big New Act." *Fortune* (December 6, 1999), pp. 152–156; Perman, Stacy, "Automate or Die." *Business Week* (July 2001); www.business2.com.

An employee tests Dell computers that are made to order on an assembly line in Austin, Texas. The results of tests of the CPU show up on the employee's monitor.

The Dell Computer Corporation provides an excellent example of designing a value chain for competitive advantage. Dell's value chain involves the coordination of key processes, such as customer relationship, order fulfillment, and supplier relationship. These are supported by finance, engineering, information systems, operations, and logistics. Value chains involve internal linkages between a firm's core processes, its supporting processes, and its external linkages with the processes of its customers and suppliers. (See Chapter 1, "Operations As a Competitive Weapon" and Chapter 2, "Operations Strategy.") Figure 9.1 shows how a firm's internal processes can be linked to those of its suppliers and its external customers. Because we have already discussed the new service/product development process in Chapter 2, "Operations Strategy," in

FIGURE 9.1   External Value-Chain Linkages

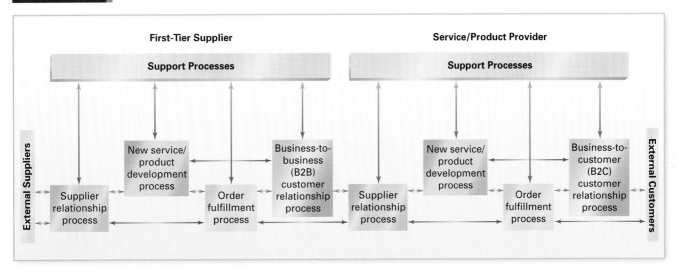

this chapter we focus on what is commonly referred to as the **supply chain,** which consists of the customer relationship, order fulfillment, and supplier relationship processes and their interconnected linkages among the suppliers of services, materials, and information, and the customers of the firm's services or products.[1] In Chapter 10, "Location," and Chapter 11, "Lean Systems," we will address two other key design decisions for competitive value chains. It is important to note, however, that a firm may have multiple supply chains, depending on the mix of services or products it produces. A supplier in one supply chain may not be a supplier in another supply chain because the service or product is different.

Supply-chain management seeks to design a firm's customer relationship, order fulfillment, and supplier relationship processes and to synchronize these processes with the key processes of its suppliers and customers in order to match the flow of services, materials, and information with customer demand. To get a better understanding of the design issues facing supply-chain managers, we begin with an overview of the nature of supply chains for service providers and for manufacturers. We then discuss dynamics in supply chains, followed by how developing integrated supply chains and designing effective customer relationship, order fulfillment, and supplier relationship processes can mitigate some of the negative effects of those dynamics. Next, we discuss the important operating and financial measures of supply-chain performance, followed by a comparison of two supply-chain designs and their strategic implications. We conclude with a discussion of supply-chain software and the implications of supply-chain design for service providers, as well as for manufacturers.

As you read this chapter, think about how the design of supply chains is important to various departments across the organization, such as . . .

> **distribution,** which determines the best way to deliver services to the customer or the best placement of finished goods inventories and modes of transportation for serving the external customers.
> **finance** and **accounting,** which must understand how the performance of the supply chain affects key financial measures and how information flows into the firm's financial statements.
> **information systems,** which designs the information flows that are essential to effective supply-chain performance.

supply chain The customer relationship, order fulfillment, and supplier relationship processes and their interconnected linkages among the suppliers of services, materials, and information, and the customers of the firm's services or products.

supply-chain management The design of a firm's customer relationship, order fulfillment, and supplier relationship processes and the synchronization of these processes with the key processes of its suppliers and customers in order to match the flow of services, materials, and information with customer demand.

---

[1]The terms *value chain* and *supply chain* are sometimes used interchangeably.

> ➤ **marketing,** which involves contact with the firm's customers and needs a supply chain that ensures responsive customer service.
> ➤ **operations,** which is responsible for major segments of the supply chain and must interface with other functional areas to ensure effective performance.
> ➤ **procurement,** which selects the suppliers for the supply chain.

SUPPLY CHAINS FOR SERVICE PROVIDERS

Supply-chain design for a service provider is driven by the need to provide support for the essential elements of the various service packages it delivers. Recall that a *service package* consists of supporting facilities, facilitating goods, explicit services, and implicit services (see Chapter 2, "Operations Strategy"). To see the connection between supply chains and service packages, consider the example of a florist with 27 retail stores in the greater Boston metropolitan area. Customers can place orders for customized floral arrangements by visiting one of the stores, using a 1-800 number, or by visiting the florist's Web page. The 1-800 number and the Web page are operated by a local Internet services company, which takes orders and relays them to the florist. The arrangements are produced at a distribution center, and deliveries are made using either local couriers, or FedEx, if the delivery is outside of the Boston area. Fresh flowers, flown in from all over the world, are used in the arrangement. The key feature that differentiates this business from floral wire services, such as Teleflora or FTD, is that this florist assembles all of the arrangements and can ship the out-of-area orders for next day delivery anywhere in the country using special packaging. The elements of its service package are

- *Supporting Facilities.* Retail stores, a delivery center, computers, point-of-sale equipment, and employees.
- *Facilitating Goods.* Flowers; arrangement materials, such as pots, baskets, greeting cards, and other items needed to fill the order; and packaging materials.
- *Explicit Services.* Arranging the flowers to customer order and delivering the arrangement as specified by the customer.
- *Implicit Services.* Convenience, which is facilitated by the location of the retail outlets and the opportunity to place orders via the Internet or the 1-800 number, and the psychological impressions derived from friendly, attentive, and helpful personnel.

The supply chain must support the florist's service package. Figure 9.2 is a simplified supply chain for the florist, showing how the suppliers support various elements of the service package. Each of the suppliers would have their own supply chains (not shown). For example, the supplier for the arrangement materials may have to get baskets from one supplier and pots from another. The focus on supply chains is important because the suppliers in the florist's supply chain play an integral role in the florist's ability to meet the competitive priorities for the service package, such as top quality, delivery speed, on-time delivery, and customization.

Generally, a service provider's supply chain must be designed so that the right resources, equipment, and personnel are available to perform a service. These supply chains can be complex. Imagine the vast number of suppliers required to run an airline, supplying materials that range from peanuts for an onboard snack to maintenance and repair items for the plane's gigantic engines. The effective design and management of supply chains offers service providers an opportunity to increase their competitiveness. Managerial Practice 9.1 shows how the Arizona Public Service company reduced costs and lowered prices by reengineering its supplier relationship process with the help of its suppliers.

FIGURE 9.2   **Supply Chain for a Florist**

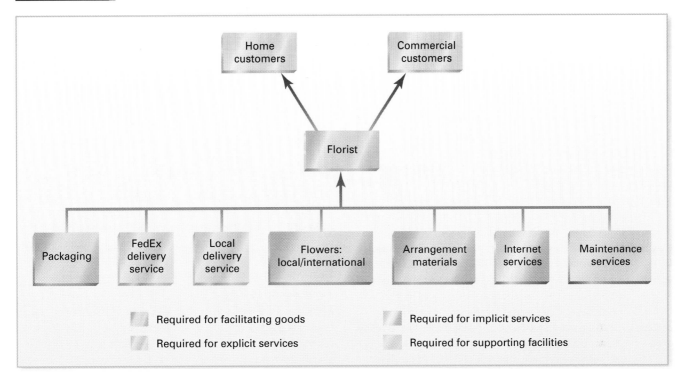

SUPPLY CHAINS FOR MANUFACTURERS

While inventories are an important part of the supply chains of service providers, a fundamental purpose of supply-chain design for manufacturers is the control of inventory by managing the flow of materials. The reason is that the typical manufacturer spends more than 60 percent of its total income from sales on purchased services and materials, while the typical service provider spends only 30 to 40 percent. Because materials comprise such a large component of the sales dollar, companies can reap large profits with a small reduction in the cost of materials. This is why supply-chain management is a key competitive weapon.

Inventory is a stock of materials used to satisfy customer demand or to support the production of services or goods. Figure 9.3 shows how inventories are created through the analogy of a water tank. The flow of water into the tank raises the water level. The inward flow of water represents input materials, such as steel, component parts, office supplies, or a finished product. The water level represents the amount of inventory held at a plant, service facility, warehouse, or retail outlet. The flow of water from the tank lowers the water level in the tank. The outward flow of water represents the demand for materials in inventory, such as customer orders for a Huffy bicycle or requirements for supplies such as soap, food, or furnishings. Another possible outward flow is that of scrap, which also lowers the level of useable inventory. Together, the rates of the input and output flows determine the level of inventory. Inventories rise when more material flows into the tank than flows out; they fall when more material flows out than flows in. Figure 9.3 also shows clearly why firms utilize Six Sigma and total quality management (TQM) to reduce defective materials: The larger the scrap flows, the larger will be the input flow of materials required for a given level of output (see Chapter 5, "Process Performance and Quality").

How is inventory created?

inventory A stock of materials used to satisfy customer demand or to support the production of services or goods.

MANAGERIAL PRACTICE 9.1

SUPPLY-CHAIN DESIGN AT ARIZONA PUBLIC SERVICE

Arizona Public Service (APS), (www.aboutapsc.com) is the largest utility company in Arizona, serving 705,000 customers and generating $1.7 billion in revenues annually. The company has three diverse business units: Generation (fossil fuel and nuclear power), Transmission, and Cooperative Services, each with very different supply-chain requirements. Even though APS is a very successful utility company, it faces new challenges. The deregulation of the generation and cooperative services segments of the industry by Congress and the states has made the $200 billion industry fully competitive. Companies such as APS are preparing for added competition by driving down operating costs and improving customer services. For example, at APS, expenditures related to the procurement of equipment and services amounted to more than 33 percent of revenues. Because of the diversity of its business units, 20 percent of the items listed in the company's inventory catalog were duplicates. The costs of duplicate orders directly affected the profitability of the utility company.

APS decided to scrutinize its supply chain for ways to increase efficiency and invest in new technology to support the management of materials and provision of services. But first it had to overcome some old practices. For example, expensive line transformers were held in inventory in case a replacement was needed in the field. In addition, the company considered large inventories of replacement parts and other items needed to support the transmission of electric power and daily office operations to be a value-added aspect of doing business. Presumably, management believed that fast replacement of failed items was desirable and that stocking allowed buyers to get the best prices. Now management views these practices as expensive and time-consuming.

APS's solution was to improve its supplier relationship process by developing an electronic system in accordance with prearranged price, quality, and delivery agreements with its suppliers. The system enables both buyers and other company personnel to buy services and products

An Arizona Public Service customer service employee works to solve a customer's problem. Excellent service depends on adequate inventories of replacement parts; however, APS finds stockpiling large quantities of all parts to be an inefficient use of resources.

through the streamlined processes of three online software modules.

MATERIALS CATALOG. This module lists items kept on hand at various warehouse locations. Personnel needing materials from this catalog merely enter the items from their PC workstations. The system keeps track of the inventories and informs buyers when replenishment orders are required.

DESCRIPTION BUY. For items not listed in the materials catalog, users can determine whether the items have already been ordered by other users. If so, another order may not be needed. Once a user has selected the needed items, a point-and-click action submits the online service and material request form, which is automatically routed to a company buyer.

EXPRESS BUY. For certain low-cost, high-volume items, APS maintains a list of approved suppliers who have entered into preestablished purchase agreements involving prices, payment terms, and delivery lead times. The module is linked to the suppliers' catalogs electronically and enables company personnel to order directly from the suppliers without involving a buyer.

The electronic system handles 50,000 to 80,000 transactions *daily,* or roughly one-half of the company's purchase orders. The time involved in obtaining services and materials has been drastically reduced to a few hours for items from the warehouse, 4 days (previously 22 days) for items ordered through the Description Buy module, and less than 48 hours for Express Buy items. The time spent on improving supply-chain performance was worthwhile. APS trimmed inventory by 20 percent, reduced materials management personnel by 25 percent, and reduced purchasing costs by 5 percent. In turn, APS reduced consumer electric rates by 5 percent.

Sources: Ettinger, Al. "Reinventing the Supply Chain: Bringing Materials Management to Light." *APICS—The Performance Advantage* (February 1997), pp. 42–45; Turdrick, James. "Supply-Chain Management: Not Just for Manufacturing Anymore." *APICS—The Performance Advantage* (December 1999), pp 39–42.

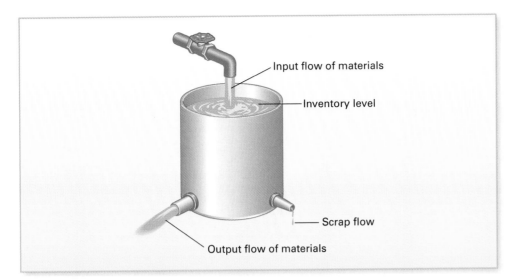

FIGURE 9.3

Creation of Inventory

Inventory exists in three aggregate categories, which are useful for accounting purposes. **Raw materials (RM)** are the inventories that are needed for the production of services or goods. They are considered to be inputs to the transformation processes of the firm, whether they produce a service or a product. **Work-in-process (WIP)** consists of items, such as components or assemblies, needed for a final product in manufacturing. WIP is also present in some service operations, such as repair shops, restaurants, check-processing centers, and package delivery services. **Finished goods (FG)** in manufacturing plants, warehouses, and retail outlets are the items sold to the firm's customers. The finished goods of one firm may actually be the raw materials for another.

Figure 9.4 shows how inventory can be held in different forms and at various stocking points. In this example, raw materials—the finished goods of the supplier—are held both by the supplier and the manufacturer. Raw materials at the plant pass through one or more processes, which transforms them into various levels of WIP inventory. Final processing of this inventory yields finished goods inventory. Finished goods can be held at the plant, the distribution center (which may be a warehouse owned by the manufacturer or the retailer), and retail locations.

The supply chain for a manufacturing firm can be very complicated, as Figure 9.5 illustrates. However, the supply chain depicted is an oversimplification because many companies have hundreds, if not thousands, of suppliers. In this example, the firm owns its distribution and transportation services. However, companies that engineer products to customer specifications normally do not have distribution centers as part of their supply chains. Such companies often ship products directly to their customers. Suppliers are often identified by their position in the supply chain. Here, tier 1

raw materials (RM) The inventories that are needed for the production of services or goods.

work-in-process (WIP) Items, such as components or assemblies, needed for a final product in manufacturing.

finished goods (FG) The items in manufacturing plants, warehouses, and retail outlets that are sold to the firm's customers.

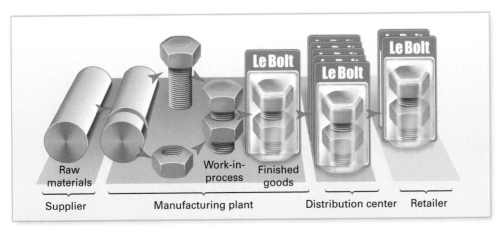

Raw materials

Supplier

Work-in-process

Finished goods

Manufacturing plant

Distribution center

Retailer

FIGURE 9.4

Inventory at Successive Stocking Points

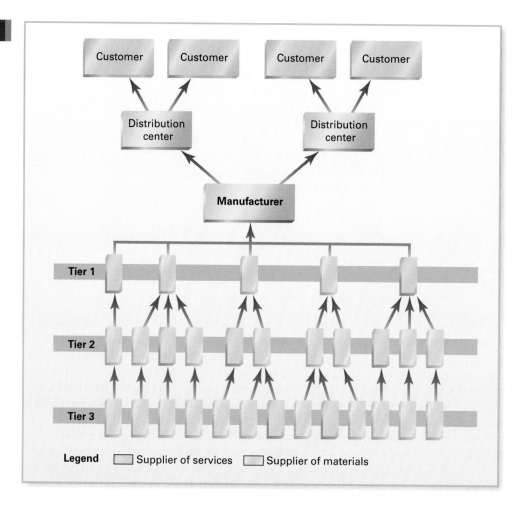

FIGURE 9.5

Supply Chain for a Manufacturing Firm

suppliers provide materials or services that are used directly by the firm, tier 2 suppliers supply tier 1 suppliers, and so on.

The value of supply-chain management becomes apparent when the complexity of the supply chain is recognized. As we showed earlier, the flow of materials determines inventory levels. The performance of numerous suppliers and the firm's supplier relationship process determines the inward flow of materials. The performance of the firm's order fulfillment and customer relationship processes determines the outward flow of products.

Imagine the chaos if all of a firm's suppliers acted independently and never adjusted to changes in the firm's schedules. Hence, management of the flow of materials is crucial, but how much control does a firm have over its suppliers? One way to gain control is to buy controlling interest in the firm's major suppliers, which is called *backward integration* (see Chapter 3, "Process Design Strategy"). The firm can then ensure its priority with the supplier and more forcefully lead efforts to improve efficiency and productivity. However, purchasing other companies takes a lot of capital, which reduces a firm's flexibility. Moreover, if demand drops, the firm cannot simply reduce the amount of materials purchased from the supplier to reduce costs because the supplier's fixed costs remain.

Another approach is to write agreements with the first-tier suppliers that hold them accountable for the performance of their own suppliers. For example, customers can provide a uniform set of guidelines to be followed throughout the supply chain. Companies, such as Ford and Chrysler in the automotive industry, have guidelines for quality, delivery, and reporting procedures to be followed by any company producing an item that ultimately becomes part of an automobile. First-tier suppliers then incorporate these guidelines in agreements with their own suppliers. This approach allows each first-tier supplier to manage its own suppliers without its customers having to do it for them.

What is the best way to control suppliers in a complex supply chain?

SUPPLY-CHAIN DYNAMICS

Each firm in a supply chain depends on other firms for services, materials, or the information needed to supply its immediate external customer in the chain. Because firms are typically owned and managed independently, the actions of downstream members (toward the ultimate user of the service or product) of the supply chain can affect the operations of upstream members (toward the lowest tier in the supply chain). The reason is that upstream members of a supply chain must react to the demands placed on them by downstream members of the chain. These demands are a function of the policies these firms have for replenishing their inventories, the actual levels of those inventories, the demands of their customers, and the accuracy of the information they have to work with. As you examine the order patterns of firms in a supply chain, you will frequently see the variability in order quantities increase as you proceed upstream. This increase in variability is referred to as the **bullwhip effect**, which gets its name from the action of a bullwhip—the handle of the whip initiates the action; however, the tip of the whip experiences the wildest action. The slightest change in customer demands can ripple through the entire chain, each member receiving more variability in demands from the member immediately downstream.

Figure 9.6 shows the bullwhip effect in a supply chain for facial tissue. The retailer's orders to the manufacturer exhibit more variability than the actual demands from the consumers of the facial tissue. The manufacturer's orders to the package supplier have more variability than the retailer's orders. Finally, the package supplier's orders to the cardboard supplier have the most variability. Because supply patterns do not match demand patterns, inventories accumulate in some firms and shortages occur in others. The firms with too much inventory stop ordering, and those that have shortages place expedite orders. The culprits are unexpected changes in demands or supplies, and there are a number of causes for these changes.

EXTERNAL CAUSES

A firm has the least amount of control over its external customers and suppliers. Consequently, a firm must design its processes with the understanding that they may have to respond to disruptions caused by suppliers or customers. Typical external disruptions include the following:

- *Volume Changes.* Customers may change the quantity of the service or product they had ordered for a specific date or unexpectedly demand more of a standard

> What causes the fluctuations in supply chains, and what are the consequences?

> **bullwhip effect** The phenomenon in supply chains whereby ordering patterns experience increasing variance as you proceed upstream in the chain.

> The bullwhip effect can cause costly disruptions to upstream members of a supply chain as the variance in orders increases. Paperboard manufacturing processes, such as this one at a Weyerhaeuser Company facility, are vulnerable to the bullwhip effect.

FIGURE 9.6   Supply Chain Dynamics for Facial Tissue

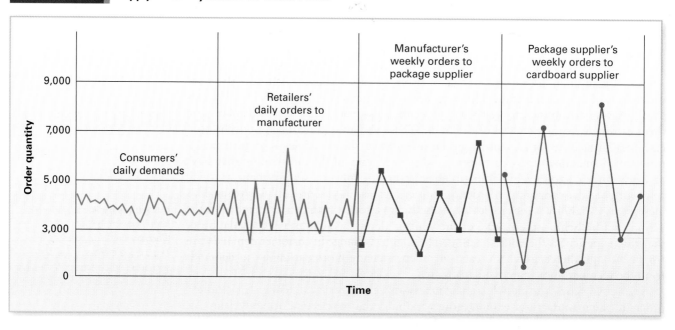

service or product. If the market demands short lead times, the firm needs quick reactions from its suppliers. For example, an electric utility experiencing an unusually warm day may require immediate power backup from another utility to avoid a brownout in its region.

• *Service and Product Mix Changes.* Customers may change the mix of items in an order and cause a ripple effect throughout the supply chain. For example, a major-appliance store chain may change the mix of washing machines in its orders from 60 percent Whirlpool brand and 40 percent Kitchen Aid brand to 40 percent Whirlpool and 60 percent Kitchen Aid. This decision changes the production schedule of the Whirlpool plant that makes both brands, causing imbalances in its inventories. Further, the company that makes the face plates for the washing machines must change its schedules, thereby affecting its suppliers.

• *Late Deliveries.* Late deliveries of materials or delays in essential services can force a firm to switch its schedule from production of one product model to another. Firms that supply model-specific items may have their schedules disrupted. For example, the Whirlpool plant may find that a component supplier for its Model A washing machine could not supply the part on time. To avoid shutting down the assembly line, which is an expensive action, Whirlpool may decide to switch to Model B production. Suddenly, there is a big demand on the suppliers for Model B-specific parts.

• *Underfilled Shipments.* Suppliers that send partial shipments do so because of disruptions at their own plants. The effects of underfilled shipments are similar to those of late shipments unless there is enough to allow the firm to operate until the next shipment.

INTERNAL CAUSES

A famous line from a Pogo cartoon is "We have seen the enemy, and it is us!" Unfortunately, this statement is true for many firms when it comes to disruptions in the supply chain. A firm's own operations can be the culprit in what becomes the source of constant dynamics in the supply chain. Typical internal disruptions include the following:

• *Internally Generated Shortages.* There may be a shortage of parts manufactured by a firm because of machine breakdowns or inexperienced workers. This shortage may cause a change in the firm's production schedule that will affect suppliers. Labor shortages, owing to strikes or high turnover, have a similar effect. A strike at a manufacturing plant will reduce the need for trucking services, for example.

* *Engineering Changes.* Changes to the design of services or products can have a direct impact on suppliers. For example, changing cable TV feed lines to fiber-optic technology increases the benefits to the cable company's customers but affects the demand for cable. Similarly, reducing the complexity of a dashboard assembly may not be noticeable (functionally) to the buyers of an automobile, but it will change demand for the outsourced parts that go into the dashboard.

* *New Service or Product Introductions.* New services or products always affect the supply chain. A firm decides how many introductions there will be, as well as their timing, and hence introduces a dynamic in the supply chain. New services or products may even require a new supply chain or addition of new members to an existing supply chain. For example, the introduction of a new refrigerated trucking service will have an impact on the suppliers of refrigerated trucks and the maintenance items for the new service.

* *Service or Product Promotions.* A common practice of firms producing standardized services or products is to use price discounts to promote sales. This practice has the effect of creating a spike in demand that is felt throughout the supply chain. That is what the Campbell Soup Company found when its annual deep-discount pricing program caused customers to buy large quantities of chicken soup, which had the effect of causing overtime production at its chicken-processing plant. (See Managerial Practice 9.4 for details.) The practice of buying in excess of immediate needs to take advantage of price discounts is called *forward buying*.

Pricing programs, however, can induce efficiencies in the supply chain if they discourage activities that increase costs. For example, Campbell initiated a *strategic pricing program* that offered customers financial incentives for ordering more efficiently by engaging in electronic ordering, accepting direct plant delivery or picking the order up themselves, buying full truckloads, and buying full pallet loads of the product. Customer orders are assigned to pricing brackets based on the cost Campbell incurs to service them. Campbell shares the savings with their customers, thereby creating a win–win situation for everyone.

* *Information Errors.* Demand forecast errors can cause a firm to order too many, or too few, services and materials. Also, forecast errors may cause expedited orders that force suppliers to react more quickly to avoid shortages in the supply chain. In addition, errors in the physical count of items in stock can cause shortages (panic purchases) or too much inventory (slowdown in purchases). Finally, communication links between buyers and suppliers can be faulty. For example, inaccurate order quantities and delays in information flows will affect supply-chain dynamics.

External and internal disruptions such as these impair the performance of any supply chain. Many disruptions are caused by ineffective coordination between supply-chain processes or poor execution. Because supply chains involve so many firms and separate operations, it is unrealistic to think that all disruptions can be eliminated. Nonetheless, the challenge for supply-chain managers is to remove as many disruptions as possible and design a supply chain that minimizes the impact of those disruptions that they cannot eliminate. A starting point is the development of an integrated supply chain.

DEVELOPING INTEGRATED SUPPLY CHAINS

Successful supply-chain management requires a high degree of functional and organizational integration. Such integration does not happen overnight. Traditionally, organizations have divided the responsibility for managing the flow of services and materials among three departments: purchasing, production, and distribution.

What is the best approach for developing an integrated supply chain?

Purchasing is the management of the acquisition process, which includes deciding which suppliers to use, negotiating contracts, and deciding whether to buy locally. Purchasing is usually responsible for working with suppliers to ensure the desired flow of services and materials for both short and long terms. Purchasing may also be responsible for the levels of raw materials and maintenance and repair inventories. **Production** is the management of the transformation processes devoted to producing the service or product. It is responsible for determining output quantities and scheduling the machines and employees directly responsible for the production of the service or good. **Distribution** is the management of the flow of services or materials from firms to external customers. It may also be responsible for finished goods inventories and the selection of transportation service providers. Typically, firms willing to undergo the rigors of developing integrated supply chains progress through a series of phases. In phase 1, a starting point for most firms, external suppliers and customers are considered to be independent of the firm. Relations with these entities are formal, and there is little sharing of operating information and costs. Internally, purchasing, production, and distribution act independently, each optimizing its own activities without considering the other entities. Each external and internal entity in the supply chain controls its own inventories and often utilizes control systems and procedures that are incompatible with those of other entities. Because of organizational and functional boundaries, large amounts of inventory exist in the supply chain and the overall flow of services and materials is ineffective.

In phase 2, the firm initiates internal integration by creating a materials management department. **Materials management** is concerned with decisions about purchasing services and materials, inventories, production levels, staffing patterns, schedules, and distribution. Figure 9.7 shows the scope of materials management and the typical domains of responsibility for purchasing, production, and distribution for a manufacturer of cookies. The flow of materials begins with the purchase of raw materials (e.g., eggs, sugar, flour, and chocolate chips) and services (e.g., maintenance) from outside suppliers. Raw materials are stored and then converted into cookies by one or more transformation processes, which involves some short-term storage of work-in-process inventory. The cookies are stored (briefly) as finished goods and then shipped by means of transportation services suppliers to large supermarket chains, which have their own distribution centers. This cycle repeats over and over, as the firm responds to customer demand.

The focus is on the integration of those aspects of the supply chain directly under the firm's control to create an *internal supply chain*. Firms in this phase utilize a seamless information and materials control system from distribution to purchasing, integrating marketing, finance, accounting, and operations. Efficiency and electronic linkages to customers and suppliers are emphasized. Nonetheless, the firm still considers its customers and suppliers to be independent entities and focuses on tactical, rather than strategic, issues. Managerial Practice 9.2 shows how Southwestern Bell Communications use an approach called *shared services* to integrate its internal supply chain.

Internal integration must precede phase 3, supply-chain integration. The internal supply chain is extended to include linkages between the firm and its suppliers and customers, as was shown in Figure 9.1. The supplier relationship, which includes purchasing; order fulfillment, which includes production and distribution; and customer relationship processes, as well as their internal and external linkages, are integrated into the normal business routine. The firm takes on a customer orientation. However, rather than merely reacting to customer demand, the firm strives to work with its customers so that everyone benefits from improved flows of services and materials. Similarly, the firm must develop a better understanding of its suppliers' organizations, capacities, strengths, and weaknesses—and include its suppliers earlier into the design of new services or products (see Chapter 2, "Operations Strategy").

The design of an integrated supply chain is complex. We have already provided some key insights into the design decisions at the process level in Part 1 and Part 2 of the text. The customer relationship, order fulfillment, and supplier relationship processes need to be analyzed from the perspective of process choice, process improvement, layout, and capacity, for example. It is important to know that the integrated supply chain provides

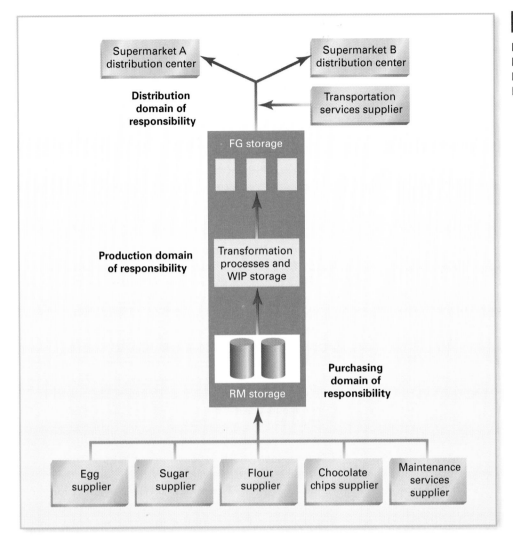

a framework for the operating decisions in a firm, which we will cover in Part 4, "Operating Value Chains." We now turn to a discussion of some additional considerations managers make in the design of the integrated supply-chain processes.

DESIGNING THE CUSTOMER RELATIONSHIP PROCESS

The customer relationship process addresses the interface between the firm and its customers downstream in the supply chain. The purpose of the customer relationship process is to identify, attract, and build relationships with customers and to facilitate the transmission and tracking of orders. Key nested processes include:

- *Marketing Process.* The marketing process focuses on such issues as determining the customers to target, how to target them, what services or products to offer and how to price them, and how to manage the promotional campaigns.
- *Order Placement Process.* The order placement process involves the activities required to execute a sale, register the specifics of the order request, confirm the acceptance of the order, and track the progress of the order until it is completed. Often the firm has a sales force that visits prospective and current customers to encourage a sale. The activities of this nested process would fall under the definition of a high customer contact process, as indicated in the customer contact model (see Chapter 3, "Process Design Strategy").

MANAGERIAL PRACTICE 9.2

USING SHARED SERVICES AS A MEANS TO INTEGRATE SUPPLY CHAINS AT SOUTHWESTERN BELL COMMUNICATIONS

Shared services is an approach that concentrates common management practices into a business unit that is focused on providing the highest-value services at the lowest possible costs to internal customers. The internal services delivered include anything that provides support to the firm's core processes, such as human resources, finance, information technology, vendor negotiation, or strategic sourcing. The rationale behind a shared services organization is to reduce the duplication of similar services being provided throughout a firm, thereby leveraging the capabilities of staff across the entire firm, and to facilitate the integration of processes within a firm. This approach is especially important for supply chains because each business unit could have its own supply chain, thereby presenting the possibility of duplication of activities and poor coordination between core processes. Leading companies, such as Alcoa, Proctor & Gamble, and Southwestern Bell Communications (SBC) have applied this approach to the integration of supply chains.

SBC (www.sbc.com), a $45.9 billion company serving 58 million access lines nationwide, provides a full range of voice, data, networking and e-business services, as well as directory advertising and publishing services. SBC is America's leading provider of high-speed DSL Internet access services. At SBC, the shared services organization ensures that business unit supply chains are operating optimally and meeting the strategic objectives of the corporation. The value of the shared services organization was demonstrated when SBC purchased Pacific Telesis, Ameritech, Southern New England Telephone, and a number of other small companies—all in a span of a few years. The result was a significant expansion in the size and scope of the company's customer base and geographic penetration. Supply-chain requirements also increased dramatically, as did the opportunity for excessive duplication of efforts. For example, while trying to integrate the supply chains of the newly acquired companies, SBC found that there were 26 different firms providing collection services across the business units. The shared services organization reduced that to just 5 companies, which increased their volumes, improved business relations, and reduced costs by 20 percent for SBC. Similar reductions were achieved in central office equipment and services and cable and transport equipment. The shared services organization has averaged more than 5 percent in cost reductions since 1997, which amounts to savings in the billions of dollars for a company the size of SBC.

The concept of shared services addresses the need to internally integrate supply chains. At SBC, another group, the supply-chain organization, provides a centralized supply-chain process, which consists of many nested processes, including processes for proposal acceptance, contract negotiation, logistics support, and monitoring the performance of the supply chain. The shared services organization, however, integrates and controls the supply-chain process by coordinating requirements across business units and presenting the units with opportunities that exist because of a collaborative effort.

This activity has strategic value. Each business unit has strategic supply initiatives for its line of business that cumulatively add up to the strategic supply-chain plan for the corporation as a whole. The shared services organization must identify those various requirements and find ways to ensure that the plans of individual business units are realized while meeting the overall strategic supply-chain plan.

Source: Forst, Leland I. "Shared Services: Four Success Stories." *Supply Chain Management Review* (November–December 2002), pp. 38–44.

The Internet has dramatically changed the way companies design their customer relationship process. Business-to-consumer (B2C) systems, which allow customers to transact business over the Internet, are commonplace. The biggest growth, however, has been in business-to-business (B2B) systems, which enable communication between the customer relationship process of one company to the supplier relationship process of another. (See Chapter 12, "Information Technology and Value Chains," for a discussion of B2C and B2B systems.) The Internet has enabled firms to reengineer their order placement process to benefit both the customer and the firm. For example, a traveler may arrive at the Ritz-Carlton on Maui and request a room without an advance reservation. An employee at the hotel will take the appropriate information regarding the order, including the dates of stay, suite or other type of room, double or single occupancy, king-size bed or double beds, smoking or nonsmoking, and then check to see which rooms (if any) are available. This is a costly approach because of the time required of the employee, particularly at busy periods, not to mention the risk that the hotel will be unable to serve the customer. Alternatively, the traveler could use the hotel's Web site several weeks in advance, provide the same information, and get confirmation of the reservation. These two versions of the order placement process for the hotel involve different amounts of employee time and provide different levels of service to the customer. The Internet provides the following advantages for a firm's order placement process.

- *Cost Reduction.* Using the Internet can reduce the costs of processing orders because it allows for greater participation by the customer (see Chapter 3, "Process Design Strategy"). Customers can select the services or products they want and place an order with the firm without actually talking to anyone. This approach reduces the need for call centers, which are labor intensive and often take longer to place orders.
- *Revenue Flow Increase.* A firm's Web page can allow customers to enter credit card information or purchase-order numbers as part of the order placement process. This approach reduces the time lags often associated with billing the customer or waiting for checks sent in the mail.
- *Global Access.* Another advantage the Internet has provided to firms is the opportunity to accept orders 24 hours a day. Traditional brick-and-mortar firms take standard orders during their normal business hours. Firms with Internet access can reduce the time it takes to satisfy a customer, thereby gaining a competitive advantage over brick-and-mortar firms.
- *Pricing Flexibility.* Firms with their services and products posted on the Web can easily change prices as the need arises, thereby avoiding the cost and delay of publishing new catalogs. Customers placing orders have current prices to consider when making their choices. From the perspective of supply chains, Dell Computer Corporation uses this capability to control for component shortages. Because of its direct-sales approach and promotional pricing, Dell can steer customers to certain configurations of computers for which ample supplies exist.

DESIGNING THE ORDER FULFILLMENT PROCESS

The order fulfillment process involves the activities required to deliver a service or product to a customer (see Chapter 1, "Operations As a Competitive Weapon"). This process might be called upon to address any of the competitive priorities falling under the categories of cost, quality, time, or flexibility. The order placement process and the order fulfillment process are tightly linked; in fact, in many instances, they occur simultaneously. For example, a customer at a Barnes and Noble store has in effect ordered a book, performing the work to actually find it in the inventory, and the store has delivered it when she checks out at the service desk. However, Barnes and Noble also has a Web page, where the order placement and the order fulfillment processes are separated. Customers doing business on its Web page must accept a delay in receiving their books, a delay Barnes and Noble seeks to minimize in its supply chain. Designing the order fulfillment process can have competitive implications.

As we mentioned earlier, many activities of the order fulfillment process associated with the internal supply chain are covered in other chapters. In this section, we will focus on virtual supply chains and the placement of inventories.

VIRTUAL SUPPLY CHAINS
The advent of the Internet has opened an entirely new set of opportunites for supply-chain design. Many companies have redesigned their supply chains to outsource some part of their entire order fulfillment process with the help of sophisticated, Web-based, information technology support packages. In effect, these companies manage the order fulfillment aspects of their business as if the process was actually in-house. Nike, for example, coordinates the manufacture and distribution of sporting apparel and athletic shoes worldwide without owning the facilities, thereby allowing the company to focus on its core processes of customer relationship and new product development. About

30 percent of all Internet retailers are also embracing the idea of virtual supply chains by using a technique called *drop shipping,* whereby a retailer passes customer orders directly to a wholesaler or manufacturer, which then ships the order directly to the customer with the retailer's label on it. These retailers have outsourced their warehouse operations to avoid the costs of holding their own inventories.

The benefits from using virtual supply chains include

- *Reduced Investment in Inventories and Order Fulfillment Infrastructure.* The investment in inventory, equipment, warehouses, and personnel is significant. The firm must generate high volumes to make it pay off.
- *Greater Service or Product Variety.* Without the overhead of one's own order fulfillment process, the firm can have the freedom to select from a wide variety of wholesalers, service providers, and manufacturers.
- *Lower Costs Due to Economies of Scale.* The supplier typically handles more volume than does the firm doing the outsourcing because the supplier may have a number of customers for the same service or product. This added volume opens the possibility that costs to the outsourcing firm will be much lower than if the order fulfillment process was done in-house.
- *Lower Transportation Costs.* Retailers realize the advantage of lower transportation costs. Traditionally, retailers pay transportation costs to acquire the goods from a wholesaler and then pay to have the goods shipped to the customer. Using drop shipping in a virtual supply chain, the only transportation cost is shipping the goods from the wholesaler to the customer.

Virtual supply chains are not a panacea for all the problems service providers or manufacturers face in the design of their supply chains. First, a lack of information transparency between a firm and its order fulfillment partner can cause customer service problems. For example, the firm needs to know if the order fulfillment partner has the inventory to transact a sale or enough capacity to provide a critical service. Acquiring the appropriate software may be prohibitive. Second, outsourcing the order fulfillment process makes the outsourcing firm vulnerable to order rationing by the order fulfillment partner. Order rationing occurs when the order fulfillment partner does not have enough capacity or inventory to satisfy all the orders from its customers, and the order fulfillment partner then imposes some rationing process across all customers. Finally, increased information transparency between the firm and its order fulfillment partner poses the risk that the order fulfillment partner could use the information to bypass the firm completely and go directly to the customers.

Supply-chain designers must choose between the traditional approach, which keeps the order fulfillment process in-house, and the virtual supply chain. The traditional approach is favored when

- *Sales Volumes Are High.* The volumes are needed to offset the high infrastructure costs. It can also be a strategic move. If a firm wants to grow and dominate their industry, such as Amazon.com in the retail business, keeping the order fulfillment process in-house is important.
- *Order Consolidation Is Important.* Virtual supply chains lose their appeal if many suppliers are needed to satisfy a single customer's order. Coordination is difficult and transportation costs increase because of inefficiencies in shipping. With the traditional approach, the firm has its own warehouses and can coordinate the supplies from a large group of suppliers. Nonetheless, the need for order consolidation in virtual supply chains opens the door of opportunity for third-party logistics providers. Some firms have taken advantage of a process called **channel assembly,** whereby members of the distribution channel act as if they were assembly stations in the factory. For example, FedEx has partnered with Cisco to coordinate the shipments of many independent suppliers, so that all components of major systems arrive at the customer within a small window of time.
- *Small-Order Fulfillment Capability of Suppliers Is Important.* Retaining the order fulfillment process, particularly in warehouse operations, may be necessary if it is important for customers to deal in small quantities, and the suppliers do not

channel assembly The process of using members of the distribution channel as if they were assembly stations in the factory.

have the capability to handle small orders. Small-order fulfillment technology is becoming more common; however, manufacturers in many industries still do not have the capability. The durable goods industry is a good example.

The virtual supply chain approach is favored when

- *Demands Are Highly Volatile.* Volatile demands present risks for holding inventories, which can prove costly for a firm (see Chapter 15, "Inventory Management"). A more cost-effective approach may be to find a supplier that is supplying the same stock item for other firms with similar demand uncertainties. The suppliers can smooth the random fluctuations in demands from multiple customers and provide the item at a cost-effective price, with less risk of stockouts.
- *High Service or Product Variety Is Important.* Partnering with a supplier can broaden the provision of services or products dramatically. For example, a typical Circuit City store carries 500 to 3,000 movie titles. When designing the Internet presence for the company, management discovered that Internet shoppers expected to have about 55,000 titles to choose from. The solution was to partner with another company to provide the product variety. Shoppers using **CircuitCity.com** can now place orders for movie titles, which will be fulfilled through virtual inventories.

The trade-offs between a traditional approach to the order fulfillment process and virtual supply chains are important considerations for a firm. There are two other implications of the choice. First, virtual supply chains relinquish direct control of the order fulfillment process to other firms. Consequently, it is important to have the appropriate contractual relationship with members of the virtual supply chain. Strategic alliances, partnerships, and long-term contracts provide much more control than do short-term contracts. The more important an activity is for the achievement of the firm's competitive priorities, the greater the degree of control the firm will want. Second, virtual supply chains provide the firm with more flexibility to change the design of its service packages or its products because it does not have the heavy overhead investment in the order fulfillment process. The firm needs to balance the need for control against the need for flexibility in choosing its supply-chain design.

The concept of virtual supply chains carries over to value chains, which include linkages to supporting processes. Managerial Practice 9.3 shows how one company has found a niche by supplying services to major corporations, and thereby becoming an important supplier in their customer's value chain.

INVENTORY PLACEMENT

A fundamental supply-chain decision is where to locate an inventory of finished goods. Placing inventories can have strategic implications, as in the case of international companies locating *distribution centers* (DC) in foreign countries to preempt local competition by reducing delivery times to its customers. However, the issue for any firm producing standardized products is where to position the inventory in the supply chain. At one extreme, the firm could keep all the finished-goods inventory at the manufacturing plant and ship directly to each of its customers. The advantage would come from what is referred to as **inventory pooling,** which is a reduction in inventory and safety stock because of the merging of variable demands from the customers. A higher-than-expected demand from one customer can be offset by a lower-than-expected demand from another. We discuss the methods for determining the amount of safety stock in Chapter 15 "Inventory Management." A disadvantage of placing inventory at the plant, however, is the added cost of shipping smaller, uneconomical quantities directly to the customers, typically over long distances.

Another approach is to use **forward placement,** which means locating stock closer to customers at a warehouse, DC, wholesaler, or retailer. Forward placement can have two advantages for the order fulfillment process—faster delivery times and reduced transportation costs—that can stimulate sales. As inventory is placed closer to the customer, such as at a DC, the pooling effect of the inventories is reduced, but the time to

inventory pooling A reduction in inventory and safety stock because of the merging of variable demands from customers.

Should distribution centers be added to position inventory closer to the customer?

forward placement Locating stock closer to customers at a warehouse, DC, wholesaler, or retailer.

MANAGERIAL PRACTICE 9.3

HCL CORPORATION PROVIDES SERVICE PROCESSES IN VIRTUAL VALUE CHAINS

HCL Corporation (www.hcltech.com) is a $600 million transnational group with interests in computers, networking, office automation, systems integration, software services, consulting, and computer-based education. With major technology centers located in India, the company has joint ventures, partnerships, and strategic alliances with a host of international giants, including Hewlett-Packard, Perot Systems Corporation, Microsoft, Cisco, and Cigna Corporation. HCL works with its customers to design certain business processes and then operates them from remote locations around the world. With the help of advanced technology and high-speed Internet connections, the processes become part of the customer's virtual value chain. Processes that HCL has managed for clients in virtual value chains include process support services and contact center services, among many others in sales and marketing and software development.

Process Support

HCL provides customers the opportunity to outsource process support services, such as human resource services, accounting, and transaction services.

HUMAN RESOURCE SERVICES. Country service representatives from HCL have knowledge about country-specific human resource policies, rules and regulations, in addition to communication and language skills. The services HCL can provide include health and benefits administration, employee record management, visa filing and administration, resume management, and payroll. HCL can also provide a complete Web-enabled secretarial assistance service for customers. For example, a work task from a customer of a client of HCL, an online secretarial services company in the United Kingdom, goes to an HCL *back office* located in India, where it follows a defined process and is sent back to a team at the client's firm, and then finally goes back

to the client's customer. These services are provided around the clock by using a center located in India; however, the center could have been located anywhere in the world.

ACCOUNTING SERVICES. Customers can completely outsource their accounting processes and have the services performed anywhere in the world. To accomplish this feat, HCL must be skilled at understanding the customer-specific regulatory and compliance requirements. Typical services include accounts payable, general accounting, customer invoicing, credit and collections, accounts receivables, fixed-asset accounting, and travel and expense accounting.

TRANSACTION SERVICES. Speed and accuracy are important for these services. HCL needs to be responsive to the requests of the customers of their customer. Typical services include customer database maintenance, customer e-mail responses, customer correspondence, application capture, claims processing, and underwriting.

Contact Center Services

Companies can outsource their customer contact services; however, it is a major decision because of the high level of personal interaction with customers. HCL, and other companies in this business, must have personnel with high levels of language, interaction, and accent-sensitive skills. A major advantage of Web-enabled contact center services is that the customer has 24 × 7 × 365 access, which nicely supports global businesses. Typical services include surveys, help desks, order capture, collection, verification, authorization calls, and customer inquiries.

HCL Corporation is but one example of a firm that has found a niche making virtual value chains feasible for a number of leading companies.

Many companies outsource their transaction process services, which may be provided from locations anywhere in the world. Here, employees process health insurance data from a U.S. firm at an office in Accra, the capital city of Ghana.

Sources: www.hclperot.com/e-integration_casestudy2.htm, 2001 HCL Perot Systems; www.hcltech.com/IT_Enabled.asp.

get the product to the customer is also reduced. Consequently, service to the customer is quicker, and the firm can take advantage of larger, less costly shipments to the DCs. The extreme application of forward placement is to locate the inventories at the customer. This tactic is referred to as **vendor-managed inventories (VMI)**. Some manufacturers, such as Dell Computer, have inventories of materials on consignment from their suppliers. Dell pays for the materials, as noted earlier, only when they are used. In deciding where to place inventories, firms must balance the inventory and transportation costs against the need to reduce the time to fulfill orders. Managerial Practice 9.4 explains a VMI method used by Campbell Soup Company called **continuous replenishment program (CRP)**, where the supplier monitors inventory levels at the customer and replenishes the stock as needed to avoid shortages. IBM, Heinz Pet Products, and Purina are among the many companies that utilize this approach to forward inventory placement. CRP helps reduce inventories and boost efficiencies in warehousing and transportation.

The successes with CRP have spurred the development of a process called *collaborative planning, forecasting, and replenishment (CPFR)*, which allows the supplier and the customer to develop replenishment quantities jointly. In an iterative process, the customer and the supplier fine-tune and coordinate their forecasts of demands for each individual item. See Chapter 13, "Forecasting," for more details on CPFR.

vendor-managed inventories (VMI) An extreme application of the forward placement tactic, which involves locating the inventories at the customer.

continuous replenishment program (CRP) A VMI method in which the supplier monitors inventory levels at the customer and replenishes the stock as needed to avoid shortages.

DESIGNING THE SUPPLIER RELATIONSHIP PROCESS

The supplier relationship process focuses on the interaction of the firm and upstream suppliers. The major nested processes include

- *Design Collaboration Process.* The design collaboration process focuses on jointly designing new services or products with key suppliers. This process seeks to eliminate costly delays and mistakes incurred when many suppliers concurrently, but independently, design service packages or manufactured components. Without sharing information between the suppliers, the end result can be far off the mark.
- *Sourcing Process.* The sourcing process qualifies, selects, manages the contracts, and evaluates suppliers.
- *Negotiation Process.* The negotiation process focuses on obtaining an effective contract that meets the price, quality, and delivery requirements of the supplier relationship process's internal customers.
- *Buying Process.* The buying process executes the actual procurement of the service or material from the supplier. This process includes the creation, management, and approval of purchase orders. (See Chapter 12, "Information Technology and Value Chains," for a discussion of various forms of e-purchasing.)
- *Information Exchange Process.* The information exchange process facilitates the exchange of pertinent operating information, such as forecasts, schedules, and inventory levels between the firm and its supplier.

In this section we focus on several important decision areas that affect the design of the supplier relationship process. First we discuss the considerations firms make in selecting and certifying suppliers, an important activity in the sourcing process. Next, we discuss the nature of supplier relations, which reflects on the design collaboration and negotiation processes. We then discuss the implications of centralized versus localized buying, which affects the negotiation and buying processes. Finally, we discuss the technique of value analysis, which lies at the heart of the design collaboration process.

SUPPLIER SELECTION AND CERTIFICATION

Purchasing is the eyes and ears of the organization in the supplier marketplace, continuously seeking better buys and new materials from suppliers. Consequently, purchasing is in a good position to select suppliers for the supply chain and to conduct certification programs.

MANAGERIAL PRACTICE 9.4

CONTINUOUS REPLENISHMENT AT THE CAMPBELL SOUP COMPANY

The Campbell Soup Company (www.campbellsoup.com) makes products that are very price sensitive. An important competitive priority for the company is low-cost operations, which extends to the entire supply chain. Campbell operates in an environment with a high degree of certainty. Only 5 percent of its products are new each year; the rest have been on the market for years, making forecasting demand easy. Even though Campbell already had high levels of customer service—98 percent of the time, Campbell's products were available in retailers' inventories—management believed that improvements in costs were possible. It scrutinized the entire supply chain to determine where performance could be improved.

The outcome was a program called the *continuous replenishment program (CRP)*, which reduced the inventories of retailers from an average of four to two weeks' supply. This reduction amounts to savings on the order of 1 percent of retail sales. As the average retailer's profits are only 2 percent of sales, the result was a 50 percent increase in the average retailer's profits. Because of that increase in profitability, retailers purchased a broader line of Campbell products, thereby increasing Campbell's sales. The program works in the following way.

- Each morning Campbell uses Electronic Data Interchange to link with retailers.
- Retailers inform Campbell of demands for Campbell products and the current inventory levels in their distribution centers.
- Campbell determines which products need replenishment based on upper and lower inventory limits established with each retailer.
- Campbell makes daily deliveries of needed products.

Campbell must avoid actions that would disrupt the supply chain. For example, retailers on the continuous replenishment program had to forgo forward buying, whereby retailers in the industry often buy excess stock at dis-counted prices so that they can offer price promotions. Forward buying causes ripples in the supply chain, increasing everyone's costs. That was the case with chicken soup. Campbell would offer deep discounts once a year and retailers would take advantage of them, sometimes buying an entire year's supply. Because of the bulge in demand, the chicken-processing plant would have to go on overtime. When that happened, costs in the entire supply chain increased—Campbell's production costs increased, and retailers had to pay for warehousing large stocks of chicken soup. With the continuous replenishment system, those extra costs are eliminated and everyone wins.

The success of CRP has led Campbell to pursue additional ways to improve efficiency in the supply chain. One improvement is quicker order turnaround for those customers who participate in a new program, called the continuous planning, forecasting, and replenishment (CPFR) program, which is a movement gaining ground in the grocery industry. The program allows Campbell to determine replenishment quantities in concert with the retailer and thereby remove redundant inventory and improve customer service.

To combat inefficient customer-ordering patterns, Campbell has also initiated a "strategic-pricing program" that rewards customers for ordering electronically and in quantities that fill trucks and pallets, rather than by the case. Customers get allowances or price breaks for picking up the goods themselves. Campbell has observed a significant change in the ordering patterns of its customers because of the program, with about two-thirds of its customers now meeting the criteria for the best pricing bracket. The strategic-pricing program has netted several million dollars in savings for Campbell and its trading partners.

Forward buying poses problems for Campbell's high-volume, standardized, low-cost operations. Here, employees at the end of the automated can-making line inspect cans before they are filled with soup. Changing volumes is very difficult on such a process.

Sources; Fisher, Marshall L. "What Is the Right Supply Chain for Your Product?" *Harvard Business Review* (March–April 1997), pp. 105–116; www.campbell soup.com, 2003.

SUPPLIER SELECTION. To make supplier selection decisions and to review the performance of current suppliers, management must review the market segments it wants to serve and relate their needs to the supply chain. Competitive priorities (see Chapter 2, "Operations Strategy") are a starting point in developing a list of performance criteria to be used. For example, food-service firms use on-time delivery and quality as the top two criteria for selecting suppliers. These criteria reflect the requirements that food-service supply chains need to meet.

Three criteria most often considered by firms selecting new suppliers are price, quality, and delivery. Because firms spend a large percentage of their total income on purchased items, finding suppliers that charge low *prices* is a key objective. However, the *quality* of a supplier's materials also is important. The hidden costs of poor quality can be high, particularly if defects are not detected until after considerable value has been added by subsequent operations (see Chapter 5, "Process Performance and Quality"). For a retailer, poor merchandise quality can mean loss of customer goodwill and future sales. Finally, shorter lead times and on-time *delivery* help the buying firm maintain acceptable customer service with less inventory. For example, Maimonides Medical Center, a 700-bed hospital in Brooklyn, buys many of its materials from one supplier. The supplier offers very short lead times from a nearby warehouse, which allowed Maimonides to pare its inventory from about $1,200 to only $150 per bed.

The benefits of fast, on-time deliveries also apply to the manufacturing sector. Many manufacturers demand quick, dependable deliveries from their suppliers to minimize inventory levels. This constraint forces suppliers to have nearby plants or warehouses. Kasle Steel Corporation built a steel-processing plant adjacent to GM's Buick facility in Flint, Michigan, even though it already had two plants only 70 miles away. This new plant is part of a complex (called "Buick City") in which all parts are supplied to the GM facility by nearby plants. These clustered suppliers ship small quantities frequently to minimize the assembly plant's inventory. There is a 20-minute window during which a quantity of a particular part must be delivered; otherwise, the production line may have to be shut down. Kasle Steel was selected as a supplier in part because of its willingness to provide quick, dependable deliveries.

A fourth criterion is becoming very important in the selection of suppliers—environmental impact. Many firms are engaging in **green purchasing,** which involves identifying, assessing, and managing the flow of environmental waste and finding ways to reduce it and minimize its impact on the environment. Suppliers are being asked to be environmentally conscious when designing and manufacturing their products, and claims such as *green, biodegradable, natural,* and *recycled* must be substantiated when bidding on a contract. In the not-too-distant future, this criterion could be one of the most important in the selection of suppliers.

green purchasing The process of identifying, assessing, and managing the flow of environmental waste and finding ways to reduce it and minimize its impact on the environment.

SUPPLIER CERTIFICATION. Supplier certification programs verify that potential suppliers have the capability to provide the services or materials the buying firm requires. Certification typically involves site visits by a cross-functional team from the buying firm who do an in-depth evaluation of the supplier's capability to meet cost, quality, delivery, and flexibility targets from process and information system perspectives. The team may consist of members from operations, purchasing, engineering, information systems, and accounting. Every aspect of producing the services or materials is explored through observation of the processes in action and review of documentation for completeness and accuracy. Once certified, the supplier can be used by purchasing without its having to make background checks. Performance is monitored and performance records are kept. After a certain period of time, or if performance declines, the supplier may have to be recertified.

SUPPLIER RELATIONS

The nature of relations maintained with suppliers can affect the quality, timeliness, and price of a firm's services and products.

What criteria should be used to select suppliers and how should suppliers be certified?

competitive orientation   A supplier relation that views negotiations between buyer and seller as a zero-sum game: Whatever one side loses, the other side gains and short-term advantages are prized over long-term commitments.

How can purchasing power be used effectively in a supply chain?

COMPETITIVE ORIENTATION. The **competitive orientation** to supplier relations views negotiations between buyer and seller as a zero-sum game: Whatever one side loses, the other side gains. Short-term advantages are prized over long-term commitments. The buyer may try to beat the supplier's price down to the lowest survival level or to push demand to high levels during boom times and order almost nothing during recessions. In contrast, the supplier presses for higher prices for specific levels of quality, customer service, and volume flexibility. Which party wins depends largely on who has the most clout.

Purchasing power determines the clout that a firm has. A firm has purchasing power when its purchasing volume represents a significant share of the supplier's sales or the purchased service or item is standardized and many substitutes are available. For example, Staples merged with Office Depot to create a chain of 1,100 office supply stores in the United States and Canada. The buying power of the new company is enormous. Clout is also used in the health care industry. Premier, Inc., a cooperative with 1,759 member hospitals, spends $10 billion a year on services and materials for its members. Suppliers are uneasy because they have to give Premier prices far lower than they do their other customers to keep its business, reflecting Premier's purchasing power. For example, Premier got a 30 percent savings in dye used in medical imaging and a 25 percent savings in the film for that process. Premier will buy from the lowest bidder without much loyalty to any supplier. Analysts estimate that Premier has helped reduce the cost of health care by $2 billion a year because of its efforts.

cooperative orientation   A supplier relation in which the buyer and seller are partners, each helping the other as much as possible.

COOPERATIVE ORIENTATION. With the **cooperative orientation** to supplier relations, the buyer and seller are partners, each helping the other as much as possible. A cooperative orientation means long-term commitment, joint work on quality, and support by the buyer of the supplier's managerial, technological, and capacity development. A cooperative orientation favors few suppliers of a particular service or item, with just one or two suppliers being the ideal number. As order volumes increase, the supplier gains repeatability, which helps movement toward high-volume operations at a low cost. When contracts are large and a long-term relationship is ensured, the supplier might even build a new facility and hire a new workforce, perhaps relocating close to the buyer's plant, as in the case of GM and Kasle Steel. Reducing the number of suppliers also can help the buyer, as suppliers become almost an extension of the buyer.

A cooperative orientation means that the buyer shares more information with the supplier on its future buying intentions. This forward visibility allows suppliers to make better, more reliable forecasts of future demand. The buyer visits suppliers' plants and cultivates cooperative attitudes. The buyer may even suggest ways to improve the suppliers' operations. This close cooperation with suppliers could even mean that the buyer does not need to inspect incoming materials. It also could mean giving the supplier more latitude in specifications, involving the supplier more in designing parts, implementing cost-reduction ideas, and sharing in savings.

A cooperative orientation has opened the door for innovative arrangements with suppliers. One extreme example of such an arrangement is the DaimlerChrysler Smart car plant in France's Alsace region. Just about everything at the plant is outsourced, from nuts and bolts on the assembly line to the delivery of cars to Europe and Japan. The unique car, which is a two-seater that is five feet shorter and a foot narrower than the Volkswagen Beetle, is built in an equally unique factory. The plant is a cross-shaped building, with assembly lines moving through a "U" up and down each wing. Major suppliers have constructed plants along each of the wings in close proximity to the point where their products would be needed in the assembly of the Smart car. The suppliers own all of the equipment and hire all of the employees—DaimlerChrysler only owns the assembly building. DaimlerChrysler's policy is to "pay on build," which means that the suppliers must carry the cost of work-in-progress inventory until the units are accepted for sale by inspectors. Nonetheless, the suppliers are guaranteed a certain volume of units each year to reduce their risk in the venture.

One advantage of reducing the number of suppliers in the supply chain is a reduction in the complexity of managing them. However, reducing the number of suppliers

VIDEO CLIP 9.1
Video Clip 9.1 on the Student CD-ROM addresses supplier relations and the testing and evaluation of new products.

for a service or item may have the disadvantage of increased risk of an interruption in supply. Also, there is less opportunity to drive a good bargain in prices unless the buyer has a lot of clout. **Sole sourcing,** which is the awarding of a contract for a service or item to only one supplier, can amplify any problems with the supplier that may crop up.

Both the competitive and cooperative orientations have their advantages and disadvantages. The key is to use the approach that serves the firm's competitive priorities best. Some companies utilize a mixed strategy. A company can pursue a competitive orientation by seeking price reductions from its suppliers of common supplies and infrequently purchased items on an electronic marketplace; a company can also use a cooperative orientation with suppliers of higher volume services and materials and negotiate long-term contracts with them. However, a cooperative orientation does not preclude the obligation to reduce costs. For example, automakers make long-term commitments to selected suppliers but require continuous improvement programs to gain annual price reductions from them (see Chapter 5, "Process Performance and Quality"). Such commitments can give suppliers enough volume to invest in cost-saving equipment and new capacity.

CENTRALIZED VERSUS LOCALIZED BUYING

When an organization has several facilities (e.g., stores, hospitals, or plants), management must decide whether to buy locally or centrally. This decision has implications for the control of supply-chain flows.

Centralized buying has the advantage of increasing purchasing clout. Savings can be significant, often on the order of 10 percent or more. Increased buying power can mean getting better service, ensuring long-term supply availability, or developing new supplier capability. Companies with overseas suppliers favor centralization because of the specialized skills (e.g., understanding of foreign languages and cultures) needed to buy from foreign sources. Buyers also need to understand international commercial and contract law regarding the transfer of services and goods. Another trend that favors centralization is the growth of computer-based information systems and the Internet, which give specialists at headquarters access to data previously available only at the local level.

Probably the biggest disadvantage of centralized buying is loss of control at the local level. When plants or divisions are evaluated as profit or cost centers, centralized buying is undesirable for items unique to a particular facility. These items should be purchased locally whenever possible. The same holds for purchases that must be closely meshed with production schedules. Further, localized buying is an advantage when the firm has major facilities in foreign countries because the managers there, often foreign nationals, have a much better understanding of the culture than a staff would at the home office. Also, centralized purchasing often means longer lead times and another level in the firm's hierarchy. Perhaps the best solution is a compromise strategy, whereby both local autonomy and centralized buying are possible. For example, the corporate purchasing group at IBM negotiates contracts on a centralized basis only at the request of local plants. Then management at one of the facilities monitors the contract for all the participating plants.

VALUE ANALYSIS

A systematic effort to reduce the cost or improve the performance of services or products, either purchased or produced, is referred to as **value analysis.** It is an intensive examination of the services, materials, processes, information systems, and flows of material involved in the production of a service or an item. Benefits include reduced production, materials, and distribution costs; improved profit margins; and increased customer satisfaction. Because teams involving purchasing, production, and engineering personnel from both the firm and its major suppliers play a key role in value analysis, another potential benefit is increased employee morale.

Value analysis encourages employees of the firm and its suppliers to address questions such as the following: What is the function of the service or the item? Is the

sole sourcing The awarding of a contract for a service or item to only one supplier.

value analysis A systematic effort to reduce the cost or improve the performace of services or products, either purchased or produced.

How can suppliers get involved in value analysis to benefit the supply chain?

function necessary? Can a lower-cost standard part that serves the purpose be identified? Can the service or the item be simplified, or its specifications relaxed, to achieve a lower price? Can the service or the item be designed so that it can be produced more efficiently or more quickly? Can features that the customer values highly be added to the service or the item? Value analysis should be part of a continual effort to improve the performance of the supply chain and increase the value of the service or the item to the customer.

Value analysis can focus solely on the *internal* supply chain with some success, but its true potential lies in applying it to the entire value chain as well. An approach that many firms are using is called **early supplier involvement**, which is a program that includes suppliers in the design phase of a service or product. Suppliers provide suggestions for design changes and materials choices that will result in more efficient operations and higher quality. In the automotive industry, an even higher level of early supplier involvement is known as **presourcing**, whereby suppliers are selected early in a vehicle's concept development stage and are given significant, if not total, responsibility for the design of certain components or systems. Presourced suppliers also take responsibility for the cost, quality, and on-time delivery of the items they produce.

early supplier involvement
A program that includes suppliers in the design phase of a service or product.

presourcing   In the automotive industry, a level of supplier involvement in which suppliers are selected early in a vehicle's concept development stage and are given significant, if not total, responsibility for the design of certain components or systems.

● MEASURES OF SUPPLY-CHAIN PERFORMANCE

As we have shown, supply-chain management involves managing the flow of services, materials, and information in a supply chain. This flow also affects various financial measures of concern to the firm. In this section, we first define the typical inventory measures used to monitor supply-chain performance. We then present some process measures. Finally, we relate some commonly used supply-chain performance measures to several important financial measures.

INVENTORY MEASURES

All methods of measuring inventory begin with a physical count of units, volume, or weight. However, measures of inventories are reported in three basic ways: (1) average aggregate inventory value, (2) weeks of supply, and (3) inventory turnover.

The **average aggregate inventory value** is the total value of all items held in inventory for a firm. We express all the dollar values in this inventory measure at cost because we can then sum the values of individual items in raw materials, work-in-process, and finished goods: Final sales dollars have meaning only for final services or products and cannot be used for all inventory items. It is an average because it usually represents the inventory investment over some period of time. Suppose a retailer holds items A and B in stock. One unit of item A may be worth only a few dollars, whereas one unit of item B may be valued in the hundreds of dollars because of the labor, technology, and other value-added operations performed in manufacturing the product. This measure for an inventory consisting of only items A and B is

What measures of inventory are important to supply-chain management?

average aggregate inventory value   The total value of all items held in inventory for a firm.

$$
\begin{aligned}
\text{Average aggregate} \atop \text{inventory value} = & \left(\begin{array}{c} \text{Number of units of item A} \\ \text{typically on hand} \end{array} \right) \left(\begin{array}{c} \text{Value of each} \\ \text{unit of item A} \end{array} \right) \\
& + \left(\begin{array}{c} \text{Number of units of item B} \\ \text{typically on hand} \end{array} \right) \left(\begin{array}{c} \text{Value of each} \\ \text{unit of item B} \end{array} \right)
\end{aligned}
$$

Summed over all items in an inventory, this total value tells managers how much of a firm's assets are tied up in inventory. Manufacturing firms typically have about 25 percent of their total assets in inventory, whereas wholesalers and retailers average about 75 percent.

To some extent, managers can decide whether the aggregate inventory value is too low or too high by historical or industry comparison or by managerial judgment. However, a better performance measure would take demand into account. **Weeks of supply** is an inventory measure obtained by dividing the average aggregate inventory value by sales per week at cost. (In some low-inventory operations, days or even hours are a better unit of time for measuring inventory.) The formula (expressed in weeks) is

weeks of supply   An Inventory measure obtained by dividing the average aggregate inventory value by sales per week at cost.

$$\text{Weeks of supply} = \frac{\text{Average aggregate inventory value}}{\text{Weekly sales (at cost)}}$$

Although the numerator includes the value of all items a firm holds in inventory (raw materials, WIP, and finished goods), the denominator represents only the finished goods sold—at cost rather than the sale price after markups or discounts. This cost is referred to as the *cost of goods sold*.

Inventory turnover (or *turns*) is an inventory measure obtained by dividing annual sales at cost by the average aggregate inventory value maintained during the year, or

inventory turnover   An inventory measure obtained by dividing annual sales at cost by the average aggregate inventory value maintained during the year.

$$\text{Inventory turnover} = \frac{\text{Annual sales (at cost)}}{\text{Average aggregate inventory value}}$$

The "best" inventory level, even when expressed as turnover, cannot be determined easily. A good starting point is to benchmark the leading firms in an industry.

Calculating Inventory Measures   EXAMPLE 9.1

The Eagle Machine Company averaged $2 million in inventory last year, and the cost of goods sold was $10 million. Figure 9.8 shows the breakout of raw materials, work-in-process, and finished goods inventories. The best inventory turnover in the company's industry is six turns per year. If the company has 52 business weeks per year, how many weeks of supply were held in inventory? What was the inventory turnover? What should the company do?

SOLUTION

The average aggregate inventory value of $2 million translates into 10.4 weeks of supply and five turns per year, calculated as follows:

$$\text{Weeks of supply} = \frac{\$2 \text{ million}}{(\$10 \text{ million})/(52 \text{ weeks})} = 10.4 \text{ weeks}$$

$$\text{Inventory turns} = \frac{\$10 \text{ million}}{\$2 \text{ million}} = 5 \text{ turns/year}$$

TUTOR 9.1

Tutor 9.1 on the Student CD-ROM provides a new example to practice the calculation of inventory measures.

DECISION POINT   The analysis indicates that management must improve the inventory turns by 20 percent. Management should improve its order fulfillment process to reduce finished goods inventory assets through postponement (see Chapter 2, "Operations Strategy"), better placement of the inventories to increase the pooling effect, or improved information flows between the company and its customers. Internal supply-chain operations can be improved to reduce the need to have so much raw materials and work-in-process inventory stock. It will take an inventory reduction of about 16 percent to achieve the target of six turns per year. However, inventories would not have to be reduced as much if there was an increase in sales. If the sales department targets an increase in sales of 8 percent ($10.8 million), inventories need only be reduced by 10 percent ($1.8 million) to get six turns a year. Management can now do sensitivity analyses with OM Explorer to see what effect reductions in the inventory of specific items or increases in the annual sales have on weeks of supply or inventory turns.

FIGURE 9.8

Calculating Inventory
Measures using Inventory
Estimator Solver

Solver - Inventory Estimator
Enter data in yellow - shaded areas.

Cost of Goods Sold $10,000,000
Weeks of Operation 52

	Item Number	Average Level	Unit Value	Total Value
Raw Materials	1	1,400	$50.00	$70,000
	2	1,000	$32.00	$32,000
	3	400	$60.00	$24,000
	4	2,400	$10.00	$24,000
	5	800	$15.00	$12,000
Work in Process	6	320	$700.00	$224,000
	7	160	$900.00	$144,000
	8	280	$750.00	$210,000
	9	240	$800.00	$192,000
	10	400	$1,000.00	$400,000
Finished Goods	11	60	$2,000.00	$120,000
	12	40	$3,500.00	$140,000
	13	50	$2,800.00	$140,000
	14	20	$5,000.00	$100,000
	15	40	$4,200.00	$168,000
Total				$2,000,000

Average Weekly Sales at Cost $192,308

Weeks of Supply   10.4

Inventory Turnover   5.0

PROCESS MEASURES

We have discussed three major processes related to supply-chain management: customer relationship, order fulfillment, and supplier relationship. Supply-chain managers monitor performance by measuring costs, time, and quality. Table 9.1 contains examples of operating measures for the three processes.

Managers periodically collect data on measures such as these and track them to note changes in level or direction. Statistical process control charts can be used to determine if the changes are statistically significant, thereby prompting management's attention (see Chapter 5, "Process Performance and Quality"). The impact of improvements to the three processes can be monitored using control charts.

TABLE 9.1 SUPPLY-CHAIN PROCESS MEASURES

Customer Relationship	Order Fulfillment	Supplier Relationship
• Percent of orders taken accurately • Time to complete the order placement process • Customer satisfaction with the order placement process	• Percent of incomplete orders shipped • Percent of orders shipped on time • Time to fulfill the order • Percent of botched services or returned items • Cost to produce the service or item • Customer satisfaction with the order fulfillment process	• Percent of suppliers' deliveries on time • Suppliers' lead times • Percent defects in services and purchased materials • Cost of services and purchased materials

LINKS TO FINANCIAL MEASURES

Effective management of the supply chain has a fundamental impact on the financial status of a firm. Inventory should be considered an investment because it is created for future use. However, inventory ties up funds that might be used more profitably in other operations.

How are operating measures of supply-chain performance related to a firm's typical financial measures?

RETURN ON ASSETS. Managing the supply chain so as to reduce the aggregate inventory investment will reduce the *total assets* portion of the firm's balance sheet. An important financial measure is *return on assets (ROA)*, which is net income divided by total assets. Consequently, reducing aggregate inventory investment will increase ROA. Nonetheless, the objective should be to have the proper amount of inventory, not the least amount of inventory.

WORKING CAPITAL. Weeks of inventory and inventory turns are reflected in another financial measure, *working capital*, which is money used to finance ongoing operations. Increases in inventory investment require increased payments to suppliers, for example. Decreasing weeks of supply or increasing inventory turns reduces the pressure on working capital by reducing inventories. Increasing inventory turns can be accomplished by improving the customer relationship, order fulfillment, or supplier relationship processes. For example, reducing supplier lead times has the effect of reducing weeks of supply and increasing inventory turns: Matching the input and output flows of materials is easier because shorter-range, more reliable forecasts of demand can be used. Similarly, improvements in the other measures in Table 9.1 can be traced to improvements in working capital.

COST OF GOODS SOLD. Managers can also reduce production and material costs through effective supply-chain management. Costs of materials are determined through the financial arrangements with suppliers, and production costs are a result of the design and execution of the internal supply chain. In addition, the percent of defects, experienced anywhere in the supply chain, also affects the costs of operation. Improvements in these measures are reflected in the *cost of goods sold* and ultimately in the *net income* of the firm. They also have an effect on *contribution margin*, which is the difference between price and the variable costs to produce a service or good. Reducing production and material costs, and quality defect costs, increases the contribution margin, allowing for greater profits. Contribution margins are often used as inputs to decisions regarding the portfolio of services or products the firm offers.

TOTAL REVENUE. Supply-chain performance measures related to time also have financial implications. Many service providers and manufacturers measure the percent of on-time deliveries of their services or product to their customers, as well as services and materials from their suppliers. Increasing the percent of on-time deliveries to customers will increase *total revenue* because satisfied customers will buy more services and products from the firm. Increasing the percent of on-time deliveries from suppliers has the effect of reducing the costs of inventories, which has implications for the cost of goods sold and contribution margins.

CASH FLOW. The Internet has brought another financial measure related to time to the forefront: *cash-to-cash,* which is the time lag between paying for the services and materials needed to produce a service or product and receiving payment for it. The shorter the time lag, the better the *cash flow* position of the firm. There is less need for working capital; therefore, the firm can use the freed-up funds for projects or investments. Reengineering the order placement process, so that payment for the service or product is made at the time the order is placed, can reduce the time lag. Billing the customer after the service is performed or the order is shipped increases the need for working capital. The ultimate is to have a negative cash-to-cash situation, which is possible when the customer pays for the service or product before the firm has to pay for the resources and materials needed to produce it. In such a case, the firm must have supplier inventories on consignment, which allows the firm to pay for materials as it uses them. Dell Computer, in the chapter opener, is a prime example of a negative cash-to-cash situation.

SUPPLY-CHAIN LINKS TO OPERATIONS STRATEGY

What is the appropriate supply-chain design for a particular competitive environment?

Operations strategy seeks to link the design and use of a firm's infrastructure and processes to the competitive priorities of each of its services or products, so as to maximize its potential in the marketplace. A supply chain is a network of firms. Thus, each firm in the chain should build its own supply chain to support the competitive priorities of its services or products. In this section, we discuss two distinct supply-chain designs and demonstrate how they can support the operations strategies of firms.

EFFICIENT VERSUS RESPONSIVE SUPPLY CHAINS

Even though extensive technologies such as electronic data interchange (EDI), the Internet, computer-assisted design, flexible manufacturing, and automated warehousing have been applied to all stages of the supply chain, the performance of many supply chains has been dismal. A recent study of the U.S. food industry estimated that poor coordination among supply-chain partners was wasting $30 billion annually. One possible cause for failures is that managers do not understand the nature of the demand for their services or products and, therefore, cannot devise a supply chain that would best satisfy that demand. Two distinct designs used to competitive advantage are *efficient supply chains* and *responsive supply chains* (Fisher, 1997). The purpose of efficient supply chains is to coordinate the flow of services and materials, so as to minimize inventories and maximize the efficiency of the service providers and manufacturers in the chain. Responsive supply chains are designed to react quickly to market demands by positioning inventories and capacities in order to hedge against uncertainties in demand. Table 9.2 shows the environments that best suit each design.

The nature of demand for the firm's services or products is a key factor in the best choice of supply-chain design. Efficient supply chains work best in environments where demand is highly predictable, such as demand for staple items purchased at grocery stores or demand for a package delivery service. The focus of the supply chain is on the efficient flows of services and materials and keeping inventories to a minimum. Because of the markets the firms serve, service or product designs last a long time, new introductions are infrequent, and variety is small. Such firms typically produce for markets in which price is crucial to winning an order; therefore, contribution margins are low and efficiency is important. Consequently, the firm's competitive priorities are low-cost operations, consistent quality, and on-time delivery.

TABLE 9.2 ENVIRONMENTS BEST SUITED FOR EFFICIENT AND RESPONSIVE SUPPLY CHAINS

Factor	Efficient Supply Chains	Responsive Supply Chains
Demand	Predictable, low forecast errors	Unpredictable, high forecast errors
Competitive priorities	Low cost, consistent quality, on-time delivery	Development speed, fast delivery times, customization, volume flexibility, variety, top quality
New-service/ product introduction	Infrequent	Frequent
Contribution margins	Low	High
Product variety	Low	High

Responsive supply chains work best when firms offer a great variety of services or products and demand predictability is low. The firms may not know what services or products they need to provide until customers place orders. In addition, demand may be short-lived, as in the case of fashion goods. The focus of responsive supply chains is reaction time, so as to avoid keeping costly inventories that ultimately must be sold at deep discounts. Such is the operating environment of mass customizers (see Chapter 2, "Operations Strategy"). To be competitive, such firms must frequently introduce new services or products. Nonetheless, because of the innovativeness of their services or products, these firms enjoy high contribution margins. Typical competitive priorities are development speed, fast delivery times, customization, variety, volume flexibility, and top quality.

A firm may need to utilize both types of supply chains, especially when it focuses its operations on specific market segments or when it uses postponement (see Chapter 2, "Operations Strategy"). For example, the supply chain for a standard product, such as an oil tanker, has different requirements than that for a customized product, such as a luxury liner, even though both are ocean-going vessels and both may be manufactured by the same company. You might also see elements of efficiency and responsiveness in the same supply chain. For example, Gillette uses an efficient supply chain to manufacture its products so that it can utilize a capital-intensive manufacturing process, and then postpones the packaging of the products until the very last moment to be responsive to the needs at the retail level. The packaging operation involves customization in the form of printing in different languages. Just as processes can be broken into parts, with different process choices for each (see Chapter 3, "Process Design Strategy"), so can supply-chain processes be segmented to achieve optimal performance.

DESIGN OF EFFICIENT AND RESPONSIVE SUPPLY CHAINS

Table 9.3 contains the basic design features for efficient and responsive supply chains. The more downstream in an efficient supply chain that a firm is, the more likely it is to have a line-flow strategy that supports high volumes of standardized services or products. Consequently, suppliers in efficient supply chains should have low capacity cushions because high utilization keeps the cost per unit low. High inventory turns are desired because inventory investment must be kept low to achieve low costs. Firms should work with their suppliers to shorten lead times, but care must be taken to use tactics that do not appreciably increase costs. For example, lead times for a supplier could be shortened by switching from rail to air transportation; however, the added cost may offset the savings obtained from the shorter lead times. Suppliers should be selected with emphasis on low prices, consistent quality, and on-time delivery. Because of low capacity cushions, disruptions in an efficient supply chain can be costly and must be avoided.

TABLE 9.3 DESIGN FEATURES FOR EFFICIENT AND RESPONSIVE SUPPLY CHAINS

Factor	Efficient Supply Chains	Responsive Supply Chains
Operation strategy	Make-to-stock or standardized services or products; emphasize high-volumes	Assemble-to-order, make-to-order, or customized services or products; emphasize variety
Capacity cushion	Low	High
Inventory investment	Low, enable high inventory turns	As needed to enable fast delivery time
Lead time	Shorten, but do not increase costs	Shorten aggressively
Supplier selection	Emphasize low prices, consistent quality, on-time delivery	Emphasize fast delivery time, customization, variety, volume flexibility, top quality

Because of the need for quick reactions and the high levels of service or product variety, firms in a responsive supply chain should be flexible and have high capacity cushions. Inventories should be positioned in the chain to support delivery speed, but inventories of expensive finished goods should be avoided. Firms should aggressively work with their suppliers to shorten lead times because it allows firms to wait longer before committing to customer orders. Firms should select suppliers to support the competitive priorities of the services or products provided, which in this case would include the ability to provide quick deliveries, customize services or components, adjust volumes quickly to match demand cycles in the market, offer variety and provide top quality. Our discussion of the Dell Computer Company at the beginning of this chapter is an example of the use of a responsive supply chain for competitive advantage. Managerial Practice 9.5 shows how a clothing retailer has used a responsive supply chain to competitive advantage.

Poor supply-chain performance often is the result of using the wrong supply-chain design for the services or products provided. A common mistake is to use an efficient supply chain in an environment that calls for a responsive supply chain. Over time, a firm may add options to its basic service or product, or introduce variations, so that the variety of its offerings increases dramatically and demand for any given service or product predictability drops. Yet, the firm continues to measure the performance of its supply chain as it always has, emphasizing efficiency, even when contribution margins would allow a responsive supply-chain design. Clearly, effective alignment of supply-chain operations to its competitive priorities has strategic implications for a firm.

SUPPLY-CHAIN SOFTWARE

Supply-chain software provides the capability to share information with suppliers and customers and to make decisions affecting the performance of the integrated supply chain. The software options available today offer many sophisticated features; however, the benefit to the organization depends upon how people use them.

This "rolling chassis" is built by Dana Corporation in Curitiba, Brazil, and then shipped to a nearby DaimlerChysler plant where the Dakota pickup truck is assembled. Sophisticated supply-chain software is needed to coordinate the production and delivery of these expensive units.

MANAGERIAL PRACTICE 9.5

EUROPEAN CLOTHING RETAILER USES A RESPONSIVE SUPPLY CHAIN TO DELIGHT CUSTOMERS

Suppose you are shopping for the latest hip fashions in a men's knit vest or a black dress with red and beige accents at a quality level closer to Banana Republic than Gap, and at prices in line with Old Navy. You are in luck if you are shopping at Zara, a chain of 519 clothing retail stores in Europe, the Americas, and the Middle East that caters to the dressier European tastes. Zara is a part of Inditex, a $2.8 billion retail conglomerate, which has 1,315 stores in 40 countries. Zara contributes 75 percent of Inditex's sales, which grew at an annual rate of 31 percent in 2001, and continues to grow when competitors, such as Gap and Sweden's H&M, retrench. What is the secret?

In fashion retailing, nothing is as important as time to market—not advertising (Zara advertises twice a year), sales promotions (Zara uses promotions sparingly), or labor costs. Rather than going to Third World countries to manufacture their items at low cost, management designed a supply chain that can react very quickly to changes in customer preferences. The factories had to be flexible and geared for quick response—something that would be difficult to manage if the plants were in South America or Asia. It all begins at the new product development group, which is located at Zara headquarters in La Coruna, Spain. There, some 200 designers and product managers decide what to create, given inputs from the 519 store managers worldwide. The group develops more than 10,000 new items each year, far more than the competition does. The designers draw up their ideas on computers and send them along to the factories, which are located across the highway from the headquarters. Within days, the cutting, dyeing, stitching, and pressing operations begin.

A key element of the supply chain is a four story, five-million-square-foot (the equivalent of 90 football fields) warehouse that is connected to 14 factories through a series of tunnels, each equipped with a rail and cable system. Coats, pants, dresses, and other products produced in the plants are put on racks and moved by cables through the tunnels to the warehouse, where the merchandise is selected, sorted, rerouted, resorted, and then taken to a special area where each Zara store has its own staging area. As soon as a store's order is complete, it is packed and shipped to its destination—by truck if it is a European destination or by plane if it is outside of Europe. The vast majority of the items are in the warehouse in only a few hours.

Zara's management believes that flexibility and speed are the two top competitive priorities for their supply chain. The elapsed time from developing a new garment to hanging it up in a store for sale is just three weeks. In contrast, it takes Gap nine months for the same cycle. Such performance, however, comes at a price. Zara's manufacturing costs run 15 to 20 percent higher than those of its rivals. The key point is that the business is still very profitable. Zara maintains a profit margin of 10 percent, which is on par with the best in the industry.

Sources: Helft, Miguel. "Fashion Fast Forward." *Business Week* (May 2002); www.business2.com.

Consideration should be given to the following questions:

- *Which Processes Should Be Fixed with the Software?* Massive redesigns of the supply-chain processes to fit a software package do not always pay off. A better approach is to focus on fixing the processes with the most immediate economic impact. Such processes might include forecasting, setting inventory levels, and ensuring that delivery schedules are met. The systematic approach to process analysis should be used to identify the processes most in need of redesign. (See Chapter 4, "Process Analysis").

- *What Should Be Promised to Win the Support of Users?* A typical mistake is to promise more than the software can deliver or that the implementation team can accomplish in a given time frame. Expectations rise, only to be dashed when reality sets in. The realistic setting of expectations will avoid the trap of promising everything to everybody just to win support.

- *What Training Is Required?* The greatest value of the new software packages is their ability to improve decision making. Training should go beyond merely showing how to move old processes based on telephones or fax machines to the computer and the Internet. Training should also include how to make effective decisions with the added information flows and powerful decision aids normally provided by these packages. This is more training than most companies anticipate.

- *Who Should Be Held Accountable for the Software's Success?* To avoid finger-pointing if something goes wrong, vendors, IT departments, and users should all be held accountable. Vendors should be held accountable for how well the software does its job. The IT department should be held accountable for delivering the software on time and on budget, and the users, supply-chain managers, should be held accountable for performance improvements in the supply-chain processes.

Supply-chain applications are often a part of enterprise resource planning (ERP) systems (see Chapter 12, "Information Technology and Value Chains") or can be purchased independently from a variety of vendors. For example, Pepperidge Farm purchased a supply-chain management system to improve customer service, reduce costs in finished goods inventory, and gain efficiencies in materials purchasing. Pepperidge Farm produces fresh breads made-to-order, as well as a number of other products that are made-to-stock.

The system has the following modules:

- *Order Commitment.* Accepts customer orders, allocates resources to ensure that delivery is possible, and commits the firm to a specified delivery date.
- *Transportation Management.* Schedules freight movements, provides routing capability, allocates resources, and tracks shipments worldwide.
- *Purchasing Management.* Links to suppliers to share information and manage procurement contracts.
- *Demand Management.* Provides multiple forecasting algorithms and causal modeling to assist in estimating demands, allowing for management overrides to incorporate real-time customer information (see Chapter 13, "Forecasting").
- *Vendor-Managed Inventory.* Coordinates the replenishment of inventories stored at the customer's site.
- *Replenishment Planning.* Facilitates the order fulfillment process by orchestrating the flow of inventory through the various stocking points in the distribution channel and allocates inventories among customers when shortages exist.
- *Configuration.* Enables the assemble-to-order strategy by checking for the availability of all components before accepting an order and facilitates the substitution of components or features based on availability.
- *Material Planning.* Determines the replenishment of components and assemblies to support the master schedule of finished products (see Chapter 16, "Resource Planning").
- *Scheduling.* Provides multisite schedules with the capability to reschedule as needed (see Chapter 17, "Scheduling").
- *Master Planning.* Offers optimization tools to allocate and coordinate limited resources across the distribution network based upon user strategies.
- *Strategic Planning.* Provides tools for designing global supply chains, which assist in deciding inventory levels and the appropriate product mix across the distribution network and the best production and storage locations subject to customer and resource constraints.

The Pepperidge Farm supply-chain management system is representative of the software packages available from a number of vendors. Most companies will purchase the software rather than create their own.

SUPPLY-CHAIN DESIGN ACROSS THE ORGANIZATION

Supply chains permeate the entire organization. It is hard to envision a process in a firm that is not in some way affected by a supply chain. Supply chains must be managed to coordinate the inputs with the outputs in a firm so as to achieve the appropriate competitive priorities of the firm's enterprise processes. The Internet has offered firms an alternative to traditional methods for managing the supply chain.

However, the firm must be committed to reengineering its information flows throughout the organization. The supply-chain processes most affected are the customer relationship, order fulfillment (including the internal supply chain), and supplier relationship processes. These processes intersect all of the traditional functional areas of the firm.

Supply-chain management is essential for service as well as manufacturing firms. In fact, service providers are beginning to realize the potential for organizational benefits through the reengineering of supply-chain processes. For example, hospitals have notoriously held to old-fashioned approaches for purchasing and materials management. Even with the advent of group purchasing organizations and centralized buying groups, such as Premier, Inc., the materials management department in a typical hospital collects orders from throughout the hospital for medical supplies and equipment ranging from latex gloves to operating tables from a stack of often-outdated catalogs. Prices must be checked and the orders sent by phone or fax to literally thousands of distributors and suppliers. Can this process be improved? Columbia/HCA Health Care Corporation and Tenet Health Care Corporation think so. They are funding separate ventures that will create an electronic marketplace for placing orders online. The systems will link to the suppliers of several hundred-thousand medical and surgical supplies. Of course, to take full advantage of the marketplace, the hospitals will have to reengineer their supplier relationship processes to realize the benefits. The potential benefits to the health care industry for improved supply-chain practices are enormous. It is estimated that of the $83 billion hospitals spend annually on supplies, $11 billion could be eliminated by improved supply-chain design.

CHAPTER HIGHLIGHTS

- A supply chain consists of a firm's customer relationship, order fulfillment, and supplier relationship processes and their interconnected linkages among the firm's suppliers and customers. The purpose of supply-chain management is to design the supply chain and to synchronize the key processes of the firm's suppliers and customers, so as to match the flow of services, materials, and information with customer demand.

- Supply chains can be very complex. A key purpose for the supply chains of service providers is to provide support for the key elements of the various service packages it delivers. The supply chains of manufacturers focus on the efficient and timely flow of materials because the purchase of materials and services are a major expense item. Inventory can be categorized as raw materials, work-in-process, or finished goods.

- Because supply chains consist of many independent firms linked to other firms, disruptions from downstream members spread through the entire supply chain, causing firms upstream in the supply chain to experience significant swings in demand known as the bullwhip effect. Such disruptions can be caused by processes both internal and external to a firm.

- Firms that develop an integrated supply chain link purchasing, production, and distribution to create an internal supply chain that is the responsibility of a materials management department. Then, they link suppliers and customers to the internal supply chain to form an integrated supply chain.

- The Internet has dramatically changed the way companies design their supply chains. The order placement process, which is a nested process within the customer relationship process, can be reengineered to allow for more customer involvement and less employee involvement, to remain open for business 24 hours per day, and to enable a firm to use pricing as a means to control material or product shortages.

- Designing the order fulfillment process involves decisions regarding the use of virtual supply chains and the placement of inventories. The choice between keeping the order fulfillment process in-house versus using a virtual supply-chain design depends on the capabilities of the suppliers and the strategic needs of the firm.

- Key decisions in the design of the supplier relationship process include supplier selection and certification and supplier relations. Buyers can take two approaches in dealing with their suppliers. The competitive orientation pits supplier against supplier in an effort to get the buyer's business. Bargaining clout often determines the outcome of the negotiations. The cooperative orientation seeks to make long-term commitments to a small number of suppliers with advantages accruing to both parties. The ultimate form of a cooperative orientation is sole sourcing. Centralization of the purchasing in an organization also affects the way the supplier relationship process is designed.

- Value analysis is used to reduce the cost or improve the performance of services or products, either purchased or produced. It is an intensive examination of the services, materials, process, and information flows involved in the production of a service or an item. Programs such as early suppplier involvement and presourcing involve suppliers in the value analysis.

• Supply-chain performance is tracked with inventory measures, such as aggregate inventory level, weeks of supply, and inventory turnover. Supply-chain process measures include production and material costs, percent defects, percent on-time delivery, and supplier lead times. These measures are related to financial measures, such as return on

total assets (ROA), working capital, cost of goods sold, total revenue, and cash flow.

• Efficient supply chains are designed to coordinate the flows of services and materials, so as to minimize inventories and maximize the efficiency of the firms in the supply chain. Responsive supply chains are designed to react quickly to market demand through judicious use of inventories and capacities.

STUDENT CD-ROM AND INTERNET RESOURCES

The Student CD-ROM and the Companion Website at **www.prenhall.com/krajewski** contain many tools, activities, and resources designed for this chapter. The following items are recommended to enhance your skills and improve your understanding of the material in this chapter.

STUDENT CD-ROM RESOURCES

➤ **PowerPoint Slides.** View the comprehensive set of slides customized for this chapter's concepts and techniques.
➤ **Video Clip.** See the video clip customized for this chapter to learn more about the importance of supplier relations.
➤ **OM Explorer Tutors.** OM Explorer contains a tutor program to enhance your understanding of how to calculate inventory measures. See the Chapter 9 folder in the OM Explorer menu. See also the Tutor Exercise requiring the use of this tutor program.
➤ **OM Explorer Solvers.** The Inventory Estimator in OM Explorer can be used to solve general problems involving common inventory measures. See the Supply-Chain Design folder in the OM Explorer menu.

➤ **SimQuick.** Learn the basics of building simulation models for supply chains by working through Example 15 in *SlimQuick: Process Simulation with Excel*. This example, which is described in the Simulation Exercises box, is one of many examples addressing waiting lines, inventory management, manufacturing, and project management.

INTERNET RESOURCES

➤ **Self-Study Quizzes.** See the compendium of true or false, multiple choice, and essay questions that allows online tests or gives you feedback on how well you have mastered the concepts of this chapter.
➤ **In the News.** See the articles that apply to this chapter.
➤ **Internet Exercises.** Try out five different links to supply-chain topics including supplier requirements, supplier collaboration, and supply-chain design strategies.
➤ **Virtual Tours.** Explore the link between operations and supply-chain design at Yamaha's musical instruments factory. Also see the "Web Links to Company Facility Tours" for additional tours of company facilities.

KEY EQUATIONS

1. Weeks of supply $= \dfrac{\text{Average aggregate inventory value}}{\text{Weekly sales (at cost)}}$

2. Inventory turnover $= \dfrac{\text{Annual sales (at cost)}}{\text{Average aggregate inventory value}}$

KEY TERMS

average aggregate inventory value 416
bullwhip effect 401
channel assembly 408
competitive orientation 414
continuous replenishment program (CRP) 411
cooperative orientation 414
distribution 404
early supplier involvement 416

finished goods (FG) 399
forward placement 409
green purchasing 413
inventory 397
inventory pooling 409
inventory turnover 417
materials management 404
presourcing 416
production 404

purchasing 404
raw materials (RM) 399
sole sourcing 415
supply chain 395
supply-chain management 395
value analysis 415
vendor-managed inventories (VMI) 411
weeks of supply 417
work-in-process (WIP) 399

SOLVED PROBLEM 1

A firm's cost of goods sold last year was $3,410,000, and the firm operates 52 weeks per year. It carries seven items in inventory: three raw materials, two work-in-process items, and two finished goods. The following table contains last year's average inventory level for each item, along with its value.

    a. What is the average aggregate inventory value?
    b. What weeks of supply does the firm maintain?
    c. What was the inventory turnover last year?

CATEGORY	PART NUMBER	AVERAGE LEVEL	UNIT VALUE
Raw materials	1	15,000	$ 3.00
	2	2,500	5.00
	3	3,000	1.00
Work-in-process	4	5,000	14.00
	5	4,000	18.00
Finished goods	6	2,000	48.00
	7	1,000	62.00

SOLUTION

a.

PART NUMBER	AVERAGE LEVEL	UNIT VALUE		TOTAL VALUE
1	15,000	× $ 3.00	=	$ 45,000
2	2,500	× $ 5.00	=	$ 12,500
3	3,000	× $ 1.00	=	$ 3,000
4	5,000	× $14.00	=	$ 70,000
5	4,000	× $18.00	=	$ 72,000
6	2,000	× $48.00	=	$ 96,000
7	1,000	× $62.00	=	$ 62,000
	Average aggregate inventory value		=	$360,500

b. Average weekly sales at cost = $3,410,000/52 weeks = $65,577/week

$$\text{Weeks of supply} = \frac{\text{Average aggregate inventory value}}{\text{Weekly sales (at cost)}} = \frac{\$360,500}{\$65,577} = 5.5 \text{ weeks}$$

c. $$\text{Inventory turnover} = \frac{\text{Annual sales (at cost)}}{\text{Average aggregate inventory value}} = \frac{\$3,410,000}{\$360,500} = 9.5 \text{ turns}$$

DISCUSSION QUESTIONS

1. Under the Defense Industry Initiative on Business Ethics and Conduct, 46 contractors agreed to establish internal codes of ethics, to conduct training sessions, and to report suspected abuses.

    a. Is this initiative an example of moving toward competitive or cooperative supplier relations?

    b. Suppose that you are a defense contracts manager. You have a friend in the military whom you have known for 20 years. As a gesture of friendship, she offers useful inside information about a competing contractor's bid. What would you do if your company were part of the industry's ethics project? What would you do if your company were not part of it?

    c. To build a win–win relationship with its suppliers, the armed forces made agreements calling for suppliers to be reimbursed for the costs of supplier training and employee morale-building programs. According to that agreement, your company decided to hold a private party for employees to "build morale." Because the expenses were to be reimbursed, the party planners were not very careful in making the arrangements and got carried away. They rented the city auditorium and hired a nationally known music group to provide entertainment. Furthermore, the planners did not do a good job of contract negotiation and ended up paying five times the going rate for these services. The bill for the party now reaches your desk . . . $250,000! Under the terms of your agreement, your company is entitled to reimbursement of the entire amount. What should you do?

2. DaimlerChrysler and General Motors vigorously compete with each other in many automobile and truck markets. When Jose Ignacio Lopez was vice president of purchasing for GM, he made it very clear that his buyers were not to accept luncheon invitations from suppliers. Thomas Stalcamp, head of purchasing for Chrysler before the merger with Daimler, instructed his buyers to take suppliers to lunch. Rationalize these two directives in light of supply-chain design and management.

3. The Wal-Mart retail chain has great purchasing clout with its suppliers. The Limited retail chain owns Mast Industries, which is responsible for producing many of the fashion items sold in The Limited stores. The Limited boasts that it can go from the concept for a new garment to the store shelf in 1,000 hours. Compare and contrast the implications for supply-chain management for these two retail systems.

4. Consider the Lower Florida Keys Health System and the Chaparral Steel tours on the Student CD-ROM. Both organizations represent very different approaches to doing business in their respective industries. Compare and contrast the opportunities each organization has to engage in electronic purchasing. Also, compare them with respect to the nature of their relationships with suppliers.

PROBLEMS

An icon next to a problem identifies the software that can be helpful, but is not mandatory. The software is available on the Student CD-ROM that is packaged with every new copy of the textbook.

1. **OM Explorer** Buzzrite, a retailer of casual clothes, ended the current year with annual sales (at cost) of $48 million. During the year, the inventory of apparal turned over six times. For the next year, Buzzrite plans to increase annual sales (at cost) by 25 percent.

   a. What is the increase in the average aggregate inventory value required if Buzzrite maintains the same inventory turnover during the next year?

   b. What change in inventory turns must Buzzrite achieve if, through better supply-chain management, it wants to support next year's sales with no increase in the average aggregate inventory value?

2. **OM Explorer** Jack Jones, the materials manager at Precision Enterprises, is beginning to look for ways to reduce inventories. A recent accounting statement shows the following inventory investment by category: raw materials, $3,129,500; work-in-process, $6,237,000; and finished goods, $2,686,500. This year's cost of goods sold will be about $32.5 million. Assuming 52 business weeks per year, express total inventory as

   a. weeks of supply
   b. inventory turns

3. **OM Explorer** One product line has 10 turns per year and an annual sales volume (at cost) of $985,000. How much inventory is being held, on average?

4. **OM Explorer** The Bawl Corporation supplies alloy ball bearings to auto manufacturers in Detroit. Because of its specialized manufacturing process, considerable work-in-process and raw materials are needed. The current inventory levels are $2,470,000 and $1,566,000, respectively. In addition, finished goods inventory is $1,200,000 and sales (at cost) for the current year are expected to be about $48 million. Express total inventory as

   a. weeks of supply
   b. inventory turns

5. The following data have been collected for a retailer:

Cost of goods sold	$3,500,000
Gross profit	$ 700,000
Operating costs	$ 500,000
Operating profit	$ 200,000
Total inventory	$1,200,000
Fixed assets	$ 750,000
Long-term debt	$ 300,000

   Assuming 52 business weeks per year, express total inventory as

   a. weeks of supply
   b. inventory turns

TABLE 9.4
SUPPLIER PERFORMANCE SCORES

Performance Criterion	Weight	Rating		
		Supplier A	Supplier B	Supplier C
1. Price	0.2	0.6	0.5	0.9
2. Quality	0.2	0.6	0.4	0.8
3. Delivery	0.3	0.6	0.3	0.8
4. Production facilities	0.1	0.5	0.9	0.6
5. Warranty and claims policy	0.1	0.7	0.8	0.6
6. Financial position	0.1	0.9	0.9	0.7

Advanced Problems

Problems 6 and 7 require prior reading of Supplement A, "Decision Making."

6. **OM Explorer** The Bennet Company purchases one of its essential raw materials from three suppliers. Bennet's current policy is to distribute purchases equally among the three. The owner's son, Benjamin Bennet, has just graduated from business college. He proposes that these suppliers be rated (high numbers mean good performance) on six performance criteria weighted as shown in Table 9.4. A hurdle total score of 0.60 is proposed to screen suppliers. Purchasing policy would be revised to order raw materials from suppliers with performance scores greater than the hurdle total score, in proportion to their performance rating scores.

   a. Use a preference matrix to calculate the total weighted score for each supplier.

   b. Which supplier(s) survived the hurdle total score? Under the younger Bennet's proposed policy, what proportion of orders would each supplier receive?

   c. What advantages does the proposed policy have over the current policy?

7. **OM Explorer** Beagle clothiers uses a weighted score for the evaluation and selection of its suppliers of trendy fashion garments. Each supplier is rated on a 10-point scale (10 = highest) for four different criteria: price, quality, delivery, and flexibility (to accommodate changes in quantity and timing). Because of the volatility of the business in which Beagle operates, flexibility is given twice the weight of each of the other three criteria, which are equally weighted. Table 9.5 shows the scores for three potential suppliers for the four performance criteria. Based on the highest weighted score, which supplier should be selected?

8. **OM Explorer** Sterling, Inc. operates 52 weeks per year, and its cost of goods sold last year was $6,500,000. The firm carries eight items in inventory: four raw materials, two work-in-process items, and two finished goods. Table 9.6 shows last year's average inventory levels for these items, along with their unit values.

   a. What is the average aggregate inventory value?

   b. How many weeks of supply does the firm have?

   c. What was the inventory turnover last year?

TABLE 9.5
SUPPLIER PERFORMANCE SCORES

Criteria	Supplier A	Supplier B	Supplier C
Price	8	6	6
Quality	9	7	7
Delivery	7	9	6
Flexibility	5	8	9

TABLE 9.6
INVENTORY ITEMS

Category	Part Number	Average Inventory Units	Value per Unit
Raw materials	RM-1	20,000	$ 1
	RM-2	5,000	5
	RM-3	3,000	6
	RM-4	1,000	8
Work-in-process	WIP-1	6,000	10
	WIP-2	8,000	12
Finished goods	FG-1	1,000	65
	FG-2	500	88

SIMULATION EXERCISES

These simulation exercises require the use of the SimQuick and Extend simulation packages. SimQuick is on the Student CD-ROM that is packaged with every new copy of the textbook. Extend is an optional simulation package that your instructor may or may not have ordered.

1. **SimQuick** A company owns two retail stores that sell the same handheld computer. Orders are placed to a regional warehouse, also owned by the company. The regional warehouse places orders to a manufacturer. The management of the company wants to determine the best ordering and inventory placement policies at the retail stores and the warehouse to achieve good customer service at minimum cost. Use SimQuick to determine the best policies to use. See Example 15 in *SimQuick: Process Simulation with Excel* for more details of this problem and additional exercises.

2. **Extend** Like many producers of computer peripheral devices, Compware Peripherals subcontracts the manufacturing of its low-cost, high-volume products to firms in China for subsequent shipment to distribution centers in Asia, Europe, and North America. Management is exploring options to improve both the cost and timeliness of Compware's supply chain for a standard product, a basic ink-jet printer. The supply chain is shown in Figure 9.9.

   Competition on price and service has grown tremendously over the last few years. Use the Extend simulator to identify opportunities to improve the performance of Compware's supply chain. See the *Managing the Supply Chain at Compware Peripherals* case on the Student CD-ROM, which includes the basic model and how to use it. Answer the various questions asked about improving the supply chain.

FIGURE 9.9   Simplified Supply Chain for Compware's Ink-Jet Printer

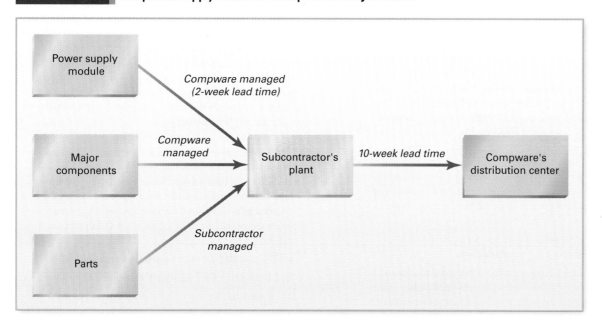

EXPERIENTIAL LEARNING SONIC DISTRIBUTORS

SCENARIO

Sonic Distributors produces and sells music CDs. The CDs are pressed at a single facility (factory), issued through the company's distribution center, and sold to the public from various retail stores. The goal is to operate the distribution chain at the lowest total cost.

Materials (available from instructor)

Retail and distributor purchase order forms
Factory work order forms
Factory and distributor materials delivery forms
Inventory position worksheets
A means of generating random demand (typically a pair of dice)

Setup

Each team is in the business of manufacturing music CDs and distributing them to retail stores where they are sold. Two or more people play the role of retail outlet buyers. Their task is to determine the demand for the CDs and order replenishment stock from the distributor. The distributor carries forward-placed stock obtained from the factory. The factory produces in lot sizes either to customer order or to stock.

Tasks

Divide into teams of four or five.
Two or three people operate the retail stores.
One person operates the distribution center.
One person schedules production at the factory.

Every day, as play progresses, the participants at each level of the supply chain determine demand, fill customer orders,

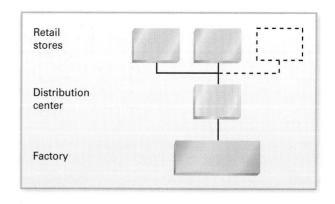

record inventory levels, and decide how much to order or produce and when to place orders with their supplier.

COSTS AND CONDITIONS

Unless your instructor indicates otherwise, the following costs and conditions hold.

Costs

Holding cost per unit per day	Retail outlets: $1.00/CD/day Distribution Center: $0.50/CD/day Factory: $0.25/CD/day
Pipeline inventory cost	Because plant space is no longer tied up, this cost is small and can be ignored (consider it zero).

Ordering cost (retailers and distributors)	$20/order
Factory setup cost (to run an order)	$50 (*Note:* Cost is per order, not per day, because even though successive orders from distributors are for the same item, the factory is busy fabricating other things between orders.)
Stockout (lost margin) cost	Retail Store: $8 per CD sale lost in a period. $0 for backorders for shortages from the factory or shipping new orders.
Shipping cost	Since other products are already being distributed through this chain and because CDs are light and take up little volume, consider the cost to be zero.

Conditions

Starting inventory	Retail stores each have 15 CDs Distribution center has 25 CDs Factory has 100 CDs
Lot-sizing restrictions	Retail outlets and distribution centers—no minimum order. Any amount may be stored. Factory production lot sizes and capacity—produce in minimum lots of 20. Maximum capacity, 200/day.
Outstanding orders	None

Delays

Ordering Delay. One day to send an order from a retail store to the distributor and from the distributor to the factory (i.e., one day is lost between placing an order and acting on it).

There is no delay to start up production once an order has been received (but one day is needed for delivery of an order from the distributor to the factory).

Delivery Delay. One-day shipping time between the distributor and a retail store and between the factory and the distributor (i.e., one day is lost between shipping an order and receiving it).

RUN THE EXERCISE

For simplicity sake, assume all transactions take place simultaneously at the middle of the day. For every simulated day, the sequence of play goes as follows.

Retailers

a. Each retailer receives any shipment due in from its distributor (one day after shipment) and places it in sales inventory (adds the quantity indicated on any incoming Material Delivery Form from the distributor—after its one-day delay—to the previous day's ending inventory level on the Retailer's Inventory Position Worksheet).

(*Note:* For the first day of the exercise, no order will be coming in.)

b. The retailers each determine the day's retail demand (the quantity of CDs requested) by rolling a pair of dice. The roll determines the number demanded.

c. Retailers fill demand from available stock, if possible. Demand is filled by subtracting it from the current inventory level to develop the ending inventory level, which is recorded. If demand exceeds supply, sales are lost. Record all lost sales on the worksheet.

d. Retailers determine whether an order should be placed. If an order is required, the desired quantity of CDs is written on a Retail Store Purchase Order, which is forwarded to the distributor (who receives it after a one-day delay). If an order is made, it should be noted on the worksheet. Retailers may also desire to keep track of outstanding orders separately.

Distributor

a. The distributor receives any shipment due in from the factory and places the CDs in available inventory (adds the quantity indicated on any incoming Material Delivery Form from the factory—after its one-day delay—to the previous day's ending inventory level on the distributor's inventory position worksheet).

b. All outstanding backorders are filled (the quantity is subtracted from the current inventory level indicated on the worksheet) and prepared for shipment. CDs are shipped by filling out a Distribution Center Material Delivery Form indicating the quantity of CDs to be delivered.

c. The distributor uses the purchase orders received from the retail stores (after the designated one-day delay) to prepare shipments for delivery from available inventory. Quantities shipped are subtracted from the current level to develop the ending inventory level, which is recorded. If insufficient supply exists, backorders are generated.

d. The distributor determines whether a replenishment order should be placed. If an order is required, the quantity of CDs is written on a Distribution Center Purchase Order, which is forwarded to the factory (after a one-day delay). If an order is made, it should be noted on the worksheet. The distributor may also desire to keep track of outstanding orders separately.

Factory

a. The factory places any available new production into inventory (adds the items produced the previous day to the previous day's ending inventory level on the Factory Inventory Position Worksheet).

b. All outstanding backorders are filled (the quantity is subtracted from the current inventory level indicated on the worksheet) and prepared for shipment. CDs are shipped by filling out a Factory Material Delivery Form, indicating the quantity of CDs to be delivered.

c. The factory obtains the incoming distributor's purchase orders (after the designated one-day delay) and ships them from stock, if it can. These amounts are subtracted from the current values on the inventory worksheet. Any unfilled orders become backorders for the next day.

d. The factory decides whether to issue a work order to produce CDs either to stock or to order. If production is required, a Factory Work Order is issued, and the order is noted on the inventory worksheet. Remember that there is a setup cost for each *production* order. It is important to keep careful track of all production in process.

Remember that, once an order has been placed, it cannot be changed and no partial shipments can be made. For each day, record your ending inventory position, backorder or lost sales amount, and whether an order was made (or a production run initiated). When everyone has completed the transactions for the day, the sequence repeats (go to retailer step a). Your instructor will tell you how many simulated days to run the exercise.

When the play is stopped, find the cumulative amount of inventory and other costs. You can do so by summing up the numbers in each column and then multiplying these totals by the costs previously listed. Use the total of these costs to assess how well your team operated the distribution chain.

Source: This exercise was developed by Larry Meile, Carroll School of Management, Boston College.

CASE   WOLF MOTORS

John Wolf, president of Wolf Motors, had just returned to his office after visiting the company's newly acquired automotive dealership. It was the fourth Wolf Motors' dealership in a network that served a metropolitan area of 400,000 people. Beyond the metropolitan area, but within a 45-minute drive, were another 500,000 people. Each of the dealerships in the network marketed a different make of automobile and historically had operated autonomously.

Wolf was particularly excited about this new dealership because it was the first "auto supermarket" in the network. Auto supermarkets differ from traditional auto dealerships in that they sell multiple makes of automobiles at the same location. The new dealership sold a full line of Chevrolets, Nissans, and Volkswagens.

Starting 15 years ago with the purchase of a bankrupt Dodge dealership, Wolf Motors had grown steadily in size and in reputation. Wolf attributed this success to three highly interdependent factors. The first was volume. By maintaining a high volume of sales and turning over inventory rapidly, economies of scale could be achieved, which reduced costs and provided customers with a large selection. The second factor was a marketing approach called the "hassle-free buying experience." Listed on each automobile was the "one price–lowest price." Customers came in, browsed, and compared prices without being approached by pushy salespeople. If they had questions or were ready to buy, a walk to a customer service desk produced a knowledgeable salesperson to assist them. Finally, and Wolf thought perhaps most important, was the after-sale service. Wolf Motors had established a solid reputation for servicing, diagnosing, and repairing vehicles correctly and in a timely manner—the first time.

High-quality service after the sale depended on three essential components. First was the presence of a highly qualified, well-trained staff of service technicians. Second was the use of the latest tools and technologies to support diagnosis and repair activities. And third was the availability of the full range of parts and materials necessary to complete the service and repairs without delay. Wolf invested in training and equipment to ensure that the trained personnel and technology were provided. What he worried about, as Wolf Motors grew, was the continued availability of the right parts and materials. This concern caused him to focus on the supplier relationship process and management of the service parts and materials flows in the supply chain.

Wolf thought back on the stories in the newspaper's business pages describing the failure of companies that had not planned appropriately for growth. These companies outgrew their existing policies, procedures, and control systems. Lacking a plan to update their systems, the companies experienced myriad problems that led to inefficiencies and an inability to compete effectively. He did not want that to happen to Wolf Motors.

Each of the four dealerships purchased its own service parts and materials. Purchases were based on forecasts derived from historical demand data, which accounted for factors such as seasonality. Batteries and alternators had a high failure rate in the winter, and air-conditioner parts were in great demand during the summer. Similarly, coolant was needed in the spring to service air conditioners for the summer months, whereas antifreeze was needed in the fall to winterize automobiles. Forecasts also were adjusted for special vehicle sales and service promotions, which increased the need for materials used to prep new cars and service other cars.

One thing that made the purchase of service parts and materials so difficult was the tremendous number of different parts that had to be kept on hand. Some of these parts would be used to service customer automobiles, and others would be sold over the counter. Some had to be purchased from the automobile manufacturers or their certified wholesalers, and to support, for example, the "guaranteed GM parts" promotion. Still, other parts and materials such as oils, lubricants, and fan belts could be purchased from any number of suppliers. The purchasing department had to remember that the success of the dealership depended on (1) lowering costs to support the hassle-free, one price–lowest price concept and (2) providing the right parts at the right time to support fast, reliable after-sale service.

As Wolf thought about the purchasing of parts and materials, two things kept going through his mind: the amount of space available for parts storage and the level of financial resources available to invest in parts and materials. The acquisition of the auto supermarket dealership put an increased strain on both finances and space, with the need to support three different automobile lines at the same facility. Investment dollars were becoming scarce, and space was at a premium. Wolf wondered what could be done in the purchasing area to address some of these concerns and alleviate some of the pressures.

QUESTIONS

1. What recommendations would you make to John Wolf with respect to structuring the supplier relationship process for the Wolf Motors dealership network?
2. How might purchasing policies and procedures differ as the dealerships purchase different types of service parts and materials (e.g., lubricants versus genuine GM parts)?
3. How can supply-chain management concepts help John Wolf reduce investment and space requirements while maintaining adequate service levels?

Source: This case was prepared by Dr. Brooke Saladin, Wake Forest University, as a basis for classroom discussion.

CASE   BRUNSWICK DISTRIBUTION, INC.

James Brunswick, CEO of Brunswick Distribution, Inc. (BDI), looked out of his office window at another sweltering day and wondered what could have gone wrong at his company. He had just finished reviewing his company's recent financial performance and noticed something that worried him. Brunswick Distribution, Inc. had experienced a period of robust growth over the last four years. "What could be going wrong?" he thought to himself. "Our sales have been growing at an average rate of eight percent over the last four years but we still appear to be worse off than before." He sat back in his chair with a heavy sigh and continued reviewing the report on his desk.

Sales had risen consistently over the past four years but the future was uncertain. James Brunswick was aware that part of the past growth had largely been the result of a few competitors in the region going out of business. This was unlikely to continue. Net earnings, however, exhibited an inconsistent trend in the opposite direction and had been declining for the last three years.

Brunswick was determined to turn his company around within the next three years. He sat back from his desk and buzzed his personal assistant. "Carla, could you ask Lew and Frank to come up?"

BACKGROUND

The distribution business, in its simplest form, involves the purchase of inventory from a variety of manufacturers and its resale to retailers. Over the last three to five years, demands on inventory have changed considerably; neither manufacturers nor retailers want to handle inventory, leaving distributors to pick up the slack. In addition, an increased tendency of retailers to order directly from manufacturers has placed further strain on the profitability of distributorships in general.

BDI was started as a simple distributor of products from local manufacturers, which resold them to small customers in and around the town of Moline. James Brunswick had been the senior logistics officer at a large freight company based in Chicago that operated in seven midwestern states. After five years with the freight company, he left to open up his own distribution business in his hometown using his personal finances and a small line of credit from his local bank.

With the help of two of his old college buddies, Lew Jackson and Frank Pulaski, Brunswick Distribution, Inc. was founded as a small but profitable distribution company. In the first nine months, the trio operated from a shed behind Brunswick's grandmother's house. Brunswick had been able to convince the local bank to issue him a small-business loan, which he used to purchase two used vans.

As business increased, BDI had to relocate from the shed to larger premises in the outskirts of the town. The company moved to a 10,000 square foot leased facility. In 1997, BDI entered into an agreement with KitchenAid Corp., a large manufacturer of high-end kitchen appliances, located 35 miles from Moline, to distribute KitchenAid appliances to local customers. Over the years BDI enjoyed steady growth and expanded its area of coverage. As of December 2005, Brunswick was covering an area with a radius of 60 miles from the company's main facility. Given the rapid growth, BDI purchased the leased facility and made additions to it to bring its capacity to 30,000 square feet. The company also dropped most of the low-margin products and now deals exclusively in high-end kitchen appliances.

The demise of several of its competitors resulted in the acquisition of new retailer customers and some new product lines. Traditional ordering in the retailer–distributor–manufacturer chain has been done via fax or phone. Brunswick considered implementing an Internet-based ordering system but was unsure of the potential operational and marketing benefits that it could provide.

CONCERNS

Market

Direct competition from distributors has decreased over the past five years. There has also been an increased tendency for retailers to get some products directly from manufacturers. As a result, the most successful distributors deal in high-end, high-margin products and have had to adopt a value-added strategy in order to remain competitive.

Financial

Manufacturers commonly demand payment in 30 to 60 days and provide no financing considerations. Retailers, on the other hand, pay in 45 to 50 days. This has often left BDI in a cash-poor situation that puts an unnecessary strain on its current operating loan. The company's borrowing capacity has almost been exhausted. Any additional financing will have to be sought from alternative sources. Given BDI's financial situation, any additional financing will be issued at a higher charge than existing debt.

Operations

Historically, BDI has maintained 8 to 12 weeks of inventory. Ideally, inventory turnover should be approximately 8, with 10 as a target. The past two years, however, have seen turnover significantly less than ideal. This trend seems likely to continue.

Orders from retailers come in as their customers near completion of construction or renovations. While historical information has been a good benchmark of future sales, the changing market has lessened the reliability of the information. This also affects BDI's ordering. Manufacturers require projections 60, 90, and 120 days out in order to budget their production.

STRATEGIC ISSUES

As Lew and Frank walked into Brunswick's office, he was still pondering the report. "Grab a seat, gentlemen," he grunted. They knew they were going to have a long day.

Brunswick quickly briefed the men on why he had summoned them and they all immediately dived into a spirited discussion. Brunswick pointed out that BDI would need to be properly structured to deal with the recession and the reality of today's market. "We will have to be well-positioned for growth as the market stabilizes," he said. In order to meet this challenge, BDI must evaluate a number of alternative options. Some of the possible options might include expanding current systems and, when necessary, developing new systems, which interface with suppliers, customers, and commercial transportation resources to gain total asset visibility.

Before making any investment decision, Brunswick reminded them that BDI would have to evaluate any new capital requirements, as well as the expected contribution to the company's bottom line and market share, that any option might provide. Exhibit 1 shows financial statements covering the past four years, with projections for 2006.

Investing in New Infrastructure

Frank Pulaski, vice president of operations, said, "Since Associated Business Distribution Corp. ceased operations, we have been inundated with phone calls and e-mails from potential customers across the Midwest looking for an alternative to ABD's services. These requests have come not only from former ABD customers but also from potential customers that have not dealt with either ABD or us in the past. This would require us to construct a new storage facility to complement our already strained resources." The financing resources for this option would be a challenge, given that BDI was almost approaching its credit limit with its principle bank. "We are challenged by an inadequate infrastructure far too small for our requirements. We have only one warehouse." The addition of new facilities would provide Brunswick Distribution, Inc. with an opportunity for increased penetration in key industrial markets in the upper Midwest where BDI has had a limited presence before.

Additional financing from larger banks in Chicago, however, was not ruled out. It would be expensive (current interest rates for long term loans start at 11 percent). According to Frank, this option would cost $2 million for property and $10 million for plant and equipment. The additional facilities would be depreciated over 20 years. With the additional infrastructure, BDI would be able to increase annual sales by $3,600,000. However, certain operating costs would also increase. The shipping of materials from current suppliers to the new location would increase shipping costs by $955,000. Materials costs (for the added inventories) and labor costs would each increase by 6 percent. Accounts receivable would increase by $1,500,000. Other liabilities are expected to increase by the annual interest payments on the new loan.

Streamlining the Order Fulfillment System

Lew Jackson, the vice president of logistics, stated, "I believe there is an opportunity to capitalize on the void left by our fallen rivals by utilizing a cost-efficient distribution system. We do not need a new facility. What we need is an efficient distribution system. We are holding a considerable amount of stock that has not moved simply because we are unable to get it to customers. One of our top priorities is working diligently with the inventory control department to keep what we need and dispose of what we do not need. This will allow us to reduce our infrastructure and become more efficient, while becoming more effective as well. Everything we do and every dollar we spend affects our customers. Our cost of operations is our customers' cost. Our goal is to enable customers to spend their resources on readiness and the tools of their trade, not logistics."

The option of having a fully integrated center, composed of sophisticated automation systems, advanced materials-handling equipment, and specially developed information technology, will provide BDI with both the versatility and capacity to offer improved products and services to Brunswick's customers. The new system would support real-time ordering, after-sales service, and warehousing equipped with an automatic storage and retrieval system (AS/RS). The system could be installed in the present warehouse facilities. When an order is received through a call center at Brunswick's offices in Moline, it will be forwarded to a logistic center for processing. The capital costs of this system would be either $4.7 million for a basic level implementation or $7 million for a fully integrated system. These costs would be amortized over a 10-year period. The operating costs including training would be $0.5 million each year for either system. These costs are considered fixed expenses by Brunswick. The improved system, however, would have tremendous cost savings. The basic implementation would result in 10 percent savings in direct shipping, as well as labor expenses, while the fully integrated system would save up to 16 percent in each. BDI could finance this option using a 5-year loan at a 10 percent rate of interest. Other liabilities would increase by the annual interest payments on the loan.

These savings would come from more efficient handling of customers orders by the call center and improved communication with the warehouse, as well as a dramatic reduction in the shipping costs in the supply chain. There would also be savings from the resulting reduction in personnel costs, as fewer operators would be required, thus reducing short-term liabilities.

THE DECISION

James Brunswick pondered the two options posed by Frank and Lew. Frank's option enabled the firm to increase its revenues by serving more customers. The capital outlay was sizable, however. Lew's option focused on serving the firm's existing customers better and more efficiently. The value of that option was its dramatic reduction in costs, although—at least for the present—the customer base would stay the same. Brunswick realized that he could not undertake both options, given the company's current financial position. How will each option affect the firm's financial ratios, which investors watch very closely? Which one would be better for the company?

Exhibits 2 through 4 show the worksheets from the Financial Measures Analyzer, a program on the Student CD-ROM in OM Explorer (see the Supply-Chain Design folder). They contain the 2006 data as a starting point. Changes, or "shocks" to the starting position, resulting from an investment option can be entered in the center column. The program computes the effects of the shocks in the right-hand column.

EXHIBIT I   **Company Financial Statements**

Brunswick Balance Sheet					
(in thousands of dollars)					
	2006	2005	2004	2003	2002
Assets					
Current assets					
Inventory	6,789	6,813	5,961	6,214	5,942
Accounts receivable	5,603	5,531	4,989	6,261	6,862
Other current assets	1,381	907	981	1,242	921
Cash	3,223	2,841	2,756	2,912	3,105
	16,996	16,092	14,687	16,629	16,830
Long-term assets					
Net PP&E	12,174	13,968	15,762	17,556	19,350
Long-term investments	1,000	1,000	1,000	1,000	750
	13,174	14,968	16,762	18,556	20,100
Total assets	**30,170**	**31,060**	**31,449**	**35,185**	**36,930**
Liabilities					
Current liabilities					
Accounts payable	2,582	2,654	2,811	3,480	3,510
Notes payable	1,099	894	964	1,263	1,522
Other liabilities	2,859	3,050	3,320	3,061	3,650
	6,540	6,598	7,095	7,804	8,682
Long-term liabilities					
Long-term loans	7,523	8,260	8,460	7,839	8,960
Total debt	14,063	14,858	15,555	15,643	17,642
Total equity	16,107	16,202	15,894	19,542	19,288
Total debt and equity	**30,170**	**31,060**	**31,449**	**35,185**	**36,930**

Brunswick Income Statement					
(in thousands of dollars)					
	2006	2005	2004	2003	2002
Sales	33,074	30,428	27,994	25,754	23,694
Cost of sales	21,620	19,840	18,065	16,345	15,065
Gross profit	11,454	10,588	9,929	9,409	8,629
SG&A	8,049	7,384	6,813	6,295	5,468
Depreciation	1,794	1,794	1,794	1,794	1,794
Operating income	1,611	1,410	1,322	1,320	1,367
Interest	96	96	94	72	72
Taxable income	980	1,314	1,228	1,248	1,295
Taxes	392	526	491	499	518
Net income	588	788	737	749	777

EXHIBIT 2   **Profit and Loss**

	Without Shock		Shock	With Shock
Income Statement	$000's	$000's	$000's	
Revenue		$33,074		$33,074
Cost of goods sold				
Shipping costs	$8,931			$8,931
Direct materials	$5,963			$5,963
Direct labor and other	$6,726			$6,726
Total	$21,620			$21,620
Gross profit		$11,454		$11,454
Operating expenses				
Selling expenses	$3,820			$3,820
Fixed expenses	$4,229			$4,229
Depreciation	$1,794			$1,794
Total	$9,843			$9,843
Earnings before interest and taxes		$1,611		$1,611
Interest expense	$96			$96
Earnings before taxes		$1,515		$1,515
Taxes @ 40%	$606			$606
Net income		$909		$909
Dividends	$0			$0
Contribution to retained earnings		$909		$909
Number of shares outstanding	350			350
Stock prices as of 1/31/2006	$5.00			$5.00

EXHIBIT 3   Balance Sheet

Assets	Without Shock	Shock	With Shock	Liabilities	Without Shock	Shock	With Shock
Current assets				Current liabilities			
				Accounts payable	$2,582		$1,282
Inventory	$6,789		$6,789	Short-term liabilities			$0
Total inventory		$6,789		$6,789	Notes payable	$1,099		$1,099
				Other liabilities	$2,859		$4,159
Cash	$3,223		$3,223	Total STL		$6,540		$6,540
Accounts receivable	$5,603		$5,603				
Other current assets	$1,381		$1,381	Long-term liabilities			
Total CA		$16,996		$16,996	Long-term loans	$7,523		$7,523
				Bonds			$0
Long-term assets				Other liabilities			$0
Property	$3,179		$3,179	Total LTL		$7,523		$7,523
Plant and equipment, net	$8,995		$8,995				
Long-term investments	$1,000		$1,000	Total debt		$14,063		$14,063
Total LTA		$13,174		$13,174				
				Equity	$1,750		$1,750
Total assets		$30,170		$30,170	Common stock			$0
				Paid-In-Excess	$428		$428
				Retained earnings	$13,929		$13,929
				Total equity		$16,107		$16,107
				Total debt and equity		$30,170		$30,170

EXHIBIT 4   Ratios

DuPont Analysis and ROA	Without Shock	With Shock	Change
ROE	5.6%		No change = Net income/Equity
ROA	5.3%		No change = EBIT/Total assets
NPM	2.7%		No change = Net income/Sales
TATO	109.6%		No change = Sales/Total assets

Operational Measures

Current ratio	2.60		No change = Current assets/Current operating liabilities
Inventory turns	3.2		No change = COGS/Inventory
WC to sales	31.6%		No change = Operating WC/Sales
Fixed asset turnover	271.7%		No change = Sales/Net property, plant, equipment

Liquidity

A/R days	61.8		No change = Accounts Rec./(Sales/365) = number of days to collect credit charges
A/P days	158.0		No change = Accounts Pay./(Direct materials/365)
Inventory days	114.6		No change = Inventory/(COGS/365)
Cash cycle	18.4		No change = A/R days - A/P days + Inventory days

Financial Performance

Debt-asset ratio	46.6%		No change = Debt/Total assets
Debt-equity ratio	87.3%		No change = Debt/Equity
Times interest earned	16.78		No change = EBIT/Interest
Gross profit margin	34.6%		No change = Gross profit/Sales
Materials %	27.6%		No change = Direct materials/COGS
Labor %	31.1%		No change = Direct labor/COGS

Stock Market Performance

EPS	2.60		No change = Earnings/Number of shares outstanding
Earnings/Price	0.52		No change = EPS/Market price
Market value/Book value	0.11		No change = Market value/Book value of equity

SELECTED REFERENCES

Bowersox, D.J., and D. J. Closs. *Logistical Management: The Integrated Supply Chain Process.* New York: McGraw-Hill, 1996.

Bridleman, Dan, and Jeff Herrmann. "Supply-Chain Management in a Make-to-Order World." *APICS—The Performance Advantage* (March 1997), pp. 32–38.

Champion, David. "Mastering the Value Chain." *Harvard Business Review* (June 2001), pp. 109–115.

Chopra, Sunil, and Peter Meindl. "What Will Drive the Enterprise Software Shakeout?" *Supply Chain Management Review* (January–February 2003), pp. 51–56.

Chopra, Sunil, and Jan A. Van Mieghem. "Which E-Business Is Right for Your Supply Chain?" Working Paper, Northwestern University. Kellogg Graduate School of Management, 2000.

Dyer, Jeffrey H. "How Chrysler Created an American Keiretsu." *Harvard Business Review* (July–August 1996), pp. 42–56.

Ellram, Lisa M., and Baohong Liu. "The Financial Impact of Supply Management." *Supply Chain Management Review* (November–December 2002), pp. 30–37.

Fisher, Marshall L. "What is the Right Supply Chain for Your Product?" *Harvard Business Review* (March–April 1997), pp. 105–116.

Gurusami, Senthil A. "Ford's Wrenching Decision." *OR/MS Today* (December 1998), pp. 36–39.

Hammer, Michael. "The Superefficient Company." *Harvard Business Review* (September 2001), pp. 82–91.

Handfield, Robert, S. Walton, Robert Sroufe, and Steven Melnyk. "Applying Environmental Criteria to Supplier Assessment: A Study of the Application of the Analytical Hierarchy Process." *European Journal of Operational Research,* vol. 41, no. 1 (2002), pp. 70–87.

Hartvigsen, David. *SimQuick: Process Simulation with Excel.* 2d ed. Upper Saddle River, NJ: Prentice Hall, 2004.

Harwick, Tom. "Optimal Decision Making for the Supply Chain." *APICS—The Performance Advantage* (January 1997), pp. 42–44.

Kanakamedala, Kishore, Glenn Ramsdell, and Vats Srivatsan. *"Getting Supply Chain Software Right."* The McKinsey Quarterly, no. 1 (2003).

Latamore G-Benton. "Supply Chain Optimization at Internet Speed." *APICS—The Performance Advantage* (May 2000), pp. 37–40.

Lee, Hau L., and Corey Billington. "Managing Supply Chain Inventory: Pitfalls and Opportunities." *Sloan Management Review* (Spring 1992), pp. 65–73.

Maloni, M., and W. C. Benton. "Power Influences in the Supply Chain." *Journal of Business Logistics,* vol. 21 (2000), pp. 49–73.

Melnyk, Steven, and Robert Handfield. "Green Speak." *Purchasing Today,* vol. 7, no.7 (1996), pp. 32–36.

Melnyk, Steven, Robert Sroufe, and Roger Calantone, "Assessing the Impact of Environmental Management Systems on Corporate and Environmental Performance," *Journal of Operations Management,* vol. 21, no.3 (2003).

Randall, Taylor, Serguei Netessine, and Nils Rudi. "Should You Take the Virtual Fulfillment Path?" *Supply Chain Management Review* (November–December 2002), pp. 54–58.

Ross, David F. "Meeting the Challenge of Supply-Chain Management." *APICS—The Performance Advantage* (September 1996), pp. 38–63.

Siekman, Philip. "The Smart Car Is Looking More So." *Fortune* (April 15, 2002), pp. 310I–310P.

Venkatesan, Ravi. "Strategic Sourcing: To Make or Not to Make." *Harvard Business Review* (November–December 1992), pp. 98–107.

Location

CHAPTER OUTLINE

LEARNING GOALS   *After reading this chapter, you should be able to . . .*

IDENTIFY OR DEFINE
1. factors leading to globalization.
2. factors affecting location choices.

DESCRIBE OR EXPLAIN
3. how location decisions relate to the design of value chains.
4. managerial challenges in global operations.
5. how to apply the load-distance method, break-even analysis, and the transportation method to location decisions.

STARBUCKS

An important aspect of the Starbucks service strategy (see the Chapter 2 opener about Starbucks) is its location strategy and how it analyzes potential sites. Last year alone the chain opened over 1,100 stores, bringing the total to over 5,600 stores. This phenomenal growth has been aided by a site selection technology that strengthens the decision-making process of strategic planning and market development. Starbucks (www.starbucks.com) relies on location analysis to evaluate where to place new stores. Early on, a relatively small number of people participated in new store decisions, which was more of an experiential than a systematic process. As Starbucks grew, however, more planners became involved in the process and used a more standard, formal analysis. Despite Starbucks's scale, the company continues to grow very rapidly. Because Starbucks does not have unlimited resources, its planners must make good choices on where they are looking in the first place. So, if a site's potential is not within certain parameters, they do not even waste their time giving it any additional consideration. For example, Starbucks already has taken the premium locations in some markets, so the company now looks at stores that have lower volume but essentially the same type of investment. Location analysis helps limit Starbucks's risk, given that the margin for error is smaller, because the lower volume locations provide lower paybacks.

Starbucks's original strategy in store locations was to expand in major urban areas, clustering in prime locations and placing outlets across from one another, sometimes even in the same block, which maximized market share in areas with the highest volume potential and built Starbucks's regional reputation. Although Starbucks used to locate its stores in affluent areas, low-profile regions and rural areas began demanding for Starbucks to be located there as a status symbol that would upgrade the area's image. Over the past five to seven years, Starbucks's domestic expansion strategy has definitely evolved, and previously under served areas, such as Harlem, NY, are now targeted. Another change to the original strategy has been the implementation of a geodemographic system as a productivity and process tool. It determines the impact over the course of a year of opening an additional store one day sooner. Starbuck's site-acquisition process includes a number of elements where spatial models, geodemographics, as well as the sales-forecasting models based upon them are employed. To identify potential locations, maps, such as the map shown to the left, are used by the company to show walk-time trade areas that pinpoint hotspots for gourmet coffee consumption.

In addition to growing domestically, Starbucks has also expanded internationally, opening stores in the United Kingdom, Japan, China, Canada, and Hong Kong. However, this expansion has not been easy. When seeking potentially viable sites abroad, Starbucks has encountered additional challenges, such as the lack of available and accurate data. Internationally, there is not a countrywide collection of information. In addition, the systems available to use those data vary. There is no central place to get information about data availability in certain countries, which translates into comparability issues and increases the risks of erring in expansion analyses.

As Starbucks continues to rapidly expand both domestically and abroad, more than ever before the use of location analysis becomes paramount to the firm. According to Mr. Schults, "people need that kind of 'third place' where they can escape, reflect, read, chat, or listen." He conceived Starbucks to satisfy those needs and, in order to do so, each Starbucks store must be perfectly located. For Starbucks, it all boils down to three key words: location, location, location.

Sources: "Location Analysis Tools Help Starbucks Brew Up New Ideas." *Business Geographics,* www.geoplace.com; Vishwanath, Vijay, and David Hardling. "The Starbucks Effect." *Harvard Business Review* (March–April 2000), pp. 17–18.

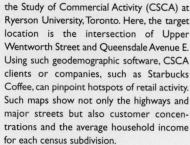

TRADE AREA MAP - HAMILTON, ON

A sample trade area map from the Centre for the Study of Commercial Activity (CSCA) at Ryerson University, Toronto. Here, the target location is the intersection of Upper Wentworth Street and Queensdale Avenue E. Using such geodemographic software, CSCA clients or companies, such as Starbucks Coffee, can pinpoint hotspots of retail activity. Such maps show not only the highways and major streets but also customer concentrations and the average household income for each census subdivision.

An important decision in value-chain design is where to locate an organization's facilities. The external supplier interface process and the customer interface process can be directly affected by facility locations. They can affect the supplier relationship process, for example, because the global economy opens up many new options for suppliers across the world. These options may offer lower labor costs or better quality of outsourced services or products. At the same time, greater distances may mean higher transportation costs or difficulties in coordinating with suppliers. The customer relationship process can also be affected. If the customer must be physically present at the process, it is unlikely that a location will be acceptable if the time or distance between the service provider and customer is great. On the other hand, if customer contact is more passive and impersonal, or if possessions or information is processed rather than people (see Figure 3.2), then location is less of an issue. Information technology might support an effective customer relationship process, even if the customer or service facility is at a remote location. One thing is clear: The location of a business's facilities has a significant impact on the company's operating costs, the prices it charges for services and goods, and its ability to compete in the marketplace.

Analyzing location patterns to discover a firm's underlying strategy is fascinating. For example, why does White Castle often locate restaurants near manufacturing plants? Why do competing new-car sales showrooms cluster near one another? White Castle's strategy is to cater to blue-collar workers. As a result, it tends to locate near the target population and away from competitors, such as Wendy's and McDonald's. In contrast, managers of new-car showrooms deliberately locate near one another because customers prefer to do their comparison shopping in one area. In each case, management's location decision reflects a particular strategy.

Recognizing the strategic impact of location decisions on value-chain design, we first examine the most important trend in location patterns: the globalization of operations. We then consider qualitative factors that influence location choices. We end by presenting some analytic techniques for making single- or multiple-facility location decisions.

As you read about location and how it is a part of the design of value chains, think about why it is important to the various departments and functions across the organization, such as . . .

> **accounting,** which prepares cost estimates for operating at new locations.
> **finance,** which performs the financial analysis for investments in facilities at new locations and raises funds to support them.
> **human resources,** which hires and trains employees to support new or relocated operations.
> **management information systems,** which provides information technologies that link operations at different locations along the value chain.
> **marketing,** which assesses how new locations will appeal to customers and possibly open up entirely new markets.
> **operations,** which locates its facilities where they can meet current customer demand most effectively and provide the right amount of customer contact for both external and internal customers.

THE GLOBALIZATION AND GEOGRAPHIC DISPERSION OF OPERATIONS

In the past, industries tended to concentrate in specific areas—for example, fabricated metals manufacturers were concentrated in the industrial belt of the United States and international banking firms were concentrated in London and New York City. Today, this tendency to concentrate in certain geographic regions is lessening. Although electric machinery and electronics remain key industries in New England, and sports shoes remain a key industry in South Korea, these industries and many others have become

Should facilities be opened overseas?

more geographically diversified. Geography and distance are becoming increasingly irrelevant in location decisions, owing to improved communication technologies, such as e-mail, faxes, video conferencing, and overnight delivery. An important exception is manufacturing firms that utilize just-in-time systems (see Chapter 11, "Lean Systems"), which rely on supplier proximity. The trend of separating operations and putting thousands of miles between them applies to large corporations, medium-sized companies, and small businesses alike. For example, a high-fashion designer may choose to locate its headquarters in New York City because it is the center of fashion, its warehouses in Ohio because it is centrally located, customer service toll-free numbers in Des Moines because Iowans speak with an all-American accent, and manufacturing facilities in Hong Kong because people in Asia are skilled in textile work and receive lower wages.

globalization The description of businesses' deployment of facilities and operations around the world.

The term **globalization** describes businesses' deployment of facilities and operations around the world. Worldwide exports now account for more than 30 percent of worldwide gross national product. For years, U.S. firms have built production facilities overseas. That trend continues, and foreign businesses have begun building facilities in the United States.

Globalization results in more exports to and imports from other countries, often called *offshore* sales and imports. Offshore sales and purchases by U.S. manufacturers have increased to 14 percent of total sales and 10 percent of total purchases. The volume of corporate voice, data, and teleconferencing traffic between countries is growing at an annual rate of 15 to 20 percent—about double the corporate domestic rate—indicating how businesses are increasingly bridging national boundaries.

Globalization of services is also widespread. The value of world trade in services is roughly 20 percent of total world trade. Banking, law, information services, airlines, education, consulting, and restaurant services are particularly active globally. For example, McDonald's opened a record 220 restaurants in foreign countries in just one year. Wal-Mart Stores, the world's largest retailer, paid $10.8 billion in 1999 for the United Kingdom's Asda Group PLC, whose large stores and selection of goods closely mirror its own. The purchase is part of Wal-Mart's push to expand across Europe. Small companies also are beginning to export their services. The Tokyo city government awarded a $50 million contract to a New York architect to design and build a $1 billion International Forum complex in downtown Tokyo. India's Steel Authority hired a Silver Spring, Maryland consulting firm to design and implement quality systems for its five major steel plants.

Wal-Mart Stores, the world's largest retailer, has gone global. Here, two customers leave a Wal-Mart store in Mexico City. Wal-Mart's trademark yellow smiley face, low prices, and focus on customer service was first introduced to larger U.S. cities and then abroad, to Canada, Puerto Rico, Brazil, the United Kingdom, Germany, South Korea, Japan, China, as well as Mexico.

REASONS FOR GLOBALIZATION
Four developments have spurred the trend toward globalization: (1) improved transportation and communication technologies, (2) loosened regulations on financial institutions, (3) increased demand for imported services and goods, and (4) reduced import quotas and other international trade barriers.

IMPROVED TRANSPORTATION AND COMMUNICATION TECHNOLOGIES. Improvements in communications technology and transportation have broken down the barriers of time and space between countries. For example, air transportation can move goods quickly from Kansas City to New York or even from Osaka, Japan to Kansas City. Telecommunications (voice and data) technology—including e-mail, facsimile machines, the Internet, and sophisticated toll-free telephone arrangements—allows facilities to serve larger market areas and allows firms to centralize some operations and provide support to branches located near their customers. It also permits managers around the world to communicate quickly, increasing the opportunities for cooperation and coordination.

LOOSENED REGULATIONS ON FINANCIAL INSTITUTIONS. During the 1980s, U.S. banking regulators removed interest rate ceilings, which allowed banks to attract more foreign investors by offering higher rates. At the same time, foreign banks removed barriers to entry. As a result, the world's financial systems have become more open, making it easier for firms to locate where capital, supplies, and resources are cheapest.

INCREASED DEMAND FOR IMPORTED SERVICES AND GOODS. Import penetration of the major economies has increased, as political barriers to international trade have crumbled. Imported services and goods now are the equivalent of about 13 percent of total output in the United States and 14 percent in Japan, up considerably from earlier decades. Penetration has been increased by locating production facilities in foreign countries because a local presence reduces customer aversion to buying imports. For example, Elasticos Selectos, a Mexico City-based elastics concern, built a plant in the United States primarily to gain customers who demand a "made-in-the-USA" label.

REDUCED IMPORT QUOTAS AND OTHER INTERNATIONAL TRADE BARRIERS. Producing services or goods in the country where the customers live also circumvents import quotas and other trade barriers, such as India's restrictions on certain imports. During the 1980s, Japanese automakers located production facilities in the United States to avoid import quotas and negative public opinion. The development of regional trading blocks, such as the European Union (EU) and the North American Free Trade Agreement (NAFTA), also make trade between countries easier. So does the General Agreement on Tariffs and Trade (GATT), a tariff-cutting world trade agreement, and the U.S.–China Trade Relations Act of 2000 that helps restore normal trade relations with China. Japanese and Chinese markets are far more open to foreign entrants than in the past, creating an explosion of partnership opportunities that were unthinkable just a decade ago. Lastly, the World Trade Organization (WTO) facilitates free trade. Created in 1995 after massive negotiations over new trade rules among 123 nations, the WTO has powers to hear trade disputes and to issue binding rulings. WTO's goals are free trade, open markets, and an unrestricted flow of capital.

Free trade is not without critics, however. Some unions and environmentalists argue that it is unfair for a low-wage country to suppress unions and thus keep wages artificially low, to undercut environmental laws, or to have factories using child labor. Free trade, they argue, should not make such practices part of a country's natural competitive advantage.

DISADVANTAGES TO GLOBALIZATION
Of course, operations in other countries can have disadvantages. A firm may have to relinquish proprietary technology if it turns over some of its component manufacturing to offshore suppliers or if suppliers need the firm's technology to achieve desired quality and cost goals.

There may be political risks. Each nation can exercise its sovereignty over the people and property within its borders. The extreme case is nationalization, in which a government may take over a firm's assets without paying compensation. Also, a firm may alienate customers back home if jobs are lost to offshore operations.

Employee skills may be lower in foreign countries, requiring additional training time. South Korean firms moved much of their sports shoe production to low-wage Indonesia and China, but they still manufacture hiking shoes and in-line roller skates in South Korea because of the greater skills required.

When a firm's operations are scattered, customer response times can be longer. Effective cross-functional connections also may be more difficult if face-to-face discussions are needed.

MANAGING GLOBAL OPERATIONS

How should global operations be managed, and what are their biggest challenges?

All the concepts and techniques described in this textbook apply to operations throughout the world. However, location decisions involve added complexities when a firm sets up facilities abroad. One study (see Klassen and Whybark, 1994) revealed that the most important barrier to effective global manufacturing operations is that many firms do not take a global view of their market opportunities and competitors. Global markets impose new standards on quality and time. Managers should not think about domestic markets first and then global markets later, if at all. Also, managers must have a good understanding of their competitors, which requires greater appraisal capabilities when the competitors are global, rather than domestic. Other important challenges of managing multinational operations include other languages and customs, different management styles, unfamiliar laws and regulations, and different costs. The Radisson Slavjanskaya faced all these challenges, as Managerial Practice 10.1 illustrates.

OTHER LANGUAGES. The ability to communicate effectively is important to all organizations. Most U.S. managers are fluent only in English and, thus, are at a disadvantage when dealing with managers in Europe or Asia who are fluent in several languages. For example, despite the vast potential for trade with Russia, few U.S. students and managers are studying Russian.

DIFFERENT NORMS AND CUSTOMS. Several U.S. franchisers, such as Century 21 Real Estate, Levi Strauss, and Quality Inns International, found that even when the same language is spoken, different countries have unique norms and customs that shape their business values. The goals, attitudes toward work, customer expectations, desire for risk taking, and other business values can vary dramatically from one part of the world to another. For example, a survey showed that more than two-thirds of Japanese managers believed that business should take an active role in environmental protection, whereas only 25 percent of Mexican managers agreed.

WORKFORCE MANAGEMENT. Employees in different countries prefer different management styles. Managers moving to operations in another country often must reevaluate their on-the-job behaviors (e.g., superior–subordinate relationships), assumptions about workers' attitudes, and hiring and promotion practices. Practices that work well in one country may be ineffective in another.

UNFAMILIAR LAWS AND REGULATIONS. Managers in charge of overseas plants must deal with unfamiliar labor laws, tax laws, and regulatory requirements. The after-tax consequences of an automation project, for instance, can be quite different from country to country because of different tax laws. Legal systems also differ. Some policies and practices that are illegal in one country might be acceptable, or even mandated, elsewhere in the world.

MANAGERIAL PRACTICE 10.1

MANAGERIAL CHALLENGES AT THE RADISSON SLAVJANSKAYA

The Radisson Hotels International, with headquarters in Minneapolis, Minnesota, had become by 1995 one of the world's fastest-growing upscale hotel companies. Its global expansion program was adding one new location every 10 days, on average. In 1991, it opened the four-star Radisson Slavjanskaya Hotel in Moscow, which has become a very successful hospitality oasis for Western business travelers. However, opening the Slavjanskaya forced Radisson to weather many storms and deal with every conceivable managerial challenge. The hotel has since been purchased by the Radisson SAS Hotels & Resorts (www.radissonsas.com), a European hotel chain. While ownership has changed, the lessons learned still apply today.

Multiple Languages

There is great diversity in the language of the hotel's managers, employees, suppliers, and customers. Most of the managers are expatriates, and most of the employees are Russians. The customer mix is American (55 percent), Western European (20 percent), Eastern European (15 percent), Asian (5 percent), and Russian (5 percent).

Different Norms and Customs

Russian standards of service quality were much lower than those expected by management. To attain and maintain top-service quality, employees had to participate in intensive training. Employee attitudes toward work and ethical norms also were different. For example, employees often missed work because of sick leaves, maternal leaves, and vacations. Russian laws allow 24-day vacations and sick leaves of up to four months with pay, which can be renewed by returning to work for only a few days. Security requirements were demanding, with theft being commonplace. Once, the entire payroll was "lost" in a Russian bank. On another occasion, about 500 of the 600 champagne glasses were missing. The nearby train station was said to be controlled by gangs who offered "protection" to the vendors. Some 70 security guards were employed, many more than at a typical Radisson hotel.

Workforce Management

Staffing and training issues arose unexpectedly. For example, the Russian employees were offended by being rotated through various jobs to gain wider experience, viewing rotation as a lack of confidence in their abilities. They believed that Americans were too quick to punish and too slow to understand cultural differences. An important hiring requirement was that the applicant had smiled sometime during the interview and had expressed a willingness to reject bribes. The notion of linking pay and bonuses with performance was a radically new idea to Russian employees.

Unfamiliar Laws and Regulations

Communist-era "job-for-life" laws were still in effect, and firing an employee was difficult. The housekeeping people were paid for 8½ hours per day, regardless of the actual hours worked. Tax laws were extremely complicated and sometimes were changed retroactively. Russian employees were paid in rubles at a time when inflation was 18 percent per month.

Unexpected Cost Mix

Labor productivity was low, relative to a comparable Western hotel, but salary rates were even lower. The net result was a savings because salaries accounted for only 13.5 percent of total costs, in contrast to the 35 percent in the United States. However, local suppliers were unreliable and procurement costs were quite high. About 93 percent of all products were imported from the West—shipped to Helsinki or St. Petersburg and then trucked to Moscow. This importing process was slowed by problems with customs, Russian fuel, truck breakdowns, and the need for "expediting payments." These uncertainties and delays created unusually large inventories. The infrastructure, including mail, telephone, banking, and city services, also was inadequate. For example, hot water came from city-run, water-heating plants. Because this source was not always reliable, Slavjanskaya had to pay for the construction of a second hot water pipe to guarantee both heat and hot water.

Sources: "The Radisson Slavjanskaya Hotel and Business Center." International Institute for Management Development (IMD), Lausanne, Switzerland, 1996, distributed by ECCH at Babson, Ltd., Case 696-007-1; "Murder in Moscow." *Fortune* (March 3, 1997), p. 128.

UNEXPECTED COST MIX. Firms may shift some of their operations to another country because of lower inventory, labor, materials, and real estate costs. However, these same differences may mean that policies that worked well in one economic environment—such as automating a process—might be a mistake in the new environment.

In dealing with global operations, managers must decide how much of the firm's operations to shift overseas and how much control the home office should retain. At one extreme, firms can rely on their home offices for strategic direction and are highly centralized. At the other extreme, firms can have a worldwide vision but allow each subsidiary to operate independently. Here the manager must be able to manage highly decentralized organizations that have a complex mix of product strategies, cultures, and consumer needs.

FACTORS AFFECTING LOCATION DECISIONS

Which factors are dominant in picking a new location? Which factors are secondary?

facility location The process of determining a geographic site for a firm's operations.

Facility location is the process of determining a geographic site for a firm's operations. Managers of both service and manufacturing organizations must weigh many factors when assessing the desirability of a particular site, including proximity to customers and suppliers, labor costs, and transportation costs. Managers generally can disregard factors that fail to meet at least one of the following two conditions.

I. *The Factor Must Be Sensitive to Location.* That is, managers should not consider a factor that is not affected by the location decision. For example, if community attitudes are uniformly good at all the locations under consideration, community attitudes should not be considered as a factor.

2. *The Factor Must Have a High Impact on the Company's Ability to Meet Its Goals.* For example, although different locations will be at different distances from suppliers, if shipments and communication can take place by overnight delivery, faxing, and other means, distance to suppliers should not be considered as a factor.

Managers can divide location factors into dominant and secondary factors. Dominant factors are those that are derived from competitive priorities (cost, quality, time, and flexibility) and that have a particularly strong impact on sales or costs. For example, a favorable labor climate and monetary incentives are dominant factors when locating call centers in Texas, as Managerial Practice 10.2 demonstrates. Secondary factors also are important, but management may downplay or even ignore some of these secondary factors if other factors are more important. Thus, for GM's Saturn plant, which makes many parts on site, inbound transportation costs were considered to be a secondary factor.

DOMINANT FACTORS IN MANUFACTURING

Six groups of factors dominate location decisions for new manufacturing plants. Listed in order of importance, they are

1. favorable labor climate,
2. proximity to markets,
3. quality of life,
4. proximity to suppliers and resources,
5. proximity to the parent company's facilities, and
6. utilities, taxes, and real estate costs.

FAVORABLE LABOR CLIMATE. A favorable labor climate may be the most important factor in location decisions for labor-intensive firms in industries such as textiles, furniture, and consumer electronics. Labor climate is a function of wage rates, training requirements, attitudes toward work, worker productivity, and union strength. Many executives perceive weak unions or a low probability of union organizing efforts as a distinct advantage.

Having a favorable climate applies not only to the workforce already on site, but in the case of relocation decisions, to the employees that a firm hopes will transfer or will be attracted to the new site. A good example is MCI Communications Corporation's

MANAGERIAL PRACTICE 10.2

LOCATION FACTORS FOR CALL CENTERS

Call centers are frequently mistaken for telemarketing operations, when in fact they are not. Most are "inbound" facilities that take reservations and orders or provide customer service. The industry has boomed during the last decade as more firms decided to outsource such customer service processes. There are currently over 60,000 call centers in the United States. A survey by Dallas-based Trammell Crow Company found that call centers spend more than 70 percent of their annual expenses on labor and less than 5 percent on real estate. Furthermore, labor costs could be shaved by 50 percent if corporations were to relocate away from high-cost metropolitan areas or away from saturated call-center environments. Some suggest that if over 2 percent of an area's workforce is employed in call-center operations, then that area is at saturation. Because the call-center industry has matured, many metropolitan areas might be approaching the saturation level. Therefore, areas with populations of less than 50,000 are enjoying tremendous popularity. In most cases, the call center is one of the largest employers in the area, which creates tremendous employee loyalty and significantly fewer problems for recruitment and retention. Hence, an added bonus for relocating to these areas is lower training costs due to minimal employee turnover.

Texas leads the United States in the number of new centers over the past decade—its number of call centers doubled in the last decade. By one estimate, 113 centers located there in the 1990s, compared with 81 in Florida, the runner-up. In the past, the vast majority of call centers went to the state's large metropolitan areas, but now smaller cities such as Big Spring, McAllen, and Brownsville are getting in on the act.

Two dominant factors favoring small Texas cities are their ample supply of inexpensive labor and the incentives that they are tossing in to land the companies. Before Denver-based StarTek opened a call center in

Employees of a StarTek call center chat across the partitions between their office spaces. Small Texas cities have become a favorite location for call centers because of the ample supply of inexpensive labor and the incentives offered to land companies that require such service processes.

Big Spring, a West Texas town of 23,000 where unemployment had been about 6 percent, a job fair attracted 1,200 applicants. Employees started at $6.50 per hour, far less than what would be paid in a bigger city. To seal the deal, Big Springs gave StarTek $2.3 million in interest-free loans. Smaller cities are more likely to get state funds for this type of economic development because the call centers are such an economic-development bonanza for them. In larger cities, companies usually do not qualify for incentives unless they make a substantial capital investment—and many do not, choosing to lease office space. The smaller cities need the jobs more. Call centers employ several hundred people, bringing jobs and a level of technical training and giving smaller cities a foot in the door to the new high-tech economy. Particularly, if labor stays in short supply, call centers could be the first step for smaller cities to draw other burgeoning business, such as the distribution centers for e-commerce companies. Indeed, an interesting Web site to visit is www.callcentersites.net, which provides detailed information on call-center locations in the United States and worldwide.

Other factors that favor Texas are the central time zone (making it convenient to reach markets on both coasts), the availability of advanced telecommunications structures (such as fiber-optic lines and digital switching systems), and the favorable regulatory climate. It is a one-party-consent state, meaning customers do not need to be notified if their conversations are being recorded; getting permission slows down the calling process. And the state also does not levy excise or sales taxes on out-of-state long-distance calls, as some states do. Border cities also offer a supply of bilingual workers—to take calls from Spanish-speaking customers. This advantage is particularly important as more companies expand their markets into Latin America.

(continued)

Sources: "Call Centers are Booming in Small Cities." *Wall Street Journal* (March 3, 2000); "Labor, Labor, Labor: The Three Top Criteria for Call-Center Site Selection." (March 2000), www.summitcircuit.com; Beatty, James R. "Site Selection in North America: Key Components to Consider."

President, NCS International. (December 2001), www.summitcircuit.com; Craven, Karen T. "Site Selection—Before Asking Where, Consider Who." *CC News Magazine* (May 2001).

decision to relocate its Systems Engineering division from its Washington, DC head-quarters to Colorado Springs. This 4,000-employee division was MCI's brain trust that had created numerous breakthrough products. Management reasoned that this location would inspire the workers and that the mountains, low crime rate, healthy climate, and rock-bottom real estate prices would surely attract the best and brightest computer software engineers. The results were quite different than expected. Numerous executives and engineers and hundreds of the division's 51 percent minority population said "no" to the transfer or fled MCI soon after relocating. Colorado Springs' isolated and politically conservative setting repelled many employees who were used to living in larger, ethnically diverse urban areas. The relocated engineers also felt isolated from top management and the marketing staff. That prevented the daily, informal contact that had spawned many successful innovations. Whereas Colorado Springs seemed destined to become a major center for MCI, it ended up being just a branch.

PROXIMITY TO MARKETS. After determining where the demand for services and goods is greatest, management must select a location for the facility that will supply that demand. Locating near markets is particularly important when the final goods are bulky or heavy and *outbound* transportation rates are high. For example, manufacturers of products, such as plastic pipe and heavy metals, all emphasize proximity to their markets.

quality of life A factor that considers the availability of good schools, recreational facilities, cultural events, and an attractive lifestyle.

QUALITY OF LIFE. Good schools, recreational facilities, cultural events, and an attractive lifestyle contribute to **quality of life.** This factor is relatively unimportant on its own, but it can make the difference in location decisions. In the United States during the past two decades, more than 50 percent of new industrial jobs went to nonurban regions. A similar shift is taking place in Japan and Europe. Reasons for this movement include high costs of living, high crime rates, and general decline in the quality of life in many large cities.

PROXIMITY TO SUPPLIERS AND RESOURCES. Firms dependent on inputs of bulky, perishable, or heavy raw materials emphasize proximity to suppliers and resources. In such cases, *inbound* transportation costs become a dominant factor, encouraging such firms to locate facilities near suppliers. For example, locating paper mills near forests, and food processing facilities near farms is practical. Another advantage of locating near suppliers is the ability to maintain lower inventories.

PROXIMITY TO THE PARENT COMPANY'S FACILITIES. In many companies, plants supply parts to other facilities or rely on other facilities for management and staff support. These ties require frequent coordination and communication, which can become more difficult as distance increases.

UTILITIES, TAXES, AND REAL ESTATE COSTS. Other important factors that may emerge include utility costs (telephone, energy, and water), local and state taxes, financing incentives offered by local or state governments, relocation costs, and land costs. For example, MCI was attracted by being able to buy an abandoned 220,000 square foot IBM factory for its new Colorado Springs facility for just $13.5 million, a bargain by Washington standards. MCI was also able to wrangle $3.5 million in incentives from local governments. These strong attractions were much less important, in retrospect, than finding a favorable labor climate for its employees.

OTHER FACTORS. Still other factors may need to be considered, including room for expansion, construction costs, accessibility to multiple modes of transportation, the cost of shuffling people and materials between plants, insurance costs, competition from other firms for the workforce, local ordinances (such as pollution or noise control regulations), community attitudes, and many others. For global operations, firms are emphasizing local employee skills and education and the local infrastructure. Many firms are concluding that large, centralized manufacturing facilities in low-cost countries with poorly trained workers are not sustainable. Smaller, flexible facilities serving multiple markets allow the firm to deal with nontariff barriers such as sales-volume limitations, regional trading blocs, political risks, and exchange rates.

DOMINANT FACTORS IN SERVICES

The factors mentioned for manufacturers also apply to service providers with one important addition: the impact that the location might have on sales and customer satisfaction. Customers usually care about how close a service facility is, particularly if the process requires considerable customer contact.

> How does the location decision for service facilities differ from that for manufacturing facilities?

PROXIMITY TO CUSTOMERS. Location is a key factor in determining how conveniently customers can carry on business with a firm. For example, few people will patronize a remotely located dry cleaner or supermarket if another is more convenient. Thus, the influence of location on revenues tends to be the dominant factor. Managerial Practice 10.3 demonstrates that customer proximity is not enough—the key is proximity to customers who will patronize the facility and seek its services.

TRANSPORTATION COSTS AND PROXIMITY TO MARKETS. For warehousing and distribution operations, transportation costs and proximity to markets are extremely important. With a warehouse nearby, many firms can hold inventory closer to the customer, thus reducing delivery time and promoting sales. For example, Invacare Corporation of Elyria, Ohio gained a competitive edge in the distribution of home health care products by decentralizing inventory into 32 warehouses across the country. Invacare sells wheelchairs, hospital beds, and other patient aids, some of which it produces and some of which it buys from other firms, to small dealers who sell to consumers. Previously the dealers, often small mom-and-pop operations, had to wait three weeks for deliveries, which meant that a lot of their cash was tied up in excess inventory. With Invacare's new distribution network, the dealers get daily deliveries of products from one source. Invacare's location strategy shows how timely delivery can be a competitive advantage.

LOCATION OF COMPETITORS. One complication in estimating the sales potential at different locations is the impact of competitors. Management must not only consider the current location of competitors but also try to anticipate their reaction to the firm's new location. Avoiding areas where competitors are already well established often pays. However, in some industries, such as new-car sales showrooms and fast-food chains, locating near competitors is actually advantageous. The strategy is to create a **critical mass**, whereby several competing firms clustered in one location attract more customers than the total number who would shop at the same stores at scattered locations. Recognizing this effect, some firms use a follow-the-leader strategy when selecting new sites.

> Should a firm be a leader or a follower in picking locations for new retail outlets?

critical mass A situation whereby several competing firms clustered in one location attract more customers than the total number who would shop at the same stores at scattered locations.

SITE-SPECIFIC FACTORS. Retailers also must consider the level of retail activity, residential density, traffic flow, and site visibility. Retail activity in the area is important, as shoppers often decide on impulse to go shopping or to eat in a restaurant. Traffic

MANAGERIAL PRACTICE 10.3

MARBLE BATHS VERSUS BARBECUE FOR CASINO LOCATIONS

Mirage Resorts, Inc., (www.mirageresorts.com) reinvented Las Vegas with lush new casinos, including the $730 million Mirage, built in 1989, and the $1.8 billion Bellagio, which opened in 1998. In 1999, Mirage opened the Beau Rivage casino (www.beaurivage.com) in Biloxi, Mississippi as its first big casino located outside of Nevada. Management believed that the location would allow Mirage to join the nationwide expansion of casinos. The location scored high on many important location factors: The region offered low taxes, high population growth, state officials keen for investment, and an eager and plentiful workforce supply.

Aiming for high-paying customers as in Las Vegas, the goal was to build a high-end resort that would appeal to wealthy southeasterners. Every detail sought perfection. Fifteen 75-year-old live-oak trees were painstakingly transplanted from a local farm to grace the drive of the casino. Seven pairs of live finches flutter in magnolia trees in the hotel's lobby, and 250 yards of fine silk line the spa's walls. The sushi bar is Rosso Verona marble. The resort invested in fine linens and marble bathrooms, and it promised nightly turn-down service and triple sheeting. Concrete ceilings were sanded to a perfect smoothness. The construction adapted offshore-oil-platform technology, floating the casino on five barges anchored by nine million pounds of structural steel. The projected costs metamorphosed when management added a $10-million, 31-slip floating marina built of Brazilian ipe hardwood. The resort claims that, per slip, it is the world's most expensive marina. Before the grand opening, Wall Street was enthusiastic: Upbeat analysts predicted annual returns of as much as 20 percent—well above industry averages.

But Beau Rivage failed spectacularly to draw the high-paying customers it sought and produced about half the cash flow that investors expected. The $1.6 billion property cost is at least double its original budget. Beau Rivage failed to comprehend several vital differences between Las Vegas and the Southeast region. Beau Rivage was not designed with southerners in mind. The community on which it depends wants a good southern buffet, friendly card dealers, and a sense of accessibility. Mirage did not understand the passions for barbecue, country-rock music, the value of valet parking, the high cost of flying in from surrounding areas, and the training needed for an inexperienced local workforce. Biloxi is a day-trippers market, where gamblers blow their $40 budgets before driving home. Biloxi customers, spiffed up for an evening on the town, place a high value on handing their car keys to a valet, but the resort was short on capacity, and long waiting lines developed. The resorts' creators proved right on one count—visitors flocked to Biloxi to gawk at the new place. But then they went elsewhere to gamble, where they were more comfortable. Casino revenues on the Gulf Coast rose 43 percent from the year before, but the increase was mainly enjoyed by the resort's rivals.

Changes have been made since the grand opening to correct many missteps. Costs have been slashed. Plans for "hands-free" luggage delivery to the airport, which cost $21 a customer, were cancelled. The night turn-down service was discontinued in standard rooms, saving $6 per room per customer. Soft rock replaced opera and Frank Sinatra elevator music. A second valet area was added, and the parking valets received scripts on greeting guests. Waiters were tutored in the pronunciation of foods such as foie gras. New restaurant managers made the crab cakes bigger, banned lobster crepes, and added an 11.5-ounce T-bone. There's prime rib on Mondays, and on Tuesdays, all-you-can-eat ribs. The improvements seem to be paying off, and Beau Rivage has enjoyed much stronger operating numbers in recent quarters. However, its occupancy rate in December is only 80 percent. Even though

The location of the Beau Rivage casino in Biloxi, Mississippi was selected because the region offered low taxes, high population growth, government officials keen on investment, and a plentiful workforce supply. The hotel has made some adjustments in its service processes and image to reconcile the vital differences between Las Vegas and the Southeast region.

(continued)

MANAGERIAL PRACTICE 10.3 *continued*

that rate is outstanding for Biloxi for that time of year, it is low in an industry that shoots for at least 95 percent capacity utilization.

Sources: "Mississippi Gamble." *Wall Street Journal* (February 2, 2000); "Biloxi Celebrates Tenth Anniversary of Casino-Induced Prosperity." *Gaming Magazine* (May 23, 2002), www.gamingmagazine.com.

flows and visibility are important because businesses' customers arrive in cars. Management considers possible traffic tie-ups, traffic volume and direction by time of day, traffic signals, intersections, and the position of traffic medians. Visibility involves distance from the street and the size of nearby buildings and signs. High residential density ensures nighttime and weekend business when the population in the area fits the firm's competitive priorities and target market segment.

LOCATING A SINGLE FACILITY

Having examined trends and important factors in location, we now consider more specifically how a firm can make location decisions. In this section, we consider the case of locating only one new facility. When the facility is part of a firm's larger network of facilities, we assume that there is no interdependence; that is, a decision to open a restaurant in Tampa, Florida is independent of whether the chain has a restaurant in Austin, Texas. Let us begin by considering how to decide whether a new location is needed, and then examine a systematic selection process aided by the load–distance method to deal with proximity.

SELECTING ON-SITE EXPANSION, NEW LOCATION, OR RELOCATION

Management must first decide whether to expand on-site, build another facility, or relocate to another site. A survey of Fortune 500 firms showed that 45 percent of expansions were on-site, 43 percent were in new plants at new locations, and only 12 percent were relocations of all facilities. On-site expansion has the advantage of keeping management together, reducing construction time and costs, and avoiding splitting up operations. However, a firm may overexpand a facility, at which point diseconomies of scale set in (see Chapter 6, "Process Capacity"). Poor materials handling, increasingly complex production control, and simple lack of space are reasons for building a new plant or relocating the existing plant.

Should a firm expand on-site, add a new facility, or relocate the existing facility?

The advantages of building a new plant or moving to a new retail or office space are that the firm does not have to rely on production from a single plant, it can hire new and possibly more productive labor, the firm can modernize with new technology, and it can reduce transportation costs. Most firms that choose to relocate are small (less than 10 employees). They tend to be single-location companies cramped for space and needing to redesign their production processes and layouts. More than 80 percent of all relocations are within 20 miles of the first location, which enables the firm to retain its current workforce.

COMPARING SEVERAL SITES

A systematic selection process begins after there is a perception or evidence that opening a retail outlet, warehouse, office, or plant in a new location will increase profits. A team may be responsible for the selection decision in a large corporation, or an individual may make the decision in a small company. The process of selecting a new facility location involves a series of steps.

1. Identify the important location factors and categorize them as dominant or secondary.

2. Consider alternative regions; then narrow the choices to alternative communities and finally to specific sites.

3. Collect data on the alternatives from location consultants, state development agencies, city and county planning departments, chambers of commerce, land developers, electric power companies, banks, and on-site visits. Governmental data provide a statistical mother lode. For example, the U.S. Census Bureau has a minutely detailed computerized map of the entire United States—the so-called Tiger file. Its formal name is the Topologically Integrated Geographic Encoding and Reference file (tiger .census.gov). It lists in digital form every highway, street, bridge, and tunnel in the 50 states. When combined with a database, such as the results of the 2000 census or a company's own customer files, Tiger gives desktop computer users the ability to ask various "what-if" questions about different location alternatives. The Internet also has Web sites (see **maps.yahoo.com/yahoo;www.mapquest.com**; and **www.expediamaps .com**) that provide maps, distances and travel time, and routes between any two locations, such as between Toronto, Ontario and San Diego, California.

4. Analyze the data collected, beginning with the *quantitative* factors—factors that can be measured in dollars, such as annual transportation costs or taxes. These dollar values may be broken into separate cost categories (e.g., inbound and outbound transportation, labor, construction, and utilities) and separate revenue sources (e.g., sales, stock or bond issues, and interest income). These financial factors can then be converted to a single measure of financial merit and used to compare two or more sites.

5. Bring the qualitative factors pertaining to each site into the evaluation. A *qualitative* factor is one that cannot be evaluated in dollar terms, such as community attitudes or quality of life. To merge quantitative and qualitative factors, some managers review the expected performance of each factor, while others assign each factor a weight of relative importance and calculate a weighted score for each site, using a preference matrix. What is important in one situation may be unimportant or less important in another. The site with the highest weighted score is best.

After thoroughly evaluating between 5 and 15 sites, those making the study prepare a final report containing site recommendations, along with a summary of the data and analyses on which they are based. An audiovisual presentation of the key findings usually is delivered to top management in large firms.

EXAMPLE 10.1   Calculating Weighted Scores in a Preference Matrix

TUTOR 10.1

Tutor 10.1 on the Student CD-ROM provides another example to practice with a preference matrix for location decisions.

A new medical facility, Health-Watch, is to be located in Erie, Pennsylvania. The following table shows the location factors, weights, and scores (1 = poor, 5 = excellent) for one potential site. The weights in this case add up to 100 percent. A weighted score (*WS*) will be calculated for each site. What is the *WS* for this site?

LOCATION FACTOR	WEIGHT	SCORE
Total patient miles per month	25	4
Facility utilization	20	3
Average time per emergency trip	20	3
Expressway accessibility	15	4
Land and construction costs	10	1
Employee preferences	10	5

SOLUTION

The WS for this particular site is calculated by multiplying each factor's weight by its score and adding the results:

$$WS = (25 \times 4) + (20 \times 3) + (20 \times 3) + (15 \times 4) + (10 \times 1) + (10 \times 5)$$
$$= 100 + 60 + 60 + 60 + 10 + 50$$
$$= 340$$

The total WS of 340 can be compared with the total weighted scores for other sites being evaluated.

APPLYING THE LOAD–DISTANCE METHOD

In the systematic selection process, the analyst must identify attractive candidate locations and compare them on the basis of quantitative factors. The load–distance method is one way to facilitate this step. It works much like the weighted-distance method does for designing flexible-flow layouts (see Chapter 7, "Process Layout"). Several location factors relate directly to distance: proximity to markets, average distance to target customers, proximity to suppliers and resources, and proximity to other company facilities. The **load–distance method** is a mathematical model used to evaluate locations based on proximity factors. The objective is to select a location that minimizes the total weighted loads moving into and out of the facility. The distance between two points is expressed by assigning the points to grid coordinates on a map. An alternative approach is to use time rather than distance.

Should a firm locate near its suppliers, workforce, or customers?

load–distance method   A mathematical model used to evaluate locations based on proximity factors.

CALCULATING A LOAD–DISTANCE SCORE. Suppose that a firm planning a new location wants to select a site that minimizes the distances that loads, particularly the larger ones, must travel to and from the site. Depending on the industry, a *load* may be shipments from suppliers, between plants, or to customers, or it may be customers or employees traveling to or from the facility. The firm seeks to minimize its load–distance (*ld*) score, generally by choosing a location, so that large loads go short distances.

To calculate *ld* score for any potential location, we use either the Euclidean or rectilinear distance measure and simply multiply the loads flowing to and from the facility by the distances traveled. The formula for the *ld* score is

$$ld = \sum_i l_i d_i$$

These loads may be expressed as the number of potential customers needing physical presence for a service facility; loads may be tons or number of trips per week for a manufacturing facility. The score is the sum of these load–distance products. By selecting a new location based on *ld* scores, customer service is improved or transportation costs reduced. (For assistance in calculating distances, see Tutor 7.1 and Chapter 7, "Process Layout.")

The goal is to find one acceptable facility location that minimizes the score, where the location is defined by its *x*-coordinate and *y*-coordinate. Practical considerations rarely allow managers to select the exact location with the lowest possible score. For example, land may not be available there at a reasonable price, or other location factors may make the site undesirable.

CENTER OF GRAVITY. Testing different locations with the load–distance model is relatively simple if some systematic search process is followed. A good starting point is the **center of gravity** of the target area. The center of gravity's *x*-coordinate, denoted x^*, is found by multiplying each point's *x*-coordinate (x_i) by its load (l_i), summing these products $(\Sigma\, l_i x_i)$, and then dividing by the sum of the loads $(\Sigma\, l_i)$. The *y*-coordinate,

center of gravity   A good starting point in evaluating locations is with the load–distance model; the center of gravity's *x*-coordinate (x^*) is found by multiplying each point's *x*-coordinate (x_i) by its load (l_i), summing these products, and then dividing by the sum of the loads.

denoted y^*, is found the same way, with the y-coordinates used in the numerator. The formulas are

$$x^* = \frac{\sum_i l_i x_i}{\sum_i l_i} \quad \text{and} \quad y^* = \frac{\sum_i l_i y_i}{\sum_i l_i}$$

This location usually is not the optimal one for the Euclidean or rectilinear distance measures, but it still is an excellent starting point. Calculate the load–distance scores for locations in its vicinity until you are satisfied that your solution is near optimal.

EXAMPLE 10.2   Finding the Center of Gravity

ACTIVE MODEL 10.1

Active Model 10.1 on the Student CD-ROM explores the *ld* scores of locations in the vicinity of the center of gravity.

TUTOR 10.2

Tutor 10.2 on the Student CD-ROM provides another example on how to calculate the center of gravity.

The new Health-Watch facility is targeted to serve seven census tracts in Erie, Pennsylvania. Customers will travel from the seven census tract centers to the new facility when they need health care. What is the target area's center of gravity for the Health-Watch medical facility?

SOLUTION

To calculate the center of gravity, we begin with the information in the following table, in which population is given in thousands:

CENSUS TRACT	(x, y)	Population (*l*)	lx	ly
A	(2.5, 4.5)	2	5	9
B	(2.5, 2.5)	5	12.5	12.5
C	(5.5, 4.5)	10	55	45
D	(5, 2)	7	35	14
E	(8, 5)	10	80	50
F	(7, 2)	20	140	40
G	(9, 2.5)	14	126	35
	Totals	68	453.5	205.5

Next we solve for x^* and y^*.

$$x^* = \frac{453.5}{68} = 6.67$$

$$y^* = \frac{205.5}{68} = 3.02$$

Figure 10.1, from OM Explorer, confirms these calculations.

DECISION POINT   The center of gravity is (6.67, 3.02), which is not necessarily optimal. Using the center of gravity as a starting point, managers can now search in its vicinity for the optimal location.

USING BREAK-EVEN ANALYSIS

How does the expected output level of the facility affect location choice?

Break-even analysis (see Supplement A, "Decision Making") can help a manager compare location alternatives on the basis of quantitative factors that can be expressed in terms of total cost. It is particularly useful when the manager wants to define the ranges over which each alternative is best. The basic steps for graphic and algebraic solutions are as follows.

1. Determine the variable costs and fixed costs for each site. Recall that *variable costs* are the portion of the total cost that varies directly with the volume of output. Recall that *fixed costs* are the portion of the total cost that remains constant regardless of output levels.

Solver - Center of Gravity

Enter data in yellow - shaded areas.

Enter the names of the towns and the coordinates (*x* and *y*) and population (or load, *l*) of each town.

| Add A Town | | Remove A Town | | | |

City/Town Name	x	y	l	lx	ly
A	2.5	4.5	2	5	9
B	2.5	2.5	5	12.5	12.5
C	5.5	4.5	10	55	45
D	5	2	7	35	14
E	8	5	10	80	50
F	7	2	20	140	40
G	9	2.5	14	126	35
			68	453.5	205.5

Center-of-Gravity Coordinates	x*	6.67
	y*	3.02

FIGURE 10.1

Location Analysis with Center-of-Gravity Solver

2. Plot the total cost lines—the sum of variable and fixed costs—for all the sites on a single graph (for assistance, see Tutors A.1 and A.2 in OM Explorer).
3. Identify the approximate ranges for which each location has the lowest cost.
4. Solve algebraically for the break-even points over the relevant ranges.

Break-Even Analysis for Location

EXAMPLE 10.3

An operations manager has narrowed the search for a new facility location to four communities. The annual fixed costs (land, property taxes, insurance, equipment, and buildings) and the variable costs (labor, materials, transportation, and variable overhead) are

COMMUNITY	FIXED COSTS PER YEAR	VARIABLE COSTS PER UNIT
A	$150,000	$62
B	$300,000	$38
C	$500,000	$24
D	$600,000	$30

ACTIVE MODEL 10.2
Active Model 10.2 on the Student CD-ROM provides insight on defining the three relevant ranges for this example.

Step 1. Plot the total cost curves for all the communities on a single graph. Identify on the graph the approximate range over which each community provides the lowest cost.

Step 2. Using break-even analysis, calculate the break-even quantities over the relevant ranges. If the expected demand is 15,000 units per year, what is the best location?

TUTOR 10.3
Tutor 10.3 on the Student CD-ROM provides another example to practice break-even analysis for location decisions.

SOLUTION

Step 1. To plot a community's total cost line, let us first compute the total cost for two output levels: $Q = 0$ and $Q = 20,000$ units per year. For the $Q = 0$ level, the total cost is simply the fixed costs. For the $Q = 20,000$ level, the total cost (fixed plus variable costs) is

COMMUNITY	FIXED COSTS	VARIABLE COSTS (COST PER UNIT) (NO. OF UNITS)	TOTAL COST (FIXED + VARIABLE)
A	$150,000	$62(20,000) = $1,240,000	$1,390,000
B	$300,000	$38(20,000) = $ 760,000	$1,060,000
C	$500,000	$24(20,000) = $ 480,000	$ 980,000
D	$600,000	$30(20,000) = $ 600,000	$1,200,000

Figure 10.2 shows the graph of the total cost lines. The line for community A goes from (0, 150) to (20, 1,390). The graph indicates that community A is best for low volumes, B for intermediate volumes, and C for high volumes. We should no longer consider community D, as both its fixed *and* its variable costs are higher than community C's.

Step 2. The break-even quantity between A and B lies at the end of the first range, where A is best, and the beginning of the second range, where B is best. We find it by setting their total cost equations equal to each other and solving:

$$\text{(A)} \qquad \qquad \text{(B)}$$

$$\$150{,}000 + \$62Q = \$300{,}000 + \$38Q$$
$$Q = 6{,}250 \text{ units}$$

The break-even quantity between B and C lies at the end of the range over which B is best and the beginning of the final range where C is best. It is

$$\text{(B)} \qquad \qquad \text{(C)}$$

$$\$300{,}000 + \$38Q = \$500{,}000 + \$24Q$$
$$Q = 14{,}286 \text{ units}$$

No other break-even quantities are needed. The break-even point between A and C lies above the shaded area, which does not mark either the start or the end of one of the three relevant ranges.

DECISION POINT   Management located the new facility at Community C, because the 15,000 units-per-year demand forecast lies in the high-volume range.

FIGURE 10.2

Break-Even Analysis of Four Candidate Locations

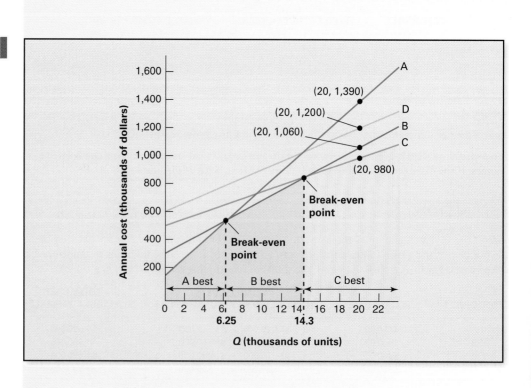

◉ LOCATING A FACILITY WITHIN A NETWORK OF FACILITIES

When a firm with a network of existing facilities plans a new facility, one of two conditions exists: Either the facilities operate independently (e.g., a chain of restaurants, health clinics, banks, or retail establishments) or the facilities interact (e.g., component manufacturing plants, assembly plants, and warehouses). Independently operating units can be located by treating each as a separate single facility, as described in the preceding section. Locating interacting facilities introduces new issues, such as how to allocate work between the facilities and how to determine the best capacity for each. Changing work allocations in turn affects the size (or capacity utilization) of the facilities. Thus, the multiple-facility location problem has three dimensions—location, allocation, and capacity—that must be solved simultaneously. In many cases, the analyst can identify a workable solution merely by looking for patterns in the cost, demand, and capacity data and using trial-and-error calculations. In other cases, more formal approaches are needed.

THE TRANSPORTATION METHOD

The **transportation method** is a quantitative approach that can help solve multiple-facility location problems. We use it here to determine the allocation pattern that minimizes the cost of shipping products from two or more plants, or *sources of supply*, to two or more warehouses, or *destinations*.[1] We focus on the setup and interpretation of the problem, leaving the rest of the solution process to a software package on a computer. The transportation method is based on linear programming (see Supplement D, "Linear Programming"). More efficient algorithms for solving this problem can be found in textbooks covering quantitative methods and management science.

The transportation method does not solve *all* facets of the multiple-facility location problem. It only finds the *best* shipping pattern between plants and warehouses for a particular set of plant locations, each with a given capacity. The analyst must try a variety of location–capacity combinations and use the transportation method to find the optimal distribution for each one. Distribution costs (variable shipping and possibly variable production costs) are but one important input in evaluating a particular location–allocation combination. Investment costs and other fixed costs also must be considered, along with various qualitative factors. This complete analysis must be made for each reasonable location–capacity combination. Because of the importance of making a good decision, this extra effort is well worth its cost.

SETTING UP THE INITIAL TABLEAU. The first step in solving a transportation problem is to format it in a standard matrix, sometimes called a *tableau*. The basic steps in setting up an initial tableau are as follows:

1. Create a row for each plant (existing or new) being considered and a column for each warehouse.
2. Add a column for plant capacities and a row for warehouse demands and insert their specific numerical values.
3. Each cell not in the requirements row or capacity column represents a shipping route from a plant to a warehouse. Insert the unit costs in the upper right-hand corner of each of these cells.

The Sunbelt Pool Company is considering building a new 500-unit plant, because business is booming. One possible location is Atlanta. Figure 10.3 shows a tableau with its plant capacity, warehouse requirements, and shipping costs. The tableau shows, for example, that shipping one unit from the existing Phoenix plant to warehouse 1 costs

What is the best way to partition work among various facilities?

transportation method A quantitative approach that can help solve multiple-facility location problems.

---

[1]It can also be used to determine an optimal production plan (see Chapter 14, "Aggregate Planning") or an optimal allocation of service accounts to service centers.

FIGURE 10.3

Initial Tableau

Plant	Warehouse			Capacity
	1	2	3	
Phoenix	$5.00	$6.00	$5.40	400
Atlanta	$7.00	$4.60	$6.60	500
Requirements	200	400	300	900 / 900

$5.00. Costs are assumed to increase linearly with the size of the shipment; that is, the cost is the same *per unit* regardless of the size of the total shipment.

In the transportation method, the sum of the shipments in a row must equal the corresponding plant's capacity. For example, in Figure 10.3, the total shipments from the Atlanta plant to warehouses 1, 2, and 3 must add up to 500. Similarly, the sum of shipments to a column must equal the corresponding warehouse's demand requirements. Thus, shipments to warehouse 1 from Phoenix and Atlanta must total 200 units.

DUMMY PLANTS OR WAREHOUSES. The transportation method also requires that the sum of capacities equal the sum of demands, which happens to be the case at 900 units (see Figure 10.3). In many real problems, total capacity may exceed requirements, or vice versa. If capacity exceeds requirements by *r* units, we add an extra column (a *dummy warehouse*) with a demand of *r* units and make the shipping costs in the newly created cells $0. Shipments are not actually made, so they represent unused plant capacity. Similarly, if requirements exceed capacity by *r* units, we add an extra row (a *dummy plant*) with a capacity of *r* units. We assign shipping costs equal to the stockout costs of the new cells. If stockout costs are unknown or are the same for all warehouses, we simply assign shipping costs of $0 per unit to each cell in the dummy row. The optimal solution will not be affected because the shortage of *r* units is required in all cases. Adding a dummy warehouse or dummy plant ensures that the sum of capacities equals the sum of demands. Some software packages automatically add them when we make the data inputs.

FINDING A SOLUTION. After the initial tableau has been set up, the goal is to find the least-cost allocation pattern that satisfies all demands and exhausts all capacities. This pattern can be found by using the transportation method, which guarantees the optimal solution. The initial tableau is filled in with a feasible solution that satisfies all warehouse demands and exhausts all plant capacities. Then a new tableau is created, defining a new solution that has a lower total cost. This iterative process continues until no improvements can be made in the current solution, signaling that the optimal solution has been found. When using a computer package, all that you have to input is the information for the initial tableau.

Another procedure is the simplex method (see Supplement D, "Linear Programming"), although more inputs are required. The transportation problem is actually a special case of linear programming, which can be modeled with a decision variable for each cell in the tableau, a constraint for each row in the tableau (requiring that each plant's capacity be fully utilized), and a constraint for each column in the tableau (requiring that each warehouse's demand be satisfied).

Whichever method is used, the number of nonzero shipments in the optimal solution will never exceed the sum of the numbers of plants and warehouses minus 1. The Sunbelt Pool Company has 2 plants and 3 warehouses, so there need not be more than 4 (or $3 + 2 - 1$) shipments in the optimal solution.

| **Interpreting the Optimal Solution** | **EXAMPLE** 10.4 |

The printout in Figure 10.4 from OM Explorer is for the Sunbelt Pool Company. Tutor 10.4 is set up to handle up to three sources and four destinations (for larger problems, use the *Transportation Method* Solver). With only two sources, we make the third row a "dummy" with a capacity of 0, and the fourth warehouse a "dummy" with a demand of 0. The bold numbers show the optimal shipments. Verify that each plant's capacity is exhausted and that each warehouse's demand is filled. Also confirm that the total transportation cost of the solution is $4,580.

FIGURE 10.4

Optimal Tableau for Sunbelt Pool Company Using Tutor 10.4

Enter data in yellow shaded areas.

Solve

Sources	Destinations				Capacity
	Warehouse 1	Warehouse 2	Warehouse 3	Dummy	
Phoenix	5 **200**	6	5.4 **200**	0	400
Atlanta	7	4.6 **400**	6.6 **100**	0	500
Dummy	0	0	0	0	0
					900
Requirements	200	400	300	0	900

| Costs | $1,000 | $1,840 | $1,740 | $0 | |
| Total Cost | | | | | $4,580 |

SOLUTION

Phoenix ships 200 units to warehouse 1 and 200 units to warehouse 3, exhausting its 400-unit capacity. Atlanta ships 400 units of its 500-unit capacity to warehouse 2 and the remaining 100 units to warehouse 3. All warehouse demand is satisfied: Warehouse 1 is fully supplied by Phoenix and warehouse 2 by Atlanta. Warehouse 3 receives 200 units from Phoenix and 100 units from Atlanta, satisfying its 300-unit demand. The total transportation cost is 200($5.00) + 200($5.40) + 400($4.60) + 100($6.60) = $4,580.

DECISION POINT   Management must evaluate other plant locations before deciding on the best one. The optimal solution does not necessarily mean that the best choice is to open an Atlanta plant. It just means that the best allocation pattern for the current choices on the other two dimensions of this multiple-facility location problem (i.e., a capacity of 400 units at Phoenix and the new plant's location at Atlanta) results in total *transportation* costs of $4,580.

TUTOR 10.4

Tutor 10.4 on the Student CD-ROM provides another example of how to apply the transportation method to location decisions.

THE LARGER SOLUTION PROCESS. Other costs and various qualitative factors also must be considered as additional parts of a complete evaluation. For example, the annual profits earned from the expansion must be balanced against the land and construction costs of a new plant in Atlanta. Thus, management might use the preference matrix approach (see Example 10.1) to account for the full set of location factors.

The analyst should also evaluate other capacity and location combinations. For example, one possibility is to expand at Phoenix and build a smaller plant at Atlanta. Alternatively, a new plant could be built at another location, or several new plants could be built. The analyst must repeat the analysis for each such likely location strategy.

OTHER METHODS OF LOCATION ANALYSIS

Many location analysis problems are even more complex than those discussed so far. Consider the complexity that a medium-sized manufacturer faces when distributing products through warehouses, or *distribution centers*, to various demand centers. The problem is to determine the number, size, allocation pattern, and location of the warehouses. There could be thousands of demand centers, hundreds of potential warehouse locations, several plants, and multiple product lines. Transportation rates depend on the direction of shipment, product, quantity, rate breaks, and geographic area.

Such complexity requires the use of a computer for a comprehensive evaluation. Three basic types of computer models have been developed for this purpose: (1) heuristics, (2) simulation, and (3) optimization.

HEURISTICS. Solution guidelines, or rules of thumb, that find feasible—but not necessarily the best—solutions to problems are called **heuristics**. Their advantages include efficiency and an ability to handle general views of a problem. The systematic search procedure utilizing a target area's center of gravity, described earlier for single-facility location problems, is a typical heuristic procedure. One of the first heuristics to be computerized for location problems was proposed four decades ago to handle several hundred potential warehouse sites and several thousand demand centers (Kuehn and Hamburger, 1963). Many other heuristic models are available today for analyzing a variety of situations.

> **heuristics**   Solution guidelines, or rules of thumb, that find feasible—but not necessarily the best—solutions to problems.

SIMULATION. A modeling technique that reproduces the behavior of a system is called **simulation**. Simulation allows manipulation of certain variables and shows the effect on selected operating characteristics (see Supplement B, "Simulation"). Simulation models allow the analyst to evaluate different location alternatives by trial and error. It is up to the analyst to propose the most reasonable alternatives. Simulation handles more realistic views of a problem and involves the analyst in the solution process itself. For each run, the analyst inputs the facilities to be opened, and the simulator typically makes the allocation decisions based on some reasonable assumptions that have been written into the computer program. The Ralston-Purina Company used simulation to assist the company in locating warehouses to serve 137 demand centers, 5 field warehouses, and 4 plants. Random demand at each demand center by product type was simulated over a period of time. Demand was met by the closest warehouse that had available inventory. Data were produced by simulating inventory levels, transportation costs, warehouse operating costs, and backorders. Ralston-Purina implemented the result of the simulation, which showed that the least-cost alternative would be to consolidate the five field warehouses into only three.

> **simulation**   A modeling technique that reproduces the behavior of a system.

OPTIMIZATION. The transportation method was one of the first optimization procedures for solving one part (the allocation pattern) of multiple-facility location problems. In contrast to heuristics and simulation, **optimization** involves procedures to determine the *best* solution. Even though this approach might appear to be preferable, it has a limitation: Optimization procedures generally utilize simplified and less realistic views of a problem. However, the payoffs can be substantial.

> **optimization**   A procedure used to determine the "best" solution; generally utilizes simplified and less realistic views of a problem.

For an example of computer software support for location analysis, see the Northwestern University Production and Logistics Laboratory at **primal.iems.nwu .edu/~levi/location.html**. There are a variety of logistics-related software applications for various clients. Collaborating with a group of computer analysts, they develop software for supply-chain/logistics/vehicle-routing applications fully integrated within a geographic information system (GIS). For example, they have worked with the New York City Board of Education on a project to improve their school bus transportation. They have integrated their algorithms with the geographic information system called *MapInfo,* which has been a very useful tool for the transportation planners there.

● MANAGING LOCATION ACROSS THE ORGANIZATION

Location decisions affect processes and departments throughout the organization. When locating new retail facilities, such as Starbucks stores, marketing must carefully assess how the location will appeal to customers and possibly open up new markets.

Relocating the whole or part of an organization can significantly affect workforce attitudes and ability to operate effectively across department lines, as MCI's move of its Systems Engineering division from its Washington, DC headquarters to Colorado Springs. Locating new facilities or relocating existing facilities can involve significant investment requirements, which must be carefully evaluated by the organization's accounting and finance departments. Human resources must be attuned to the hiring and training needs, such as at StarTek's call center in Texas. Finally, operations also has an important stake in location decisions. The choices can significantly affect supply-chain effectiveness, workforce productivity, and the ability to provide quality services and products. International operations, such as at the Radisson Slavjanskaya hotel, introduce a new set of challenges and opportunities.

CHAPTER HIGHLIGHTS

- The globalization of operations affects both service and manufacturing industries. More facilities are being located in other countries, and offshore sales (and imports) are increasing. Four factors that spur globalization are improved transportation and communications technologies, opened financial systems, increased demand for imports, and fewer import quotas and other trade barriers. Offsetting the advantages of global operations are differences in language, regulations, and culture that create new management problems.

- Location decisions depend on many factors. For any situation some factors may be disregarded entirely; the remainder may be divided into dominant and secondary factors.

- Favorable labor climate; proximity to markets; quality of life; proximity to suppliers and resources; proximity to other company facilities; and utilities, taxes, and real estate costs are important factors in most manufacturing plant location decisions. Proximity to markets, clients, or customers usually is the most important factor in service industry location decisions. Competition is a complicating factor in estimating the sales potential of a location. Having competitors' facilities nearby may be an asset or a liability, depending on the type of business.

- One way of evaluating qualitative factors is to calculate a weighted score for each alternative location by using the preference matrix approach.

- The load–distance method brings together concerns of proximity (to markets, suppliers, resources, and other company facilities) during the early stages of location analysis. By making a systematic search of an area, an analyst identifies locations resulting in lower *ld* scores. The center of gravity of an area is a good starting point for making a search. Break-even analysis can help compare location alternatives when location factors can be expressed in terms of variable and fixed costs.

- Multiple-facility problems have three dimensions: location, allocation, and capacity. The transportation method is a basic tool for finding the best allocation pattern for a particular combination of location–capacity choices. Transportation costs are recalculated for each location–capacity combination under consideration. The transportation method's single criterion for determining the best shipping pattern is minimum transportation costs. To complete the location study, the analysis must be expanded to account for the full set of location factors.

- Location analysis can become complex for multiple facilities. A variety of computerized heuristic, simulation, and optimization models have been developed over the last four decades to help analysts deal with this complexity.

STUDENT CD-ROM AND INTERNET RESOURCES

The Student CD-ROM and the Companion Website at **www.prenhall.com/krajewski** contain many tools, activities, and resources designed for this chapter. The following items are recommended to enhance your skills and improve your understanding of the material in this chapter.

STUDENT CD-ROM RESOURCES

- **PowerPoint Slides:** View this comprehensive set of slides customized for this chapter's concepts and techniques.
- **OM Explorer Tutors:** OM Explorer contains five tutor spreadsheets that will help you learn about the preference matrix for location, center of gravity, break-even analysis

for location, the transportation method, and distance measures. See Chapter 10, Supplement A, and Chapter 7 in the OM Explorer menu. See also the three Tutor Exercises on making location decisions.

- **OM Explorer Solvers:** OM Explorer contains spreadsheets to find the center of gravity, to solve with the transportation method, and to calculate *WS* scores in a preference matrix. See Location and Decision Making in the OM Explorer menu for these routines.
- **Active Models:** There are active model spreadsheets that provide additional insights on the center of gravity and break-even analysis applied to location decisions. See Location in the Active Models menu for these two routines.

➤ **Supplement J:** "Financial Analysis." Learn about several tools for evaluating location decisions that involve large capital investments.

INTERNET RESOURCES

➤ **Self-Study Quizzes:** See the compendium of true or false, multiple choice, and essay questions that give you feedback on how well you have mastered the concepts in this chapter.

➤ **In the News:** See the articles that apply to this chapter.
➤ **Internet Exercises:** Try out six different links to location topics, including how McDonald's and Dunkin' Donuts use partnering arrangements and how to use map sites.
➤ **Virtual Tours:** Check out location decisions by a cheese-making plant and a distillery. Also see the "Web Links to Company Facility Tours" for additional tours of company facilities.

KEY EQUATIONS

1. Load–distance score: $ld = \sum_i l_i d_i$

2. Center of gravity: $x^* = \dfrac{\sum_i l_i x_i}{\sum_i l_i}$ and $y^* = \dfrac{\sum_i l_i y_i}{\sum_i l_i}$

KEY TERMS

center of gravity 455
critical mass 451
facility location 448
globalization 444

heuristics 462
load–distance method 455
optimization 462
quality of life 450

simulation 462
transportation method 459

SOLVED PROBLEM I

An electronics manufacturer must expand by building a second facility. The search has been narrowed to four locations, all of which are acceptable to management in terms of dominant factors. Assessment of these sites in terms of seven location factors is shown in Table 10.1. For example, location A has a factor score of 5 (excellent) for labor climate; the weight for this factor (20) is the highest of any.

TABLE 10.1   FACTOR INFORMATION FOR ELECTRONICS MANUFACTURER

LOCATION FACTOR	FACTOR WEIGHT	A	B	C	D
1. Labor climate	20	5	4	4	5
2. Quality of life	16	2	3	4	1
3. Transportation system	16	3	4	3	2
4. Proximity to markets	14	5	3	4	4
5. Proximity to materials	12	2	3	3	4
6. Taxes	12	2	5	5	4
7. Utilities	10	5	4	3	3

Calculate the weighted score for each location. Which location should be recommended?

SOLUTION

Based on the weighted scores shown in Table 10.2, location C is the preferred site, although location B is a close second.

		WEIGHTED SCORE FOR EACH LOCATION			
LOCATION FACTOR	**FACTOR WEIGHT**	**A**	**B**	**C**	**D**
1. Labor climate	20	100	80	80	100
2. Quality of life	16	32	48	64	16
3. Transportation system	16	48	64	48	32
4. Proximity to markets	14	70	42	56	56
5. Proximity to materials	12	24	36	36	48
6. Taxes	12	24	60	60	48
7. Utilities	10	50	40	30	30
Totals	100	348	370	374	330

TABLE 10.2 CALCULATING WEIGHTED SCORES FOR ELECTRONICS MANUFACTURER

SOLVED PROBLEM 2

The operations manager for Mile-High Beer has narrowed the search for a new facility location to seven communities. Annual fixed costs (land, property taxes, insurance, equipment, and buildings) and variable costs (labor, materials, transportation, and variable overhead) are shown in Table 10.3.

TABLE 10.3 FIXED AND VARIABLE COSTS FOR MILE-HIGH BEER

COMMUNITY	FIXED COSTS PER YEAR	VARIABLE COSTS PER BARREL
Aurora	$1,600,000	$17.00
Boulder	$2,000,000	$12.00
Colorado Springs	$1,500,000	$16.00
Denver	$3,000,000	$10.00
Englewood	$1,800,000	$15.00
Fort Collins	$1,200,000	$15.00
Golden	$1,700,000	$14.00

a. Which of the communities can be eliminated from further consideration because they are dominated (both variable and fixed costs are higher) by another community?
b. Plot the total cost curves for all remaining communities on a single graph. Identify on the graph the approximate range over which each community provides the lowest cost.
c. Using break-even analysis (see Supplement A, "Decision Making"), calculate the break-even quantities to determine the range over which each community provides the lowest cost.

SOLUTION

a. Aurora and Colorado Springs are dominated by Fort Collins, as both fixed and variable costs are higher for those communities than for Fort Collins. Englewood is dominated by Golden.
b. Figure 10.5 shows that Fort Collins is best for low volumes, Boulder for intermediate volumes, and Denver for high volumes. Although Golden is not dominated by any community, it is the second or third choice over the entire range. Golden does not become the lowest cost choice at any volume.
c. The break-even point between Fort Collins and Boulder is

$$\$1,200,000 + \$15Q = \$2,000,000 + \$12Q$$
$$Q = 266,667 \text{ barrels per year}$$

The break-even point between Denver and Boulder is

$$\$3,000,000 + \$10Q = \$2,000,000 + \$12Q$$
$$Q = 500,000 \text{ barrels per year}$$

FIGURE 10.5

Break-Even Analysis of Four Candidate Locations

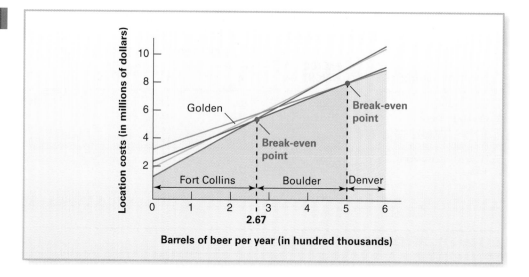

SOLVED PROBLEM 3

A supplier to the electric utility industry has a heavy product, and the transportation costs are high. One market area includes the lower part of the Great Lakes region and the upper portion of the southeastern region. More than 600,000 tons are to be shipped to eight major customer locations as shown in Table 10.4.

TABLE 10.4 MARKETS FOR ELECTRIC UTILITIES SUPPLIER		
CUSTOMER LOCATION	**TONS SHIPPED**	**xy-COORDINATES**
Three Rivers, MI	5,000	(7, 13)
Fort Wayne, IN	92,000	(8, 12)
Columbus, OH	70,000	(11, 10)
Ashland, KY	35,000	(11, 7)
Kingsport, TN	9,000	(12, 4)
Akron, OH	227,000	(13, 11)
Wheeling, WV	16,000	(14, 10)
Roanoke, VA	153,000	(15, 5)

a. Calculate the center of gravity, rounding distance to the nearest tenth.
b. Calculate the load–distance score for this location, using rectilinear distance.

SOLUTION

a. The center of gravity is (12.4, 9.2).

$$\sum_i l_i = 5 + 92 + 70 + 35 + 9 + 227 + 16 + 153 = 607$$

$$\sum_i l_i x_i = 5(7) + 92(8) + 70(11) + 35(11) + 9(12) + 227(13) + 16(14) + 153(15)$$

$$= 7,504$$

$$x^* = \frac{\sum_i l_i y_i}{\sum_i l_i} = \frac{7,504}{607} = 12.4$$

$$\sum_i l_i y_i = 5(13) + 92(12) + 70(10) + 35(7) + 9(4) + 227(11) + 16(10) + 153(5) = 5,572$$

$$y^* = \frac{\sum_i l_i y_i}{\sum_i l_i} = \frac{5,572}{607} = 9.2$$

b. The load–distance score is

$$ld = \sum_i l_i d_i = 5(5.4 + 3.8) + 92(4.4 + 2.8) + 70(1.4 + 0.8) + 35(1.4 + 2.2)$$

$$+ 9(0.4 + 5.2) + 227(0.6 + 1.8) + 16(1.6 + 0.8) + 153(2.6 + 4.2)$$

$$= 2{,}662.4$$

where

$$d_i = \left| x_i - x^* \right| + \left| y_i - y^* \right|$$

SOLVED PROBLEM 4

The Arid Company makes canoe paddles to serve distribution centers in Worchester, Rochester, and Dorchester from existing plants in Battle Creek and Cherry Creek. Annual demand is expected to increase as projected in the bottom row of the tableau shown in Figure 10.6. Arid is considering locating a plant near the headwaters of Dee Creek. Annual capacity for each plant is shown in the right-hand column of the tableau. Transportation costs per paddle are shown in the tableau in the small boxes. For example, the cost to ship one paddle from Battle Creek to Worchester is $4.37. The optimal allocations are also shown. For example, Battle Creek ships 12,000 units to Rochester. What are the estimated transportation costs associated with this allocation pattern?

SOLUTION

The total cost is $167,000.

Ship 12,000 units from Battle Creek to Rochester @ $4.25.	Cost = $ 51,000
Ship 6,000 units from Cherry Creek to Worchester @ $4.00.	Cost = $ 24,000
Ship 4,000 units from Cherry Creek to Rochester @ $5.00.	Cost = $ 20,000
Ship 6,000 units from Dee Creek to Rochester @ $4.50.	Cost = $ 27,000
Ship 12,000 units from Dee Creek to Dorchester @ $3.75.	Cost = $ 45,000
	Total $167,000

FIGURE 10.6

Optimal Solution for Arid Company

Source	Destination			Capacity
	Worchester	Rochester	Dorchester	
Battle Creek	$4.37	$4.25 **12,000**	$4.89	12,000
Cherry Creek	$4.00 **6,000**	$5.00 **4,000**	$5.27	10,000
Dee Creek	$4.13	$4.50 **6,000**	$3.75 **12,000**	18,000
Demand	6,000	22,000	12,000	40,000

DISCUSSION QUESTIONS

1. Break into teams. Select two organizations, one in services and one in manufacturing, that are known to some of your team members. What are the key factors that each organization would consider in locating a new facility? What data would you want to collect before evaluating the location options, and how would you collect the data? Would additional factors or data be needed if some of the location options were in another country? Explain.

2. The owner of a major league baseball team is considering moving his team from its current city in the Rust Belt to a city in the Sun Belt. The Sun Belt city offers a larger television market and a new stadium and holds the potential for greater fan support. What ethical obligations, if any, does the owner have to the city in which the team is presently located?

PROBLEMS

An icon next to a problem identifies the software that can be helpful, but is not mandatory. The software is available on the Student CD-ROM that is packaged with every new copy of the textbook.

1. **OM Explorer** Calculate the weighted score for each location (A, B, C, and D) shown in Table 10.5. Which location would you recommend?

2. **OM Explorer** John and Jane Darling are newlyweds trying to decide among several available rentals. Alternatives were scored on a scale of 1 to 5 (5 = best) against weighted performance criteria, as shown in Table 10.6. The criteria included rent, proximity to work and recreational opportunities, security, and other neighborhood characteristics associated with the couple's values and lifestyle. Alternative A is an apartment, B is a bungalow, C is a condo, and D is a downstairs apartment in Jane's parents' home.
   Which location is indicated by the preference matrix? What qualitative factors might cause this preference to change?

3. **OM Explorer** Two alternative locations are under consideration for a new plant: Jackson, Mississippi and Dayton, Ohio. The Jackson location is superior in terms of costs. However, management believes that sales volume would decline if this location were chosen because it is farther from the market, and the firm's customers

TABLE 10.6
FACTORS FOR NEWLYWEDS

Location Factor	Factor Weight	Factor Score for Each Location			
		A	B	C	D
1. Rent	25	3	1	2	5
2. Quality of life	20	2	5	5	4
3. Schools	5	3	5	3	1
4. Proximity to work	10	5	3	4	3
5. Proximity to recreation	15	4	4	5	2
6. Neighborhood security	15	2	4	4	4
7. Utilities	10	4	2	3	5
Total	100				

prefer local suppliers. The selling price of the product is $250 per unit in either case. Use the following information to determine which location yields the higher total profit contribution per year.

Location	Annual Fixed Cost	Variable Cost per Unit	Forecast Demand per Year
Jackson	$1,500,000	$50	30,000 units
Dayton	$2,800,000	$85	40,000 units

4. **OM Explorer** Fall-Line, Inc. is a Great Falls, Montana manufacturer of a variety of downhill skis. Fall-Line is considering four locations for a new plant: Aspen, Colorado; Medicine Lodge, Kansas; Broken Bow, Nebraska; and Wounded Knee, South Dakota. Annual fixed costs and variable costs per pair of skis are shown in the following table.

Location	Annual Fixed Costs	Variable Costs per Pair
Aspen	$8,000,000	$250
Medicine Lodge	$2,400,000	$130
Broken Bow	$3,400,000	$ 90
Wounded Knee	$4,500,000	$ 65

   a. Plot the total cost curves for all the communities on a single graph (see Solved Problem 2). Identify on

TABLE 10.5
FACTORS FOR LOCATIONS A–D

Location Factor	Factor Weight	Factor Score for Each Location			
		A	B	C	D
1. Labor climate	5	5	4	3	5
2. Quality of life	30	2	3	5	1
3. Transportation system	5	3	4	3	5
4. Proximity to markets	25	5	3	4	4
5. Proximity to materials	5	3	2	3	5
6. Taxes	15	2	5	5	4
7. Utilities	15	5	4	2	1
Total	100				

the graph the range in volume over which each location would be best.

b. What break-even quantity defines each range?

Although Aspen's fixed and variable costs are dominated by those of the other communities, Fall-Line believes that both the demand and the price would be higher for skis made in Aspen than for skis made in the other locations. The following table shows those projections.

Location	Price per Pair	Forecast Demand per Year
Aspen	$500	60,000 pairs
Medicine Lodge	$350	45,000 pairs
Broken Bow	$350	43,000 pairs
Wounded Knee	$350	40,000 pairs

c. Determine which location yields the highest total profit contribution per year.

d. Is this location decision sensitive to forecast accuracy? At what minimum sales volume does Aspen become the location of choice?

5. ◆ OM Explorer Wiebe Trucking, Inc. is planning a new warehouse to serve the West. Denver, Santa Fe, and Salt Lake City are under consideration. For each location, annual fixed costs (rent, equipment, and insurance) and average variable costs per shipment (labor, transportation, and utilities) are listed in the following table. Sales projections range from 550,000 to 600,000 shipments per year.

Location	Annual Fixed Costs	Variable Costs per Shipment
Denver	$5,000,000	$4.65
Santa Fe	$4,200,000	$6.25
Salt Lake City	$3,500,000	$7.25

a. Plot the total cost curves for all the locations on a single graph.

b. Which city provides the lowest overall costs?

6. The operations manager for Hot House Roses has narrowed the search for a new facility location to seven communities. Annual fixed costs (land, property taxes, insurance, equipment, and buildings) and variable costs (labor, materials, transportation, and variable overhead) are shown in the following table.

Community	Fixed Costs per Year	Variable Costs per Dozen
Aurora, CO	$210,000	$7.20
Flora, IL	$200,000	$7.00
Garden City, KS	$150,000	$9.00
Greensboro, NC	$280,000	$6.20
Roseland, LA	$260,000	$6.00
Sunnyvale, CA	$420,000	$5.00
Watertown, MA	$370,000	$8.00

a. Which of the communities can be eliminated from further consideration because they are dominated (both variable and fixed costs are higher) by another community?

b. Plot the total cost curves for the remaining communities on a single graph. Identify on the graph the approximate range over which each community provides the lowest cost.

c. Using break-even analysis (see Supplement A, "Decision Making"), calculate the break-even quantities to determine the range over which each community provides the lowest cost.

7. ◆ OM Explorer Ethel and Earl Griese narrowed their choice for a new oil refinery to three locations. Fixed and variable costs are as follows.

Location	Fixed Costs per Year	Variable Costs per Unit
Albany	$ 350,000	$980
Baltimore	$1,500,500	$240
Chattanooga	$1,100,000	$500

a. Plot the total cost curves for all the communities on a single graph. Identify on the graph the range in volume over which each location would be best.

b. What break-even quantities define each range?

8. Sam Bagelstein is planning to operate a specialty bagel sandwich kiosk but is undecided about whether to locate in the downtown shopping plaza or in a suburban shopping mall. Based on the following data, which location would you recommend?

Location	Downtown	Suburban
Annual rent including utilities	$12,000	$8,000
Expected annual demand (sandwiches)	30,000	25,000
Average variable costs per sandwich	$1.50	$1.00
Average selling price per sandwich	$3.25	$2.85

9. ◆ OM Explorer The following three points are the locations of important facilities in a transportation network: (20, 20), (30, 50), and (60, 0). The coordinates are in miles.

a. Calculate the Euclidean distances (in miles) between each of the three pairs of facilities.

b. Calculate these distances using rectilinear distances.

10. ◆ OM Explorer The following three points are the locations of important facilities in a transportation network: (20, 20), (50, 10), and (50, 60). The coordinates are in miles.

a. Calculate the Euclidean distances (in miles) between each of the three pairs of facilities.

b. Calculate these distances using rectilinear distances.

11. ◆ OM Explorer Centura High School is to be located at the population center of gravity of three communities:

FIGURE 10.7   **Coordinates for Three Communities**

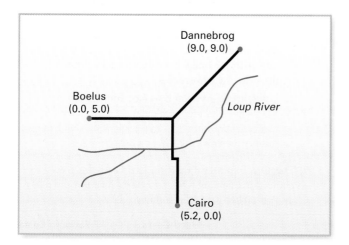

Boelus, population 228; Cairo, population 737; and Dannebrog, population 356. The coordinates (on a grid of square miles) for the communities are provided in Figure 10.7. Where should Centura High School be located? (Round to 0.1 mile.) What factors may result in locating at the site indicated by this technique?

12. **OM Explorer** Val's Pizza is looking for a single central location to make pizza for delivery only. This college town is arranged on a grid with arterial streets, as shown in Figure 10.8. The main campus (A), located at 14th and R, is the source of 4,000 pizza orders per week. Three smaller campuses (B, C, and D) are located at 52nd and V, at 67th and Z, and at 70th and South. Orders from the smaller campuses average 1,000 pizzas a week. In addition, the State Patrol headquarters (E) at 10th and A orders 500 pizzas per week.

a. At about what intersection should Val start looking for a suitable site? (Estimate coordinates for the major demands accurate to the nearest one-quarter mile, and then find the center of gravity.)

b. What is the rectilinear weekly load–distance score for this location?

c. If the delivery person can travel one mile in two minutes on arterial streets and one-quarter mile per minute on residential streets, going from the center of gravity location to the farthest demand location will take how long?

13. **OM Explorer** Oakmont Manufacturing Company is considering where to locate its new plant relative to its two suppliers (in cities A and B) and two market areas (locations X and Y). Management wants to limit its search to these four locations. The following information has been collected.

Location	xy-Coordinates (miles)	Tons per Year	Freight Rate ($/ton-mile)
A	(200, 500)	4,000	$3.00
B	(400, 300)	2,000	$3.00
C	(300, 200)	5,000	$2.00
D	(600, 400)	3,000	$2.00

a. Which of these four locations gives the lowest total cost based on Euclidean distances? [*Hint:* The annual cost of inbound shipments from supplier A to the new plant is $12,000 per mile traveled (4,000 tons per year × $3.00 per ton-mile).]

b. Which location is best, based on rectilinear distances?

c. What are the coordinates of the center of gravity of the four locations?

FIGURE 10.8   **Map of Campus Area**

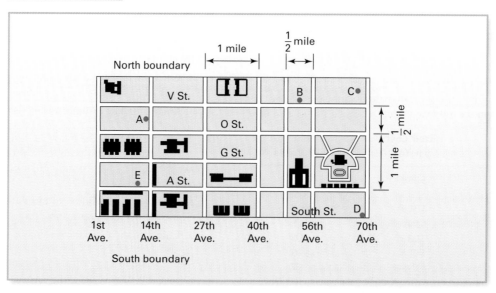

14. **OM Explorer** A larger and more modern main post office is to be constructed at a new location in Davis, California. Growing suburbs have shifted the population density from where it was 40 years ago, when the current facility was built. Annette Werk, the postmaster, asked her assistants to draw a grid map of the seven points where mail is picked up and delivered in bulk. The coordinates and trips per day to and from the seven mail source points and the current main post office, M, are shown in the following table. M will continue to act as a mail source point after relocation.

Mail Source Point	Bound Trips per Day (l)	xy-Coordinates (miles)
1	6	(2, 8)
2	3	(6, 1)
3	3	(8, 5)
4	3	(13, 3)
5	2	(15, 10)
6	7	(6, 14)
7	5	(18, 1)
M	3	(10, 3)

a. Calculate the center of gravity as a possible location for the new facility (round to the nearest whole number).

b. Compare the load–distance scores for the location in part (a) and the current location, using rectilinear distance.

15. **OM Explorer** Paramount Manufacturing is investigating which location would best position its new plant relative to two suppliers (located in cities A and B) and one market area (represented by city C). Management has limited the search for this plant to those three locations. The following information has been collected.

Location	Coordinates (miles)	Tons per Year	Freight Rate ($/ton-mile)
A	(100,200)	4,000	$3.00
B	(400,100)	3,000	$1.00
C	(100,100)	4,000	$3.00

a. Which of the three locations gives the lowest total cost, based on Euclidean distances? [*Hint:* The annual cost of inbound shipments from supplier A to the new plant is $12,000 per mile (4,000 tons per year × $3.00 per ton-mile).]

b. Which location is best, based on rectilinear distances?

c. What are the coordinates of the center of gravity?

16. A personal computer manufacturer plans to locate its assembly plant in Taiwan and to ship its computers back to the United States through either Los Angeles or San Francisco. It has distribution centers in Atlanta, New York, and Chicago and will ship to them from whichever city is chosen as the port of entry on the West Coast. Overall transportation cost is the only criterion for choosing the port. Use the load–distance model and the information in Table 10.7 to select the more cost-effective city.

Advanced Problems

17. **OM Explorer** Fire Brand makes picante sauce in El Paso and New York City. Distribution centers are located in Atlanta, Omaha, and Seattle. For the capacities, locations, and shipment costs per case shown in Figure 10.9, determine the shipping pattern that will minimize transportation costs. What are the estimated transportation costs associated with this optimal allocation pattern?

18. **OM Explorer** The Pelican Company has four distribution centers (A, B, C, and D) that require 40,000, 60,000, 30,000, and 50,000 gallons of diesel fuel, respectively, per month for their long-haul trucks. Three fuel wholesalers (1, 2, and 3) have indicated their willingness to supply as many as 50,000, 70,000, and 60,000 gallons of fuel, respectively. The total cost (shipping plus price) of delivering 1,000 gallons of fuel from each wholesaler to each distribution center is shown in the following table.

	TABLE 10.7		
	DISTANCES AND COSTS FOR PC MANUFACTURER		

		Distribution Center (units/year)		
		Chicago (10,000)	Atlanta (7,500)	New York (12,500)
Port of Entry	Los Angeles			
	Distance (miles)	1,800	2,600	3,200
	Shipping cost ($/unit)	0.0017/mile	0.0017/mile	0.0017/mile
	San Francisco			
	Distance (miles)	1,700	2,800	3,000
	Shipping cost ($/unit)	0.0020/mile	0.0020/mile	0.0020/mile

FIGURE 10.9   **Transportation Tableau for Fire Brand**

Source	Destination			Capacity
	Atlanta	Omaha	Seattle	
El Paso	$4	$5	$6	12,000
New York City	$3	$7	$9	10,000
Demand	8,000	10,000	4,000	22,000

	Distribution Center			
Wholesaler	A	B	C	D
I	$1.30	$1.40	$1.80	$1.60
2	$1.30	$1.50	$1.80	$1.60
3	$1.60	$1.40	$1.70	$1.50

a. Determine the optimal solution. Show that all capacities have been exhausted and that all demands can be met with this solution.

b. What is the total cost of the solution?

19. ● OM Explorer The Acme Company has four factories that ship products to five warehouses. The shipping costs, requirements capacities, and optimal allocations are shown in Figure 10.10. What is the total cost of the optimal solution?

20. ● OM Explorer The Giant Farmer Company processes food for sale in discount food stores. It has two plants: one in Chicago and one in Houston. The company also operates warehouses in Miami, Denver, Lincoln, and Jackson. Forecasts indicate that demand soon will exceed supply and that a new plant with a capacity of 8,000 cases per week is needed. The question is where to locate the new plant. Two potential sites are Buffalo and Atlanta. The following data on capacities, forecasted demand, and shipping costs have been gathered.

FIGURE 10.10   **Optimal Solution for Acme Company**

Factory	Shipping Cost per Case to Warehouse					Capacity
	W1	W2	W3	W4	W5	
F1	$1 60,000	$3 20,000	$4	$5	$6	80,000
F2	$2	$2	$1 50,000	$4 10,000	$5	60,000
F3	$1	$5	$1	$3 20,000	$1 40,000	60,000
F4	$5	$2 50,000	$4	$5	$4	50,000
Demand	60,000	70,000	50,000	30,000	40,000	250,000

Plant	Capacity (cases per week)	Warehouse	Demand (cases per week)
Chicago	10,000	Miami	7,000
Houston	7,500	Denver	9,000
New plant	8,000	Lincoln	4,500
Total	25,500	Jackson	5,000
		Total	25,500

Shipping Cost to Warehouse (per case)

Plant	Miami	Denver	Lincoln	Jackson
Chicago	$7.00	$ 2.00	$4.00	$5.00
Houston	$3.00	$ 1.00	$5.00	$2.00
Buffalo (alternative 1)	$6.00	$ 9.00	$7.00	$4.00
Atlanta (alternative 2)	$2.00	$10.00	$8.00	$3.00

For each alternative new plant location, determine the shipping pattern that will minimize total transportation costs. Where should the new plant be located?

21. ◗ **OM Explorer** Pucchi, Inc. makes designer dog collars in Chihuahua, Mexico; Saint Bernard, Ohio; and Yorkshire, New York. Distribution centers are located in Baustin, Vegas, Nawlns, and New Yawk. The shipping costs, requirements, and capacities are shown in Figure 10.11. Use the transportation method to find the shipping schedule that minimizes shipping cost.

22. ◗ **OM Explorer** The Ajax International Company has four factories that ship products to five warehouses. The shipping costs, requirements, and capacities are shown in Figure 10.12. Use the transportation method to find the shipping schedule that minimizes shipping cost.

23. ◗ **OM Explorer** Consider further the Ajax International Company situation described in Problem 22. Ajax has decided to close F3 because of high operating costs. In addition, the company has decided to add 50,000 units of capacity to F4. The logistics manager is worried about the effect of this move on transportation costs. Presently, F3 is shipping 30,000 units to W4 and 50,000 units to W5 at a cost of $140,000 [or 30,000(3) + 50,000(1)]. If these warehouses were to be served by F4, the cost would increase to $350,000 [or 30,000(5) + 50,000(4)]. As a result, the Ajax logistics manager has requested a budget increase of $210,000 (or $350,000 − $140,000).

    a. Should the logistics manager get the budget increase?

    b. If not, how much would you budget for the increase in shipping costs?

24. ◗ **OM Explorer** Consider the facility location problem at the Giant Farmer Company described in Problem 20. Management is considering a third site, at Memphis. The shipping costs per case from Memphis are $3 to Miami, $11 to Denver, $6 to Lincoln, and $5 to Jackson. Find the minimum-cost plan for an alternative plant in Memphis. Would this result change the decision in Problem 20?

25. ◗ **OM Explorer** The Bright Paint Company has four factories (A, B, C, and D) that require 30,000, 20,000, 10,000, and 20,000 paint cans, respectively, per month. Three paint-can suppliers (1, 2, and 3) have indicated their willingness to supply as many as 40,000, 30,000, and 20,000 cans per month, respectively. The shipping costs per 100 cans are shown in Figure 10.13, along with capacity and demand quantities in hundreds of cans.

FIGURE 10.11   **Transportation Tableau for Pucchi, Inc.**

Factory	Shipping Cost per Collar to Distribution Centers					Capacity
	Baustin	Vegas	Nawlns	New Yawk	Dummy	
Chihuahua	$8	$5	$4	$9	$0	12,000
Saint Bernard	$4	$6	$3	$3	$0	7,000
Yorkshire	$2	$8	$6	$1	$0	4,000
Demand	4,000	6,000	3,000	8,000	2,000	23,000

FIGURE 10.12   **Transportation Tableau for Ajax International**

Factory	Shipping Cost per Case to Warehouse						Capacity
	W1	W2	W3	W4	W5	Dummy	
F1	$1	$3	$3	$5	$6	$0	50,000
F2	$2	$2	$1	$4	$5	$0	80,000
F3	$1	$5	$1	$3	$1	$0	80,000
F4	$5	$2	$4	$5	$4	$0	40,000
Demand	45,000	30,000	30,000	35,000	50,000	60,000	250,000

Currently supplier 1 is shipping 20,000 cans to plant B and 20,000 cans to D. Supplier 2 is shipping 30,000 cans to A, and supplier 3 is shipping 10,000 gallons to C. Does the present delivery arrangement minimize the total cost to the Bright Paint Company? If not, find a plan that does so.

26. ◗ **OM Explorer** The Chambers Corporation produces and markets an automotive theft-deterrent product, which it stocks in various warehouses throughout the country. Recently, its market research group compiled a forecast indicating that a significant increase in demand will occur in the near future, after which demand will level off for the foreseeable future. The company has decided to satisfy this demand by constructing new plant capacity. Chambers already has plants in Baltimore and Milwaukee and has no desire to relocate those facilities. Each plant is capable of producing 600,000 units per year.

After a thorough search, the company developed three site and capacity alternatives. *Alternative 1* is to build a 600,000-unit plant in Portland. *Alternative 2* is to build a 600,000-unit plant in San Antonio. *Alternative 3* is to build a 300,000-unit plant in Portland and a 300,000-unit plant in San Antonio. The company has four warehouses that distribute the product to retailers. The market research study provided the following data.

FIGURE 10.13   **Transportation Tableau for Bright Paint Company**

Supplier	Shipping Cost per 100 Cans to Plant					Capacity
	A	B	C	D	Dummy	
S1	$54	$48	$50	$46		400
S2	$52	$50	$54	$48		300
S3	$46	$48	$50	$52		200
Demand	300	200	100	200	100	900

Warehouse	Expected Annual Demand
Atlanta (AT)	500,000
Columbus (CO)	300,000
Los Angeles (LA)	600,000
Seattle (SE)	400,000

The logistics department compiled the following cost table that specified the cost per unit to ship the product from each plant to each warehouse in the most economical manner, subject to the reliability of the various carriers involved.

	Warehouse			
Plant	AT	CO	LA	SE
Baltimore	$0.35	$0.20	$0.85	$0.75
Milwaukee	$0.55	$0.15	$0.70	$0.65
Portland	$0.85	$0.60	$0.30	$0.10
San Antonio	$0.55	$0.40	$0.40	$0.55

As one part of the location decision, management wants an estimate of the total distribution cost for each alternative. Use the transportation method to calculate these estimates.

ACTIVE MODEL EXERCISE

This Active Model appears on the Student CD-ROM. It allows you to find the location that minimizes the total load–distance score.

QUESTIONS

1. What is the total load–distance score to the new Health-Watch medical facility if it is located at the center of gravity?
2. Fix the *y*-coordinate, and use the scroll bar to modify the *x*-coordinate. Can you reduce the total load–distance score?
3. Fix the *x*-coordinate, and use the scroll bar to modify the *y*- coordinate. Can you reduce the total load–distance score?
4. The center of gravity does not necessarily find the site with the minimum total load–distance score. Use both scroll bars to move the trial location, and see if you can improve (lower) the total load–distance score.

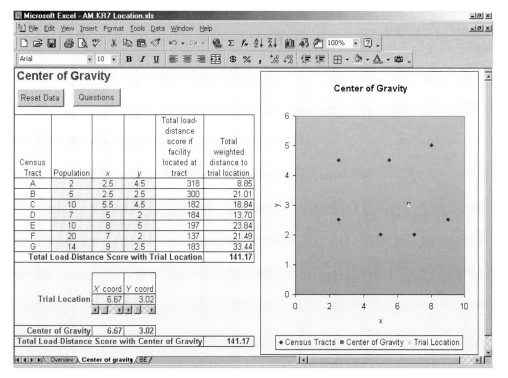

ACTIVE MODEL 10.1

Center of Gravity Using Data from Example 10.2

CASE   IMAGINATIVE TOYS

When Gerald Kramb arrived at the company offices early on Monday, July 1, 1991, to review the end-of-the-year sales and operating figures, several pressing matters commanded his attention. Sales had been much stronger than projected in 1990 to 1991, and existing production capacity had been fully utilized, with excessive overtime, to meet demand. Sales forecasts for the coming year indicated further rapid growth in demand, and Kramb knew that added capacity was needed. Several alternatives were available to the company, and he wanted to be sure that all the key factors were considered in making the decision.

Imaginative Toys was founded in Seattle, Washington in 1975. When he founded the company, Gerald Kramb envisioned that Imaginative Toys would develop and produce toys that "reach children's imagination and bring out their creativity." He liked to call these toys "learning toys." Two product lines quickly emerged as the mainstays of the company: construction toys that were similar to Lincoln Logs and Legos and maze and mind toys that focused on solving puzzles and developing hand–eye coordination. The toys were quickly accepted in the marketplace and became a popular choice for day care centers, preschool facilities, and elementary schools, as well as for parents.

Keys to success in this market were continual development of innovative products and a high level of product quality. Toys needed to be both creative and durable. Two other important factors were timing and availability. New products had to be ready to be introduced at the spring toy shows. Then, sufficient capacity was needed to fill retail orders by late summer in order to be ready for the Christmas buying season. Hence, Kramb knew that any capacity expansion decisions had to be made soon to meet next spring's production needs.

Because of the long-term nature of the decision, Kramb had asked Pat Namura, the marketing director, to prepare a four-year sales forecast. This forecast projected strong growth in sales during the four-year period for several reasons. First, the 1960s baby-boomers' children were reaching preschool and elementary school age, and child care facilities were rapidly expanding to accommodate these children, whose parents typically both worked. A second factor was the growth of international markets. Domestic sales remained strong, but international sales were growing at the rate of 25 percent per year. An important factor to consider was that, in a trendy business such as toys, the European market was one to two years behind the U.S. market. Namura attributed this lag to less developed television programming targeted toward children.

Finally, Imaginative Toys had just launched a new line of toys, and initial sales figures were very promising. The new line of toys was called Transformers. Much like a puzzle, each of the transformers could be rearranged and snapped together to form from two to four different toys. Designs were patterned after the robotic characters in children's Saturday morning cartoon shows. Namura was sure that this new line was just beginning to take off.

As Kramb reviewed the alternatives, he wished that expanding existing facilities were a viable option. Were the necessary space available, adding to the Seattle facilities would put much less pressure on the company's already thin management structure. As it was, suitable space was nowhere to be found in the Seattle area. However, the processes used to manufacture the three product lines could be replicated easily at any location. All three line processes were labor intensive, with plastic parts molding being the only skilled position. The construction toys consisted of molded plastic parts that were assembled into kits and packaged for shipment. The maze and mind toys required some parts fabrication from wood and metal materials. Then these parts were assembled into toys that were packed for shipment. The transformers were made from molded plastic parts that were then assembled with various fasteners and packed for shipment. The operating costs breakdown across all three toy lines was estimated to be 30 percent materials, 30 percent labor, 20 percent overhead, and 20 percent transportation and distribution. Obtaining the raw materials used to manufacture the toys would not be a problem for any location.

Kramb and his staff had researched two alternative locations for expansion. One was in a maquiladora in Nogales, Mexico, across the border from Tucson, Arizona. The improving trade relations and projected relaxation of tariffs and duties made this an attractive alternative. Labor costs also could be substantially reduced. If skilled labor was not available to mold and fabricate the parts, these operations could be done in the United States and the parts could be shipped across the border to Nogales for assembly and packaging.

The second alternative was to locate in Europe. A plastic injection molding company outside Brussels had decided to close and was looking for a buyer. Labor costs would be comparable to those in Seattle, but transportation cost would be 10 to 15 percent higher on toys shipped back to the U.S. market. However, the Brussels location was attractive because of the European Community's projected single-market program. It was designed to bring free movement of people, goods, capital, and services to the EC by January 1, 1993. The 1988 Cecchini report developed for the European Commission forecasted an increase of 5 percent in the gross EC product from this program. By producing in Brussels, Imaginative Toys also could avoid the 6 percent tariff on goods entering the EC.

As Kramb prepared to meet with his staff, he wondered how the company would be affected by expanding to a multisite operation. Conceivably, the decision would be to expand into both Mexico and Europe. If the sales projections held, the demand would support a three-plant network.

QUESTIONS

1. In making the location decision, what factors would you consider to be dominant? What factors would you consider secondary?

2. What role, if any, do the competitive priorities of Imaginative Toys play in the location decision?

Source: This case was prepared by Dr. Brooke Saladin, Wake Forest University, as a basis for classroom discussion.

CASE   R. U. REDDIE FOR LOCATION

The R. U. Reddie Corporation, located in Chicago, manufactures clothing specially designed for stuffed cartoon animals such as Snoopy and Wile-E-Coyote. Among the popular products are a wedding tuxedo for Snoopy and a flak jacket for Wile-E-Coyote. The latter is capable of stopping an Acme Rocket at close range . . . sometimes.

For many sales, the company relies upon the help of spoiled children who refuse to leave the toy store until their parents purchase a wardrobe for their stuffed toys. Rhonda Ulysses Reddie, owner of the company, is concerned over the market projections that indicate demand for the product is substantially greater than current plant capacity. The "most likely" projections indicate that the company will be short by 400,000 units next year, and thereafter 700,000 units annually. As such, Rhonda is considering opening a new plant to produce additional units.

BACKGROUND

The R. U. Reddie Corporation currently has three plants, which are located in Boston, Cleveland, and Chicago, respectively. The company's first plant was the Chicago plant, but as sales grew in the Midwest and Northeast, the Cleveland and Boston plants were built in short order. As the demand for wardrobes for stuffed animals moved west, warehouse centers were opened in St. Louis and Denver. The capacities of the three plants were increased to accommodate the demand. Each plant has its own warehouse to satisfy demands in its own area. Extra capacity left over was used to ship the product to St. Louis or Denver.

The new long-term forecasts provided by the sales department were both good news and bad news. The added revenues would certainly help Rhonda's profitability, but the company would have to buy another plant to realize the added profits. Space is not available at the existing plants, and the benefits of the new technology for manufacturing stuffed animal wardrobes are tantalizing. These factors motivated the search for the best location for a new plant. Rhonda has identified Denver and St. Louis as possible locations for the new plant.

RHONDA'S CONCERNS

A plant addition is a big decision. Rhonda started to think about the accuracy of the data she was able to obtain. She had market, financial, and operations concerns.

Market

The projected demands for years 2 through 10 show an annual increase of 700,000 units to a total of 2,000,000 units for each year. She had two concerns here. First, what if the projections for each city were off plus or minus 10 percent equally across the board? That is, total annual demands could be as low as 1,800,000 or as high as 2,200,000, with each city being affected the same as the others. Second, the marketing manager expressed a concern over a possible market shift from the Midwest and Northeast to the West. Under this scenario, there would be an additional demand of 50,000 units in St. Louis and 150,000 units in Denver, with the other cities staying at the "most likely" demand projections.

Financial

Rhonda realized that the net present value (NPV) of each alternative is an important input to the final decision. However, the accuracy of the estimates for the various costs is critical to determining good estimates of cash flows. She wondered if her decision would change if the COGS (variable production plus transportation costs) for each option was off by ± 10 percent. That is, what if the variable production costs and transportation costs of St. Louis are 10 percent higher than estimated while the variable production costs and transportation costs for Denver are 10 percent lower than estimated? Or vice versa? Further, what if the estimate for fixed costs is off by ±} 10 percent? For example, suppose St. Louis is 10 percent higher while Denver is 10 percent lower, or vice versa. Would the recommendation change under any of these situations?

Operations

The ultimate location of the new plant will determine the distribution assignments and the level of utilization of each plant in the network. Cutting back production in any of the plants will change the distribution assignments of all plants. Since there will be excess capacity in the system with a new plant under the assumption of the "most likely" demand projections, the capacity of the Cleveland plant could be cut in year 2 and beyond. Suppose Cleveland cuts back production by 50 (000) units a year from year 2 and beyond. Will this affect the choice between Denver and St. Louis? What is the impact on the distribution assignments of the plant? Further, there are some nonquantifiable concerns. First, the availability of a good workforce is much better in Denver than St. Louis because of the recent shutdown of a beanie baby factory. The labor market is much tighter in St. Louis and the prognosis is for continued short supply in the foreseeable future. Second, Denver metropolitan area has just instituted strict environmental regulations. Rhonda's new plant would adhere to existing laws, but the area is very environmentally conscious and more regulations may be coming in the future. It is very costly to modify a plant once operations have begun. Finally, Denver has a number of good suppliers with the capability to assist in production design (new wardrobe fashions). St. Louis also has suppliers but they cannot help with product development. Proximity to suppliers with product development capability is a "plus" for this industry.

DATA

The following data have been gathered for Rhonda:

1. The per-unit shipping cost based on the average ton-mile rates for the most efficient carriers is $0.0005 per mile. The average revenue per outfit is $8.00.

2. The company presently has the following capacity constraints:

	CAPACITY[1]
(i) Boston	400
(ii) Cleveland	400
(iii) Chicago	500

3. Data concerning the various locations is as follows:

CITY	MOST LIKELY DEMAND[1] FIRST YEAR	MOST LIKELY DEMAND AFTER[1] YEARS 2–10	CURRENT COSTS BUILDING AND EQUIPMENT[1,2]	ANNUAL FIXED COSTS (SGA)[1,3]	VARIABLE PRODUCTION COSTS/UNIT	LAND[1]
Boston	80	140	$9,500	$600	$3.80	$500
Cleveland	200	260	7,700	300	3.00	400
Chicago	370	430	8,600	400	3.25	600
St. Louis	440	500				
Denver	610	670				

[1] In 000s.

[2] Net book value of plant and equipment with remaining depreciable life of 10 years.

[3] Annual fixed costs do not include depreciation on plant and equipment.

4. New plant information:

ALTERNATIVE	BUILDING AND EQUIPMENT[1]	ANNUAL FIXED COSTS (SGA)[1,3]	VARIABLE PRODUCTION COSTS/UNIT	LAND[1]
Denver	$12,100	$550	$3.15	$1,200
St. Louis	10,800	750	3.05	800

[1] In 000s.

[2] Net book value of plant and equipment with remaining depreciable life of 10 years.

[3] Annual fixed costs do not include depreciation on plant and equipment.

5. The road mileage between the cities is:

	BOSTON	CLEVELAND	CHICAGO	ST. LOUIS	DENVER
Boston	—	650	1,000	1,200	2,000
Cleveland		—	350	600	1,400
Chicago			—	300	1,000
St. Louis				—	850
Denver					—

6. Basic assumptions you should follow:

- Terminal value (in 10 years) of the new investment is 50 percent of plant, equipment, and land cost.
- Tax rate of 40 percent.
- Straight-line depreciation for all assets over a 10-year life.
- R. U. Reddie is a 100 percent equity company with all equity financing and a weighted average cost of capital (WACC) of 11 percent.
- Capacity of the new plant production for the first year will be 500 (000) units.
- Capacity of the new plant production thereafter will be 900 (000) units.
- Cost of goods sold (COGS) equals variable costs of production plus total transportation costs.
- There is no cost to ship from a plant to its own warehouse. There is a production cost, however.

7. R. U. Reddie operations and logistics managers determined the shipping plan and cost of goods sold for the option of *not* building a new plant and simply using the existing capacities to their fullest extent (status quo solution):

Year 1	COGS = $4,692,000
Boston to Boston	80
Boston to St. Louis	320
Cleveland to Chicago	80
Cleveland to Cleveland	200
Cleveland to St. Louis	120
Chicago to Chicago	290
Chicago to Denver	210

Years 2–10	COGS = $4,554,000
Boston to Boston	140
Boston to St. Louis	260
Cleveland to Cleveland	260
Cleveland to St. Louis	140
Chicago to Chicago	430
Chicago to St. Louis	70

QUESTIONS

Your team has been asked to determine whether or not R. U. Reddie should build a new plant and, if so, where it should be located. Your report should consist of six parts.

1. A memo from your team to R. U. Reddie indicating your recommendation and a brief overview of the supporting evidence.

2. Model the location decision as a linear model. The objective function should be to minimize the total variable costs (production plus transportation costs). The variables should be the quantity to ship from each of the plants (including one of the alternative new plants) to each of the warehouses. You should have 20 variables (four plants and five warehouses). You should also have 9 constraints (four plant capacity constraints and five warehouse demand constraints). See the addendum for hints. You will need two models—one for Denver and one for St. Louis.

3. Use the Linear Programming Solver or the Transportation Method Solver in OM Explorer to solve for the optimal distribution plan for each alternative (i.e., Denver and St. Louis).

4. Compute the NPV of each alternative. Use the results from the linear models for the COGS for each alternative. (*Hint:* Your analysis will be simplified if you think in terms of incremental cash flows.) Create an easy-to-read spreadsheet for each alternative.

5. Do a sensitivity analysis of the quantitative factors mentioned in the case: Forecast errors (across the board and market shift), errors in COGS estimate, and errors in fixed cost estimates. Do each factor independent of the others and use the "most likely" projections as the base case. Summarize the results in one table.

6. Use the analysis in (5) to identify the key quantitative variables that determine the superiority of one alternative over another. Rationalize your final recommendation in light of all the considerations R. U. Reddie must make.

ADDENDUM

Here are some hints for your model.

1. The capacity constraint for Boston would look like this:

$$1B\text{-}B + 1B\text{-}CL + 1B\text{-}CH + 1B\text{-}D + 1B\text{-}SL \leq 400$$

The variable B-CH means Boston to Chicago in this example. You will need a total of four capacity constraints, one for each of the existing sites and one for the alternative site you are evaluating.

Remember that the new site will have a capacity limit of 500 in the first year, and 900 in the second year.

2. The demand constraint for Boston would look like this:

$$1B\text{-}B + 1CL\text{-}B + 1CH\text{-}B + 1D\text{-}B = 140$$

The Denver location alternative is depicted in this example (D-B represents the number of units produced in Denver and shipped to Boston). You will need a total of five demand constraints, one for each warehouse location. Notice that the demand constraints have equal signs to indicate that exactly that quantity must be received at each warehouse.

3. There is no need to put three zeros after each demand and capacity value. Define your variables to be "thou-sands of units shipped." Remember to multiply your final decisions and total variable costs by a thousand after you get your solution from the model.

4. Since the capacity and demand changes from year 1 to year 2, you will have to run your model twice for each location to get the data you need. You will also need to run the model and spreadsheets multiple times to do part (5) of the report.

SELECTED REFERENCES

Andel, T. "Site Selection Tools Dig Data." *Transportation & Distribution*, vol. 37, no. 6 (1996), pp. 77–81.

Bartlett, Christopher, and Sumantra Ghoshal. *Managing Across Borders*. Boston: Harvard Business School Press, 1989.

Bartness, A. D. "The Plant Location Puzzle." *Harvard Business Review* (March–April 1994), pp. 20–30.

"The Best Cities for Business." *Fortune* (November 4, 1991), pp. 52–84.

"The Boom Belt." *Business Week* (September 27, 1993), pp. 98–104.

Cook, David P., Chon-Huat Goh, and Chen H. Chung. "Service Typologies: A State of the Art Survey." *Production and Operations Management*, vol. 8, no. 3 (1999), pp. 318–338.

Cook, Thomas M., and Robert A. Russell. *Introduction to Management Sciences*. Englewood Cliffs, NJ: Prentice Hall, 1993.

DeForest, M. E. "Thinking of a Plant in Mexico?" *The Academy of Management Executive*, vol. 8, no. 1 (1994), pp. 33–40.

"Doing Well by Doing Good." *The Economist* (April 22, 2000), pp. 65–67.

Drezner, Z. *Facility Location: A Survey of Applications and Methods*. Secaucus, NJ: Springer-Verlag, 1995.

Ferdows, Kasra. "Making the Most of Foreign Factories." *Fortune* (March–April 1997), pp. 73–88.

Harris, Philip R., and Robert T. Moran. *Managing Cultural Differences*. Houston: Gulf, 1987.

"How Legend Lives Up to Its Name." *Business Week* (February 15, 1999), pp. 75–78.

Kanter, Rosabeth Moss. "Transcending Business Boundaries: 12,000 World Managers View Change." *Harvard Business Review* (May–June 1991), pp. 151–164.

"Korea." *Business Week* (July 31, 1995), pp. 56–64.

Klassen, Robert D., and D. Clay Whybark. "Barriers to the Management of International Operations." *Journal of Operations Management*, vol. 11, no. 4 (1994), pp. 385–396.

Kuehn, Alfred A., and Michael J. Hamburger. "A Heuristic Program for Locating Warehouses." *Management Science*, vol. 9, no. 4 (1963), pp. 643–666.

"Location Analysis Tools Help Starbucks Brew Up New Ideas." *Business Geographics*, www.geoplace.com.

"Long Distance: Innovative MCI Unit Finds Culture Shock in Colorado Springs." *Wall Street Journal* (June 25, 1996).

Love, Robert F., James G. Morris, and George O. Weslowsky. *Facilities Location: Models and Methods*. New York: North-Holland, 1988.

Lovelock, Christopher H., and George S. Yip. "Developing Global Strategies for Service Businesses." *California Management Review*, vol. 38, no. 2 (1996), pp. 64–86.

MacCormack, Alan D., Lawrence James Newman III, and David B. Rosenfield. "The New Dynamics of Global Manufacturing Site Location." *Sloan Management Review* (Summer 1994), pp. 69–77.

Markland, Robert E., and James R. Sweigart. *Quantitative Methods: Applications to Managerial Decision Making*. New York: John Wiley & Sons, 1987.

"Mexico: A Rough Road Back." *Business Week* (November 13, 1995), pp. 104–107.

Porter, Michael E. "The Competitive Advantage of Nations." *Harvard Business Review* (March–April 1990), pp. 73–93.

Roth, Aleda. "The Second Generation of Quality: Global Supply-Chain Integration in Japan and the United States." *The Quality Yearbook: 1998 Edition*. Edited by J. W. Cortada and J. A. Woods. New York: McGraw-Hill, 1998.

Schmenner, Roger W. *Making Business Location Decisions*. Englewood Cliffs, NJ: Prentice Hall, 1982.

"Spanning the Globe." *Wall Street Journal* (October 4, 1991).

Sugiura, Hideo. "How Honda Localizes Its Global Strategy." *Sloan Management Review* (Fall 1990), pp. 77–82.

"The Science of Site Selection." *National Real Estate Investor* (October 11, 2002).

Vargos, G. A., and T. W. Johnson. "An Analysis of Operational Experience in the U.S./Mexico Production Sharing (Maquiladora) Program." *Journal of Operations Management*, vol. 11, no. 1 (1993), pp. 17–34.

Vishwanath, Vijay, and David Hardling. "The Starbucks Effect." *Harvard Business Review* (March–April 2000), pp. 17–18.

Lean Systems

LEARNING GOALS   *After reading this chapter, you should be able to . . .*

IDENTIFY OR DEFINE

1. the characteristics of lean systems.
2. the strategic advantages of lean systems.
3. the implementation issues associated with the application of lean systems.

DESCRIBE OR EXPLAIN

4. how lean systems can facilitate the continuous improvement of processes.
5. how to calculate the number of containers of a specific item required for a production schedule in a lean system.
6. how the principles of lean systems can be applied to service processes.

TOYOTA PRODUCTION SYSTEM

If you were to select one company that is exemplary of excellence in automobile manufacturing, it would probably be Toyota (www.toyota.com). Worldwide in its presence, it has a total investment of $13.1 billion in 12 manufacturing plants that employ 32,500 associates in North America alone. Toyota was at the forefront of firms developing lean systems for manufacturing, and today the Toyota Production System (TPS) is one of the most admired lean manufacturing systems in existence. Replicating the system, however, is fraught with difficulties. What makes the system tick, and why could Toyota employ the system in so many different plants when others have difficulty?

Most outsiders see the TPS as a set of tools and procedures that are readily visible during a plant tour. While they are important for the success of the TPS, they are not the keys to the heart of the system. What most people overlook is that Toyota has built a learning organization over the course of 50 years. Lean systems require constant improvements to increase efficiency and reduce waste. Toyota has created a system that stimulates employees to experiment with their environment by seeking better ways whenever things go wrong. Toyota sets up all operations as experiments and teaches employees at all levels how to use the scientific method of problem solving.

There are four underlying principles of the TPS. First, all work must be completely specified as to content, sequence, timing, and outcome. Detail is important, otherwise there is no foundation for improvements. Second, every customer–supplier connection must be direct, unambiguously specifying the people involved, the form and quantity of the services or goods to be provided, the way the requests are made by each customer, and the expected time in which the requests will be met. Customer–supplier connections can be internal—employee to employee—or external—company to company.

Third, the pathway for every service and product must be simple and direct. That is, services and goods do not flow to the next available person or machine, but to a *specific* person or machine. With this principle, employees can determine, for example, that there is a capacity problem at a particular workstation and then analyze ways to resolve it.

The first three principles define the system in detail by specifying how employees do work, interact with each other, and design work flows. These specifications actually are "hypotheses" about the way the system should work. For example, if something goes wrong at a workstation enough times, the hypothesis about the methods the employee uses to do work is rejected. The fourth principle, then, is that any improvement to the system must be made in accordance with the scientific method, under the guidance of a teacher, at the lowest possible organizational level. The scientific method involves clearly stating a verifiable hypothesis of the form, "If we make the following specific changes, we expect to achieve this specific outcome." The hypothesis must then be tested under a variety of conditions. Working with a teacher, who is often the employees' supervisor, is a key to becoming a learning organization. Employees learn the scientific method and eventually become teachers of others. Finally, making improvements at the lowest level of the organization means that the employees who are actually doing the work are actively involved in making improvements.

These four principles are deceptively simple; however, they are difficult to replicate. Nonetheless, those organizations that have successfully implemented them have enjoyed the benefits of a lean system that adapts to change.

Source: Spear, Steven, and H. Kent Bowen. "Decoding the DNA of the Toyota Production System." *Harvard Business Review* (September–October 1999), pp. 97–106. Updated March 2003.

A Toyota Motor Corporation employee works on the assembly line at the Tsutsumi Plant in Tokyo. The TPS stimulates employees to experiment with their environment by seeking better ways when things go wrong.

Value chains involve internal linkages between a firm's core and supporting processes and external linkages with the processes of its customers and suppliers. In the preceding chapters in Part 3 of the text, we have seen how these linkages manifest themselves in the customer relationship, order fulfillment, and supplier relationship processes, and how these relationships are extended globally through effective location decisions. The Toyota Production System (TPS) is an excellent example of an approach for designing value chains known as **lean systems,** which are operations systems that maximize the value added of each of their activities. Value is created by paring unnecessary resources and delays from activities. Lean systems embody a total systems view that incorporates operations strategy, process design, quality management, capacity planning, layout design, supply-chain design, and technology and inventory management to create efficient processes. Lean systems can be applied to the provision of services as well as to the manufacture of products. As in manufacturing, each service business has to take an order from a customer, deliver a service, and collect revenue. Each service business has to purchase services or items, receive them, and pay for them. The firm may want to develop new services or hire and pay employees. Each of these processes bears considerable similarity to those in manufacturing firms, and they also typically contain huge amounts of waste. In Part 2 of this text we have discussed many ways to improve processes, regardless of whether they are manufacturing or nonmanufacturing processes. These same principles can be applied to make service processes lean, whether they are front-office, hybrid-office, or back-office designs (see Chapter 3, "Process Design Strategy").

One of the most popular systems that incorporate the generic elements of lean systems is the just-in-time (JIT) system. The **just-in-time (JIT) philosophy** is simple but powerful—*eliminate waste* by cutting excess capacity or inventory and removing non-value-added activities in operations. The goals are to produce services and products as needed and to continuously improve the value-added benefits of operations. A **JIT system** is the organization of resources, information flows, and decision rules that can enable an organization to realize the benefits of the JIT philosophy. We begin by identifying the characteristics of lean systems for service and manufacturing processes as embodied in the TPS or JIT systems, and then discuss how they can be used for continuous improvement of operations. We also address the operational benefits of lean systems and some of the implementation issues that companies face.

As you read this chapter, think about how the design of value chains using the lean systems approach is important to various departments across the organization, such as . . .

> ➤ **accounting,** which often must adjust its billing and cost accounting practices to take advantage of lean systems.
> ➤ **engineering,** which must design products that use more common parts so that fewer setups are required and focused factories and group technology can be used.
> ➤ **finance,** which must secure the working capital needed for a lean system.
> ➤ **human resources,** which must recruit, train, and evaluate the employees needed to successfully operate a lean system.
> ➤ **management information systems,** which must integrate the lean system with other information systems in the firm.
> ➤ **marketing,** which relies on lean systems to deliver high-quality services or products on time, at reasonable prices.
> ➤ **operations,** which is responsible for using the lean system in the production of services or goods.

lean systems Operations systems that maximize the value added of each of their activities by paring unnecessary resources and delays from them.

just-in-time (JIT) philosophy The belief that waste can be eliminated by cutting unnecessary capacity or inventory and removing non-value-added activities in operations.

JIT system The organization of resources, information flows, and decision rules that can enable an organization to realize the benefits of a JIT philosophy.

◉ CHARACTERISTICS OF LEAN SYSTEMS FOR SERVICES AND MANUFACTURING

Lean systems focus on reducing inefficiency and unproductive time in processes to improve continuously the process and the quality of the services or products they produce. Employee involvement and the reduction of non-value-added activities are essential to lean systems. In this section, we discuss the following characteristics of lean systems: pull method of work flow, consistent quality, small lot sizes, uniform workstation loads, standardized components and work methods, close supplier ties, flexible workforce, line flows, automation, and preventive maintenance.

How can lean systems be used in a service environment?

PULL METHOD OF WORK FLOW

Lean systems utilize the pull method of work flow. However, another popular method is the push method of work flow. To differentiate between these two methods, let us use a service example that involves a favorite pastime, eating. Consider a cafeteria on a busy downtown corner. During the busy periods around 12 P.M. and 5 P.M. lines develop, with hungry patrons eager to eat and then move on to other activities. The cafeteria offers choices of chicken (roasted or deep fried), roast beef, pork chops, hamburgers, hot dogs, salad, soup (chicken, pea, and clam chowder), bread (three types), beverages, and desserts (pies, ice cream, and cookies). Close coordination is required between the cafeteria "front office," where the service process interfaces with the customer, and the "back office," where the food is prepared in the kitchen. Shortages in food could cause riotous conditions, while excess food is wasteful. However, since it takes quite a while to cook some of the food items, the cafeteria uses a **push method,** in which the production of items begins in advance of customer needs. The kitchen produces to a forecast of actual customer needs for the various food items. The selection of food items in the cafeteria is actually an inventory of food, and the push method is geared to make sure that an adequate inventory is available.

Now consider a five-star restaurant where you are seated at a table and offered a menu of exquisite dishes, appetizers, soups, salads, and desserts. You can choose from pheasant (under glass, if you wish), filet mignon, porterhouse steak, yellowfin tuna, grouper, and lamb chops. There are several salad choices, which are prepared at your table. While some appetizers, soups, and desserts can be prepared in advance and brought to temperature just before serving, the main course and salads cannot. Your order for the salad and the main course becomes the signal for the server and the chef to begin preparation of your specific requests. For these items, the restaurant is using the **pull method,** in which customer demand activates the production of the service or item. Firms using the pull method must be able to fulfill the customer's demands within an acceptable amount of time. The cafeteria would have a difficult time using the pull method because it could not wait until an item was nearly gone before asking the kitchen to begin processing another batch.

The choice between the push and pull methods is often situational. Firms that have highly repetitive processes and well-defined work flows of standardized items often use the pull method because it allows closer control of inventory and output at the workstations. The five-star restaurant uses the pull method to control inventory costs (and the freshness and taste of the meal). Firms that have processes with long lead times, reasonably accurate forecasts of demand, a variety of products that require common processes, and customers who will not wait long for the product tend to produce to stock and use a push method. That is the case with the cafeteria and many manufacturing firms. Firms using an assemble-to-order strategy sometimes use both methods: the push method to produce the standardized components and the pull method to fulfill the customer's request for a particular combination of the components.

push method A method in which the production of the item begins in advance of customer needs.

pull method A method in which customer demand activates production of the service or item.

Diners fill their plates at a restaurant buffet. Since the food items must be prepared in advance, the restaurant uses a push method of work flow.

CONSISTENT QUALITY

Lean systems seek to eliminate process errors and rework in order to achieve a uniform flow of work. Efficient operations consistently meet the customer's expectations for the service or product by adhering to advertised or customer-requested specifications even if it involves dimensions of top quality. Consistently hitting the target is an important characteristic of lean systems. Implementing the behavioral and statistical methods of total quality management and Six Sigma help to maintain consistency in operations (see Chapter 5, "Process Performance and Quality"). Lean systems incorporate *quality at the source*, with employees acting as their own quality inspectors.

For example, a soldering operation at the Texas Instruments antenna department had a defect rate that varied from zero to 50 percent on a daily basis, averaging about 20 percent. To compensate, production planners increased the lot sizes, which only increased inventory levels and did nothing to reduce the number of defective items. Engineers discovered through experimentation that gas temperature was a critical variable in producing defect-free items. They devised statistical control charts for the operators to use to monitor gas temperature and adjust it themselves. Process yields immediately improved and stabilized at 95 percent, eventually enabling management to implement a lean system.

One approach for implementing quality at the source is a practice the Japanese call *andon*, which authorizes employees to stop a production line by pulling a cord if quality problems arise at their stations. Stopping a production line is a costly action that brings a problem to everyone's attention. Such stoppages can amount to thousands of dollars per minute. Employees often have the option to signal a need for help without actually stopping the line. Needless to say, management must realize the enormous responsibility this method places on the employees and must prepare them properly.

SMALL LOT SIZES

Lean systems use lot sizes that are as small as possible. A **lot** is a quantity of items that are processed together. Small lots have the advantage of reducing the average level of inventory relative to large lots (see Chapter 15, "Inventory Management"). Small lots pass through the system faster than large lots. In addition, if any defective items are discovered, large lots cause longer delays because the entire lot must be examined to find all the items that need rework. Finally, small lots help achieve a uniform workload on the system. Large lots consume large chunks of capacity at workstations and, therefore, complicate scheduling. Small lots can be juggled more effectively, enabling schedulers to efficiently utilize capacities.

> **lot** A quantity of items that are processed together.

Although small lots are beneficial to operations, they have the disadvantage of increased setup frequency. A **setup** is the group of activities needed to readjust a process between successive lots of items, sometimes referred to as a *changeover*. Typically, a setup takes the same time regardless of the lot size. Consequently, many small lots, in lieu of several large lots, may result in waste in the form of idle employees and equipment. Setup times must be brief to realize the benefits of small-lot production.

> **setup** The group of activities needed to readjust a process between successive lots of items, sometimes referred to as a *changeover*.

Achieving brief setup times often requires close cooperation among engineering, management, and labor. For example, changing dies on large presses to form automobile parts from sheet metal can take three to four hours. At Honda's Marysville, Ohio plant—where four stamping lines stamp all the exterior and major interior body panels for Accord production—teams worked on ways to reduce the changeover time for the massive dies. As a result, a complete change of dies for a giant 2,400-ton press now takes less than 8 minutes. The goal of **single-digit setup** means having setup times of less than 10 minutes. Some techniques to reduce setup times include using conveyors for die storage, moving large dies with cranes, simplifying dies, enacting machine controls, using microcomputers to automatically feed and position work, and preparing for changeovers while the current job is being processed.

> **single-digit setup** The goal of having a setup time of less than 10 minutes.

UNIFORM WORKSTATION LOADS

A lean system works best if the daily load on individual workstations is relatively uniform. Service processes can achieve uniform workstation loads by using reservation systems. For example, hospitals schedule surgeries in advance of the actual service so that the facilities and facilitating goods can be ready when the time comes. The load on the surgery rooms and surgeons can be leveled to make the best use of these resources. Another approach is to use differential pricing of the service to manage the demand for it. Uniform loads is the rationale behind airlines promoting weekend travel or red-eye flights that begin late in the day and end in the early morning. Efficiencies can be realized when the load on the resources can be managed.

For manufacturing processes, uniform loads can be achieved by assembling the same type and number of units each day, thus creating a uniform daily demand at all workstations. Capacity planning, which recognizes capacity constraints at critical workstations, and line balancing are used to develop the master production schedule. (See Supplement F, "Master Production Scheduling", on the Student CD-ROM, for details.) For example, at Toyota, the production plan may call for 4,500 vehicles per week for the next month. That requires two full shifts, five days per week, producing 900 vehicles each day, or 450 per shift. Three models are produced: Camry (C), Avalon (A), and Sienna (S). Suppose that Toyota needs 200 Camrys, 150 Avalons, and 100 Siennas per shift to satisfy market demand. To produce 450 units in one shift of 480 minutes, the line must roll out a vehicle every 480/450 = 1.067 minutes.

Three ways of devising a master production schedule for the vehicles are of interest here. First, with big-lot production, all daily requirements of a model are produced in one batch before another model is started. The sequence of 200 Cs, 150 As, and 100 Ss would be repeated once per shift. Not only would these big lots increase the average cycle inventory level but they also would cause lumpy requirements on all the workstations feeding the assembly line.

mixed-model assembly A type of assembly that produces a mix of models in smaller lots.

The second option uses **mixed-model assembly**, producing a mix of models in smaller lots. Note that the production requirements are in the ratio of 4 Cs to 3 As to 2 Ss, found by dividing the model's production requirements by the greatest common divisor, or 50. Thus, the Toyota planner could develop a production cycle consisting of 9 units: 4 Cs, 3 As, and 2 Ss. The cycle would repeat in 9(1.067) = 9.60 minutes, for a total of 50 times per shift (480 min/9.60 min = 50).

A sequence of C–S–C–A–C–A–C–S–A, repeated 50 times per shift, would achieve the same total output as the other options. This third option is feasible only if the setup times are very brief. The sequence generates a steady rate of component requirements for the various models and allows the use of small lot sizes at the feeder workstations. Consequently, the capacity requirements at those stations are greatly smoothed. These requirements can be compared to actual capacities during the planning phase, and modifications to the production cycle, production requirements, or capacities can be made as necessary.

STANDARDIZED COMPONENTS AND WORK METHODS

In highly repetitive service operations, great efficiencies can be gained by analyzing work methods and documenting the improvements for all employees to use. For example, UPS consistently monitors work methods and revises them as necessary to improve service. In manufacturing, the standardization of components, called *part commonality* or *modularity*, increases repeatability. For example, a firm producing 10 products from 1,000 different components could redesign its products so that they consist of only 100 different components with larger daily requirements. Because the requirements per component increase, so does repeatability; that is, each worker performs a standardized task or work method more often each day. Productivity tends to increase because, with increased repetition, workers learn to do the task more efficiently. Standardization of components and work methods aids in achieving the high-productivity, low-inventory objectives of lean systems.

CLOSE SUPPLIER TIES

Because lean systems operate with very low levels of capacity slack or inventory, close relationships with suppliers are necessary. Stock shipments must be frequent, have short lead times, arrive on schedule, and be of high quality. A contract might require a supplier to deliver goods to a facility as often as several times per day. Purchasing managers focus on three areas: reducing the number of suppliers, using local suppliers, and improving supplier relations (see Chapter 9, "Supply-Chain Design").

Typically, one of the first actions undertaken when a lean system is implemented is to pare the number of suppliers. Xerox, for example, reduced the number of its suppliers from 5,000 to just 300. This approach puts a lot of pressure on these suppliers to deliver high-quality components on time. To compensate, lean system users extend their contracts with these suppliers and give them firm advance-order information. In addition, they include their suppliers in the early phases of product design to avoid problems after production has begun. They also work with their suppliers' vendors, trying to achieve synchronized inventory flows throughout the entire supply chain.

Manufacturers using lean systems generally utilize local suppliers. For instance, when GM located its Saturn complex in Tennessee, many suppliers clustered nearby. Harley-Davidson reduced the number of its suppliers and gave preference to those close to its plants—for example, three-fourths of the suppliers for the Milwaukee engine plant are located within a 175-mile radius. Geographic proximity means that the company can reduce the need for safety stocks. Companies that have no suppliers close by must rely on a finely tuned supplier delivery system. For example, New United Motor Manufacturing, Incorporated (NUMMI), the joint venture between GM and Toyota in California, has suppliers in Indiana, Ohio, and Michigan. Through a carefully coordinated system involving trains and piggyback truck trailers, suppliers deliver enough parts for exactly one day's production each day.

Users of lean systems also find that a cooperative orientation with suppliers is essential. The lean system philosophy is to look for ways to improve efficiency and reduce inventories throughout the supply chain. Close cooperation between companies and their suppliers can be a win–win situation for everyone. Better communication of component requirements, for example, enables more efficient inventory planning and delivery scheduling by suppliers, thereby improving supplier profit margins. Customers can then negotiate lower component prices. Suppliers also should be included in the design of new services or products so that inefficient designs can be avoided before production begins. Close supplier relations cannot be established and maintained if companies view their suppliers as adversaries whenever contracts are negotiated. Rather, they should consider suppliers to be partners in a venture, wherein both parties have an interest in maintaining a long-term, profitable relationship.

FLEXIBLE WORKFORCE

Workers in flexible workforces can be trained to perform more than one job. The more customized the service, as in front-office and hybrid-office process designs, the greater is the need for a multiskilled workforce. For example, stereo repair shops require broadly trained personnel who can identify a wide variety of component problems when the customer brings the defective unit into the shop and who then can repair the unit. Alternatively, back-office designs, such as the mail-processing operations at a large post office have employees with more narrowly defined jobs because of the repetitive nature of the tasks they must perform. These employees do not have to acquire as many alternative skills. In situations such as at the Texas Instruments antenna department, shifting workers to other jobs may require extensive, costly training. Flexibility can be very beneficial: Workers can be shifted among workstations to help relieve bottlenecks as they arise without resorting to inventory buffers—an important aspect of the uniform flow of lean systems. Also, workers can step in and do the job for those who are on vacation or who are out sick. Although assigning workers to tasks they do not usually perform may reduce efficiency, some rotation relieves boredom and refreshes workers.

LINE FLOWS

Managers of hybrid-office and back-office service processes can organize their employees and equipment to provide uniform work flows through the process and, thereby,

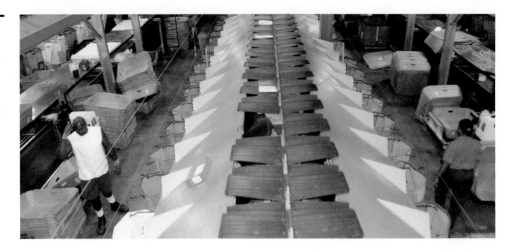

Employees of United Parcel Service work on a small package line in the $1 billion air hub in Louisville, Kentucky. The packages (in the center of the photo) are automatically deposited in the bin dedicated to their destination.

eliminate wasted employee time. Banks use this strategy in their check-processing operations, as does UPS in its parcel-sorting process. Line flows can reduce the frequency of setups. If volumes of specific products are large enough, groups of machines and workers can be organized into a line-flow layout (see Chapter 7, "Process Layout") to eliminate setups entirely. If volume is insufficient to keep a production line of similar products busy, *group technology* can be used to design small production lines that manufacture, in volume, families of components with common attributes. Changeovers from a component in one product family to the next component in the same family are minimal.

Another tactic used to reduce or eliminate setups is the one-worker, multiple-machines (OWMM) approach, which essentially is a one-person line. One worker operates several machines, with each machine advancing the process a step at a time. Because the same product is made repeatedly, setups are eliminated.

AUTOMATION

Automation plays a big role in lean systems and is a key to low-cost operations. Money freed up because of inventory reductions or other efficiencies can be invested in automation to reduce costs. The benefits, of course, are greater profits, greater market share (because prices can be cut), or both. Automation can play a big role in providing lean services. For example, banks offer ATMs that provide various bank services on demand 24 hours a day. Automation should be planned carefully, however. Many managers believe that if some automation is good, more is better. That is not always the case. When GM initiated Buick City, for example, it installed 250 robots, some with vision systems for mounting windshields. Unfortunately, the robots skipped black cars because they could not "see" them. New software eventually solved the problem; however, GM management found that humans could do some jobs better than robots and replaced 30 robots with humans.

PREVENTIVE MAINTENANCE

Because lean systems emphasize finely tuned flows of work and little capacity slack or buffer inventory between workstations, unplanned machine downtime can be disruptive. Preventive maintenance can reduce the frequency and duration of machine downtime. After performing routine maintenance activities, the technician can test other parts that might need to be replaced. Replacement during regularly scheduled maintenance periods is easier and quicker than dealing with machine failures during production. Maintenance is done on a schedule that balances the cost of the preventive maintenance program against the risks and costs of machine failure. Services that are highly dependent on machinery can make good use of routine preventive maintenance. For example, entertainment services, such as Walt Disney World, must have dependable people-moving apparatus to accommodate large volumes of customers.

A monorail heads toward Cinderella's Castle and Space Mountain in Florida's Disney World. Preventive maintenance ensures reliable service to customers.

Another tactic is to make workers responsible for routinely maintaining their own equipment and develop employee pride in keeping their machines in top condition. This tactic, however, typically is limited to general housekeeping chores, minor lubrication, and adjustments. Maintenance of high-tech machines needs trained specialists. Nonetheless, performing even simple maintenance tasks goes a long way toward improving machine performance.

Managerial Practice 11.1 shows how Internet grocers have used the principles of lean systems to advantage.

CONTINUOUS IMPROVEMENT USING A LEAN SYSTEMS APPROACH

By spotlighting areas that need improvement, lean systems lead to continuous improvement in quality and productivity. The Japanese term for this approach to process improvement is *kaizen* (see Chapter 5, "Process Performance and Quality"). The key to kaizen is the understanding that excess capacity or inventory hides underlying problems with the processes that produce a service or product. Lean systems provide the mechanism for management to reveal the problems by systematically lowering capacities or inventories until the problems are exposed. For example, Figure 11.1, characterizes the philosophy behind continuous improvement with lean systems. In services, the water surface represents service system capacity, such as staff levels. In manufacturing, the water surface represents product and component inventory levels. The rocks represent problems encountered in the provision of services or products. When the water surface is high enough, the boat passes over the rocks because the high level of capacity or inventory covers up problems. As capacity or inventory shrinks, rocks are exposed. Ultimately, the boat will hit a rock if the water surface falls far enough. Through lean systems, workers, supervisors, engineers, and analysts apply methods for

How can lean systems facilitate continuous improvement?

MANAGERIAL PRACTICE 11.1

INTERNET GROCERS USE LEAN SYSTEMS FOR THEIR ORDER FULFILLMENT PROCESSES

Do you need to stock your kitchen but have no time to go to the grocery store? Now you can solve that problem over the Internet. Today, online grocers service customers who prefer to use the Internet to do their shopping. Not surprisingly, the online shopping option is rapidly gaining popularity. Web grocery sales were estimated to triple from 2000 to 2003, and a quarter of all grocery stores now offer Web shopping. Whereas many Internet grocers failed in their first attempt at online grocery service during the Internet boom, e-grocers today are keeping costs down by limiting when and where they deliver. As a result, companies such as FreshDirect have created successful operations that offer low-cost, high-quality groceries with dependable, on-time delivery.

FreshDirect competes for online business with other Internet grocers, including MyWebGrocer.com, Peapod, Safeway.com, and Netgrocer.com. Although fundamentally built around the same core competencies, each e-grocer has different delivery and cost-cutting methods. For instance, MyWebGrocer.com partnered with over 200 stores nationwide. Customers pick which store they prefer and MyWebGrocer.com handles the delivery of the order. Conversely, Safeway.com leverages their own vast inventory and nationwide availability to meet customer needs. Many companies cover delivery costs by offering a sliding delivery price scale depending on the amount ordered—the more ordered, the less the customer pays for delivery.

In the case of FreshDirect, which services only New York City, customers can log onto its Web site and order from a selection of over 3,000 fresh foods stored in a 300,000 square foot warehouse located in Long Island City. Customers pick a convenient time for delivery as early as the next day, and FreshDirect guarantees the quality of the food. FreshDirect, like other online grocers, requires a $40 minimum order but charges a flat $3.95 delivery fee. In order to meet the promise of delivery and freshness, FreshDirect relies on lean-system principles for its order fulfillment process, which are applied in the following way:

- Nothing happens until a customer places an order on the Web site (*pull method*).
- An automated conveyor belt moves through the warehouse (*automation*), which is separated into climate zones to ensure freshness.
- At each station, an expert in that department places the groceries in a box before the conveyor belt moves the box to the next station (*line flow*).
- The boxes are scanned for accuracy before being loaded onto a refrigerated truck (*high quality, consistent quality*).

E-grocers are wary of the pitfalls that befell their predecessors; consequently, companies like FreshDirect are limited in their service area. In an industry where the average online bill is $125 compared to $25 per visit to a regular store, however, the competition to offer JIT delivery to wider regions is growing.

Source: McLaughlin, Katy. "Back from the Dead: Buying Groceries Online—Armchair Shoppers Embrace Revamped Web Supermarkets; Which Ones Deliver?" *Wall Street Journal* (February 25, 2003), page D1.

continuous improvement to demolish the exposed rock. The coordination required for the pull system of material flows in lean systems identifies problems in time for corrective action to be taken.

Service processes, such as scheduling, billing, order taking, accounting, and financial planning can be improved with lean systems. Continuous improvement means that employees and managers continue to seek ways to improve operations. In service operations, a common approach used by managers is to place stress on the system by reducing the number of employees doing a particular activity or series of activities until the process begins to slow or come to a halt. The problems can be identified, and ways for overcoming the problems can be explored.

In manufacturing, eliminating the problem of too much scrap might require improving work methods, employee quality training, and supplier quality. The desire to eliminate capacity imbalances might focus attention on the master production schedule and workforce flexibility. Reducing unreliable deliveries calls for cooperating better with suppliers or replacing suppliers. Maintaining low inventories, periodically stressing the system to identify problems, and focusing on the elements of the lean system lie at the heart of continuous improvement. For example, the Kawasaki plant in Nebraska periodically cuts safety stocks almost to zero.

FIGURE 11.1

**Continuous Improvement
with Lean Systems**

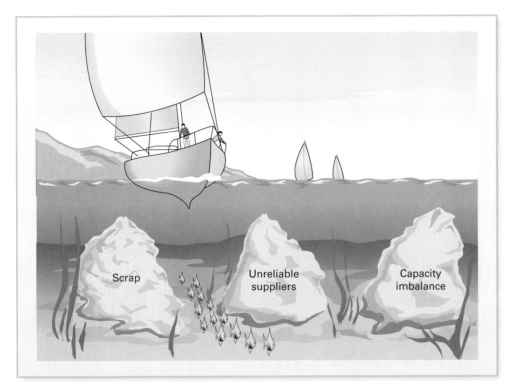

Problems are exposed, recorded, and later assigned as improvement projects. After
the improvements have been made, inventories are permanently cut to the new level.
Many firms have used this trial-and-error process to develop more efficient manufacturing operations.

⬤ THE KANBAN SYSTEM

One of the most publicized aspects of lean systems, and the TPS in particular, is the
kanban system developed by Toyota. **Kanban**, meaning "card" or "visible record" in
Japanese, refers to cards used to control the flow of production through a factory. In
the most basic kanban system, a card is attached to each container of items that have
been produced. The container holds a given percent of the daily requirements for an
item. When the user of the parts empties a container, the card is removed from the container and put on a receiving post. The empty container is taken to the storage area.
The card signals the need to produce another container of the part. When a container
has been refilled, the card is put back on the container, which is then returned to a storage area. The cycle begins again when the user of the parts retrieves the container with
the card attached.

Figure 11.2 shows how a single-card kanban system works when a fabrication cell
feeds two assembly lines. As an assembly line needs more parts, the kanban card for
those parts is taken to the receiving post and a full container of parts is removed from
the storage area. The receiving post accumulates cards for assembly lines and a scheduler sequences the production of replenishment parts. In this example, the fabrication
cell will produce product 2 (red) before it produces product 1 (green). The cell consists
of three different operations, but operation 2 has two workstations. Once production
has been initiated in the cell, the product begins on operation 1, but could be routed
to either of the workstations performing operation 2, depending on the workload at
the time. Finally, the product is processed on operation 3 before being taken to the
storage area.

How is the flow of materials in a
factory controlled in a lean system?

kanban A word meaning "card"
or "visible record" in Japanese;
refers to cards used to control the
flow of production through a
factory.

FIGURE 11.2   Single-Card Kanban System

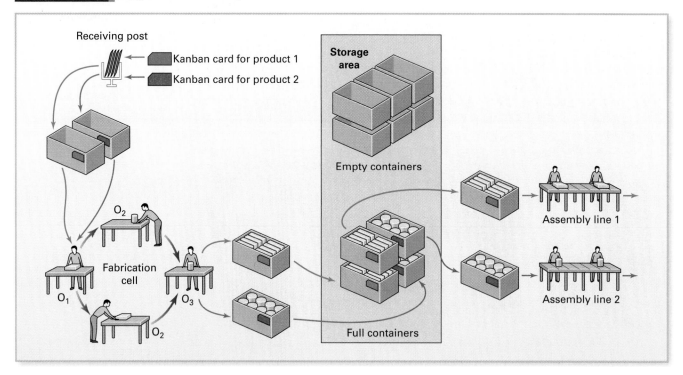

GENERAL OPERATING RULES

The operating rules for the single-card system are simple and are designed to facilitate the flow of materials while maintaining control of inventory levels.

  1. Each container must have a card.
  2. The assembly line always withdraws materials from the fabrication cell. The fabrication cell never pushes parts to the assembly line because, sooner or later, parts will be supplied that are not yet needed for production.
  3. Containers of parts must never be removed from a storage area without a kanban first being posted on the receiving post.
  4. The containers should always contain the same number of good parts. The use of nonstandard containers or irregularly filled containers disrupts the production flow of the assembly line.
  5. Only nondefective parts should be passed along to the assembly line to make the best use of materials and workers' time.
  6. Total production should not exceed the total amount authorized on the kanbans in the system.

Toyota uses a two-card system, based on a withdrawal card and a production-order card, to control withdrawal quantities more closely. The withdrawal card specifies the item and the quantity the user of the item should withdraw from the producer of the item, as well as the stocking locations for both the user and the producer. The production-order card specifies the item and the production quantity to be produced, the materials required and where to find them, and where to store the finished item. Materials cannot be withdrawn without a withdrawal card, and production cannot begin without a production-order card. The cards are attached to containers when production commences.

DETERMINING THE NUMBER OF CONTAINERS

The number of authorized containers in the TPS determines the amount of authorized inventory. Management must make two determinations: (1) the number of units to be held by each container and (2) the number of containers flowing back and forth between the supplier station and the user station. The first decision amounts to determining the lot size, which requires balancing the cost of setup with the cost of holding inventory in stock, among other considerations (see Chapter 15, "Inventory Management" and Chapter 16, "Resource Planning").

The number of containers flowing back and forth between two stations directly affects the quantities of work-in-process inventory and safety stock. The containers spend some time in production, in a line waiting, in a storage location, or in transit. The key to determining the number of containers required is to estimate accurately the average lead time needed to produce a container of parts. The lead time is a function of the processing time per container at the supplier station, the waiting time during the production process, and the time required for materials handling. The number of containers needed to support the user station equals the average demand during the lead time, plus some safety stock to account for unexpected circumstances, divided by the number of units in one container. Therefore, the number of containers is

$$\kappa = \frac{\text{Average demand during lead time + safety stock}}{\text{Number of units per container}}$$

$$= \frac{d(\overline{\omega} + \overline{\rho})(1 + \alpha)}{c}$$

where

κ = number of containers for a part

d = expected daily demand for the part, in units

$\overline{\omega}$ = average waiting time during the production process plus materials handling time per container, in fractions of a day

$\overline{\rho}$ = average processing time per container, in fractions of a day

c = quantity in a standard container of the part

α = a policy variable that adds safety stock to cover for unexpected circumstances (Toyota uses a value of no more than 10 percent)

The number of containers must, of course, be an integer. Rounding κ up provides more inventory than desired, whereas rounding κ down provides less.

The kanban system allows management to fine-tune the flow of materials in the system in a straightforward way. For example, removing cards from the system reduces the number of authorized containers of the part, thus reducing the inventory of the part.

The container quantity, c, and the efficiency factor, α, are variables that management can use to control inventory. Adjusting c changes the lot sizes, and adjusting α changes the amount of safety stock.

Determining the Appropriate Number of Containers

EXAMPLE 11.1

The Westerville Auto Parts Company produces rocker-arm assemblies for use in the steering and suspension systems of four-wheel-drive trucks. A typical container of parts spends 0.02 day in processing and 0.08 day in materials handling and waiting during its manufacturing cycle. The daily demand for the part is 2,000 units. Management believes that demand for the rocker-arm assembly is uncertain enough to warrant a safety stock equivalent of 10 percent of its authorized inventory.

a. If there are 22 parts in each container, how many containers should be authorized?

b. Suppose that a proposal to revise the plant layout would cut materials handling and waiting time per container to 0.06 day. How many containers would be needed?

TUTOR 11.1

Tutor 11.1 on the Student CD-ROM provides a new example of using the model to determine the number of containers.

SOLUTION

a. If $d = 2,000$ units/day, $\bar{\rho} = 0.02$ day, $\alpha = 0.10$, $\bar{\omega} = 0.08$ day, and $c = 22$ units,

$$\kappa = \frac{2,000(0.08 + 0.02)(1.10)}{22} = \frac{220}{22} = 10 \text{ containers}$$

b. Figure 11.3 from OM Explorer shows that the number of containers drops to 8.

FIGURE 11.3

OM Explorer Solver for Number of Containers

Solver - Number of Containers

Enter data in yellow-shaded areas.

Daily Expected Demand	2000
Quantity in Standard Container	22
Container Waiting Time (days)	0.06
Processing Time (days)	0.02
Policy Variable	10%
Containers Required	8

DECISION POINT The average lead time per container is $\bar{\omega} + \bar{\rho}$. With a lead time of 0.10 day, 10 containers are needed. However, if the improved facility layout reduces the materials handling time and waiting time, $\bar{\omega}$, to 0.06 day, only 8 containers are needed. The maximum authorized inventory of the rocker-arm assembly is κc units. Thus, in part (a), the maximum authorized inventory is 220 units, but in part (b), it is only 176 units. Reducing $\bar{\omega} + \bar{\rho}$ by 20 percent has reduced the inventory of the part by 20 percent. Management must balance the cost of the relayout (a one-time charge) against the long-term benefits of inventory reduction.

OTHER KANBAN SIGNALS

Cards are not the only way to signal the need for more production of a part. Other, less formal methods are possible, including container and containerless systems.

CONTAINER SYSTEM. Sometimes, the container itself can be used as a signal device: An empty container signals the need to fill it. Unisys took this approach for low-value items. The amount of inventory of the part is adjusted by adding or removing containers. This system works well when the container is specially designed for a particular part and no other parts could accidentally be put in the container. Such is the case when the container is actually a pallet or fixture used to position the part during precision processing.

CONTAINERLESS SYSTEM. Systems requiring no containers have been devised. In assembly-line operations, operators having their own workbench areas put completed units on painted squares, one unit per square. Each painted square represents a container, and the number of painted squares on each operator's bench is calculated to balance the line flow. When the subsequent user removes a unit from one of the producer's squares, the empty square signals the need to produce another unit.

McDonald's uses a containerless system. Information entered by the order taker at the cash register is transmitted to the cooks and assemblers, who produce the sandwiches requested by the customer.

JIT II

The JIT II concept was conceived and implemented by the Bose Corporation, a producer of high-quality professional sound and speaker systems. In a JIT II system, the supplier is brought into the plant to be an active member of the purchasing office of the customer. The *in-plant representative* is on site full-time at the supplier's expense and is empowered to plan and schedule the replenishment of materials from the supplier. This is an example of vendor-managed inventories (see Chapter 9, "Supply-Chain Design"). Typically, the representative's duties include

- issuing purchase orders to his or her own firm on behalf of Bose;
- working on design ideas to help save costs and improve manufacturing processes; and
- managing production schedules for suppliers, materials contractors, and other subcontractors.

The in-plant representative replaces the buyer, the salesperson, and sometimes the materials planner in a typical JIT arrangement. Thus, JIT II fosters extremely close interaction with suppliers. The qualifications for a supplier to be included in the program are stringent.

In general, JIT II offers the following benefits to the customer:

- Liberated from administrative tasks, the purchasing staff is able to work on improving efficiencies in other areas of procurement.
- Communication and purchase order placement are improved dramatically.
- The cost of materials is reduced immediately, and the savings are ongoing.
- Preferred suppliers are brought into the product design process earlier.
- A natural foundation is provided for electronic data interchange (EDI), effective paperwork, and administrative savings.

In general, JIT II offers the following benefits to the supplier:

- It eliminates sales effort.
- Communication and purchase order placement are improved dramatically.
- The volume of business rises at the start of the program and continues to grow as new products are introduced.
- A renewable contract is provided, with no end date and no rebidding.
- The supplier can communicate with, and sell directly to, engineering.
- Invoicing and payment administration are efficient.

Several large corporations have implemented JIT II in their supply chains. IBM and Intel have more than 50 on-site JIT II suppliers. AT&T, Honeywell, Roadway Express, Ingersoll-Rand, and Westinghouse also use the system. JIT II is an advance over other lean systems because it provides the organizational structure needed to improve supplier coordination by integrating the logistics, production, and purchasing processes.

OPERATIONAL BENEFITS OF LEAN SYSTEMS

When corporate strategy centers on dramatic improvements in inventory turnover and labor productivity, a lean system can be the solution. For example, lean systems, such as just-in-time, form an integral part of corporate strategies emphasizing time-based competition because they focus on cutting cycle times, improving inventory turnover, and increasing labor productivity.

Lean systems have many operational benefits. They

- reduce space requirements;
- reduce inventory investment in purchased parts, raw materials, work-in-process, and finished goods;

What are the benefits of lean systems?

- reduce lead times;
- increase the productivity of direct-labor employees, indirect-support employees, and clerical staff;
- increase equipment utilization;
- reduce paperwork and require only simple planning systems;
- set valid priorities for scheduling;
- encourage participation by the workforce; and
- increase service or product quality.

One goal is to drive setup times so low that production of one end unit or part becomes economical. Although this goal is rarely achieved, the focus still is on small-lot production. In addition, constant attention is given to removing non-value-added activities in processes. The result is less need for storage space, inventory investment, or capacity. Smaller lot sizes and smoothed flows of materials help reduce lead times, increase employee productivity, and improve equipment utilization.

A primary operational benefit is the simplicity of the system. For example, in manufacturing, product mix or volume changes can be accomplished by adjusting the number of kanbans in the system. The priority of each production order is reflected in the sequence of the kanbans on the post. Production orders for parts that are running low are placed before those for parts that have more supply.

Lean systems also involve a considerable amount of employee participation through small-group interaction sessions, which have resulted in improvements in many aspects of operations, not the least of which is service or product quality. Overall, the advantages of lean systems have caused many managers to reevaluate their own systems and consider redesigning processes to achieve many of the characteristics of lean systems.

IMPLEMENTATION ISSUES

What can be done to make employees more receptive to the changes associated with lean systems?

The benefits of lean systems seem to be outstanding, yet problems can arise even after a lean system has long been operational. Even the Japanese, who pioneered JIT practices in the automobile industry, are not immune to problems: Tokyo is experiencing monumental traffic jams owing in large measure to truck deliveries to JIT manufacturers—small trucks make up 47 percent of Tokyo's traffic. In this section, we address some of the issues managers should be aware of when implementing a lean system.

ORGANIZATIONAL CONSIDERATIONS

Implementing a lean system requires management to consider issues of worker stress, cooperation and trust among workers and management, and reward systems and labor classifications.

HUMAN COSTS OF LEAN SYSTEMS. Lean systems can be coupled with statistical process control (SPC) to reduce variations in outputs. However, this combination requires a high degree of regimentation and sometimes causes stress in the workforce. For example, in the Toyota Production System, workers must meet specified cycle times, and, with SPC, they must follow prescribed problem-solving methods. Such systems might make workers feel pushed and stressed, causing productivity losses or quality reductions. In addition, workers might feel that they have lost some autonomy because of the close linkages in work flows between stations with little or no excess capacity or safety stocks. Managers can mitigate some of these effects by allowing slack in the system through the judicious use of safety stock inventories or capacity slack and by emphasizing work flows instead of worker pace. Managers also can promote the use of work teams and allow them to determine their task assignments or rotations within the team's domain of responsibility.

COOPERATION AND TRUST. In a lean system, workers and first-line supervisors must take on responsibilities formerly assigned to middle managers and support staff. Activities such as scheduling, expediting, and improving productivity become part of the duties of lower-level personnel. Consequently, organizational relationships must be reoriented to build close cooperation and mutual trust between the workforce and management. Such cooperation and trust may be difficult to achieve, particularly in light of the typical adversarial positions taken by labor and management in the past.

REWARD SYSTEMS AND LABOR CLASSIFICATIONS. In some instances, the reward system must be revamped when a lean system is implemented. At General Motors, for example, a plan to reduce stock at one plant ran into trouble because the production superintendent refused to cut back production of unneeded parts; his salary was based on his plant's production volume.

The realignment of reward systems is not the only hurdle. Labor contracts traditionally have reduced management's flexibility in reassigning workers as the need arises. A typical automobile plant in the United States has several unions and dozens of labor classifications. To gain more flexibility, management in some cases has obtained union concessions by granting other types of benefits. In other cases, management has relocated plants to take advantage of nonunion or foreign labor.

PROCESS CONSIDERATIONS

Firms using lean systems typically have some dominant work flows. To take advantage of lean practices, firms might have to change their existing layouts. Certain workstations might have to be moved closer together, and cells of machines devoted to particular families of components may have to be established. A survey of 68 firms using lean systems indicated that the single most important factor in successful implementation is changing product flows and layout to a cellular design (Billesbach, 1991). However, rearranging a plant to conform to lean practices can be costly. For example, whereas many plants now receive raw materials and purchased parts by rail, to facilitate smaller, more frequent shipments, truck deliveries would be preferable. Loading docks might have to be reconstructed or expanded and certain operations relocated to accommodate the change in transportation mode and quantities of arriving materials.

INVENTORY AND SCHEDULING

Manufacturing firms need to have stable master production schedules, short setups, and frequent, reliable supplies of materials and components to achieve the full potential of the lean systems concept.

SCHEDULE STABILITY. Daily production schedules in high-volume, make-to-stock environments must be stable for extended periods. At Toyota, the master production schedule is stated in fractions of days over a three-month period and is revised only once a month. The first month of the schedule is frozen to avoid disruptive changes in the daily production schedule for each workstation; that is, the workstations execute the same work schedule each day of the month. At the beginning of each month, kanbans are reissued for the new daily production rate. Stable schedules are needed so that production lines can be balanced and new assignments found for employees who otherwise would be underutilized. Lean systems used in high-volume, make-to-stock environments cannot respond quickly to scheduling changes because little slack inventory or capacity is available to absorb these changes.

SETUPS. If the inventory advantages of a lean system are to be realized, small lot sizes must be used. However, because small lots require a large number of setups, companies must significantly reduce setup times. Some companies have not been able to achieve short setup times and, therefore, have to use large-lot production, negating some of the advantages of lean practices. Also, lean systems are vulnerable to lengthy changeovers to new products because the low levels of finished goods inventory will be insufficient to cover demand while the system is down. If changeover times cannot be reduced, large finished goods inventories of the old product must be accumulated to compensate. In the automobile industry, every week that a plant is shut down for new-model changeover costs between $16 million and $20 million in pretax profits.

PURCHASING AND LOGISTICS. If frequent, small shipments of purchased items cannot be arranged with suppliers, large inventory savings for these items cannot be realized. For example, in the United States, such arrangements may prove difficult because of the geographic dispersion of suppliers.

The shipments of raw materials and components must be reliable because of the low inventory levels in lean systems. A plant can be shut down because of a lack of materials. For example, a strike at the GM plant in Lordstown, Ohio caused the Saturn plant in Spring Hill, Tennessee to shut down, losing the production of 1,000 cars per day. Lordstown supplies parts to Saturn, which does not stockpile the parts because of lean practices.

Managerial Practice 11.2 shows that implementing a lean system can take a long time.

LEAN SYSTEMS ACROSS THE ORGANIZATION

The philosophy of lean systems has application throughout the organization. A theme of this text is that organizations create services or products with processes, which cut across functional boundaries to create value for customers—who can be internal or external. Lean systems focus on efficient value creation, which applies to any process in the organization.

To take advantage of lean systems, companies must clearly define the value of their services or products as perceived by their customers (see Chapter 5, "Process Performance and Quality"). Every service or product category must be carefully scrutinized for excessive complexity or unnecessary features and options. The goal should be to deliver services or products that precisely match the customer's needs without waste. Then, the company must identify the sequence of activities and the processes involved that are *essential* to the creation of the service or product by drawing flow diagrams and developing process charts (see Chapter 4, "Process Analysis"). Activities that are value-added (those tasks that transform the service or product in some measurable way) should be clearly differentiated from those that are non-valued-added (wasted effort that could be eliminated without any impact on the customer).

Once the activities are identified and the flows are charted, the barriers to the flow of value must be eliminated. For example, these barriers can be found in the factory in the form of large batches and excessive inventory; in the product development process in the form of excessive documentation, approvals, and meetings; or in the order placement process in the form of incomplete service or product information or poorly designed Web pages. These barriers are examples of the rocks in Figure 11.1. Once these rocks are removed, the firm is free to allow its customers to "pull" value, which is the real market demand that becomes the trigger for all activities to follow. Lean systems certainly are important to all processes in the organization.

MANAGERIAL PRACTICE 11.2

IMPLEMENTING LEAN MANUFACTURING PRINCIPLES AT CESSNA

Cessna Aircraft (www.cessna.com) is a leading manufacturer of business jets; utility planes; and single-engine, piston-powered personal aircraft. The planes range in price from $150,000 for a single-engine, piston-powered aircraft to over $17 million for a business jet. However, 15 years ago, the company decided to abandon the production of single-engine, piston-powered planes because of the liability the company incurred for just about any accident involving a Cessna, regardless of the circumstances. After legislation in 1994 limited the liability of aircraft manufacturers, Cessna decided to get back into the manufacture of small planes by building a new plant in Independence, Kansas. It was an opportunity to incorporate a new, lean manufacturing system to a product line that had not changed much over the years, with the exception of the avionics in the cockpit and a new, efficient engine, which was outsourced. To do so, however, Cessna had to learn how to go from a craftwork mentality, which is what they had when they last produced small aircraft, to a modern manufacturing mentality that involves a whole new way of doing things.

Cessna adopted three lean manufacturing practices in its new plant. First, management committed to the team concept. Teamwork fosters workforce flexibility because team members learn the duties of other team members and can shift across assembly lines as needed. However, because of a shortage of technically qualified employees, Cessna had to hire employees short on sheet metal skills but willing to work as a team and to assume responsibility. Productivity initially suffered, but retired assembly-line workers were recalled to serve as mentors to teach the new employees the skills and confidence they needed to do their jobs. It has taken four years to bring the teams to the point of learning about conflict resolution, problem solving, and flexibility.

Second, Cessna initiated vendor-managed inventories with several of its suppliers. For example, two Honeywell field engineers who also help with problems after installation maintain a 30-day avionics inventory worth $30 million on-site. In addition, a warehouse nearby was opened to house the inventories of several suppliers. The warehouse operations are being integrated with the plant schedule so that inventory will be delivered daily to the production line. Suppliers initially balked at the idea, but eventually saw its advantages.

Finally, Cessna has incorporated manufacturing cells and group technology in their manufacturing process and has moved away from a batch process approach that supported a make-to-stock strategy. In the past, Cessna had a network of dealers who took what was sent to them, maintained large inventories to support the dealers, and had to give incentives to get rid of excess inventories. Today, Cessna assembles to order. This change in manufacturing strategy required a change in the manufacturing process as well as a change in the way Cessna does business with its dealers.

Cessna has made the transition from craftwork to modern manufacturing, but not without hard work. Although inventory investment has shown improvement, it still takes twice as many hours to build a model 172 than it did in the 1980s. The theoretical capacity of the plant is 2,000 planes a year, but the annual target four years after the start of operations was only 975 planes a year. Much of the slow start-up was due to initiating a brand-new workforce. This experience at Cessna shows that switching to lean manufacturing is a long-term commitment.

Single-engine Cessna airplanes roll off the assembly line at Independence, Kansas. Three versions of single-engine planes are built at the southeast Kansas plant, using the concepts of lean manufacturing systems.

Source: Siekman, Phillip. "Cessna Tackles Lean Manufacturing." *Fortune* (May 1, 2000), pp. 1222 B–1222 Z.

CHAPTER HIGHLIGHTS

- Lean systems focus on the efficient delivery of services or products. A just-in-time (JIT) system, a popular lean system, is designed to produce or deliver just the right services or products in just the right quantities just in time to serve subsequent processes or customers.

- Some of the key elements of lean systems for service and manufacturing processes are a pull method to manage work flow, consistently high quality, small lot sizes, uniform workstation loads, standardized components and work methods, close supplier ties, flexible workforce, line flow strategy, automation, preventive maintenance, and continuous improvement.

- A single-card JIT system uses a kanban to control production flow. The authorized inventory of a part is a function of the number of authorized cards for that item. The number of cards depends on average demand during manufacturing lead time, the container size, and a policy variable to adjust for unexpected occurrences. Many other methods may be used to signal the need for material replenishment and production.

- The JIT II system provides an organizational structure for improved supplier coordination by integrating the logistics, production, and purchasing processes.

- The benefits of lean systems include reductions in inventory, space requirements, and paperwork and increases in productivity, employee participation, and quality. Lean systems require fundamental changes in the way *all* of the firm's business functions are performed. Increasing cooperation and trust between management and labor, basing rewards on team rather than individual performance, and replacing adversarial supplier relationships with partnerships are some of the basic cultural changes involved in lean system implementation.

STUDENT CD-ROM AND INTERNET RESOURCES

The Student CD-ROM and the Companion Website at **www.prenhall.com/krajewski** contain many tools, activities, and resources designed for this chapter. The following items are recommended to enhance your skills and improve your understanding of the material in this chapter.

STUDENT CD-ROM RESOURCES

➤ **PowerPoint Slides.** View the comprehensive set of slides customized for this chapter's concepts and techniques.
➤ **OM Explorer Tutors.** OM Explorer contains a tutor program to enhance your understanding of how to apply the equation for determining the number of containers in a kanban system. See Chapter 11 in the OM Explorer menu. See also the Tutor Exercise requiring the use of this tutor program.
➤ **OM Explorer Solvers.** Number of Containers in OM Explorer can be used to solve general problems involving the determination of the correct number of containers for a kanban system. See Lean Systems in the OM Explorer menu.

INTERNET RESOURCES

➤ **Self-Study Quizzes.** See the compendium of true or false, multiple choice, and essay questions that allows online tests or gives you feedback on how well you have mastered the concepts of this chapter.
➤ **In the News.** See the articles that apply to this chapter.
➤ **Internet Exercises.** Try out three links to lean systems topics including lean production, logistic support for JIT, and component modularity.
➤ **Virtual Tours.** Explore lean system practices at New United Motors Manufacturing, Inc. Also see the "Web Links to Company Facility Tours" for additional tours of company facilities.

KEY EQUATION

1. Number of containers:

$$\kappa = \frac{\text{Average demand during lead time + Safety stock}}{\text{Number of units per container}}$$

$$= \frac{d(\overline{\omega} + \overline{\rho})(1 + \alpha)}{c}$$

KEY TERMS

just-in-time (JIT) philosophy 483
JIT system 483
kanban 491
lean systems 483

lot 485
mixed-model assembly 486
pull method 484
push method 484

setup 485
single-digit setup 485

SOLVED PROBLEM

A company using a kanban system has an inefficient machine group. For example, the daily demand for part L105A is 3,000 units. The average waiting time for a container of parts is 0.8 day. The processing time for a container of L105A is 0.2 day, and a container holds 270 units. Currently, there are 20 containers for this item.

    a. What is the value of the policy variable, α?
    b. What is the total planned inventory (work-in-process and finished goods) for item L105A?
    c. Suppose that the policy variable, α, were 0. How many containers would be needed now? What is the effect of the policy variable in this example?

SOLUTION

    a. We use the equation for the number of containers and then solve for α:

$$\kappa = \frac{d(\overline{\omega} + \overline{\rho})(1 + \alpha)}{c}$$

$$= \frac{3,000(0.8 + 0.2)(1 + \alpha)}{270} = 20$$

and

$$(1 + \alpha) = \frac{20(270)}{3,000(0.8 + 0.2)} = 1.8$$

$$\alpha = 1.8 - 1 = 0.8$$

    b. With 20 containers in the system and each container holding 270 units, the total planned inventory is 20(270) = 5,400 units.
    c. If $\alpha = 0$

$$\kappa = \frac{3,000(0.8 + 0.2)(1 + 0)}{270} = 11.11 \quad \text{or} \quad 12 \text{ containers}$$

The policy variable adjusts the number of containers. In this case, the difference is quite dramatic because $\overline{\omega} + \overline{\rho}$ is fairly large and the number of units per container is small relative to daily demand.

DISCUSSION QUESTIONS

1. Compare and contrast the following two situations:

    a. A company's lean system stresses teamwork. Employees feel more involved and, therefore productivity and quality have increased. Yet, one of the problems in implementing the lean system has been the loss of individual autonomy.
    b. A humanities professor believes that all students desire to learn. To encourage students to work together and learn from each other, thereby increasing involvement, productivity, and the quality of the learning experience, the professor announces that all students in the class will receive the same grade and that it will be based on the performance of the group.

2. Which elements of lean systems would be most troublesome for manufacturers to implement? Why?

PROBLEMS

An icon next to a problem identifies the software that can be helpful, but is not mandatory. The software is available on the Student CD-ROM that is packaged with every new copy of the textbook.

1. The Harvey motorcycle company produces three models: the Tiger, a sure-footed dirt bike; the LX2000, a nimble cafe racer; and the Golden, a large interstate tourer. This month's master production schedule calls for the production of 54 Goldens, 42 LX2000s, and 30 Tigers per seven-hour shift.

   a. What average cycle time is required for the assembly line to achieve the production quota in seven hours?

   b. If mixed-model scheduling is used, how many of each model will be produced before the production cycle is repeated?

   c. Determine a satisfactory production sequence for the ultimate in small-lot production: one unit.

   d. The design of a new model, the Cheetah, includes features from the Tiger, LX2000, and Golden models. The resulting blended design has an indecisive character and is expected to attract some sales from the other models. Determine a mixed-model schedule resulting in 52 Goldens, 39 LX2000s, 26 Tigers, and 13 Cheetahs per seven-hour shift. Although the total number of motorcycles produced per day will increase only slightly, what problem might be anticipated in implementing this change from the production schedule indicated in part (b)?

2. ◆ **OM Explorer** A fabrication cell at Spradley's Sprockets uses the pull method to supply gears to an assembly line. George Jitson is in charge of the assembly line, which requires 500 gears per day. Containers typically wait 0.20 day in the fabrication cell. Each container holds 20 gears, and one container requires 1.8 days in machine time. Setup times are negligible. If the policy variable for unforeseen contingencies is set at 5 percent, how many containers should Jitson authorize for the gear replenishment system?

3. ◆ **OM Explorer** You have been asked to analyze the kanban system of LeWin, a French manufacturer of gaming devices. One of the workstations feeding the assembly line produces part M670N. The daily demand

for M670N is 1,800 units. The average processing time per unit is 0.003 day. LeWin's records show that the average container spends 1.05 days waiting at the feeder workstation. The container for M670N can hold 300 units. Twelve containers are authorized for the part. Recall that $\bar{\rho}$ is the average processing time per container, not per individual part.

   a. Find the value of the policy variable, α, that expresses the amount of implied safety stock in this system.

   b. Use the implied value of α from part (a) to determine the required reduction in waiting time if one container was removed. Assume that all other parameters remain constant.

4. ◆ **OM Explorer** An assembly line requires two components: gadjits and widjits. Gadjits are produced by center 1 and widjits by center 2. Each unit of the end item, called a jit-together, requires 3 gadjits and 2 widjits, as shown in Figure 11.4. The daily production quota on the assembly line is 800 jit-togethers.
   The container for gadjits holds 80 units. The policy variable for center 1 is set at 0.09. The average waiting time for a container of gadjits is 0.09 day, and 0.06 day is needed to produce a container. The container for widjits holds 50 units, and the policy variable for center 2 is 0.08. The average waiting time per container of widgits is 0.14 day, and the time required to process a container is 0.20 day.

   a. How many containers are needed for gadjits?

   b. How many containers are needed for widjits?

5. ◆ **OM Explorer** Gestalt, Inc. uses a kanban system in its automobile production facility in Germany. This facility operates eight hours per day to produce the Jitterbug, a replacement for the obsolete but immensely popular Jitney Beetle. Suppose that a certain part requires 150 seconds of processing at machine cell 33B and a container of parts averages 1.6 hours of waiting time there. Management has allowed a 10 percent buffer for unexpected occurrences. Each container holds 30 parts, and 8 containers are authorized. How much daily demand can be satisfied with this system? (*Hint:* Recall that $\bar{\rho}$ is the average processing time per container, not per individual part.)

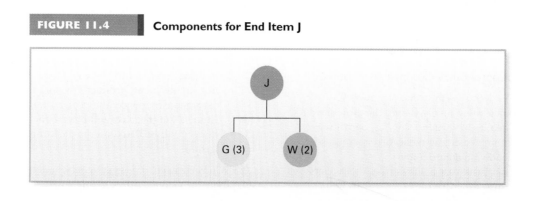

FIGURE 11.4   **Components for End Item J**

6. ◗ **OM Explorer** A jittery U.S. Postal Service supervisor is looking for ways to reduce stress in the sorting department. With the existing arrangement, stamped letters are machine-canceled and loaded into tubs with 375 letters per tub. The tubs are then pushed to postal clerks, who read and key zip codes into an automated sorting machine at the rate of one tub per 375 seconds. To overcome the stress caused when the stamp canceling machine outpaces the sorting clerks, a pull system is proposed. When the clerks are ready to process another tub of mail, they will pull the tub from the canceling machine area. How many tubs should circulate between the sorting clerks and the canceling machine if 90,000 letters are to be sorted during an eight-hour shift, the safety stock policy variable, α, is 0.18, and the average waiting time plus materials handling time is 25 minutes per tub?

7. ◗ **OM Explorer** The production schedule at Mazda calls for 1,200 Mazdas to be produced during each of 22 production days in January and 900 Mazdas to be produced during each of 20 production days in February. Mazda uses a kanban system to communicate with Gesundheit, a nearby supplier of tires. Mazda purchases four tires per vehicle from Gesundheit. The safety stock policy variable, α, is 0.15. The container (a delivery truck) size is 200 tires. The average waiting time plus materials handling time is 0.16 day per container. Assembly lines are rebalanced at the beginning of each month. The average processing time per container in January is 0.10 day. February processing time will average 0.125 day per container. How many containers should be authorized for January? How many for February?

8. ◗ **OM Explorer** Jitsmart is a retailer of plastic action-figure toys. The action figures are purchased from Tacky Toys, Inc. and arrive in boxes of 48. Full boxes are stored on high shelves out of reach of customers. A small inventory is maintained on child-level shelves. Depletion of the lower-shelf inventory signals the need to take down a box of action figures to replenish the inventory. A reorder card is then removed from the box and sent to Tacky Toys to authorize replenishment of a container of action figures. The average demand rate for a popular action figure, Agent 99, is 36 units per day. The total lead time (waiting plus processing) is 11 days. Jitsmart's safety stock policy variable, α is 0.25. What is the authorized stock level for Jitsmart?

C ~ d in std cont. of port

SIMULATION EXERCISE

This simulation exercise requires the use of the Extend software, which is an optional simulation package that your instructor may or may not have ordered.

1. **Extend** Heritage Furniture is a medium-sized regional supplier of bedroom furniture. Heritage's products include the full range of dressers, commonly referred to as case goods in the trade. The plant manager is reviewing the process for manufacturing drawers. The process has nine basic steps, with operations divided between manual steps and more automated operations. Use the Extend simulator to evaluate the impact of adopting a lean system and identify bottlenecks. See the *Just-in-Time Production at Heritage Furniture* case on the optional Student CD-ROM, which includes the basic model and how to use it. Answer the various questions and indicate how performance changes with the different changes in the system and process.

CASE   COPPER KETTLE CATERING

Copper Kettle Catering (CKC) is a full-service catering company that provides services ranging from box lunches for picnics or luncheon meetings to large wedding, dinner, or office parties. Established as a lunch delivery service for offices in 1972 by Wayne and Janet Williams, CKC has grown to be one of the largest catering businesses in Raleigh, North Carolina. The Williamses divide customer demand into two categories: *deliver only* and *deliver and serve*.

The deliver-only side of the business provides delivery of boxed meals consisting of a sandwich, salad, dessert, and fruit. The menu for this service is limited to six sandwich selections, three salads or potato chips, and a brownie or fruit bar. Grapes and an orange slice are included with every meal, and iced tea can be ordered to accompany the meals. The overall level of demand for this service throughout the year is fairly constant, although the mix of menu items delivered varies. The planning horizon for this segment of the business is short: Customers usually call no more than a day ahead of time. CKC requires customers to call deliver-only orders in by 10:00 A.M. to guarantee delivery the same day.

The deliver-and-serve side of the business focuses on catering large parties, dinners, and weddings. The extensive range of menu items includes a full selection of hors d'oeuvres, entrées, beverages, and special-request items. The demand for these services is much more seasonal, with heavier demands occurring in the late spring–early summer for weddings and the late fall–early winter for holiday parties. However, this segment also has a longer planning horizon. Customers book dates and choose menu items weeks or months ahead of time.

Copper Kettle Company's food preparation facilities support both operations. The physical facilities layout resembles that of a job shop. There are five major work areas: a stove–oven area for hot food preparation, a cold area for salad preparation, an hors d'oeuvre preparation area, a sandwich preparation area, and an assembly area where deliver-only orders are boxed and deliver-and-serve orders are assembled and trayed. Three walk-in coolers store foods requiring refrigeration, and a large pantry houses nonperishable goods. Space limitations and the risk of spoilage limit the amount of raw materials and prepared food items that can be carried in inventory at any one time. CKC purchases desserts from outside vendors. Some deliver the desserts to CKC; others require CKC to send someone to pick up desserts at their facilities.

The scheduling of orders is a two-stage process. Each Monday, the Williamses develop the schedule of deliver-and-serve orders to be processed each day. CKC typically has multiple deliver-and-serve orders to fill each day of the week. This level of demand allows a certain efficiency in preparation of multiple orders. The deliver-only orders are sched-

uled day to day, owing to the short-order lead times. CKC sometimes runs out of ingredients for deliver-only menu items because of the limited inventory space.

Wayne and Janet Williams have 10 full-time employees: 2 cooks and 8 food preparation workers, who also work as servers for the deliver-and-serve orders. In periods of high demand, the Williamses hire additional part-time servers. The position of cook is specialized and requires a high degree of training and skill. The rest of the employees are flexible and move between tasks as needed.

The business environment for catering is competitive. The competitive priorities are high-quality food, delivery reliability, flexibility, and cost—in that order. "The quality of the food and its preparation is paramount," states Wayne Williams. "Caterers with poor-quality food will not stay in business long." Quality is measured by both freshness and taste. Delivery reliability encompasses both on-time delivery and the time required to respond to customer orders (in effect, the order lead time). Flexibility focuses on both the range of catering requests that a company can satisfy and menu variety.

Recently, CKC has begun to feel the competitive pressures of increasingly demanding customers and several new specialty caterers. Customers are demanding more menu flexibility and faster response times. Small specialty caterers have entered the market and have targeted specific well-defined market segments. One example is a small caterer called Lunches-R-US, which located a facility in the middle of a large office complex to serve the lunch trade and competes with CKC on cost.

Wayne and Janet Williams have been impressed by the concepts of lean operating systems, especially the ideas of increasing flexibility, reducing lead times, and lowering costs. They sound like what CKC needs to do to remain competitive. But the Williamses wonder whether lean concepts and practices are transferable to a service business.

QUESTIONS

1. Are the operations of Copper Kettle Catering conducive to the application of lean concepts and practices? Explain.
2. What, if any, are the major barriers to implementing a lean system at Copper Kettle Catering?
3. What would you recommend that Wayne and Janet Williams do to take advantage of lean concepts in operating CKC?

Source: This case was prepared by Dr. Brooke Saladin, Wake Forest University, as a basis for classroom discussion.

SELECTED REFERENCES

Ansberry, Clare. "Hurry-Up Inventory Method Hurts Where It Once Helped." *Wall Street Journal Online* (June 25, 2002).

Beckett, W.K., and K. Dang. "Synchronous Manufacturing, New Methods, New Mind Set." *Journal of Business Strategy,* vol. 12 (1992), pp. 53–56.

Billesbach, Thomas J. "A Study of the Implementation of Just-in-Time in the United States." *Production and Inventory Management Journal* (Third Quarter 1991), pp. 1–4.

Billesbach, Thomas J., and M.J. Schniederjans. "Applicability of Just-in-Time Techniques in Administration." *Production and Inventory Management Journal* (Third Quarter 1989), pp. 40–44.

Dixon, Lance. "Tomorrow's Ideas Take Flight in Today's Leading Edge Corporations." *APICS—The Performance Advantage* (July 1996), p.60.

Fuime, Orrest. "Lean Accounting and Finance." *Target,* vol. 18, no. 4 (Fourth Quarter 2002), pp. 6–14.

Golhar, D.Y., and C.L. Stam. "The Just-in-Time Philosophy: A Literature Review." *International Journal of Production Research*, vol. 29 (1991), pp. 657–676.

Greenblatt, Sherwin. "Continous Improvement in Supply Chain Management." *Chief Executive* (June 1993), pp. 40–43.

Hall, Robert W. "The Americanization of the Toyota System." *Target*, vol. 15, no.1 (First Quarter 1999), pp. 52–54.

Klein, J.A. "The Human Costs of Manufacturing Reform." *Harvard Business Review* (March–April 1989), pp. 60–66.

Mascitelli, Ron. "Lean Thinking: It's About Efficient Value Creation." *Target*, vol. 16 no. 2 (Second Quarter 2000), pp. 22–26.

McClenahen, John S. "So Long, Salespeople, and Good-bye, Buyers—JIT II is Here." *Industry Week* (February 18, 1991). pp. 48–65.

Millstein, Mitchell. "How to Make Your MRP System Flow." *APICS—The Performance Advantage* (July 2000). pp. 47–49.

Moody, Patricia E. "Bose Corporation: Hi-Fi Leader Stretches to Meet Growth Challenges." *Target* (Winter 1991), pp. 17–22.

Schaller, Jeff. "A 'Just Do It Now' Philosophy Rapidly Creates a Lean Culture, Produces Dramatic Results at Novametix Medical Systems." *Target*, vol. 18, no. 2 (Second Quarter 2002), pp. 48–54.

Syberg, Keith. "Best Practices (BP) Program: Honda of America Manufacturing." *Target*, vol. 15, no. 2 (Second Quarter 1999), pp. 46–48.

Tonkin, Lea. "System Sensor's Lean Journey." *Target*, vol. 18, no.2 (Second Quarter 2002), pp. 44–47.

Information Technology and Value Chains

CHAPTER OUTLINE

LEARNING GOALS   *After reading this chapter, you should be able to . . .*

IDENTIFY OR DEFINE

1. the primary areas of technology.
2. information technology and its components.
3. B2B and B2C e-commerce.
4. four approaches to e-purchasing.
5. the key factors in formulating technology strategy.

DESCRIBE OR EXPLAIN

6. how information technology can improve a firm's value chain.
7. real examples of the impact of information technology in service and manufacturing industries.
8. how the Internet, e-commerce, and ERP change the ways companies manage their customer and supplier interfaces.

SEVEN-ELEVEN JAPAN

Technology needs to be managed, like any other aspect of processes and value chains. Such is the case at Seven-Eleven Japan (www.sej.co.jp), which has invested aggressively in information technology (IT) over the years. Since Seven-Eleven Japan began in the early 1970s, founder Toshifumi Suzuki has sought to upgrade processes that better satisfy customers' demand for convenience, quality, and service. Achieving these competitive priorities has led to the continual application of information technology. The company's information system rivals any in the West for just-in-time logistics excellence and deep knowledge of customers. It allows stores to be very responsive to consumers' shifting tastes. If a particular type of *bento* (take-out lunch box) sells out by midday, extra stock can be in the stores by early afternoon. If it is raining and *bentos* will not be in high demand, deliveries are reduced. However, the information system reminds operators to put umbrellas on sale next to the cash register.

This responsiveness to customer needs is made possible by a sophisti-

A mother and son leave one of the Seven-Eleven Japan stores with their purchases. The company has significantly upgraded its information systems. Its process and value-chain performance have improved, and it can better satisfy customer needs.

cated point-of-sale data-collection system and an electronic ordering system that link individual stores to a central distribution area. Because Japanese customers place a high premium on freshness, the company makes multiple daily deliveries. Now stores receive four batches of fresh inventory each day, and fresh food turns over entirely three times a day.

Seven-Eleven Japan's early investments in such systems, and its constant additions to them, have paid off. The company is now the largest and most profitable retailer in Japan. It has continually increased the number of stores, each store's average profit margin, and average daily sales, while reducing the average turnover time of its stock. Seven-Eleven Japan has been so successful that it took over its troubled parent, the Southland Corporation, owner of the U.S. Seven-Eleven chain.

Several lessons can be learned from Seven-Eleven Japan on the task of managing technology. Its managers see IT as just one competitive lever among many and, as such, a way to improve its value-chain performance. They choose technology, whether old or new, that helps them achieve process performance goals. Investments are chosen to add customer value to processes and to help managers learn how to understand their customers better. IT projects are not assessed primarily by financial metrics and "value for money" thinking. Instead, performance-improvement goals drive investments. Rather than seeking "technology solutions" and "technology for technology's sake," Seven-Eleven Japan executives prefer "appropriate technology" to "first-mover" advantages. They identify the tasks to be done and desired performance levels. Then they pick a technology that suits the people doing the work. The goal is enhancing the contribution of people rather than boasting the latest tech-

nological solution. For example, with hardware from NEC and software from Microsoft, Seven-Eleven Japan installed in 1998 a new system based on proprietary technology rather than on the trendier open structure of the Internet, which was being adopted by most retailers. This proprietary system allowed the company to establish the system it needed: an easy-to-use multimedia system with pictures and sound, a system that could quickly repair itself if something went wrong, a common system for all companies in its value chain, and a system that could be easily updated to take advantage of technological advances.

Its new technology has four advantages. First, it allows Seven-Eleven Japan to better monitor customer needs. Second, it improves quality control, pricing, and product development through better use of sales data. For example, Seven-Eleven Japan collects sales information from all its stores three times a day, and analyzes it in roughly 20 minutes. Third, it helps predict daily trends. Finally, it also improves the efficiency of its value chain. For example, orders can be electronically processed in less than 7 minutes and sent to 230 distribution centers that work exclusively for Seven-Eleven Japan. Truck drivers carry cards with bar codes that are scanned into store computers when they arrive with a delivery. If a driver is often late, the operator will review his route and might add another truck to lighten the load.

The company is also expanding its e-commerce initiatives, both in the United States and Japan. The process is envisioned somewhat differently in Japan, where there is a widespread preference for cash payments and money transfers instead of credit cards. The shopper in Tokyo would browse on the Web and place the order electronically, just as in the United States. The difference is that, a few days later, the shopper will traipse to his or her local Seven-

Eleven, fork over some yen to the clerk, and receive his or her purchases.

Nowadays, Seven-Eleven Japan's latest development is the launch of its Internet site, 7dream.com, a joint venture with seven other companies that offers a wide range of goods and services, including books, CDs, concert tickets, and travel. Time will soon tell us whether this venture is successful in the future or not.

Sources: Earl, Michael, and M. M. Bensaou. "The Right Mind-Set for Managing Informa-tion Technology." *Harvard Business Review* (September–October, 1998), pp. 119–129; "E-Commerce Japanese Style." *Wired* (June 1999); "Seven-Eleven: Over the Counter E-Commerce." *The Economist* (May 27, 2001); "Demand Chain Excellence: A Tale of Two Retailers." *Supply Chain Management Review* (March 1, 2001), p. 40.

Technological change is a major factor in gaining competitive advantage. It can create whole new industries and dramatically alter the landscape in existing industries. The development and innovative use of technology can give a firm a distinctive competence that is difficult to match, as with Seven-Eleven Japan. Competitive advantage comes not just from creating new technology but also by applying and integrating existing technologies. Advances in technology spawn new services and products and reshape processes. Thus, technology takes many forms, beginning with ideas, knowledge, and experience, and then uses them to create new and better ways of doing things.

In this chapter, we explore how technology can create a competitive advantage. We begin with a general definition of technology and apply it specifically to products, processes, and information. We then focus on information technology and how it helps operate value chains. Information technology is becoming an important component of customer relationship processes and supplier relationship processes in external value-chain linkages (see Figure 9.1). We single out three high-growth information technologies: e-commerce, e-purchasing, and enterprise resource planning. Finally, we examine technology strategy, offering guidelines on choosing new technologies.

As you read about information technology and value chains, think about why they are important to the various departments and functions across the organization, such as . . .

➤ **accounting**, which can use new technologies to perform its work better and provide important information on new technology proposals.

➤ **finance**, which seeks better ways to perform its work, provides inputs to top management on the financial advisability of new technologies, and looks for ways to finance technological change.

➤ **human resources**, which needs to anticipate and manage the impact that technological change has on the workforce.

➤ **management information systems**, which helps identify new information technologies and implements them when approved.

➤ **marketing**, which seeks better technologies for its customer relationship processes and how new product possibilities can better meet customer needs.

➤ **operations**, which needs new technologies to manage the value chain most effectively.

➤ **purchasing**, which seeks better technologies for its supplier relationship processes.

THE MEANING AND ROLE OF TECHNOLOGY

We define **technology** as the know-how, physical equipment, and procedures used to produce services and products. Know-how is the knowledge and judgment of how, when, and why to employ equipment and procedures. Craftsmanship and experience are embodied in this knowledge and often cannot be written into manuals or routines. Equipment consists of such tools as computers, scanners, ATMs, or robots. Procedures are the rules and techniques for operating equipment and performing the work. All three components work together, as illustrated by air-travel technology. Knowledge is reflected in scheduling, routing, and pricing decisions. The airplane is the equipment, consisting of many components and assemblies. The procedures are rules and manuals

What are the key aspects of technology and its management?

technology The know-how, physical equipment, and procedures used to produce services and products.

on aircraft maintenance and how to operate the airplane under many different conditions. Technologies do not occur in a vacuum but are embedded in support networks. A **support network** comprises the physical, informational, and organizational relationships that make a technology complete and allow it to function as intended. Thus, the support network for air-travel technology includes the infrastructure of airports, baggage-handling facilities, travel agencies, air traffic control operations, and the communication systems that connect them.

support network   A network comprised of the physical, informational, and organizational relationships that make a technology complete and allow it to function as intended.

THREE PRIMARY AREAS OF TECHNOLOGY

Within an organization, technologies reflect what people are working on and what they are using to do that work. The most widespread view of technology is that of *product technology*, which a firm's engineering and research groups develop when creating new services and products. Another view is that of *process technology*, which a firm's employees use to do their work. A third area, which has become increasingly important, is *information technology*, which a firm's employees use to acquire, process, and communicate information. The way in which a specific technology is classified depends on its application. A product technology to one firm may be part of the process technology of another firm.

Operations managers are interested in all three aspects of technology. Product technology is important because a firm's processes must be designed to produce services and products spawned by technological advances. Process technology is important because it can improve methods currently used in the production system. Information technology is important because it can improve the way information is used to operate the firm's processes. Moving from individual processes to the whole firm's value chain, information technology also is often essential to managing it well.

product technology   Ideas that are developed within the organization and translated into new services and products.

PRODUCT TECHNOLOGY. Developed within the organization, **product technology** translates ideas into new services and products. Product technology is developed primarily by engineers and researchers. They develop new knowledge and ways of doing things, merge them with and extend conventional capabilities, and translate them into specific services and products with features that customers value. Developing new product technologies requires close cooperation with marketing, to find out what customers really want, and with operations, to determine how services or goods can be produced effectively.

What process technologies are used in a supply chain?

process technology   The methods by which an organization does things.

PROCESS TECHNOLOGY. The methods by which an organization does things rely on the application of **process technology**. Some of the large number of process technologies used by an organization are unique to a functional area; others are used more universally. Of interest are the many technologies used in a firm's value chain (see Chapter 3, "Process Design Strategy" and Chapter 9, "Supply-Chain Design").

Figure 12.1 shows how technologies support the processes in the value chain for both service providers and manufacturers. Each technology can be broken further into still more technologies.

Supplement K, "Computer-Integrated Manufacturing," on the Student CD-ROM describes a new family of manufacturing technologies and will give you a sense of the widening array of possibilities. All functional areas, not just those areas directly involved with the value chain, rely on process technologies. Figure 12.2 identifies the process technologies commonly used in these other functional areas.

Developments in process technology for each area can be dramatic. Consider sales processes that use vending machines to distribute products. This process technology is shedding its low-tech image. New electronic vending machines are loaded with circuit boards and microprocessors rather than gears and chains. They determine how much product is left, audit coin boxes, and make sure that the mechanisms work properly. These capabilities simplify product ordering and inventory control processes.

With more sophisticated versions, vending machine communication may even allow companies at distant locations to change product prices, reset thermostats, and verify credit cards. Handheld computers have also caught on, and some drivers tending

FIGURE 12.1   Process Technologies Along the Value Chain

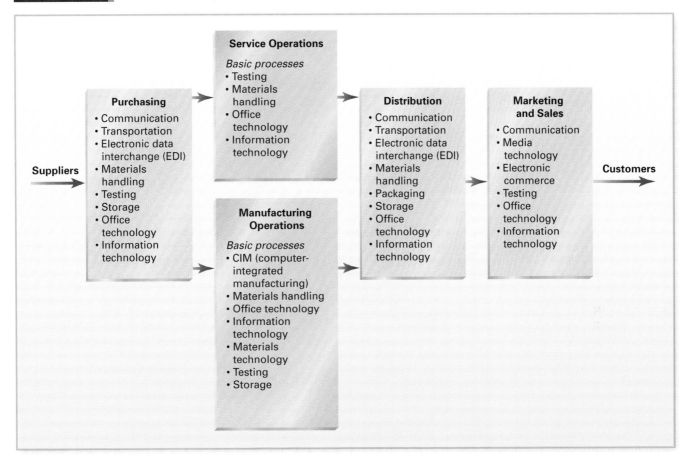

vending machines use them to "read" the status of certain machines in just seconds. When the data are processed, the computers prepare restocking lists for route drivers. Now that replenishments can be made more quickly and accurately, some customers are reporting inventory reductions of 20 percent with no loss in service—a reduction that amounts to a significant savings, in addition to the time savings for the drivers.

INFORMATION TECHNOLOGY. Managers and employees use **information technology** to acquire, process, and transmit information with which to make more effective decisions. Information technology pervades every functional area in the workplace (see Figures 12.1 and 12.2). Nowhere is it more revolutionary than in services, whether front, hybrid, or back offices. Information technologies include various types of telecommunication systems, word processing, computer spreadsheets, computer graphics, e-mail, online databases, the Internet, and intranets.

information technology
Technology used to acquire, process, and transmit information with which to make more effective decisions.

TECHNOLOGY'S ROLE IN IMPROVING BUSINESS PERFORMANCE

Technology is probably the most important force driving the increase in global competition. As various studies show, companies that invest in and apply new technologies tend to have stronger financial positions than those that do not. One study of more than 1,300 manufacturers in Europe, Japan, and North America focused on process technologies and revealed a strong link between financial performance and technological innovation. Companies with stellar performance in annual sales, inventory turns, and profits had more experience with multiple advanced manufacturing technologies and demonstrated more leadership in technological change than their underperforming counterparts. Even small firms that have more technological know-how and use

Why is technology so important to operations managers?

FIGURE 12.2   Technologies for Other Functional Areas

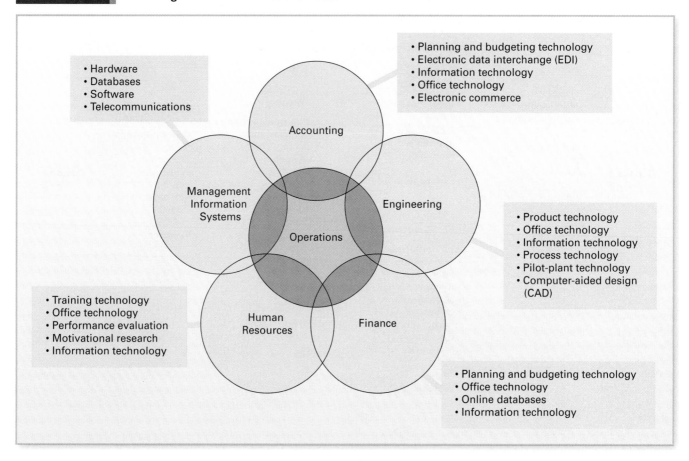

computer-based information and manufacturing technologies more intensively enjoy stronger competitive positions.

At the same time, the relationship between technology and competitive advantage is often misunderstood. High technology and technological change for its own sake are not always best. They might not create a competitive advantage, be economically justifiable, fit with the desired profile of competitive priorities, or add to the firm's core competencies. In other words, being a high-tech firm is not necessarily the appropriate use of technology. For many jobs, a simple handsaw is a better choice than a computer-controlled laser.

INFORMATION TECHNOLOGY

Information technology is crucial to operations everywhere along the value chain and to every functional area (see Figures 12.1 and 12.2). Computers have spawned a huge proportion of current technological changes and innovations, either directly or indirectly. Computer-based information technology, in particular, has greatly influenced how operations are managed and how offices work. Office workers now do things that were not even possible before, such as accessing information simultaneously from several locations and diverse functional areas. Information technology makes cross-functional coordination easier and links a firm's basic processes. In a manufacturing plant, information technologies link people with the work centers, databases, and computers. For software support in using information technology to manage value chains, see iCat (**www.icat.com**); CAPS Logistics, Inc. (**www.caps.com**); Sabre, Inc. (**www.sabre.com**); Manugistics (**www.manugistics.com**); User Solutions, Inc.

(www.usersol.com); TCI (www.tcisolutions.com); Prophet 21 (www.p21.com); SAP AG (www.sap.com); Baan (www.baan.com); Oracle (www.oracle.com); PeopleSoft (www.peoplesoft.com); and J.D. Edwards (www.jdedwards.com).

Let us first examine the four basic building blocks of information technology. Then we show how they are being used in three of the fastest-growing areas of information technology: e-commerce, e-purchasing and enterprise resource planning.

COMPONENTS OF INFORMATION TECHNOLOGY

Information technology is made up of four subtechnologies: (1) *hardware*, (2) *software*, (3) *databases*, and (4) *telecommunications*.

What are the components of information technology?

HARDWARE. A computer and the devices connected to it, which can include (among other things) an Intel semiconductor or a PixelVision flat-panel monitor, are called **hardware**. Improved hardware memory, processing capability, and speed have, in large part, driven recent technological change. Scientists and engineers at computer and telecommunications companies and academics are the primary sources of these advances.

hardware A computer and the devices connected to it.

SOFTWARE. The computer programs that make hardware work and carry out different application tasks are called **software**. It has become such an important technology that people often get the mistaken impression that software is the sum total of information systems. Application software, such as that provided by Microsoft, Sun Microsystems, and others, is what computer users work with. It allows information to be recorded, manipulated, and presented as output that is invaluable in performing work and managing operations. Information systems specialists, both inside and outside a firm, work with the managers who ultimately must decide what the firm's systems should do, who should have access to them, and how the information should be used.

software The computer programs that make hardware work and carry out different application tasks.

Software is available for use with almost all the decision tools described in this text, including flowcharting, statistical process control techniques, learning curves, simulation, queuing models, location and layout techniques, forecasting models, linear programming, production and inventory control systems, and scheduling techniques. Software is essential to many manufacturing processes, such as computer-aided design and manufacturing; robots; automated materials handling; computerized, numerically controlled machines; automated guided vehicles; and flexible manufacturing systems (see Supplement K, "Computer-Integrated Manufacturing," on the Student CD-ROM). Software also provides various executive support systems, including management information systems and decision support systems. These software tools allow managers to evaluate business issues quickly and effectively.

DATABASES. A **database** is a collection of interrelated data or information stored on a data storage device, such as a computer hard drive, a floppy disk, or tape. A database can be a firm's inventory records, time standards for different kinds of processes, cost data, or customer demand information. For example, a database helps the New York Police Department target its assault on neighborhood drug trafficking by keeping track of drug-selling locations and activity. Thousands of online databases are also available commercially. Some are organized according to numbers: economic indicators, stock market prices, and the like. Others are built on collections of key subjects or words: weather data, ski conditions, and full texts of major newspapers and journals around the world, to name a few.

database A collection of interrelated data or information stored on a data storage device, such as a computer hard drive, a floppy disk, or tape.

American Express uses its database of some 30 million cardholders to offer an innovative marketing program called CustomExtras. Marketing information contains customers' purchase records and other information. Using proprietary software with this database allows American Express to add personalized offers and messages to the invoices of selected customers. The database tracks customer reactions to these offers and eligibility for reward programs and redemptions. This one-to-one marketing process is based on the notion that different customers should be treated differently and that the best customers should get the most attention. This approach has relevance for airlines, mutual fund companies, mass-customization manufacturers, and many other types of business.

telecommunications The final component of information technology that makes electronic networks possible.

TELECOMMUNICATIONS. The final component of information technology, which many believe might be the most important, is **telecommunications**. Fiber optics, telephones, modems, fax machines, and their related components make electronic networks possible. Such networks, and the use of compatible software, allow computer users at one location to communicate directly with computer users at another location and can pay big dividends. Sun Microsystems, Inc. used to need almost a month to close its financial books after each quarter ended. Now, all transactions are made on one network of Sun computers, permitting the quarterly accounting process to be completed in only 24 hours. Sun also has cut in half the time it required to receive payment after an order is delivered. General Electric set up a corporate **intranet**—an internal Internet network, surrounded by a firewall for security purposes—that connects the organization's various electronic systems. An employee at GE's Motors Business Division in Indiana, for example, can use the intranet to find out how buyers in other divisions rate a potential supplier. To help draw employees into using the system, the company's home page displays a particularly popular piece of data: GE's current stock price.

intranet An internal Internet network, surrounded by a "firewall" for security purposes, that connects an organization's various electronic systems.

Connecting different organizations by computer has also paid dividends. Wal-Mart Stores, Inc. revolutionized retailing by linking its computers with those of its suppliers. Its pioneering use of computer networks to conduct business electronically squeezed cost and time from its value chains (see Chapter 9, "Supply-Chain Design"). Such private networks are now about to move to the wide-open Internet as components of the information superhighway.

◗ ELECTRONIC COMMERCE

electronic commerce (e-commerce) The application of information and communication technology anywhere along the entire value chain of business processes.

Global access to the Internet gives organizations unprecedented market and process information. The Web has a huge impact on how firms interact with their suppliers, customers, employees, and investors. **Electronic commerce (e-commerce)** is the application of information and communication technology anywhere along the entire value chain of business processes. Both whole processes and subprocesses nested within them can be conducted as e-commerce. E-commerce encompasses business-to-business as well as business-to-consumer and consumer-to-business transactions. It is the sharing

A Wal-Mart distribution center, where boxes are being routed to their different destinations. Wal-Mart has revolutionized retailing by linking its computers with those of its suppliers and by improving the performance of its value chain. Higher inventory turnover is one such benefit.

of business information, maintaining business relationships, and conducting business transactions by means of telecommunications networks. It is, however, more than simply buying and selling goods electronically and includes the use of network communications technology to perform processes up and down the value chain, both within and outside the organization. E-commerce—the paperless exchange of business information—allows firms to improve their processes that give competitive advantage by cutting costs, improving quality, and increasing the speed of service delivery.

THE INTERNET

E-commerce is not limited to the Internet and Web-based systems to perform transactions, because it includes proprietary services such as electronic data interchange (EDI), covered later in this chapter. However, the Internet is the fundamental enabling technology for e-commerce, and so we begin our discussion with it. The **Internet** is a network of networks—thousands of interconnected communications networks and millions of users. It is a medium to exchange all forms of digital data, including text, graphics, audio, video, programs, and faxes. It is also an infrastructure for providing various services, such as e-mail, EDI, file transfer protocol (FTP), UserNet News, and the World Wide Web. It works because Internet software is designed according to a common set of protocols (TCP/IP) for routing and transporting data. This protocol suite sets standards by which computers communicate with each other.

> What is the Internet?

> **Internet** A network of networks; a medium to exchange all forms of digital data, including text, graphics, audio, video, programs, and faxes.

THE WORLD WIDE WEB

One of the most popular Internet services is the World Wide Web, which emerged in 1993. The **World Wide Web** consists of software called *Web servers* running on thousands of independently owned computers and computer networks that work together as part of this Internet service. All information on the Web originates within computers dedicated to the role of serving every imaginable type of data and information. Users request information from the Web using software called Web browsers. **Web browsers**, such as Microsoft's Internet Explorer and Netscape's Navigator, are software that allow users to view documents at Web sites. The Web is user friendly because the user has several tools from which to select Web sites. *Search engines* are navigational services that allow users to search the Web. Most search engines have developed into *portals*—Web sites that provide a variety of services in addition to search, including chat, free e-mail, bulletin boards, news, stock quotes, and games. Yahoo! (**www.yahoo.com**) is a good example of a widely used portal, with 50 million visitors to its site each month. Each visitor is counted only once, regardless of how many times he or she visits the site. The open protocols of the Internet allow anyone with an Internet connection to share data with other users, regardless of the type of access device employed. Of course, some sites might prohibit unauthorized access or transmission.

> **World Wide Web** An Internet service that consists of software called *Web servers* running on thousands of independently owned computers and computer networks that work together.

> **Web browsers** Software that allows users to view documents at Web sites.

HOW E-COMMERCE AFFECTS PROCESSES

It is no secret that e-commerce is growing and changing at breathtaking speed. For example, it took Sam Walton 12 years to reach $150 million in sales at Wal-Mart, but Amazon.com did it in 3 years. GE was the first firm to do $1 billion of business on the Internet, and Intel sold its first billion in goods online in less than a week. Relative to the size of the whole economy, the dollar value of e-commerce transactions is still small, but both the new Internet-based companies (the so-called dot-coms) and the traditional producers of services and goods are increasingly turning to the Web. E-commerce cuts costs because it links companies to their customers and suppliers, improves inventory management, automates fax-and-phone procurement processes, and provides inexpensive sales, marketing, and customer support channels. Managerial Practice 12.1 describes how eBay has become a leader in e-commerce with its online auctions.

> How does e-commerce affect business processes?

MANAGERIAL PRACTICE 12.1

ONLINE AUCTIONS AT EBAY

In order to attract a large number of buyers to an auction, there must be a large number of items to be auctioned. Similarly, to attract suppliers, there must be a large number of buyers (otherwise suppliers will choose a different distribution channel). The Internet clearly has the potential to bring together a large number of buyers and sellers. Just a few years ago, a new company created an online auctioning site for rare goods. Not facing much competition, it grew and began to attract more and more suppliers and buyers and to post large number of products for auctioning. Eventually, the customer base grew so large that this company gained network effects. (Also known as Metzcalf's Law, network effects simply means that the usefulness or utility of a network increases as the number of users increase.) Finally, when this company created high switching costs, it virtually assured that most of its customers would not leave it. In the end, a perfect model for online auctions was created. Ah, the name of the company? eBay (www.ebay.com).

With 2001 sales of over $750 million, eBay is one of the few Internet success stories. Despite attempts by Yahoo and Amazon to dominate this market, eBay holds roughly 80 percent of the online auction market. eBay succeeded in defending its position due to its first-mover advantage, in which it gained many customers. However, eBay perfected it by creating high switching costs through an online rating mechanism that lowers the risk associated with doing business on eBay. As a seller builds up a rating and reputation, a switching cost is established, for if the seller were to start selling in a different company, the seller would have to build their credentials from scratch.

In addition, eBay stayed close to its customers, receiving feedback and acting upon it to improve the efficiency of the network. In turn, this improved customer satisfaction, increased loyalty, and attracted more suppliers and buyers. This system is beneficial to all. Buyers prefer a large number of suppliers because they can find more items at lower prices. Likewise, suppliers prefer a large number of buyers because prices will be bid up higher. Hence, eBay is a market of first choice for both sellers and buyers.

Two issues that affect many e-commerce sites are fraud and system reliability, yet eBay has been successful at managing both. Clearly, without a system that is sound, customers would not be willing to trade on eBay. As the customer base increases, however, eBay must adopt more stringent rules to ensure the reliability and security of the network.

Consider June 1999, when eBay was shut down for a full 22 hours. If this sort of event were to occur periodically, customers would likely look for a substitute to eBay, despite the switching costs already mentioned. Realizing the potential negative consequences of shutdowns, eBay improved its system, and currently its average nonfunctionality is no more than 42 minutes per month.

Suddenly, what began as a market for rare items evolved into a market for virtually every item. As an example, consider the fact that eBay is now the biggest car dealer in the United States, with over $1 billion in yearly car and car parts sales. Looking forward, eBay is moving its e-commerce system outside the realm of its own Web site. In other words, eBay aims at creating an e-commerce platform by encouraging other firms to set up applications based on eBay's technologies, with the ultimate goal of becoming the operating system for e-commerce, much like Windows is for PCs. That is, eBay aspires to become the preeminent place for people and businesses to sell online. This new territory is both very promising and risky, as many other firms—think Yahoo, Amazon, and Microsoft—share similar objectives. Finally, as eBay continues to grow, it faces the problem of losing the culture that helped it reach its current status. That is, the close contact with its customers will be very difficult as its consumer

Online auctions at eBay attract a large number of sellers and buyers and offer a wide variety of products ranging from rare items to cars. Here, talk show host Jay Leno displays his 2001 Harley-Davidson during his TV show, featuring signatures from Hollywood's biggest celebrities. The proceeds from the auction on eBay benefited the Twin Towers Fund.

(continued)

MANAGERIAL PRACTICE 12.1 (continued)

base increases. Could eBay continue to outperform without it? Time will share the answer with us in a few years. Stay tuned!

Sources: Gallaugher, John. "E-Commerce and the Undulating Distribution Channel." *Communications of the ACM*, vol. 45, no. 7 (July 2002), pp. 89–95; Hof, Robert D. "The People's Company." *Business Week* (December 3, 2001).

BUSINESS-TO-CONSUMER E-COMMERCE

Many of the advantages of e-commerce were first exploited by retail "e-businesses," such as Amazon.com, E*Trade, and Auto-by-tel. These three companies created Internet versions of traditional bookstores, brokerage firms, and auto dealerships. Business-to-consumer (B2C) e-commerce, sometimes called "B2C e-commerce," offers individual consumers a new buying alternative. The Internet is changing operations, processes, and cost structures for many retailers, and the overall growth in usage has been dramatic. Online business sales to individual customers reached over $30 billion in 2000, more than double the total for the previous year.

However, the mix of companies using B2C e-commerce is shifting. It is no longer limited to the original dot-com retailers, because their emergence forced their "brick-and-mortar" competitors to reconsider their own e-commerce options. Now many of these more established companies are operating their own online stores and putting pressure on dot-com retailers. A shakeout is occurring for those online retailers that face slim profit margins, too little product differentiation, and not enough size to control their own order fulfillment processes and guarantee customer satisfaction. Anyone with an Internet connection can open a store in cyberspace, but delivering the goods to consumers has proven to be a much more complicated task.

B2C e-commerce offers a new distribution channel, and consumers can avoid shopping at crowded department stores, with their checkout lines and parking-space shortages. A business can publish information using hypertext markup language (HTML) not only on the World Wide Web but also on major online services. Many leading retailers and catalog companies have opened Web "stores" where consumers can browse thousands of virtual aisles and millions of items. Such methods allow customers to do much more shopping in an hour than they could possibly do in person at a traditional retail outlet. Browsers can find intriguing products at exotic sites, such as an authentic turn-of-the-century rocking horse from a London antiques broker, a gift pack of 7-ounce portions of beef Wellington, and a personalized Louisville Slugger baseball bat. The most popular online purchases are books, travel arrangements, CDs, computer software, health and beauty products, and clothing. Banking and financial services are further down the line but are growing. E-commerce is particularly attractive for products that the consumer does not have to look at carefully or touch. The Internet has an advantage with higher-value branded convenience goods over the in-store experience.

The Internet also has potential in "greening" the environment. There is less need for building retail space, warehouse space, and commercial office space. Energy saved means less pollution from power plants, which release greenhouse gases into the atmosphere. Furthermore, fewer trips to malls and stores would mean savings on gasoline. Less reliance on catalogs would save millions of tons of paper.

The question of security, primarily involving credit card numbers, continues to make many people reluctant to buy over the Internet. However, a card number follows a prescribed path and is encrypted the moment it leaves the computer. **Encryption** is the process of coding customer information and sending it over the Internet in scrambled form. Although no credit card transaction is entirely secure, the risk of fraud on the Internet is no higher than giving a credit card number over the phone or handing a credit card to a salesclerk.

encryption The process of coding customer information and sending it over the Internet in scrambled form.

BUSINESS-TO-BUSINESS E-COMMERCE

Many of the same advantages that arise from B2C e-commerce hold for business-to-business (B2B) e-commerce. E-commerce helps businesses enhance the services they offer to customers. Business-to-business transactions continue to outpace business-to-consumer transactions in e-commerce. Because trade between businesses makes up more than 70 percent of the regular economy, it is no surprise that B2B e-commerce also dwarfs the B2C variety.

Consider Fruit of the Loom, Inc., an apparel maker that depends on its wholesalers to ship products to various retailer customers. It put its wholesalers on the Web and gave each one a complete computer system that displays colorful catalogs, processes electronic orders around the clock, and manages inventories. If one of its distributors is out of stock, the company's central warehouse is notified to ship replacement stock directly to the customer. Building such an integrated e-commerce system took only a few months, using software from Connect, Inc., called OneServer, and a catalog program from Snickleways Interactive to get online. The firm's retailer customers need only an Internet connection and some Web-browsing software.

E-commerce can transform almost all B2B processes, not just their sales processes, as Managerial Practice 12.2 demonstrates. Even more impressive is how the Web is streamlining the value chain. It can dramatically reduce a firm's purchasing costs, as transactions move away from the numbing pace of paper to the lightning speed of electronics. By eliminating paper forms, firms spend less time and money rekeying information into different computers and correcting the inevitable errors. E-commerce previously operated primarily on private links. However, software and security measures have allowed the Web to become the global infrastructure for e-commerce. Moving from private networks to the Internet allows a company to reach thousands of new businesses around the world.

Currently, e-commerce is dominated by the model of one seller to many buyers, as is the case with Fruit of the Loom. However, e-commerce is beginning to take place in *virtual marketplaces*. These trading posts allow buyers and sellers who may not know each other to meet electronically and trade services and products without the aid or cost of traditional agents and brokers. Web marketplaces are growing for B2B trade. Analogies in the B2C world include eBay and Priceline.com, although the B2B customers are companies. For example, Ford, GM, and DaimlerChrysler have put together a marketplace to procure parts from suppliers. Similar marketplaces are forming around the buying and selling of paper, plastic, steel, bandwidth, chemicals, and the like.

● ELECTRONIC PURCHASING

The emergence of virtual marketplaces, enabled by Internet technologies, has provided firms with many opportunities to improve their purchasing processes. Not all e-purchasing opportunities, however, involve the Internet. In this section, we will discuss four approaches to e-purchasing: (1) electronic data interchange, (2) catalog hubs, (3) exchanges, and (4) auctions.

ELECTRONIC DATA INTERCHANGE

electronic data interchange (EDI) A technology that enables the transmission of routine business documents having a standard format from computer to computer over telephone or direct leased lines.

The most used form of e-purchasing today is **electronic data interchange (EDI),** a technology that enables the transmission of routine business documents having a standard format from computer to computer over telephone or direct leased lines. Special communications software translates documents into and out of a generic form, allowing organizations to exchange information even if they have different hardware and software components. Invoices, purchase orders, and payments are some of the routine documents that EDI can handle—it replaces the phone call or mailed document. An e-purchasing system with EDI might work as follows. Buyers browse an electronic catalog and click on items to purchase from a supplier. A computer sends the order directly to the supplier. The supplier's computer checks the buyer's credit and determines that

MANAGERIAL PRACTICE 12.2

INTERNET BUILDER CISCO USES THE INTERNET TO BUY, SELL, AND HIRE

Cisco Pre-2000

Cisco System, Inc. (www.cisco.com) prospers by building the Internet. The name *Cisco* is synonymous with the Internet. It supplies Internet service providers with 80 percent of their routers and switches—the equipment that directs data to the right destination on the Internet. It is also the biggest supplier of Internet plumbing, including the equipment that directs data around big corporate networks and corporate data-networking equipment for small and medium business. Cisco's revenues have exploded from $1.3 billion in 1994 to $19 billion in 2002.

Less well known is how Cisco uses the Internet in almost every phase of its own value chain—an approach known in the tech industry as "eating its own dog food." With the company's state-of-the-art Internet programs, every employee, customer, and supplier can use browsers for instant access to Cisco's vast storehouses of data. All told, the typical employee taps Cisco's internal Web site more than 30 times per day. Most human resources functions, from expense reports to benefit changes and employee evaluations, are handled online. Cisco encourages job aspirants to apply online, and 85 percent do. Most new-hire orientation and 80 percent of all sales training are now conducted online. Managers can pull up staff records and information on competitors.

Cisco also gets over 80 percent of its sales orders over the Internet. Its Web site is chock-full of information and free software, and most customer service issues are handled electronically, shaving millions off product support costs. Cisco's online system uses software that dramatically reduces the cost of configuring the product, because each sales order is a potentially customized product.

Finally, the Internet is woven deeply into Cisco's manufacturing operations. Orders from the Internet are fed directly into the software programs that run Cisco's business—scheduling products to be built, ordering parts, and arranging shipments. The company outsources most of its production to manufacturers like Flextronics, Inc. (www.flextronics.com), and half of all customer orders placed on Cisco's Web site flow directly to contractors who ship to customers. By build-

ing products assemble-to-order rather than to stock, Flextronics lowers inventory costs. By revamping its operations around Internet technologies, Cisco created a blueprint by which other companies can do the same. That is, Cisco functioned without virtually any inventory, with just-in-time delivery and an impressive value chain.

Cisco Post-2000

Unfortunately for Cisco, things changed quickly. The dot-com and tele-com meltdowns of 2000 seriously affected the company. But more importantly, it was probably due to certain choices made at Cisco that the company suffered so much, particularly with regards to inventory management and forecasting. Cisco failed to spot the meltdown until it was too late. Given that Cisco was experiencing backlogs in the late 1990s due to its booming business, Cisco attempted to solve this problem by securing large, long-term contracts with suppliers. This decision was supported by forecasts at Cisco that indicated growth rates of 50 to 70 percent in the early 2000 years. As the meltdown occurred, demand for Cisco's products decreased. Thus, Cisco, the company with virtually no inventory on hand, was left with the burden of having to take ownership of very short-lived inventory in the months and years to come. Hence, Cisco has been forced to write off large sums of inventory.

Although these errors in forecasting and inventory management have seriously affected the company, Cisco continues to be the dominant player in its industry. The fact that Cisco had large amounts of cash available to ride the downturn has certainly helped. As it looks into the future, management is paying special attention to inventory and value-chain management issues to ensure that the errors that occurred a few years ago are not repeated in the future.

Sources: "Meet Mr. Internet." *Business Week* (September 13, 1999), pp. 129–140; Thurm, Scott. "Behind Cisco's Woes Are Some Wounds of Its Own Making." *Wall Street Journal* (April 18, 2001), pp. A1, A8.

the items are available. The supplier's warehouse and shipping departments are notified electronically, and the items are readied for shipment. Finally, the supplier's accounting department bills the buyer electronically. For example, Chaparral Steel allows customers to have computer access to its sales database, to check inventory, and to place orders. EDI saves the cost of opening mail, directing it to the right department, checking the document for accuracy, and reentering the information in a computer system. It also improves accuracy, shortens response times, and can even reduce inventory. Savings (ranging from $5 to $125 per document) are considerable in light of the hundreds to thousands of documents many firms typically handle daily.

CATALOG HUBS

catalog hubs An approach to e-purchasing that is used to reduce the costs of placing orders to suppliers as well as the costs of the services or goods themselves.

Catalog hubs can be used to reduce the costs of placing orders to suppliers as well as the costs of the services or goods themselves. Suppliers post their catalog of items on the hub, and buyers select what they need and purchase them electronically. However, a buying firm can negotiate prices with specific suppliers for items, such as office supplies, technical equipment, specialized items, services, or furniture. The catalog that the buying firm's employees see consists only of the approved items and their negotiated prices. Employees use their PCs to select the items they need, and the system generates the purchase orders, which are electronically dispatched to the suppliers. The hub connects the firm to potentially hundreds of suppliers through the Internet, saving the costs of EDI, which requires one-to-one connections to individual suppliers.

EXCHANGES

exchange An electronic marketplace where buying firms and selling firms come together to do business.

An **exchange** is an electronic marketplace where buying firms and selling firms come together to do business. The exchange maintains relationships with buyers and sellers, making it easy to do business without the aspect of contract negotiations or other types of long-term conditions. Exchanges are often used for "spot" purchases, which are needed to satisfy an immediate need at the lowest possible cost. Commodity items such as oil, steel, or energy fit this category. However, exchanges can also be used for most any item. For example, Marriott International and Hyatt Corporation formed an exchange for hotels. Hotels traditionally have bought supplies from thousands of firms, with each firm focusing on selected items, such as soap, food, and equipment. The hotels have used faxes, telephones, and forms that were made in quadruplicate. Placing orders was expensive, and there was little opportunity to do comparison shopping. The new exchange has one-stop shopping for hotels using the service.

AUCTIONS

auction An extension of the exchange in which firms place competitive bids to buy something.

An extension of the exchange is the **auction,** where firms place competitive bids to buy something. For example, a site may be formed for a particular industry at which firms with excess capacity or materials can offer them for sale to the highest bidder. Bids can either be closed or open to the competition. Industries where auctions have value include steel; chemicals; and the home mortgage industry, where financial institutions can bid for mortgages.

An approach that has received considerable attention is the so-called reverse auction, where suppliers bid for contracts with buyers. One such site is FreeMarkets, an electronic marketplace where Fortune 500 companies offer supply contracts for open bidding. Each bid is posted, so suppliers can see how much lower their next bid must be to remain in the running for the contract. Each contract has an electronic prospectus that provides all the specifications, conditions, and other requirements that are nonnegotiable. The only thing left to determine is the cost to the buyer. Savings can be dramatic. For example, a company posted a contract for plastic parts with a benchmark starting price of $745,000, which was the most recent price for that contract. Twenty-five suppliers vied for the contract over a 20 minute bidding period. Within minutes of opening, the price was $738,000, then it plummeted to $612,000. With 30 seconds remaining in the auction, the price went to $585,000, then finally to $518,000 after 13 minutes of overtime bidding. In little more than a half-hour, the company saved about 31 percent.

Our discussion of these electronic approaches in purchasing should not leave the impression that cost is the only consideration in selecting a supplier. Exchanges and auctions are more useful for commodities, near-commodities, or infrequently needed items that require only short-term relationships with suppliers. The past two decades have proven that suppliers should be thought of as partners when the needed supply is significant and steady over extended periods of time. Supplier involvement in service or product design and supply-chain performance improvement requires long-term relationships not found by competitive pricing on the Internet.

◉ ENTERPRISE RESOURCE PLANNING

Enterprise resource planning (ERP) refers to a large, integrated information system that supports many enterprise processes and data storage needs. An **enterprise process** is a companywide process that cuts across functional areas, business units, geographic regions, and product lines. Also known as an *enterprise system*, ERP is essentially a collection of compatible software modules, possibly interfacing to existing (sometimes called "legacy") information systems, that allow a company to have one comprehensive, fully integrated information system.

We cover different aspects of ERP in several places throughout this text. For example, we describe the process decisions about how work is to be performed in Chapter 4, "Process Analysis." Designing an ERP system requires that a company carefully define its major processes so that appropriate decisions about the coordination of legacy systems and new software modules can be made. Processes to be used by ERP applications must also be fully specified. In many cases, a company's processes must be reengineered before the company can enjoy the benefits of an integrated information system. In Chapter 9, "Supply-Chain Design," we describe how ERP systems help coordinate relations among customers, internal operations, and suppliers. Finally, in Chapter 16, "Resource Planning," we examine ERP from the perspective of what it has to offer by way of resource planning, both in manufacturing and service organizations.

> **What is ERP?**
>
> **enterprise resource planning (ERP)**   A large, integrated information system that supports many enterprise processes and data storage needs.
>
> **enterprise process**   A companywide process that cuts across functional areas, business units, geographic regions, and product lines.

WHAT ERP DOES

By integrating functional areas, ERP systems allow a firm to concentrate on enterprise processes rather than on functional boundaries. For example, suppose that a U.S. manufacturer of telecommunication products has an ERP system and that an Athens-based sales representative wants to prepare a customer quote. When the salesperson enters information about the customer's needs into a laptop computer, the ERP system automatically generates a formal contract, in Greek, giving the product's specifications, delivery date, and price. After the customer accepts it, the salesperson makes an entry, whereupon ERP verifies the customer's credit limit and records the order. The next application takes over to schedule shipment using the best routing. Backing up from the delivery date, it reserves the necessary materials from inventory and determines when to release production orders to its factories and purchase orders to its suppliers. Another application updates the sales and production forecasts, while still another credits the sales representative's payroll account with the appropriate commission, in drachma. The accounting application calculates the actual product cost and profitability, in U.S. dollars, and reflects the transaction in the accounts payable and accounts receivable ledgers. Divisional and corporate balance sheets are updated, as are cash levels. In short, the system supports all of the enterprise processes that are activated as a result of the sale.

ERP APPLICATIONS

ERP revolves around a single comprehensive database that can be made available across the entire organization (or enterprise). Of course, security locks are possible and highly recommended to protect sensitive data from accidental or malicious damage. It provides visibility to relevant data enterprisewide, for all products, at all locations, and at all times. The database collects data from and feeds it into the various modular applications (or suites) of the software system. As new information is entered as a *transaction* in one application, related information is automatically updated in the other applications, including (but not limited to) financial and accounting information, human resource and payroll information, value-chain information, and customer information. ERP streamlines data flows throughout the organization and allows management direct access to a wealth of real-time operating information. It seamlessly connects information among different enterprise processes and can eliminate many of the

FIGURE 12.3

ERP Application Modules

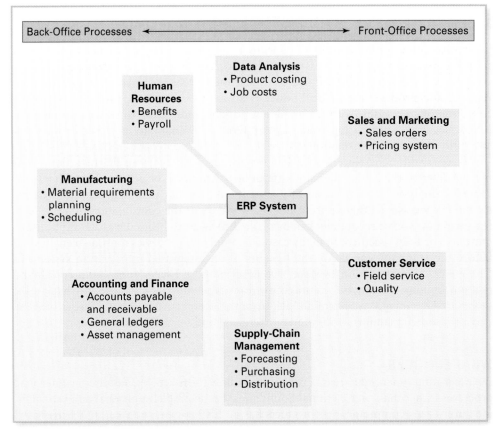

Source: Scalle, Cedric X., and Mark J. Cotteleer. *Enterprise Resource Planning (ERP)*. Boston, MA: Harvard Business School Publishing, No. 9-699-020, 1999.

cross-functional coordination problems that existed under prior poorly integrated and noninterfaced legacy systems. Figure 12.3 shows some of the typical applications, with a few subprocesses nested within each one. Some of the applications are for back-office operations such as manufacturing and payroll, while others are for front-office operations such as customer service and employee self-service.

ERP is used by both service providers and manufacturers. Amazon.com is a value-added reseller that uses ERP. The supply-chain application is of particular importance because it allows Amazon.com to link customer orders to warehouse shipments and, ultimately, to supplier-replenishment orders. Universities put particular emphasis on the human resources and accounting and finance applications, and manufacturers have an interest in almost every application suite. Not all applications in Figure 12.3 need be integrated into an ERP system, but those left out will not share their information in the corporate database.

HOW TO USE ERP

Managerial Practice 12.3 describes how ATOFINA Chemicals, Inc. made its choices on using ERP. Most ERP systems today use a graphical user interface, although the older keyboard-driven, text-based systems are still very popular because of their dependability and technical simplicity. Users navigate through various screens and menus. When they are trained, such as during ERP implementation, the focus is on these screens and how to use them to get their jobs done. The biggest supplier of these off-the-shelf commercial ERP packages is Germany's SAP AG followed by Oracle, PeopleSoft, J.D. Edwards, and Baan. Figure 12.4 shows screen shots of the J.D. Edwards ERP software, called OneWorld. Figure 12.4 (a) shows the menu for the various applications. Within the Distribution suite, for example, a user may select the Sales Order Entry process. Figure 12.4 (b) shows the screen for entering a sales order.

MANAGERIAL PRACTICE 12.3

IMPLEMENTING ERP AT ATOFINA CHEMICALS, INC.

Sometimes, implementing ERP is almost mandatory, as in the chemical industry. So thoroughly do companies share information electronically throughout the supply chain that it is difficult to do business without it. ATOFINA Chemicals (www.atofinachemicals.com) is a $1.4 billion regional chemicals subsidiary of the French company Total Fino Elf. ATOFINA Chemicals had a highly fragmented information system among its 12 different business units. Ordering was not integrated with production, and sales forecasting was not tied to budgeting systems or financial systems. Each unit tracked its own financial data independently.

The company decided to implement SAP's R/3 system for ERP but did not regard ERP as simply a technology solution. Rather, it seized an opportunity to reconfigure itself and its corporate strategy. It saw its problem not just as fragmentation of its information system but fragmentation of the organization as a whole. Customers perceived up to 12 different businesses, each managed independently. To place an order, a customer would frequently have to call many different businesses and process many different invoices. Even inside a given business unit, numerous handoffs were needed to process an order, and response time was slow.

ATOFINA Chemicals chose to implement modules for four key processes: materials management, production planning, order management, and financial reporting. These processes cut across many units, were the most fragmented, and had the biggest impact on good customer relations. At the same time, organizational structure was revised. In the financial area, the accounts receivable and credit departments were combined as a single companywide function. Thus, all customer orders would be handled as one account and with a single invoice. Another change was to create a "demand manager" responsible for integrating the sales process with the production planning process. Implementation was overseen by a 60-person project team, consisting of business analysts, IT specialists, and software users from different functions. This broadly representative team installed ERP one business unit at a time, and the same set of procedures for the four selected processes were implemented for all.

Once implemented at 9 of the company's 12 units, the benefits of ERP were already apparent. Customer satisfaction was up dramatically, now that most customer orders were completed with just one call. Inventory levels, receivables, and production and distribution costs were down, saving millions of dollars each year.

A team of three employees at ATOFINA Chemicals, Inc. keep things under control using various computer technologies after implementing ERP. Previously, it took many more people, more handoffs between people, and more time delays to get an order processed.

Source: Davenport, Thomas H. "Putting the Enterprise into the Enterprise System." *Harvard Business Review* (July–August 1998), pp. 121–131.

INTEROPERABILITY. ERP has changed a good deal over the last several years. One important direction is **interoperability**—the ability of one piece of software to interact with others. Electronic data interchange, a system that allows data interchange between companies on a batch basis, has been a major workhorse over the years. However, there is increasing interest in moving to the new economy of e-commerce. Thus, considerable attention is now being given to XML (extensible markup language), IBM's WebSphere MQ, and Microsoft's MSMQ as vehicles for this new approach. XML, for example, lets companies structure and exchange information without rewriting existing systems or adding large amounts of heavyweight middleware. These enablers of collaborative commerce are shaping the ways in which previously disparate and possibly competing

interoperability The ability of one piece of software to interact with others.

FIGURE 12.4   J.D. Edwards ERP Package

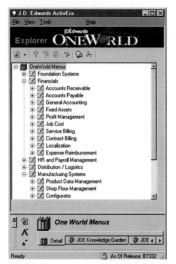

(a) Menu for various
applications.

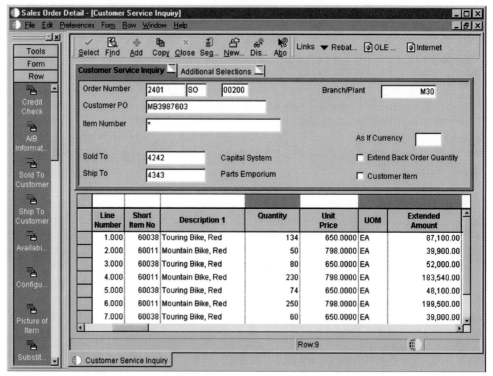

(b) Entering a sales order.

pieces of software are working together to add value and reduce costs. The goal of all such methods is to automate, in almost real time, the sharing of information across enterprise boundaries.

TECHNOLOGY STRATEGY

Which technologies should be pursued and when?

Because technology is changing so rapidly and because of the many technologies available, operations managers must more than ever make intelligent, informed decisions about new product and process technologies. The stakes are high because such choices affect the human as well as the technical aspects of operations. Here we examine how technologies should be chosen and how these choices link with strategy to create a competitive advantage. An appropriate technology is one that fits corporate and operations strategies and gives the firm a sustainable advantage. Several tests of a potential technological change should be made. If the change being considered fails these tests, it should not be pursued, even if the change represents an impressive technological accomplishment. Tests leading to *technological choice* are valid for both manufacturers and service providers.

Technology strategy deals with more than just technological choice. It also determines whether an organization should be a leader or a follower in technological change and aids in evaluating radically new technologies when conventional financial analyses would not do the job.

TECHNOLOGY AS A COMPETITIVE ADVANTAGE

A new technology should create some kind of competitive advantage. *Competitive advantage* is created by increasing the value of a product to a customer or by reducing the costs of bringing the product to market. The potential for increasing value and reducing costs from a new technology is vast. The most obvious cost-reduction strategy is that of reducing the *direct costs* of labor and materials. Labor savings are still used to justify most automation projects, but labor is a shrinking component—only 10 to 15 percent—of total costs. Therefore, to understand a new technology's true value, a manager should assess factors other than cost savings.

For example, *sales* can increase, as MCI Communications found when it spent $300 million to update its computer systems and offer innovative residential calling services. *Quality* can improve, as illustrated by magnetic resonance imaging (MRI) machines that can diagnose heart and liver diseases without using X rays and radioactive materials. With MRIs, scanning times are reduced from about 45 to 20 minutes, thus increasing the number of patients who can be served, reducing costs per patient, and increasing patient comfort. In manufacturing, Giddings & Lewis makes groups of machine tools by using automated materials handling equipment and computer control. These systems reduce human error and, thus, improve product quality. In addition, they yield *quicker delivery times* by reducing processing times. These reductions allow for *smaller inventories*, with less inventory held on the shop floor.

The *environment* might even improve: CSX Corporation replaced the mufflers on some of its unloading machinery with a noise-cancellation system that eliminates engine noise completely. The system, consisting of tiny speakers, a microphone, and a small signal processor, analyzes noise and instantly generates identical waves that are 180° out of phase with the sound waves. This technology eliminates the need for ear protection in a workplace that used to produce a noise level equivalent to that of a commercial jet during takeoff.

Of course, new technology also can have its downside. Investment in new technology can be forbidding, particularly for complex and expensive projects that require new facilities or extensive facility overhaul. The investment also can be risky because of uncertainties in demand and in per-unit benefits. Finally, technology may have hidden costs, requiring different employee knowledge and skills to maintain and operate the new equipment. Such requirements may generate employee resistance, lower morale, and increase turnover. Thus, the operations manager must sort out the many benefits and costs of different technological choices.

FIT WITH COMPETITIVE PRIORITIES

Another important test is how technological change will help a firm achieve the competitive priorities of cost, quality, time, and flexibility. Such a change should have a positive impact on one or more of these priorities, particularly on those that are emphasized for the service or product in question and on determining whether this advantage can be protected from imitation. For example, FedEx promises fast delivery time (overnight delivery) and that parcels will be "absolutely, positively" delivered on time. FedEx chose bar code technology to give it an early ability to track packages throughout the handling cycle—a capability possessed by none of its competitors at the time. Combining this technology with its own fleet of airplanes allowed its operations to support its strategic orientation and gave FedEx a large market share. Its competitors could not easily match FedEx's differentiation strategy on the basis of time.

FIRST-MOVER CONSIDERATIONS

This strategic consideration deals with *when* to adopt a new technology rather than which technology to choose. Being the first to market with a new technology offers a firm numerous advantages that can outweigh the financial investment needed. Technological leaders lay down the competitive rules that others will follow with regard to a new product or process. A "first-mover" may be able to gain an early, large market share that creates an entry barrier for other firms. Even if competitors are able to match the new technology, the first-mover's initial advantage in the market can endure.

Of course, a company that pursues a first-mover strategy faces risks that can jeopardize its financial and market position. First, pioneering costs can be high, with research and development costs exceeding the firm's financial capabilities.

Should the firm be a technology leader or follower?

Second, market demand for a new technology is speculative, and estimates of future financial gains may be overstated. Third, a new product or process technology may well become outdated quickly because of new technological breakthroughs. Thus, managers must carefully analyze these risks and benefits before deciding which technologies to pursue.

ECONOMIC JUSTIFICATION

Managers should make every effort to translate considerations of sources of competitive advantages, fit with competitive priorities, existence of core competencies, and first-mover strategy into a financial analysis to estimate whether investment in a new technology is economically justified. Operations managers should state precisely what they expect from a new technology and then quantify costs and performance goals. They should determine whether the expected after-tax cash flows resulting from the investment are likely to outweigh the costs, after accounting for the time value of money. Traditional techniques, such as the net present value method, internal rate of return method, and the payback method can be used to estimate financial impact (see Supplement J, "Financial Analysis" on the Student CD-ROM).

However, uncertainties and intangibles must also be considered, even though they cannot be easily measured. For example, there may be uncertainty about whether a new technology can be successfully developed. If it is a known technology, uncertainty may exist about how well it can be adapted to current processes or vice versa. Certain downstream benefits may be hard to quantify. For example, flexible automation might be of value for products that will be introduced well into the future, long after the life of the product for which it was first implemented. For these reasons, financial analyses should be augmented by qualitative judgments.

Operations managers must look beyond the direct costs of a new technology to its impact on customer service, delivery times, inventories, and resource flexibility. These are often the most important considerations. Quantifying such intangible goals as the ability to move quickly into a new market may be difficult. However, a firm that fails to make technological changes along with its competitors can quickly lose its competitive advantage and face declining revenues and layoffs. Justification should begin with financial analyses recognizing all quantifiable factors that can be translated into dollar values. The resulting financial measures should then be merged with an evaluation of the qualitative factors and intangibles involved. The manager can then estimate the risks associated with uncertain cost and revenue estimates. Decision-making tools, such as the preference matrix approach, decision theory, and decision trees, can help the manager make a final decision (see Supplement A, "Decision Making").

DISRUPTIVE TECHNOLOGIES

What is a disruptive technology and how can it be dealt with?

Many companies have invested aggressively and successfully in technologies to retain current customers and to improve current processes. They have done all the right things in terms of seeking a competitive advantage and funding the technology projects that should lead to the highest profit margins and largest market share, relative to their *current* customers. They have pursued new process technologies that address the next-generation performance requirements of their customers. And yet, paradoxically, what seems like good business practice may be devastating and prevent many firms from investing in the technologies that *future* customers will want and need.

This paradox is likely to occur because of disruptive technologies, which occur infrequently and are nearly impossible to justify on the basis of rational, analytical investment techniques. A **disruptive technology** is one that

disruptive technology A technology that has performance attributes that are not valued yet by *existing* customers or for current products, or performs much worse on some performance attributes that existing or future customers value but will quickly surpass existing technologies on such attributes when it is refined.

- has performance attributes that are not valued yet by *existing* customers or for current products, or
- performs much worse on some performance attributes that existing or future customers value but will quickly surpass existing technologies on such attributes when it is refined.

COUNTERING DISRUPTIVE TECHNOLOGIES. How can a company deal with the paradox of disruptive technology? The first step is to recognize that it is a disruptive rather than a sustaining technology. One indicator could be internal disagreement over the advisability of producing the new technology. Marketing and financial managers will rarely support a disruptive technology, but technical personnel may argue forcibly that a new technology market can be achieved. A second indicator is to compare the likely slope of performance improvement of the technology with market demand. If its performance trajectory, as judged by knowledgeable analysts, is much faster than market expectations, it might be a disruptive technology that could become strategically crucial. It might best meet future market needs even though it is currently an inferior product.

Managers must be willing to undertake major and rapid change with disruptive technologies that are strategically crucial, even if doing so means initially serving emerging markets and realizing low profit margins. When both technology and customers change rapidly, as at many high-tech firms, one of two conflicting methods can be used to manage disruptive technologies. One method is to develop these technologies in a different part of the organization, with one part of the firm pursuing innovation and the other parts pursuing efficiency and continual improvement of technologies for existing customer bases. A team, sometimes referred to as a *skunk works*, can be formed to develop the new technology without disrupting normal operations. Such teams often work in close quarters, without many amenities, but band together in almost missionary zeal.

The other method is to use different methods of management at different times in the course of technological development. Firms can alternate periods of consolidation and continuity with sharp reorientation, interspersing periods of action and change with periods of evaluation and efficiency. With either method, the operations manager must seek ways to improve continually the existing technologies driving the production system, while being alert for radical innovations and discontinuities that can make technologies obsolete.

MANAGING INFORMATION TECHNOLOGY AND VALUE CHAINS ACROSS THE ORGANIZATION

Technologies are embedded in processes throughout an organization (see Figure 12.2) and across its value chain. In each of their functional areas and business units, both service providers and manufacturers use many technologies. For example, Seven-Eleven Japan uses point-of-sale technology to assess customers' needs (*marketing*) and to control inventory in its value chain (*operations*). Technology also creates special needs for training and supporting employees (*human resources*). The New York Stock Exchange uses computer equipment and software (*management information systems*) to streamline trading processes (*finance*). *Engineering* is heavily involved in research and development, creating new services and products and applying them to the organization's processes. eBay's online auctions show how e-commerce can thrive, and Cisco shows how the Internet can establish connections throughout the entire organization as well as to its suppliers. The very essence of ERP illustrates many of the ways in which this chapter's topic, information technology and value chains, is important to all business areas. ERP makes connections among applications in sales and marketing, customer service, supply chain management, accounting and finance, manufacturing, and human resources.

CHAPTER HIGHLIGHTS

- Technology consists of physical equipment, procedures, know-how, and the support network used at operations to produce services and products. Managers must make informed decisions about which technological possibilities to pursue and how best to implement those that are chosen.

- Innovation and technological change is a primary source of productivity improvement and a driver of global competition. Organizations more experienced at adapting to changing technologies tend to enjoy stronger competitive positions worldwide.

- Technologies are involved in all the processes along a firm's value chain and in each of the firm's functional areas. Managers need to invest the time to learn about the technologies that are used or could be used at their organizations.

- Information technology deals with how managers use and communicate information to make decisions effectively. Hardware, software, databases, and telecommunications are the main components that make up information technology.

- The Internet is a network of networks, allowing the exchange of text, graphics, audio, video, programs, and faxes.

- E-commerce, both B2C and B2B, has created totally new ways for a firm to relate to customers, suppliers, employees, and investors.

- E-purchasing is changing the way that many firms are handling their supplier-relationship processes in external value-chain linkages. Electronic data interchange (EDI) has been used since the 1970s. It is now more accessible through the Internet and enables firms to include more suppliers in their value chains. Catalog hubs, exchanges, and auctions are among the innovations brought on by the Internet.

- ERP is a large, integrated information system. Its applications cut across many processes, functional areas, business units, regions, and products.

- High-tech options are not necessarily appropriate solutions to operations problems. Tests of the advisability of technological change include competitive advantages measured in terms of costs, sales, quality, delivery times, inventory, and the environment; financial analyses; first-mover or follower considerations; identifying disruptive technologies; and fit with competitive priorities.

STUDENT CD-ROM AND INTERNET RESOURCES

The Student CD-ROM and the Companion Website at **www.prenhall.com/krajewski** contain many tools, activities, and resources designed for this chapter. The following items are recommended to enhance your skills and improve your understanding of the material in this chapter.

STUDENT CD-ROM RESOURCES

➤ **PowerPoint Slides:** View the comprehensive set of slides customized for this chapter's concepts and techniques.
➤ **OM Explorer Tutors:** OM Explorer contains four tutor spreadsheets that will help you learn about financial analysis. See Supplement J in the OM Explorer menu.
➤ **OM Explorer Solver:** OM Explorer contains one spreadsheet to help with general financial analysis, such as for investments in new technology. See Financial Analysis in the OM Explorer menu for this routine.
➤ **Written Tours:** See how process technology is used by the Lower Florida Keys Health System to treat patients and by Chaparral Steel to produce steel.

➤ **Supplement K:** "Computer-Integrated Manufacturing." See how to integrate product design and engineering, process planning, and manufacturing by means of complex computer systems.

INTERNET RESOURCES

➤ **Self-Study Quizzes:** See the compendium of true or false, multiple choice, and essay questions that give feedback on how well you have mastered the concepts in this chapter.
➤ **In the News:** See the articles that apply to this chapter.
➤ **Internet Exercises:** Try out seven different links to product and information technology at ZDNet, CDNOW, Wal-Mart, Internet Ventures, Hewitt Associates, and Cable & Wireless Networks. Other exercises are available on additional aspects of information technology and value chains.
➤ **Virtual Tours:** Check out the use of process technology in manufacturing circuit boards and in making trades at the New York Stock Exchange. Also see the "Web Links to Company Facility Tours" for additional tours of company facilities.

KEY TERMS

auction 520
catalog hubs 520
database 513
disruptive technology 526
electronic commerce (e-commerce) 514
electronic data interchange (EDI) 518
encryption 517
enterprise process 521

enterprise resource planning (ERP) 521
exchange 520
hardware 513
information technology 511
Internet 515
interoperability 523
intranet 514
process technology 510

product technology 510
software 513
support network 510
technology 509
telecommunications 514
Web browsers 515
World Wide Web 515

DISCUSSION QUESTIONS

1. Why are traditional financial analysis techniques criticized when they are used to justify new technologies? Must such projects just be accepted as a leap of faith and an act of hope? Explain.

2. Chip "Hacker" Snerdly works for the sales department of Farr and Wyde, an office equipment supplier in a cut-throat competitive market. Farr and Wyde's competitors use voice mailboxes to receive messages while calling on other customers. Snerdly discovers that a surprising number of voice-mailbox occupants do not bother to use passwords and that others rarely change their passwords.

So he listens to, copies, and deletes messages left for his competitors by their customers. Snerdly calls on those customers himself, knowing that they are in the market for office equipment. What are the ethical issues here? What policies are necessary to foil Snerdly?

3. Discuss how increased Internet use of business-to-business interactions would affect customer–supplier relationships.

4. For an organization of your choice, such as where you previously worked, discuss how an ERP system could be used and whether it would increase value-chain effectiveness.

PROBLEMS

An icon in the margin next to a problem identifies the software that can be helpful, but is not mandatory. The software is available on the Student CD-ROM that is packaged with every new copy of the textbook. Problems 1 through 4 require reading Supplement A, "Decision Making." Problems 6 through 8 require reading Supplement J, "Financial Analysis." Problem 9 should be solved as a team exercise.

Advanced Problems

1. **OM Explorer** You have been asked to analyze four new advanced technologies and recommend the best one for adoption by your company. Management has rated these technologies with respect to seven criteria, using a 0 through 100 scale (0 = worst; 100 = best). Management has given the performance criteria different weights. Table 12.1 summarizes the relevant information. Which technology would you recommend?

TABLE 12.1
ANALYSIS OF NEW TECHNOLOGIES

Criterion	Weight	Technology Rating			
		A	B	C	D
Financial measures	25	60	70	10	100
Volume flexibility	15	90	25	60	80
Quality of output	20	70	90	75	90
Required facility space	5	60	20	40	50
Market share	10	60	70	90	90
Product mix flexibility	20	90	80	30	90
Required labor skills	5	80	40	20	10

2. **OM Explorer** Hitech Manufacturing Company must select a process technology for one of its new products from among three different alternatives. The following cost data have been obtained for the three process technologies.

Cost	Process A	Process B	Process C
Fixed costs per year	$20,000	$40,000	$100,000
Variable costs per unit	$15	$10	$6

a. Find the range for the annual production volume in which each process will be preferred.

b. If the expected annual production volume is 12,000 units, which process should be selected?

3. **OM Explorer** Technology Enterprises Company is evaluating three different manufacturing technologies to choose the best one for manufacturing its new product line. The payoffs from the technologies will depend on market conditions for the new product line, which is uncertain but could be buoyant, moderate, or dismal. Although management is unable to estimate the probabilities for these market conditions because of the nature of the new products, it has developed the following payoff table.

Alternative	Market Condition		
	Buoyant	Moderate	Dismal
Technology A	$500,000	$150,000	($200,000)
Technology B	$200,000	$50,000	$20,000
Technology C	$900,000	$25,000	($300,000)

Which alternative would you recommend for each of the following decision criteria?

a. Maximin

b. Maximax

c. Laplace

d. Minimax regret

4. **SmartDraw** Super Innovators, Inc. is faced with the decision of switching its production facilities to new (promising, but not yet completely tried) processing technology. The technology may be implemented in one

or two steps, with the option to stop after the initial step. Because the benefits from the new technology (cost savings and productivity improvements) are subject to uncertainty, the firm is considering two options. The first option is to make the full switchover in one step to take advantage of economies of scale in investment and opportunities to gain a larger market share. For this choice the investment cost is $5 million. The expected present value of the cash flows is $20 million if the new processing technology works as well as expected and $6 million if it does not work as well as expected. The second option is to implement part of the system as a first step and then extend the system to full capability. If the technology does not work as well as expected and the firm had decided to go for the full switchover, the total investment cost could be higher (because of diseconomies of scale) and the payoff could be lower. The investment cost for the initial step is $2 million, and the present value of the combined investment in two steps will be $6 million. If both steps are implemented, the expected present value of the cash flows is $15 million if the new processing technology works as well as expected and $8 million otherwise. If only the first step is implemented, the expected present value of the cash flows is $4 million if the new processing technology works as well as expected and $2 million otherwise. The firm estimates that there is a 40 percent chance that the new technology will work as well as expected.

a. Draw a decision tree to solve this problem.

b. What should the firm do to achieve the highest expected payoff?

5. The GSX Company is considering an automated manufacturing system to replace its current system. At present, the monthly cost of goods sold is $1 million. Direct labor accounts for 40 percent of this cost. Scrap and rework costs are $200,000. Working capital (primarily inventories) required for the smooth operation of the current system averages four months' cost of goods sold. The anticipated benefits of the proposed automated system are (1) a reduction of 25 percent in direct labor and 75 percent in scrap and rework costs and (2) a 50 percent reduction in the working capital investment resulting from a one-time reduction in work-in-process inventories.

a. Estimate the annual savings from the automated system in dollars per year.

b. What is the reduction in the dollar amount invested in working capital?

6. **OM Explorer** Riverbend Hospital is considering two different computerized information systems to improve pharmacy productivity. The first alternative is a computer system that will require a one-time investment of $80,000 for the computer hardware, software, and necessary employee training. After-tax cash flows attributable to the investment are expected to be $20,000 per year for the next eight years. Savings would accrue from increased pharmacist productivity and the value of having timely and accurate information. The second alternative is to install a different computer system linked to bedside terminals that would allow doctors to prescribe

treatments directly to the pharmacy from patients' rooms. This system would require an investment of $170,000, but is expected to generate after-tax cash flows of $40,000 per year for eight years. The hospital seeks to earn 16 percent on its investments. Assume that both systems will have no salvage value at the end of eight years.

a. Calculate the net present value, internal rate of return (IRR), and payback period for each alternative.

b. Based on your financial analysis, what do you recommend?

c. Are there any valid considerations other than financial? If so, what are they?

7. **OM Explorer** First State Bank is considering installing a new automatic teller machine (ATM) at either of two new locations: inside a supermarket or inside the bank itself. An initial investment of $60,000 is required for the ATM regardless of location. The operating costs of the ATM at the supermarket would be $15,000 per year and of the ATM inside the bank $10,000 per year. The higher costs of the supermarket ATM reflect the additional cost of leasing supermarket space and transportation. Revenue generated from new accounts because of the installation of each ATM should also differ, with the supermarket ATM generating $55,000 per year and the bank ATM $52,000 per year. Assume a tax rate of 30 percent and a desired rate of return of 18 percent on investment. The ATMs have an expected life of eight years, with no salvage value at the end of that time. Use MACRS depreciation allowances (see Supplement J, "Financial Analysis" on the Student CD-ROM) noting that the ATMs may be considered as assets in the five-year class.

a. Calculate the net present value for each alternative.

b. Based on your analysis, which location do you recommend?

8. **OM Explorer** New England Power and Electric, a supplier of electric power to the northeast United States, is considering the purchase of a robot to repair welds in nuclear reactors. Two types of vision-system robots are being considered: a "smart" robot, whose actions in the reactor would be controlled by what it "sees," and a different kind of robot, whose actions in the reactor would be controlled by an external operator. The "smart" robot requires an initial investment of $300,000, and the operator-controlled robot requires an initial investment of $200,000. Both robots have an expected life of five years and no salvage value at the end of that time. Welds are currently repaired by a human welder. The job is hazardous, so the welder's annual pay and fringe benefits total $150,000. Buying either robot eliminates the need for the human welder, but the operator-controlled robot requires an operator whose annual salary (and benefits) would be $50,000. The "smart" robot requires an extra $15,000 in technical support. New England Power and Electric seeks at least 18 percent on its investments, and its tax rate is 50 percent. As these robots are specially designed tools, treat them as assets in the three-year class and use MACRS depreciation allowances.

a. Calculate the net present value for each alternative

b. Based on your financial analysis, which do you recommend?

9. Imagine that you are a member of the operations management team in a firm that manufactures flashlights. Your firm is faced with the problem of choosing the equipment and process technology for manufacturing the casings for the flashlights. After an evaluation of several alternative technologies, the choice has been narrowed to two technologies: (1) deep drawing of metal bars on a press using a die and (2) injection molding of a variety of plastic materials. Compare the two technologies in terms of how each one will influence various elements of the operating system.

a. First, make a list of the various elements (e.g., equipment, raw materials, building, operators, safety) and then indicate how the two technologies influence each element.

b. For which of these elements is the contrast between the influences of the two technologies most striking?

CASE   BILL'S HARDWARE

It had been a very busy week at Bill Murton's hardware store. A storm had blown through early in the week, and sales of tools and repair parts had been brisk. This morning was relatively quiet, however, so Murton was using it as an opportunity to look over his shelves to get an idea of inventory levels. Some items had sold much less than he would have expected; others had sold out completely.

I sure wish I could predict what will be sold each week, he mused. It seems like I always have too much of some things and not enough of others. I wonder if the POS system that our cooperative is considering would help me deal with this uncertainty.

Bill's Hardware is a member of a hardware store cooperative, a group of more than 300 independently owned hardware stores that banded together for greater buying power and better merchandise distribution. Many of the items carried by a typical hardware store are similar. By buying these items as a group and storing them at a few centrally located distribution centers, individual stores can achieve economies of scale, allowing them to compete better with large nationwide chains. The cooperative is member owned. An annual membership fee and a service charge are applied to the cost of the items that a store purchases through the cooperative. Any revenues generated beyond the cooperative's operating costs are returned to members as a dividend.

Typically, a member store reviews inventory once a week and places orders that will bring stock back up to a target level. That level is the quantity of an item that, based on the time of year, the store owner wants to have on the shelf. Owners place orders by using a PC-based software program and a modem over a dial-up telephone connection to the cooperative's computer. The cooperative leases a fleet of trucks to deliver goods weekly to member stores from one of three distribution centers. Each geographic area receives shipments on a designated day. Surges in demand, if detected, can be met by midcycle orders shipped via UPS.

Target inventory levels are based on forecasts made from historical information kept in the store's inventory database. These forecasts are adjusted by the owner's past experience and information gleaned from trade journals and from listening to customers. Additionally, the cooperative makes aggregate sales data from member stores available, along with projected demand trends. The challenge for the store owner is to project weekly requirements accurately and to detect unusual demand for items that exceed inventory in time to avoid stockouts.

THE POS SYSTEM

The cooperative's directors have formulated a plan to obtain and install point-of-sale (POS) technology in members' stores. The motivation is to take advantage of technology that can allow the distribution center to know, in real time, what items are being sold in various stores. Armed with this information, the cooperative can improve its product forecasting, make better purchasing decisions, and reduce the chance that an item will be out of stock at distribution centers. Although the original plan was to make installation of the system mandatory, the cooperative's directors decided that such a requirement could place an excessive burden on some of the smaller or less profitable stores. Consequently, installation will be optional.

The POS system is to comprise a scanning device attached to a cash register that operates with a microprocessor. This cash register will be networked to a PC so that an item's current price can be obtained for checkout and a perpetual inventory maintained. Each night, the distribution center will telephone the store's computer, which will answer and download the day's sales. At the end of the business day, the store owner can also review the day's sales and determine current inventory levels. The system will be designed to detect any items likely to sell out. The owner can tag any item, permitting an order to be placed that night (when the distribution center calls) for midcycle delivery.

The cost of the POS system will be borne by individual stores but, because of combined purchasing power, systems can be obtained for 40 percent less than list price. The cooperative's directors propose that each distribution center contract with an installer to do on-site equipment installation at individual stores. However, individual store owners would be allowed to have local technicians do the installation. The cost of system installation at the distribution center will be borne by a one-time assessment of all member stores, whether or not they install and use the system.

A two-day training session will be conducted at distribution centers whenever five or more store owners have installed the system and are ready to learn how to use it. Optionally, store owners can travel to the POS vendor's home office in Atlanta at their own expense for a two-day training session, which is to be offered once a month.

A vote has been scheduled prior to the cooperative's annual members' meeting. Members are asked to vote "yes" or "no" on the proposal, and a majority of those voting will determine the outcome.

As Bill Murton completes his shelf scan and returns to his office, he thinks to himself: Since the new POS system will automatically track inventory, I wonder if I will still be able to get a gut feel for what is selling and what is not. There is nothing like examining the shelves like I just did and talking to customers to understand what I should be stocking. And, I wonder how much it will cost to run the system once it is installed?

QUESTIONS

1. How will a POS system enhance the operations of Bill's Hardware? How will it enhance the operations of the cooperative?
2. What strategic advantages will the system confer on Bill's Hardware? What strategic advantages will accrue to the cooperative?
3. What criteria should be considered when assessing the benefits of the POS technology? What costs should be included?
4. How should Bill Murton vote?

Source: This case was prepared by Larry Meile, Boston College, as a basis for classroom discussion.

SELECTED REFERENCES

Alsop, Stewart. "Sun's Java: What's Hype and What's Real." *Fortune* (July 7, 1997), pp. 191–192.

"AT&T IP Backbone Network," www.ipservices.att.com/backbone/.

Beeter-Schmelz, D. R., and R. Graham. "Business-to-Business Online Purchasing: Suppliers' Impact on Buyers' Adoption and Usage Intent." *Journal of Supply Chain Management*, vol. 6 (2001), pp. 4–10.

Bower, Joseph L., and Clayton M. Christensen. "Disruptive Technologies: Catching the Wave." *Harvard Business Review* (January–February 1995), pp. 43–53.

Boyer, K. K. "E-Operations: A Guide to Streamlining with the Internet." *Business Horizons* (January–February 2001), pp. 47–54.

Burgelman, Robert A., Modesto A. Maidique, and Steven C. Wheelwright. *Strategic Management of Technology and Innovation*. Chicago: Irwin, 1996.

Cheng, E. W. L., H. Li, P. E. D. Love, and A. Irani. "An E-Business Model to Support Supply-Chain Activities in Construction." *Logistics Information Management*, vol. 14, no. 1 (2001), pp. 68–78.

Cohen, Morris A., and Uday M. Apte. *Manufacturing Automation*. Chicago: Irwin, 1997.

Collier, David A. *Service Management: The Automation of Services*. Reston, VA: Reston, 1985.

Davenport, Thomas H. "Putting the Enterprise into the Enterprise System." *Harvard Business Review* (July–August 1998), pp. 121–131.

Dinning, M., and E. W. Shuster. "Fighting Friction: Using Low-Cost Passive Tags, Auto-ID Technology Seeks to Speed Up the Flow of Goods." *APICS–The Performance Advantage*, vol. 14, no. 1 (February 2003), pp. 27–31.

Earl, Michael, and M. M. Bensaou. "The Right Mind-Set of Managing Information Technology." *Harvard Business Review* (September–October 1998), pp. 119–129.

"The Emerging Digital Economy II," 1999. (www.ecommerce.gov/ede).

Emiliani, M. L. "Business-to Business Online Auctions: Key Issues for Purchasing Process Improvement." *Supply Chain Management*, vol. 5, no. 4 (2000), pp. 176–186.

Gallaugher, John. "E-Commerce and the Undulating Distribution Channel." *Communications of the ACM*, vol. 45, no. 7 (July 2002), pp. 89–95.

Helft, Miguel. "Fashion Fast Forward." *Business 2.0* (May 2002).

How the Internet Works, *Internet World*, vol. 8, no. 10 (1996).

How the Internet Works: All You Really Need to Know, *Business Week* (July 20, 1998).

Iansiti, Marco, and Jonathan West. "Technology Integration: Turning Great Research into Great Products." *Harvard Business Review* (May–June 1997), pp. 69–79.

Jacobs, F. Robert, and D. Clay Whybark. *Why ERP?* New York: Irwin McGraw-Hill, 2000.

Kanakamedala, Hishore, Glenn Ramsdell, and Vats Srivatsan. "Getting Supply Chain Software Right." *McKinsey Quarterly*, no. 1 (2003).

Lefebvre, Louis A., Ann Langley, Jean Harvey, and Elisabeth Lefebvre, "Exploring the Strategy Technology Connection in Small Manufacturing Firms." *Production and Operations Management*, vol. 1, no. 3 (1992), pp. 269–285.

Moe, W. W. and P. S. Fader. "Uncovering Patterns in Cybershopping." *California Management Review*, vol. 43, no. 4 (2001), pp. 106–117.

Noori, Hamid. *Managing the Dynamics of New Technology*. Englewood Cliffs, NJ: Prentice Hall, 1990.

Noori, Hamid, and Russell W. Radford. *Readings and Cases in the Management of New Technology*. Englewood Cliffs, NJ: Prentice Hall, 1990.

Prahalad, C. K., and Gary Hamel. "The Core Competence of the Corporation." *Harvard Business Review* (May–June 1990), pp. 79–91.

Quinn, James B., and Penny C. Paquette. "Technology in Services: Creating Organizational Revolutions." *Sloan Management Review* (Winter 1990), pp. 67–78.

Roth, Aleda V. "Neo-Operations Strategy: Linking Capabilities-Based Competition to Technology." In *Handbook of Technology Management*, G. H. Gaynor (ed.). New York: McGraw-Hill, 1996, pp. 38.1–38.44.

Scalle, Cedric X., and Mark J. Cotteleer. *Enterprise Resource Planning (ERP)*. Boston, MA: Harvard Business School Publishing, No. 9-699-020, 1999.

Schneiderjans, Marc J., and Quing Cao. *E-Commerce Operations Management*. New Jersey: World Scientific, 2002.

Seifert, Dirk. *Collaborative Planning Forecasting and Replenishment: How to Create a Supply Chain Advantage*. Krefeld, Germany: Galileo Business, 2002.

Shah, J., and N. Singh. "Benchmarking Internal Supply Chain Performance Development of a Framework." *Journal of Supply Chain Management* (Winter 2001), pp. 37–47.

Skinner, Wickham. "Operations Technology: Blind Spot in Strategic Management." *Interfaces*, vol. 14 (January–February 1984). pp. 116–125.

Surowiecki, James. "The Most Devastating Retailer in the World," *New Yorker* (September 18, 2000), p. 74.

Thurm, Scott. "Behind Cisco's Woes Are Some Wounds of Its Own Making." *Wall Street Journal* (April 18, 2001), pp. A1, A8.

"Wireless in Cyberspace." *Business Week Online* (May 22, 2000). www.businessweek.com/common_frames/bws.htm?http://www.businessweek.com/2000/00_21/b3682029.htm.

Wymbs, C. "How E-Commerce Is Transforming and Internationalizing Service Industries." *Journal of Services Marketing*, vol. 14, no. 6 (2000), pp. 463–478.

Zsidisin, G. A., M. Jun, and L. L. Adams. "The Relationship Between Information Technology and Service Quality in the Dual-Direction Supply Chain." *International Journal of Service Industry Management*, vol. 11, no. 4 (2000), pp. 312–328.

Forecasting

LEARNING GOALS   *After reading this chapter, you should be able to . . .*

IDENTIFY OR DEFINE

1. the basic demand patterns that combine to produce a demand time series.
2. collaborative planning, forecasting, and replenishment (CPFR).
3. the various judgmental forecasting approaches.
4. the various measures of forecast errors.

DESCRIBE OR EXPLAIN

5. how to choose the appropriate forecasting technique for a given situation.
6. the use of regression to make forecasts.
7. how to compute forecasts using the most common approaches for time-series analysis.
8. how forecast errors are used to monitor and control forecast performance.

UNILEVER

One of the critical drivers in managing value chains is effective customer demand planning (CDP), which begins with accurate forecasts. CDP is a business-planning process that enables sales teams (and customers) to develop demand forecasts as input to service-planning processes, production and inventory planning, and revenue planning. *Forecasting* is generally seen as the process of developing the most probable view of what future demand will be, given a set of assumptions about technology, competitors, pricing, marketing, expenditures, and sales effort. *Planning*, on the other hand, is the process of making management decisions on how to deploy resources to best respond to the demand forecasts. Forecasts must generally precede plans: It is not possible to make decisions on staffing levels, purchasing commitments, and inventory levels until forecasts are developed that give reasonably accurate views of demand over the forecasting time horizon.

Unilever (www.unilever.com), the fast-moving consumer products supplier, has a state-of-the-art CDP system. Using software from Manugistics (www.manugistics.com), the current system blends historical shipment data with promotional data, allowing information sharing and collaboration with important customers. The system begins with shipment history and current order information, the foundation upon which Unilever's system is built. This baseline forecast depends solely on past and present information, so reliable data is a critical requirement. Because data frequently is collected from disparate legacy systems, it may contain errors and may not necessarily lead to the best forecast. Moreover, statistical information is not useful in forecasting the outcomes of certain events, promotions, rollouts, and special packages, which are very common in the industry. To overcome this problem, planners at Unilever must adjust the statistical forecasts with planned promotion predictions conducted by special sales teams. For each promotion, the sales-planning system predicts the "lift," or projected increase in sales, and routes it to the demand-planning system, which applies it to appropriate *stock-keeping units (SKUs)* and distribution centers each week. In turn, these forecasts are reviewed and adjusted if needed. Furthermore, Unilever conducts external market research and internal sales projections that are analyzed, combined with the retail customer promotions, and fed into the demand-planning system. To further improve the accuracy of its forecasts and reduce inventory lead times, Unilever—the purveyor of

Dove, Lipton, Hellmann's, and hundreds of other brands—compares point-of-sale (POS) data with its own forecasts. Unfortunately, not all customers provide POS data. Moreover, integrating the data is not easy because it comes in different formats, which forces the company to build interfaces in order to manage it. Because creating these interfaces is expensive and time consuming, most companies, including Unilever, only collect POS data from its largest customers. Ultimately, planners at Unilever negotiate the final numbers each week and feed these forecasts into the demand-planning system.

Overall, the current system has been a success. Unilever has reduced its inventory and improved its customer service. However, if collaboration and the usage of POS data were to increase, Unilever would likely reap even larger benefits from its more accurate forecasts. The next step for Unilever is to collaborate with its customers and suppliers, a process by which forecasts, promotion plans, and other data are shared among these firms to determine the final forecast. This process is known as *collaborative planning, forecasting, and replenishment (CPFR)*.

Sources: Mitchell, Robert L. "Case Study: Unilever Crosses the Data Streams." *Computerworld* (December 17, 2001); **www.computerworld .com/softwaretopics/erp/story/0,10801,6657 4,00.html;** Mitchell, Robert L. "Tech Check: Getting Demand Planning Right." *Computerworld* (December 17, 2001); **www.computerworld .com/softwaretopics/erp/story/0,10001,6657 6,00.html;** Schoenberger, Chana R. "The Weakest Link." *Forbes* (October 1, 2001). **www.forbes .com/forbes/2001/1001/114_print.html.**

Lipton tea is one of the many Unilever products, and its demand must be forecast for around the world. Here tourists walk past a souvenir and food stall in Beijing, China, which offers cups of Lipton tea. For centuries, globalism's story traveled with merchants who shepherded spice along Eurasian trade routes. Now it travels over wires and radio waves, satellites, airplanes, and gigabytes.

Why is forecasting important?

forecast A prediction of future events used for planning purposes.

Unilever's success to date demonstrates the value of forecasting. A **forecast** is a prediction of future events used for planning purposes. At Unilever, management needed accurate forecasts to ensure value-chain success. Changing business conditions resulting from global competition, rapid technological change, and increasing environmental concerns exert pressure on a firm's capability to generate accurate forecasts.

Forecasts aid in determining what resources are needed, in scheduling existing resources, and in acquiring additional resources. Accurate forecasts allow schedulers to increase customer satisfaction, reduce customer response times, use capacity efficiently, and cut inventories.

Forecasting methods may be based on mathematical models that use available historical data, on qualitative methods that draw on managerial experience and customer judgments, or they may be based on a combination of both. Unilever's CDP system combines these methods and CPFR (see Managerial Practice 13.1) promises even more improvements in its forecasting process. Variations of these methods are valuable in estimating future processing times and learning-curve effects (see Supplement G, "Learning Curve Analysis" and Supplement H, "Measuring Output Rates"). In this chapter, our focus is on demand forecasts. We will explore several forecasting methods commonly used today and their advantages and limitations. We also identify the decisions that managers should make in designing a forecasting system.

As you read about forecasting, think about why it is important to the various departments and functions across the organization, such as . . .

> ➤ **finance**, which uses long-term forecasts to project cash flow and capital requirements.
> ➤ **human resources**, which uses forecasts to anticipate employee hiring and training needs.
> ➤ **management information systems**, which designs and implements forecasting systems.
> ➤ **marketing**, which develops sales forecasts that are used for medium- and long-range plans and the customer relationship process.
> ➤ **operations**, which develops and uses forecasts for decisions, such as workforce and output scheduling, short-term inventory replenishment, managing the supplier relationship process, and long-term capacity planning.

◐ DEMAND CHARACTERISTICS

At the root of most business decisions is the challenge of forecasting customer demand. It is a difficult task because the demand for services and goods can vary greatly. For example, demand for lawn fertilizer predictably increases in the spring and summer months; however, the particular weekends when demand is heaviest may depend on uncontrollable factors such as the weather. Sometimes patterns are more predictable. Thus, the peak hours of the day for a large bank's call center is from 9:00 A.M. to 12:00 P.M., and the peak day of the week is Monday. For its statement-rendering processes, the peak months are January, April, July, and October, which is when the quarterly statements are sent out. Forecasting demand in such situations requires uncovering the underlying patterns from available information. In this section, we discuss the basic patterns of demand.

The repeated observations of demand for a service or product in their order of occurrence form a pattern known as a **time series**. There are five basic patterns of most demand time series.

time series The repeated observations of demand for a service or product in their order of occurrence.

1. *Horizontal.* The fluctuation of data around a constant mean.
2. *Trend.* The systematic increase or decrease in the mean of the series over time.
3. *Seasonal.* A repeatable pattern of increases or decreases in demand, depending on the time of day, week, month, or season.
4. *Cyclical.* The less predictable gradual increases or decreases in demand over longer periods of time (years or decades).
5. *Random.* The unforecastable variation in demand.

Cyclical patterns arise from two influences. The first is the business cycle, which includes factors that cause the economy to go from recession to expansion over a number of years. The other influence is the service or product life cycle, which reflects the stages of demand from development through decline. Business cycle movement is difficult to predict because it is affected by national or international events, such as presidential elections or political turmoil in other countries. Predicting the rate of demand buildup or decline in the life cycle also is difficult. Sometimes firms estimate demand for a new product by starting with the demand history for the product it is replacing.

Four of the patterns of demand—horizontal, trend, seasonal, and cyclical—combine in varying degrees to define the underlying time pattern of demand for a service or product. The fifth pattern, random variation, results from chance causes and thus cannot be predicted. Random variation is an aspect of demand that makes every forecast wrong. Figure 13.1 shows the first four patterns of a demand time series, all of which contain random variation. A time series may comprise any combination of these patterns.

DESIGNING THE FORECASTING SYSTEM

Before using forecasting techniques to analyze operations management problems, a manager must make three decisions: (1) what to forecast, (2) what type of forecasting technique to use, and (3) what type of computer hardware or software (or both) to use. We discuss each of these decisions before examining specific forecasting techniques.

DECIDING WHAT TO FORECAST

What makes a forecasting system best for any particular situation?

Although some sort of demand estimate is needed for the individual services or goods produced by a company, forecasting total demand for groups or clusters and then deriving individual service or product forecasts may be easiest. Also, selecting the correct unit of measurement (e.g., service or product units or machine hours) for forecasting may be as important as choosing the best method.

aggregation The act of clustering several similar services or products so that companies can obtain more accurate forecasts.

LEVEL OF AGGREGATION. Few companies err by more than 5 percent when forecasting total demand for all their services or products. However, errors in forecasts for individual items may be much higher. By clustering several similar services or products in a process called **aggregation**, companies can obtain more accurate forecasts. Many compa-

---

FIGURE 13.1

Patterns of Demand

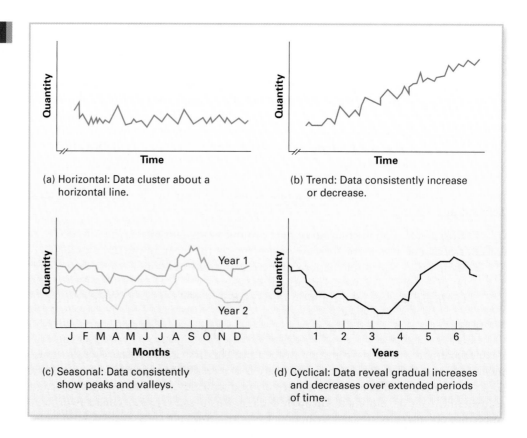

(a) Horizontal: Data cluster about a horizontal line.

(b) Trend: Data consistently increase or decrease.

(c) Seasonal: Data consistently show peaks and valleys.

(d) Cyclical: Data reveal gradual increases and decreases over extended periods of time.

nies utilize a two-tier forecasting system, first making forecasts for families of services or goods that have similar demand requirements and common processing, labor, and materials requirements and then deriving forecasts for individual items, which are sometimes called stock-keeping units. A **stock-keeping unit (SKU)** is an individual item or product that has an identifying code and is held in inventory somewhere along the value chain, such as a distribution center or hospital. This two-tier approach maintains consistency between planning for the final stages of manufacturing (which requires the unit forecasts) and longer-term planning for sales, profit, and capacity (which requires the product family forecasts). We return to this point later (see Chapter 14, "Aggregate Planning").

UNITS OF MEASUREMENT. The most useful forecasts for planning and analyzing operations problems are those based on service or product units, such as SKUs, express packages to deliver, or customers needing maintenance service or repairs for their cars, rather than dollars. Forecasts of sales revenue are not very helpful because prices often fluctuate. Forecasting the number of units of demand—and then translating these estimates to sales revenue estimates by multiplying them by the price—often is the better method. If accurately forecasting the number of units of demand for a service or product is not possible, forecasting the standard labor or machine *hours* required of each of the critical resources, based on historical patterns, often is better. For companies that produce services or goods to customer order, estimates of labor or machine hours are important to scheduling and capacity planning.

CHOOSING THE TYPE OF FORECASTING TECHNIQUE

The forecaster's objective is to develop a useful forecast from the information at hand with the technique that is appropriate for the different characteristics of demand. This choice sometimes involves a trade-off between forecast accuracy and costs, such as software purchases, the time required to develop a forecast, and personnel training. Two general types of forecasting techniques are used for demand forecasting: qualitative methods and quantitative methods. Unilever's CDP process uses a combination of both methods. Qualitative methods include **judgment methods**, which translate the opinions of managers, expert opinions, consumer surveys, and sales-force estimates into quantitative estimates. Quantitative methods include causal methods and time-series analysis. **Causal methods** use historical data on independent variables, such as promotional campaigns, economic conditions, and competitors' actions, to predict demand. **Time-series analysis** is a statistical approach that relies heavily on historical demand data to project the future size of demand and recognizes trends and seasonal patterns.

A key factor in choosing the proper forecasting approach is the time horizon for the decision requiring forecasts. Forecasts can be made for the short term, medium term, and long term. Table 13.1 contains examples of demand-forecasting applications and the typical planning horizon for each.

FORECASTING WITH COMPUTERS

In many short-term forecasting applications, computers are a necessity. Often companies must prepare forecasts for hundreds or even thousands of services or products repeatedly. For example, a large network of health care facilities must calculate demand forecasts for each of its services for every department. This undertaking involves voluminous data that must be manipulated frequently. Analysts must examine the time series for each service or product and arrive at a forecast. However, new software can ease the burden of making these forecasts and coordinating the forecasts between retailers and suppliers.

Many forecasting software packages are available for all sizes of computers and offer a wide variety of forecasting capabilities and report formats. To explore the options available, see Manugistics (**www.manugistics.com**), Forecast Pro (**www.forecastpro.com**), and SAS (**www.sas.com**). A more comprehensive list, including a recent survey of available software can be found at (**www.lionhrtpub.com/orms/surveys/FSS/fss-fr.html**) and (**www.morris.wharton.upenn.edu/forecast/programs.html**). As you will learn when we

stock-keeping unit (SKU) An individual item or product that has an identifying code and is held in inventory somewhere along the value chain.

When are time-series methods best and when are causal or judgment methods best?

judgment methods A type of qualitative method that translates the opinions of managers, expert opinions, consumer surveys, and sales-force estimates into quantitative estimates.

causal methods A type of quantitative method that uses historical data on independent variables, such as promotional campaigns, economic conditions, and competitors' actions, to predict demand.

time-series analysis A statistical approach that relies heavily on historical demand data to project the future size of demand and recognizes trends and seasonal patterns.

TABLE 13.1   DEMAND FORECAST APPLICATIONS

Application	Time Horizon		
	Short Term (0 to 3 months)	**Medium Term (3 months to 2 years)**	**Long Term (more than 2 years)**
Forecast quantity	Individual services or products	Total sales Groups or families of services or products	Total sales
Decision area	Inventory management Final assembly scheduling Workforce scheduling Master production scheduling	Staff planning Production planning Master production scheduling Purchasing Distribution	Facility location Capacity planning Process management
Forecasting technique	Time series Causal Judgment	Causal Judgment	Causal Judgment

discuss forecasting techniques, one important task associated with developing a good forecasting model is "fitting" it to the data. This task involves determining the values of certain model parameters, so that the forecasts are as accurate as possible. Software packages provide varying degrees of assistance in this regard. There are three categories of software packages (Yurkiewicz 2000).

1. *Manual Systems.* The user chooses the forecasting technique and specifies the parameters needed for a specific forcasting model.
2. *Semiautomatic Systems.* The user specifies the forecasting technique but the software determines the parameters for the model, so that the most accurate forecasts are provided.
3. *Automatic Systems.* The software examines the data and suggests not only the appropriate technique but also the best parameters for the model.

Software packages for forecasting typically can read data inputs from spreadsheet files, plot graphs of the data and the forecasts, and save forecast files for spreadsheet display of results. The prices of these programs range from $150 to more than $10,000, depending on the data analysis functions they provide. The design of these programs for personal computers and their relatively low price place these packages within the reach of any business.

An important development in forecasting is the general approach taken by Unilever, which uses software to allow information sharing and collaboration with customers. Managerial Practice 13.1 describes a formal approach to doing so and Wal-Mart's experience with this new process. **Collaborative planning, forecasting, and replenishment (CPFR)** is a nine-step process for value-chain management, in which forecasting plays a pivotal role, that allows a manufacturer and its customers to collaborate on making the forecast by using the Internet. Companies are giving this approach careful attention, with promising pilot studies reported. However, factors such as legacy systems, mutual trust, and geography have caused uneven adoption of CPFR to date.

collaborative planning, forecasting, and replenishment (CPFR) A nine-step process for value-chain management that allows a manufacturer and its customers to collaborate on making the forecast by using the Internet.

JUDGMENT METHODS

Forecasts from quantitative methods are possible only when there is adequate historical data, often called the *history file* by various commercial software packages. However, the history file may be nonexistent when a new product is introduced or when technology is

MANAGERIAL PRACTICE 13.1

WAL-MART USES CPFR AND THE INTERNET TO IMPROVE FORECAST PERFORMANCE

Wal-Mart has long been known for its careful analysis of cash register receipts and for working with suppliers to reduce inventories. In the past, like many other retailers, Wal-Mart did not share its forecasts with its suppliers. The result was forecast errors as much as 60 percent of actual demand. Retailers ordered more than they needed in order to avoid product shortages and lost sales, and suppliers produced more than they could sell. To combat the ill effects of forecast errors on inventories, Benchmarking Partners, Inc. (www.benchmarking.com) was funded in the mid-1990s by Wal-Mart, IBM, SAP, and Manugistics to develop a software package called CFAR (pronounced "see far"), which stands for collaborative forecasting and replenishment. A key benefit of the package was the capability of providing more reliable medium-term forecasts. The system allowed manufacturers and merchants to work together on forecasts by using the Internet rather than fax or phone, which would have been a heavy burden with the thousands of items stocked at each store requiring weekly forecasts.

Wal-Mart initiated CFAR with Warner-Lambert's Listerine product. The system worked in the following way. Wal-Mart and Warner-Lambert independently calculated the demand they expected for Listerine six months into the future, taking into consideration factors such as past sales trends and promotion plans. They then exchanged their forecasts over the Internet. If the forecasts differed by more than a predetermined percentage, the retailer and the manufacturer used the Internet to exchange written comments and supporting data. The parties went through as many cycles as needed to converge on an acceptable forecast. After the pilot ended, the benefits to Wal-Mart included an improvement in in-stock position from 85 percent to 98 percent as well as significant increases in sales and reductions in inventory costs. Likewise, Warner-Lambert benefited by having a smoother production plan and lower average costs.

The project was overseen by the Voluntary Interindustry Commerce Standards association (VICS), which later generalized CFAR into a model dubbed CPFR, which stands for collaborative planning, forecasting, and replenishment. CPFR is a nine-step process for supply management, and as in CFAR, forecasting plays a major role. The goal of CPFR is to change the relationship paradigm and create significantly more accurate information that can drive the value chain to greater sales and profits. In other words, CPFR can remove costs from the value chain and improve profitability. Following the pilot with Warner-Lambert, Wal-Mart had a CPFR pilot with Sara Lee in which the firms both exchanged information, such as forecasts and replenishment data. In return, Wal-Mart benefited by ensuring that it had the right item at the right time and at the right place, thus increasing customer satisfaction and profitability. Much like CFAR, the more general CPFR model calls for the comparison of two forecasts (one for each partner). However, it should be noted that the process is still valuable when one forecast is compared to actual sales or when the current forecast is compared to the previous forecast. Either way, collaboration improves forecast accuracy and ensures that it agrees with the company's future plans and objectives.

In addition to Wal-Mart, several other leading companies have already engaged in pilot plans to test CPFR. Examples include Kimberly-Clark and Kmart, Walgreens and Schering-Plough, and Nabisco and Wegmans Food Markets among others. In general, companies that participated in pilots contend that the investment committed to CPFR was relatively small because the Internet and communications standards already existed and human resources implications were few. In return, companies adopting CPFR can reduce working capital, so that funds can be invested in more productive uses, such as new product development and marketing, the reduction of fixed capital and infrastructure expenses, the reduction of operating expenses, and the growth of sales each year.

Despite promising pilots, CPFR's adoption rate has been slower than predicted. Research indicates that only 41 percent of consumer goods companies and 25 percent of retailers will have implemented any degree of CPFR by the end of 2003. First, many companies still have legacy systems that delay implementation. Second, information sharing, which is critical to the success of CPFR, requires that partners trust that they are working in each other's best interests. Without this trust, complete information sharing will not materialize, and CPFR will not be successful. Lastly, implementation of CPFR differs in terms of geography. For instance, in Europe CPFR has encountered different barriers than in the United States, leading some practitioners to consider regional models of CPFR rather than one general approach.

Sources: VICS (2002). "Collaborative Planning, Forecasting, and Replenishment" Version 2.0, www.cpfr.org; Smaros, Johanna. "Collaborative Forecasting in Practice." www.tai.hut.fi/ecomlog/publications/CF_in_practice.pdf, "Collaboratiive Planning and Forecasting," www.consumergoods.com/b2b_2002/collaborative_planning_forecasting.htm; Bowman, Robert J. "Access to Data in Real Time: Seeing Isn't Everything." Global Logistics and Supply-Chain Strategies. (May 2002) www.glsccs.com/archives/5.02.demand.htm?adcode=35; Schachtman, Noah. "Trading Partners Collaborate to Increase Sales." InformationWeek.com (October 9, 2000); "Clearing the Cobwebs from the Stockroom." Business Week (October 21, 1996), p. 140.

expected to change. The history file might exist but be less useful when certain events (such as rollouts or special packages) are reflected in the past data, or when certain events are expected to occur in the future. The experience of Unilever is a good example. In some cases, judgment methods are the only practical way to make a forecast. In other cases, judgment methods can also be used to modify forecasts that are generated by quantitative methods to anticipate upcoming special events that otherwise would not be reflected in the forecast. Finally, judgment methods can be used to adjust the history file that will be analyzed with quantitative methods to discount the impact of special one-time events that occurred in the past. If judgment methods are not utilized, the quantitative methods would give unreliable forecasts. In this section, we discuss four of the more successful judgment methods currently in use: (1) sales-force estimates, (2) executive opinion, (3) market research, and (4) the Delphi method.

SALES-FORCE ESTIMATES

sales-force estimates The forecasts that are compiled from estimates of future demands made periodically by members of a company's sales force.

How can reasonable forecasts be obtained when no historical information is available?

Sometimes the best information about future demand comes from the people closest to the external customer. **Sales-force estimates** are forecasts compiled from estimates of future demands made periodically by members of a company's sales force. This approach has several advantages.

- The sales force is the group most likely to know which services or products customers will be buying in the near future and in what quantities.
- Sales territories often are divided by district or region. Information broken down in this manner can be useful for inventory management, distribution, and sales-force staffing purposes.
- The forecasts of individual sales-force members can be combined easily to get regional or national sales.

But it also has several disadvantages.

- Individual biases of the salespeople may taint the forecast; moreover, some people are naturally optimistic, whereas others are more cautious.
- Salespeople may not always be able to detect the difference between what a customer "wants" (a wish list) and what a customer "needs" (a necessary purchase).
- If the firm uses individual sales as a performance measure, salespeople may underestimate their forecasts so that their performance will look good when they exceed their projections or they may work hard only until they reach their required minimum sales.

EXECUTIVE OPINION

executive opinion A forecasting method in which the opinions, experience, and technical knowledge of one or more managers are summarized to arrive at a single forecast.

technological forecasting An application of executive opinion in light of the difficulties in keeping abreast of the latest advances in technology.

When a new service or product is contemplated, the sales force may not be able to make accurate demand estimates. **Executive opinion** is a forecasting method in which the opinions, experience, and technical knowledge of one or more managers are summarized to arrive at a single forecast. As we discuss later, executive opinion can be used to modify an existing sales forecast to account for unusual circumstances, such as a new sales promotion or unexpected international events. Executive opinion can also be used for **technological forecasting**. The quick pace of technological change makes keeping abreast of the latest advances difficult.

This method of forecasting has several disadvantages. Executive opinion can be costly because it takes valuable executive time. Although that may be warranted under certain circumstances, it sometimes gets out of control. In addition, if executives are allowed to modify a forecast without collectively agreeing to the changes, the resulting forecast will not be useful. The key to effective use of executive opinion is to ensure that the forecast reflects not a series of independent modifications but consensus among executives on a single forecast.

MARKET RESEARCH

market research A systematic approach to determine external consumer interest in a service or product by creating and testing hypotheses through data-gathering surveys.

Market research is a systematic approach to determine external consumer interest in a service or product by creating and testing hypotheses through data-gathering surveys.

Conducting a market research study includes

- designing a questionnaire that requests economic and demographic information from each person interviewed and asks whether the interviewed would be interested in the service or product;
- deciding how to administer the survey, whether by telephone polling, mailings, or personal interviews;
- selecting a representative sample of households to survey, which should include a random selection within the market area of the proposed service or product; and
- analyzing the information using judgment and statistical tools to interpret the responses, determine their adequacy, make allowance for economic or competitive factors not included in the questionnaire, and analyze whether the survey represents a random sample of the potential market.

Market research may be used to forecast demand for the short, medium, and long term. Accuracy is excellent for the short term, good for the medium term, and only fair for the long term. Although market research yields important information, one shortcoming is the numerous qualifications and hedges typically included in the findings. Another shortcoming is that the typical response rate for mailed questionnaires is poor (30 percent is often considered high). Yet another shortcoming is the possibility that the survey results do not reflect the opinions of the market. Finally, the survey might produce imitative, rather than innovative, ideas because the customer's reference point is often limited.

DELPHI METHOD

The **Delphi method** is a process of gaining consensus from a group of experts while maintaining their anonymity. This form of forecasting is useful when there are no historical data from which to develop statistial models and when managers inside the firm have no experience on which to base informed projections. A coordinator sends questions to each member of the group of outside experts, who may not even know who else is participating. Anonymity is important when some members of the group tend to dominate discussion or command a high degree of respect in their fields. In an anonymous group, the members tend to respond to the questions and support their responses freely. The coordinator prepares a statistical summary of the responses along with a summary of arguments for particular responses. The report is sent to the same group for another round, and the participants may choose to modify their previous responses. These rounds continue until consensus is obtained.

The Delphi method can be used to develop long-range forecasts of product demand and new-product sales projections. It can also be used for technological forecasting. The Delphi method can be used to obtain a consensus from a panel of experts who can devote their attention to following scientific advances, changes in society, governmental regulations, and the competitive environment. The results can provide direction for a firm's research and development staff.

Delphi method   A process of gaining consensus from a group of experts while maintaining their anonymity.

GUIDELINES FOR USING JUDGMENT FORECASTS

Judgment forecasting is clearly needed when no quantitative data are available to use quantitative forecasting approaches. However, judgment approaches can be used in concert with quantitative approaches to improve forecast quality. Among the guidelines for the use of judgment to adjust the results of quantitative forecasts are the following (Sanders and Ritzman 1992):

- *Adjust quantitative forecasts when their track record is poor and the decision maker has important contextual knowledge.* Contextual knowledge is knowledge that practitioners gain through experience, such as cause-and-effect relationships, environmental cues, and organizational information that may have an effect on the variable being forecast. Often, these factors cannot be incorporated into quantitative forecasting approaches. The quality of forecasts generated by quantitative approaches also deteriorates as the variability of the data increases, particularly for time series. The more variable the data, the more likely it is that judgment forecasting will improve the forecasts. Consequently, the decision maker can bring valuable contextual information to the forecasting process when the quantitative approaches alone are inadequate.

• *Make adjustments to quantitative forecasts to compensate for specific events.* Specific events, such as advertising campaigns, the actions of competitors, or international developments often are not recognized in quantitative forecasting and should be acknowledged when a final forecast is being made.

In the remainder of this chapter, we focus on the commonly used quantitative forecasting approaches.

CAUSAL METHODS: LINEAR REGRESSION

Causal methods are used when historical data are available and the relationship between the factor to be forecasted and other external or internal factors (e.g., government actions or advertising promotions) can be identified. These relationships are expressed in mathematical terms and can be very complex. Causal methods provide the most sophisticated forecasting tools and are very good for predicting turning points in demand and for preparing long-range forecasts. Although many causal methods are available, we focus here on linear regression, one of the best-known and most commonly used causal methods.

linear regression   A causal method in which one variable (the dependent variable) is related to one or more independent variables by a linear equation.

In **linear regression**, one variable, called a dependent variable, is related to one or more independent variables by a linear equation. The **dependent variable** (such as demand for doorknobs) is the one the manager wants to forecast. The **independent variables** (such as advertising expenditures and new housing starts) are assumed to affect the dependent variable and thereby "cause" the results observed in the past. Figure 13.2 shows how a linear regression line relates to the data. In technical terms, the regression line minimizes the squared deviations from the actual data.

dependent variable   The variable that one wants to forecast.

independent variables
Variables that are assumed to affect the dependent variable and thereby "cause" the results observed in the past.

In the simplest linear regression models, the dependent variable is a function of only one independent variable and, therefore, the theoretical relationship is a straight line:

$$Y = a + bX$$

FIGURE 13.2

Linear Regression Line Relative to Actual Data

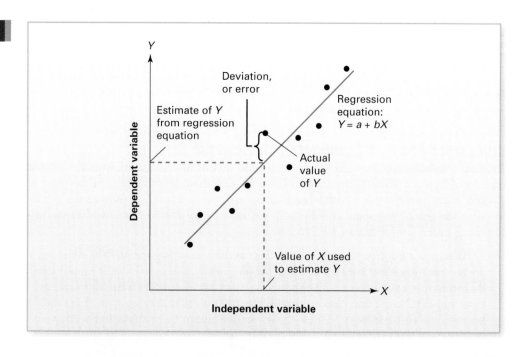

where

$$Y = \text{dependent variable}$$

$$X = \text{independent variable}$$

$$a = Y\text{-intercept of the line}$$

$$b = \text{slope of the line}$$

The objective of linear regression analysis is to find values of a and b that minimize the sum of the squared deviations of the actual data points from the graphed line. Computer programs are used for this purpose. For any set of matched observations for Y and X, the program computes the values of a and b and provides measures of forecast accuracy. Three measures commonly reported are the sample correlation coefficient, the sample coefficient of determination, and the standard error of the estimate.

The *sample correlation coefficient, r*, measures the direction and strength of the relationship between the independent variable and the dependent variable. The value of r can range from -1.00 to $+1.00$. A correlation coefficient of $+1.00$ implies that period-by-period changes in direction (increases or decreases) of the independent variable are always accompanied by changes in the same direction by the dependent variable. An r of -1.00 means that decreases in the independent variable are always accompanied by increases in the dependent variable, and vice versa. A zero value of r means that there is no relationship between the variables. The closer the value of r is to ± 1.00, the better the regression line fits the points.

The *sample coefficient of determination* measures the amount of variation in the dependent variable about its mean that is explained by the regression line. The coefficient of determination is the square of the correlation coefficient, or r^2. The value of r^2 ranges from 0.00 to 1.00. Regression equations with a value of r^2 close to 1.00 are desirable because the variations in the dependent variable and the forecast generated by the regression equation are closely related.

The *standard error of the estimate*, s_{yx}, measures how closely the data on the dependent variable cluster around the regression line. Although it is similar to the sample standard deviation, it measures the error from the dependent variable, Y, to the regression line, rather than to the mean. Thus, it is the standard deviation of the difference between the actual demand and the estimate provided by the regression equation. When determining which independent variable to include in the regression equation, you should choose the one with the smallest standard error of the estimate.

Using Linear Regression to Forecast Product Demand

EXAMPLE 13.1

The person in charge of production scheduling for a company must prepare forecasts of product demand in order to plan for appropriate production quantities. During a luncheon meeting, the marketing manager gives her information about the advertising budget for a brass door hinge. The following are sales and advertising data for the past five months:

ACTIVE MODEL 13.1
Active Model 13.1 on the Student CD-ROM provides insight on varying the intercept and slope of the model.

MONTH	SALES (THOUSANDS OF UNITS)	ADVERTISING (THOUSANDS OF $)
1	264	2.5
2	116	1.3
3	165	1.4
4	101	1.0
5	209	2.0

The marketing manager says that next month the company will spend $1,750 on advertising for the product. Use linear regression to develop an equation and a forecast for this product.

SOLUTION

We assume that sales are linearly related to advertising expenditures. In other words, sales are the dependent variable, Y, and advertising expenditures are the independent variable, X. Using the paired monthly observations of sales and advertising expenditures supplied by the marketing manager, we use the computer to determine the best values of a, b, the correlation coefficient, the coefficient of determination, and the standard error of the estimate.

$$
\begin{aligned}
a &= -8.135 \\
b &= 109.229X \\
r &= 0.980 \\
r^2 &= 0.960 \\
s_{yx} &= 15.603
\end{aligned}
$$

The regression equation is

$$Y = -8.137 + 109.229X$$

and the regression line is shown in Figure 13.3.

Are advertising expenditures a good choice to use in forecasting sales? Note that the sample correlation coefficient, r, is 0.98. Because the value of r is very close to 1.00, we conclude that there is a strong positive relationship between sales and advertising expenditures and that the choice was a good one.

Next, we examine the sample coefficient of determination, r^2, or 0.96. This value of r^2 implies that 96 percent of the variation in sales is explained by advertising expenditures. Most relationships between advertising and sales in practice are not this strong because other variables, such as general economic conditions and the strategies of competitors, often combine to affect sales.

As the advertising expenditure will be $1,750, the forecast for month 6 is

$$
\begin{aligned}
Y &= -8.137 + 109.229(1.75) \\
&= 183.016 \quad \text{or} \quad 183,016 \text{ units}
\end{aligned}
$$

FIGURE 13.3

Linear Regression Line for the Sales and Advertising Data

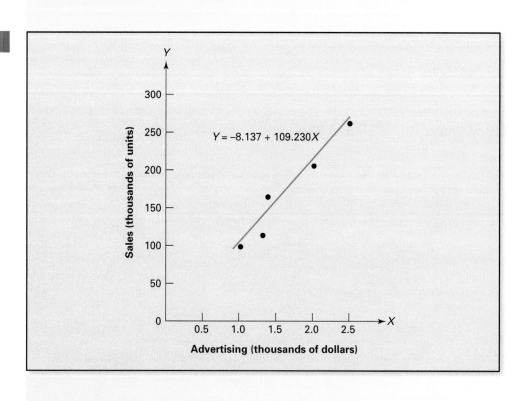

The Regression Analysis Solver of OM Explorer confirms these calculations and the forecast for month 6 (the expenditure is the trial value highlighted in yellow), as Figure 13.4 shows.

R-squared	0.960		
R	0.980		
Constant	-8.135		
Standard Error of Estimate	15.603		
Trial X1 Value	1.75	X1 Coefficient	109.229
		Predicted Y Value	183.016

FIGURE 13.4

The Regression Analysis Solver from OM Explorer Showing the Forecast for Month Six

DECISION POINT   The production scheduler can use this forecast to determine the quantity of brass door hinges needed for month six. Suppose that she has 62,500 units in stock. The requirement to be filled from production is $183{,}016 - 62{,}500 = 120{,}016$ units, assuming that she does not want to lose any sales.

Often several independent variables may affect the dependent variable. For example, advertising expenditures, new corporation start-ups, and residential building contracts may be important for estimating the demand for door hinges. In such cases, *multiple regression analysis* is helpful in determining a forecasting equation for the dependent variable as a function of several independent variables. Such models can be analyzed with OM Explorer and can be quite useful for predicting turning points and solving many planning problems.

TIME-SERIES METHODS

Rather than using independent variables for the forecast as regression models do, time-series methods use historical information regarding only the dependent variable. These methods are based on the assumption that the dependent variable's past pattern will continue in the future. Time-series analysis identifies the underlying patterns of demand that combine to produce an observed historical pattern of the dependent variable and then develops a model to replicate it. In this section, we focus on time-series methods that address the horizontal, trend, and seasonal patterns of demand. Before we discuss statistical methods, let us take a look at the simplest time-series method for addressing all patterns of demand—the naive forecast.

NAIVE FORECAST

A method often used in practice is the **naive forecast**, whereby the forecast for the next period equals the demand for the current period (D_t). So, if the actual demand for Wednesday is 35 customers, the forecasted demand for Thursday is 35 customers. If the actual demand on Thursday is 42 customers, the forecasted demand for Friday is 42 customers.

The naive-forecast method may be adapted to take into account a demand trend. The increase (or decrease) in demand observed between the last two periods is used to adjust the current demand to arrive at a forecast. Suppose that last week the demand was 120 units and the week before it was 108 units. Demand increased 12 units in one

naive forecast A time-series method whereby the forecast for the next period equals the demand for the current period, or Forecast = D_t.

week, so the forecast for next week would be 120 + 12 = 132 units. If the actual demand next week turned out to be 127 units, the next forecast would be 127 + 7 = 134 units. The naive-forecast method also may be used to account for seasonal patterns. If the demand last July was 50,000 units, the forecast for this July would be 50,000 units. Similarly, forecasts of demand for each month of the coming year may simply reflect actual demand in the same month last year.

The advantages of the naive-forecast method are its simplicity and low cost. The method works best when the horizontal, trend, or seasonal patterns are stable and random variation is small. If random variation is large, using last period's demand to estimate next period's demand can result in highly variable forecasts that are not useful for planning purposes. Nonetheless, if its level of accuracy is acceptable, the naive forecast is an attractive approach for time-series forecasting.

ESTIMATING THE AVERAGE

Every demand time series has at least two of the five patterns of demand: horizontal and random. It *may* have trend, seasonal, or cyclical patterns. We begin our discussion of statistical methods of time-series forecasting with demand that has no trend, seasonal, or cyclical patterns. The horizontal pattern in a time series is based on the mean of the demands, so we focus on forecasting methods that estimate the average of a time series of data. Consequently, for all the methods of forecasting we discuss in this section, the forecast of demand for *any* period in the future is the average of the time series computed in the current period. For example, if the average of past demand calculated on Tuesday is 65 customers, the forecasts for Wednesday, Thursday, and Friday are 65 customers each day.

Consider Figure 13.5, which shows patient arrivals at a medical clinic over the past 28 weeks. Assume that the demand pattern for patient arrivals has no trend, seasonal, or cyclical pattern. The time series has only a horizontal and random pattern. As no one can predict random error, we focus on estimating the average. The statistical techniques useful for forecasting such a time series are (1) simple moving averages, (2) weighted moving averages, and (3) exponential smoothing.

simple moving average method   A time-series method used to estimate the average of a demand time series by averaging the demand for the *n* most recent time periods.

SIMPLE MOVING AVERAGES. The **simple moving average method** is used to estimate the average of a demand time series and thereby remove the effects of random fluctuation. It is most useful when demand has no pronounced trend or seasonal influences. Applying a moving average model simply involves calculating the average demand for the *n* most recent time periods and using it as the forecast for the next time period. For the next period, after the demand is known, the oldest demand from the previous average is replaced with the most recent demand and the average is

FIGURE 13.5

Weekly Patient Arrivals at a Medical Clinic

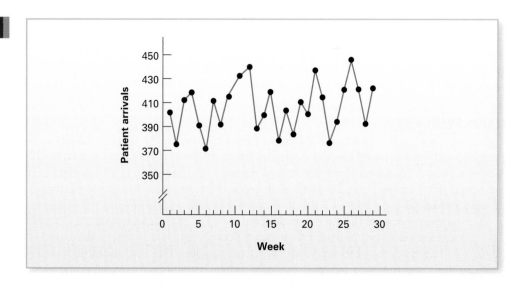

recalculated. In this way, the *n* most recent demands are used, and the average "moves" from period to period.

Specifically, the forecast for period *t* + 1, can be calculated as

$$F_{t+1} = \frac{\text{Sum of last } n \text{ demands}}{n} = \frac{D_t + D_{t-1} + D_{t-2} + \cdots + D_{t-n+1}}{n}$$

where

D_t = actual demand in period *t*

n = total number of periods in the average

F_{t+1} = forecast for period *t* + 1

With the moving average method, the forecast of next period's demand equals the average calculated at the end of this period.

Using the Moving Average Method to Estimate Average Demand

✓ **a.** Compute a *three-week* moving average forecast for the arrival of medical clinic patients in week 4. The numbers of arrivals for the past three weeks were

WEEK	PATIENT ARRIVALS
1	400
2	380
3	411

ACTIVE MODEL 13.2
Active Model 13.2 on the Student CD-ROM provides insight on the impact of varying *n*, using the example in Figures 13.5 and 13.11.

TUTOR 13.1
Tutor 13.1 on the Student CD-ROM provides another example to practice making forecasts with the moving average method.

✓ **b.** If the actual number of patient arrivals in week 4 is 415, what is the forecast for week 5?

SOLUTION

a. The moving average forecast at the end of week 3 is

$$F_4 = \frac{411 + 380 + 400}{3} = 397.0$$

b. The forecast for week 5 requires the actual arrivals from weeks 2 through 4, the three most recent weeks of data.

$$F_5 = \frac{415 + 411 + 380}{3} = 402.0$$

DECISION POINT Thus, the forecast at the end of week 3 would have been 397 patients for week 4. The forecast for week 5, made at the end of week 4, would have been 402 patients. In addition, at the end of week 4, the forecast for week 6 and beyond is also 402 patients.

The moving average method may involve the use of as many periods of past demand as desired. The stability of the demand series generally determines how many periods to include (i.e., the value of *n*). Stable demand series are those for which the average (to be estimated by the forecasting method) only infrequently experiences changes. Large values of *n* should be used for demand series that are stable and small values of *n* should be used for those that are susceptible to changes in the underlying average.

Consider Figure 13.6, which compares actual patient arrivals to a three-week and a six-week moving average forecast for the medical clinic data. Note that the three-week moving average forecast varies more and reacts more quickly to large swings in demand. Conversely, the six-week moving average forecast is more stable because large swings in demand tend to cancel each other. We defer discussion of which of the two forecast methods is better for this problem until we discuss the criteria for choosing time-series methods later in the chapter.

Including more historical data in the average by increasing the number of periods results in a forecast that is less susceptible to random variations. If the underlying average in the series is changing, however, the forecasts will tend to lag behind the changes for a longer time interval because of the additional time required to remove the old data from the forecast. We address other considerations in the choice of n when we discuss choosing a time-series method.

weighted moving average method   A time-series method in which each historical demand in the average can have its own weight; the sum of the weights equals 1.0.

WEIGHTED MOVING AVERAGES. In the simple moving average method, each demand has the same weight in the average—namely, $1/n$. In the **weighted moving average method**, each historical demand in the average can have its own weight. The sum of the weights equals 1.0. For example, in a *three-period* weighted moving average model, the most recent period might be assigned a weight of 0.50, the second most recent might be weighted 0.30, and the third most recent might be weighted 0.20. The average is obtained by multiplying the weight of each period by the value for that period and adding the products together:

$$F_{t+1} = 0.50D_t + 0.30D_{t-1} + 0.20D_{t-2}$$

TUTOR 13.2

Tutor 13.2 on the Student CD-ROM provides a new practice example for making forecasts with the weighted moving average method.

For a numerical example of using the weighted moving average method to estimate average demand, see Solved Problem 2 and Tutor 13.2 in the OM Explorer.

The advantage of a weighted moving average method is that it allows you to emphasize recent demand over earlier demand. (It can even handle seasonal effects by putting higher weights on prior periods in the same season.) The forecast will be more responsive to changes in the underlying average of the demand series than the simple moving average forecast. Nonetheless, the weighted moving average forecast will still lag behind demand because it merely averages *past* demands. This lag is especially

FIGURE 13.6

Comparison of Three- and Six-Week Moving Average Forecasts

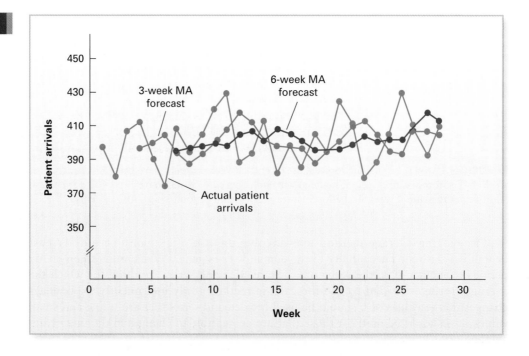

noticeable with a trend because the average of the time series is systematically increasing or decreasing.

The weighted moving average method has the same shortcomings as the simple moving average method: Data must be retained for n periods of demand to allow calculation of the average for each period. Keeping this amount of data is not a great burden in simple situations, such as the preceding three- and six-week examples.

EXPONENTIAL SMOOTHING. The **exponential smoothing method** is a sophisticated weighted moving average method that calculates the average of a time series by giving recent demands more weight than earlier demands. It is the most frequently used formal forecasting method because of its simplicity and the small amount of data needed to support it. Unlike the weighted moving average method, which requires n periods of past demand and n weights, exponential smoothing requires only three items of data: the last period's forecast; the demand for this period; and a smoothing parameter, alpha (α), which has a value between 0 and 1.0. To obtain an exponentially smoothed forecast, we simply calculate a weighted average of the most recent demand and the forecast calculated last period. The equation for the forecast is

$$F_{t+1} = \alpha \text{ (Demand this period)} + (1 - \alpha)(\text{Forecast calculated last period})$$
$$= \alpha D_t + (1 - \alpha)F_t$$

An equivalent equation is

$$F_{t+1} = F_t + \alpha \, (D_t - F_t)$$

exponential smoothing method A weighted moving average method that calculates the average of a time series by giving recent demands more weight than earlier demands.

This form of the equation shows that the forecast for the next period equals the forecast for the current period plus a proportion of the forecast error for the current period.

The emphasis given to the most recent demand levels can be adjusted by changing the smoothing parameter. Larger α values emphasize recent levels of demand and result in forecasts more responsive to changes in the underlying average. Smaller α values treat past demand more uniformly and result in more stable forecasts. This approach is analogous to adjusting the value of n in the moving average methods except, there, smaller values of n emphasize recent demand and larger values give greater weight to past demand. In practice, various values of α are tried and the one producing the best forecasts is chosen.

Exponential smoothing requires an initial forecast to get started. There are two ways to get this initial forecast: Either use last period's demand or, if some historical data are available, calculate the average of several recent periods of demand. The effect of the initial estimate of the average on successive estimates of the average diminishes over time because, with exponential smoothing, the weights given to successive historical demands used to calculate the average decay exponentially. We can illustrate this effect with an example. If we let $\alpha = 0.20$, the forecast for period $t + 1$ is

$$F_{t+1} = 0.20D_t + 0.80F_t$$

Using the equation for F_t, we expand the equation for F_{t+1}:

$$F_{t+1} = 0.20D_t + 0.80 \, (0.20D_{t-1} + 0.80F_{t-1}) = 0.20D_t + 0.16D_{t-1} + 0.64F_{t-1}$$

Continuing to expand, we get

$$F_{t+1} = 0.20D_t + 0.16D_{t-1} + 0.128D_{t-2} + 0.1024D_{t-3} + \cdots$$

Eventually, the weights of demands many periods ago approach zero. As with the weighted moving average method, the sum of the weights must equal 1.0, which is implicit in the exponential smoothing equation.

EXAMPLE 13.3   Using Exponential Smoothing to Estimate Average Demand

ACTIVE MODEL 13.3
Active Model 13.3 on the Student CD-ROM provides insight on the impact of varying α, using the example in Figures 13.5 and 13.11.

TUTOR 13.3
Tutor 13.3 on the Student CD-ROM provides a new practice example of how to make forecasts with the exponential smoothing method.

Reconsider the patient arrival data in Example 13.2. It is now the end of week 3. Using $\alpha = 0.10$, calculate the exponential smoothing forecast for week 4.

SOLUTION

The exponential smoothing method requires an initial forecast. Suppose that we take the demand data for the first two weeks and average them, obtaining $(400 + 380)/2 = 390$ as an initial forecast. To obtain the forecast for week 4, using exponential smoothing with $\alpha = 0.10$, we calculate the average at the end of week 3 as

$$F_4 = 0.10(411) + 0.90(390) = 392.1$$

Thus, the forecast for week 4 would be 392 patients. If the actual demand for week 4 proved to be 415, the new forecast for week 5 would be

$$F_5 = 0.10(415) + 0.90(392.1) = 394.4$$

or 394 patients. Note that we used F_4, not the integer-value forecast for week 4, in the computation for F_5. In general, we round off (when it is appropriate) only the final result to maintain as much accuracy as possible in the calculations.

DECISION POINT   Using this exponential smoothing model, the analyst's forecasts would have been 392 patients for week 4 and then 394 patients for week 5 and beyond. As soon as the actual demand for week 5 is known, then the forecast for week 6 will be updated.

Exponential smoothing has the advantages of simplicity and minimal data requirements. It is inexpensive to use and therefore, very attractive to firms that make thousands of forecasts for each time period. However, its simplicity also is a disadvantage when the underlying average is changing, as in the case of a demand series with a trend. Like any method geared solely to the assumption of a stable average, exponential smoothing results will lag behind changes in the underlying average of demand. Higher α values may help reduce forecast errors when there is a change in the average of the time series; however, the lags will still be there if the average is changing systematically. Typically, if large α values (e.g., >0.50) are required for an exponential smoothing application, chances are good that a more sophisticated model is needed because of a significant trend or seasonal influence in the demand series.

INCLUDING A TREND

Let us now consider a demand time series that has a trend. A *trend* in a time series is a systematic increase or decrease in the average of the series over time. Where a significant trend is present, exponential smoothing approaches must be modified; otherwise, the forecasts tend to be below or above the actual demand.

To improve the forecast, we need to calculate an estimate of the trend. We start by calculating the *current* estimate of the trend, which is the difference between the average of the series computed in the current period and the average computed last period. To obtain an estimate of the long-term trend, you can average the current estimates. The method for estimating a trend is similar to that used for estimating the demand average with exponential smoothing.

The method for incorporating a trend in an exponentially smoothed forecast is called the **trend-adjusted exponential smoothing method**. With this approach, the estimates for both the average and the trend are smoothed, requiring two smoothing constants. For each period, we calculate the average and the trend:

trend-adjusted exponential smoothing method   The method for incorporating a trend in an exponentially smoothed forecast.

$$A_t = \alpha(\text{Demand this period}) + (1 - \alpha)(\text{Average} + \text{Trend estimate last period})$$
$$= \alpha D_t + (1 - \alpha)(A_{t-1} + T_{t-1})$$
$$T_t = \beta(\text{Average this period} - \text{Average last period})$$
$$+ (1 - \beta)(\text{Trend estimate last period})$$
$$= \beta(A_t - A_{t-1}) + (1 - \beta)T_{t-1}$$
$$F_{t+1} = A_t + T_t$$

where

A_t = exponentially smoothed average of the series in period t

T_t = exponentially smoothed average of the trend in period t

α = smoothing parameter for the average, with a value between 0 and 1

β = smoothing parameter for the trend, with a value between 0 and 1

F_{t+1} = forecast for period $t + 1$

To make forecasts for periods beyond the next period, we multiply the trend estimate (T_t) by the number of additional periods that we want in the forecast, and add the results to the current average (A_t). Thus, trend-adjusted exponential smoothing differs from the previous methods covered. For those methods, the forecast for all future periods is the same as the forecast for the next period.

Estimates for last period's average and trend needed for the first forecast can be derived from past data or they can be based on an educated guess if no historical data exist. To find values for α and β, often an analyst systematically adjusts α and β until the forecast errors are lowest. This process can be carried out in an experimental setting with the model used to forecast historical demands.

Using Trend-Adjusted Exponential Smoothing to Forecast a Demand Series with a Trend

EXAMPLE 13.4

Medanalysis, Inc. provides medical laboratory services to patients of Health Providers, a group of 10 family-practice doctors associated with a new health maintenance program. Managers are interested in forecasting the number of patients requesting blood analysis per week. Supplies must be purchased and a decision made regarding the number of blood samples to be sent to another laboratory because of capacity limitations at the main laboratory. Recent publicity about the damaging effects of cholesterol on the heart has caused a national increase in requests for standard blood tests. Medanalysis ran an average of 28 blood tests per week during the past four weeks. The trend over that period was 3 additional patients per week. This week's demand was for 27 blood tests. We use $\alpha = 0.20$ and $\beta = 0.20$ to calculate the forecast for next week.

ACTIVE MODEL 13.4
Active Model 13.4 on the Student CD-ROM provides insight on varying α and β, using the example in Figure 13.7.

SOLUTION

$$A_0 = 28 \text{ patients} \quad \text{and} \quad T_0 = 3 \text{ patients}$$

The forecast for week 2 (next week) is

$$A_1 = 0.20(27) + 0.80(28 + 3) = 30.2$$
$$T_1 = 0.20(30.2 - 28) + 0.80(3) = 2.8$$
$$F_2 = 30.2 + 2.8 = 33 \text{ blood tests}$$

If the actual number of blood tests requested in week 2 proved to be 44, the updated forecast for week 3 would be

$$A_2 = 0.20(44) + 0.80(30.2 + 2.8) = 35.2$$
$$T_2 = 0.2(35.2 - 30.2) + 0.80(2.8) = 3.2$$
$$F_3 = 35.2 + 3.2 = 38.4 \quad \text{or} \quad 38 \text{ blood tests}$$

TUTOR 13.4
Tutor 13.4 on the Student CD-ROM provides another practice example and explanation of how to make forecasts with the trend-adjusted exponential smoothing method.

DECISION POINT Using this trend-adjusted exponential smoothing model, the forecast for week 2 was 33 blood tests, and then 38 blood tests for week 3. If the analyst makes forecasts at the end of week 2 for periods beyond week 3, the forecast would be even greater because of the upward trend estimated to be 3.2 blood tests per week.

Figure 13.7 shows the trend-adjusted forecast (the blue line) for Medanalysis for a period of 15 weeks. At the end of each week, we calculated a forecast for the next week, using the number of blood tests for the current week. Note that the forecasts (shown in the following lists and in Table 13.2) vary less than actual demand because of the smoothing effect of the procedure for calculating the estimates for the average and the trend. By adjusting α and β, we may be able to come up with a better forecast.

To make forecasts for periods beyond the next period, we multiply the trend estimate by the number of additional periods that we want in the forecast and add the result to the current average. For example, if we were at the end of week 2 and wanted to estimate the demand for blood tests in week 6 (i.e., 4 weeks ahead), the forecast would be $35.2 + 4(3.2) = 48$ tests.

Number of time periods	15
Demand smoothing coefficient (α)	0.20
Initial demand value	28
Trend-smoothing coefficient (β)	0.20
Estimate of trend	3

Summary

Average demand	49.80
Mean square error	76.13
Mean absolute deviation	7.36
Forecast for week 16	68.67
Forecast for week 17	70.95
Forecast for week 18	73.24

The summary list shows the forecasts for periods 16, 17, and 18. The trend-adjusted exponential smoothing method has the advantage of being able to adjust the forecast to *changes* in the trend. Nonetheless, when the trend is changing, the farther ahead we project the trend estimate, the more tenuous the forecast becomes. Thus, the use of times-series methods should be restricted to short-term forecasting.

FIGURE 13.7

Trend-Adjusted Forecast for Medanalysis

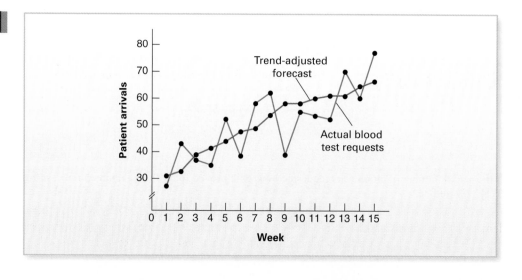

TABLE 13.2   FORECASTS FOR MEDANALYSIS USING THE TREND-ADJUSTED EXPONENTIAL SMOOTHING MODEL

Week	Arrivals	Smoothed Average	Trend Average	Forecast	Forecast Error
0	28	28	3	0	0
1	27	30.20	2.84	31	−4
2	44	35.23	3.28	33.04	10.96
3	37	38.21	3.22	38.51	−1.51
4	35	40.14	2.96	41.43	−6.43
5	53	45.08	3.36	43.10	9.90
6	38	46.35	2.94	48.44	−10.44
7	57	50.83	3.25	49.29	7.71
8	61	55.46	3.52	54.08	6.92
9	39	54.99	2.72	58.99	−19.99
10	55	57.17	2.62	57.72	−2.72
11	54	58.63	2.38	59.79	−5.79
12	52	59.21	2.02	61.02	−9.02
13	60	60.99	1.97	61.24	−1.24
14	60	62.37	1.86	62.96	−2.96
15	75	66.38	2.29	64.23	10.78

SEASONAL PATTERNS

Many organizations experience seasonal demand for their services or goods. Seasonal patterns are regularly repeating upward or downward movements in demand measured in periods of less than one year (hours, days, weeks, months, or quarters). In this context, the time periods are called *seasons*. For example, customer arrivals at a fast-food shop on any day may peak between 11 A.M. and 1 P.M. and again from 5 P.M. to 7 P.M. Here, the seasonal pattern lasts a day, and each hour of the day is a season. Similarly, the demand for haircuts may peak on Saturday, week to week. In this case, the seasonal pattern lasts a week, and the seasons are the days of the week. Seasonal patterns may last a month, as in the weekly applications for driver's license renewals, or a year, as in the monthly volumes of mail processed and the monthly demand for automobile tires.

An easy way to account for seasonal effects is to use one of the techniques already described but to limit the data in the time series to those time periods in the same season. For example, if there is day-of-the-week seasonal effect, then one time series would be for Mondays, one for Tuesdays, and so on. If the naive forecast is used, then the forecast for this Tuesday is the actual demand seven days ago (last Tuesday), rather than the actual demand one day ago (Monday). If the weighted moving average method is used, high weights are placed on prior periods belonging to the same season. These approaches account for seasonal effects but have the disadvantage of discarding considerable information on past demand.

Other methods are available that analyze all past data, using one model to forecast demand for all of the seasons. We describe only the **multiplicative seasonal method,** whereby seasonal factors are multiplied by an estimate of average demand to arrive at a seasonal forecast. The four-step procedure presented here involves the use of simple averages of past demand, although more sophisticated methods for calculating averages, such as a moving average or exponential smoothing approach, could be used. The following description is based on a seasonal pattern lasting one year and seasons of one month, although the procedure can be used for any seasonal pattern and season of any length.

multiplicative seasonal method   A method whereby seasonal factors are multiplied by an estimate of average demand to arrive at a seasonal forecast.

1. For each year, calculate the average demand per season by dividing annual demand by the number of seasons per year. For example, if the total demand for a year is 6,000 units and each month is a season, the average demand per season is 6,000/12 = 500 units.

2. For each year, divide the actual demand for a season by the average demand per season. The result is a *seasonal index* for each season in the year, which indicates the level of demand relative to the average demand. For example, suppose that the demand for March was 400 units. The seasonal index for March then is 400/500 = 0.80, which indicates that March's demand is 20 percent below the average demand per month. Similarly, a seasonal index of 1.14 for April implies that April's demand is 14 percent greater than the average demand per month.

3. Calculate the average seasonal index for each season, using the results from step 2. Add the seasonal indices for a season and divide by the number of years of data. For example, suppose that we have calculated three seasonal indices for April: 1.14, 1.18, and 1.04. The average seasonal index for April is (1.14 + 1.18 + 1.04)/3 = 1.12. This is the index we will use for forecasting April's demand.

4. Calculate each season's forecast for next year. Begin by estimating the average demand per season for next year. Use the naive method, moving averages, exponential smoothing, trend-adjusted exponential smoothing, or linear regression to forecast annual demand. Divide annual demand by the number of seasons per year. Then obtain the seasonal forecast by multiplying the seasonal index by the average demand per season.

At the end of each year, the average seasonal factor for each quarter can be updated. We calculate the average of all historical factors for the quarter or, if we want some control over the relevance of past demand patterns, we calculate a moving average or single exponential smoothed average.

EXAMPLE 13.5   Using the Multiplicative Seasonal Method to Forecast the Number of Custom

The manager of the Stanley Steemer carpet cleaning company needs a quarterly forecast of the number of customers expected next year. The carpet cleaning business is seasonal, with a peak in the third quarter and a trough in the first quarter. Following are the quarterly demand data from the past four years:

QUARTER	YEAR 1	YEAR 2	YEAR 3	YEAR 4
1	45	70	100	100
2	335	370	585	725
3	520	590	830	1,160
4	100	170	285	215
Total	1,000	1,200	1,800	2,200

The manager wants to forecast customer demand for each quarter of year 5, based on her estimate of total year 5 demand of 2,600 customers.

SOLUTION

Figure 13.8 shows the solution using the Seasonal Forecasting solver. (For a numerical example calculated manually, see Solved Problem 5 at the end of this chapter.) For the Inputs sheet, a forecast for the total demand in year 5 is needed. The annual demand has been increasing by an average of 400 customers each year (from 1,000 in year 1 to 2,200 in year 4, or 1,200/3 = 400). The computed forecast demand is found by extending that trend, and projecting an annual demand in year 5 of 2,200 + 400 = 2,600 customers. The option of a user-supplied forecast is also available if the manager wishes to make a judgmental forecast based on additional information.

The Results sheet shows quarterly forecasts by multiplying the seasonal factors by the average demand per quarter. For example, the average demand forecast in year 5 is 650 customers (or 2,600/4 = 650). Multiplying that by the seasonal index computed for the first quarter gives a forecast of 133 customers (or 650 × 0.2043 = 132.795).

DECISION POINT Using this seasonal method, the analyst makes a demand forecast as low as 130 customers in the first quarter and as high as 1,300 customers in the third quarter. The season of the year clearly makes a difference.

FIGURE 13.8

Demand Forecasts Using the Seasonal Forecast Solver

Period	Quarters ▼			
Starting Year	1	Years	4 ▲▼	
Computed Forecast Demand for Year 5			2600	
User-supplied Forecast Demand for Year 5			2600	

		Year		
Quarter	**1**	**2**	**3**	**4**
1	45	70	100	100
2	335	370	585	725
3	520	590	830	1160
4	100	170	285	215

(a)   Inputs sheet

Quarter	**Seasonal Index**	**Forecast**
1	0.2043	132.795
2	1.2979	843.635
3	2.0001	1300.065
4	0.4977	323.505

(b)   Results

The multiplicative seasonal method gets its name from the way seasonal factors are calculated and used. Multiplying the seasonal factor by an estimate of the average period demand implies that the seasonal pattern depends on the level of demand. The peaks and valleys are more extreme when average demand is high, a situation faced most often by firms that produce services and goods having a seasonal demand. Figure 13.9 (a) shows a time series with a multiplicative seasonal pattern. Note how the amplitude of the seasons increases, reflecting an upward trend in demand. The reverse occurs with a downward trend in demand. An alternative to the multiplicative seasonal method is the **additive seasonal method**, whereby seasonal forecasts are generated by adding a constant (say, 50 units) to the estimate of average demand per season. This approach is based on the assumption that the seasonal pattern is constant, regardless of average demand. Figure 13.9 (b) shows a time series with an additive seasonal pattern. Here, the amplitude of the seasons remains the same regardless of the level of demand.

additive seasonal method   A method in which seasonal forecasts are generated by adding a constant to the estimate of average demand per season.

FIGURE 13.9

Comparison of Seasonal Patterns

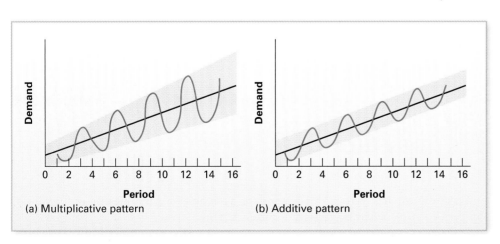

(a) Multiplicative pattern

(b) Additive pattern

CHOOSING A TIME-SERIES METHOD

We now turn to factors that managers must consider in selecting a method for time-series forecasting. One important consideration is forecast performance, as determined by forecast errors. Managers need to know how to measure forecast errors and how to detect when something is going wrong with the forecasting system. After examining forecast errors and their detection, we discuss criteria that managers can use to choose an appropriate time-series forecasting method.

FORECAST ERROR

Forecasts almost always contain errors. Forecast errors can be classified as either *bias errors* or *random errors*. Bias errors are the result of consistent mistakes—the forecast is always too high or too low. These errors often are the result of neglecting or not accurately estimating patterns of demand, such as a trend, seasonal, or cyclical pattern.

The other type of forecast error, random error, results from unpredictable factors that cause the forecast to deviate from the actual demand. Forecasting analysts try to minimize the effects of bias and random errors by selecting appropriate forecasting models, but eliminating all forms of errors is impossible.

MEASURES OF FORECAST ERROR. Before they can think about minimizing forecast error, managers must have some way to measure it. **Forecast error** is simply the difference found by subtracting the forecast from actual demand for a given period, or

forecast error The difference found by subtracting the forecast from actual demand for a given period.

$$E_t = D_t - F_t$$

where

$$E_t = \text{forecast error for period } t$$
$$D_t = \text{actual demand for period } t$$
$$F_t = \text{forecast for period } t$$

However, managers usually are more interested in measuring forecast error over a relatively long period of time.

The **cumulative sum of forecast errors** (CFE) measures the total forecast error:

cumulative sum of forecast errors (CFE) A measurement of the total forecast error that assesses the bias in a forecast.

$$\text{CFE} = \Sigma E_t$$

Large positive errors tend to be offset by large negative errors in the CFE measure. Nonetheless, CFE is useful in assessing *bias* in a forecast. For example, if a forecast is always lower than actual demand, the value of CFE will gradually get larger and larger. This increasingly large error indicates some systematic deficiency in the forecasting approach. Perhaps the analyst omitted a trend element or a cyclical pattern, or perhaps seasonal influences changed from their historical pattern. Note that the average forecast error is simply

mean squared error (MSE) A measurement of the dispersion of forecast errors.

standard deviation (σ) A measurement of the dispersion of forecast errors.

$$\overline{E} = \frac{\text{CFE}}{n}$$

The **mean squared error (MSE), standard deviation (σ),** and **mean absolute deviation (MAD)** measure the dispersion of forecast errors:

mean absolute deviation (MAD) A measurement of the dispersion of forecast errors.

$$MSE = \frac{\Sigma E_t^2}{n}$$

$$\sigma = \sqrt{\frac{\Sigma(E_t - \overline{E})^2}{n-1}}$$

$$MAD = \frac{\Sigma|E_t|}{n}$$

The mathematical symbol || is used to indicate the absolute value—that is, it tells you to disregard positive or negative signs. If MSE, σ, or MAD is small, the forecast is typically close to actual demand; a large value indicates the possibility of large forecast errors. The measures differ in the way they emphasize errors. Large errors get far more weight in MSE and σ because the errors are squared. MAD is a widely used measure of forecast error because managers can easily understand it; it is merely the mean of the forecast errors over a series of time periods, without regard to whether the error was an overestimate or an underestimate. MAD also is used in tracking signals and inventory control. Later, we discuss how MAD or σ can be used to determine safety stocks for inventory items (see Chapter 15, "Inventory Management").

The **mean absolute percent error (MAPE)** relates the forecast error to the level of demand and is useful for putting forecast performance in the proper perspective:

mean absolute percent error (MAPE) A measurement that relates the forecast error to the level of demand and is useful for putting forecast performance in the proper perspective.

$$MAPE = \frac{(\Sigma|E_t|/D_t)(100)}{n} \quad \text{(expressed as a percent)}$$

For example, an absolute forecast error of 100 results in a larger percentage error when the demand is 200 units than when the demand is 10,000 units. MAPE is the best error measure to use when making comparisons between different time series or SKUs.

Calculating Forecast Error Measures

EXAMPLE 13.6

The following table shows the actual sales of upholstered chairs for a furniture manufacturer and the forecasts made for each of the last eight months. Calculate CFE, MSE, σ, MAD, and MAPE for this product.

MONTH, t	DEMAND, D_t	FORECAST, F_t	ERROR E_t	ERROR SQUARED, E_t^2	ABSOLUTE ERROR, $|E_t|$	ABSOLUTE PRECENT ERROR, $(|E_t|/D_t)(100)$
1	200	225	−25	625	25	12.5%
2	240	220	20	400	20	8.3
3	300	285	15	225	15	5.0
4	270	290	−20	400	20	7.4
5	230	250	−20	400	20	8.7
6	260	240	20	400	20	7.7
7	210	250	−40	1,600	40	19.0
8	275	240	35	1,225	35	12.7
		Total	−15	5,275	195	81.3%

SOLUTION

Using the formulas for the measures, we get

Cumulative forecast error: $\text{CFE} = -15$

Average forecast error: $\overline{E} = \dfrac{\text{CFE}}{8} = -1.875$

Mean squared error: $\text{MSE} = \dfrac{\Sigma E_t^2}{n} = \dfrac{5,275}{8} = 659.4$

Standard deviation: $\sigma = \sqrt{\dfrac{\Sigma[E_t - (-1.875)]^2}{7}} = 27.4$

Mean absolute deviation: $\text{MAD} = \dfrac{\Sigma|E_t|}{n} = \dfrac{195}{8} = 24.4$

Mean absolute percent error: $\text{MAPE} = \dfrac{[\Sigma|E_t|/D_t]\,100}{n} = \dfrac{81.3\%}{8} = 10.2\%$

A CFE of -15 indicates that the forecast has a slight tendency to overestimate demand. The MSE, σ, and MAD statistics provide measures of forecast error variability. A MAD of 24.4 means that the average forecast error was 24.4 units in absolute value. The value of σ, 27.4, indicates that the sample distribution of forecast errors has a standard deviation of 27.4 units. A MAPE of 10.2 percent implies that, on average, the forecast error was about 10 percent of actual demand. These measures become more reliable as the number of periods of data increases.

DECISION POINT   Although reasonably satisfied with these forecast performance results, the analyst decided to test out a few more forecasting methods before reaching a final forecasting method to use for the future.

tracking signal A measure that indicates whether a method of forecasting is accurately predicting actual changes in demand.

TRACKING SIGNALS. A **tracking signal** is a measure that indicates whether a method of forecasting is accurately predicting actual changes in demand. The tracking signal measures the number of MADs represented by the cumulative sum of forecast errors, the CFE. The CFE tends to be 0 when a correct forecasting system is being used. At any time, however, random errors can cause the CFE to be a nonzero number. The tracking signal formula is

$$\text{Tracking signal} = \frac{\text{CFE}}{\text{MAD}}$$

What types of controls are needed for the forecasting system?

Each period, the CFE and MAD are updated to reflect current error, and the tracking signal is compared to some predetermined limits. The MAD can be calculated in one of two ways: (1) as the simple average of all absolute errors (as demonstrated in Example 13.6) or (2) as a weighted average determined by the exponential smoothing method:

$$\text{MAD}_t = \alpha|E_t| + (1 - \alpha)\text{MAD}_{t-1}$$

If forecast errors are normally distributed with a mean of 0, there is a simple relationship between σ and MAD:

$$\sigma = (\sqrt{\pi/2})(\text{MAD}) \cong 1.25(\text{MAD})$$
$$\text{MAD} = 0.7978\sigma \cong 0.8\sigma$$

where

$$\pi = 3.1416$$

This relationship allows use of the normal probability tables to specify limits for the tracking signal. If the tracking signal falls outside those limits, the forecasting model no

TABLE 13.3   PERCENTAGE OF THE AREA OF THE NORMAL PROBABILITY DISTRIBUTION WITHIN THE CONTROL LIMITS OF THE TRACKING SIGNAL

Control Limit Spread (number of MAD)	Equivalent Number of σ*	Percent of Area Within Control Limits†
±1.0	±0.80	57.62
±1.5	±1.20	76.98
±2.0	±1.60	89.04
±2.5	±2.00	95.44
±3.0	±2.40	98.36
±3.5	±2.80	99.48
±4.0	±3.20	99.86

*The equivalent number of standard deviations is found by using the approximation of MAD = 0.8σ.

†The area of the normal curve included within the control limits is found in Appendix 1. For example, the cumulative area from $-\infty$ to 0.80σ is 0.7881. The area between 0 and $+0.80\sigma$ is $0.7881 - 0.5000 = 0.2881$. Since the normal curve is symmetric, the area between -0.80σ and 0 is also 0.2881. Therefore, the area between $\pm0.80s$ is $0.2881 + 0.2881 = 0.5762$.

longer is tracking demand adequately. A tracking system is useful when forecasting systems are computerized because it alerts analysts when forecasts are getting far from desirable limits. Table 13.3 shows the area of the normal probability distribution within the control limits of 1 to 4 MAD.

Figure 13.10 shows tracking signal results for 23 periods plotted in a *control chart*. The control chart is useful for determining whether any action needs to be taken to improve the forecasting model. In the example, the first 20 points cluster around 0, as we would expect if the forecasts are not biased. The CFE will tend toward 0. When the underlying characteristics of demand change but the forecasting model does not, the tracking signal eventually goes out of control. The steady increase after the 20th point in Figure 13.10 indicates that the process is going out of control. The 21st and 22nd points are acceptable, but the 23rd point is not.

FORECAST ERROR RANGES. Calculating MAD can also provide additional information. Forecasts that are stated as a single value, such as 1,200 units or 26 customers, can be less useful because they do not indicate the range of likely errors that the forecast typically generates. A better approach can be to provide the manager with a forecasted value and an error range. For example, suppose that the forecasted value for a product is 1,000 units, with a MAD of 20 units. Table 13.3 shows that there is about a

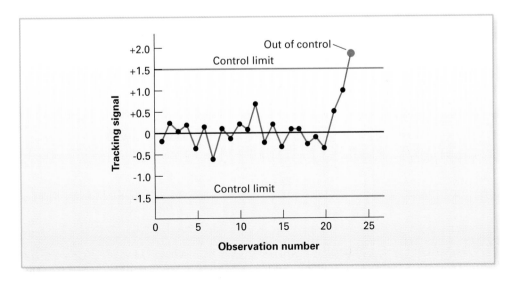

FIGURE 13.10

Tracking Signal

95 percent chance that actual demand will fall within ±2.5 MAD of the forecast; that is, for a forecast of 1,000 units, we can say with a 95 percent confidence level that actual demand will fall in the range of 950 to 1,050 units.

COMPUTER SUPPORT. Computer support, such as from *OM Explorer*, makes error calculations easy when evaluating how well forecasting models fit with past data (i.e., the *history file*). Figure 13.11 shows the output from the Time-Series Forecasting Solver, when applied to the medical clinic patient arrivals (see the original plot in Figure 13.5). Four different models are evaluated: naive forecasts (obtained with moving averages when $n = 1$), weighted moving averages ($n = 3$), exponential smoothing ($\alpha = 0.10$), and trend-adjusted exponential smoothing ($\alpha = 0.10$, $\beta = 0.10$). Figure 13.11 (a) is a worksheet that allows you to select the methods to be evaluated and then calculates the resulting errors for each method on a period-by-period basis. Initial forecasts must be selected for the exponential smoothing method and the trend-adjusted exponential smoothing method. Here we simply equated them to the actual demand for the week of January 1, 2003. Other reasonable starting points would not affect the results in a significant way.

Figure 13.11 (b) shows the various error measures across the entire history file for each method evaluated. For the medical clinic, the exponential smoothing model provides the best fit with past data in terms of MAPE (3.54 percent), MSE (293.39), and MAD (14.42). It is worse than the weighted moving average on CFE (75.26 versus 14.10). Other versions of these models could be evaluated by testing other reasonable values for n, α, and β.

FIGURE 13.11   **Output from Time-Series Forecasting Solver for Medical Clinic Patient Arrivals**

(a) Worksheet

1-Period Moving Average	3-Period Weighted Moving Average	Exponential Smoothing	Trend-Adj. Exp. Smoothing
	Enter weights	α 0.10	α 0.10
	Most recent 0.70	Initial Forecast 400	β 0.10
	2rd most recent 0.20		Initial Average 400
	3rd most recent 0.10	Initial Forecast = av. Of 1st 3 pds.	Initial Trend 0

Actual Data		1-Period Moving Average			3-Period Weighted Moving Average			Exponential Smoothing			Trend-adj. Exp. Smoothing		
		Forecast	Error	CFE	Forecast	Error	CFE	Forecast	Error	CFE	Forecast	Error	CFE
1/1/2003	400							400.00	0.00	0.00	400.00	0.00	0.00
1/8/2003	380	400.00	-20.00	-20.00				400.00	-20.00	-20.00	400.00	-20.00	-20.00
1/15/2003	411	380.00	31.00	11.00				398.00	13.00	-7.00	397.80	13.20	-6.80
1/22/2003	415	411.00	4.00	15.00	403.70	11.30	11.30	399.30	15.70	8.70	399.05	15.95	9.15
1/29/2003	393	415.00	-22.00	-7.00	410.70	-17.70	-6.40	400.87	-7.87	0.83	400.74	-7.74	1.41
2/5/2003	375	393.00	-18.00	-25.00	399.20	-24.20	-30.60	400.08	-25.08	-24.25	399.98	-24.98	-23.57
2/12/2003	410	375.00	35.00	10.00	382.60	27.40	-3.20	397.57	12.43	-11.83	397.25	12.75	-10.81
2/19/2003	395	410.00	-15.00	-5.00	401.30	-6.30	-9.50	398.82	-3.82	-15.64	398.41	-3.41	-14.23
2/26/2003	406	395.00	11.00	6.00	396.00	10.00	0.50	398.44	7.56	-8.08	397.93	8.07	-6.16
3/5/2003	424	406.00	18.00	24.00	404.20	19.80	20.30	399.19	24.81	16.73	398.67	25.33	19.17
3/12/2003	433	424.00	9.00	33.00	417.50	15.50	35.80	401.67	31.33	48.05	401.40	31.60	50.77
3/19/2003	391	433.00	-42.00	-9.00	428.50	-37.50	-1.70	404.81	-13.81	34.25	405.07	-14.07	36.71
3/26/2003	396	391.00	5.00	-4.00	402.70	-6.70	-8.40	403.42	-7.42	26.82	404.03	-8.03	28.68
4/2/2003	417	396.00	21.00	17.00	398.70	18.30	9.90	402.68	14.32	41.14	403.51	13.49	42.17
4/9/2003	383	417.00	-34.00	-17.00	410.20	-27.20	-17.30	404.11	-21.11	20.03	405.28	-22.28	19.89
4/16/2003	402	383.00	19.00	2.00	391.10	10.90	-6.40	402.00	0.00	20.03	403.25	-1.25	18.63
4/23/2003	387	402.00	-15.00	-13.00	399.70	-12.70	-19.10	402.00	-15.00	5.02	403.31	-16.31	2.32
4/30/2003	410	387.00	23.00	10.00	389.60	20.40	1.30	400.50	9.50	14.52	401.71	8.29	10.61
5/7/2003	398	410.00	-12.00	-2.00	404.60	-6.60	-5.30	401.45	-3.45	11.07	402.64	-4.64	5.97
5/14/2003	433	398.00	35.00	33.00	399.30	33.70	28.40	401.11	31.89	42.96	402.24	30.76	36.74
5/21/2003	415	433.00	-18.00	15.00	423.70	-8.70	19.70	404.30	10.70	53.67	405.68	9.32	46.06
5/28/2003	380	415.00	-35.00	-20.00	416.90	-36.90	-17.20	405.37	-25.37	28.30	407.07	-27.07	18.98
6/4/2003	394	380.00	14.00	-6.00	392.30	1.70	-15.50	402.83	-8.83	19.47	404.56	-10.56	8.43
6/11/2003	412	394.00	18.00	12.00	393.30	18.70	3.20	401.95	10.05	29.52	403.58	8.42	16.84
6/18/2003	439	412.00	27.00	39.00	405.20	33.80	37.00	402.95	36.05	65.57	404.59	34.41	51.25
6/25/2003	416	439.00	-23.00	16.00	429.10	-13.10	23.90	406.56	9.44	75.01	408.55	7.45	58.70
7/2/2003	395	416.00	-21.00	-5.00	420.20	-25.20	-1.30	407.50	-12.50	62.51	409.88	-14.88	43.82
7/9/2003	419	395.00	24.00	19.00	403.60	15.40	14.10	406.25	12.75	75.26	408.83	10.17	53.99

(b) Results sheet

Method 1 - Moving Average:

1 -Period Moving Average

Forecast for 7/16/03	419.00
CFE	19.00
MAD	21.07
MSE	532.41
MAPE	5.22%

Method 2 - Weighted Moving Average:

3 -Period Weighted Moving Average

Forecast for 7/16/03	413.90
CFE	14.10
MAD	18.39
MSE	437.07
MAPE	4.54%

Method 3 - Exponential Smoothing:

α	0.10
Initial Forecast	400.00
Forecast for 7/16/03	407.53
CFE	75.26
MAD	14.42
MSE	293.39
MAPE	3.54%

Method 4 - Trend-Adjusted Exponential Smoothing:

α	0.10
β	0.10
Initial Average	400.00
Initial Trend	0.00
Average for last period	409.85
Trend for last period	0.54
Forecast for 7/16/03	410.39
Forecast for 7/23/03	410.93
Forecast for 7/30/03	411.47
Forecast for 8/6/03	412.01
Forecast for 8/13/03	412.55
Forecast for 8/20/03	413.09
CFE	53.99
MAD	14.44
MSE	303.82
MAPE	3.69%

Figure 13.11 (b) also makes forecasts for the next period. Forecasts for all future periods made at this point of time (the end of the history file) would be identical to next period's forecasts. The only exception is for the trend-adjusted exponential smoothing method, which provides forecasts for several periods in the future that

account for the latest trend estimate (0.54 per week). If the exponential smoothing method is selected to make next period's forecast (because of its good performance to date), the expectation would be for 408 patients (calculated as 407.53). The forecast would be 414 patients (calculated as 413.90) using the weighted moving average method. Averaging these two numbers (see *combination forecasts* in the next section) would give a forecast of 411 patients.

CRITERIA FOR SELECTING TIME-SERIES METHODS

What is involved in choosing the best time-series forecasting method?

Forecast error measures provide important information for choosing the best forecasting method for a service or product. They also guide managers in selecting the best values for the parameters needed for the method: n for the moving average method, the weights for the weighted moving average method, and α for the exponential smoothing method. The criteria to use in making forecast method and parameter choices include (1) minimizing bias; (2) minimizing MAPE, MAD, or MSE; (3) meeting managerial expectations of changes in the components of demand; and (4) minimizing the forecast error last period. The first two criteria relate to statistical measures based on historical performance, the third reflects expectations of the future that may not be rooted in the past, and the fourth is a way to use whatever method seems to be working best at the time a forecast must be made.

USING STATISTICAL CRITERIA. Statistical performance measures can be used in the selection of a forecasting method. The use of the following guidelines will help when searching for the best time-series models.

1. For projections of more stable demand patterns, use lower α and β values or larger n values to emphasize historical experience.
2. For projections of more dynamic demand patterns, using the models covered in this chapter, try higher α and β values or smaller n values. When historical demand patterns are changing, recent history should be emphasized.

Often, the forecaster must make trade-offs between bias (CFE) and the measures of forecast error dispersion (MAPE, MAD, and MSE). Managers also must recognize that the best technique in explaining the past data is not necessarily the best technique to predict the future, and that "overfitting" past data can be deceptive. A forecasting method may have small errors, relative to the history file, but may generate high errors for future time periods. For this reason, some analysts prefer to use a **holdout set** as a final test. To do so, they set aside some of the more recent periods from the time series and use only the earlier time periods to develop and test different models. Once the final models have been selected in the first phase, then they are tested again with the holdout set. Performance measures, such as MAPE and CFE, would still be used but they would be applied to the holdout sample. Whether this idea is used or not, managers should monitor future forecast errors, perhaps with tracking signals, and modify their forecasting approaches as needed. Maintaining data on forecast performance is the ultimate test of forecasting power—rather than how well a model fits past data or holdout samples.

holdout set   Actual demands from the more recent time periods in the time series, which are set aside to test different models developed from the earlier time periods.

USING MULTIPLE TECHNIQUES

We have described several individual forecasting methods and shown how to assess their forecast performance. However, there is no need to rely on only a single forecasting method. The forecasting process of Unilever and Wal-Mart brings together several different forecasts when arriving at a final forecast. Initial statistical forecasts using several time-series methods and regression are distributed to knowledgeable individuals, such as marketing directors and sales teams, for their adjustments. They can account for current market and customer conditions that are not necessarily reflected in past data. There can be multiple forecasts from different sales teams, and some teams may have a better record on forecast errors than others. Finally, the collaborative process of CPFR introduces forecasts from suppliers and even customers. There are two approaches to using several forecasting techniques in unison: (1) combination forecasts and (2) focus forecasting.

COMBINATION FORECASTS

Research during the last two decades suggest that combining forecasts from multiple sources often produces more accurate forecasts. **Combination forecasts** are forecasts that are produced by averaging independent forecasts based on different methods or different data or both. It is intriguing that combination forecasts often perform better over time than do even the *best* single forecasting procedure. For example, suppose that the forecast for next period is 100 units from technique 1 and 120 units from technique 2 and that technique 1 has provided more accurate forecasts to date. The combination forecast for next period, giving equal weight to each technique, is 110 units (or $0.5 \times 100 + 0.5 \times 120$). When this averaging technique is used consistently into the future, its combination forecasts often will be much more accurate than those of any single best forecasting technique (in this example, technique 1). Combining is most effective when the individual forecasts bring different kinds of information into the forecasting process. Forecasters have achieved excellent results by weighting forecasts equally, and this is a good starting point. However, unequal weights may provide better results under some conditions.

> **combination forecasts** Forecasts that are produced by averaging independent forecasts based on different methods or different data or both.

OM Explorer allows you to evaluate several forecasting models, and then create combination forecasts from them. The models can be the ones evaluated separately in Figure 13.11 but they can also include forecasts from regression, judgment, or the naive method. To evaluate the judgment method, the forecaster should be given actual demand just one period at a time, preferably as the actual events are happening, and then commit to a forecast for the next period. To be informed, the forecaster should also be aware of how well the other forecasting methods have been performing, particularly in the recent past.

FOCUS FORECASTING

Another way to take advantage of multiple techniques is **focus forecasting**, which selects the best forecast from a group of forecasts generated by individual techniques. Every period, all techniques are used to make forecasts for each item. The forecasts are made with a computer because there can be 100,000 SKUs at a company. Using the history file as the starting point for each method, the computer generates forecasts for the current period. The forecasts are compared to actual demand, and the method that produces the forecast with the least error is used to make the forecast for the next period. The method used for each item may change from period to period.

> Is the most sophisticiated forecasting system always the best one to use?

> **focus forecasting** A method of forecasting, which selects the best forecast from a group of forecasts generated by individual techniques.

⊙ FORECASTING ACROSS THE ORGANIZATION

The organization-wide forecasting process cuts across functional areas. Forecasting overall demand typically originates with marketing, but internal customers throughout the organization depend on forecasts to formulate and execute their plans. Forecasts are critical inputs to business plans, annual plans, and budgets. Finance needs forecasts to project cash flows and capital requirements. Human resources needs forecasts to anticipate hiring and training needs. Marketing is a primary source for sales forecast information, because they are closest to external customers. Operations needs forecasts to plan output levels, purchases of services and materials, workforce and output schedules, inventories, and long-term capacities.

Managers throughout the organization make forecasts on many variables other than future demand, such as competitor strategies, regulatory changes, technological change, processing times, supplier lead times, and quality losses. Tools for making these forecasts are basically the same tools covered here for demand: judgment, opinions of knowledgeable people, averages of past experience, regression, and time-series techniques. Using them, forecasting performance can be improved. But forecasts are rarely perfect. As Samuel Clemens (Mark Twain) said in *Following the Equator*, "prophesy is a good line of business, but it is full of risks." Smart managers recognize this reality and find ways to update their plans when the inevitable forecast error or unexpected event occurs.

CHAPTER HIGHLIGHTS

- The five basic patterns of demand are the horizontal, trend, seasonal, cyclical, and random variation.

- Designing a forecasting system involves determining what to forecast, which forecasting technique to use, and how computerized forecasting systems can assist managerial decision making.

- Level of data aggregation and units of measure are important considerations in managerial decisions about what to forecast. Two general types of demand forecasting are used: qualitative methods and quantitative methods. Qualitative methods include judgment methods, and quantitative methods include causal methods and time-series analysis.

- Judgment methods of forecasting are useful in situations where relevant historical data are lacking. Sales-force estimates, executive opinion, market research, and the Delphi method are judgment methods. Judgment methods require the most human interaction and, therefore, are the most costly of these methods.

- Causal forecasting methods hypothesize a functional relationship between the factor to be forecasted and other internal or external factors. Causal methods identify turning points in demand patterns but require more extensive analysis to determine the appropriate relationships between the item to be forecast and the external and internal factors. Linear regression is one of the more popular causal forecasting methods.

- Time-series analysis is often used with computer systems to generate quickly the large number of short-term forecasts required for scheduling services or products. Simple moving averages, weighted moving averages, and exponential smoothing are used to estimate the average of a time series. The exponential smoothing technique has the advantage of requiring that only a minimal amount of data be kept for use in updating the forecast. Trend-adjusted exponential smoothing is a method for including a trend estimate in exponentially smoothed forecasts. Estimates for the series average and the trend are smoothed to provide the forecast.

- Although many techniques allow for seasonal influences, a simple approach is the multiplicative seasonal method, which is based on the assumption that the seasonal influence is proportional to the level of average demand.

- The cumulative sum of forecast errors (CFE), mean squared error (MSE), standard deviation of forecast errors (σ), mean absolute deviation (MAD), and mean absolute percent error (MAPE) are all measures of forecast error used in practice. The CFE and MAD are used to develop a tracking signal that determines when a forecasting method no longer is yielding acceptable forecasts. Forecast error measures also are used to select the best forecast methods from available alternatives.

- Combination forecasts produced by averaging two or more independent forecasts often provide more accurate forecasts.

- Unilever's CDP process, and the recent initiatives with CPFR, are compatible with combination forecasting.

STUDENT CD-ROM AND INTERNET RESOURCES

The Student CD-ROM and the Companion Website at **www.prenhall.com/krajewski** contain many tools, activities, and resources designed for this chapter. The following items are recommended to enhance your skills and improve your understanding of the material in this chapter.

STUDENT CD-ROM RESOURCES

- ► **PowerPoint Slides:** View this comprehensive set of slides customized for this chapter's concepts and techniques.
- ► **OM Explorer Tutors:** OM Explorer contains four tutor spreadsheets that will help you learn how to use the moving average, weighted moving average, exponential

smoothing, and trend-adjusted exponential smoothing techniques. See Chapter 13 in the OM Explorer menu. See also the Tutor exercise that uses three tutors to forecast newspaper subscriptions.

- ► **OM Explorer Solvers:** OM Explorer contains three spreadsheets to help with general problems involving regression analysis, seasonal forecasting, and time-series models. See Forecasting in the OM Explorer menu for these routines.
- ► **Active Models:** There are four active model spreadsheets that provide additional insights on making forecasts with regression, moving averages, exponential smoothing, and trend-adjusted exponential smoothing. See Forecasting in the Active Models menu for these four routines.

➤ **Supplement G:** "Learning Curve Analysis." See how variations of forecasting techniques are used to analyze learning curves.

➤ **Supplement H:** "Measuring Output Rates." See how variations of forecasting techniques are used to estimate future processing times.

INTERNET RESOURCES

➤ **Self-Study Quizzes:** See the compendium of true or false, multiple choice, and essay questions that give feedback on how well you have mastered the concepts in this chapter.

➤ **In the News:** See the articles that apply to this chapter.
➤ **Internet Exercises:** Try out four different links to forecasting topics, including global warming, government data, and a forecasting pool. Other exercises are available on additional aspects of forecasting.
➤ **Virtual Tours:** Check out the manufacturing process at Ferrara Pan Candy Company and the forecasting issues involved. Also see the "Web Links to Company Facility Tours" for additional tours of company facilities.

KEY EQUATIONS

1. Linear regression: $Y = a + bX$

2. Naive forecasting: Forecast $= D_t$

3. Simple moving average:
$$F_{t+1} = \frac{D_t + D_{t-1} + D_{t-2} + \cdots + D_{t-n+1}}{n}$$

4. Weighted moving average:
$$F_{t+1} = \text{Weight}_1(D_t) + \text{Weight}_2(D_{t-1}) + \text{Weight}_3(D_{t-2}) + \cdots + \text{Weight}_n(D_{t-n+1})$$

5. Exponential smoothing: $F_{t+1} = \alpha D_t + (1-\alpha)F_t$

6. Trend-adjusted exponential smoothing:
$$A_t = \alpha D_t + (1-\alpha)(A_{t-1} + T_{t-1})$$
$$T_t = \beta(A_t - A_{t-1}) + (1-\beta)T_{t-1}$$
$$F_{t+1} = A_t + T_t$$

7. Forecast error:
$$E_t = D_t - F_t$$
$$\text{CFE} = \Sigma E_t$$
$$\overline{E} = \frac{\text{CFE}}{n}$$
$$\text{MSE} = \frac{\Sigma E_t^2}{n}$$
$$\sigma = \sqrt{\frac{\Sigma(E_t - \overline{E})^2}{n-1}}$$
$$\text{MAD} = \frac{\Sigma|E_t|}{n}$$
$$\text{MAPE} = \frac{(\Sigma|E_t|/D_t)(100\%)}{n}$$

8. Tracking signal: $\dfrac{\text{CFE}}{\text{MAD}}$ or $\dfrac{\text{CFE}}{\text{MAD}_t}$

9. Exponentially smoothed error:
$$\text{MAD}_t = \alpha|E_t| + (1-\alpha)\text{MAD}_{t-1}$$

KEY TERMS

additive seasonal method 557
aggregation 538
causal methods 539
collaborative planning, forecasting, and replenishment (CPFR) 540
combination forecasts 565
cumulative sum of forecast errors (CFE) 558
Delphi method 543
dependent variable 544
executive opinion 542
exponential smoothing method 551
focus forecasting 565

forecast 536
forecast error 558
holdout set 564
independent variables 544
judgment methods 539
linear regression 544
market research 542
mean absolute deviation (MAD) 558
mean absolute percent error (MAPE) 559
mean squared error (MSE) 558
multiplicative seasonal method 555
naive forecast 547

sales-force estimates 542
simple moving average method 548
standard deviation (σ) 558
stock-keeping unit (SKU) 539
technological forecasting 542
time series 537
time-series analysis 539
tracking signal 560
trend-adjusted exponential smoothing method 552
weighted moving average method 550

SOLVED PROBLEM I

Chicken Palace periodically offers carryout five-piece chicken dinners at special prices. Let Y be the number of dinners sold and X be the price. Based on the historical observations and calculations in the following table, determine the regression equation, correlation coefficient, and coefficient of determination. How many dinners can Chicken Palace expect to sell at $3.00 each?

Observation	Price(X)	Dinners Sold (Y)
1	$ 2.70	760
2	$ 3.50	510
3	$ 2.00	980
4	$ 4.20	250
5	$ 3.10	320
6	$ 4.05	480
Total	$19.55	3,300
Average	$ 3.258	550

SOLUTION

We use the computer to calculate the best values of a, b, the correlation coefficient, and the coefficient of determination.

$$a = 1,450.13$$
$$b = -276.28$$
$$r = -0.84$$
$$r^2 = 0.71$$

The regression line is

$$Y = a + bX = 1,450.13 - 276.28X$$

The correlation coefficient ($r = -0.84$) shows a negative correlation between the variables. The coefficient of determination ($r^2 = 0.71$) indicates that other variables (in addition to price) appreciably affect sales.

If the regression equation is satisfactory to the manager, estimated sales at a price of $3.00 per dinner may be calculated as follows:

$$Y = a + bX = 1,450.13 - 276.28(3.00)$$
$$= 621.28 \quad \text{or} \quad 621 \text{ dinners}$$

SOLVED PROBLEM 2

The Polish General's Pizza Parlor is a small restaurant catering to patrons with a taste for European pizza. One of its specialties is Polish Prize pizza. The manager must forecast weekly demand for these special pizzas so that he can order pizza shells weekly. Recently, demand has been as follows:

Week	Pizzas	Week	Pizzas
June 2	50	June 23	56
June 9	65	June 30	55
June 16	52	July 7	60

a. Forecast the demand for pizza for June 23 to July 14 by using the simple moving average method with $n = 3$. Then repeat the forecast by using the weighted moving average method with $n = 3$ and weights of 0.50, 0.30, and 0.20, with 0.50 applying to the most recent demand.

b. Calculate the MAD for each method.

SOLUTION

a. The simple moving average method and the weighted moving average method give the following results.

CURRENT WEEK	SIMPLE MOVING AVERAGE FORECAST FOR NEXT WEEK	WEIGHTED MOVING AVERAGE FORECAST FOR NEXT WEEK
June 16	$\dfrac{52 + 65 + 50}{3} = 55.7$ or 56	$[(0.5 \times 52) + (0.3 \times 65) + (0.2 \times 50)] = 55.5$ or 56
June 23	$\dfrac{56 + 52 + 65}{3} = 57.7$ or 58	$[(0.5 \times 56) + (0.3 \times 52) + (0.2 \times 65)] = 56.6$ or 57
June 30	$\dfrac{55 + 56 + 52}{3} = 54.3$ or 54	$[(0.5 \times 55) + (0.3 \times 56) + (0.2 \times 52)] = 54.7$ or 55
July 7	$\dfrac{60 + 55 + 56}{3} = 57.0$ or 57	$[(0.5 \times 60) + (0.3 \times 55) + (0.2 \times 56)] = 57.7$ or 58

b. The mean absolute deviation is calculated as follows:

WEEK	ACTUAL DEMAND	SIMPLE MOVING AVERAGE FORECAST	ABSOLUTE ERRORS $|E_t|$	WEIGHTED MOVING AVERAGE FORECAST	ABSOLUTE ERRORS $|E_t|$
June 23	56	56	$|56 - 56| = 0$	56	$|56 - 56| = 0$
June 30	55	58	$|55 - 58| = 3$	57	$|55 - 57| = 2$
July 7	60	54	$|60 - 54| = 6$	55	$|60 - 55| = 5$
			$\text{MAD} = \dfrac{0 + 3 + 6}{3} = 3$		$\text{MAD} = \dfrac{0 + 2 + 5}{3} = 2.3$

For this limited set of data, the weighted moving average method resulted in a slightly lower mean absolute deviation. However, final conclusions can be made only after analyzing much more data.

SOLVED PROBLEM 3

The monthly demand for units manufactured by the Acme Rocket Company has been as follows:

MONTH	UNITS	MONTH	UNITS
May	100	September	105
June	80	October	110
July	110	November	125
August	115	December	120

a. Use the exponential smoothing method to forecast the number of units for June to January. The initial forecast for May was 105 units; $\alpha = 0.2$.

b. Calculate the absolute percentage error for each month from June through December and the MAD and MAPE of forecast error as of the end of December.

c. Calculate the tracking signal as of the end of December. What can you say about the performance of your forecasting method?

SOLUTION

a.

CURRENT MONTH, t	$F_{t+1} = \alpha D_t + (1 - \alpha)F_t$	FORECAST, MONTH $t + 1$
May	$0.2(100) + 0.8(105) = 104.0$ or 104	June
June	$0.2(80) + 0.8(104.0) = 99.2$ or 99	July
July	$0.2(110) + 0.8(99.2) = 101.4$ or 101	August
August	$0.2(115) + 0.8(101.4) = 104.1$ or 104	September
September	$0.2(105) + 0.8(104.1) = 104.3$ or 104	October
October	$0.2(110) + 0.8(104.3) = 105.4$ or 105	November
November	$0.2(125) + 0.8(105.4) = 109.3$ or 109	December
December	$0.2(120) + 0.8(109.3) = 111.4$ or 111	January

b.

MONTH, t	ACTUAL DEMAND, D_t	FORECAST, F_t	ERROR $E_t = D_t - F_t$	ABSOLUTE ERROR $|E_t|$	ABSOLUTE PERCENTAGE ERROR, $(|E_t|/D_t)$ (100%)
June	80	104	−24	24	30.0%
July	110	99	11	11	10.0
August	115	101	14	14	12.2
September	105	104	1	1	0.9
October	110	104	6	6	5.4
November	125	105	20	20	16.0
December	120	109	11	11	9.2
Total	765		39	87	83.7%

$$\text{MAD} = \frac{\Sigma |E_t|}{n} = \frac{87}{7} = 12.4 \quad \text{and} \quad \text{MAPE} = \frac{(\Sigma |E_t|/D_t)(100)}{n} = \frac{83.7\%}{7} = 11.9$$

c. As of the end of December, the cumulative sum of forecast errors (CFE) is 39. Using the mean absolute deviation calculated in part (b), we calculate the tracking signal:

$$\text{Tracking signal} = \frac{\text{CFE}}{\text{MAD}} = \frac{39}{12.4} = 3.14$$

The probability that a tracking signal value of 3.14 could be generated completely by chance is very small. Consequently, we should revise our approach. The long string of forecasts lower than actual demand suggests use of a trend method.

SOLVED PROBLEM 4

The demand for Krispee Crunchies, a favorite breakfast cereal of people born in the 1940s, is experiencing a decline. The company wants to monitor demand for this product closely as it nears the end of its life cycle. The trend-adjusted exponential smoothing method is used with $\alpha = 0.1$ and $\beta = 0.2$. At the end of December, the January estimate for the average number of cases sold per month, A_t, was 900,000 and the trend, T_t, was −50,000 per month. The following table shows the actual sales history for January, February, and March. Generate forecasts for February, March, and April.

MONTH	SALES
January	890,000
February	800,000
March	825,000

SOLUTION

We know the initial condition at the end of December and actual demand for January, February, and March. We must now update the forecast method and prepare a forecast for April. All data are expressed in thousands of cases. Our equations for use with trend-adjusted exponential smoothing are

$$A_t = \alpha D_t + (1 - \alpha)(A_{t-1} + T_{t-1})$$
$$T_t = \beta(A_t - A_{t-1}) + (1 - \beta)T_{t-1}$$
$$F_{t+1} = A_t + T_t$$

For January, we have

$$A_{Jan} = 0.1(890,000) + 0.9(900,000 - 50,000)$$
$$= 854,000 \text{ cases}$$
$$T_{Jan} = 0.2(854,000 - 900,000) + 0.8(-50,000)$$
$$= -49,200 \text{ cases}$$
$$F_{Feb} = A_{Jan} + T_{Jan} = 854,000 - 49,200 = 804,800 \text{ cases}$$

For February, we have

$$A_{Feb} = 0.1(800,000) + 0.9(854,000 - 49,200)$$
$$= 804,320 \text{ cases}$$
$$T_{Feb} = 0.2(804,320 - 854,000) + 0.8(-49,200)$$
$$= -49,296 \text{ cases}$$
$$F_{Mar} = A_{Feb} + T_{Feb} = 804,320 - 49,296 = 755,024 \text{ cases}$$

For March, we have

$$A_{Mar} = 0.1(825,000) + 0.9(804,320 - 49,296)$$
$$= 762,021.6 \text{ or } 762,022 \text{ cases}$$
$$T_{Mar} = 0.2(762,022 - 804,320) + 0.8(-49,296)$$
$$= -47,896.4 \text{ or } -47,897 \text{ cases}$$
$$F_{Apr} = A_{Mar} + T_{Mar} = 762,022 - 47,897 = 714,125 \text{ cases}$$

SOLVED PROBLEM 5

The Northville Post Office experiences a seasonal pattern of daily mail volume every week. The following data for two representative weeks are expressed in thousands of pieces of mail:

DAY		WEEK 1	WEEK 2
Sunday		5	8
Monday		20	15
Tuesday		30	32
Wednesday		35	30
Thursday		49	45
Friday		70	70
Saturday		15	10
	Total	224	210

a. Calculate a seasonal factor for each day of the week.
b. If the postmaster estimates that there will be 230,000 pieces of mail to sort next week, forecast the volume for each day of the week.

SOLUTION

a. Calculate the average daily mail volume for each week. Then for each day of the week divide the mail volume by the week's average to get the seasonal factor. Finally, for each day, add the two seasonal factors and divide by 2 to obtain the average seasonal factor to use in the forecast (see part (b)).

DAY	WEEK 1 MAIL VOLUME	WEEK 1 SEASONAL FACTOR (1)	WEEK 2 MAIL VOLUME	WEEK 2 SEASONAL FACTOR (2)	AVERAGE SEASONAL FACTOR [(1) + (2)]/2
Sunday	5	5/32 = 0.15625	8	8/30 = 0.26667	0.21146
Monday	20	20/32 = 0.62500	15	15/30 = 0.50000	0.56250
Tuesday	30	30/32 = 0.93750	32	32/30 = 1.06667	1.00209
Wednesday	35	35/32 = 1.09375	30	30/30 = 1.00000	1.04688
Thursday	49	49/32 = 1.53125	45	45/30 = 1.50000	1.51563
Friday	70	70/32 = 2.18750	70	70/30 = 2.33333	2.26042
Saturday	15	15/32 = 0.46875	10	10/30 = 0.33333	0.40104
Total	224		210		
Average	224/7 = 32		210/7 = 30		

b. The average daily mail volume is expected to be 230,000/7 = 32,857 pieces of mail. Using the average seasonal factors calculated in part (a), we obtain the following forecasts:

DAY	CALCULATION	FORECAST
Sunday	0.21146(32,857) =	6,948
Monday	0.56250(32,857) =	18,482
Tuesday	1.00209(32,857) =	32,926
Wednesday	1.04688(32,857) =	34,397
Thursday	1.51563(32,857) =	49,799
Friday	2.26042(32,857) =	74,271
Saturday	0.40104(32,857) =	13,177
	Total	230,000

DISCUSSION QUESTIONS

1. Figure 13.12 shows summer air visibility measurements for Denver. The acceptable visibility standard is 100, with readings above 100 indicating clean air and good visibility and readings below 100 indicating temperature inversions, forest fires, volcanic eruptions, or collisions with comets.

   a. Is there a trend in the data? Which time-series techniques might be appropriate for estimating the average of these data?

   b. A medical center for asthma and respiratory diseases located in Denver has great demand for its services when air quality is poor. If you were in charge of developing a short-term (say, 3-day) forecast of visibility, which causal factor(s) would you analyze? In other words, which external factors hold the potential to significantly affect visibility in the *short term?*

   c. Tourism, an important factor in Denver's economy, is affected by the city's image. Air quality, as measured by visibility, affects the city's image. If you were responsible for development of tourism, which causal factor(s) would you analyze to forecast visibility for the *medium term* (say, the next two summers)?

   d. The federal government threatens to withhold several hundred million dollars in Department of Transportation funds unless Denver meets visibility standards within eight years. How would you proceed to generate a *long-term* judgment forecast of technologies that will be available to improve visibility in the next 10 years?

2. Kay and Michael Passe publish *What's Happening?*—a biweekly newspaper to publicize local events. *What's Happening?* has few subscribers; it typically is sold at checkout stands. Much of the revenue comes from advertisers of garage sales and supermarket specials. In an effort to reduce costs associated with printing too many papers or delivering them to the wrong location, Michael implemented a computerized system to collect sales data. Sales-counter scanners accurately record sales data for each location. Since the system was implemented, total sales volume has steadily declined. Selling advertising space and maintaining shelf space at supermarkets are getting more difficult.

   Reduced revenue makes controlling costs all the more important. For each issue, Michael carefully makes a forecast based on sales data collected at each location. Then he orders papers to be printed and distributed in quantities matching the forecast. Michael's forecast reflects a downward trend, which *is* present in the sales data. Now only a few papers are left over at only a few locations. Although the sales forecast accurately predicts the actual sales at most locations, *What's Happening?* is spiraling toward oblivion. Kay suspects that Michael is doing something wrong in preparing the forecast but can find no mathematical errors. Tell her what is happening.

FIGURE 13.12

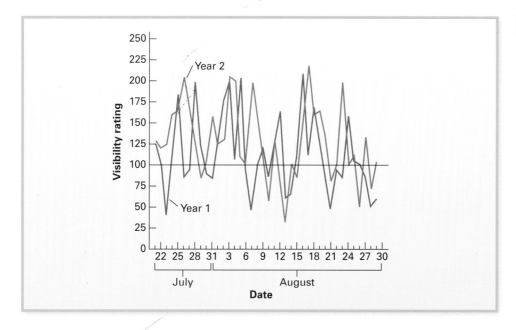

PROBLEMS

An icon next to a problem identifies the software that can be helpful, but is not mandatory. The software is available on the Student CD-ROM that is packaged with every new copy of the textbook.

Problem 7(vi) and Problems 12 through 14 involve considerable computations. The use of regression software or a spreadsheet is recommended.

1. **OM Explorer** The owner of a computer store rents printers to some of her preferred customers. She is interested in arriving at a forecast of rentals so that she can order the correct quantities of supplies that go with the printers. Data for the last 10 weeks are shown here.

Week	Rentals	Week	Rentals
1	23	6	28
2	24	7	32
3	32	8	35
4	26	9	26
5	31	10	24

a. Prepare a forecast for weeks 6 through 10 by using a five-week moving average. What is the forecast for week 11?

b. Calculate the mean absolute deviation as of the end of week 10.

2. **OM Explorer** Sales for the past 12 months at Dalworth Company are given here.

Month	Sales ($ millions)	Month	Sales ($ million)
January	20	July	53
February	24	August	62
March	27	September	54
April	31	October	36
May	37	November	32
June	47	December	29

a. Use a three-month moving average to forecast the sales for the months April through December.

b. Use a four-month moving average to forecast the sales for the months May through December.

c. Compare the performance of the two methods by using the mean absolute deviation as the performance criterion. Which method would you recommend?

d. Compare the performance of the two methods by using the mean absolute percent error as the performance criterion. Which method would you recommend?

e. Compare the performance of the two methods by using the mean squared error as the performance criterion. Which method would you recommend?

3. **OM Explorer** Karl's Copiers sells and repairs photocopy machines. The manager needs weekly forecasts of service calls so that he can schedule service personnel. The forecast for the week of July 3 was 24 calls. The manager uses exponential smoothing with $\alpha = 0.20$. Forecast the number of calls for the week of August 7, which is next week.

Week	Actual Service Calls
July 3	24
July 10	32
July 17	36
July 24	23
July 31	25

4. **OM Explorer** Consider the sales data for Dalworth Company given in Problem 2.

   a. Use a three-month weighted moving average to forecast the sales for the months April through December. Use weights of (3/6), (2/6), and (1/6), giving more weight to more recent data.

   b. Use exponential smoothing with $\alpha = 0.6$ to forecast the sales for the months April through December. Assume that the initial forecast for January was $22 million.

   c. Compare the performance of the two methods by using the mean absolute deviation as the performance criterion. Which method would you recommend?

   d. Compare the performance of the two methods by using the mean absolute percent error as the performance criterion. Which method would you recommend?

   e. Compare the performance of the two methods by using the mean squared error as the performance criterion. Which method would you recommend?

5. A convenience store recently started to carry a new brand of soft drink in its territory. Management is interested in estimating future sales volume to determine whether it should continue to carry the new brand or replace it with another brand. At the end of April, the average monthly sales volume of the new soft drink was 700 cans and the trend was +50 cans per month. The actual sales volume figures for May, June, and July are 760, 800, and 820, respectively. Use trend-adjusted exponential smoothing with $\alpha = 0.2$ and $\beta = 0.1$ to forecast usage for June, July, and August.

6. Dixie Bank in Dothan, Alabama, recently installed a new automatic teller machine to perform the standard banking services and handle loan applications and investment transactions. The new machine is a bit complicated to use, so management is interested in tracking its past use and projecting its future use. Additional machines may be needed if projected use is high enough.

   At the end of April, the average monthly use was 600 customers and the trend was +60 customers per month. The actual use figures for May, June, and July are 680, 710, and 790, respectively. Use trend-adjusted exponential smoothing with $\alpha = 0.3$ and $\beta = 0.2$ to forecast usage for June, July, and August.

7. **OM Explorer** The number of heart surgeries performed at Heartville General Hospital has increased steadily over the past years. The hospital's administration is seeking the best method to forecast the demand for such surgeries in year 6. The data for the past five years are shown. Six years ago, the forecast for year 1

was 41 surgeries, and the estimated trend was an increase of 2 per year.

Year	Demand
1	45
2	50
3	52
4	56
5	58

The hospital's administration is considering the following forecasting methods.

   (i) Exponential smoothing, with $\alpha = 0.6$. ✔

   (ii) Exponential smoothing, with $\alpha = 0.9$. ✔

   (iii) Trend-adjusted exponential smoothing, with $\alpha = 0.6$ and $\beta = 0.1$.

   (iv) Three-year moving average.

   (v) Three-year weighted moving average, using weights (3/6), (2/6), and (1/6), with more recent data given more weight.

   (vi) Regression model, $Y = 42.6 + 3.2X$, where Y is the number of surgeries and X is the index for the year (e.g., $X = 1$ for year 1, $X = 2$ for year 2, etc.).

   a. If MAD is the performance criterion chosen by the administration, which forecasting method should it choose?

   b. If MSE is the performance criterion chosen by the administration, which forecasting method should it choose?

   c. If MAPE is the performance criterion chosen by the administration, which forecasting method should it choose?

8. The following data are for calculator sales in units at an electronics store over the past five weeks:

Week	Sales
1	46
2	49
3	43
4	50
5	53

Use trend-adjusted exponential smoothing with $\alpha = 0.2$ and $\beta = 0.2$ to forecast sales for weeks 3 through 6. Assume that the average of the time series was 45 units and that the average trend was +2 units per week just before week 1.

9. **OM Explorer** Forrest and Dan make boxes of chocolates for which the demand is uncertain. Forrest says, "That's life." But Dan believes that some demand patterns exist that could be useful for planning the purchase of sugar, chocolate, and shrimp. Forrest insists on placing a surprise chocolate-covered shrimp in some boxes so that "You never know what you'll get." Quarterly demand (in boxes of chocolates) for the last three years follows:

Quarter	Year 1	Year 2	Year 3
1	3,000	3,300	3,502
2	1,700	2,100	2,448
3	900	1,500	1,768
4	4,400	5,100	5,882
Total	10,000	12,000	13,600

a. Use intuition and judgment to estimate quarterly demand for the fourth year.

b. If the expected sales for chocolates are 14,800 cases for year 4, use the multiplicative seasonal method to prepare a forecast for each quarter of the year. Are any of the quarterly forecasts different from what you thought you would get in part (a)?

10. **OM Explorer** The manager of Snyder's Garden Center must make her annual purchasing plans for rakes, gloves, and other gardening items. One of the items she stocks is Fast-Grow, a liquid fertilizer. The sales of this item are seasonal, with peaks in the spring, summer, and fall months. Quarterly demand (in cases) for the past two years follows:

Quarter	Year 1	Year 2
1	40	60
2	350	440
3	290	320
4	210	280
Total	890	1,100

If the expected sales for Fast-Grow are 1,150 cases for year 3, use the multiplicative seasonal method to prepare a forecast for each quarter of the year.

11. **OM Explorer** The manager of a utility company in the Texas panhandle wants to develop quarterly forecasts of power loads for the next year. The power loads are seasonal, and the data on the quarterly loads in megawatts (MW) for the last four years are as follows:

Quarter	Year 1	Year 2	Year 3	Year 4
1	103.5	94.7	118.6	109.3
2	126.1	116.0	141.2	131.6
3	144.5	137.1	159.0	149.5
4	166.1	152.5	178.2	169.0

The manager has estimated the total demand for the next year at 600 MW. Use the multiplicative seasonal method to develop the forecast for each quarter.

12. **OM Explorer** Demand for oil changes at Garcia's Garage has been as follows:

Month	Number of Oil Changes
January	41
February	46
March	57
April	52
May	59
June	51
July	60
August	62

a. Use simple linear regression analysis to develop a forecasting model for monthly demand. In this application, the dependent variable, Y, is monthly demand and the independent variable, X, is the month. For January, let $X = 1$; for February, let $X = 2$; and so on.

b. Use the model to forecast demand for September, October, and November. Here, $X = 9$, 10, and 11, respectively.

13. **OM Explorer** At a hydrocarbon processing factory, process control involves periodic analysis of samples for a certain process quality parameter. The analytic procedure currently used is costly and time consuming. A faster and more economical alternative procedure has been proposed. However, the numbers for the quality parameter given by the alternative procedure are somewhat different from those given by the current procedure, not because of any inherent errors but because of changes in the nature of the chemical analysis.

Management believes that, if the numbers from the new procedure can be used to forecast reliably the corresponding numbers from the current procedure, switching to the new procedure would be reasonable and cost effective. The following data were obtained for the quality parameter by analyzing samples using both procedures:

Current (Y)	Proposed (X)	Current (Y)	Proposed (X)
3.0	3.1	3.1	3.1
3.1	3.9	2.7	2.9
3.0	3.4	3.3	3.6
3.6	4.0	3.2	4.1
3.8	3.6	2.1	2.6
2.7	3.6	3.0	3.1
2.7	3.6	2.6	2.8

a. Use linear regression to find a relation to forecast Y, which is the quality parameter from the current procedure, using the values from the proposed procedure, X.

b. Is there a strong relationship between Y and X? Explain.

14. **OM Explorer** Ohio Swiss Milk Products manufactures and distributes ice cream in Ohio, Kentucky, and West Virginia. The company wants to expand operations by locating another plant in northern Ohio. The size of the new plant will be a function of the expected

demand for ice cream within the area served by the plant. A market survey is currently under way to determine that demand.

Ohio Swiss wants to estimate the relationship between the manufacturing cost per gallon and the number of gallons sold in a year to determine the demand for ice cream and, thus, the size of the new plant. The following data have been collected:

Plant	Cost per Thousand Gallons (Y)	Thousands of Gallons Sold (X)
1	$ 1,015	416.9
2	973	472.5
3	1,046	250.0
4	1,006	372.1
5	1,058	238.1
6	1,068	258.6
7	967	597.0
8	997	414.0
9	1,044	263.2
10	1,008	372.0
Total	$10,182	3,654.4

a. Develop a regression equation to forecast the cost per gallon as a function of the number of gallons produced.

b. What are the correlation coefficient and the coefficient of determination? Comment on your regression equation in light of these measures.

c. Suppose that the market survey indicates a demand of 325,000 gallons in the Bucyrus, Ohio area. Estimate the manufacturing cost per gallon for a plant producing 325,000 gallons per year.

Advanced Problems

15. **OM Explorer** The director of a large public library must schedule employees to reshelve books and periodicals checked out of the library. The number of items checked out will determine the labor requirements. The following data reflect the numbers of items checked out of the library for the past three years:

Month	Year 1	Year 2	Year 3
January	1,847	2,045	1,986
February	2,669	2,321	2,564
March	2,467	2,419	2,635
April	2,432	2,088	2,150
May	2,464	2,667	2,201
June	2,378	2,122	2,663
July	2,217	2,206	2,055
August	2,445	1,869	1,678
September	1,894	2,441	1,845
October	1,922	2,291	2,065
November	2,431	2,364	2,147
December	2,274	2,189	2,451

The director needs a time-series method for forecasting the number of items to be checked out during the next month. Find the best simple moving average forecast

you can. Decide what is meant by "best" and justify your decision.

16. **OM Explorer** Using the data in Problem 15, find the best exponential smoothing solution you can. Justify your choice.

17. **OM Explorer** Using the data in Problem 15, find the best trend-adjusted exponential smoothing solution you can. Compare the performance of this method with those of the best moving average method and the exponential smoothing method. Which of the three methods would you choose?

18. **OM Explorer** Cannister, Inc. specializes in the manufacture of plastic containers. The data on the monthly sales of 10-ounce shampoo bottles for the last five years are as follows:

Year	1	2	3	4	5
January	742	741	896	951	1,030
February	697	700	793	861	1,032
March	776	774	885	938	1,126
April	898	932	1,055	1,109	1,285
May	1,030	1,099	1,204	1,274	1,468
June	1,107	1,223	1,326	1,422	1,637
July	1,165	1,290	1,303	1,486	1,611
August	1,216	1,349	1,436	1,555	1,608
September	1,208	1,341	1,473	1,604	1,528
October	1,131	1,296	1,453	1,600	1,420
November	971	1,066	1,170	1,403	1,119
December	783	901	1,023	1,209	1,013

a. Using the multiplicative seasonal method, calculate the monthly seasonal indices.

b. Develop a simple linear regression equation to forecast annual sales. For this regression, the dependent variable, Y, is the demand in each year and the independent variable, X, is the index for the year (i.e., X = 1 for year 1, X = 2 for year 2, and so on until X = 5 for year 5).

c. Forecast the annual sales for year 6 by using the regression model you developed in part (b).

d. Prepare the seasonal forecast for each month by using the monthly seasonal indices calculated in part (a).

19. **OM Explorer** The Midwest Computer Company serves a large number of businesses in the Great Lakes region. The company sells supplies and replacements and performs service on all computers sold through seven sales offices. Many items are stocked, so close inventory control is necessary to assure customers of efficient service. Recently, business has been increasing, and management is concerned about stockouts. A forecasting method is needed to estimate requirements several months in advance so that adequate replenishment quantities can be purchased. An example of the sales growth experienced during the last 50 months is the growth in demand for item EP-37, a laser printer cartridge, shown in Table 13.4.

| | TABLE 13.4 | | | | |
| | EP-37 SALES AND LEASE DATA | | | | |
Month	EP-37 Sales	Leases	Month	EP-37 Sales	Leases
1	80	32	26	1,296	281
2	132	29	27	1,199	298
3	143	32	28	1,267	314
4	180	54	29	1,300	323
5	200	53	30	1,370	309
6	168	89	31	1,489	343
7	212	74	32	1,499	357
8	254	93	33	1,669	353
9	397	120	34	1,716	360
10	385	113	35	1,603	370
11	472	147	36	1,812	386
12	397	126	37	1,817	389
13	476	138	38	1,798	399
14	699	145	39	1,873	409
15	545	160	40	1,923	410
16	837	196	41	2,028	413
17	743	180	42	2,049	439
18	722	197	43	2,084	454
19	735	203	44	2,083	441
20	838	223	45	2,121	470
21	1,057	247	46	2,072	469
22	930	242	47	2,262	490
23	1,085	234	48	2,371	496
24	1,090	254	49	2,309	509
25	1,218	271	50	2,422	522

a. Develop a trend-adjusted exponential smoothing solution for forecasting demand. Find the "best" parameters and justify your choices. Forecast demand for months 51 through 53.

b. A consultant to Midwest's management suggested that new office building leases would be a good leading indicator for company sales. He quoted a recent university study finding that new office building leases precede office equipment and supply sales by three months. According to the study findings, leases in month 1 would affect sales in month 4; leases in month 2 would affect sales in month 5; and so on. Use linear regression to develop a forecasting model for sales, with leases as the independent variable. Forecast sales for months 51 through 53.

c. Which of the two models provides better forecasts? Explain.

20. ◆ OM Explorer A certain food item at P&Q Supermarkets has the demand pattern shown in the following table. Find the "best" forecast you can for month 25 and justify your methodology. You may use some of the data to find the best parameter value(s) for your method and the rest to test the forecast model. Your justification should include both quantitative and qualitative considerations.

Month	Demand	Month	Demand
1	33	13	37
2	37	14	43
3	31	15	56
4	39	16	41
5	54	17	36
6	38	18	39
7	42	19	41
8	40	20	58
9	41	21	42
10	54	22	45
11	43	23	41
12	39	24	38

21. ◆ OM Explorer The data for the visibility chart in Discussion Question 1 are shown in Table 13.5. The visibility standard is set at 100. Readings below 100 indicate that air pollution has reduced visibility, and readings above 100 indicate that the air is clearer.

| | TABLE 13.5 | | | | | | | |
| | VISIBILITY DATA | | | | | | | |
Date	Year 1	Year 2	Date	Year 1	Year 2	Date	Year 1	Year 2
July 22	125	130	Aug. 5	105	200	Aug. 19	170	160
23	100	120	6	205	110	20	125	165
24	40	125	7	90	100	21	85	135
25	100	160	8	45	200	22	45	80
26	185	165	9	100	160	23	95	100
27	85	205	10	120	100	24	85	200
28	95	165	11	85	55	25	160	100
29	200	125	12	125	130	26	105	110
30	125	85	13	165	75	27	100	50
31	90	105	14	60	30	28	95	135
Aug. 1	85	160	15	65	100	29	50	70
2	135	125	16	110	85	30	60	105
3	175	130	17	210	150			
4	200	205	18	110	220			

a. Use several methods to generate a visibility forecast for August 31 of the second year. Which method seems to produce the best forecast?

b. Use several methods to forecast the visibility index for the summer of the third year. Which method seems to produce the best forecast? Support your choice.

22. ◗ **OM Explorer** Tom Glass forecasts electrical demand for the Flatlands Public Power District (FPPD). The FPPD wants to take its Comstock power plant out of service for maintenance when demand is expected to be low. After shutdown, performing maintenance and getting the plant back on line takes two weeks. The utility has enough other generating capacity to satisfy 1,550 megawatts (MW) of demand while Comstock is out of service. Table 13.6 shows weekly peak demands (in MW) for the past several autumns. When next fall should the Comstock plant be scheduled for maintenance?

23. ◗ **OM Explorer** A manufacturing firm has developed a skills test, the scores from which can be used to predict workers' production rating factors. Data on the test scores of various workers and their subsequent production ratings are shown.

Worker	Test Score	Production Rating	Worker	Test Score	Production Rating
A	53	45	K	54	59
B	36	43	L	73	77
C	88	89	M	65	56
D	84	79	N	29	28
E	86	84	O	52	51
F	64	66	P	22	27
G	45	49	Q	76	76
H	48	48	R	32	34
I	39	43	S	51	60
J	67	76	T	37	32

a. Using linear regression, develop a relationship to forecast production ratings from test scores.

b. If a worker's test score was 80, what would be your forecast of the worker's production rating?

c. Comment on the strength of the relationship between the test scores and production ratings.

24. ◗ **OM Explorer** The materials handling manager of a manufacturing company is trying to forecast the cost of maintenance for the company's fleet of over-the-road tractors. He believes that the cost of maintaining the tractors increases with their age. He has collected the following data:

Age (years)	Yearly Maintenance Cost ($)
4.5	619
4.5	1,049
4.5	1,033
4.0	495
4.0	723
4.0	681
5.0	890
5.0	1,522
5.5	987
5.0	1,194
0.5	163
0.5	182
6.0	764
6.0	1,373
1.0	978
1.0	466
1.0	549

a. Use linear regression to develop a relationship to forecast to yearly maintenance cost based on the age of a tractor.

b. If a section has 20 three-year-old tractors, what is the forecast for the annual maintenance cost?

TABLE 13.6
WEEKLY PEAK POWER DEMANDS

	August		September				October					November	
Year	1	2	3	4	5	6	7	8	9	10	11	12	13
1	2,050	1,925	1,825	1,525	1,050	1,300	1,200	1,175	1,350	1,525	1,725	1,575	1,925
2	2,000	2,075	2,225	1,800	1,175	1,050	1,250	1,025	1,300	1,425	1,625	1,950	1,950
3	1,950	1,800	2,150	1,725	1,575	1,275	1,325	1,100	1,500	1,550	1,375	1,825	2,000
4	2,100	2,400	1,975	1,675	1,350	1,525	1,500	1,150	1,350	1,225	1,225	1,475	1,850
5	2,275	2,300	2,150	1,525	1,350	1,475	1,475	1,175	1,375	1,400	1,425	1,550	1,900

ACTIVE MODEL EXERCISE

This Active Model appears on the Student CD-ROM. It allows you to see the effects of the intercept (*a*) and slope (*b*) of a linear regression line on the standard error of estimate and on MAD.

QUESTIONS

1. How many units are sold for each dollar spent in advertisting, according to the regression model?
2. Use the scroll bar to lower the intercept. What happens to the standard error? What happens to the MAD?
3. Use the scroll bar to lower the slope. What happens to the standard error? What happens to the MAD?
4. Use the scroll bars for the slope and intercept to determine the values that minimize the MAD. Are these the same values that regression yields?

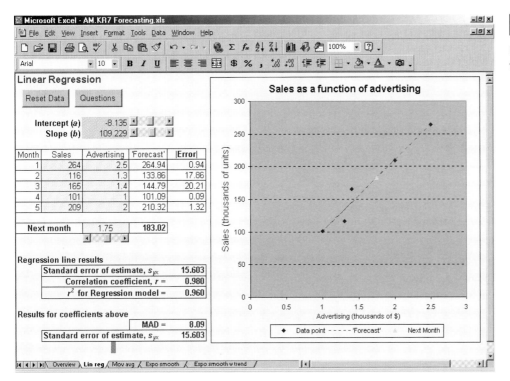

ACTIVE MODEL 13.1

Linear Regression Using Data from Example 13.1

CASE   YANKEE FORK AND HOE COMPANY

The Yankee Fork and Hoe Company is a leading producer of garden tools ranging from wheelbarrows, mortar pans, and hand trucks to shovels, rakes, and trowels. The tools are sold in four different product lines ranging from the top-of-the-line Hercules products, which are rugged tools for the toughest jobs, to the Garden Helper products, which are economy tools for the occasional user. The market for garden tools is extremely competitive because of the simple design of the products and the large number of competing producers. In addition, more people are using power tools, such as lawn edgers, hedge trimmers, and thatchers, reducing demand for their manual counterparts. These factors compel Yankee to maintain low prices while retaining high quality and dependable delivery.

Garden tools represent a mature industry. Unless new manual products can be developed or there is a sudden resurgence in home gardening, the prospects for large increases in sales are not bright. Keeping ahead of the competition is a constant battle. No one knows this better than Alan Roberts, president of Yankee.

The types of tools sold today are, by and large, the same ones sold 30 years ago. The only way to generate new sales and retain old customers is to provide superior customer service and produce a product with high customer value. This approach puts pressure on the manufacturing system, which has been having difficulties lately. Recently, Roberts has been receiving calls from long-time customers, such as Sears and Tru-Value Hardware Stores, complaining about late shipments. These customers advertise promotions for garden tools and require on-time delivery.

Roberts knows that losing customers like Sears and Tru-Value would be disastrous. He decides to ask consultant Sharon Place to look into the matter and report to him in one week. Roberts suggests that she focus on the bow rake as a case in point because it is a high-volume product and has been a major source of customer complaints of late.

PLANNING BOW RAKE PRODUCTION

A bow rake consists of a head with 12 teeth spaced one inch apart, a hardwood handle, a bow that attaches the head to the handle, and a metal ferrule that reinforces the area where the bow inserts into the handle. The bow is a metal strip that is welded to the ends of the rake head and bent in the middle to form a flat tab for insertion into the handle. The rake is about 64 inches long.

Place decides to find out how Yankee plans bow rake production. She goes straight to Phil Stanton, who gives the following account:

Planning is informal around here. To begin, marketing determines the forecast for bow rakes by month for the next year. Then they pass it along to me. Quite frankly, the forecasts are usually inflated—must be their big egos over there. I have to be careful

because we enter into long-term purchasing agreements for steel, and having it just sitting around is expensive. So, I usually reduce the forecast by 10 percent or so. I use the modified forecast to generate a monthly final-assembly schedule, which determines what I need to have from the forging and woodworking areas. The system works well if the forecasts are good. But when marketing comes to me and says they are behind on customer orders, as they often do near the end of the year, it wreaks havoc with the schedules. Forging gets hit the hardest. For example, the presses that stamp the rake heads from blanks of steel can handle only 7,000 heads per day, and the bow rolling machine can do only 5,000 per day. Both operations are also required for many other products.

Because the marketing department provides crucial information to Stanton, Place decides to see the marketing manager, Ron Adams. Adams explains how he arrives at the bow rake forecasts.

Things don't change much from year to year. Sure, sometimes we put on a sales promotion of some kind, but we try to give Phil enough warning before the demand kicks in—usually a month or so. I meet with several managers from the various sales regions to go over shipping data from last year and discuss anticipated promotions, changes in the economy, and shortages we experienced last year. Based on these meetings, I generate a monthly forecast for the next year. Even though we take a lot of time getting the forecast, it never seems to help us avoid customer problems.

THE PROBLEM

Place ponders the comments from Stanton and Adams. She understands Stanton's concerns about costs and keeping inventory low and Adams's concern about having enough rakes on hand to make timely shipments. Both are also somewhat concerned about capacity. Yet, she decides to check actual customer demand for the bow rake over the past four years (in Table 13.7) before making her final report to Roberts.

QUESTIONS

1. Comment on the forecasting system being used by Yankee. Suggest changes or improvements that you believe are justified.
2. Develop your own forecast for bow rakes for each month of the next year (year 5). Justify your forecast and the method you used.

TABLE 13.7   FOUR-YEAR DEMAND HISTORY FOR THE BOW RAKE

	Demand			
Month	**Year 1**	**Year 2**	**Year 3**	**Year 4**
1	55,220	39,875	32,180	62,377
2	57,350	64,128	38,600	66,501
3	15,445	47,653	25,020	31,404
4	27,776	43,050	51,300	36,504
5	21,408	39,359	31,790	16,888
6	17,118	10,317	32,100	18,909
7	18,028	45,194	59,832	35,500
8	19,883	46,530	30,740	51,250
9	15,796	22,105	47,800	34,443
10	53,665	41,350	73,890	68,088
11	83,269	46,024	60,202	68,175
12	72,991	41,856	55,200	61,100

Note: The demand figures shown in the table are the number of units promised for delivery each month. Actual delivery quantities differed because of capacity or shortages of materials.

SELECTED REFERENCES

Armstrong. J. S. *Long-Range Forecasting: From Crystal Ball to Computer*. New York: John Wiley & Sons, 1995.

Armstrong. J. Scott, and F. Collopy. "Integration of Statistical Methods and Judgment for Time Series Forecasting: Principles from Empirical Research," in G. Wright and P. Goodwin (eds.), *Forecasting with Judgement*. New York: John Wiley and Sons, 1998.

Bowman, Robert J. "Access to Data in Real Time: Seeing Isn't Everything." *Global Logistics and Supply-Chain Strategies* (May 2002). **www.glscs.com/archives/5.02.demand .htm?adcode¯35.**

Blattberg, R. C., and S. J. Hoch. "Database Models and Managerial Intuition: 50% Model + 50% Manager." *Management Science*, vol. 36 (1990), pp. 887–899.

Bowerman, Bruce L., and Richard T. O'Connell. *Forcasting and Time Series: An Applied Approach*, 3d ed., Belmont, CA: Duxbury Press, 1993.

Chambers, John C., Satinder K. Mullick, and Donald D. Smith. "How to Choose the Right Forecasting Technique." *Harvard Business Review* (July–August 1971), pp. 45–74.

"Clearing the Cobwebs from the Stockroom." *Business Week* (October 21, 1996), p. 140.

Clemen, R. T. "Combining Forecasts: A Review and Annotated Bibliography." *International Journal of Forecasting*, vol. 5 (1989), pp. 559–583.

Hudson, William J. *Executive Economics: Forecasting and Planning for the Real World of Business*. New York: John Wiley & Sons, 1993.

Jenkins, Carolyn. "Accurate Forecasting Reduces Inventory and Increases Output at Henredon." *APIC—The Performance Advantage* (September 1992), pp. 37–39.

Kimes, Sheryl E, and James A. Fitzsimmons. "Selecting Profitable Hotel Sites at La Quinta Motor Inns." *Interfaces*, vol. 20, no. 2 (1990), pp. 12–20.

Li, X. "An Intelligent Business Forecaster for Strategic Business Planning." *Journal of Forecasting*, vol. 18, no. 3(1999), pp. 181–205.

Lim, J. S., and M. O'Connor. "Judgmental Forecasting with Time Series and Causal Information." *International Journal of Forecasting*, vol. 12(1996), pp. 139–153.

Melnyk, Steven. "1997 Forecasting Software Product Listing." *APICS—The Performance Advantage* (April 1997), pp. 62–65.

Mitchell, Robert L. "Case Study: Unilever Crosses the Data Streams." *Computerworld* (December 17, 2001). **www .computerworld.com/softwaretopics/erp/story/0.10801 .66574.00.html**

Moon, Mark A., John T. Mentzer, and Dwight E. Thomas Jr. "Customer Demand Planning at Lucent Technologies; A Case Study in Continuous Improvement Through Sales Forecast Auditing." *Industrial Marketing Management*, vol. 29, no. 1 (2000).

Principles of Forecasting: A Handbook for Researchers and Practitioners. J. Scott Armstrong (ed.). Norwell, MA: Kluwer Academic Publishers, 2001. Also visit **www-marketing .wharton.upenn.edu/forecast.** for valuable information on forecasting, including frequently asked questions, forecasting methodology tree, and dictionary.

Raghunathan, Srinivasan. "Interorganizational Collaborative Forecasting and Replenishment Systems and Supply-Chain Implications." *Decision Sciences*, vol. 30, no. 5 (1999), pp. 1053–1067.

Sanders, Nada R., and L. P. Ritzman. "Bringing Judgment into Combination Forecasts." *Journal of Operations Management*, vol. 13 (1995), pp. 311–321.

Sanders, Nada R., and K. B. Manrodt. "Forecasting Practices in U.S. Corporations: Survey Results." *Interfaces*, vol. 24 (1994), pp. 91–100.

Sanders, Nada R., and Larry P. Ritzman. "The Need for Contextual and Technical Knowledge in Judgmental Forecasting." *Journal of Behavioral Decision Making*, vol. 5, no. 1 (1992), pp. 39–52.

Schachtman, Noah. "Trading Partners Collaborate to Increase Sales." *InformationWeek.com* (October 9, 2000), www.informationweek.com/807/cpfr.htm.

Schoenberger, Chana R. "The Weakest Link." *Forbes* (October 1, 2001). www.forbes.com/forbes/2001/1001/114 print.html.

Seifert, Dirk. *Collaborative Planning, Forecasting, and Replenishment: How to Create a Supply-Chain Advantage.* Bonn, Germany: Galileo Press, 2002.

Smith, Bernard. *Focus Forecasting: Computer Techniques for Inventory Control.* Boston: CBI Publishing, 1984.

VICS (2002) "Collaborative Planning, Forecasting, and Replenishment" Version 2.0, www.cpfr.org.

Yurkiewicz, Jack. "Forecasting 2000." *OR/MS Today*, vol. 27, no. 1 (2000), pp. 58–65.

Yurkiewicz, Jack. "2003 Forecasting Software Survey." *OR/MS Today* (February 2003). **www.lionhrtpub.com/orms/surveys/FSS/fss=fr.html.**

Aggregate Planning

LEARNING GOALS   *After reading this chapter, you should be able to . . .*

IDENTIFY OR DEFINE

1. the dimensions of aggregation.
2. the pros and cons of different reactive and aggressive alternatives.
3. the process of developing an acceptable plan.

DESCRIBE OR EXPLAIN

4. how aggregate plans relate to a firm's long- and short-term plans.
5. why aggregation helps in the planning process.
6. the spreadsheet approach to evaluating different strategies.
7. how the transportation method and the linear programming method assist in aggregate planning.

WHIRLPOOL CORPORATION

Whirlpool Corporation (www.whirlpoolcorp.com) is a leading producer of room air conditioners. The demand for window units is highly seasonal and also depends on variations in the weather. Typically, Whirlpool begins production of room air conditioners in the fall and holds them as inventory until they are shipped in the spring. Building inventory in the slack season allows the company to level production rates over much of the year and yet satisfy demand in the peak periods (spring and summer) when retailers are placing most of their orders. However, when summers are hotter than usual, demand increases dramatically and stockouts can occur. If Whirlpool increases output and the summer is hot, it stands to increase its sales and market share. But if the summer is cool, the company is stuck with expensive inventories of unsold machines. Whirlpool prefers to make its production plans based on the average year, taking into account industry forecasts for total sales and traditional seasonalities. Because of Whirlpool's increasingly global operations, its aggregate demand smooths out regional variations in demand. For example, the particularly strong results in North America and Europe more than offset weak economic and business conditions in Latin America and Asia.

Seasonality patterns depend on the weather and the product, and in turn affect aggregate plans. Aggregate plans for processes further downstream in the value chain can also be affected. Here a sales associate talks on the phone to a customer near two Whirlpool dryers in the appliance department of a Sears store.

Source: **www.whirlpoolcorp.com/wh**, January 10, 2000.

---

aggregate plan   A statement of a company's production rates, workforce levels, and inventory holdings based on estimates of customer requirements and capacity limitations.

staffing plan   A service firm's aggregate plan, which centers on staffing and other labor-related factors.

production plan   A manufacturing firm's aggregate plan, which generally focuses on production rates and inventory holdings.

Operating value chains effectively requires not just good forecasts, but also wise choices on deploying resources to best satisfy customer demand. These choices are not easy for complex processes and value chains, in part because customer demand is uneven over time. Uneven demand is certainly the case with Whirlpool, which experiences seasonal shifts in demand for its products. Its strategy, called an **aggregate plan,** is a statement of the company's production rates, workforce levels, and inventory holdings based on estimates of customer requirements and capacity limitations. This statement is time-phased, meaning that the plan is projected for several time periods (such as months) into the future.

A service firm's aggregate plan, called a **staffing plan,** centers on staffing and other labor-related factors; whereas a manufacturing firm's aggregate plan, called a **production plan,** generally focuses on production rates and inventory holdings. For both types of companies, the plan must balance conflicting objectives involving customer service, workforce stability, cost, and profit.

Based on the broad, long-term goals of a company, the aggregate plan specifies how the company will work, for the next year or more, toward those goals within existing equipment and facility capacity constraints. From these medium-range plans, managers prepare detailed operating plans. For service providers, the aggregate plan links strategic goals with detailed workforce schedules. We discuss this linkage in Chapter 17, "Scheduling." For manufacturing companies, the aggregate plan links strategic goals and objectives with production plans for individual products and the specific components that go into them. In this chapter and Chapter 16, "Resource Planning," we demonstrate how this linkage is achieved.

As you read about aggregate planning, think about why it is important to the various departments and functions across the organization, such as . . .

➤ **accounting,** which prepares cost accounting information needed to evaluate aggregate plans.

➤ **distribution,** which coordinates the outbound flow of materials in the value chain with the aggregate plan.

➤ **finance,** which knows the financial condition of the firm, seeks ways to contain expensive inventory accumulations, and develops plans to finance the cash flows created by the aggregate plan.

➤ **human resources,** which is aware of how labor-market conditions and training capacities constrain aggregate plans.

➤ **management information systems,** which develops information systems and decision support systems for developing production and staffing plans.

➤ **marketing,** which makes inputs for demand forecasts and provides information on competition and customer preferences.

➤ **operations,** which develops plans that are the best compromise among cost, customer service, inventory investment, stable workforce levels, and facility utilization.

➤ **purchasing,** which provides information on supplier capabilities and coordinates the inbound flow of services and materials in the value chain with the aggregate plan.

THE PURPOSE OF AGGREGATE PLANS

In this section, we explain why companies need aggregate plans and how they use them to take a macro, or big picture, view of their business. We also discuss how the aggregate plan relates to a company's long- and short-term plans.

AGGREGATION

The aggregate plan is useful because it focuses on a general course of action, consistent with the company's strategic goals and objectives, without getting bogged down in details. For example, the aggregate plan allows Whirlpool's managers to determine whether they can satisfy budgetary goals without having to schedule each of the company's thousands of products and employees. Even if a planner could prepare such a detailed plan, the time and effort required to update the plan would make it uneconomical. For this reason, production and staffing plans are prepared by grouping, or aggregating, similar services, products, units of labor, or units of time. For instance, a manufacturer of bicycles that produces 12 different models of bikes might divide them into two groups, mountain bikes and road bikes, for the purpose of preparing the aggregate plan. The manufacturer might also consider its workforce needs in terms of units of labor needed per month. In general, companies perform aggregation along three dimensions: services or products, labor, and time. Managerial Practice 14.1 shows one aggregate planning issue encountered in package delivery services, which is to find the best mix of full- and part-time employees.

What items should be aggregated?

PRODUCT FAMILIES. A group of customers, services, or products that have similar demand requirements and common process, labor, and materials requirements is called a **product family.** Sometimes, product families relate to market groupings or to specific processes. A firm can aggregate its services or products into a set of relatively broad families, avoiding too much detail at this stage of the planning process. Common and relevant measurements, such as number of customers, dollars, standard hours, gallons, or units, should be used. For example, consider the bicycle manufacturer that has aggregated all products into two families: mountain bikes and road bikes.

product family A group of customers, services, or products that have similar demand requirements and common process, labor, and materials requirements.

LABOR. A company can aggregate the workforce in various ways, depending on workforce flexibility. For example, if workers at the bicycle manufacturer are trained to work on either mountain bikes or road bikes, for planning purposes management can consider its workforce to be a single aggregate group, even though the skills of individual workers may differ.

MANAGERIAL PRACTICE 14.1

AGGREGATE PLANNING IN DELIVERY SERVICES

One aggregate planning decision is the best mix of full- and part-time employees. Part-time workers offer more flexibility in meeting peak demands, less reliance on expensive overtime, and the possibility of lower fringe benefits. However, there are also disadvantages. In the delivery services industry, United Parcel Service and FedEx opt for different strategies.

United Parcel Service (www.ups.com) utilizes a large number of employees for its package-sorting hub. The work is hard and routine, and the hours are long. The high level of productivity demanded by UPS occasionally generates complaints from Teamsters Union members. When faced with the alternatives of hiring full- or part-time employees, UPS managers prefer full-time employees for many jobs so that they can train them and, by means of thoroughly researched process and job designs, instill a strong sense of teamwork and job satisfaction. At the same time, UPS does have a part-time workforce, which was the cause of a union strike in 1997.

By the time the 15-day strike was settled, UPS had lost more than 7 percent of its average prestrike daily volume of 12 million packages and was faced with a backlog of some 90 million packages. In addition to the foregone revenues during the strike, UPS also had to win many of its customers back who, because of the strike, had chosen to work with a different company. After all the costs were considered, UPS attributed $775 million in lost revenues in 1997 to the strike.

FedEx (www.fedex.com) also requires large numbers of employees for its package-sorting facilities. Its managers, however, prefer part-time employees. To enable next-day delivery, FedEx's facilities are designed and staffed to sort more than a million pieces of freight and express mail in only four hours during the middle of the night. A full complement of full-time employees could not be effectively utilized all day long, whereas part-time employees, with high energy levels, can be used to meet daily peak demands.

To attract part-time employees, FedEx offers the same benefits package to its full- and part-time workers. College students are a good source for these sorting facilities. To attract them, FedEx gives generous educational allowances to both its full-time and part-time employees. Working mothers are another good source. FedEx won an award in 1998 as being a great place for working mothers, who match well with the company's need for part-time workers and flexible work schedules. Finally, FedEx was named one of the top 100 employers by *Fortune* during the period from 1998 to 2001.

A FedEx employee uses a computer as other employees load packages from conveyor belts to trucks. FedEx prefers to use large numbers of part-time employees at its package-sorting facilities. To attract employees, FexEx offers the same benefits package to its full- and part-time workers. Working mothers are also attracted to the flexible working schedule.

Sources: www.upsjobs.com; www.fedex.com/us/about/express/pressreleases/pressrelease090898.html; Jedd, Marcia. "Big Battle for Small Packages." *Logistics Management* (February 1, 1999); www.manufacturing.net/lm/index.asp?layout_articleCurrentWeb &articleid-CA123199; Johnson, Paul B, "FedEx Ranks High." *High Point Enterprise* (March 3, 2001); www.hpe.com/2001/03/05/news/305news2 .html.

Alternatively, management can aggregate employees along product family lines by splitting the workforce into subgroups and assigning a different group to the production of each product family. In service operations, such as a city government, workers are aggregated by the type of service they provide: firefighters, police officers, sanitation workers, and administrators.

TIME. The planning horizon covered by an aggregate plan typically is one year, although it can differ in various situations. To avoid the expense and disruptive effect of frequent changes in output rates and the workforce, adjustments usually are made monthly or quarterly. In other words, the company looks at time in the aggregate—months, quarters, or seasons—rather than in days or hours. Some companies use monthly planning periods for the near portion of the planning horizon and quarterly periods for the later portion. In practice, planning periods reflect a balance between the needs for (1) a limited number of decision points to reduce planning complexity and (2) flexibility to adjust output rates and workforce levels when demand forecasts exhibit seasonal variations. The bicycle manufacturer, for example, may choose monthly planning periods so that timely adjustments to inventory levels can be made without excessively disruptive changes to the workforce.

RELATIONSHIP TO OTHER PLANS

A financial assessment of the organization's near future—that is, for one or two years ahead—is called either a business plan (in for-profit firms) or an annual plan (in nonprofit services). A **business plan** is a projected statement of income, costs, and profits. It usually is accompanied by budgets, a projected (pro forma) balance sheet, and a projected cash-flow statement, showing sources and allocations of funds. The business plan unifies the plans and expectations of a firm's operations, finance, sales, and marketing managers. In particular, it reflects plans for market penetration, new product introduction, and capital investment. Manufacturing firms and for-profit service organizations, such as a retail store, a firm of attorneys, or a hospital, prepare such plans. A nonprofit service organization, such as the United Way or a municipal government, prepares a different type of plan for financial assessment, called an **annual plan or financial plan.**

Figure 14.1 illustrates the relationships among the business or annual plan, production or staffing plan (aggregate plan), and detailed production or workforce schedules. For service providers in the value chain, top management sets the organization's direction and objectives in the business plan (for-profit organization) or annual plan (nonprofit organization). In either case, the plan provides the framework for the staffing plan and workforce schedule. The staffing plan presents the number and types of employees needed to meet the objectives of the business or annual plan. The **workforce schedule,** in turn, details the specific work schedule for each category of employee. For example, a staffing plan might allocate 10 police officers for the day shift in a particular district; the workforce schedule might assign 5 of them to work Monday through Friday and the other 5 to work Wednesday through Sunday to meet the varying daily needs for police protection in that district. (We present a more complete discussion of workforce scheduling in Chapter 17, "Scheduling".)

> How should an aggregate plan fit with other plans?

> **business plan**   A projected statement of income, costs, and profits.

> **annual plan or financial plan**   A plan for financial assessment used by a nonprofit service organization.

> **workforce schedule**   A schedule that details the specific work schedule for each category of employee.

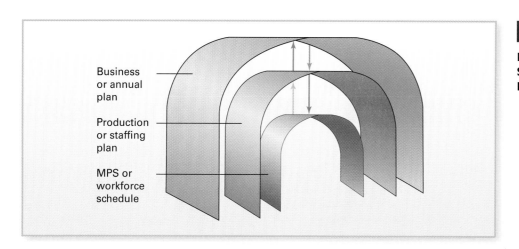

FIGURE 14.1

Relationship of Production or Staffing Plan (Aggregate Plan) to Other Plans

Business or annual plan

Production or staffing plan

MPS or workforce schedule

master production schedule
A schedule that specifies the timing and size of production quantities for each product in the product families.

For manufacturing firms in the value chain, top management sets the company's strategic objectives for at least the next year in the business plan. It provides the overall framework of demand projections, functional area inputs, and capital budget from which the aggregate plan and the master production schedule (MPS) are developed. The production plan specifies corresponding product family production rates, inventory levels, and workforce levels. The **master production schedule,** in turn, specifies the timing and size of production quantities for each product in the product families. Thus, the aggregate plan plays a key role in translating the strategies of the business plan into an operational plan for the manufacturing process.

As the arrows in Figure 14.1 indicate, information flows in two directions: from the top down (broad to detailed) and from the bottom up (detailed to broad). If an aggregate plan cannot be developed to satisfy the objectives of the business or annual plan, the business or annual plan might have to be adjusted. Similarly, if a feasible master production schedule or workforce schedule cannot be developed, the aggregate plan might have to be adjusted. The planning process is dynamic, with periodic plan revisions or adjustments based on two-way information flows.

An analogy for the three levels of plans in Figure 14.1 is a student's calendar. Basing the choice of a school on career goals—a plan covering four or five years—corresponds to the highest planning level. Basing the choice of classes on that school's requirements—a plan for the next school year—corresponds to the middle planning level (or aggregate plan). Finally, scheduling group meetings and study times around work requirements in current classes—a plan for the next few weeks—corresponds to the most detailed planning level.

MANAGERIAL IMPORTANCE OF AGGREGATE PLANS

In this section, we concentrate on the managerial inputs, objectives, alternatives, and strategies associated with aggregate plans.

MANAGERIAL INPUTS

What kind of cross-functional coordination is needed?

Figure 14.2 shows the types of information that managers from various functional areas supply to aggregate plans. One way of ensuring the necessary cross-functional coordination and supply of information is to create a committee of functional-area representatives. Chaired by a general manager, the committee has the overall responsi-

FIGURE 14.2

Managerial Inputs from Functional Areas to Aggregate Plans

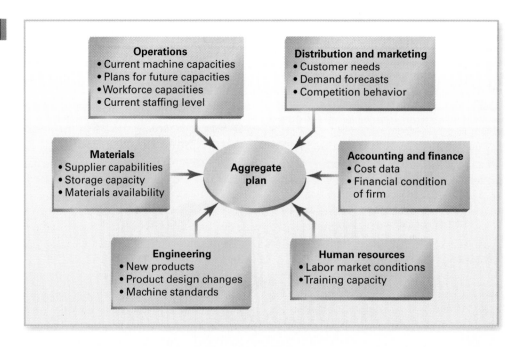

bility to make sure that company policies are followed, conflicts are resolved, and a final plan is approved. Coordinating the firm's functions, either in this way or less formally, helps synchronize the flow of services, materials, and information through the value chain and best meet customer demand.

TYPICAL OBJECTIVES

The many functional areas in an organization that give input to the aggregate plan typically have conflicting objectives for the use of the organization's resources. Six objectives usually are considered during development of a production or staffing plan, and conflicts among them may have to be resolved.

1. *Minimize Costs/Maximize Profits.* If customer demand is not affected by the plan, minimizing costs will also maximize profits.
2. *Maximize Customer Service.* Improving delivery time and on-time delivery may require additional workforce, machine capacity, or inventory resources.
3. *Minimize Inventory Investment.* Inventory accumulations are expensive because the money could be used for more productive investments.
4. *Minimize Changes in Production Rates.* Frequent changes in production rates can cause difficulties in coordinating the supply of materials and require production line rebalancing.
5. *Minimize Changes in Workforce Levels.* Fluctuating workforce levels may cause lower productivity because new employees typically need time to become fully productive.
6. *Maximize Utilization of Plant and Equipment.* Capital-intensive line processes require uniformly high utilization of plant and equipment.

The weight given to each objective in the plan involves cost trade-offs and consideration of nonquantifiable factors. For example, maximizing customer service with fast, on-time delivery can be improved by increasing—not minimizing—the stock of finished goods in a production plan; or, for example, a staffing plan that minimizes costs may not minimize changes in workforce levels or maximize customer service.

Balancing these various objectives to arrive at an acceptable aggregate plan involves consideration of various alternatives. The two basic types of alternatives are (1) reactive and (2) aggressive. Reactive alternatives are actions that respond to given demand patterns, whereas aggressive alternatives are actions that attempt to modify demand patterns and, consequently, resource requirements.

REACTIVE ALTERNATIVES

Reactive alternatives are actions that can be taken to cope with demand requirements. Typically, an operations manager controls reactive alternatives. That is, the operations manager accepts forecasted demand as a given and modifies workforce levels, overtime, vacation schedules, inventory levels, subcontracting, and planned backlogs to meet that demand.

What options should be considered in responding to uneven demand?

reactive alternatives Actions that can be taken to cope with demand requirements.

WORKFORCE ADJUSTMENT. Management can adjust workforce levels by hiring or laying off employees. The use of this alternative can be attractive if the workforce is largely unskilled or semiskilled and the labor pool is large. However, for a particular company, the size of the qualified labor pool may limit the number of new employees that can be hired at any one time. Also, new employees must be trained, and the capacity of the training facilities themselves might limit the number of new hires at any one time. In some industries, laying off employees is difficult or unusual for contractual reasons (unions); in other industries, such as tourism and agriculture, seasonal layoffs and hirings are the norm.

ANTICIPATION INVENTORY. **Anticipation inventory** can be used to absorb uneven rates of demand or supply. For example, a plant facing seasonal demand can stock anticipation inventory during light demand periods and use it during heavy demand

anticipation inventory Inventory that can be used to absorb uneven rates of demand or supply.

periods. Manufacturers of air conditioners, such as Whirlpool, can experience 90 percent of their annual demand during just three months of a year. Smoothing output rates with inventory can increase productivity because workforce adjustments can be costly. Anticipation inventory also can help when supply, rather than demand, is uneven. A company can stock up on a certain purchased item if the company's suppliers expect severe capacity limitations. Despite its advantages, anticipation inventory can be costly to hold, particularly if stocked in its finished state. Stocking components and subassemblies that can be assembled quickly when customer orders come in might be preferable to stocking finished goods.

Service providers in the value chain generally cannot use anticipation inventory because services cannot be stocked. In some instances, however, services can be performed prior to actual need. For example, telephone company workers usually lay cables for service to a new subdivision before housing construction begins. They can do this work during a period when the workload for scheduled services is low.

overtime The time that employees work that is longer than the regular workday or workweek, for which they receive additional pay for the extra hours.

WORKFORCE UTILIZATION. An alternative to workforce adjustment is workforce utilization, involving overtime and undertime. **Overtime** means that employees work longer than the regular workday or workweek and receive additional pay for the extra hours. It can be used to satisfy output requirements that cannot be completed on regular time. However, overtime is expensive (typically 150 percent of the regular-time pay rate). Moreover, workers often do not want to work a lot of overtime for an extended period of time, and excessive overtime may result in declining quality and productivity.

undertime The situation that occurs when employees do not work *productively* for the regular-time workday or workweek.

Undertime means that employees do not work *productively* for the regular-time workday or workweek. For example, they do not work productively for eight hours per day or for five days per week. Undertime occurs when labor capacity exceeds a period's demand requirements (net of anticipation inventory), and this excess capacity cannot or should not be used productively to build up inventory or to satisfy customer orders earlier than the delivery dates already promised. When services or products are customized, anticipation inventory is not usually an option. A product cannot be produced to inventory if its specifications are unknown or if customers are unlikely to want what has been produced in advance because it does not meet their exact requirements.

Undertime can either be paid or unpaid. An example of *unpaid undertime* is when part-time employees are paid only for the hours or days worked. Perhaps they only work during the peak times of the day or peak days of the week. Sometimes, part-time arrangements provide predictable work schedules, such as the same hours each day for five consecutive days each week. At other times, such as with stockpickers at some warehouse operations, worker schedules are unpredictable and depend on customer shipments expected for the next day. If the workload is light, some workers are not called in to work. Such arrangements are more common in low-skill positions or when the supply of workers seeking such an arrangement is sufficient. An example of this arrangement includes college students near a FedEx package-sorting facility (see Managerial Practice 14.1). Although unpaid undertime may minimize costs, the firm must balance cost considerations against the ethical issues of being a good employer.

An example of *paid undertime* is when employees are kept on the payroll rather than being laid off. In this scenario, employees work a full day and receive their full salary but are not as productive because of the light workload. Some companies use paid undertime (though they do not call it that) during slack periods, particularly with highly skilled, hard-to-replace employees or when there are obstacles to laying off workers. The disadvantages of paid undertime include the cost of paying for work not performed and lowered productivity.

VACATION SCHEDULES. A manufacturer can shut down during an annual lull in sales, leaving a skeleton crew to cover operations and perform maintenance. Hospital employees might be encouraged to take all or part of their allowed vacation time during slack periods. Use of this alternative depends on whether the employer can mandate the vacation schedules of its employees. In any case, employees may be strongly discouraged from taking vacations during peak periods or encouraged to take vacations during periods when replacement part-time labor is most abundant.

SUBCONTRACTORS. Subcontractors can be used to overcome short-term capacity shortages, such as during peaks of the season or business cycle. Subcontractors can supply services, make components and subassemblies, or even assemble an entire product. If the subcontractor can supply components or services of equal or better quality less expensively than the company can produce them itself, these arrangements may become permanent.

BACKLOGS, BACKORDERS, AND STOCKOUTS. Firms in the value chain that maintain a backlog of orders as a normal business practice can allow the backlog to grow during periods of high demand and then reduce it during periods of low demand. A **backlog** is an accumulation of customer orders that have been promised for delivery at some future date. Firms that use backlogs do not promise instantaneous delivery, as do wholesalers or retailers farther forward in the value chain. Instead, they impose a lead time between when the order is placed and when it is delivered. Firms that are most likely to use backlogs—and increase the size of them during periods of heavy demand—make customized products and provide customized services. They tend to have a make-to-order or customized services strategy and include dental offices, TV repair shops, and automobile repair shops. Backlogs reduce the uncertainty of future production requirements and also can be used to level these requirements. However, they become a competitive disadvantage if they get too big. Delivery speed often is an important competitive priority (see Chapter 2, "Operations Strategy"), but large backlogs mean long delivery times.

Service providers that offer standardized services with little customer contact and manufacturers with a make-to-stock strategy (see Chapter 3, "Process Design Strategy") are expected to provide immediate delivery. For them, poor customer service during peak demand periods takes the form of backorders and stockouts rather than large backlogs. A **backorder** is a customer order that cannot be filled immediately but is filled as soon as possible. Although the customer is not pleased with the delay, the customer order is not lost and it is filled at a later date. A **stockout** is much the same, except that the order is lost and the customer goes elsewhere. A backorder adds to the next period's requirement, whereas a stockout does not increase future requirements. Backorders and stockouts can lead dissatisfied customers to do their future business with another firm. Generally, backorders and stockouts are to be avoided. Planned stockouts may be used, but only when the expected loss in sales and customer goodwill is less than the cost of using other reactive alternatives or aggressive alternatives or adding the capacity needed to satisfy demand.

In conclusion, decisions about the use of each alternative for each period of the planning horizon specify the output rate for each period. In other words, the output rate is a function of the choices among these alternatives.

AGGRESSIVE ALTERNATIVES

Coping with seasonal or volatile demand by using reactive alternatives can be costly. Another approach is to attempt to change demand patterns to achieve efficiency and reduce costs. **Aggressive alternatives** are actions that attempt to modify demand and, consequently, resource requirements. Typically, marketing managers are responsible for specifying these actions in the marketing plan.

COMPLEMENTARY PRODUCTS. One way a company can even out the load on resources is to produce **complementary products** or services that have similar resource requirements but different demand cycles. For example, a city parks and recreation department can counterbalance seasonal staffing requirements for summer activities by offering ice skating, tobogganing, or indoor activities during the winter months. The

backlog An accumulation of customer orders that have been promised for delivery at some future date.

backorder A customer order that cannot be filled immediately but is filled as soon as possible.

stockout An order that is lost and causes the customer to go elsewhere.

How can demand be leveled to reduce operating costs?

aggressive alternatives Actions that attempt to modify demand and, consequently, resource requirements.

complementary products Services or products that have similar resource requirements but different demand cycles.

key is to find services and products that can be produced with the existing resources and can level off the need for resources over the year.

CREATIVE PRICING. Promotional campaigns are designed to increase sales with creative pricing. Examples include automobile rebate programs, price reductions for winter clothing in the late summer months, reduced prices on airline tickets for travel during off-peak periods, and "two for the price of one" automobile tire sales.

PLANNING STRATEGIES

Managers often combine reactive and aggressive alternatives in various ways to arrive at an acceptable aggregate plan. For the remainder of this chapter, let us assume that the expected results of the aggressive alternatives have already been incorporated into the demand forecasts of services or product families. This assumption allows us to focus on the reactive alternatives that define output rates and workforce levels. Countless aggregate plans are possible even when just a few reactive alternatives are allowed. Four very different strategies, two chase strategies and two level strategies, are useful starting points in searching for the best aggregate plan. These strategies can be implemented with a limited or expanded set of reactive alternatives, as shown in Table 14.1. The specific reactive alternatives allowed, and how they are mixed together, must be stated before a chase strategy or a level strategy can be translated into a unique aggregate plan.

chase strategy A strategy that *matches* demand during the planning horizon by varying either the workforce level or the output rate.

CHASE STRATEGIES. A **chase strategy** *matches* demand during the planning horizon by varying either (1) the workforce level or (2) the output rate. When a chase strategy uses the first method, varying the *workforce level* to match demand, it relies on just one reactive alternative—workforce variation. Sometimes called the *capacity strategy*, it uses hiring and layoffs to keep the workforce's regular-time capacity equal to demand. This chase strategy has the advantages of no inventory investment, overtime, or undertime. However, it has some drawbacks, including the expense of continually adjusting workforce levels, the potential alienation of the workforce, and the loss of productivity and quality because of constant changes in the workforce.

The second chase strategy, varying the *output rate* to match demand, opens up additional reactive alternatives beyond changing the workforce level. Sometimes called the *utilization strategy*, the extent and timing of the workforce's utilization are changed through overtime, undertime, and when vacations are taken. Subcontracting, including temporary help during the peak season, is another way of matching demand.

level strategy A strategy that maintains a constant workforce level or constant output rate during the planning horizon.

LEVEL STRATEGIES. A **level strategy** maintains (1) a constant workforce level or (2) a constant output rate during the planning horizon. These two strategies differ from chase strategies not only because either the workforce or output rate is held constant

TABLE 14.1	**PLANNING STRATEGIES FOR AGGREGATE PLANS**	
Strategy	**Possible Alternatives During Slack Season**	**Possible Alternatives During Peak Season**
Chase 1: Vary workforce level to match demand	Layoffs	Hiring
Chase 2: Vary output rate to match demand	Layoffs, undertime, vacations	Hiring, overtime, subcontracting
Level 1: Constant workforce level	No layoffs, building anticipation inventory, undertime, vacations	No hiring, depleting anticipation inventory, overtime, subcontracting, backorders, stockouts
Level 2: Constant output rate	Layoffs, building anticipation inventory, undertime, vacations	Hiring, depleting anticipation inventory, overtime, subcontracting, backorders, stockouts

but also because anticipation inventory, backorders, and stockouts are added to the list of possible reactive alternatives. For this reason, they are sometimes called *inventory strategies*.

When a level strategy uses the first method, maintaining a constant *workforce level*, it might consist of not hiring or laying off workers (except at the beginning of the planning horizon), building up anticipation inventories to absorb seasonal demand fluctuations, using undertime in slack periods and overtime up to contracted limits for peak periods, using subcontractors for additional needs as necessary, and scheduling vacation timing to match slack periods.

Even though a constant workforce must be maintained with this first level strategy, many aggregate plans are possible. The constant workforce can be sized many ways. It can be so large as to minimize the planned use of overtime and subcontractors (which creates considerable undertime) or so small as to rely heavily on overtime and subcontractors during the peak seasons (which places a strain on the workforce and endangers quality). Thus, the advantages of a stable workforce must be weighted against the

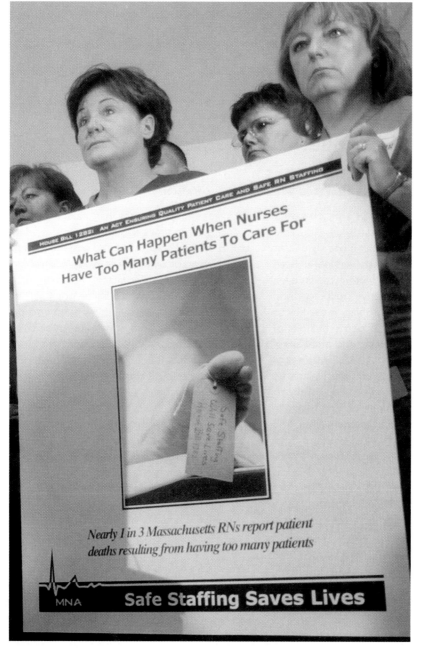

Overtime and subcontracting (using part-time employees) are two reactive alternatives used extensively in the health industry to keep costs in check. However, excessive use of these alternatives is opposed by nurses. Here, registered nurses hold a poster during a news conference at the state house in Boston, where a survey was released saying nurse-staffing levels in hospitals across the state is threatening proper patient care. Similar protests have occurred recently in other states, such as California, Hawaii, Minnesota, Ohio, and Pennsylvania.

disadvantages of the other alternatives allowed, such as increased undertime, overtime, and inventory. Managerial Practice 14.2 shows how Hallmark uses a level strategy for competitive advantage.

When a level strategy uses the second method, maintaining a constant *output rate*, it allows hiring and layoffs in addition to the other alternatives of the first level strategy. The output rate can be level even if the workforce fluctuates, depending on the set of alternatives that is used in the strategy. The key to identifying a level strategy is whether the workforce or output rate is constant.

MIXED STRATEGIES. Used alone, chase and level strategies are unlikely to produce the best acceptable aggregate plan. Improvements are likely by considering plans that are neither pure level nor pure chase strategies. The workforce (or output rate) is not exactly level, and yet it does not exactly match demand. Instead, the best strategy for a process is a **mixed strategy** that considers and implements a fuller range of reactive alternatives and goes beyond a "pure" chase or level strategy. Whether management chooses a pure strategy or some mix, the strategy should reflect the organization's environment and planning objectives. For example, for a municipal street repair department, which faces seasonal demand shifts and needs an ample supply of unskilled labor, possible strategies include varying the workforce level, reducing overtime, and eliminating subcontracting.

mixed strategy   A strategy that considers and implements a fuller range of reactive alternatives and goes beyond a "pure" chase or level strategy.

MANAGERIAL PRACTICE 14.2

HALLMARK'S LEVEL STRATEGY

Hallmark (www.hallmark.com), a $4.2 billion-a-year producer of greeting cards, spends considerable sums to improve efficiency and has made significant gains—all without imposing layoffs. Hallmark has never used layoffs to adjust production rates of greeting cards, even though the business is highly competitive, exhibits little growth, and is very seasonal. Employee flexibility is the key to this strategy. The company's four plants produce millions of cards each day, along with gift wrapping paper and other party goods. Even though technology in the industry has made production processes increasingly more labor efficient, Hallmark's philosophy has been to retrain its employees continually to make them more flexible. For example, a cutting machine operator might also be a custom card imprinter, a painter, or a modular office assembler as needed. To keep workers busy, Hallmark shifts production from its Kansas City plant to branch plants in Topeka, Leavenworth, and Lawrence, Kansas to keep those plants fully utilized. It uses the Kansas City plant as its "swing facility"—when demand is down, these employees may take jobs in clerical positions, all at factory pay rates. They might also be in classrooms learning new skills.

According to former CEO Irvine O. Hockaday, Hallmark must protect its employees from cyclical markets and other unexpected happenings beyond their control. The added job security, however, carries the expectation that employees' performance will be commensurate with their compensation package. The philosophy has paid dividends. For example, reducing setup times to support short production runs is crucial to keeping inventories and costs low. Employees have suggested ways to cut setup times significantly. A stable workforce policy has been a major factor in allowing Hallmark to capture some 57 percent of the $8 billion domestic card market.

Although a no-layoff policy seems to be the exception rather than the rule in corporate America, executives at no-layoff companies, such as Hallmark and Southwest Airlines, argue that maintaining their ranks even in terrible times breeds fierce loyalty, higher productivity, and the innovation needed to enable their companies to snap back once the economy recovers. In addition, companies that avoid downsizing also tend to have a recruiting edge over companies that routinely lay off employees. On the other hand, when companies choose to implement massive layoffs, the results can backfire. When severance and rehiring costs, potential lawsuits from aggrieved workers, lack of staffers when the economy rebounds, and distrust in management are taken into account, the benefits of downsizing seem to disappear.

Sources: "Loyal to a Fault." *Forbes* (March 14, 1994), pp. 58–60; www.hallmark.com; Armour, Stephanie. "Some Companies Choose No-Layoff Policy." *USA Today* (December 17, 2001), p. 1B; Conlin, Michelle. "Where Layoffs Are a Last Resort." *Business Week* (October 8, 2001), p. 42.

THE PLANNING PROCESS

Figure 14.3 shows the process for preparing aggregate plans. It is dynamic and continuing, as aspects of the plan are updated periodically when new information becomes available and new opportunities emerge.

DETERMINING DEMAND REQUIREMENTS

The first step in the planning process is to determine the demand requirements for each period of the planning horizon, using one of the many methods that we have already discussed. For staffing plans, the planner bases forecasts of staff requirements for each workforce group on historical levels of demand, managerial judgment, and existing backlogs for services. For example, a director of nursing in a hospital can develop a direct-care index for a nursing staff and translate a projection of the month-to-month patient census into an equivalent total amount of nursing care time—and thus the number of nurses—required for each month of the year.

For production plans, however, the requirements represent the demand for finished goods and the external demand for replacement parts. The planner can derive future requirements for finished goods from backlogs (for make-to-order operations) or from forecasts for product families made to stock (for make-to-stock operations). Sometimes distributors or dealers indicate their requirements for finished goods in advance of actual orders, providing a reliable forecast of requirements from those sources.

IDENTIFYING ALTERNATIVES, CONSTRAINTS, AND COSTS

The second step in the planning process is to identify the alternatives, constraints, and costs for the plan. We presented the reactive alternatives used in aggregate plans earlier, so we now focus on constraints and costs.

Constraints represent physical limitations or managerial policies associated with the aggregate plan. Examples of physical constraints might include training facilities capable of handling only so many new hires at a time, machine capacities that limit maximum output, or inadequate inventory storage space. Policy constraints might include limitations on the amount of backorders or the use of subcontractors or overtime, as well as the minimum inventory levels needed to achieve desired safety stocks.

Typically, many plans can satisfy a specific set of constraints. The planner usually considers several types of costs when preparing aggregate plans.

1. *Regular-Time Costs.* These costs include regular-time wages paid to employees plus contributions to benefits, such as health insurance; dental care; Social Security; retirement funds; and pay for vacations, holidays, and certain other types of absence.

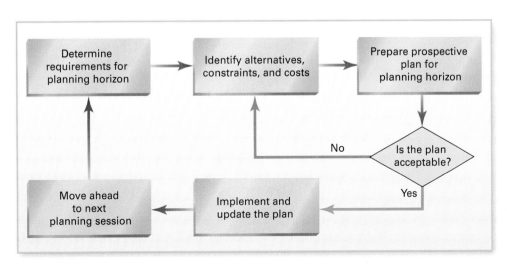

FIGURE 14.3

The Process for Preparing Aggregate Plans

2. *Overtime Costs.* Overtime wages typically are 150 percent of regular-time wages, exclusive of fringe benefits. Some companies offer a 200 percent rate for working overtime on Sundays and holidays.

3. *Hiring and Layoff Costs.* Hiring costs include the costs of advertising jobs, interviews, training programs for new employees, scrap caused by the inexperience of new employees, loss of productivity, and initial paperwork. Layoff costs include the costs of exit interviews, severance pay, retraining remaining workers and managers, and lost productivity.

4. *Inventory Holding Costs.* Inventory holding costs include costs that vary with the *level* of inventory investment: the costs of capital tied up in inventory, variable storage and warehousing costs, pilferage and obsolescence costs, insurance costs, and taxes.

5. *Backorder and Stockout Costs.* As discussed earlier, the use of backorders and stockouts involves costs of expediting past-due orders, costs of lost sales, and the potential cost of losing the customer's sales to competitors in the future (sometimes called loss of goodwill).

PREPARING AN ACCEPTABLE PLAN

The third step in the planning process is to prepare the aggregate plan. Developing an acceptable plan is an iterative process; that is, plans may need to go through several revisions and adjustments (see Figure 14.3). A prospective, or tentative, plan is developed to start. A production plan with monthly periods, for example, must specify monthly production rates, inventory and backorder accumulations, subcontracted production, and monthly workforce levels (including hires, layoffs, and overtime). The plan must then be checked against constraints and evaluated in terms of strategic objectives. If the prospective plan is not acceptable for either of those reasons, a new prospective plan must be developed.

IMPLEMENTING AND UPDATING THE PLAN

The final step in the planning process is to implement and update the aggregate plan. Implementation requires the commitment of managers in all functional areas. The planning committee may recommend changes in the plan during implementation or they may recommend updating the plan to balance conflicting objectives better. Acceptance of the plan does not necessarily mean that everyone is in total agreement, but it does imply that everyone will work to achieve the plan.

AGGREGATE PLANNING WITH SPREADSHEETS

Should a level workforce strategy or some variable workforce strategy be used in providing services?

Here we use a *spreadsheet* approach of stating a strategy, developing a plan, comparing the developed plan to other plans, and finally modifying the plan or strategy as necessary until we are satisfied with the results. We demonstrate this approach by developing two staffing plans, the first plan based on a level strategy and the second plan on a chase strategy. We then consider a mixed strategy for a manufacturer facing a different demand pattern and cost structure.

After a plan has been formulated, it is evaluated by use of a spreadsheet. One part of the spreadsheet shows the *input values* that give the demand requirements and the reactive alternative choices period by period. Another part of the spreadsheet shows the *derived values* that must follow from the input values. The final part of the spreadsheet shows the *calculated costs* of the plan. Along with qualitative considerations, the calculated cost of each plan determines whether the plan is satisfactory or whether a revised plan should be considered. When seeking clues about how to improve a plan already evaluated, we identify its highest cost elements. Revisions that would reduce these specific costs might produce a new plan with lower overall costs. Spreadsheet programs make analyzing these plans easy, and they present a whole new set of possibilities for developing sound aggregate plans.

LEVEL STRATEGY WITH OVERTIME AND UNDERTIME

One possible level strategy, which uses a constant number of employees that will satisfy demand during the planning horizon, is determined by using the maximum amount of overtime in the peak period. Undertime is used in slack periods. The workforce level does not change, except possibly for hires or layoffs at the beginning of the first period if the current and desired constant workforce levels do not match. The level strategy can lead to considerable undertime, which is the amount of time by which capacity exceeds demand requirements, summed over all periods for the time horizon. The cost of this unused capacity depends on whether undertime is paid or unpaid.

| A Level Strategy with Overtime and Undertime | EXAMPLE 14.1 |

The manager of a large distribution center must determine how many part-time stockpickers to maintain on the payroll. She wants to develop a staffing plan with a level workforce, implemented with overtime and undertime. Her objective is to keep the part-time workforce stable and to minimize undertime usage. She will achieve this goal by using the maximum amount of overtime possible in the peak period.

The manager divides the next year into six time periods, each one two months long. Each part-time employee can work a maximum of 20 hours per week on regular time, but the actual number can be less. The distribution center shortens each worker's day during slack periods, rather than pay undertime. Once on the payroll, each worker is used each day, but they may work only a few hours. Overtime can be used during peak periods to avoid excessive undertime.

Workforce requirements are shown as the number of part-time employees required for each time period at the maximum regular time of 20 hours per week. For example, in period 3, an estimated 18 part-time employees working 20 hours per week on regular time will be needed.

ACTIVE MODEL 14.1

Active Model 14.1 on the Student CD-ROM shows the impact of changing the workforce level, the cost structure, and overtime capacity.

TUTOR 14.1

Tutor 14.1 on the Student CD-ROM provides a new example for planning using the level strategy with overtime and undertime.

	TIME PERIOD						
	1	**2**	**3**	**4**	**5**	**6**	**TOTAL**
Requirement*	6	12	18	15	13	14	78

*Number of part-time employees

Currently, 10 part-time clerks are employed. They have not been subtracted from the requirements shown. Constraints on employment and cost information are as follows:

   a. The size of training facilities limits the number of new hires in any period to no more than 10.
   b. No backorders are permitted; demand must be met each period.
   c. Overtime cannot exceed 20 percent of the regular-time capacity (that is, 4 hours) in any period. Therefore, the most that any part-time employee can work is 1.20(20) = 24 hours per week.

Framed by thousands of ski poles, a part-time worker sorts and inventories new products in the receiving department of REI's Distribution Center in Sumner, Washington. REI has 400 workers moving roughly $700 million in inventory through this 521,000-square-foot distribution center. REI employs a high percentage of part-time workers, many of whom are college students. They tend to be young people who participate in outdoor sports and are very familiar with the equipment that REI sells.

d. The following costs can be assigned:

Regular-time wage rate	$2,000 per time period at 20 hours per week
Overtime wages	150 percent of the regular-time rate
Hires	$1,000 per person
Layoffs	$500 per person

SOLUTION

For this particular level strategy, the manager begins by finding the number of part-time employees, at 24 hours per week (20×1.20) needed to meet the peak requirement. The most overtime that she can use is 20 percent of the regular-time capacity, w, so

$$120w = 18 \text{ employees required in peak period (period 3)}$$
$$w = \frac{18}{1.20} = 15 \text{ employees}$$

A 15-employee staff size minimizes the amount of undertime for this level strategy. As there already are 10 part-time employees, the manager should immediately hire 5 more. The complete plan is shown in Figure 14.4.

The input values are the requirement, a 15-person workforce level, undertime, and overtime for each period. The first row of derived values is called *productive time*, which is that portion of the workforce's regular time that is paid for and used productively. In any period, the productive time equals the workforce level minus undertime. The hires and layoffs rows can be derived from the workforce levels. In this example, the workforce is increased for period 1 from its initial size of 10 employees to 15, which means that 5 employees are hired. Because the workforce size remains constant throughout the planning horizon, there are no other hirings or layoffs.

For this particular example, overtime and undertime can be derived directly from the first two rows of input values. When a period's workforce level exceeds the requirement, overtime is zero and undertime equals the difference. When a period's workforce level is less than the requirements, undertime is zero and overtime equals the difference. For the general case when other alternatives (such as vacations, inventory, and backorders) are possible, however, the overtime and undertime cannot be derived just from information on requirements and workforce levels. Thus, undertime and overtime are shown as input values (rather than derived values) in the spreadsheet, and the user must be careful to specify consistent input values.

Another decision to be made is how to apportion undertime and overtime to employees. Except for periods 3 and 4, the employees will have some undertime or work less than the maximum 20 hours per week, because the requirement for those periods is less than 15 employees. In period 1, for example, 15 employees are on the payroll, but only 120 hours, or 6(20), per week are needed. Consequently, each employee might work only 8 hours per week. Alternatively, the

FIGURE 14.4

Spreadsheet for a Level Strategy with Overtime and Minimum Undertime

	1	2	3	4	5	6	Total
Requirement	6	12	18	15	13	14	78
Workforce level	15	15	15	15	15	15	90
Undertime	9	3	0	0	2	1	15
Overtime	0	0	3	0	0	0	3
Productive time	6	12	15	15	13	14	75
Hires	5	0	0	0	0	0	5
Layoffs	0	0	0	0	0	0	0
Costs	1	2	3	4	5	6	Totals
Productive time	$12,000	24,000	30,000	30,000	26,000	28,000	$150,000
Undertime	$0	0	0	0	0	0	$0
Overtime	$0	0	9,000	0	0	0	$9,000
Hires	$5,000	0	0	0	0	0	$5,000
Layoffs	$0	0	0	0	0	0	$0
Total cost	$17,000	24,000	39,000	30,000	26,000	28,000	$164,000

manager could assign 5 employees to 4 hours per week and 10 employees to 10 hours per week. A similar approach can be applied to overtime.

The calculated costs for this plan are $164,000, which seems reasonable because the minimum conceivable cost is only $156,000 (78 periods × $2,000/period). This cost could be achieved only if the manager found a way to cover the requirement for all 78 periods with regular time. This plan seems reasonable primarily because it involves the use of large amounts of undertime (15 periods), which in this example are unpaid. The only way to reduce costs are somehow to reduce the premium for 3 overtime periods (3 periods × $1,000/period) or to reduce the hiring cost of 5 employees (5 hires × $1,000/person). Nonetheless, better solutions may be possible. For example, undertime can be reduced by delaying the hiring until period 2 because the current workforce is sufficient until then. This delay would decrease the amount of unpaid undertime, which is a qualitative improvement. However, this modification creates mixed strategy rather than a level strategy with a constant workforce out to the horizon, which is the one illustrated here.

DECISION POINT The manager, now having a point of reference with which to compare other plans, decided to evaluate some other plans before making a final choice, beginning with the chase strategy.

CHASE STRATEGY WITH HIRING AND LAYOFFS

Consider the chase strategy that adjusts workforce levels as needed to achieve requirements without using overtime, undertime, or subcontractors. This chase strategy can result in a large number of hirings and layoffs. However, many employees, such as college students, prefer part-time work. With this chase strategy, the workforce level row is identical to the requirement row, with no overtime in any period.

A Chase Strategy with Hiring and Layoffs

EXAMPLE 14.2

The manager now wants to determine the staffing plan for the distribution center, using the chase strategy to avoid all overtime and undertime.

SOLUTION

This strategy simply involves adjusting the workforce as needed to meet demand, as shown in Figure 14.5.

	1	2	3	4	5	6	Total
Requirement	6	12	18	15	13	14	78
Workforce level	6	12	18	15	13	14	78
Undertime	0	0	0	0	0	0	0
Overtime	0	0	0	0	0	0	0
Productive time	6	12	18	15	13	14	78
Hires	0	6	6	0	0	1	13
Layoffs	4	0	0	3	2	0	9
Costs	1	2	3	4	5	6	Totals
Productive time	$12,000	24,000	36,000	30,000	26,000	28,000	$156,000
Undertime	$0	0	0	0	0	0	$0
Overtime	$0	0	0	0	0	0	$0
Hires	$0	6,000	6,000	0	0	1,000	$13,000
Layoffs	$2,000	0	0	1,500	1,000	0	$4,500
Total cost	$14,000	30,000	42,000	31,500	27,000	29,000	$173,500

FIGURE 14.5

Spreadsheet for a Chase Strategy with Hiring and Layoffs

TUTOR 14.2

Tutor 14.2 on the Student CD-ROM provides a new example to plan using the chase strategy with hiring and layoffs.

The manager should plan to lay off 4 part-time employees immediately because the current staff is 10 and the staff level required in period 1 is only 6. The workforce then should steadily build to 18 by period 3. After that, the manager can reduce the workforce except for the secondary peak in period 6, when she should hire 1 more employee.

The $173,500 cost of this plan is considerably higher than for the level strategy. The spreadsheet shows that most of the cost increase comes from frequent hiring and layoffs, which add $17,500 to the cost of productive regular-time costs. Clearly, a low-cost solution must avoid frequent workforce adjustments by using more overtime and undertime, particularly because part-time employees offer flexible work hours and because undertime is not a payroll cost.

DECISION POINT   Having found this chase strategy worse than the level strategy, the manager decided to formulate some mixed strategies that keep more of the elements of a level strategy.

MIXED STRATEGIES

The manager of the distribution center in Example 14.1 might find even better solutions with a mixed strategy, which varies the workforce level or output rate somewhat but not to the extreme of a chase strategy. She might also consider a fuller range of reactive alternatives, such as vacations, subcontracting, and even customer service reductions (increased backlogs, backorders, or stockouts).

Manufacturers often have still another alternative, building up anticipation inventory to help smooth the output rate. When inventory is introduced, however, care must be taken to recognize differences in how requirements and reactive alternatives are measured. The workforce level might be expressed as the number of employees, but the requirements and inventory are expressed as units of the product. Relationships between the requirements and reactive alternatives must account for these differences. The OM Explorer spreadsheets require a common unit of measure, so we must translate some of the data prior to entering the input values. Perhaps the easiest approach is to express the requirements and reactive alternatives as *employee-period equivalents*. If demand requirements are given as units of product, we can convert them to employee-period equivalents by *dividing* them by the productivity of a worker. For example, if the demand is for 1,500 units of product and the average employee produces 100 units in one period, the demand requirement is 15 employee-period equivalents.

This translation from product units to employee-period equivalents also applies to the initial inventory or backorders at the beginning of period 1, if they are given as product units. To convert the spreadsheet results back to product units, we simply *multiply* employee-period equivalents by the productivity rate. For example, an ending inventory of 20 employee-period equivalents would translate back to 2,000 units of product, or 20 × 100.

Figure 14.6 demonstrates a mixed strategy for a manufacturer using the *Aggregate Planning with Spreadsheets Solver* of OM Explorer. It demonstrates the full range of reactive alternatives. The plan calls for expanding the workforce in periods 2 and 3, varying the anticipation inventory level, scheduling vacations during slack periods, and planning no backorders or subcontracting. We know it is a mixed strategy because (1) neither the workforce nor output rate matches the requirements, as with a chase strategy (note that inventory varies from one period to the next) and (2) neither the workforce nor output rate is constant, as with a level strategy.

AGGREGATE PLANNING WITH MATHEMATICAL METHODS

The major advantage of the spreadsheet approach is its simplicity; however, the planner still must make many choices for each period of the planning horizon. The large costs involved with aggregate plans are a motivation to seek the best possible plan. Several mathematical methods can help with this search process. We begin with the transportation method.

	1	2	3	4	5	6	Total
Requirement	24	142	220	180	136	168	870
Workforce level	120	158	158	158	158	158	910
Undertime	6	0	0	0	0	0	6
Overtime	0	0	0	0	0	0	0
Vacation time	20	6	0	0	4	10	40
Subcontracting time	0	0	0	0	0	6	6
Backorders	0	0	0	4	0	0	4
Productive time	94	152	158	158	154	148	864
Inventory	70	80	18	0	14	0	182
Hires	0	38	0	0	0	0	38
Layoffs	0	0	0	0	0	0	0

Costs	1	2	3	4	5	6	Totals
Productive time	$376,000	608,000	632,000	632,000	616,000	592,000	$3,456,000
Undertime	$24,000	0	0	0	0	0	$24,000
Overtime	$0	0	0	0	0	0	$0
Vacation time	$80,000	24,000	0	0	16,000	40,000	$160,000
Inventory	$2,800	3,200	720	0	560	0	$7,280
Backorders	$0	0	0	4,000	0	0	$4,000
Hires	$0	91,200	0	0	0	0	$91,200
Layoffs	$0	0	0	0	0	0	$0
Subcontracting	$0	0	0	0	0	43,200	$43,200
Total cost	$482,800	726,400	632,720	636,000	632,560	675,200	$3,785,680

FIGURE 14.6

Mixed Strategy for a Manufacturer

TRANSPORTATION METHOD OF PRODUCTION PLANNING

In this section, we present and demonstrate the **transportation method of production planning.** Earlier, we applied it to locating a facility within a network of facilities (see Chapter 10, "Location"). The transportation method, when applied to aggregate planning, is particularly helpful in determining anticipation inventories. Thus, it relates more to manufacturers' production plans than to service providers' staffing plans. In fact, the workforce levels for each period are inputs to the transportation method rather than outputs from it. Different workforce adjustment plans, ranging from the chase strategy to the level strategy, must be tried. Thus, several transportation method solutions may be obtained before a final plan is selected.

Use of the transportation method for production planning is based on the assumption that a demand forecast is available for each period, along with a workforce level plan for regular time. Capacity limits on overtime and subcontractor production also are needed for each period. Another assumption is that all costs are linearly related to the amount of goods produced; that is, a change in the amount of goods produced creates a proportionate change in costs.

With these assumptions, the transportation method yields the optimal mixed-strategy production plan for the planning horizon.

PRODUCTION PLANNING WITHOUT BACKORDERS. We start with a table—called a *tableau*—of the workforce levels, capacity limits, demand forecast quantities, beginning inventory level, and costs for each period of the planning horizon. Figure 14.7 shows such a tableau for a four-period production plan, where

h = holding cost per unit per period
r = cost per unit to produce on regular time
c = cost per unit to produce on overtime
s = cost per unit to subcontract
u = undertime cost per unit
b = backorder cost per unit per period

Should subcontracting be used to achieve short-term capacity increases or should some combination of inventory accumulation and overtime be used?

transportation method of production planning The use of the transportation method to solve production planning problems, assuming that a demand forecast is available for each period, along with a workforce level plan for regular time.

FIGURE 14.7

Transportation Method of Production Planning

Alternatives		Time Period 1	Time Period 2	Time Period 3	Time Period 4	Unused Capacity	Total Capacity
Period	Beginning inventory	0	h	$2h$	$3h$	$4h$	I_0
1	Regular time	r	$r+h$	$r+2h$	$r+3h$	u	R_1
1	Overtime	c	$c+h$	$c+2h$	$c+3h$	0	O_1
1	Subcontract	s	$s+h$	$s+2h$	$s+3h$	0	S_1
2	Regular time	$r+b$	r	$r+h$	$r+2h$	u	R_2
2	Overtime	$c+b$	c	$c+h$	$c+2h$	0	O_2
2	Subcontract	$s+b$	s	$s+h$	$s+2h$	0	S_2
3	Regular time	$r+2b$	$r+b$	r	$r+h$	u	R_3
3	Overtime	$c+2b$	$c+b$	c	$c+h$	0	O_3
3	Subcontract	$s+2b$	$s+b$	s	$s+h$	0	S_3
4	Regular time	$r+3b$	$r+2b$	$r+b$	r	u	R_4
4	Overtime	$c+3b$	$c+2b$	$c+b$	c	0	O_4
4	Subcontract	$s+3b$	$s+2b$	$s+b$	s	0	S_4
Requirements		D_1	D_2	D_3	$D_4 + I_4$	U	

I_0 = beginning inventory level
I_4 = desired inventory level at the end of period 4
R_t = regular-time capacity in period t
O_t = overtime capacity in period t
S_t = subcontracting capacity in period t
D_t = forecasted demand for period t
U = total unused capacities

Note that each row in the tableau represents an alternative for supplying output. For example, the first row shows the beginning inventory (the amount currently on hand) for the present time (period 0), which can be used to satisfy demand in any of the four periods. The second row is for regular-time production in period 1, which can also be used to satisfy demand in any of the four periods the plan will cover. The third and fourth rows are for two other production alternatives (overtime and subcontracting) in period 1, for meeting demand in any of the four periods.

The columns represent the periods that the plan must cover, plus the unused and total capacities available. The box in the upper right-hand corner of each cell shows the cost of producing a unit in one period and, in some cases, carrying the unit in inventory for sale in a future period. For example, in period 1 the regular-time cost to produce one unit is r (column 1). To produce the unit in period 1 for sale in period 2, the cost is $r + h$ (column 2) because we must hold the unit in inventory for one period. Satisfying a unit of demand in period 3 by producing in period 1 on regular time and carrying the unit for two periods costs $r + 2h$ (column 3), and so on. The cells in color at the bottom left of the tableau imply backorders (or producing in a period to satisfy in a past period). We can disallow backorders by making the back-order cost an arbitrarily large number. If backorder costs are so large, the transportation method will try to avoid backorders because it seeks a solution that minimizes total cost. If that is not possible, we increase the staffing plan and the overtime and subcontracting capacities.

The least expensive alternatives are those in which the output is produced and sold in the same period. However, we may not always be able to use those alternatives exclusively because of capacity restrictions. Finally, the per-unit holding cost for the beginning inventory in period 1 is 0 because it is a function of previous production-planning decisions. Similarly, the target inventory at the end of the planning horizon is added to the forecasted demand for the last period. No holding cost is charged because we have already decided to have a specified ending inventory; in this regard, it is a sunk cost.[1]

Use the following procedure to develop an acceptable aggregate plan.

Step 1. Select a workforce adjustment plan (or R_t values), using a chase strategy, level strategy, or a mixed strategy. Identify the capacity constraints on overtime (O_t values) and on subcontracting (S_t values). Usually, a period's overtime capacity is a percentage of its regular-time capacity. Also identify the on-hand anticipation inventory (I_0 values) currently available before the start of period 1. Input these values to the computer routine, which in turn inserts these values in the last column of the transportation tableau.

Step 2. Input the cost parameters (h, r, c, s, u, and b) for the different reactive alternatives. The computer software uses them to compute the values in the box of the upper right-hand corner of each cell.

Step 3. Forecast the demand for each future period, and insert the forecasts as the values in the tableau's last row. The last period's requirement should be increased to account for any desired inventory at the end of the planning horizon. The unused capacity cell in the last row equals the total demand requirements in the last row, minus the total capacity in the tableau's last column.

Step 4. Solve the transportation problem just formulated with a computer routine to find the optimal solution (based on the workforce adjustment plan). The sum of all entries in a row equals the total capacity for that row, and the sum of all entries in a column must equal the requirements for that column.

Step 5. Return to step 1 and try other staffing plans until you find the solution that best balances cost and qualitative considerations.

---

[1]If we were analyzing the implications of different ending inventory levels, the holding cost of the ending inventory would have to be added to the costs because ending inventory level would be a decision variable.

EXAMPLE 14.3   Preparing a Production Plan with the Transportation Method

TUTOR 14.3

Tutor 14.3 on the Student CD-ROM provides another example of production planning with the transportation method.

The Tru-Rainbow Company produces a variety of paint products for both commercial and private use. The demand for paint is highly seasonal, peaking in the third quarter. Current inventory is 250,000 gallons, and ending inventory should be 300,000 gallons.

Tru-Rainbow's manufacturing manager wants to determine the best production plan, using the following demand requirements and capacity plan. Demands and capacities here are expressed in thousands of gallons (rather than employee-period equivalents). The manager knows that the regular-time cost is $1.00 per unit, overtime cost is $1.50 per unit, subcontracting cost is $1.90 per unit, and inventory holding cost is $0.30 per gallon per quarter.

	QUARTER				
	1	2	3	4	TOTAL
Demand	300	850	1,500	350	3,000
Capacities					
Regular time	450	450	750	450	2,100
Overtime	90	90	150	90	420
Subcontracting	200	200	200	200	800

The following constraints apply:

a. Maximum allowable overtime in any quarter is 20 percent of the regular-time capacity in that quarter.

b. The subcontractor can supply a maximum of 200,000 gallons in any quarter. Production can be subcontracted in one period and the excess held in inventory for a future period to avoid a stockout.

c. No backorders or stockouts are permitted.

SOLUTION

Figure 14.8 graphically shows the inventory accumulation and consumption over the planning horizon that the tableau solution provides. Inventory accumulates whenever production plus subcontracting exceeds quarterly demand. Conversely, anticipation inventories are consumed when production plus subcontracting is less than quarterly demand. Quarter 2 illustrates this scenario when total production (including subcontracting) is only 740,000 gallons, but requirements are for 850,000 gallons, calling for consumption of 110,000 gallons from inventory.

FIGURE 14.8

Prospective Tru-Rainbow Company Production Plan

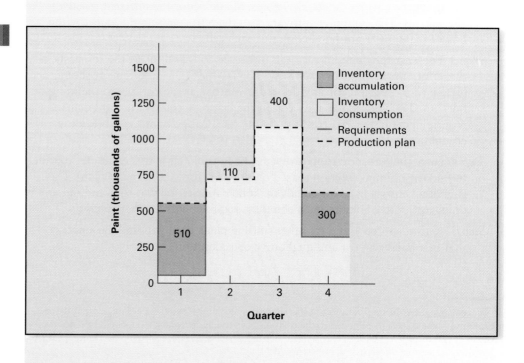

The tableau solution from which this graph is derived is found using OM Explorer's Tutor 14.3. Figure 14.9 shows the computer output. The *Results Worksheet* summarizes the costs of this prospective production plan, as shown in the two rows below the tableau. These numbers can be confirmed as the sum of the products calculated by multiplying the allocation in each cell by the cost per unit in that cell. Computing the cost column by column, as done by Tutor 14.3, yields a total cost of $4,010,000, or $4,010 × 1,000.

COST CALCULATIONS BY COLUMN

Quarter 1	250($0) + 30($1.00) + 20($1.90)	= $ 68
Quarter 2	420($1.30) + 90($1.80) + 340($1.00)	= 1,048
Quarter 3	110($1.30) + 90($1.80) + 200($2.20) + 750($1.00) + 150($1.50) + 200($1.90)	= 2,100
Quarter 4	450($1.00) + 90($1.50) + 110($1.90)	= 794
		Total = $4,010

To interpret the solution, we can convert the tableau solution into the following table. For example, the total regular-time production in quarter 1 is 450,000 gallons (30,000 gallons to meet demand in quarter 1 and 420,000 gallons to help satisfy demand in quarter 2).

QUARTER	REGULAR-TIME PRODUCTION	OVERTIME PRODUCTION	SUBCON-TRACTING	TOTAL PRODUCTION	ANTICIPATION INVENTORY
1	450	90	20	560	250 + 560 − 300 = 510
2	450	90	200	740	510 + 740 − 850 = 400
3	750	150	200	1,100	400 + 1,100 − 1,500 = 0
4	450	90	110	650	0 + 650 − 350 = 300
Totals	2,100	420	530	3,050	

Note: Anticipation inventory is the amount at the end of each quarter, where Beginning inventory + Total production − Demand = Ending inventory.

FIGURE 14.9

OM Explorer Results Worksheet for Tru-Rainbow Production Plan

	Period	Quarter 1	Quarter 2	Quarter 3	Quarter 4	Unused Capacity	Total Capacity
	Beginning Inventory	0 / 250	$0.30	$0.60	$0.90	0	250
1	Regular Time	$1.00 / 30	$1.30 / 420	$1.60 / -	$1.90 / -	-	450
1	Overtime	$1.50 / -	$1.80 / 90	$2.10 / -	$2.40 / -	-	90
	Subcontract	$1.90 / 20	$2.20 / -	$2.50 / -	$2.80 / -	180	200
2	Regular Time	999	$1.00 / 340	$1.30 / 110	$1.60 / -	-	450
2	Overtime	999	$1.50 / -	$1.80 / 90	$2.10 / -	-	90
	Subcontract	999	$1.90 / -	$2.20 / 200	$2.50 / -	-	200
3	Regular Time	999	999	$1.00 / 750	$1.30 / -	-	750
3	Overtime	999	999	$1.50 / 150	$1.80 / -	-	150
	Subcontract	999	999	$1.90 / 200	$2.20 / -	-	200
4	Regular Time	999	999	999	$1.00 / 450	-	450
4	Overtime	999	999	999	$1.50 / 90	-	90
	Subcontract	999	999	999	$1.90 / 110	90	200
	Requirements	300	850	1500	650	270	3570

	Q1	Q2	Q3	Q4
Costs	68	1,048	2,100	794
Total Cost				4,010

Solve

The anticipation inventory held at the end of each quarter is obtained in the last column. For any quarter, it is the quarter's beginning inventory plus total production (regular-time and over-time production, plus subcontracting) minus demand. For example, for quarter 1 the beginning inventory (250,000) plus the total from production and subcontracting (560,000) minus quarter 1 demand (300,000) results in an ending inventory of 510,000, which also is the beginning inventory for quarter 2.

DECISION POINT This plan requires too much overtime and subcontracting. The manager decided to search for a better capacity plan—with increases in the workforce to boost regular-time production capacity—that could lower production costs, perhaps even low enough to offset the added capacity costs.

ADDITIONAL CAPACITY PLANS A series of capacity plans can be tried and compared to find the best plan. Even though this process involves trial and error, the transportation method yields the best mix of regular time, overtime, and subcontracting for each capacity plan.

LINEAR PROGRAMMING FOR PRODUCTION PLANNING

The transportation method just discussed actually is a specialized form of linear programming (see Supplement D, "Linear Programming"). Linear programming models for production planning seek the optimal production plan for a linear objective function and a set of linear constraints; that is, there can be no cross products or powers of decision variables or other types of nonlinear terms in the problem formulation. Linear programming models are capable of handling a large number of variables and constraints and, unlike the transportation method, are not limited to the use of a specific capacity plan. Linear programming models can be used to determine optimal inventory levels, backorders, subcontractor quantities, production quantities, overtime production, hires, and layoffs. The main drawbacks are that all relationships between variables must be linear and that the optimal values of the decision variables may be fractional. The assumption of linearity is violated when certain costs (e.g., setup costs) are incurred only when specific product families are produced in a time period and do not get larger as the production quantity increases. Also, fractional values of the decision variables may cause difficulties when the variables represent discrete items, such as workers, bicycles, or trucks.

Suppose that you must plan the production of a certain product family and do not want to use backorders. Each worker produces 5,000 units per month if used productively on regular time or overtime. Subcontracting and overtime production are possible options to supplement regular-time production, and undertime is paid. Overtime is limited to 15 percent of the regular-time production in any month. Let

D_t = demand as product units in month t (presumed known, not a variable)
W_t = workers on hand at the start of month t
H_t = hires at the start of month t
L_t = layoffs at the start of month t
I_t = inventory as product units at the end of month t
S_t = subcontracted production as product units in month t
O_t = overtime production as product units in month t

Then, for each month, the following constraints are required:

$W_t = W_{t-1} + H_t - L_t$ (relationship for the number of workers)
$I_t = I_{t-1} + 5,000\,W_t + O_t + S_t - D_t$ (relationship for the inventory level)
$O_t \le 0.15(5,000\,W_t)$ (relationship for the overtime limit)

There are six variables (D_t is not a decision variable) and three constraints for each month. If the production plan is to cover 12 months, you need 72 decision variables and 36 constraints. In addition, you need to specify an objective function for minimizing costs or maximizing profits. For example, let

c_w = regular-time wages per worker per month

c_h = cost to hire one worker

c_L = cost to lay off one worker

c_I = cost to hold one unit of product for one month

c_s = cost to subcontract one unit of product

c_o = cost to produce one unit of product on overtime

An objective function for minimizing costs would be

$$TC = \sum_{t=1}^{12} (c_w W_t + c_h H_t + c_L L_t + c_I I_t + c_s S_t + c_o O_t)$$

Obviously, even for simple problems, this approach requires a considerable number of variables and constraints. Hence, a computer is mandatory for production-planning applications of linear programming. Nonetheless, the method is versatile in its ability to handle a wide variety and large number of variables and constraints.

MANAGERIAL CONSIDERATIONS

Such mathematical techniques can be useful in developing sound aggregate plans, but they are only aids to the planning process. As you have seen in this chapter, the planning process is dynamic and often complicated by conflicting objectives. Analytic techniques can help managers evaluate plans and resolve conflicting objectives, but managers—not techniques—make the decisions.

After arriving at an acceptable production plan, management must implement the plan. However, the aggregate plan is stated in aggregate terms. The first step in implementation, therefore, is to disaggregate the plan; that is, break the plan down into specific products, work centers, and dates (see Chapter 16, "Resource Planning," Chapter 17, "Scheduling," as well as Supplement F, "Master Production Scheduling" on the Student CD-ROM).

AGGREGATE PLANNING ACROSS THE ORGANIZATION

Aggregate planning is meaningful for each organization along the value chain. *First,* the aggregate-planning process requires managerial inputs from all of a firm's functions and must sometimes reconcile conflicting needs and objectives. Marketing provides inputs on demand and customer requirements, and accounting provides important cost data and a firm's financial condition. One of finance's objectives might be to cut inventory, whereas operations might argue for a more stable workforce and for less reliance on overtime. *Second,* each function is affected by the plan. An aggregate plan puts into effect decisions on expanding or reducing the size of the workforce, which has a direct impact on the hiring and training requirements for the human resources function. As an aggregate plan is implemented, it creates revenue and cost streams that finance must deal with as it manages the firm's cash flows. *Third,* each department and group in a firm has its own workforce. Managers of its processes must make choices on hiring, overtime, and vacations. Aggregate planning is an activity for the whole organization.

CHAPTER HIGHLIGHTS

- Aggregate plans (staffing plans or production plans) are statements of strategy that specify time-phased service or production rates, workforce levels, and (in manufacturing) inventory investment. These plans show how the organization will work toward longer-term objectives while considering the demand and capacity that are likely to exist during a planning horizon of only a year or two. In service organizations, the staffing plan links strategic goals to the workforce schedule. In manufacturing organizations, the plan that links strategic goals to the master production schedule is called the production plan.

- To reduce the level of detail required in the planning process, services or products are aggregated into families, and labor is aggregated along product family lines or according to the general services or skills provided. Time is aggregated into periods of months or quarters.

- Managerial inputs are required from the various functional areas in the organization. This approach typically raises conflicting objectives, such as high customer service, a stable workforce, and low inventory investment. Creativity and cross-functional compromise are required to reconcile these conflicts.

- The two basic types of alternatives are reactive and aggressive. Reactive alternatives take customer demand as a given. Aggressive alternatives attempt to change the timing or quantity of customer demand to stabilize service or production rates and reduce inventory requirements.

- Four pure, but generally high-cost planning strategies are the two level strategies, which maintain a constant workforce size or production rate, and the two chase strategies, which vary workforce level or production rate to match fluctuations in demand.

- Developing aggregate plans is an iterative process of determining demand requirements; identifying relevant constraints, alternatives, and costs; preparing and approving a plan; and implementing and updating the plan.

- Although spreadsheets, the transportation method, and linear programming can help analyze complicated alternatives, aggregate planning is primarily an exercise in conflict resolution and compromise. Ultimately, decisions are made by managers, not by quantitative methods.

STUDENT CD-ROM AND INTERNET RESOURCES

The Student CD-ROM and the Companion Website at **www.prenhall.com/krajewski** contain many tools, activities, and resources designed for this chapter. The following items are recommended to enhance your skills and improve your understanding of the material in this chapter.

STUDENT CD-ROM RESOURCES

- **PowerPoint Slides:** View this comprehensive set of slides customized for this chapter's concepts and techniques.
- **OM Explorer Tutors:** OM Explorer contains four tutor spreadsheets that will help you learn how to implement a level strategy, a chase strategy, the transportation method, and various staffing strategies. See Chapter 14 in the OM Explorer menu. See also the Tutor Exercise on developing a level strategy.
- **OM Explorer Solvers:** OM Explorer contains two spreadsheets to help with general problems involving aggregate-planning problems with spreadsheets and production planning with the transportation method. See Aggregate Planning in the OM Explorer menu for these routines.
- **Active Model:** There is an active model spreadsheet that provides additional insights on aggregate planning with the

Level 1 strategy. See Aggregate Planning in the Active Models menu for this routine.
- **Supplement F:** "Master Production Scheduling." See how the production plan gets broken down into plans for individual products.

INTERNET RESOURCES

- **Self-Study Quizzes:** See the compendium of true or false, multiple choice, and essay questions that give you feedback on how well you have mastered the concepts in this chapter.
- **In the News:** See the articles that apply to this chapter.
- **Internet Exercises:** Try out five different links to aggregate-planning topics, including job opportunities at UPS and handling seasonal demands at H&R Block. Other exercises are available on additional aspects of aggregate planning.
- **Virtual Tours:** Check out the aggregate-planning strategies at Statton Furniture Company. Also see the "Web Links to Company Facility Tours" for additional tours of company facilities.

KEY TERMS

aggregate plan 584
aggressive alternatives 591
annual plan or financial plan 587
anticipation inventory 589
backlog 591
backorder 591
business plan 587
chase strategy 592

complementary products 591
level strategy 592
master production schedule 588
mixed strategy 594
overtime 590
product family 585
production plan 584
reactive alternatives 589

staffing plan 584
stockout 591
transportation method of production
planning 601
undertime 590
workforce schedule 587

SOLVED PROBLEM I

The Cranston Telephone Company employs workers who lay telephone cables and perform various other construction tasks. The company prides itself on good service and strives to complete all service orders within the planning period in which they are received.

Each worker puts in 600 hours of regular time per planning period and can work as much as an additional 100 hours overtime. The operations department has estimated the following workforce requirements for such services over the next four planning periods:

Tutor 14.4 on the Student CD-ROM provides another example for practicing aggregate planning using a variety of strategies.

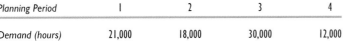

Planning Period	I	2	3	4
Demand (hours)	21,000	18,000	30,000	12,000

Cranston pays regular-time wages of $6,000 per employee per period for any time worked up to 600 hours (including undertime). The overtime pay rate is $15 per hour over 600 hours. Hiring, training, and outfitting a new employee costs $8,000. Layoff costs are $2,000 per employee. Currently, 40 employees work for Cranston in this capacity. No delays in service, or backorders, are allowed. Use the spreadsheet approach to answer the following questions:

a. Develop a level workforce plan that uses only the overtime and undertime alternatives. Maximize the use of overtime during the peak period so as to minimize the workforce level and amount of undertime.
b. Prepare a chase strategy using only the workforce adjustment alternative of hiring and layoffs. What are the total numbers of employees hired and laid off?
c. Propose an effective mixed-strategy plan.
d. Compare the total costs of the three plans.

SOLUTION

a. The peak demand is 30,000 hours in period 3. As each employee can work 700 hours per period (600 on regular time and 100 on overtime), the level workforce that minimizes undertime is 30,000/700 = 42.86, or 43, employees. The level strategy calls for three employees to be hired in the first quarter and for none to be laid off. To convert the demand requirements into employee-period equivalents, divide the demand in hours by 600. For example, the demand of 21,000 hours in period 1 translates into 35 employee-period equivalents (21,000/600) and demand in the third period translates into 50 employee-period equivalents (30,000/600). Figure 14.10 shows one solution using the "level strategy" option of Tutor 14.4.
b. The chase strategy workforce is calculated by dividing the demand for each period by 600 hours, or the amount or regular-time work for one employee during one period. This strategy calls for a total of 20 workers to be hired and 40 to be laid off during the four period plan. Figure 14.11 shows the "chase strategy" solution that Tutor 14.4 produces.
c. The mixed-strategy plan that we propose uses a combination of hires, layoffs, and overtime to reduce total costs. The workforce is reduced by 5 at the beginning of the first period, increased by 8 in the third period, and reduced by 13 in the fourth period. Switching to the general-purpose *Aggregate Planning with Spreadsheets Solver* for this mixed strategy, and hiding any unneeded columns and rows, we get the results shown

FIGURE 14.10

Chase Staffing Strategy Spreadsheet

Starting workforce	40
Regular-time wages	$6,000
(per worker per quarter)	
☑ Employees paid for undertime	
Level Strategy ▼	
Required staff level	43

Regular-time hrs per worker	600
Max overtime hrs per worker	100
Overtime rate ($/hour)	$15
Cost to hire one worker	$8,000
Cost to lay off one worker	$2,000

	Quarter				
	1	2	3	4	Total
Requirement (hrs)	21,000	18,000	30,000	12,000	81000
Workforce level (workers)	43	43	43	43	172
Undertime (hours)	4,800	7,800	0	13,800	26400
Overtime (hours)	0	0	4,200	0	4200
Productive time (hours)	21,000	18,000	25,800	12,000	76800
Hires (workers)	3	0	0	0	3
Layoffs (workers)	0	0	0	0	0
Costs					
Productive time	$210,000	$180,000	$258,000	$120,000	$768,000
Undertime	48,000	78,000	0	138,000	264,000
Overtime	0	0	63,000	0	63,000
Hires	24,000	0	0	0	24,000
Layoffs	0	0	0	0	0
Total Cost					$1,119,000

FIGURE 14.11

Chase Staffing Strategy Spreadsheet

Starting workforce	40
Regular-time wages	$6,000
(per worker per quarter)	
☑ Employees paid for undertime	
Chase Strategy ▼	
Required staff level	---

Regular-time hrs per worker	600
Max overtime hrs per worker	100
Overtime rate ($/hour)	$15
Cost to hire one worker	$8,000
Cost to lay off one worker	$2,000

	Quarter				
	1	2	3	4	Total
Requirement (hrs)	21,000	18,000	30,000	12,000	81,000
Workforce level (workers)	35	30	50	20	135
Undertime (hours)	0	0	0	0	0
Overtime (hours)	0	0	0	0	0
Productive time (hours)	21,000	18,000	30,000	12,000	81,000
Hires (workers)	0	0	20	0	20
Layoffs (workers)	5	5	0	30	40
Costs					
Productive time	$210,000	$180,000	$300,000	$120,000	$810,000
Undertime	0	0	0	0	0
Overtime	0	0	0	0	0
Hires	0	0	160,000	0	160,000
Layoffs	10,000	10,000	0	60,000	80,000
Total Cost					$1,050,000

FIGURE 14.12

OM Explorer Solver Spreadsheet for Aggregate Planning

☑ Employees Paid for Undertime

	1	2	3	4	Total
Requirement	35	30	50	20	135
Workforce level	35	35	43	30	143
Undertime	0	5	0	10	15
Overtime	0	0	7	0	7
Productive time	35	30	43	20	128
Hires	0	0	8	0	8
Layoffs	5	0	0	13	18

Costs	1	2	3	4	Totals
Productive time	$210,000	180,000	258,000	120,000	$768,000
Undertime	$0	30,000	0	60,000	$90,000
Overtime	$0	0	63,000	0	$63,000
Hires	$0	0	64,000	0	$64,000
Layoffs	$10,000	0	0	26,000	$36,000
Total cost	$220,000	210,000	385,000	206,000	$1,021,000

in Figure 14.12. The solver can evaluate any aggregate plan that is proposed. Its format is much the same as that for Tutor 14.4, except that the data in the top half of the spreadsheet (above the cost data) are expressed as employee-period equivalents, rather than as hours.

d. The total cost of the level strategy is $1,119,000. The chase strategy results in a total cost of $1,050,000. The mixed-strategy plan was developed by trial and error and results in a total cost of $1,021,000. Further improvements to the mixed strategy are possible.

SOLVED PROBLEM 2

The Arctic Air Company produces residential air conditioners. The manufacturing manager wants to develop a production plan for the next year based on the following demand and capacity data (in hundreds of product units):

	PERIOD					
	JAN–FEB (1)	MAR–APR (2)	MAY–JUNE (3)	JUL–AUG (4)	SEP–OCT (5)	NOV–DEC (6)
Demand	50	60	90	120	70	40
Capacities						
Regular time	65	65	65	80	80	65
Overtime	13	13	13	16	16	13
Subcontractor	10	10	10	10	10	10

Undertime is unpaid, and no cost is associated with unused overtime or subcontractor capacity. Producing one air conditioning unit on regular time costs $1,000, including $300 for labor. Producing a unit on overtime costs $1,150. A subcontractor can produce a unit to Arctic Air specifications for $1,250. Holding an air conditioner in stock costs $60 for each two-month period, and 200 air conditioners are currently in stock. The plan calls for 400 units to be in stock at the end of period 6. No backorders are allowed. Use the transportation method to develop the aggregate plan that minimizes costs.

SOLUTION

The following table identifies the optimal production and inventory plans and concludes with a cost summary. Figure 14.13 shows the tableau that corresponds to this solution. An arbitrarily large cost ($99,999 per period) was used for backorders, which effectively ruled them out. Again, all production quantities are in hundreds of units. Note that demand in period 6 is 4,400. That amount is the period 6 demand plus the desired ending inventory of 400. The anticipation inventory is measured as the amount at the end of each period. Cost calculations are based on the assumption that workers are not paid for undertime or are productively put to work elsewhere in the organization whenever they are not needed for this work. The total cost of this plan is $44,287,000.

	PRODUCTION PLAN			
PERIOD	REGULAR-TIME PRODUCTION	OVERTIME PRODUCTION	SUBCONTRACTING	TOTAL
1	6,500	—	—	6,500
2	6,500	400	—	6,900
3	6,500	1,300	—	7,800
4	8,000	1,600	1,000	10,600
5	7,000	—	—	7,000
6	4,400	—	—	4,400

	ANTICIPATION INVENTORY	
PERIOD	BEGINNING INVENTORY PLUS TOTAL PRODUCTION MINUS DEMAND	ANTICIPATION (ENDING) INVENTORY
1	200 + 6,500 − 5,000	1,700
2	1,700 + 6,900 − 6,000	2,600
3	2,600 + 7,800 − 9,000	1,400
4	1,400 + 10,600 − 12,000	0
5	0 + 7,000 − 7,000	0
6	0 + 4,400 − 4,000	400

DISCUSSION QUESTIONS

1. Quantitative methods can help managers evaluate alternative production plans on the basis of cost. These methods require cost estimates for each of the controllable variables, such as overtime, subcontracting, hiring, firing, and inventory investment. Say that the existing workforce is made up of 10,000 direct-labor employees, each having skills valued at $40,000 per year. The production plan calls for "creating alternative career opportunities"—in other words, laying off 500 employees. List the types of costs incurred when employees are laid off, and make a rough estimate of the length of time required for payroll savings to recover restructuring costs. If business is expected to improve in one year, are layoffs financially justified? What costs are incurred in a layoff that are difficult to estimate in monetary terms?

2. In your community, some employers maintain stable workforces at all costs, and others furlough and recall workers seemingly at the drop of a hat. What are the differences in markets, management, products, financial position, skills, costs, and competition that could explain these two extremes in personnel policy?

FIGURE 14.13   Tableau for Optimal Production and Inventory Plans

Period	Alternatives	1	2	3	4	5	6	Unused Capacity	Total Capacity
	I_0	0	60	120	180	240	300	0	2
					2				
1	R_1	1,000	1,060	1,120	1,180	1,240	1,300	0	65
		50	15						
	O_1	1,150	1,210	1,270	1,330	1,390	1,450	13	13
	S_1	1,250	1,310	1,370	1,430	1,490	1,550	10	10
2	R_2	99,999	1,000	1,060	1,120	1,180	1,240	0	65
			41	12	12				
	O_2	99,999	1,150	1,210	1,270	1,330	1,390	9	13
			4						
	S_2	99,999	1,250	1,310	1,370	1,430	1,490	10	10
3	R_3	99,999	99,999	1,000	1,060	1,120	1,180	0	65
				65					
	O_3	99,999	99,999	1,150	1,210	1,270	1,330	0	13
				13					
	S_3	99,999	99,999	1,250	1,310	1,370	1,430	10	10
4	R_4	99,999	99,999	99,999	1,000	1,060	1,120	0	80
					80				
	R_4	99,999	99,999	99,999	1,150	1,210	1,270	0	16
					16				
	S_4	99,999	99,999	99,999	1,250	1,310	1,370	0	10
					10				
5	R_5	99,999	99,999	99,999	99,999	1,000	1,060	10	80
						70			
	O_5	99,999	99,999	99,999	99,999	1,150	1,210	16	16
	S_5	99,999	99,999	99,999	99,999	1,250	1,310	10	10
6	R_6	99,999	99,999	99,999	99,999	99,999	1,000	21	65
							44		
	O_6	99,999	99,999	99,999	99,999	99,999	1,150	13	13
	S_6	99,999	99,999	99,999	99,999	99,999	1,250	10	10
	D	50	60	90	120	70	44	132	566

3. As the fortunes of the Big Three domestic automakers improved in the mid-1990s, workers at one GM plant went on strike. The striking workers produced transmissions used in other GM plants. Almost immediately, many other GM plants shut down for lack of transmissions. Facing lost production during a hot market, GM management quickly acceded to labor's demands to recall more furloughed workers and schedule less overtime. What production-planning decisions regarding the controllable variables (listed in Discussion Question 1) are apparent in this situation?

PROBLEMS

An icon next to a problem identifies the software that can be helpful, but is not mandatory. The software is available on the Student CD-ROM that is packaged with every new copy of the textbook.

1. **OM Explorer** The Barberton Municipal Division of Road Maintenance is charged with road repair in the city of Barberton and the surrounding area. Cindy Kramer, road maintenance director, must submit a staffing plan for the next year based on a set schedule for repairs and on the city budget. Kramer estimates that the labor hours required for the next four quarters are 6,000, 12,000, 19,000, and 9,000, respectively. Each of the 11 workers on the workforce can contribute 500 hours per quarter. Payroll costs are $6,000 in wages per worker for regular time worked up to 500 hours, with an overtime pay rate of $18 for each overtime hour. Overtime is limited to 20 percent of the regular-time capacity in any quarter. Although unused overtime capacity has no cost, unused regular time is paid at $12 per hour. The cost of hiring a worker is $3,000, and the cost of laying off a worker is $2,000. Subcontracting is not permitted.

   a. Find a level workforce plan that allows no delay in road repair and minimizes undertime. Overtime can be used to its limits in any quarter. What is the total cost of the plan and how many undertime hours does it call for?

   b. Use a chase strategy that varies the workforce level without using overtime or undertime. What is the total cost of this plan?

   c. Propose a plan of your own. Compare your plan with those in part (a) and part (b) and discuss its comparative merits.

2. **OM Explorer** Bob Carlton's golf camp estimates the following workforce requirements for its services over the next two years.

Quarter	1	2	3	4
Demand (hours)	4,200	6,400	3,000	4,800

Quarter	5	6	7	8
Demand (hours)	4,400	6,240	3,600	4,800

Each certified instructor puts in 480 hours per quarter regular time and can work an additional 120 hours overtime. Regular-time wages and benefits cost Carlton $7,200 per employee per quarter for regular time worked up to 480 hours, with an overtime cost of $20 per hour. Unused regular time for certified instructors is paid at $15 per hour. There is no cost for unused overtime capacity. The cost of hiring, training, and certifying a new employee is $10,000. Layoff costs are $4,000 per employee. Currently, eight employees work in this capacity.

   a. Find a level workforce plan that allows for no delay in service and minimizes undertime. What is the total cost of this plan?

   b. Use a chase strategy that varies the workforce level without using overtime or undertime. What is the total cost of this plan?

   c. Propose a low-cost, mixed-strategy plan and calculate its total cost.

3. Continuing Problem 2, now assume that Carlton is permitted to employ some uncertified, part-time instructors, provided they represent no more than 15 percent of the total workforce hours in any quarter. Each part-time instructor can work up to 240 hours per quarter, with no overtime or undertime cost. Labor costs for part-time instructors are $12 per hour. Hiring and training costs are $2,000 per uncertified instructor, and there are no layoff costs.

   a. Propose a low-cost, mixed-strategy plan and calculate its total cost.

   b. What are the primary advantages and disadvantages of having a workforce consisting of both regular and temporary employees?

4. The Donald Fertilizer Company produces industrial chemical fertilizers. The projected manufacturing requirements (in thousands of gallons) for the next four quarters are 80, 50, 80, and 130, respectively. Stockouts and backorders are to be avoided. A level production strategy is desired.

   a. Determine the quarterly production rate required to meet total demand for the year, without resorting to backorders or stockouts. Use the Level 2 (constant output rate) strategy that mimimizes the anticipation inventory that would be left over at the end of the year. (*Hint: You need not specify how the constant output rate is achieved relative to hiring, layoffs, overtime, undertime, subcontracting, and vacations*). Beginning inventory is zero.

   b. Specify the anticipation inventories that will be produced.

   c. Suppose that the requirements for the next four quarters are revised to 80, 130, 50, and 80, respectively. If total demand is the same, what level of production rate is needed now, using the same strategy as part (a)?

5. **OM Explorer** Management at the Davis Corporation has determined the following demand schedule (in units).

Month	1	2	3	4
Demand	500	800	1,000	1,400

Month	5	6	7	8
Demand	2,000	1,600	1,400	1,200

Month	9	10	11	12
Demand	1,000	2,400	3,000	1,000

An employee can produce an average of 10 units per month. Each worker on the payroll costs $2,000 in regular-time wages per month. Undertime is paid at the same rate as regular time. In accordance with the labor contract in force, Davis Corporation does not work overtime or use subcontracting. Davis can hire and train a new employee for $2,000 and lay one off for $500. Inventory costs $32 per unit on hand at the end of each month. At present, 140 employees are on the payroll and anticipation inventory is zero.

a. Prepare a production plan with the Level 1 (constant workforce level) strategy that only uses hires and anticipation inventory as possible alternatives, and minimizes the inventory left over at the end of the year. Layoffs, undertime, vacations, subcontracting, backorders, and stockouts are not options. The plan may call for a one-time adjustment of the workforce before month 1.

b. Prepare a production plan with the Chase 1 strategy, relying only on hires and layoffs.

c. Compare and contrast these two plans on the basis of annual costs and other factors that you believe to be important.

d. Propose a mixed-strategy plan that is better than these two plans. Explain why you believe that your plan is better.

6. 🔴 **OM Explorer** The Flying Frisbee Company has forecasted the following staffing requirements for full-time employees. Demand is seasonal, and management wants three alternative staffing plans to be developed.

Month	1	2	3	4
Requirement	2	2	4	6

Month	5	6	7	8
Requirement	18	20	12	18

Month	9	10	11	12
Requirement	7	3	2	1

The company currently has 10 employees. No more than 10 new hires can be accommodated in any month because of limited training facilities. No backorders are allowed, and overtime cannot exceed 25 percent of regular-time capacity in any month. There is no cost for unused overtime capacity. Regular-time wages are $1,500 per month, and overtime wages are 150 percent of regular-time wages. Undertime is paid at the same rate as regular time. The hiring cost is $2,500 per person, and the layoff cost is $2,000 per person.

a. Prepare a staffing plan utilizing a level workforce strategy. The plan may call for a one-time adjustment of the workforce before month 1.

b. Using a chase strategy, prepare a plan that is consistent with the constraint on hiring and minimizes use of overtime.

c. Prepare a low-cost, mixed-strategy plan.

d. Which strategy is most cost-effective? What are the advantages and disadvantages of each plan?

7. 🔴 **OM Explorer** The Twilight Clothing Company makes jeans for children. Management has just prepared a forecast of sales (in pairs of jeans) for next year and now must prepare a production plan. The company has traditionally maintained a level workforce strategy. Currently, there are eight workers, who have been with the company for a number of years. Each employee can produce 2,000 pairs of jeans during a two-month planning period. Every year management authorizes overtime in periods 1, 5, and 6, up to a maximum of 20 percent of regular-time capacity. Management wants to avoid stockouts and backorders and will not accept any plan that calls for such shortages. At present, there are 12,000 pairs of jeans in finished goods inventory. The demand forecast is as follows:

Period	1	2	3
Sales	25,000	6,500	15,000

Period	4	5	6
Sales	19,000	32,000	29,000

a. Is the level workforce strategy feasible with the current workforce assuming that overtime is used only in periods 1, 5, and 6 ? Explain.

b. Find two alternative plans that would satisfy management's concern over stockouts and backorders, disregarding costs. What trade-offs between these two plans must be considered?

Advanced Problems

Linear programming approaches, including the transportation method, are recommended for solving Advanced Problems 8 through 10. Additional applications of these production-planning problems may be found in Supplement D, "Linear Programming" for Problems 16, 17, and 20.

8. 🔴 **OM Explorer** The Bull Grin Company makes a supplement for the animal feed produced by a number of companies. Sales are seasonal, but Bull Grin's customers refuse to stockpile the supplement during slack sales periods. In other words, the customers want to minimize their inventory investments, insist on shipments according to their schedules, and will not accept backorders.

Bull Grin employs manual, unskilled laborers who require little or not training. Producing 1,000 pounds of supplement costs $830 on regular time and $910 on overtime. There is no cost for unused regular time, overtime, or subcontractor capacity. These figures include materials, which account for 80 percent of the cost. Overtime is limited to production of a total of 20,000 pounds per quarter. In addition, subcontractors can be hired at $1,000 per thousand pounds, but only 30,000 pounds per quarter can be produced this way.

The current level of inventory is 40,000 pounds, and management wants to end the year at that level. Holding 1,000 pounds of feed supplement in inventory per quarter costs $100. The latest annual forecast is shown in Table 14.2.

Use the transportation method of production planning to find the optimal production plan and calculate

TABLE 14.2
FORECASTS AND CAPACITIES

	Period				
	Quarter 1	**Quarter 2**	**Quarter 3**	**Quarter 4**	**Total**
Demand (pounds)	130,000	400,000	800,000	470,000	1,800,000
Capacities (pounds)					
Regular time	390,000	400,000	460,000	380,000	1,630,000
Overtime	20,000	20,000	20,000	20,000	80,000
Subcontract	30,000	30,000	30,000	30,000	30,000

its cost, or use the spreadsheet approach to find a good production plan and calculate its cost.

9. ◗ OM Explorer The Cut Rite Company is a major producer of industrial lawn mowers. The cost to Cut Rite for hiring a semiskilled worker for its assembly plant is $3,000, and the cost for laying one off is $2,000. The plant averages an output of 36,000 mowers per quarter, with its current workforce of 720 employees. Regular-time capacity is directly proportional to the number of employees. Overtime is limited to a maximum of 3,000 mowers per quarter, and subcontracting is limited to 1,000 mowers per quarter. The costs to produce one mower are $2,430 on regular time (including materials), $2,700 on overtime, and $3,300 via subcontracting. Unused regular-time capacity costs $270 per mower. There is no cost for unused overtime or subcontractor capacity. The current level of inventory is 4,000 mowers, and management wants to end the year at that level. Customers do not tolerate backorders, and holding a mower in inventory per quarter costs $300. The demand for mowers this coming year is

Quarter	1	2	3	4
Demand	10,000	41,000	77,000	44,000

Two workforce plans have been proposed, and management is uncertain as to which one to use. The following table shows the number of employees per quarter under each plan.

Quarter	1	2	3	4
Plan 1	720	780	920	720
Plan 2	860	860	860	860

a. Which plan would you recommend to management? Explain, supporting your recommendation with an analysis using the transportation method of production planning.

b. If management used creative pricing to get customers to buy mowers in nontraditional time periods, the following demand schedule would result:

Quarter	1	2	3	4
Demand	20,000	54,000	54,000	44,000

Which workforce plan would you recommend now?

10. ◗ OM Explorer Gretchen's Kitchen is a fast-food restaurant located in an ideal spot near the local high school. Gretchen Lowe must prepare an annual staffing plan. The only menu items are hamburgers, chili, soft drinks, shakes, and french fries. A sample of 1,000 customers taken at random revealed that they purchased 2,100 hamburgers, 200 pints of chili, 1,000 soft drinks and shakes, and 1,000 bags of french fries. Thus, for purposes of estimating staffing requirements, Lowe assumes that each customer purchases 2.1 hamburgers, 0.2 pint of chili, 1 soft drink or shake, and 1 bag of french fries. Each hamburger requires four minutes of labor, a pint of chili requires three minutes, and a soft drink or shake and a bag of fries each take two minutes of labor.

The restaurant currently has 10 part-time employees who work 80 hours a month on staggered shifts. Wages are $400 per month for regular time and $7.50 per hour for overtime. Hiring and training costs are $250 per new employee, and layoff costs are $50 per employee.

Lowe realizes that building up seasonal inventories of hamburgers (or any of the products) would not be wise because of shelf-life considerations. Also, any demand not satisfied is a lost sale and must be avoided. Three strategies come to mind.

• Utilize a level workforce strategy and use up to 20 percent of regular-time capacity on overtime.

• Maintain a base of 10 employees, hiring and laying off as needed to avoid any overtime.

• Utilize a chase strategy, hiring and firing employees as demand changes to avoid overtime.

When performing her calculations, Lowe always rounds to the next highest integer for the number of employees. She also follows a policy of not using an employee more than 80 hours per month, except when ovetime is needed. The projected demand by month (number of customers) for next year is as follows:

Jan.	3,200	July	4,800
Feb.	2,600	Aug.	4,200
Mar.	3,300	Sept.	3,800
Apr.	3,900	Oct.	3,600
May	3,600	Nov.	3,500
June	4,200	Dec.	3,000

a. Develop the schedule of service requirements for the next year.

b. Which of the strategies is most effective?

c. Suppose that an arrangement with the high school enables the manager to identify good prospective employees without having to advertise in the local newspaper. This source reduces the hiring cost to $50, which is mainly the cost of charred hamburgers during training. If cost is her only concern, will this method of hiring change Gretchen Lowe's strategy? Considering other objectives that may be appropriate, do you think she should change strategies?

11. **OM Explorer** The Holloway Calendar Company produces a variety of printed calendars for both commercial and private use. The demand for calendars is highly seasonal, peaking in the third quarter. Current inventory is 165,000 calendars, and ending inventory should be 200,000 calendars.

Ann Ritter, Holloway's manufacturing manager, wants to determine the best production plan for the demand requirements and capacity plan shown in the following table. (Here, demand and capacities are expressed as thousands of calendars rather than as employee-period equivalents.) Ritter knows that the regular-time costs is $0.50 per unit, overtime cost is $0.75 per unit, subcontracting cost is $0.90 per unit, and inventory holding cost is $0.10 per calendar per quarter.

	Quarter				
	1	**2**	**3**	**4**	**Total**
Demand	250	515	1,200	325	2,290
Capacities					
Regular Time	300	300	600	300	1,500
Overtime	75	75	150	75	375
Subcontracting	150	150	150	150	600

a. Recommend a production plan to Ritter, using the transportation method of production planning. (Do not allow any stockouts or backorders to occur.)

b. Interpret and explain your recommendation.

c. Calculate the total cost of your recommended production plan.

12. The Alexis Golf Company produces three major lines of premium golf clubs. The demand for their products is highly seasonal, peaking in the second quarter. Kyle Stone, Alexis's manufacturing manager, has presented the tableau, shown in Figure 14.14, based on the transportation method of production planning. All quantities are in 000s.

Use the information shown in Figure 14.14 to answer the following questions.

a. How much regular-time production is expected during the third period? How much subcontracting is expected during the third period?

b. How much regular-time production is expected during the first period? How much anticipatory inventory is expected to be held at the end of the first period?

c. As shown, the firm has no ending inventory for period 4. If the firm decided to hold 250,000 units in inventory at the end of period 4, how could it do so?

FIGURE 14.14

Transportion Method Tableau for the Alexis Golf Company

Alternatives		Quarter 1	Quarter 2	Quarter 3	Quarter 4	Unused Capacity	Total Capacity
Quarter	Beginning inventory	0.00 / 200	3.00	6.00	9.00	0	200
1	Regular time	10.00 / 350	13.00 / 150	16.00	19.00	0	500
1	Overtime	15.00	18.00 / 100	21.00	24.00	0	100
1	Subcontract	19.00	22.00 / 50	25.00	28.00	150	200
2	Regular time	999	10.00 / 1,000	13.00	16.00	0	1,000
2	Overtime	999	15.00 / 200	18.00	21.00	0	200
2	Subcontract	999	19.00 / 200	22.00	25.00	0	200
3	Regular time	999	999	10.00 / 500	13.00	0	500
3	Overtime	999	999	15.00 / 100	18.00	0	100
3	Subcontract	999	999	19.00 / 100	22.00	100	200
4	Regular time	999	999	999	10.00 / 500	0	500
4	Overtime	999	999	999	15.00 / 100	0	100
4	Subcontract	999	999	999	19.00 / 50	150	200
Requirements		550	1,700	700	650		

ACTIVE MODEL EXERCISE

This Active Model appears on the Student CD-ROM. It allows you to evaluate the effects of modifying the size of a constant workforce.

QUESTIONS

1. If we use the same number of workers in each period, what happens as the number of workers increases from 15?
2. If we use the same number of workers in each period, what happens as the number of workers decreases from 15?
3. Suppose the hiring cost is $1,100, what happens as the number of workers increases?
4. Suppose the overtime cost is $3,300, what happens as the number of workers increases?
5. Suppose the undertime cost is the same as the regular-time cost (i.e., paid undertime). What is the best number of workers to have in each month and still meet the demand?
6. If the overtime capacity increases to 30 percent, what is the minimum number of workers that meets the demand in every month?

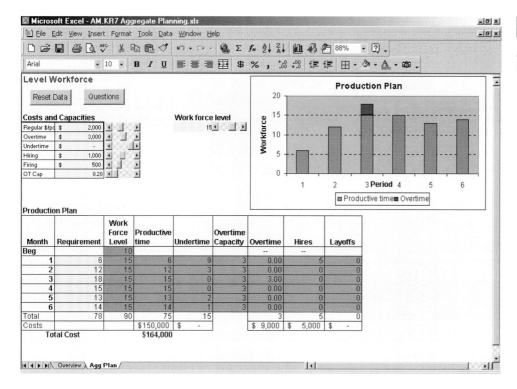

ACTIVE MODEL 14.1

Aggregate Planning Using Data from Example 14.3

CASE   MEMORIAL HOSPITAL

Memorial Hospital is a 265-bed regional health care facility located in the mountains of western North Carolina. The mission of the hospital is to provide quality health care to the people of Ashe County and the six surrounding counties. To accomplish this mission, Memorial Hospital's CEO has outlined three objectives: (1) maximize customer service to increase customer satisfaction, (2) minimize costs to remain competitive, and (3) minimize fluctuations in workforce levels to help stabilize area employment.

The hospital's operations are segmented into eight major wards for the purposes of planning and scheduling the nursing staff. These wards are listed in Table 14.3, along with the number of beds, targeted patient-to-nurse ratios, and average patient census for each ward. The overall demand for hospital services has remained relatively constant over the past few years even though the population of the seven counties served has increased. This stable demand can be attributed to increased competition from other hospitals in the area and

the rise in alternative health care delivery systems, such as health maintenance organizations (HMOs). However, demand for Memorial Hospital's services does vary considerably by type of ward and time of year. Table 14.4 provides an historical monthly breakdown of the average daily patient census per ward.

The director of nursing for Memorial Hospital is Darlene Fry. Each fall she confronts one of the most challenging aspects of her job: planning the nurse-staffing levels for the next calendar year. Although the average demand for nurses has remained relatively stable over the past couple of years, the staffing plan usually changes because of changing work policies, changing pay structures, and temporary nurse availability and cost. With fall quickly approaching, Fry has begun to collect information to plan next year's staffing levels.

The nurses at Memorial Hospital work a regular schedule of four 10-hour days per week. The average regular-time pay across all nursing grades is $12.00 per hour. Overtime

TABLE 14.3   WARD CAPACITY DATA

Ward	Number of Beds	Patients per Nurse	Patient Census*
Intensive care	20	2	10
Cardiac	25	4	15
Maternity	30	4	10
Pediatric	40	4	22
Surgery	5	†	†
Post-Op	15	5	8 (T–F daily equivalent)‡
Emergency	10	3	5 (daily equivalent)‡
General	120	8	98

* Yearly average per day.

  † The hospital employs 20 surgical nurses. Routine surgery is scheduled on Tuesdays and Fridays; five surgeries can be scheduled per day per operating room (bed) on these days. Emergency surgery is scheduled as needed.

  ‡ Daily equivalents are used to schedule nurses because patients flow through these wards in relatively short periods of time. A daily equivalent of 5 indicates that throughout a typical day, an average of five patients are treated in the ward.

TABLE 14.4   AVERAGE DAILY PATIENT CENSUS PER MONTH

	Month											
Ward	J	F	M	A	M	J	J	A	S	O	N	D
Intensive care	13	10	8	7	7	6	11	13	9	10	12	14
Cardiac	18	16	15	13	14	12	13	12	13	15	18	20
Maternity	8	8	12	13	10	8	13	13	14	10	8	7
Pediatric	22	23	24	24	25	21	22	20	18	20	21	19
Surgery*	20	18	18	17	16	16	22	21	17	18	20	22
Post-Op†	10	8	7	7	6	6	10	10	7	8	9	10
Emergency†	6	4	4	7	8	5	5	4	4	3	4	6
General	110	108	100	98	95	90	88	92	98	102	107	94

  *Average surgeries per day.

  †Daily equivalents.

may be scheduled when necessary. However, because of the intensity of the demands placed on nurses, only a limited amount of overtime is permitted per week. Nurses may be scheduled for as many as 12 hours per day, for a maximum of five days per week. Overtime is compensated at a rate of $18.00 per hour. In periods of extremely high demand, temporary part-time nurses may be hired for a limited period of time. Temporary nurses are paid $15.00 per hour. Memorial Hospital has a policy that limits the proportion of temporary nurses to 15 percent of the total nursing staff.

Finding, hiring, and retaining qualified nurses is a problem that hospitals have been facing for years. One reason is that various forms of private practice are luring many nurses away from hospitals with higher pay and greater flexibility. This situation has caused Memorial to guarantee its full-time staff nurses pay for a minimum of 30 hours per week, regardless of the demand placed on nursing services. In addition, each nurse receives a four-week paid vacation each year. However, vacation scheduling may be somewhat restricted by the projected demand for nurses during particular times of the year.

At present, the hospital employs 130 nurses, including 20 surgical nurses. The other 110 nurses are assigned to the remaining seven major areas of the hospital. The personnel department has told Fry that the average cost to the hospital for hiring a new full-time nurse is $400 and for laying off or firing a nurse is $150. Although layoffs are an option, Fry is aware of the hospital's objective of maintaining a level workforce.

After looking over the information that she has collected, Darlene Fry decides that it is time to roll up her sleeves and get started. She wants to consider staffing changes in all areas except the surgery ward, which is already correctly staffed.

QUESTIONS

1. Explain the alternatives available to Darlene Fry as she develops a nurse-staffing plan for Memorial Hospital. How does each meet the objectives stated by the CEO?
2. Based on the data presented, develop a nurse staffing plan for Memorial Hospital. Explain your rationale for this plan.

Source: This case was prepared by Dr. Brooke Saladin, Wake Forest University, as a basis for classroom discussion.

SELECTED REFERENCES

Armacost, R. L., R. L. Penlesky, and S. C. Ross. "Avoiding Problems Inherent in Spreadsheet-Based Simulation Models—An Aggregate Planning Application." *Production and Inventory Management,* vol. 31(1990), pp. 62–68.

Bowman, E. H. "Production Planning by the Transportation Method of Linear Programming." *Journal of the Operations Research Society,* vol. 4 (1956), pp. 100–103.

Buxey, G. "Production Planning and Scheduling for Seasonal Demand." *International Journal of Operations and Production Management,* vol. 13, no. 7 (1993), pp. 4–21.

Fisher, M. L., J. H. Hammond, W. R. Obermeyer, and A. Raman. "Making Supply Meet Demand in an Uncertain World." *Harvard Business Review,* vol. 72, no. 3 (1994), pp. 83–93.

Hanssman, F., and S. W. Hess. "A Linear Programming Approach to Production and Employment Scheduling." *Management Technology,* vol. 1 (1960), pp. 46–51.

Heskett, J., W. E. Sasser, and C. Hart. *Service Breakthroughs: Changing the Rules of the Game.* New York: The Free Press, 1990.

Krajewski, L., and H. Thompson. "Efficient Employment Planning in Public Utilities." *Bell Journal of Economics and Management Science,* vol. 6, no. 1 (1975), pp. 314–326.

Lee, S. M., and L. J. Moore. "A Practical Approach to Production Scheduling." *Production and Inventory Management* (First Quarter 1974), pp. 79–92.

Lee, W. B., and B. M. Khumawala. "Simulation Testing of Aggregate Production Planning Models in an Implementation Methodology." *Management Science,* vol. 20, no. 6 (1974), pp. 903–911.

Ryan, D. M. "Optimization Earns Its Wings." *OR/MS Today,* vol. 27, no. 2 (2000), pp. 26–30.

Silver, E. A. "A Tutorial on Production Smoothing and Workforce Balancing." *Operations Research* (November–December 1967), pp. 985–1010.

Sipper, D., and R. Bulfin. *Production: Planning, Control, and Integration.* New York: McGraw-Hill, 1997.

Vollmann, T. E., W. L. Berry, and D. C. Whybark. *Manufacturing Planning and Control Systems,* 3d ed. Homewood, IL: Irwin, 1992.

Linear Programming

LEARNING GOALS *After reading this supplement, you should be able to . . .*

IDENTIFY OR DEFINE

1. the characteristics and assumptions of linear programming models.
2. slack and surplus variables.
3. sensitivity analysis on the objective function coefficients and right-hand-side parameters.

DESCRIBE OR EXPLAIN

4. formulating models for various problems.
5. graphic analysis for two-variable problems.
6. the algebraic solution for corner points in two-variable problems.
7. computer output of a linear programming solution.

In many business situations, resources are limited and demand for them is great. For example, a limited number of vehicles may have to be scheduled to make multiple trips to customers, or a staffing plan may have to be developed to cover expected variable demand with the fewest employees. In this supplement, we describe a technique called **linear programming**, which is useful for allocating scarce resources among competing demands. The resources may be time, money, or materials, and the limitations are known as constraints. Linear programming can help managers find the best allocation solution and provide information about the value of additional resources.

linear programming   A technique that is useful for allocating scarce resources among competing demands.

BASIC CONCEPTS

Before we can demonstrate how to solve problems in operations management with linear programming, we must first explain several characteristics of all linear programming models and mathematical assumptions that apply to them: (1) *objective function*, (2) *decision variables*, (3) *constraints*, (4) *feasible region*, (5) *parameters*, (6) *linearity*, and (7) *nonnegativity*.

Linear programming is an *optimization* process. A single **objective function** states mathematically what is being maximized (e.g., profit or present value) or minimized (e.g., cost or scrap). The objective function provides the scorecard on which the attractiveness of different solutions is judged.

Decision variables represent choices that the decision maker can control. Solving the problem yields their optimal values. For example, a decision variable could be the number of units of a product to make next month or the number of units of inventory to hold next month. Linear programming is based on the assumption that decision variables are *continuous;* they can be fractional quantities and need not be whole numbers. Often, this assumption is realistic, as when the decision variable is expressed in dollars, hours, or some other continuous measure. Even when the decision variables represent nondivisible units, such as workers, tables, or trucks, we sometimes can simply round the linear programming solution up or down to get a reasonable solution that does not violate any constraints, or we can use a more advanced technique, called *integer programming*.

Constraints are limitations that restrict the permissible choices for the decision variables. Each limitation can be expressed mathematically in one of three ways: a less-than-or-equal-to ($\leq$), an equal-to ($=$), or a greater-than-or-equal-to ($\geq$) constraint. A $\leq$ constraint puts an upper limit on some function of decision variables and most often is used with maximization problems. For example, a $\leq$ constraint may specify the maximum number of customers who can be served or the capacity limit of a machine. An $=$ constraint means that the function must equal some value. For example, 100 (not 99 or 101) units of one product must be made. An $=$ constraint often is used for certain mandatory relationships, such as the fact that ending inventory always equals beginning inventory plus production minus sales. A $\geq$ constraint puts a lower limit on some function of decision variables. For example, a $\geq$ constraint may specify that production of a product must exceed or equal demand.

Every linear programming problem must have one or more constraints. Taken together, the constraints define a **feasible region,** which represents all permissible combinations of the decision variables. In some unusual situations, the problem is so tightly constrained that there is only one possible solution—or perhaps none. However, in the usual case, the feasibility region contains infinitely many possible solutions, assuming that the feasible combinations of the decision variables can be fractional values. The goal of the decision maker is to find the best possible solution.

The objective function and constraints are functions of decision variables and parameters. A **parameter,** also known as a *coefficient* or *given constant,* is a value that the decision maker cannot control and that does not change when the solution is

objective function   An expression in linear programming models that states mathematically what is being maximized (e.g., profit or present value) or minimized (e.g., cost or scrap).

decision variables   The variables that represent choices the decision maker can control.

constraints   The limitations that restrict the permissible choices for the decision variables.

feasible region   A region that represents all permissible combinations of the decision variables in a linear programming model.

parameter   A value that the decision maker cannot control and that does not change when the solution is implemented.

implemented. Each parameter is assumed to be known with **certainty.** For example, a computer programmer may know that running a software program will take three hours—no more, no less.

The objective function and constraint equations are assumed to be linear. **Linearity** implies proportionality and additivity, there can be no products (e.g., $10x_1x_2$) or powers (e.g., x_1^3) of decision variables. Suppose that the profit gained by producing two types of products (represented by decision variables x_1 and x_2) is $2x + 3x_2$. Proportionality implies that one unit of x_1 contributes $2 to profits and two units contribute $4, regardless of how much of x_2 is produced. Similarly, each unit of x_2 contributes $3, whether it is the first or the tenth unit produced. Additivity means that the total objective function value equals the profits from x_1 plus the profits from x_2.

Finally, we make an assumption of **nonnegativity,** which means that the decision variables must be positive or zero. A firm that makes spaghetti sauce, for example, cannot produce a negative number of jars. To be formally correct, a linear programming formulation should show a ≥ 0 constraint for each decision variable.

Although the assumptions of linearity, certainty, and continuous variables are restrictive, linear programming can help managers analyze many complex resource allocation problems. The process of building the model forces managers to identify the important decision variables and constraints, which is a useful step in its own right. Identifying the nature and scope of the problem represents a major step toward solving it. In a later section, we show how sensitivity analysis can help the manager deal with uncertainties in the parameters and answer "what-if" questions.

FORMULATING A PROBLEM

Linear programming applications begin with the formulation of a *model* of the problem with the general characteristics just described. We illustrate the modeling process here with the **product-mix problem,** which is a one-period type of aggregate-planning problem, the solution of which yields optimal output quantities (or product mix) of a group of services or products subject to resource capacity and market demand constraints. Formulating a model to represent each unique problem, using the following three-step sequence, is the most creative and perhaps the most difficult part of linear programming.

Step 1. Define the Decision Variables. What must be decided? Define each decision variable specifically, remembering that the definitions used in the objective function must be equally useful in the constraints. The definitions should be as specific as possible. Consider the following two alternative definitions:

x_1 = product 1
x_1 = number of units of product 1 to be produced and sold next month

The second definition is much more specific than the first, making the remaining steps easier.

Step 2. Write Out the Objective Function. What is to be maximized or minimized? If it is next month's profits, write out an objective function that makes next month's profits a linear function of the decision variables. Identify parameters to go with each decision variable. For example, if each unit of x_1 sold yields a profit of $7, the total profit from product $x_1 = 7x_1$. If a variable has no impact on the objective function, its objective function coefficient is 0. The objective function often is set equal to Z, and the goal is to maximize or minimize Z.

Step 3. Write Out the Constraints. What limits the values of the decision variables? Identify the constraints and the parameters for each decision variable in them. As with the objective function, the parameter for a variable that has no impact in a constraint is 0. To be formally correct, also write out the nonnegativity constraints.

---

certainty The word that is used to describe that a fact is known without doubt.

linearity A characteristic of linear programming models that implies proportionality and additivity—there can be no products or powers of decision variables.

nonnegativity An assumption that the decision variables must be positive or zero.

product-mix problem A one-period type of aggregate-planning problem, the solution of which yields optimal output quantities (or product mix) of a group of services or products subject to resource capacity and market demand constraints.

As a consistency check, make sure that the same unit of measure is being used on both sides of each constraint and in the objective function. For example, suppose that the right-hand side of a constraint is hours of capacity per month. Then, if a decision variable on the left-hand side of the constraint measures the number of units produced per month, the dimensions of the parameter that is multiplied by the decision variable must be hours per unit because

$$\left(\frac{\text{Hours}}{\text{Unit}}\right)\left(\frac{\text{Units}}{\text{Month}}\right) = \left(\frac{\text{Hours}}{\text{Month}}\right)$$

Of course, you can also skip around from one step to another, depending on the part of the problem that has your attention. If you cannot get past step 1, try a new set of definitions for the decision variables. There may be more than one way to model a problem correctly.

EXAMPLE D.1   Formulating a Linear Programming Model

The Stratton Company produces two basic types of plastic pipe. Three resources are crucial to the output of pipe: extrusion hours, packaging hours, and a special additive to the plastic raw material. The following data represent next week's situation. All data are expressed in units of 100 feet of pipe.

	PRODUCT		RESOURCE AVAILABILITY
RESOURCE	**TYPE 1**	**TYPE 2**	
Extrusion	4 hr	6 hr	48 hr
Packaging	2 hr	2 hr	18 hr
Additive mix	2 lb	1 lb	16 lb

The contribution to profits and overhead per 100 feet of pipe is $34 for type 1 and $40 for type 2. Formulate a linear programming model to determine how much of each type of pipe should be produced to maximize contribution to profits and to overhead.

SOLUTION

Step 1. To define the decision variables that determine product mix, we let

$x_1 =$ amount of type 1 pipe to be produced and sold next week, measured in 100-foot increments (e.g., $x_1 = 2$ means 200 feet of type 1 pipe)

and

$x_2 =$ amount of type 2 pipe to be produced and sold next week, measured in 100-foot increments

Step 2. Next, we define the objective function. The goal is to maximize the total contribution that the two products make to profits and overhead. Each unit of x_1 yields $34, and each unit of x_2 yields $40. For specific values of x_1 and x_2, we find the total profit by multiplying the number of units of each product produced by the profit per unit and adding them. Thus, our objective function becomes

$$\text{Maximize: } \$34x_1 + \$40x_2 = Z$$

Step 3. The final step is to formulate the constraints. Each unit of x_1 and x_2 produced consumes some of the critical resources. In the extrusion department, a unit of x_1 requires 4 hours and a unit of x_2 requires 6 hours. The total must not exceed the 48 hours of capacity available, so we use the $\leq$ sign. Thus, the first constraint is

$$4x_1 + 6x_2 \leq 48 \text{ (extrusion)}$$

Similarly, we can formulate constraints for packaging and raw materials:

$$2x_1 + 2x_2 \leq 18 \text{ (packaging)}$$
$$2x_1 + x_2 \leq 16 \text{ (additive mix)}$$

These three constraints restrict our choice of values for the decision variables because the values we choose for x_1 and x_2 must satisfy all of the constraints. Negative values for x_1 and x_2 do not make sense, so we add nonnegativity restrictions to the model:

$$x_1 \geq 0 \quad \text{and} \quad x_2 \geq 0 \text{ (nonnegativity restrictions)}$$

We can now state the entire model, made complete with the definitions of variables.

$$\text{Maximize: } \$34x_1 + \$40x_2 = Z$$
$$\text{Subject to: } 4x_1 + 6x_2 \leq 48$$
$$2x_1 + 2x_2 \leq 18$$
$$2x_1 + x_2 \leq 16$$
$$x_1 \geq 0 \quad \text{and} \quad x_2 \geq 0$$

where

x_1 = amount of type 1 pipe to be produced and sold next week, measured in 100-foot increments

x_2 = amount of type 2 pipe to be produced and sold next week, measured in 100-foot increments

● GRAPHIC ANALYSIS

With the model formulated, we now seek the optimal solution. In practice, most linear programming problems are solved with a computer. However, insight into the meaning of the computer output—and linear programming concepts in general—can be gained by analyzing a simple two-variable problem with the **graphic method of linear programming.** Hence, we begin with the graphic method, even though it is not a practical technique for solving problems that have three or more decision variables. The five basic steps are (1) *plot the constraints,* (2) *identify the feasible region,* (3) *plot an objective function line,* (4) *find the visual solution,* and (5) *find the algebraic solution.*

graphic method of linear programming A type of graphic analysis that involves the following five steps: plotting the constraints, identifying the feasible region, plotting an objective function line, finding a visual solution, and finding the algebraic solution.

PLOT THE CONSTRAINTS

We begin by plotting the constraint equations, disregarding the inequality portion of the constraints ($<$ or $>$). Making each constraint an equality ($=$) transforms it into the equation for a straight line. The line can be drawn as soon as we identify two points on it. Any two points reasonably spread out may be chosen; the easiest ones to find are the *axis intercepts,* where the line intersects each axis. To find the x_1 axis intercept, set x_2 equal to 0 and solve the equation for x_1. For the Stratton Company in Example D.1, the equation of the line for the extrusion process is

$$4x_1 + 6x_2 = 48$$

For the x_1 axis intercept, $x_2 = 0$, so

$$4x_1 + 6(0) = 48$$
$$x_1 = 12$$

To find the x_2 axis intercept, set $x_1 = 0$ and solve for x_2:

$$4(0) + 6x_2 = 48$$
$$x_2 = 8$$

We connect points (0, 8) and (12, 0) with a straight line, as shown in Figure D.1.

FIGURE D.1

Graph of the Extrusion Constraint

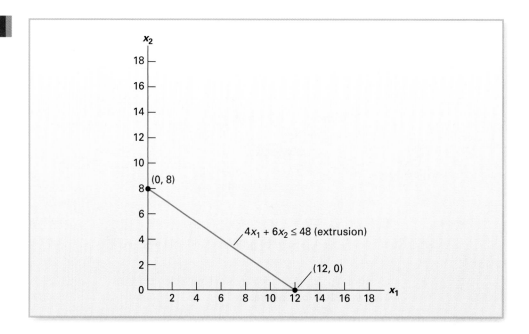

EXAMPLE D.2   **Plotting the Constraints**

ACTIVE MODEL D.1
Active Model D.1 on the Student CD-ROM offers many insights on graphic analysis and sensitivity analysis. Use it when studying Examples D.2 through D.7.

TUTOR D.1
Tutor D.1 on the Student CD-ROM provides a new practice example for plotting the constraints.

For the Stratton Company problem, plot the other constraints: one constraint for packaging and one constraint for the additive mix.

SOLUTION

The equation for the packaging process's line is $2x_1 + 2x_2 = 18$. To find the x_1 intercept, set $x_2 = 0$:

$$2x_1 + 2(0) = 18$$
$$x_1 = 9$$

To find the x_2 axis intercept, set $x_1 = 0$:

$$2(0) + 2x_2 = 18$$
$$x_2 = 9$$

The equation for the additive mix's line is $2x_1 + x_2 = 16$. To find the x_1 intercept, set $x_2 = 0$:

$$2x_1 + 0 = 16$$
$$x_1 = 8$$

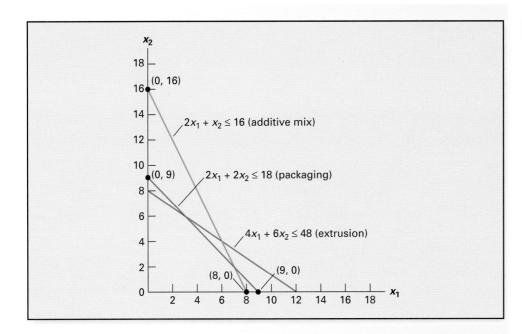

To find the x_2 axis intercept, set $x_1 = 0$:

$$2(0) + x_2 = 16$$
$$x_2 = 16$$

With a straight line, we connect points $(0, 9)$ and $(9, 0)$ for the packaging constraint and points $(0, 16)$ and $(8, 0)$ for the additive mix constraint. Figure D.2 shows the graph with all three constraints plotted.

IDENTIFY THE FEASIBLE REGION

The feasible region is the area on the graph that contains the solutions that satisfy all the constraints simultaneously, including the nonnegativity restrictions. To find the feasible region, first locate the feasible points for each constraint and then the area that satisfies all constraints. *Generally,* the following three rules identify the feasible points for a given constraint:

1. For the = constraint, only the points on the line are feasible solutions.
2. For the ≤ constraint, the points on the line and the points below or to the left of the line are feasible solutions.
3. For the ≥ constraint, the points on the line and the points above or to the right of the line are feasible solutions.

Exceptions to these rules occur when one or more of the parameters on the left-hand side of a constraint are negative. In such cases, we draw the constraint line and test a point on one side of it. If the point does not satisfy the constraint, it is in the infeasible part of the graph. Suppose that a linear programming model has the following five constraints plus the nonnegativity constraints:

$$
\begin{aligned}
2x_1 + x_2 &\ge 10 \\
2x_1 + 3x_2 &\ge 18 \\
x_1 &\le 7 \\
x_2 &\le 5 \\
6x_1 + 5x_2 &\le 5 \\
x_1, x_2 &\ge 0
\end{aligned}
$$

FIGURE D.3

Identifying the Feasible Region

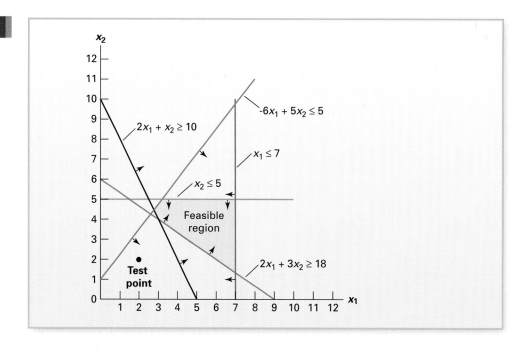

The feasible region is the shaded portion of Figure D.3. The arrows shown on each constraint identify which side of each line is feasible. The rules work for all but the fifth constraint, which has a negative parameter, -6, for x_1. We arbitrarily select (2, 2) as the test point, which Figure D.3 shows is below the line and to the right. At this point, we find $-6(2) + 5(2) = -2$. Because -2 does not exceed 5, the portion of the figure containing (2, 2) is feasible, at least for this fifth constraint.

EXAMPLE D.3   Identifying the Feasible Region

Identify the feasible region for the Stratton Company problem.

SOLUTION

Because there are only $\leq$ constraints, and the parameters on the left-hand side of each constraint are not negative, the feasible portions are to the left of and below each constraint. The feasible region, shaded in Figure D.4, satisfies all three constraints simultaneously.

PLOT AN OBJECTIVE FUNCTION LINE

Now we want to find the solution that optimizes the objective function. Even though all the points in the feasible region represent possible solutions, we can limit our search to the corner points. A **corner point** lies at the intersection of two (or possibly more) constraint lines on the boundary of the feasible region. No interior points in the feasible region need be considered because at least one corner point is better than any interior point. Similarly, other points on the boundary of the feasible region can be ignored because there is a corner point that is at least as good as any of them.

In Figure D.4 the five corner points are marked A, B, C, D, and E. Point A is the origin (0, 0) and can be ignored because any other feasible point is a better solution. We could try each of the other corner points in the objective function and select the one that maximizes Z. For example, corner point B lies at (0, 8). If we substitute these values into the objective function, the resulting Z value is 320:

corner point A point that lies at the intersection of two (or possibly more) constraint lines on the boundary of the feasible region.

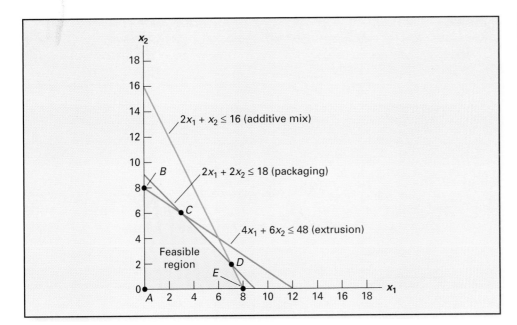

$$34x_1 + 40x_2 = Z$$
$$34(0) + 40(8) = 320$$

However, we may not be able to read accurately the values of x_1 and x_2 for some of the points (e.g., C or D) on the graph. Algebraically solving two linear equations for each corner point also is inefficient when there are many constraints and, thus, many corner points.

The best approach is to plot the objective function on the graph of the feasible region for some arbitrary Z values. From these objective function lines, we can spot the best solution visually. If the objective function is profits, each line is called an *iso-profit line* and every point on that line will yield the same profit. If Z measures cost, the line is called an *iso-cost line* and every point on it represents the same cost. We can simplify the search by plotting the first line in the feasible region—somewhere near the optimal solution, we hope. For the Stratton Company example, let us pass a line through point E (8, 0). This point is a corner point. It might even be the optimal solution because it is far from the origin. To draw the line, we first identify its Z value as $34(8) + 40(0) = 272$. Therefore, the equation for the objective function line passing through E is

$$34x_1 + 40x_2 = 272$$

Every point on the line defined by this equation has an objective function Z value of 272. To draw the line, we need to identify a second point on it, and then connect the two points. Let us use the x_2 intercept, where $x_1 = 0$:

$$34(0) + 40x_2 = 272$$
$$x_2 = 6.8$$

Figure D.5 shows the iso-profit line that connects points (8, 0) and (0, 6.8). A series of other dashed lines could be drawn parallel to this first line. Each would have its own Z value. Lines above the first line we drew would have higher Z values. Lines below it would have lower Z values.

FIND THE VISUAL SOLUTION

We now eliminate corner points A and E from consideration as the optimal solution because better points lie above and to the right of the $Z = 272$ iso-profit line. Our goal

FIGURE D.5

Passing an Iso-Profit Line Through (8, 0)

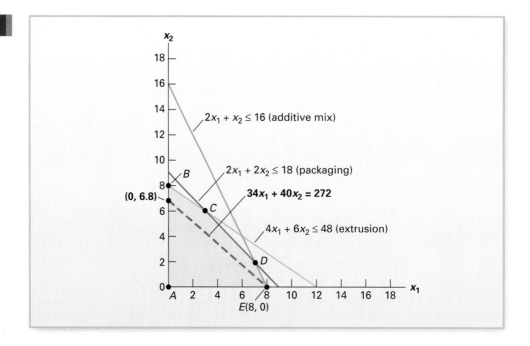

is to maximize profits, so the best solution is a point on the iso-profit line *farthest* from the origin but still touching the feasible region. (For minimization problems, it is a point in the feasible region on the iso-cost line *closest* to the origin.) To identify which of the remaining corner points is optimal (B, C, or D), we draw, parallel to the first line, one or more iso-profit lines that give better Z values (higher for maximization and lower for minimization). The line that just touches the feasible region identifies the optimal solution. For the Stratton Company problem, Figure D.6 shows the second iso-profit line. The optimal solution is the last point touching the feasible region: point C. It appears to be in the vicinity of (3, 6), but the visual solution is not exact.

A linear programming problem can have more than one optimal solution. This situation occurs when the objective function is parallel to one of the faces of the feasible region. Such would be the case if our objective function in the Stratton Company problem were $38x_1 + $38x_2. Points (3, 6) and (7, 2) would be optimal, as would any other

FIGURE D.6

Drawing the Second Iso-Profit Line

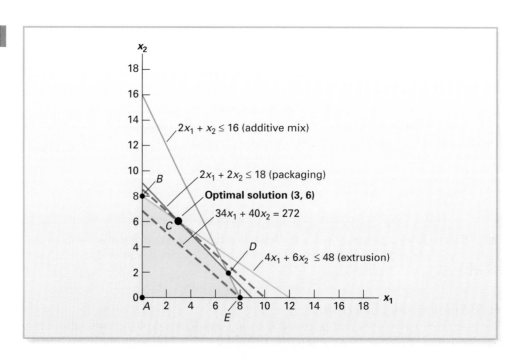

point on the line connecting these two corner points. In such a case, management probably would base a final decision on nonquantifiable factors. It is important to understand, however, that we need to consider only the corner points of the feasible region when optimizing an objective function.

FIND THE ALGEBRAIC SOLUTION

To find an exact solution, we must use algebra. We begin by identifying the pair of constraints that define the corner point at their intersection. We then list the constraints as equations and solve them simultaneously to find the coordinates (x_1, x_2) of the corner point. Simultaneous equations can be solved several ways. For small problems, the easiest way is as follows:

Step 1. Develop an equation with just one unknown. Start by multiplying both sides of one equation by a constant so that the coefficient for one of the two decision variables is *identical* in both equations. Then subtract one equation from the other and solve the resulting equation for its single unknown variable.

Step 2. Insert this decision variable's value into either one of the original constraints and solve for the other decision variable.

Finding the Optimal Solution Algebraically

EXAMPLE D.4

Find the optimal solution algebraically for the Stratton Company problem. What is the value of Z when the decision variables have optimal values?

TUTOR D.2

Tutor D.2 on the Student CD-ROM provides a new practice example for finding the optimal solution.

SOLUTION

Step 1. Figure D.6 showed that the optimal corner point lies at the intersection of the extrusion and packaging constraints. Listing the constraints as equalities, we have

$$4x_1 + 6x_2 = 48 \text{ (extrusion)}$$
$$2x_1 + 2x_2 = 18 \text{ (packaging)}$$

We multiply each term in the packaging constraint by 2. The packaging constraint now is $4x_1 + 4x_2 = 36$. Next, we subtract the packaging constraint from the extrusion constraint. The result will be an equation from which x_1 has dropped out. (Alternatively, we could multiply the second equation by 3 so that x_2 drops out after the subtraction.) Thus,

$$
\begin{array}{r}
4x_1 + 6x_2 = 48 \\
-(4x_1 + 4x_2 = 36) \\
\hline
2x_2 = 12 \\
x_2 = 6
\end{array}
$$

Step 2. Substituting the value of x_2 into the extrusion equation, we get

$$4x_1 + 6(6) = 48$$
$$4x_1 = 12$$
$$x_1 = 3$$

Thus, the optimal point is (3, 6). This solution gives a total profit of $34(3) + 40(6) = \$342$.

DECISION POINT   Management at the Stratton Company decided to produce 300 feet of type 1 pipe and 600 feet of type 2 pipe for the next week.

SLACK AND SURPLUS VARIABLES

Figure D.6 showed that the optimal product mix will exhaust all the extrusion and packaging resources because at the optimal corner point (3, 6) the two constraints are equalities. Substituting the values of x_1 and x_2 into these constraints shows that the left-hand sides equal the right-hand sides:

$$4(3) + 6(6) = 48 \text{ (extrusion)}$$
$$2(3) + 2(6) = 18 \text{ (packaging)}$$

binding constraint   A constraint that helps form the optimal corner point; it limits the ability to improve the objective function.

A constraint (such as the one for extrusion) that helps form the optimal corner point is called a **binding constraint** because it limits the ability to improve the objective function. If a binding constraint is *relaxed,* or made less restrictive, a better solution is possible. Relaxing a constraint means increasing the right-hand-side parameter for a ≤ constraint or decreasing it for a ≥ constraint. No improvement is possible from relaxing a constraint that is not binding, such as the additive mix constraint in Figure D.6. If the right-hand side were increased from 16 to 17 and the problem solved again, the optimal solution would not change. In other words, there is already more additive mix than needed.

For nonbinding inequality constraints, knowing how much the left and right sides differ is helpful. Such information tells us how close the constraint is to becoming binding. For a ≤ constraint, the amount by which the left-hand side falls short of the right-hand side is called **slack**. For a ≥ constraint, the amount by which the left-hand side exceeds the right-hand side is called **surplus**. To find the slack for a ≤ constraint algebraically, we *add* a slack variable to the constraint and convert it to an equality. Then we substitute in the values of the decision variables and solve for the slack. For example, the additive mix constraint in Figure D.6, $2x_1 + x_2 \le 16$, can be rewritten by adding slack variable s_1:

slack   The amount by which the left-hand side falls short of the right-hand side.

surplus   The amount by which the left-hand side exceeds the right-hand side.

$$2x_1 + x_2 + s_1 = 16$$

We then find the slack at the optimal solution (3, 6):

$$2(3) + 6 + s_1 = 16$$
$$s_1 = 4$$

TUTOR D.3

Tutor D.3 on the Student CD-ROM provides another practice example for finding slack.

The procedure is much the same to find the surplus for a ≥ constraint, except that we *subtract* a surplus variable from the left-hand side. Suppose that $x_1 + x_2 \ge 6$ was another constraint in the Stratton Company problem, representing a lower bound on the number of units produced. We would then rewrite the constraint by subtracting a surplus variable s_2:

$$x_1 + x_2 - s_2 = 6$$

The slack at the optimal solution (3, 6) would be

$$3 + 6 - s_2 = 6$$
$$s_2 = 3$$

SENSITIVITY ANALYSIS

Rarely are the parameters in the objective function and constraints known with certainty. Often, they are just estimates of actual values. For example, the available packaging and extrusion hours for the Stratton Company are estimates that do not reflect the uncertainties associated with absenteeism or personnel transfers, and the required hours per unit to package and extrude may be work standards that essentially are averages. Likewise, profit contributions used for the objective function coefficients do not reflect uncertainties in selling prices and such variable costs as wages, raw materials, and shipping.

Despite such uncertainties, initial estimates are needed to solve the problem. Accounting, marketing, and work-standard information systems often provide these initial estimates. After solving the problem using these estimated values, the analyst can determine how much the optimal values of the decision variables and the objective function value Z would be affected if certain parameters had different values. This type of postsolution analysis for answering "what-if" questions is called *sensitivity analysis*.

One way of conducting sensitivity analysis for linear programming problems is the brute-force approach of changing one or more parameter values and re-solving the entire problem. This approach may be acceptable for small problems, but it is inefficient if there are many parameters. For example, brute-force sensitivity analysis using 3 separate values for each of 20 objective function coefficients requires 3^{20}; or 3,486,784,401, separate solutions! Fortunately, efficient methods are available for getting sensitivity information without re-solving the entire problem, and they are routinely used in most linear programming computer software packages. Here, we do sensitivity analysis on the objective function coefficients and the right-hand-side parameters of the constraints for a one-parameter-at-a-time change.

OBJECTIVE FUNCTION COEFFICIENTS

We begin sensitivity analysis on the objective function of a two-variable problem by calculating the slope of the iso-profit (or iso-cost) lines. The equation of any straight line can be written as $y = mx + b$, where m is the slope of the line. In our graphic solution in Figure D.6, we used x_2 rather than y, and x_1 rather than x. Thus, the equation that reveals a line's slope will be $x_2 = mx_1 + b$. To put the objective function in this form, we solve the objective function for x_2 in terms of x_1 and Z:

$$34x_1 + 40x_2 = Z$$
$$40x_2 = -34x_1 + Z$$
$$x_2 = -\frac{34x_1}{40} + \frac{Z}{40}$$

Thus, the slope m of the iso-profit lines for Stratton Company is $-34/40$, or -0.85. In general, it is the negative of the ratio found by dividing the objective function coefficient of x_1 by the objective function coefficient of x_2.

Now, let us see what happens when an objective function coefficient changes. We define c_1 to be the profit contribution per 100 feet of x_1 and c_2 to be the profit contribution per 100 feet of x_2. The equation of the iso-profit line becomes

$$x_2 = -\frac{c_1 x_1}{c_2} + \frac{Z}{c_2}$$

If c_1 *increases* while c_2 stays constant, the slope becomes more negative (steeper), and the line rotates clockwise. For example, if c_1 increases to \$40, the slope becomes -1.00, or $-40/40$. But if c_1 *decreases,* the slope becomes less negative and the line rotates counterclockwise. If the reduction is substantial enough, the slope of the objective function will equal the slope of the extrusion constraint. When this happens, point B becomes an optimal corner point. If c_1 instead increases so that the slope of the objective function becomes more negative than the slope of the packaging constraint, corner point D becomes optimal. Similar conclusions also can be drawn about changes in c_2.

RANGE OF OPTIMALITY. If the objective function coefficient makes the slope of the objective function greater than the slope of the packaging constraint but less than the slope of the extrusion constraint, point C remains the optimal solution. In Figure D.7,

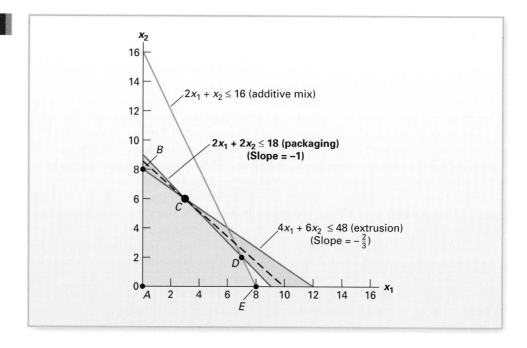

the area between the two binding constraints, extrusion and packaging, is shaded. Note that point C remains optimal if the objective function slope is greater than -1.00, the slope of the packaging constraint, and less than $-2/3$, the slope of the extrusion constraint. Thus, the following relationship holds:

$$-1 \le -\frac{c_1}{c_2} \le -\frac{2}{3}$$

We use this relationship to find the range over which c_1 can vary without changing the optimality of point C, holding c_2 constant at $40:

$$-1 \le -\frac{c_1}{40} \le -\frac{2}{3}$$

Because we seek the range for c_1, rather than $-c_1/40$, we multiply by -40. Multiplying by a negative number reverses the direction of the inequalities, so we get

$$40 \ge c_1 \ge 26.67$$

Rearranging terms for ease of reading yields

$$26.67 \le c_1 \le 40$$

range of optimality The lower and upper limit over which the optimal values of the decision variables remain unchanged.

Thus, the objective function coefficient for x_1 ranges from a *lower limit* of $26.67 through an *upper limit* of $40. This **range of optimality** defines a lower and upper limit over which the optimal values of the decision variables remain unchanged. Of course, the value of Z would change as c_1 changed. For example, if c_1 increased from $34 to $40, the value of Z at point C would become 360:

$$40x_1 + 40x_2 = Z$$
$$40(3) + 40(6) = 360$$

Finding the Range of Optimality for c_2

EXAMPLE D.5

What is the range of optimality for c_2 in the Stratton Company problem?

SOLUTION

If we hold c_1 constant at \$34, the relationship for the slope of the iso-profit lines is

$$-1 \leq -\frac{34}{c_2} \leq -\frac{2}{3}$$

Because c_2 is in the denominator, defining one limit at a time is easiest. For the limit on the left, we get

$$-1 \leq -\frac{34}{c_2}$$

Multiplying by $-c_2$, we find the lower limit:

$$c_2 \geq 34$$

Now, taking the second relationship on the right, we have

$$-\frac{34}{c_2} \leq -\frac{2}{3}$$

Multiplying by $-c_2$, we obtain the upper limit:

$$34 \geq \frac{2c_2}{3}$$
$$51 \geq c_2$$

Putting both limits into one final expression, we find that c_2 can be as low as \$34 or as high as \$51 without changing the optimality of point C, or

$$34 \leq c_2 \leq 51$$

COEFFICIENT SENSITIVITY. In the Stratton Company problem, the optimal point makes both decision variables greater than 0 (3 and 6). If c_1 were low enough (below 26.67), point B would be optimal, and the optimal value of x_1 would be 0. Sensitivity analysis can give us additional information about variables that have optimal values of 0. **Coefficient sensitivity** measures how much the objective function coefficient of a decision variable must *improve* (increase for maximization or decrease for minimization) before the optimal solution changes and the decision variable becomes some positive number. The coefficient sensitivity for c_1 can be found in the following manner:

coefficient sensitivity The measurement of how much the objective function coefficient of a decision variable must *improve* (increase for maximization or decrease for minimization) before the optimal solution changes and the decision variable becomes some positive number.

   Step 1. Identify the direction of rotation (clockwise or counterclockwise) of the iso-profit (or iso-cost) line that improves c_1. Rotate the iso-profit (or iso-cost) line in this direction until it reaches a new optimal corner point that makes x_1 greater than 0.

   Step 2. Determine which binding constraint has the same slope as the rotated iso-profit (or iso-cost) line at this new point. Solve for the value of c_1 that makes the objective function slope equal to the slope of this binding constraint.

Step 3. Set the coefficient sensitivity equal to the difference between this value and the current value of c_1.

EXAMPLE D.6   Finding the Coefficient Sensitivity for a Revised Problem

Suppose that the Stratton Company problem is changed so that c_1 is $20 rather than $34. Figure D.8 shows that the highest iso-profit line now passes through point B, making it the optimal solution rather than point C. At point B, the optimal value of x_1 is 0. What is the coefficient sensitivity for c_1?

FIGURE D.8

Coefficient Sensitivity for the Revised Problem

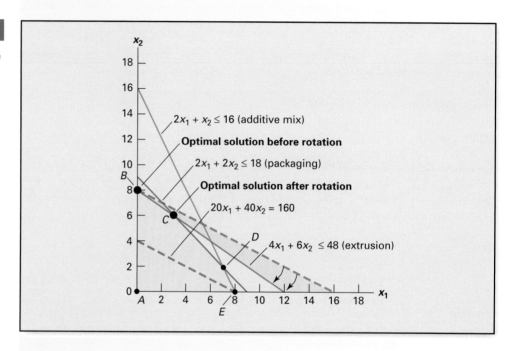

SOLUTION

We apply the three solution steps to the revised Stratton problem.

Step 1. This is a maximization problem, so c_1 improves as it *increases*. Increasing c_1 rotates the iso-profit line clockwise. Rotation continues until point C is reached—a corner point that makes x_1 a positive number (3).

Step 2. The binding constraint that has the same slope is extrusion. Solving for the c_1 that makes the two slopes equal, we get

$$-\frac{c_1}{40} = -\frac{2}{3}$$
$$c_1 = 26.67$$

Step 3. The coefficient sensitivity is $6.67 or $26.67 − $20.

Therefore, c_1 must increase by $6.67 before it is optimal to make x_1 greater than 0.

RIGHT-HAND-SIDE PARAMETERS

Now consider how a change in the right-hand-side parameter for a constraint may affect the feasible region and perhaps cause a change in the optimal solution. Let us return to the original Stratton Company problem, changing c_1 back from $20 to $34.

However, we now consider adding one more hour to the packaging resource, increasing it from 18 to 19 hours.

SHADOW PRICES. As Figure D.9 demonstrates, this change expands the feasible region, and the optimal solution changes from point C to point C'. Point C' is better in terms of Z because the added unit of a binding constraint will be used to make more product. To find the amount of improvement, we first find the new values of x_1 and x_2 by simultaneously solving the two binding constraints at point C', where

$$4x_1 + 6x_2 = 48 \text{ (extrusion)}$$
$$2x_1 + 2x_2 = 19 \text{ (packaging)}$$

The optimal values are $x_1 = 4.5$ and $x_2 = 5$, and the new Z value is $\$34(4.5) + \$40(5) = \$353$. Because the value of Z was $\$342$ with 18 hours of packaging, the value of one more hour of packaging is $\$11$ (or $\$353 - \$342$).

The change in Z per unit of change in the value of the right-hand-side parameter of a constraint is called the shadow price. The **shadow price** is the marginal *improvement* in Z (increase for maximization and decrease for minimization) caused by relaxing the constraint by one unit. Relaxation means making the constraint less restrictive, which involves increasing the right-hand side for a $\leq$ constraint or decreasing it for a $\geq$ constraint. The shadow price also is the marginal loss in Z caused by making the constraint more restrictive by one unit. In our example, the shadow price for the packaging resource is $\$11$ per hour. Thus, if scheduling additional packaging hours is possible, Stratton's management should be willing to pay a premium of up to $\$11$ per hour over and above the normal cost for a packaging hour. However, if capacity is cut by one hour, profits will fall by $\$11$.

RANGE OF FEASIBILITY. A lower limit and an upper limit define the **range of feasibility,** which is the interval over which the right-hand-side parameter can vary while its shadow price remains valid. If the right-hand side is increased beyond the upper limit or reduced beyond the lower limit, at least one other constraint becomes binding, which in turn alters the rate of change in Z. These two limits are established when, as the constraint line is relaxed or tightened, a new corner point on the feasible region is reached that makes a different constraint binding.

shadow price The marginal *improvement* in Z (increase for maximization and decrease for minimization) caused by relaxing the constraint by one unit.

range of feasibility The interval over which the right-hand-side parameter can vary while its shadow price remains valid.

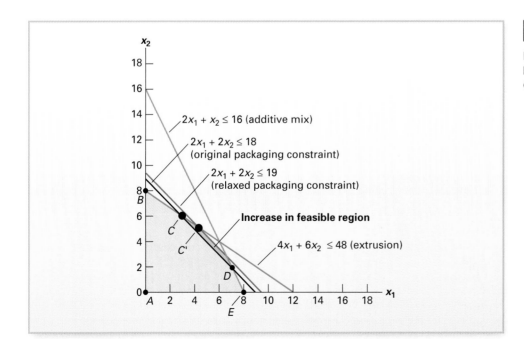

FIGURE D.9

Enlarging the Feasible Region by Relaxing the Packaging Constraint by One Hour

FIGURE D.10

Defining the Upper and
Lower Limits to Packaging's
Range of Feasibility

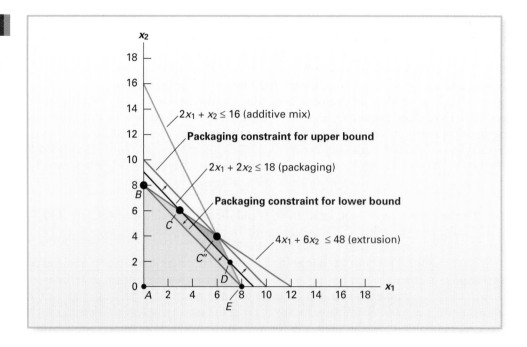

With 18 packaging hours, the optimal solution for the Stratton Company is $x_1 = 3$, $x_2 = 6$, 4 pounds of slack in the additive mix, and 0 slack for the other two constraints. We found that each additional packaging hour would increase profit by \$11 (minus any premium cost of adding this additional capacity). Similarly, one fewer packaging hour would reduce profits by \$11. However, \$11 is the shadow price over a limited range of packaging hours. Let us begin by finding the *upper* limit over which this shadow price is valid. Figure D.10 shows the packaging constraint being relaxed and shifted to the right, away from the origin. When it reaches point C'', where it intersects the extrusion and additive mix constraints, the additive mix constraint and the extrusion constraint become binding. Until the packaging constraint reaches C'', relaxing it will expand the feasible region, as shown by the pink shading in the feasible region. With this expansion comes the improvement in Z, which is \$11 per packaging hour added. However, any increase in packaging hours beyond what is used at point C'' will be worth \$0 because the constraint will no longer be binding.

To find how many hours are used at point C'', we solve the additive mix and extrusion constraints simultaneously because C'' lies at their intersection. Doing so, we get $x_1 = 6$ and $x_2 = 4$. Substituting these values into the packaging constraint, we find that the upper limit on the shadow price of \$11 is 20 packaging hours, or $2(6) + 2(4) = 20$.

EXAMPLE D.7   Finding the Lower Limit on the \$11 Shadow Price

What is the lower limit on the \$11 shadow price for packaging hours?

SOLUTION

Figure D.10 showed that reducing the packaging hours shifts the constraint to the left, toward the origin, reducing the feasible region and, thus, the value of Z. Eventually, the constraint reaches corner point B, defined by the extrusion constraint and the x_1 nonnegativity constraint. Because a new constraint is binding (the x_1 nonnegativity constraint), B defines the lower limit on packaging's shadow price. We found earlier that, at point B, $x_1 = 0$ and $x_2 = 8$. Substituting these values into the packaging constraint, we determine the *lower* limit on the shadow price of \$11 to be 16 packaging hours, or $2(0) + 2(8) = 16$.

In some cases, there may be no lower or upper limit to the range of feasibility. The additive mix constraint provides one example. Figure D.6 shows that this constraint is not binding. Shifting the constraint further upward does not expand the feasible region or improve Z. Thus, the shadow price of the additive mix is 0. The right-hand side can be increased without limit—to infinity—and the shadow price remains at 0.

The additive mix constraint illustrates a final principle that always holds: When a constraint's slack or surplus variable is greater than 0, its shadow price is 0. In every optimal solution, either a constraint's slack (or surplus) variable is 0 or its shadow price is 0. For the additive mix, with its shadow price of 0, there are 4 pounds of slack at the optimal point C. Because $x_1 = 3$ and $x_2 = 6$ at C, only $2(3) + 1(6) = 12$ pounds of the additive mix are needed. The slack is 4 pounds $(16 - 12)$ because 16 pounds of the mix are available.

COMPUTER SOLUTION

Most real-world linear programming problems are solved on a computer, so we concentrate here on understanding the use of linear programming and the logic on which it is based. The solution procedure in computer codes is some form of the **simplex method,** which is an iterative algebraic procedure for solving linear programming problems.

simplex method An iterative algebraic procedure for solving linear programming problems.

SIMPLEX METHOD

The graphic analysis gives insight into the logic of the simplex method, beginning with the focus on corner points. One corner point will always be the optimum, even when there are multiple optimal solutions. Thus, the simplex method starts with an initial corner point and then systematically evaluates other corner points in such a way that the objective function improves (or, at worst, stays the same) at each iteration. In the Stratton Company problem, an improvement would be an increase in profits. When no more improvements are possible, the optimal solution has been found.[1] The simplex method also helps generate the sensitivity analysis information that we developed graphically.

Each corner point has no more than m variables that are greater than 0, where m is the number of constraints (not counting the nonnegativity constraints). The m variables include slack and surplus variables, not just the original decision variables. Because of this property, we can find a corner point by simultaneously solving m constraints, where all but m variables are set equal to 0. For example, point B in Figure D.6 has three nonzero variables: x_2, the slack variable for packaging, and the slack variable for the additive mix. Their values can be found by solving simultaneously the three constraints, with x_1 and the slack variable for extrusion equal to 0. After finding this corner point, the simplex method applies information similar to the coefficient sensitivity to decide which new corner point to find next that gives an even better Z value. It continues in this way until no better corner point is possible. The final corner point evaluated is the optimal one.

COMPUTER OUTPUT

Computer programs dramatically reduce the amount of time required to solve linear programming problems. Special-purpose programs can be developed for applications that must be repeated frequently. Such programs simplify data input and generate the objective function and constraints for the problem. In addition, they can prepare customized managerial reports.

The capabilities and displays of software packages are not uniform. For example, OM Explorer can handle small- to medium-sized linear programming problems. It relies

---

[1]For more information on how to perform the simplex method manually, see Render, Stair, and Hanna (2003) or any other current textbook on management science.

on Microsoft's *Excel Solver* to find the optimal solutions, and, thus, Excel's "Solver Add-In" must be installed so that it is compatible with OM Explorer's linear programming spreadsheet. Solving linear programming problems with OM Explorer, rather than using Excel's Solver directly, is more convenient for two reasons. First, inputs are easily made and nonnegativity constraints need not be entered. Second, the output's interpretation and format corresponds exactly to the graphic analysis that we just presented. For other software for linear programming, see ILOG Optimization Suite (**www.ilog .com/products/optimization**), Lindo Systems (**www.lindo.com**), IBM's Optimization Subroutine Library (**www.research.ibm.com/osl**), FrontLine's Premium Solver Products for Microsoft Excel (**www.frontsys.com/xlprod.htm**), and Lionheart's latest linear programming software survey (**lionhrtpub.com/orms/surveys/LP/LP-survey.html**).

OM Explorer has three worksheets of output, which we illustrate for the Stratton Company. The output from the first two worksheets is shown in Figure D.11.

The *Inputs Worksheet* asks for the number of decision variables and constraints, and also whether it is a maximization or minimization problem. After making these inputs and clicking the Setup Problem button, the *Work Area Worksheet* is opened. The user may choose to enter labels for the decision variables, right-hand-side values, objective function, and constraints. Here, the first decision variable is labeled as "X1," the right-hand-side values as "RHV," the objective function as "Max-Z," and the extrusion constraint as "Extrusion." For convenience in specifying the type of constraint ($\leq$, $=$, or $\geq$), just enter "<" for a $\leq$ constraint and ">" for a $\geq$ constraint. Slack and surplus variables will be added automatically as needed. When all of the inputs are made, click the "Find Optimal Solution" button.

The *Results Worksheet,* shown in Figure D.12, gives the optimal solution for the Stratton Company problem. OM Explorer begins by showing the optimal values of the decision variables (X1 = 3.0000 and X2 = 6.0000), their objective function coefficients, and their coefficient sensitivities. There is a coefficient sensitivity number for each decision variable's objective function coefficient. Two tips on interpreting its value are

1. The sensitivity number is relevant only for a decision variable that is 0 in the optimal solution. If the decision variable is greater than 0, ignore the coefficient sensitivity number.

FIGURE D.11

Inputs Worksheet

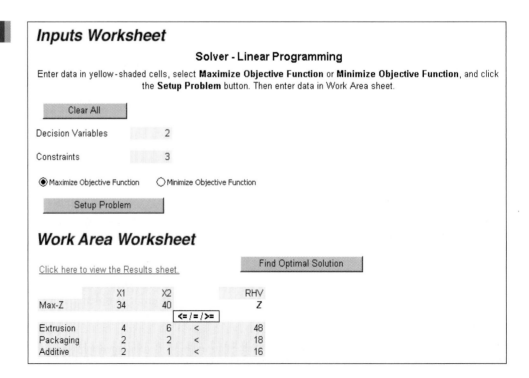

FIGURE D.12

Results Worksheet

Solution

Variable Label	Variable Value	Original Coefficient	Coefficient Sensitivity
X1	3.0000	34.0000	0
X2	6.0000	40.0000	0

Constraint Label	Original RHV	Slack or Surplus	Shadow Price
Extrusion	48	0	3.0000
Packaging	18	0	11.0000
Additive	16	4	0

Objective Function Value: 342

Sensitivity Analysis and Ranges

Objective Function Coefficients

Variable Label	Lower Limit	Original Coefficient	Upper Limit
X1	26.66666667	34	40
X2	34	40	51

Right-Hand-Side Values

Constraint Label	Lower Limit	Original Value	Upper Limit
Extrusion	40	48	54
Packaging	16	18	20
Additive	12	16	No Limit

2. OM Explorer reports the absolute value of the coefficient sensitivity number, ignoring any minus sign. Thus, the value always tells how much the objective function coefficient must *improve* (increase for maximization problems or decrease for minimization problems) before the optimal solution would change. At that point, the decision variable associated with the coefficient enters the optimal solution at some positive level. To learn the new solution, apply OM Explorer again with a coefficient improved by slightly more than the coefficient sensitivity number.

Thus, for the Stratton Company problem, the coefficient sensitivities provide no new insight because they are always 0 when decision variables have positive values in the optimal solution. Look instead at the lower and upper limits on the objective function coefficients, given in a following output section.

For the constraints, Figure D.12 shows the original right-hand-side values, the slack or surplus variables, and the shadow prices. There is a shadow price for each right-hand-side value or, more specifically, the constraint's slack or surplus variable. Two tips on interpreting its value follow:

1. The number is relevant only for a binding constraint, where the slack or surplus variable is 0 in the optimal solution. For a nonbinding constraint, the shadow price is 0.

2. OM Explorer reports the absolute value of the shadow price numbers, ignoring any minus sign. Thus, the value always tells how much the objective function's Z value *improves* (increases for maximization problems or decreases for minimization problems) by "relaxing" the constraint by one unit. Relaxing means increasing the right-hand-side value for a $\leq$ constraint or decreasing it for a $\geq$ constraint. The shadow price can also be interpreted as the marginal loss (or penalty) in Z caused by making the constraint more restrictive by one unit.

Thus, for the Stratton Company problem, there are 4 pounds of the additive mix slack, so the shadow price is 0. Packaging, on the other hand, is a binding constraint because it has no slack. The shadow price of one more packaging hour is $11.

Finally, at the end of the top half of the output (as shown in Figure D.12), OM Explorer reports the optimal objective function Z value as $342. All output confirms our earlier calculations and the graphic analysis.

The bottom half of the *Results Worksheet*, shown in Figure D.12, begins with the range over which the objective function coefficients can vary without changing the optimal values of the decision variables. Note that c_1, which currently has a value of $34, has a range of optimality from $26.67 to $40. The objection function's Z value would change with coefficient changes over this range, but the optimal values of the decision variables remain the same. Finally, OM Explorer reports the range of feasibility, over which the right-hand-side parameters can range without changing the shadow prices. For example, the $11 shadow price for packaging is valid over the range from 16 to 20 hours. Again, these findings are identical to the sensitivity analysis done graphically. The difference is that OM Explorer can handle more than two decision variables (up to 99) and can be solved much more quickly.

The number of variables in the optimal solution (counting the decision variables, slack variables, and surplus variables) that are greater than 0 never exceeds the number of constraints. Such is the case for the Stratton Company problem, where there are three constraints (not counting the implicit nonnegativity constraints) and three nonzero variables in the optimal solution (X1, X2, and the additive mix slack variable). On some rare occasions, the number of nonzero variables in the optimal solution can be less than the number of constraints—a condition called **degeneracy**. When degeneracy occurs, the sensitivity analysis information is suspect. Ignore the sensitivity analysis portion of the OM Explorer's output that is suspect. If you want more "what-if" information, simply run OM Explorer again using the new parameter values that you want to investigate.

degeneracy A condition that occurs when the number of nonzero variables in the optimal solution is less than the number of constraints.

EXAMPLE D.8   Using Shadow Prices for Decision Making

The Stratton Company needs answers to three important questions: Would increasing capacities in the extrusion or packaging area pay if it cost an extra $8 per hour over and above the normal costs already reflected in the objective function coefficients? Would increasing packaging capacity pay if it cost an additional $6 per hour? Would buying more raw materials pay?

SOLUTION

Expanding extrusion capacity would cost a premium of $8 per hour, but the shadow price for that capacity is only $3 per hour. However, expanding packaging hours would cost only $6 per hour more than the price reflected in the objective function, and the shadow price is $11 per hour. Finally, buying more raw materials would not pay because there is already a surplus of 4 pounds; the shadow price is 0 for that resource.

DECISION POINT   Management decided to increase its packaging hours capacity but not to expand extrusion capacity or buy more raw materials.

APPLICATIONS

Many problems in operations management, and in other functional areas, have been modeled as linear programming problems. Knowing how to formulate a problem generally, the decision maker can then adapt it to the situation at hand.

The following list identifies some problems that can be solved with linear programming. The review problems at the end of this supplement and at the end of other chapters illustrate many of these types of problems.

- **Aggregate Planning**
  Production. Find the minimum-cost production schedule, taking into account hiring and layoffs, inventory carrying, overtime, and subcontracting costs, subject to various capacity and policy constraints.
  Staffing. Find the optimal staffing levels for various categories of workers, subject to various demand and policy constraints.
  Blends. Find the optimal proportions of various ingredients used to make products, such as gasoline, paints, and food, subject to certain minimal requirements.
- **Distribution**
  Shipping. Find the optimal shipping assignments from factories to distribution centers or from warehouses to retailers.
- **Inventory**
  Stock Control. Determine the optimal mix of products to hold in inventory in a warehouse.
  Supplier Selection. Find the optimal combination of suppliers to minimize the amount of unwanted inventory.
- **Location**
  Plants or Warehouses. Determine the optimal location of a plant or warehouse, with respect to total transportation costs between various alternative locations and existing supply and demand sources.
- **Process Management**
  Stock Cutting. Given the dimensions of a roll or sheet of raw material, find the cutting pattern that minimizes the amount of scrap material.
- **Scheduling**
  Shifts. Determine the minimum-cost assignment of workers to shifts, subject to varying demand.
  Vehicles. Assign vehicles to products or customers and determine the number of trips to make, subject to vehicle size, vehicle availability, and demand constraints.
  Routing. Find the optimal routing of a service or product through several sequential processes, with each having its own capacity and other characteristics.

SUPPLEMENT HIGHLIGHTS

- Linear programming is an effective tool for solving complex resource allocation problems when the objective and constraints can be approximated by linear equations. Skill and creativity often are required to model a situation with a set of linear equations. After the model has been formulated, one of several available computer programs may be used to identify the optimal solution.

- Although only simple linear programming problems can be solved by using graphic analysis, the technique provides valuable insight into the way optimal solutions to complex problems are generated.

- In addition to identifying the optimal combination of decision variables, analysis of the solution will determine shadow price, coefficient sensitivity, and ranging information. Shadow prices are the values of additional resources. Coefficient sensitivity indicates the penalties associated with nonoptimal solutions. Ranging describes either how much coefficients can change without invalidating the solution or how much of a resource can be acquired without changing the value of its shadow price.

STUDENT CD-ROM AND INTERNET RESOURCES

The Student CD-ROM and the Companion Website at **www.prenhall.com/krajewski** contain many tools, activities, and resources designed for this supplement. The following items are recommended to enhance your skills and improve your understanding of the material in this supplement.

STUDENT CD-ROM RESOURCES

➤ **PowerPoint Slides:** View the comprehensive set of slides customized for this supplement's concepts and techniques.
➤ **OM Explorer Tutors:** OM Explorer contains four tutor spreadsheets to help you learn about plotting constraints, finding the optimal solution, finding slack, and graphic and algebraic solutions. See Supplement D in the OM Explorer menu.
➤ **OM Explorer Solvers:** OM Explorer contains one spreadsheet designed to solve general linear programming problems and one spreadsheet for the solution of transportation problems. See Linear Programming and

Location/Transportation Method in the OM Explorer menu for these routines.
➤ **Active Model:** There is an active model spreadsheet that provides many insights on graphic analysis and sensitivity analysis. See Linear Programming in the Active Models menu for this routine.

INTERNET RESOURCES

➤ **Self-Study Quizzes:** See the compendium of true or false, multiple choice, and essay questions that give you feedback on how well you have mastered the concepts of this supplement.
➤ **In the News:** See the articles that apply to this supplement.
➤ **Internet Exercises:** Try out the exercises available on various aspects of linear programming.
➤ **Virtual Tours:** See the "Web Links to Company Facility Tours" for various tours of company facilities.

KEY TERMS

binding constraint 634
certainty 625
coefficient sensitivity 637
constraints 624
corner point 630
decision variables 624
degeneracy 644
feasible region 624

graphic method of linear
    programming 627
linear programming 624
linearity 625
nonnegativity 625
objective function 624
parameter 624
product-mix problem 625

range of feasibility 639
range of optimality 636
shadow price 639
simplex method 641
slack 634
surplus 634

SOLVED PROBLEM I

TUTOR D.4

Tutor D.4 on the Student CD-ROM provides a practice example for finding the graphic and algebraic solution.

O'Connel Airlines is considering air service from its hub of operations in Cicely, Alaska, to Rome, Wisconsin, and Seattle, Washington. O'Connel has one gate at the Cicely Airport. which operates 12 hours per day. Each flight requires 1 hour of gate time. Each flight to Rome consumes 15 hours of pilot crew time and is expected to produce a profit of $2,500. Serving Seattle uses 10 hours of pilot crew time per flight and will result in a profit of $2,000 per flight. Pilot crew labor is limited to 150 hours per day. The market for service to Rome is limited to nine flights per day.

    a. Use the graphic method of linear programming to maximize profits for O'Connel Airlines.
    b. Identify slack and surplus constraints, if any.
    c. Find the range of optimality for c_1, the profit per flight to Rome.
    d. Chris Hoover says that radio advertising would increase the demand for travel to Rome. What is the value of increasing demand (relaxing the market constraint) by one flight to Rome?
    e. By how much would O'Connel's objective function increase if the Cicely Airport operated an extra hour per day? Would increased hours of operation result in increased service to Rome, Seattle, or both?
    f. Maurice Foster strongly voices his opinion that O'Connel would benefit from hiring additional experienced pilots. What is the value of one additional hour of flight crew resources? What is the upper limit on the range of feasibility for flight crew time?

SOLUTION

a. The objective function is to maximize profits, Z:

$$\text{Maximize: } \$2,500x_1 + \$2,000x_2 = Z$$

where

x_1 = number of flights per day to Rome, Wisconsin
x_2 = number of flights per day to Seattle, Washington

The constraints are

$$x_1 + x_2 \leq 12 \text{ (gate capacity)}$$
$$15x_1 + 10x_2 \leq 150 \text{ (labor)}$$
$$x_1 \leq 9 \text{ (market)}$$
$$x_1 \geq 0 \quad \text{and} \quad x_2 \geq 0$$

A careful drawing of iso-profit lines parallel to the one shown in Figure D.13 will indicate that point D is the optimal solution. It is at the intersection of the labor and gate capacity constraints. Solving algebraically, we get

$$15x_1 + 10x_2 = 150 \text{ (labor)}$$
$$\frac{-10x_1 - 10x_2}{5x_1 + 0x_2} = \frac{-120}{30} \text{ (gate} \times -10)$$
$$x_1 = 6$$
$$6 + x_2 = 12 \text{ (gate)}$$
$$x_2 = 6$$

The maximum profit results from making six flights to Rome and six flights to Seattle:

$$\$2,500(6) + \$2,000(6) = \$27,000$$

b. The market constraint has three units of slack, so the demand for flights to Rome is not fully met:

$$x_1 \leq 9$$
$$x_1 + s_3 = 9$$
$$6 + s_3 = 9$$
$$s_3 = 3$$

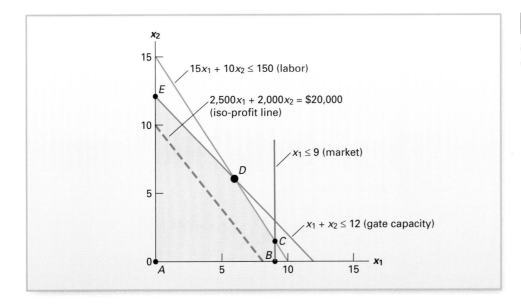

FIGURE D.13

Graphic Solution for O'Connel Airlines

c. Point D remains optimal as long as the objective function slope $(-c_1/c_2)$ is between $-3/2$, the slope of the labor constraint, and -1.00, the slope of the gate capacity constraint, or

$$-\frac{3}{2} \le -\frac{c_1}{c_2} \le -1$$

Holding c_2 constant at 2,000 yields

$$-\frac{3}{2} \le -\frac{c_1}{2,000} \le -1$$

and multiplying by $-2,000$ gives

$$3,000 \ge c_1 \ge 2,000 \quad \text{or} \quad 2,000 \le c_1 \le 3,000$$

d. As the market constraint already has slack, the optimal solution would not improve with an increase in demand for service to Rome.

e. Figure D.14 shows what would happen if the gate were open for 13 hours instead of 12 hours. One increased hour of operation would increase service to Seattle from six to nine flights, but it would decrease service to Rome from six to four flights. The intersecting constraints are

$$x_1 + x_2 \le \ 13 \text{ (gate capacity)}$$
$$15x_1 + 10x_2 \le 150 \text{ (labor)}$$

Solving algebraically, we have

$$15x_1 + 10x_2 = 150 \text{ (labor)}$$
$$\underline{-10x_1 - 10x_2 = 130} \text{ (gate} \times -10)$$
$$5x_1 + 0x_2 = 20$$
$$x_1 = 4$$
$$4 + x_2 = 13 \text{ (\textbf{gate})}$$
$$x_2 = 9$$

The objective function would be $\$2,500(4) + \$2,000(9) = \$28,000$, an increase of $\$1,000$ over the previous solution. The shadow price for gate capacity is $\$1,000$ per hour.

f. The intersecting constraints are

$$x_1 + \ x_2 \le 12 \text{ (gate capacity)}$$
$$15x_1 + 10x_2 \le 151 \text{ (labor)}$$

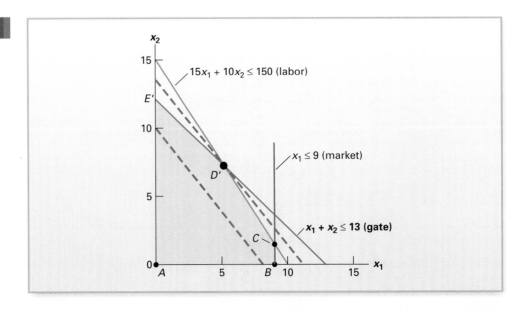

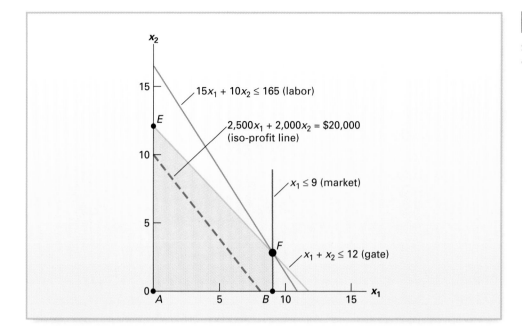

Solving algebraically, we get

$$15x_1 + 10x_2 = 151 \text{ (labor)}$$
$$\underline{-10x_1 - 10x_2 = -120} \text{ (gate} \times -10)$$
$$5x_1 + 0x_2 = 31$$
$$x_1 = 6.2$$
$$6.2 + x_2 = 12 \text{ (gate)}$$
$$x_2 = 5.8$$

The objective function would be \$2,500(6.2) + \$2,000(5.8) = \$27,100, an increase of \$100 over the previous solution. The shadow price for flight crew time is \$100 per hour. Increasing flight crew time would increase service to Rome and decrease service to Seattle. However, a one-hour change in flight crew time does not result in an integer change in the number of flights.

As more hours of flight crew time become available, the optimal solution shifts toward point F. Eventually, as Figure D.15 shows, the market limit on flights to Rome (≤ 9) will bind the solution. Point F is at the intersection of the market and gate constraints, located at (9, 3). You may prove this result by algebraically solving for the intersection of those two constraints. Now we find the labor constraint that will also go through that point. When $x_1 = 9$ and $x_2 = 3$,

$$15x_1 + 10x_2 = 15(9) + 10(3) = 165$$

The labor constraint that passes through point (9, 3) is

$$15x_1 + 10x_2 \leq 165$$

The right-hand side of the labor constraint has increased by $165 - 150 = 15$ hours. Therefore, 15 more flight crew hours would improve the solution by (15)(\$100 shadow price) = \$1,500. Beyond this point, additional flight crew time would merely become a slack resource and not further improve the solution.

SOLVED PROBLEM 2

Holling desires to minimize the cost of preparing at least 750 hors d'oeuvres for a celebration. Holling is considering two recipes: Dave's crab cakes (x_1) and Shelly's seafood surprise (x_2). The cost per unit is \$0.30 for the crab cakes and \$0.20 for the seafood surprise. Holling has a

FIGURE D.16

Graphic Solution for Holling

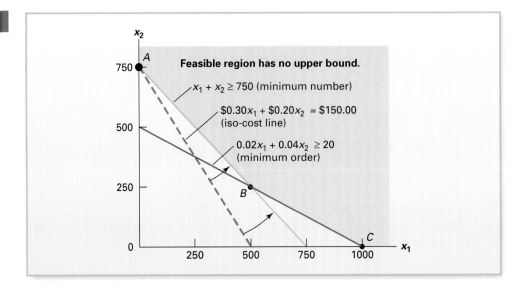

good supply of Alaskan king crab but must order at least 20 pounds at a time to obtain it at a reasonable price. The crab cake recipe requires 0.02 pound of crabmeat per unit. Seafood surprise requires 0.04 pound per unit. Because of crabmeat's short shelf life, Holling wants to use an entire order of crabmeat in preparing the hors d'oeuvres. Again, at least 20 pounds of crabmeat must be consumed.

  a. Use the graphic method of linear programming to minimize Holling's costs.
  b. Use coefficient sensitivity to determine the value of c_1, the cost of crab cakes, that would bring x_1 into the solution (make x_1 greater than 0).

SOLUTION

  a. The graphic solution (Figure D.16) shows that the optimal solution occurs at point A. Thus, 750 units of Shelly's seafood surprise and no crab cakes would be produced.
  b. The per-unit cost of crab cakes would have to be reduced to $0.20 to bring x_1 into the optimal solution. Improving c_1 results in a counterclockwise rotation of the iso-cost line. The objective function becomes parallel to the quantity constraint (at least 750 hors d'oeuvres produced). The slope of that constraint is -1.00. Solving for the value of c_1 that makes the objective function slope, $-c_1/c_2$, equal to -1.00 yields

$$-\frac{c_1}{c_2} = -1.00$$

$$-\frac{c_1}{\$0.20} = -1.00$$

$$c_1 = \$0.20$$

The coefficient sensitivity equals the difference between this value and the current value of c_1: $\$0.30 - \$0.20 = \$0.10$. In other words, forcing the production of one crab cake into the solution incurs a penalty of $0.10.

DISCUSSION QUESTIONS

  1. A company wants to use linear programming for production planning but finds that the cost of firing workers is not linear. Rather, it is approximated by the equation

$$\text{Firing cost} = \$4,000F^{1.25}$$

where F is the number of workers fired during a month. How could this relation be modified to permit linear program formulation and modeling of this situation?

2. A particular linear programming maximization problem has the following less-than-or-equal-to constraints: (1) raw materials, (2) labor hours, and (3) storage space. The optimal solution occurs at the intersection of the raw materials and labor hours constraints, so those constraints are binding. Management is considering whether to authorize over-time. What useful information could the linear programming solution provide to management in making this decision? Suppose a warehouse becomes available for rent at bargain rates. What would management need to know in order to decide whether to rent the warehouse? How could the linear programming model be helpful?

PROBLEMS

An icon next to a problem identifies the software that can be helpful, and in some cases is mandatory. The software is available on the Student CD-ROM that is packaged with every new copy of the textbook.

1. ⬛ **OM Explorer** The Really Big Shoe is a manufacturer of basketball and football shoes. Ed Sullivan, the manager of marketing, must decide the best way to spend advertising resources. Each football team sponsored requires 120 pairs of shoes. Each basketball team requires 32 pairs of shoes. Football coaches receive $300,000 for shoe sponsorship, and basketball coaches receive $1,000,000. Sullivan's promotional budget is $30,000,000. The Really Big Shoe has a limited supply (4 liters or 4000 cubic centimeters) of flubber, a rare and costly compound used in promotional athletic shoes. Each pair of basketball shoes requires 3 cc of flubber, and each pair of football shoes requires 1 cc. Sullivan wants to sponsor as many basketball and football teams as resources allow.

  a. Create a set of linear equations to describe the objective function and the constraints.

  b. Use graphic analysis to find the visual solution.

  c. What is the maximum number of each type of team The Really Big Shoe can sponsor?

2. A business student at Nowledge College must complete a total of 65 courses to graduate. The number of business courses must be greater than or equal to 23. The number of nonbusiness courses must be greater than or equal to 20. The average business course requires a textbook costing $60 and 120 hours of study. Nonbusiness courses require a textbook costing $24 and 200 hours of study. The student has $3,000 to spend on books.

  a. Create a set of linear equations to describe the objective function and the constraints.

  b. Use graphic analysis to find the visual solution.

  c. What combination of business and nonbusiness courses minimizes total hours of study?

  d. Identify the slack or surplus variables.

3. In Problem 2, suppose that the objective is to minimize the cost of books and that the student's total study time is limited to 12,600 hours.

  a. Use graphic analysis to determine the combination of courses that minimizes the total cost of books.

  b. Identify the slack or surplus variables.

4. Mile-High Microbrewery makes a light beer and a dark beer. Mile-High has a limited supply of barley, limited bottling capacity, and a limited market for light beer.

Profits are $0.20 per bottle of light beer and $0.50 per bottle of dark beer.

  a. The following table shows resource availability of products at the Mile-High Microbrewery. Use the graphic method of linear programming to maximize profits. How many bottles of each product should be produced per month?

	Product		
Resource	Light Beer (x_1)	Dark Beer (x_2)	Resource Availability (per month)
Barley	0.1 gram	0.6 gram	2,000 grams
Bottling	1 bottle	1 bottle	6,000 bottles
Market	1 bottle	—	4,000 bottles

  b. Identify any constraints with slack or surplus.

  c. Find the range of optimality for c_2, the profit per bottle of dark beer.

  d. Beth Richards says that sponsoring sporting events would increase the demand for Mile-High's light beer. What is the value of increasing demand for light beer?

  e. Jorge Gallegos suggests that the bottling constraint could be alleviated by subcontracting for additional bottling capacity. By how much would Mile-High's objective function increase if bottling capacity increased by one bottle per month? Would increased hours of operation result in increased production of light beer, dark beer, or both?

  f. What is the upper limit on the range of feasibility for bottling capacity?

5. The plant manager of a plastic pipe manufacturer has the opportunity to use two different routings for a particular type of plastic pipe. Routing 1 uses extruder A, and routing 2 uses extruder B. Both routings require the same melting process. The following table shows the time requirements and capacities of these processes:

	Time Requirements (hr/100 ft)		
Process	Routing 1	Routing 2	Capacity (hr)
Melting	1	1	45
Extruder A	3	0	90
Extruder B	0	1	160

Each 100 feet of pipe processed on routing 1 uses 5 pounds of raw material, whereas each 100 feet of pipe processed on routing 2 uses only 4 pounds. This difference results from differing scrap rates of the extruding machines. Consequently, the profit per 100 feet of pipe processed on routing 1 is $60 and on routing 2 is $80. A total of 200 pounds of raw material is available.

a. Create a set of linear equations to describe the objective function and the constraints.

b. Use graphic analysis to find the visual solution.

c. What is the maximum profit?

d. Use coefficient sensitivity to determine the value of c_1, the profit per unit processed on routing 1, that would bring x_1 into the solution (make x_1 greater than 0).

6. A manufacturer of textile dyes can use two different processing routings for a particular type of dye. Routing 1 uses drying press A, and routing 2 uses drying press B. Both routings require the same mixing vat to blend chemicals for the dye before drying. The following table shows the time requirements and capacities of these processes:

Time Requirements (hr/kg)

Process	Routing 1	Routing 2	Capacity (hr)
Mixing	2	2	54
Dryer A	6	0	120
Dryer B	0	8	180

Each kilogram of dye processed on routing 1 uses 20 liters of chemicals, whereas each kilogram of dye processed on routing 2 uses only 15 liters. The difference results from differing yield rates of the drying presses. Consequently, the profit per kilogram processed on routing 1 is $50 and on routing 2 is $65. A total of 450 liters of input chemicals is available.

a. Write the constraints and objective function to maximize profits.

b. Use the graphic method of linear programming to find the optimal solution.

c. Identify any constraints with slack or surplus.

d. What is the value of an additional hour of mixing time? What is the upper limit of the range for which this shadow price is valid?

7. **OM Explorer** The Trim-Look Company makes several lines of skirts, dresses, and sport coats. Recently, a consultant suggested that the company reevaluate its South Islander line and allocate its resources to products that would maximize contribution to profits and to overhead. Each product requires the same polyester fabric and must pass through the cutting and sewing departments. The following data were collected for the study:

Processing Time (hr)

Product	Cutting	Sewing	Material (yd)
Skirt	1	1	1
Dress	3	4	1
Sport coat	4	6	4

The cutting department has 100 hours of capacity, sewing has 180 hours of capacity, and 60 yards of material are available. Each skirt contributes $5 to profits and overhead; each dress, $17; and each sport coat, $30.

a. Specify the objective function and constraints for this problem.

b. Use a computer package to solve the problem.

8. **OM Explorer** Consider Problem 7 further.

a. How much would you be willing to pay for an extra hour of cutting time? For an extra hour of sewing time? For an extra yard of material? Explain your response to each question.

b. Determine the range of right-hand-side values over which the shadow price would be valid for the cutting constraint and for the material constraint.

9. **OM Explorer** Polly Astaire makes fine clothing for big and tall men. A few years ago Astaire entered the sportswear market with the Sunset line of shorts, pants, and shirts. Management wants to make the amount of each product that will maximize profits. Each type of clothing is routed through two departments, A and B. The relevant data for each product are as follows:

Processing Time (hr)

Product	Department A	Department B	Material (yd)
Shirt	2	1	2
Shorts	2	3	1
Pants	3	4	4

Department A has 120 hours of capacity, department B has 160 hours of capacity, and 90 yards of material are available. Each shirt contributes $10 to profits and overhead; each pair of shorts, $10; and each pair of pants, $23.

a. Specify the objective function and constraints for this problem.

b. Use a computer package to solve the problem.

c. How much should Astaire be willing to pay for an extra hour of department A capacity? How much for an extra hour of department B capacity? For what range of right-hand values are these shadow prices valid?

10. **OM Explorer** The Butterfield Company makes a variety of hunting knives. Each knife is processed on four machines. The processing times required are as follows. Machine capacities (in hours) are 1,500 for machine 1, 1,400 for machine 2, 1,600 for machine 3, and 1,500 for machine 4.

Processing Time (hr)

Knife	Machine 1	Machine 2	Machine 3	Machine 4
A	0.05	0.10	0.15	0.05
B	0.15	0.10	0.05	0.05
C	0.20	0.05	0.10	0.20
D	0.15	0.10	0.10	0.10
E	0.05	0.10	0.10	0.05

Each product contains a different amount of two basic raw materials. Raw material 1 costs $0.50 per ounce, and raw material 2 costs $1.50 per ounce. There are 75,000 ounces of raw material 1 and 100,000 ounces of raw material 2 available.

Requirements (oz/unit)

Knife	Raw Material 1	Raw Material 2	Selling Price ($/unit)
A	4	2	15.00
B	6	8	25.50
C	1	3	14.00
D	2	5	19.50
E	6	10	27.00

a. If the objective is to maximize profit, specify the objective function and constraints for the problem. Assume that labor costs are negligible.

b. Solve the problem with a computer package.

11. **OM Explorer** The Nutmeg Corporation produces five different nut and mixed nut products: almond pack, walnut pack, gourmet pack, fancy pack, and thrifty pack. Each product (individual or mix) comes in a one-pound can. The firm can purchase almonds at $0.80 per pound, walnuts at $0.60 per pound, and peanuts at $0.35 per pound. Peanuts are used to complete each mix, and the company has an unlimited supply of them. The supply of almonds and walnuts is limited. The company can buy up to 3,000 pounds of almonds and 2,000 pounds of walnuts. The resource requirements and forecasted demand for the products follow. Use a computer package to solve this problem.

Minimum Requirements (%)

Product	Almonds	Walnuts	Demand (cans)
Almonds	100	—	1,250
Walnuts	—	100	750
Gourmet	45	45	1,000
Fancy	30	30	500
Thrifty	20	20	1,500

a. What mix minimizes the cost of meeting the demand for all five products?

b. What is the impact on the product mix if only 2,000 pounds of peanuts are available?

c. What is the impact on the product mix if the gourmet pack requires 50 percent almonds and 50 percent walnuts?

d. What is the impact on the product mix if demand for the fancy pack doubles?

12. **OM Explorer** A problem often of concern to managers in processing industries is blending. Consider the task facing Lisa Rankin, procurement manager of a company that manufactures special additives. She must determine the proper amount of each raw material to purchase for the production of a certain product. Each gallon of the finished product must have a combustion point of at least 220°F. In addition, the product's gamma content (which causes hydrocarbon pollution) cannot exceed 6 percent of volume, and the product's zeta content (which cleans the internal moving parts of engines) must be at least 12 percent by volume. Three raw materials are available. Each raw material has a different rating on these characteristics.

	Raw Material		
Characteristic	A	B	C
Combustion point (°F)	200	180	280
Gamma content (%)	4	3	10
Zeta content (%)	20	10	8

Raw material A costs $0.60 per gallon; raw materials B and C cost $0.40 and $0.50 per gallon, respectively. The procurement manager wants to minimize the cost of raw materials per gallon of product. Use linear programming to find the optimal proportion of each raw material for a gallon of finished product. (*Hint:* Express the decision variables in terms of fractions of a gallon; the sum of the fractions must equal 1.00.)

13. **OM Explorer** A small fabrication firm makes three basic types of components for use by other companies. Each component is processed on three machines. The processing times follow. Total capacities (in hours) are 1,600 for machine 1, 1,400 for machine 2, and 1,500 for machine 3.

Processing Time (hr)

Component	Machine 1	Machine 2	Machine 3
A	0.25	0.10	0.05
B	0.20	0.15	0.10
C	0.10	0.05	0.15

Each component contains a different amount of two basic raw materials. Raw material 1 costs $0.20 per ounce, and raw material 2 costs $0.35 per ounce. There are 200,000 ounces of raw material 1 and 85,000 ounces of raw material 2 available.

Requirement (oz/unit)

Component	Raw Material 1	Raw Material 2	Selling Price ($/unit)
A	32	12	40
B	26	16	28
C	19	9	24

a. Assume that the company must make at least 1,200 units of component B, that labor costs are negligible, and that the objective is to maximize profits. Specify the objective function and constraints for the problem.

b. Use a computer package to solve the problem.

14. The following is a linear programming model for analyzing the product mix of Maxine's Hat Company, which produces three hat styles:

Maximize: $\$7x_1 + \$5x_2 + \$2x_3 = Z$

Subject to:
$$3x_1 + 5x_2 + x_3 \leq 150 \text{ (machine A time)}$$
$$5x_1 + 3x_2 + 2x_3 \leq 100 \text{ (machine B time)}$$
$$x_1 + 2x_2 + x_3 \leq 160 \text{ (machine C time)}$$
$$x_1 \geq 0, \quad x_2 \geq 0, \quad \text{and} \quad x_3 \geq 0$$

The OM Explorer printout in Figure D.17 shows the optimal solution to the problem. Consider each of the following statements independently, and state whether it is true or false. Explain each answer.

a. If the price of hat 3 were increased to $2.50, it would be part of the optimal product mix.

b. The capacity of machine C can be reduced to 65 hours without affecting profits.

c. If machine A had a capacity of 170 hours, the production output would remain unchanged.

15. ◗ **OM Explorer** The Washington Chemical Company produces chemicals and solvents for the glue industry. The production process is divided into several "focused factories," each producing a specific set of products. The time has come to prepare the production plan for one of the focused factories. This particular factory produces five products, which must pass through both the reactor and the separator. Each product also requires a certain combination of raw materials. Production data are shown in Table D.1.

The Washington Chemical Company has a long-term contract with a major glue manufacturer that requires annual production of 3,000 pounds of both products 3 and 4. More of these products could be produced because there is a demand for them.

FIGURE D.17   **OM Explorer Solver Output for Maxine's Hat Company**

Solution

Variable Label	Variable Value	Original Coefficient	Coefficient Sensitivity
X1	3.1250	7.0000	0
X2	28.1250	5.0000	0
X3	0.0000	2.0000	0.7500

Constraint Label	Original RHV	Slack or Surplus	Shadow Price
Machine A	150	0	0.2500
Machine B	100	0	1.2500
Machine C	160	100.6250	0

Objective Function Value:			162.5

Sensitivity Analysis and Ranges

Objective Function Coefficients

Variable Label	Lower Limit	Original Coefficient	Upper Limit
X1	5.2857	7	8.3333
X2	4.2000	5	11.6667
X3	No Limit	2	2.75

Right-Hand-Side Values

Constraint Label	Lower Limit	Original Value	Upper Limit
Machine A	60	150	166.6667
Machine B	90	100	250
Machine C	59.3750	160	No Limit

TABLE D.1
PRODUCTION DATA FOR WASHINGTON CHEMICAL

Resource	Product 1	2	3	4	5	Total Resources Available
Reactor (hr/lb)	0.05	0.10	0.80	0.57	0.15	7,500 hr*
Separator (hr/lb)	0.20	0.02	0.20	0.09	0.30	7,500 hr*
Raw material 1 (lb)	0.20	0.50	0.10	0.40	0.18	10,000 lb
Raw material 2 (lb)	—	0.70	—	0.50	—	6,000 lb
Raw material 3 (lb)	0.10	0.20	0.40	—	—	7,000 lb
Profit contribution ($/lb)	4.00	7.00	3.50	4.00	5.70	

*The total time available has been adjusted to account for setups. The five products have a prescribed sequence owing to the cost of changeovers between products. The company has a 35-day cycle (or 10 changeovers per year per product). Consequently, the time for these changeovers has been deducted from the total time available for these machines.

a. Determine the annual production quantity of each product that maximizes contribution to profits. Assume the company can sell all it can produce.

b. Specify the lot size for each product.

16. **OM Explorer** The Warwick Manufacturing Company produces shovels for industrial and home use. Sales of the shovels are seasonal, and Warwick's customers refuse to stockpile them during slack periods. In other words, the customers want to minimize inventory, insist on shipments according to their schedules, and will not accept backorders.

   Warwick employs manual, unskilled laborers who require only very basic training. Producing 1,000 shovels costs $3,500 on regular time and $3,700 on overtime. These amounts include materials, which account for over 85 percent of the cost. Overtime is limited to production of 15,000 shovels per quarter. In addition, subcontractors can be hired at $4,200 per thousand shovels, but Warwick's labor contract restricts this type of production to 5,000 shovels per quarter.

   The current level of inventory is 30,000 shovels, and management wants to end the year at that level. Holding 1,000 shovels in inventory costs $280 per quarter. The latest annual demand forecast is

Quarter	Demand
1	70,000
2	150,000
3	320,000
4	100,000
Totals	640,000

   Build a linear programming model to determine the *best* regular-time capacity plan. Assume that

   • the firm has 30 workers now, and management wants to have the same number in quarter 4,

   • each worker can produce 4,000 shovels per quarter, and

   • hiring a worker costs $1,000, and laying off a worker costs $600.

17. **OM Explorer** The management of Warwick Manufacturing Company is willing to give price breaks to its customers as an incentive to purchase shovels in advance of the traditional seasons. Warwick's sales and marketing staff estimates that the demand for shovels resulting from the price breaks would be

Quarter	Demand	Original Demand
1	120,000	70,000
2	180,000	150,000
3	180,000	320,000
4	160,000	100,000
Totals	640,000	640,000

   Calculate the optimal production plan (including the workforce staffing plan) under the new demand schedule. Compare it to the optimal production plan under the original demand schedule. Evaluate the potential effects of demand management.

18. The Bull Grin Company produces a feed supplement for animal foods produced by a number of companies. Sales are seasonal, and Bull Grin's customers refuse to stockpile the supplement during slack sales periods. In other words, the customers want to minimize inventory, insist on shipments according to their schedules, and will not accept backorders.

   Bull Grin employs manual, unskilled laborers who require little or no training. Producing 1,000 pounds of supplement costs $810 on regular time and $900 on overtime. These amounts include materials, which account for over 80 percent of the cost. Overtime is limited to production of 30,000 pounds per quarter. In addition, subcontractors can be hired at $1,100 per thousand pounds, but only 10,000 pounds per quarter can be produced this way.

   The current level of inventory is 40,000 pounds, and management wants to end the year at that level. Holding 1,000 pounds of feed supplement in inventory costs $110 per quarter. The latest annual forecast follows:

Quarter	Demand (lb)
1	100,000
2	410,000
3	770,000
4	440,000
Total	1,720,000

   The firm currently has 180 workers, a number that management wants to keep in quarter 4. Each worker can produce 2,000 pounds per quarter, so regular-time production costs $1,620 per worker. Idle workers must be paid at that same rate. Hiring one worker costs $1,000, and laying off a worker costs $600.

   Write the objective function and constraints describing this production planning problem after fully defining the decision variables.

19. Insight Traders, Inc. invests in various types of securities. The firm has $5 million for immediate investment and wants to maximize the interest earned over the next year. Four investment possibilities are presented in the following table. To further structure the portfolio, the board of directors has specified that at least 40 percent of the investment must be in corporate bonds and common stock. Furthermore, no more than 20 percent of the investment may be in real estate.

Investment	Expected Interest Earned (%)
Corporate bonds	8.5
Common stock	9.0
Gold certificates	10.0
Real estate	13.0

   Write the objective function and constraints for this portfolio investment problem after fully defining the decision variables.

20. JPMorgan Chase has a scheduling problem. Operators work eight-hour shifts and can begin work at midnight. 4 A.M., 8 A.M., noon, 4 P.M., or 8 P.M. Operators are needed to satisfy the following demand pattern. Formulate a linear programming model to cover the demand requirements with the minimum number of operators.

Time Period	Operators Needed
Midnight to 4 A.M.	4
4 A.M. to 8 A.M.	6
8 A.M. to noon	90
Noon to 4 P.M.	85
4 P.M. to 8 P.M.	55
8 P.M. to 12 midnight	20

SELECTED REFERENCES

Asim, R., E. De Falomir, and L. Lasdon. "An Optimization-Based Decision Support System for a Product-Mix Problem." *Interfaces*, vol. 12, no. 2(1982), pp. 26–33.

Bonini, Charles P., Warren H. Hausman, and Harold Bierman, Jr. *Quantitative Analysis for Management*, 9th ed. Chicago: Irwin, 1997.

Cook, Thomas M., and Robert A. Russell. *Introduction to Management Sciences*. Englewood Cliffs, NJ: Prentice Hall, 1993.

Eppen, G. D., F. J. Gould, C. P. Schmidt, Jeffrey H. Moore, and Larry R. Weatherford. *Introductory Management Science: Decision Modeling with Spreadsheets*, 5th ed. Upper Saddle River, NJ: Prentice Hall, 1998.

Fourer, Robert. "Software Survey: Linear Programming." *OR/MS Today* (April 1997), pp. 54–63.

Greenberg, H. J. "How to Analyze the Results of Linear Programs—Part 2: Price Interpretation." *Interfaces*, vol. 23, no. 5 (1993), pp. 97–114.

Hess, Rick. *Managerial Spreadsheet Modeling and Analysis*. Chicago: Irwin, 1997.

Jayaraman, V., R. Srivastava, and W. C. Benton. "Supplier Selection and Order Quantity Allocation." *Journal of Supply Chain Management*, vol. 35, no. 2 (1999), pp. 50–58.

Krajewski, L. J., and H. E. Thompson. *Management Science: Quantitative Methods in Context*. New York: John Wiley & Sons, 1981.

Markland, Robert E., and James R. Sweigart. *Quantitative Methods: Applications to Managerial Decision Making*. New York: John Wiley & Sons, 1987.

Perry, C., and K. C. Crellin. "The Precise Management Meaning of a Shadow Price." *Interfaces*, vol. 12, no. 2 (1982), pp. 61–63.

Ragsdale, Cliff T., and Rick Hess. *Spreadsheet Modeling and Decision Analysis; A Practical Introduction to Management Science*, 2d ed. Cincinnati, OH: South-Western, 1998.

Render, B., R.M. Stair, and Michael Hanna. *Quantitative Analysis for Management*, 8th ed. Upper Saddle River, NJ: Prentice Hall, 2003.

Taylor, Bernard W., Ill. *Introduction to Management Science*. Needham Heights, MA: Allyn & Bacon, 1990.

Verma, Rohit. "My Operations Management Students Love Linear Programming." *Decision Line* (July 1997), pp. 9–12.

Winston, Wayne L., S. Christian Albright, and Mark Broadie. *Practical Management Science: Spreadsheet Modeling and Applications*. Pacific Grove, CA: Duxbury, 1996.

Inventory Management

LEARNING GOALS
After reading this chapter, you should be able to . . .

IDENTIFY OR DEFINE

1. the differences between the various types of inventory and how to manage their quantities.
2. the key factors that determine the appropriate choice of an inventory system.
3. the ways to maintain accurate inventory records.

DESCRIBE OR EXPLAIN

4. the cost and service trade-offs involved in inventory decisions.
5. how to calculate the economic order quantity and apply it to various situations.
6. how to develop policies for both the continuous review and periodic review inventory control systems.

INVENTORY MANAGEMENT AT INTERNET COMPANIES

The Internet has opened a realm of business opportunities not even dreamed about 10 years ago. Many Internet companies, however, were formed under the assumption that customers, retailers, manufacturers, distributors, and service providers can be linked electronically in a seamless network, thereby eliminating the need for costly warehouses and retail stores. They thought that inventory management and distribution can be outsourced to someone else. If that assumption is true, then why have some major Internet companies gone against that conventional Internet wisdom? For example, Amazon.com (www.amazon.com) invested $300 million for 3 million square feet of warehouse space.

The answer is that Internet companies are learning the lessons learned earlier by their brick-and-mortar cousins—excellent customer service requires control over inventories. The Christmas of 1999 was a disaster for many "e-tailers." Etoys (www.etoys.com), while achieving on-time delivery for 96 percent of its orders, still got a black eye for shipping thousands of orders late. Now, Etoys must restore investor confidence by increasing total revenues and profitability. Its stock fell 90 percent in one year, placing its very existence in jeopardy. Toysrus.com (www.toysrus.com) was unable to ship many orders on time, which prompted the Federal Trade Commission to impose a fine for not informing its customers of the delayed shipments. Low revenues from Internet operations caused Toysrus.com to seek an alliance with Amazon, whereby Amazon would manage the customer service, warehousing, and shipping and Toysrus.com would buy and manage the inventory of toys. The alliance builds on the Toys "R" Us competence for managing toy inventories through traditional brick-and-mortar operations that support its retail stores and Amazon.com's competence for customer service management. Even Amazon, however, had a difficult time. Most of its customers were happy, but it bought far too much inventory—including such things as a 50-week supply of Kermit the Frog telephones—leading to a major charge against earnings for unsold goods. Consequently, it is clear that inventory management is just as important now as it has ever been.

An Amazon.com employee loads a copy of the book *Harry Potter and the Order of the Phoenix* onto a packaging machine in a fulfillment center near Reno, Nevada. Automation such as the packaging machine enabled Amazon.com to ship over 600,000 copies of the book on the first day it was released for sale.

Sources: Bannon, Lisa and Joseph Pereira. "Two Big Online Toy Sellers Fight over Delivery Speed and Exclusive Rights." *Wall Street Journal* (September 26, 2000), p. B1; Hof, Robert D. "What's with All the Warehouses?" *Business Week* (November 1, 1999), p. EB 88.

Inventory Management is an important concern for managers in all types of businesses. Effective inventory management is essential for realizing the full potential of any value chain. For companies that operate on relatively low profit margins, poor inventory management can seriously undermine the business. The challenge is not to pare inventories to the bone to reduce costs or to have plenty around to satisfy all demands, but to have the right amount to achieve the competitive priorities for the business most efficiently. In this chapter, we first introduce the basic concepts of inventory management for all types of businesses and then discuss inventory control systems appropriate for retail and distribution inventories.

As you read this chapter, think about how effective inventory management is important to various departments across the organization, such as . . .

> **accounting,** which provides the cost estimates used in inventory control, pays suppliers, and bills customers.

> **finance,** which deals with the implications of interest or investment opportunity costs on inventory management and anticipates how best to finance inventory and the cash flows related to inventory.

> **management information systems,** which develops and maintains the systems for managing inventories.

➤ **marketing and sales,** which create the need for inventory systems and rely on inventories to satisfy customers.

➤ **operations,** which has the responsibility to control the firm's inventories.

INVENTORY CONCEPTS

Inventory is created when the receipt of materials, parts, or finished goods exceeds their disbursement; it is depleted when their disbursement exceeds their receipt (see Chapter 9, "Supply-Chain Design"). In this section, we identify the pressures for low and high inventories, define the different types of inventory, discuss tactics that can be used to reduce inventories when appropriate, identify the trade-offs involved in making inventory placement decisions, and discuss how to identify the inventory items that need the most attention.

PRESSURES FOR LOW INVENTORIES

An inventory manager's job is to balance the conflicting costs and pressures that argue for both low and high inventories and determine appropriate inventory levels. The primary reason for keeping inventories low is that inventory represents a temporary monetary investment in goods on which a firm must pay (rather than receive) interest. **Inventory holding cost** (or carrying cost) is the variable cost of keeping items on hand, including interest, storage and handling, taxes, insurance, and shrinkage. When these components change with inventory levels, so does the holding cost. Companies usually state an item's holding cost per period of time as a percent of its value. The annual cost to maintain one unit in inventory typically ranges from 20 to 40 percent of its value. Suppose that a firm's holding cost is 30 percent. If the average value of total inventory is 20 percent of sales, the average annual cost to hold inventory is 6 percent [0.30(0.20)] of total sales. This cost is sizable in terms of gross profit margins, which often are less than 10 percent. Thus, the components of holding cost create pressures for low inventories.

> What are the costs for holding inventories?

> **inventory holding cost** The variable cost of keeping items on hand, including interest, storage and handling, taxes, insurance, and shrinkage.

INTEREST OR OPPORTUNITY COST. To finance inventory, a company may obtain a loan or forgo the opportunity of an investment that promises an attractive return. Interest or opportunity cost, whichever is greater, usually is the largest component of holding cost, often as high as 15 percent. For example, a car dealer may obtain a loan to finance an inventory of cars at an annual interest rate of 11 percent, or the dealer may pay cash and forgo the opportunity to invest the money in the stock market at an expected return of 13 percent.

STORAGE AND HANDLING COSTS. Inventory takes up space and must be moved into and out of storage. Storage and handling costs may be incurred when a firm rents space on either a long- or short-term basis. There also is an opportunity cost for storage when a firm could use storage space productively in some other way.

TAXES, INSURANCE, AND SHRINKAGE. More taxes are paid if end-of-year inventories are high, and insurance on assets increases when there is more to insure. Shrinkage takes three forms. The first, *pilferage,* or theft of inventory by customers or employees, is a significant percentage of sales for some businesses. The second form of shrinkage, called *obsolescence,* occurs when inventory cannot be used or sold at full value, owing to model changes, engineering modifications, or unexpectedly low demand. Obsolescence is a big expense in retail clothing, where drastic discounts on seasonal clothing are offered at the end of a season. Finally, *deterioration* through physical spoilage or damage results in lost value. Food and beverages, for example, lose value and might even have to be discarded when their shelf life is reached. When the rate of deterioration is high, building large inventories may be unwise.

PRESSURES FOR HIGH INVENTORIES

Why are inventories necessary?

The fact that inventory held in the U.S. economy exceeds the $1.3 trillion mark suggests that there are pressures for large inventories, despite the expense. Let us look briefly at each type of pressure.

CUSTOMER SERVICE. Creating inventory can speed delivery and improve on-time delivery. Inventory reduces the potential for stockouts and backorders, which are key concerns of wholesalers and retailers. A stockout occurs when an item that is typically stocked is not available to satisfy a demand the moment it occurs, resulting in loss of the sale. A backorder is a customer order that cannot be filled when promised or demanded but is filled later. Customers may be willing to wait for a backorder but next time may take their business elsewhere. Sometimes, customers are given discounts for the inconvenience of waiting.

ordering cost The cost of preparing a purchase order for a supplier or a production order for the shop.

ORDERING COST. Each time a firm places a new order, it incurs an **ordering cost,** or the cost of preparing a purchase order for a supplier or a production order for the shop. For the same item, the ordering cost is the same, regardless of the order size: The purchasing agent must take the time to decide how much to order and, perhaps, select a supplier and negotiate terms. Time also is spent on paperwork, follow-up, and receiving. In the case of a production order for a manufactured item, a blueprint and routing instructions often must accompany the shop order. The Internet (see Chapter 12, "Information Technology and Value Chains" and Chapter 9, "Supply-Chain Design") can help streamline the order process and reduce the costs of placing orders.

setup cost The cost involved in changing over a machine to produce a different item.

SETUP COST. The cost involved in changing over a machine to produce a different item is the **setup cost.** It includes labor and time to make the changeover, cleaning, and new tools or fixtures. Scrap or rework costs can be substantially higher at the start of the production run. Setup cost also is independent of order size, so there is pressure to order a large supply of the items and hold them in inventory.

LABOR AND EQUIPMENT UTILIZATION. By creating more inventory, management can increase workforce productivity and facility utilization in three ways. First, placing larger, less frequent production orders reduces the number of unproductive setups, which add no value to a service or product. Second, holding inventory reduces the chance of costly rescheduling of production orders because the components needed to make the product are not in inventory. Third, building inventories improves resource utilization by stabilizing the output rate when demand is cyclical or seasonal. The firm uses inventory built during slack periods to handle extra demand in peak seasons and minimizes the need for extra shifts, hiring, layoffs, overtime, and additional equipment.

TRANSPORTATION COST. Sometimes, outbound transportation cost can be reduced by increasing inventory levels. Having inventory on hand allows more carload shipments and minimizes the need to expedite shipments by more expensive modes of transportation. Forward placement of inventory can also reduce outbound transportation cost, even though the pooling effect is lessened and more inventory is necessary (see Chapter 9, "Supply-Chain Design"). Inbound transportation cost also may be reduced by creating more inventory. Sometimes, several items are ordered from the same supplier. Combining these orders and placing them at the same time may lead to rate discounts, thereby decreasing the costs of transportation and raw materials.

quantity discount A drop in the price per unit when the order is sufficiently large.

PAYMENTS TO SUPPLIERS. A firm often can reduce total payments to suppliers if it can tolerate higher inventory levels. Suppose that a firm learns that a key supplier is about to increase prices. It might be cheaper for the firm to order a larger quantity than usual—in effect delaying the price increase—even though inventory will increase temporarily. Similarly, a firm can take advantage of quantity discounts. A **quantity discount,** whereby the price per unit drops when the order is sufficiently large, is an incentive to order larger quantities.

TYPES OF INVENTORY

Another perspective on inventory is to classify it by how it is created. In this context, there are four types of inventory for an item: (1) cycle, (2) safety stock, (3) anticipation, and (4) pipeline. They cannot be identified physically; that is, an inventory manager cannot look at a pile of widgets and identify which ones are cycle inventory and which ones are pipeline inventory. However, conceptually, each of the four types comes into being in an entirely different way. Once you understand these differences, you can prescribe different ways to reduce inventory, which we discuss in the next section.

CYCLE INVENTORY. The portion of total inventory that varies directly with lot size is called **cycle inventory.** Determining how frequently to order, and in what quantity, is called **lot sizing.** Two principles apply.

1. The lot size, Q, varies directly with the elapsed time (or cycle) between orders. If a lot is ordered every five weeks, the average lot size must equal five weeks' demand.
2. The longer the time between orders for a given item, the greater the cycle inventory must be.

At the beginning of the interval, the cycle inventory is at its maximum, or Q. At the end of the interval, just before a new lot arrives, cycle inventory drops to its minimum, or 0. The average cycle inventory is the average of these two extremes:

$$\text{Average cycle inventory} = \frac{Q + 0}{2} = \frac{Q}{2}$$

This formula is exact only when the demand rate is constant and uniform. However, it does provide a reasonably good estimate even when demand rates are not constant. Factors other than the demand rate (e.g., scrap losses) also may cause estimating errors when this simple formula is used.

SAFETY STOCK INVENTORY. To avoid customer service problems and the hidden costs of unavailable components, companies hold safety stock. **Safety stock inventory** is surplus inventory that protects against uncertainties in demand, lead time, and supply. Safety stocks are desirable when suppliers fail to deliver the desired quantity on the specified date with acceptable quality or when manufactured items have significant amounts of scrap or rework. Safety stock inventory ensures that operations are not disrupted when such problems occur, allowing subsequent operations to continue.

To create safety stock, a firm places an order for delivery earlier than when the item is typically needed.[1] The replenishment order therefore arrives ahead of time, giving a cushion against uncertainty. For example, suppose that the average lead time from a supplier is three weeks but a firm orders five weeks in advance just to be safe. This policy creates a safety stock equal to a two weeks' supply (5—3).

ANTICIPATION INVENTORY. Inventory used to absorb uneven rates of demand or supply, which businesses often face, is referred to as anticipation inventory (see Chapter 14, "Aggregate Planning"). Predictable, seasonal demand patterns lend themselves to the use of anticipation inventory. Uneven demand may lead a manufacturer to stockpile anticipation inventory during periods of low demand so that output levels do not have to be increased much when demand peaks. Anticipation inventory also can help when suppliers are threatened with a strike or have severe capacity limitations.

---

[1]When orders are placed at fixed intervals, there is a second way. Each new order placed is larger than the quantity typically needed through the next delivery date.

What types of inventory does a business own?

cycle inventory The portion of total inventory that varies directly with lot size.

lot sizing The determination of how frequently and in what quantity to order inventory.

VIDEO CLIP 15.1
Video Clip 15.1 on the Student CD-ROM summarizes the various types of inventory and inventory costs.

safety stock inventory
Surplus inventory that a company holds to protect against uncertainties in demand, lead time, and supply.

Inventory management begins with knowing how much inventory you have on hand. Here a grocer uses a handheld scanner to check inventory on supermarket shelves.

pipeline inventory   Inventory moving from point to point in the materials flow system.

PIPELINE INVENTORY. Inventory moving from point to point in the materials flow system is called **pipeline inventory.** Materials move from suppliers to a plant, from one operation to the next in the plant, from the plant to a distribution center or customer, and from the distribution center to a retailer. Pipeline inventory consists of orders that have been placed but not yet received. For example, NUMMI, the joint venture between General Motors and Toyota in California, uses parts produced in the Midwest. Shipments arrive daily at the plant, but the transportation lead time requires a pipeline inventory of parts in rail cars enroute from the Midwest at all times. Pipeline inventory between two points, for either transportation or production, can be measured as the average demand during lead time, $\overline{D}_L$, which is the average demand for the item per period (d) times the number of periods in the item's lead time (L) to move between the two points, or

$$\text{Pipeline inventory} = \overline{D}_L = dL$$

MANAGERIAL PRACTICE 15.1

IMPROVING CUSTOMER SERVICE THROUGH INVENTORY MANAGEMENT AT AMAZON.COM

As alluded to in the chapter opener, Amazon.com (www.amazon.com) had a rough holiday season in 1999, owing primarily to mismanaged inventories and chaotic warehouse operations that resulted in major charges to earnings for unsold goods. Since then Amazon has changed its ways. For example, it had housed items such as DVDs and DVD players in different states, which complicated collecting orders for a single customer. Now the items are grouped together in its shipping facilities. Also, Amazon has started to forecast demands by areas of the country. Palm hand-held computers are forecasted by zip code and the proper inventories are sent to the warehouse serving that area. This approach will reduce the time it takes to get a product to the customer, but it will increase the amount of inventory of the item in the distribution system (see the discussion of inventory pooling in Chapter 9, "Supply-Chain Design").

Jeffrey Wilke, vice president and general manager of operations at Amazon, identified four things Amazon has done to improve customer service through inventory management.

- Increased warehouse capacity quickly. Three million square feet of warehouse capacity in less than a year, which enabled Amazon to develop the appropriate amount of cycle, safety stock, and anticipation inventories to service its customers.
- Introduced state-of-the-art automation and mechanization. The warehouses are efficient and flexible enough to move items in container sizes, pallet sizes, or lot sizes of one, thereby reducing handling costs.

- Linked order information to a customer archive through information technology. When a customer places an order for a particular basket of goods, the system captures the data and adds it to a database of past purchases from that customer. This capability enables Amazon to forecast future purchases and tailor the shopping experience the customer receives.
- Replicated the system across the distribution centers where possible. Linking capacity, automation, and information technology allows Amazon to expand in terms of product breadth and in terms of partnerships and alliances. Because the system can be replicated, Amazon has the capability to expand in modular fashion as new warehouses are added.

Amazon's approach is to control inventories themselves, rather than to delegate this important function to another company. While the use of the Internet is expanding at a blistering pace, the dream of a seamless interface between suppliers, retailers, and customers must still await the development of the enabling technology.

Sources: Wingsfield, Nick. "Amazon Vows to Avoid Mess of 1999 Christmas Rush: Too Many Kermit Phones." *Wall Street Journal* (September 25, 2000), p. B1; "Q&A with Jeffrey Wilke." *Business Week* (November 1, 1999), www.ebiz.businessweek.com.

Note that the lot size does not directly affect the average level of the pipeline inventory. Increasing Q inflates the size of each order, so if an order has been placed but not received, there is more pipeline inventory for that lead time. However, that increase is canceled by a proportionate decrease in the number of orders placed per year. The lot size can *indirectly* affect pipeline inventory, however, if increasing Q causes the lead time to increase. Here $\bar{D}_L$, and therefore pipeline inventory, will increase.

Managerial Practice 15.1 shows how Amazon.com has designed an inventory system to improve customer service.

Estimating Inventory Levels

EXAMPLE 15.1

A plant makes monthly shipments of electric drills to a wholesaler in average lot sizes of 280 drills. The wholesaler's average demand is 70 drills a week, and the lead time from the plant is three weeks. The wholesaler must pay for the inventory from the moment the plant makes a shipment. If the wholesaler is willing to increase its purchase quantity to 350 units, the plant will guarantee a lead time of two weeks. What is the effect on cycle and pipeline inventories?

Tutor 15.1 on the Student CD-ROM provides a new example to practice the estimation of inventory levels.

SOLUTION

The current cycle and pipeline inventories are

$$\text{Cycle inventory} = \frac{Q}{2} = \frac{280}{2} = 140 \text{ drills}$$

$$\text{Pipeline inventory} = \overline{D}_L = dL = (70 \text{ drills/week})(3 \text{ weeks}) = 210 \text{ drills}$$

Figure 15.1 shows the cycle and pipeline inventories if the wholesaler accepts the new proposal.

FIGURE 15.1

Estimating Inventory Levels for Cycle and Pipeline Inventories

Tutor—Estimating Inventory Levels

1. Enter the average lot size, average demand during a period, and the number of periods of lead time:

Average lot size	350
Average demand	70
Lead time	2

2. To compute cycle inventory, simply divide average lot size by 2. To compute pipeline inventory, multipy average demand by lead time:

Cycle inventory	175
Pipeline inventory	140

DECISION POINT   The effect of the new proposal on cycle inventories is to increase them by 35 units, or 25 percent. The reduction in pipeline inventories, however, is 70 units, or 33 percent. The proposal would reduce the total investment in cycle and pipeline inventories. Also, it is advantageous to have shorter lead times because the wholesaler only has to commit to purchases two weeks in advance, rather than three.

INVENTORY REDUCTION TACTICS

What are the options for reducing inventory prudently?

Managers always are eager to find cost-effective ways to reduce inventory. Later in this chapter, we examine various ways for finding optimal lot sizes (see also Supplement E, "Special Inventory Models"). Here, we discuss something more fundamental—the basic tactics (which we call *levers*) for reducing inventory. A primary lever is one that must be activated if inventory is to be reduced. A secondary lever reduces the penalty cost of applying the primary lever and the need for having inventory in the first place.

CYCLE INVENTORY.   The primary lever to reduce cycle inventory is simply to reduce the lot size. A key aspect of lean systems (see Chapter 11, "Lean Systems") is to use extremely small lots, compared to traditional lot sizes equaling several weeks' (or even months') supply. However, making such reductions in *Q* without making any other changes can be devastating. For example, setup costs can skyrocket, which leads to use of the two secondary levers.

   1. Streamline methods for placing orders and making setups, which reduces ordering and setup costs and allows *Q* to be reduced.

   2. Increase repeatability to eliminate the need for changeovers. **Repeatability** is the degree to which the same work can be done again. It can be increased through high product demand; the use of specialization; the devotion of resources exclusively to a product; the use of the same part in many different products; through flexible automation; the use of the one-worker, multiple-machines concept; or through group technology (see Chapter 3, "Process Design Strategy," and Chapter 7, "Process Layout"). Increased repeatability may justify new setup methods, reduce transportation costs, and allow quantity discounts from suppliers.

repeatability   The degree to which the same work can be done again.

SAFETY STOCK INVENTORY. The primary lever to reduce safety stock inventory is to place orders closer to the time when they must be received. However, this approach can lead to unacceptable customer service unless demand, supply, and delivery uncertainties can be minimized. Four secondary levers can be used.

1. Improve demand forecasts so that there are fewer surprises from customers. Perhaps customers can even be encouraged to order items before they need them.

2. Cut lead times of purchased or produced items to reduce demand uncertainty during lead time. For example, local suppliers with short lead times could be selected whenever possible.

3. Reduce supply uncertainties. Suppliers may be more reliable if production plans are shared with them, permitting the suppliers to make more realistic forecasts. Surprises from unexpected scrap or rework can be reduced by improving manufacturing processes. Preventive maintenance can minimize unexpected downtime caused by equipment failure.

4. Rely more on equipment and labor buffers, such as capacity cushions and cross-trained workers. These are the only buffers available to businesses in the service sector because they cannot inventory their services.

ANTICIPATION INVENTORY. The primary lever to reduce anticipation inventory is simply to match demand rate with production rate. Secondary levers are used to level customer demand in one of the following ways:

1. Add new products with different demand cycles so that a peak in the demand for one product compensates for the seasonal low for another.

2. Provide off-season promotional campaigns.

3. Offer seasonal pricing plans.

PIPELINE INVENTORY. An operations manager has direct control over lead time but not demand rate. Because pipeline inventory is a function of demand during lead time, the primary lever is to reduce the lead time. Two secondary levers can help managers cut lead times.

1. Find more responsive suppliers and select new carriers for shipments between stocking locations or improve materials handling within the plant. Introducing a computer system could overcome information delays between a distribution center and retailer.

2. Decrease Q, at least in those cases where lead time depends on lot size. Smaller jobs generally require less time to complete.

PLACEMENT OF INVENTORIES

The positioning of a firm's inventories supports its competitive priorities. Inventories can be held at the raw materials, work-in-process, and finished goods levels. Managers make inventory placement decisions by designating an item as either a special or a standard. A **special** is an item made to order or, if purchased, it is bought to order. Just enough are ordered to cover the latest customer request. A **standard** is an item that is made to stock, or ordered to stock, and normally the item is available upon request. For example, retailers typically deal with standard items and hold them in stock on the store's shelves to satisfy customer demand. Such is the case at Wal-Mart or Marshall Field's, although occasionally you can order items not normally in stock. Expect to wait a while for delivery if the item is unique to your needs. Cafeterias also display standard food items from which customers can choose to make a meal. Alternatively, a tailor deals with special items because he would not know your exact measurements or your cloth preferences until you arrive at the store. Dealing with special items is also the case at a fine restaurant, where your specific meal cannot be prepared until you discuss it with the server. The ingredients for the meal are available, but the meal itself is considered a special item.

Should most inventory be held at the raw materials, work-in-process, or finished goods level? Which items should be standards?

special An item made to order; if purchased, it is bought to order.

standard An item that is made to stock or ordered to stock, and normally is available upon request.

Inventory held toward the finished goods level means short delivery times—but a higher dollar investment in inventory. Inventory placement at Shamrock Chemicals, a Newark, New Jersey, manufacturer of materials used in printing inks, illustrates this trade-off. Shamrock enjoys annual sales of more than $15 million because it can ship a product the same day a customer orders it. However, because finished goods are treated as standards rather than specials, Shamrock is forced to maintain a large inventory. Holding inventory at the raw materials level would reduce the cost of carrying inventory—but at the expense of the quick customer response time that gives Shamrock its competitive advantage. R. R. Donnelley, a large manufacturer of books and other printed materials, chooses an opposite strategy by positioning inventory back at the raw materials level (e.g., in rolled paper stock and ink). The reason is that the products Donnelley produces are made to order and, therefore, considered specials. Stocking the products based on a forecast would be very expensive. Placing inventories closer to the raw materials level gives Donnelley great flexibility in meeting a variety of customer demands.

IDENTIFYING CRITICAL INVENTORY ITEMS WITH ABC ANALYSIS

Which items demand the closest attention and control?

ABC analysis   The process of dividing items into three classes, according to their dollar usage, so that managers can focus on items that have the highest dollar value.

TUTOR 15.2

Tutor 15.2 on the Student CD-ROM provides an example to practice ABC analysis.

Thousands of items are held in inventory by a typical organization, but only a small percentage of them deserve management's closest attention and tightest control. **ABC analysis** is the process of dividing items into three classes, according to their dollar usage, so that managers can focus on items that have the highest dollar value. This method is the equivalent of creating a Pareto chart (see Chapter 4, "Process Analysis") except that it is applied to inventory rather than to process errors. As Figure 15.2 shows, class A items typically represent only about 20 percent of the items but account for 80 percent of the dollar usage. Class B items account for another 30 percent of the items but only 15 percent of the dollar usage. Finally, 50 percent of the items fall in class C, representing a mere 5 percent of the dollar usage.

The goal of ABC analysis is to identify the inventory levels of class A items and enable management to control them tightly by using the levers just discussed. The analyst begins by multiplying the annual demand rate for one item by the dollar value (cost) of one unit to determine its dollar usage. After ranking the items on the basis of dollar usage and creating the Pareto chart, the analyst looks for "natural" changes in slope. The dividing lines in Figure 15.2 between classes are inexact. Class A items could be somewhat higher or lower than 20 percent of all items but normally account for the bulk of the dollar usage.

FIGURE 15.2

Typical Chart from ABC Analysis

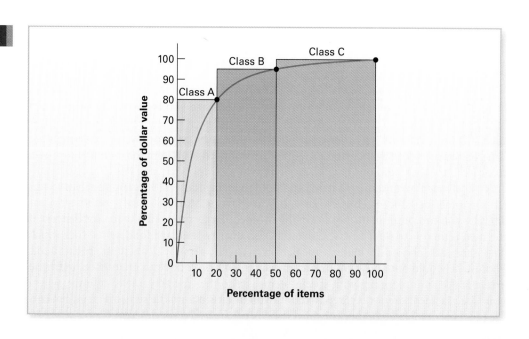

A manager can direct that class A items be reviewed frequently to reduce the average lot size and keep inventory records current. If the records show an on-hand balance of 100 units but the actual balance is 200 units, costly inventory is being carried needlessly. If a class A item is bought outside the firm, the purchasing department may be able to reduce its cost through centralized buying, switching suppliers, or more effective contract negotiation.

For class C items, much looser control is appropriate. A stockout of a class C item can be as crucial as for a class A item, but the inventory holding cost of class C items tends to be low. These features suggest that higher inventory levels can be tolerated and that more safety stock, larger lot sizes, and perhaps even a visual system, which we discuss later, may suffice for class C items. See Solved Problem 2 for a detailed example of ABC analysis.

VIDEO CLIP 15.2
Video Clip 15.2 on the Student CD-ROM shows how a book distribution center uses ABC analysis to organize its inventories.

⬤ ECONOMIC ORDER QUANTITY

Recall that managers face conflicting pressures to keep inventories low enough to avoid excess inventory holding costs but high enough to reduce the frequency of orders and setups. A good starting point for balancing these conflicting pressures and determining the best cycle-inventory level for an item is finding the **economic order quantity (EOQ)**, which is the lot size that minimizes total annual inventory holding and ordering costs. The approach to determining the EOQ is based on the following assumptions:

economic order quantity (EOQ) The lot size that minimizes total annual inventory holding and ordering costs.

1. The demand rate for the item is constant (e.g., always 10 units per day) and known with certainty.
2. There are no constraints (e.g., truck capacity or materials handling limitations) on the size of each lot.
3. The only two relevant costs are the inventory holding cost and the fixed cost per lot for ordering or setup.
4. Decisions for one item can be made independently of decisions for other items (i.e., no advantage is gained in combining several orders going to the same supplier).
5. There is no uncertainty in lead time or supply. The lead time is constant (e.g., always 14 days) and known with certainty. The amount received is exactly what was ordered and it arrives all at once rather than piecemeal.

The economic order quantity will be optimal when the five assumptions are satisfied. In reality, few situations are so simple and well behaved. In fact, different lot-sizing approaches are needed to reflect quantity discounts, uneven demand rates, or interactions between items (see Supplement E, "Special Inventory Models"). However, the EOQ often is a reasonable first approximation of average lot sizes, even when one or more of the assumptions do not quite apply.

CALCULATING THE EOQ

We begin by formulating the total cost for any lot size Q. Next, we derive the EOQ, which is the Q that minimizes total cost. Finally, we describe how to convert the EOQ into a companion measure, the elapsed time between orders.

How much should be ordered?

When the EOQ assumptions are satisfied, cycle inventory behaves as shown in Figure 15.3. A cycle begins with Q units held in inventory, which happens when a new order is received. During the cycle, on-hand inventory is used at a constant rate and, because demand is known with certainty and the lead time is a constant, a new lot can be ordered so that inventory falls to 0 precisely when the new lot is received. Because inventory varies uniformly between Q and 0, the average cycle inventory equals half the lot size, Q.

The annual holding cost for this amount of inventory, which increases linearly with Q, as Figure 15.4 (a) shows, is

Annual holding cost = (Average cycle inventory)(Unit holding cost)

FIGURE 15.3

Cycle-Inventory Levels

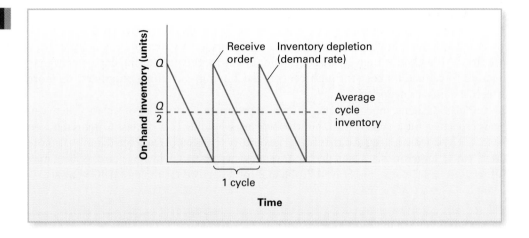

The annual ordering cost is

Annual ordering cost = (Number of orders/year)(Ordering or setup cost)

The average number of orders per year equals annual demand divided by Q. For example, if 1,200 units must be ordered each year and the average lot size is 100 units, then 12 orders will be placed during the year. The annual ordering or setup cost decreases nonlinearly as Q increases, as shown in Figure 15.4(b), because fewer orders are placed.

The total annual cost,[2] as graphed in Figure 15.4(c), is the sum of the two cost components:

Total cost = Annual holding cost + Annual ordering or setup cost[3]

$$C = \frac{Q}{2}(H) + \frac{D}{Q}(S)$$

FIGURE 15.4   **Graphs of Annual Holding, Ordering, and Total Costs**

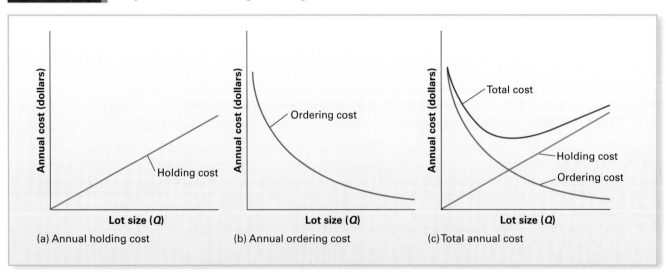

(a) Annual holding cost

(b) Annual ordering cost

(c) Total annual cost

---

[2]Expressing the total cost on an annual basis usually is convenient (although not necessary). Any time horizon can be selected, as long as D and H cover the same time period. If the total cost is calculated on a monthly basis, D must be monthly demand and H must be the cost of holding a unit for one month.

[3]The number of orders actually placed in any year is always a whole number, although the formula allows the use of fractional values. However, rounding is not needed because what is being calculated is an average for multiple years. Such averages often are nonintegers.

where

C = total annual cost

Q = lot size, in units

H = cost of holding one unit in inventory for a year,
      often calculated as a proportion of the item's value

D = annual demand, in units per year

S = cost of ordering or setting up one lot, in dollars per lot

---

Costing Out a Lot-Sizing Policy   **EXAMPLE** 15.2

A museum of natural history opened a gift shop two years ago. Managing inventories has become a problem. Low inventory turnover is squeezing profit margins and causing cash-flow problems.

One of the top-selling items in the container group at the museum's gift shop is a bird feeder. Sales are 18 units per week, and the supplier charges $60 per unit. The cost of placing an order with the supplier is $45. Annual holding cost is 25 percent of a feeder's value, and the museum operates 52 weeks per year. Management chose a 390-unit lot size so that new orders could be placed less frequently. What is the annual cost of the current policy of using a 390-unit lot size? Would a lot size of 468 be better?

SOLUTION

We begin by computing the annual demand and holding cost as

$$D = (18 \text{ units}/\text{week})(52 \text{ weeks}/\text{year}) = 936 \text{ units}$$
$$H = 0.25(\$60/\text{unit}) = \$15$$

The total annual cost for the current policy is

$$C = \frac{Q}{2}(H) + \frac{D}{Q}(S)$$

$$= \frac{390}{2}(\$15) + \frac{936}{390}(\$45) = \$2,925 + \$108 = \$3,033$$

The total annual cost for the alternative lot size is

$$C = \frac{468}{2}(\$15) + \frac{936}{468}(\$45) = \$3,510 + \$90 = \$3,600$$

DECISION POINT   The lot size of 468 units, which is a half-year supply, would be a more expensive option than the current policy. The savings in order costs are more than offset by the increase in holding costs. Management should use the total annual cost equation to explore other lot-size alternatives.

Figure 15.5 displays the impact of using several Q values for the bird feeder in Example 15.2. Eight different lot sizes were evaluated in addition to the current one. Both holding and ordering costs were plotted, but their sum—the total annual cost curve—is the important feature. The graph shows that the best lot size, or EOQ, is the lowest point on the total annual cost curve, or between 50 and

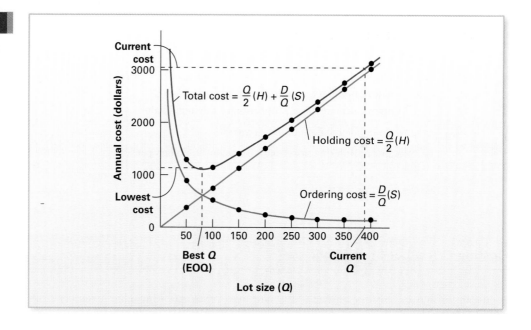

FIGURE 15.5

Total Annual Cost Function for Bird Feeder

VIDEO CLIP 15.3

Video Clip 15.3 on the Student CD-ROM shows an example of a process with high setup costs resulting in a large economic run size.

100 units. Obviously, reducing the current lot-size policy ($Q = 390$) can result in significant savings.

A more efficient approach is to use the EOQ formula:

$$EOQ = \sqrt{\frac{2DS}{H}}$$

We use calculus to obtain the EOQ formula from the total cost formula. We take the first derivative of the total cost function with respect to Q, set it equal to 0, and solve for Q. As Figure 15.5 indicates, the EOQ is the order quantity for which annual holding cost equals annual ordering cost. Using this insight, we can also obtain the EOQ formula by equating the formulas for annual ordering cost and annual holding cost and solving for Q. The graph in Figure 15.5 also reveals that when the annual holding cost for any Q exceeds the annual ordering cost, as with the 390-unit order, we can immediately conclude that Q is too big. A smaller Q reduces holding cost and increases ordering cost, bringing them into balance. Similarly, if the annual ordering cost exceeds the annual holding cost, Q should be increased.

Sometimes, inventory policies are based on the time between replenishment orders, rather than on the number of units in the lot size. The **time between orders (TBO)** for a particular lot size is the average elapsed time between receiving (or placing) replenishment orders of Q units. Expressed as a fraction of a year, the TBO is simply Q divided by annual demand. When we use the EOQ and express time in terms of months, the TBO is

$$TBO_{EOQ} = \frac{EOQ}{D}(12 \text{ months/year})$$

In Example 15.3, we show how to calculate TBO for years, months, weeks, and days.

time between orders (TBO)
The average elapsed time between receiving (or placing) replenishment orders of Q units for a particular lot size.

Finding the EOQ, Total Cost, and TBO

EXAMPLE 15.3

For the bird feeders in Example 15.2, calculate the EOQ and its total annual cost. How frequently will orders be placed if the EOQ is used?

SOLUTION

Using the formulas for EOQ and annual cost, we get

$$EOQ = \sqrt{\frac{2DS}{H}} = \sqrt{\frac{2(936)(45)}{15}} = 74.94 \quad or \quad 75 \text{ units}$$

Figure 15.6 shows that the total annual cost is much less than the $3,033 cost of the current policy of placing 390-unit orders.

TUTOR 15.3

Tutor 15.3 on the Student CD-ROM provides a new example to practice the application of the EOQ model.

ACTIVE MODEL 15.1

Active Model 15.1 on the Student CD-ROM provides additional insight on the EOQ model and its uses.

FIGURE 15.6

Total Annual Costs Based on EOQ using Tutor 15.3

Parameters		Economic Order Quantity	75
Current Lot Size (Q)	390		
Demand (D)	936		
Order Cost (S)	$45		
Unit Holding Cost (H)	$15		
Annual Costs		**Annual Costs based on EOQ**	
Orders per Year	2.4	Orders per Year	12.48
Annual Ordering Cost	$108.00	Annual Ordering Cost	$561.60
Annual Holding Cost	$2,925.00	Annual Holding Cost	$562.50
Annual Inventory Cost	$3,033.00	Annual Inventory Cost	$1,124.10

When the EOQ is used, the time between orders (TBO) can be expressed in various ways for the same time period.

$$TBO_{EOQ} = \frac{EOQ}{D} = \frac{75}{936} = 0.080 \text{ year}$$

$$TBO_{EOQ} = \frac{EOQ}{D}(12 \text{ months/year}) = \frac{75}{936}(12) = 0.96 \text{ month}$$

$$TBO_{EOQ} = \frac{EOQ}{D}(52 \text{ weeks/year}) = \frac{75}{936}(52) = 4.17 \text{ weeks}$$

$$TBO_{EOQ} = \frac{EOQ}{D}(365 \text{ days/year}) = \frac{75}{936}(365) = 29.25 \text{ days}$$

DECISION POINT Using the EOQ, about 12 orders per year will be required. Using the current policy of 390 units per order, an average of 2.4 orders will be needed each year (every five months). The current policy saves on ordering costs but incurs a much larger cost for carrying the cycle inventory. While it is easy to see which option is best on the basis of total ordering and holding costs, other factors may affect the final decision. For example, if the supplier would reduce the price per unit for large orders, it may be better to order the larger quantity (see Supplement E, "Special Inventory Models").

UNDERSTANDING THE EFFECT OF CHANGES

Subjecting the EOQ formula to sensitivity analysis can yield valuable insights into the management of inventories. Sensitivity analysis is a technique for systematically changing crucial parameters to determine the effects of change (see Supplement A, "Decision Making"). Let us consider the effects on the EOQ when we substitute different values into the numerator or denominator of the formula.

How often should demand estimates, cost estimates, and lot sizes be updated?

A CHANGE IN THE DEMAND RATE. Because *D* is in the numerator, the EOQ (and, therefore, the best cycle-inventory level) increases in proportion to the square root of the annual demand. Therefore, when demand rises, the lot size also should rise, but more slowly than actual demand.

A CHANGE IN THE SETUP COSTS. Because *S* is in the numerator, increasing *S* increases the EOQ and, consequently, the average cycle inventory. Conversely, reducing *S* reduces the EOQ, allowing smaller lot sizes to be produced economically. This relationship explains why manufacturers are so concerned about cutting setup time and costs. When weeks of supply decline, inventory turns increase. When setup cost and setup time become trivial, a major impediment to small-lot production is removed.

A CHANGE IN THE HOLDING COSTS. Because *H* is in the denominator, the EOQ declines when *H* increases. Conversely, when *H* declines, the EOQ increases. Larger lot sizes are justified by lower holding costs.

ERRORS IN ESTIMATING *D*, *H*, AND *S*. Total cost is fairly insensitive to errors, even when the estimates are wrong by a large margin. The reasons are that errors tend to cancel each other out and that the square root reduces the effect of the error. Suppose that we incorrectly estimate the holding cost to be double its true value; that is, we calculate EOQ using *2H*, instead of *H*. For Example 15.3, this 100 percent error increases total cost by only 6 percent, from $1,124 to $1,192. Thus, the EOQ lies in a fairly large zone of acceptable lot sizes, allowing managers to deviate somewhat from the EOQ to accommodate supplier contracts or storage constraints.

INVENTORY CONTROL SYSTEMS

The EOQ and other lot-sizing methods (see Supplement E, "Special Inventory Models") answer the important question: How much should we order? Another important question that needs an answer is: When should we place the order? An inventory control system responds to both questions. In selecting an inventory control system for a particular application, the nature of the demands imposed on the inventory items is crucial. An important distinction between types of inventory is whether an item is subject to dependent or independent demand. Retailers, such as JCPenney, and distributors must manage **independent demand items**—that is, items for which demand is influenced by market conditions and is not related to the inventory decisions for any other item held in stock. Independent demand inventory includes

independent demand items
Items for which demand is influenced by market conditions and is not related to the inventory decisions for any other item held in stock.

- wholesale and retail merchandise;
- service support inventory, such as stamps and mailing labels for post offices, office supplies for law firms, and laboratory supplies for research universities;
- product and replacement-part distribution inventories; and
- maintenance, repair, and operating (MRO) supplies—that is, items that do not become part of the final service or product, such as employee uniforms, fuel, paint, and machine repair parts.

How can inventory be controlled if fixing the lot-size quantity is advantageous?

Managing independent demand inventory can be tricky because demand is influenced by external factors. For example, the owner of a bookstore may not be sure how many copies of the latest best-seller novel customers will purchase during the coming month. As a result, the manager may decide to stock extra copies as a safeguard. Independent demand such as the demand for various book titles, must be forecasted (see Chapter 13, "Forecasting").

In this chapter, we focus on inventory control systems for independent demand items, which is the type of demand the bookstore owner, other retailers, service providers, and distributors face. Even though demand from any one customer is difficult to predict, low demand from some customers often is offset by high demand from others. Thus, total demand for any independent demand item may follow a relatively smooth pattern, with some random fluctuations. *Dependent demand items* are those required as components or inputs to a service or product. Dependent demand exhibits a pattern very different from that of independent demand and must be managed with different techniques (see Chapter 16, "Resource Planning").

In this section, we discuss and compare two inventory control systems: (1) the continuous review system, called a Q system, and (2) the periodic review system, called a P system. We close with a look at hybrid systems, which incorporate features of both the P and Q systems.

CONTINUOUS REVIEW SYSTEM

A **continuous review (Q) system**, sometimes called a **reorder point (ROP) system** or fixed order-quantity system, tracks the remaining inventory of an item each time a withdrawal is made to determine whether it is time to reorder. In practice, these reviews are done frequently (e.g., daily) and often continuously (after each withdrawal). The advent of computers and electronic cash registers linked to inventory records has made continuous reviews easy. At each review, a decision is made about an item's inventory position. If it is judged to be too low, the system triggers a new order. The **inventory position (IP)** measures the item's ability to satisfy future demand. It includes **scheduled receipts (SR)**, which are orders that have been placed but have not yet been received, plus on-hand inventory (OH) minus backorders (BO). Sometimes, scheduled receipts are called **open orders**. More specifically,

$$\text{Inventory position} = \text{On-hand inventory} + \text{Scheduled receipts} - \text{Backorders}$$
$$\text{IP} = \text{OH} + \text{SR} - \text{BO}$$

When the inventory position reaches a predetermined minimum level, called the **reorder point (R)**, a fixed quantity Q of the item is ordered. In a continuous review system, although the order quantity Q is fixed, the time between orders can vary. Hence, Q can be based on the EOQ, a price break quantity (the minimum lot size that qualifies for a quantity discount), a container size (such as a truckload), or some other quantity selected by management.

SELECTING THE REORDER POINT WHEN DEMAND IS CERTAIN. To demonstrate the concept of a reorder point, suppose that the demand for feeders at the museum gift shop in Example 15.3 is always 18 per week, the lead time is a constant two weeks, and the supplier always ships the exact amount ordered on time. With both demand and lead time certain, the museum's buyer can wait until the inventory position drops to 36 units, or (18 units/week) (2 weeks), to place a new order. Thus, in this case, the reorder point, R, equals the *demand during lead time,* with no added allowance for safety stock.

Figure 15.7 shows how the system operates when demand and lead time are constant. The downward-sloping line represents the on-hand inventory, which is being depleted at a constant rate. When it reaches reorder point R (the horizontal line), a new order for Q units is placed. The on-hand inventory continues to drop throughout lead time L until the order is received. At that time, which marks the end of the lead time, on-hand inventory jumps by Q units. A new order arrives just when inventory drops to 0. The time between orders (TBO) is the same for each cycle.

The inventory position, IP, shown in Figure 15.7 corresponds to the on-hand inventory, except during the lead time. Just after a new order is placed, at the start of the lead time, IP increases by Q, as shown by the dashed line. The IP exceeds OH by this same margin throughout the lead time.[4] At the end of the lead time, when the

continuous review (Q) system
A system designed to track the remaining inventory of an item each time a withdrawal is made to determine whether it is time to reorder.

reorder point (ROP) system
See **continuous review (Q) system.**

inventory position (IP) The measurement of an item's ability to satisfy future demand.

scheduled receipts (SR) Orders that have been placed but have not yet been received.

open orders See **scheduled receipts (SR).**

reorder point (R) The predetermined minimum level that an inventory position must reach before a fixed quantity Q of the item is ordered.

---

[4]A possible exception is the unlikely situation when more than one scheduled receipt is open at the same time because of long lead times.

FIGURE 15.7

Q System When Demand and Lead Time Are Constant and Certain

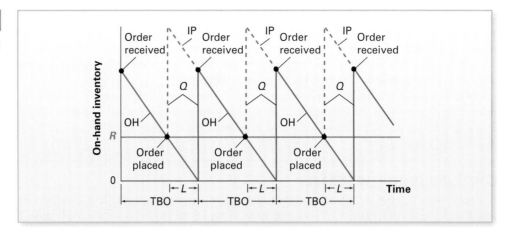

scheduled receipts convert to on-hand inventory, IP = OH once again. The key point here is to compare IP, not OH, with R in deciding whether to reorder. A common error is to ignore scheduled receipts or backorders.

EXAMPLE 15.7   Determining Whether to Place an Order

Demand for chicken soup at a supermarket is always 25 cases a day and the lead time is always four days. The shelves were just restocked with chicken soup, leaving an on-hand inventory of only 10 cases. There are no backorders, but there is one open order for 200 cases. What is the inventory position? Should a new order be placed?

SOLUTION

$$R = \text{Average demand during lead time} = (25)(4) = 100 \text{ cases}$$
$$\text{IP} = \text{OH} + \text{SR} - \text{BO}$$
$$= 10 + 200 - 0 = 210 \text{ cases}$$

DECISION POINT   Because IP exceeds R (210 versus 100), do not reorder. Inventory is almost depleted, but there is no need to place a new order because the scheduled receipt is on the way.

SELECTING THE REORDER POINT WHEN DEMAND IS UNCERTAIN. In reality, demand and lead times are not always predictable. For instance, the museum's buyer knows that *average* demand is 18 feeders per week and that the *average* lead time is two weeks. That is, a variable number of feeders may be purchased during the lead time, with an average demand during lead time of 36 feeders (assuming that each week's demand is identically distributed). This situation gives rise to the need for safety stocks. Suppose that the museum's buyer sets R at 46 units, thereby placing orders before they typically are needed. This approach will create a safety stock, or stock held in excess of expected demand, of 10 units (46 − 36) to buffer against uncertain demand. In general,

Reorder point = Average demand during lead time + Safety stock

Figure 15.8 shows how the Q system operates when demand is variable and uncertain. We assume that the variability in lead times is negligible and, therefore, can be treated as a constant, as we did in the development of the EOQ model. The wavy downward-sloping line indicates that demand varies from day to day. Its slope is steeper in the second cycle, which means that the demand rate is higher during this time

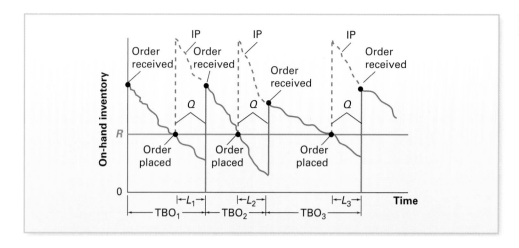

FIGURE 15.8

Q System When Demand Is Uncertain

period. The changing demand rate means that the time between orders changes, so $TBO_1 \neq TBO_2 \neq TBO_3$. Because of uncertain demand, sales during lead time are unpredictable, and safety stock is added to hedge against lost sales. This addition is why R is higher in Figure 15.8 than in Figure 15.7. It also explains why the on-hand inventory usually does not drop to 0 by the time a replenishment order arrives. The greater the safety stock, and thus the higher reorder point R, the less likely a stockout.

Because the average demand during lead time is variable and uncertain, the real decision to be made when selecting R concerns the safety stock level. Deciding on a small or large safety stock is a trade-off between customer service and inventory holding costs. Cost minimization models can be used to find the best safety stock, but they require estimates of stockout and backorder costs, which are usually difficult to make with any precision. The usual approach for determining R is for management—based on judgment—to set a reasonable service-level policy for the inventory and then determine the safety stock level that satisfies this policy.

CHOOSING AN APPROPRIATE SERVICE-LEVEL POLICY. Managers must weigh the benefits of holding safety stock against the cost of holding it. One way to determine the safety stock is to set a **service level,** or cycle-service level—the desired probability of not running out of stock in any one ordering cycle, which begins at the time an order is placed and ends when it arrives in stock. In a bookstore, the manager may select a 90 percent cycle-service level for a book. In other words, the probability is 90 percent that demand will not exceed the supply during the lead time. For the Q system, the lead time is also the **protection interval,** or the period over which safety stock must protect the user from running out of stock. The probability of running short *during the protection interval*, creating a stockout or backorder, is only 10 percent $(100 - 90)$. This stockout risk, which occurs only during the lead time in the Q system, is greater than the overall risk of stockout because the risk is nonexistent outside the ordering cycle.

To translate this policy into a specific safety stock level, we must know how demand during the lead time is distributed. If demand varies little around its average, safety stock can be small. Conversely, if demand during the lead time varies greatly from one order cycle to the next, the safety stock must be large. Variability is measured with probability distributions, which are specified by a mean and a variance.

FINDING THE SAFETY STOCK. When selecting the safety stock, the inventory planner often assumes that demand during lead time is normally distributed, as shown in Figure 15.9. The average demand during the lead time is the centerline of the graph, with 50 percent of the area under the curve to the left and 50 percent to the right. Thus, if a cycle-service level of 50 percent were chosen, the reorder point R would be the quantity represented by this centerline. As R equals the average demand during the lead time plus the safety stock, the safety stock is 0 when R equals this average

service level The desired probability of not running out of stock in any one ordering cycle, which begins at the time an order is placed and ends when it arrives in stock.

cycle-service level See **service level.**

protection interval The period over which safety stock must protect the user from running out of stock.

FIGURE 15.9

Finding Safety Stock with a Normal Probability Distribution for an 85 Percent Cycle-Service Level

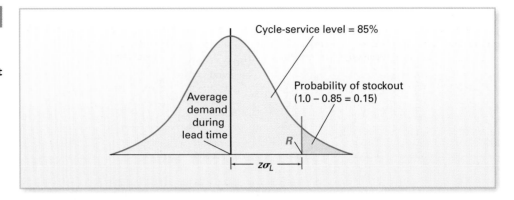

demand. Demand is less than average 50 percent of the time and, thus, having no safety stock will be sufficient only 50 percent of the time.

To provide a service level above 50 percent, the reorder point must be greater than the average demand during the lead time. In Figure 15.9 that requires moving the reorder point to the right of the centerline so that more than 50 percent of the area under the curve is to the left of R. An 85 percent cycle-service level is achieved in Figure 15.9 with 85 percent of the area under the curve to the left of R (in blue) and only 15 percent to the right (in pink). We compute the safety stock by multiplying the number of standard deviations from the mean needed to implement the cycle-service level, z, by the standard deviation of demand during lead time probability distribution,[5] σ_L:

$$\text{Safety stock} = z\sigma_L$$

The higher the value of z, the higher the safety stock and the cycle-service level should be. If $z = 0$, there is no safety stock, and stockouts will occur during 50 percent of the order cycles.

EXAMPLE 15.5   Finding the Safety Stock and R

Records show that the demand for dishwasher detergent during the lead time is normally distributed, with an average of 250 boxes and $\sigma_L = 22$. What safety stock should be carried for a 99 percent cycle-service level? What is R?

SOLUTION

The first step is to find z, the number of standard deviations to the right of average demand during the lead time that places 99 percent of the area under the curve to the left of that point (0.9900 in the body of the table in the Normal Distribution appendix). The closest number in the table is 0.9901, which corresponds to 2.3 in the row heading and 0.03 in the column heading. Adding these values gives a z of 2.33. With this information, you can calculate the safety stock and reorder point:

$$\text{Safety stock} = z\sigma_L = 2.33(22) = 51.3 \quad \text{or} \quad 51 \text{ boxes}$$
$$\text{Reorder point} = \text{Average demand during lead time} + \text{Safety stock}$$
$$= 250 + 51 = 301 \text{ boxes}$$

---

[5]Some inventory planners who use manual systems prefer to work with the mean absolute deviation (MAD) rather than the standard deviation because it is easier to calculate. Recall that to approximate the standard deviation you simply multiply the MAD by 1.25 (see Chapter 13, "Forecasting"). Then, proceed to calculate the safety stock.

We rounded the safety stock to the nearest whole number. In this case, the theoretical cycle-service level will be less than 99 percent. Raising the safety stock to 52 boxes will yield a cycle-service level greater than 99 percent.

DECISION POINT Management can control the quantity of safety stock by choosing a service level. Another approach to reducing safety stock is to reduce the standard deviation of demand during the lead time, which can be accomplished by closer coordination with major customers through information technology.

Finding the appropriate reorder point and safety stock in practice requires estimating the distribution for the demand during the lead time. Sometimes average demand during the lead time and the standard deviation of demand during the lead time, σ_L, are not directly available and must be calculated by combining information on the demand rate with information on the lead time. There are two reasons for this additional calculation.

1. It may be easier to develop estimates for demand first and then to develop estimates for the lead time. Demand information comes from the customer, whereas lead times come from the supplier.

2. Records are not likely to be collected for a time interval that is exactly the same as the lead time. The same inventory control system may be used to manage thousands of different items, each with a different lead time. For example, if demand is reported *weekly,* records can be used directly to compute the average and the standard deviation of demand during the lead time if the lead time is exactly one week. However, the average and standard deviation of demand during the lead time for a lead time of three weeks are more difficult to determine.

We can get at the more difficult case by making some reasonable assumptions. Suppose that the average demand, d, is known along with the standard deviation of demand, σ_t, over some time interval t (say, days or weeks), where t does not equal the lead time. Also, suppose that the probability distributions of demand for each time interval t are identical and independent of each other. For example, if the time interval is a week, the probability distributions of demand are the same each week (identical d and σ_t), and the total demand in one week does not affect the total demand in another week. Let L be the constant lead time, expressed as a multiple (or fraction) of t. If t represents a week and the lead time is three weeks, $L = 3$. Under these assumptions, average demand during the lead time will be the sum of the averages for each of the L identical and independent distributions of demand, or $d + d + d + \cdots = dL$. In addition, the variance of the demand distribution for the lead time will be the sum of the variances of the L identical and independent distributions of demand, or $\sigma_t^2 + \sigma_t^2 + \sigma_t^2 + \cdots = \sigma_t^2 L$. Finally, the standard deviation of the sum of two or more identically distributed independent random variables is the square root of the sum of their variances, or

$$\sigma_L = \sqrt{\sigma_t^2 L} = \sigma_t \sqrt{L}$$

Figure 15.10 shows how the demand distribution for the lead time is developed from the individual distributions of weekly demands, where $d = 75$, $\sigma_t = 15$, and $L = 3$ weeks. In this case, average demand during the lead time is $(75)(3) = 225$ units and $\sigma_L = 15\sqrt{3} = 25.98$, or 26.

CALCULATING TOTAL Q SYSTEM COSTS. Total costs for the continuous review (Q) system is the sum of three cost components:

Total cost = Annual cycle inventory holding cost + Annual ordering cost
        + Annual safety stock holding cost

$$C = \frac{Q}{2}(H) + \frac{D}{Q}(S) + Hz\sigma_L$$

FIGURE 15.10   Development of Demand Distribution for the Lead Time

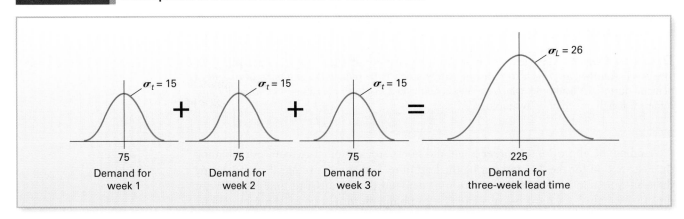

The annual cycle inventory holding cost and annual ordering costs are the same equations we used for computing the annual cost in Examples 15.2 and 15.3. The annual cost of holding the safety stock is computed under the assumption that the safety stock is on hand all the time. Referring to Figure 15.8 in each order cycle, sometimes, we will have experienced a demand greater than the average demand during lead time, and sometimes we will have experienced less. On average over the year, we can assume the safety stock will be on hand.

EXAMPLE 15.6   **Finding the Safety Stock and R When the Demand Distribution for the Lead Time Must Be Developed**

TUTOR 15.4

Tutor 15.4 on the Student CD-ROM provides a new example to determine the safety stock and the reorder point for a Q system.

Let us return to the bird feeder example. Suppose that the average demand is 18 units per week with a standard deviation of 5 units. The lead time is constant at two weeks. Determine the safety stock and reorder point if management wants a 90 percent cycle-service level. What is the total cost of the Q system?

SOLUTION

In this case, $t = 1$ week, $d = 18$ units, and $L = 2$ weeks, so

$$\sigma_L = \sigma_t \sqrt{L} = 5\sqrt{2} = 7.1$$

Consult the body of the table in the Normal Distribution appendix for 0.9000, which corresponds to a 90 percent cycle-service level. The closest number is 0.8997, which corresponds to a z value of 1.28. With this information, we calculate the safety stock and reorder point as follows:

$$\text{Safety stock} = z\sigma_L = 1.28(7.1) = 9.1 \quad \text{or} \quad 9 \text{ units}$$
$$\text{Reorder point} = dL + \text{Safety stock}$$
$$= 2(18) + 9 = 45 \text{ units}$$

Hence, the Q system for the bird feeder operates as follows: Whenever the inventory position reaches 45 units, order 75 units. The total Q system cost for the bird feeder is

$$C = \frac{75}{2}(\$15) + \frac{936}{75}(\$45) + 9(\$15) = \$562.50 + \$561.60 + \$135.00 = \$1,259.10$$

DECISION POINT   Various order quantities and safety stock levels can be used in the Q system. For example, management could specify a different order quantity (because of shipping constraints) or a different safety stock (because of storage limitations). The total costs of such systems can be calculated, and the trade-off between costs and service levels could be assessed.

SELECTING THE REORDER POINT WHEN DEMAND AND LEAD TIME ARE UNCERTAIN. In practice, it is often the case that both demand and lead time are uncertain. The key to determining the reorder point is to develop the demand during the protection interval probability distribution under these more complicated conditions. However, once the distribution is known and a desired cycle-service level is specified, we can select the reorder point as we did before for the case where the lead time was constant. If the theoretical distributions for demand per unit of time and the lead time are known, the joint probability distribution of demand during lead time can be analytically derived with a lot of work. A more practical approach is to use computer simulation (see Supplement B, "Simulation"). A lead time is randomly drawn from the lead time distribution, and then demands for each period of the lead time are randomly drawn from the demand distribution. The total demand for that lead time is recorded, and the procedure is repeated a large number of times to arrive at a demand during lead time distribution.

We will demonstrate this approach using discrete probability distributions for the demand and lead time distributions. Discrete probability distributions can be used to approximate theoretical probability distributions, and they can be used in situations where actual demands or lead times do not follow any of the known theoretical distributions. A discrete probability distribution for lead time lists each possible lead time in time intervals t (say, days or weeks) and its probability. A discrete probability distribution for demand lists each possible demand that could occur during a time interval of length t and its probability. Consider the following information, which is based on the bird feeder data from Example 15.6. Suppose that the lead time has the probability distribution shown in Table 15.1. The average lead time is 2 weeks, as it is in Example 15.6. However, now there is considerable variability in the actual lead times that could be experienced.

Now consider the following distribution for demand as shown in Table 15.2. The average demand per week is 18 units, and the standard deviation is 5 units (rounded to the nearest whole number), as in Example 15.6. The demand during the protection interval probability distribution can be estimated using an Excel spreadsheet, as shown in Figure 15.11.

With a normal distribution, the safety stock is computed first and then is added to the average demand during lead time to get the reorder point; whereas with a

TABLE 15.1   PROBABILITY DISTRIBUTION FOR LEAD TIME

Lead Time (weeks)	Probability for Lead Time
1	0.35
2	0.45
3	0.10
4	0.05
5	0.05

TABLE 15.2   PROBABILITY DISTRIBUTION FOR DEMAND

Demand (units per week)	Probability of Demand
10	0.10
13	0.20
18	0.40
23	0.20
26	0.10

FIGURE 15.11   Excel Spreadsheet Showing How to Simulate Demand During the Protection Interval for a Q System

Demand Probability Distribution
(Units Per Period)

Probability of Demand	Lower Range Probability	Demand (Units)
0.10	0.00	10
0.20	0.10	13
0.40	0.30	18
0.20	0.70	23
0.10	0.90	26

Lead Time Probability Distribution

Probability of Lead Time	Lower Range	Protection Interval
0.35	0.00	1
0.45	0.35	2
0.10	0.80	3
0.05	0.90	4
0.05	0.95	5

Demand During Protection Interval Distribution

BINS	Demand	Frequency	Cumulative Percentage
10	10	24	0.05
22	16	84	0.22
34	28	141	0.50
46	40	145	0.79
58	52	49	0.89
70	64	23	0.93
82	76	17	0.97
94	88	10	0.99
106	100	5	1.00
118	112	2	1.00
130	More	0	1.00
	Total	500	

Lower Bound	10
Upper Bound	130
Range	120
Bins	10
Bin Range	12

Random Numbers

Demand Per Period in Protection Interval

Lead Time	Period 1	Period 2	Period 3	Period 4	Period 5	Period 6	Period 7	Period 8	Period 9	Period 10
0.1637	0.0833	0.5102	0.2518	0.5184	0.2025	0.7836	0.1628	0.5987	0.3116	0.4781
0.6769	0.8404	0.6872	0.0135	0.1993	0.6971	0.3746	0.4923	0.4031	0.1828	0.5277
0.6847	0.7367	0.9619	0.9626	0.5671	0.5760	0.6335	0.1021	0.6465	0.1341	0.3566
0.2129	0.6666	0.7249	0.4595	0.2043	0.6652	0.6160	0.9479	0.7499	0.5985	0.0808
0.2541	0.0365	0.4230	0.2839	0.7738	0.3001	0.8734	0.0667	0.8477	0.7052	0.0513
0.5016	0.6766	0.6239	0.3281	0.6489	0.4644	0.6653	0.5601	0.9461	0.5983	0.6157
				0.7195	0.0047	0.6908	0.5194	0.4332	0.1357	0.9932
				0.3818	0.7743	0.9017	0.2498	0.8027	0.1885	0.7843
				0.2327	0.6862	0.2880	0.2900	0.1826	0.0995	0.1947
				0.9474	0.1487	0.0656	0.8645	0.4554	0.1548	0.6615
				0.6635	0.1279	0.5530	0.1295	0.0743	0.8928	0.2884
				0.7150	0.6383	0.4391	0.5368	0.7860	0.0648	0.5368
0.7255	0.8283	0.0344	0.8689	0.2304	0.4721	0.5777	0.0694	0.0299	0.4083	0.1546
0.0536	0.3992	0.1281	0.8438	0.1844	0.7781	0.6994	0.8040	0.5647	0.2609	0.2157
0.7607	0.6912	0.8048	0.3671	0.8267	0.8732	0.2523	0.0433	0.2588	0.4854	0.2447
0.2107	0.7238	0.9769	0.4767	0.4132	0.0630	0.7979	0.6091	0.5206	0.8320	0.5991
0.2335	0.4533	0.6874	0.9631	0.6808	0.8151	0.3555	0.5553	0.7274	0.4522	0.3312
0.0386	0.3003	0.4065	0.3505	0.9062	0.5987	0.4494	0.8158	0.4851	0.2432	0.2846
0.5019	0.9661	0.2541	0.6851	0.2483	0.0343	0.4933	0.2734	0.1725	0.7055	0.5887
0.4108	0.8023	0.0978	0.0657	0.9296	0.6807	0.9976	0.2785	0.5228	0.2677	0.6724
0.3744	0.5385	0.7282	0.7645	0.8855	0.0943	0.6941	0.2202	0.0919	0.0393	0.0131
0.2122	0.7615	0.7820	0.0261	0.1679	0.0716	0.2459	0.2291	0.6456	0.6446	0.5195
0.0925	0.8525	0.2320	0.0427	0.7376	0.6809	0.4502	0.7044	0.5545	0.8276	0.4048
0.8343	0.6395	0.7648	0.8997	0.3425	0.3840	0.6041	0.8482	0.3168	0.8569	0.2660
						0.9964	0.9124	0.9332	0.0995	0.1204
						0.2084	0.4818	0.2383	0.0342	0.9235
						0.2432	0.6588	0.2063	0.1991	0.6926
						0.5117	0.1409	0.9094	0.3037	0.1828
						0.1725	0.3838	0.6962	0.9058	0.6118
0.6475	0.7993	0.6954	0.2517	0.8252	0.0122	0.2091	0.0821	0.2956	0.7970	0.6666
0.2870	0.2413	0.1980	0.9134	0.7304	0.5016	0.5433	0.5863	0.9347	0.7322	0.9262
0.1155	0.4369	0.6033	0.6577	0.9506	0.6063	0.8189	0.2593	0.5367	0.7205	0.6265
0.8156	0.0910	0.8654	0.3667	0.7712	0.5901	0.1183	0.2655	0.1137	0.7680	0.2330
			0.5130	0.9228	0.5766	0.9350	0.9113	0.5257	0.7750	0.9551
			0.0563	0.4335	0.2733	0.4960	0.8591	0.6733	0.7491	0.8072
			0.0315	0.7549	0.6415	0.0524	0.6159	0.9905	0.7097	0.1597
			0.0015	0.4733	0.8386	0.3708	0.7001	0.1249	0.6756	0.9454
			0.3777	0.0219	0.9943	0.2587	0.8397	0.3581	0.4197	0.1695
			0.0735	0.4363	0.7587	0.3205	0.4638	0.7741	0.4405	0.2971
			0.1646	0.4396	0.0534	0.1325	0.2512	0.5349	0.0922	0.6232
			0.2910	0.4212	0.0393	0.0922	0.7903	0.9088	0.2052	0.2047
0.7387	0.4376	0.0762	0.8870	0.1202	0.7112	0.6327	0.7573	0.9966	0.0188	0.2281
0.3492	0.9502	0.0280	0.7639	0.8914	0.5056	0.3405	0.4324	0.1394	0.1070	0.0724
0.5814	0.5982	0.5455	0.7837	0.4116	0.5398	0.8612	0.8702	0.3948	0.6403	0.1019
0.3771	0.2760	0.9884	0.8313	0.5897	0.6728	0.4663	0.5004	0.2913	0.9015	0.6352

Callout: Random numbers are generated by using the Random Number generator function RAND (). These numbers are frozen by copying the numbers and pasting them as values from cell F4:P503.

Callout: Frequencies are calculated by using the FREQUENCY ARRAY function: =FREQUENCY(AD4:AD503,A23:A33) Cells AD4:AD503 are the data array inputs and cells A23:A33 are the bin array input of the function.

Callout: "Bins" are the upper bounds of the intervals that we need to group the total demand during the protection interval.

Callout: They are obtained by subtracting the lower bound from the upper bound and dividing it by 10. This will be the range of each bin, thus allowing 10 bins of the same size. Simply start with the lower bound and add to it the Bin Range (cell B44, which is cell B40/cell B42, in this case).

discrete distribution, the sequence is reversed. We assume that the demand levels listed in Figure 15.11 are the only demand levels that can occur (nothing in between). We then select R from the list of demand levels in the distribution. The cumulative probability of demands at or less than the chosen value for R must equal or exceed the desired cycle-service level, and R is the smallest such quantity. This is a conservative approach that assures we will meet or exceed our inventory service goals. For example, since the desired cycle-service level for the bird feeder is 90 percent, we would set R equal to 64 units in Figure 15.11, which actually will give us a cycle-service level of 93 percent. To calculate the level of safety stock, subtract the average demand during the lead time in the simulation from R. In our example, the safety stock is 64 − 36 = 28 units.

We can now specify the complete continuous review (Q) system. The order quantity is determined as before; here, as in Example 15.6, we use an EOQ of 75 units. The reorder point is 64 units, and the safety stock is 28 units. The total cost, C, of this system is

$$C = \frac{75}{2}(\$15) + \frac{936}{75}(\$45) + 28(\$15) = \$562.50 + \$561.60 + \$420.00 = \$1,544.10$$

FIGURE 15.11   continued

Simulation

Inventory Cycle	Lead Time (# Periods)	Period 1	Period 2	Period 3	Period 4	Period 5	Period 6	Period 7	Period 8	Period 9	Period 10	Total During Protection Interval
					Demand Per Period in Protection Interval							
1	1	10	0	0	0	0	0	0	0	0	0	10
2	2	23	18	0	0	0	0	0	0	0	0	41
3	2	23	26	0	0	0	0	0	0	0	0	49
4	1	18									0	18
5	1	10									0	10
6	2	18									0	36
7	1	10									0	10
8	1	10									0	10
9	1	18									0	18
10	2	13									0	36
11	1	13									0	13
12	3	23									0	54
13	2	23									0	33
14	1	18	0	0	0	0	0	0	0	0	0	18
15	2	18	23	0	0	0	0	0	0	0	0	41
16	1	23	0	0	0	0	0	0	0	0	0	23
17	1	18	0	0	0						0	18
18	1	18	0	0	0						0	18
19	2	26	13	0	0						0	39
20	2	23	10	0	0						0	33
21	2	18	23	0	0						0	41
22	1	23	0	0	0						0	23
23	1	23	0	0	0						0	23
24	3	18	23	23	0	0	0	0	0	0	0	64
25	2	18	18	0	0	0	0	0	0	0	0	36
26	1	13	0	0	0	0	0	0	0	0	0	13
27	3	18	26	18	0	0	0	0	0	0	0	62
28	3	18	18	18	0	0	0	0	0	0	0	54
29	1	18	0	0	0	0	0	0	0	0	0	18
30	2	23	18	0	0	0	0	0	0	0	0	41
31	1	13	0	0	0	0	0	0	0	0	0	13
32	1	18	0	0	0	0	0	0	0	0	0	18
33	3	10	23	18	0	0	0	0	0	0	0	51
34	3	13	18	18	0	0	0	0	0	0	0	49
35	2	26	18	0	0	0	0	0	0	0	0	44
36	1	23	0	0	0	0	0	0	0	0	0	23
37	2	13	23	0	0	0	0	0	0	0	0	36
38	2	18	18	0	0	0	0	0	0	0	0	36
39	4	18	13	10	18	0	0	0	0	0	0	59
40	2	23	26	0	0	0	0	0	0	0	0	49
41	2	13	18	0	0	0	0	0	0	0	0	31
42	2	18	10	0	0	0	0	0	0	0	0	28
43	1	26	0	0	0	0	0	0	0	0	0	26
44	2	18	18	0	0	0	0	0	0	0	0	36
45	2	13	26	0	0	0	0	0	0	0	0	39

Callout: To obtain the demand per period, it is necessary to use the **value look up function**. With this function the corresponding demand value will be based on the random number and the match up of that number with the probability distribution of demand. Enter the formula: **IF($S4>=1,VLOOKUP(G4,$B$4:$C$8,2),0)** into cell T4. This formula will look up the value in Lower Range Probability and the units of Demand assigned to each probability. The units demanded will be assigned based on the value of the Random Number in the specific period. Enter the formula: **IF($S4>=2,VLOOKUP(H4,$B$4:$C$8,2),0)** into cell U4. Copy this relationship in cells T4:AC503.

Callout: The total demand is simply the summation of the demand at every individual period, which can be obtained by using the sumation function: **=SUM(T4:AC4)** Copy it and paste it as a formula through cells AD4:AD503

OM Explorer has two spreadsheet solvers that can be used to analyze *Q* systems when both the demand and the lead time are uncertain. The Demand During the Protection Interval Simulator can be used to develop the probability distribution for the protection interval from which you can choose an appropriate value of *R* for a given cycle-service level. Once the reorder point and the order quantity have been specified, the *Q* system can be simulated using the *Q* System Simulator. (Solved Problem 8 shows an application of this Solver.) See Supplement B, "Simulation," for details on how to develop your own inventory simulator.

TWO-BIN SYSTEM. The concept of a *Q* system can be incorporated in a **visual system,** that is, a system that allows employees to place orders when inventory visibly reaches a certain marker. Visual systems are easy to administer because records are not kept on the current inventory position. The historical usage rate can simply be reconstructed from past purchase orders. Visual systems are intended for use with low-value items that have a steady demand, such as nuts and bolts or office supplies. Overstocking is common, but the extra inventory holding cost is minimal because the items have relatively little value.

visual system A system that allows employees to place orders when inventory visibly reaches a certain marker.

A visual system version of the Q system is the **two-bin system** in which an item's inventory is stored at two different locations. Inventory is first withdrawn from one bin. If the first bin is empty, the second bin provides backup to cover demand until a replenishment order arrives. An empty first bin signals the need to place a new order. Premade order forms placed near the bins let workers send one to purchasing or even directly to the supplier. When the new order arrives, the second bin is restored to its normal level and the rest is put in the first bin. The two-bin system operates like a Q system, with the normal level in the second bin being the reorder point R. The system also may be implemented with just one bin by marking the bin at the reorder point level.

PERIODIC REVIEW SYSTEM

An alternative inventory control system is the **periodic review (P) system**, sometimes called a *fixed interval reorder system* or *periodic reorder system,* in which an item's inventory position is reviewed periodically rather than continuously. Such a system can simplify delivery scheduling because it establishes a routine. A new order is always placed at the end of each review, and the time between orders (TBO) is fixed at P. Demand is a random variable, so total demand between reviews varies. In a P system, the lot size, Q, may change from one order to the next, but the time between orders is fixed. An example of a periodic review system is that of a soft-drink supplier making weekly rounds of grocery stores. Each week, the supplier reviews the store's inventory of soft drinks and restocks the store with enough items to meet demand and safety stock requirements until the next week.

Four of the original EOQ assumptions are maintained: (1) there are no constraints on the size of the lot, (2) the relevant costs are holding and ordering costs, (3) decisions for one item are independent of decisions for other items, and (4) there is no uncertainty in lead times or supply. However, demand uncertainty is again allowed for. We will allow for lead time uncertainty later. Figure 15.12 shows the periodic review system under these assumptions. The downward-sloping line again represents on-hand inventory. When the predetermined time, P, has elapsed since the last review, an order is placed to bring the inventory position, represented by the dashed line, up to the target inventory level, T. The lot size for the first review is Q_1, or the difference between inventory position IP_1 and T. As with the continuous review system, IP and OH differ only during the lead time. When the order arrives, at the end of the lead time, OH and IP again are identical. Figure 15.12 shows that lot sizes vary from one order cycle to the next. Because the inventory position is lower at the second review, a greater quantity is needed to achieve an inventory level of T.

FIGURE 15.12

P System When Demand Is Uncertain

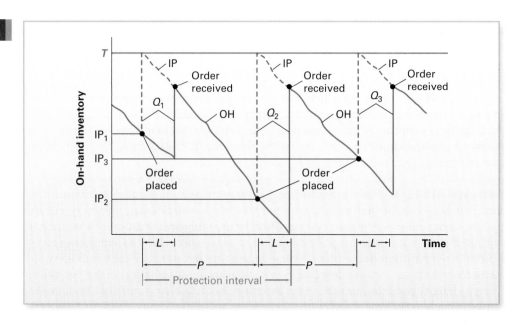

Determining How Much to Reorder in a P System

EXAMPLE 15.7

There is a backorder of five 36-inch color TV sets at a distribution center. There is no on-hand inventory, and now is the time to review. How much should be reordered if $T = 400$ and there are no scheduled receipts?

SOLUTION

$$IP = OH + SR - BO$$
$$= 0 + 0 - 5 = -5 \text{ sets}$$
$$T - IP = 400 - (-5) = 405 \text{ sets}$$

That is, 405 sets must be ordered to bring the inventory position up to T sets.

SELECTING THE TIME BETWEEN REVIEWS. To run a P system, managers must make two decisions: the length of time between reviews, P, and the target inventory level, T. Let us first consider the time between reviews, P. It can be any convenient interval, such as each Friday or every other Friday. Another option is to base P on the cost trade-offs of the EOQ. In other words, P can be set equal to the average time between orders for the economic order quantity, or TBO_{EOQ}. Because demand is variable, some orders will be larger than the EOQ and some will be smaller. However, over an extended period of time, the average lot size should equal the EOQ. If other models are used to determine the lot size (e.g., those described in Supplement E, "Special Inventory Models"), we divide the lot size chosen by the annual demand, D, and use this ratio as P. It will be expressed as the fraction of a year between orders, which can be converted into months, weeks, or days as needed.

SELECTING THE TARGET INVENTORY LEVEL WHEN DEMAND IS UNCERTAIN. Now let us consider how to calculate the target inventory level, T, when demand is uncertain but the lead time is constant. Figure 15.12 reveals that an order must be large enough to make the inventory position, IP, last beyond the next review, which is P time periods away. The checker must wait P periods to revise, correct, and reestablish the inventory position. Then, a new order is placed, but it does not arrive until after the lead time, L. Therefore, as Figure 15.12 shows, a protection interval of $P + L$ periods is needed. A fundamental difference between the Q and P systems is the length of time needed for stockout protection. A Q system needs stockout protection only during the lead time because orders can be placed as soon as they are needed and will be received L periods later. A P system, however, needs stockout protection for the longer $P + L$ protection interval because orders are placed only at fixed intervals, and the inventory is not checked until the next designated review time.

As with the Q system, we need to develop the appropriate distribution of demand during the protection interval to specify the system fully. In a P system, we must develop the distribution of demand for $P + L$ time periods. The target inventory level T must equal the expected demand during the protection interval of $P + L$ periods, plus enough safety stock to protect against demand uncertainty over this same protection interval. We use the same statistical assumptions that we made for the Q system. Thus, the average demand during the protection interval is $d(P + L)$, or

$$T = d(P + L) + \text{Safety stock for protection interval}$$

We compute safety stock for a P system much as we did for the Q system. However, the safety stock must cover demand uncertainty for a longer period of time. When using a normal probability distribution, we multiply the desired standard deviations to implement the cycle-service level, z, by the standard deviation of demand during the protection interval, σ_{P+L}. The value of z is the same as for a Q system with the same cycle-service level. Thus,

$$\text{Safety stock} = z\sigma_{P+L}$$

Based on our earlier logic for calculating σ_L, we know that the standard deviation of the distribution of demand during the protection interval is

$$\sigma_{P+L} = \sigma_t \sqrt{P + L}$$

Because a P system requires safety stock to cover demand uncertainty over a longer time period than a Q system, a P system requires more safety stock; that is, σ_{P+L} exceeds σ_L. Hence, to gain the convenience of a P system requires that overall inventory levels be somewhat higher than those for a Q system.

CALCULATING TOTAL P SYSTEM COSTS. The total costs for the P system are the sum of the same three cost elements as for the Q system. The differences are in the calculation of the order quantity and the safety stock. Referring to Figure 15.12, the average order quantity will be the average consumption of inventory during the P periods between orders. Consequently, $Q = dP$. Total costs for the P system are

$$C = \frac{dP}{2}(H) + \frac{D}{dP}(S) + Hz\sigma_{P+L}$$

Managerial Practice 15.2 shows how Hewlett-Packard implemented a periodic review inventory system for many of their business units.

EXAMPLE 15.8   Calculating P and T

TUTOR 15.5

Tutor 15.5 on the Student CD-ROM provides a new example to determine the review interval and the target inventory for a P system.

Again, let us return to the bird feeder example. Recall that demand for the bird feeder is normally distributed with a mean of 18 units per week and a standard deviation in weekly demand of 5 units. The lead time is 2 weeks, and the business operates 52 weeks per year. The Q system developed in Example 15.6 called for an EOQ of 75 units and a safety stock of 9 units for a cycle-service level of 90 percent. What is the equivalent P system? What is the total cost? Answers are to be rounded to the nearest integer.

SOLUTION

We first define D and then P. Here, P is the time between reviews, expressed as a multiple (or fraction) of time interval t ($t = 1$ week because the data are expressed as demand *per week*):

$$D = (18 \text{ units/week})(52 \text{ weeks/year}) = 936 \text{ units}$$
$$P = \frac{\text{EOQ}}{D}(52) = \frac{75}{936}(52) = 4.2 \quad \text{or} \quad 4 \text{ weeks}$$

With $d = 18$ units per week, we can also calculate P by dividing the EOQ by d to get $75/18 = 4.2$ or 4 weeks. Hence, we would review the bird feeder inventory every 4 weeks. We now find the standard deviation of demand over the protection interval ($P + L = 6$):

$$\sigma_{P+L} = \sigma_t \sqrt{P + L} = 5\sqrt{6} = 12 \text{ units}$$

Before calculating T, we also need a z value. For a 90 percent cycle-service level, $z = 1.28$ (see the Normal Distribution appendix). We now solve for T:

MANAGERIAL PRACTICE 15.2

IMPLEMENTING A PERIODIC REVIEW INVENTORY SYSTEM AT HEWLETT-PACKARD

Hewlett-Packard (www.hp.com) manufactures computers, accessories, and a wide variety of instrumentation devices in more than 100 separate businesses, each responsible for its own product designing, marketing, and manufacturing processes as well as the required inventories to service its customers. At most HP businesses, inventory-driven costs (which include currency devaluation, obsolescence, price protection, and financing) are now the biggest control lever that the manufacturing organization has on business performance, measured in terms of return on assets or economic value added. Inventory is a major cost driver and the most variable element on the balance sheet.

Most of HP's business units were inefficient, carrying more inventory than needed in order to achieve a desired level of product delivery performance. They often used simplified approaches, such as ABC analysis, to determine their safety stocks for independent demand items, ignoring supply or demand uncertainty, part commonality, desired part availability, or cost. The solution was to develop a periodic review system that used part availability targets and included as many uncertainties as possible. The system, although in principle similar to the *P* system discussed in this chapter, uses complex equations to determine the review interval and target inventory parameters. The complexity arises from considering uncertainties in supply as well as demand in the determination of the safety stocks.

Even though the system could be shown to reduce inventories and improve customer service, no benefits would be realized until the planning and procurement staff actually used it. Since each business unit had some unique characteristics, the results had to be easily understandable and credible, and the system had to be easily configurable to each situation. Consequently, HP developed a software wizard that allows the user to enter product data and costs in a friendly environment, develops the equations for the periodic review system, and then translates the results to the user's format requirements. The wizard is programmed in Excel, which allows users access to all of Excel's functionality for conducting their own analyses.

The periodic review system and the software wizard have been very successful. At HP's Integrated Circuit Manufacturing Division, for example, planners cut inventories by $1.6 million while simultaneously improving on-time delivery performance from 93 percent to 97 percent. Other benefits included less expediting, fewer disagreements about operating policy, and more control of the production system. The system is used across a wide variety of product lines and geographies wordwide. HP believes that, without exception, the product lines how have more efficient operations.

Source: Cargille, Brian, Steve Kakouros, and Robert Hall. "Part Tool, Part Process: Inventory Optimization at Hewlett-Packard Co." *OR/MS/TODAY* (October 1999), pp. 18–24.

$$T = \text{Average demand during the protection interval} + \text{Safety stock}$$
$$= d(P + L) + z\sigma_{P+L}$$
$$= (18 \text{ units/week})(6 \text{ weeks}) + 1.28(12 \text{ units}) = 123 \text{ units}$$

Every 4 weeks we would order the number of units needed to bring inventory position IP (counting the new order) up to the target inventory level of 123 units. The safety stock for this *P* system is 1.28(12) = 15 units.

The total *P* system cost for the bird feeder is

$$C = \frac{4(18)}{2}(\$15) + \frac{936}{4(18)}(\$45) + 15(\$15) = \$540 + \$585 + \$225 = \$1,350$$

DECISION POINT The *P* system requires 15 units in safety stock, while the *Q* system only needs 9 units. If cost were the only criterion, the *Q* system would be the choice for the bird feeder. As we discuss in the next section, there are other factors that may sway the decision in favor of the *P* system.

SELECTING THE TARGET INVENTORY LEVEL WHEN DEMAND AND LEAD TIME ARE UNCERTAIN.
The procedure for selecting the target inventory level when both demand and lead times are uncertain is similar to the approach we used for the continuous review system. The difference is that now we must consider the demand

over the protection interval, $P + L$. Computer simulation is a practical approach, given the probability distributions for demand and lead times. The review period, P, is considered a constant. The simulation proceeds by randomly drawing a lead time L and adding it to P to arrive at a protection interval. Next, demands are randomly drawn from the demand distribution for each period in the protection interval. The total demand is recorded, and the procedure is repeated.

Consider the bird feeder data that we used previously to demonstrate the use of simulation for the development of the demand during the protection interval probability distribution in the continuous review system. Example 15.8 showed that the best review interval, P, is four weeks. Figure 15.13 shows the distribution of the demand during the protection interval for the bird feeder data using the Demand During the Protection Interval Simulator in OM Explorer. We select T from the list of demand levels in the distribution. The cumulative probability of demands at or less than the selected T must equal or exceed the desired cycle-service level. In this example, the desired cycle-service level is 90 percent; the best choice is $T = 136$. The amount of safety stock required for that level of service is found by subtracting the average demand during the protection level from T. Here, the safety stock is $136 - 108 = 28$ units.[6]

FIGURE 15.13   **Demand During the Protection Interval Probability Distribution for a P System**

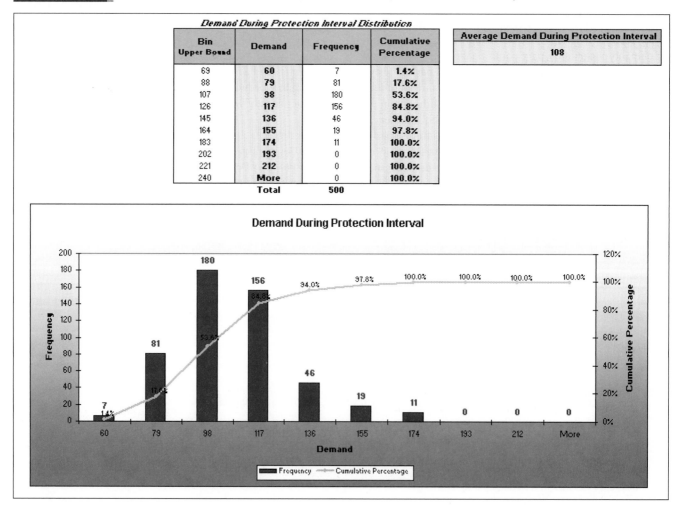

---

[6]Recall that our development of the Q system using the Demand During the Protection Interval Simulator resulted in the same safety stock quantity. Simulations of this sort should be run multiple times before drawing conclusions. Typically, the safety stock required for a P system exceeds that the Q system.

The total cost for the *P* system when both demands and lead times are uncertain is

$$C = \frac{4(18)}{2}(\$15) + \frac{936}{4(18)}(\$45) + 28(\$15) = \$540.00 + \$585.00 + \$420.00 = \$1,545.00$$

The Demand During the Protection Interval Simulator in OM Explorer can be used to develop the demand distribution for periodic review systems when both demand and lead times are uncertain.

SINGLE-BIN SYSTEM. The concept of a *P* system can be translated into a simple visual system of inventory control. In the **single-bin system**, a maximum level is marked on the storage shelf or bin on a measuring rod, and the inventory is brought up to the mark periodically—say, once a week. The single bin may be, for example, a gasoline storage tank at a service station or a storage bin for small parts at a manufacturing plant.

single-bin system A system of inventory control in which a maximum level is marked on the storage shelf or bin on a measuring rod, and the inventory is brought up to the mark periodically.

COMPARATIVE ADVANTAGES OF THE *Q* AND *P* SYSTEMS
Neither the *Q* nor *P* system is best for all situations. Three *P*-system advantages must be balanced against three *Q*-system advantages. The advantages of one system are implicitly disadvantages of the other system. The primary advantages of *P* systems are the following:

Which type of system—a *Q* or *P* system—should be used to control inventories?

1. Administration of the system is convenient because replenishments are made at fixed intervals. Employees can regularly set aside a day or part of a day to concentrate on this particular task. Fixed replenishment intervals also allow for standardized pickup and delivery times.

2. Orders for multiple items from the same supplier may be combined into a single purchase order. This approach reduces ordering and transportation costs and may result in a price break from the supplier.

3. The inventory position, IP, needs to be known only when a review is made (not continuously, as in a *Q* system). However, this advantage is moot for firms using computerized record-keeping systems, in which a transaction is reported upon each receipt or withdrawal. When inventory records are always current, the system is called a **perpetual inventory system**.

perpetual inventory system A system of inventory control in which the inventory records are always current.

The primary advantages of *Q* systems are the following:

1. The review frequency of each item may be individualized. Tailoring the review frequency to the item can reduce total ordering and holding costs.

2. Fixed lot sizes, if large enough, may result in quantity discounts. Physical limitations, such as truckload capacities, materials handling methods, and shelf space also may require a fixed lot size.

3. Lower safety stocks result in savings.

In conclusion, the choice between *Q* and *P* systems is not clear cut. Which system is better depends on the relative importance of its advantages in various situations. Management must weigh each alternative carefully in selecting the best system.

What other types of systems are possible?

HYBRID SYSTEMS
Various hybrid inventory control systems merge some but not all the features of the *P* and *Q* systems. We briefly examine two such systems: (1) optional replenishment and (2) base stock.

optional replenishment system A system used to review the inventory position at fixed time intervals and, if the position has dropped to (or below) a predetermined level, to place a variable-sized order to cover expected needs.

OPTIONAL REPLENISHMENT SYSTEM. Sometimes called the optional review, min–max, or (*s*, *S*) system, the **optional replenishment system** is much like the *P* system. It is used to review the inventory position at fixed time intervals and, if the position has dropped to (or below) a predetermined level, to place a variable-sized order to cover expected needs. The new order is large enough to bring the inventory position up to a target inventory, similar to T for the P system. However, orders are not placed after a review unless the inventory position has dropped to the predetermined minimum level. The minimum level acts as reorder point R does in a Q system. If the target is 100 and the minimum level is 60, the minimum order size is 40 (or $100 - 60$). The optional review system avoids continuous reviews and, therfore, it is particularly attractive when both review and ordering costs are significant.

base-stock system An inventory control system that issues a replenishment order, Q, each time a withdrawal is made, for the same amount of the withdrawal.

BASE-STOCK SYSTEM. In its simplest form, the **base-stock system** issues a replenishment order, Q, each time a withdrawal is made, for the same amount as the withdrawal. This one-for-one replacement policy maintains the inventory position at a base-stock level equal to expected demand during the lead time plus safety stock. The base-stock level, therefore, is equivalent to the reorder point in a Q system. However, order quantities now vary to keep the inventory position at R at all times. Because this position is the lowest IP possible that will maintain a specified service level, the base-stock system may be used to minimize cycle inventory. More orders are placed, but each order is smaller. This system is appropriate for very expensive items, such as replacement engines for jet airplanes. No more inventory is held than the maximum demand expected until a replacement order can be received. The base-stock system is also used in just-in-time systems. The average demand during lead time plus safety stock, used in the calculation of the number of containers in a kanban system, is actually the base-stock level (see Chapter 11, "Lean Systems").

INVENTORY RECORD ACCURACY

Regardless of the inventory system in use, record accuracy is crucial to its success. One method of achieving and maintaining accuracy is to assign responsibility to specific employees for issuing and receiving materials and accurately reporting each transaction. A second method is to secure inventory behind locked doors or gates to prevent unauthorized or unreported withdrawals. This method also guards against storing new receipts in the wrong locations, where they can be lost for months. **Cycle counting** is a third method, whereby storeroom personnel physically count a small percentage of the total number of items each day, correcting errors that they find. Class A items are counted most frequently. A final method, for computerized systems, is to make logic error checks on each transaction reported and fully investigate any discrepancies. Discrepancies may include (1) actual receipts when there is no record of scheduled receipts, (2) disbursements that exceed the current on-hand balance, and (3) receipts with an inaccurate (nonexistent) part number.

cycle counting An inventory control method, whereby storeroom personnel physically count a small percentage of the total number of items each day, correcting errors that they find.

These four methods can keep inventory record accuracy within acceptable bounds. Accuracy pays off mainly through better customer service, although some inventory reductions can be achieved by improving accuracy. A side benefit is that auditors may not require end-of-year counts if records prove to be sufficiently accurate.

INVENTORY MANAGEMENT ACROSS THE ORGANIZATION

Inventories are important to all types of organizations and their employees. Inventories affect everyday operations because they must be counted, paid for, used in operations, used to satisfy customers, and managed. Inventories require an investment of funds, as does the purchase of a new machine. Monies invested in inventory are not available for investment in other things; thus, they represent a drain on the cash flows of an organization. Carrying that notion to its extreme, one may conclude that inventories should be eliminated. Not only is that idea impossible, it is hazardous to the financial health of an organization.

We have focused on independent demand inventories in this chapter. These inventories are often found in retail and distribution operations. Consequently, independent demand inventories are often the last stocking point before the consumer. Companies concerned with customer service know that availability of products is a key selling point in many markets. Earlier, we discussed Internet retail companies that have discovered a competitive advantage by controlling their own inventories, rather than outsourcing that function to someone else. The consequences in Internet markets for lack of supply are dire—plummeting stock prices, financial restructuring, outsider acquisition, or bankruptcy.

Is inventory a boon or a bane? Certainly, profitability is reduced if there is too much inventory, and customer confidence is damaged if there is too little inventory. The goal should not be to minimize inventory or to maximize customer service, but rather to have the right amount of inventory to support the competitive priorities of the company. The Internet has provided many alternatives for a successful business model. To date, we have seen pure Internet companies, combinations of Internet and brick-and-mortar companies, and totally brick-and-mortar companies.

Each of these models provides a different set of capabilities and opportunities to exploit different competitive priorities. Regardless of the model, inventory management plays a major role.

CHAPTER HIGHLIGHTS

- Inventory investment decisions involve trade-offs among the conflicting objectives of low inventory investment, good customer service, and high resource utilization. Benefits of good customer service and high resource utilization may be outweighed by the cost of carrying large inventories, including interest or opportunity costs, storage and handling costs, taxes, insurance, shrinkage, and obsolescence. Order quantity decisions are guided by a trade-off between the cost of holding inventories and the combined costs of ordering, setup, transportation, and purchased materials.

- Cycle, safety stock, anticipation, and pipeline inventories vary in size with order quantity, uncertainty, production rate flexibility, and lead time, respectively.

- Inventory placement depends on whether an item is a standard or a special and on the trade-off between short customer response time and low inventory costs.

- ABC analysis helps managers focus on the few significant items that account for the bulk of investment in inventory. Class A items deserve the most attention, with less attention justified for class B and class C items.

- A basic inventory management question is whether to order large quantities infrequently or to order small quantities frequently. The EOQ provides guidance for this choice by indicating the lot size that minimizes (subject to several assumptions) the sum of holding and ordering costs over some period of time, such as a year.

- Independent demand inventory management methods are appropriate for wholesale and retail merchandise, service industry supplies, finished goods and service parts replenishment, and maintenance, repair, and operating supplies.

- In the continuous review (Q) system, the buyer places orders of a fixed lot size Q when the inventory position drops to the reorder point. In the periodic review (P) system, every P fixed time interval the buyer places an order to replenish the quantity consumed since the last order.

- The base-stock system minimizes cycle inventory by maintaining the inventory position at the base-stock level. Visual systems, such as single-bin and two-bin systems, are adaptations of the P and Q systems that eliminate the need for inventory-position records.

STUDENT CD-ROM AND INTERNET RESOURCES

The Student CD-ROM and the Companion Website at **www.prenhall.com/krajewski** contain many tools, activities, and resources designed for this chapter. The following items are recommended to enhance your skills and improve your understanding of the material in this chapter.

STUDENT CD-ROM RESOURCES

➤ **PowerPoint Slides:** View the comprehensive set of slides customized for this chapter's concepts and techniques.

➤ **Video Clips:** See the three video clips customized for this chapter to learn more about inventory types, ABC analysis, and the effect of setup costs on lot sizes.

➤ **OM Explorer Tutors:** OM Explorer contains five tutor spreadsheets to enhance your understanding of how to estimate inventory levels, calculate EOQs and total costs,

determine the safety stock and reorder point for Q systems, calculate the review period and target inventory level for P systems, and perform ABC analysis. See Chapter 15 in the OM Explorer menu. See also the Tutor Exercise on inventory management.

➤ **OM Explorer Solvers:** OM Explorer has seven programs that can be used to solve general problems involving inventory level estimation, Q or P system development, economic production lot size calculation, quantity discount analysis, one-period inventory decisions, simulating the demand during the protection interval, and simulating the Q system. See Inventory Management in the OM Explorer menu.

➤ **Active Model:** There is an Active Model spreadsheet that provides additional insights on inventory management decisions. See Economic Order Quantity Model in the Active Models menu for this spreadsheet. Also see the

Active Model exercise in this chapter for an example of its use.

➤ **SimQuick Exercise:** Learn how to build simulation models and improve the performance of inventory processes in supply chains. Examples in Chapter 3 of *SimQuick: Process Simulation with Excel* include periodic review, reorder point, and base-stock inventory systems.

 INTERNET RESOURCES

➤ **Self-Study Quizzes:** See the compendium of true or false, multiple choice, and essay questions that allows online

tests or gives you feedback on how well you have mastered the concepts of this chapter.

➤ **In the News:** See the articles that apply to this chapter.

➤ **Internet Exercises:** Try out five different links to inventory topics, including field service inventories, supplier relationships, software support, and safety stocks.

➤ **Virtual Tours:** Explore inventory issues for a high-volume batch process at the Stickley Furniture Factory. Also see the "Web Links to Company Facility Tours" for additional tours of company facilities.

KEY EQUATIONS

1. Cycle inventory $= \dfrac{Q}{2}$

2. Pipeline inventory $= dL$

3. Total annual cost $=$ Annual holding cost + Annual ordering or setup cost

$$C = \frac{Q}{2}(H) + \frac{D}{Q}(S)$$

4. Economic order quantity: $\text{EOQ} = \sqrt{\dfrac{2DS}{H}}$

5. Time between orders, expressed in weeks:

$$\text{TBO}_{\text{EOQ}} = \frac{\text{EOQ}}{D}(52 \text{ weeks/year})$$

6. Inventory position $=$ On-hand inventory + Scheduled receipts − Backorders

$$\text{IP} = \text{OH} + \text{SR} - \text{BO}$$

7. Continuous review system:

Reorder point(R) $=$ Average demand during the protection interval + Safety stock

$$= dL + z\sigma_{\text{L}}$$

Protection interval $=$ Lead time(L)

Standard deviation of demand during the lead time $= \sigma_{\text{L}}$

$$= \sigma_t \sqrt{L}$$

Order quantity $=$ EOQ

Replenishment rule: Order EOQ units when IP $\leq$ R.

Total Q system cost: $C = \dfrac{Q}{2}(H) + \dfrac{D}{Q}(S) + Hz\sigma_{\text{L}}$

8. Periodic review system:

Target inventory level (T) $=$ Average demand during the protection interval + Safety stock

$$= d(P + L) + z\sigma_{\text{P}+\text{L}}$$

Protection interval $=$ Time between orders + Lead time

$$= P + L$$

Review interval $=$ Time between orders $= P$

Standard deviation of demand during the protection interval $= \sigma_{\text{P}+\text{L}} = \sigma_t \sqrt{P + L}$

Order quantity $=$ Target inventory level − Inventory position $= T - \text{IP}$

Replenishment rule: Every P time periods order $T - \text{IP}$ units.

Total P system cost: $C = \dfrac{dP}{2}(H) + \dfrac{D}{dP}(S) + Hz\sigma_{\text{P}+\text{L}}$

KEY TERMS

SOLVED PROBLEM 1

A distribution center (DC) experiences an average weekly demand of 50 units for one of its items. The product is valued at $650 per unit. Average inbound shipments from the factory warehouse average 350 units. Average lead time (including ordering delays and transit time) is 2 weeks. The DC operates 52 weeks per year; it carries a 1-week supply of inventory as safety stock and no anticipation inventory. What is the average aggregate inventory being held by the DC?

SOLUTION

TYPE OF INVENTORY	CALCULATION OF AVERAGE INVENTORY QUANTITY	
Cycle	$\dfrac{Q}{2} = \dfrac{350}{2} =$	175 units
Safety stock	1-week supply =	50 units
Anticipation	None	
Pipeline	dL = (50 units/week)(2 weeks)	= 100 units
	Average aggregate inventory	= 325 units

SOLVED PROBLEM 2

Booker's Book Bindery divides inventory items into three classes, according to their dollar usage. Calculate the usage values of the following inventory items and determine which is most likely to be classified as an A item.

PART NUMBER	DESCRIPTION	QUANTITY USED PER YEAR	UNIT VALUE ($)
1	Boxes	500	3.00
2	Cardboard (square feet)	18,000	0.02
3	Cover stock	10,000	0.75
4	Glue (gallons)	75	40.00
5	Inside covers	20,000	0.05
6	Reinforcing tape (meters)	3,000	0.15
7	Signatures	150,000	0.45

SOLUTION

PART NUMBER	DESCRIPTION	QUANTITY USED PER YEAR		UNIT VALUE($)		ANNUAL DOLLAR USAGE($)
1	Boxes	500	×	3.00	=	1,500
2	Cardboard (square feet)	18,000	×	0.02	=	360
3	Cover stock	10,000	×	0.75	=	7,500
4	Glue (gallons)	75	×	40.00	=	3,000
5	Inside covers	20,000	×	0.05	=	1,000
6	Reinforcing tape (meters)	3,000	×	0.15	=	450
7	Signatures	150,000	×	0.45	=	67,500
					Total	81,310

The annual dollar usage for each item is determined by multiplying the annual usage quantity by the value per unit, as shown in Figure 15.14. The items are sorted by annual dollar usage, in declining order. Finally, A–B and B–C class lines are drawn roughly, according to the guidelines presented in the text. Here, class A includes only one item (signatures), which represents only 1/7, or 14 percent, of the items but accounts for 83 percent of annual dollar usage. Class B includes the next two items, which taken together represent 28 percent of the items and account for 13 percent of annual dollar usage. The final four items, class C, represent over half the number of items but only 4 percent of total annual dollar usage.

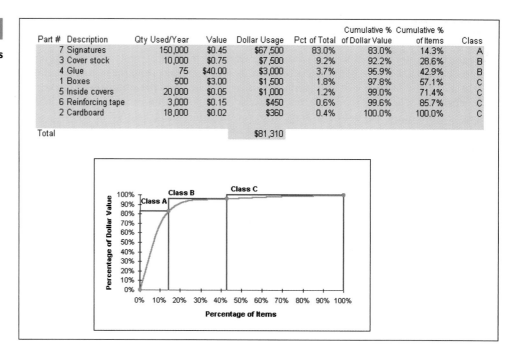

Part #	Description	Qty Used/Year	Value	Dollar Usage	Pct of Total	Cumulative % of Dollar Value	Cumulative % of Items	Class
7	Signatures	150,000	$0.45	$67,500	83.0%	83.0%	14.3%	A
3	Cover stock	10,000	$0.75	$7,500	9.2%	92.2%	28.6%	B
4	Glue	75	$40.00	$3,000	3.7%	95.9%	42.9%	B
1	Boxes	500	$3.00	$1,500	1.8%	97.8%	57.1%	C
5	Inside covers	20,000	$0.05	$1,000	1.2%	99.0%	71.4%	C
6	Reinforcing tape	3,000	$0.15	$450	0.6%	99.6%	85.7%	C
2	Cardboard	18,000	$0.02	$360	0.4%	100.0%	100.0%	C
Total				$81,310				

SOLVED PROBLEM 3

In Example 15.3, the economic order quantity, EOQ, is 75 units when annual demand, D, is 936 units/year, setup cost, S, is $45, and holding cost, H, is $15/unit/year. Suppose that we mistakenly estimate inventory holding cost to be $30/unit/year.

a. What is the new order quantity, Q, if $D = 936$ units/year, $S = 45, and $H = $30/unit/year?

b. What is the change in order quantity, expressed as a percentage of the economic order quantity (75 units)?

SOLUTION

a. The new order quantity is

$$\text{EOQ} = \sqrt{\frac{2DS}{H}} = \sqrt{\frac{2(936)($45)}{$30}} = \sqrt{2,808} = 52.99 \quad \text{or} \quad 53 \text{ units}$$

b. The change in percentage is

$$\left(\frac{53 - 75}{75}\right)(100) = -29.33 \text{ percent}$$

The new order quantity (53) is about 29 percent smaller than the correct order quantity (75).

SOLVED PROBLEM 4

In Example 15.3, the total annual cost, C, is $1,124.

a. What is the annual total cost when $D = 936$ units/year, $S = 45, $H = $15/unit/year, and Q is the result from Solved Problem 3(a)?

b. What is the change in total cost, expressed as a percentage of the total cost ($1,124)?

SOLUTION

a. With 53 as the order quantity, the annual cost is

$$C = \frac{Q}{2}(H) + \frac{D}{Q}(S) = \frac{53}{2}(\$15) + \frac{936}{53}(\$45) = \$397.50 + \$794.72$$
$$= \$1,192.22 \quad \text{or} \quad \text{about } \$1,192$$

b. The change expressed as a percentage is

$$\left(\frac{\$1,192 - \$1,124}{\$1,124}\right)(100) = 6.05 \text{ percent or about 6 percent}$$

A 100 percent error in estimating the holding cost caused the order quantity to be 29 percent too small, and that in turn increased annual costs by about 6 percent.

SOLVED PROBLEM 5

A regional warehouse purchases hand tools from various suppliers and then distributes them on demand to retailers in the region. The warehouse operates five days per week, 52 weeks per year. Only when it is open can orders be received. The following data are estimated for 3/8-inch hand drills with double insulation and variable speeds:

> Average daily demand = 100 drills
> Standard deviation of daily demand (σ_t) = 30 drills
> Lead time (L) = 3 days
> Holding cost (H) = \$9.40/unit/year
> Ordering cost (S) = \$35/order
> Cycle-service level = 92 percent

The warehouse uses a continuous review (Q) system.

a. What order quantity, Q and reorder point, R, should be used?
b. If on-hand inventory is 40 units, there is one open order for 440 drills, and there are no backorders, should a new order be placed?

SOLUTION

a. Annual demand is

$$D = (5 \text{ days/week})(52 \text{ weeks/year})(100 \text{ drills/day}) = 26,000 \text{ drills/year}$$

The order quantity is

$$EOQ = \sqrt{\frac{2DS}{H}} = \sqrt{\frac{2(26,000)(\$35)}{\$9.40}} = \sqrt{193,167} = 440.02 \quad \text{or} \quad 440 \text{ drills}$$

and the standard deviation is

$$s_L = s_t\sqrt{L} = (30 \text{ drills})\sqrt{3} = 51.96 \quad \text{or} \quad 52 \text{ drills}$$

A 92 percent cycle-service level corresponds to $z = 1.41$ (see the Normal Distribution appendix). Therefore,

$$\text{Safety stock} = z\sigma_L = 1.41(52 \text{ drills}) = 73.38 \quad \text{or} \quad 73 \text{ drills}$$
$$\text{Average demand during the lead time} = 100(3) = 300 \text{ drills}$$
$$\text{Reorder point} = \text{Average demand during the lead time} + \text{Safety stock}$$
$$= 300 \text{ drills} + 73 \text{ drills} = 373 \text{ drills}$$

With a continuous review system, $Q = 440$ and $R = 373$.

b. Inventory position = On-hand inventory + Scheduled receipts − Backorders

$$\text{IP} = \text{OH} + \text{SR} - \text{BO} = 40 + 440 - 0 = 480 \text{ drills}$$

Since IP(480) exceeds R(373), do not place a new order.

SOLVED PROBLEM 6

Suppose that a periodic review (P) system is used at the warehouse, but otherwise the data are the same as in Solved Problem 5.

    a. Calculate the P (in workdays, rounded to the nearest day) that gives approximately the same number of orders per year as the EOQ.

    b. What is the value of the target inventory level, T? Compare the P system to the Q system in Solved Problem 5.

    c. It is time to review the item. On-hand inventory is 40 drills; there is a scheduled receipt of 440 drills and no backorders. How much should be reordered?

SOLUTION

    a. The time between orders is

$$P = \frac{\text{EOQ}}{D}(260 \text{ days/year}) = \frac{440}{26,000}(260) = 4.4 \quad \text{or} \quad 4 \text{ days}$$

    b. Figure 15.15 shows that $T = 812$. The corresponding Q system for the hand drill requires less safety stock.

    c. Inventory position is the amount on hand plus scheduled receipts minus backorders, or

$$\text{IP} = \text{OH} + \text{SR} - \text{BO} = 40 + 440 - 0 = 480 \text{ drills}$$

FIGURE 15.15

OM Explorer Solver for Inventory Systems

Solver - Inventory Systems

Continuous Review (Q) System		Periodic Review (P) System	
z	1.41	Time Between Reviews (P)	4.00 Days
			☑ Enter manually
Safety Stock	73	Standard Deviation of Demand During Protection Interval	79.37
Reorder Point	373	Safety Stock	112
Annual Cost	$4,822.38	Average Demand During Protection Interval	700
		Target Inventory Level (T)	812
		Annual Cost	$5,207.80

The order quantity is the target inventory level minus the inventory position, or

$$Q = T - IP = 812 \text{ drills} - 480 \text{ drills} = 332 \text{ drills}$$

In a periodic review system, the order quantity for this review period is 332 drills.

SOLVED PROBLEM 7

Zeke's Hardware Store sells furnace filters. The cost to place an order to the distributor is $25 and the annual cost to hold a filter in stock is $2. The average demand per week for the filters is 32 units, and the store operates 50 weeks per year. The weekly demand for filters has the following probability distribution:

DEMAND	PROBABILITY
24	0.15
28	0.20
32	0.30
36	0.20
40	0.15

The delivery lead time from the distributor is uncertain and has the following probability distribution:

LEAD TIME (WKS)	PROBABILITY
1	0.05
2	0.25
3	0.40
4	0.25
5	0.05

Suppose Zeke wants to use a P system with $P = 6$ weeks and a cycle-service level of 90 percent. What is the appropriate value for T and the associated annual cost of the system?

SOLUTION

Figure 15.16 contains output from the Demand During the Protection Interval Simulator from OM Explorer.

Given the desired cycle-service level of 90 percent, the appropriate T value is 322 units. The simulation estimated the average demand during the protection interval to be 289 units, consequently the safety stock is $322 - 289 = 33$ units.

The annual cost of this P system is

$$C = \frac{6(32)}{2}(\$2) + \frac{50(32)}{6(32)}(\$25) + 33(\$2) = \$192.00 + \$208.33 + \$66.00 = \$466.33$$

Demand During Protection Interval Distribution

Bin Upper Bound	Demand	Frequency	Cumulative Percentage
196	182	0	0.0%
224	210	17	3.4%
252	238	66	16.6%
280	266	135	43.6%
308	294	140	71.6%
336	322	109	93.4%
364	350	30	99.4%
392	378	3	100.0%
420	406	0	100.0%
448	More	0	100.0%
Total		**500**	

Average Demand During Protection Interval
289

FIGURE 15.16

OM Explorer Solver for Demand During the Protection Interval

SOLVED PROBLEM 8

Consider Zeke's inventory in Solved Problem 7. Suppose that he wants to use a continuous review (Q) system for the filter, with an order quantity of 200 and a reorder point of 140. Initial inventory is 170 units. If the stockout cost is \$5 per unit, and all of the other data in Solved Problem 7 are the same, what is the expected cost per week of using the Q system?

SOLUTION

Figure 15.17 shows output from the Q System Simulator in OM Explorer. Only weeks 1 through 13 and weeks 41 through 50 are shown in the figure. The average total cost per week is \$305.62. Notice that no stockouts occurred in this simulation. These results are dependent on Zeke's choices for the reorder point and lot size. It is possible that stockouts would occur if the simulation were run for more than 50 weeks.

FIGURE 15.17   **OM Explorer Q System Simulator**

Week	Beginning Inventory	Simulated Demand	Ending Inventory	Stockout Units	Place Order?	Simulated Lead Time	Weeks to Receive Order	Holding Cost	Ordering Cost	Stockout Cost	Total Cost
1	170	36	134	0	Yes	4	4	\$ 304	\$ 25	\$ -	\$ 329
2	134	32	102	0	No	-	3	\$ 236	\$ -	\$ -	\$ 236
3	102	40	62	0	No	-	2	\$ 164	\$ -	\$ -	\$ 164
4	62	28	34	0	No	-	1	\$ 96	\$ -	\$ -	\$ 96
5	234	32	202	0	No	-	0	\$ 436	\$ -	\$ -	\$ 436
6	202	40	162	0	No	-	-	\$ 364	\$ -	\$ -	\$ 364
7	162	28	134	0	Yes	2	2	\$ 296	\$ 25	\$ -	\$ 321
8	134	40	94	0	No	-	1	\$ 228	\$ -	\$ -	\$ 228
9	294	32	262	0	No	-	0	\$ 556	\$ -	\$ -	\$ 556
10	262	24	238	0	No	-	-	\$ 500	\$ -	\$ -	\$ 500
11	238	32	206	0	No	-	-	\$ 444	\$ -	\$ -	\$ 444
12	206	40	166	0	No	-	-	\$ 372	\$ -	\$ -	\$ 372
13	166	24	142	0	No	-	-	\$ 308	\$ -	\$ -	\$ 308
41	262	28	234	0	No	-	0	\$ 496	\$ -	\$ -	\$ 496
42	234	40	194	0	No	-	-	\$ 428	\$ -	\$ -	\$ 428
43	194	36	158	0	No	-	-	\$ 352	\$ -	\$ -	\$ 352
44	158	36	122	0	Yes	3	3	\$ 280	\$ 25	\$ -	\$ 305
45	122	36	86	0	No	-	2	\$ 208	\$ -	\$ -	\$ 208
46	86	28	58	0	No	-	1	\$ 144	\$ -	\$ -	\$ 144
47	258	36	222	0	No	-	0	\$ 480	\$ -	\$ -	\$ 480
48	222	36	186	0	No	-	-	\$ 408	\$ -	\$ -	\$ 408
49	186	40	146	0	No	-	-	\$ 332	\$ -	\$ -	\$ 332
50	146	32	114	0	Yes	2	2	\$ 260	\$ 25	\$ -	\$ 285
Averages	**167.12**	**33.12**	**134.00**	**0.00**		**3.00**		**\$301.12**	**\$4.50**	**\$0.00**	**\$305.62**

DISCUSSION QUESTIONS

1. What is the relationship between inventory and the nine competitive priorities? (See Chapter 2, "Operations Strategy".) Suppose that two competing manufacturers, Company H and Company L, are similar except that Company H has much higher investments in raw materials, work-in-process, and finished goods inventory than Company L. In which of the nine competitive priorities will Company H have an advantage?

2. Form a discussion group in which each member represents a different functional area of a retailer. Suppose that cycle inventories are to be reduced. Discuss the implications of that decision for each functional area.

3. Will organizations ever get to the point where they will no longer need inventories? Why or why not?

PROBLEMS

An icon next to a problem identifies the software that can be helpful, but is not mandatory. The software is available on the Student CD-ROM that is packaged with every new copy of the textbook.

1. **OM Explorer** A part is produced in lots of 1,000 units. It is assembled from two components worth $50 total. The value added in production (for labor and variable overhead) is $60 per unit, bringing total costs per completed unit to $110. The average lead time for the part is 6 weeks and annual demand is 3,800 units. There are 50 business weeks per year.

   a. How many units of the part are held, on average, in cycle inventory? What is the dollar value of this inventory?

   b. How many units of the part are held, on average, in pipeline inventory? What is the dollar value of this inventory? (*Hint.* Assume that the typical part in pipeline inventory is 50 percent completed. Thus, half the labor and variable overhead costs has been added, bringing the unit cost to $80 or $50 + $60/2.)

2. **OM Explorer** Prince Electronics, a manufacturer of consumer electronic goods, has five distribution centers (DCs) in different regions of the country. For one of its products, a high-speed modem priced at $350 per unit, the average weekly demand at *each* DC is 75 units. Average shipment size to each DC is 400 units, and average lead time for delivery is two weeks. Each DC carries two week's supply as safety stock but holds no anticipation inventory.

   a. On average, how many dollars of pipeline inventory will be in transit to each DC?

   b. How much total inventory (cycle, safety, and pipeline) does Prince hold for all five DCs?

3. **OM Explorer** Lockwood Industries is considering the use of ABC analysis to focus on the most critical items in its inventory. For a random sample of eight items, the following table shows the annual dollar usage. Rank the items, and assign them to the A, B, or C class.

Item	Dollar Value	Annual Usage
1	$0.01	1,200
2	$0.03	120,000
3	$0.45	100
4	$1.00	44,000
5	$4.50	900
6	$0.90	350
7	$0.30	70,000
8	$1.50	200

4. **OM Explorer** Terminator, Inc. manufactures a motorcycle part in lots of 250 units. The raw materials cost for the part is $150, and the value added in manufacturing one unit from its components is $300, for a total cost per completed unit of $450. The lead time to make the part is 3 weeks; and the annual demand is 4,000 units. Assume 50 working weeks per year.

   a. How many units of the part are held, on average, as cycle inventory? What is its value?

   b. How many units of the part are held, on average, as pipeline inventory? What is its value?

5. **OM Explorer** Stock-Rite, Inc. is considering the use of ABC analysis to focus on the most critical items in its inventory. For a random sample of eight items, the following table shows the item's unit value and annual demand. Categorize these items as A, B, and C classes.

Item Code	Unit Value	Demand (units)
A104	$40.25	80
D205	80.75	120
X104	10.00	150
U404	40.50	150
L205	60.70	50
S104	80.20	20
X205	80.15	20
L104	20.05	100

6. **OM Explorer** Yellow Press, Inc. buys slick paper in 1,500-pound rolls for textbook printing. Annual demand is 2,500 rolls. The cost per roll is $800, and the annual holding cost is 15 percent of the cost. Each order costs $50.

a. How many rolls should Yellow Press order at a time?

b. What is the time between orders?

7. **OM Explorer** Babble, Inc. buys 400 blank cassette tapes per month for use in producing foreign language courseware. The ordering cost is $12.50. Holding cost is $0.12 per cassette per year.

a. How many tapes should Babble order at a time?

b. What is the time between orders?

8. **OM Explorer** At Dot Com, a large retailer of popular books, demand is constant at 32,000 books per year. The cost of placing an order to replenish stock is $10, and the annual cost of holding is $4 per book. Stock is received 5 working days after an order has been placed. No backordering is allowed. Assume 300 working days a year.

a. What is Dot Com's optimal ordering quantity?

b. What is the optimal number of orders per year?

c. What is the optimal interval (in working days) between orders?

d. What is demand during the lead time?

e. What is the reorder point?

f. What is the inventory position immediately after an order has been placed?

9. **OM Explorer** Leaky Pipe, a local retailer of plumbing supplies, faces demand for one of its inventoried items at a constant rate of 30,000 units per year. It costs Leaky Pipe $10 to process an order to replenish stock and $1 per unit per year to carry the item in stock. Stock is received 4 working days after an order is placed. No backordering is allowed. Assume 300 working days a year.

a. What is Leaky Pipe's optimal ordering quantity?

b. What is the optimal number of orders per year?

c. What is the optimal interval (in working days) between orders?

d. What is the demand during the lead time?

e. What is the reorder point?

f. What is the inventory position immediately after an order has been placed?

10. **OM Explorer** Sam's Cat Hotel operates 52 weeks per year, 6 days per week, and uses a continuous review inventory system. It purchases kitty litter for $11.70 per bag. The following information is available about these bags.

Demand = 90 bags/week
Order cost = $54/order
Annual holding cost = 27 percent of cost
Desired cycle-service level = 80 percent
Lead time = 3 weeks (18 working days)
Standard deviation of weekly demand = 15 bags

Current on-hand inventory is 320 bags, with no open orders or backorders.

a. What is the EOQ? What would be the average time between orders (in weeks)?

b. What should R be?

c. An inventory withdrawal of 10 bags was just made. Is it time to reorder?

d. The store currently uses a lot size of 500 bags (i.e., $Q = 500$). What is the annual holding cost of this policy? Annual ordering cost? Without calculating the EOQ, how can you conclude from these two calculations that the current lot size is too large?

e. What would be the annual cost saved by shifting from the 500-bag lot size to the EOQ?

11. **OM Explorer** Consider again the kitty litter ordering policy for Sam's Cat Hotel in Problem 10.

a. Suppose that the weekly demand forecast of 90 bags is incorrect and actual demand averages only 60 bags per week. How much higher will total costs be, owing to the distorted EOQ caused by this forecast error?

b. Suppose that actual demand is 60 bags but that ordering costs are cut to only $6 by using the Internet to automate order placing. However, the buyer does not tell anyone, and the EOQ is not adjusted to reflect this reduction in S. How much higher will total costs be, compared to what they could be if the EOQ were adjusted?

12. **OM Explorer** In a Q system, the demand rate for gizmos is normally distributed, with an average of 300 units *per week*. The lead time is nine weeks. The standard deviation of *weekly* demand is 15 units.

a. What is the standard deviation of demand during the nine-week lead time?

b. What is the average demand during the nine-week lead time?

c. What reorder point results in a cycle-service level of 99 percent?

13. **OM Explorer** Petromax Enterprises uses a continuous review inventory control system for one of its inventory items. The following information is available on the item. The firm operates 50 weeks in a year.

Demand = 50,000 units/year
Ordering cost = $35/order
Holding cost = $2/unit/year
Average lead time = 3 weeks
Standard deviation of weekly demand = 125 units

a. What is the economic order quantity for this item?

b. If Petromax wants to provide a 90 percent cycle-service level, what should be the safety stock and the reorder point?

14. **OM Explorer** In a perpetual inventory system, the lead time for dohickies is five weeks. The standard

deviation of demand during the lead time is 85 units. The desired cycle-service level is 99 percent. The supplier of dohickies has streamlined operations and now quotes a one-week lead time. How much can safety stock be reduced without reducing the 99 percent cycle-service level?

15. **OM Explorer** In a two-bin inventory system, the demand for whatchamacallits during the two-week lead time is normally distributed, with an average of 53 units per week. The standard deviation of weekly demand is 5 units. What cycle-service level is provided when the normal level in the second bin is set at 120 units?

16. **OM Explorer** Nationwide Auto Parts uses a periodic review inventory control system for one of its stock items. The review interval is six weeks, and the lead time for receiving the materials ordered from its wholesaler is three weeks. Weekly demand is normally distributed, with a mean of 100 units and a standard deviation of 20 units.

   a. What is the average and the standard deviation of demand during the protection interval?

   b. What should be the target inventory level if the firm desires 97.5 percent stockout protection?

   c. If 350 units were in stock at the time of a certain periodic review, how many units should be ordered?

17. In a P system, the lead time for gadgets is two weeks and the review period is one week. Demand during the protection interval averages 218 units, with a standard deviation of 40 units. What is the cycle-service level when the target inventory level is set at 300 units?

18. **OM Explorer** You are in charge of inventory control of a highly successful product retailed by your firm. Weekly demand for this item varies, with an average of 200 units and a standard deviation of 16 units. It is purchased from a wholesaler at a cost of $12.50 per unit. The supply lead time is 4 weeks. Placing an order costs $50, and the inventory carrying rate per year is 20 percent of the item's cost. Your firm operates 5 days per week, 50 weeks per year.

   a. What is the optimal ordering quantity for this item?

   b. How many units of the item should be maintained as safety stock for 99 percent protection against stockouts during an order cycle?

   c. If supply lead time can be reduced to 2 weeks, what is the percent reduction in the number of units maintained as safety stock for the same 99 percent stockout protection?

   d. If through appropriate sales promotions, the demand variability is reduced so that the standard deviation of weekly demand is 8 units instead of 16, what is the percent reduction [compared to that in part (b)] in the number of units maintained as safety stock for the same 99 percent stockout protection?

19. **OM Explorer** Suppose that Sam's Cat Hotel in Problem 10 uses a P system instead of a Q system. The average daily demand is 15 bags (90/6), and the standard deviation of *daily* demand is 6.124 bags $(15/\sqrt{6})$.

   a. What P (in working days) and T should be used to approximate the cost trade-offs of the EOQ?

   b. How much more safety stock is needed than with a Q system?

   c. It is time for the periodic review. How much kitty litter should be ordered?

20. **OM Explorer** Your firm uses a continuous review system and operates 52 weeks per year. One of the items handled has the following characteristics.

   Demand $(D) = 20,000$ units/year
   Ordering cost $(S) = \$40$/order
   Holding cost $(H) = \$2$/unit/year
   Lead time $(L) = 2$ weeks
   Cycle-service level = 95 percent

   Demand is normally distributed, with a standard deviation of *weekly* demand of 100 units.

   Current on-hand inventory is 1,040 units, with no scheduled receipts and no backorders.

   a. Calculate the item's EOQ. What is the average time, in weeks, between orders?

   b. Find the safety stock and reorder point that provide a 95 percent cycle-service level.

   c. For these policies, what are the annual costs of (i) holding the cycle inventory and (ii) placing orders?

   d. A withdrawal of 15 units just occurred. Is it time to reorder? If so, how much should be ordered?

21. **OM Explorer** Suppose that your firm uses a periodic review system, but otherwise the data are the same as in Problem 20.

   a. Calculate the P that gives approximately the same number of orders per year as the EOQ. Round your answer to the nearest week.

   b. Find the safety stock and the target inventory level that provide a 95 percent cycle-service level.

   c. How much larger is the safety stock than with a Q system?

22. **OM Explorer** A company begins a review of ordering policies for its continuous review system by checking the current policies for a sample of items. Following are the characteristics of one item.

   Demand $(D) = 64$ units/week (Assume 52 weeks per year)
   Ordering and setup cost $(S) = \$50$/order
   Holding cost $(H) = \$13$/unit/year
   Lead time $(L) = 2$ weeks
   Standard deviation of *weekly* demand = 12 units
   Cycle-service level = 88 percent

   a. What is the EOQ for this item?

   b. What is the desired safety stock?

c. What is the reorder point?

d. What are the cost implications if the current policy for this item is $Q = 200$ and $R = 180$?

23. **OM Explorer** Using the same information as in Problem 22, develop the best policies for a periodic review system.

a. What value of P gives the same approximate number of orders per year as the EOQ? Round to the nearest week.

b. What safety stock and target inventory level provide an 88 percent cycle-service level?

24. **OM Explorer** Wood County Hospital consumes 1,000 boxes of bandages per week. The price of bandages is $35 per box, and the hospital operates 52 weeks per year. The cost of processing an order is $15, and the cost of holding one box for a year is 15 percent of the value of the material.

a. The hospital orders bandages in lot sizes of 900 boxes. What *extra cost* does the hospital incur, which it could save by using the EOQ method?

b. Demand is normally distributed, with a standard deviation of weekly demand of 100 boxes. The lead time is 2 weeks. What safety stock is necessary if the hospital uses a continuous review system and a 97 percent cycle-service level is desired? What should be the reorder point?

c. If the hospital uses a periodic review system, with $P = 2$ weeks, what should be the target inventory level, T?

25. **OM Explorer** A golf specialty wholesaler operates 50 weeks per year. Management is trying to determine an inventory policy for its 1-irons, which have the following characteristics:

Demand $(D) = 2,000$ units/year
Demand is normally distributed.
Standard deviation of *weekly* demand = 3 units
Ordering cost = $40/order
Annual holding cost $(H) = $5/unit
Desired cycle-service level = 90 percent
Lead time $(L) = 4$ weeks

a. If the company uses a periodic review system, what should P and T be? Round P to the nearest week.

b. If the company uses a continuous review system, what should R be?

Advanced Problems

It may be helpful to review Supplement B, "Simulation," before working Problems 26-29.

26. **OM Explorer** The Office Supply Shop estimates that the monthly demand for ballpoint pens has the following distribution:

Demand (thousands)	Probability
5	0.1
10	0.3
15	0.4
20	0.1
25	0.1

Furthermore, the lead time for the ballpoint pens from the distributor has the following distribution:

Lead Time (weeks)	Probability
1	0.2
2	0.4
3	0.2
4	0.1
5	0.1

a. If management wants to have a cycle-service level of 95 percent for their continuous review system, what should the reorder point be?

b. What quantity of safety stock must be held?

27. **OM Explorer** The manager of a grocery store orders health care items from a regional distributor every three weeks. One item, Happy Breath Toothpaste, has the following weekly demand distribution:

Demand	Probability
10	0.08
15	0.12
20	0.35
25	0.25
30	0.20

The service the manager gets from the distributor has not been consistent. The lead time for a resupply of Happy Breath has the following distribution:

Lead Time (weeks)	Probability
1	0.10
2	0.25
3	0.30
4	0.25
5	0.10

a. If the manager wants to maintain a cycle-service level of 85 percent on Happy Breath Toothpaste, what target level (T) would he have to use?

b. Suppose the manager could redesign his order placement process and work more closely with the distributor so that the lead time was a constant three weeks. That is, in the table for lead time, the probability for a three-week lead time would be 1.0, and for all other options it would be zero. What would the cycle-service level be for the same target inventory level you found for part (a)?

28. **OM Explorer** The manager of a floral shop sells 2,550 flower baskets per year. The baskets provide a nice souvenir to the recipients of the floral arrangements. The floral shop is open 50 weeks a year. The baskets must be ordered from a supplier whose lead times have been erratic in the past. The cost to place an order to the supplier is $30, and the cost to hold a basket in inventory for a year is $1. The manager has estimated that the cost to the floral shop is $10 for each basket she does not have in stock when a customer demands one.

The probability distribution for weekly demand is as follows:

Demand	Probability
40	0.40
50	0.30
60	0.15
70	0.10
80	0.05

The distribution for lead times is

Lead Time (weeks)	Probability
1	0.3
2	0.4
3	0.2
4	0.1
5	0.0

a. Specify the order quantity and reorder point for a continuous review system that will provide at least a 90 percent cycle-service level. Use the Demand During the Protection Interval Simulator in OM Explorer.

b. Use the Q System Simulator in OM Explorer to estimate the average cost per day of using the Q system you developed. Assume the beginning inventory is 300 baskets.

29. The Georgia Lighting Center stocks more than 3,000 lighting fixtures, including chandeliers, swags, wall lamps, and track lights. The store sells at retail, operates 6 days per week, and advertises itself as the "brightest spot in town." One expensive fixture is selling at an average rate of 5 units per day. The reorder policy is $Q = 40$ and $R = 15$. A new order is placed on the day the reorder point is reached. The lead time is 3 business days. For example, an order placed on Monday will be delivered on Thursday. Simulate the performance of this Q system for the next 3 weeks (18 workdays). Any stockouts result in lost sales (rather than backorders). The beginning inventory is 19 units, and there are no scheduled receipts. Table 15.3 simulates the first week of operation. Extend Table 15.3 to simulate operations for the next 2 weeks if demand for the next 12 business days is 7, 4, 2, 7, 3, 6, 10, 0, 5, 10, 4, and 7.

a. What is the average daily ending inventory over the 18 days?

b. How many stockouts occurred?

	TABLE 15.3					
	FIRST WEEK OF OPERATION					
Workday	Beginning Inventory	Orders Received	Daily Demand	Ending Inventory	Inventory Position	Order Quantity
1. Monday	19	—	5	14	14	40
2. Tuesday	14	—	3	11	51	—
3. Wednesday	11	—	4	7	47	—
4. Thursday	7	40	1	46	46	—
5. Friday	46	—	10	36	36	—
6. Saturday	36	—	9	27	27	—

ACTIVE MODEL EXERCISE

This Active Model appears on the Student CD-ROM. It allows you to evaluate the sensitivity of the EOQ and associated costs to changes in the demand and cost parameters.

QUESTIONS

1. What is the EOQ and what is the lowest total cost?
2. What is the annual cost of holding inventory at the EOQ and the annual cost of ordering inventory at the EOQ?
3. From the graph, what can you conclude about the relationship between the lowest total cost and the costs of ordering and holding inventory?

ACTIVE MODEL 15.1

The Economic Order Quantity Model Using Data from Example 15.3

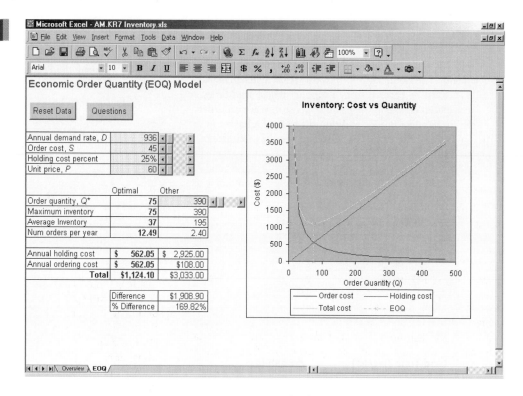

4. How much does the total cost increase if the store manager orders twice as many bird feeders as the EOQ? How much does the total cost increase if the store manager orders half as many bird feeders as the EOQ?
5. What happens to the EOQ and the total cost when demand is doubled? What happens to the EOQ and the total cost when unit price is doubled?
6. Scroll through the lower order cost values and describe the changes to the graph. What happens to the EOQ?
7. Comment on the sensitivity of the EOQ model to errors in demand or cost estimates.

SIMULATION EXERCISES

These simulation exercises require the use of the SimQuick and Extend simulation packages. SimQuick is on the Student CD-ROM that is packaged with every new copy of the textbook. Extend is an optional simulation package that your instructor may or may not have ordered.

1. **SimQuick** A large electronics superstore sells a popular handheld computer. Whenever the number of computers in stock reaches 25, the store places an order for 35 to the manufacturer. The time it takes to receive an order varies according to a normal distribution, with a mean of 5 days and a standard deviation of 0.3 days. The mean demand is 5 computers a day. Management would like to maintain a 90 percent service level on its inventory of computers. Use SimQuick to determine the best reorder point and order size. See Example 22 in *SimQuick: Process Simulation with Excel* for more details of this problem and additional exercises.

2. **Extend** Ready Hardware is a midsize regional distributor of hardware for construction firms, small manufacturers, and independent retailers. The purchasing manager is reviewing replenishment policies for the different product lines. One particular product is a standard door lock set, which has fairly steady sales with approximately 15 sold each day. Use the Extend simulator to evaluate different lot sizing and replenishment policies. See the *Inventory Management at Ready Hardware* case on the optional CD-ROM, which includes the basic model and how to use it. Answer the various questions asked in Sections A to D. Section E, on quantity discounts, should be done after reading Supplement E, "Special Inventory Models."

EXPERIENTIAL LEARNING SWIFT ELECTRONIC SUPPLY, INC.

It was a typical fall afternoon in southern California. Thousands of tourists headed to the beaches to have fun. About 40 miles away, however, Steven Holland, the CEO of the Swift Electronic Supply, Inc. faced a severe problem with Swift's inventory management.

An Intel veteran, Steven Holland has worked in the electronic components distribution industry for over twenty years. Seven years ago, he founded the Swift Electronic Supply, Inc. an electronic distributor. After a couple of successful years, the company is now troubled with eroding profit margins. Recent economic downturns worsened the situation further. Factors such as the growth of B2B e-commerce, the globalization of markets, the increased popularity of value-added services, and ongoing consolidations among electronic distributors affect the future of Swift. To reverse these influences, Holland talked to a prestigious local university. After consultation, Holland found the most effective way to increase profitability is to cut inventory costs. As a starting point, he studied in detail a representative product, dynamic random access memory (DRAM), as the basis for his plan.

INDUSTRY AND COMPANY PREVIEW

Electronics distribution is a $200 billion industry worldwide, according to a report by San Jose-based Semiconductor Industry Association (SIA).* The United States is the largest single market. The primary product mix includes semiconductors, computer products, connectors and cable assemblies, electron mechanical products (e.g., small motors), passive components, and wires and cables.

Owing to a boom in the telecommunications industry and the information technology revolution, electronics distributors have experienced double-digit annual growth over the last decade. To cut the cost of direct purchasing forces, large component manufacturers like Intel, Cisco, and Texas Instruments decided to outsource their procurement so that they could focus on product development and manufacturing. Therefore, independent electronic distributors like Swift started offering procurement services to these companies.

Swift serves component manufacturers in California and Arizona. Working as the intermediary between its customers and overseas original equipment manufacturers (OEMs), Swift's business model is quite simple. Forecasting customer demand, Swift places orders to a number of OEMs, stocks those products, breaks the quantities down, and delivers the products to its end customers. Recently, due to more intense competition and declines in demand, Swift offered more flexibility in delivery schedules and was willing to accommodate small order quantities. However, customers can always shift to Swift's competitors should Swift not fulfill their orders. Steven Holland was in a dilemma: The intangible costs of losing customers can be enormous; however, maintaining high levels of inventory can also be very costly.

DRAM

Steven Holland turned his attention to DRAM as a representative product. Previously, the company ordered a big amount every time it felt it was necessary. Holland's assistant developed a table (Table 15.4), which has two months of demand history. From Holland's experience, the demand for DRAM is relatively stable in the company's product line and it had no sales seasonality. The sales staff agrees that conditions in the current year will not be different from those of past years, and historical demand will be a good indicator of what to expect in the future.

The primary manufacturers of DRAM are those in "Asian Tiger" nations. Currently, one unit of 64M DRAM is sold to Swift Electronic Supply for $10. After negotiation with a reputable supplier, Holland managed to sign a long-term agreement, which kept the price at $10 and allowed Swift to place orders at any time. The supplier also supplies other items in Swift's inventory. In addition, it takes the supplier of the DRAM two days to deliver the goods to Swift's warehouse using air carriers.

When Swift does not have enough inventory to fill a customer's order, the sales are lost; that is, Swift was not able to backorder the shortage because its customers apparently fill their requirements through competitors. The customers will accept partial shipments, however.

It costs Swift $200 to place an order with the suppliers. This covers the corresponding internal ordering costs and the costs of delivering the products to the company. Holland estimates that the cost of lost sales amounts to $2 per unit of DRAM. This is a very rough estimate that includes the loss of profits, as well as the intangible damage to customer goodwill.

| TABLE 15.4 | | | | | |
| HISTORICAL DEMAND DATA FOR THE DRAM (UNITS) | | | | | |
Day	Demand	Day	Demand	Day	Demand
1	869	21	663	41	959
2	902	22	1,146	42	703
3	1,109	23	1,016	43	823
4	947	24	1,166	44	862
5	968	25	829	45	966
6	917	26	723	46	1,042
7	1,069	27	749	47	889
8	1,086	28	766	48	1,002
9	1,066	29	996	49	763
10	929	30	1,122	50	932
11	1,022	31	962	51	1,052
12	959	32	829	52	1,062
13	756	33	862	53	989
14	882	34	793	54	1,029
15	829	35	1,039	55	823
16	726	36	1,009	56	942
17	666	37	979	57	986
18	879	38	976	58	736
19	1,086	39	856	59	1,009
20	992	40	1,036	60	852

*Electronic Business Online, www.e-insite.net/eb-mag/index.asp?layout=article&articleId=CA93826.

Consequently, to simplify the design of inventory management system, Swift has a policy of maintaining a cycle service level of 95 percent. The holding cost per day per unit is estimated to be 0.5 percent of the cost of goods, regardless of the product. Inventory holding costs are calculated on the basis of the ending inventory each day. There is presently a balance of 1,700 units of DRAM in stock.

The daily purchasing routine is as follows. Orders are placed at the *beginning* of the day, before Swift is open for customer business. The orders arrive at the beginning of the day, two days later, and can be used for sales that day. For example, an order placed at the beginning of day 1 will arrive at Swift before Swift is open for business on day 3. The actual daily demand is always recorded at the *end* of the day, after Swift has closed for customer business. All cost computations are done at the end of the day after the total demand has been recorded.

SIMULATION

Steven Holland believes that simulation is a useful approach to assess various inventory control alternatives. The historical data from Table 15.4 could be used to develop attractive inventory policies. The table was developed to record various costs and evaluate different alternatives. An example showing some recent DRAM inventory decisions is shown in Table 15.5.

1. Design an inventory system for Swift Electronic Supply, Inc., using the data provided.
2. Provide the rationale for your system, which should include the decision rules you would follow to determine how much to order and when to order.
3. Simulate the use of your inventory system and record the costs using Table 15.6. You may need to bring several copies of Table 15.6 to class so that all the periods of the simulation will be covered. Your instructor will provide actual demands on a day-to-day basis during the simulation.

TABLE 15.5 EXAMPLE SIMULATION										
Day Number	1	2	3	4	5	6	7	8	9	10
Beginning Inventory Position	1,700	831	1,500	391	3,000	3,232	2,315			
Number Ordered	1,500		3,000	1,200			1,900			
Daily Demand	869	902	1,109	947	968	917	1,069			
Day-Ending Inventory	831	-71	391	-556	2,032	2,315	1,246			
Ordering Costs ($200 per order)	200		200	200			200			
Holding Costs ($0.05 per piece per day)	41.55	0.00	19.55	0.00	101.60	115.75	62.30			
Shortage Costs ($2 per piece)	0	142	0	1112	0	0	0			
Total Cost for Day	241.55	142.00	219.55	1,312.00	101.60	115.75	262.30			
Cumulative Cost from Last Day	0.00	241.55	383.55	603.10	1,915.10	2,016.70	2,132.45			
Cumulative Costs to Date	241.55	383.55	603.10	1,915.10	2,016.70	2,132.45	2,394.75			

TABLE 15.6 SIMULATION EVALUATION SHEET										
Day Number	1	2	3	4	5	6	7	8	9	10
Beginning Inventory Position										
Number Ordered										
Daily Demand										
Day-Ending Inventory										
Ordering Costs ($200 per order)										
Holding Costs ($0.05 per piece per day)										
Shortage Costs ($2 per piece)										
Total Cost for Day										
Cumulative Cost from Last Day										
Cumulative Costs to Date										

CASE PARTS EMPORIUM

It is June 6, Sue McCaskey's first day in the newly created position of materials manager for Parts Emporium. A recent graduate of a prominent business school, McCaskey is eagerly awaiting her first real-world problem. At approximately 8:30 A.M., it arrives in the form of status reports on inventory and orders shipped. At the top of an extensive computer printout is a handwritten note from Joe Donnell, the purchasing manager: "Attached you will find the inventory and customer service performance data. Rest assured that the individual inventory levels are accurate because we took a complete physical inventory count at the end of last week. Unfortunately, we do not keep compiled records in some of the areas as you requested. However, you are welcome to do so yourself. Welcome aboard!"

A little upset that aggregate information is not available, McCaskey decides to randomly select a small sample of approximately 100 items and compile inventory and customer service characteristics to get a feel for the "total picture." The results of this experiment reveal to her why Parts Emporium decided to create the position she now fills. It seems that the inventory is in all the wrong places. Although there is an *average* of approximately 60 days of inventory, customer service is inadequate. Parts Emporium tries to backorder the customer orders not immediately filled from stock, but some 10 percent of demand is being lost to competing distributorships. Because stockouts are costly, relative to inventory holding costs, McCaskey believes that a cycle-service level of at least 95 percent should be achieved.

Parts Emporium, Inc. was formed in 1973 as a wholesale distributor of automobile parts by two disenchanted auto mechanics, Dan Block and Ed Spriggs. Originally located in Block's garage, the firm showed slow but steady growth until 1976, when it relocated to an old, abandoned meat-packing warehouse on Chicago's South Side. With increased space for inventory storage, the company was able to begin offering an expanded line of auto parts. This increased selection, combined with the trend toward longer car ownership, led to an explosive growth of the business. By 1998, Parts Emporium was the largest independent distributor of auto parts in the north central region.

Recently, Parts Emporium relocated in a sparkling new office and warehouse complex off Interstate 55 in suburban Chicago. The warehouse space alone occupied more than 100,000 square feet. Although only a handful of new products have been added since the warehouse was constructed, its utilization has increased from 65 percent to more than 90 percent of capacity. During this same period, however, sales growth has stagnated. These conditions motivated Block and Spriggs to hire the first manager from outside the company in the firm's history.

Sue McCaskey knows that although her influence to initiate changes will be limited, she must produce positive results immediately. Thus, she decides to concentrate on two products from the extensive product line: the EG151 exhaust gasket and the DB032 drive belt. If she can demonstrate significant gains from proper inventory managment for just two

products, perhaps Block and Spriggs will give her the backing needed to change the total inventory management system.

The EG151 exhaust gasket is purchased from an overseas supplier, Haipei, Inc. Actual demand for the first 21 weeks of this year is shown in the following table:

WEEK	ACTUAL DEMAND	WEEK	ACTUAL DEMAND
1	104	12	97
2	103	13	99
3	107	14	102
4	105	15	99
5	102	16	103
6	102	17	101
7	101	18	101
8	104	19	104
9	100	20	108
10	100	21	97
11	103		

A quick review of past orders, shown in another document, indicates that a lot size of 150 units is being used and that the lead time from Haipei is fairly constant at two weeks. Currently, at the end of week 21, no inventory is on hand; 11 units are backordered, and there is a scheduled receipt of 150 units.

The DB032 drive belt is purchased from the Bendox Corporation of Grand Rapids, Michigan. Actual demand so far this year is shown in the following table:

WEEK	ACTUAL DEMAND	WEEK	ACTUAL DEMAND
11	18	17	50
12	33	18	53
13	53	19	54
14	54	20	49
15	51	21	52
16	53		

Because this product is new, data are available only since its introduction in week 11. Currently, 324 units are on hand; there are no backorders and no scheduled receipts. A lot size of 1,000 units is being used, with the lead time fairly constant at three weeks.

The wholesale prices that Parts Emporium charges its customers are $12.99 for the EG151 exhaust gasket and $8.89 for the DB032 drive belt. Because no quantity discounts are offered on these two highly profitable items, gross margins based on current purchasing practices are 32 percent of the wholesale price for the exhaust gasket and 48 percent of the wholesale price for the drive belt.

Parts Emporium estimates its cost to hold inventory at 21 percent of its inventory investment. This percent recognizes the opportunity cost of tying money up in inventory and the variable costs of taxes, insurance, and shrinkage. The annual report notes other warehousing expenditures for utilities and maintenance and debt service on the 100,000-square-foot warehouse, which was built for $1.5 million. However, McCaskey reasons that these warehousing costs can be ignored because they will not change for the range of inventory policies that she is considering.

Out-of-pocket costs for Parts Emporium to place an order with suppliers are estimated to be $20 per order for exhaust gaskets and $10 per order for drive belts. On the outbound side, there can be delivery charges. Although most customers pick up their parts at Parts Emporium, some orders are delivered to customers. To provide this service, Parts Emporium contracts with a local company for a flat fee of $21.40 per order, which is added to the customer's bill. McCaskey is unsure whether to increase the ordering costs for Parts Emporium to include delivery charges.

QUESTIONS

1. Put yourself in Sue McCaskey's position and prepare a detailed report to Dan Block and Ed Spriggs on managing the inventory of the EG151 exhaust gasket and the DB032 drive belt. Be sure to present a proper inventory system and recognize all relevant costs.
2. By how much do your recommendations for these two items reduce annual cycle inventory, stockout, and ordering costs?

Source: This case was provided by Professor Robert Bregman, University of Houston.

SELECTED REFERENCES

Berlin, Bob. "Solving the OEM Puzzle at Valleylab." *APICS—The Performance Advantage* (March 1997), pp. 58–63.

Chikan, A., A. Milne, and L. G. Sprague. "Reflections on Firm and National Inventories." Budapest: International Society for Inventory Research, 1996.

"Factors That Make or Break Season Sales." *Wall Street Journal* (December 9, 1991).

Greene, James H. *Production and Inventory Control Handbook*, 3d ed. New York: McGraw-Hill, 1997.

Hartvigsen, David. *SimQuick: Process Simulation with Excel*. 2d ed. Upper Saddle River, NJ: Prentice Hall, 2004.

Inventory Management Reprints. Falls Church, VA: American Production and Inventory Control Society, 1993.

Krupp, James A. G. "Are ABC Codes an Obsolete Technology?" *APICS—The Performance Advantage* (April 1994), pp. 34–35.

Silver, Edward A. "Changing the Givens in Modeling Inventory Problems: The Example of Just-in-Time Systems." *International Journal of Production Economics*, vol. 26 (1996), pp. 347–351.

Silver, Edward A., D. E. Pyke, and Rein Peterson. *Inventory Management, Production Planning, and Scheduling*, 3d ed. New York: John Wiley & Sons, 1998.

Tersine, Richard J. *Principles of Inventory and Materials Management*, 4th ed. Saddlebrook, NJ: Prentice Hall, 1994.

Special Inventory Models

LEARNING GOALS

After reading this supplement, you should be able to . . .

IDENTIFY OR DEFINE

1. the relevant costs that should be considered to determine the order quantity when discounts are available.
2. the situations where the economic lot size should be used in lieu of the economic order quantity.

DESCRIBE OR EXPLAIN

3. how to calculate the optimal lot size when replenishment is not instantaneous.
4. how to determine the optimal order quantity when materials are subject to quantity discounts.
5. how to calculate the order quantity that maximizes the expected profits for a one-period inventory decision.

Many real world problems require relaxation of certain assumptions on which the EOQ model is based. This supplement addresses three realistic situations that require going beyond the simple EOQ formulation.

1. *Noninstantaneous Replenishment.* Particularly in situations in which manufacturers use a continuous process to make a primary material, such as a liquid, gas, or powder, production is not instantaneous. Thus, inventory is replenished gradually, rather than in lots.

2. *Quantity Discounts.* There are three relevant annual costs: the inventory holding cost, the fixed cost for ordering and setup, and the cost of materials. For service providers and for manufacturers alike, the unit cost of purchased materials sometimes depends on the order quantity.

3. *One-Period Decisions.* Retailers and manufacturers of fashion goods often face a situation in which demand is uncertain and occurs during just one period or season.

NONINSTANTANEOUS REPLENISHMENT

If an item is being produced internally rather than purchased, finished units may be used or sold as soon as they are completed, without waiting until a full lot has been completed. For example, a restaurant that bakes its own dinner rolls begins to use some of the rolls from the first pan even before the baker finishes a five-pan batch. The inventory of rolls never reaches the full five-pan level, the way it would if the rolls all arrived at once on a truck sent by an external supplier or a cart driven by an internal materials handler.

Figure E.1 depicts the usual case, in which the production rate, p, exceeds the demand rate, d.[1] Cycle inventory accumulates faster than demand occurs; that is, there

FIGURE E.1
Lot Sizing with Noninstantaneous Replenishment

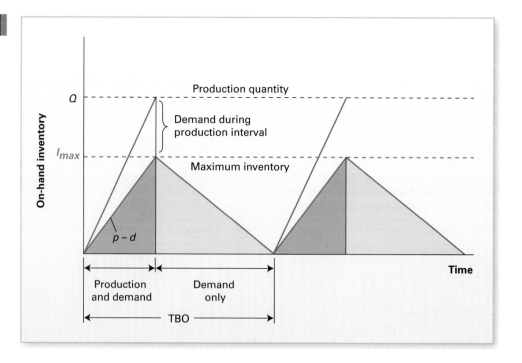

---

[1]If they were equal, production would be continuous with no buildup of cycle inventory. If the production rate is lower than the demand rate, sales opportunities are being missed on an ongoing basis. We assume that $p > d$ in this supplement.

is a buildup of $p - d$ units during the time when both production and demand occur. For example, if the production rate is 100 units per day and the demand is 5 units per day, the buildup is 95 (or $100 - 5$) units each day. This buildup continues until the lot size, Q, has been produced, after which the inventory depletes at a rate of 5 units per day. Just as the inventory reaches 0, the next production interval begins. To be consistent, both p and d must be expressed in units of the same time interval, such as units per day or units per week. Here, we assume that they are expressed in units per day.

The $p - d$ buildup continues for Q/p days because Q is the lot size and p units are produced each day. In our example, if the lot size is 300 units, the production interval is 3 days (300/100). For the given rate of buildup over the production interval, the maximum cycle inventory, I_{max}, is

$$I_{max} = \frac{Q}{p}(p - d) = Q\left(\frac{p - d}{p}\right)$$

Cycle inventory is no longer $Q/2$, as it was with the basic EOQ method (see Chapter 15, "Inventory Management"); instead, it is $I_{max}/2$. Setting up the total annual cost equation for this production situation, where D is annual demand, as before, and d is daily demand, we get

Total annual cost = Annual holding cost + Annual ordering or setup cost

$$C = \frac{I_{max}}{2}(H) + \frac{D}{Q}(S) = \frac{Q}{2}\left(\frac{p - d}{p}\right)(H) + \frac{D}{Q}(S)$$

Based on this cost function, the optimal lot size, often called the **economic production lot size (ELS)**, is

$$ELS = \sqrt{\frac{2DS}{H}}\sqrt{\frac{p}{p - d}}$$

economic production lot size (ELS)   The optimal lot size in a situation in which replenishment is not instantaneous.

Because the second term is a ratio greater than 1, the ELS results in a larger lot size than the EOQ.

Finding the Economic Production Lot Size

EXAMPLE E.1

A plant manager of a chemical plant must determine the lot size for a particular chemical that has a steady demand of 30 barrels per day. The production rate is 190 barrels per day, annual demand is 10,500 barrels, setup cost is $200, annual holding cost is $0.21 per barrel, and the plant operates 350 days per year.

   a. Determine the economic production lot size (ELS).
   b. Determine the total annual setup and inventory holding cost for this item.
   c. Determine the TBO, or cycle length, for the ELS.
   d. Determine the production time per lot.

What are the advantages of reducing the setup time by 10 percent?

TUTOR E.1

Tutor E.1 on the Student CD-ROM provides a new example to determine the ELS.

SOLUTION

   a. Solving first for the ELS, we get

$$ELS = \sqrt{\frac{2DS}{H}}\sqrt{\frac{p}{p - d}} = \sqrt{\frac{2(10,500)(\$200)}{\$0.21}}\sqrt{\frac{190}{190 - 30}}$$
$$= 4,873.4 \text{ barrels}$$

ACTIVE MODEL E.1

Active Model E.1 on the Student CD-ROM provides additional insight on the ELS model and its uses.

b. The total annual cost with the ELS is

$$C = \frac{Q}{2}\left(\frac{p-d}{p}\right)(H) + \frac{D}{Q}(S)$$

$$= \frac{4,873.4}{2}\left(\frac{190-30}{190}\right)(\$0.21) + \frac{10,500}{4,873.4}(\$200)$$

$$= \$430.91 + \$430.91 = \$861.82$$

c. Applying the TBO formula (see Chapter 15, "Inventory Management") to the ELS, we get

$$\text{TBO}_{\text{ELS}} = \frac{\text{ELS}}{D}(350 \text{ days/year}) = \frac{4,873.4}{10,500}(350)$$

$$= 162.4 \quad \text{or} \quad 162 \text{ days}$$

d. The production time during each cycle is the lot size divided by the production rate:

$$\frac{\text{ELS}}{p} = \frac{4,873.4}{190} = 25.6 \quad \text{or} \quad 26 \text{ days}$$

FIGURE E.2	

OM Explorer Solver Showing the Effect of a Ten Percent Reduction in Setup Cost

Solver - Economic Production Lot Size

Period Used in Calculations	Day
Demand per Day	30
Production Rate/Day	190
Annual Demand	10,500
Setup Cost	$180
Annual Holding Cost ($)	$0.21 ⦿ Enter Holding Cost Manually ○ Holding Cost As % of Value
Operating Days per Year	350
Economic Lot Size (ELS)	4,623
Annual Total Cost	$817.60
Time Between Orders (days)	154.1
Production Time	24.3

DECISION POINT As OM Explorer shows in Figure E.2, the net effect of reducing the setup cost by 10 percent is to reduce the lot size, the time between orders, and the production cycle time. Consequently, total annual costs are also reduced. This adds flexibility to the manufacturing process because items can be made quicker with less expense. Management must decide whether the added cost of improving the setup process is worth the added flexibility and inventory cost reductions.

QUANTITY DISCOUNTS

Quantity discounts, which are price incentives to purchase large quantities, create pressure to maintain a large inventory. For example, a supplier may offer a price of $4.00 per unit for orders between 1 and 99 units, a price of $3.50 per unit for orders between 100 and 199 units, and a price of $3.00 per unit for orders of more than 200 units. The item's price is no longer fixed, as assumed in the EOQ derivation; instead, if the order quantity is increased enough, the price is discounted. Hence, a new approach is needed to find the best lot size—one that balances the advantages of lower prices for purchased materials and fewer orders (which are benefits of large order quantities) against the disadvantage of the increased cost of holding more inventory.

The total annual cost now includes not only the holding cost, $(Q/2)(H)$, and the ordering cost, $(D/Q)(S)$, but also the cost of purchased materials. For any per-unit price level, P, the total cost is

Total annual cost = Annual holding cost + Annual ordering cost + Annual cost of materials

$$C = \frac{Q}{2}(H) + \frac{D}{Q}(S) + PD$$

The unit holding cost, H, usually is expressed as a percent of the unit price because the more valuable the item held in inventory, the higher the holding cost is. Thus, the lower the unit price, P, is, the lower H is. Conversely, the higher P is, the higher H is.

As when we calculated total cost previously (see Chapter 15, "Inventory Management"), the total cost equation yields U-shaped total cost curves. Adding the annual cost of materials to the total cost equation raises each total cost curve by a fixed amount, as shown in Figure E.3(a). There are three cost curves—one for each price level. The top curve applies when no discounts are received; the lower curves reflect the discounted price levels. No single curve is relevant to all purchase quantities. The relevant, or *feasible*, total cost begins with the top curve, then drops down, curve by curve, at the price breaks. A *price break* is the minimum quantity needed to get a discount. In Figure E.3, there are two price breaks: at $Q = 100$ and $Q = 200$. The result is a total cost curve, with steps at the price breaks.

Figure E.3(b) also shows three additional points—the minimum point on each curve, obtained with the EOQ formula at each price level. These EOQs do not necessarily produce the best lot size for two reasons.

 1. The EOQ at a particular price level may not be feasible: The lot size may not lie in the range corresponding to its per-unit price. Figure E.3(b) illustrates two instances of an infeasible EOQ. First, the minimum point for the $3.00 curve appears to be less than 200 units. However, the supplier's quantity discount schedule does not allow

| FIGURE E.3 | Total Cost Curves with Quantity Discounts |

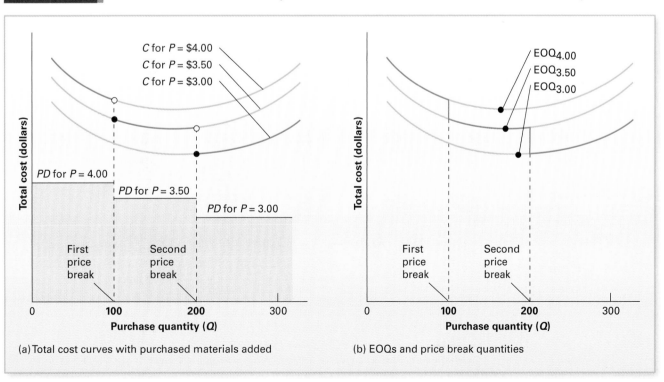

(a) Total cost curves with purchased materials added

(b) EOQs and price break quantities

purchases of that small a quantity at the $3.00 unit price. Similarly, the EOQ for the $4.00 price level is greater than the first price break, so the price charged would be only $3.50.

2. The EOQ at a particular price level may be feasible but may not be the best lot size: The feasible EOQ may have a *higher* cost than is achieved by the EOQ or price break quantity on a *lower* price curve. In Figure E.3(b), for example, the 200-unit price break quantity for the $3.00 price level has a lower total cost than the feasible EOQ for the $3.50 price level. A feasible EOQ always is better than any feasible point on cost curves with higher price levels, but not necessarily those with lower levels. Thus, the only time we can immediately conclude, without comparing total costs, that a feasible EOQ is the best order quantity is when it is on the curve for the *lowest* price level. This conclusion is not possible in Figure E.3(b) because the only feasible EOQ is at the middle price level, $P = \$3.50$.

We must therefore pay attention only to feasible price–quantity combinations, shown as solid lines in Figure E.3(b), as we search for the best lot size. The following two-step procedure may be used to find the best lot size.[2]

Step 1. Beginning with the *lowest* price, calculate the EOQ for each price level until a feasible EOQ is found. It is feasible if it lies in the range corresponding to its price. Each subsequent EOQ is smaller than the previous one because *P*, and thus *H*, gets larger and because the larger *H* is in the denominator of the EOQ formula.

Step 2. If the first feasible EOQ found is for the *lowest* price level, this quantity is the best lot size. Otherwise, calculate the total cost for the first feasible EOQ and for the larger price break quantity at each *lower* price level. The quantity with the lowest total cost is optimal.

EXAMPLE E.2   Finding Q with Quantity Discounts at St. LeRoy Hospital

TUTOR E.2

Tutor E.2 on the Student CD-ROM provides a new example for choosing the best order quantity when discounts are available.

ACTIVE MODEL E.2

Active Model E.2 on the Student CD-ROM provides additional insight on the quantity discount model and its uses.

A supplier for St. LeRoy Hospital has introduced quantity discounts to encourage larger order quantities of a special catheter. The price schedule is

ORDER QUANTITY	PRICE PER UNIT
0 to 299	$60.00
300 to 499	$58.80
500 or more	$57.00

The hospital estimates that its annual demand for this item is 936 units, its ordering cost is $45.00 per order, and its annual holding cost is 25 percent of the catheter's unit price. What quantity of this catheter should the hospital order to minimize total costs? Suppose the price for quantities between 300 and 499 is reduced to $58.00. Should the order quantity change?

SOLUTION

Step 1. Find the first feasible EOQ, starting with the lowest price level:

$$\text{EOQ}_{57.00} = \sqrt{\frac{2DS}{H}} = \sqrt{\frac{2(936)(\$45.00)}{0.25(\$57.00)}} = 77 \text{ units}$$

---

[2]Another approach that often reduces the number of iterations can be found in Goyal, S. K. "A Simple Procedure for Price Break Models." *Production Planning and Control*, vol. 6, no. 6 (1995), pp. 584–585.

A 77-unit order actually costs $60.00 per unit, instead of the $57.00 per unit used in the EOQ calculation, so this EOQ is infeasible. Now try the $58.80 level:

$$\text{EOQ}_{58.80} = \sqrt{\frac{2DS}{H}} = \sqrt{\frac{2(936)(\$45.00)}{0.25(\$58.80)}} = 76 \text{ units}$$

This quantity also is infeasible because a 76-unit order is too small to qualify for the $58.80 price. Try the highest price level:

$$\text{EOQ}_{60.00} = \sqrt{\frac{2DS}{H}} = \sqrt{\frac{2(936)(\$45.00)}{0.25(\$60.00)}} = 75 \text{ units}$$

This quantity is feasible, because it lies in the range corresponding to its price, $P = \$60.00$.

Step 2. The first feasible EOQ of 75 does not correspond to the lowest price level. Hence, we must compare its total cost with the price break quantities (300 and 500 units) at the *lower* price levels ($58.80 and $57.00):

$$C = \frac{Q}{2}(H) + \frac{D}{Q}(S) + PD$$

$$C_{75} = \frac{75}{2}[(0.25)(\$60.00)] + \frac{936}{75}(\$45.00) + \$60.00(936) = \$57,284$$

$$C_{300} = \frac{300}{2}[(0.25)(\$58.80)] + \frac{936}{300}(\$45.00) + \$58.80(936) = \$57,382$$

$$C_{500} = \frac{500}{2}[(0.25)(\$57.00)] + \frac{936}{500}(\$45.00) + \$57.00(936) = \$56,999$$

The best purchase quantity is 500 units, which qualifies for the deepest discount.

DECISION POINT   If the price per unit for the range of 300 to 499 units is reduced to $58.00, the best decision is to order 300 catheters, as shown by OM Explorer in Figure E.4. This result shows that the decision is sensitive to the price schedule. A reduction of slightly more than 1 percent is enough to make the difference in this example. In general, however, it is not always the case that you should order more than the economic order quantity when given price discounts. When discounts are small, holding cost H is large, and demand D is small, small lot sizes are better even though price discounts are forgone.

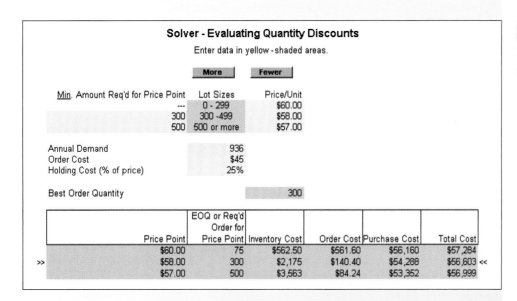

FIGURE E.4

OM Explorer Solver Showing the Best Order Quantity

Solver - Evaluating Quantity Discounts

Enter data in yellow-shaded areas.

Min. Amount Req'd for Price Point	Lot Sizes	Price/Unit
---	0 - 299	$60.00
300	300 - 499	$58.00
500	500 or more	$57.00

Annual Demand	936
Order Cost	$45
Holding Cost (% of price)	25%

Best Order Quantity	300

Price Point	EOQ or Req'd Order for Price Point	Inventory Cost	Order Cost	Purchase Cost	Total Cost
$60.00	75	$562.50	$561.60	$56,160	$57,284
$58.00	300	$2,175	$140.40	$54,288	$56,603 <<
$57.00	500	$3,563	$84.24	$53,352	$56,999

ONE PERIOD DECISIONS

One of the dilemmas facing many retailers is how to handle seasonal goods, such as winter coats. Often, they cannot be sold at full markup next year because of changes in styles. Furthermore, the lead time can be longer than the selling season, allowing no second chance to rush through another order to cover unexpectedly high demand. A similar problem exists for manufacturers of fashion goods.

This type of situation is often called the *newsboy problem*. If the newspaper seller does not buy enough newspapers to resell on the street corner, sales opportunities are lost. If the seller buys too many newspapers, the overage cannot be sold because nobody wants yesterday's newspaper.

The following process is a straightforward way to analyze such problems and decide on the best order quantity.

1. List the different levels of demand that are possible, along with the estimated probability of each.

2. Develop a *payoff table* (see Supplement A, "Decision Making") that shows the profit for each purchase quantity, Q, at each assumed demand level, D. Each row in the table represents a different order quantity, and each column represents a different demand level. The payoff for a given quantity–demand combination depends on whether all units are sold at the regular profit margin during the regular season. There are two possible cases.

a. If demand is high enough ($Q \le D$), then all units are sold at the full profit margin, p, during the regular season,

$$\text{Payoff} = (\text{Profit per unit})(\text{Purchase quantity}) = pQ$$

b. If the purchase quantity exceeds the eventual demand ($Q > D$), only D units are sold at the full profit margin, and the remaining units purchased must be disposed of at a loss, l, after the season. In this case,

$$\text{Payoff} = \left(\begin{array}{c}\text{Profit per unit sold} \\ \text{during season}\end{array}\right)(\text{Demand}) - \left(\begin{array}{c}\text{Loss per} \\ \text{unit}\end{array}\right)\left(\begin{array}{c}\text{Amount disposed of} \\ \text{after season}\end{array}\right)$$
$$= pD - l(Q - D)$$

3. Calculate the expected payoff for each Q (or row in the payoff table) by using the *expected value* decision rule (see Supplement A, "Decision Making"). For a specific Q, first multiply each payoff in the row by the demand probability associated with the payoff, and then add these products.

4. Choose the order quantity Q with the highest expected payoff.

Using this decision process for all such items over many selling seasons will maximize profits. However, it is not foolproof, and it can result in an occasional bad outcome.

EXAMPLE E.3   Finding Q for One-Time Inventory Decisions

One of many items sold at a museum of natural history is a Christmas ornament carved from wood. The gift shop makes a $10 profit per unit sold during the season, but it takes a $5 loss per unit after the season is over. The following discrete probability distribution for the season's demand has been identified:

Demand	10	20	30	40	50
Demand Probability	0.2	0.3	0.3	0.1	0.1

How many ornaments should the museum's buyer order?

SOLUTION

Each demand level is a candidate for best order quantity, so the payoff table should have five rows. For the first row, where $Q = 10$, demand is at least as great as the purchase quantity. Thus, all five payoffs in this row are

$$\text{Payoff} = pQ = (\$10)(10) = \$100$$

This formula can be used in other rows but only for those quantity–demand combinations where all units are sold during the season. These combinations lie in the upper-right portion of the pay-off table, where $Q \le D$. For example, the payoff when $Q = 40$ and $D = 50$ is

$$\text{Payoff} = pQ = (\$10)(40) = \$400$$

The payoffs in the lower-left portion of the table represent quantity-demand combinations where some units must be disposed of after the season ($Q > D$). For this case, the payoff must be calculated with the second formula. For example, when $Q = 40$ and $D = 30$,

$$\text{Payoff} = pD - l(Q - D) = (\$10)(30) - (\$5)(40 - 30) = \$250$$

Using OM Explorer, we obtain the payoff table in Figure E.5.

Solver - One-Period Inventory Decisions

Enter data in yellow-shaded areas.

Profit	$10.00	(if sold during preferred period)
Loss	$5.00	(if sold after preferred period)

Enter the possible demands along with the probability of each occurring. Use the buttons to increase or decrease the number of allowable demand forecasts. NOTE: Be sure to enter demand forecasts and probabilities in all tinted cells, and be sure probabilities add up to 1.

	<	>			
Demand	10	20	30	40	50
Probability	0.2	0.3	0.3	0.1	0.1

Payoff Table

		Demand				
		10	20	30	40	50
Quantity	10	100	100	100	100	100
	20	50	200	200	200	200
	30	0	150	300	300	300
	40	-50	100	250	400	400
	50	-100	50	200	350	500

FIGURE E.5

OM Explorer Solver Showing the Payoff Table

Now we calculate the expected payoff for each Q by multiplying the payoff for each demand quantity by the probability of that demand and then adding the results. For example, for $Q = 30$,

$$\text{Payoff} = 0.2(\$0) + 0.3(\$150) + 0.3(\$300) + 0.1(\$300) + 0.1(\$300) = \$195$$

Using OM Explorer, Figure E.6 shows the expected payoffs.

FIGURE E.6

FIGURE E.6

OM Explorer Solver Showing the Expected Payoffs

Weighted Payoffs		
Order Quantity	Expected Payoff	
10	100	
20	170	
30	195	Greatest Expected Payoff 195
40	175	Associated with Order Quantity 30
50	140	

DECISION POINT Because $Q = 30$ has the highest payoff at $195, it is the best order quantity. Management can use OM Explorer to do sensitivity analysis on the demands and their probabilities to see how confident they are with that decision.

The need for one-time inventory decisions also can arise in manufacturing plants when (1) customized items (specials) are made (or purchased) to a single order *and* (2) scrap quantities are high.[3] A special item produced for a single order is never intentionally held in stock because the demand for it is too unpredictable. In fact, it may never be ordered again so the manufacturer would like to make just the amount requested by the customer—no more, no less. The manufacturer also would like to satisfy an order in just one run to avoid an extra setup and a delay in delivering goods ordered. These two goals may conflict if the likelihood of some units being scrapped is high. Suppose that a customer places an order for 20 units. If the manager orders 20 units from the shop or from the supplier, one or two units may have to be scrapped. This shortage will force the manager to place a second (or even third) order to replace the defective units. Replacement can be costly if setup time is high and can also delay shipment to the customer. To avoid such problems, the manager could order more than 20 units the first time. If some units are left over, the customer might be willing to buy the extras or the manager might find an internal use for them. For example, some manufacturing companies set up a special account for obsolete materials. These materials can be "bought" by departments within the company at less than their normal cost, as an incentive to use them.

SUPPLEMENT HIGHLIGHTS

- When inventory items are made instead of bought, inventory is replenished gradually over some production period. This condition is called *noninstantaneous replenishment*. The amount of inventory accumulated during the production period is reduced by concurrent sales. Hence, the maximum amount in inventory will be less than the production lot size. The economic production lot size is a balance between annual holding and annual ordering costs. Sales during the production period have the effect of lowering the average inventory and annual holding costs, so balance is restored by increasing the size of each order. Larger orders reduce the number of orders placed during a year.

- When quantity discounts are available, the total relevant cost includes annual holding, ordering, and materials costs. Purchasing larger quantities to achieve price discounts reduces annual ordering and materials costs but usually increases annual holding costs. The order quantity is based on minimizing the total of relevant costs per year, instead of obtaining the minimum purchase price per unit.

- Retailers, as well as manufacturers of customized products, often face one-time inventory decisions. Demand uncertainty can lead to ordering too much or too little, which can result in cost or customer service penalties. A straightforward approach to one-time inventory decisions is to calculate the expected payoff over a range of reasonable alternatives and choose the one with the best expected payoff.

---

[3]One goal of TQM is to eliminate scrap. Achievement of that TQM goal makes this discussion moot.

STUDENT CD-ROM AND INTERNET RESOURCES

The Student CD-ROM and the Companion Website at **www.prenhall.com/krajewski** contain many tools, activities, and resources designed for this supplement. The following items are recommended to enhance your skills and improve your understanding of the material in this supplement.

STUDENT CD-ROM RESOURCES

➤ **PowerPoint Slides:** View the comprehensive set of slides customized for this supplement's concepts and techniques.
➤ **OM Explorer Tutors:** OM Explorer contains three tutor programs to enhance your understanding of how to calculate the economic production lot size, determine the best order quantity when discounts are available, and calculate the best one-period order quantity. See Supplement E in the OM Explorer menu.
➤ **OM Explorer Solvers:** OM Explorer has three programs that can be used to solve general problems involving economic production lot size calculation, quantity discount

analysis, and one-period inventory decisions. See Inventory Management in the OM Explorer menu.
➤ **Active Models:** There are three active model spreadsheets that provide additional insight on special inventory models. See Special Inventory Models in the Active Models menu for these routines.

INTERNET RESOURCES

➤ **Self-Study Quizzes:** See the compendium of true or false, multiple choice, and essay questions that allows online tests or gives you feedback on how well you have mastered the concepts of this supplement.
➤ **In the News:** See the articles that apply to this supplement.
➤ **Internet Exercises:** Compare the tire production processes and inventory issues at Goodyear and Pirelli.
➤ **Virtual Tours:** See the "Web Links to Company Facility Tours" for tours of company facilities.

KEY EQUATIONS

1. Noninstantaneous replenishment:

    Maximum inventory: $I_{\max} = Q\left(\dfrac{p-d}{p}\right)$

    Economic production lot size: $\text{ELS} = \sqrt{\dfrac{2DS}{H}}\sqrt{\dfrac{p}{p-d}}$

    Total annual cost = Annual holding costs + Annual ordering or setup cost

    $$C = \frac{Q}{2}\left(\frac{p-d}{p}\right)(H) + \frac{D}{Q}(S)$$

    Time between orders, expressed in years: $\text{TBO}_{\text{ELS}} = \dfrac{\text{ELS}}{D}$

2. Quantity discounts:

    Total annual cost = Annual holding cost + Annual setup cost + Annual cost of material

    $$C = \frac{Q}{2}(H) + \frac{D}{Q}(S) + PD$$

3. One-period decisions:

    Payoff matrix: $\text{Payoff} = \begin{cases} pQ & \text{if } Q \le D \\ pD - I(Q-D) & \text{if } Q > D \end{cases}$

KEY TERM

economic production lot size (ELS) 709

SOLVED PROBLEM 1

Peachy Keen, Inc. makes mohair sweaters, blouses with Peter Pan collars, pedal pushers, poodle skirts, and other popular clothing styles of the 1950s. The average demand for mohair sweaters is 100 per week. Peachy's production facility has the capacity to sew 400 sweaters per week. Setup cost is $351. The value of finished goods inventory is $40 per sweater. The annual per-unit inventory holding cost is 20 percent of the item's value.

a. What is the economic production lot size (ELS)?
b. What is the average time between orders (TBO)?
c. What is the total of the annual holding costs and setup costs?

SOLUTION

a. The production lot size that minimizes total costs is

$$\text{ELS} = \sqrt{\frac{2DS}{H}}\sqrt{\frac{p}{p-d}} = \sqrt{\frac{2(100 \times 52)(\$351)}{0.20(\$40)}}\sqrt{\frac{400}{(400-100)}}$$

$$= \sqrt{456,300}\sqrt{\frac{4}{3}} = 780 \text{ sweaters}$$

b. The average time between orders is

$$\text{TBO}_{\text{ELS}} = \frac{\text{ELS}}{D} = \frac{780}{5,200} = 0.15 \text{ year}$$

Converting to weeks, we get

$$\text{TBO}_{\text{ELS}} = (0.15 \text{ year})(52 \text{ weeks/year}) = 7.8 \text{weeks}$$

c. The minimum total of ordering and holding costs is

$$C = \frac{Q}{2}\left(\frac{p-d}{p}\right)(H) + \frac{D}{Q}(S) = \frac{780}{2}\left(\frac{400-100}{400}\right)(0.20 \times \$40) + \frac{5,200}{780}(\$351)$$

$$= \$2,340/\text{year} + \$2,340/\text{year} = \$4,680/\text{year}$$

SOLVED PROBLEM 2

A hospital buys disposable surgical packages from Pfisher, Inc. Pfisher's price schedule is $50.25 per package on orders of 1 to 199 packages and $49.00 per package on orders of 200 or more packages. Ordering cost is $64 per order, and annual holding cost is 20 percent of the per-unit purchase price. Annual demand is 490 packages. What is the best purchase quantity?

SOLUTION

We first calculate the EOQ at the *lowest* price:

$$\text{EOQ}_{49.00} = \sqrt{\frac{2DS}{H}} = \sqrt{\frac{2(490)(\$64.00)}{0.20(\$49.00)}} = \sqrt{6,400} = 80 \text{ packages}$$

This solution is infeasible because, according to the price schedule, we cannot purchase 80 packages at a price of $49.00 each. Therefore, we calculate the EOQ at the next lowest price ($50.25):

$$\text{EOQ}_{50.25} = \sqrt{\frac{2DS}{H}} = \sqrt{\frac{2(490)(\$64.00)}{0.20(\$50.25)}} = \sqrt{6,241} = 79 \text{ packages}$$

This EOQ is feasible, but $50.25 per package is not the lowest price. Hence, we have to determine whether total costs can be reduced by purchasing 200 units and thereby obtaining a quantity discount.

$$C = \frac{Q}{2}(H) + \frac{D}{Q}(S) + PD$$

$$C_{79} = \frac{79}{2}(0.20 \times \$50.25) + \frac{490}{79}(\$64.00) + \$50.25(490)$$
$$= \$396.98/\text{year} + \$396.98/\text{year} + \$24,622.50/\text{year} = \$25,416.44/\text{year}$$

$$C_{200} = \frac{200}{2}(0.20 \times \$49.00) + \frac{490}{200}(\$64.00) + \$49.00(490)$$
$$= \$980.00/\text{year} + \$156.80/\text{year} + \$24,010.00/\text{year} = \$25,146.80/\text{year}$$

Purchasing 200 units per order will save \$269.64/year, compared to buying 79 units at a time.

SOLVED PROBLEM 3

Swell Productions is sponsoring an outdoor conclave for owners of collectible and classic Fords. The concession stand in the T-Bird area will sell T-shirts, poodle skirts, and other souvenirs of the 1950s. Poodle skirts are purchased from Peachy Keen, Inc. for \$40 each and are sold during the event for \$75 each. If any skirts are left over, they can be returned to Peachy for a refund of \$30 each. Poodle skirt sales depend on the weather, attendance, and other variables. The following table shows the probability of various sales quantities. How many poodle skirts should Swell Productions order from Peachy Keen for this one-time event?

SALES QUANTITY	PROBABILITY	SALES QUANTITY	PROBABILITY
100	0.05	400	0.34
200	0.11	500	0.11
300	0.34	600	0.05

SOLUTION

Table E.1 is the payoff table that describes this one-period inventory decision. The upper-right portion of the table shows the payoffs when the demand, D, is greater than or equal to the order quantity, Q. The payoff is equal to the per-unit profit (the difference between price and cost) multiplied by the order quantity. For example, when the order quantity is 100 and the demand is 200,

$$\text{Payoff} = (p - c)Q = (\$75 - \$40)100 = \$3,500$$

The lower-left portion of the payoff table shows the payoffs when the order quantity exceeds the demand. Here the payoff is the profit from sales, pD, minus the loss associated with returning overstock, $I(Q - D)$, where I is the difference between the cost and the amount refunded for each poodle skirt returned and $Q - D$ is the number of skirts returned. For example, when the order quantity is 500 and the demand is 200,

$$\text{Payoff} = pD - l(Q - D) = (\$75 - \$40)200 - (\$40 - \$30)(500 - 200) = \$4,000$$

The highest expected payoff occurs when 400 poodle skirts are ordered:

$$\text{Expected payoff}_{400} = (\$500 \times 0.05) + (\$5,000 \times 0.11) + (\$9,500 \times 0.34)$$
$$+ (\$14,000 \times 0.34) + (\$14,000 \times 0.11) + (\$14,000 \times 0.05)$$
$$= \$10,805$$

TABLE 5.1
PAYOFFS

	DEMAND, D						
Q	100	200	300	400	500	600	EXPECTED PAYOFF
100	$3,500	$3,500	$ 3,500	$ 3,500	$ 3,500	$ 3,500	$ 3,500
200	$2,500	$7,000	$ 7,000	$ 7,000	$ 7,000	$ 7,000	$ 6,775
300	$1,500	$6,000	$10,500	$10,500	$10,500	$10,500	$ 9,555
400	$ 500	$5,000	$ 9,500	$14,000	$14,000	$14,000	$10,805
500	($ 500)	$4,000	$ 8,500	$13,000	$17,500	$17,500	$10,525
600	($1,500)	$3,000	$ 7,500	$12,000	$16,500	$21,000	$ 9,750

PROBLEMS

1. **OM Explorer** Bold Vision, Inc. makes laser printer and photocopier toner cartridges. The demand rate is 625 EP cartridges per week. The production rate is 1,736 EP cartridges per week, and the setup cost is $100. The value of inventory is $130 per unit, and the holding cost is 20 percent of the inventory value. What is the economic production lot size?

2. **OM Explorer** Sharpe Cutter is a small company that produces specialty knives for paper cutting machinery. The annual demand for a particular type of knife is 100,000 units. The demand is uniform over the 250 working days in a year. Sharpe Cutter produces this type of knife in lots and, on average, can produce 450 knives a day. The cost to set up a production lot is $300, and the annual holding cost is $1.20 per knife.
   a. Determine the economic production lot size (ELS).
   b. Determine the total annual setup and inventory holding cost for this item.
   c. Determine the TBO, or cycle length, for the ELS.
   d. Determine the production time per lot.

3. **OM Explorer** Suds's Bottling Company does bottling, labeling, and distribution work for several local microbreweries. The demand rate for Wortman's beer is 600 cases (24 bottles each) per week. Suds's bottling production rate is 2,400 cases per week, and the setup cost is $800. The value of inventory is $12.50 per case, and the annual holding cost is 30 percent of the inventory value. What is the economic production lot size?

4. **OM Explorer** The Bucks Grande major league baseball team breaks an average of four bats per week. The team orders baseball bats from Corky's, a bat manufacturer noted for its access to the finest hardwood. The order cost is $70, and the annual holding cost per bat per year is 38 percent of the purchase price. Corky's price structure is

Order Quantity	Price per Unit
0 to 11	$54.00
12 to 143	$51.00
144 or more	$48.50

a. How many bats should the team buy per order?
b. What are the total annual costs associated with the best order quantity?
c. Corky discovers that, owing to special manufacturing processes required for the Bucks' bats, it has underestimated setup costs. Rather than raise prices, Corky adds another category to the price structure to provide an incentive for larger orders and reduce the number of setups required. If the Bucks buy 180 bats or more, the price will drop to $45.00 each. Should the Bucks revise the order quantity to 180 bats?

5. **OM Explorer** To boost sales, Pfisher (refer to Solved Problem 2) announces a new price structure for disposable surgical packages. Although the price break no longer is available at 200 units, Pfisher now offers an even greater discount if larger quantities are purchased. On orders of 1 to 499 packages, the price is $50.25 per package. For orders of 500 or more, the price per unit is $47.80. Ordering costs, annual holding costs, and annual demand remain at $64 per order, 20 percent of the per-unit cost, and 490 packages per year, respectively. What is the new lot size?

6. **OM Explorer** The University Bookstore at a prestigious private university buys mechanical pencils from a wholesaler. The wholesaler offers discounts for large orders according to the following price schedule:

Order Quantity	Price per Unit
0 to 200	$4.00
201 to 2,000	$3.50
2,001 or more	$3.25

The bookstore expects an annual demand of 2,500 units. It costs $10 to place an order, and the annual cost of holding a unit in stock is 30 percent of the unit's price. Determine the best order quantity.

7. **OM Explorer** Mac-in-the-Box, Inc. sells computer equipment by mail and telephone order. Mac sells 1,200 flat-bed scanners per year. Ordering cost is $300, and annual holding cost is 16 percent of the item's price. The

scanner manufacturer offers the following price structure to Mac-in-the-Box:

Order Quantity	Price per Unit
0 to 11	$520.00
12 to 143	$500.00
144 or more	$400.00

What order quantity minimizes total annual costs?

8. **OM Explorer** As inventory manager, you must decide on the order quantity for an item that has an annual demand of 2,000 units. Placing an order costs you $20 each time. Your annual holding cost, expressed as a percentage of average inventory value, is 20 percent. Your supplier has provided the following price schedule:

Minimum Order Quantity	Price per Unit
1	$2.50
200	$2.40
300	$2.25
1,000	$2.00

What ordering policy do you recommend?

9. **OM Explorer** National Printing Company must decide how many wall calendars it should produce for sale during the upcoming sale season. Each calendar sells for $8.50 and costs $2.50 to produce. The local school district has agreed to buy all unsold calendars at a unit price of $1.50. National estimates the following probability distribution for the season's demand:

Demand	Probability
2,000	0.05
3,000	0.20
4,000	0.25
5,000	0.40
6,000	0.10

How many calendars should National produce to maximize its expected profit?

10. **OM Explorer** Dorothy's pastries are freshly baked and sold at several specialty shops throughout Dallas. When they are a day old, they must be sold at reduced prices. Daily demand is distributed as follows:

Demand	Probability
50	0.25
150	0.50
200	0.25

Each pastry sells for $1.00 and costs $0.60 to make. Each one not sold at the end of the day can be sold the next day for $0.30 as day-old merchandise. How many pastries should be baked each day?

11. **OM Explorer** The Aggies will host Tech in this year's homecoming football game. Based on advance ticket sales, the athletic department has forecast hot dog sales as shown in the following table. The school buys premium hot dogs for $1.50 and sells them during the game at $3.00 each. Hot dogs left over after the game will be sold for $0.50 each to the Aggie student cafeteria to be used in making beanie weenie casserole.

Sales Quantity	Probability
2,000	0.10
3,000	0.30
4,000	0.30
5,000	0.20
6,000	0.10

Use a payoff matrix to determine the number of hot dogs to buy for the game.

SIMULATION EXERCISE

This simulation exercise requires the use of the Extend software, which is an optional package your instructor may or may not have ordered.

1. **Extend** Revisit the case on Ready Hardware, a midsize regional distributor of hardware that was introduced in the Simulation Exercise at the end of Chapter 15, "Inventory Management." Given the supplier's quantity discount schedule for the lockset, what lot sizing policy do you recommend, using the Extend simulator? See Section E of the *Inventory Management at Ready Hardware* case on the optional CD-ROM, which includes the basic model and how to use it.

SELECTED REFERENCES

"Factors That Make or Break Season Sales." *Wall Street Journal* (December 9, 1991).

Greene, James H. *Production and Inventory Control Handbook,* 3d ed. New York: McGraw-Hill, 1997.

Inventory Management Reprints. Falls Church, VA: American Production and Inventory Control Society, 1993.

Silver, Edward A., D. F. Pyke, and Rein Peterson. *Inventory Management, Production Planning, and Scheduling,* 3d ed. New York: John Wiley & Sons, 1998.

Sipper, Daniel, and Robert L. Bulfin, Jr. *Production Planning, Control, and Integration.* New York: McGraw-Hill, 1997.

Tersine, Richard J. *Principles of Inventory and Materials Management,* 4th ed. Saddlebrook, NJ: Prentice Hall, 1994.

Resource Planning

LEARNING GOALS   *After reading this chapter, you should be able to . . .*

IDENTIFY OR DEFINE

1. the key outputs from the resource planning process and how they are used.
2. the benefits of manufacturing resource planning to core and supporting processes in the firm.
3. the key planning factors that management can use to control the performance of a material requirements planning system.

DESCRIBE OR EXPLAIN

4. the logic of material requirements planning.
5. how to schedule the receipt of services and materials to meet future deadlines.
6. how the principles of material requirements planning can be applied to the provision of services and distribution inventories.

VF CORPORATION

What do Wrangler or Lee jeans, Timber Creek khakis, Vanity Fair underwear, Healthtex clothes for kids, Jantzen bathing suits, and JanSport backpacks have in common, other than that you can find them in diverse retail outlets such as Wal-Mart, Target, and Macy's? One-hundred-and-two year-old VF Corporation (www.vfc.com), a $5.5 billion-a-year company in Greensboro, North Carolina, and the world's largest apparel producer, manufactures all of these products and many more. In 1999, VF's stock had been a steady performer; however, its sales were flat and management realized that the corporation needed shaking up. VF's 14 divisions were operated as independent entities, each with its own purchasing, production, marketing, and computer systems. Management initiated a drive to

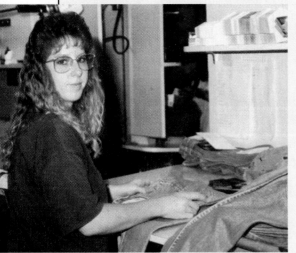

Data on quality are important inputs for VF's ERP system. Here an employee inspects jeans to assure they conform to VF's quality standards and meet customer expectations.

focus its key business processes on identifying and fulfilling customer needs. The restructuring resulted in five "coalitions": jeanswear, intimates, playwear, knitwear, and international operations and marketing. Each coalition will phase into the integrated system over time.

The coalitions need to work together to take advantage of common resources. However, resource planning across such a complex environment poses major challenges. To establish the critical information links between the coalitions, VF decided to install a modified version of the R/3 ERP system from SAP AG specifically designed for apparel and footwear manufacturers as the core integrating system (www.sap.com). However, VF also decided to use the *best of breed* implementation strategy, which allowed VF to choose the best applications modules from any vendor or retain some of its own legacy systems. For example, the heart of the system has only four R/3 modules: order management, production planning, materials management, and finance. However, each coalition has its favorite applications from other vendors that have to be included. Intimates uses WebPDM from Gerber to cut product design costs and Rhythm from i2 to optimize materials utilization and assembly-line space. Information from Rhythm is fed back to the R/3 production planning module. Jeanswear is using software from Logility to make customer forecasts, which are fed back to the production planning and financial modules in R/3. VF's own customized software tracks production in the plants, using

information from the R/3 production planning, order management, and materials management modules and then reports back to R/3 for the fine-tuning of production plans. VF also has developed a "micromarketing" system that forecasts the need for a specific size and color of Wrangler jeans (say), for the beginning of summer, at a particular Wal-Mart store.

Key modules in the new system for resource planning are material requirements planning and capacity planning. The material requirements planning system is contained in the production planning module and uses forecasts from the Logility sales and demand planning module to determine the purchase quantities and delivery dates for supplies and materials, such as leather, fabric, or linings; the production of finished goods, such as jeans, backpacks, or shirts; and the manufacture of assemblies, such as shoe soles or bootlegs. The output from material requirements planning is useful for planning production as well as financial resources. For example, the timing of planned purchase quantities can be translated into the need for funds to pay for them. The output can also be used by the capacity planning module, which facilitates the planning for critical resources, such as skilled employees or specialized equipment, to support the production plan.

Sources: Brown, Eryn. "VF Corp. Changes Its Underware." *Fortune* (December 7, 1998), pp. 115–118; "SAP Consumer Products for Apparel and Footwear." (July 2000); VFC Press Release. "VF Corporation Launches First Large Scale Apparel Industry-Specific SAP Solution." (May 31, 2000).

The VF Corporation demonstrates that companies can gain a competitive edge by integrating processes through an effective operations information system. Maintaining an efficient flow of services and materials from suppliers and managing internal activities relating to materials and other resources are essential to the smooth operation of value chains. The order fulfillment process must ensure that all resources needed to produce finished services or products are available at the right time. For a manufacturer, this task may mean keeping track of thousands of subassemblies, components, and raw materials as well as the capacities of key equipment. For a service provider, this task may mean keeping track of various materials and supplies and time requirements for many different categories of employees and equipment.

We begin this chapter with a discussion of material requirements planning (MRP), which is a key element of manufacturing resource planning systems. We discuss the important concept of dependent demand and all the information inputs to MRP that are used to generate the reports needed for managing manufacturing and distribution inventories as well as other resources. We introduce these topics from a manufacturing perspective because the terminology is often easier to understand when we can use tangible, commonly recognized products. MRP evolved into a system called manufacturing resource planning, which provides valuable information to core and supporting processes based on a firm's production plans. The success of manufacturing resource planning led the way for the application of these concepts to the provision of services. Consequently, we devote an entire section of this chapter to resource planning for service providers and demonstrate how the concept of dependent demands can be used to manage the supplies, human resources, equipment, financial resources, and inventories for service providers. The resource planning techniques in this chapter are important elements of enterprise resource planning (ERP) systems for service providers and manufacturers alike (see Chapter 12, "Information Technology and Value Chains").

As you read this chapter, think about how effective resource planning is important to various departments across the organization, such as . . .

➤ **accounting,** which coordinates the payments to suppliers and billings to customers with the resource plan.

➤ **finance,** which plans for adequate working capital to support the schedules generated in the resource plan.

➤ **human resources,** which determines the implications of the resource plan on personnel requirements.

➤ **management information systems,** which must identify the information requirements of managers and the information that can be generated from the resource plan.

➤ **marketing,** which makes reliable delivery commitments to customers.

➤ **operations,** which is responsible for inventories and the utilization of the resources required by the firm's processes to meet customer demand.

● OVERVIEW OF MATERIAL REQUIREMENTS PLANNING

Material requirements planning (MRP), which is a computerized information system, was developed specifically to aid companies in managing dependent demand inventory and scheduling replenishment orders. MRP systems have proven to be beneficial to many companies. In this section, we discuss the nature of dependent demands and identify some of the benefits firms have experienced with these systems.

material requirements planning (MRP) A computerized information system developed specifically to aid in managing dependent demand inventory and scheduling replenishment orders.

DEPENDENT DEMAND

To illustrate the concept of dependent demand, let us consider a Huffy bicycle produced for retail outlets. The bicycle, one of many different types held in inventory at Huffy's plant, has a high-volume demand rate over time. Demand for a final product, such as a bicycle, is called *independent demand* because it is influenced only by market conditions and not by demand for any other type of bicycle held in inventory (see Chapter 15, "Inventory Management"). Huffy must *forecast* that demand (see Chapter 13, "Forecasting"). However, Huffy also keeps many other items in inventory, including handlebars, pedals, frames, and wheel rims, used to make completed bicycles. Each of these items has a **dependent demand** because the quantity required is a function of the demand for other items held in inventory. For example, the demand for frames,

dependent demand A demand that occurs because the quantity required is a function of the demand for other items held in inventory.

pedals, and wheel rims is *dependent* on the production of completed bicycles. Operations can *calculate* the demand for dependent demand items once the bicycle production levels are announced. For example, every bicycle needs two wheel rims, so 1,000 completed bicycles need 1,000(2) = 2,000 rims. Statistical forecasting techniques are not needed for these items.

The bicycle, or any other product that is manufactured from one or more components, is called a **parent**. The wheel rim is an example of a **component**—an item that may go through one or more operations to be transformed into, or become, part of one or more parents. The wheel rim may have several different parents because it might be used for more than one style of bicycle. The parent–component relationship can cause erratic dependent demand patterns for components. Suppose that every time inventory falls to 500 units (a reorder point), an order for 1,000 more bicycles is placed, as shown in Figure 16.1(a). The assembly supervisor then authorizes the withdrawal of 2,000 rims from inventory, along with other components for the finished product; demand for the rim is shown in Figure 16.1(b). So, even though customer demand for the finished bicycle is continuous and reasonably uniform, the production demand for wheel rims is "lumpy"; that is, it occurs sporadically, usually in relatively large quantities. Thus, the *production* decisions for the assembly of bicycles, which account for the costs of assembling the bicycles and the projected assembly capacities at the time the decisions are made, determine the demand for wheel rims.

Managing dependent demand inventories is complicated because some components may be subject to both dependent and independent demand. For example, operations needs 2,000 wheel rims for the new bicycles, but the company also sells replacement rims for old bicycles directly to retail outlets. This practice places an independent demand on the inventory of wheel rims. Material requirements planning can be used in complex situations involving components that may have independent demand as well as dependent demand inventories.

parent   Any product that is manufactured from one or more components.

component   An item that may go through one or more operations to be transformed into, or become, part of one or more parents.

BENEFITS OF MRP

Why should companies invest in an MRP system?

For years, many companies tried to manage production and delivery of dependent demand inventories with independent demand systems, but the outcome was seldom satisfactory. However, because it recognizes dependent demands, the MRP system enables businesses to reduce inventory levels, utilize labor and facilities better, and improve customer service. These successes are due to three advantages of material requirements planning.

FIGURE 16.1

Lumpy Dependent Demand Resulting from Continuous Independent Demand

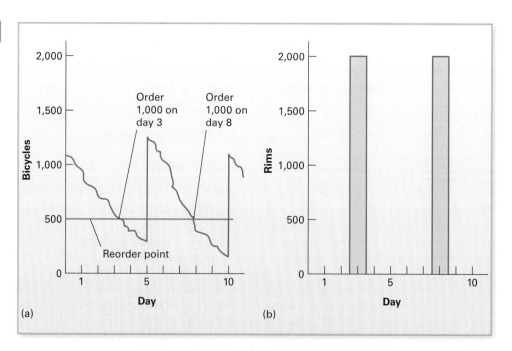

1. Statistical forecasting for components with lumpy demand results in large forecasting errors. Compensating for such errors by increasing safety stock is costly, with no guarantee that stockouts can be avoided. MRP calculates the dependent demand of components from the production schedules of their parents, thereby providing a better forecast of component requirements.

2. MRP systems provide managers with information that is useful for planning capacities and estimating financial requirements. Production schedules and materials purchases can be translated into capacity requirements and dollar amounts and can be projected in the time periods when they will appear. Planners can use the information on parent item schedules to identify times when needed components may be unavailable because of capacity shortages, supplier delivery delays, and the like.

3. MRP systems automatically update the dependent demand and inventory replenishment schedules of components when the production schedules of parent items change. The MRP system alerts the planners whenever action is needed on any component.

INPUTS TO MRP

The key inputs of an MRP system are a bill of materials database, a master production schedule, and an inventory record database, as shown in Figure 16.2. Using this information, the MRP system identifies actions that operations must take to stay on schedule, such as releasing new production orders, adjusting order quantities, and expediting late orders.

An MRP system translates the master production schedule and other sources of demand, such as independent demand for replacement parts and maintenance items, into the requirements for all subassemblies, components, and raw materials needed to produce the required parent items. This process is called an **MRP explosion** because it converts the requirements of various final products into a *material requirements plan* that specifies the replenishment schedules of all the subassemblies, components, and raw materials needed by the final products.

BILL OF MATERIALS

The replenishment schedule for a component is determined from the production schedules of its parents. Hence, the system needs accurate information on parent–component relationships. A **bill of materials (BOM)** is a record of all the components of an item,

MRP explosion A process that converts the requirements of various final products into a *material requirements plan* that specifies the replenishment schedules of all the subassemblies, components, and raw materials needed by the final products.

bill of materials (BOM) A record of all the components of an item, the parent–component relationships, and the usage quantities derived from engineering and process designs.

| **FIGURE 16.2** | **Material Requirements Plan Inputs** |

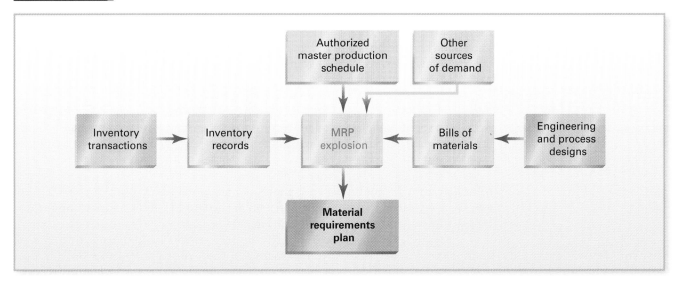

VIDEO CLIP 16.1
Video Clip 16.1 on the Student CD-ROM introduces the concept of dependent demand and shows a simple bill of materials.

Figure 16.3 diagram: BOM for a Ladder-Back Chair

Back slats

Seat cushion

Leg supports

Seat-frame boards

Back legs

Front legs

A
Ladder-back chair

B (1)
Ladder-back subassembly

C (1)
Seat subassembly

D (2)
Front legs

E (4)
Leg supports

F(2)
Back legs

G (4)
Back slats

H (1)
Seat frame

I (1)
Seat cushion

J (4)
Seat-frame boards

usage quantity The number of units of a component that are needed to make one unit of its immediate parent.

the parent–component relationships, and the usage quantities derived from engineering and process designs. In Figure 16.3, the BOM of a simple ladder-back chair shows that the chair is made from a ladder-back subassembly, a seat subassembly, front legs, and leg supports. In turn, the ladder-back subassembly is made from back legs and back slats, and the seat subassembly is made from a seat frame and a seat cushion. Finally, the seat frame is made from seat-frame boards. For convenience, we refer to these items by the letters shown in Figure 16.3.

All items except item A are components because they are needed to make a parent. Items A, B, C, and H are parents because they all have at least one component. The BOM also specifies the **usage quantity,** or the number of units of a component that are needed to make one unit of its immediate parent. Figure 16.3 shows usage quantities for each parent–component relationship in parentheses. Note that one chair (item A) is made from one ladder-back subassembly (item B), one seat subassembly (item C), two front legs (item D), and four leg supports (item E). In addition, item B is made from two back legs (item F) and four back slats (item G). Item C needs one seat frame (item H) and one seat cushion (item I). Finally, item H needs four seat-frame boards (item J).

Four terms frequently used to describe inventory items are end items, intermediate items, subassemblies, and purchased items. An **end item** typically is the final product sold to the customer; it is a parent but not a component. Item A in Figure 16.3, the

end item The final product sold to a customer.

completed ladder-back chair, is an end item. Accounting statements classify inventory of end items as either work-in-process (WIP), if work remains to be done, or finished goods. An **intermediate item** is one such as item B, C, or H that has at least one parent and at least one component. Some products have several levels of intermediate items; the parent of one intermediate item also is an intermediate item. Inventory of intermediate items—whether completed or still on the shop floor—is classified as WIP. A **subassembly** is an intermediate item that is *assembled* (as opposed to being transformed by other means) from *more* than one component. Items B and C are subassemblies. A **purchased item** has no components because it comes from a supplier, but it has one or more parents. Examples are items D, E, F, G, I, and J in Figure 16.3. Inventory of purchased items is treated as raw materials in accounting statements.

A component may have more than one parent. **Part commonality**, sometimes called *standardization of parts* or *modularity*, is the degree to which a component has more than one immediate parent. As a result of commonality, the same item may appear in several places in the bill of materials for a product, or it may appear in the bills of materials for several different products. For example, the seat subassembly in Figure 16.3 is a component of the ladder-back chair and of a kitchen chair that is part of the same family of products. The usage quantity specified in the bill of materials relates to a specific parent–component relationship. The usage quantity for any component can change, depending on the parent item. Part commonality increases volume and repeatability for some items, which has several advantages for process design (see Chapter 3, "Process Design Strategy"), and helps minimize inventory costs. Today, with the need for greater efficiency in all firms, part commonality is used extensively.

intermediate item   An item that has at least one parent and at least one component.

subassembly   An intermediate item that is *assembled* (as opposed to being transformed by other means) from *more* than one component.

purchased item   An item that has one or more parents but no components because it comes from a supplier.

part commonality   The degree to which a component has more than one immediate parent.

MASTER PRODUCTION SCHEDULE

The second input into a material requirements plan is the **master production schedule** (**MPS**), which details how many end items will be produced within specified periods of time. It breaks the aggregate production plan (see Chapter 14, "Aggregate Planning") into specific product schedules. Figure 16.4 shows how an aggregate plan for a family of chairs breaks down into the weekly MPS for each specific chair type (the time period can be hours, days, weeks, or months). Here, the scheduled quantities are shown in the week they must be released to the shop to start final assembly so as to meet customer delivery promises. We use the MPS "start" quantities throughout this chapter. The chair example demonstrates the following aspects of master scheduling:

Why is the master production schedule important to the material requirements plan?

master production schedule (MPS)   A part of the material requirements plan that details how many end items will be produced within specified periods of time.

1. The sums of the quantities in the MPS must equal those in the aggregate production plan. This consistency between the plans is desirable because of the economic analysis done to arrive at the aggregate plan.

2. The aggregate production quantities must be allocated efficiently over time. The specific mix of chair types—the amount of each type as a percent of the total aggregate

FIGURE 16.4
MPS for a Family of Chairs

	April				May			
	1	2	3	4	5	6	7	8
Ladder-back chair	150					150		
Kitchen chair			120				120	
Desk chair		200	200		200			200
Aggregate production plan for chair family			670				670	

quantity—is based on historic demand and marketing and promotional considerations. The planner must select lot sizes for each chair type, taking into consideration economic factors, such as production setup costs and inventory carrying costs.

3. Capacity limitations, such as machine or labor capacity, storage space, or working capital, may determine the timing and size of MPS quantities. The planner must acknowledge these limitations by recognizing that some chair styles require more resources than others and setting the timing and size of the production quantities accordingly.

The MPS start quantities are used in the MRP system to determine the components needed to support the schedule. Details of how to develop the MPS are contained in Supplement F, "Master Production Scheduling" on the Student CD-ROM.

INVENTORY RECORD

Inventory records are a third major input to MRP, and inventory transactions are the basic building blocks of up-to-date records (see Figure 16.2). Transactions include releasing new orders, receiving scheduled receipts, adjusting due dates for scheduled receipts, withdrawing inventory, canceling orders, correcting inventory errors, rejecting shipments, and verifying scrap losses and stock returns. Recording such transactions is essential for maintaining the accurate records of on-hand inventory balances and scheduled receipts necessary for an effective MRP system.

inventory record *A record that shows an item's lot-size policy, lead time, and various time-phased data.*

The **inventory record** divides the future into time periods called *time buckets*. In our discussion, we use weekly time buckets for consistency with our MPS example, although other time periods could as easily be used. The inventory record shows an item's lot-size policy, lead time, and various time-phased data. The purpose of the inventory record is to keep track of inventory levels and component replenishment needs. The time-phased information contained in the inventory record consists of (1) *gross requirements*, (2) *scheduled receipts*, (3) *projected on-hand inventory*, (4) *planned receipts,* and (5) *planned order releases.*

We illustrate the discussion of inventory records with the seat subassembly, item C, that was shown in Figure 16.3. It is used in two products: a ladder-back chair and a kitchen chair.

gross requirements *The total demand derived from* all *parent production plans.*

GROSS REQUIREMENTS. The **gross requirements** are the total demand derived from *all* parent production plans. They also include demand not otherwise accounted for, such as demand for replacement parts for units already sold. Figure 16.5 shows an inventory record for item C, the seat subassembly. Item C is produced in lots of 230 units and has a lead time of two weeks. The inventory record also shows item C's gross requirements for the next eight weeks, which come from the master production schedule for the ladder-back and kitchen chairs (see Figure 16.4). The MPS start quantities for each parent are added to arrive at each week's gross requirements. The seat subassembly's gross requirements exhibit lumpy demand: Operations will withdraw seat subassemblies from inventory in only four of the eight weeks.

The MRP system works with release dates to schedule production and delivery for components and subassemblies. Its program logic anticipates the removal of all materials required by a parent's production order from inventory at the *beginning* of the parent item's lead time—when the scheduler first releases the order to the shop.

SCHEDULED RECEIPTS. Recall that *scheduled receipts* (sometimes called *open orders*) are orders that have been placed but not yet completed. For a purchased item, the scheduled receipt could be in one of several stages: being processed by a supplier, being transported to the purchaser, or being inspected by the purchaser's receiving department. If the firm is making the item in-house, the order could be on the shop floor being processed, waiting for components, waiting for a machine to become available, or waiting to be moved to its next operation. According to Figure 16.5 one 230-unit order of item C is due in week 1. Given the two-week lead time, the inventory planner released the order two weeks ago.

FIGURE 16.5

MRP Record for the Seat
Subassembly

Item: C				Lot Size: 230 units				
Description: Seat subassembly				Lead Time: 2 weeks				

	Week							
	1	2	3	4	5	6	7	8
Gross requirements	150	0	0	120	0	150	120	0
Scheduled receipts	230	0	0	0	0	0	0	0
Projected on-hand inventory 37	117	117	117	−3	−3	−153	−273	−273
Planned receipts								
Planned order releases								

Explanation:
Gross requirements are the total demand for the two chairs. Projected on-hand inventory in week 1 is 37 + 230 − 150 = 117 units.

PROJECTED ON-HAND INVENTORY. The **projected on-hand inventory** is an estimate of the amount of inventory available each week after gross requirements have been satisfied. The beginning inventory, shown as the first entry (37) in Figure 16.5, indicates the on-hand inventory available at the time the record was computed. As with scheduled receipts, entries are made for each actual withdrawal and receipt to update the MRP database. Then, when the MRP system produces the revised record, the correct inventory will appear.

Other entries in the row show inventory expected in future weeks. Projected on-hand inventory is calculated as

$$\begin{pmatrix} \text{Projected on-hand} \\ \text{inventory balance} \\ \text{at end of week } t \end{pmatrix} = \begin{pmatrix} \text{Inventory on} \\ \text{hand at end of} \\ \text{week } t-1 \end{pmatrix} + \begin{pmatrix} \text{Scheduled} \\ \text{or planned} \\ \text{receipts in} \\ \text{week } t \end{pmatrix} - \begin{pmatrix} \text{Gross} \\ \text{requirements} \\ \text{in week } t \end{pmatrix}$$

The projected on-hand calculation includes the consideration of **planned receipts,** which are orders not yet released to the shop or the supplier. In Figure 16.5, the planned receipts are all zero. The on-hand inventory calculations for each week are

Week 1:	37 + 230 − 150	= 117
Weeks 2 and 3:	117 + 0 − 0	= 117
Week 4:	117 + 0 − 120	= −3
Week 5:	−3 + 0 − 0	= −3
Week 6:	−3 + 0 − 150	= −153
Week 7:	−153 + 0 − 120	= −273
Week 8:	−273 + 0 − 0	= −273

projected on-hand inventory
An estimate of the amount of inventory available each week after gross requirements have been satisfied.

planned receipts Orders that are not yet released to the shop or the supplier.

In week 4, the balance drops to −3 units, which indicates that a shortage of 3 units will occur unless more seat subassemblies are built. This condition signals the need for a planned receipt to arrive in week 4. In addition, unless more stock is received, the shortage will grow to 273 units in weeks 7 and 8.

PLANNED RECEIPTS. Planning for receipt of new orders will keep the projected on-hand balance from dropping below zero. The planned receipt row is developed as follows:

1. Weekly on-hand inventory is projected until a shortage appears. Completion of the initial planned receipt is scheduled for the week when the shortage is projected. The addition of the newly planned receipt should raise the projected on-hand balance so that it equals or exceeds zero. It will exceed zero when the lot size exceeds requirements in the week it is planned to arrive.

2. The projection of on-hand inventory continues until the next shortage occurs. This shortage signals the need for the second planned receipt.

This process is repeated until the end of the planning horizon by proceeding column by column through the MRP record—filling in planned receipts as needed and completing the projected on-hand inventory row. Figure 16.6 shows the planned receipts for the seat subassembly. In week 4, the projected on-hand inventory will drop below zero, so a planned receipt of 230 units is scheduled for week 4. The updated inventory on-hand balance is 117 (inventory at end of week 3) + 230 (planned receipts) − 120 (gross requirements) = 227 units. The projected on-hand inventory remains at 227 for week 5 because there are no scheduled receipts of gross requirements. In week 6, the projected on-hand inventory is 227 (inventory at end of week 5) − 150 (gross requirements) = 77 units. This quantity is greater than zero, so no new planned receipt is needed. In week 7, however, a shortage will occur unless more seat subassemblies are received. With a planned receipt in week 7, the updated inventory balance is 77 (inventory at end of week 6) + 230 (planned receipts) − 120 (gross requirements) = 187 units.

planned order release An indication of when an order for a specified quantity of an item is to be issued.

PLANNED ORDER RELEASES. A **planned order release** indicates when an order for a specified quantity of an item is to be issued. We must place the planned order release quantity in the proper time bucket. To do so, we must assume that all inventory flows—scheduled receipts, planned receipts, and gross requirements—occur at the same point of time in a time period. Some firms assume that all flows occur at the beginning of a time period; other firms assume that they occur at the end of a time period or at the middle of the time period. Regardless of when the flows are assumed to occur, we find the release date by subtracting the lead time from the receipt date. For example, the release date for the first planned order release in Figure 16.6 is: 4 (planned receipt date) − 2 (lead time) = 2 (planned order release date). Figure 16.6 shows the planned order releases for the seat subassembly. If all goes according to the plan, we will release an order for 230 seat assemblies in week 2. This order release sets off a series of updates to the inventory record. First, the planned order release for the order is removed. Next, the planned receipt for 230 units in week 4 is also removed. Finally, a new scheduled receipt for 230 units will appear in the scheduled receipt row for week 4.

PLANNING FACTORS

The planning factors in a MRP inventory record play an important role in the overall performance of the MRP system. By manipulating these factors, managers can fine-tune inventory operations. In this section, we discuss planning lead time, lot-sizing rules, and safety stock.

FIGURE 16.6

Completed Inventory Record for the Seat Subassembly

Item: C
Description: Seat subassembly

Lot Size: 230 units
Lead Time: 2 weeks

	Week							
	1	2	3	4	5	6	7	8
Gross requirements	150	0	0	120	0	150	120	0
Scheduled receipts	230	0	0	0	0	0	0	0
Projected on-hand inventory 37	117	117	117	227	227	77	187	187
Planned receipts				230			230	
Planned order releases		230			230			

Explanation:
Without a new order in week 4, there will be a shortage of 3 units: $117 + 0 + 0 - 120 = -3$ units. Adding the planned receipt brings the balance to $117 + 0 + 230 - 120 = 227$ units. Offsetting for a two-week lead time puts the corresponding planned order release back to week 2.

Explanation:
The first planned order lasts until week 7, when projected inventory would drop to $77 + 0 + 0 - 120 = -43$ units. Adding the second planned receipt brings the balance to $77 + 0 + 230 - 120 = 187$ units. The corresponding planned order release is for week 5 (or week 7 minus 2 weeks).

PLANNING LEAD TIME

Planning lead time is an estimate of the time between placing an order for an item and receiving the item in inventory. Accuracy is important in planning lead time. If an item arrives in inventory sooner than needed, inventory holding costs increase. If an item arrives too late, stockouts, excessive expediting costs, or both may occur.

For purchased items, the planning lead time is the time allowed for receiving a shipment from the supplier after the order has been sent, including the normal time to place the order. Often, the purchasing contract stipulates the delivery date. For items manufactured in-house, the planning lead time consists of estimates for

- setup time,
- processing time,
- materials handling time between operations, and
- waiting time.

Each of these times must be estimated for every operation along the item's route. Estimating setup, processing, and materials handling time may be relatively easy, but estimating the waiting time for materials handling equipment or for a machine to perform a particular operation may be more difficult. In a facility that uses a make-to-order strategy, such as a machine shop, the load on the shop varies considerably over time, causing actual waiting times for a particular order to fluctuate widely. Therefore, estimating waiting time in such a facility is very important in estimating the planning lead time. However, in a facility that uses a make-to-stock strategy, such as an assembly plant, product routings are more standard and waiting time is more predictable; hence, waiting time generally is a less significant proportion of planning lead times.

LOT-SIZING RULES

How important is the choice of lot-sizing rules?

A lot-sizing rule determines the timing and size of order quantities. A lot-sizing rule must be assigned to each item before planned receipts and planned order releases can be computed. The choice of lot-sizing rules is important because they determine the number of setups required and the inventory holding costs for each item. We present three lot-sizing rules: (1) fixed order quantity, (2) periodic order quantity, and (3) lot for lot.

fixed order quantity (FOQ)
A rule that maintains the same order quantity each time an order is issued.

FIXED ORDER QUANTITY. The **fixed order quantity (FOQ)** rule maintains the same order quantity each time an order is issued. For example, the lot size might be the size dictated by equipment capacity limits, as when a full lot must be loaded into a furnace at one time. For purchased items, the FOQ could be determined by the quantity discount level, truckload capacity, or minimum purchase quantity. Alternatively, the lot size could be determined by the economic order quantity (EOQ) formula (see Chapter 15, "Inventory Management"). Figure 16.6 illustrates the FOQ rule. However, if an item's gross requirement within a week is particularly large, the FOQ might be insufficient to avoid a shortage. In such unusual cases, the inventory planner must increase the lot size beyond the FOQ, typically to a size large enough to avoid a shortage. Another option is to make the order quantity an integer multiple of the FOQ. This option is appropriate when capacity constraints limit production to FOQ sizes (at most) and setup costs are high.

periodic order quantity (POQ)
A rule that allows a different order quantity for each order issued but tends to issue the order at predetermined time intervals.

PERIODIC ORDER QUANTITY. The **periodic order quantity (POQ)** rule allows a different order quantity for each order issued but tends to issue the order at predetermined time intervals, such as every two weeks. The order quantity equals the amount of the item needed during the predetermined time between orders and must be large enough to prevent shortages. Specifically, the POQ is

$$\begin{pmatrix} \text{POQ lot size} \\ \text{to arrive in} \\ \text{week } t \end{pmatrix} = \begin{pmatrix} \text{Total gross requirements} \\ \text{for } P \text{ weeks, including} \\ \text{week } t \end{pmatrix} - \begin{pmatrix} \text{Projected on-hand} \\ \text{inventory balance at} \\ \text{end of week } t - 1 \end{pmatrix}$$

TUTOR 16.1

Tutor 16.1 on the Student CD-ROM provides a new example to practice lot-sizing decisions using the FOQ, POQ, and L4L rules.

This amount exactly covers P weeks worth of gross requirements. That is, the projected on-hand inventory should equal zero at the end of the Pth week.

Suppose that we want to switch from the FOQ rule used in Figure 16.6 to the POQ rule. Figure 16.7 shows the application of the POQ rule, with $P = 3$ weeks, to the seat

FIGURE 16.7

The POQ ($P = 3$) Rule for the Seat Subassembly

Solver - Single-Item MRP											
Enter data in yellow-shaded areas.											
Periods		8									
Item		Seat Assembly		Period (P) for POQ		3	Lot Size (FOQ)				
Description							Lead Time				2
POQ Rule											
			1	2	3	4	5	6	7	8	
Gross Requirements			150			120		150	120		
Scheduled Receipts			230								
Projected On-Hand Inventory	37		117	117	117	150	150				
Planned Receipts						153			120		
Planned Order Releases				153			120				

subassembly inventory. The first order is required in week 4 because that is the first week when the projected inventory balance will fall below zero. The first order using $P = 3$ weeks is

$$\begin{pmatrix} \text{POQ lot size} \end{pmatrix} = \begin{pmatrix} \text{Gross requirements} \\ \text{for weeks} \\ 4,\ 5,\ \text{and } 6 \end{pmatrix} - \begin{pmatrix} \text{Inventory at} \\ \text{end of week 3} \end{pmatrix}$$
$$= (120 + 0 + 150) - 117 = 153 \text{ units}$$

The second order must arrive in week 7, with a lot size of $(120 + 0) - 0 = 120$ units. This second order reflects only two weeks' worth of gross requirements—to the end of the planning horizon.

The POQ rule does *not* mean that operations must issue a new order every P weeks. Rather, when an order *is* planned, its lot size must be enough to cover P successive weeks. One way to select a P value is to divide the average lot size desired, such as the EOQ (see Chapter 15, "Inventory Management"), or some other applicable lot size, by the average weekly demand. That is, express the target lot size as a desired weeks of supply (P) and round to the nearest integer.

LOT FOR LOT. A special case of the POQ rule is the **lot-for-lot (L4L)** rule, under which the lot size ordered covers the gross requirements of a single week. Thus, $P = 1$, and the goal is to minimize inventory levels. This rule ensures that the planned order is just large enough to prevent a shortage in the single week it covers. The L4L lot size is

lot for lot (L4L) A rule under which the lot size ordered covers the gross requirements of a single week.

$$\begin{pmatrix} \text{L4L lot size} \\ \text{to arrive in} \\ \text{week } t \end{pmatrix} = \begin{pmatrix} \text{Gross requirements} \\ \text{for week } t \end{pmatrix} - \begin{pmatrix} \text{Projected on-hand} \\ \text{inventory balance at} \\ \text{the end of week } t-1 \end{pmatrix}$$

The projected on-hand inventory combined with the new order will equal zero at the end of week t. Following the first planned order, an additional planned order will be used to match each subsequent gross requirement.

This time we want to switch from the FOQ rule to the L4L rule. Figure 16.8 shows the application of the L4L rule to the seat subassembly inventory. As before, the first order is needed in week 4:

$$\begin{pmatrix} \text{L4L lot size} \end{pmatrix} = \begin{pmatrix} \text{Gross requirements} \\ \text{in week 4} \end{pmatrix} - \begin{pmatrix} \text{Inventory balance} \\ \text{at end of week 3} \end{pmatrix}$$
$$= 120 - 117 = 3$$

The stockroom must receive additional orders in weeks 6 and 7 to satisfy each of the subsequent gross requirements. The planned receipt for week 6 is 150 and for week 7 is 120.

Solver - Single-Item MRP

Enter data in yellow-shaded areas.

Periods	8								
Item	Seat Assembly			Period (P) for POQ			Lot Size (FOQ)		
Description							Lead Time		2
L4L Rule ▼		1	2	3	4	5	6	7	8
Gross Requirements		150			120		150	120	
Scheduled Receipts		230							
Projected On-Hand Inventory	37	117	117	117					
Planned Receipts					3		150	120	
Planned Order Releases			3		150	120			

FIGURE 16.8

The L4L Rule for the Seat Subassembly

COMPARISON OF LOT-SIZING RULES. Choosing a lot-sizing rule can have important implications for inventory management. Lot-sizing rules affect inventory costs and setup or ordering costs. The FOQ, POQ, and L4L rules differ from one another in one or both respects. In our example, each rule took effect in week 4, when the first order was placed. Let us compare the projected on-hand inventory averaged over weeks 4 through 8 of the planning horizon. The data are shown in Figures 16.6, 16.7, and 16.8 respectively.

$$\text{FOQ: } \frac{227 + 227 + 77 + 187 + 187}{5} = 181 \text{ units}$$

$$\text{POQ: } \frac{150 + 150 + 0 + 0 + 0}{5} = 60 \text{ units}$$

$$\text{L4L: } \frac{0 + 0 + 0 + 0 + 0}{5} = 0 \text{ units}$$

The performance of the L4L rule with respect to average inventory levels comes at the expense of an additional planned order and its accompanying setup time and cost. We can draw three conclusions from this comparison.

1. The FOQ rule generates a high level of average inventory because it creates inventory *remnants*. A remnant is inventory carried into a week, but it is too small to prevent a shortage. Remnants occur because the FOQ does not match requirements exactly. For example, according to Figure 16.6, the stockroom must receive a planned order in week 7, even though 77 units are on hand at the beginning of that week. The remnant is the 77 units that the stockroom will carry for three weeks, beginning with receipt of the first planned order in week 4. Although they increase average inventory levels, inventory remnants introduce stability into the production process by buffering unexpected scrap losses, capacity bottlenecks, inaccurate inventory records, or unstable gross requirements.

2. The POQ rule reduces the amount of average on-hand inventory because it does a better job of matching order quantity to requirements. It adjusts lot sizes as requirements increase or decrease. Figure 16.7 shows that in week 7, when the POQ rule has fully taken effect, the projected on-hand inventory is zero. There are no remnants.

3. The L4L rule minimizes inventory investment, but it also maximizes the number of orders placed. This rule is most applicable to expensive items or items with small ordering or setup costs. It is the only rule that can be used for a low-volume item made to order.

By avoiding remnants, both the POQ and the L4L rule may introduce instability by tying the lot-sizing decision so closely to requirements. If any requirement changes, so must the lot size, which can disrupt component schedules. Last-minute increases in parent orders may be hindered by missing components.

SAFETY STOCK

An important managerial decision is the quantity of safety stock to carry. It is more complex for dependent demand items than for independent demand items. Safety stock for dependent demand items with lumpy demand (gross requirements) is valuable only when future gross requirements, the timing or size of scheduled receipts, and the amount of scrap are uncertain. Safety stock should be reduced and ultimately removed as the causes of the uncertainty are eliminated. The usual policy is to use safety stock for end items and purchased items to protect against fluctuating customer orders and unreliable suppliers of components and to avoid using it as much as possible for intermediate items. Safety stocks can be incorporated in the MRP logic by using the following rule: schedule a planned receipt whenever the projected on-hand inventory balance drops below the desired safety stock level (rather than zero, as before). The objective is to keep a minimum level of planned inventories equal to the safety stock quantity. Figure 16.9 shows what happens when there is a requirement for 80 units of safety stock for the seat assembly using a FOQ of 230 units. Compare these results to Figure 16.6 . The net effect is to move the second planned order release from week 5 to week 4 to avoid going below 80 units in week 6.

Tutor - FOQ, POQ, and L4L Rules

FOQ Rule						Lot Size		230
						Lead Time		2
						Safety Stock		80
	1	2	3	4	5	6	7	8
Gross Requirements	150	0	0	120	0	150	120	0
Scheduled Receipts	230	0	0	0	0	0	0	0
Projected On-Hand Inventory 37	117	117	117	227	227	307	187	187
Planned Receipts	0	0	0	230	0	230	0	0
Planned Order Releases	0	230	0	230	0	0	0	0

Inventory Record for the Seat Subassembly Showing the Application of a Safety Stock.

OUTPUTS FROM MRP

MRP systems provide many reports, schedules, and notices to help managers control dependent demand inventories, as indicated in Figure 16.10. In this section, we discuss the MRP explosion process, action notices that alert managers to items needing attention, and capacity reports that project the capacity requirements implied by the material requirements plan.

MRP EXPLOSION

MRP translates, or *explodes*, the MPS and other sources of demand into the requirements for all subassemblies, components, and raw materials needed to produce parent items. This process generates the material requirements plan for each component item.

What information is available from MRP systems that will provide help in managing materials better?

FIGURE 16.10 **MRP Outputs**

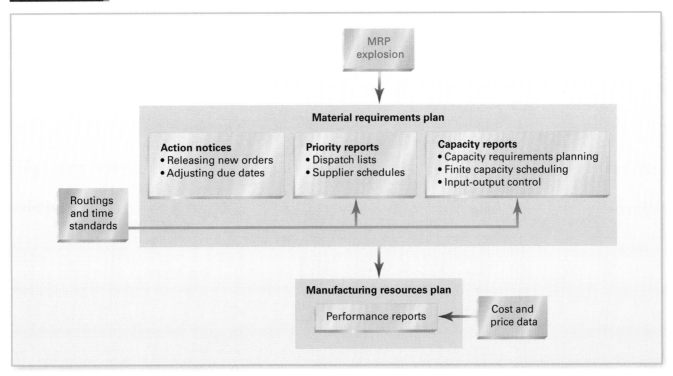

An item's gross requirements are derived from three sources:

• the MPS for immediate parents that are end items,
• the planned order releases for parents below the MPS level, and
• any other requirements not originating in the MPS, such as the demand for replacement parts.

Consider the seat subassembly for which we have developed the inventory record shown in Figure 16.6. The seat subassembly requires a seat cushion and a seat frame, which in turn needs four seat-frame boards. Its BOM is shown in Figure 16.11 (see also Figure 16.3, which shows how the seat subassembly BOM relates to the product as a whole). How many seat cushions should we order from the supplier? How many seat frames should we produce to support the seat subassembly schedule? How many seat-frame boards do we need to make? The answers to these questions depend on the inventories we already have of these items and the replenishment orders already in progress. MRP can help answer these questions through the explosion process.

Figure 16.12 shows the MRP records for the seat subassembly and its components. We have already shown how to develop the MRP record for the seat subassembly. We now concentrate on the MRP records of its components. The lot-size rules are an FOQ of 300 units for the seat frame, L4L for the seat cushion, and an FOQ of 1,500 for the seat-frame boards. All three components have a one-week lead time. The key to the explosion process is to determine the proper timing and size of the gross requirements for each component. When we have done that, we can derive the planned order release schedule for each component by using the logic we have already demonstrated.

In our example, the components have no independent demand for replacement parts. Consequently, in Figure 16.12, the gross requirements of a component come from the planned order releases of its parents. The seat frame and the seat cushion get their gross requirements from the planned order release schedule of the seat subassembly. Both components have gross requirements of 230 units in weeks 2 and 5, the same weeks in which we will be releasing orders to make more seat subassemblies. In week 2, for example, the materials handler for the assembly department will withdraw 230 seat frames and 230 seat cushions from inventory so that the assembly department can produce the seat subassemblies in time to avoid a stockout in week 4. The materials plans for the seat frame and the seat cushion must allow for that.

Using the gross requirements in weeks 2 and 5, we can develop the MRP records for the seat frame and the seat cushion, as shown in Figure 16.12. For a scheduled

FIGURE 16.11

BOM for the Seat Subassembly

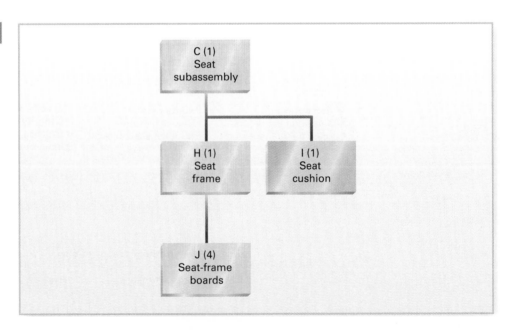

FIGURE 16.12   **MRP Explosion of Seat Assembly Components**

Item: Seat subassembly
Lot size: 230 units

Lead time: 2 weeks	Week							
	1	2	3	4	5	6	7	8
Gross requirements	150	0	0	120	0	150	120	0
Scheduled receipts	230	0	0	0	0	0	0	0
Projected inventory 37	117	117	117	227	227	77	187	187
Planned receipts				230			230	
Planned order releases		230			230			

Usage quantity: 1 ⟩   ⟨ Usage quantity: 1

Item: Seat frames
Lot size: 300 units

Lead time: 1 week	Week							
	1	2	3	4	5	6	7	8
Gross requirements	0	230	0	0	230	0	0	0
Scheduled receipts	0	300	0	0	0	0	0	0
Projected inventory 40	40	110	110	110	180	180	180	180
Planned receipts					300			
Planned order releases				300				

Item: Seat cushion
Lot size: L4L

Lead time: 1 week	Week							
	1	2	3	4	5	6	7	8
Gross requirements	0	230	0	0	230	0	0	0
Scheduled receipts	0	0	0	0	0	0	0	0
Projected inventory 0	0	0	0	0	0	0	0	0
Planned receipts		230			230			
Planned order releases	230			230				

Usage quantity: 4 ⟩

Item: Seat-frame boards
Lot size: 1,500 units

Lead time: 1 week	Week							
	1	2	3	4	5	6	7	8
Gross requirements	0	0	0	1,200	0	0	0	0
Scheduled receipts	0	0	0	0	0	0	0	0
Projected inventory 200	200	200	200	500	500	500	500	500
Planned receipts				1,500				
Planned order releases			1,500					

receipt of 300 seat frames in week 2, an on-hand quantity of 40 units, and a lead time of one week, we need to release an order of 300 seat frames in week 4 to cover the assembly schedule for the seat subassembly. The seat cushion has no scheduled receipts and no inventory on hand; consequently, we must place orders for 230 units in weeks 1 and 4, using the L4L logic with a lead time of one week.

Once we have determined the replenishment schedule for the seat frame, we can calculate the gross requirements for the seat-frame boards. We plan to begin producing 300 seat frames in week 4. Each frame requires 4 boards, so we need to have 300(4) = 1,200 boards available in week 4. Consequently, the gross requirement for seat-frame boards is 1,200 in week 4. Given no scheduled receipts, 200 boards in stock, a lead time of one week, and an FOQ of 1,500 units, we need a planned order release of 1,500 in week 3.

The questions we posed earlier can now be answered. The following orders must be released: 300 seat frames in week 4, 230 seat cushions in each of weeks 1 and 4, and 1,500 seat-frame boards in week 3.

ACTION NOTICES

action notice A computer-generated memo used by inventory planners to make decisions about releasing new orders and adjusting the due dates of scheduled receipts.

Once computed, inventory records for any item appearing in the BOM can be printed in hard copy or displayed on a computer video screen. Inventory planners use a computer-generated memo called an **action notice** to make decisions about releasing new orders and adjusting the due dates of scheduled receipts. These notices are generated every time the system is updated. The action notice alerts planners to only the items that need their attention, such as those items that have a planned order release in the current period or those that need their due dates adjusted because of changes to parent item schedules or the unavailability of components. Planners can then view the full records for those items and take the necessary actions. An action notice can simply be a list of part numbers for items that need attention; or it can be the full record for such items, with a note at the bottom identifying the action needed. See Solved Problem 2 for an example of action notices.

CAPACITY REPORTS

How can capacity constraints be recognized in the material requirements plan?

By itself, the MRP system does not recognize capacity limitations when computing planned orders. That is, it may call for a planned order release that exceeds the amount that can be physically produced. An essential role of managers is to monitor the capacity requirements of material requirements plans, adjusting a plan when it cannot be met. In this section, we discuss three sources of information for short-term decisions that materials managers continually make: (1) *capacity requirements planning reports*, (2) *finite capacity scheduling reports*, and (3) *input–output reports*.

capacity requirements planning (CRP) A technique used for projecting time-phased capacity requirements for workstations; its purpose is to match the material requirements plan with the capacity of key processes.

CAPACITY REQUIREMENTS PLANNING. One technique for projecting time-phased capacity requirements for workstations is **capacity requirements planning (CRP)**. Its purpose is to match the material requirements plan with the capacity of key processes. The technique is used to calculate workload according to the work required to complete the scheduled receipts already in the shop and to complete the planned order releases not yet released. This task involves the use of the inventory records, which supply the planned order releases and the status of the scheduled receipts; the item's routing, which specifies the workstations that must process the item; average lead times between each workstation; and the average processing and setup times at each workstation. Using the MRP dates for the arrival of replenishment orders for an item to avoid shortages, CRP traces back through the item's routing to estimate when the scheduled receipt or planned order will reach each workstation. The system uses the processing and setup times to estimate the load that the item will impose on each station for each planned order and scheduled receipt of the item. The workloads for each workstation are obtained by adding the time that each item needs at a particular workstation. Critical workstations are those at which the projected loads exceed station capacities.

FIGURE 16.13

CRP Report

Date: **Week:** 32
Plant 01 Dept. 03: Lathe Station
Capacity: 320 hours per week

	Week					
	32	33	34	35	36	37
Planned hours	90	156	349	210	360	280
Actual hours	210	104	41	0	0	0
Total hours	300	260	390	210	360	280

Explanation:
Projected capacity requirements
exceed weekly hours of capacity.

Figure 16.13 shows a CRP report for a lathe station that turns wooden table legs. Each of four lathes is scheduled for two shifts per day. The lathe station has a maximum capacity of 320 hours per week. The *planned* hours represent the labor requirements for all planned orders for items that need to be routed through the lathe station. The *actual* hours represent the backlog of work visible on the shop floor (i.e., scheduled receipts). Combining requirements from both sources gives *total* hours. Comparing total hours to actual capacity constraints gives advance warning of any potential problems. The planner must manually resolve any capacity problems that are uncovered.

For example, the CRP report shown in Figure 16.13 would alert the planner to the need for scheduling adjustments. Unless something is done, the current capacity of 320 hours per week will be exceeded in week 34 and again in week 36. Requirements for all other time periods are well below the capacity limit. Perhaps the best choice is to release some orders earlier than planned so that they will arrive at the lathe station in weeks 32, 33, and 35 rather than in weeks 34 and 36. This adjustment will help smooth capacity and alleviate bottlenecks. Other options might be to change the lot sizes of some items, use overtime, subcontract, off-load to another workstation, or simply let the bottlenecks occur.

FINITE CAPACITY SCHEDULING. In large production facilities, thousands of orders may be in progress at any one time. Manually adjusting the timing of these orders with the use of spreadsheets or wall-mounted magnetic schedule boards is virtually impossible. The best solutions—those that meet the MRP schedule due dates and do not violate any constraints—may never be identified because of the time needed to explore the alternatives. A useful tool for these situations is a **finite capacity scheduling (FCS)** system, which is an algorithm designed to schedule a group of orders appropriately across an entire shop. The system utilizes routings for the items manufactured, resource constraints, available capacity, shift patterns, and a scheduling rule to be used at each workstation to determine the priorities for orders (see Chapter 17, "Scheduling").

finite capacity scheduling (FCS) An algorithm designed to schedule a group of orders appropriately across an entire shop.

To be effective, the FCS system needs to be integrated with MRP. The MRP system can download the orders that need to be scheduled, but the FCS system needs much more than that. An FCS system operates at a finer level of detail than MRP and needs to know the status of each machine and when the current order will finish processing, the maintenance schedule, the routings, the setup times, machine speeds and capabilities, and resource capacities, for example. The FCS system uses that information to determine actual, realistic start and end times of jobs and uploads the results to MRP for subsequent replanning. The FCS system provides a more accurate picture than MRP of when the orders will be completed because MRP uses estimates for job waiting times in job lead times, does not recognize capacities when making the materials plans, and often uses aggregated time buckets (e.g., weeks). If these realistic completion times conflict with the MRP schedule, it may have to be revised and the FCS system rerun. Many companies are using advanced planning and scheduling (APS) systems that link their FCS and MRP systems to their ERP and supply-chain management systems (see Chapter 17, "Scheduling").

input–output control report
A report that compares planned input (from prior CRP or FCS reports) with actual input and compares planned output with actual output.

INPUT–OUTPUT CONTROL. An **input–output control report** compares planned input (from prior CRP or FCS reports) with actual input and compares planned output with actual output. Inputs and outputs are expressed in common units, usually labor or machine hours. Information in the report indicates whether workstations have been performing as expected and helps management pinpoint the source of capacity problems. Actual outputs can fall behind planned outputs for two reasons:

1. *Insufficient Inputs.* Output may lag when inputs are insufficient to support the planned output rates. The problem can lie upstream at a prior operation, or it may be caused by missing purchased parts. In effect, not enough work arrives to keep the operation busy.
2. *Insufficient Capacity.* Output may lag at the station itself. Even though input rates keep pace, output may slip below expected levels because of absenteeism, equipment failures, inadequate staffing levels, or low productivity rates.

The input–output control report shown in Figure 16.14 was prepared for a rough mill workstation at which desk chair components are machined. Management established a tolerance of ±25 hours of cumulative deviations from plans. As long as cumulative deviations do not exceed this threshold, there is no cause for concern. However, the report shows that in week 31 actual outputs fell behind planned outputs by a total of 32 hours. This cumulative deviation exceeds the 25-hour tolerance, so there is a problem. Actual inputs are keeping pace with planned inputs, so the lag results from insufficient capacity at the rough mill station itself. The temporary use of overtime may be necessary to increase the output rate.

FIGURE 16.14

Input–Output Control Report

Workstation: Rough Mill					Week: 32
Tolerance: ±25 hours					

	Week Ending				
	28	29	30	31	32
Inputs					
Planned	160	155	170	160	165
Actual	145	160	168	177	
Cumulative deviation	−15	−10	−12	+5	
Outputs					
Planned	170	170	160	160	160
Actual	165	165	150	148	
Cumulative deviation	−5	−10	−20	−32	

Explanation:
Cumulative deviations between −25 hours and +25 hours are allowed.

Explanation:
Cumulative deviation exceeds lower tolerance limit, indicating actual hours of output have fallen too far below planned hours of output and some action is required.

MRP AND THE ENVIRONMENT

Consumer and governmental concern about the deterioration of the natural environment has driven manufacturers to reengineer their processes to become more environmentally friendly. Recycling of base materials is becoming more commonplace and products are being designed for ease of remanufacturing after their useful lives. Nonetheless, manufacturing processes often produce a number of wastes that need to be properly disposed. Wastes come in many forms, including

- effluents, such as carbon monoxide, sulfur dioxide, and hazardous chemicals, that are associated with the processes used to manufacture the product;
- materials, such as metal shavings, oils, and chemicals, that are associated with specific operations;
- packaging materials, such as unusable cardboard and plastics associated with certain products or purchased items; and
- scrap associated with unusable product or component defects generated by the manufacturing process.

Companies can modify their MRP systems to assist them in tracking these wastes and in planning for their disposition. The type and amount of waste associated with each item can be entered into its BOM by treating the waste much like you would a component of the item. When the MPS is developed for a product, reports can be generated that project the amount of waste that is expected and when it will occur. Although this approach requires substantial modification of a firm's BOM, the benefits are also substantial. Firms can identify their waste problems in advance and consequently plan for the proper disposal of them. The firms also have a means to generate any formal documentation required by the government to verify compliance with environmental laws and policies.

MANUFACTURING RESOURCE PLANNING

The basic MRP system has its roots in the batch manufacturing of discrete parts involving assemblies that must be stocked to support future manufacturing needs. The focus is on producing schedules that meet the materials needs identified in the MPS. When managers realized that the information in an MRP system would be useful to functional areas other than operations, MRP evolved into **manufacturing resource planning (MRP II)**, a system that ties the basic MRP system to the company's financial system and to other core and supporting processes. Figure 16.15 shows an overview of an MRP II system. The focus of MRP II is to aid the management of a firm's resources by providing information based on the production plan to all functional areas. MRP II enables managers to test "what-if" scenarios by using simulation. For example, managers can see the effect of changing the MPS on the purchasing requirements for certain critical suppliers or the workload on bottleneck work centers without actually authorizing the schedule. In addition, management can project the dollar value of shipments, product costs, overhead allocations, inventories, backlogs, and profits by using the MRP plan along with prices and product and activity costs from the accounting system. Also, information from the MPS, scheduled receipts, and planned orders can be converted into cash flow projections, which are broken down by product families. For example, the projected on-hand quantities in MRP inventory records allow the computation of future levels of inventory investment. These levels are obtained simply by multiplying the quantities by the per-unit value of each item and adding these amounts for all items belonging to the same product family. Similar computations are possible for other performance measures of interest to management.

Information from MRP II is used by managers in manufacturing, purchasing, marketing, finance, accounting, and engineering. MRP II reports help these managers

manufacturing resource planning (MRP II) A system that ties the basic MRP system to the company's financial system and to other core and supporting processes.

FIGURE 16.15   Overview of an MRP II System

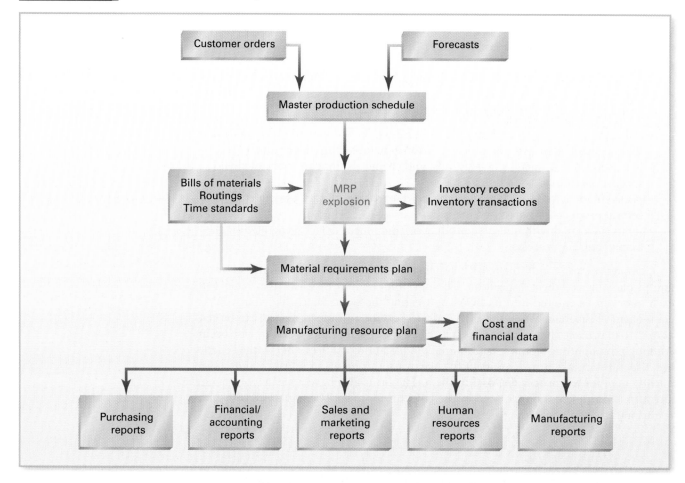

develop and monitor the overall business plan and recognize sales objectives, manufacturing capabilities, and cash flow constraints. MRP II is used extensively and it provides benefits beyond that of MRP alone. For example, the Colorado Springs Division of Hewlett-Packard has used MRP II successfully. This division, which makes a variety of complex electronic instruments, modified its MRP system to coordinate its financial reports with its operational plans. As a result, production costs are within 1 percent of predictions. Managerial Practice 16.1 shows how MRP II can support a firm's strategy in the computer industry. MRP II ultimately evolved into enterprise resource planning (ERP), see Chapter 12, "Information Technology and Value Chains."

SERVICE RESOURCE PLANNING

Service providers must plan for resources just as manufacturers do. We have seen how manufacturing companies can disaggregate an MPS of finished products, which in turn must be translated into the needs for resources, such as staff, equipment, supporting materials, and financial assets. The driver for these resource requirements is a material plan. Service providers must plan for the same resources; however, services cannot be inventoried and often must be provided on demand. The focus is on maintaining the capacity to serve, which may involve planning for supporting inventories as well as personnel and capital assets. The utilization of resources is important because the investment in capital and personnel is often significant for a service provider. In this section, we will discuss the concept of dependent demand for services, the use of a bill of resources, and distribution requirements planning.

MANAGERIAL PRACTICE 16.1

IBM'S ROCHESTER PLANT USES MRP II TO EXECUTE ITS FAST TURNAROUND STRATEGY

IBM's Rochester, Minnesota, plant (www.research.ibm.com) is responsible for the final assembly of IBM's AS/400 midrange computers. The complex includes a printed circuit board assembly and testing facility that provides subassemblies to the final assembly lines. Each AS/400 computer is assembled to customer order, which the plant does more than 50,000 times per year. There are more than 10,000 different configurations. The plant must manage over 57,000 parts and assemblies no matter where they might be in the 3.6 million square feet of space the facility occupies, a daunting task without the help of modern systems. To remain competitive in this industry, IBM must promise delivery of complete computers within 96 hours of receiving the order. In addition, because of the short lead times, the plant must procure materials before firm customer orders are received, which requires careful management of inventory levels and shortages.

A core element of the plant's fast turnaround strategy is a MAPICS MRP II system (www.mapics.com), which took 18 months to install. In addition, IBM developed an application called Production Resource Manager (PRM), which interfaces with a firm's MRP II or ERP systems. In addition to typical inputs to an MRP II system, PRM requires *bills of capacity*, production, suppliers and inventory constraints, and optimization objectives, such as maximizing profits, minimizing costs, or minimizing inventories. The bills of capacity are analogous to bills of material, except they contain the amounts of specific capacities that are needed by a particular configuration of the final product and when they are needed. PRM takes the MRP II plan for component and purchased material replenishment orders and modifies it as needed to account for supply and component availability, capacity constraints, and objectives. The many outputs include a master production schedule, an optimal component production schedule, a revised shipment schedule, and a critical parts list.

The system has enabled the Rochester plant to improve its inventory accuracy to 99 percent and reduce safety stocks by 15 to 25 percent. The system also includes a cost accounting module, which makes costing information that used to take more than a week to obtain immediately available. In addition, planners can simulate "what-if" scenarios quickly to see the impacts of various events on the production schedule. MRP II and the PRM application have enabled IBM's Rochester plant to execute its fast turnaround strategy.

The IBM eServer i825 has a revolutionary on–off capacity on-demand feature that allows smaller customers to turn on extra processing power when needed. The Rochester, Minnesota plant produces the AS/400 and iServer midrange computers.

Sources: "Success Stories: IBM Rochester, Minnesota, USA." MAPICS, Inc. (2000); Weaver, Russ. "PRM in Action at Rochester, MN." IBM Corporation (1996); Weaver, Russ. "Production Resource Manager." IBM Corporation (1996).

DEPENDENT DEMAND FOR SERVICES

When we discussed MRP earlier in this chapter, we introduced the concept of *dependent demand*, which is demand for an item that is a function of the demand for some other item the company produces. For service resource planning, it is useful to define the concept of dependent demand to include demands for resources that are driven by forecasts of customer requests for services or by plans for various activities in support of the services the company provides. For example, a resource every service provider manages closely is cash. Forecasts of customer requests for services drive the need to purchase supporting materials and outside services. Staffing levels, a function of the forecasts, and employee schedules, a function of the forecasts and the staffing

How can the concept of dependent demand be useful to service providers?

A couple enjoys eating at a fine restaurant. Each meal initiates the need for facilitating goods, staff, and equipment.

plan, drive the payroll (see Chapter 14, "Aggregate Planning" and Chapter 17, "Scheduling"). These actions increase the firm's accounts payable. As services are actually completed, the accounts receivable increase. Both the accounts receivable and the accounts payable help predict the amount and timing of cash flows for the firm. Here are some other examples of dependent demands for service providers.

RESTAURANTS. Every time you order from the menu at a restaurant, you initiate the need for facilitating goods (uncooked food items, plates, and napkins), staff (chef, servers, and dishwashers), and equipment (stoves, ovens, and cooking utensils). Using a forecast of the demand for each type of meal, the manager of the restaurant can estimate the need for resources. Many restaurants have "specials" on certain days, such as fish frys on Fridays or prime ribs on Saturdays. Specials improve the accuracy of the forecast for meal types and typically signal the need for above-average levels of staff help.

AIRLINES. Whenever an airline schedules a flight, there are requirements for facilitating goods (meals, beverages, and fuel), staff (pilots, flight attendants, and airport services), and equipment (plane and airport gate). Forecasts of customer patronage of each flight help determine the amount of facilitating goods and the type of plane needed. A master schedule of flights based on the forecasts can be exploded to determine the resources needed to support the schedule.

HOSPITALS. With the exception of the emergency room, appointments, which are a form of master schedule for specific services, generally drive the short-term need for health care resources in hospitals. Forecasts of requests for various services provided by the hospital drive the long-term needs. When you schedule a surgical procedure, you generate a need for facilitating goods (medicines, surgical gowns, and linens), staff (surgeon, nurses, and anesthesiologist), and equipment (operating room, surgical tools, and recovery bed). Hospitals must take care so that certain equipment or personnel do not become overcommitted. That is why an appointment for a kidney operation is put off until the surgeon is available, even though the appropriate operating room, nurses, and other resources are available.

HOTELS. The major fixed assets at a hotel are the rooms where guests stay. Given the high capital costs involved, hotels try to maintain as high a utilization rate as possible by offering group rates or special promotions at certain times of the year. Reservations, supplemented by forecasts of "walk-in" customers, provide a master schedule of needs for the hotel's services. When a traveler makes a reservation at a hotel, a need is generated for facilitating goods (soap and towels), staff (front desk, housekeeping, and concierge), and equipment (fax, television, and exercise bicycle). Managerial Practice 16.2 shows that resource planning for a large hotel management and holding company can be a complex problem.

MANAGERIAL PRACTICE 16.2

RESOURCE PLANNING AT STARWOOD HOTELS AND RESORTS WORLDWIDE

Starwood Hotels and Resorts Worldwide (www.starwood.com) is one of the largest hotel and gambling companies in the world, with more than 750 hotels and resorts in more than 80 countries worldwide. It owns international hotel chains, such as Sheraton Hotels, CIGA Hotels, Four Points Hotels, and The Luxury Collection, which includes the St. Regis in New York, the Prince de Gaulle in Paris, the Hotel Gritti Palace in Venice, and the Hotel Imperial in Vienna. It also owns Caesar's Palace in Las Vegas and other casinos in Cairo, Egypt and Atlantic City. Over 50 million travelers a year visit Starwood's properties.

Resource planning at a company such as Starwood is complex, not only because of the size of the business, but also because of the variety of its holdings. As in any service environment, resources, such as employees, equipment, and supplies, must be managed so as to ensure that the needs and expectations of the customers are met. Information technology can help by providing the means for centralized information flows while allowing decision making to take place at the most appropriate level. An important concept for resource planning in services is *dependent demand* for key resources. Starwood makes use of that concept in two ways. First, Starwood's reservation system builds profiles of its customers' preferences so that they can be better served each time they stay at a hotel or resort. For example, the profile would include infor-

A concierge for the Hotel Gritti Palace greets a rowing team competing in the Volgalonga. Boaters must row from the Piazza San Marco to Buranoa and back, a total distance of 20 miles. The Hotel Gritti Palace is one of many properties of Starwood Hotels and Resorts Worldwide that faces complex resource planning issues.

mation, such as whether they like a feather or foam pillow, what types of newspapers they like, whether they want a low floor or a high floor, if they want suites, or even if they are handicapped. The profile is used at the time a reservation is made to estimate the requirements for various types of rooms and locations, newspapers, pillows, and any other resource affected by the customer's preferences. Such a capability provides a "customized" experience for each guest.

Second, Starwood has linked its worldwide reservation system to its property management system for resource planning at a particular property. The property management system schedules staff and housekeepers and projects requirements for the food-preparation department. Given expected occupancies for weeks in advance, property managers can plan for the needed resources to make their customers' stay enjoyable.

The ERP system Starwood uses for managing the resources of this worldwide enterprise has a centralized database and common modules, including payroll, accounts payable, general ledger, and fixed assets, from Oracle as well as some legacy systems. Given the enormity of this application, various parts of the enterprise will be phased into the integrated system over time.

Source: Baum, David. "Setting the Standard for Service." *Profit Magazine* (1999); www.oracle.com (updated 2003).

BILL OF RESOURCES

bill of resources (BOR)   A record of all the required materials, equipment time, staff, and other resources needed to provide a service, the parent–component relationships, and the usage quantities.

The service analogy to the BOM in a manufacturing company is the **bill of resources (BOR),** which is a record of all the required materials, equipment time, staff, and other resources needed to provide a service, the parent–component relationships, and the usage quantities. Given a master schedule of services, the BOR can be used to derive the time-phased requirements for the firm's critical resources, as we did for the inventory records in MRP. A BOR for a service provider can be as complex as a BOM for a manufacturer. Consider a hospital that has just scheduled treatment of a patient with an aneurysm. As shown in Figure 16.16, the BOR for treatment of an aneurysm has seven

FIGURE 16.16

BOR for Treating an Aneurysm

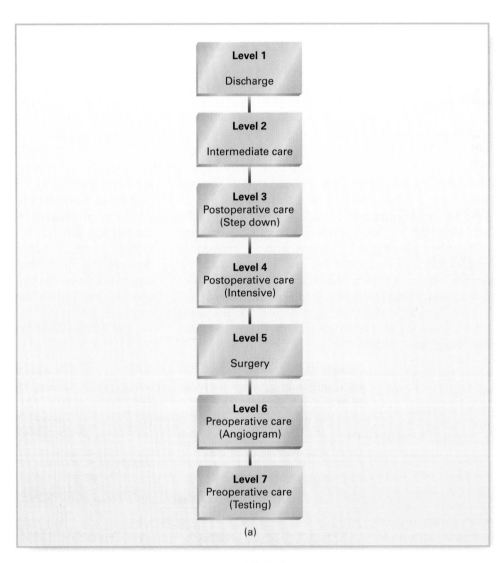

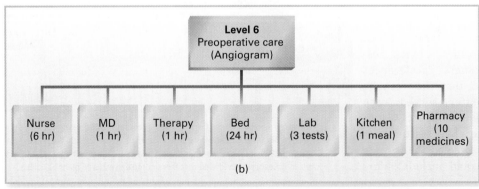

levels, starting at the top (end item): (1) discharge; (2) intermediate care; (3)postoperative care (step down); (4) postoperative care (intensive); (5)surgery; (6)preoperative care (angiogram); and (7)preoperative care (testing). Each level of the BOR has a set of material and resource requirements and a lead time. For example, at level 6, shown in Figure 16.16 (b), the patient needs 6 hours of nurses' time, 1 hour of the primary MD's time, 1 hour of the respiratory therapist's time, 24 hours of bed time, 3 different lab tests, 1 dietary meal, and 10 different medicines from the pharmacy. The lead time for this level is 1 day. The lead time for the entire stay for treatment of the aneurysm is 12.2 days. A master schedule of patient admissions and the BORs for each illness enable the hospital to manage their critical resources. Reports analogous to those we discussed for MRP II can be generated for the managers of the major processes in the hospital.

DISTRIBUTION REQUIREMENTS PLANNING

The principles of MRP can also be applied to nonmanufacturing inventories, such as distribution inventories, which are stocks of items held at retailers and distribution centers. Consider the distribution system in Figure 16.17. The top level represents retail stores at various locations throughout the country. At the middle level are regional distribution centers (DCs) that replenish retail store inventories on request. The bottom level consists of one or more plants that supply the DCs. In the past, plants tended to schedule production to meet the forecasted demand patterns of the DCs. The DCs, in turn, replenished their inventories based on past demand patterns of the retail stores, reordering stocks from the factory whenever the inventory position reached a predetermined reorder point. The retailers followed a similar procedure, ordering stock from the distributor.

To illustrate the shortcomings of this approach, let us suppose that customer demand for a product suddenly increases by 10 percent. What will happen? Because the retailers carry some inventory, there will be some delay before the DCs feel the impact of the full 10 percent increase. Still more time passes before the plants feel the effect of the full increase, reflected as higher demand from the DCs. Thus, for months, the plants could continue underproducing at their normal rate. When the deficiency finally becomes apparent, the plants must increase their output by much more than 10 percent to replenish inventory levels. This is one cause of the bullwhip effect in supply chains (see Chapter 9, "Supply-Chain Design").

Distribution requirements planning (DRP) is an inventory control and scheduling technique that applies MRP principles to distribution inventories. It helps avoid self-induced swings in demand. An inventory record is maintained for each item at each location. The planned order releases projected at the retail level are used to derive the gross requirements for each item at the DC level from standard MRP logic and bills of resources.

Can MRP be used for distribution inventories?

distribution requirements planning (DRP) An inventory control and scheduling technique that applies MRP principles to distribution inventories.

FIGURE 16.17   **Distribution System, Showing Supply Links from Plants to Distribution Centers and Retail Stores**

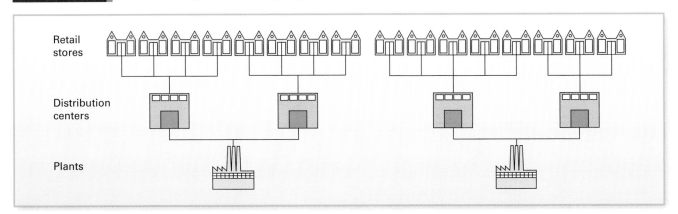

Next, planned order releases at the DC are computed and transmitted to the manufacturer through the DC's supplier relationship process. The order releases are used for updating the master production schedule at the manufacturer and are used by the order fulfillment process to provide the items requested by the DC.

Use of DRP requires an integrated information system. If the manufacturer operates its own DCs and retail stores, called *forward integration,* gathering demand information and relaying it back to the plants is easy. If the manufacturer does not own the DCs and retail stores, all three levels must agree to convey planned order releases from one level to the next. Open communication can be extended from manufacturers to their suppliers, giving suppliers a better idea of future demand. Reducing demand uncertainty can pay off in lower inventories, better service, or both.

RESOURCE PLANNING ACROSS THE ORGANIZATION

Resource planning lies at the heart of any organization. We have seen examples of how traditional brick-and-mortar organizations, such as manufacturers, restaurants, airlines, hospitals, and hotels, organize their resource planning efforts by utilizing integrated information systems that connect the organization's enterprise processes and functional areas. But what about the Internet companies, which rely extensively on Internet connectivity to customers and suppliers? They too have resource planning concerns that permeate the organization. For example, consider online grocers, which do not have the retail outlets and checkout counters their brick-and-mortar competitors do. What resource planning must online grocers do? To be competitive in a very competitive industry where profit margins are low, they must make it easy for the customer to shop on the Internet, provide a wide variety of goods, and make sure the deliveries of groceries are on time and cost efficient. Often, they partner with traditional grocery chains to take advantage of the existing distribution infrastructure. Their Web pages must be designed to keep track of customers' preferences so that weekly shopping is easier and shoppers are apprised of specials and promotions that sometimes are keyed to the availability of goods in stock. The demands for goods at their partner's stores or their own warehouses are derived from the orders placed by customers at their Web sites. They must manage their resources to ensure a wide variety of grocery options for customers, enough stock to minimize stockouts, and adequate personnel to fill orders. Online grocers must coordinate the order picking, packing, and handling that customers normally do at traditional supermarkets. In addition, the delivery of customer orders is derived from the delivery time requested by the customers as well as the completion of the packing process. The delivery of groceries is complicated by the fact that they cannot be left at the door if the customer is not home, and rural deliveries are usually far apart from each other and difficult to efficiently schedule. This operation needs a specialized delivery fleet, capable of moving perishable, bulky items over short distances. Effective management of the delivery service is critical to an online grocery's success. Finally, online grocers are also concerned with planning their cash flows, which are derived from the timing between its sales of groceries and their payments to suppliers and employees. Internet companies have very important resource planning problems that affect all the major processes of the firm.

CHAPTER HIGHLIGHTS

- Dependent demand for component items can be calculated from production schedules of parent items in a manufacturing company. Dependent demands can be calculated from forecasts and other resource plans in a service company.

- Material requirements planning (MRP) is a computerized scheduling and information system that offers benefits in managing dependent demand inventories because it (1) recognizes the relationship between production schedules and the demand for component items, (2) provides forward visibility for planning and problem solving, and (3) provides a way to change materials plans in concert with production schedule changes. MRP has three basic inputs: bills of materials, the master production schedule, and inventory records.

- A bill of materials is a diagram or structured list of all the components of an item, the parent–component relationships, and the usage quantities.

- A master production schedule (MPS) states the number of end items to be produced during specific time periods within an intermediate planning horizon. The MPS is developed within the overall guidelines of the production plan.

- The MRP is also prepared from the most recent inventory records for all items. The basic elements in each record are gross requirements, scheduled receipts, projected on-hand inventory, planned receipts, and planned order releases. Several quantities must be determined for each inventory record, including lot size, lead time, and safety stock.

- The MRP explosion procedure determines the production schedules of the components that are needed to support the MPS. The planned order releases of a parent, modified by usage quantities shown in the bill of materials, become the gross requirements of its components.

- MRP systems provide outputs, such as the material requirements plan, action notices, capacity reports, and performance reports. Action notices bring to a planner's attention new orders that need to be released or items that have open orders with misaligned due dates.

- Capacity requirements planning (CRP) is a technique for estimating the workload required by a master schedule. CRP uses routing information to identify the workstations involved and MRP information about existing inventory, lead-time offset, and replacement part requirements to calculate accurate workload projections. Finite capacity scheduling (FCS) determines a schedule for production orders that recognizes resource constraints. The input–output control report monitors activity at the workstations and compares actual workloads to those planned by CRP or FCS. Discrepancies between the actual and the plan indicate the need for corrective action.

- MRP can be a useful tool in protecting the environment by managing the waste produced by manufacturing processes.

- Manufacturing resource planning (MRP II) ties the basic MRP system to the financial and accounting systems. Advanced systems integrate management decision support for all business functions.

- Service providers can take advantage of MRP principles by developing bills of resources that include requirements for materials, labor, and equipment.

STUDENT CD-ROM AND INTERNET RESOURCES

The Student CD-ROM and the Companion Website at **www.prenhall.com/krajewski** contain many tools, activities, and resources designed for this chapter. The following items are recommended to enhance your skills and improve your understanding of the material in this chapter.

STUDENT CD-ROM RESOURCES

➤ **PowerPoint Slides:** View the comprehensive set of slides customized for this chapter's concepts and techniques.
➤ **Video Clips:** See the video clip customized for this chapter to learn more about dependent demand.
➤ **OM Explorer Tutors:** OM Explorer contains two tutor programs to enhance your understanding of the use of FOQ, POQ, and L4L decision rules for inventory lot-sizing decisions and how to develop a master production schedule. See Chapter 16 and Supplement F in the OM Explorer menu. See also the Tutor Exercise requiring the use of these tutor programs.
➤ **OM Explorer Solvers:** OM Explorer has three programs that can be used to solve general problems involving single-item MRP inventory records, MRP records for multiple-level bills of materials, and master production schedules. See Resource Planning in the OM Explorer menu.

➤ **Active Models:** There is an Active Model spreadsheet that provides additional insight on lot-sizing decisions using the FOQ, POQ, and L4L rules. See Resource Planning in the Active Models menu for this routine. Also see the Active Model exercise at the end of this chapter.
➤ **Written Tours:** See the Lower Florida Keys Health System and Chaparral Steel tours for situations where resource planning can be used.
➤ **Supplement F:** "Master Production Scheduling." Learn how to develop master production schedules and how customer due-date promises are linked to production schedules.

INTERNET RESOURCES

➤ **Self-Study Quizzes:** See the compendium of true or false, multiple choice, and essay questions that allows online tests or gives you feedback on how well you have mastered the concepts of this chapter.
➤ **In the News:** See the articles that apply to this chapter.
➤ **Internet Exercises:** Try out three different links to resource planning topics including part commonality, MRP II, and service resource management.
➤ **Virtual Tours:** See the "Web Links to Company Facility Tours" for tours of company facilities.

KEY TERMS

SOLVED PROBLEM 1

Refer to the bill of materials for product A shown in Figure 16.18.

If there is no existing inventory, how many units of items G, E, and D must be purchased to produce five units of end item A?

SOLUTION

Five units of item G, 30 units of item E, and 20 units of item D must be purchased to make 5 units of A. The usage quantities shown in Figure 16.18 indicate that 2 units of E are needed to make 1 unit of B and that 3 units of B are needed to make 1 unit of A; therefore, 5 units of A require 30 units of E ($2 \times 3 \times 5 = 30$). One unit of D is consumed to make 1 unit of B, and 3 units of B per unit of A result in 15 units of D ($1 \times 3 \times 5 = 15$); plus 1 unit of D in each unit of C and 1 unit of C per unit of A result in another 5 units of D ($1 \times 1 \times 5 = 5$). The total requirements to make 5 units of A are 20 units of D ($15 + 5$). The calculation of requirements for G is simply $1 \times 1 \times 1 \times 5 = 5$ units.

FIGURE 16.18

BOM for Product A

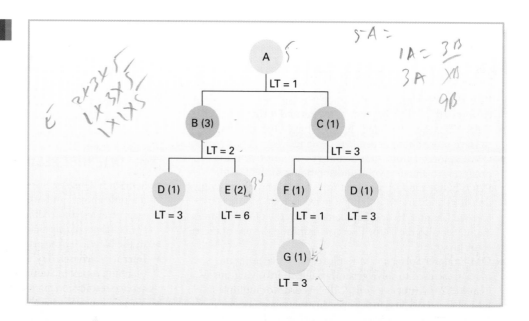

SOLVED PROBLEM 2

The MPS for product A calls for the assembly department to begin final assembly according to the following schedule: 100 units in week 2; 200 units in week 4; 120 units in week 6; 180 units in week 7; and 60 units in week 8. Develop a material requirements plan for the next eight weeks for items B, C, and D, identifying any action notices that would be provided. The BOM for A is shown in Figure 16.19, and data from the inventory records are shown in Table 16.1.

SOLUTION

We begin with items B and C and develop their inventory records, as shown in Figure 16.20. The MPS for product A must be multiplied by 2 to derive the gross requirements for item C because of the usage quantity. Once the planned order releases for item C are found, the gross requirements for item D can be calculated.

Notice that an action notice would call for delaying the scheduled receipt for item C from week 1 to week 2. Other action notices would notify planners that items B and D have a planned order release in the current week, which is week 1.

ACTIVE MODEL 16.1

Active Model 16.1 on the Student CD-ROM provides additional insight on lot-sizing decisions for MRP.

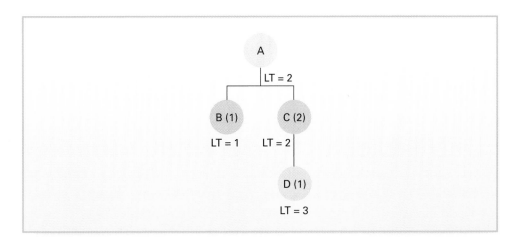

FIGURE 16.19

BOM for Product A

$1A = 365 \quad 6E5 \quad 3D5$
$5A = 5(3) \quad 5(6) \quad 5(3)$

TABLE 16.1
INVENTORY RECORD DATA

Data Category	Item		
	B	C	D
Lot-sizing rule	POQ (P = 3)	L4L	FOQ = 500 units
Lead time (LT)	1 week	2 weeks	3 weeks
Scheduled receipts	None	200 (week 1)	None
Beginning (on-hand) inventory	20	0	425

DISCUSSION QUESTIONS

1. Form a group in which each member represents a different functional area. Identify the nature and importance of the information that a material requirements plan can provide to each of the functional areas.

2. Consider the tours of Lower Florida Keys Health System (LFKHS) and Chapparel Steel on the Student CD-ROM.

Explain how the concept of a bill of resources (BOR) can help LFKHS plan for medical resources. Could Chapparal Steel use the BOR concept as well?

3. Consider a service provider that is in the delivery business, such as UPS or FedEx. How can the principles of MRP be useful to such a company?

FIGURE 16.20

Inventory Records for Items B, C, and D

Item: B
Description:
Lot Size: POQ ($P = 3$)
Lead Time: 1 week

	Week									
	1	2	3	4	5	6	7	8	9	10
Gross requirements		100		200		120	180	60		
Scheduled receipts										
Projected on-hand inventory 20	20	200	200	0	0	240	60	0	0	0
Planned receipts		280				360				
Planned order releases	280				360					

Item: C
Description:
Lot Size: L4L
Lead Time: 2 weeks

	Week									
	1	2	3	4	5	6	7	8	9	10
Gross requirements		200		400		240	360	120		
Scheduled receipts	200 →									
Projected on-hand inventory 0	200	0	0	0	0	0	0	0	0	0
Planned receipts				400		240	360	120		
Planned order releases		400		240	360	120				

Item: D
Description:
Lot Size: FOQ = 500 units
Lead Time: 3 weeks

	Week									
	1	2	3	4	5	6	7	8	9	10
Gross requirements		400		240	360	120				
Scheduled receipts										
Projected on-hand inventory 425	425	25	25	285	425	305	305	305	305	305
Planned receipts				500	500					
Planned order releases	500	500								

PROBLEMS

1. Consider the bill of materials (BOM) in Figure 16.21.

   a. How many immediate parents (one level above) does item I have? How many immediate parents does item E have?

   b. How many unique components does product A have at all levels?

   c. Which of the components are purchased items?

   d. How many intermediate items does product A have at all levels?

   e. Given the lead times (LT) noted on Figure 16.21, how far in advance of shipment is the earliest purchase commitment required?

2. Product A is made from components B, C, and D. Item B is a subassembly that requires 2 units of C and 1 unit of E. Item D also is an intermediate item, made from F. All other usage quantities are 2. Draw the BOM for product A.

3. What is the lead time (in weeks) to respond to a customer order for product A, based on the BOM shown in Figure 16.22 and assuming that there are no existing inventories?

4. Product A is made from components B and C. Item B, in turn, is made from D and E. Item C also is an intermediate item, made from F and H. Finally, intermediate item E is made from H and G. Note that item H has two parents. The following are item lead times:

Item	A	B	C	D	E	F	G	H
Lead Time (weeks)	1	2	2	6	5	6	4	3

   a. What lead time (in weeks) is needed to respond to a customer order for product A, assuming that there are no existing inventories?

   b. What is the customer response time if all purchased items (i.e., D, F, G, and H) are in inventory?

   c. If you are allowed to keep just one purchased item in stock, which one would you choose?

5. Refer to Figure 16.18 and Solved Problem 1. If there are 2 units of B, 1 unit of F, and 3 units of G in inventory, how many units of G, E, and D must be purchased to produce 5 units of product A?

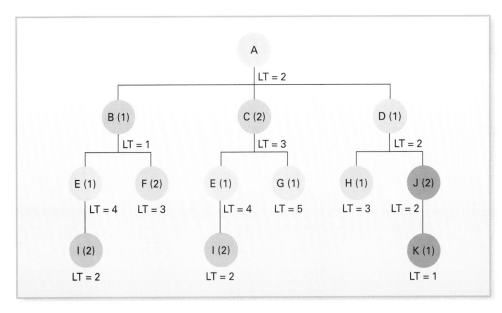

FIGURE 16.21

BOM for Product A

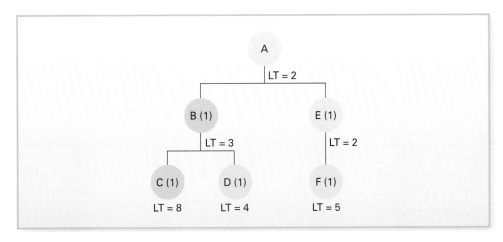

FIGURE 16.22

BOM for Product A

6. A milling machine workstation makes small gears used in a transmission gear box. As of week 22, the capacity requirements planning (CRP) report for the workstation revealed the following information. The planned hours for weeks 22, 23, 24, 25, 26, and 27 were 40, 60, 100, 120, 175, and 160, respectively. The actual hours for the same weeks were 90, 75, 80, 0, 0, and 0. Each of two machines at the workstation is scheduled for two shifts per day. The workstation has a maximum capacity of 160 hours per week. Does the CRP report reveal any problems at the workstation? If so, what are they and what should be done to correct them?

7. The partially completed inventory record for the tabletop subassembly in Figure 16.23 shows gross requirements, scheduled receipts, lead time, and current on-hand inventory.

   a. Complete the last three rows of the record for an FOQ of 110 units.

   b. Complete the last three rows of the record by using the L4L lot-sizing rule.

   c. Complete the last three rows of the record by using the POQ lot-sizing rule, with $P = 2$.

8. 🖎 OM Explorer The partially completed inventory record for the rotor subassembly in Figure 16.24 shows gross requirements, scheduled receipts, lead time, and current on-hand inventory.

FIGURE 16.23

Inventory Record for the Tabletop Subassembly

| Item: M405−X | | | | | | | | | | Lot Size: | |
| Description: Tabletop subassembly | | | | | | | | | | Lead Time: 2 weeks | |

		Week									
	1	2	3	4	5	6	7	8	9	10
Gross requirements	90		85		80		45	90		
Scheduled receipts	110									
Projected on-hand inventory 40										
Planned receipts										
Planned order releases										

FIGURE 16.24

Inventory Record for the Rotor Subassembly

| Item: Rotor subassembly | | | | | | | | Lot Size: | |
| | | | | | | | | Lead Time: 2 weeks | |

		Week						
	1	2	3	4	5	6	7	8
Gross requirements	65	15	45	40	80	80	80	80
Scheduled receipts	150							
Projected on-hand inventory 20								
Planned receipts								
Planned order releases								

a. Complete the last three rows of the record for an FOQ of 150 units.

b. Complete the last three rows of the record by using the L4L lot-sizing rule.

c. Complete the last three rows of the record by using the POQ lot-sizing rule, with $P = 2$.

9. **OM Explorer** The partially completed inventory record for the driveshaft subassembly in Figure 16.25 shows gross requirements, scheduled receipts, lead time, and current on-hand inventory.

a. Complete the last three rows of the record for an FOQ of 50 units.

b. Complete the last three rows of the record by using the L4L lot-sizing rule.

c. Complete the last three rows of the record by using the POQ lot-sizing rule, with $P=4$.

10. **OM Explorer** Figure 16.26 shows a partially completed inventory record for the rear wheel subassembly. Gross requirements, scheduled receipts, lead time, and current on-hand inventory, are shown.

a. Complete the last three rows of the record for an FOQ of 300 units.

b. Complete the last three rows of the record by using the L4L rule.

FIGURE 16.25

Inventory Record for the Driveshaft Subassembly

Item: Driveshaft subassembly				Lot Size: Lead Time: 3 weeks				
	Week							
	1	2	3	4	5	6	7	8
Gross requirements	35	25	15	20	40	40	50	50
Scheduled receipts	80							
Projected on-hand inventory 10								
Planned receipts								
Planned order releases								

FIGURE 16.26

Inventory Record for the Rear Wheel Subassembly

Item: MQ—09 Description: Rear wheel subassembly					Lot Size: Lead Time: 1 week					
	Week									
	1	2	3	4	5	6	7	8	9	10
Gross requirements	205		130	85		70	60	95		
Scheduled receipts	300									
Projected on-hand inventory 100										
Planned receipts										
Planned order releases										

c. Complete the last three rows of the record by using the POQ rule, with $P = 4$.

11. ◗ OM Explorer The inventory record for the motor subassembly in Figure 16.27 has been partially completed.

 a. Complete the last three rows of the record for an FOQ of 60 units. If there are action notices, what factors should you consider in responding to them?

 b. Revise the planned order release row by using the L4L rule.

 c. Revise the planned order release row by using the POQ rule. Find the value of P that should (in the long run) yield an average lot size of 60 units. Assume that the average weekly demand for the foreseeable future is 15 units.

12. ◗ OM Explorer The BOM for product A is shown in Figure 16.28, and data from the inventory records are shown in Table 16.2. In the master production schedule for product A, the MPS start row has 500 units in week 6. The lead time for production of A is two weeks. Develop the material requirements plan for the next six weeks for items B, C, and D.

 After completing the plan, identify any action notices that would be issued. (*Hint:* You cannot derive an item's gross requirements unless you know the planned order releases of all its parents.)

13. ◗ OM Explorer The BOMs for products A and B are shown in Figure 16.29. Data from inventory records are shown in Table 16.3. The MPS calls for 85 units of product A to be started in week 3 and 100 units in week

---

FIGURE 16.27   **Inventory Record for the Motor Subassembly**

Item: GF—4
Description: Motor subassembly

Lot Size:
Lead Time: 3 weeks

	Week											
	1	2	3	4	5	6	7	8	9	10	11	12
Gross requirements		50		35		55		30		10		25
Scheduled receipts		60										
Projected on-hand inventory 40												
Planned receipts												
Planned order releases												

FIGURE 16.28

BOM for Product A

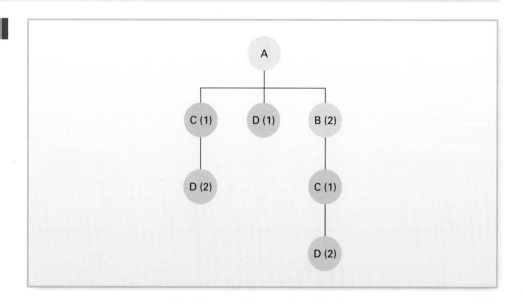

6. The MPS for product B calls for 180 units to be started in week 5. Develop the material requirements plan for the next six weeks for items C, D, E, and F. Identify any action notices.

14. **OM Explorer** Figure 16.30 illustrates the BOM for product A. The MPS start row in the master production schedule for product A calls for 50 units in week 2, 65 units in week 5, and 80 units in week 8. Item C is produced to make A and to meet the forecasted demand for replacement parts. Past replacement part demand has been 20 units per week (add 20 units to C's gross requirements). The lead times for items F and C are one week, and for the other items the lead time is two weeks. No safety stock is required for items B, C, D, E, and F. The L4L lot-sizing rule is used for items B and F; the POQ lot-sizing rule ($P = 3$) is used for C. Item E has an FOQ of 600 units, and D has an FOQ of 250 units. On-hand inventories are 50 units of B, 50 units of C, 120 units of D, 70 units of E, and 250 units of F. Item B has a scheduled receipt of 50 units in week 2.

Develop a material requirements plan for the next eight weeks for items B, C, D, E, and F. What action notices will be generated?

TABLE 16.2
INVENTORY RECORD DATA

	Item		
Data Category	B	C	D
Lot-sizing rule	L4L	L4L	FOQ = 2,000
Lead time	3 weeks	1 week	1 week
Scheduled receipts	None	None	2,000 (week 1)
Beginning inventory	0	0	200

TABLE 16.3
INVENTORY RECORD DATA

	Item			
Data Category	C	D	E	F
Lot-sizing rule	FOQ = 220	L4L	FOQ = 300	POQ ($P = 2$)
Lead time	3 weeks	2 weeks	3 weeks	2 weeks
Scheduled receipts	280 (week 1)	None	300 (week 3)	None
Beginning inventory	25	0	150	600

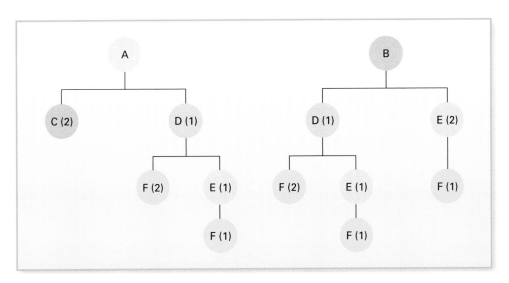

FIGURE 16.29

BOMs for Product A and Product B

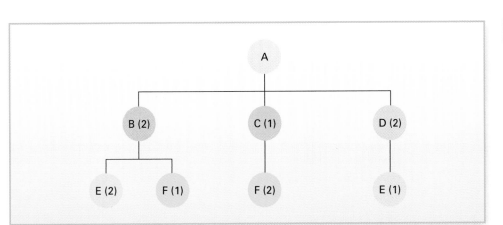

FIGURE 16.30

BOM for Product A

15. The following information is available for three MPS items.

Product A   An 80-unit order is to be started in week 3. A 55-unit order is to be started in week 6.
Product B   A 125-unit order is to be started in week 5.
Product C   A 60-unit order is to be started in week 4.

Develop the material requirements plan for the next six weeks for items D, E, and F, identifying any action notices that would be provided. The BOMs are shown in Figure 16.31, and data from the inventory records are shown in Table 16.4. (*Warning:* There is a safety stock requirement for item F. Be sure to plan a receipt for any week in which the projected on-hand inventory becomes less than the safety stock.)

TABLE 16.4
INVENTORY RECORD DATA

Data Category	Item		
	D	**E**	**F**
Lot-sizing rule	FOQ = 150	L4L	POQ ($P = 2$)
Lead time	3 weeks	1 week	2 weeks
Safety stock	0	0	30
Scheduled receipts	150 (week 3)	120 (week 2)	None
Beginning inventory	150	0	100

16. At the beginning of week 45, production schedules at the chair assembly workstation called for the existing 60-hour backlog of work to be gradually reduced to 20 hours by the end of week 48. This reduction was to be accomplished by releasing an average of 310 hours of work per week to chair assembly while providing resources sufficient to complete 320 hours per week. At the beginning of week 49, the input–output control report represented by Figure 16.32 is brought to your attention.

   a. What triggered this report? (*Hint:* Complete the cumulative deviation rows.)

   b. What problem is indicated by the data in the input–output control report? (*Hint:* Calculate the actual backlog row and compare it to the planned backlog row.)

   c. What might be done to resolve this problem?

17. ◆ **OM Explorer** Items A and B are dependent demand items. Item B's only parent is A. The current material requirements plan for A is shown in Figure 16.33. Three units of B are needed to make one unit of A. Item B has zero inventory on hand. The order policy for item B is L4L and the lead time is three weeks. A scheduled receipt of 270 units for item B is to arrive in week 2.

FIGURE 16.31

BOMs for Products A, B, and C

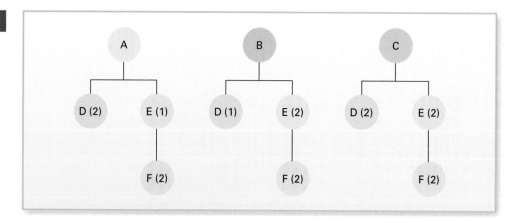

FIGURE 16.32

Input–Output Control Report for a Chair Assembly Workstation

Workstation: Chair assembly				Week: 49	
Tolerance: ±50 hours					
		Week			
	45	46	47	48	49
Inputs					
Planned	310	310	310	310	320
Actual	305	285	295	270	
Cumulative deviation					
Outputs					
Planned	320	320	320	320	320
Actual	320	305	300	290	
Cumulative deviation					
Planned ending backlog (hr)	50	40	30	20	20
Actual backlog 60 hr					

Item: A Description:						Lot Size: 90 units Lead Time: 2 weeks		
		Week						
		1	2	3	4	5	6	7
Gross requirements		65		70			110	60
Scheduled receipts		90						
Projected on-hand inventory	20	45	45	65	65	65	45	75
Planned receipts				90			90	90
Planned order releases		90			90	90		

a. Today the planner responsible for items A and B learned some good news and some bad news. Although the scheduled receipt of 90 units of A has been finished (the good news), only 45 units were put in the storeroom; the other 45 units were scrapped (the bad news). Prepare the inventory records for items A and B to reflect this event. (*Hint:* A scheduled receipt should no longer be shown for A, but its on-hand balance now is 65 units.)

b. What action notices would be issued relative to the new material requirements plan?

18. ✏ **OM Explorer** Figure 16.34 shows the BOMs for two products, A and B. Table 16.5 shows the MPS quantity start date for each one. Table 16.6 contains data from inventory records for items C, D, and E. There are no safety stock requirements for any of the items. Determine the material requirements plan for items C, D, and E for the next eight weeks. Identify any action notices that would be provided.

19. ✏ **OM Explorer** The BOM for product A is shown in Figure 16.35. The MPS for product A calls for 120 units to be started in weeks 2, 4, 5, and 8. Table 16.7

MPS QUANTITY START DATES

				Date				
Product	1	2	3	4	5	6	7	8
A		125		95		150		130
B			80			70		

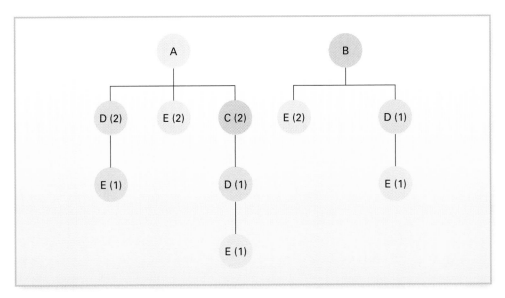

TABLE 16.6
INVENTORY RECORD DATA

Data Category	Item		
	C	D	E
Lot-sizing rule	L4L	POQ ($P = 3$)	FOQ = 800
Lead time	3 weeks	2 weeks	1 week
Scheduled receipts	200 (week 2)	None	800 (week 1)
Beginning inventory	85	625	350

shows data from the inventory records. Develop the material requirements plan for the next eight weeks for each item. Would any action notices be issued? If so, identify them. (*Warning:* Note that item E has a safety stock requirement.)

20.   **OM Explorer** Develop the material requirements plan for all components and intermediate items associated with product A for the next ten weeks. Refer to Solved Problem 1 (Figure 16.18) for the bill of materials and Table 16.8 for component inventory record information. The MPS for product A calls for 50 units to be started in weeks 2, 6, 8, and 9. (*Warning:* Note that items B and C have safety stock requirements.)

TABLE 16.7
INVENTORY RECORD DATA

Data Category	Item				
	B	C	D	E	F
Lot-sizing rule	L4L	FOQ = 700	FOQ = 700	L4L	L4L
Lead time	3 weeks	3 weeks	4 weeks	2 weeks	1 week
Safety stock	0	0	0	50	0
Scheduled receipts	150 (week 2)	450 (week 2)	700 (week 1)	None	1,400 (week 1)
Beginning inventory	125	0	235	750	0

TABLE 16.8
INVENTORY RECORD DATA

Data Category	Item					
	B	C	D	E	F	G
Lot-sizing rule	L4L	L4L	POQ ($P = 2$)	L4L	L4L	FOQ = 100
Lead time	2 weeks	3 weeks	3 weeks	6 weeks	1 week	3 weeks
Safety stock	30	10	0	0	0	0
Scheduled receipts	150 (week 2)	50 (week 2)	None	400 (week 6)	40 (week 3)	None
Beginning inventory	30	20	60	400	0	0

FIGURE 16.35

BOM for Product A

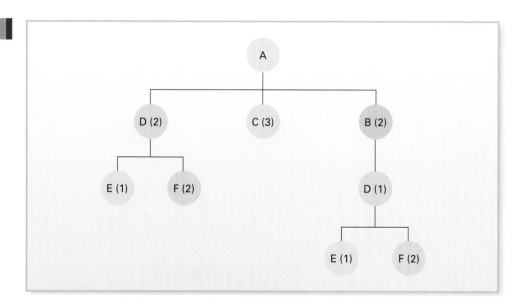

21. **OM Explorer** Items X and Y are dependent demand items. One unit of Y is needed to make one unit of X. Item Y's only parent is X. The current material requirements plans for X and Y are shown in Figure 16.36. Complete the records to determine the planned order releases for items X and Y.

FIGURE 16.36

MRP Records for Item X and Item Y

Item: X
Description:

Lot Size: L4L
Lead Time: 1 week
Safety Stock: 0 units

	Week									
	1	2	3	4	5	6	7	8	9	10
Gross requirements	20	110	50		80	50	100	40		
Scheduled receipts	25									
Projected on-hand inventory 0										
Planned receipts										
Planned order releases										

Item: Y
Description:

Lot Size: POQ (P = 2 weeks)
Lead Time: 3 weeks
Safety Stock: 0 units

	Week									
	1	2	3	4	5	6	7	8	9	10
Gross requirements										
Scheduled receipts	100									
Projected on-hand inventory 55										
Planned receipts										
Planned order releases										

ACTIVE MODEL EXERCISE

This Active Model appears on the Student CD-ROM. It allows you to evaluate the relationship between the inventory record data and the planned order releases.

QUESTIONS

1. Suppose that the POQ for item B is changed from three weeks to two weeks. How does this affect the order releases for items B, C, and D?

2. As the on-hand inventory for item C increases from 0 to 200, what happens to the order releases for items B, C, and D?

3. As the fixed order quantity (FOQ) for item D increases from 500 to 750, what happens to the order releases for items B, C, and D?

4. As the lead time for item C changes, what happens to the order releases for items B, C, and D?

ACTIVE MODEL 16.1

Material Requirements Planning Using Data from Solved Problem 2 and Table 16.1

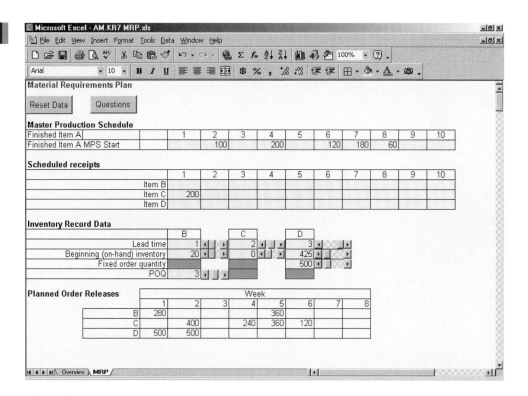

CASE FLASHY FLASHERS, INC.

Jack Jacobs, the Production and Inventory Management manager of Flashy Flashers Inc., stopped for a moment to adjust his tie knot and run his fingers through his hair before entering the office of Ollie Prout, the vice president of operations. From the tone of Prout's voice over the telephone, Jacobs knew that he was not being called for a social tête-à-tête.

COMPANY BACKGROUND

Flashy Flashers is a medium-sized firm employing 500 persons and 75 managerial and administrative personnel. The firm produces a line of automotive electrical components. It supplies about 75 auto parts stores and "Moonbird Silverstreak" car dealers in its region.

Johnny Bennett, who serves as the president, founded the company. Bennett is a great entrepreneur who started producing cable assemblies in his garage. Through hard work, consistent product quality, and high customer service, he expanded his business to produce a variety of electrical components. Bennett's commitment to customer service is so strong that his company motto, "Love Thy Customers As Thyself," is etched on a big cast-iron plaque under his giant oil portrait in the building's front lobby.

The company's two most profitable products are the automotive front sidelamp and the headlamp. With the recent boom in the auto industry and the rising popularity of Eurosport sedans, such as the Moonbird Silverstreak, Flashy Flashers has enjoyed substantial demand for these two lamp items.

Last year, on Prout's recommendation—and for better management of the inventory system—Bennett approved the installation of a new MRP system. Prout worked closely with the task force that was created to bring MRP online. He frequently attended the training sessions for selected employees, emphasizing how MRP should help Flashy Flashers secure a better competitive edge. On the day the system "went up," there was an aura of tranquility and goodwill. The days of the informal system of firefighting were over!

A year later, Prout's mood is quite different. Inventory and overtime levels had not dropped as much as expected, customer service was getting worse, and there were too many complaints about late shipments. Convinced that this should not happen with MRP, Prout is attempting to find out what is going wrong.

THE PROBLEMS

Jacobs had barely taken two steps inside Prout's office when his voice cut across the room. "Jack, what's going on out there? I've just received another call from a customer complaining that we've fallen back on our lamp shipment to them again! This is the umpteenth time I've received complaints about late shipments. Johnny has been on my back about this. Why isn't our system working as it is supposed to and what do we have to do to hold onto valuable customers and stay in business?"

Jacobs gulped and took a moment to regain his composure before answering Prout. "We're trying our best to maintain the inventory records and BOM files. With our system, there's a new explosion each week. This gives us an updated material requirements plan and action notices for launching new orders. Some of my group think we should extend our outputs to get priority and capacity reports. As you know, we decided to get the order-launching capability well established first. However, we don't seem to have a formal system of priority planning, and that's creating scheduling problems on the shop floor.

"I think our purchasing and marketing departments also are at fault. We seem to experience too many stockouts of purchased parts even though we've worked closely with Jayne Spring's group to get realistic lead-time estimates. And marketing keeps taking last-minute orders from favorite customers. This plays havoc with our master production schedule."

"Well, I'm really getting fed up with this," Prout cut in. "Talk with the people concerned and find out what exactly is going wrong. I'll expect a complete report from you in two weeks, giving me all the details and recommendations for improvement."

Jacobs decided to get to the bottom of things, as he walked out of Prout's office. He first called on Sam McKenzie, the shop superintendent.

PRODUCTION

Jacobs's conversation with McKenzie suggested that the pre-MRP informal system is still alive and well. "I'm starting to wonder about this MRP system, even though it looks great on paper," McKenzie commented. "Last week we hardly had any work, and I was forced to overproduce on several orders just to keep everyone busy. This week is just the opposite, so many new orders were released with short fuses that almost everyone will need to work overtime. It's either feast or famine! Our priority planners don't seem to update the due dates assigned to each order, but things change pretty quickly around here.

"Another thing is the inventory records. When I get an order, I first check the inventory record for that item to find out the current stock situation. More often than not, the actual number of units is less than what the records indicate. This means that I often have to produce more than planned. This plays havoc with our capacity plans. We can't stick to our lead times when things are so fluid around here!"

PURCHASING

Jacobs's next conversation was with Jayne Spring, the purchasing manager. It was equally disconcerting. "Our buyers are really getting frustrated with this new system. There's no time for creative buying. Almost all of their time is spent following up on late orders because of constant expediting action notices. For example, the other day the system told us to bring in 200 units of part HL222P in just two weeks. We tried all possible vendors but they said that a delivery in two weeks was impossible. What are the planners doing? The perplexing thing is that the planned lead time in the inventory record for this part is correctly stated as four weeks. Doesn't MRP offset for lead time? On top of this, we also have some problems with unreliable vendor lead times. This requires us to carry more safety stock for some items than is necessary."

Jacobs tried to assimilate all this information. He then proceeded to collect all the required information about the sidelamps and headlamps (shown in Table 16.9 through Table 16.13 and in Figure 16.37) and decided to gain further insights into the problem by working out the MRP explosion manually for the next six weeks.

TABLE 16.9 PART NUMBERS AND DESCRIPTIONS

Part Number	Description
C206P	Screws
C310P	Back rubber gasket
HL200E	Headlamp
HL211A	Head frame subassembly
HL212P	Head lens
HL222P	Headlamp module
HL223F	Head frame
SL100E	Sidelamp
SL111P	Side lens
SL112A	Side frame subassembly
SL113P	Side lens rubber gasket
SL121F	Side frame
SL122A	Side bulb subassembly
SL123A	Flasher bulb subassembly
SL131F	Side cable grommet and receptacle
SL132P	Side bulb
SL133F	Flasher cable grommet and receptacle
SL134P	Flasher bulb

TABLE 16.10 MASTER PRODUCTION SCHEDULE

Item Description and Part Number	Quantity	MPS Start Date
Headlamp (HL200E)	120	Week 14
	90	Week 15
	75	Week 16
Sidelamp (SL100E)	100	Week 13
	80	Week 15
	110	Week 16

TABLE 16.11	REPLACEMENT PART DEMAND	
Item Description and Part Number	Quantity	Date
Side lens (SL111P)	40	Week 13
	35	Week 16

TABLE 16.12	SELECTED DATA FROM INVENTORY RECORDS				
Part Number	Lead Time (weeks)	Safety Stock (units)	Lot-Sizing Rule	On-Hand (units)	Scheduled Receipt (units and due dates)
C206P	1	30	FOQ = 2,500	150	—
C310P	1	20	FOQ = 180	30	180 (week 12)
HL211A	2	0	L4L	10	50 (week 12)
HL212P	2	15	FOQ = 350	15	—
HL222P	4	10	POQ (P = 4 weeks)	50	110 (week 14)
HL223F	1	0	L4L	70	—
SL111P	2	0	FOQ = 350	15	—
SL112A	3	0	L4L	20	100 (week 13)
SL113P	1	20	FOQ = 100	20	—
SL121F	3	0	L4L	0	70 (week 13)
SL122A	1	0	L4L	10	50 (week 12)
SL123A	1	0	L4L	0	—
SL131F	2	0	POQ (P = 2 weeks)	0	—
SL132P	1	25	FOQ = 100	35	100 (week 12)
SL133F	2	0	POQ (P = 2 weeks)	0	180 (week 12)
SL134P	1	25	FOQ = 100	20	100 (week 11)

FIGURE 16.37   **BOMS for Headlamps and Sidelamps**

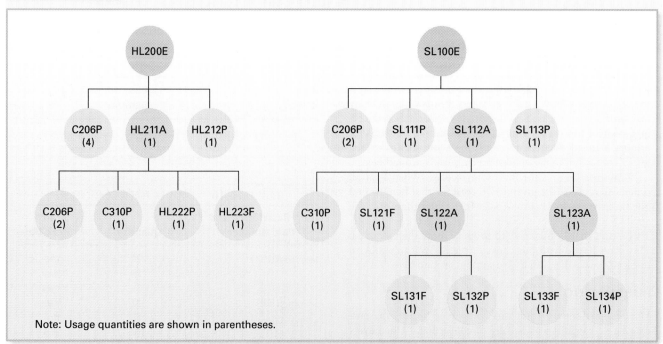

Note: Usage quantities are shown in parentheses.

TABLE 16.13   PLANNED ORDER RELEASE FORM

Fill in the planned order releases for all components.

	Week					
Item Description and Part Number	**11**	**12**	**13**	**14**	**15**	**16**
Side lens (SL111P)						
Side lens rubber gasket (SL113P)						
Side frame subassembly (SL112A)						
Side frame (SL121F)						
Side bulb subassembly (SL122A)						
Flasher bulb subassembly (SL123A)						
Side cable grommet and receptacle (SL131F)						
Flasher cable grommet and receptacle (SL133F)						
Side bulb (SL132P)						
Flasher bulb (SL134P)						
Head frame subassembly (HL211A)						
Head lens (HL212P)						
Headlamp module (HL222P)						
Head frame (HL223F)						
Back rubber gasket (C310P)						
Screws (C206P)						

YOUR ASSIGNMENT

Put yourself in Jacobs's place and write the report to your boss, Ollie Prout. Specifically, you are required to do a manual MRP explosion for the sidelamps and headlamps for the next six weeks (beginning with the current week). Assume that it is now the start of week 11. Fill in the planned order releases form provided in Table 16.13. It should show the planned order releases for all items for the next six weeks. Include it in your report.

Your report should identify the good and bad points of MRP implementation at Flashy Flashers. Supplement your report with worksheets on the manual MRP explosion, indicating where adjustments must be made for order releases and scheduled receipts. Conclude by making suggestions for change.

Source: This case was prepared by Professor Soumen Ghosh, Georgia Institute of Technology, for the purpose of classroom discussion only.

SELECTED REFERENCES

Blackstone, J. H. *Capacity Management.* Cincinnati: South-Western, 1989.

Conway, Richard W. "Linking MRP II and FCS." *APICS—The Performance Advantage* (June 1996), pp. 40–44.

Cotten, Jim. "Starting from Scratch." *APICS—The Performance Advantage* (November 1996), pp. 34–37.

Dollries, Joseph. "Don't Pick a Package—Match One." *APICS—The Performance Advantage* (May 1996), pp. 50–52.

Goddard, Walter, and James Correll. "MRP II in the Year 2000." *APICS—The Performance Advantage* (March 1994), pp. 38–42.

Haddock, Jorge, and Donald E. Hubicki. "Which Lot-Sizing Techniques Are Used in Material Requirements Planning?" *Production and Inventory Management Journal,* vol. 30, no. 3 (1989), pp. 53–56.

Hoy, Paul A. "The Changing Role of MRP II." *APICS—The Performance Advantage* (June 1996), pp. 50–53.

Jemigan, Jeff. "Comprehensiveness, Cost-Effectiveness Sweep Aside Operations Challenges." *APICS—The Performance Advantage* (March 1993), pp. 44–45.

Lunn, Terry, and Susan Neff. *MRP: Integrating Material Requirements Planning and Modern Business.* Homewood, IL: Irwin Professional Publication, 1992.

Meinyk, Steven A., Robert Sroufe, Frank Montabon, Roger Calantone, R. Lal Tummala, and Timothy J. Hinds. "Integrating Environmental Issues into Material Planning: 'Green' MRP." *Production and Inventory Management Journal* (Third Quarter 1999). pp. 36–45.

Ormsby, Joseph G., Susan Y. Ormsby, and Carl R. Ruthstrom. "MRP II Implementation: A Case Study." *Production and Inventory Management,* vol. 31, no. 4 (1990), pp. 77–82.

Prouty, Dave. "Shiva Finite Capacity Scheduling System." *APICS—The Performance Advantage* (April 1997), pp. 58–61.

Ptak, Carol. *MRP and Beyond.* Homewood IL: Irwin Professional Publication, 1996.

Roth, Aleda V., and Roland Van Dierdonck. "Hospital Resource Planning: Concepts, Feasibility, and Framework." *Production and Operations Management,* vol. 4, no. 1 (1995), pp. 2–29.

Turbide, David A. "This is Not Your Father's MRP!" *APICS—The Performance Advantage* (March 1994), pp. 28–37.

Vollmann, T. E., W. L. Berry, and D. C. Whybark. *Manufacturing Planning and Control Systems,* 4th ed. Homewood, IL: Irwin Professional Publications, 1997.

Wallace, Tom. *MRP II: Making It Happen.* Essex Junction, VT: Oliver Wight Ltd. Publishers, 1994.

Scheduling

LEARNING GOALS   *After reading this chapter, you should be able to . . .*

IDENTIFY OR DEFINE

1. the key performance measures to consider when selecting a schedule.
2. the situations where demands can be scheduled by appointments, reservations, or backlogs.
3. the components of advanced planning systems that link operations schedules to the supply chain.

DESCRIBE OR EXPLAIN

4. the importance of scheduling to the performance of the firm.
5. how to schedule employees to allow for two consecutive days off.
6. how to create schedules for single and multiple workstations.

AIR NEW ZEALAND

How important is scheduling to an airline company? Certainly, customer satisfaction regarding on-time schedule performance is critical in a highly competitive industry, such as air transportation. In addition, airlines lose a lot of money when expensive equipment, such as an aircraft, is idle. Flight and crew scheduling, however, is a very complex process. For example, Air New Zealand (www.airnz.com) has 9,000 employees and operates more than 85 domestic and 50 international flights daily. Scheduling begins with a 5-year market plan that identifies the new and existing flight segments that are needed to remain competitive in the industry. This general plan is further refined to a three-year plan, and then is put into an annual budget, where the flight segments have specific departure and arrival times.

Next, crew availability must be matched to the flight schedules. There are two types of crews, pilots and attendants, each with their own set of constraints. Pilots, for example, cannot be scheduled for more than 35 hours in a 7-day week and no more than 100 hours in a 28-day cycle, and they must have a 36-hour break every 7 days and 30 days off in an 84-day cycle. Sophisticated optimization models are used to design generic minimum-cost tours of duty that cover every flight and recognize all the constraints. Each tour of duty begins and ends at a crew base and consists of an alternating sequence of duty periods and rest periods, with duty periods including one or more flights. The tours of duty are posted, and crew members bid on them within a specified period of time. Actual crew rosters are constructed from the bids received. The roster must ensure that each flight has a qualified crew complement and that each crew member has a feasible line of work over the roster period.

From the crew's point of view, it is also important to satisfy as many crew requests and preferences as possible.

Scheduling does not end with the definition of the flights and crew rosters. Daily disruptions, such as severe weather conditions or mechanical failures, can cause schedule changes to attendants, pilots, and even aircraft. Customers expect a fast resolution of the problem, and the company needs to find the least-cost solution. In the airline industry, the scheduling process can determine a company's long-term competitive strength.

The scheduling of cabin attendants must recognize many constraints. Here, a cabin attendant serves dinner to passengers on an Air New Zealand flight.

Sources: Ryan, David M. "Optimization Earns Its Wings". *OR/MS Today* (April 2000), pp. 26–30; "Service Scheduling at Air New Zealand." *Operations Management in Action Video Series.* Upper Saddle River, NJ: Prentice Hall, 2000.

scheduling The allocation of resources over time to accomplish specific tasks.

As the crew scheduling example at Air New Zealand demonstrates, effective scheduling is essential to successful operations. **Scheduling** allocates resources over time to accomplish specific tasks. Up to this point in the text, we have discussed the design of processes, how they are linked to form value chains, and the key planning techniques for effectively operating them. Scheduling is the activity that brings all of these design and planning activities to fruition. For example, police protection services must have low cost, consistent quality, fast delivery, and variety and volume flexibility. Decisions are required about the location of police stations and the quantity of patrol cars at each location. The information technology must be decided; forecasting methods must be selected for estimating the requirements for police services on an hourly, daily, weekly, monthly, and annual basis; and a staffing plan must be determined for each station. All of these design and planning activities, however, will not achieve the competitive priorities unless effective work schedules can be devised for the police officers. Scheduling is a critical link between the planning and execution phases of operations. Without effective scheduling, value chains will not meet their potential. For this reason, supply-chain management software and enterprise resource planning systems that include scheduling applications are becoming more common.

In this chapter, we begin with a discussion of scheduling for service and manufacturing processes, focusing on useful performance measures and the application of Gantt charts. We then discuss approaches for **demand scheduling**, which assigns customers to a definite time for order fulfillment. Next, we discuss a technique for **workforce scheduling**, which determines when employees work. Finally, we explore several techniques for **operations scheduling**, which assigns jobs to workstations or employees to jobs for specified time periods. Effectively solving these three scheduling problems will help managers achieve the full potential of their value chains.

As you read this chapter, think about how effective scheduling is important to various departments across the organization, such as . . .

> **accounting,** which administers the billing process that is driven by the scheduling of services or products.
> **finance,** which manages the cash flows in the firm that, in turn, are a function of the effectiveness of service and product scheduling.
> **human resources,** which hires and trains employees needed to support workforce schedules.
> **marketing,** which depends on meeting due dates promised to customers.
> **management information systems,** which designs the software and databases to support the scheduling process.
> **operations,** which is responsible for effective scheduling of production systems.

demand scheduling A type of scheduling that assigns customers to a definite time for order fulfillment.

workforce scheduling A type of scheduling that determines when employees work.

operations scheduling A type of scheduling that assigns jobs to workstations or employees to jobs for specified time periods.

SCHEDULING SERVICE AND MANUFACTURING PROCESSES

The scheduling techniques we discuss in this chapter cut across the various process types found in services and manufacturing (see Chapter 3, "Process Design Strategy"). In services, a front-office process is characterized by high customer contact and involvement, jumbled work flows, customization and, consequently, a complex scheduling environment. Inventories cannot be used to buffer demand uncertainties. This puts a premium on scheduling employees to handle the varied needs of customers. Demand scheduling and workforce scheduling are two useful techniques. At the other extreme, a back-office process has low customer involvement, uses more line work flows, and provides standardized services. Inanimate objects are processed; these processes take on the appearance of manufacturing processes. While workforce schedules are important, operations scheduling techniques also have application.

Manufacturing processes also benefit from demand scheduling, workforce scheduling, and operations scheduling techniques. We have already discussed techniques for scheduling project processes in Chapter 8, "Planning and Managing Projects." Our discussion of the operations scheduling techniques in this chapter has application for job, batch, and line processes in services as well as in manufacturing. Schedules for continuous processes can be developed with linear programming (see Supplement D, "Linear Programming"). While the scheduling techniques in this chapter provide some structure to the selection of good schedules, there are typically many alternatives to evaluate. Before we explore the techniques for generating job and employee schedules, let us look at the performance measures managers use to select good schedules.

VIDEO CLIP 17.1
Video Clip 17.1 explains how the scheduling process at Air New Zealand starts with a long-term plan.

PERFORMANCE MEASURES

From the manager's perspective, identifying the performance measures to be used in selecting a schedule is important. If the competitive priorities of a process are to be achieved, the schedules should reflect managerially acceptable performance measures that are consistent with those competitive priorities. The following performance measures are commonly used in scheduling services and manufacturing processes. In this regard, a *job* is the object receiving service or being manufactured. For example, a job may be a customer waiting for service at a state licensing bureau or it may be a batch of pistons waiting for a manufacturing process.

job flow time   The amount of time a job spends in the service or manufacturing system.

- *Job Flow Time.* The amount of time a job spends in the service or manufacturing system is called **job flow time.** It is the sum of the waiting time for servers or machines; the process time, including setups; the time spent moving between operations; and delays resulting from machine breakdowns, unavailability of facilitating goods or components, and the like. Minimizing job flow times supports the competitive priorities of cost (lower inventory) and time (delivery speed).

$$\text{Job flow time} = \text{Time of completion} - \text{Time job was available for first processing operation}$$

Note that the starting time is the time the job was available for its first processing operation, not necessarily when the job began its first operation. Job flow time is sometimes referred to as *throughput time* or *time spent in the system, including service* (see Supplement C, "Waiting Lines").

makespan   The total amount of time required to complete a *group* of jobs.

- *Makespan.* The total amount of time required to complete a *group* of jobs is called **makespan.** Minimizing makespan supports the competitive priorities of cost (lower inventory) and time (delivery speed).

$$\text{Makespan} = \text{Time of completion of last job} - \text{Starting time of first job}$$

past due   The amount of time by which a job missed its due date or the percentage of total jobs processed over some period of time that missed their due dates.

tardiness   See **past due.**

work-in-process (WIP) inventory   Any job that is waiting in line, moving from one operation to the next, being delayed for some reason, being processed, or residing in some inventory in a semifinished state.

total inventory   The sum of scheduled receipts and on-hand inventories.

- *Past Due.* The measure **past due** can be expressed as the amount of time by which a job missed its due date (also referred to as **tardiness**) or as the percentage of total jobs processed over some period of time that missed their due dates. Minimizing the past due measure supports competitive priorities of cost (penalties for missing due dates), quality (perceptions of poor service), and time (on time delivery).
- *Work-in-Process Inventory.* Any job that is waiting in line, moving from one operation to the next, being delayed for some reason, being processed, or residing in some inventory in a semifinished state is considered to be **work-in-process (WIP) inventory.** WIP is also referred to as *pipeline inventory* (see Chapter 15, "Inventory Management") or as *number of customers in the service system* (see Supplement C, "Waiting Lines"). Minimizing the WIP inventory supports the competitive priority of cost (inventory holding costs).
- *Total Inventory.* This performance measure is used to measure the effectiveness of schedules for manufacturing processes. The sum of scheduled receipts and on-hand inventories is the **total inventory** (see Chapter 16, "Resource Planning").

$$\text{Total inventory} = \text{Scheduled receipts for all items} + \text{On-hand inventories of all items}$$

Minimizing total inventory supports the competitive priority of cost (inventory holding costs). Essentially, total inventory is the sum of WIP and finished goods inventories.

- *Utilization.* The percentage of work time that is productively spent by an employee or a machine is called utilization (see Chapter 6, "Process Capacity"). Maximizing the utilization of a process supports the competitive priority of cost (slack capacity).

These performance measures often are interrelated. For example, minimizing the average job flow time tends to reduce WIP inventory and increase utilization. Minimizing the makespan for a group of jobs tends to increase process utilization. An understanding of the interactions of job flow time, makespan, past due, WIP inventory, total inventory, and utilization can make the selection of good schedules easier.

GANTT CHARTS

The Gantt chart, which we introduced in Chapter 8, "Planning and Managing Projects," can be used as a tool to monitor the progress of work and to view the load on workstations. The chart takes two basic forms: (1) the job or activity progress chart and (2) the workstation chart. The Gantt *progress chart* graphically displays the current status of each job or activity relative to its scheduled completion date. For example, suppose that an automobile parts manufacturer has three jobs under way, one each for Ford, Plymouth, and Pontiac. The actual status of these orders is shown by the colored bars in Figure 17.1; the red lines indicate the desired schedule for the start and finish of each job. For the current date, April 21, this Gantt chart shows that the Ford order is behind schedule because operations has completed only the work scheduled through April 18. The Plymouth order is exactly on schedule, and the Pontiac order is ahead of schedule.

Figure 17.2 shows a Gantt *workstation chart* of the operating rooms at a hospital for a particular day. Using the same notation as in Figure 17.1, the chart shows the

FIGURE 17.1 Gantt Progress Chart for an Auto Parts Company

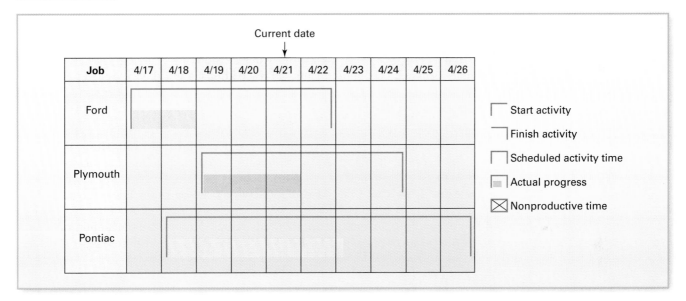

FIGURE 17.2 Gantt Workstation Chart for Operating Rooms at a Hospital

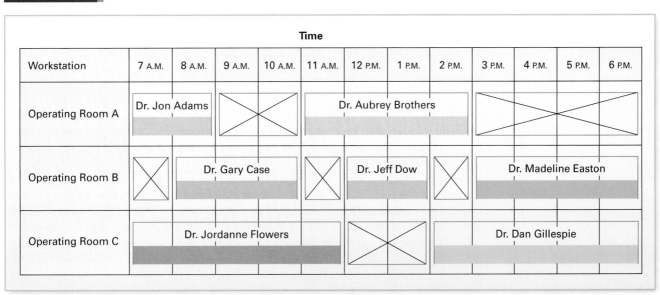

load on the operating rooms and the nonproductive time. The time slots assigned to each doctor include the time needed to clean the room for the next surgery. The work-station chart shows that operating room A is the least effectively utilized. The chart can be used to identify time slots for unscheduled emergency surgeries. It can also be used to accommodate requests to change the time of surgeries. For example, Dr. Flowers may be able to change the start of her surgery to 2 P.M. by swapping time slots with Dr. Gillespie in operating room C or by asking Dr. Brothers to start her surgery one hour earlier in operating room A. In any event, the hospital administrator would have to get involved in rescheduling the surgeries.

Gantt charts can be used to generate schedules for employees or workstations; however, the approach would be on a trial-and-error basis. We now turn to some techniques that can be used to arrive at good schedules.

● SCHEDULING CUSTOMER DEMAND

Capacity, which can be in the form of employees or equipment, is crucial for service providers and manufacturers. One way to manage capacity with a scheduling system is to schedule customers for definite periods of order fulfillment. With this approach, capacity is assumed to be fixed and demand is leveled to provide timely order fulfillment and a desired capacity utilization. Three methods are commonly used to schedule customer demand: (1) appointments, (2) reservations, and (3) backlogs.

APPOINTMENTS

What scheduling methods can be used to manage the capacity of a service system?

An appointment system assigns specific times for service to customers. The advantages of this method are timely customer service and high utilization of servers. Doctors, dentists, lawyers, and automobile repair shops are examples of service providers that use appointment systems. Doctors can use the system to schedule parts of their day to visit hospital patients, and lawyers can set aside time to prepare cases. If timely service is to be provided, however, care must be taken to tailor the length of appointments to individual customer needs rather than merely scheduling customers at equal time intervals.

RESERVATIONS

Reservation systems, although quite similar to appointment systems, are used when the customer actually occupies or uses facilities associated with the service. For example, customers reserve hotel rooms, automobiles, airline seats, and concert seats. The major advantage of reservation systems is the lead time they give service managers to plan the efficient use of facilities. Often, reservations require some form of down payment to reduce the problem of no-shows.

BACKLOGS

There are two forms of backlogs. In the first form, the customer is given a *due date* for the fulfillment of an ordered product. For example, the repair department of a car dealer may agree with an automotive parts manufacturer to receive delivery of a batch of 100 door latches for a particular car model next Tuesday. The parts manufacturer uses that due date to plan its production of door latches within its capacity limits. The equivalent of the due date for services is the use of appointments or reservations.

The second form of backlog is to simply allow a backlog to develop as customers arrive at the system. Customers may never know exactly when their orders will be fulfilled. Their order request is presented to an order taker, who adds the customer's new order request to the waiting line of orders already in the system. Television repair shops, restaurants, banks, grocery stores, or any waiting line situation are examples of the use of this system of demand scheduling (see Supplement C, "Waiting Lines").

Hundreds of fans camp out to get tickets for a Radiohead concert in New York. The tickets serve as a reservation system for the seats at the concert.

SCHEDULING EMPLOYEES

Another way to manage capacity with a scheduling system is to specify the on-duty and off-duty periods for each employee over a certain time period, as in assigning postal clerks, nurses, pilots, attendants, or police officers to specific workdays and shifts. This approach is used when customers demand quick response and total demand can be forecasted with reasonable accuracy. In these instances, capacity is adjusted to meet the expected loads on the service system.

Recall that workforce schedules translate the staffing plan into specific schedules of work for each employee (see Chapter 14, "Aggregate Planning"). Determining the workdays for each employee in itself does not make the staffing plan operational. Daily workforce requirements, stated in aggregate terms in the staffing plan, must be satisfied. The workforce capacity available each day must meet or exceed daily workforce requirements. If it does not, the scheduler must try to rearrange days off until the requirements are met. If no such schedule can be found, management might have to change the staffing plan and authorize more employees, overtime hours, or larger backlogs.

VIDEO CLIP 17.2
Video Clip 17.2 summarizes the scheduling process at Air New Zealand.

CONSTRAINTS

The technical constraints imposed on the workforce schedule are the resources provided by the staffing plan and the requirements placed on the operating system. However, other constraints, including legal and behavioral considerations, also can be imposed. For example, Air New Zealand is required to have at least a minimum number of flight attendants on duty at all times. Similarly, a minimum number of fire and safety personnel must be on duty at a fire station at all times. Such constraints limit management's flexibility in developing workforce schedules.

The constraints imposed by the psychological needs of workers complicate scheduling even more. Some of these constraints are written into labor agreements. For example, an employer may agree to give employees a certain number of consecutive days off per week or to limit employees' consecutive workdays to a certain maximum. Other provisions might govern the allocation of vacation, days off for holidays, or rotating shift assignments. In addition, the preferences of the employees themselves need to be considered.

One way that managers deal with certain undesirable aspects of scheduling is to use a **rotating schedule,** which rotates employees through a series of workdays or hours. Thus, over a period of time, each person has the same opportunity to have weekends and holidays off and to work days, as well as evenings and nights. A rotating schedule gives each employee the next employee's schedule the following week. In contrast, a **fixed schedule** calls for each employee to work the same days and hours each week.

DEVELOPING A WORKFORCE SCHEDULE

Suppose that we are interested in developing a workforce schedule for a company that operates seven days a week and provides each employee with two consecutive days off. In this section, we demonstrate a method that recognizes this constraint.[1] The objective is to identify the two consecutive days off for each employee that will minimize the amount of total slack capacity, thereby maximizing the utilization of the workforce. The work schedule for each employee, then, is the five days that remain after the two days off have been determined. The procedure involves the following steps.

Step 1. From the schedule of net requirements for the week, find all the pairs of consecutive days that exclude the maximum daily requirements. Select the unique pair that has the lowest total requirements for the two days. In some unusual situations, all pairs may contain a day with the maximum requirements. If so, select the pair with the lowest total requirements. Suppose that the numbers of employees required are

Monday: 8	Thursday: 12	Saturday: 4
Tuesday: 9	Friday: 7	Sunday: 2
Wednesday: 2		

The maximum capacity requirement is 12 employees, on Thursday. The pair with the lowest total requirements is Saturday and Sunday, with $4 + 2 = 6$.

Step 2. If a tie occurs, choose one of the tied pairs, consistent with the provisions written into the labor agreement, if any. Alternatively, the tie could be broken by asking the employee being scheduled to make the choice. As a last resort, the tie could be broken arbitrarily. For example, preference could be given to Saturday–Sunday pairs.

Step 3. Assign the employee the selected pair of days off. Subtract the requirements satisfied by the employee from the net requirements for each day the employee is to work. In this example, the employee is assigned Saturday and Sunday off. After requirements are subtracted, Monday's requirement is 7, Tuesday's is 8, Wednesday's is 1, Thursday's is 11, and Friday's is 6. Saturday's and Sunday's requirements do not change because no employee is yet scheduled to work those days.

Step 4. Repeat steps 1 through 3 until all the requirements have been satisfied or a certain number of employees have been scheduled.

---

rotating schedule A schedule that rotates employees through a series of workdays or hours.

fixed schedule A schedule that calls for each employee to work the same days and hours each week.

How can an effective workforce schedule be developed for a service system?

---

[1]See Tibrewala, Philippe, and Browne (1972) for an optimizing approach.

This method reduces the amount of slack capacity assigned to days with low requirements and forces the days with high requirements to be scheduled first. It also recognizes some of the behavioral and contractual aspects of workforce scheduling in the tie-breaking rules. However, the schedules produced might *not* minimize total slack capacity. Different rules for finding the days-off pair and breaking ties are needed to ensure minimal total slack capacity.

Developing a Workforce Schedule

EXAMPLE 17.1

The Amalgamated Parcel Service is open seven days a week. The schedule of requirements is

Day	M	T	W	Th	F	S	Su
Number of Employees	6	4	8	9	10*	3	2

The manager needs a workforce schedule that provides two consecutive days off and minimizes the amount of total slack capacity. To break ties in the selection of off days, the scheduler gives preference to Saturday and Sunday if it is one of the tied pairs. If not, she selects one of the tied pairs arbitrarily.

TUTOR 17.1

Tutor 17.1 on the Student CD-ROM provides a new example to practice workforce scheduling.

SOLUTION

Friday contains the maximum requirements (designated by an *), and the pair S–Su has the lowest total requirements. Therefore, employee 1 is scheduled to work Monday through Friday. The revised set of requirements, after scheduling employee 1, is

Day	M	T	W	Th	F	S	Su
Number of Employees	5	3	7	8	9*	3	2

SCHEDULING DAYS OFF								
M	T	W	Th	F	S	Su	EMPLOYEE	COMMENTS
4	2	6	7	8*	3	2	3	The S–Su pair has the lowest total requirements. Assign employee 3 to a Monday through Friday schedule and update the requirements.
3	1	5	6	7*	3	2	4	The M–T pair has the lowest total requirements. Assign employee 4 to a Wednesday through Sunday schedule and update the requirements.
3	1	4	5	6*	2	1	5	The S–Su pair has the lowest total requirements. Assign employee 5 to a Monday through Friday schedule and update the requirements.
2	0	3	4	5*	2	1	6	The M–T pair has the lowest total requirements. Assign employee 6 to a Wednesday through Sunday schedule and update the requirements.
2	0	2	3	4*	1	0	7	The S–Su pair has the lowest total requirements. Assign employee 7 to a Monday through Friday schedule and update the requirements.
1	0	1	2	3*	1	0	8	Four pairs have the minimum requirement and the lowest total: S–Su, Su–M, M–T, and T–W. Choose the S–Su pair according to the tie-breakinging rule. Assign employee 8 to a Monday through Friday schedule and update the require-
0	0	0	1	2*	1	0	9	ments. Arbitrarily choose the Su–M pair to break ties because the S–Su pair does not have the lowest total requirements. Assign employee 9 to a Tuesday through Saturday schedule and update the requirements.
0	0	0	0	1*	0	0	10	Choose the S–Su pair according to the tie-breaking rule. Assign employee 10 to a Monday through Friday schedule.

Note that Friday still has the maximum requirements and that the requirements for the S–Su pair are carried forward because these are employee 1's days off. These updated requirements are the ones the scheduler uses for the next employee.

The unique minimum again is for the S–Su pair, so the scheduler assigns employee 2 to a Monday through Friday schedule. She then reduces the requirements for Monday through Friday to reflect the assignment of employee 2.

The day-off assignments for the remaining employees are shown in the following table.

In this example, Friday always has the maximum requirements and should be avoided as a day off. The final schedule for the employees is shown in the following table.

FINAL SCHEDULE								
EMPLOYEE	**M**	**T**	**W**	**Th**	**F**	**S**	**Su**	**TOTAL**
1	X	X	X	X	X	off	off	
2	X	X	X	X	X	off	off	
3	X	X	X	X	X	off	off	
4	off	off	X	X	X	X	X	
5	X	X	X	X	X	off	off	
6	off	off	X	X	X	X	X	
7	X	X	X	X	X	off	off	
8	X	X	X	X	X	off	off	
9	off	X	X	X	X	X	off	
10	X	X	X	X	X	off	off	
Capacity, C	7	8	10	10	10	3	2	50
Requirements, R	6	4	8	9	10	3	2	42
Slack, C–R	1	4	2	1	0	0	0	8

DECISION POINT   With its substantial amount of slack capacity, the schedule is not unique. Employee 9, for example, could have Sunday and Monday, Monday and Tuesday, or Tuesday and Wednesday off without causing a capacity shortage. Indeed, the company might be able to get by with one fewer employee because of the total of eight slack days of capacity. However, all 10 employees are needed on Fridays. If the manager were willing to get by with only 9 employees on Fridays or if someone could work one day of overtime on a rotating basis, he would not need employee 10. As indicated in the table, the net requirement left for employee 10 to satisfy amounts to only one day, Friday. Thus, employee 10 can be used to fill in for vacationing or sick employees.

COMPUTERIZED WORKFORCE SCHEDULING SYSTEMS

Workforce scheduling often entails myriad constraints and concerns. In some types of firms, such as telephone companies, mail-order catalog houses, or emergency hot line agencies, employees must be on duty 24 hours a day, seven days a week. Sometimes a portion of the staff is part-time, allowing management a great deal of flexibility in developing schedules but adding considerable complexity to the requirements. The flexibility comes from the opportunity to match anticipated loads closely through the use of overlapping shifts or odd shift lengths; the complexity comes from the need to evaluate the numerous possible alternatives. Management also must consider the timing of lunch breaks and rest periods, the number and starting times of shift schedules, and the days off for each employee. An additional typical concern is that the number of employees on duty at any particular time be sufficient to answer calls within a reasonable amount of time.

Computerized scheduling systems are available to cope with the complexity of workforce scheduling. For example, L.L.Bean's telephone service center must be staffed with telephone operators seven days a week, 24 hours a day. The company uses 350 permanent and temporary employees. The permanent workers are guaranteed a minimum weekly workload apportioned over a seven-day week on a rotating schedule. The temporary staff works a variety of schedules, ranging from a full six-day week to a guaranteed weekly minimum of 20 hours. The company uses a computer program to forecast the hourly load for the telephone service center, to translate the workload into capacity requirements, and then to generate week-long staffing schedules for the permanent and temporary telephone operators to meet these demand requirements. The program selects the schedule that minimizes the sum of expected costs of over- and understaffing. Managerial Practice 17.1 describes the computerized scheduling system used by the Anderson Graduate School of Management at the University of California, Los Angeles.

OPERATIONS SCHEDULING

Operations schedules are short-term plans designed to implement the master production schedule. Operations scheduling focuses on how best to use existing capacity, taking into account technical production constraints. Often, several jobs must be processed at one or more workstations. Typically, a variety of tasks can be performed at each workstation. If schedules are not carefully planned to avoid bottlenecks, waiting lines may develop. For example, Figure 17.3 depicts the complexity of scheduling a manufacturing process. When a job order is received for a part, the raw materials are collected and the batch is moved to its first operation. The colored arrows show that jobs follow different routes through the manufacturing process, depending on the product being made. At each workstation, someone must determine the next job to process because the arrival rate of jobs at a workstation often differs from the processing rate of the jobs at a workstation, thereby creating a waiting line. In addition, new jobs can enter the process at any time, thereby creating a dynamic environment. Such complexity puts pressure on managers to develop scheduling procedures that will handle the workload efficiently.

MANAGERIAL PRACTICE 17.1

COURSE SCHEDULING AT THE UNIVERSITY OF CALIFORNIA, LOS ANGELES

Manually scheduling undergraduate, MBA, and doctoral courses at the Anderson Graduate School of Management at the University of California, Los Angeles (www.agsm.ucr.edu), used to take two people as many as three days each quarter. The complexity comes from myriad faculty preferences and facility and administrative constraints. For example, teachers may prefer to teach their assigned courses back-to-back, on the same days, and in the afternoon. In addition, there are only eight time slots in a day to start core MBA classes and limits to the number of rooms that can handle case discussions, large lectures, or computer access. Courses taught by the same instructor must not overlap, and courses must be scheduled at times so that students can take all required courses offered each quarter. Scheduling the 25 core MBA courses and 120 noncore courses to maximize faculty preferences, meet student needs, and satisfy all the constraints obviously is difficult.

Scheduling of the courses is now done with computer assistance. Core courses are scheduled first because they have limited starting times and all MBA students must enroll in them. Data on the number of sections of the core courses to be offered, facility and administrative constraints, and the teaching preferences of the faculty who will teach the core courses are entered into a computer model that assigns faculty to courses and courses to time slots that maximizes teaching preferences and meets all constraints. Not all teaching preferences can be satisfied. If the teacher's time preferences can be changed, however, the model can be used again to produce a completely new schedule in seconds.

Another model was developed to assign noncore courses to times and teachers to courses so that faculty preferences are maximized. Inputs to the model include the teaching assignments of the core courses, as a teacher can teach both a core and noncore course, the schedule of the core courses, classroom availability, and faculty preferences.

The system has been implemented and is running smoothly. The scheduling system improves the quality of the final course schedule and saves time. The entire schedule of courses can now be produced in only three hours, which includes the time needed to resolve conflicts with faculty preferences.

Source: Stallaert, Jan. "Automated Timetabling Improves Course Scheduling at UCLA." Interfaces, vol. 27, no. 4 (July-August 1997), pp. 67-81.

FIGURE 17.3   **Diagram of a Manufacturing Process**

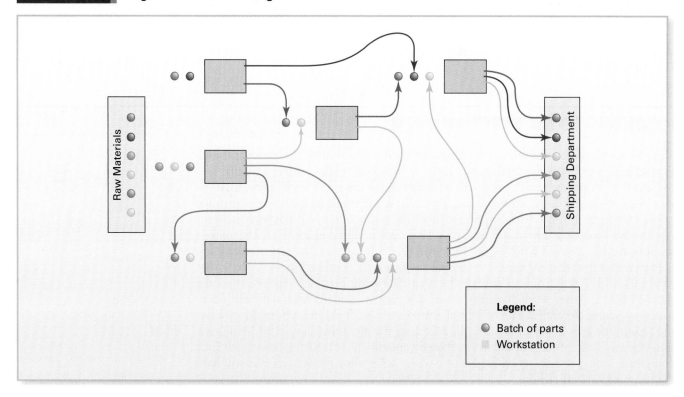

Legend:
● Batch of parts
■ Workstation

job shop   A firm that specializes in low- to medium-volume production and utilizes job or batch processes.

flow shop   A firm that specializes in medium- to high-volume production and utilizes line or continuous processes.

In this section, we focus on scheduling approaches used in two environments: (1) job shops and (2) flow shops. A **job shop** is a firm that specializes in low- to medium-volume production and utilizes job or batch processes (see Chapter 3, "Process Design Strategy"). Tasks in this type of flexible flow environment are difficult to schedule because of the variability in job routings and the continual introduction of new jobs to be processed. Figure 17.3 depicts a job shop environment. A **flow shop** specializes in medium- to high-volume production and utilizes line or continuous processes. Tasks are easier to schedule because the jobs in a line flow facility have a common flow pattern through the system. Nonetheless, scheduling mistakes can be costly in either situation.

Which jobs should have top priority?

JOB SHOP DISPATCHING

dispatching   A method of generating schedules in job shops that allows the schedule for a workstation to evolve over a period of time.

Just as there are many feasible schedules for a specific group of jobs on a particular set of workstations, there also are many ways to generate schedules. They range from straightforward manual methods, such as manipulating Gantt charts, to sophisticated computer models for developing optimal schedules. One way to generate schedules in job shops is with **dispatching**, which allows the schedule for a workstation to evolve over a period of time. The decision about which job to process next (or whether to let the station remain idle) is made with simple priority rules whenever the workstation becomes available for further processing. One advantage of this method is that last-minute information on operating conditions can be incorporated into the schedule as it evolves.

priority sequencing rules   The rules that specify the job processing sequence when several jobs are waiting in line at a workstation.

Dispatching determines the job to process next with the help of **priority sequencing rules.** When several jobs are waiting in line at a workstation, priority rules specify the job processing sequence. These rules can be applied by a worker or incorporated into a computerized scheduling system that generates a dispatch list of jobs and priorities for each workstation. The following priority sequencing rules are commonly used in practice.

- *Critical Ratio.* The **critical ratio (CR)** is calculated by dividing the time remaining until a job's due date by the total shop time remaining for the job, which is defined as the setup, processing, move, and expected waiting times of all remaining operations, including the operation being scheduled. The formula is

$$CR = \frac{\text{Due date} - \text{Today's date}}{\text{Total shop time remaining}}$$

  The difference between the due date and today's date must be in the same time units as the total shop time remaining. A ratio less than 1.0 implies that the job is behind schedule, and a ratio greater than 1.0 implies that the job is ahead of schedule. The job with the lowest CR is scheduled next.
- *Earliest Due Date.* The job with the **earliest due date (EDD)** is the next job to be processed.
- *First Come, First Served.* The job arriving at the workstation first has the highest priority under a **first come, first served (FCFS)** rule.
- *Shortest Processing Time.* The job requiring the **shortest processing time (SPT)** at the workstation is processed next.
- *Slack per Remaining Operations.* Slack is the difference between the time remaining until a job's due date and the total shop time remaining, including that of the operation being scheduled. A job's priority is determined by dividing the slack by the number of operations that remain, including the one being scheduled, to arrive at the **slack per remaining operations (S/RO)**.

$$S/RO = \frac{(\text{Due date} - \text{Today's date}) - \text{Total shop time remaining}}{\text{Number of operations remaining}}$$

  The job with the lowest S/RO is scheduled next. There are many ways to break ties if two or more jobs have the same top priority. One way is to arbitrarily choose one of the tied jobs for processing next.

Although the priority sequencing rules seem simple, the actual task of scheduling hundreds of jobs through hundreds of workstations requires intensive data gathering and manipulation. The scheduler needs information on each job's processing requirements: the job's due date; its routing; the standard setup, processing, and expected waiting times at each operation; whether alternative workstations could be used at each operation; and the components and raw materials needed at each operation. In addition, the scheduler needs to know the job's current status: its location (waiting in line for a workstation or being processed on a workstation), how much of the operation has been completed, the actual arrival and departure times at each operation or waiting line, and the actual processing and setup times. The scheduler uses the priority sequencing rules to determine the processing sequence of jobs at a workstation and the remaining information for estimating job arrival times at the next workstation, determining whether an alternative workstation should be used when the primary one is busy, and predicting the need for materials-handling equipment. Because this information may change throughout the day, computers are needed to track the data and to maintain valid priorities.

SCHEDULING JOBS FOR ONE WORKSTATION

Any priority sequencing rule can be used to schedule any number of workstations with the dispatching procedure. For the purpose of illustrating the rules, however, we focus on scheduling several jobs on a single machine. We divide the rules into two categories: (1) single-dimension rules and (2) multiple-dimension rules.

SINGLE-DIMENSION RULES. Some priority sequencing rules (e.g., FCFS, EDD, and SPT) base a job's priority assignment only on information on the jobs waiting for processing at the individual workstation. We call these rules **single-dimension rules** because they

critical ratio (CR) A ratio that is calculated by dividing the time remaining until a job's due date by the total shop time remaining for the job, which is defined as the setup, processing, move, and expected waiting times of all remaining operations, including the operation being scheduled.

earliest due date (EDD) A priority sequencing rule that specifies that the job with the earliest due date is the next job to be processed.

first come, first served (FCFS) A priority sequencing rule that specifies that the job arriving at the workstation first has the highest priority.

shortest processing time (SPT) A priority sequencing rule that specifies that the job requiring the shortest processing time is the next job to be processed.

slack per remaining operations (S/RO) A priority sequencing rule that determines priority by dividing the slack by the number of operations that remain, including the one being scheduled.

single-dimension rules A set of rules that bases the priority of a job on a single aspect of the job, such as arrival time at the workstation, the due date, or the processing time.

base the priority on a single aspect of the job, such as arrival time at the workstation, the due date, or the processing time. We begin with an example of single-dimension rules.

EXAMPLE 17.2   Comparing the EDD and SPT Rules

TUTOR 17.2

Tutor 17.2 on the Student CD-ROM provides a new example to practice EDD and SPT rules.

ACTIVE MODEL 17.1

Active Model 17.1 on the Student CD-ROM provides additional insight on the use of single-dimension rules.

The Taylor Machine Shop rebores engine blocks. Currently, five engine blocks are waiting for processing. At any time, the company has only one engine expert on duty who can do this type of work. The engine problems have been diagnosed, and the processing times for the jobs have been estimated. Expected completion times have been agreed upon with the shops' customers. The accompanying table shows the situation as of Monday morning. Because the Taylor Machine Shop is open from 8 A.M. until 5 P.M. each weekday, plus weekend hours as needed, the customer pickup times are measured in business hours from Monday morning. Determine the schedule for the engine expert by using (a) the EDD rule and (b) the SPT rule. For each rule, calculate the average hours early, the hours past due, the WIP inventory, and the total inventory. If low job flow times and WIP inventories are critical, which rule should be chosen?

ENGINE BLOCK	PROCESSING TIME, INCLUDING SETUP (HR)	SCHEDULED CUSTOMER PICKUP TIME (BUSINESS HR FROM NOW)
Ranger	8	10
Explorer	6	12
Bronco	15	20
Econoline 150	3	18
Thunderbird	12	22

SOLUTION

a. The EDD rule states that the first engine block in the sequence is the one with the closest due date. Consequently, the Ranger engine block is processed first. The Thunderbird engine block, with its due date furthest in the future, is processed last. The sequence is shown in the following table, along with the job flow times, the hours early, and the hours past due.

ENGINE BLOCK SEQUENCE	BEGIN WORK		PROCESSING TIME (hr)		JOB FLOW TIME (hr)	SCHEDULED CUSTOMER PICKUP TIME	ACTUAL CUSTOMER PICKUP TIME	HOURS EARLY	HOURS PAST DUE
Ranger	0	+	8	=	8	10	10	2	—
Explorer	8	+	6	=	14	12	14	—	2
Econoline 150	14	+	3	=	17	18	18	1	—
Bronco	17	+	15	=	32	20	32	—	12
Thunderbird	32	+	12	=	44	22	44	—	22

The flow time for each job equals the waiting time plus the processing time. For example, the Explorer engine block had to wait 8 hours before the engine expert started to work on it. The process time for the job is 6 hours, so its flow time is 14 hours. The average flow time and the other performance measures for the EDD schedule for the five engine blocks are

$$\text{Average job flow time} = \frac{8 + 14 + 17 + 32 + 44}{5} = 23 \text{ hours}$$

$$\text{Average hours early} = \frac{2 + 0 + 1 + 0 + 0}{5} = 0.6 \text{ hours}$$

$$\text{Average hours past due} = \frac{0 + 2 + 0 + 12 + 22}{5} = 7.2 \text{ hours}$$

$$\text{Average WIP inventory} = \frac{\text{Sum of flow times}}{\text{Makespan}} = \frac{8 + 14 + 17 + 32 + 44}{44}$$

$$= 2.61 \text{ engine blocks}$$

You might think of the sum of flow times as the total *job hours* spent by the engine blocks waiting for the engine expert and being processed. (In this example, there are no component or subassembly inventories, so WIP inventory consists only of those engine blocks waiting or being processed.) Dividing this sum by the makespan, or the total elapsed time required to complete work on all the engine blocks, provides the average WIP inventory.

Finally,

$$\text{Average total inventory} = \frac{\text{Sum of time in system}}{\text{Makespan}} = \frac{10 + 14 + 18 + 32 + 44}{44}$$
$$= 2.68 \text{ engine blocks}$$

Total inventory is the sum of the WIP inventory and the completed jobs waiting to be picked up by customers. The average total inventory equals the sum of the times each job spent in the shop—in this example, the total job hours spent waiting for the engine expert, being processed, and waiting for pickup—divided by the makespan. For example, the first job to be picked up is the Ranger engine block, which spent 10 hours in the system. Then the Explorer engine block is picked up, after spending 14 job hours in the system. The time spent by any job in the system equals its actual customer pickup time because all jobs were available for processing at time zero.

b. Under the SPT rule, the sequence starts with the engine block that has the shortest processing time, the Econoline 150, and it ends with the engine block that has the longest processing time, the Bronco. The sequence, along with the job flow times, early hours, and past due hours, is contained in the following table.

ENGINE BLOCK SEQUENCE	BEGIN WORK		PROCESSING TIME (hr)		JOB FLOW TIME (hr)	SCHEDULED CUSTOMER PICKUP TIME	ACTUAL CUSTOMER PICKUP TIME	HOURS EARLY	HOURS PAST DUE
Econoline 150	0	+	3	=	3	18	18	15	—
Explorer	3	+	6	=	9	12	12	3	—
Ranger	9	+	8	=	17	10	17	—	7
Thunderbird	17	+	12	=	29	22	29	—	7
Bronco	29	+	15	=	44	20	44	—	24

The performance measures are

$$\text{Average job flow time} = \frac{3 + 9 + 17 + 29 + 44}{5} = 20.4 \text{ hours}$$

$$\text{Average hours early} = \frac{15 + 3 + 0 + 0 + 0}{5} = 3.6 \text{ hours}$$

$$\text{Average past due hours} = \frac{0 + 0 + 7 + 7 + 24}{5} = 7.6 \text{ hours}$$

$$\text{Average WIP inventory} = \frac{3 + 9 + 17 + 29 + 44}{44} = 2.32 \text{ engine blocks}$$

$$\text{Average total inventory} = \frac{18 + 12 + 17 + 29 + 44}{44} = 2.73 \text{ engine blocks}$$

DECISION POINT The SPT rule is clearly superior to the EDD rule with respect to average job flow time and average WIP inventory. If these criteria outweigh all others, management should use SPT.

As the solution of Example 17.2 shows, the SPT schedule provided a lower average job flow time and lower WIP inventory. The EDD schedule, however, gave better customer service, as measured by the average hours past due, and a lower maximum hours past due (22 versus 24). It also provided a lower total inventory because fewer job hours were spent waiting for customers to pick up their engine blocks after they had been completed. The SPT priority rule will push jobs through the system to completion

How important is the choice of priority dispatching rules to the effectiveness of the operating system?

more quickly than will the other rules. Speed can be an advantage—but only if jobs can be delivered sooner than promised and revenue collected earlier. If they cannot, the completed job must stay in finished inventory, canceling the advantage of minimizing the average WIP inventory. Consequently, the priority rule chosen can help or hinder the firm in meeting its competitive priorities.

In Example 17.2, SPT and EDD provided schedules that resulted in different values for the performance criteria; however, both schedules have the same makespan of 44 hours. This result always will occur in single-operation scheduling for a *fixed number* of jobs available for processing—regardless of the priority rule used—because there are no idle workstation times between any two jobs.

Researchers have studied the implications of the single-dimension rules for various performance measures. In most of these studies, all jobs were considered to be independent, and the assumption was made that sufficient capacity generally was available. These studies found that the EDD rule performs well with respect to the percentage of jobs past due and the variance of hours past due. For any set of jobs to be processed at a single workstation, it minimizes the maximum of the past due hours of any job in the set. The EDD rule is popular with firms that are sensitive to due date changes, although it does not perform very well with respect to flow time, WIP inventory, or utilization.

Often referred to as the *world champion,* the SPT rule tends to minimize the mean flow time, the WIP inventory, and the percentage of jobs past due and it tends to maximize shop utilization. For the single-workstation case, the SPT rule always will provide the lowest mean flow time. However, it could increase total inventory because it tends to push all work to the finished state. In addition, it tends to produce a large variance in past due hours because the larger jobs might have to wait a long time for processing. Also, it provides no opportunity to adjust schedules when due dates change. The advantage of this rule over others diminishes as the load on the shop increases.

Finally, though the FCFS rule is considered fair to the jobs (or customers), it performs poorly with respect to all performance measures. This result is to be expected because FCFS does not acknowledge any job (or customer) characteristics.

MULTIPLE-DIMENSION RULES. Priority rules, such as CR and S/RO, incorporate information about the remaining workstations at which the job must be processed, in addition to the processing time at the present workstation or the due date considered by single-dimension rules. We call these rules **multiple-dimension rules** because they apply to more than one aspect of the job. Example 17.3 demonstrates their use for sequencing jobs.

multiple-dimension rules   A set of rules that apply to more than one aspect of a job.

EXAMPLE 17.3   **Sequencing with the CR and S/RO Rules**

TUTOR 17.3

Tutor 17.3 on the Student CD-ROM provides a new example to practice CR and S/RO rules.

The first five columns of the following table contain information about a set of four jobs presently waiting at an engine lathe. Several operations, including the one at the engine lathe, remain to be done on each job. Determine the schedule by using (a) the CR rule and (b) the S/RO rule. Compare these schedules to those generated by FCFS, SPT, and EDD.

JOB	OPERATION TIME AT ENGINE LATHE (hr)	TIME REMAINING UNTIL DUE DATE (days)	NUMBER OF OPERATIONS REMAINING	SHOP TIME REMAINING (days)	CR	S/RO
1	2.3	15	10	6.1	2.46	0.89
2	10.5	10	2	7.8	1.28	1.10
3	6.2	20	12	14.5	1.38	0.46
4	15.6	8	5	10.2	0.78	−0.44

SOLUTION

a. Using CR to schedule the machine, we divide the time remaining until the due date by the shop time remaining to get the priority index for each job. For job 1,

$$CR = \frac{\text{Time remaining until the due date}}{\text{Shop time remaining}} = \frac{15}{6.1} = 2.46$$

By arranging the jobs in sequence with the lowest critical ratio first, we determine that the sequence of jobs to be processed by the engine lathe is 4, 2, 3, and finally 1, assuming that no other jobs arrive in the meantime.

b. Using S/RO, we divide the difference between the time remaining until the due date and the shop time remaining by the number of remaining operations. For job 1,

$$S/RO = \frac{\text{Time remaining until the due date} - \text{Shop time remaining}}{\text{Number of operations remaining}} = \frac{15 - 6.1}{10} = 0.89$$

Arranging the jobs by starting with the lowest S/RO yields a 4, 3, 1, 2 sequence of jobs.

DECISION POINT Note that the application of the two priority rules gives two different schedules. Moreover, the SPT sequence, based on operation times (measured in hours) at the engine lathe only, is 1, 3, 2, and 4. No preference is given to job 4 in the SPT schedule, even though it may not be finished by its due date. The FCFS sequence is 1, 2, 3, and 4; and the EDD sequence is 4, 2, 1, and 3. The following table shows the comparative performance of the five dispatching rules at the engine lathe.

PRIORITY RULE SUMMARY					
	FCFS	**SPT**	**EDD**	**CR**	**S/RO**
Average Flow Time	17.175	16.100	26.175	27.150	24.025
Average Early Time	3.425	6.050	0	0	0
Average Past Due	7.350	8.900	12.925	13.900	10.775
Average WIP	1.986	1.861	3.026	3.139	2.777
Average Total Inventory	2.382	2.561	3.026	3.139	2.777

The S/RO rule is better than the EDD rule and the CR rule but it is much worse than the SPT rule and the FCFS rule for this example. However, the S/RO has the advantage of allowing schedule changes when due dates change. These results cannot be generalized to other situations because only four jobs are being processed.

Research studies have shown that S/RO is better than EDD with respect to the percentage of jobs past due but worse than SPT and EDD with respect to average job flow times. These studies also indicate that CR results in longer job flow times than SPT but CR also results in less variance in the distribution of past due hours. Consequently, even though the use of the multiple-dimension rules requires more information, there is no clear-cut best choice. Each rule should be tested in the environment for which it is intended.

SCHEDULING JOBS FOR MULTIPLE WORKSTATIONS

Priority sequencing rules may be used to schedule more than one operation with the dispatching procedure. Each operation is treated independently. When a workstation becomes idle, the priority rule is applied to the jobs waiting for that operation, and the job with the highest priority is selected. When that operation is finished, the job is moved to the next operation in its routing, where it waits until it again has the highest priority. At any workstation, the jobs in the waiting line change over a period of time, so the choice of a priority rule can make quite a difference in the processing sequence. Schedules can be evaluated with the performance measures already discussed.

Identifying the best priority rule to use at a particular operation in a process is a complex problem because the output from one operation becomes the input to another. The priority rule at a workstation determines the sequence of work the workstation will perform, which in turn determines the arrival of work at the next workstation downstream. Computer simulation models are effective tools to determine which priority rules work best in a given situation (see Supplement B, "Simulation"). Once the current process is modeled, the analyst can make changes to the priority rules at various operations and measure the impact on performance measures, such as past due, work-in-progress, job flow time, and utilization. Example 17.4 demonstrates the use of simulation using Extend, which is the simulation software that is on the optional CD-ROM. To learn more about Extend, see its tutorials and work through the simulation exercises with the preprogrammed model at the end of this chapter. SimQuick, included on the Student CD-ROM that is packaged with each new textbook, is also very useful.

EXAMPLE 17.4   Simulation of Precision AutoBody Operations

Precision AutoBody has an excellent reputation in the local market for doing high-quality autobody repair work. Repair of a vehicle body consists of two general steps: body repair and finishing. For body repair, vehicles are classified as having either minor or major damage. Those with minor damage require, on average, one eight-hour day to complete, and two-thirds of the vehicles serviced by Precision fell into this category. In contrast, vehicles with major damage require more extensive repairs that extend beyond the surface sheet metal, and damages often include hidden problems that are not evident when first inspected. As a result, this repair work averages two days. Of those vehicles with major damage, about half need to have the underlying frame of the vehicle straightened on special hydraulic equipment in a dedicated area adjacent to the repair bays. This extra operation tends to add an average of one additional day to the completion time.

After body repair, the vehicle is moved to the finishing area. A small percentage of vehicles, 25 percent of those with minor damage, move directly to the finishing area. Here, an apprentice prepares the vehicle by doing final sanding and masking off areas that are not to be painted. Next, the vehicle is moved to one of several paint booths, where the painter mixes the paint color to match the vehicle, taking into account any fading that has occurred. Virtually all vehicles require two coats, a colored base coat followed by a clear coat applied the next day. After completion, the vehicle's exterior and interior are thoroughly cleaned to give that "just new" impression to the customer when the vehicle is delivered. The times to complete each operation are summarized in the following table.

PRECISION AUTOBODY PROCESS TIMES		
	TIME TO PERFORM	
OPERATION	**AVERAGE (hr)**	**STANDARD DEVIATION**
1. Frame straightening*	8	2
2a. Body repair, major damage*	16	4
2b. Body repair, minor damage*	8	2
3. Paint preparation	$1\frac{1}{4}$	$\frac{1}{3}$
4. Paint application (two coats)	$1\frac{1}{2}$	$\frac{1}{2}$
5. Clean up	3	$\frac{1}{2}$

*Not necessary for all vehicles.

The operations times all can be approximated by a log-normal distribution.

Bill Curtis, manager at Precision, schedules each vehicle at the body repair and paint operations on a first come, first served basis—an equitable approach—with a quoted delivery time of about one week (i.e., five business days), plus any lead time needed for delivery of the parts. A review of the last month's data indicated that 18.17 percent of the jobs were delivered late and the average throughput time (flow time) per auto was 30.49 hours. In addition, the average number of vehicles in the system (work-in-process) was 9.6 autos. Curtis wanted to know if the application of the SPT rule to the body repair and paint operations would improve delivery performance and reduce flow times and work-in-process.

SOLUTION

The Extend software, contained on the optional CD-ROM, is used to model and simulate the Precision AutoBody operations. Figure 17.4 shows the simulation model. The five operations are boxed in the diagram. As the simulation proceeds, vehicles arrive and require major repair with a 33 percent chance. If major repair is needed, there is a 50 percent chance that the vehicle will need the frame work operation before the body repair operation. If minor repair is needed, there is a 25 percent chance that the vehicle will go straight to the paint preparation operation. After body repair, all vehicles go through paint preparation, painting, and clean up. The activities after clean up are needed to gather the statistics for each vehicle before it exits the simulation. The SPT priority rule for each operation was selected in the Controls box (not shown).

The results of the simulation using the SPT rule for the body repair operation and the finishing operations (paint preparation, paint, and clean up) are shown in Figure 17.5, using the

FIGURE 17.4   **Precision AutoBody Operations Using Extend Software**

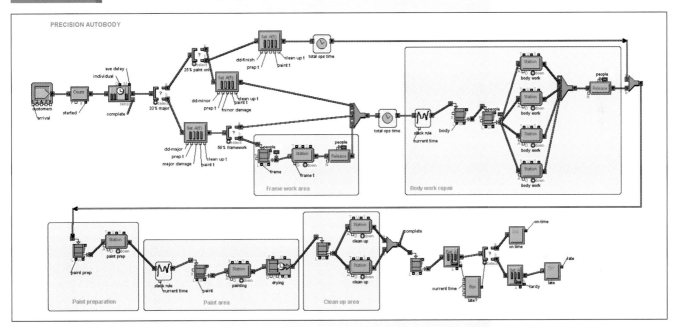

FIGURE 17.5

Results of the SPT Rule for the Body Repair and Finishing Operations for Precision AutoBody

DELIVERY PERFORMANCE	
Late (%)	17.35
Average tardiness (hr)	7.896
System performance	
Average number of vehicles in system	9.422
Overall throughput time (hr)	
average	29.67
standard deviation	10.92
Operation utilization	
Body repair	0.8338
Paint operation	0.7687

Number of Vehicles in the System for a 2,500 Hour Period

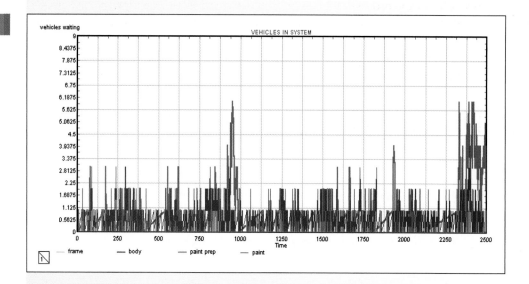

Notebook feature of Extend. Notice that the percentage of late deliveries, the average number of vehicles in the system, and the average throughput time have been improved with the use of SPT. The average tardiness statistic, shown in Figure 17.5, is another form of the past-due measure of performance. It is the average number of hours past the due date for those vehicles that were delivered late.

Figure 17.6 shows the number of vehicles in the system for a simulated period of 2,500 hours. Each of the operations is color coded to show how the work-in-process at each operation changes over the time period simulated.

DECISION POINT   The results show that SPT is superior to the FCFS priority rule for Precision AutoBody. Curtis should consider changing the priority rule. However, Figure 17.6 indicates that the body repair operation will have sizeable swings in WIP inventory. Management should explore increasing resources at that operation. Further improvements in the percentage of late deliveries might be achieved by increasing the lead time in setting the due dates or by changing the priority rules. The simulation model can help determine the best solution.

Source: This case and simulation experience was provided by Professor Robert Klassen, University of Western Ontario.

SCHEDULING JOBS FOR A TWO-STATION FLOW SHOP

Suppose that a flow shop has several jobs ready for processing at two workstations and that the routings of all jobs are identical. Whereas in single-workstation scheduling the makespan is the same regardless of the priority rule chosen; in the scheduling of two or more workstations in a flow shop, the makespan varies according to the sequence chosen. Determining a production sequence for a group of jobs to minimize the makespan has two advantages.

1. The group of jobs is completed in minimum time.
2. The utilization of the two-station flow shop is maximized. Utilizing the first workstation continuously until it processes the last job minimizes the idle time on the *second* workstation.

Johnson's rule   A procedure that minimizes makespan in scheduling a group of jobs on two workstations.

Johnson's rule is a procedure that minimizes makespan in scheduling a group of jobs on two workstations. S. M. Johnson showed that the sequence of jobs at the two stations should be identical and that the priority assigned to a job should therefore be the same at both. The procedure is based on the assumption of a known set of jobs, each with a known processing time and available to begin processing on the first workstation. The procedure is as follows.

Step 1. Scan the processing times at each workstation and find the shortest processing time among the jobs not yet scheduled. If there is a tie, choose one job arbitrarily.

Step 2. If the shortest processing time is on workstation 1, schedule the corresponding job as early as possible. If the shortest processing time is on workstation 2, schedule the corresponding job as late as possible.

Step 3. Eliminate the last job scheduled from further consideration. Repeat steps 1 and 2 until all jobs have been scheduled.

Scheduling a Group of Jobs on Two Workstations

EXAMPLE 17.5

TUTOR 17.4

Tutor 17.4 on the Student CD-ROM provides a new example to practice Johnson's rule.

The Morris Machine Company just received an order to refurbish five motors for materials handling equipment that were damaged in a fire. The motors will be repaired at two workstations in the following manner.

Workstation 1   Dismantle the motor and clean the parts.
Workstation 2   Replace the parts as necessary, test the motor, and make adjustments.

The customer's shop will be inoperable until all the motors have been repaired, so the plant manager is interested in developing a schedule that minimizes the makespan and has authorized around-the-clock operations until the motors have been repaired. The estimated time to repair each motor is shown in the following table.

	TIME (hr)	
MOTOR	**WORKSTATION 1**	**WORKSTATION 2**
M1	12	22
M2	4	5
M3	5	3
M4	15	16
M5	10	8

SOLUTION

The logic for the optimal sequence is shown in the following table.

ESTABLISHING A JOB SEQUENCE					
ITERATION	**JOB SEQUENCE**				**COMMENTS**
1				M3	The shortest processing time is 3 hours for M3 at workstation 2. Therefore, M3 is scheduled as late as possible.
2	M2			M3	Eliminate M3's time from the table of estimated times. The next shortest processing time is 4 hours for M2 at workstation 1. M2 is therefore scheduled first.
3	M2		M5	M3	Eliminate M2 from the table. The next shortest processing time is eight hours for M5 at workstation 2. Therefore, M5 is scheduled as late as possible.
4	M2	M1	M5	M3	Eliminate M5 from the table. The next shortest processing time is 12 hours for M1 at workstation 1. M1 is scheduled as early as possible.
5	M2	M1	M4	M5	M3	The last motor to be scheduled is M4. It is placed in the last remaining position, in the middle of the schedule.

FIGURE 17.7   **Workstation Chart for the Morris Machine Company Repair Schedule**

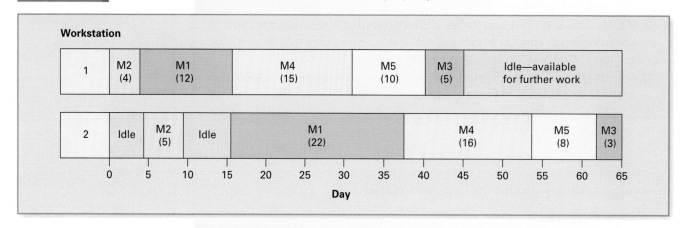

DECISION POINT   No other sequence of jobs will produce a lower makespan. To determine the makespan, we have to draw a Gantt chart, as shown in Figure 17.7. In this case, refurbishing and reinstalling all five motors will take 65 hours. This schedule minimizes the idle time of work-station 2 and gives the fastest repair time for all five motors. Note that the schedule recognizes that a job cannot begin at workstation 2 until it has been completed at workstation 1.

LABOR-LIMITED ENVIRONMENTS

labor-limited environment
An environment in which the resource constraint is the amount of labor available, not the number of machines or workstations.

Thus far, we have assumed that a job never has to wait for lack of a worker; that is, the limiting resource is the number of machines or workstations available. More typi-cal, however, is a **labor-limited environment** in which the resource constraint is the amount of labor available, not the number of machines or workstations. In this case, workers are trained to work on a variety of machines or tasks to increase the flexibil-ity of operations.

In a labor-limited environment, the scheduler not only must decide which job to process next at a particular workstation but also must assign workers to their next workstations. The scheduler can use priority rules to make these decisions, as we used them to schedule engine blocks in Example 17.2. In labor-limited environments, the labor-assignment policies, as well as the dispatching priority rules, affect performance. The following examples provide some labor-assignment rules.

- Assign personnel to the workstation with the job that has been in the system longest.
- Assign personnel to the workstation with the most jobs waiting for processing.
- Assign personnel to the workstation with the largest standard work content.
- Assign personnel to the workstation with the job that has the earliest due date.

LINKING OPERATIONS SCHEDULING TO THE SUPPLY CHAIN

advanced planning and scheduling (APS) systems
Systems that seek to optimize resources across the supply chain and align daily operations with strategic goals.

In Chapter 9, "Supply-Chain Design", we discussed how firms design and manage the linkages between customers and suppliers with the concept of an integrated supply chain. True integration requires the manipulation of large amounts of complex data in real time because the customer order work flow must be synchronized with the required material, manufacturing, and distribution activity. Attempting to accomplish this integration with piecemeal systems can be resource-intensive and ultimately less than satisfactory. The Internet, new computer software, and improved data storage and manipulation methods have given rise to **advanced planning and scheduling (APS) systems,** which seek to optimize resources across the supply chain and align daily oper-ations with strategic goals. These systems typically have four major components.

1. *Demand Planning.* This capability enables companies in a supply chain to share demand forecasts, thereby providing more visibility of future requirements. A broad range of forecasting techniques is provided (see Chapter 13 "Forecasting").

2. *Supply Network Planning.* Optimization models based on linear programming can be used to make long-term decisions, such as the number and location of plants and distribution centers, which suppliers to use, and the optimal location and amounts of inventory (see Chapter 10, "Location" and Supplement D, "Linear Programming").

3. *Available-to-Promise.* Firms can use this capability to promise delivery to customers by checking the availability of components and materials at its suppliers, who may be located anywhere in the world (see Supplement F, "Master Production Scheduling"). Variants of this capability include *capable-to-promise*—for suppliers who produce to customer order and reserve capacity—and *capable-to-deliver*—for suppliers of transportation services.

4. *Manufacturing Scheduling.* This module attempts to determine an optimal grouping and sequencing of manufacturing orders based on detailed product attributes, production line capacities, and material flows. In some applications, schedules for material, labor, and equipment can be determined minute-by-minute. Gantt charts can be used to view the schedule and make adjustments (see Figure 17.1 and Figure 17.2). The schedules are "constraint-based" and use the *theory of constraints* to schedule bottlenecks in the manufacturing process (see Chapter 6, "Process Capacity").

The manufacturing scheduling process is a key element of an integrated supply chain. APS systems attempt to link to the scheduling process demand data and forecasts, supply-chain facility and inventory decisions, and the capability of suppliers so that the entire supply chain can operate as efficiently as possible. The ability to change schedules quickly while recognizing the implications on the rest of the supply chain can provide a competitive edge. Managerial Practice 17.2 demonstrates the advantages of real-time scheduling at Chrysler.

⬤ SCHEDULING ACROSS THE ORGANIZATION

In this chapter, we have shown the importance of the scheduling process for service and manufacturing processes. Whether the business is an airline, hotel, computer manufacturer, or university, schedules are a part of everyday life. Schedules involve an enormous amount of detail and affect every process in a firm. For example, service product and employee schedules determine specific cash flow requirements, trigger the billing process into action, and initiate requirements for the employee training process. The order fulfillment process depends on good performance in terms of due dates for promised services or products, which is the result of a good scheduling process. In addition, when customers place orders using a Web-based order-entry process, the scheduling process determines when they can expect to receive the service or product. Certainly, regardless of the discipline, schedules affect everyone in a firm.

Given the development of computer hardware and software and the availability of the Internet, firms have elevated the scheduling process to a level where it can be used as a competitive weapon. As we have seen in Managerial Practice 17.2, Chrysler used the scheduling process to decrease costs and improve responsiveness to supply-chain dynamics by finding a way to produce complex schedules quickly. These schedules affect operations in plants worldwide. The scheduling process can provide any firm with a capability it can use to compete successfully, whether it is in services or manufacturing.

MANAGERIAL PRACTICE 17.2

REAL-TIME SCHEDULING IN CHRYSLER'S APS SYSTEM

Vehicle painting operations are typically a bottleneck to the assembly process. Every auto must go through the paint process, which involves special application sequences depending on the required finish. When an auto requires a different color than the auto just before it in sequence, the paint guns must be purged and cleaned with special solvents. The time to accomplish this activity depends on the sequence of colors. Typically, production orders are sequenced from lighter to darker colors to minimize the time to clean the paint guns between color changes. The problem is much more complex than simply deciding how many autos should be included in each batch of a particular color. Each auto has particular options selected by the customer that have to be assembled to the auto after the paint operation. Disregarding the implications of the paint schedule on the other processes can cause bottlenecks elsewhere in the plant. For example, a batch of blue cars ordered by a governmental agency might all be ordered with diesel engines. If all of these cars are included in the same batch of blue cars, an overload may occur on the limited manpower available to mount diesel engines. Delays in mounting diesel engines may cause delays in the entire production line, which in turn can affect global supplies of autos. The challenge is to optimize the paint sequence while recognizing the constraints imposed by other processes in the plant.

At Chrysler (daimlerchrysler.com), the vehicle painting operations were a major bottleneck that affected operations throughout the plant. Operations at the paint booth had to be optimized; however, overloading or underutilizing other parts of the production line had to be avoided. Chrysler developed its own paint sequencing application as part of an APS system and employed it in 18 assembly plants. The new system eliminated the bottleneck at the paint operations, reducing paint purges in the 18 plants from 383 to 191 per day, which resulted in more than $7 million in savings per year. In addition, the time to produce a one-day schedule of 1,200 vehicles was cut from four to six hours to only two and one-half minutes. This capability allows Chrysler to adjust schedules in real time, making the production process much more responsive to customer needs and supply-chain constraints.

Marion Boone, Chrysler's paint manufacturing manager, shows the results of a new environmentally friendly paint technology at the Newark assembly plant. Chrysler developed its own software to sequence vehicles along the assembly line, with particular attention to the painting process.

Source: Berger, Llana. "Optimizing the Supply Chain with APS." *APICS—The Performance Advantage* (December 1999), pp. 24–27.

CHAPTER HIGHLIGHTS

- Scheduling is the allocation of resources over a period of time to accomplish a specific set of tasks. Three basic types of scheduling are demand scheduling, workforce scheduling, and operations scheduling. Scheduling applications are becoming more common in ERP systems.

- Gantt charts are useful for depicting the sequence of work at a particular workstation and for monitoring the progress of jobs in the system.

- No approach to scheduling is best for all situations. Performance measures that can be used to evaluate schedules include average job flow time, makespan, percentage of jobs past due, average amount of time past due per job, average WIP inventory, average investment in total inventory, and utilization of equipment and workers.

- Capacity considerations are important for scheduling services and manufacturing processes. If the capacity of the operating system is fixed, loads can be leveled by using approaches, such as appointments, reservations, and backlogs. If service is determined by labor availability, workforce scheduling may be appropriate.

- A workforce schedule translates a staffing plan into a specific work schedule for each employee. Typical workforce scheduling considerations include capacity limits, service targets, consecutive days off, maximum number of workdays in a row, type of schedule (fixed or rotating), and vacation and holiday time.

- Dispatching allows a schedule to evolve from new information about operating conditions. Priority rules are used to make these decisions. The choice of priority rule can affect the schedule performance measures that are of concern to management.

- Labor-limited systems add another dimension to operations scheduling. In addition to determining which job to process next, the scheduler also must assign the work to an available operator with the required skills.

- The impact of scheduling can be increased by focusing on the schedules of bottleneck resources to maximize the flow of total value-added funds.

STUDENT CD-ROM AND INTERNET RESOURCES

The Student CD-ROM and the Companion Website at **www.prenhall.com/krajewski** contain many tools, activities, and resources designed for this chapter. The following items are recommended to enhance your skills and improve your understanding of the material in this chapter.

STUDENT CD-ROM RESOURCES

- ➤ **PowerPoint Slides:** View the comprehensive set of slides customized for this chapter's concepts and techniques.
- ➤ **Video Clips:** See the two video clips customized for this chapter to learn more about the scheduling process at Air New Zealand.
- ➤ **OM Explorer Tutors:** OM Explorer has four tutor programs that will help you learn how to develop workforce schedules or job schedules at a single workstation or at a two-station flow shop. See Chapter 17 in the OM Explorer menu. See also the Tutor Exercise requiring the use of these tutor programs.
- ➤ **OM Explorer Solvers:** OM Explorer has three programs that can be used to solve general problems involving workforce schedules and operations schedules at a single workstation and at a two-workstation flow shop. See Scheduling in the OM Explorer menu.
- ➤ **Active Models:** There is an Active Model spreadsheet that provides additional insight on the use of single-dimension

rules for scheduling operations. See Scheduling in the Active Models menu for this routine. Also see the Active Model exercise at the end of this chapter.

- ➤ **SimQuick Exercise:** Learn the basics of building simulation models to schedule batch and job shop processes by working through example 21 and example 22 in *SimQuick: Process Simulation with Excel*. These are just a few of the many examples in the text, which include waiting lines, inventory in supply chains, manufacturing, and project management.

INTERNET RESOURCES

- ➤ **Self-Study Quizzes:** See the compendium of true or false, multiple choice, and essay questions that allows online tests or gives you feedback on how well you have mastered the concepts of this chapter.
- ➤ **In the News:** See the articles that apply to this chapter.
- ➤ **Internet Exercises:** Try out two different links to scheduling topics, including automobile production scheduling and airline assistance in scheduling business and vacation trips.
- ➤ **Virtual Tours:** See how d'Elegant schedules vans for custom conversions. See also the "Web Links to Company Facility Tours" for tours of company facilities.

KEY EQUATIONS

1. Performance measures:

Job flow time = Time of completion − Time job was available for first processing operation

Makespan = Time of completion of last job − Starting time of first job

$$\text{Average WIP inventory} = \frac{\text{Sum of flow times}}{\text{Makespan}}$$

$$\text{Average inventory} = \frac{\text{Sum of time in system}}{\text{Makespan}}$$

Total inventory = Scheduled receipts for all items + On-hand inventories of all items

$$\text{Utilization} = \frac{\text{Productive work time}}{\text{Total work time available}}$$

2. Critical ratio: $CR = \dfrac{\text{Due date} - \text{Today's date}}{\text{Total shop time remaining}}$

3. Slack per remaining operations: $S/RO = \dfrac{(\text{Due date} - \text{Today's date}) - \text{Total time remaining}}{\text{Number of operations remaining}}$

KEY TERMS

advanced planning and scheduling (APS) systems 790
critical ratio (CR) 781
demand scheduling 771
dispatching 780
earliest due date (EDD) 781
first come, first served (FCFS) 781
fixed schedule 776
flow shop 780
job flow time 772

job shop 780
Johnson's rule 788
labor-limited environment 790
makespan 772
multiple-dimension rules 784
operations scheduling 771
past due 772
priority sequencing rules 780
rotating schedule 776
scheduling 770

shortest processing time (SPT) 781
single-dimension rules 781
slack per remaining operations (S/RO) 781
tardiness 772
total inventory 772
workforce scheduling 771
work-in-process (WIP) inventory 772

SOLVED PROBLEM 1

The Food Bin grocery store operates 24 hours per day, seven days per week. Fred Bulger, the store manager, has been analyzing the efficiency and productivity of store operations recently. Bulger decided to observe the need for checkout clerks on the first shift for a one-month period. At the end of the month, he calculated the average number of checkout registers that should be open during the first shift each day. His results showed peak needs on Saturdays and Sundays.

Day	M	T	W	Th	F	S	Su
Number of Employees	3	4	5	5	4	7	8

Bulger now has to come up with a workforce schedule that guarantees each checkout clerk two consecutive days off but still covers all requirements.

    a. Develop a workforce schedule that covers all requirements while giving two consecutive days off to each clerk. How many clerks are needed? Assume that the clerks have no preference regarding which days they have off.

    b. Plans can be made to use the clerks for other duties if slack or idle time resulting from this schedule can be determined. How much idle time will result from this schedule and on what days?

SOLUTION

a. We use the method demonstrated in Example 17.1 to determine the number of clerks needed.

	DAY						
	M	T	W	Th	F	S	Su
Requirements	3	4	5	5	4	7	8*
Clerk 1	off	off	X	X	X	X	X
Requirements	3	4	4	4	3	6	7*
Clerk 2	off	off	X	X	X	X	X
Requirements	3	4	3	3	2	5	6*
Clerk 3	X	X	X	off	off	X	X
Requirements	2	3	2	3	2	4	5*
Clerk 4	X	X	X	off	off	X	X
Requirements	1	2	1	3	2	3	4*
Clerk 5	X	off	off	X	X	X	X
Requirements	0	2	1	2	1	2	3*
Clerk 6	off	off	X	X	X	X	X
Requirements	0	2*	0	1	0	1	2*
Clerk 7	X	X	off	off	X	X	X
Requirements	0	1*	0	1*	0	0	1*
Clerk 8	X	X	X	X	off	off	X
Requirements	0	0	0	0	0	0	0

*Maximum requirements.

The minimum number of clerks is eight.

b. Based on the results in part (a), the number of clerks on duty minus the requirements is the number of idle clerks available for other duties:

	DAY						
	M	T	W	Th	F	S	Su
Number on Duty	5	4	6	5	5	7	8
Requirements	3	4	5	5	4	7	8
Idle Clerks	2	0	1	0	1	0	0

The slack in this schedule would indicate to Bulger the number of employees he might ask to work part-time (fewer than five days per week). For example, clerk 7 might work Tuesday, Saturday, and Sunday and clerk 8 might work Tuesday, Thursday, and Sunday. That would eliminate slack from the schedule.

SOLVED PROBLEM 2

The Neptune's Den Machine Shop specializes in overhauling outboard marine engines. Some engines require replacement of broken parts, whereas others need a complete overhaul. Currently, five engines with varying problems are awaiting service. The best estimates for the labor times involved and the promise dates (in number of days from today) are shown in the following table. Customers usually do not pick up their engines early.

ENGINE	ESTIMATED LABOR TIME (days)	PROMISE DATE (days from now)
50-hp Evinrude	5	8
7-hp Chrysler	4	15
100-hp Mercury	10	12
4-hp Sportsman	1	20
75-hp Nautique	3	10

a. Develop separate schedules by using the SPT and EDD rules. Compare the two schedules on the basis of average job flow time, percentage of past due jobs, and maximum past due days for any engine.

b. For each schedule, calculate average WIP inventory (in engines) and average total inventory (in engines).

SOLUTION

a. Using the SPT rule, we obtain the following schedule:

REPAIR SEQUENCE	PROCESSING TIME	JOB FLOW TIME	PROMISE DATE	ACTUAL PICKUP DATE	DAYS EARLY	DAYS PAST DUE
4-hp Sportsman	1	1	20	20	19	—
75-hp Nautique	3	4	10	10	6	—
7-hp Chrysler	4	8	15	15	7	—
50-hp Evinrude	5	13	8	13	—	5
100-hp Mercury	10	23	12	23	—	11
		Total 49		81		

Using the EDD we obtain this schedule:

REPAIR SEQUENCE	PROCESSING TIME	JOB FLOW TIME	PROMISE DATE	ACTUAL PICKUP DATE	DAYS EARLY	DAYS PAST DUE
50-hp Evinrude	5	5	8	8	3	—
75-hp Nautique	3	8	10	10	2	—
100-hp Mercury	10	18	12	18	—	6
7-hp Chrysler	4	22	15	22	—	7
4-hp Sportsman	1	23	20	23	—	3
		Total 76		81		

Average job flow time is 9.8 (or 49/5) days for SPT and 15.2 (or 76/5) days for EDD. The percentage of past due jobs is 40 percent (2/5) for SPT and 60 percent (3/5) for EDD. The EDD schedule minimizes the maximum days past due but has a greater flow time and causes more jobs to be past due.

b. For SPT, inventory averages are as follows:

$$\text{Average WIP inventory} = \frac{\text{Sum of flow times}}{\text{Makespan}} = \frac{49}{23} = 2.13 \text{ engines}$$

$$\text{Average total inventory} = \frac{\text{Sum of time in system}}{\text{Makespan}} = \frac{81}{23} = 3.52 \text{ engines}$$

For EDD, they are

$$\text{Average WIP inventory} = \frac{76}{23} = 3.30 \text{ engines}$$

$$\text{Average total inventory} = \frac{81}{23} = 3.52 \text{ engines}$$

SOLVED PROBLEM 3

The following data were reported by the shop floor control system for order processing at the edge grinder. The current date is day 150. The number of remaining operations and the total work remaining include the operation at the edge grinder. All orders are available for processing, and none have been started yet.

CURRENT ORDER	PROCESSING TIME (HR)	DUE DATE (DAY)	REMAINING OPERATIONS	SHOP TIME REMAINING (DAYS)
A101	10	162	10	9
B272	7	158	9	6
C105	15	152	1	1
D707	4	170	8	18
E555	8	154	5	8

a. Specify the priorities for each job if the shop floor control system uses slack per remaining operations (S/RO) or critical ratio (CR).

b. For each priority rule, calculate the average job flow time per job at the edge grinder.

SOLUTION

a. We specify the priorities for each job using the two dispatching rules.

$$S/RO = \frac{(\text{Due date} - \text{Today's date}) - \text{Shop time remaining}}{\text{Number of operations remaining}}$$

$$\text{E555: } S/RO = \frac{(154 - 150) - 8}{5} = -0.80 \quad [1]$$

$$\text{B272: } S/RO = \frac{(158 - 150) - 6}{9} = 0.22 \quad [2]$$

$$\text{D707: } S/RO = \frac{(170 - 150) - 18}{8} = 0.25 \quad [3]$$

$$\text{A101: } S/RO = \frac{(162 - 150) - 9}{10} = 0.30 \quad [4]$$

$$\text{C105: } S/RO = \frac{(152 - 150) - 1}{1} = 1.00 \quad [5]$$

The sequence of production for S/RO is shown above in brackets.

$$CR = \frac{\text{Due date} - \text{Today's date}}{\text{Shop time remaining}}$$

$$\text{E555: } CR = \frac{154 - 150}{8} = 0.50 \quad [1]$$

$$\text{D707: } CR = \frac{170 - 150}{18} = 1.11 \quad [2]$$

$$\text{B272: } CR = \frac{158 - 150}{6} = 1.33 \quad [3]$$

$$\text{A101: } CR = \frac{162 - 150}{9} = 1.33 \quad [4]$$

$$\text{C105: } CR = \frac{152 - 150}{1} = 2.00 \quad [5]$$

The sequence of production for CR is shown above in brackets.

b. We are looking for the flow time of a set of jobs at a single machine, so each job's flow time equals the flow time of the job just prior to it in sequence plus its own processing time. Consequently, the average flow times are

$$\text{S/RO: } \frac{8 + 15 + 19 + 29 + 44}{5} = 23.0 \text{ hours}$$

$$\text{CR: } \frac{8 + 12 + 19 + 29 + 44}{5} = 22.4 \text{ hours}$$

In this example, the average flow time per job is lower for the CR rule, which is not always the case. For example, the critical ratios for B272 and A101 are tied at 1.33. If we arbitrarily assigned A101 before B272, the average flow time would increase to (8 + 12 + 22 + 29 + 44)/5 = 23.0 hours.

SOLVED PROBLEM 4

The Rocky Mountain Arsenal, formerly a chemical warfare manufacturing site, is said to be one of the most polluted locations in the United States. Cleanup of chemical waste storage basins will involve two operations.

Operation 1: Drain and dredge basin.
Operation 2: Incinerate materials.

Management has estimated that each operation will require the following amounts of time (in days):

					STORAGE BASIN					
	A	B	C	D	E	F	G	H	I	J
Dredge	3	4	3	6	1	3	2	1	8	4
Incinerate	1	4	2	1	2	6	4	1	2	8

Because of the health danger, human access to the area has been severely restricted for decades. As an unintended result, the Rocky Mountain Arsenal has now become a prolific wildlife refuge, which now supports several endangered species. Management's objective is to clean up the area while minimizing disruption to wildlife. This objective can be translated as minimizing the makespan of the cleanup operations. First, find a schedule that minimizes the makespan. Then, calculate the average job flow time of a storage basin through the two operations. What is the total elapsed time for cleaning all 10 basins? Display the schedule in a Gantt machine chart.

SOLUTION

We can use Johnson's rule to find the schedule that minimizes the total makespan. Four jobs are tied for the shortest process time: A, D, E, and H. We arbitrarily choose to start with basin E, the first on the list for the drain and dredge operation. The 10 steps used to arrive at a sequence are as follows:

1. Select basin E first (tied with basin H); put at the front.   E — — — — — — — — —
2. Select basin H next; put toward the front.   E H — — — — — — — —
3. Select basin A next (tied with basin D); put at the end.   E H — — — — — — — A
4. Put basin D toward the end.   E H — — — — — — D A
5. Put basin G toward the front.   E H G — — — — — D A
6. Put basin C toward the end.   E H G — — — — C D A
7. Put basin I toward the end.   E H G — — — I C D A
8. Put basin F toward the front.   E H G F — — I C D A
9. Put basin B toward the front.   E H G F B — I C D A
10. Put basin J in the remaining space.   E H G F B J I C D A

There are several optimal solutions to this problem because of the ties at the start of the scheduling procedure. However, all have the same makespan. The schedule would be as follows:

	OPERATION I		OPERATION 2	
BASIN	START	FINISH	START	FINISH
E	0	1	1	3
H	1	2	3	4
G	2	4	4	8
F	4	7	8	14
B	7	11	14	18
J	11	15	18	26
I	15	23	26	28
C	23	26	28	30
D	26	32	32	33
A	32	35	35	36
			Total	200

FIGURE 17.8

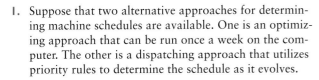

Storage basin

| Dredge | E | H | G | | F | | B | | J | | | I | | C | | D | | | A | |
| Incinerate | | E | H | | G | | F | | B | | J | | | I | C | | D | | A |

The makespan is 36 days. The average job flow time is the sum of incineration finish times divided by 10, or 200/10 = 20 days. The Gantt machine chart for this schedule is given in Figure 17.8.

DISCUSSION QUESTIONS

1. Suppose that two alternative approaches for determining machine schedules are available. One is an optimizing approach that can be run once a week on the computer. The other is a dispatching approach that utilizes priority rules to determine the schedule as it evolves. Discuss the advantages and disadvantages of each approach and the conditions under which each approach is likely to be better.

2. Explain why management should be concerned about priority systems in service and manufacturing organizations.

PROBLEMS

1. ✒ **OM Explorer** Gerald Glynn manages the Michaels Distribution Center. After careful examination of his database information, he has determined the daily requirements for part-time loading dock personnel. The distribution center operates seven days a week, and the daily part-time staffing requirements are

Day	M	T	W	Th	F	S	Su
Requirements	6	3	5	3	7	2	3

Find the minimum number of workers Glynn must hire. Prepare a workforce schedule for these individuals so that each will have two consecutive days off per week and all staffing requirements will be satisfied. Give preference to the S–Su pair in case of a tie.

2. Cara Ryder manages a ski school in a large resort and is trying to develop a schedule for instructors. The instructors receive little salary and work just enough to earn room and board. They do receive free skiing, spending most of their free time tackling the resort's notorious double black diamond slopes. Hence, the instructors work only four days a week. One of the lesson packages offered at the resort is a four-day beginner package. Ryder likes to keep the same instructor with a group over the four-day period, so she schedules the instructors for four consecutive days and then three days off. Ryder uses years of experience with demand forecasts provided by management to formulate her instructor requirements for the upcoming month.

Day	M	T	W	Th	F	S	Su
Requirements	7	5	4	5	6	9	8

a. Determine how many instructors Ryder needs to employ. Give preference to Saturday and Sunday off. (*Hint:* Look for the group of three days with lowest requirements.)

b. Specify the work schedule for each employee. How much slack does your schedule generate for each day?

3. ✒ **OM Explorer** The mayor of Massilon, Ohio, wanting to be environmentally progressive, has decided to implement a recycling plan. All residents of the city will receive a special three-part bin to separate their glass, plastic, and aluminum, and the city will be responsible for picking up the materials. A young city and regional planning graduate, Michael Duffy, has been hired to manage the recycling program. After carefully studying the city's population density, Duffy decides that the following numbers of recycling collectors will be needed.

Day	M	T	W	Th	F	S	Su
Requirements	12	7	9	9	5	3	6

The requirements are based on the populations of the various housing developments and subdivisions in the city and surrounding communities. To motivate residents of some areas to have their pickups scheduled on weekends, a special tax break will be given.

a. Find the minimum number of recycling collectors required if each employee works five days a week and has two consecutive days off. Give preference to the S–Su pair when that pair is involved in a tie.

b. Specify the work schedule for each employee. How much slack does your schedule generate for each day?

c. Suppose that Duffy can smooth the requirements further through greater tax incentives. The requirements then will be eight collectors on Monday and seven on the other days of the week. How many collectors will be needed now? Find the optimal solution in terms of minimal total slack capacity. Does smoothing of requirements have capital investment implications? If so, what are they?

4. ◗ OM Explorer The Hickory Company manufactures wooden desks. Management schedules overtime every weekend to reduce the backlog on the most popular models. The automatic routing machine is used to cut certain types of edges on the desktops. The following orders need to be scheduled for the routing machine:

Order	Estimated Machine Time (hr)	Due Date (hr from now)
1	10	12
2	3	8
3	15	18
4	9	20
5	7	21

The due dates reflect the need for the order to be at its next operation.

a. Develop separate schedules by using the FCFS, SPT, and EDD rules. Compare the schedules on the basis of average flow time, the average early time, and average past due hours for any order.

b. For each schedule, calculate the average WIP inventory (in orders) and the average total inventory (in orders).

c. Comment on the performance of the two rules relative to these measures.

5. ◗ OM Explorer The drill press is a bottleneck operation in a production system. Currently, five jobs are waiting to be processed. Following are the available operations data. Assume that the current date is week 5 and that the number of remaining operations and the

shop time remaining include the operation at the drill press.

Job	Processing Time	Due Date	Operations Remaining	Shop Time Remaining (wk)
AA	4	10	3	4
BB	8	16	4	6
CC	13	21	10	9
DD	6	23	3	12
EE	2	12	5	3

a. Specify the priority for each job if the shop floor control system uses each of the following priority rules: SPT, S/RO, EDD, and CR.

b. For each priority rule, calculate the average flow time per job at the drill press.

c. Which of these priority rules would work best for priority planning with an MRP system? Why?

6. The machine shop at Bycraft Enterprises operates 24 hours a day and uses a numerically controlled (NC) welding machine. The load on the machine is monitored, and no more than 24 hours of work is released to the welding operators in one day. The data for a typical set of jobs are shown in Table 17.1. Management has been investigating scheduling procedures that would reduce inventory and increase customer service in the shop. Assume that at 8:00 A.M. on Monday the NC welding machine was idle.

a. Develop schedules for SPT and EDD priority rules, and draw a Gantt machine chart for each schedule.

b. For each schedule in part (a), calculate the average past due hours per job and the average flow time per job. Keep in mind that the jobs are available for processing at different times.

c. Comment on the customer service and inventory performance of the two rules. What trade-offs should management consider in selecting rules for scheduling the welding machine in the future?

7. ◗ OM Explorer Refer to the Gantt machine chart in Figure 17.9.

a. Suppose that a routing requirement is that each job must be processed on machine A first. Can the makespan be improved? If so, draw a Gantt chart with the improved schedule. If not, state why not.

	TABLE 17.1
	MANUFACTURING DATA

Job	Release Time	Lot Size	Processing Time (hr/unit)	Setup Time (hr)	Due Date
1	9:00 A.M. Monday	50	0.06	4	9:00 P.M. Monday
2	10:00 A.M. Monday	120	0.05	3	10:00 P.M. Monday
3	11:00 A.M. Monday	260	0.03	5	11:00 P.M. Monday
4	12:00 P.M. Monday	200	0.04	2	2:00 A.M. Tuesday

FIGURE 17.9

b. Suppose that there is no routing restriction on machine sequence, and that jobs can be processed in any sequence on the machines. Can the makespan in the chart be improved in this case? If so, draw a Gantt chart with your schedule. If not, state why not.

8. OM Explorer A manufacturer of sails for small boats has a group of custom sails awaiting the last two processing operations before the sails are sent to the customers. Operation 1 must be performed before operation 2, and the jobs have different time requirements for each operation. The hours required are as follows:

	Job									
	1	**2**	**3**	**4**	**5**	**6**	**7**	**8**	**9**	**10**
Operation 1	1	5	8	3	9	4	7	2	4	9
Operation 2	8	3	1	2	8	6	7	2	4	1

a. Use Johnson's rule to determine the optimal sequence.

b. Draw a Gantt chart for each operation.

9. OM Explorer McGee Parts Company is under tremendous pressure to complete a government contract for six orders in 31 working days. The orders are for spare parts for highway maintenance equipment. According to the government contract, a late penalty of $1,000 is imposed each day the order is late. Owing to a nationwide increase in highway construction, McGee Parts has received many orders for spare parts replacement and the shop has been extremely busy. To complete the government contract, the parts must be deburred and heat treated. The production control manager has suggested the following schedule:

	Debur		Heat Treat	
Job	**Start**	**Finish**	**Start**	**Finish**
1	0	2	2	8
2	2	5	8	13
3	5	12	13	17
4	12	15	17	25
5	15	16	25	30
6	16	24	30	32

a. Use Johnson's rule to determine the optimal sequence.

b. Draw a Gantt chart for each operation.

10. OM Explorer Carolyn Roberts is the operations manager of the machine shop of Reliable Manufacturing. She has to schedule eight jobs that are to be sent to final assembly for an important customer order. Currently, all eight jobs are in department 12 and must be routed to department 22 next. Jason Mangano, supervisor for department 12, is concerned about keeping his WIP inventory low and is adamant about processing the jobs through his department on the basis of shortest processing time. Pat Mooney, supervisor for department 22, pointed out that if Mangano were more flexible the orders could be finished and shipped earlier. The processing times (in days) for each job in each department follow:

	Job							
	1	**2**	**3**	**4**	**5**	**6**	**7**	**8**
Department 12	2	4	7	5	4	10	8	2
Department 22	3	6	3	8	2	6	6	5

a. Determine a schedule for the operation in each department. Use SPT for department 12 and the same sequence for department 22. What is the average job flow time for department 12? What is the makespan through both departments? What is the sum of jobs times days spent in the system?

b. Find a schedule that will minimize the makespan through both departments, and then calculate the average job flow time for department 12. What is the sum of jobs times days spent in the system?

c. Discuss the trade-offs represented by these two schedules. What implications do they have for centralized scheduling?

Advanced Problems

11. OM Explorer Little 6, Inc., an accounting firm, forecasts the following weekly workload during the tax season:

		Day					
	M	T	W	Th	F	S	Su
Personal Tax Returns	24	14	18	18	10	28	16
Corporate Tax Returns	18	10	12	15	24	12	4

Corporate tax returns each require 4 hours of an accountant's time, and personal returns each require 90 minutes. During tax season, each accountant can work up to 10 hours per day. However, error rates increase to unacceptable levels when accountants work more than five consecutive days per week.

a. Create an effective and efficient work schedule.

b. Assume that Little 6 has three part-time employees available to work three days per week. How could these employees be effectively utilized?

12. Return to Problem 1 and the workforce schedule for part-time loading dock workers. Suppose that each part-time worker can work only three days, but the days must be consecutive. Devise an approach to this workforce scheduling problem. Your objective is to minimize total slack capacity. What is the minimum number of clerks needed now and what are their schedules?

13. **OM Explorer** The repair manager at Standard Components needs to develop a priority schedule for repairing eight Dell PCs. Each job requires analysis using the same diagnostic system. Furthermore, each job will require additional processing after the diagnostic evaluation. The manager does not expect any rescheduling delays, and the jobs are to move directly to the next process after the diagnostic work has been completed. The manager has collected the following processing time and scheduling data for each repair job:

Job	Work Time (days)	Due Date (days)	Shop Time Remaining (days)	Operations Remaining
1	1.25	6	2.5	5
2	2.75	5	3.5	7
3	2.50	7	4.0	9
4	3.00	6	4.5	12
5	2.50	5	3.0	8
6	1.75	8	2.5	6
7	2.25	7	3.0	9
8	2.00	5	2.5	3

a. Compare the relative performance of the FCFS, SPT, EDD, S/RO, and CR rules.

b. Discuss the selection of one of the rules for this company. What criteria do you consider most important in the selection of a rule in this situation?

14. **OM Explorer** Penultimate Support Systems makes fairly good speaker and equipment support stands for music groups. The assembly process involves two operations: (1) fabrication, or cutting aluminum tubing to the correct lengths, and (2) assembly, with purchased fasteners and injection-molded plastic parts. Setup time for assembly is negligible. Fabrication setup time and

run time per unit, assembly run time per unit, and the production schedule for next week follow. Organize the work to minimize makespan, and create a Gantt chart. Can this work be accomplished within two 40-hour shifts?

		Fabrication		**Assembly**
Model	Quantity	Setup (hr)	Run Time (hr/unit)	Run Time (hr/unit)
A	200	2	0.050	0.04
B	300	3	0.070	0.10
C	100	1	0.050	0.12
D	250	2	0.064	0.60

15. Eight jobs must be processed on three machines in the sequence M1, M2, and M3. The processing times (in hours) are

				Job				
	1	2	3	4	5	6	7	8
Machine 1	2	5	2	3	1	2	4	2
Machine 2	4	1	3	5	5	6	2	1
Machine 3	6	4	5	2	3	2	6	2

Machine M2 is a bottleneck, and management wants to maximize its use. Consequently, the schedule for the eight jobs, through the three machines, was based on the SPT rule on M2. The proposed schedule is 2, 8, 7, 3, 1, 4, 5, and 6.

a. It is now 4 P.M. on Monday. Suppose that processing on M2 is to begin at 7 A.M. on Tuesday. Use the proposed schedule to determine the schedules for M1 and M3 so that job 2 begins processing on M2 at 7 A.M. on Tuesday. Draw Gantt charts for M1, M2, and M3. What is the makespan for the eight jobs?

b. Find a schedule that utilizes M2 better and yields a shorter makespan.

16. The last few steps of a production process require two operations. Some jobs require processing on M1 before processing on M3. Other jobs require processing on M2 before M3. Currently, six jobs are waiting at M1 and four jobs are waiting at M2. The following data have been supplied by the shop floor control system:

	Processing Time (hr)			Due Date
Job	M1	M2	M3	(hr from now)
1	6	—	4	13
2	2	—	1	18
3	4	—	7	22
4	5	—	3	16
5	7	—	4	30
6	3	—	1	29
7	—	4	6	42
8	—	2	10	31
9	—	6	9	48
10	—	8	2	40

a. Schedule this shop by using the following rules: SPT, EDD, S/RO, and CR.

b. Discuss the operating implications of each of the schedules you developed in part (a).

 ACTIVE MODEL EXERCISE

This Active Model appears on the Student CD-ROM. It allows you to evaluate the application of single-dimension priority rules for scheduling jobs at one workstation.

QUESTIONS

1. Which rule minimizes the average job flow time and the average WIP in the system for this example?
2. Use the scroll bars to change the five processing times and the five due dates. Does the same rule always minimize the average flow time and average WIP?
3. Which rule minimizes the average hours past due for this example?
4. Use the scroll bar to change the processing time for the Thunderbird and to modify the due date for the Thunderbird. Does the same rule always minimize the average hours past due?
5. Which rule minimizes the average hours early for this example?
6. Use the scroll bar to change the processing time for the Econoline and to modify the due date for the Econoline. Does the same rule always minimize the average hours past due?

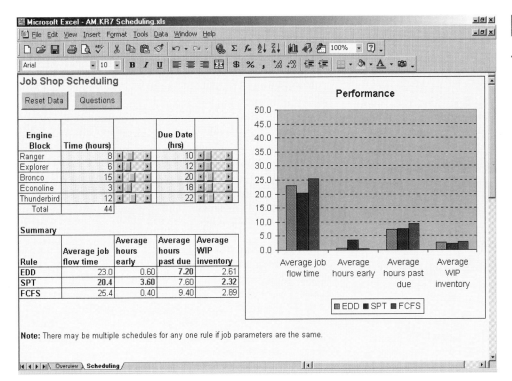

ACTIVE MODEL 17.1

Job Shop Scheduling Using Data from Example 17.2

SIMULATION EXERCISES

These simulation exercises require the use of the SimQuick and Extend simulation packages. SimQuick is on the Student CD-ROM that is packaged with every new copy of the textbook. Extend is an optional simulation package that your instructor may or may not have ordered.

1. **SimQuick** A small company has a single machine that processes four types of products, each with its own processing time distributions and arrival time distributions. It is important to schedule the machine so as to reduce the average work-in-process of the

products and the tardiness in delivering the products to the customers. Use SimQuick to determine the mean flow time and overall tardiness of the products processed by the machine when the shortest processing time (SPT) and the earliest due date (EDD) rules are used to schedule the machine. See Example 22 in *SimQuick: Process Simulation with Excel* for more details about this problem and additional exercises.

2. **Extend** Recall Precision AutoBody in Example 17.3. Customers are increasingly frustrated with long delivery times and unmet delivery promises. Use the Extend simulator to evaluate the current process and other priority dispatching rules such as first come, first served (FCFS), shortest process time (SPT), earliest due date (EDD), and minimum slack time. See the *Scheduling Vehicle Repair at Precision AutoBody* case on the optional CD-ROM, which includes the basic model and how to use it. Answer the various questions about scheduling rules, increased customer demand, and adjusted due dates.

CASE   FOOD KING

Based in Charlotte, North Carolina, the Food King grocery supermarket chain stretches from the Virginias down the East Coast into Florida. As in the rest of the country, the grocery supermarket industry in the Southeast is very competitive, with average profit margins running at about 2 percent of revenues. Historically, the overriding competitive priority for all grocery chains was low prices. With profit margins so small, stores were continually looking for ways to reduce costs and utilize facilities efficiently. Several grocery chains still focus on low prices as their main competitive priority.

Food King, however, recently decided to focus its competitive positioning on enhancing the consumer's shopping experience. Food King's target market is the upscale food shopper, who has the following shopping priorities:

1. **Cleanliness.** The facility is clean and orderly, with items well marked and easy to find.
2. **Availability.** The selection of items is broad, and the customer has several choices for any one item.
3. **Timely Service.** The store is open at convenient times, and customers do not have to wait in long checkout lines.
4. **Reasonable Prices.** Although customers are willing to pay a small premium for cleanliness, availability, and good service, prices still must be competitive.

Marty Moyer had been the store manager of the Food King supermarket in Rock Hill, South Carolina, for the past three years. He had worked his way up from stockboy to manager of this medium-sized facility. Because of his success managing the Rock Hill facility, Moyer was promoted to the store manager's position at the large, flagship Food King store in Columbia. This facility had just instituted 24-hours-per-day, seven-days-a-week hours in response to competitive pressures.

After a month as manager at the Columbia store, Moyer has become familiar with the local market characteristics, store operations, and store personnel. His major challenge for the future is to align the store with the new competitive priorities established for the chain. An area he has identified as a particular concern is the scheduling of stockers and baggers. The cleanliness, availability, and service time priorities

put added pressure on Moyer to have the appropriate number of stocking and bagging personnel available. Maintaining a high level of cleanliness requires more stocking personnel to keep the stock orderly on the shelves and the aisles clear and swept. The availability priority requires more frequent replenishment of shelves because the greater selection of items means less space is allocated to any one brand or item. Finally, the need for fast service requires baggers to be available to assist the cashier in serving customers quickly, especially during peak shopping periods when long waits could occur if cashiers had to bag and ring up the groceries.

Moyer knows that he cannot solve the cleanliness, availability, and timely service issues just by adding stocking and bagging personnel to the payroll. To make a profit in a low-margin business environment, he has to control costs so that prices remain competitive. The trick is to develop a work schedule for the stocking and bagging personnel that satisfies competitive requirements, conforms to a reasonable set of work policies, and utilizes the personnel efficiently to minimize labor costs.

Moyer begins to address this problem by collecting information on existing scheduling policies and procedures along with a forecasted level of demand for personnel. The stocking and bagging positions can be filled with either full- or part-time employees. Full-time employees work eight hours per day five days a week, with two consecutive days off each week. The eight-hour shifts usually are scheduled as consecutive eight-hour blocks of time; however, he can schedule an employee to two four-hour time blocks (with four hours off between them) within a particular day if there is a stocker and a bagger for the four-hour period between scheduled blocks of time.

All part-time employees are scheduled in four-hour blocks of time for up to 20 hours per week. Food King limits the number of part-time employees to 50 percent of the total number of full-time employees for each category of worker. Most of the part-time employees are utilized as baggers because they tend to be retired people who have difficulty with the heavy lifting required in stocking shelves. Food King likes to hire retired people because they are dependable, reliable, and more willing to work weekends than are teenagers. Full-time employees earn $5.25 per hour; part-time employees earn only $4.50 per hour.

For scheduling purposes, each day is divided into six four-hour time blocks beginning with 8:00 A.M. to 12:00 P.M. Demand for stocking and bagging personnel varies quite a bit within a 24-hour period. Moyer developed a forecast of personnel needs by four-hour time blocks by analyzing customer activity data and supplier delivery schedules. The following table gives his estimate of the total number of stockers and baggers required for each four-hour block of time starting at the time indicated:

	Day						
HOUR	**M**	**T**	**W**	**Th**	**F**	**S**	**Su**
8:00 A.M.	6	8	5	5	8	15	4
12:00 P.M.	6	8	5	5	10	15	6
4:00 P.M.	5	6	5	5	15	15	6
8:00 P.M.	4	4	4	4	8	6	4
12:00 A.M.	4	4	4	4	5	4	4
4:00 A.M.	8	4	4	8	5	4	4

The peak requirements occur during the heavy shopping periods on Friday and Saturday. More stocking personnel are required on Monday and Thursday evenings because of the large number of supplier deliveries on those days.

Moyer wants to determine the number of stocking and bagging personnel needed, the appropriate mix of full-time and part-time employees, and the work schedule for each employee. Going to a 24-hours-a-day operation has certainly complicated the scheduling task. He knows that younger, full-time employees probably will be best for the late night and early morning blocks of time. But the younger employees dislike working these hours. Somehow the schedule has to convey fairness for all.

QUESTIONS

1. Translate the four priorities of the shoppers into a set of competitive priorities for operations at the Rock Hill Food King store.
2. Develop a schedule of full-time and part-time stockers and baggers for Marty Moyer. Explain the strategy you used and the trade-offs you made to satisfy the Rock Hill store's competitive priorities.
3. What measures would you take to ensure that the schedule is fair to all employees?

Source: This case was prepared by Dr. Brooke Saladin, Wake Forest University, as a basis for classroom discussion.

SELECTED REFERENCES

Andrews, B.H., and H.L. Parsons. "L.L.Bean Chooses a Telephone Agent Scheduling System." *Interfaces* (November–December 1989), pp. 1–9.

Ashton, James E., and Frank X. Cook, Jr. "Time to Reform Job Shop Manufacturing." *Harvard Business Review* (March–April 1989), pp. 106–111.

Baker, K. R. *Elements of Sequencing and Scheduling.* Hanover, NH: Baker Press, 1995.

Browne, J.J. "Simplified Scheduling of Routine Work Hours and Days Off." *Industrial Engineering* (December 1979), pp. 27–29.

Browne, J. J., and J. Prop. "Supplement to Scheduling Routine Work Hours." *Industrial Engineering* (July 1989), p. 12.

Dillon, Jeffrey E, and Spyros Kontogiorgis. "US Airways Optimizes the Scheduling of Reserve Flight Crews." *Interfaces* (September–October 1999), pp. 123–131.

Hartvigsen, David. *SimQuick: Process Simulation with Excel.* 2d ed. Upper Saddle River, NJ: Prentice Hall, 2004.

Johnson, S. M. "Optimal Two Stage and Three Stage Production Schedules with Setup Times Included." *Naval Logistics Quarterly,* vol. 1, no. 1 (1954), pp. 61–68.

Kiran, Ali S., and Thomas H. Willingham. "Simulation: Help for Your Scheduling Problems." *APICS—The Performance Advantage* (August 1992), pp. 26–28.

LaForge, R. Lawrence, and Christopher W. Craighead. "Computer-Based Scheduling in Manufacturing Firms: Some Indicators of Successful Practice." *Production and Inventory Management Journal* (First Quarter 2000), pp. 29–34.

Lesaint, David, Christos Voudouris, and Nader Azarmi. "Dynamic Workforce Scheduling for British Telecommunications plc." *Interfaces* (January–February 2000), pp. 45–56.

Metters, Richard, and Vincente Vargas. "A Comparison of Production Scheduling Policies on Costs, Service Levels, and Schedule Changes." *Production and Operations Management,* vol. 17, no. 3 (1999), pp. 76–91.

Pinedo, M., and X. Chao. *Operations Scheduling with Applications in Manufacturing and Services.* Boston: McGraw-Hill/Irwin, 1998.

Port, Otis. "Customers Move into the Driver's Seat." *Business Week* (October 4, 1999), pp. 103–106.

Ramani, K. V. "Scheduling Doctors' Activities at a Large Teaching Hospital." *Production and Inventory Management Journal* (First/Second Quarter 2002), pp. 56–62.

Rhodes, Phillip. "Modern Job Shop Manufacturing Systems." *APICS—The Performance Advantage* (January 1992), pp. 27–28.

Simons, Jacob, Jr., and Wendell P. Simpson, III. "An Exposition of Multiple Constraint Scheduling as Implemented in the Goal System (Formerly Disaster™)." *Production and Operations Management,* vol. 6, no. 1 (Spring 1997), pp. 3–22.

Suresh, V., and D. Chaudhuri. "Dynamic Scheduling—A Survey of Research." *International Journal of Production Economics,* vol. 32 (1993), pp. 52–63.

Tibrewala, R. K., D. Philippe, and J. J. Browne. "Optimal Scheduling of Two Consecutive Idle Periods." *Management Science,* vol. 19, no. 1 (1972), pp. 71–75.

Vollmann, Thomas E., William Berry, and D. Clay Whybark. *Manufacturing Planning and Control Systems,* 4th ed. Homewood, IL: Irwin Professional Publication, 1997.

APPENDIX I:
Normal Distribution

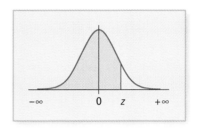

	.00	.01	.02	.03	.04	.05	.06	.07	.08	.09
.0	.5000	.5040	.5080	.5120	.5160	.5199	.5239	.5279	.5319	.5359
.1	.5398	.5438	.5478	.5517	.5557	.5596	.5636	.5675	.5714	.5753
.2	.5793	.5832	.5871	.5910	.5948	.5987	.6026	.6064	.6103	.6141
.3	.6179	.6217	.6255	.6293	.6331	.6368	.6406	.6443	.6480	.6517
.4	.6554	.6591	.6628	.6664	.6700	.6736	.6772	.6808	.6844	.6879
.5	.6915	.6950	.6985	.7019	.7054	.7088	.7123	.7157	.7190	.7224
.6	.7257	.7291	.7324	.7357	.7389	.7422	.7454	.7486	.7517	.7549
.7	.7580	.7611	.7642	.7673	.7704	.7734	.7764	.7794	.7823	.7852
.8	.7881	.7910	.7939	.7967	.7995	.8023	.8051	.8078	.8106	.8133
.9	.8159	.8186	.8212	.8238	.8264	.8289	.8315	.8340	.8365	.8389
1.0	.8413	.8438	.8461	.8485	.8508	.8531	.8554	.8577	.8599	.8621
1.1	.8643	.8665	.8686	.8708	.8729	.8749	.8770	.8790	.8810	.8830
1.2	.8849	.8869	.8888	.8907	.8925	.8944	.8962	.8980	.8997	.9015
1.3	.9032	.9049	.9066	.9082	.9099	.9115	.9131	.9147	.9162	.9177
1.4	.9192	.9207	.9222	.9236	.9251	.9265	.9279	.9292	.9306	.9319
1.5	.9332	.9345	.9357	.9370	.9382	.9394	.9406	.9418	.9429	.9441
1.6	.9452	.9463	.9474	.9484	.9495	.9505	.9515	.9525	.9535	.9545
1.7	.9554	.9564	.9573	.9582	.9591	.9599	.9608	.9616	.9625	.9633
1.8	.9641	.9649	.9656	.9664	.9671	.9678	.9686	.9693	.9699	.9706
1.9	.9713	.9719	.9726	.9732	.9738	.9744	.9750	.9756	.9761	.9767
2.0	.9772	.9778	.9783	.9788	.9793	.9798	.9803	.9808	.9812	.9817
2.1	.9821	.9826	.9830	.9834	.9838	.9842	.9846	.9850	.9854	.9857
2.2	.9861	.9864	.9868	.9871	.9875	.9878	.9881	.9884	.9887	.9890
2.3	.9893	.9896	.9898	.9901	.9904	.9906	.9909	.9911	.9913	.9916
2.4	.9918	.9920	.9922	.9925	.9927	.9929	.9931	.9932	.9934	.9936
2.5	.9938	.9940	.9941	.9943	.9945	.9946	.9948	.9949	.9951	.9952
2.6	.9953	.9955	.9956	.9957	.9959	.9960	.9961	.9962	.9963	.9964
2.7	.9965	.9966	.9967	.9968	.9969	.9970	.9971	.9972	.9973	.9974
2.8	.9974	.9975	.9976	.9977	.9977	.9978	.9979	.9979	.9980	.9981
2.9	.9981	.9982	.9982	.9983	.9984	.9984	.9985	.9985	.9986	.9986
3.0	.9987	.9987	.9987	.9988	.9988	.9989	.9989	.9989	.9990	.9990
3.1	.9990	.9991	.9991	.9991	.9992	.9992	.9992	.9992	.9993	.9993
3.2	.9993	.9993	.9994	.9994	.9994	.9994	.9994	.9995	.9995	.9995
3.3	.9995	.9995	.9995	.9996	.9996	.9996	.9996	.9996	.9996	.9997
3.4	.9997	.9997	.9997	.9997	.9997	.9997	.9997	.9997	.9997	.9998

APPENDIX 2:
Table of Random Numbers

71509	68310	48213	99928	64650	13229	36921	58732	13459	93487
21949	30920	23287	89514	58502	46185	00368	82613	02668	37444
50639	54968	11409	36148	82090	87298	41396	71111	00076	60029
47837	76716	09653	54466	87987	82362	17933	52793	17641	19502
31735	36901	92295	19293	57582	86043	69502	12601	00535	82697
04174	32342	66532	07875	54445	08795	63563	42295	74646	73120
96980	68728	21154	56181	71843	66134	52396	89723	96435	17871
21823	04027	76402	04655	87276	32593	17097	06913	05136	05115
25922	07122	31485	52166	07645	85122	20945	06369	70254	22806
32530	98882	19105	01769	20276	59401	60426	03316	41438	22012
00159	08461	51810	14650	45119	97920	08063	70819	01832	53295
66574	21384	75357	55888	83429	96916	73977	87883	13249	28870
00995	28829	15048	49573	65277	61493	44031	88719	73057	66010
55114	79226	27929	23392	06432	50200	39054	15528	53483	33972
10614	25190	52647	62580	51183	31338	60008	66595	64357	14985
31359	77469	58126	59192	23371	25190	37841	44386	92420	42965
09736	51873	94595	61367	82091	63835	86858	10677	58209	59820
24709	23224	45788	21426	63353	29874	51058	29958	61220	61199
79957	67598	74102	49824	39305	15069	56327	26905	34453	53964
66616	22137	72805	64420	58711	68435	60301	28620	91919	96080
01413	27281	19397	36231	05010	42003	99865	20924	76151	54089
88238	80731	20777	45725	41480	48277	45704	96457	13918	52375
57457	87883	64273	26236	61095	01309	48632	00431	63730	18917
21614	06412	71007	20255	39890	75336	89451	88091	61011	38072
26466	03735	39891	26361	86816	48193	33492	70484	77322	01016
97314	03944	04509	46143	88908	55261	73433	62538	63187	57352
91207	33555	75942	41668	64650	38741	86189	38197	99112	59694
46791	78974	01999	78891	16177	95746	78076	75001	51309	18791
34161	32258	05345	79267	75607	29916	37005	09213	10991	50451
02376	40372	45077	73705	56076	01853	83512	81567	55951	27156
33994	56809	58377	45976	01581	78389	18268	90057	93382	28494
92588	92024	15048	87841	38008	80689	73098	39201	10907	88092
73767	61534	66197	47147	22994	38197	60844	86962	27595	49907
51517	39870	94094	77092	94595	37904	27553	02229	44993	10468
33910	05156	60844	89012	21154	68937	96477	05867	95809	72827
09444	93069	61764	99301	55826	78849	26131	28201	91417	98172
96896	43760	72890	78682	78243	24061	55449	53587	77574	51580
97523	54633	99656	08503	52563	12099	52479	74374	79581	57143
42568	30794	32613	21802	73809	60237	70087	36650	54487	43718
45453	33136	90246	61953	17724	42421	87611	95369	42108	95369
52814	26445	73516	24897	90622	35018	70087	60112	09025	05324
87318	33345	14546	15445	81588	75461	12246	47858	08983	18205
08063	83575	26294	93027	09988	04487	88364	31087	22200	91019
53400	82078	52103	25650	75315	18916	06809	88217	12245	33053
90789	60614	20862	34475	11744	24437	55198	55219	74730	59820
73684	25859	86858	48946	30941	79017	53776	72534	83638	44680
82007	12183	89326	53713	77782	50368	01748	39033	47042	65758
80208	30920	97774	41417	79038	60531	32990	57770	53441	58732
62434	96122	63019	58439	89702	38657	60049	88761	22785	66093
04718	83199	65863	58857	49886	70275	27511	99426	53985	84077

NAME INDEX

SUBJECT INDEX

Page numbers followed by f *have figures. Page numbers followed by* t *have tables.*

PHOTO CREDITS

CHAPTER 1: p. 2: Mary Katz/The Image Works, p. 4: Dana White/PhotoEdit, p. 7: Amy Etra/PhotoEdit, p. 8: Honeywell International, p. 17: Rob Lewine/CORBIS BETTMANN, p. 23: David K. Crow/PhotoEdit.

CHAPTER 2: p. 56: AP/Wide World Photos, p. 59: Ron Watts/CORBIS BETTMANN, p. 63: AP/Wide World Photos, p. 66: AP/Wide World Photos, p. 68: Najlah Feanny/CORBIS BETTMANN, p. 76: © 1992 The Ritz-Carlton Hotel Company. All rights reserved. Reprinted with the permission of The Ritz-Carlton Hotel Company, L.L.C. The Ritz-Carlton®is a federally registered trademark of The Ritz-Carlton Hotel Company, L.L.C., p. 78: Kit Kittle/CORBIS BETTMANN.

CHAPTER 3: p. 88: John Feingersh/Corbis/Stock Market, p. 90: Netscape Communications, p. 93: Bonnie Kamin/PhotoEdit, p. 98: David Young-Wolff/PhotoEdit, p. 100: AP/Wide World Photos, p. 108: David Young-Wolff/PhotoEdit.

CHAPTER 4: p. 132: Intermarket, p. 137: Frank Herholdt/Getty Images Inc.-Stone Allstock, p. 153: Xerox Corporation.

CHAPTER 5: p. 194: SuperStock, Inc., p. 197: Corbis Royalty Free, p. 203: Archer Daniels Midland Company, p. 205: Reuters NewMedia Inc/ CORBIS BETTMANN, p. 207: Ronnie Kaufman/Corbis/Stock Market, p. 223: Corbis Royalty Free.

CHAPTER 6: p. 244: JP Morgan Chase & Company, p. 247: AP/Wide World Photos, p. 251: Staff Sgt. Tony R. Tolley/U.S. Air Force, p. 252: Mark Wagner/Aviation-images.com.

SUPPLEMENT C: p. 279: David Young-Wolff/PhotoEdit, p. 287: Tom Carter/PhotoEdit.

CHAPTER 7: p. 298: Scott McDonald/Hedrich Blessing, p. 301: Color Kinetics Incorporated, p. 304: Myrleen Ferguson Cate/PhotoEdit, page 315 (top and bottom): Pearson Education/PH College, p. 317: Microsoft Corporation, p. 318: DKM, Inc., p. 319: Kevin R. Morris/CORBIS BETTMAN.

CHAPTER 8: p. 342: Bechtel Corporation, Inc., p. 359: AP/Wide World Photos.

CHAPTER 9: p. 394: Greg Smith/CORBIS BETTMANN, P. 398: Arizona Public Service Corporate Communications, p. 401: Matthew Mc Vay/CORBIS BETTMANN, p. 410: © Reuters New Media, Inc./CORBIS BETTMANN, p. 412: Will and Deni McIntyre/Photo Researchers, Inc., p. 423: Dana Corporation.

CHAPTER 10: p. 442: MapInfo Corporation, p. 444; AP/Wide World Photos, p. 449: Startek, Inc., p. 452: D. Donne Bryant Stock Photography.

CHAPTER 11: p. 482: Photo by Junko Kimura/Getty Images, Inc., p. 484: Owen Franken/CORBIS BETTMANN, p. 488: AP/Wide World Photos, p. 489: Nik Wheeler/CORBIS BETTMANN, p. 499: Cessna Aircraft Company.

CHAPTER 12: p. 508: 7-Eleven Inc., p.514: Wal Mart, p. 516: NBC/Getty Images Inc., p. 523: ATOFINA Chemicals, Inc.

CHAPTER 13: p. 536: AP/Wide World Photos.

CHAPTER 14: p. 584: Tim Boyle/Getty Images, Inc., p. 586: Mark Richards/PhotoEdit, p. 593: AP/Wide World Photos, p. 597: AP/Wide World Photos.

CHAPTER 15: p. 658: AP/Wide World Photos, p. 662: Michael Newman/PhotoEdit.

CHAPTER 16: p. 724: VF Corporation, p. 745: Courtesy of International Business Machines Corporation. Unauthorized use not permitted, p. 746: Jon Feingersh/Corbis/Stock Market, p. 747: Todd Gipstein/CORBIS BETTMANN.

CHAPTER 17: p. 770: Mark Wagner/Aviation-images.com, p. 775: Lawrence Lucier/Getty Images, Inc., p. 792: Don Murray/Getty Images, Inc.

SUPPLEMENT K: (on Student CD-ROM) p. K.2: AP/Wide World Photos, p. K.4: Charles O'Rear/CORBIS BETTMANN.